Kerr and Hunter on Receivers and Administrators

KERR AND HUNTER ON RECEIVERS AND ADMINISTRATORS

TWENTIETH EDITION

Supreme Courts

Library

EDITED BY

THOMAS ROBINSON M.A. (Oxon)
Barrister of Wilberforce Chambers, Lincoln's Inn

PROFESSOR PETER WALTON LL.B., Ph.D. (Wolv.)
Professor of Insolvency Law, University of Wolverhampton, and General Editor of Totty, Moss and Segal: Insolvency

SWEET & MAXWELL

 THOMSON REUTERS

First Edition (1869) by W. W. Kerr
Tenth Edition (1935) by F. C. Watmough
Eleventh Edition (1946) by F. C. Watmough
Twelfth Edition (1952) by R. Walton and A. W. Sanson
Thirteenth Edition (1963) by R. Walton
Fourteenth Edition (1972) by R. Walton
Fifteenth Edition (1978) by R. Walton
Sixteenth Edition (1983) by R. Walton
Seventeenth Edition (1989) by R. Walton with Muir Hunter
Eighteenth Edition (2005) by Muir Hunter
Nineteenth Edition (2010) by M. Davis-White and S. Frisby
Twentieth Edition (2018) by P. Walton and T. Robinson

Published in 2018 by Thomson Reuters, trading as Sweet & Maxwell.
Registered in England & Wales, Company No.1679046.
Registered Office and address for service: 5 Canada Square, Canary Wharf,
London, E14 5AQ.

For further information on our products and services, visit *http://
www.sweetandmaxwell.co.uk*

Computerset by Sweet & Maxwell.
Printed and bound by CPI Group (UK) Ltd, Croydon, CR0 4YY.
No natural forests were destroyed to make this product; only farmed timber
was used and re-planted.
A CIP catalogue record of this book is available from the British Library.

ISBN: 9780414046436

Full list of contributors

Edited with the expert assistance of
Marcia Shekerdemian Q.C., B.A. (Cantab)
Barrister of Wilberforce Chambers, Lincoln's Inn

Anna Littler M.A. (Oxon)
Barrister of Wilberforce Chambers, Lincoln's Inn

Bobby Friedman B.A. (Cantab)
Barrister of Wilberforce Chambers, Lincoln's Inn

Reuben Comiskey B.A. (Oxon)
Barrister of Radcliffe Chambers, Lincoln's Inn

David Montague LL.B (Liv.)
Senior Editor, Practical Law Restructuring and Insolvency

And the Taxation expertise of
Sally Mann B.A. (Oxon)
Senior Editor, Practical Law Tax

Gary Richards LL.B., M.A. (Cantab)
Partner, Mishcon de Reya LLP

PREFACE

The twentieth edition of *Kerr and Hunter on Receivers and Administrators* appears at a time of continuing change in its specialist areas and in English law more widely. Since the previous edition in 2010, much has happened in the world of receivership, administration and insolvency law generally. Administrative receivership is less and less frequently encountered, but retains significant advantages where available to creditors and remains important. Court appointed receivership remains a highly useful tool, mainly due to its acting in personam. It continues to be used frequently in relation to equitable execution especially where there are assets overseas or held in less transparent structures. It is an important resource in fraud cases. Pre-packaged administration has become subject to greater scrutiny. The powers of administrators have become further aligned with those of liquidators with more potential actions available to administrators as well as the ability to assign statutory causes of action. Case law in recent years has considered the commencement of an administration; the consequences of invalid appointments; termination, including by contested removal of administrators by creditors, and all points in between. We have seen the Insolvency Rules 2016 come into force which have revolutionised how creditors make decisions. Cost estimating is a new challenge and forms one of a number of areas where creditor challenges to the decisions of administrators can be expected. At a time when the decision of the UK to leave the EU leaves many questions unanswered we have a new recast EU Regulation on Insolvency Proceedings.

In bringing this august publication up to date, we have sought to address these changes with the law stated being that available to us as at 1 August 2017.

We would like to thank Matt Seys-Llewellyn of Sweet & Maxwell for his commitment and assistance in encouraging us to bring about this new edition. We would also like to thank Elisabeth Rangeley for her editorial skills and assistance. Peter Walton would like to thank his wife Deborah and son Caleb for their support during the updating of this work. He would also like to thank the Rolling Bones Hot Rod Team for providing a most invigorating oasis break during its production. Thomas Robinson's work on this edition would no doubt have progressed much more smoothly had he too been lucky enough to spend time with the Rolling Bones Hot Rod Team. However he is extremely grateful to a team of expert contributors from the Bar who are responsible for all the improvements to chapters in the administration section. Any errors are his own. He would like to thank his wife Ellen and sons Wilfred, Francis and Jeremy for their patience and support.

Thomas Robinson and Professor Peter Walton, 9 October 2017

TABLE OF CONTENTS

PART I: THE APPOINTMENT OF RECEIVERS BY THE COURT IN ENGLAND AND WALES

CHAPTER 1   PRINCIPLES ON WHICH A RECEIVER IS APPOINTED BY THE COURT

CHAPTER 2   IN WHAT CASES A RECEIVER WILL BE APPOINTED

CHAPTER 3   OVER WHAT PROPERTY A RECEIVER MAY BE APPOINTED

CHAPTER 4   WHO MAY BE APPOINTED RECEIVER

CHAPTER 5   MODES OF APPOINTING A RECEIVER OF THE COURT

PART II: THE STRUCTURE OF COURT-APPOINTED RECEIVERSHIPS IN ENGLAND AND WALES

CHAPTER 6   EFFECT OF APPOINTMENT AND POSSESSION OF A RECEIVER

CHAPTER 7   POWERS AND DUTIES OF A RECEIVER

PART IV: RECEIVERS APPOINTED OUT OF COURT

CHAPTER 18   RECEIVERS APPOINTED UNDER AN AGREEMENT

CHAPTER 19   RECEIVERS APPOINTED UNDER STATUTORY POWERS

CHAPTER 20   RECEIVERS APPOINTED OVER PROPERTY OF A COMPANY
              (OTHER THAN ADMINISTRATIVE RECEIVERS)

PART V: ADMINISTRATIVE RECEIVERS

CHAPTER 21   APPOINTMENT, STATUS AND POWERS OF AN ADMINISTRATIVE
              RECEIVER

CHAPTER 22   ADMINISTRATIVE RECEIVER'S RELATIONSHIP WITH THE
              UNSECURED CREDITORS

CHAPTER 23   ADMINISTRATIVE RECEIVER'S RELATIONSHIP WITH THE
              COMPANY AND ITS STAFF: CONTRACTS OF EMPLOYMENT;
              RESIDUAL POWERS OF THE DIRECTORS

CHAPTER 24   EXTRA-TERRITORIAL EXTENT OF FLOATING CHARGES AND OF
              RECEIVERSHIPS

CHAPTER 25   RELATIONSHIP BETWEEN ADMINISTRATIVE RECEIVERSHIP AND
              OTHER INSOLVENCY PROCESSES

CHAPTER 26   TERMINATION OF ADMINISTRATIVE RECEIVERSHIP

PART VI: TAXATION

Chapter 27   The Taxation of Receivers and Administrators

PART VII: CROSS-BORDER PROCEEDINGS

Chapter 28   The EU Regulations on Insolvency Proceedings and
the Cross-Border Insolvency Regulations 2006

TABLE OF CASES

TABLE OF STATUTES

(All references are to paragraph number)

TABLE OF STATUTORY INSTRUMENTS

(All references are to paragraph number)

TABLE OF CIVIL PROCEDURE RULES

(All references are to paragraph number)

PART I: THE APPOINTMENT OF RECEIVERS BY THE COURT IN ENGLAND AND WALES

CHAPTER 1

PRINCIPLES ON WHICH A RECEIVER IS APPOINTED BY THE COURT

1-1   **Procedure in England and Wales.**   The introduction of the Civil Procedure Rules 1998 (SI 1998/3132) ("CPR") in England and Wales abolished a number of long-established court procedures and reconstructed others. In an ever decreasing number of fields, a small number of the former Rules of the Supreme Court ("RSC") and County Court Rules ("CCR") have been retained in schedules to the CPR, with or without amendments, as rules still to be generally applicable; they are referred to, and cited, in this work as "CPR Sch.1 (former RSC number)" or as "CPR Sch.2 (former CCR number)". Part 69 of the CPR contains provisions specifically applicable to receivers appointed by the court.

1-2   **Nature of the office.**   A receiver in a claim or other proceeding is an impartial person, appointed by the court to collect, protect and receive, pending the proceedings, the rents, issues and profits of land, personal estate or any other kind of asset, which it does not seem reasonable to the Court that either party should collect or receive, or for enabling the same to be distributed among the persons entitled.

1-3   **Jurisdiction.**   The jurisdiction of the Court of Chancery to appoint a receiver was founded on the inadequacy of the remedy to be obtained in the courts of ordinary jurisdiction; where that remedy was inadequate for the purposes of justice, the Court of Chancery would, on a proper case being made out, appoint a receiver.[1]

The courts of common law had not, under the former procedure, jurisdiction to appoint a receiver. But under the Supreme Court of Judicature Act 1873 s.16 (see now Senior Courts Act 1981[2] s.19 preserving the same position), all the jurisdiction of the Court of Chancery became vested in the High Court of Justice; and under s.25(8) of that Act (now s.37(1), (2) of the Act of 1981) a receiver may be appointed by order (originally an "interlocutory order," but in the 1981 Act expressed as "interlocutory or final"), in all cases in which it appears to the court to be just and convenient that such an order should be made; and any such order may be made either unconditionally, or upon such terms and conditions as the court thinks fit.

A receiver may now be appointed in any division of the High Court, the family court and the County Court. In one sense, the jurisdiction to appoint a receiver is enlarged[3]; under the CPR inconvenient rules have been relaxed and there is no

---

[1]   *Hopkins v Worcester, etc. Canal Co* (1868) L.R. 6 Eq. 437, 447 per Giffard LJ; *Cupit v Jackson* (1824) 13 Price 721, 734 per Alexander CB.

[2]   Formerly the Supreme Court Act 1981 and renamed by the Constitutional Reform Act 2005 s.59(5) Sch.11 Pt 1 para.1 and s.148(1).

[3]   *Anglo-Italian Bank v Davies* (1878) 9 Ch. D. 275, 293.

longer any limit to the jurisdiction to appoint a receiver upon application for an interim remedy.[4]

The main general powers of the courts to appoint a receiver which are derived from statute are set out in s.37 of the Act of 1981, Pt V of the Proceeds of Crime Act 2002 (the High Court) and ss.38 and 107 of the County Courts Act 1984 (the County Court). It has been stated that these statutory powers do not curtail the inherent power of the court to appoint receivers, they enlarge it.[5]

Principles governing the exercise of the jurisdiction. The appointment of a receiver has always been for the purpose of getting in and holding, or securing, funds or other property for the benefit of those entitled to such property. The appointment is inherently a temporary appointment pending payment. The question arises as to the principles upon which the jurisdiction should be exercised. Until 1986, it was thought that this had been settled, in the sense that the principles were those upon which the Court of Chancery was accustomed to proceed.[6] In accordance with this view of the matter, a receiver could be appointed in any proceedings, without the commencement of special proceedings being necessary. It was no longer necessary for a judgment creditor to commence proceedings in the Chancery Division before obtaining the appointment of a receiver over an equitable interest,[7] but no receiver would be appointed in cases where the Court of Chancery would have had no jurisdiction to make the appointment, after the special proceedings had been instituted.[8] However, in *Parker v the London Borough of Camden*,[9] the Master of the Rolls departed from this view of the matter, and did not accept that the pre-Judicature Act practices of the Court of Chancery, or of any other court, "still ruled us from their graves". As he saw the matter, the jurisdiction, as a jurisdiction, was quite general, and in terms unlimited.[10] The other members of the court agreed with him as to the unlimited nature of the jurisdiction, and would have been ready and willing to appoint a receiver for the purpose of receiving rents due from a tenant, in order to enable breaches of landlords' covenants contained in the lease to be remedied, had not special circumstances been present affecting the landlord in that case.[11]

The decision in *Parker v London Borough of Camden*[12] therefore left the legal position in a state of uncertainty.

These uncertainties appear to have been largely resolved by the subsequent landmark decision of the Court of Appeal in *Masri v Consolidated Contractors International (UK) Ltd (No.2)*.[13] *Masri* decided that in considering the appointment of a receiver the demands of justice are the overriding consideration but that

1-4

4 CPR Pt 23.
5 *Cummins v Perkins* [1899]1 Ch. 16 at 20 per Lindley LJ.
6 *Holmes v Millage* [1893] 1 Q.B. 551; *Harris v Beauchamp* [1894] 1 Q.B. 801; *Edwards & Co v Picard* [1909] 2 K.B. 903; cf. *Smith v Tsakyris* [1929] W.N. 39.
7 *Smith v Cowell* (1880) 6 Q.B.D. 75.
8 *Holmes v Millage*, n.6, above; *Morgan v Hart* [1914] 2 K.B. 183.
9 *Parker v London Borough of Camden* [1986] Ch. 162 CA.
10 *Parker v London Borough of Camden*, 172–3.
11 *Parker v London Borough of Camden*, 177, 179.
12 *Parker v London Borough of Camden*, 177, 179.
13 *Masri v Consolidated Contractors International (UK) Ltd (No.2)* [2009] Q.B. 450. For a discussion of the principles laid down in *Masri* see *JSC VTB Bank v Skurikhin* [2015] EWHC 2131 (Comm) at [35]; and for an example where the appointment of a receiver would have exceeded the permissible limits of the jurisdiction, see *Taurus Petroleum Ltd v State Oil Marketing Co of the Ministry of Oil, Iraq* [2015] EWCA Civ 835 at [36]–[37].

the court does not have an unfettered power. The court is not bound by pre-Judicature Act 1873 jurisprudence which would prevent incremental development. The jurisdiction may be exercised by applying old principles to new situations. This jurisdiction allowed the court to appoint receivers in situations where no such receivers would have been possible before 1873. On the facts of *Masri* the court ordered the appointment of a receiver over future receipts from a defined asset. There is no longer a rule that an order can only be made in relation to property which is presently amenable to legal execution and may therefore include whatever is considered in equity to be an asset.

1-5   **Limitations on the court's discretion.**   However, the court is not now likely, any more than it would formerly have been, to appoint a receiver by way of equitable execution, over property the title to which is legal, merely because it affords a more convenient method of obtaining payment,[14] save under its statutory powers in this regard.[15] The jurisdiction will not be used unless there is some hindrance or difficulty in using normal processes of execution.[16] Nor will it appoint a receiver, merely because the property is not amenable to legal execution for reasons other than the equitable nature of the debtor's title[17]; nor will the court appoint a receiver, except in aid of existing rights.[18] A receiver may be appointed over an asset whether or not it is at the time amenable to execution at law.[19] A receiver will not be appointed over property associated with the charged property, but not itself charged, merely for convenience.[20]

The words "interlocutory order" (a term now no longer employed) in the successive statutory provisions were never confined in their meaning to an order made between commencement of action and final judgment, but meant an order other than an order made by way of final judgment in an action, whether such order was made before judgment or after.[21] The court cannot properly order disclosure, on an application for a receiver after judgment, though it may order production of documents necessary for working out the judgment.[22]

The court always had the same power of appointing a receiver at the trial of the action, as it had on interlocutory application.[23]

The jurisdiction of the court relative of the appointment of receivers, and the

---

[14]   *Morgan v Hart*, n.8, above and *Maclaine Watson & Co Ltd v International Tin Council* [1988] Ch. 1. See also *Cruz City I Mauritius Holdings v Unitech Ltd* [2014] EWHC 3131 (Comm) at [47]; and *JSC VTB Bank v Skurikhin* [2015] EWHC 2131 (Comm) at [35] where it was explained that "convenience" is a relevant consideration in deciding whether or not to appoint a receiver but it not the only one.

[15]   See Senior Courts Act 1981 s.37(4).

[16]   *Cruz City I Mauritius Holdings v Unitech Ltd* [2014] EWHC 3131 (Comm).

[17]   *Edwards & Co v Picard*, n.6, above.

[18]   *Philips v Jones* (1884) 28 S.J. 360. The local authority was charged with the duty of maintenance of the houses under the Housing Acts, so that a receiver of the houses could not be appointed by the court.

[19]   *Tasurruf Mevduati Sigorta Fonu v Merrill Lynch Bank and Trust Co (Cayman) Ltd* [2012] 1 W.L.R. 1721 at [56].

[20]   *Britannia Building Society v Crammer* [1997] B.P.I.R. 596.

[21]   *Smith v Cowell* (1880) 6 Q.B.D. 75, 78. They are new orders made in conferring "interim remedies" under CPR Pt 23.

[22]   *Korkis v Andrew Weir & Co* [1914] W.N. 99; if accounts have been referred to a special referee, application should be made to him or her.

[23]   *Re Prytherch* (1889) 42 Ch. D. 590.

authority to be given them, was further enlarged by the CPR,[24] where it is necessary to preserve property which is in dispute in pending actions,[25] or where it is the subject-matter of an arbitration.[26]

The court also has express power, under statutes, to appoint a receiver or a person upon whom the powers of a receiver may be conferred[27]; see also the Proceeds of Crime Act 2002,[28] under which various types of receiver can be appointed in aid of confiscation orders or to make a restraint order effective.

The court will not in general[29] entertain a claim by an encumbrancer in which a receiver only is claimed; there must be a claim for foreclosure or sale.[30] In other cases, substantive relief, in addition to a receiver, must be claimed, save in a few exceptional cases, e.g. where the appointment is made under the express provisions of a statute, or, semble, where the appointment is sought to preserve the assets of a deceased person, and the nominal defendant has not intermeddled with the assets.[31] The jurisdiction to appoint a receiver, like the jurisdiction to grant an injunction, is only exercisable for the purpose of protecting, or enforcing, a legal or equitable right, which will usually need to be represented by, or identifiable as, a cause of action.[32]

Object of appointment.   A receiver can only be properly appointed in a claim for the purpose of getting in and holding or securing funds or other property, which the court at the trial, or in the course of the claim, will have the power, and the means to distribute amongst, or making over to, the persons or person entitled thereto the property in dispute.[33] The object sought by such appointment is therefore the safeguarding of property for the benefit of those entitled to it.[34] There are two main classes of cases in which the appointment is made: **1-6**

(1)   to enable persons who possess rights over property to obtain the benefit of those rights and to preserve the property pending realisation, where ordinary legal remedies are defective[35]; and

(2)   to preserve property from some danger which threatens it.

Appointment to enforce right.   In the first class of cases are included those in which the court appoints a receiver at the instance of a mortgagee, whose principal is immediately payable or whose interest is in arrear.[36] Cases of equitable execution, i.e. where the appointment is made to enable a judgment creditor to obtain pay-   **1-7**

---

[24]   See now CPR Pt 69 and PD 69, and CPR Pt 23 and r.25.1(c).
[25]   *Leney & Sons Ltd v Callingham & John Thompson* [1908] 1 K.B. 79 at 84 per Farwell LJ.
[26]   Arbitration Act 1996 s.44(2)(e).
[27]   e.g. Railway Companies Act 1867 s.4 and Landlord and Tenant Act 1987 s.24(1)(b).
[28]   See e.g. Pinto and Evans, *Corporate Criminal Responsibility*, 3rd edn (Sweet & Maxwell, 2013), especially ch.9: "Confiscation, Restraint and Receivership – The Criminal Confiscation Regime".
[29]   See *Re Newport Construction Co Ltd* [1948] Ch. 217.
[30]   *Gasson and Hallagan v Jell* [1940] Ch. 248; *Re Newport, etc. Co*, n.29, above.
[31]   This exception is more apparent than real; for in most cases accounts should be asked for in the first instance.
[32]   *Channel Tunnel Group and France Manche SA v Balfour Beatty Construction* [1993] A.C. 334 HL, applied in *Mercantile Group (Europe) AG v Aiyela* [1994] Q.B. 366 CA.
[33]   *Evans v Coventry* (1854) 3 Drew 75; see, too, *Wright v Vernon* (1855) 3 Drew. 112.
[34]   *Tullett v Armstrong* (1836) 1 Keen 428; *Owen v Homan* (1853) 4 H.L.C. 997, 1032.
[35]   *Cummins v Perkins* [1899] 1 Ch. 16, 19.
[36]   *Re Crompton & Co Ltd* [1914] 1 Ch. 954.

ment out of property which cannot be reached by legal execution,[37] are within this class. In such cases, the appointment is made as a matter of course, as soon as the applicant's right is established; it is unnecessary to allege any danger to the property,[38] for the appointment of a receiver is necessary to enable the applicant to obtain that to which he is entitled. Cases in which the appointment is made under a statutory provision also fall within this class: so do cases where a receiver is appointed over the assets of a dissolved partnership. Where there is an alternative legal remedy, as in the case of legal mortgages,[39] the court has a discretion; but the appointment is now frequently made without proof of jeopardy.

1-8 **Appointment to preserve property.** The second class of cases includes those in which the appointment is made to preserve property and, where required, to ensure its proper management, pending litigation to decide the rights of the parties,[40] ; or

> (1) to prevent a scramble among those entitled, as where a receiver is appointed, pending a grant of probate or administration; or
> (2) to preserve property of persons under disability; or
> (3) where there is danger of the property being damaged or dissipated by those with the legal title, such as executors or trustees,[41] tenants for life, persons with a partial interest, such as partners, or the persons in control, as where the directors of a company with equal powers are at variance.[42]

In all cases within this second class, it is necessary to allege and prove some peril to the property; the appointment then rests on the discretion of the court.[43] In exercising its discretion, the court proceeds with caution, and is governed by a view of all the circumstances. No rule can be laid down as to whether the court will or will not interfere by this kind of interim protection of the property. Where, indeed, the property is, as it were, *in medio*, in the enjoyment of no one, it is the common interest of all parties that the court should prevent a scramble, and a receiver will readily be appointed: as, for instance, over the property of a deceased person, pending litigation as to the right to probate or administration.

1-9 **Balancing the rights claimed by the parties.** Where the object of the claimant is to assert a right to property of which the defendant is in enjoyment, the case presents more difficulty. The court, if it takes possession at the instance of the claimant, may be doing a wrong to the defendant; in some cases an irreparable wrong. If the claimant should eventually fail in establishing his right against the defendant, the court may by its interim interference have caused mischief to the defendant, for which the subsequent restoration of the property may afford no adequate

---

[37] The court has always had jurisdiction to protect a fund for the benefit of a person entitled to be paid out of it *Cummins v Perkins* [1899] 1 Ch. 16.

[38] *Re Crompton & Co Ltd* [1914] 1 Ch. 954.

[39] *Pratchett v Drew* [1924] 1 Ch. 280; and para.2-21, below.

[40] *Tullett v Armstrong*, at 138; *Owen v Homan* 1032, see at n.34, above; *Att.-Gen. v Schonfeld*, unreported, 1979: Order of Walton J of 13 July 1979, referred to S.C. [1980] 1 W.L.R. 1182.

[41] Ch.2, s.2.

[42] *Stanfield v Gibbon* [1925] W.N. 11. See also *Featherstone v Cooke* (1873) L.R. 16 Eq. 298; *Trade Auxiliary Co v Vicker* (1873) L.R. 16 Eq. 303; *Re a Company (No.00596 of 1986)* (1986) 2 B.C.C. 99063.

[43] *Greville v Fleming* (1845) 2 J. & L. 335; *Re Prytherch* (1889) 42 Ch. D. 590; *Re Henry Pound, Son & Hutchins* (1889) 42 Ch. D. 402.

compensation.[44] Where the evidence on which the court is to act is very clearly in favour of the claimant, then the risk of eventual injury to the defendant is very small, and the court does not hesitate to interfere. Where there is more doubt, there is, of course, more difficulty. The question is one of degree, as to which, therefore, it is impossible to lay down any precise or unvarying rule.[45] To avoid damage capable of being caused by the appointment, the court may appoint a protective regime, supervised by an independent accountant.[46]

If the court is satisfied, upon the materials it has before it, that the applicant has established a good prima facie title, and:

(1) that the property the subject-matter of the proceedings will be in danger, if left until the trial in the possession or under the control[47] of the party against whom the appointment of the receiver is asked for,[48] or

(2) that there is at least some reason to apprehend that the party who makes the application will be in a worse situation if the appointment of a receiver be delayed,[49]

the appointment of a receiver is almost a matter of course.[50] If there is no danger to the property, and no fact is in evidence to show the necessity or expediency of appointing a receiver, a receiver will not be appointed.[51]

The duty of the court, upon an application for a receiver, is merely to protect the property for the benefit of the person or persons to whom the court, when it has all the materials necessary for a determination, shall think it properly belongs.[52] On application for a receiver, the court will not prejudice the claim,[53] or say what view it will take at the trial.[54] Indeed, the court will not appoint a receiver at the instance of a person whose right is disputed, where the effect of the order would be to establish that right, even if the court be satisfied that the person against whom the demand is made is fencing off the claim.[55] Nor will the appointment be made where it might affect legal rights: formerly a receiver would not, for instance, have been appointed merely to prevent an executor exercising his right of retainer.[56]

Postponed operation of appointment. In an appropriate case, an appointment **1-10** of a receiver may be made immediately, but with directions that the receiver shall not give security, nor take possession of the assets, until the expiration of a limited

---

44 See *Marshall v Charteris* [1920] 1 Ch. 520.
45 *Owen v Homan*, n.34 above, 1932 per Lord Lanworth; see also *Don King Productions Inc v Warren (No.3)* [2000] B.C.C. 263.
46 See n.45.
47 *Cummins v Perkins* [1899] 1 Ch. 16; *Leney & Sons Ltd v Callingham & Thompson* [1908] 1 K.B. 79.
48 *Evans v Coventry* (1854) 5 D.M. & G. 911.
49 *Thomas v Davies* (1847) 11 Beav. 29.
50 *Real and Personal Advance Co v M'Carthy & Smith* (1879) 27 W.R. 706.
51 See *Whitworth v Whyddon* (1850) 2 Mac. & G. 52; *Wright v Vernon* (1855) 3 Drew 112; *Micklethwait v Micklethwait* (1857) 1 De. G. & J. 504.
52 *Blakeney v Dufaur* (1851) 15 Beav. 40.
53 *Huguenin v Baseley* (1808) 13 Ves. 105.
54 *Fripp v Chard Ry* (1853) 11 Hare. 241; *Skinner's Company v Irish Society* (1836) 1 My. & Cr. 162.
55 *Greville v Fleming* (1845) 2 J. & L. 335: see *Marshall v Charteris* [1920] 1 Ch. 520.
56 *Re Wells* (1890) 45 Ch. D. 569. The right of retainer was abolished by the Administration of Estates Act 1971 s.10.

time.[57] Normally, however, the appointment *will not be made until there are moneys for the receiver to receive.*[58]

1-11 **Conduct of applicant.** The court, on the application for a receiver, always looks at the conduct of the party who makes the application, and will usually refuse to interfere, unless that person's conduct has been free from blame.[59] Parties who have acquiesced in property being enjoyed against their own alleged rights cannot, except in special circumstances, come to the court for a receiver.[60]

1-12 **Defendant submitting to order.** The court may abstain from appointing a receiver, on the submission of the defendant to an order to pay money into court,[61] or to the claimant,[62] or to deal with moneys as the court shall direct,[63] or to pay an occupation rent.[64]

1-13 **Pleading and practice.** The practice in respect of applications by mortgagees for possession on the appointment of a receiver is prescribed by the provisions of Pt 55 of the CPR.[65]

Provided the proper parties are before the court,[66] technical objections as to parties are not an answer to the application for a receiver, if a case for the appointment of a receiver is shown[67]: if the objection is a formal one, and such as may be removed by amendment,[68] the court will not stay its hand.

The written evidence should show that all parties with an interest in the property are before the court[69]; but if a sufficient case is made out, the appointment may be made in the absence of some of the persons interested.

If the subject of the action, in respect of which a receiver is sought, is a matter of public interest, the Attorney-General should be made a party.[70]

If a receiver is claimed generally, the court may grant the claim so far as is proper, or in a limited form.[71]

Where a receiver has been appointed generally, it is unnecessary, when the action comes on upon further consideration, to insert in the minutes a direction to continue the receiver.[72] So, also, a receiver appointed on an interim application

---

[57] *Re Crompton & Co Ltd* [1914] 1 Ch. 954 per Warrington J at 967.
[58] *Re Knott End Railway Act 1898* [1901] 2 Ch. 8 (railway not yet open for public traffic).
[59] See *Baxter v West* (1858) 28 L.J. Ch. 169; *Wood v Hitchings* (1840) 2 Beav. 289.
[60] *Gray v Chaplin* (1826) 2 Russ. 126, 147; *Skinners' Company v Irish Society*, n.54.
[61] *Curling v Marquis Townshend* (1816) 19 Ves. 628; *Palmer v Vaughan* (1818) 3 Swans. 173.
[62] *Pritchard v Fleetwood* (1815) 1 Mer. 54.
[63] *Earl Talbot v Hope Scott* (1858) 4 K. & J. 96.
[64] *Porter v Lopes* (1877) 7 Ch. D. 358; *Real and Personal Advance Co v M'Carthy* (1879) 27 W.R. 706.
[65] See the Civil Procedure (Amendment) Rules 2001 (SI 2001/256), revoking RSC Ord.88.
[66] See *Mukjerjee v Giri* (1927) 55 L.R. Ind. App. 131.
[67] *Evans v Coventry* (1854) 5 D.M. & G. 911; *Hamp v Robinson* (1865) 3 D.J. & S 97; *Re Johnson* (1866) L.R. 1 Ch. App. 325.
[68] Under CPR Pt 17.
[69] *Gray v Chaplin* (1826) 2 Russ. 126.
[70] *Gray v Chaplin* (1826) 2 Russ. 147, n.69, above; *Skinners' Company v Irish Society* (1836) 1 My & Cr. 162; see also *Re Chamberlain's Settlement* [1921] 2 Ch. 533.
[71] *Major v Major* (1844) 8 Jur. 797.
[72] See *Re Underwood* (1889) 37 W.R. 428; but if the further consideration disposes of the matter, provision should be made for discharge of the receiver.

before judgment need not be continued by the judgment,[73] unless the appointment was in the first instance an interim appointment only.[74] If the judgment continues a receiver who has been appointed until judgment or further order, this is virtually a new appointment, and further security must be given.[75]

The practice on the appointment, the effect of the order, and other topics are dealt with at length in subsequent chapters.[76] The procedure of the Queen's Bench Division in relation to the appointment of a receiver is, as far as possible, analogous to the procedure in like circumstances of the Chancery Division.[77]

Concurrent claims.   The High Court (and the county court in mortgage cases)   **1-14**
have jurisdiction to appoint a receiver in a proper case, although another court has already appointed a receiver over the same property in a concurrent claim,[78] and will stay further proceedings in such concurrent claim if in the circumstances of the case they are vexatious.[79] Thus in one case an equitable mortgagee had commenced an action in the Palatine Court and obtained a receiver therein ex parte, after a writ had, to his knowledge, been issued in a debenture holder's action in the Chancery Division relative to the same, amongst other, property. Parker J, who had appointed a receiver in the Chancery action, without knowledge of the order made in the Palatine action, restrained the plaintiff in the latter action from further proceeding therewith, on the ground that all matters in dispute could be adjusted in the Chancery action, whereas some only of them could be dealt with in the Palatine action, and that the conduct of the plaintiff in the latter action was in the circumstances vexatious: this decision was affirmed by the Court of Appeal.[80]

The Crown.   No receiver by way of equitable execution can be appointed against   **1-15**
the Crown.[81] For relief, analogous to attachment, which may be obtained against the Crown, see Ch.2 below.

Foreign Sovereigns.   The submission to arbitration of a foreign Sovereign does   **1-16**
not enable the court to appoint a receiver over property of the Sovereign within the jurisdiction to enforce payment of money or costs; but it is submitted that a receiver might be appointed over property which is the subject of litigation to which the Sovereign is a party,[82] or which is the subject-matter of the arbitration.

Costs.   The court, in its discretion, may either: **1-17**

   (1)   deal with the costs of an application for a receiver at the time of the application[83]; or
   (2)   order the costs of the application to be costs in the claim; or

---

[73]   *Davies v Vale of Evesham Preserves* [1895] W.N. 105; 73 L.T. 150; 43 W.R. 645.
[74]   *Cruse v Smith* (1879) 24 S.J. 121.
[75]   *Brinsley v Lynton Hotel Co* [1895] W.N. 53.
[76]   See Chs 4, 5 and 6, below.
[77]   *Walmsley v Mundy* (1884) 13 Q.B.D. 807. As to appointment in matrimonial causes, see Ch.2, below.
[78]   *Nothard v Proctor* (1875) 1 Ch. D. 4.
[79]   *Re Connolly Bros Ltd* [1911] 1 Ch. 731.
[80]   *Re Connolly Bros Ltd*, n.79, above; the proper course where such an order has been made is to apply in the concurrent action for the discharge of the receiver appointed therein.
[81]   Crown Proceedings Act 1947 s.25(4).
[82]   See *Duff Development Co v Kelantan Government* [1923] 1 Ch. 385 CA; on appeal [1924] A.C. 797; cf. *Re Suarez* [1917] 2 Ch. 131.
[83]   *Goodman v Whitcomb* (1820) 1 J. & W. 589; *Wilson v Wilson* (1838) 2 Keen 249; *Wood v Hitch-*

(3)   reserve the costs,[84] even although the application is refused.[85]

The former practice[86] was that where no direction as to costs was given, the party making a successful motion was entitled to costs as costs in the action, but the party opposing was not; where the motion failed, the party moving was not, in the absence of express direction, but the party opposing was, entitled to costs as costs in the action; where the motion was not opposed, the costs of both parties were costs in the action.[87] Although an express order of the court is now necessary in every case,[88] these principles are still usually followed.[89]

The respondent to an abandoned application is entitled to the costs thereof, although he or she has given no notice of his or her claim to such costs.[90]

Where, at the trial, an application for a receiver was unsuccessful, but the plaintiff was successful on another claim, he was ordered to pay the costs, so far as increased by the application for a receiver.[91]

1-18   **Courts having jurisdiction in claims by mortgagees.**   Until October 2001, possession claims by mortgagees were all assigned to the Chancery Division.[92] By virtue of the amendment of the CPR,[93] such proceedings (now defined as possession claims, that is claims for the recovery of possession of land (including buildings or part of buildings)[94]) commenced on or after that date must normally be commenced in the county court for the district where the property is situated, unless justified by exceptional circumstances.[95] Circumstances which may, in an appropriate case, justify starting a claim in the High Court are if:

(1)   there are complicated disputes of fact;
(2)   there are points of law of general importance; or
(3)   the claim is against trespassers, and there is a substantial risk of public disturbance or of serious harm to persons or property, which properly require immediate determination.[96]

The value of the property, or the amount of the financial claim, may also be relevant factors, but these factors alone will not normally justify starting the claim in the High Court.[97]

1-19   **Appeals.**   In most cases an appeal lies to the Court of Appeal (but now only with

---

ings (1840) 4 Jur. 858.

84   *Hewett v Murray* (1885) 54 L.J. Ch. 572; *Tillett v Nixon* (1883) 25 Ch. D. 238.
85   *Chaplin v Young* (1862) 6 L.T. 97.
86   *Baxter v West* (1858) 28 L.J. Ch. 169; *Coope v Cresswell* (1863) 12 W.R. 299.
87   See *Corcoran v Witt* (1872) L.R. 13 Eq. 53; cf. *Grimston v Timms* (1870) 18 W.R. 747, 781. See also Morgan and Wurzburg, *Law of Costs in the Chancery Division*, pp.47–55. As to county court practice, see *Friis v Paramount Bagwash Co (No.2)* [1940] 2 K.B. 654, 657.
88   See former RSC Ord.62 r.3 and the structure of the costs provisions of Pt 44 and following of the CPR.
89   In the CPR context, references to "motion" can be treated as references to an application and references to "an action" as references to a claim.
90   *Hinde v Power* [1913] W.N. 184.
91   *Re New York Taxicab Co* [1913] 1 Ch.1.
92   See the now revoked CPR Sch.1 RSC Ord.88 r.2.
93   RSC Ord.88 was revoked, with effect from 15 October 2001, by the Civil Procedure (Amendment No.4) Rules 2001 (SI 2001/2792), and replaced by CPR Pt 55.
94   CPR r.55.1(1).
95   CPR PD 55A at 55.3 para.1.1.
96   CPR PD 55A at 55.3 para.1.3.
97   CPR PD 55A at 55.3 para.1.4.

permission) from an order granting or refusing the appointment of a receiver.[98] For an order of the Court of Appeal appointing a receiver, see *Hyde v Warden*:[99] and for an order of the House of Lords, see *Houlditch v Donegall (Marquess)*.[100] An appeal will equally lie, where it is the personality of the receiver which is in question; but it requires a very strong case before the court will interfere with the discretion of the judge in this respect.[101]

---

[98] Part IV of Access to Justice Act 1999; CPR Pt 52. In certain types of proceedings the CPR do not apply or apply only to a limited extent, see, e.g. proceedings to which the Insolvency Rules 2016 apply.

[99] (1876) 1 Ex.D. 309.

[100] (1834) 2 Cl. & F. 470.

[101] *Re New Zealand Midland Ry Co* (1879) 13 T.L.R. 212.

Chapter 2

IN WHAT CASES A RECEIVER WILL BE APPOINTED

Section 1: In the Case of Minors[1]

2-1   A legal estate in land cannot be vested in a minor[2]: it must be vested either in trustees of land[3] or in Settled Land Act trustees as statutory owners.[4] No new Settled Land Act settlements can be created after commencement of the Trusts of Land and Appointment of Trustees Act 1996.[5] Any land which as at the date of commencement of the 1996 Act remained vested in the grantor by reason of the Settled Land Act 1925 s.27(1)[6] will be held on trust for the minor, the conveyance ceasing to be treated as an agreement to execute a settlement.[7] The principles and practice relating to the appointment of a receiver against trustees and executors will, therefore, apply where the protection of a minor's property is necessary. A "trust of land" (which replaced the "trust for sale") means any trust of property which consists of or includes land, and its trustees are termed "trustees of land".[8]

Where a minor is beneficially entitled to any property, the court, with a view to the application of the capital or income for his or her maintenance, may by statute appoint a person to convey, or to vest the right to transfer, stock or shares or things in action, or to receive dividends or to sue to recover a thing in action.[9] Where this provision could apply, application should be made under this provision, and not for the appointment of a receiver generally.

Section 2: In The Case of Executors and Trustees

2-2   **Grounds of appointment.**   The court will, upon a proper case being made out, dispossess an executor or trustee of the trust estate by appointing a receiver, but it

---

[1]   That is to say, a person who has not attained the age of 18 (formerly entitled "infants"): Family Law Reform Act 1969 s.1.

[2]   Law of Property Act 1925 s.1(6).

[3]   See Trusts of Land and Appointment of Trustees Act 1996 s.2 and Sch.1 paras 1 and 2.

[4]   Settled Land Act 1925 ss.1(1)(ii)(d), (2), 26, and Sch.2 para.3.

[5]   Trusts of Land and Appointment of Trustees Act 1996 s.2.

[6]   Prior to that date a conveyance to a minor operated as an agreement to execute a settlement in favour of the minor: Law of Property Act 1925 s.19(1); Settled Land Act 1925 s.27(1).

[7]   Trusts of Land and Appointment of Trustees Act 1996 s.2 and Sch.1 para.1(3).

[8]   Formerly under Law of Property Act 1925, now under Trusts of Land and Appointment of Trustees Act 1996 s.1; the Act repeals much of Law of Property Act 1925.

[9]   Trustee Act 1925 s.53, which enables a disentailing assurance to be executed for enabling money to be raised for the benefit of the minor tenant in tail: *Re Gower's Settlement* [1934] Ch. 365, and cf. *Re Meux* [1958] Ch. 154. Where there is capital money, an order may be made for its application for advancement or education of a minor tenant in tail under Settled Land Act 1925 s.64; cf. *Re Scarisbrick's Resettlement Estates* [1944] Ch. 229.

will only do so on substantial grounds. It is for the testator or creator of the trust, and not for the court, to say in whom the trust for the administration of the property shall be reposed. A strong case must be made out to induce the court to dispossess a trustee or executor who is willing to act.[10] It must clearly be shown that the nature and position of the property is such as to warrant the interference of the court.[11] Thus, the court will not, at the instance of one of several parties interested in an estate, displace a competent trustee, or take possession from him, unless he or she has wilfully or ignorantly permitted the property to be placed in a state of insecurity, which due care or conduct would have prevented. It is not enough that the estate may have depreciated in value, and that the incumbrances thereon may have been increasing, if the management of the trustees does not appear to have been improper.[12]

It is not sufficient cause for the appointment of a receiver that one of several trustees has disclaimed, unless the remaining trustees consent to such appointment[13]; nor that the trustees or executors are "poor men in mean circumstances"[14]; nor that, being trustees for sale, they have let the purchaser into possession before they received the purchase-moneys, for the court will not necessarily infer this to be misconduct.[15]

Nor is it a sufficient cause for the appointment of a receiver that one of several trustees is inactive,[16] or has gone abroad, though where a sole executor or trustee, or all the trustees, are out of the jurisdiction, a receiver may be appointed where there is default by the agent here in rendering accounts.[17] Where a sole trustee, or one of several trustees, is an enemy or in enemy territory, a receiver can be appointed in case of urgency to protect the property: but this is rarely necessary; the proper course is to appoint or apply for the appointment of a new trustee and for a vesting order. This jurisdiction has been exercised in the case of a foreign testator, even if the trustees, who were in enemy territory, had been appointed by a foreign court, where there were assets within the jurisdiction. For a fuller discussion on this subject, see note on "Enemies" at para.2-124, below.

Misconduct, etc. a ground for a receiver.   If any misconduct, waste, or improper   2-3
disposition of the assets can be shown,[18] or if it appears that the trust property has been improperly managed, or is in danger of being lost[19]—e.g. owing to the

---

[10]   *Middleton v Dodswell* (1806) 13 Ves. 266; *Smith v Smith* (1836) 2 Y. & C. 361; *Bainbridge v Blair* (1841) 4 L.J. Ch. 207.

[11]   *Whitworth v Whyddon* (1850) 2 Mac. & G. 52.

[12]   *Barkley v Lord Reay* (1843) 2 Hare. 306.

[13]   *Browell v Reed* (1842) 1 Hare. 434.

[14]   *Anon.* (1806) 12 Ves. 4; *Howard v Papera* (1815) 1 Madd. 142.

[15]   *Browell v Reed*, n.13, above.

[16]   See n.15 but cf. *Tait v Jenkins* (1842) 1 Y. & C. Ch. 492. If he is absent from the UK for 12 months, a new trustee may be appointed: see Trustee Act 1925 s.36.

[17]   *Noad v Backhouse* (1843) 2 Y. & C.Ch. 529; *Smith v Smith* (1853) 10 Hare 71; *Westby v Westby* (1847) 2 Coop.t.Cott. 210; *Dickins v Harris* [1866] W.N. 93; 14 L.T. 98.

[18]   *Anon.* (1806) 12 Ves. 4 per Sir W. Grant; see, too, *Oldfield v Cobbett* (1835) 4 L.J. Ch. 272. Query whether this would include distribution of the estate in accordance with the terms of the will within six months from the grant, without making provision for a possible claim under the Inheritance (Provision for Family and Dependants) Act 1975 (see *Re Simson* [1950] Ch. 38), or s.31 of the Matrimonial Causes Act 1973.

[19]   *Middleton v Dodswell* (1806) 13 Ves. 266, 276; *Colebourne v Colebourne* (1876) 1 Ch. D. 690.

insolvency of the executor[20]—or if it can be satisfactorily established that parties in a fiduciary position have been guilty of a breach of duty, there is a sufficient foundation for the appointment of a receiver.[21]

In exceptional circumstances where trustees of property of a trade union, which had been fined for contempt of court, transferred funds overseas to avoid sequestration for contempt of court, the court, on a without notice application, removed the trustees and appointed a receiver.[22]

Similarly, a receiver may be appointed at the instance of sureties to an administration guarantee, where the administrator threatens to distribute the estate without providing for a contingent liability.[23]

The appointment of a receiver pending a grant of probate or letters of administration is dealt with below.[24]

Where a portion of a trust fund has been lost, the loss is prima facie evidence of a breach of duty on the part of the trustees, sufficient to authorise the interference of the court by the appointment of a receiver.[25] So, also, it has been held to be a good ground for the appointment of a receiver that an executor or trustee has omitted to raise a certain sum as, according to the will of the testator, the executor should have done for the maintenance and education of infant legatees,[26] or that the executor has left a considerable portion of it outstanding on improper securities[27]; though in all these cases the matter may be dealt with by the appointment of new trustees, or in a proper case by a vesting order under various statutory provisions.[28] So, also, a receiver will be appointed, if it appears that the trustee has an undue bias towards or against one of the contending parties,[29] or where, in consequence of disputes among the trustees, the payment of rents has been permitted to fall into arrear,[30] or where a trustee, in spite of repeated applications, with no proper excuse refuses or neglects to render an account to the beneficiaries.[31]

Where a man, who had accepted and held moneys for particular persons upon certain trusts, afterwards denied the legality of the trusts on which he held the moneys, the court appointed a receiver.[32]

A creditor in an administration action cannot, unless a case of waste of assets be shown or some other special case be made out, have a receiver appointed, merely because the administrator will not admit assets, or, formerly, had been paying debts and preferring creditors when the estate was insolvent,[33] though the case would have

---

[20] *Gawthorpe v Gawthorpe* [1878] W.N. 91; *Re H's Estate, H v H* (1876) Ch. D. 276.
[21] *Evans v Coventry* (1854) 5 D.M. & G. 911; *Bainbridge v Blair* (1841) 10 L.J. Ch. 193; Beav. 421; *Nothard v Proctor* (1875) 1 Ch. D. 4; *Hamilton v Girdlestone* [1876] W.N. 202.
[22] *Clarke v Heathfield* [1985] I.C.R. 203; *Clarke v Heathfield (No.2)* [1985] I.C.R. 606.
[23] *Re Anderson-Berry, Harris v Griffith* [1928] Ch. 290, where, under the old procedure, an administration bond had been given.
[24] See para.2-13, below.
[25] *Evans v Coventry* (1854) 5 D.M. & G. 911.
[26] *Richards v Perkins* (1839) 3 Y. & C. 299; *Hart v Tulk* (1849) 6 Hare. 611.
[27] See n.26, above.
[28] e.g. Settled Land Act 1925 ss.12(1), 16(7): Administration of Estates Act 1925 s.43(2).
[29] *Earl Talbot v Hope Scott* (1858) 4 K. & J. 96.
[30] *Wilson v Wilson* (1837) 2 Keen 249.
[31] See also CPR Pt 64 and PD6A—Estates, Trusts and Charities, para.3.2.
[32] *Sheppard v Oxenford* (1855) 1 K. & J. 491.
[33] *Phillips v Jones* (1884) 28 S.J. 360; *Re Harris* (1887) 35 W.R. 710; 56 L.J. Ch. 754. The dictum of Jessel MR to the contrary in *Re Radcliffe* (1878) 7 Ch. D. 733, cannot be regarded as good law; *Re Wells* (1890) 45 Ch. D. 569, 574. The right of preference was abolished by Administration of Estates

been otherwise, if any preferential debts[34] were being disregarded. Nor would the court formerly have interfered with an executor's legal right of retainer by the appointment of a receiver, in cases where it was not shown that the assets were being wasted.[35] It is only in cases of improper conduct, or danger to the assets reasonably proved, that the court will interfere by appointing a receiver.[36]

Bankruptcy, etc. of trustee.   If a sole executor or trustee becomes bankrupt, (or, it would seem, enters into any form of insolvency arrangement with his creditors) there is a case for the appointment of a receiver.[37] But if a testator has selected an insolvent debtor as his executor, with full knowledge of his insolvency, the court will not, on the bare fact of the insolvency alone, interfere by appointing a receiver,[38] though the fact that a testator has not altered a will made before the insolvency, after knowledge of the insolvency, is not in itself sufficient to deter the court from appointing a receiver[39]; and the court may make the appointment where the estate is barely sufficient for creditors.[40] An interim order may be refused where some parties refuse to join in the application, although the personal representative was not nominated by the testator but is the administrator of an executrix.[41]

2-4

Poverty, etc. of trustee.   Although it is not a sufficient cause for the appointment of a receiver that an executor or trustee is poor or in mean circumstances,[42] the case was held to be different if an executor or administrator be proved to be of bad character and drunken habits, as well as poor.[43]

2-5

Early cases, where a receiver was appointed on the sole ground that an executrix was married to a man who was insolvent or out of the jurisdiction,[44] are obsolete.[45] But, as in any other case of undue influence, if either an executor or an executrix is proved to be under the influence of a fraudulent, or possibly even a necessitous, spouse or civil partner,[46] this would presumably be a factor influencing the court on an application to appoint a receiver on the ground of jeopardy.

Receiver appointed by consent.   If all the *cestuis que trust*, or parties beneficially interested in an estate, concur in the application for a receiver, and the trustee

2-6

Act 1971 s.10. An order for administration can now be speedily obtained under CPR Pt 64, or in bankruptcy under Insolvency Act 1986 s.421 (and s.421A); see the Administration of Insolvent Estates of Deceased Persons Order 1986 (SI 1986/1999).

[34] See Insolvency Act 1986 s.386 and Sch.6.

[35] *Re Wells*, n.33, approved in *Re Stevens* [1898] Ch. 162, 173. The right of retainer was abolished by Administration of Estates Act 1971 s.10.

[36] *Baird v Walker* (1890) 35 S.J. 56; 90 L.T. 56.

[37] *Re Johnson* (1886) L.R. 1 Ch. App. 325; *Re Hopkins* (1881) 19 Ch. D. 61; or an injunction may be granted: *Bowen v Phillips* [1897] 1 Ch. 164. The court may, if it considers it expedient, appoint a receiver, instead of directing the return of effects alleged to be vested in an executor which have been taken possession of by a trustee in bankruptcy.

[38] *Gladdon v Stoneman* (1808) 1 Madd. 143n.; *Stainton v Carron Co* (1864) 18 Beav. 146, 161.

[39] *Langley v Hawke* (1820) 5 Madd. 46.

[40] *Oldfield v Cobbett* (1835) 4 L.J. Ch. 272.

[41] *Smith v Smith* (1836) 2 Y. & C. 361.

[42] See para.2-2, above.

[43] *Everett v Prytherch* (1841) 12 Sim. 363; and see *Dillon v Lord Mountcashell* (1727) 4 Bro.P.C. 306.

[44] *Taylor v Allen* (1741) 1 Atk. 213; see *Bathe v Bank of England* (1858) 4 K. J. 564.

[45] Law Reform (Married Women and Tortfeasors) Act 1935 Pt 1; Law of Property Act 1925 s.170, repealed by the Statute Law (Repeal) Act 1969.

[46] See Civil Partnership Act 2004.

consents, the court will make the order[47]; and will also so order if the only acting trustee consents, the others being abroad[48] or guilty of misconduct.[49] Similarly, where, of two trustees, one had died and the survivor refused to act, a receiver was appointed, in spite of the opposition of the representative of the deceased trustee, who had advanced money out of his own pocket to an annuitant under the will, in expectation of repayment out of the assets.[50]

2-7   **Other cases.**   Where two out of three trustees chose to act separately, and took securities in their own names, omitting that of the third trustee, a cestui que trust was held entitled to a receiver.[51] A receiver may also be appointed where the co-trustees cannot act through disagreement among themselves.[52] So too, where the trustees had to manage a business and were themselves not qualified to do so, but could not agree on appointing some person as manager, a receiver was appointed.[53]

2-8   **Settled land.**   Land which is subject to a settlement, within the meaning of the Settled Land Act 1925, is vested in the tenant for life upon the trusts of the settlement, or, if there is no tenant for life of full age, in the trustees as statutory owners; or on the death of a tenant for life, where the settlement continues to exist, in his special personal representatives. The appointment of a receiver against a tenant for life will still, as under the old law, be made where he does not apply the income in keeping down incumbrances,[54] or omits to keep leaseholds in repair according to the covenants in the leases.[55] In cases where a tenant for life does not fulfil his obligations to maintain and insure improvements under s.88 of the Settled Land Act 1925, it is conceived that a receiver will be appointed.[56] A receiver has been refused where a tenant for life pulled down houses, but was rebuilding them.[57]

Under the old law, a receiver was appointed where a tenant for life refused to produce deeds to enable a term for raising portions to be created. A vesting order can now be obtained, where the tenant for life refuses or neglects to create a legal estate required for giving effect to any provision of the settlement,[58] and a similar provision applies in the case of personal representatives[59]; similarly, where a tenant for life or other person refuses to execute any instrument required for vesting the land in the person entitled to have the land vested in him[60]; where a tenant for life has ceased, due to bankruptcy, assignment or otherwise, to have a substantial

---

[47]   *Brodie v Barry* (1811) 3 Mer. 695.
[48]   *Tidd v Lister* (1854) 5 Madd. 433.
[49]   *Middleton v Dodswell* (1806) 13 Ves. 266.
[50]   *Palmer v Wright* (1846) 10 Beav. 234.
[51]   *Swale v Swale* (1856) 22 Beav. 584.
[52]   *Bagot v Bagot* (1841) 10 L.J. Ch. 116; *Day v Croft* 1839 (unreported); *Lewin on Trusts*, 16th edn, p.646; as to the power of the majority (who may be assisted by injunction), see *Re Whiteley* [1910] 1 Ch. 600.
[53]   *Hart v Denham* [1871] W.N. 2.
[54]   See note (a) to *Giffard v Hort* (1804) 1 Sch. & Lef. 386, 407, and *Gresley v Adderley* (1818) 1 Swans. 573; *Bertie v Abingdon* (1817) 3 Mer. 560; *Shore v Shore* (1859) 4 Drew. 501.
[55]   *Re Fowler* (1881) 16 Ch. D. 723.
[56]   An injunction and damages would be an alternative remedy.
[57]   *Micklethwait v Micklethwait* (1857) 1 De G. & J. 504.
[58]   Or, if he is outside the UK, or cannot be found: Settled Land Act 1925 s.16(7).
[59]   Administration of Estates Act 1925 s.43(2).
[60]   Settled Land Act 1925 s.12: e.g. where a tenant for life, who has surrendered his or her life interest, (or this has been done by the tenant for life's trustee in bankruptcy), to the next remainderman,

interest, the trustees can be authorised to exercise his powers.[61] These provisions usually enable an application of a receiver to be dispensed with, but pending the making of a vesting order, a receiver may be appointed in urgent cases.

Trust of land.   Land can no longer be held in undivided shares, and the interests of tenants in common now take effect behind "a trust of land".[62] The Trusts of Land and Appointment of Trustees Act 1996 substantially changed the law, where land is held by more than one person and where the interest of one co-owner (or more than one, but not all) has been charged to an outside party.[63] The former principle[64] that, save in exceptional circumstances, the wish of a trustee in bankruptcy or of a chargee of a co-owner to sell the property should prevail over the interests of the other co-owner or co-owners or their chargees, has been repealed, although it remains substantially in operation in the context of trustees in bankruptcy.[65]

2-9

On any application to the court by a chargee under the 1996 Act, to deal with land subject to a trust of land, the court has to have regard to four matters: (a) the intention of the creators of the trust; (b) the purposes for which the trust was created; (c) the welfare of minors occupying, or reasonably likely to occupy, the land; and (d) the interests of a secured creditor or of any beneficiary of the trust. The interest of a trustee in bankruptcy of a person holding an interest in land as co-owner is excluded from the ambit of the 1996 Act. If the application is made by the trustee in bankruptcy the considerations listed in s.335A of the Insolvency Act 1986 are taken into account.

Where the trustees of land are also the beneficiaries, and one is in possession and retaining the whole of the rents, a receiver may be appointed, as under the old law[66]; or the trustee in occupation might presumably be ordered to pay an occupation rent[67]; or give security[68]; similarly with joint tenants both in law and equity, whose equitable interests are subject to a trust of land.

Where land is held for the purposes of trade, a receiver is appointed on the same principle as in partnership cases.[69] There may be a partnership in the trade, though not in land vested in one or more of the partners. Where the land is the subject-matter of the claim, a receiver may be appointed over both the land and the business, when that is the convenient course.[70]

Voluntary arrangements.   Under the previous law, a receiver was appointed

2-10

---

      refuses to convey: see *Re Shawdon Estates* [1930] 2 Ch. 24.
[61] See n.56, s.24, cf. *Re Thornhill's Settlement* [1941] Ch. 24.
[62] See the Trusts of Land and Appointment of Trustees Act 1996 ss.14, 15, replacing Law of Property Act 1925 s.30. Partition actions have been abolished.
[63] *Mortgage Corporation v Shaire* [2001] Ch. 747; [2000] B.P.I.R. 483, where Neuberger J considered that the decisions in *Re Citro* [1991] Ch. 142; CA; and *Lloyd's Bank v Byrne & Byrne* [1993] 1 F.L.R. 369 CA, did not apply to the 1996 Act s.15 of which had changed the law, giving the court "greater flexibility". However, a powerful consideration will be whether the creditor is receiving proper recompense for being kept out of his money, repayment of which is overdue (*Bank Of Ireland Home Mortgages Ltd v Bell* (2001) 2 All E.R. (Comm) 920: (2001) 2 F.L.R. 809: (2000) EG 151 (CS), CA. and *Pritchard Englefield (A Firm) v Steinberg* [2004] EWHC 1908 Ch.
[64] Law of Property Act 1925 s.30 (now repealed).
[65] Insolvency Act 1986 ss.335A, 336, 337 and cf. s.283A.
[66] *Norway v Rowe* (1816) 19 Ves. 144; *Sandford v Ballard* (1861) 30 Beav. 109.
[67] *Porter v Lopes* (1877) 7 Ch. D. 358.
[68] *Street v Anderton* (1793) 4 Bro.C.C. 414; *Murray v Cockerell* [1866] W.N. 223.
[69] *Jefferys v Smith* (1820) 1 Jac. & W. 298, 302.
[70] See *Roberts v Eberhardt* (1853) Kay 148, 159.

when the property of a debtor had been vested in trustees, under a deed of arrangement, for the benefit of his or her creditors, and the appointment was necessary for the protection of the property.[71] Although deeds of arrangement have now been abolished,[72] it is possible that where an individual or corporate debtor has entered into a voluntary arrangement with creditors, if property held by the supervisor or some other person is in need of protection, the appointment of a receiver may be necessary where mere replacement of the supervisor would not resolve the risk to the assets in question. Application would be made to the court having jurisdiction in bankruptcy or with jurisdiction to wind up the company (as the case may be).[73]

2-11   **Implied trusts.** In the case of misconduct by trustees, the court will appoint a receiver, as well where the trust arises by implication as where it is express.[74] An order for the appointment of a receiver of the rents and profits of an estate, for the purpose of accumulating a fund, was made where the tenant for life had fraudulently obtained a sum of stock to which the trustees of the settlement were entitled.[75]

In a case where, on proof of a secret trust, the court was satisfied that real and personal estate had been bequeathed on the faith of a promise made by the legatee that she would dispose of the property in favour of the plaintiffs, a receiver was appointed.[76]

2-12   **Pending proceedings abroad.** If one of the next-of-kin of a foreigner obtains administration here, pending proceedings abroad to ascertain who are entitled, an action for a receiver was held to be maintainable by a person also claiming as next-of-kin.[77]

SECTION 3: PENDING GRANT OF PROBATE OR LETTERS OF ADMINISTRATION

2-13   Formerly, during litigation in the Ecclesiastical Court as to probate or administration, the Court of Chancery would entertain a bill for the mere preservation of the property of the deceased until the litigation was determined, and would appoint a receiver, although the Ecclesiastical Court might itself, by appointing an administrator, have provided for the collection of the effects *pendente lite*.[78] It was, indeed, a matter of course, where no probate or administration had been granted, for the Court of Chancery to appoint a receiver, pending bona fide litigation in the Ecclesiastical Court to determine the right to probate or administration, unless a special case was made out for not doing so.[79] In cases where the representation was in contest, and no person had been appointed executor, or administrator, the court would

---

71   *Waterlow v Sharp* [1867] W.N. 64.

72   The Deeds of Arrangement Act 1914 was repealed by the Deregulation Act 2015.

73   For the statutory procedure for a remedy in the context of voluntary arrangements, see generally Pts 1 (Companies) and 8 (Individuals) of the Insolvency Act 1986.

74   See *Re One and All Sickness Association, The Times,* 12 and 18 December 1908, where a receiver of the property of an unregistered friendly society was appointed, it being held that the relationship of trustee and beneficiary existed. As to winding up, see *Re Victoria Society* [1913] 1 Ch. 167.

75   *Woodyatt v Gresley* (1836) 8 Sim. 180.

76   *Podmore v Gunning* (1836) 7 Sim. 644.

77   *Transatlantic Co v Pietroni* (1860) John 604. This would now be in proceedings for administration.

78   *Watkins v Brent* (1835) 1 Myl. & Cr. 97; *Wood v Hitchings* (1840) 2 Beav. 289; on appeal, 4 Jur. 858; *De FeuchÉres v Dawes* (1842) 5 Beav. 110.

79   *Watkins v Brent*, n.78, above; *Grimston v Turner* (1870) 18 W.R. 724; [1870] W.N. 93. Before the grant of administration, a receiver and manager may be appointed to carry on the business of an intestate: *Blackett v Blackett* (1871) 19 W.R. 559; *Re Wright* (1888) 32 S.J. 721.

interfere, not because of the contest, but because there was no proper person to receive the assets.[80] But the appointment was refused where the property was of trifling value or where no sufficient ground had been shown to warrant the interference of the court.[81]

Appointment of receiver before probate.   Under the CPR, probate proceedings in the High Court are assigned to the Chancery Division and probate claims in the County Court must only be started at a County Court hearing centre where there is also a Chancery district registry (or the County Court at Central London).[82] In order to protect the assets, the court will, in proceedings by a beneficiary or creditor against the persons named as executors in the will or entitled to a grant of letters of administration,[83] claiming a receiver, appoint one, pending the grant.[84] The probate claim form may claim administration after the grant has been made,[85] or after accounts; though of course no order for administration can be made before a grant has been obtained by the defendant. Where there is already a *lis pendens*,[86] the application should, prima facie, be made in that claim for an administrator *pendente lite*[87]; but the existence of such proceedings does not displace the jurisdiction to appoint a receiver.[88] But after an administrator pendente lite has been appointed, a receiver will only be appointed in special circumstances.[89] The appointment is an interim appointment only, and is usually termed to expire within a few days of a grant being obtained.[90]

2-14

In order to found jurisdiction to make the appointment, a claim must have been commenced, and the claim form must specifically claim a receiver[91]; the person named in the will as executor,[92] or the person entitled to take out administration,[93] and any other person who has intermeddled with the estate, should be made defendants. Where no will is known to exist and no successor on intestacy is known,

---

[80]   *Rendall v Rendall* (1841) 1 Hare. 152 per Wigram V-C; *Parkin v Seddons* (1873) L.R. 16 Eq. 34.

[81]   *Whitworth v Whyddon* (1850) 2 Mac. & G. 52.

[82]   CPR Pt 57 and CPR Practice Direction 57.

[83]   See further paras 2-16 ff, below.

[84]   *Re Oakes* [1917] 1 Ch. 230; *Re Wenge* [1911] W.N. 129; and see *Re Shephard* (1889) 43 Ch. D. 131; *Macleod v Lane* (1886) 2 T.L.R. 322; *Re Dawson* (1906) 75 L.J. Ch. 201; In the goods of *Pryse* [1904] P. 301; *Re Clark* [1910] 55 S.J. 64; [1910] W.N. 234. Under the old practice, it was held that an action to protect and also to administer the estate was irregular: *Overington v Ward* (1865) 34 Beav. 175.

[85]   per Eve J in *Re Wenge*, n.84, above. But, semble, this only applies where the defendant is an executor: cf. *Ingall v Moran* [1944] K.B. 160 CA.

[86]   A caveat, though warned, is not a *lis pendens* for this purpose: *Salter v Salter* [1896] P. 291.

[87]   *Re Parker* (1885) 54 L.J. Ch. 694; and see *In the goods of Moore* (1888) 13 P. D. 36; *Re Green* [1895] W.N. 69.

[88]   *Re Oakes*, n.84, above.

[89]   *Veret v Duprez* (1868) L.R. 6 Eq. 329; *Parkin v Seddons*, n.80, above. Both these cases were decided when the administrator *pendente lite* was appointed by the Probate Division of the High Court of Justice. The practice has now hardened against the appointment of a receiver in such circumstances. As to practice, where the receiver was appointed before the administrator *pendente lite*, see para.2-17, above.

[90]   *Re Clark*, n.84, above; but even under the old practice, a bill was not demurrable in such a case because it asked for a receiver generally: *Major v Major* (1844) 8 Jur. 797; the appointment may be extended if there is jeopardy, on the proper parties being added.

[91]   *Re Wenge*, n.84, above; *Re Oakes*, n.84, above.

[92]   *Re Sutcliffe* [1942] Ch. 453.

[93]   *Re Leask* (1891) 65 L.T. 199.

a person who has intermeddled with the estate would, it seems, be a sufficient defendant.[94]

On the other hand, if the proceedings are not directed to obtaining administration of the estate—for example, if they are based upon the allegation that the defendant is a constructive trustee—then such an appointment will not be made. The claimant must wait until there is a properly constituted representative, or there has been intermeddling by somebody in the estate.[95]

2-15   **Death of executor sole defendant.**   Upon the death of a sole executor against whom an action had been commenced for the administration of the estate of the testator, an interim receiver was appointed, pending a fresh grant being obtained, where the assets were in peril.[96] In such cases, a receiver will be appointed either before[97] or after[98] judgment, even though there is no living defendant on the record.[99]

2-16   **Pending proceedings to recall probate.**   If probate or administration has been granted, the circumstance that proceedings are pending to recall or revoke probate or administration, is not of itself a sufficient ground justifying the court, as of course, to interfere to prevent the parties, to whom probate or administration has been granted, from using their powers. In such a case, it is only in special circumstances that the court will make the appointment[100]; for where there is a legal title to receive, the court ought not to interfere, unless the legal title is abused, or there is evidence of intention to abuse it[101]: as, for instance, where a prima facie case of fraud is made out,[102] or where peril to the assets is shown, whether from insolvency or otherwise.[103]

A grant is neither impounded, nor withheld, on the ground of jeopardy; in such cases, therefore, application should be made for a receiver.[104] Such application was successfully made, where there appeared to be no executor or administrator in existence with power to act as such, notwithstanding that there was no ground laid for interference in respect of any improper conduct of the parties.[105] Where, accordingly, an executor, by agreeing with his opponents that the question as to the validity of the supposed testamentary papers should be tried in the suit to recall probate, had treated himself as not being a complete executor, a receiver was appointed. "If the question be whether the party claiming to be executor is so de jure or not, a receiver will be appointed."[106] A receiver was appointed upon the application of the actual executor, pending a suit to annul probate, upon the ground that the opposing party, by having given notice to the debtors to the estate not to pay to the ap-

---

[94]   cf. *Re Chalmers* [1921] W.N. 129.

[95]   *Fanto v Monteverde, The Times,* 26 April 1972.

[96]   *Re Clark*, n.84 above, following *Cash v Parker* (1879) 12 Ch. D. 293; *Re Shephard* (1889) 43 Ch. D. 131; and see *Mullane v Ahern* (1891) 28 L.R. Ir. 105.

[97]   *Re Clark*, n.84, above.

[98]   *Cash v Parker*, n.96, above.

[99]   *Re Clark*, n.84, above.

[100]   *Watkins v Brent* (1835) 1 Myl. & Cr. 97; *Newton v Ricketts* (1847) 11 Jur. 662; *Rendall v Rendall* (1841) 1 Hare. 152.

[101]   *Devey v Thornton* (1851) 9 Hare.222.

[102]   *Rutherford v Douglas* (1822) 1 Sim. & St. 111n.; *Watkins v Brent*, n.79, above.

[103]   *Ball v Oliver* (1813) 2 Ves. & B.; *Newton v Ricketts*, n.100; *Devey v Thornton*, n.101, above.

[104]   *In the Goods of Moxley* [1916] 2 Ir.R. 145.

[105]   *Watkins v Brent*, n.100, above.

[106]   *Rendall v Rendall* (1841) 1 Hare. 152 per Wigram V-C.

plicant, had by his own act produced an incapacity on the part of the executor to collect and preserve the assets.[107]

Upon these principles, a receiver would be granted, pending an application to revoke a grant of probate or administration to the estate of a tenant for life, as regards land continuing to be settled after his or her death,[108] where the grant has been obtained for an improper purpose or is being improperly employed. This will, however, rarely be necessary, as revocation is speedily obtained. Alternatively, a special or additional personal representative may be appointed under s.23 of the Administration of Estates Act 1925.

Administrator "pendente lite".   Under s.117 of the Senior Courts Act 1981,[109]   **2-17**
where any legal proceedings touching the validity of a will, or for obtaining, recalling or revoking any grant are pending, the High Court[110] may grant administration to an administrator who has all the powers of a general administrator,[111] other than the right of distributing the residue, and every such administrator is to be subject to the immediate control of the court and to act under its direction. Remuneration may be allowed.[112] Even if there is a life interest in the estate, it is not necessary to appoint more than one administrator *pendente lite*.[113] For the Chancery Division to have jurisdiction under this Act, there must be an actual *lis pendens* before it: the entering of a caveat, though warned by the executor, is not sufficient.[114] In either case, the difference is minimal: if there is a pending claim, the application will be made by application notice.

The appointment may be made on the application of a person not a party, e.g. a creditor, where the proceedings are likely to be prolonged,[115] or where the parties to the testamentary suit take no steps to bring it to trial.[116] In a case where there was a contest as to the validity of several wills made by a tenant for life, none of which affected the beneficial interest in the settled land, and the litigation was likely to be prolonged, the Settled Land Act trustees were appointed administrators *pendente lite* of the settled land without security, and with liberty to exercise all powers without leave of the court.[117]

The court has jurisdiction under the section to appoint the same person administrator and receiver *pendente lite* of the estates of a person whose sole executor has died, and of such executor, where a claim pending as to the testamentary dispositions of such executor, although there is no litigation pending relative to the estate of the original testator.[118]

Where the deceased died after 1897, a grant *pendente lite* has included both real

---

[107] *Marr v Littlewood* (1837) 2 Myl. & Cr. 454.
[108] See *Re Bridgett and Hayes' Contract* [1928] Ch. 163.
[109] Replacing Judicature Act 1925 s.63.
[110] See CPR Pt 57 and CPR PD 57.
[111] As to such powers, see Administration of Estates Act 1925 ss.2, 32-34. When such jurisdiction was exercised by the Probate Division, it followed the settled practice of the Chancery Division in appointing receivers: *Re Bevan, Bevan v Holdsworth* [1948] 1 All E.R. 271.
[112] See *Neale v Bailey* (1875) 23 W.R. 418; and, as to costs of administrator and receiver, *Taylor v Taylor* (1881) 6 P.D. 29.
[113] *Re Price* (1931) 75 S.J. 295.
[114] *Salter v Salter* [1896] P. 291: see now CPR PD 57.
[115] *Tichborne v Tichborne* (1869) L.R. 1 P. & D. 730.
[116] *In the goods of Evans* (1890) 15 P.D. 215; *In the estate of Cleaver* [1905] P. 319.
[117] *Re St Germans* 1943 (unreported); in such a case a special grant of administration limited to the settled land, might now be made to the trustees under the Senior Courts Act 1981 s.116.
[118] *Shorter v Shorter* [1911] P. 184: see, however, *Salter v Salter*, n.114, above.

and personal estate; but if the deceased died before 1926, only on notice to the heir, unless this citation is dispensed with.[119] The grant terminates with the decree,[120] or the decision of an appeal therefrom, before the actual grant of probate or letters of administration.[121]

A party to the litigation will not in general be appointed receiver, except by consent,[122] though there is no absolute rule to this effect.[123] If the parties to the litigation do not agree upon a nominee, the court may refer it to the Master to nominate a person to act.

As soon as the court clothes anybody with the character of an administrator, even although he or she is only appointed *pendente lite*, it will usually discharge the order for a receiver; it will allow the administrator to receive the estate, but will hold its hand over his dealings with it, and make such orders upon the administrator as it may think proper. Where the appointment of an administrator *pendente lite* is made, the provisions of the CPR r.69.5 (relating to security), r.69.8 (relating to accounts), and r.69.9 (relating to non-compliance)[124] and (subject to s.117(3) of the Senior Courts Act 1981, which empowers the court to fix such reasonable remuneration as it thinks fit for the administrator), r.69.7 (relating to remuneration)[125] will apply.[126] Where the probate litigation may be prolonged, and it is necessary to deal by sale, lease or mortgage with the property, the appointment of an administrator *pendente lite* is essential: the receiver cannot make title. The receiver appointed will sometimes be appointed administrator *pendente lite*[127]; and a grant outright may be made to him or her, e.g. where the next-of-kin, though cited, are unable to find security,[128] or do not apply for a grant.[129]

2-18   **Pleading.**   The court, though it may appoint a receiver to get in a testator's estate in aid of an administrator *pendente lite*, will not appoint a receiver over property of a testator claimed by a party independently of the will, even though that person's title may be sought to be impeached on the ground of fraud. Where, pending a contest between the plaintiff and the defendant as to the validity of two wills, the plaintiff filed a bill for a receiver of the testatrix's estate, and to set aside an assignment made by her to the defendant, the court refused to appoint a receiver of the property comprised in the assignment, that relief being claimed by the defendant independently of either will.[130]

Although a receiver has been appointed during litigation in the proper court respecting the validity of a will, the court will not, on that account alone, order the person named as executor to pay into court money in his or her hands belonging to the testator's estate, received previously to the appointment of the receiver.[131]

2-19   **Practice.**   It has been said that an action to appoint a receiver pending litigation

---

[119] *Wiggins v Hudson* (1890) 80 L.T. 296; *Re Messiter Terry* (1908) 24 T.L.R. 465.
[120] *Wieland v Bird* [1894] P. 262.
[121] *Taylor v Taylor* (1881) 6 P. D. 29.
[122] *De Chatelain v Pontigny* (1858) 1 Sw. & Tr. 34.
[123] *Re Griffin* [1925] P. 38.
[124] See Ch.11, below.
[125] See Ch.12, below.
[126] See Ch.10, below, and CPR Pt 64.
[127] *In the goods of Evans* (1890) 15 P.D. 215; *In the estate of Cleaver* [1905] P. 319.
[128] *In the goods of G Moore* [1892] P. 145.
[129] *In the goods of Mayer* (1873) 3 P. & M. 39.
[130] *Jones v Goodrich* (1840) 10 Sim. 327; on appeal, 4 Jur. 98.
[131] *Reed v Harris* (1836) 7 Sim. 638; *Edwards v Edwards* (1852) 10 Hare 63.

as to probate or administration should not be brought to a hearing.[132] An application, therefore, to dismiss such action for want of prosecution will be refused with costs.[133] But where the grant of probate or administration has been made to the defendant, and the claim form claims administration, or is amended so as to claim administration after grant, there appears to be no reason why an order for administration should not be made in the action. The court will, after grant, make an order by consent for the continuance of the receiver, and for payment of costs, and the investment of the fund in court.[134] Normally, after the probate litigation is over, it is the practice to discharge the receiver and dispose of the costs; and, if it appears that there was no reasonable ground for the action at all, the court may order the claimant to pay all the costs, although a receiver has been appointed.[135]

Estate of a British subject dying abroad. If a foreign personal representative **2-20** brings assets of the estate into this country, the court may appoint a receiver at the instance of the personal representative instituted here, to prevent those assets being removed elsewhere.[136] If the foreign personal representative collects English assets, such as debts due in England, he is apparently executor *de son tort*, and a receiver would be appointed at the instance of a beneficiary or an English personal representative.

Section 4: In Cases between Mortgagor and Mortgagee

Legal mortgages. Before the Judicature Acts, a mortgagee having the legal estate **2-21** could not, except under special circumstances, obtain from the Court of Chancery the appointment of a receiver over the mortgaged property, because he could take possession under his legal title.[137] But since the Judicature Acts, the court[138] will appoint a receiver at the instance of a legal mortgagee, after default in payment of principal or interest.[139] The court does this, not because the mortgagee has in fact less power than he or she formerly had to take possession,[140] but because there is an obvious convenience in appointing a receiver, so as to prevent a mortgagee from taking up the unpleasant position of a mortgagee in possession.[141] Since 1925, a mortgagor always retains a legal estate if he or she had one when the mortgage was created[142]; and a mortgagee under a charge by way of legal mortgage is to be treated as in the same position as a mortgagee by demise.[143]

The appointment of a receiver at the instance of a legal mortgagee is not a matter of course, and the court has a discretion in the matter[144]; but under the present practice, where an action for foreclosure is pending, the court will usually appoint

---

[132] *Anderson v Guichard* (1851) 9 Hare 275; but see *Carrow v Ferrior* (1868) 16 W.R. 922.

[133] *Edwards v Edwards*, n.131, above.

[134] *Anderson v Guichard*, n.132, above.

[135] *Barton v Rock* (1856) 22 Beav. 81, 376.

[136] *Hervey v Fitzpatrick* (1854) Kay 421. As to position of an administrator-attorney for a foreign principal, see *Re Achillopoulos* [1928] Ch. 433.

[137] *Berney v Sewell* (1820) 1 Jac. & W. 648; *Pease v Fletcher* (1875) 1 Ch. D. 273.

[138] As to mortgages of metalliferous mines in Cornwall, see statutes referred to below at 2-99.

[139] *Tillett v Nixon* (1883) 25 Ch. D. 238.

[140] As to the exclusive jurisdiction of the county court in certain mortgage actions for possession, see County Courts Act 1984 s.21(3), (4), and *Manchester Unity Trustees v Sadler* [1974] 1 W.L.R. 770.

[141] *Re Pope* (1886) 17 Q.B.D. 749; *Re Prytherch* (1889) 42 Ch. D. 590.

[142] See *Smith v Tsakyris* (1929) W.N. 39.

[143] Law of Property Act 1925 s.87.

[144] *Mason v Westoby* (1886) 32 Ch. D. 206; *Re Prytherch*, n.141, above.

a receiver at the instance of a legal mortgagee, and will do so, on interim application, where the mortgagor is in possession; possession is usually directed to be given to the receiver, but the mortgagor may be allowed to attorn tenant at a rent.[145]

2-22   **Court in which possession proceedings are to be brought.**   Under the RSC, before the reforms effected by the CPR 1998, all claims by a mortgagee for possession were assigned to the Chancery Division, and were to be commenced by originating summons.[146] But with the coming into force of CPR 55, all actions by a mortgagee in which possession of the property is sought are normally to be heard in the County Court hearing centre which serves the address where the land is situated,[147] unless special issues are raised, which justify, or necessitate, the action being brought in the High Court: such issues are where there are complicated disputes of fact, points of law of general importance, or the claim is against trespassers, and there is a substantial risk of public disturbance or of serious harm to persons or property which properly require immediate determination.[148] See Ch.1, above.

Such actions are to be commenced, and defences are to be drafted, in the prescribed forms.[149] Applications for foreclosure or sale are to be made to the district judge or to the Master, as the case may be.

The fact that the legal mortgagee has taken possession does not prevent the court from appointing a receiver at his or her instance,[150] though in such a case the mortgagee may be required to show some special circumstances to induce the court to relieve him or her from the position in which he or she has chosen.[151] The fact that a mortgagee has an express power to appoint a receiver under his or her security or by statute (see Ch.15, below) will not deter the court from making the appointment[152]: nor will the fact that the mortgagee has exercised the power, at all events where the mortgagor is in possession. Where more than one mortgagee is interested, if the power of appointing a receiver is not exercised by the mortgagee to whom it is confided bona fide, the court will appoint its own receiver.[153]

2-23   **Rentcharge.**   The remedies of the owner of a rentcharge, or other yearly sum charged on land or the income of land, and created since 1881, are, subject to any contrary intention contained in the instrument creating it,[154] contained in s.121 of the Law of Property Act 1925, and include possession and the creation of a term under subss.(3) and (4).[155] It is conceived that the court has jurisdiction to appoint a receiver to enforce payment of arrears,[156] except where the rentcharge was cre-

---

[145] *Pratchett v Drew* [1924] 1 Ch. 280. *Re Burchnall, Walker v Lacey* (1893) 38 Sol. J. 59.
[146] RSC Ord.88 r.2 (revoked).
[147] CPR PD 55A, 55.3, para.1.1.
[148] CPR PD 55A, 55.3, para.1.3.
[149] CPR PD 55A, 55.3, para.1.5.
[150] *County of Gloucester Bank v Rudry Merthyr Co* [1895] 1 Ch. 629.
[151] *County of Gloucester Bank v Rudry Merthyr Co* [1895] 1 Ch. 629.
[152] *Tillett v Nixon* (1883) 25 Ch. D. 238.
[153] See *Re Maskelyne British Typewriter* (1898) 1 Ch. 133; and below, Ch.15; see also *Re Slogger Automatic Feeder Co* [1915] 1 Ch. 478.
[154] Law of Property Act 1925 s.121(5).
[155] A legal term can only be created if the rentcharge is held for a legal estate, i.e. it must be perpetual or for a term of years absolute.
[156] Under Senior Courts Act 1981 s.37(1). cf. *Pease v Fletcher* (1875) 1 Ch. D. 273; *Mason v Westoby* (1886) 32 Ch. D. 206; *Re Prytherch* (1889) 42 Ch. D. 590; *Re Tucker* [1893] 2 Ch. 323; *Hambro v Hambro* [1894] 2 Ch. 364.

ated under the Improvement of Land Act 1864 or any special Improvement Act[157]; but there appears to be no reported case where this has been done. Where a rentcharge is charged upon another rentcharge, and is in arrear, the owner of the former may appoint a receiver of the latter under s.122.

Since the Rentcharges Act 1977 prohibited, in general, the creation of any new rentcharges subsequent to 22 August 1977[158] and provided for the extinguishment[159] of all rentcharges (except of a kind which may still be created) at the expiration of 60 years from the passing of that Act, or from the date on which the rentcharge first became payable,[160] whichever is the later, these provisions are obsolete except that, until a rentcharge is so extinguished, they will continue to apply to it.

After foreclosure. After judgment for foreclosure absolute, the action being at an end, the claimant cannot obtain an order for a receiver, even though the conveyance of the foreclosed property has not been settled. In a proper case, however, the court may open a foreclosure, where special circumstances are shown for the reconsideration of the judgment.[161] **2-24**

Mortgagee of tolls, etc. Receivers have been appointed at the instance of mortgagees of turnpike and other tolls.[162] The Turnpike Roads Act 1822 provided that there should be no priority between mortgagees of such tolls. So, when a mortgagee took possession upon not being paid, and retained the whole proceeds in discharge of his own demand, a receiver was appointed at the instance of another mortgagee.[163] "Under an ordinary mortgage," said Turner LJ[164]: **2-25**

> "the mortgage when he enters into possession holds for his own benefit. Under a mortgage of this description he becomes, when he enters into possession, liable to the other mortgagees to the extent of their interest. This liability would entitle him, upon possession taken, to come to the court to have it ascertained what is due upon the other mortgages, and for a receiver to aid him in the due application of the tolls; and if this court can be called upon to appoint a receiver immediately after the possession recovered at law, it can hardly be necessary that the proceedings at law should first be taken."

Equitable mortgagee. The right to the appointment of a receiver is one of the rights which accrue to an equitable mortgagee,[165] whose security has become enforceable, as one of the steps in realisation.[166] An equitable mortgagee has, in the absence of express agreement, no means of taking possession[167]: he or she cannot **2-26**

---

[157] See e.g. the now repealed Improvement of Land Act 1899 s.3 (which limited the remedies available in relation to certain rentcharges).

[158] Rentcharges Act 1977 s.2. For the exceptions, see Rentcharges Act 1977 s.2(3).

[159] Rentcharges Act 1977 s.3.

[160] As to the meaning of this date, in the case of a variable rentcharge, see Rentcharges Act 1977 s.3(4).

[161] *Wills v Luff* (1888) 38 Ch. D. 197.

[162] *Lord Crewe v Edleston* (1857) 1 De G. & J. 93.

[163] *Dumville v Ashbrooke* (1829) 3 Russ. 98n.

[164] *Lord Crewe v Edleston*, n.162, above.

[165] A second or subsequent mortgagee is no longer necessarily an equitable mortgagee: see Law of Property Act 1925 ss. 85(2), 86(2).

[166] See *Re Crompton & Co Ltd* [1914] 1 Ch. 954; as to debenture-holders, see paras 2-62 ff, below.

[167] Although the court can order the mortgagor to give up possession to the mortgagee: *Barclays Bank v Bird* [1954] Ch. 274.

by notice to tenants enforce payment of their rents to him or her.[168] If, therefore, there is no prior legal incumbrancer in possession, the court as a matter of right appoints a receiver upon the application of an equitable mortgagee, whose security has become enforceable, either under its express terms or by operation of law.[169]

A receiver will be appointed at the instance of an equitable incumbrancer, if the principal has become payable,[170] or if the payment of interest is in arrear, though the principal is not payable,[171] or if there is reason to apprehend that the property is in peril or insufficient to pay the charges on it.[172]

The existence of a prior legal mortgage forms no bar to the appointment of a receiver at the instance of a subsequent incumbrancer, unless the legal mortgagee is in possession.[173] The court will not allow a prior legal incumbrancer to object to the appointment by anything short of an assertion of his legal right of taking possession or appointing a receiver[174]; and the fact that the legal mortgagee has a right to appoint a receiver by the express terms of his or her security makes no difference to this rule.[175] Except in the case of debentures secured by a floating charge, second mortgagees in most cases have a legal estate.[176]

If a subsequent incumbrancer or judgment creditor were in possession of the estate, the Court of Chancery would appoint a receiver at the instance of a prior incumbrancer, if by reason of a prior legal estate the latter could not recover in ejectment[177]; but a prior incumbrancer, having the legal estate and right in law to recover possession, was left to his remedy in ejectment.[178] Under the present practice, receivers are freely appointed at the instance of legal mortgagees, and possession is ordered to be given to such receivers.[179]

2-27   **Parties: joinder of prior encumbrancers.**   Where second or third incumbrancers apply for a receiver in foreclosure proceedings, it is not essential to make the prior mortgagee or mortgagees parties, though the court will see that their rights are not prejudiced[180]: subsequent incumbrancers, including judgment creditors who have obtained a charge, as well as the mortgagor, must be made defendants.[181] In an order for the appointment of a receiver at the instance of a second or later

---

[168] *Vacuum Oil Co v Ellis* [1914] 1 K.B. 693; though, if the mortgage is by deed, a receiver may be appointed under Law of Property Act 1925 s.101(1)(iii). See paras 19-1 ff, below.

[169] See *Re Crompton & Co Ltd*, n.166; *Dalmer v Dashwood* (1973) 2 Cox 378; *Davis v Duke of Marlborough* (1818) 2 Swans. 108, 137; *Hopkins v Worcester, etc. Canal Co* (1868) L.R. 6 Eq. 437 per Giffard V-C at 447.

[170] Where there is an express provision that the principal is not to be called in, as long as interest is punctually paid, "punctually" means on the day fixed for payments: *Maclaine v Gatty* [1921] A.C. 376.

[171] *Burrowes v Molloy* (1845) 2 Jo. & Lat. 521; *Wilson v Wilson* (1837) 2 Keen 249; *Hopkins v Worcester and Birmingham Canal Co* (1868) L.R. 6 Eq. 447. In mortgage transactions, prima facie, "month" means "calendar month"; *Schiller v Peterson & Co Ltd* [1924] 1 Ch. 394.

[172] See para.2-71, below, and *Herbert v Greene* (1889) 3 Ir.Ch. 270; *Moore v Malyon* (1889) 33 S.J. 699.

[173] See para.2-29, below and *Norway v Rowe* (1812) 10 Ves. 144.

[174] *Silver v Bishop of Norwich* (1816) 3 Swans 112n; *Re Metropolitan Amalgamated Estates* [1912] 2 Ch. 497.

[175] *Bord v Tollemache* (1862) 1 New Rep. 177; *Re Metropolitan Amalgamated Estates*, n.174.

[176] See n.165, para.2-25, above.

[177] *White v Bishop of Peterborough* (1818) 3 Swans. 109; *Silver v Bishop of Norwich*, n.174, above.

[178] *Silver v Bishop of Norwich* n.174, above.

[179] See para.2-23, above.

[180] See para.2-23, above. *Norway v Rowe* (1816) 19 Ves. 144, 152. See article by Master Mosse in *Law Notes* (1934), p.917.

[181] *Dalmer v Dashwood* (1793) 2 Cox 378; *Rose v Page* (1829) 2 Sim. 471; but see *Price v Williams*

incumbrancer, there should be inserted the words "without prejudice to the rights of prior incumbrancers who may think fit to take possession by virtue of their respective securities."[182] If these words are inserted, a prior incumbrancer who has taken possession, or a receiver appointed by him, is not displaced, and it appears that a legal mortgagee could take possession without applying for leave to the court.[183]

If the above words are omitted, the rights of a prior legal mortgagee to take possession or appoint a receiver remain unaffected[184]; but he must obtain the leave of the court before enforcing those rights,[185] and where the security is deficient or nearly so, he or she has in effect to bear the costs of such an application. Though a legal mortgagee may have appointed a receiver at the date when the court, in ignorance of that fact, appoints a receiver at the instance of a subsequent incumbrancer, the later appointment is effective, though the court's receiver will be at once displaced upon the application of the legal mortgagee, as from the date of service of such application.[186]

Prior encumbrancer applying later than subsequent encumbrancer. If a receiver has already been appointed at the instance of a subsequent incumbrancer, the prior incumbrancer may apply for a receiver; but if the security of the subsequent incumbrancer includes other property, the receiver already appointed will be treated as receiver also for the prior incumbrancer without respect to the property included in his or her security, in order to avoid the expense of two receivers. If the security of the prior incumbrancer includes property other than that included in the security of the subsequent incumbrancer, fresh proceedings by the former are necessary; but if it does not, he or she can apply to be added as a defendant in the subsequent incumbrancer's claim and apply in the claim. Similarly, if a receiver has been appointed in a partnership claim, an incumbrancer who intervenes should commence fresh proceedings if his or security contains property additional to the assets of the partnership.

2-28

Instances of exercise of jurisdiction. A receiver may be appointed, on the application of an equitable mortgagee of leasehold property, against a person in possession under an agreement with the mortgagor for an assignment of the latter's interest in the property.[187] Although the security of the applicant may be one which gave no right to be considered a mortgagee of the estate, but only made the rents a fund for payment of interest and of premiums under a policy of insurance, out of the produce of which the principal was to be paid, a receiver will still be appointed.[188]

Undivided shares in land can no longer exist: accordingly, a mortgage of the

2-29

(1806) G. Coop. 31; a receiver may, however, be appointed in the absence of some of the subsequent incumbrancers: see *Re Crigglestone Coal Co* [1906] 1 Ch. 523.

[182] Seton, *Forms of Judgments and Orders* (7th ed.), pp.765, 798; *Lewis v Zouche* (1828) 2 Sim. 388; *Smith v Lord Effingham* (1839) 2 Beav. 232; *Underhay v Read* (1887) 20 Q.B.D. 209.

[183] *Underhay v Read*, n.182; see *Re Metropolitan Amalgamated Estates*, n.174, above, where the point was raised, but *Underhay v Read*, n.182, above, was not referred to.

[184] See *Davis v Duke of Marlborough* (1818) 2 Swans. 108, 137, 138.

[185] *Re Metropolitan Amalgamated Estates*, n.174, above.

[186] *Re Metropolitan Amalgamated Estates*, n.174, above, and see paras 6-29, 6-48, below.

[187] *Reid v Middleton* (1823) T. & R. 455; but only if the equitable mortgagee has registered his mortgage as a land charge, unless he holds the deeds.

[188] *Taylor v Emerson* (1843) 4 Dr. & War. 117; see also *Cummins v Perkins* [1899] 1 Ch. 16; as to the

interest of a tenant in common in possession is a mortgage of an interest under a trust of land.[189] Although, therefore, a receiver will be appointed at the instance of a mortgagee of an undivided share of the interest of the tenant in common in the proceeds of sale, and of the rents and profits until sale, a receiver of the rents and profits of the land will only be appointed in case of such misconduct by the trustees in whom the legal estate is vested as justifies such appointment,[190] e.g. where the trustees of land omit to hand over the mortgaged share of the rents or proceeds of sale to the mortgage after notice requiring them to do so.[191] In cases where mortgages of all the undivided shares made before 1926 for securing the same mortgage money are vested in the same mortgagees,[192] the mortgage becomes a legal mortgage; but in the case of mortgages made after the Act this is not so. Where, however, all the undivided shares are not mortgaged to the same mortgagee, and the mortgagors are themselves the trustees in whom the legal estate is vested, it is possible that a receiver might be appointed of the rents and profits of the estate, at all events where there are no subsequent mortgagees; in such a case the mortgagee has not the legal estate.[193]

2-30   **Prior legal mortgagee in possession.**   The court will not appoint a receiver, at the instance of a subsequent incumbrancer, against a prior[194] legal mortgagee in possession,[195] as long as anything remains due to the latter on the mortgage security, for he or she is entitled to retain that possession until fully paid. In the absence of misconduct,[196] a receiver will not be appointed against him or her, except on his or her own admission, that he or she has been paid off, or on his or her refusal to accept what is due.[197] If he or she swears that something is due on the mortgage security, no receiver will be appointed against him or her,[198] and the only course is to pay him or her off according to his or her own statement of the debt.[199]

It is not necessary, in order to preserve his or her possession, that he or she should be able to state with great precision what sum is due. It is enough if he or she can swear that something is due (however small it may be) on the security[200]; the court will not try the truth of the statement by written evidence against it.[201] If, however,

---

right of creditor of a building society, see *Baker v Landport, etc. Building Society* (1912) 56 S.J. 224.

[189] See now the Trusts of Land and Appointment of Trustees Act 1996 ss.14, 15. There remains the unusual case, under para.4 of Pt 4 of Sch.1 to Law of Property Act 1925, as amended by Law of Property (Amendment) Act 1926, (as to which see *Re Barratt* [1929] 1 Ch. 336), where the beneficial interest of the tenant in common is an equitable interest in the land, vested in the tenants in common as joint tenants.

[190] See s.2 of this Chapter.

[191] See *Pawson's Settlement* [1917] 1 Ch. 541. As to power of sale and to appoint receiver, see Law of Property Act 1925 s.102.

[192] Law of Property Act 1925 Sch.1 Pt 4 para.1(7).

[193] For a case under the old law, where a receiver was appointed over the estate at the instance of a mortgage of an undivided share, see *Sumsion v Crutwell* (1833) 31 W.R. 399. In *Holmes v Bell* (1840) 2 Beav. 298, a receiver of the rents and profits of an estate belonging to mortgagors as tenants in common was appointed, where one of them was out of the jurisdiction.

[194] See, as to the restrictions upon obtaining priority by tacking, Law of Property Act 1925 s.94.

[195] *Richards v Gould* (1827) 1 Mol. 22.

[196] See para.2-31, below.

[197] *Berney v Sewell* (1820) 1 Jac. & W. 647.

[198] *Quarrell v Beckford* (1807) 13 Ves. 377.

[199] *Berney v Sewell*, n.197, above.

[200] *Quarrell v Beckford*, n.198, above.

[201] *Rowe v Wood* (1822), 2 Jac. & W. 553.

he or she will not state that something is due, the court will appoint a receiver.[202] The statement must be a distinct and positive statement, not a vague assertion,[203] such as of a belief that, when the accounts are taken, some particular sum will be found due.[204] Nor can the incomplete state of accounts be admitted as an excuse for not being able to say that something is due. If a mortgagee in possession keeps accounts so negligently that neither he nor she, nor a subsequent incumbrancer, nor the owner of the estate, can ascertain what is due, the court may assume that nothing is due.[205] Time, however, may be given to file written evidence of the debt.[206]

The rule, as to not appointing a receiver against a prior legal mortgagee in possession, has been held to apply in favour of persons in possession entitled to a mortgage and prior charges on the estate, though they had applied part of the rents in payment of the interest on those charges, instead of discharging the principal of the mortgage; it being the proper course, as between the tenant for life and the owners of the inheritance, to keep down such interest out of the rents, and not to treat the surplus rents, after payment of the interest on the unpaid part of the principal, as applicable to the discharge of such unpaid principal.[207]

In order to deprive an equitable mortgagee of his or her right to a receiver, the possession of the party must be such a possession as invests him or her with a title to receive the rents and profits in the capacity of mortgagee. A mere possession as tenant is not sufficient[208]

Exceptional cases. Still, although a receiver will not, as a general rule, be appointed against a prior legal mortgagee in possession, the court may, if a case of gross mismanagement of the estate is made out, deprive a mortgagee of possession by appointing a receiver; but to warrant such an interference the mismanagement must be of a clear and specific nature.[209] **2-31**

Manager. If a mortgagee's security includes (either expressly or by clear implication) not only land, but a business carried on upon the land, the court may, upon the mortgagee's application, appoint a manager as well as a receiver.[210] **2-32**

In such cases, if the mortgagee elects to have the receiver also appointed manager, the goodwill of the business forms part of the property entrusted to the receiver, who must do all acts necessary to preserve it: the receiver cannot, therefore, without the express permission of the court,[211] disregard contracts entered into by the mortgagor, because to do so would result in the destruction of the goodwill.[212]. If, however, the mortgagee elects to have a receiver only, and possession is taken by the receiver, the latter may disregard contracts entered into by the

---

[202] *Quarrell v Beckford*, n.198, above; *Rowe v Wood*, n.201, above.

[203] *Hiles v Moore* (1825) 15 Beav. 175.

[204] See n.203, above.

[205] *Codrington v Parker* (1810) 16 Ves. 469; *Hiles v Moore* (1852) 15 Beav. 175.

[206] *Codrington v Parker*, n.205, above.

[207] *Faulkner v Daniel* (1843) 3 Hare 199n.; 10 L.J. Ch. 34. The old cases must be read in the light of the present law, which enables a second mortgagee under a legal mortgage to take a legal estate.

[208] *Archdeacon v Bowes* (1796) 3 Anst. 752. Where an equitable mortgagee had taken possession under the mistaken impression that he was the owner, payment of interest was presumed, to prevent the charge becoming barred by the Statute of Limitations: *Re Battersby* [1911] 1 Ir.R. 543.

[209] *Rowe v Wood* (1822) 2 Jac. & W. 553.

[210] *County of Gloucester Bank v Rudry, Merthyr Colliery Co* [1895] 1 Ch. 629; and see Ch.9.

[211] See paras 9-12 ff, below.

[212] See *Re Newdigate Colliery Co* [1912] 1 Ch. 468; and paras.9-12 ff, below

mortgagor, because he or she is under no obligation to preserve the goodwill.[213] It is, as a rule, useless to appoint a manager, unless he or she can utilise or acquire the chattels employed in the business. It must be remembered that, except in the case of incorporated companies and certain statutory bodies, a charge on chattels is void, unless registered as a bill of sale, though it may be valid as to the remainder of the property comprised therein.[214]

It seems that, although the court will not appoint a manager of licensed premises at the instance of a mortgagee whose security does not include the goodwill,[215] it may, where the licences are in jeopardy, authorise the receiver to keep the house open as licensed premises, and to do all acts necessary to preserve the licences.[216]

2-33   **Rent acts.**   In the case of regulated mortgages on dwelling-houses to which the Rent Restriction Acts[217] formerly applied,[218] the court has certain powers to mitigate hardship caused by the taking of steps (one of which might be an application for the appointment of a receiver) to enforce the security.[219]

2-34   **Reserve and auxiliary forces.**   See Reserve and Auxiliary Forces (Protection of Civil Interests) Act 1951 s.2, as amended, which places limits on the ability within England and Wales to appoint a receiver unless the leave of the court is first obtained.[220]

Section 5: In Cases between Debtor and Creditor

2-35   **General creditors.**   General creditors may, like specific incumbrancers, obtain the appointment of a receiver of the property of their debtor,[221] provided they can show to the court the existence of circumstances creating the equity from which alone the jurisdiction arises.[222] Thus, where it is made to appear that an executor or devisee is wasting the personal or real estate, a receiver may be appointed in administration proceedings commenced by simple contract creditors,[223] who may also obtain

---

[213] See *Re Newdigate Colliery Co*, n.212, above per Cozens-Hardy MR and Moulton LJ.

[214] *Re North Wales Produce etc. Co* [1922] 2 Ch. 340: see Bills of Sale Act (1878), Amendment Act 1882.

[215] *Whitley v Challis* [1892] 1 Ch. 64.

[216] See *Charrington v Camp* [1902] 1 Ch. 386; *Leney & Sons Ltd v Callingham* [1908] 1 K.B. 79, where such an order was made on the application of lessors seeking to recover possession: but cf. *Britannia Building Society v Crammer* [1997] B.P.I.R. 596, para.1-5, above.

[217] Now Rent Act 1977.

[218] See Rent Act 1977 s.129.

[219] Rent Act 1977 s.132.

[220] As regards Scotland, see s.8.

[221] *Owen v Homan* (1853) 4 H.L.C. 997; *Oldfield v Cobbett* (1835) 4 L.J. Ch. 272. For an instance, where a receiver was appointed to collect the plaintiff's agreed 50% of royalties payable by sub-licensees, following a dispute as to whether the licence had been repudiated, see *Mordechai Meirowitz v Invicta Plastics Ltd* (1982) 18 December, Court of Appeal Transcripts, UB 704.

[222] See *Re Shephard* (1889) 43 Ch. D. 131, 138.

[223] By a creditor's petition for an insolvency administration order, Insolvency Act 1986 s.421, and the Administration of Insolvent Estates of Deceased Persons Order 1986 (SI 1986/1999), as amended. Under the former Bankruptcy Act 1914, an administration order on a bankruptcy petition against a deceased debtor could not be made, unless the personal representative had been served, or the debtor had presented the petition himself or herself: see *Re a Debtor (1035 of 1938)* [1939] Ch. 594. Under Sch.I Pt II para.2 of the 1986 Order, the court may now dispense with such service, or may order service of the petition to be made on other parties.

the appointment of a receiver of real and personal estate, pending a grant of probate.[224]

Independently of the powers enacted by the Senior Courts Act 1981, where a claimant has a right to be paid out of a particular fund, the court will appoint a receiver in order to prevent that fund from being dissipated so as to defeat his rights. The appointment of a receiver in such a case is not by way of equitable execution, but is analogous to it.[225] Another remedy is applied by the court in divorce, which will interfere by injunction to restrain a spouse from disposing of property so as to defeat an order for payment of alimony or maintenance accrued due.[226]

The fact that the real estate, over which a receiver is sought, is in mortgage will not prevent the appointment of a receiver, unless the mortgagee is in possession.[227]

Still, although general creditors may obtain a receiver of the property of the debtor, a strong case must be made out to warrant the interference of the court. The court will not, unless a clear case is established, deprive a person of property over which the claimant has no specific claim, in order that, if the claim as a creditor is established, there may be assets wherewith to satisfy it.[228]

Judgment creditors. Before the Judicature Acts, the Court of Chancery exercised a jurisdiction in aid of judgments at law. A judgment creditor, who had sued out a writ of *elegit* or *fi. fa.*, but was precluded from obtaining execution at law, on the ground that the debtor had no lands, goods or chattels out of which the judgment could be satisfied at law, had a right to come to the Court of Chancery for the appointment of a receiver of the proceeds of the estate of the debtor which could be reached in equity.[229] The Court of Chancery, before exercising the jurisdiction, required to be satisfied of two things: first, that the plaintiff in the action had tried all he or she could to get satisfaction at law; and then, that the debtor was possessed of a particular interest which could not be attached at law.[230] Since the Judicature Act 1873, the first of these conditions has ceased to apply: but the second still holds good as a general principle, although modified in relation to interests in

2-36

---

[224] See Section 3, para.2-13, above.
[225] *Cummins v Perkins* [1899] 1 Ch. 16, 19 per Lindley MR. Where persons, against whom the claimant has a money demand, have an equitable interest in property, the persons with the legal title might be joined as defendants, though no substantive relief is claimed against them, other than payment out of the property of sums recovered from their codefendant; but where inconvenience would be caused by the joinder, the trustees will be struck out: *Ideal Films v Richards* [1927] 2 K.B. 374.
[226] *Fanshawe v Fanshawe* [1927] P. 238. See also Matrimonial Causes Act 1973 s.37.
[227] *Rhodes v Mostyn* (1853) 17 Jr. 1007; *Bryan v Cormick* (1788) 1 Cox. 422; *Berney v Sewell* (1820) 1 Jac. & W. 647; *Cadogan v Lyric Theatre* [1894] 3 Ch. 338, 340.
[228] *Owen v Homan*, n.221, above at 1036. Quaere, however, whether in all cases in which the courts would now grant a freezing injunction (formerly a "*Mareva*" injunction), as to which see Senior Courts Act 1981 s.37(3)), it would not equally, if required, appoint a receiver to further safeguard the assets therein comprised. Alternatively, the courts might do so in those cases in which, prior to Senior Courts Act 1981 (since s.37(3) only speaks of injunctions), it would have granted such an injunction. See generally, as to the grant of such injunctions, CPR r.25.1(1) and for some recent examples where the courts have been asked to grant an injunction and/or appoint a receiver see e.g. *Masri v Consolidated Contractors International (UK) Ltd (No.2)* [2009] Q.B. 450; *JSC VTB Bank v Skurikhin* [2015] EWHC 2131 (Comm); *Taurus Petroleum Ltd v State Oil Marketing Co of the Ministry of Oil, Iraq* [2015] EWCA Civ 835; and *Cruz City I Mauritius Holdings v Unitech Ltd* [2014] EWHC 3131 (Comm).
[229] *Smith v Hurst* (1845) 1 Coll. 705; 10 Hare. 48; *Smith v Cowell* (1880) 6 Q.B.D. 75; *R. v Charrington* (1888) 22 Q.B.D. 187; see, as to form of order, *Wells v Kilpin* (1874) L.R. 18 Eq. 298.
[230] per Jessel MR in *Salt v Cooper* (1880) 16 Ch. D. 544, 552; *Re Pope* (1886) 17 Q.B.D. 743.

land and certain other assets.[231] The former obligation on a judgment creditor, before obtaining an order for equitable execution, to issue an *elegit* had disappeared,[232] even before elegits had been abolished.[233]

But neither the Judicature Acts, nor subsequent legislation, such as the conversion of the equitable interest of a mortgagor into a legal estate,[234] affected the practice of the Court of Chancery, by which a receiver was only appointed in aid of a judgment at law, where there was a legal (or practical) impediment to ordinary execution.[235] Special provision was later made by statute for the enforcement of judgments against the debtor's land or interests in land and certain other assets, by the appointment of a receiver.[236]

2-37   **Equitable relief distinguished from equitable execution.**   In appointing a receiver in aid of a legal judgment for a legal debt, the Court of Chancery, it has been very commonly said, granted "equitable execution"; but the expression is not correct.[237] The appointment of a receiver is not execution, but equitable relief, granted under circumstances which make it right that legal difficulties should be removed out of the creditor's way. What a judgment creditor gets by the appointment of a receiver is not execution, but equitable relief, which is granted on the ground that there is no practical remedy by execution at law.[238]

This distinction between equitable relief and execution is of importance, because the creditor who applies to have a receiver appointed stands in many respects in a very different position from a creditor who issues execution.[239] Thus, an order cannot be made appointing a receiver by way of equitable execution, after the death of the judgment debtor, even though he was alive when the application was first made,[240] for this would amount to preferring one creditor of a deceased person to another[241]; and the executors of a deceased judgment creditor are not entitled to apply for a receiver under CPR 83.2, because this does not amount to asking for leave to issue execution within that rule.[242]

---

[231] Senior Courts Act 1981 s.37(4). See para.3-20 ff, below.
[232] *Re Whitley* (1887) 56 L.T. 846; see too, *Coney v Bennett* (1885) 22 Q.B.D. 173; and below. Nor was it necessary, under the old practice, to sue out an *elegit*: *Ex p. Evans* (1879) 13 Ch. D. 252; *Re Pope*, n.230; see, too, *Hills v Webber* (1901) 17 T.L.R. 513.
[233] Elegits were abolished by the Administration of Justice Act 1956 s.34.
[234] *Smith v Tsakyris* [1929] W.N. 39.
[235] See para.1-7, above. See the discussion in the landmark case of *Masri v Consolidated Contractors International (UK) Ltd (No.2)* [2009] Q.B. 450 at [164-167].
[236] Administration of Justice Act 1956 s.36 (repealed by the Charging Orders Act 1979 s.7, see now paras 3-15 ff, below).
[237] *Morgan v Hart* [1914] 2 K.B. 183; *Re A Company* [1915] 1 Ch. 526.
[238] *Re Shephard* (1889) 43 Ch. D. 131, 135; *Levasseur v Mason & Barry* (1891) 2 Q.B. 73. See, too, *Re Marquis of Anglesey* [1903] 2 Ch. 727, 731; *Thompson v Gill* [1903] 1 K.B. 760, 765; *Re Bond* [1911] 2 K.B. 988.
[239] See further, para.6-21, below.
[240] *Re Shephard*, n.238, above.
[241] *Re Cave* [1892] W.N. 142. The appointment of a receiver in *Waddell v Waddell* [1892] P. 226, over the estate of a deceased co-respondent, at the instance of a petitioner in a divorce suit to enforce payment of costs, appears to have been made without jurisdiction, as the suit had lapsed by the death, and there was no power to add the legal personal representatives: *Brydges v Brydges* [1909] P. 187; *Coleman v Coleman* [1920] P. 71.
[242] *Norburn v Norburn* [1894] 1 Q.B. 448. It appears that the proper course is for the executors to apply to be added as parties under CPR r.19.2.

A judgment creditor who has obtained equitable execution subject to existing incumbrances does not obtain priority by giving notice to trustees of the debtor.[243]

The cases in which the court will appoint a receiver at the instance of a judgment creditor depend mainly upon the nature of the property and of the judgment debtor's interest in it: this matter, and the principles which guide the court in the exercise of its jurisdiction, are dealt with in Ch.3,[244] and the practice on appointment in Ch.4.[245]

Principles governing exercise of power. The powers of equitable execution should not be exercised, except in cases where the judgment debt is sufficiently large to justify this expensive procedure,[246] and the property sought to be charged in execution is not only of a fitting character, but likely to satisfy a reasonable proportion of the debt.[247] In some cases, receivership orders have been granted over contingent and reversionary interests, whereas the sounder practice would have been to grant orders over that class of property by way of charge only, so as to avoid costs being incurred in settling security, etc. for what is at the moment, if granted, a mere dry receivership.[248] The following rule of court was accordingly made, for the purpose of limiting the cases in which a receiver can be appointed:

2-38

> "Where an application is made for the appointment of a receiver by way of equitable execution, the court, in determining whether it is just or convenient that the appointment should be made, shall have regard to the amount claimed by the judgment creditor, to the amount likely to be obtained by the receiver and to the probable costs of his appointment, and may direct an inquiry on any of these matters or any other matter before making the appointment."[249]

This provision has since been replaced by para.5 of PD 69 which provides that where a judgment creditor applies for the appointment of a receiver as a method of enforcing a judgment, in considering whether to make the appointment the court will have regard to: (1) the amount claimed by the judgment creditor; (2) the amount likely to be obtained by the receiver; and (3) the probable costs of the appointment.

The court has jurisdiction to appoint a receiver by way of equitable execution, for the purpose of enforcing orders for the payment of money due, for example, to a trustee in bankruptcy,[250] or to appoint an interim receiver for protecting the assets of a debtor against whom a bankruptcy petition has been presented.[251] But such an order will not, as a general rule, be made upon an application without notice.[252]

The court may appoint the official receiver or an insolvency practitioner as interim receiver of the property of the debtor or any part of it.[253]

---

[243] *Arden v Arden* (1885) 29 Ch. D. 702; and see *Re Ind Coope & Co* [1911] 2 Ch. 223.

[244] See para.3-1, below.

[245] See para.4-1, below.

[246] *I v K* [1884] W.N. 63.

[247] *Walls Ltd v Legge* [1923] 2 K.B. 240.

[248] The appointment will not be made at all, if it will certainly prove ineffective: *Harper v McIntyre* (1907) 51 S.J. 701.

[249] The former CPR 1998 Sch.1 -RSC Ord.51 r.1(1).

[250] *Re Goudie* [1896] 2 Q.B. 481; see CPR Pt 70 and its Practice Direction.

[251] Insolvency Act 1986, s.286 see n.253, below.

[252] See nn.249, 250, above.

[253] Insolvency Act 1986 s.286, replacing Bankruptcy Act 1914 s.8; for practice, see Insolvency Rules 2016 rr.10.49-10.54. Usually, the Official Receiver will be appointed. See *Gibson Dunn & Crutcher* [2002] EWHC 2159(Ch); [2003] B.P.I.R. 523. *Crutcher v Rio Properties Inc* [2004] EWCA Civ

2-39   Attachment of moneys payable by the Crown.   No order for the attachment of debts, or for the appointment of a sequestrator, or for the appointment of a receiver can be made in respect of any money due or accruing or alleged to be due or accruing to a judgment debtor from the Crown.[254] But where such an order could have been obtained in respect of such money, if it had been due or accruing from a subject, the court may, on the application by Pt 8 claim form of the judgment creditor, make an order restraining the judgment debtor from receiving such money, and directing payment by the Crown to the judgment creditor or to a sequestrator or receiver; and the court or a judge may appoint a sequestrator or receiver for that purpose.[255] Wages or salaries payable to officers of the Crown as such, and moneys subject to the provisions of an enactment prohibiting or restricting assigning or charging or taking in execution, were initially exempt from this jurisdiction.[256] However, on 1 January 1982, National Savings Bank deposits, previously exempt, ceased to be exempt, so that the court may order the Crown to pay such deposits to the judgment creditor.[257]

2-40   Debt not ascertained.   The court will not necessarily refuse to appoint a receiver, pending the amount of the applicant's debt being ascertained. Therefore, where an action by a married woman was dismissed with costs to be paid out of her separate property, and her only separate property consisted of a share under a will, which the trustees were about to pay over to her, the court appointed a receiver to receive the share before the costs had been taxed.[258] This was, however, a very special decision: normally, no receiver would be appointed in respect of unassessed costs.[259]

2-41   Assignee of part of debt.   The same principle which prevents the assignee of part of a judgment debt from issuing execution at law, namely, that the assignor can only issue execution for the whole debt, and cannot put the assignee in any better position than the assignor,[260] applies to prevent such an assignee from obtaining a receiver by way of equitable execution.[261]

A creditor who has obtained an order for payment of costs, and has failed to obtain a sequestration, because of the conduct of the debtor, is entitled to apply for a receiver in lieu of sequestration.[262] So also a judgment for the payment of money

---

1043; [2004] B.P.I.R. 1203. For the powers and role of an interim receiver see *Re Baars* [2002] EWHC 2159, Ch; [2003] B.P.I.R. 523.

[254] Crown Proceedings Act 1947 s.27; CPR r.66.7.

[255] Crown Proceedings Act 1947 s.27; CPR r.66.7.

[256] See CPR Pt 72 "Third Party Orders" does not apply to the Crown: CPR r.66.6.

[257] Crown Proceedings Act 1947 s. 27(1)(c), read with Post Office Act 1969 s.94 and Sch.6 Pt 3, was repealed with effect from 1 January 1982, by Senior Courts Act 1981 ss.139(1), 153 and Sch.7. See *Brooks Associates Inc v Basu* [1983] Q.B. 220, where the power was exercised, even though the Bank has its head office in Scotland, since the Crown, in right of the United Kingdom, is always within the jurisdiction of the English courts. The Lord Chancellor, by order, may re-impose the exemption in relation to any type of deposit in the National Savings Bank Senior Courts Act 1981 s.139(2). See also CPR r.66.7(5).

[258] *Cummins v Perkins* [1899] 1 Ch. 16.

[259] *Willis v Cooper* [1900] 40 S.J. 698.

[260] *Forster v Baker* [1910] 2 K.B. 636; though part of a debt can be assigned in equity: *Re Steel Wing Co* [1921] 1 Ch. 349.

[261] See *Rothschild v Fisher* [1920] 2 K.B. 243.

[262] *Bryant v Bull* (1878) 10 Ch. D. 153.

into court may be enforced by the appointment of a receiver, where service of the writ of control cannot be effected.[263]

Partnership Act 1890 s.23.   By virtue of s.23(2) of the Partnership Act 1890,[264] the High Court or a judge thereof, or the County Court, may, on the application by summons (now by application notice) of any judgment creditor of a partner, make an order charging that partner's interest in the partnership property and profits with payment of the amount of the judgment debt and interest thereon. The court may, by the same or a subsequent order, appoint a receiver of that partner's share of profits (whether already declared or accruing), and of any other money which may be coming to the partner in respect of the partnership, and may direct all accounts and inquiries and give all other orders and directions which might have been made, or given, if the charge had been made in favour of the judgment creditor by the partner, or which the circumstances of the case may require. Proceedings in insolvency by a creditor of an insolvent partnership, or in bankruptcy against a member of such a partnership, are now regulated by the Insolvent Partnerships Order 1994.[265]

2-42

Appointment of receiver over insolvent partnership.   Where a residential letting partnership collapsed, amid partners' disagreements, the High Court, at the instance of numerous landlords and tenants concerned as to the security of their rents and deposits, appointed receivers to investigate the condition of the firm, who reported that it was insolvent and unsaleable; the court, notwithstanding the absence of any petition against the firm, made a winding-up order of its own motion[266]; the receivers' costs were ordered to be a first charge on the assets.

2-43

By s.7 of the Limited Partnerships Act 1907, s.23(2) of the Act of 1890 applies to a limited partnership.

Every application under this section must be made by application notice, which must be served on the judgment debtor and on his partners, or on such of them as are within the jurisdiction see CPR PD 73, paras 6.1-6.6 and CPR r.23.1.

The application notice is to be supported by a witness statement or an affidavit which need not, as in the case of an ordinary debtor, state that the defendant has no other property available for execution, and will usually ask for a named receiver in addition to a charging order: if it is apprehended that the debtor may deal with his interest, an injunction should be applied for without notice on written evidence. The smallness of the amount due constitutes no objection to the order.[267] The order can be made by a master or district judge.[268] In the case of an application for the appointment of a receiver by way of equitable execution the written evidence must also give details of the matters set out in PD 69, para.4.1)

[263] *Stanger Leathes v Stanger Leathes* [1882] W.N. 71; *Coney v Bennett* (1885) 29 Ch. D. 993; *Re Pemberton* [1907] W.N. 118.

[264] As amended by the Courts Act 1971 Sch.2 Pt 2.

[265] SI 1994/2421, revoking Insolvency Partnership Order 1986 (as amended) made pursuant to Insolvency Act 1986 s.420. See also the Insolvent Partnerships (Amendment) Order 2005 (SI 2005/ 1516) and para.14-13.

[266] *Lancefield v Lancefield* [2002] B.P.I.R. 1108, under Insolvency Act 1986 s.122(1).

[267] See *Summers v Simpson* (1902) unreported.

[268] CPR PD 73, para.6.3.

The section has been held to apply to a foreign firm having a branch office in England.[269]

A charging order does not entitle the judgment creditor of the partner to retain the benefit of the charging order unless the execution is completed by seizure and sale prior to the commencement of the partner's bankruptcy.[270] After the appointment of a receiver, the court may give a creditor leave to issue execution, for instance by way of a charging order: but this is inconvenient, and it is preferable either: (a) to direct the receiver to pay the execution creditor out of money come to his hands[271]; or (b) to give the creditor a charge on the net assets.[272] The order should include an undertaking not to deal with the charged property, except subject to an order of the court: this enables priority to be given to the receiver's remuneration and expenses: and the creditor obtains priority over other creditors.[273]

2-44   **Council Tax and Business Rates.**   A receiver will not be appointed at the instance of a judgment creditor for the collection of sums due from a rating authority.[274]

2-45   **Family proceedings.**   Within a limited range of jurisdiction, the appointment of a receiver may be applied for to the Family Division, and granted,[275] provided that the assets sought to be protected and recovered are not unassignable. Maintenance and other analogous sums ordered to be paid in family proceedings are unassignable,[276] and in addition, as they lie within the continuing jurisdiction of the court, cannot be made the subject of a receivership order. Such an order can, however, be obtained for the purpose of protecting and recovering, in satisfaction of payment orders of the court, assets of the delinquent spouse; such assets can be recovered by sequestration.[277]

The Family Division may additionally, or in the alternative, grant an injunction to restrain the respondent from disposing of assets. Apart from those forms of property, other than maintenance, which are by their nature unassignable. As regards moneys payable by the Crown, see para.2.39 above.

It would appear to be settled practice that no court other than the Family Division has jurisdiction to make, or would make, orders for the enforcement of maintenance. After the death of the petitioner (and also the death of the co-respondent, when such parties still existed), the divorce court was held to have no jurisdiction to enforce an order against the estates of either of them for the payment of damages, costs or arrears of alimony or maintenance,[278] since the personal representatives of the deceased could not be added to the petition.[279] Neither probate

---

[269] *Brown, Janson & Co v Huchinson & Co* [1895] 1 Q.B. 737. See Lindley LJ's observations on the effect of appointing a receiver under the section.
[270] See s.346 of the Insolvency Act 1986.
[271] *Mitchell v Weise* [1892] W.N. 129.
[272] For form, see *Kewney v Attrill* (1887) 34 Ch. D. 345; Seton, *Forms of Judgments and Orders*, p.471.
[273] *Newport v Pougher* [1937] Ch. 214; A charging order can only be enforced by sale, not by foreclosure: *Daponte v Shubert* [1939] Ch. 958.
[274] There is a potential remedy by mandatory order under CPR Pt 54.
[275] See, e.g. *Livermore v Livermore* [1979] 1 W.L.R. 1277.
[276] See Ch.4, below.
[277] See *Capron v Capron* [1927] P. 243.
[278] *Brydges v Brydges* [1909] P.187, when co-respondents could be joined and sued for damages.
[279] *Waddell v Waddell* [1892] P. 226.

nor administration can be obtained, since there is no recoverable debt in respect of alimony or maintenance.[280]

For the practice and procedure in receivership applications in the Family Division, see paras 5-41 ff, below.

Foreign judgments. The effect of the Judgments Extension Act 1868 on a decree of the Court of Session in Scotland was that, when a certificate of it had been registered under that Act, it was to be treated as if it had been originally an English judgment; accordingly, the appointment of a receiver by way of equitable execution could be made upon such a certificate.[281] When the provisions of the Civil Jurisdiction and Judgments Act 1982 s.18, were brought into force on 1 January 1987,[282] these provisions were considerably widened so as to include, inter alia, judgments or orders of a Sheriff Court as well as of the Court of Sessions. At the same time, the Judgments Extension Act 1868 was repealed, without prejudice to any previous registration under that Act.[283] The registration of a judgment of a colonial court under Pt II of the Administration of Justice Act 1920[284] (as extended by the Civil Jurisdiction and Judgments Act 1982 s.35(1)), or of a foreign judgment under s.2 of the Foreign Judgments (Reciprocal Enforcement) Act 1933[285] (extended by Civil Jurisdiction and Judgments Act 1982 s.35(2)), presumably had the same effect as registration under the Act of 1868.

2-46

Equitable creditors. The case of equitable incumbrancers is dealt with in the preceding section; see para.2-26, above. There may, however, be cases in which an equitable creditor may not be an incumbrancer in the ordinary sense of the word, but may have a right to be paid out of a particular fund, or a right to the protection of certain property. The court will not appoint a receiver at the suit of an equitable creditor without an enforceable charge, however clear his claim may be, unless it is satisfied that the property is in danger, or unless there be some other equity upon which to found the application. Where a testator had devised his estate to a person for life without impeachment of waste, "except voluntary waste in pulling down houses and not rebuilding the same, or others of equal or greater degree," the tenant for life pulled down the mansion house, intending to build a better one on the site, which he was proceeding to do with all reasonable dispatch; it was contended that he was an equitable debtor for the value of the house pulled down, by virtue of the obligation imposed on him by the will to rebuild. There being no pretence for saying that he was not proceeding to fulfil his obligation, the party entitled to the next vested remainder was held not entitled to have a receiver of the rents appointed, in order to secure the rebuilding of the mansion.[286]

2-47

---

[280] *Re Hedderswick*, n.82, above; *Re Woolgan v Hopkins* [1942] Ch.318; but cf. *W v W* [1961] P. 1134 as to the mode of enforcement.
[281] *Thompson v Gill* [1903] 1 K.B. 760, 771.
[282] Civil Jurisdiction and Judgments Act 1982 (Commencement No.3) Order 1986 (SI 1986/2044).
[283] See Civil Jurisdiction and Judgments Act 1982 s.54 and Sch.14; and Sch.13 Pt II paras 2 and 3.
[284] See CPR Pt 74, as to procedure, and notes in Civil Court Practice as to which members of the Commonwealth the Act now applies to. It does not apply to the Republic of Ireland.
[285] CPR Pt 74.
[286] *Micklethwait v Micklethwait* (1857) 1 De G. & J. 504.

SECTION 6: IN THE CASE OF STATUTORY UNDERTAKINGS AND CORPORATIONS

2-48   **Mortgagee's right to receiver.**   A mortgagee from a statutory company or body of its "undertaking", or the tolls and dues arising therefrom, may, for the protection of his security, apply for a receiver.[287] The appointment of a receiver is the only remedy open to secured creditors under the Companies Clauses Acts: the right to foreclosure or sale is not open to them.[288]

So mortgages of turnpike,[289] dock,[290] or market tolls[291] have been held to have a right to apply to have a receiver appointed. And a person who has sold land to a statutory company in consideration of a rentcharge has a similar right to apply.[292]

The court has jurisdiction to appoint a receiver at the instance of a mortgagee of tolls, independently of any statute.[293] When a statute authorises a mortgage, it authorises, as incidental to it, all necessary remedies to compel payment, and in the case of tolls a power to appoint a receiver.[294] But no mortgage or assignment by a company incorporated by statute for a specific purpose with statutory privileges and obligations is valid, except to the extent and in the manner permitted by Parliament.[295]

The fact that a precise and specific remedy may be pointed out by the Act of Incorporation does not deprive a party of his right to a receiver; as, for instance, the fact that there is a provision by statute[296] for the appointment of a receiver on application to two justices of the peace. Nor is it any objection to the appointment of a receiver that the company has duties to perform, the neglect of which might subject it to indictment, for the order of the court always gives the parties liberty to apply, whereby such consequences may be averted.[297]

The court will appoint a receiver at the instances of mortgagees or debenture-

---

[287] *Fripp v Chard Ry* (1853) 11 Hare 241; *Potts v Warwick and Birmingham Canal Co* (1853) Kay 146; *Gardner v London, Chatham & Dover Ry.* (1867) 2 Ch.App. 201; *Blaker v Herts and Essex Waterworks Co* (1889) 41 Ch. D. 399; see, as to form of order, Seton, 7th edn, p.736; *Postlethwaite v Maryport Harbour Trustees* [1869] W.N. 37. In *Att. Gen. v Mersey Docks and Harbour Board*, unreported, Financial *Times,* 11 December 1970, the order provided that the receiver should only apply his receipts in discharge of the operating costs of the Board, which had other revenues available, to the extent to which such revenues were insufficient. The receivership is of the tolls, not of the profits only: *Griffin v Bishop's Castle Ry* (1867) 15 W.R. 1058.

[288] *Blaker v Herts and Essex Waterworks Co*, n.287, above. This principle also applied to the holders of debentures of a tramway company governed by the Tramways Act 1870: *Marshall v South Staffordshire Tramways Co* [1895] 2 Ch. 36.

[289] *Knapp v Williams* (1798) 4 Ves. 430n. per Lord Loughborough; *Lord Crewe v Edleston* (1857) 1 De G. & J. 93.

[290] *Ames v Birkenhead Docks* (1885) 20 Beav. 332; *Att.-Gen. v Mersey Docks and Harbour Board*, n.287, above.

[291] *De Winton v Mayor of Brecon* (1859) 26 Beav. 533.

[292] *Eyton v Denbigh, etc. Ry* (1868) L.R. 6 Eq. 14, 488.

[293] *De Winton v Mayor of Brecon*, n.291, above; *Hopkins v Worcester and Birmingham Canal Co* (1868) L.R. 6 Eq. 437.

[294] *De Winton v Mayor of Brecon*, n.291, above at 541. The Mortgage Debenture Act 1865 (ss.41, 42, 44–47) and 1870 (repealed) contained express provisions for the appointment of a receiver by the Chancery Division in the case of companies to which the Acts applied.

[295] See para.2-50, below.

[296] e.g. Companies Clauses Consolidation Act 1845 ss.53, 54; Commissioners Clauses Act 1847 ss.86, 87, and many private Acts; as to powers of such a receiver, see e.g. *Carmichael v Greenock Harbour Trustees* [1910] A.C. 274.

[297] *Fripp v Chard Ry* (1853) 11 Hare 241; and see cases cited in n.287, above, and para.2-52, below.

holders of a company formed for the conduct of a public undertaking[298]; when the interest is in arrear,[299] or when the principal is in arrear although all interest has been paid.[300] In this connection, it is to be observed that in the cases of debentures created under the Companies Clauses Acts, the principal becomes payable only on the final winding-up of the affairs of the company,[301] though redeemable debenture stock and debentures in the case of public utility companies,[302] may be issued. Although neither principal nor interest may be in arrear, the court will appoint a receiver where the whole security is in jeopardy.[303] But where the interest is not in arrear, a statutory debenture stockholder, who is an annuitant with no enforceable charge, cannot maintain an action to restrain the company from making an application of its money which is intra vires; though there may be cases in which the court will interfere to restrain acts manifestly to stockholder's injury.[304]

Pleading. A mortgagee or debenture-holder, seeking to obtain the appointment of a receiver, must sue on behalf of himself and all other mortgagees who have an interest identical with his or her own, or are in the same class.[305] **2-49**

Form of order. The court will not, at the suit of mortgagees, appoint a receiver of a public company, established by the legislature for a particular object, without providing as far as possible for the future working and continuance of the undertaking.[306] A receiver so appointed[307] has, however, no powers of management, nor will a manager be appointed, except under the express provisions of a statute.[308] The order will also be without prejudice to the rights of prior incumbrancers. **2-50**

Receiver of chattel property. Even after a receiver of the tolls had been appointed, the Court of Chancery appointed a receiver of the chattel property of a railway company on a motion by a debenture-holder, when the company had by a deed assigned its rolling stock and chattels to trustees for the general benefit of creditors.[309] **2-51**

Judgment creditor. An ordinary judgment creditor of a statutory undertaking has **2-52**

---

[298] As to what companies fall within this category, see *Re Crystal Palace Co* (1911) 104 L.T. 898, affirmed, sub nom. *Saunders v Bevan* (1912) 28 T.L.R. 518. As to the powers of such a receiver, see *Carmichael v Greenock Harbour Trustees*, n.296, above.

[299] *Bissill v Bradford Tramways Co* [1891] W.N. 51. For form of appointment over undertaking of a gas and water company, see *Re Ticehurst Gas and Water Co* (1910) 128 L.T. 516.

[300] *Hopkins v Worcester and Birmingham Canal Co* n.293, above. As to validity of a charge by a statutory company, see *Re Glyn Valley Tramway Co* [1937] Ch. 465.

[301] See *Attree v Hawe* (1878) 9 Ch. D. 337; *Cross v Imp Continental Gas Assocn* [1923] 2 Ch. 553.

[302] Statutory Companies (Redeemable Stock) Act 1915.

[303] *Legg v Mathieson* (1860) 29 L.J. Ch. 385; *Wildy v Mid-Hants Ry* (1868) 16 W.R. 409; where the creditors were proceeding by way of elegit (now abolished: see n.311, below).

[304] *Lawrence v West Somerset Mineral Ry* [1918] 2 Ch. 250; see [1918] 2 Ch. 250; see *Yorkshire Railway Wagon Co v Maclure* (1882) 21 Ch. D. 309, 314; *Re Liskeard and Caradon Ry* [1903] 2 Ch. 681, 686, 687; *Cross v Imp Cont Gas Assoc* n.301, above.

[305] *Potts v Warwick and Birmingham Canal Co* (1853) Kay 142; *Fripp v Chard Ry* (1853) 11 Hare 241, n.297, above; *Hope v Croydon Tramways Co* (1887) 34 Ch. D. 730.

[306] *Fripp v Chard Ry*, n.297, above; q.v. as to the form of the order; (also Seton, 7th edn), pp.736, 755; *Potts v Warwick and Birmingham Canal Co* n.305, above.

[307] Or under the specific powers of the Commissioners Clauses Act, see *Carmichael v Greenock Harbour Trustees* [1910] A.C. 274.

[308] See para.9-26, below.

[309] *Waterlow v Sharp* [1867] W.N. 64.

the right (except when, as in the case of railway companies, there is a statutory prohibition[310]), to obtain execution by means of a writ of control (formerly a writ of *fi. fa.*) against the chattels; and such a creditor had (before the abolition of that writ[311]) the right by means of an *elegit* to obtain possession of the lands of the company or undertakers.[312] It follows that a judgment creditor must not interfere with the working or management of the undertaking[313]; it follows that in many cases possession is useless to the execution creditor, and the court may, it seems, subject to the rights of mortgagees, appoint a receiver to enable the creditor to obtain payment from the receipts of the company.[314] A judgment creditor might formerly, under and in accordance with the provisions of the Judgments Act 1864 s.4,[315] have had an order for sale of superfluous lands of a statutory company.[316] Now the judgment creditor's remedy is by means of the imposition of a charge,[317] with or without the appointment of a receiver as well.[318]

When the unpaid vendor of land taken by a railway company commenced an action against the company to enforce his lien, the court refused to appoint a receiver before judgment had been obtained in the action, even though the company admitted liability.[319]

Where the security of the debenture-holders did not extend to the whole of the property, and the debenture-holders had also obtained a personal judgment, the court appointed the receiver in the debenture-holders' action to be receiver of all the property not included in the previous order.[320]

2-53 **Priorities between mortgagee and judgment creditor.** As between a judgment creditor and a mortgagee of the undertaking, who had obtained the mortgage before the recovery of the judgment, the right of the mortgagee is paramount.[321] Accordingly, when a receiver has been appointed at the instance of a mortgagee, the mortgagee's right is prior to the claim of a judgment creditor, whose whole interest in the land can be only that which subsists, subject to the right of the receiver and the provisions of the statutes. Notwithstanding that a receiver may have been appointed at the instance of a mortgagee, a judgment creditor may also have a receiver appointed; but the receiver who has been appointed at the instance of a judgment creditor takes without prejudice to the right of a receiver appointed at the instance of a mortgagee.[322] The fact that judgment may have been obtained before the appointment of a receiver at the instance of the mortgagee does not vary the rule.

---

310 See paras 2-59 ff, below.
311 By s.34(1) of the Administration of Justice Act 1956.
312 *Russell v East Anglian Ry* (1850) 3 Mac. & G. 104; *Potts v Warwick, etc. Canal Co*, n.305, above.
313 *Potts v Warwick, etc. Canal Co*, n.305, above. cf. *Contract Corp v Tottenham, etc. Ry* [1868] W.N. 242.
314 See *Hope v Croydon Tramways*, n.305, above; *Contract Corp v Tottenham etc. Ry*, n.313, above; *Kingston v Cowbridge Ry* (1872) 31 L.J. Ch. 152.
315 As amended by the Land Charges Act 1900 (repealed).
316 See *Re Bishop's Waltham Ry* (1866) L.R. 2 Ch. 382, 384; *Gardner v LC & D Ry Ex p. Grissell* (1867) 2 Ch. App. 201; *Re Calne Ry* (1870) L.R. 9 Eq.658; *Re Ogilvie* (1872) L.R. 7 Ch. 174; *Re Hull, Barnsley, etc. Ry* (1888) 40 Ch. D. 119, 120; *Stagg v Medway Upper Navigation Co* [1903] 1 Ch. 169, 174.
317 See the Charging Orders Act 1979.
318 See Ch.3, below.
319 *Latimer v Aylesbury and Buckingham Ry* (1878) 9 Ch. D. 385.
320 *Hope v Croydon Tramways Co*, n.305, above.
321 *Legg v Mathieson* (1860) 2 Giff. 71; *Wildy v Mid-Hants Ry* (1868) 16 W.R. 409.
322 See *Ames v Birkenhead Docks* (1855) 20 Beav. 332; *Hopkins v Worcester and Birmingham Canal*

If the mortgagee is not in possession by his receiver at the time when execution is issued, the judgment creditor's receiver may take the rates and tolls then due; but, as to the rates and tolls thereafter to become due, he may be stopped at any time by the mortgagee entering into possession by his receiver.[323]

In determining the respective rights of a mortgagee of a public undertaking, and a judgment creditor, it is necessary to bear in mind that the effect of a mortgage or debentures, secured on a company's undertaking and tolls in accordance with the provisions of the Companies Clauses Consolidation Act 1845, is to create a lien on the tolls, the unpaid calls and the undertaking as a whole. No specific charge is created on the assets, nor on the proceeds of any asset sold in the course of the company's business, nor on surplus lands of the company nor their proceeds, for it is contemplated that the company will dispose of these in the course of its business.[324] But where the company obtains statutory authority to sell its assets in bulk, the debentures constitute such a charge on the proceeds as to entitle the debenture-holders to payment thereout in priority to judgment creditors[325]; the same would appear to be the case with the land on which the undertaking is carried on, the debenture constituting a charge in the nature of a floating charge till the property is disposed of.[326]

Principles applicable.   According to these principles, where a railway company,   **2-54**
being indebted to contractors for work done, had granted to them, as a security for the debt, a specific charge upon the money to arise from the sale of the company's surplus lands, it was held that the holders of mortgage debentures of the company, made in the form given in Sch.C to the above Act of 1845, had no charge upon those lands or the proceeds of the sale of them, but that the assignees of the contractors were entitled to have a receiver of those proceeds appointed.[327] It had earlier been held that the mortgagee of the tolls arising from a company's undertaking could not obtain an injunction and a receiver against judgment creditors who were about to take, under an *elegit*,[328] the lands of the company,[329] but it appears that the court will interfere to protect the debenture-holders, where the action of the creditors would result in destroying the substratum of the company. Thus, a judgment creditor was restrained, at the instance of a mortgagee, from taking under a writ of *elegit*[330] the works, rails, etc. incidental to the working of the railway,[331] and though chattels may be seized under a writ of control (formerly a writ of *fi. fa.*)[332]; yet where the seizure would destroy the ability of the company to carry on its business, the court would

---

Co (1868) 6 Eq. 437: a judgment creditor in possession might formerly be given liberty, though not a party to the cause, to appear at the hearing of the motion, or to give a notice of motion to discharge or vary the order: *De Winton v Mayor, etc. of Brecon* (1859) 26 Beav. 533.

[323] See *Ames v Birkenhead Docks*, n.322, above at 348, 352, referring to provisions of the Common Law Procedure Act 1854. Equivalent provisions are now found in CPR Pts 70-73.

[324] *Gardner v London, Chatham and Dover Ry* (1867) L.R. 2 Ch. 201; and see *Attree v Hawe* (1878) 9 Ch. D. 337; also *Hart v Eastern Union Ry* (1852) 7 Exch. 246; *Eastern Union Ry v Hart* (1852) 8 Exch. 116.

[325] *Re Liskeard and Caradon Ry* [1903] 2 Ch. 681; see *Yorks Wagon Co v Maclure* (1882) 21 Ch. D. 309, 314–315.

[326] See *Legg v Mathieson*, n.321, above.

[327] *Gardner v London, Chatham and Dover Ry*, n.324, above.

[328] Now abolished: see Charging Orders Act 1979.

[329] *Perkins v Deptford Pier Co* (1843) 13 Sim. 277.

[330] See n.296, above.

[331] *Legg v Mathieson*, n.321, above; see now Railways Companies Act 1867, see n.336, below.

[332] *Russell v East Anglian Ry* (1850) 3 Mac. & G. 104; though now, in the case of railways, the credi-

probably appoint a receiver. But a mortgagee, with a specific charge on the proceeds of sale of lands sold by the company (not on the lands themselves), was held not entitled to a charge on the proceeds of a sale effected by judgment creditors.[333]

No mortgage or assignment by a company incorporated for a specific purpose, with statutory privileges and obligations, is valid except to the extent and in the manner permitted by Parliament.[334] But a company incorporated by statute, although it has exhausted its borrowing power in creating mortgages of its undertaking, may still create a valid security for an existing debt over all its property that may be taken in execution; and such security will be valid, if given to mortgagees who are pressing for payment. A judgment creditor will not therefore be allowed to levy execution on surplus lands or chattels which are included in such a security and of which a receiver is in possession.[335]

2-55 **Statutory bond holder as distinguished from a mortgagee.** The position of a statutory bond holder of a company governed by the Companies Clauses Act 1845[336] must be carefully distinguished from the position of a mortgagee. A statutory bond holder is not entitled to an equitable charge on the tolls and traffic receipts of the undertaking, or to have a receiver appointed over such tolls and receipts, for the purpose of paying the bond holder's claim.[337] Thus, where a receiver had been appointed by consent at the suit of a bond holder of a railway company, it was held that the order for a receiver ought not to have been made,[338] and the execution creditor was allowed to levy his writ of *fi. fa.* against the goods of the company, notwithstanding the possession of the receiver[339]; the reasoning on which the creditor was held entitled to this writ would have entitled him to a writ of *elegit*[340] (now a charging order, with or without the appointment of a receiver[341]) against the land of the company as well.[342]

2-56 **Receiver appointed at instance of statutory bond holder.** A statutory bond or debenture-holder, who has obtained judgment and execution against the company, may bring an action on his or her behalf and all the other bond holders for a receiver[343]; but is not bound to bring the action in that form. A statutory bond or debenture-holder, who has recovered judgment and issued execution against the company, is not a trustee of the money he or she may recover under the execution for himself or herself and all other bond or debenture-holders. If he or she gets paid by the company under the execution, before any of the other holders intervene or come into competition with him or her, he or she may keep what he or she has

---

tor can only obtain a receiver.

[333] *Wickham v New Brunswick, etc. Ry* (1865) L.R. 1 P.C. 64.

[334] See *Working Urban DC (Basingstoke Canal Act 1911)* [1914] 1 Ch. 300.

[335] *Stagg v Medway Upper Navigation Co* [1903] 1 Ch. 169; *Reeve v Medway Upper Navigation Co* (1905) 21 T.L.R. 400.

[336] As to railway companies, see paras 2-59 ff, below.

[337] *Imperial Mercantile Credit Assoc v Newry & Armagh Ry etc.* (1868) Ir.L.R. 2 Eq. 539; see *Lawrence v West Somerset Ry* [1918] 2 Ch. 250; *Cross v Imperial Continental Gas Assoc* [1923] 2 Ch. 553.

[338] *Russell v East Anglian Ry*, n.332, above.

[339] See *Bowen v Brecon Ry* (1867) L.R. 3 Eq. 541, 548.

[340] See n.328, above.

[341] Senior Courts Act 1981 s.37(4).

[342] *Imperial Mercantile Credit Assoc. v Newry & Armagh Ry, etc.*, n.337 per Christian LJ.

[343] At 526 per Christian LJ.

received.[344] The proper mode of giving effect to the provisions, with respect to non-priority as between bond holders, which are contained in the Companies Clauses Consolidation Act 1845 s.44, is conceived to be to let them operate after the bond holders come into competition with each other, but not so as to undo past transactions. The priority there spoken of is not a priority existing by virtue of some or one of the bonds, but a priority to be acquired by execution; in other words, a priority, not as between bonds which are not charges at all, but as between executions.[345]

Priority of mortgagees inter se.   Section 42 of the Companies Clauses   **2-57**
Consolidation Act 1845 limits and diminishes the intrinsic rights of mortgagees, imposing on them the principle of non-priority.[346] After an action had been brought by a mortgage debenture-holder, suing on behalf of himself and all other mortgage debenture-holders, against a company governed by that Act, and a receiver had been appointed, a single mortgage debenture-holder, who had recovered judgment against the company on his debenture, was held not entitled to issue execution on his judgment, otherwise than as a trustee for himself and all other mortgage debenture-holders entitled to be paid pari passu with himself.[347] Since the intent of the Act is that parity of possession shall be given to those who have parity of security, one mortgage debenture-holder is not entitled, as soon as he or she can recover judgment, to acquire an advantage over the other mortgage debenture-holders.[348] Accordingly, where a receiver had been appointed in a suit instituted on behalf of all the mortgage debenture-holders of a railway company, and a judgment was afterwards recovered against the company by one debenture-holder, an inquiry was directed whether it would be for the benefit of the debenture-holders generally that any proceedings should be taken by the receiver for the purpose of making the judgment available for them.[349]

Local authorities.[350]   Whatever the date of the borrowing, all money borrowed by   **2-58**
a local authority, and all interest thereon, is charged indifferently on all its

---

[344] *Imperial Mercantile Credit Assoc v Newry, etc. Ry* n.337, above, at 543. See, too, *Fountaine v Carmarthen Ry* (1868) L.R. 5 Eq. 316 per Lord Hatherley.

[345] See n.344, above.

[346] See n.344, above.

[347] *Bowen v Brecon Ry* (1867) L.R. 3 Eq. 541.

[348] See n.347, above, at 550.

[349] See too, *Hope v Croydon Tramways Co* (1887) 34 Ch. D. 730.

[350] As a result of the Local Government Act 2003 s.23(1) (as amended), the provisions of Pt I of that Act have effect, as regards the finances of the following local authorities: (a) a county council; (b) a county borough council; (c) a district council; (d) the Greater London Authority; (e) a functional body, within the meaning of the Greater London Authority Act 1999; (f) a London borough council; (g) the Common Council of the City of London, in its capacity as a local authority, police authority or port health authority; (h) the Council of the Isles of Scilly; (i) an authority established under s.10 of the Local Government Act 1985; (j) a joint authority established by Pt 4 of that Act (fire and rescue services and transport); (k) a joint planning board constituted for an area in Wales outside a National Park by an order under s.2(1B) of the Town and Country Planning Act 1990; (l) a fire and rescue authority constituted by a scheme under s.2 of the Fire and Rescue Services Act 2004 or a scheme to which s.4 of that Act applies; (m) a fire and rescue authority created by an order under s.4A of that Act; (n) a police and crime commissioner; (o) any other body specified for the purposes of this subsection by regulations.

revenues.[351] All securities created by a local authority shall rank equally without any priority.[352]

Apart from express statutory provision, a receiver cannot be appointed over council tax or business rates.[353] However, under the Local Government Act 2003,[354] the High Court may appoint a receiver on application by any person entitled to principal or interest due in respect of any borrowing by a local authority if the amount remains unpaid for a period of two months after demand in writing.[355] However, no application can be made unless the sum due in respect of the borrowing concerned amounts to not less than £10,000[356] or such other sum as the Secretary of State (or Welsh Ministers[357]) may by order substitute.[358] The court may confer on the receiver any powers which the local authority has in relation to collecting, receiving or recovering the revenues of the local authority, issuing levies or precepts or setting, collecting or recovering council tax.[359]

Where a local authority borrowed on the security of debentures under the provisions of the Local Loans Act 1875, and made default in payment of a sum or sums of not less than £500 for a period of 21 days, the creditors were held entitled to apply to a county court for appointment of a receiver,[360] over the local rate subject to the security.[361] These provisions were by s.13 of the Rating and Valuation Act 1925 applied to enable a precepting authority to obtain the appointment of a receiver, where a rating authority failed to meet a precept under that Act.

In addition to the remedies provided by statute, a judgment creditor may also proceed by judicial review for a mandatory order.[362]

SECTION 7: IN THE CASE OF RAILWAY COMPANIES

2-59 **Right of judgment creditor to the chattels of a railway company.** Section 4 of the Railway Companies Act 1867, made perpetual by 38 & 39 Vict. c.31, protects the plant and rolling stock of a railway company from being taken in execution.[363] Separate rules apply for railways which operate across international borders.[364] A person who has recovered judgment against a railway company for a sum of money may obtain the appointment of a receiver, and also, if necessary, of a manager of

---

[351] Local Government Act 2003 s.13(3).

[352] Local Government Act 2003 s.13(4).

[353] *Preston v Great Yarmouth Corp* (1872) 7 Ch. App. 655.

[354] See s.13.

[355] Local Government Act 2003 s.13(5).

[356] Local Government Act 2003 s.13(8).

[357] Local Government Act 2003 s.24.

[358] Local Government Act 2003 s.13(9).

[359] Local Government Act 2003 s.13(7).

[360] See the section referred to in n.361, below, as to the receiver's powers.

[361] Local Loans Act 1875 s.12. The section is without prejudice to other remedies. These provisions of the Act are incorporated into various local statutes. As to when money becomes due on a debenture issued hereunder, see *Edinburgh Corp v British Linen Bank* [1913] A.C. 133.

[362] See CPR 54 and CPR PD 54. "Mandamus" is now termed "a mandatory order".

[363] The privatisation of British Rail, whose previously unitary undertaking was split up between Railtrack Plc (now Network Rail) and a large number of train-operating companies, and the financial straits of some of those companies, has revived the relevance of the statutory provisions for the winding up of major railway companies; there are also a number of small private railway companies, operating locally. But see now the constitution of Network Rail.

[364] See the Railways (Convention on International Carriage by Rail) Regulations 2005 (SI 2005/2092).

the undertaking of the company, on application by CPR Pt 8 claim form to the Chancery Division.[365] The section further provides that:

> "all money received by such receiver or manager, after due provision for the working expenses of the railway and other proper outgoings in respect of the undertaking,[366] shall be applied and distributed under the direction of the court in payment of the debts of the company and otherwise according to the rights and priorities of the persons for the time being interested therein; and on payment of the amount due to every such judgment creditor as aforesaid, the court may, if it think fit, discharge such receiver or such receiver and manager".[367]

A judgment creditor of a railway company who obtains a receivership order under s.4 of the Act of 1867 does not thereby obtain priority over other creditors.[368]

In a case in which, after a receiver of the undertaking of a railway company had been appointed under the above s.4, the company's rolling stock and other chattels were sold to another company under an agreement, confirmed by statute, which directed the purchasing company to pay the purchase-money to the receiver, it was held that the purchase-money constituted money received by the receiver within the meaning of the section; and, further, that the holders of mortgage debentures charging the undertaking of a railway company were entitled, by virtue of s.23 of the same Act of 1867[369] (repealed) to a fund representing that money, in priority to unsecured creditors.[370]

Section 4 of the Act of 1867, though prohibiting execution against the rolling stock of a railway company, does not interfere with the right of a creditor, who has recovered judgment against a railway company, to apply under s.36 of the Companies Clauses Consolidation Act 1845, for permission to issue execution against a shareholder of the company who has been appointed receiver, to the extent of any moneys remaining due in respect of his share.[371]

Priority of mortgagees and bond holders of railway company. The priority of mortgagees and bond and debenture stock holders of a railway company against the company, and the property from time to time of the company, over all other claims on account of any debts incurred or engagements entered into by the company after 20 August 1867, was declared by s.23 (repealed) of the Railway Companies Act 1867.[372] The section gave no priority which the mortgagees and bond and debenture holders did not previously possess, except when a receiver had been appointed under s.4, or on a winding up or under a scheme.[373] It did not entitle them to priority of payment out of the proceeds of surplus lands sold on the application of judgment creditors.[374] The section, moreover, provided that this priority should not affect any claim against the company in respect of any rentcharge granted or to be granted by the company in pursuance of the Lands Clauses Consolidation Act 1845,

2-60

---

[365] *Re Manchester & Milford Ry* (1880) 14 Ch. D. 645.
[366] *Re Eastern & Midlands Ry* (1890) 45 Ch. D. 367; *Re Wrexham, Mold and Connah's Quay Ry* [1900] 1 Ch. 261; *GE Ry v East London Ry* (1881) 44 L.T. 903.
[367] *Re Manchester & Milford Ry*, n.365, above; *Re Mersey Ry* (1888) 37 Ch. D. 610.
[368] *Re Mersey Ry*, n.367, above.
[369] Repealed by the Transport Act 1962 s.95(1) and Sch.12 Pt I.
[370] *Re Liskeard & Caradon Ry* [1903] 2 Ch. 681.
[371] *Re West Lancashire Ry* [1890] W.N. 165; 63 L.T. 56.
[372] *Re Cornwall Minerals Ry* (1882) 48 L.T. 41; *Re Eastern & Midlands Ry*, n.366, above.
[373] *Re Hull, Barnsley, etc. Ry* (1888) 40 Ch. D. 119.
[374] See n.373, above; *Gardner v LC & D Ry* (1867) 2 Ch.App. 201.

or the Lands Clauses Consolidation Acts Amendment Act 1860, or in respect of any rent or sum reserved by or payable under any lease granted or made to the company by any person in pursuance of any Act relating to the company, which was entitled to rank in priority to, or pari passu with, the interest on the company's mortgages, bonds or debenture stock.

SECTION 8: COMPANIES INCORPORATED UNDER THE COMPANIES ACTS

2-61   The appointment of a receiver over the undertaking and assets of a company incorporated under the Companies Acts is usually made upon the application of mortgagees or debenture holders.[375] The appointment may, in cases of jeopardy, be made at the instance of contributories or of the company: thus a receiver and manager was appointed for a limited time, where disputes between directors had led to a dereliction in the management[376]; similarly, where there was no governing body, a receiver was appointed, pending a general meeting.[377] A receiver was also appointed in a company which was effectively a quasi-partnership, where one equal shareholder had presented a petition for relief based on unfair prejudice,[378] and there was evidence that it was likely to succeed. The appointment was made to preserve the status quo, pending judgment on the petition.[379] The appointment will not be made, where winding up is a more appropriate remedy.

2-62   **Debenture holders and mortgagees.**   The appointment is more usually made at the instance of holders of debentures, or trustees of a trust deed for securing debenture stock, or the holders of debenture stock[380] or of a mortgagee with a fixed charge. In these cases, the general principles applicable to mortgages, equitable or legal, as the case may be, apply.

A receiver will be appointed at the instance of a holder of debentures or of debenture stock which constitutes a charge[381] in the following cases:

---

[375] Foreclosure may be obtained: see *Re Corporate Equitable, etc. Society* [1940] Ch. 654, if all debenture holders are parties.

[376] *Stanfield v Gibbon* [1925] W.N. 11; application by contributories and the company: a receiver who had been previously appointed in a mortgagee's foreclosure action was appointed in the action. See also *Featherstone v Cooke* (1837) L.R. 16 Eq. 298.

[377] *Trade Auxiliary Co v Vickers* (1873) L.R. 16 Eq. 303; Seton, *Forms of Judgment and Orders*, pp.694, 695. Except in very urgent cases, a meeting will be directed under Companies Act 2006 s.306, in lieu of the appointment. Application is by claim form under CPR Pt 8, PD 8A and Form N.208.

[378] Under what is now Companies Act 2006 Pt 30 ss.994–999.

[379] *Re a Company (No.00596 of 1986)* [1986] 2 B.C.C. 99, 163; [1987] B.C.L.C. 133 at 136; the company was there regarded as a "quasi-partnership", to which the "just and equitable ground" applied. Normally the expense, damage to reputation and risk of injustice mean that appointment of a receiver in the context of unfair prejudice relief as an interim measure will not be lightly embarked upon by the court (*Jaber v Science and Information Technology Ltd* [1992] B.C.L.C. 764; and *Re Mountforest Ltd* [1993] B.C.C 565). However, in an appropriate case the court will appoint (see e.g. *Wilton-Davies v Kirk* [1998] 1 B.C.L.C. 274 where a receiver was appointed over a company and its two subsidiaries).

[380] A debenture stock holder who has no direct contract with the company is not therefore a creditor who can petition for the compulsory winding up of a company (*Re Dunderland Ore Co* [1909] 1 Ch. 446); but, as a cestui que trust entitled to the benefit of the trust deed, he can apply for a receiver, if the trustees do not (see *Re Empress Engineering Co* (1880) 16 Ch. D. 125).

[381] If the debenture is a mere bond without a charge (see *Wylie v Carlyon* [1922] 1 Ch. 51), there is no security, and the remedy is by personal judgment against the company for payment only: a receiver can only be obtained by way of equitable execution to enforce the judgment over property amenable to that remedy. The extension of the definition of debentures in Companies Act 2006 s.738, to include

(a) When the principal is in arrear,[382] or when the interest is in arrear, even though, in accordance with the terms of the debenture or trust deed, the principal has not thereby been rendered payable,[383] or when any other event has happened by which, under the terms of the debenture or trust deed, the security has become enforceable. It is sufficient if the principal has become due at the date of the application, though it was not in arrear when the proceedings were issued.[384]

(b) When the security has crystallised into a specific charge by reason of a winding-up order or resolution, even though the winding up is for purposes of reconstruction or amalgamation, and the debenture specifically provides that the security is to be enforceable, in the case of a winding up, otherwise than for purposes of reconstruction or amalgamation; since it is a characteristic of a floating security that it crystallises into a specific charge, when the company has become incapable of carrying on its business, and an equitable incumbrancer with a specific charge is entitled to a receiver.[385]

(c) Where the security is in jeopardy,[386] as, for instance:
   (i) where creditors are pressing and a winding up is imminent; or
   (ii) where the company's funds and credit are exhausted and creditors are threatening[387]; or
   (iii) where the company is threatening to dispose of its whole undertaking,[388] or to distribute among shareholders a reserve fund which is its sole asset.[389]

But the mere fact that the security is for the time being insufficient is not of itself enough to establish a case of jeopardy where no creditors are pressing[390]; where the debenture holders had a specific charge which was sufficient to answer their claim, as well as a floating charge, the appointment was limited to the property specifically charged, though a case of jeopardy was made out.[391]

---

securities not creating a charge, does not affect this principle.

[382] Even if no interest is in arrear: see *Hopkins v Worcester, etc. Canal Co* (1868) L.R. 6 Eq.437. As to when principal becomes payable, payment cannot be enforced so long as interest is punctually paid, see *Maclaine v Gatty* [1921] 1 A.C. 376.

[383] *Strong v Carlyle Press* [1893] 1 Ch. 268; as to power to issue debentures, that are irredeemable or only conditionally redeemable, see Companies Act 2006 s.739, and to reissue debentures, s.752. A different date for redemption cannot be fixed by the reissued debenture: *Re Antofagasta Ry* [1939] Ch. 732. See *Bissill v Bradford Tramways Co* [1891] W.N. 51.

[384] *Hodson v Tea Co* [1880] 14 Ch. D. 859; *Wallace v Universal Co* [1894] 2 Ch. 547; *Re Victoria Steamboats* [1897] 1 Ch. 158; *Re Carshalton Park Estate* [1908] 2 Ch. 62.

[385] *Re Crompton & Co Ltd* [1914] 1 Ch. 954.

[386] *Macmahon v North Kent Ironworks Co* [1891] 2 Ch. 148; *Edwards v Standard Rolling Stock Syndicate* [1893] 1 Ch. 574; *Thorn v Nine Reefs* (1892) 67 L.T. 93; *Re Victoria Steamboats* n.384, above; and cases below.

[387] *Re Braunstein and Marjolaine* [1914] W.N. 335. For a case where a receiver was appointed against a company in a state of suspended animation (club of enemy members), see *Higginson v German Athenaeum Ltd* (1916) 32 T.L.R. 277.

[388] *Hubbuck v Helms* (1887) 56 L.J. Ch. 536; but not where only one of several businesses is to be disposed of: see *Foster v Borax Co* [1899] 2 Ch. 130.

[389] *Re Tilt Cove Copper Co Ltd* [1913] 2 Ch. 588.

[390] *Re New York Taxicab Co Ltd* [1913] 1 Ch. 1.

[391] *Gregson v George Taplin & Co* (1916) 112 L.T. 985.

2-63   **Former limited validity of debenture.**[392]   Prior to amendments to the law made by the Companies Act 1989, the legal position was as follows. That position may be relevant regarding acts of the company prior to the coming into force of the relevant provisions of the 1989 Act on 3 February 1991.

Under the law and practice prior to 1991, the memorandum of association almost invariably conferred an express power to mortgage the undertaking. Even in the absence of an express power, a commercial or trading company had an implied power to borrow on security,[393] and such a power might be implied in other companies, as incidental to the purposes for which they were formed. A power to borrow money could however be drafted as an independent object such that no borrowing could be ultra vires the company if formally made in accordance with it. On a true construction however the express ability to borrow, set out in the memorandum of association, might simply be a power. As such, the power could only for exercised for the furtherance of the company's other objects or purposes. However, at least in the general case, a limit on a power that it must be exercised for the purposes of the company (whether express or implied) would not generally be read as a condition limiting the company's corporate capacity to exercise the power but rather as a limit on the authority of the directors. If an act was capable of being performed as reasonably incidental to the attainment or pursuit of its objects it would not be rendered ultra vires the company merely because in the particular case the directors, in performing the act in the company's name, were doing so for a purpose other than as set out in memorandum.[394]

In the case of a non-commercial company such as a club, it had been held that even a power to create debentures did not necessarily imply a power to charge the assets.[395] Uncalled capital could only be charged under an express power in the memorandum.[396]

2-64   **Amendments as to vires of limited companies effected by the Companies Act 1989.**   The law as to the nature and extent of the vires of a limited company and its directors, and the position in relation thereto of persons dealing with the company in good faith, and their potential liabilities, were substantially changed by the amendments to the 1985 Act, effected by the 1989 Act, with effect from 3 February 1991.[397] The uncertainties and complexities of the former law, as analysed in the case-law, were thereby substantially resolved.

The amendments made provided that where a company's memorandum stated that its object was to carry on business as a general commercial company, the object of the company was to carry on any trade or business whatsoever, and it had power to do all such things as were incidental or conducive to the carrying on of any trade or business.[398] The validity of the company's acts could not be called into question

---

[392] See generally Palmer, *Company Precedents*, 30th edn, Vol.III, Ch.5.
[393] See *Re Badger* [1905] 1 Ch. 568, 573; *Re Patent File Co* (1870) L.R. 6 Ch. 83.
[394] See *Rolled Steel Products (Holdings) Ltd v British Steel Corp* [1986] Ch. 246; CA.
[395] *Wylie v Carlyon* [1922] 1 Ch. 51; nor does the fact that the advance was employed in paying off a prior charge necessarily create a charge: *Wylie v Carlyon* [1922] 1 Ch. 51. See now the definition of "debenture" in Companies Act s.744.
[396] *Re Pyle Works* (1890) 44 Ch. D. 534; *Newton v Debenture-Holders' Co* [1895] A.C. 244.
[397] Transactions effected before that date were subject to the pre-existing law: transitional provisions were contained in the Commencement Orders.
[398] Companies Act 1985, new s.3A, inserted by Companies Act 1989 s.110(1), with effect from 4 February 1991.

on the ground of any lack of capacity by reason of anything in its memorandum.[399] In favour of a person dealing with the company in good faith, the directors' power to bind the company, or to authorise others to do so, was deemed to be free from any limitation under its memorandum.[400]

A party to a transaction with a company was not bound to enquire as to whether the transaction was permitted by its memorandum, or was subject to any limitation on the directors' power to bind it or to authorise others to do so.[401] A person was not be taken to have notice of any matter, merely because of it being disclosed in any document kept by the registrar of companies (and thus available for public inspection), or made available by the company for inspection.[402] Transactions by or on behalf of a company which were carried out in excess of any limitations imposed on the company or its directors were nevertheless capable of being avoided by the company.[403]

The Companies Act 2006 and the ultra vires doctrine The abrogation of the ultra vires doctrine,[404] itself first eroded by the European Communities Act 1972 s.9(1), has been completed by the Companies Act 2006. For a company formed under the Companies Act 2006, its objects are unrestricted unless the articles are drafted so as specifically to restrict them.[405] Any restriction on a company's objects is now something that will constrain the directors by reason of their duty to act in accordance with the constitution and may raise issues of directors' authority.[406] Save as regards companies which are charities,[407] the validity of an act done by a company done on or after 1 October 2009[408] is not to be called into question on the ground of lack of capacity by reason of anything in the company's constitution.[409] As regards the authority of the directors, save as regards charities[410] and transactions involving directors or their associates,[411] the general position is now that in favour of a person dealing with a company in good faith the power of the directors to bind the company, or authorise others to do so, is deemed to be free of any limitation under the company's constitution. For these purposes a person dealing with a company is not to be regarded as acting in bad faith by reason only that he knows that an act is beyond the powers of the directors or the company's constitution.

2-65

Registration under Pt XII of the Companies Act 2006. The whole of Pt XII of the Companies Act 1985 was repealed, and a new Pt XII (comprising ss.395–420) was to be substituted, by the Companies Act 1989 ss.92–104. However, these provisions were never brought into force. The Companies Act 2006 Pt 25 largely repeats

2-66

---

[399] See Companies Act 1985, new s.35.

[400] See n.399, above, new s.35A, inserted by Companies Act 1989 s.108(1).

[401] See n.399, above, new s.35B.

[402] See n.399, above, new s.711A. However, this section was never brought into force and was repealed with effect from 1 October 2009. See now Companies Act 2006 s.40(2)(b)(iii).

[403] See n.399, above, new s.322A; see n.401.

[404] It is important to distinguish acts which are illegal and which a company may not carry out. This doctrine has not been abolished. On occasion the language of "ultra vires" is used in this context: see *Aveling Barford Ltd v Perion Ltd* [1989] B.C.L.C. 626 at 631.

[405] Companies Act 2006 s.31.

[406] Companies Act 2006 s.171.

[407] As to which, see Companies Act 2006 s.42.

[408] SI 2008/2860 art.5; Sch 2 para.15(1).

[409] Companies Act 2006 s.39.

[410] Companies Act 2006 s.42.

[411] Companies Act 2006 s.41.

the provisions formerly contained in the Companies Act 1985 Pt 12 although it has amended the types of charges which need to be registered and how that registration is to take place. Under s.859A, all charges created by a company require registration unless subject to an exception (this differs from the previous system which listed the types of charge which did need to be registered). It is no longer necessary to submit the actual charge document along with the statement of particulars. A certified copy is now required.

The main relevant provisions as to registration, and the consequences of default, are:

(a) that where a charge requiring to be registered within 21 days[412] has not been so registered, it will be void against a liquidator or an administrator or a creditor of the company[413]; but

(b) the court has power to extend the period allowed for registration or to rectify any omission or mis-statement in the register on such terms as it thinks just and expedient, provided that it is satisfied that the failure to register before the end of the period allowed or that the omission or mis-statement was accidental or due to inadvertence or to some other sufficient cause or that it is not of a nature to prejudice the position of creditors or shareholders of the company or that on other grounds it is just and equitable to grant relief.[414]

As regards overseas companies the position is governed by the Overseas Companies (Execution of Documents and Registration of Charges) Regulations 2009.[415] The Regulations only apply to overseas companies whose particulars have been registered with the Registrar of Companies under the Overseas Companies Regulations 2009.[416]

The other key changes effected by the Companies Act 2006 in regard to registration of charges are to confer powers on the Secretary of State to make provision that registration of charges and mortgages by the Companies Registrar will not be necessary if they are already registered elsewhere[417] and to amend Pt 25 of the 2006 Act by introducing regulations.[418]

2-67 **Protection of charges taken in good faith and for value.** In favour of a person dealing with the company in good faith, any borrowing, like any other transaction decided upon by the directors, is now deemed to be within the power of the company's directors, whatever the contents of the company's constitution.[419] The lender is presumed to have acted in good faith unless the contrary is proved, he is not bound to make any inquiries as to any limits on the powers of the directors to bind the company or authorise others to do so and he is not regarded as acting in

---

[412] Companies Act 2006 ss.859A, 859H. The 21 days begins with the day after the day on which the charge is created or, in the case of a charge to which property acquired by a company is subject, with the day after the day on which the transaction is settled.

[413] Companies Act 2006 s.859H.

[414] Companies Act 2006 s.859F.

[415] SI 2009/1917.

[416] SI 2009/1801.

[417] Companies Act 2006 s.893.

[418] Companies Act 2006 s.894. See SI 2013/600 which exercised this power to amend the types of charge registrable and the method in which those charges are registered.

[419] See formerly Companies Act 1985 s.35A.

bad faith by reason only of knowing that an act is beyond the powers of the directors under the company's constitution.[420]

Mortgages or charges,[421] created by the company,[422] except those listed as exceptions,[423] are void against the liquidator and creditors, in so far as they purport to create a security,[424] unless particulars are registered pursuant to Pt 25 of the Companies Act 2006 within 21 days,[425] or the time for registration is extended under s.859F.[426] As regards series of debentures, the date of the trust deed creating the charge, not that of the issue of the notes, is the relevant date from which the 21-day period for registration runs. However, if there is no such deed. The 21 days begins with the day after the date on which the first debenture of the series is created.[427]

On registration, the registrar of companies issues a certificate of the registration, which is conclusive evidence that the documents required to be registered were delivered to the registrar before the end of the period allowed for delivery.[428] An out-and-out assignment of a book debt is not registrable under the Companies Act 2006 s.859A.[429]

Subsequent invalidity of debentures.   There are a number of different grounds   **2-68**
upon which a debenture, regularly granted by the company, may now be held invalid, in whole or in part, on a company entering administration or on the insolvent winding up of the company. These include provisions regarding floating charges, transactions at an undervalue and preferences (in each case England and Wales only), gratuitous alienations and unfair preferences (in each case Scotland only), extortionate credit transactions and transactions defrauding creditors (England and Wales only).

Floating Charges.   Such a charge, created at a "relevant time", as defined for the   **2-69**
purpose of this provision, will be invalid, except to the extent of:

(a)   the value of so much of the consideration for the creation of the charge as consists of money paid, or goods or services supplied,[430] to the company[431] at the same time as, or after, the creation of the charge;

---

[420] Companies Act 2006 s.40, see formerly Companies Act 1985 ss.35A, 35B: and prior to that European Communities Act 1972 s.9.

[421] See, as to what amounts to a charge, *Re David Allester Ltd* [1922] 2 Ch. 211 (deposit of bill of lading for collection); *Re Kent and Sussex Sawmills* [1947] Ch. 177 (assignment absolute in form); *Re Wallis & Simmonds (Builders) Ltd* [1974] W.L.R. 39 (deposit of title deeds to secure debt of third party); *Re Bond Worth Ltd* [1980] Ch. 228 (retention of title provision, creating a registrable floating charge).

[422] An unpaid vendor's lien, being created by law, is outside the scope of registration: *London and Cheshire Insurance Co Ltd v Laplagrene Property Co Ltd* [1917] Ch. 499.

[423] See Companies Act 2006 s.859A(6).

[424] Even against a subsequent mortgagee with notice: *Re Monolithic Building Co Ltd* [1915] 1 Ch. 643, cited with approval in *Midland Bank Trust Co Ltd v Green* [1981] A.C. 51, HL per Lord Wilberforce.

[425] Companies Act 2006 ss.859A, 859H. See formerly s.93 of the Act of 1908; s.79 of the Act of 1929; s.93 of the Companies Act 1948; Pt XII of the Companies Act 1985.

[426] In the case of a charge created out of the UK, and comprising property situated outside, the charge still needs to be registered within 21 days of creation.

[427] See now Companies Act 2006 ss.859B. For former position see *Transport and General Corp v Morgan* [1939] Ch. 531.

[428] Companies Act 2006 s.859L(6).

[429] *Ashby Warner & Co v Simmons* [1936] W.N. 212; 155 L.T. 371 CA. As to hire purchase agreements, see *Re Inglefield Ltd* [1933] Ch. 1; *Transport & General Corp v Morgan*, n.427, above.

[430] For the calculation of such value, see Insolvency Act 1986 s.245(6).

[431] In *Re Fairway Magazines Ltd* [1992] B.C.C. 924 it was held that payments directly to the company's

(b)   the value of so much of that consideration as consists of the discharge or reduction, at the same time as,[432] or after, the creation of the charge, of any debt of the company; and

(c)   the amount of such interest (if any) as is payable on the amount falling within either (a) or (b) above, in pursuance of any agreement under which the money was so paid, the goods or services were so supplied, or the debt was so discharged or reduced.[433]

This provision applies both to Scotland and to England and Wales.

Under this provision only the charge is invalidated, and money paid in discharge of the secured debt cannot be recovered by the administrator or liquidator, except on the ground of voidable preference.[434] The fact that the money is applied in discharge of a debt owing to a firm in which the lender is a partner does not prevent the money being "cash paid to the company".[435]

"Relevant time": The time between the making of an application in respect of the company for the making of an administration order and the making of such an order on that application or between the filing with the court of notice of intention to appoint an administrator under paras 14 or 22 of Sch.B1 of the Insolvency Act 1986 and the making of an appointment under either paragraph is, in each case, a "relevant time".[436] So also, in the case of a charge which is created in favour of a person connected with the company, is the period of two years ending with "the onset of insolvency".[437] In the case of a charge created in favour of any other person, the relevant period is 12 months ending with "the onset of insolvency" provided that at that time the company is unable to pay its debts within the meaning of s.123 of the Insolvency Act 1986 or becomes unable to pay its debts within the meaning of that section in consequences of the transaction under which the charge was created.[438]

For these purposes, "the onset of insolvency" is defined by reference to an appropriate commencement date of the relevant insolvency process.[439] In cases where the provision applies by reason of the making of an administration order then the relevant date is that on which the application to the court is made. If the provision

---

bank account which reduced its overdraft (and the payer's liability under a personal guarantee) were not made to the company as the company never became available to the company to be used as it wished.

[432]   Negativing *Re Columbian Mineproofing Co* [1910] 2 Ch. 120; and *Re F & E Stanton Ltd* [1929] 1 Ch. 180 (money paid before the charge held to be paid "at the time of the creation of the charge"). The money paid need not be paid unconditionally (*Re Matthew Ellis Ltd* [1933] Ch. 458), but must not be paid simply for the benefit of certain creditors (*Re Destone Fabrics Ltd* [1941] Ch. 319). For other cases raising the question, whether money has actually been "paid" to the company, see *Re Orleans Motor Company* [1911] 2 Ch. 41; and *Re Yeovil Glove Co Ltd* [1965] Ch. 148. If the money is first advanced on the obligation to grant a fixed charge, but, this proving impracticable, a floating charge is given instead, the money is not paid "at the same time as" the charge: *Re G.T. Whyte & Co Ltd* [1983] B.C.L.C. 311. See also *Re Shoe Lace Ltd, Power v Sharp Investments Ltd* [1993] B.C.C. 609.

[433]   Insolvency Act 1986 s.245(2).

[434]   *Re Parkes Garage* [1929] 1 Ch. 139; *Mace Builders (Glasgow) Ltd v Lunn* [1987] Ch. 191, CA.

[435]   *Re Matthew Ellis Ltd*, n.432, above.

[436]   Insolvency Act 1986 s.245(3)(c), (d).

[437]   Insolvency Act 1986 s.245(3)(a).

[438]   Insolvency Act 1986 s.245(3)(b), (4). For an explanation of the meaning of inability to pay debts under s.123 see *BNY Corporate Trustee Services Ltd v Eurosail-UK 2007-3BL Plc* [2013] 1 W.L.R. 1408.

[439]   Insolvency Act 1986 s.245(5).

applies as a result of an appointment pursuant to paras 14 or 22 of Sch.B1 then the relevant date is that date on which the copy of the notice of intention to appoint is filed with the court. If the provision applies as a result of appointment of an administrator by any other route, then the date is that on which the appointment takes effect. If the provision applies as a result of the company going into liquidation, then the relevant date is the commencement of the winding up. The concept of "relevant time" and the associated concept of "onset of insolvency" are very similar to the same concepts used in the context of determining whether transactions are subject to attack in England and Wales as transactions at an undervalue or preferences.[440]

Transactions at an undervalue   In England and Wales, but not Scotland, certain   **2-70**
transactions are vulnerable as transactions at an undervalue where a company later enters administration or goes into liquidation. Such transactions are ones entered into with any person at "a relevant time"[441] being a transaction where:

(a) the company makes a gift to a person, or otherwise enters into a transaction with such a person on terms that provide for the company to receive no consideration; or

(b) the company enters into a transaction with such a person for a consideration the value of which, in money or money's worth, is significantly less than the value, in money or money's worth,[442] of the consideration provided by the company.[443]

Transactions entered into in good faith and for the purpose of carrying on the business of the company, at a time when there were reasonable grounds for believing that the transaction would benefit the company, are not affected.[444]

If a company has entered into such a transaction, at the "relevant time" as referred to below, the court may make such order, as it thinks fit, restoring the position to what it would have been, if the company had not entered into that transaction.[445] Section 241 of the Insolvency Act 1986 sets down further details of the types of order that may be made and in particular the extent to which such orders may affect third parties.

Preferences.   In England and Wales, but not Scotland, certain transactions are   **2-71**
vulnerable as preferences where a company later enters administration or goes into liquidation Where the company has at a "relevant time"[446] given a preference to any person, the court may make such order as it thinks fit to restore the position to what it would have been, if the company had not given that preference.[447] For this purpose, a preference is given, if the person to whom it is given is one of the

---

[440] For comparable definitions see Insolvency Act 1986 s.240 and discussion thereof below.
[441] See further para.2-72, below.
[442] As regards the question of whether the creation of security over the company's assets will constitute a transaction at an undervalue see *Re MC Bacon Ltd* [1990] B.C.C. 78; and *Re Mistral Finance Ltd* [2001] B.C.C. 78 but cf. *Hill v Spread Trustee Co Ltd* [2006] EWCA Civ 542; [2006] B.C.C. 646.
[443] Insolvency Act 1986 s.238(4).
[444] Insolvency Act 1986 s.238(5).
[445] Insolvency Act 1986 s.238(3). The powers of the court in this regard are amplified by Insolvency Act 1986 s.241(1)–(3).
[446] Insolvency Act 1986 s.239(3). The powers of the court in this regard are amplified by Insolvency Act 1986 s.241(1)–(3).
[447] Insolvency Act 1986 s.239(4).

company's creditors, or a surety or guarantor of any of the company's debts or other liabilities, and the company does anything, or suffers anything to be done, which has the effect of putting that person into a position which, in the event of the company going into insolvent liquidation, will be better than the position the person would have been in, if that thing had not been done.[448] However, the court may not make any order unless the company, when giving the preference, was influenced in deciding to give it, by a *desire* to produce, in relation to that person (i.e. the person receiving the preference), the effect mentioned above.[449] But if the person to whom it was given was "connected with the company"[450] (otherwise than only by reason of being its employee), the company is presumed, unless the contrary is shown, to have been influenced by such consideration.[451] The fact that something has been done in pursuance of the order of a court does not, without more, prevent the doing or the suffering of that thing, from constituting the giving of a preference.[452]

2-72 **Transactions at an undervalue and preferences: "Relevant time".** "The relevant time" for the application of the Insolvency Act 1986 ss.238 and 239, is dealt with in Insolvency Act 1986 s.240. Essentially it involves a consideration of two different tests. First, the transaction must take place within a certain time period prior to the company entering the relevant formal insolvency regime of administration or liquidation; secondly, in some cases, at the time that the transaction is entered into the company must have been insolvent.

As regards the period within which the transaction must have occurred, the periods are similar to those under Insolvency Act s.245. In the case of a transaction entered into with a person connected with the company (other than by reason only of being its employee), the period within which the transaction must have taken place is any time within the period of two years ending with the "the onset of insolvency". If the transaction is a preference, and not a transaction at an undervalue, and it is not entered into with such a connected person, the period is six months ending with the "onset of insolvency". The time will also be a relevant time if the transaction is entered into at a time between the making of an administration application and the making of an administration order, and between the filing with the court of a notice of intention to appoint an administrator under paras 14 or 22 of Sch.B1 and the making of that appointment.[453]

2-73 **"Onset of insolvency".** For these purposes, "the onset of insolvency" is defined by reference to an appropriate commencement date of the relevant insolvency process.[454] In cases where the provision applies by reason of the making of an administration order then the relevant date is that on which the application to the court is made. If the provision applies as a result of an appointment pursuant to paras 14 or 22 of Sch.B1 then the relevant date is that date on which the copy of the notice of intention to appoint is filed with the court. If the provision applies as a result of appointment of an administrator by any other route, then the date is that

---

[448] Insolvency Act 1986 s.239(5).
[449] See *Re MC Bacon Ltd* [1991] Ch. 127.
[450] Insolvency Act 1986 s.239(6).
[451] Insolvency Act 1986 s.241(4).
[452] Insolvency Act 1986 s.239(7).
[453] Insolvency Act 1986 s.240(1)(c) and (d). See Ch.14, below.
[454] Insolvency Act 1986 s.240(3).

on which the appointment takes effect. If the provision applies as a result of the company going into liquidation either following conversion of administration into winding up under art.51 of the EU Regulation on Insolvency or at the time when the appointment of an administrator ceases to have effect, then the relevant date is that on which the company entered administration (or, if relevant, the date on which the application for an administration order was made or the copy of the notice of intention to appoint was filed). If the provision applies as a result of the company going into liquidation at any other time, then the relevant date is the commencement of the winding up.

Extortionate credit transactions.[455]   In circumstances where a company enters administration or liquidation and has been a party to a transaction for, or involving, the provision of, credit to the company then the court may make an order with respect to the transaction if the transaction is or was extortionate[456] and was entered into within the period of three years ending with the day on which the company entered administration or went into liquidation. The range of orders the court may make is very wide, including orders setting aside the transaction in whole or part, varying its terms, requiring sums received under the transaction to be paid to the officeholder, requiring a person to surrender property held as security for the purposes of the transaction and directing accounts to be taken.

2-74

Transactions defrauding creditors.[457]   In circumstances where there is a transaction at an undervalue, whenever entered into, the court may make such order as it thinks fit to restore the position to what it would have been if the transaction had not been entered into and protecting the interests of persons who are victims of the transaction. The definition of transaction at an undervalue, in the company context, is similar to that under Insolvency Act 1986 s.238. This is a transaction where a person enters into a transaction with another person and makes a gift to that other person or otherwise enters into a transaction with the other on terms that provide for him or her to receive no consideration or he or she enters into the transaction with the other for a consideration the value of which, in money or money's worth, is significantly less than the value, in money or money's worth, of the consideration provided. The court may only make an order under Insolvency Act 1986 s.423 where satisfied that the transaction was entered into for the purpose of putting assets beyond the reach of a person who is making or may at some time make a claim against the debtor or otherwise prejudicing the interests of such a person in relation to the claim which he or she is making or may make.

2-75

Right to appointment.   The right of debenture holders whose equitable charge has become enforceable is absolute, and does not rest in the discretion of the court[458]: thus, a receiver will be appointed, though a liquidator has already been appointed[459]; in such a case, the liquidator is sometimes appointed to be the receiver.[460] Although, where the appointment is asked for on the ground of jeopardy, the court

2-76

---

455 Insolvency Act 1986 s.244.
456 See definition in Insolvency Act 1986 s244(3).
457 Insolvency Act 1986 Pt XVI.
458 See *Strong v Carlyle Press Ltd* [1893] 1 Ch. 268; *Re Crompton & Co Ltd* [1914] 1 Ch. 954, and para.1-7, above.
459 *Strong v Carlyle Press Ltd*, n.458, above.
460 See para.4-11, below.

has a discretion, yet if a case of real jeopardy is made out, the application cannot be refused.[461]

The decision of the question whether the principal is in arrears depends upon the terms of the debentures: where no place is fixed for payment, it is the duty of the company to seek the debenture holder and tender the money[462]: but where payment is to be made at the company's office, there is no default, unless the debenture holder attends and gives the company an opportunity to pay.[463] Where the principal is payable on demand, the debtor is not entitled to more time than would be required to produce the money from safe keeping, for example at a bank.[464] The debtor is not entitled to time in which to negotiate a deal which might produce the money.[465] Where the principal is payable on demand at a certain place, but there is no such provision as to interest, and the company makes default in payment of interest, the principal becomes due, though no demand is made at the specified place.[466] If the covenant is to pay on or before a date fixed, the effect is to make the money payable on that day, with an option to the company to pay on an earlier date[467]; if the covenant is to pay on or after a date fixed, the money becomes payable on or after that date on demand by the covenantee.[468] A provision that a covenant to pay is only to be enforced at the option of the covenantor is void for repugnancy[469]; but where there is no covenant to pay, but stock is made redeemable at the option of the covenantor, there is no obligation to pay until the covenantor has exercised the option.[470]

The power to appoint may, however, be excluded by the company entering administration,[471] or inhibited by the provisions of Pt VII of the Companies Act 1989, relating to recognised investment exchanges and clearing houses, or of the Proceeds of Crime Act 2002, relating to confiscation orders.[472]

2-77 **Where receiver appointed by debenture holders.**   The fact that debenture holders, under a power contained in the debentures, appoint their own receiver, does not preclude the court from appointing its own receiver in a proper case.

The holder of a floating security cannot enforce its claim to any specific item of property over which the charge exists, until the security has crystallised.[473] A receiver should usually be asked for over the whole of the property to which the charge extends, though an item of property which is considered valueless may be

---

[461] See *Re London Pressed Hinge Co* [1905] 1 Ch. 576.

[462] *Fowler v Midland Electric Corporation* [1917] 1 Ch. 656.

[463] *Re Escalera Silver Lead Mining Co* (1908) 25 T.L.R. 87.

[464] *Cripps Ltd v Wickenden* [1973] 1 W.L.R. 944; *Bank of Baroda v Panessar* [1987] Ch. 338, and cf. *Windsor Refreigerator v Branch Nominees Ltd* (1961) Ch. 375 CA for a more detailed discussion, see para.19-5 ff, below and Ch.20.

[465] *Re Harris Calculating Machine Co* [1914] 1 Ch. 920.

[466] *Re Tewkesbury Gas Co* [1911] 2 Ch. 279; affirmed [1912] 1 Ch. 1; see also *Central Printing Works v Walker* (1907) 24 T.L.R. 88.

[467] *Re Tewkesbury Gas Co*, n.466, above. As to the currency in which the money is payable, see *Adelaide Electric Supply Co v Prudential Assurance Co* [1934] A.C. 122 (overruling *Broken Hill Co v Latham* [1933] Ch. 333); *Feist v Société Intercommunale Belge* [1934] A.C. 161; *New Brunswick Ry v British, etc. Trust Corporation* [1939] A.C. 1.

[468] *Watling v Lewis* [1911] 1 Ch. 414; *Re Tewkesbury Gas Co*, n.467, above.

[469] See *Edinburgh Corporation v British Linen Bank* [1913].

[470] *Re Slogger Automatic Feeder Co Ltd* [1915] 1 Ch. 478; see below, para.4-13, as to practice.

[471] See Chs 14 and 15, below.

[472] See e.g. Pinto and Evans *Corporate Criminal Responsibility*, 3rd edn (Sweet & Maxwell, 2013) especially Ch.9: "Confiscation, Restraint and Receivership –The Criminal Confiscation Regime".

[473] *Evans v Rival Granite Quarries* [1910] 2 K.B. 979.

excluded from the appointment.[474] But it is submitted that the court has a discretion, and if, on the application to enforce the floating charge by the appointment of a receiver, certain items are excluded, it may be that the court would refuse a subsequent application to include them.

Importance of charge over goodwill of business.   In the absence of a charge over   **2-78**
the goodwill of a business, by express words or necessary inclusion,[475] a manager of the business cannot validly be appointed by the charge-holder, and will not be appointed by the court, for there is no legal or equitable right in the charge-holder to justify it.[476]

If the charge extends to the goodwill, as it usually does in the case of debentures, the receiver will also be appointed manager; this topic is fully dealt with in Ch.9. The debenture holder may, however, elect whether he will have a receiver simply, who would be unable to fulfil the company's contracts, so destroying the goodwill, besides rendering the company liable in damages, or a receiver and manager whose duty it would be to carry out contracts.[477] If debenture holders of a prior series elect for a receiver only, being satisfied that the assets, apart from the goodwill, are sufficient to pay them in full, or if they have no charge on the goodwill, then the receiver could be appointed manager on the application of subsequent incumbrancers whose security includes the goodwill, or of the company, where this can be effected without damage to the prior incumbrancers. In similar circumstances, it appears that the only remedy of unsecured creditors would be to obtain a winding-up order and to apply to have the liquidator appointed manager.

Registration of appointment.   A person who obtains an order for the appoint-   **2-79**
ment of a receiver or manager of the property of a company, or appoints such receiver or manager under the powers of any instrument, must, under s.859K of the Companies Act 2006, within seven days give notice to the Registrar of Companies, who thereupon enters the fact on the register of charges.[478]

Statutory duties.   Any receiver so appointed is subject to numerous statutory   **2-80**
obligations, which are dealt with in Ch.8, below.

Industrial and provident societies.   Prior to the coming into force of the   **2-81**
Industrial and Provident Societies Act 1967 (now repealed),[479] such a society was unable to effect a charge upon personal chattels, without complying with the requirements of the Bills of Sale Acts 1878 and 1882.[480] The reason was that it was not an "incorporated company" within the meaning of the Bills of Sale Act (1878) Amendment Act 1882 s.17, which provides that nothing in that Act is to apply to

---

[474] See *Re Griffin Hotel* [1914] Ch. 129, where a hotel subject to a prior mortgage was excluded.
[475] *Taylor v Soper* (1890) 62 L.T. 828.
[476] *Britannia Building Society v Crammer* [1997] B.P.I.R. 242 (a 1990 decision).
[477] See *Re Newdigate Colliery Co* [1912] 1 Ch. 468.
[478] The penalty for default in complying with this requirement is on summary conviction a fine not exceeding level three on the standard scale and, for continued contravention a daily default fine not exceeding one-tenth of level three on the standard scale: Companies Act 2006 s.859K(7).
[479] See s.8(2).
[480] *Great Northern Railway Company v Coal Co-Operative Society* [1896] 1 Ch. 187; *Re North Wales Produce and Supply Society Ltd* [1922] 2 Ch. 340. Nevertheless, a foreign joint stock company, duly incorporated by its proper law, was held to be within the scope of the definition in *Clark v Balm, Hill & Co* [1908] 1 K.B. 667.

any mortgage, loan, or other incorporated company, and secured upon the capital stock or goods, chattels, and effects of such a company.

If, therefore, an Industrial and Provident Society granted a floating charge over its assets, such charge was valid as to all assets other than personal chattels, but, as to the latter, was void.[481] It is now provided by the Co-operative and Community Benefit Society Act 2014 (which repealed and replaced the 1967 Act) that any instrument executed by a registered society whose registered office is in England or Wales,[482] and which creates or is evidence of a fixed or floating charge on assets of that society, is not to be considered a bill of sale, or to be invalidated by the Bills of Sale Acts, if an application for the recording of the charge is made in the manner indicated by statute,[483] by delivering by post or otherwise to the Financial Conduct Authority,[484] within a period of 21 days[485] from the date of execution (or such extended period as may be allowed by the Financial Conduct Authority),[486] a copy of the instrument authenticated in the manner directed by the Financial Conduct Authority and with such additional authenticated particulars relating to the charge as may be required by the Financial Conduct Authority, and such fee as may be required by rules made in accordance with para.23 of Sch.1ZAS to the Financial Services and Markets Act 2000.[487] It is the duty of the Financial Conduct Authority to secure that an acknowledgement bearing the Financial Conduct Authority's seal is issued to the person by whom the application was made and that the relevant application documents are placed on a file maintained by the Financial Conduct Authority in respect of the society by whom the instrument was executed and that the file is available for public inspection.[488] The Financial Conduct Authority may under s.143 of the Co-operative and Community Benefit Society Act 2014 make provision for the giving of notice to the Financial Conduct Authority of any release, discharge or other transaction relating to any charge so registered and for the inclusion in the file maintained in respect of the society in question of such notice.[489] The holder of a qualifying floating charge created on or after 6 April 2014 may not appoint an administrative receiver of the society.[490]

Every receiver or manager of the property of a registered society, who is appointed under the powers contained in any instrument, must comply with the following requirements:

(a) he or she must, within one month from the date of appointment, notify the Financial Conduct Authority thereof[491];

(b) within one month (or such longer period as the Financial Conduct Author-

---

[481] *Re North Wales Produce and Supply Society Ltd*, n.480, above.

[482] This provision does not apply to Scotland. See ss.62-64.

[483] Co-operative and Community Benefit Society Act 2014 s.59.

[484] Previously the Financial Services Authority.

[485] The former 14-day period was extended by SI 1996/1738.

[486] Pursuant to Co-operative and Community Benefit Society Act 2014 s.60. In the case of inadvertence or other sufficient cause, an application for the recording of a charge was not made within the 21 day period or on account of matters being omitted from or mis-stated in the application, the Financial Conduct Authority may, on such terms as it thinks fit, on the application of the society or any other person claiming the benefit of the instrument, extend the period for registration or rectify the omission or mis-statement.

[487] See s.59 does not apply to a debenture registered under s.14 of the Agricultural Credits Act 1928.

[488] Co-operative and Community Benefit Society Act 2014, s.59(4).

[489] See n.488, above, s.61.

[490] See n.488, above, s.65.

[491] See n.488, above, s.66(2)(a).

ity may allow) after the expiration of the period of six months from that date, and of every subsequent period of six months, he must deliver to the Financial Conduct Authority a return showing his receipts and payments during that period of six months[492];

(c) within one month after he ceases to act as receiver or manager, he must deliver to the Financial Conduct Authority a return showing his receipts and his payments during the final period and the aggregate amount of his receipts and of his payments during all preceding periods since his appointment.[493]

Section 9: In Cases between Vendor and Purchaser

Actions for rescission. The court will, upon a proper case being made out, interfere, upon application made by application notice, and appoint a receiver, in cases between vendor and purchaser. Accordingly, where, on a bill impeaching a sale of land on the ground of fraud, and alleging gross inadequacy of consideration and undue advantage taken of the ignorance of the vendor, the court was of opinion, from the materials before it, that it was hardly possible that the transaction could stand at the hearing, a receiver was appointed in a suit instituted against the devisees of the party charged with fraud.[494] So also, where it appeared that the defendants had obtained the conveyance of the legal estate from the plaintiff upon strong suspicion of abused confidence, a receiver was appointed.[495] But where there is no clear evidence of danger to the property from neglect or misconduct, the court will not usually appoint a receiver in an action to set aside a conveyance[496]; but a receiver and manager will be appointed where necessary to preserve the property, for instance, in order to keep a coal mine in working order.[497]

2-82

Specific performance. If a fair prima facie case for the specific performance of a contract is made to appear, the court may interfere upon application and appoint a receiver.[498]

2-83

On application of purchaser. Thus, where completion was postponed for five years, upon condition that the purchaser punctually paid interest on his purchase-money out of the rents and profits, a receiver was appointed at the instance of a mortgagee of the purchaser's interest, when the vendor had re-entered upon the property in breach of the contract.[499] So also a receiver was appointed, where it was alleged that an estate under a voluntary settlement was being utilised to defeat the claim of a purchaser for value.[500] Similarly, a receiver was appointed in an action to enforce specific performance of a bill of sale of chattels, where there was

2-84

---

492 See n.488, above, s.66(2)(b).
493 See n.488, above, s.66(2)(c).
494 *Stillwell v Wilkins* (1821) Jac. 280.
495 *Huguenin v Baseley* (1808) 13 Ves. 107.
496 *George v Evans* (1840) 4 Y.C. 211, a case of a purchase by a trustee.
497 *Gibbs v David* (1875) L.R. 20 Eq. 373.
498 See *Kennedy v Lee* (1817) 3 Mer. 441; *M'Cleod v Phelps* (1838) 2 Jur. 962. The appointment may be made, in special circumstances, before the order for sale is made absolute: *Re Stafford* (1892) 31 L.R.Ir. 95.
499 *Dawson v Yates* (1839) 1 Beav. 301.
500 *Metcalfe v Pulvertoft* (1813) 1 Ves. & B. 180.

evidence of immediate danger to the chattels.[501] It is submitted that a receiver would be appointed against a vendor who, after receipt of the whole of the purchase money, has refused to execute a conveyance. Where no good title was made, and there was no fund in court, a receiver was appointed and ordered to apply the rents in discharge of the purchaser's interests and costs.[502]

2-85 **On vendor's application.** A receiver has been appointed at the instance of a vendor against a purchaser in possession, who was insolvent and endeavouring to dispose of the estate[503]; against a railway company at the instance of an unpaid vendor[504]; when considerable expenditure was necessary, for which the vendor did not wish to be responsible, where the title had been referred to the master[505]; where a purchaser in possession was dealing with the land contrary to the usual course of husbandry[506]; where, in order to avoid forfeiture, a vendor of leaseholds was obliged to pay rent by reason of default on the part of the purchaser.[507] A receiver and manager was appointed of a farm, pending an appeal by a plaintiff, in an action for specific performance of an agreement for a lease.[508]

2-86 **Indemnity of vendor.** A vendor of a business is entitled to be indemnified against losses in carrying it on, where delay in completion is due to the purchaser's default[509]; it is apprehended that, if he so desires, the vendor might, for his own protection, obtain the appointment of a receiver in such a case.[510]

SECTION 10: IN CASES BETWEEN COVENANTOR AND COVENANTEE

2-87 Where a covenantor refuses to perform his or her covenant, with the result that the covenantee is being deprived of his or her right to payment out of, or to an effective charge upon, particular property, a receiver may be appointed; such cases are equivalent to cases of relief given to an equitable mortgagee. Thus, a receiver was appointed against a tenant in tail[511] refusing to fulfil a covenant to bar his estate tail in order to secure an advance[512]; against the owner of property who refused to carry out his covenant to secure an advance by a mortgage[513]; and against a person who refused to secure an annuity on subsequently acquired property, pursuant to a covenant to do so.[514]

The court will interfere, when necessary, to prevent irreparable mischief from breach of covenant, although the property might have had to be distributed in

---

[501] *Taylor v Eckersley* (1876) 2 Ch. D. 302; (1877) 5 Ch. D. 740.
[502] *Hill v Kirwan* (1826) 1 Hog. 175.
[503] *Hall v Jenkinson* (1813) 1 Ves. & B. 125.
[504] *Munns v Isle of Wight Ry* (1807) L.R. 5 Ch. 414; see *Williams v Aylesbury Ry* (1873) 21 W.R. 819.
[505] *Boehm v Wood* (1820) 2 Jac. & W. 236; and see 1 Jac. & W. 441.
[506] *Osborne v Harvey* (1842) 1 Y. & C.Ch. Cas. 116.
[507] *Cook v Andrews* [1897] 1 Ch. 266.
[508] *Hyde v Warden* (1876) 1 Ex.D 309.
[509] See *Golden Bread Co v Hemmings* [1922] 1 Ch. 162.
[510] See *Hyde v Warden*, n.508, above.
[511] If the legal estate was not in the tenant in tail in possession, the person in whom it was vested might, semble, have been added.
[512] *Free v Hinde* (1827) 2 Sim. 7.
[513] *Shakel v Marlborough* (1819) 4 Madd. 463.
[514] *Metcalfe v Archbishop of York* (1833) 6 Sim.24; 1 M. & C. 533. This case was decided at a time when a charge on a benefice could be effected.

bankruptcy, and though the Court of Bankruptcy (as it then was) might have been able to give the same relief.[515]

Section 11: In Partnership Cases

The potentially disproportionate expense of appointing a receiver, or a receiver **2-88** and manager, means that an application for such relief should be subjected to particularly careful scrutiny, especially in light of the overriding objective under the CPR. This remedy, it has been said,[516] "should normally be regarded as a remedy of last resort".[517]

When dissolution has taken place. The readiness of the court to appoint a **2-89** receiver in partnership cases depends upon whether the partnership has been dissolved at the time when the application is made. If a dissolution has clearly been effected by the service of the claim form,[518] or if the partnership has expired by effluxion of time, a receiver will more readily be appointed, though the appointment is not a matter of course[519]; it will be enough to show that one of the former partners is delaying the winding-up and realisation of the business.[520] Conversely, if all that is shown is that a partner has retired from the partnership, leaving the remaining partners to carry on the former business, he or she will not be entitled to such an appointment.[521]

Principles on which a receiver is appointed. If, however, the partnership is a **2-90** continuing one, and may continue, the court is placed in a position of very great difficulty: if it grants the application, the effect of it is to put an end to the partnership, which one of the parties claims as a right to have continued; while if it refuses the application, it leaves the defendants at liberty to go on with the partnership business at the risk, and probably to the great loss and prejudice, of the dissenting party. Between these difficulties, it is not easy to select the course which is best to be taken; but the court must adopt some mode of proceeding to protect, according to the best view it can take of the matter, the interests of both parties.[522]

It is always a matter for the exercise of the court's discretion; there is no presumption in favour of an appointment, though there are strong persuasive factors (see below). Other forms of relief take precedence, where practicable and likely to prove effective to resolve the particular dispute.[523]

Where dissolution would be ordered at trial. The court does not therefore ap- **2-91**

---

[515] *Riches v Owen* (1868) L.R. 3 Ch. 820, 821; see also para.2-115, below.

[516] *Lindley & Banks on Partnership* (18th ed.) para.23–153.

[517] See also *Don King Productions Inc v Warren* [1999] 2 Lloyd's Rep. 392.

[518] As in the case in a partnership at will.

[519] *Pini v Roncoroni* [1892] 1 Ch. 633. A receiver and manager can be appointed, though the partnership has expired: *Taylor v Neate* (1888) 39 Ch. D. 538. The appointment was made, notwithstanding a provision in the articles for distribution of the assets with a view to the sale of the business as a going concern. The receiver was directed not to enter into contracts involving liability of more than £200, without the consent of the partners or the direction of the judge.

[520] The application notice itself may, in an urgent case, ask leave for the receiver to accept a pending offer for a specific asset, but proper evidence must be contained in the witness statements. By consent, an immediate dissolution and accounts are often ordered on the hearing of the application.

[521] *Sobell v Boston* [1975] 1 W.L.R. 1587.

[522] *Madgwick v Wimble* (1843) 6 Beav. 495 per Lord Langdale; see also, *Blakeney v Dufaur* (1851) 15 Beav. 40; *Sargant v Read* (1876) 1 Ch. D. 600.

[523] *Toker v Akgul* [1996] CLY 4540 CA.

point a receiver, unless it is reasonably clear that a dissolution will be ordered at the trial.[524] If it is not, the court will sometimes grant an injunction to restrain a partner from doing the acts which are complained of, although it will not grant a receiver[525]; for the latter course has the effect of taking the business out of the hands of the partners altogether.[526] Where complaints are made of breaches of partnership articles, it must be seen whether the complaints are urged with a view to making them the foundation of a dissolution, or of a judgment enforcing and carrying on the partnership according to the original terms, and preventing, by proper means, the recurrence of those breaches which have happened before by reason of the conduct of one of the parties.[527]

All the partners, or their representatives, must be before the court, before accounts can be ordered[528]; or, semble, before a receiver can be appointed, except in cases of extreme jeopardy, where a partner cannot be speedily served.

As the appointment is made for the purpose of preserving the assets pending realisation, and of effecting the realisation, the claim form should claim a dissolution, but it need not expressly do so. It is enough if a dissolution is plainly necessary to put an end to the concern.[529] If this be proved, the case stands upon precisely the same basis as if the action had been brought exclusively for the purpose of the dissolution.[530] The court will, in all cases, entertain an application for a receiver, if the object of the action is to wind up the partnership affairs, and the appointment of the receiver is sought with that view.[531]

If, however, it is doubtful whether there is or is not an unexpired term, a receiver will, having regard to the possible consequences of the appointment if there is in truth no partnership, not normally[532] be appointed, unless, of course, there is no danger to the assets[533]; so where a partnership is alleged on one side and denied on the other,[534] a receiver will not normally be appointed, unless the person in possession of the assets consents.

2-92   **Where dissolution not claimed.**   In certain cases, a receiver will be appointed, even where a dissolution is not expressly or impliedly claimed, as, for instance, to receive money, where there is reason to fear that, if received by any of the parties, it might be misapplied, and thus justice could not be done at the trial[535]; thus a receiver has been appointed over the takings of a theatre to secure their application in accordance with an agreement between the partners[536]; and a receiver has been appointed to secure property until a dispute between the partners has been

---

[524] *Goodman v Whitcomb* (1820) 1 Jac. & W. 589; *Smith v Jeyes* (1841) 4 Beav. 403; *Roberts v Eberhardt* (1853) Kay 148.

[525] *Hall v Hall* (1850) 3 Mac. & G. 79, 86.

[526] See *Hartz v Scharder* 1803) 8 Ves. 317; *Hall v Hall*, n.525, above.

[527] *Hall v Hall*, n.525, above.

[528] *Public Trustee v Elder* [1936] Ch. 776.

[529] *Wallworth v Holt* (1836) 4 M. & C. 619. In limited partnership cases, the remedy is by winding up: see *Re Hughes & Co* [1911] 1 Ch. 342.

[530] *Hall v Hall*, n.525, above.

[531] *Sheppard v Oxenford* (1855) 1 K. & J. 491.

[532] See *Floydd v Cheney* [1970] Ch. 602; *Tate v Barry* (1928) 28 S.R. (N.S.W.) 380.

[533] *Baxter v West* (1858) 28 L.J. Ch. 169; *Longbottom v Woodhead* (1887) 31 S.J. 796.

[534] *Peacock v Peacock* (1809) 16 Vest. 49; *Fairburn v Pearson* (1850) 2 Mac. & G. 144; *Tucker v Prior* (1889) 31 S.J. 784; cf. *Re Beard* [1915] H.B.R. 191.

[535] *Hall v Hall*, n.525, above.

[536] *Const. v Harris* (1824) T & R. 496.

determined, though dissolution was not claimed.[537] In such cases, the duties of a receiver are purely administrative.

Receiver not ordered as of course. The court will not, as a matter of course, appoint a receiver of the partnership assets, even where a case for dissolution is made.[538] Since the very basis of a partnership contract is the mutual confidence reposed in each other by the parties,[539] the court will not appoint a receiver, unless some special ground for its interference is established.[540] It must appear that the member or members of the firm against whom the appointment of a receiver is sought, has or have done acts which are inconsistent with the duty of a partner, and are of a nature to destroy the mutual confidence which ought to subsist between the parties.[541]

In the case of a professional firm, since the appointment of a receiver and manager may easily do far more harm than good, the court will be reluctant to make the appointment in such cases, unless it is unavoidable.[542]

2-93

Misconduct of partner. The ground on which the court is most commonly asked to appoint a receiver is where, by the misconduct of a partner, his or her right of personal intervention in the partnership affairs has been forfeited, and the partnership funds are in danger of being lost. Mere quarrels and disagreements between the partners, arising from infirmities of temper, are not a sufficient ground for the interference of the court.[543] The due winding up of the affairs of the concern must be shown to be endangered, to induce the court to appoint a receiver.[544] The non-co-operation of one partner, whereby the whole responsibility of management is thrown on his co-partner, is not sufficient.[545] But if the quarrels between the partners are such as to occasion a complete deadlock in carrying on the business, a receiver will be appointed.[546]

The appointment will be made, where a partner has so misconducted himself or herself as to show that he or she is no longer to be trusted; as, for example, if one partner colludes with the debtors of the firm, and allows them to delay paying their debts[547]; or if he or she is carrying on a separate trade on his or her own account with the partnership property[548]; or if a surviving partner insists on carrying on the business and employing therein the assets of the deceased partner[549]; or if, in the opinion of the court, a case has arisen for the interposition of the court to secure

2-94

---

[537] *Medwin v Ditchman* [1882] W.N. 121; 47 L.T. 250.
[538] *Harding v Glover* (1810) 18 Ves. 281; *Fairbum v Pearson*, n.534, above. cf. *Sobell v Boston* n.521, above.
[539] *Philips v Atkinson* [1787] 2 Bro. C.C. 272; see too, *Peacock v Peacock*, n.534.
[540] *Harding v Glover*, n.538, above.
[541] *Smith v Jeyes* (1841) 4 Beav. 503.
[542] *Floydd v Cheney*, n.532, above; *Sobell v Boston*, n.521, at 1593–1594.
[543] See *Goodman v Whitcombe* (1820) 1 Jac. & W. 589; *Marshall v Colman* (1820) 2 Jac. & W. 266; *Smith v Jeyes*, n.541, above at 504.
[544] See *Goodman v Whitcombe*, n.543, above; *Smith v Jeyes*, n.541, above.
[545] *Roberts v Eberhardt* [1853] Kay 148; see, too, *Rowe v Wood* (1822) 2 Jac. & W. 553, where one partner declined to advance more money to work a mine.
[546] See *Re Yenidje Tobacco Co* [1916] 2 Ch. 426.
[547] *Estwick v Conningsby* (1692) 1 Vern. 118.
[548] *Harding v Glover*, n.538, above.
[549] *Madgwick v Wimble* (1843) 6 Beav. 495.

the estate of a deceased partner against loss[550]; or if, the partnership property being abroad, one of the partners goes off there in order to do what he or she likes with it[551]; or, if the persons having the control of the partnership assets have already made away with some of them[552]; or if there has been such mismanagement as to endanger the whole concern[553]; or if one of the partners has acted in a manner inconsistent with the duties and obligations which are implied in every partnership contract.[554]

Since the unwillingness of the court, to appoint a receiver at the suit of one member of a firm against another, is based on the confidence originally reposed in each other by the parties, the ground of the rule has no longer any place, if it appears that the confidence has been misplaced[555]; as, for instance, where a prima facie case is made that the claimant has been induced to enter into partnership with the defendant by the fraudulent misrepresentations of the latter.[556]

2-95 **Partner excluded from management.**   There is a case for appointing a receiver, even although there be no misconduct endangering the partnership assets, where one partner excludes another partner from the management of the partnership affairs.[557] This doctrine is acted on, where the defendant contends that the claimant is not a partner,[558] or that he has no interest in the partnership assets,[559] or where the partnership is disputed by the defendant on the ground of illegality[560]—as, for instance, where its object is contrary to public policy.[561]

Inasmuch as the court will not appoint a receiver against a partner, unless some special ground for doing so can be shown, it follows that, in the case of a firm consisting of three or four members, there is more difficulty in obtaining a receiver than in a firm consisting of two. For since the appointment of a receiver operates as an injunction against the members, there must be some ground for excluding all who oppose the application. If the object is to exclude some or one only from intermeddling, the appropriate remedy is rather by injunction than by the appointment of a receiver.[562]

---

[550] *Baldwin v Booth* [1872] W.N. 229; *Young v Buckett* (1822) 3 W.R. 511; 46 L.T. 269.

[551] *Sheppard v Oxenford* (1855) 1 K. & J. 491.

[552] *Evans v Coventry* (1845) 5 D.M. & G. 911.

[553] See *De Tastet v Bordieu* (1805) cited in 2 Bro.C.C. 272; *Jefferys v Smith* (1820) 1 Jac. & W. 298; *Hall v Hall* (1850) 3 Mac. & G. 79; *Chaplin v Young* (1862) 6 L.T. 97.

[554] *Smith v Jeyes*, n.541, above. *Young v Buckett*, n.550, above.

[555] See *Chapman v Beach* (1820) 1 Jac. & W. 594n.

[556] See *Ex p. Broome* (1811) 1 Rose 69.

[557] See *Wilson v Greenwood* (1818) 1 Swans, 471; *Goodman v Whitcombe* (1820) 1 Jac. & W. 589; *Rowe v Wood* (1822) 2 Jac. & W. 553; *Const v Harris* (1824) T. & R. 496. A dissolution which takes place on the refusal of an appointee under a will to become a partner is not a dissolution arising from the exclusion of the appointee by the surviving partner, and therefore will not be a foundation for a receiver: *Kershaw v Matthews* (1826) 2 Russ. 62.

[558] *Peacock v Peacock* (1809) 16 Ves. 49; *Blakeney v Dufaur* (1851) 15 Beav. 40.

[559] *Wilson v Greenwood*, n.557, above, where the plaintiffs were the assignees of a bankrupt partner. See too, *Clegg v Fishwick* (1849) 1 Mac. & G. 294, where the plaintiff was the administratix of a deceased partner.

[560] *Hale v Hale* (1841) 4 Beav. 369. A partnership between two bookmakers has been held not to be, per se, illegal: *Thwaites v Coulthwaite* [1869] 1 Ch. 496; *Keen v Price* [1914] 2 Ch. 98; *Jeffrey v Bamford* [1921] 2 K.B. 351, notwithstanding the dictum of Fletcher Moulton LJ in *Hyams v Stuart-King* [1908] 2 K.B. 696, 718; and see now Gambling Act 2005; but a receiver would not be appointed to get in gambling debts.

[561] Quaere, whether a partnership to carry on a business, which would involve breach of the law of a friendly state, is illegal.

[562] *Hall v Hall* (1850) 3 Mac. & G. 79.

Partners without power of dissolution.   Another case, in which the court may   **2-96**
be called upon to appoint a receiver, is where the partners have by agreement
divested themselves more or less of their right to wind up the affairs of the concern.
In one case,[563] for instance, the plaintiff and defendant, on dissolving partnership,
appointed a third person to get in the assets of the partnership, and had agreed not
to interfere with him. After the agreement had been partially acted on, one partner
died, and, disputes arising between the executors of the deceased partner and the
surviving partner, the latter got in some of the debts of the firm in violation of the
agreement. A bill having been filed by the executors of the deceased partner for an
injunction and a receiver, the court on motion appointed a receiver, but declined to
grant an injunction, on the ground that there was no sufficient impropriety of
conduct on the part of the defendant to render such an order necessary.[564]

Death, bankruptcy, etc. of a partner.   The reasoning on which the court   **2-97**
proceeds, when it refuses to appoint a receiver at the instance of one member of a
firm against another, does not apply in the case of persons who acquire an interest
in the partnership assets by events over which the parties have no control. If a
member of a firm dies, or becomes bankrupt, the partnership is determined, as far
as his personal representatives or trustee in bankruptcy are or is concerned. The
personal representatives of a deceased partner are not strictly partners, nor is the
trustee of a bankrupt partner strictly a partner, with the surviving or solvent partners
or partner. They are only tenants in common with the surviving or solvent partners
or partner, to the extent of the interest which the deceased or bankrupt partner had
in the partnership assets at the time of death or bankruptcy, as the case may be.[565]

It is, consequently, a matter of course to appoint a receiver when all the partners
are dead, and an action is pending between their representatives[566]; or when such
appointment is sought by a partner against the personal representatives or trustee
in bankruptcy of his deceased or bankrupt co-partner.[567] *Fraser v Kershaw*[568] is a
good illustration of the doctrine. There, one partner had become bankrupt; the share
of the other partner had been taken in execution under a writ of *fi. fa.* for a separate
debt, and had been assigned to the judgment creditor by the sheriff. The creditor,
as the assignee from the sheriff of the share and interest of the non-bankrupt partner,
claimed the right of winding up the affairs of the partnership, and to exclude the
assignees of the bankrupt partner from interfering. But, on bill filed by the assignees in bankruptcy against the judgment creditor, the court granted an injunction and appointed a receiver, holding that the right of the non-bankrupt partner to
wind up the affairs was personal to himself and not transferable, and, therefore, did
not pass with his share and interest in the partnership assets.[569]

The death or bankruptcy of one of the members of a firm is not itself a ground
for the appointment of a receiver, as against the surviving or solvent partner or

---

[563] *Davis v Amer* (1854) 3 Drew. 64.

[564] See also *Turner v Major* (1836) 3 Giff. 442.

[565] *Ex p. Williams* (1805) 11 Vest. 516; *Wilson v Grenwood*, n.557, above; *Fraser v Kershaw* (1856) 2
K. & J. 499.

[566] *Philips v Atkinson* (1787) 2 Bro.C.C. 272.

[567] *Freeland v Stansfeld* (1854) 16 Jur. 792; 2 Sm. & G. 479.

[568] (1856) 2 K. & J. 496.

[569] For the procedure against partnership property for a partner's separate judgment debt, see the Partnership Act 1890 s.23, para.2-42, above.

partners.[570] If a partners dies,[571] or becomes bankrupt,[572] a right to wind up the partnership concern and collect the assets is by law vested in the surviving[573] or solvent[574] partner or partners, as the case may be. Before the court will interfere and appoint a receiver, some breach or neglect of duty on their part must be established.[575]

If it is more convenient that the affairs of the partnership should be wound up in the bankruptcy, the court will not appoint a receiver: thus, where one partner had died and the other had been adjudicated bankrupt, the court, on the application of the trustee in bankruptcy, discharged an order for a receiver made in a partnership action commenced by the executors of the dead partner, on proof that the solvency of the partnership and of the dead partner's estate was very doubtful.[576]

2-98   **Disputes referable to arbitration.**   A receiver may be appointed in an action for dissolution, notwithstanding a reference of disputes to arbitration.[577] Under s.44 of the Arbitration Act 1996, unless otherwise agreed by the parties, the court has for the purposes of and in relation to arbitral proceedings the same power of appointing a receiver as it has for the purposes of and in relation to legal proceedings. If the case is one of urgency, the court may, on the application of a party or proposed party to the arbitral proceedings, make appoint a receiver if it thinks it necessary for the purpose of preserving evidence or assets. However, if the case is not one of urgency, the court is to act only on the application of a party to the arbitral proceedings (upon notice to the other parties and to the tribunal) made with the permission of the tribunal or the agreement in writing of the other parties. In any case the court shall act only if or to the extent that the arbitral tribunal, and any arbitral or other institution or person vested by the parties with power in that regard, has no power or is unable for the time being to act effectively.

In an appropriate case, the court will, by one and the same order, appoint a receiver and stay all proceedings in the claim, except for the purpose of carrying out the order for a receiver.[578]

2-99   **Jurisdiction of courts.**   Where the value of the whole assets of the partnership do not exceed in value the county court limit, currently £350,000, the county court can exercise all the jurisdiction of the High Court in actions for dissolution or winding-up.[579] The jurisdiction of the county court may be extended by agreement in

---

[570] See *Philips v Atkinson* (1787) 2 Bro.C.C. 272, and see also Insolvent Partnerships Order 1994 (SI 1994/2421), as amended, and para.2-97, above.

[571] *Collins v Young* (1853) 1 Macq. 385.

[572] *Fraser v Kershaw* (1856) 2 K. & J. 496: see n.568, above.

[573] *Collins v Young*, n.571, above.

[574] *Freeland v Stansfeld*, n.567, above. *Fraser v Kershaw*, n.572, above.

[575] *Collins v Young*, n.571, above; see *Baldwin v Booth* [1872] W.N. 229. The court will under very special circumstances appoint an administrator pendente lite against a surviving partner: *Horrell v Witts* (1866) L.R. 1 P. 103.

[576] *Hulme v Rowbotham* [1907] W.N. 162, 189; most of the assets were situate within the jurisdiction of the county court which was the tribunal in the bankruptcy proceedings. Executors carrying on a testator's business cannot be made bankrupt as partners; *Re Fisher* [1912] 2 K.B. 491.

[577] *Halsey v Windham* [1882] W.N. 108; *Compagnie du Sénégal v Woods* [1883] W.N. 180; 53 L.J. Ch. 16.

[578] *Pini v Roncoroni* [1892] 1 Ch. 633. See also Arbitration Act 1996 s.9.

[579] County Courts Act 1984 s.23; County Courts Jurisdiction Order 2014 (SI 2014/503). As to transfers, see County Courts Act 1984 ss.38, 40-42.

writing.[580] In the High Court, proceedings normally continue in the Chancery Division or a Chancery District registry but in cases of a partnership between spouses where there are matrimonial proceedings on foot in the Family Division it may be appropriate for the dissolution proceedings also to be heard in the Family Division.[581]

A partnership formed to work metalliferous mines in Cornwall was previously a "company" within the meaning of that term in the ss.2 and 28 of the Stannaries Act 1887 (now repealed), and was by s.1(2) of the Partnership Act 1890 (now amended to remove the reference to Stannaries) excluded from the provisions of the latter Act. By virtue of s.1 of the Stannaries Court (Abolition) Act 1896, the county court now has exclusive jurisdiction to wind up such a partnership, and an application for a receiver should be made to that court.[582]

Enemy partner.   The outbreak of war causes the dissolution of a partnership, one   **2-100**
of the partners in which is an enemy[583] though the enemy partner is entitled to his share of profits made in winding up the business.[584] In such cases, a receiver will be appointed in an action in which the English partner is claimant[585]; the enemy partner can be made defendant, but cannot be a claimant.[586] After a vesting order had been made under the Trading with the Enemy Act 1939, and rules thereunder, the Custodian of Enemy Property will be the defendant in place of the enemy. Enemy character for this purpose does not depend upon nationality, but upon residence in an enemy territory.[587]

Pending action in foreign tribunal.   Where partners have agreed to refer disputes   **2-101**
to a foreign tribunal, the court will not appoint a receiver during the liquidation of the partnership affairs, unless it is shown that the rights of the partners cannot be sufficiently protected by the foreign tribunal.

Mining partnerships.   In cases of mining partnerships, a receiver will be ap-   **2-102**
pointed or refused upon the same principles as in other cases of partnership. Accordingly, if a dissolution or winding-up is not sought, a receiver will not be appointed[588]; but, where a dissolution or winding-up is sought, a receiver and manager will be appointed, if there are any such grounds for the appointment as are suf-

---

[580] County Courts Act 1984 s.24.
[581] See *Matz v Matz* (1984) 14 Fam.Law 178, where a transfer to the Family Division was refused on the facts.
[582] *Dunbar v Harvey* [1913] 2 Ch. 530.
[583] See *Kupfer v Kupfer* [1915] W.N. 397.
[584] See *Hugh Stevenson & Sons Ltd v Aktiengesellschaft für Cartonnagen Industrie* [1918] A.C. 239; as to considerations determining enemy character, see para.2-124, below.
[585] *Rombach v Rombach* [1910] W.N. 423; see *Armitage v Borgman* [1915] 84 L.J. Ch. 784, where a receiver was appointed in a case where the enemy partners retired immediately before the war.
[586] *Porter v Freudenberg* [1915] 1 K.B. 857. An alien enemy was allowed to be joined as a formal plaintiff in actions to recover debts due to the partnership: *Rodriguez v Speyer Bros.* [1919] A.C. 59. But this part of the decision will not be followed (see *Sovfracht (V10) v Van Udens Scheepvaart en Agentuur Maatschappij (N.V. Gebr.)* [1943] A.C. 203.
[587] See s.15, "Enemies", para.2-124, below.
[588] *Roberts v Eberhardt* (1853) Kay 148.

ficient in other cases,[589] or if the partners cannot agree as to the proper mode of working the mines until they are sold.[590]

Thus, a receiver was refused, although one of the partners had excluded the other from interfering in the concern; but the case was peculiar, for the partner complained of was not only a partner but also a mortgagee in possession, and his mortgage debt was unsatisfied.[591] Again, although the plaintiff had been excluded,[592] an application for a receiver of a mining concern was refused on the ground of his laches; for he had been excluded for some time, and had taken no steps to assert his right until the mines proved profitable.[593]

Again, where one of the partners in a mining concern had become mentally infirm, the court would not appoint a manager to carry on the business, but ordered a sale, and appointed an interim manager only.[594]

2-103 **Form of order.** In cases where a receiver of partnership property is appointed, the order should direct all partners and other parties to deliver over to the receiver all securities in their hands for such estate or property, and also the stock-in-trade and effects of the partnership, together with all books and papers relating thereto.[595] The court may abstain from making an order for the delivery of partnership books and papers, if there is no necessity for it, and if it would occasion inconvenience.[596]

By s.23 of the Partnership Act 1890, a judgment creditor of a partner may obtain an order appointing a receiver of that partner's share of profits, and of any other moneys which may be coming to him in respect of the partnership.[597]

Section 12: In Cases of Mental Incapacity

2-104 Receiverships due to mental incapacity were abolished in 2007. For the sake of historical completeness, there follows an account of the previous role played by receivers in mental health cases as well as an explanation of the system now in place. In cases of mental incapacity, the court had always exercised a jurisdiction to appoint a receiver, though no action was pending.[598] Under the practice prior to 1 October 2007,[599] the application was made to the Court of Protection in proceedings under the Mental Health Act 1983, and the appointment was not made by the Chancery Division,[600] except in the case of trustees.[601] After 1 October 2007, the position has been completely changed by the Mental Capacity Act 2005. All

---

[589] *Roberts v Eberhardt* (1853) Kay 148; *Sheppard v Oxenford* (1855) 1 K. & J. 491.
[590] *Jefferys v Smith* (1820) 1 Jac. & W. 298; *Roberts v Eberhardt*, n.588, above; *Lees v Jones* (1857) 3 Jur. (n.s.) 954.
[591] *Rowe v Wood* (1822) 2 Jac. & W. 553.
[592] *Norway v Rower* (1812) 19 Ves. 144, 158, 159.
[593] *Clegg v Edmondson* (1857) 8 D.M. & G. 787.
[594] *Rowlands v Williams* (1861) 30 Beav. 302.
[595] *Seton*, 7th edn, p.728.
[596] *Dacie v John* (1824) M'Cle. 206.
[597] See *Brand v Sandground* (1901) 85 L.T. 517.
[598] *Ex p. Whitfield* (1742) 2 Atk. 315. As regards the exercise of the inherent jurisdiction to appoint a receiver in respect of an incapacitated adult's financial affairs, even if there was an available statutory remedy see: *City of Sunderland v PS* [2007] EWHC 623 (Fam); [2007] 2 FLR 103.
[599] See Mental Capacity Act 2005 Sch.7 which abolished receiverships under the Mental Health Act 1983 in force 1 October 2007.
[600] As to appointment of receivers, under the practice prior to the Lunacy Act 1890, see *Ex p. Radcliffe* (1820) 1 Jac. & W. 639; *Re Birch*, in Shelford on Lunacy, p.187.
[601] See para.2-108, below.

receiverships under the Mental Health Act 1983 then came to an end but any receivers then in office continued as "deputies" under the 2005 Act, but subject to certain transitional provisions.[602] Prior to this date, the significance of receivers had already diminished by reason of the ability to create enduring powers of attorney.

Receivers under the Mental Health Act 1983. By s.99 of the Mental Health Act 1983, the judge[603]—in practice the Master of the Court of Protection,[604] or, by direction of the Master, the Public Trustee[605]—was authorised to appoint receivers, to exercise large powers of administration and management over the property of persons incapable, by reason of mental disorder, of managing and administering their property and affairs, who were comprehensively called "patients".[606] The receiver was to do all such things in relation to the property and affairs of the patient as the judge[607] ordered or directed him or her to do, and might do any such thing in relation thereto as the judge[608] might authorise him or her to do.[609] The powers of the judge[610] in this respect were very wide.   **2-105**

Wide as were the powers which could be conferred upon a receiver,[611] he or she had no powers over the person of the patient. The jurisdiction extended to patients resident abroad with property here: and under s.100, stocks registered here in the name of any person, in respect of whom a person had been appointed to exercise powers with respect to his or her property or affairs, on grounds which would render him or her a patient if resident here, might be ordered to be transferred to the foreign curator.[612] Where an English patient had property in a foreign country, it was usually necessary for the English receiver to appoint an attorney under the direction of the master. The detailed practice of the Court of Protection with regard to the appointment of so-called receivers was entirely distinct from that in the case of ordinary receivers.[613] Pursuant to the Public Trustee and Administration of Funds Act 1986,[614] the Public Trustee might have been appointed a receiver under the 1983 Act.[615]

Effect of orders under the Mental Health Act 1983. When the property of a patient became subject to the control of the Court of Protection by the appointment of a receiver, and the receiver was in physical possession, it could not be seized under a writ of *fi. fa.* by an execution creditor of the patient, for the patient's   **2-106**

---

[602] Mental Capacity Act 2005 Sch.5 para.1.

[603] For definition, see the now repealed Mental Health Act 1983 s.94(1) as amended by the Public Trustee and Administration of Funds Act 1986 ss.2(2) and 112.

[604] See the now repealed Mental Health Act 1983 s.93(2).

[605] See the now repealed Mental Health Act 1983 s.94(1A) as amended by the Public Trustee and Administration of funds Act 1986 s.2(2)(c).

[606] See for the CPR procedures, CPR 21.

[607] See n.603, above.

[608] See the now repealed Mental Health Act 1983 s.99(1).

[609] See n.608, above; and n.603, above.

[610] See n.605, above, ss.96-98.

[611] See n.603, above.

[612] See the now repealed Mental Health Act 1983 s.100.

[613] See *Heywood & Massey's Court of Protection Practice*, 11th edn.

[614] See n.612, above, s.3.

[615] For the appropriate forms of order, see the former *Practice Direction (Mental Health: Public Trustee)* [1987] 1 W.L.R. 63. The Public Trustee was appointed receiver in all cases in which the Principal of the Management Division of the Court of Protection had been (as at 2 January 1987) receiver, and the Management Division of the Court of Protection became the Receivership Division.

right to maintenance took priority over the claim of the execution creditor.[616] But where a judgment creditor, having notice of the pendency of a summons in the Court of Protection for the appointment of a receiver, issued a *fi. fa.*, under which the goods of the patient were seized before any order was made on the summons, and a receiver was afterwards appointed while the goods were in the possession of the sheriff, it was held that the creditor's claim must be satisfied before anything could be allowed for the maintenance of the patient.[617] For a receiver so appointed was only authorised to take possession of the patient's equitable interest in his property; accordingly, an order under s.99 of the Mental Health Act 1983, appointing such a receiver, did not affect any previously acquired rights of third persons against the property of the patient, which were of such a nature that effect could be given to them at law or in equity, as, for instance, a vendor's lien for unpaid purchase-money.[618] The receiver could not be authorised to sell the patient's estate tail, but could be authorised to sell the land so as to bar the estate tail.[619]

2-107   **Insolvent patients under the Mental Health Act 1983.**   A person suffering from "mental disorder", within the meaning of the Mental Health Act 1983, could only be proceeded against in bankruptcy in consequence of having failed to comply with the requirements of a statutory demand, or of having failed to satisfy in whole or in part an execution levied against his property.[620] The abolition of acts of bankruptcy eliminated the problems arising from the subjective elements formerly involved in the commission of some of such acts.[621]

The existence of an order appointing a receiver of certain specified property of a debtor was held not to prevent a receiving order in bankruptcy being made against such a debtor, after he had recovered his faculties.[622]

Under the Bankruptcy Act 1914, a direction in the order for the receiver to pay debts incurred after the date of the receivership order was held to create no charge in favour of the creditors, and the judge could not make it a term of the order for payment out to the executor of the patient that the debts should be discharged.[623]

2-108   **Dealing with patient's estate.**   Where an order authorised the receiver to receive, and give a discharge for, all dividends accrued due before lodgment, it was held that the bank must pay these dividends to the receiver.[624]

---

[616] *Re Winkle* [1894] 2 Ch. 519.

[617] *Re Clarke* [1898] 1 Ch. 336.

[618] *Davies v Thomas* [1900] 2 Ch. 462, 472, 473, explaining *Re Winkle*, n.616, above.

[619] *Re EDS* [1914] 1 Ch. 618: the proceeds were resettled on analogous trusts.

[620] *Re Belton (A Debtor)* [1913] W.N. 63; 108 L.T. 244 (under Bankruptcy Act 1883). Under Insolvency Act 1986, receiving orders in bankruptcy were abolished and replaced by bankruptcy orders, which effect the immediate adjudication of the debtor. Insolvency Act 1986 no longer includes any special provisions for bankruptcy proceedings by or against persons falling under the Mental Health Acts as mentally handicapped persons (now retitled "PLDs," i.e. "persons with learning difficulties"); but Ch.12 of the Insolvency Rules 2016 by rr.12.23–12.26, provides for the appointment by the court of representatives to appear for, represent and act for patients, therein called "incapacitated persons"; that term also includes persons physically incapacitated.

[621] *Re Belton*, n.620, above.

[622] See n.612, above.

[623] *Re Wheater* [1928].

[624] *Re Spurling* [1909] 1 Ch. 199 see 201 for form of order. It was formerly usual to order transfer into court, *Re Browne* [1894] 3 Ch. 412.

The receiver was the statutory agent of the patient[625]; a solicitor employed by the receiver therefore had an independent right against the patient's estate, and the Limitation Acts could not be pleaded by the receiver, unless the judge[626] in his or her discretion so ordered.[627]

The mere appointment did not cause a forfeiture of a protected life interest, as the receiver was a statutory agent for the patient[628]; nor did the fact that certain costs, fees and percentages were by statute[629] charged on the patient's estate cause such a forfeiture[630]; and the appointment prevented a subsequent document purporting to be a charge operating as a forfeiture, since it was wholly void.[631]

The appointment of a receiver by the Court of Protection did not prevent the Family Division in divorce from securing payment of an annual sum for a divorced spouse. Where, by an order in the Court of Protection, provision had been made for the wife, application was to be made to the Family Division for periodical payments, and for an order that they be secured at the same rate as that so ordered by the Court of Protection (if that were to be considered proper), without prejudice to any further order of the Court of Protection, the security not to be enforceable while the order of the Court of Protection was subsisting or until the death of the husband.[632]

The High Court retained its jurisdiction in the case of trustees who were patients[633]; but there was concurrent jurisdiction in the Court of Protection to make orders for the appointment of new trustees, and for vesting orders under s.54 of the Trustee Act 1925, in the cases specified in that section, including cases where the patient-trustee had any beneficial interest.[634] Where the appointment of a receiver of the trust property was required, there had to be administration proceedings in the Chancery Division.

Interim receiver. In a proper case, the judge[635] would appoint an interim receiver   **2-109**
of the estate of the supposed patient and, if the case was urgent, would do so upon an application without notice: but, unless the person appointed was the Official Solicitor, he or she was required, in default of a direction to the contrary, not to act as such until he or she had given security.[636] In such a case, if actions were pending against the supposed patient, the receiver's proper course was to apply to be ap-

---

[625] *Plumpton v Burkinshaw* [1908] 2 K.B. 572; *Re Oppenheim's Will Trust* [1950] Ch. 633.

[626] See n.612, above.

[627] *Re EG* [1914] 1 Ch. 927.

[628] *Re Marshall* [1920] 1 Ch. 284. cf. *Re Silverstone* [1949] Ch. 270 (legacy to person, if in patient's employment).

[629] See the now repealed Mental Health Act 1983 s.106(5).

[630] n.629, above, s.106(6), replacing Law Reform (Miscellaneous Provisions) Act 1949 s.8, which nullified the effect of *Re Custance's Settlements* [1946] Ch. 42; that case was, however, wrongly decided: *Re Westby's Settlement* [1950] Ch. 296.

[631] *Re Marshall*, n.628, above.

[632] *CL v CFW* [1928] P. 223. As to the proper form of Order, where it was the wife who was the patient, see *Swettenham v Swettenham* [1939] 3 All E.R. 989.

[633] See also the revoked Court of Protection Rules 2001 (SI 2001/824).

[634] See generally note "Appointment of New Trustees" in *Civil Court Practice* (2004) on the former CPR Sch.1 - RSC Ord.93. The concurrent jurisdiction extended to cases where an order of the Court of Protection had authorised the exercise of a power of appointing a trustee.

[635] See n.603, above.

[636] See the now revoked Court of Protection Rules 2001; *Re Pountain* (1888) 37 Ch. D. 609, 610, application was made to the Lords Justices, ex parte.

pointed litigation friend[637] in the several actions.[638] Where under the old practice a petition had been presented, but, pending the hearing, a coroner's jury had found a verdict of murder while of unsound mind against the supposed patient, a receiver was appointed till further order, the expression "interim" receiver being inappropriate to such a case.[639]

2-110   **Documents belonging to supposed patient in possession of receiver.** In *Re Cathcart*,[640] pending an inquiry as to the state of mind of a supposed patient, the Official Solicitor had been appointed receiver of her estate, and in that capacity had in his possession a mass of documents belonging to her. Upon an application made on her behalf for liberty to inspect and take copies of such of the documents as she might require for her defence on the inquiry, the Court of Appeal held that the proper course would be for the master, who had charge of the inquiry, to look through the documents and ascertain which of them were relevant to the inquiry; and that the parties were not at liberty to go before the master for the purpose.

Where there were no proceedings in the Court of Protection, the High Court would not, it seems, exercise its jurisdiction to order rents and profits of property belonging to a patient to be paid to a person for the benefit of the patient, if the latter was within the jurisdiction[641]; the application had to be made to the Court of Protection for a receiver. The court might have, however, made such an order, where the patient was out of the jurisdiction,[642] if a foreign court of competent jurisdiction had appointed an administrator, with authority to receive specified property of the patient in this country, the persons, in whose hands such property was, would have to hand it over to the administrator; if they insisted on an action being brought in this country, they may not have been allowed costs.[643] Such an action was brought by the foreign administrator in his own name and as "next friend" of the patient.[644] In the case of property to which the title of the person of unsound mind was equitable, the court had a discretion to limit the order to sums required for maintenance.

2-111   **Discharge of a receiver.** The receiver had to be discharged, if the judge[645] was satisfied that the former patient had become capable of managing and administering his or her property and affairs; he or she may have been discharged at any time, if the judge[646] considered it expedient in the interests of the patient[647] to do so. The receiver would be discharged (without any order) on the death of the patient.[648] It

---

[637] Under CPR 21, PD 21 and CPR PN 21, the person required to represent a child or a patient is now termed a "litigation friend".

[638] *Re Pountan*, n.636, above per Cotton LJ at 610.

[639] *Re AG* (1909) 53 S.J. 615.

[640] [1902] W.N. 80.

[641] *Re Barker's Trusts* [1904] W.N. 13.

[642] *Re Carr's Trusts* [1904] 1 Ch. 792; see also *Didisheim v London and Westminter Bank* [1900] 2 Ch. 15.

[643] *Pélégrin v Coutts & Co* [1915] 1 Ch. 696, and see the now repealed Mental Health Act 1983 s.100 and para.2-105, above, as to stock in the name of the patient.

[644] As to his appropriate title, see n.637, above.

[645] See n.603, para.2-105, above.

[646] See n.603, para.2-105, above.

[647] *Re N dec'd* [1977] 1 W.L.R. 676.

[648] See the now repealed Mental Health Act 1983 s.99(3): the administrator's title would seem not to be "litigation friend": see n.637, above.

follows that he or she could not, therefore, take credit for payments made,[649] nor could his or her sureties be made liable for rents and profits received after that date, although, of course, he or she and they remained liable in respect of all moneys received before the death.[650]

The Mental Capacity Act 2005. Under the Mental Capacity Act 2005 the of-   **2-112**
fice of the Court of Protection within the Supreme Court was abolished and in its place a new Court of Protection, being a superior court of record, was created.[651]

Almost all powers under the 2005 Act have to be exercised subject to the application of the "principles" set out in s.1 which are: (1) a person must be assumed to have capacity unless it is established that he or she lacks capacity; (2) a person is not to be treated as unable to make a decision unless all practicable steps to help him or her to do so have been taken without success; (3) a person is not to be treated as unable to make a decision merely because he or she makes an unwise decision; (4) an act done, or decision made, under this Act for or on behalf of a person who lacks capacity must be done, or made, in his or her best interests[652]; and (5) before the act is done, or the decision is made, regard must be had to whether the purpose for which it is needed can be as effectively achieved in a way that is less restrictive of the person's rights and freedom of action.

If a person ("P") lacks capacity in relation to a matter or matters concerning P's personal welfare, or P's property and affairs, the court may by making an order, make the decision or decisions on P's behalf in relation to the matter or matters, or appoint a person[653] (a "deputy") to make decisions on P's behalf in relation to the matter or matters.[654] When deciding whether it is in P's best interests to appoint a deputy, the court must have regard (in addition to the matters mentioned in s.4 dealing with determining P's best interests) to the principles that a decision by the court is to be preferred to the appointment of a deputy to make a decision, and the powers conferred on a deputy should be as limited in scope and duration as is reasonably practicable in the circumstances. The court may make such further orders or give such directions, and confer on a deputy such powers or impose on him or her such duties, as it thinks necessary or expedient for giving effect to, or otherwise in connection with, an order or appointment made by it in this respect. There are wide powers in the court to vary or revoke an appointment of a deputy. In particular, and without limitation, the court may revoke the appointment of a deputy or vary the

---

[649] See *Re Bennett* [1913] 2 Ch. 318.

[650] *Re Walker* [1907] 2 Ch. 120. The receiver, it seems, could not be made liable in the existing proceedings, though he or she could be in properly constituted proceedings: see also *Re Seager Hunt* [1906] 2 Ch. 296, and see the former r.64 of the Court of Protection Rules 2001, as to jurisdiction after the death.

[651] Mental Capacity Act 2005 Pt 2.

[652] See further, Mental Capacity Act 2005 s.4.

[653] A deputy appointed by the court must be an individual who has reached 18, or as respects powers in relation to property and affairs, an individual who has reached 18 or a trust corporation. The court may appoint an individual by appointing the holder for the time being of a specified office or position. A person may not be appointed as a deputy without his or her consent: Mental Capacity Act 1985 s.19(1)-(3).

[654] Mental Capacity Act 2005 s.16. The court may appoint two or more deputies to act jointly, jointly and severally, or jointly in respect of some matters and jointly and severally in respect of others. When appointing a deputy or deputies, the court may at the same time appoint one or more other persons to succeed the existing deputy or those deputies in such circumstances, or on the happening of such events, as may be specified by the court and for such period as may be so specified: Mental Capacity Act 1985 s.19(4)-(5).

powers conferred f it is satisfied that the deputy has behaved, or is behaving, in a way that contravenes the authority conferred by the court or is not in P's best interests, or proposes to behave in a way that would contravene that authority or would not be in P's best interests. The powers of the court regarding (among other things) the appointment of deputies are subject to the provisions of the 1983 Act and, in particular, to ss.1 (the principles) and 4 (best interests). The court may require a deputy to give to the Public Guardian such security as the court thinks fit for the due discharge of his or her functions, and to submit to the Public Guardian such reports at such times or at such intervals as the court may direct.[655]

Questions of personal welfare go beyond the scope of this work and are not dealt with further. However, as regards a person's property and affairs, there are certain restrictions on what a deputy may be appointed to do. A deputy may not be given power to make a decision on behalf of P which is inconsistent with a decision made, within the scope of his or her authority and in accordance with this Act, by the donee of a lasting power of attorney granted by P (or, if there is more than one donee, by any of them).[656] In addition, a deputy may not be given powers with respect to the settlement of any of P's property, whether for P's benefit or for the benefit of others; the execution for P of a will, or the exercise of any power (including a power to consent) vested in P whether beneficially or as trustee or otherwise.[657] Subject to this, the power of appointment extends widely to include:

(a) the control and management of P's property;
(b) the sale, exchange, charging, gift or other disposition of P's property;
(c) the acquisition of property in P's name or on P's behalf;
(d) the carrying on, on P's behalf, of any profession, trade or business;
(e) the taking of a decision which will have the effect of dissolving a partnership of which P is a member;
(f) the carrying out of any contract entered into by P;
(g) the discharge of P's debts and of any of P's obligations, whether legally enforceable or not; and
(h) the conduct of legal proceedings in P's name or on P's behalf.[658]

A deputy is to be treated as P's agent in relation to anything done or decided by him within the scope of his or her appointment. The deputy is entitled to be reimbursed out of P's property for reasonable expenses in discharging his or her functions, and, if the court so directs when appointing, to remuneration out of P's property for discharging them. The court may confer on a deputy powers to take possession or control of all or any specified part of P's property and to exercise all or any specified powers in respect of it, including such powers of investment as the court may determine.[659] However, a deputy does not have power to make a decision on behalf of P in relation to a matter if he or she knows or has reasonable grounds for believing that P has capacity in relation to the matter.[660]

---

[655] Mental Capacity Act 2005 s.19(9).
[656] Mental Capacity Act 2005 s.20(4).
[657] Mental Capacity Act 2005 s.20(3).
[658] Mental Capacity Act 2005 s.18.
[659] Mental Capacity Act 2005 s.19(6)-(8).
[660] Mental Capacity Act 2005 s.20(1).

Section 13: In the Case of Persons in Possession of Real Estate Under A Legal Title

Practice of the Court of Chancery. The Court of Chancery would not, at the **2-113** instance of a person alleging a mere legal title against another party who was in possession of real estate, and who also claimed to hold a legal title, disturb that possession by appointing a receiver. There being open to the plaintiff a full and adequate remedy at common law, he or she had no equity to come to the Court of Chancery for relief. The court would not interfere with a legal title, unless there was some equity by which it could affect the conscience of the party in possession. There might be cases in which the court would interfere to prevent absolute destructive waste, where the value of the property would be destroyed if steps were not taken, or where the contest lay between a person having a well-established pedigree and a person without any reasonable appearance of title. But, as a general rule, where one person was in possession of the rents and profits of an estate, claiming to be the holder by a legal title, and another person also claimed to hold by a legal title, the former could not be ousted in the Court of Chancery, until the true ownership of the legal title had been finally determined at law.[661]

The court would not, however, be deterred from appointing a receiver by the fact that the defendant held under a legal title, where the claimant could show a sufficient equity in his or her favour[662]; as, for instance, where a case of fraud[663] undue influence[664] was made out.

The fact that a defendant partner was in possession under a legal title did not deter the court from appointing a receiver, where a proper case was made out[665]; and similarly in the case of trustees.[666] A receiver, moreover, would be appointed at the instance of an equitable incumbrancer against a mortgagor with the legal estate,[667] or of owners of a rentcharge against a mortgagee who neglected to pay it.[668] The appointment has also been made against vendors in specific performance actions in suitable cases.

The rule, that a receiver would not be appointed when the person having the legal estate was in actual possession of the property, did not apply where the person in possession was in possession merely upon execution under a judgment. In such a case, a creditor who had taken out execution (now a receiver for such a creditor[669]) could not hold property against an estate created prior to his debt.[670]

Cases where the appointment is made pending probate or a grant of administration are dealt with in s.3 above.[671]

Judicature Act 1873. The Judicature Act 1873 did not affect the principles upon **2-114**

---

[661] *Earl Talbot v Hope Scott* (1858) 4 K. & J. 96; *Carrow v Ferrior* (1868) 3 Ch.App. 719.

[662] *Mordaunt v Hopper* (1756) Amb. 311; *Clark v Dew* (1829) 1 R. & M. 103; *Bainbridge v Baddeley* (1851) 3 Mac. & G. 413.

[663] *Hugenin v Baseley* (1807) 13 Vest. 105; *LLoyd v Passingham* (1809) 16 Ves. 59; *Mordaunt v Hooper*, n.662, above; *Woodyatt v Gresley* (1836) 8 Sim. 180.

[664] *Stilwell v Wilkins* (1821) Jac. 280.

[665] See para.2-87, above.

[666] See para.2-2, above.

[667] See Section 4, para.2-21, above.

[668] *Pritchard v Fleetwood* (1815) 1 Merc. 54; *Shee v Harris* (1844) J. & L. at 91.

[669] Senior Courts Act 1981 s.37(4).

[670] *Whitworth v Gaugain* (1841) Cr. & Ph. 325; 3 Hare 416; 1 Ph. 728; *Anderson v Kemshead* (1852) 16 Beav. 329.

[671] See para.2-13 ff, above.

which the jurisdiction of the court to appoint a receiver is exercised.[672] Although, in an action for the recovery of land, the High Court has jurisdiction[673] upon application to appoint a receiver against a person in possession, even under a legal title,[674] that jurisdiction will be exercised with the utmost care. This is because it operates to prejudice the right of a defendant in possession to plead his or her possession as a statutory defence, and put the claimant to proof of his or her paramount title, while the application compels the defendant to disclose his or her title. It also puts the court in the difficulty that the substantial issue in the action may be determined, in effect, on evidence admissible on interlocutory application, but not at the trial.[675] If the defendant is actually in occupation, the appointment will not be made, except in very special circumstances[676]: it was held not to be enough to show that the defendant was a married woman with means, and only disclosed a shadowy title.[677] Where there was vacant possession, the appointment has been made in the absence of the owner of the legal estate.[678] The occupation of tenants is an important factor since, if the defendant were found to have no title, they might not get a good discharge for their rents, and yet might be open to distress (now commercial rent arrears recovery).[679]

In such cases, if the claimant makes out a good prima facie title, and the defendant discloses only a very shadowy title, the appointment may be made.[680] When the defendant lessee has been admittedly guilty of a breach of a covenant to carry on business on the premises, the appointment has been made, even where he was in occupation: thus, in an action by a lessor for recovery of possession of an hotel, where the licences were in jeopardy, and there appeared to be a strong prima facie probability of the plaintiff succeeding in recovering possession at the trial, the court on interlocutory motion appointed a receiver of the licences (which were ordered to be handed over to him) as well as of the rents and profits, and directed that the receiver should be at liberty to keep the premises open as an hotel, and to do all acts necessary to preserve the licences.[681]

In all such cases, the court has to consider whether special interference with the possession of a defendant is required, on the basis that there is a well-founded fear that the property in question will be dissipated, or that other irreparable mischief may be done, unless the court gives its protection.[682]

Section 14: In Cases Between Landlord and Tenant

2-115   Historical development.   The appointment of a receiver to receive the rent due to the landlord from a tenant, in cases where the landlord is not fulfilling obliga-

---

[672] See paras 2-9 and 2-82, above. See also CPR Pt 23.
[673] See now Senior Courts Act 1981 s.37(1).
[674] *Foxwell v Van Grutten* [1897] 1 Ch. 64.
[675] *Marshall v Charteris* [1920] 1 Ch. 520.
[676] For an example of an appointment made against a claimant in unusual circumstances, see *Porter v Lopes* (1877) 7 Ch. D. 358, 359.
[677] *Marshall v Charteris*, n.675, above.
[678] *Berry v Keen* (1882) 51 L.J. Ch. 912.
[679] *John v John* [1898] 2 Ch. 573; see *Marshall v Charteris*, n.675, above and *Gwatkin v Bird* (1883) 52 L.J.Q.B. 263; *Percy v Thomas* (1884) 28 S.J. 533.
[680] See n.679, above.
[681] *Leney & Sons Ltd v Callingham* [1908] 1 K.B. 79, correcting form of order drawn up in *Charrington Co v Camp* [1902] 1 Ch. 386. See further for additions to order, Seton, *Form of Judgments and Orders*, 7th edn, p.732.
[682] *Mukherjee v Giri* (1927) 55 L.R.Ind.App. 131.

tions under the lease, usually if not exclusively in cases of want of repair, is a recent development of the law, as already explained.[683] It is not clear upon what basis such an appointment can be justified, for there is no doubt that the rents belong to the landlord, and that the tenant has no claim to such rents, or any part thereof, or any other interest therein.

The first case in which this relief was granted was *Hart v Emelkirk*[684]; there the appointment of a receiver was fully justified in order to preserve property, the rightful owner being unascertainable. The properties had fallen into disrepair, no attempt was being made to collect the rents, or other contributions to maintenance and other services contracted to be provided by the landlords, and in any event those contractual services were not being provided. The registered title holders had sold the property at auction and had executed a transfer in favour of the purchaser, but the purchaser had inexplicably neglected to register his title. Meanwhile, the registered proprietors had washed their hands of the property. It seems fully justifiable to have appointed a receiver to receive the rents and profits and to manage the property, in accordance with the rights and obligations of the reversioner, until trial or further order. Goulding J recognised that there was no precedent for such relief, but considered it to be, as it obviously was, "just and convenient", and that this view derived support from *Riches v Owen*.[685] However, in that case the object of the appointment of the receiver was to prevent the assets being dealt with contrary to their holder's covenants, not for the purpose of causing such convenants to be carried out.

Parker v Camden LBC.   Shortly thereafter, the two cases of *Parker v Camden LBC*[686] and *Newman v Camden LBC*[687] were decided together by the Court of Appeal. At first instance, Walton J had in the first case refused to make the appointment of a receiver, whereas Scott J had in the other case made the appointment. The Court of Appeal held that no receiver ought to have been appointed in either case, but upon the narrow ground that the court should "not ordinarily supplant those nominated by statute to manage a public undertaking by appointing a manager." In this, they followed *Gardner v London Chatham and Dover Railway Company (No.1)*.[688]   **2-116**

Although the question did not therefore directly arise, the clear impression given by the judgments in that case was that, apart from this principle, which they regarded as binding on them in the exercise of their discretions, they would have upheld the appointments. Only Mustill LJ considered what might be the proper basis for such appointment. He said:

"Furthermore. Camden's estates are not the property in dispute, or in need of safeguard until further disposal, and hence are not, in my judgment, the proper subject of an appointment."

But, he added:

---

[683]   See para.1-4, above.
[684]   [1983] 1 W.L.R. 1289; [1983] 3 All E.R. 15.
[685]   (1868) L.R. 3 Ch. 820.
[686]   [1986] Ch. 162; [1985] 2 All E.R. 141 CA.
[687]   per Browne-Wilkinson LJ at 186C, 148e.
[688]   (1867) L.R. 2 Ch.App. 201 LJJ. This decision must be regarded as having been approved by the Court of Appeal: see *Evans v Clayhope Properties Ltd* [1987] 1 W.L.R. 225 and [1988] 1 W.L.R. 358 CA, where it was described as "novel ... though clearly beneficial in the conditions of many modern residential developments": see below, n.690.

"What the tenants do claim is that a receiver should be appointed of the rents ... In itself such an order would be unobjectionable, but the ancillary powers conferred on a receiver by his appointment as manager could not, to my mind, extend beyond the rents themselves, and as such would be of no practical value to the tenants."[689]

But he entirely omitted to indicate why, having correctly identified Camden's estates as not being the property in dispute, he did not similarly denominate the rents, which were equally not in dispute.

2-117　**Evans v Clayhope Properties Ltd.**　However, his remarks on the limited nature of the receiver's powers did not deter the plaintiff in *Evans v Clayhope Properties Ltd* from obtaining (from a Master) the appointment of a receiver and manager "to receive the rents and profits and other moneys payable under the leases ... and to manage the same in accordance with the rights and obligations of the Defendant the reversioner."[690] Nor was Harman J deterred from appointing a receiver and manager of a block of flats "in the place of the landlord and to exercise all the powers, duties and authorities of the lessor as he may be advised in managing the block," in *Daiches v Bluelake Investments Ltd.*[691] In that case, the lessor had clearly not got the money to carry out the necessary repairs, the cost of which it would thereafter be entitled under the lease to recover from the tenants. The plaintiff alleged that the tenants were willing to finance the receiver to carry out the repairs, although there was no obligation on them so to do. But in this case, the power of the court to appoint a receiver was expressly conceded by counsel for the landlords, so that the case was really decided on the balance of the convenience.[692]

The reckoning came in the course of a subsequent application in *Evans v Clayhope Properties Ltd.*[693] The receiver found that his expenses exceeded his receipts, which were limited to modest ground rents. He sought an order that he should be at liberty to recoup the shortfall from the landlord, since he had no means of raising money apart from the rents; but he was held not to be so entitled, at least on any interlocutory application.

In principle, of course, there could be no objection to the appointment of a receiver of the covenant by the landlord to carry out the repairs (and usually to recover the cost of so doing from the tenants), on the basis that this particular course of action had been abandoned by the landlord, and required protection accordingly for the benefit of those whom it was intended to benefit. Clearly, however, such a receivership would be an unattractive proposition, as the receiver would have no assets with which to carry out his duties.

It would appear from the cases considered above there is jurisdiction in the court to appoint a receiver/manager in such cases; but in default of the receiver being put in funds, either (i) by the applicant tenants, or (ii) from substantial rents collectable by him from tenants, or (iii) from the exercise of a power under the leases to collect from the tenants in advance the sums required to defray the costs of necessary works of repair and maintenance,[694] appointment is likely to prove abortive.

The receiver's claims there do not appear to have included any sums expended

---

[689] At 179B-D, 150E-G.
[690] See *Evans v Clayhope Properties Ltd* at 226C, n.691.
[691] (1986) 51 P. & C.R. 51. See also *Blawdziewicz v Diadon Establishment* [1988] 2 E.G.L.R. 52.
[692] See *Blawdziewicz v Diadon Establishment*, at 57. That decision was not cited in *Evans v Clayhope Properties Ltd*, n.688, above.
[693] [1987] 1 W.L.R. 225.
[694] Such a power was present in the leases in *Hart v Emelkirk*, para.2-115; [1983] 1 W.L.R. 1289 above,

on works of repair and maintenance, but solely represented his remuneration, by way of fees for management. The point appears to have been left open, whether such fees for management could have been recouped to the receiver by their inclusion within an order for costs at the end of the litigation, wherever such costs might fall.[695]

The mischief sought to be remedied by such applications has now been replaced by statutory relief afforded by statute: see below.[696] But such statutory relief is only made available to tenants whose landlords are neither exempt nor resident[697]; accordingly, the previous non-statutory relief should still be available to tenants falling outside the scope of the Act.

Statutory provision. Applications in the most recent mould are unlikely to be made in the future, because a tenant cannot now apply for the appointment of a receiver, where he or she can apply instead to a first-tier tribunal[698] for the appointment of a manager pursuant to the Landlord and Tenant Act 1987.[699] Such applications may be made by the tenant of a flat in a building which contains two or more flats,[700] unless the interest of the landlord in the premises is held by an exempt landlord,[701] or a residential landlord[702] (unless at least one-half of the flats contained in the premises are held on long leases which are not tenancies to which Pt 2 of the

2-118

---

where the rents collectable were negligible in amount.

[695] e.g. under the Senior Courts Act 1981 s.51, where they may, in principle, be imposed on a person not a party to the proceedings.

[696] Landlord and Tenant Act 1987 s.21(2)(a); see CPR 56 and CPR P.D. 56 paras 7 and 7.1.

[697] n.696, s.21(2)(b).

[698] Landlord and Tenant Act s.21(1) and (8).

[699] Landlord and Tenant Act 1987 s.21(6).

[700] Landlord and Tenant Act 1987 s.21(1), (2).

[701] Landlord and Tenant Act 1987 s.21(3)(a). The following bodies are, under s.58(1), exempt:

(a) a district, county, county borough or London borough council, the Common Council of the City of London, a fire and rescue authority created under s.4A of the Fire and Rescue Services Act 2004, the London Fire and Emergency Planning Authority, the Council of the Isles of Scilly, a police and crime commissioner, the Mayor's Office for Policing and Crime, a joint authority established by Pt IV of the Local Government Act 1985, an economic prosperity board established under s.88 of the Local Democracy, Economic Development and Construction Act 2009 or a combined authority established under s.103 of that Act;

(b) a development corporation established by an order made (or having effect as if made) under the New Towns Act 1981;

(ba) a Mayoral development corporation;

(c) an urban development corporation within the meaning of Pt XVI of the Local Government, Planning and Land Act 1980;

(d) a housing action trust established under Pt III of the Housing Act 1988;

(e) the Homes and Communities Agency;

(f) the Broads Authority;

(g) a National Park authority;

(h) the Regulator or Social Housing;

(i) a housing trust (as defined in s.6 of the Housing Act 1985) which is a charity;

(j) a registered social landlord or a fully mutual housing association which is neither a private registered provider of social housing nor a registered social landlord; or

(k) an authority established under s.10 of the Local Government Act 1985 (joint arrangement for waste disposal functions).

[702] Landlord and Tenant Act 1987, s.21(3)(a). The landlord of any premises consisting of the whole or part of a building is a resident landlord, under s.58(1) and (2) of those premises at any time of—

(a) the premises are not, and do not form part of, a purpose-built block of flats; and

(b) at that time the landlord occupies a flat contained in the premises as his only or principal residence; and

Landlord and Tenant Act 1954 applies[703]) or the Welsh Ministers in their new towns residuary capacity,[704] or the premises are included within the functional land of any charity.[705] Nor can they be made, if the tenancy is a business tenancy.[706] But if they are joint tenants, any one or more of such tenants may make the application.[707] Tenants entitled to make individual applications may make their applications jointly in respect of two or more premises to which the Act applies.[708]

Before any such application can be made, however, unless the tribunal dispenses with this requirement,[709] the tenant must serve a preliminary notice on the landlord[710] which must:

(a) specify the tenant's name, the address of his flat and an address in England and Wales, which may be the address of the flat, at which the landlord may serve notices, including notices in proceedings, on him in connection with such application;

(b) state that the tenant intends to make such an application in respect of such premises as are specified in the notice, but (if (d) below is applicable) that he will not do so if the landlord complies with the requirement to remedy the default;

(c) specify the grounds on which the tribunal will be asked to make the order and the matters that would be relied on by the tenant for the purpose of establishing those grounds;

(d) where those matters are capable of being remedied by the landlord, require the landlord, within such reasonable period as is specified in the notice, to take such steps for the purpose of remedying them as are so specified; and

(e) contain such information (if any) as the Secretary of State may by regulations prescribe.[711]

If the landlord's interest is mortgaged, he must, as soon as reasonably practicable after receiving this notice, serve a copy on the mortgagee.[712]

The tribunal may, whether on hearing the application or prior thereto, dispense with the requirement of service of any notice under this provision; where it is satisfied that it would not be reasonably practicable to serve such notice. However, it may, when doing so, direct that such other notices be served or such other steps be taken, as it thinks fit.[713] An obvious example would be where the whereabouts of the landlord are unknown, but those of a mortgagee are. In such a case the court would doubtless direct the service of a notice on the mortgagee.

(c) he has so occupied such a flat throughout a period of not less than 12 months ending with that time.

"Purpose-built block of flats" means a building which contained as constructed, and contains, two or more flats.

[703] Landlord and Tenant Act 1987 s.21(3A) (as inserted by the Commonhold and Leasehold Reform Act 2002 s.161; SI 2002/1912; SI 2002/30123).
[704] As amended by the Housing and Regeneration Act 2008 Sch.8.
[705] Landlord and Tenant Act 1987 s.21(3)(b).
[706] Under Landlord and Tenant Act 1954 Pt II: Landlord and Tenant Act 1987 s.21(7).
[707] Landlord and Tenant Act 1987 s.21(5).
[708] Landlord and Tenant Act 1987 s.21(4).
[709] Landlord and Tenant Act 1987 s.22(3).
[710] Landlord and Tenant Act 1987 s.22(1).
[711] Landlord and Tenant Act 1987 s.22(2).
[712] Landlord and Tenant Act 1987 s.22(4).
[713] Landlord and Tenant Act 1987 s.22(3).

Jurisdiction. The jurisdiction conferred by these provisions is on a first-tier **2-119** tribunal.[714] Any order made by a tribunal under these provisions may, appoint a manager to carry out such functions in connection with the management of the premises or such functions of a receiver, or both, as the tribunal thinks fit.[715] A number of specific examples are listed which, if satisfied, may lead to an order being made. Whenever an order is made on the grounds of one of these examples it must still be just and convenient to make the order in all the circumstances of the case (which remains a separate and ground itself).[716]

No application can be made, however, unless, in a case where such a notice as aforesaid has been served, either the period specified under head (d) above has expired, or that paragraph was not, in the circumstances of the case, applicable.[717] In a case where such notice has been dispensed with, no application may be made, until any notices required to be served, and any other steps required to be taken by virtue of the order dispensing with service, have been served or taken, as the case may be, or no such direction was given anyway.[718]

Appointment of manager by the first-tier tribunal. The tribunal may, on an ap- **2-120** plication for such an order, by order (whether interlocutory or final) appoint a manager to carry out in relation to such premises such functions in connection with the management[719] of the premises, or such functions of a receiver, or both, as the tribunal thinks fit.[720]

The tribunal can only make such an order in five cases:

(a) if it is satisfied that any relevant person either is in breach of some obligation owed to the tenant under the tenancy and relating to the management of the premises in question or any part of them, or (in the case of an obligation dependent on notice) would be in breach of any such obligation, but for the fact that it has not to be reasonably practicable for the tenant to give him the appropriate notice, and that it is just and convenient to make the order in all the circumstances of the case[721];

(b) if it is satisfied that unreasonable service charges have been made, or are proposed or likely to be made, and it is just and convenient to make the order in all the circumstances of the case[722];

(c) if it is satisfied that unreasonable variable administration charges have been made, or are proposed or likely to be made, and it is just and convenient to make the order in all the circumstances of the case[723];

(c) it is satisfied that any relevant person has failed to comply with any relevant provision of a code of practice approved by the Secretary of State under s.87 of the Leasehold Reform, Housing and Urban Development Act 1993 and

---

[714] Landlord and Tenant Act 1987 s.21(8) (see SI 2013/1036).
[715] Landlord and Tenant Act 1987 s.24(1).
[716] Landlord and Tenant Act 1987 s.24(2) and see para.2-120, below.
[717] Landlord and Tenant Act 1987 s.23(1)(a).
[718] Landlord and Tenant Act 1987 s.23(1)(b).
[719] References in these provisions to the management of any premises include references to the repair, maintenance, improvement or insurance of those premises: Landlord and Tenant Act 1987 s.24(11).
[720] Landlord and Tenant Act 1987 s.24(1).
[721] Landlord and Tenant Act 1987 s.24(2)(a).
[722] Landlord and Tenant Act 1987 s.24(2)(ab). For the meaning of service charge see s.24(2A).
[723] Landlord and Tenant Act 1987 s.24(2)(aba). For the meaning of variable administrative charge see s.24(2B).

that it is just and convenient to make the order in all the circumstances of the case[724]; or

(d) if it is satisfied that other circumstances exist which make it just and convenient for the order to be made.[725]

The premises in respect of which such an order is made may, if the tribunal thinks fit, be either more or less extensive than the premises specified in the application therefore.[726]

An order may make provision with respect to any matters relating to the exercise by the manager of his or her functions, and such incidental or ancillary matters as the tribunal thinks fit.[727] It may also provide for rights and liabilities, arising under contracts to which the manager is not a party, to become rights and liabilities of the manager; for the manager to be entitled to prosecute claims in respect of causes of action (whether contractual or tortious) accruing before or after the date of appointment; for remuneration to be paid to the manager by any relevant person, or by the tenants of the premises in respect of which the order is made, or by all or any of those persons: and for the manager's functions to be exercisable, either during a specified period or without limit of time.[728] On any subsequent application made for the purpose by the manager, the tribunal may give the manager appropriate directions.[729]

Any such order may be granted subject to such conditions as the tribunal thinks fit, and in particular its operation may be suspended on terms fixed by the tribunal.[730] Where an application for an order under this section is preceded by the service of a preliminary notice,[731] the tribunal may, if it thinks fit, make such an order, notwithstanding that any period specified therein was not a reasonable period, or that the notice failed in any other respect to comply with an requirement contained in the 1987 Act, or in any regulations applying to the notice.[732]

The Land Charges Act 1972 and the Land Registration Act 1925 apply in relation to an order made under this section as they apply in relation to an order appointing a receiver, or sequestrator of land.[733]

The tribunal may, on the application of any person interested, vary or discharge (whether conditionally or unconditionally) any such order; and if the order has been protected by an entry registered under the Land Charges Act 1972 or the Land Registration Act 1925, the tribunal may be order direct that the entry shall be cancelled.[734] However, the tribunal shall not vary or discharge an order on the ap-

---

[724] Landlord and Tenant Act 1987 s.24(2)(ac).
[725] Landlord and Tenant Act 1987 s.24(2)(b).
[726] Landlord and Tenant Act 1987 s.24(3).
[727] Landlord and Tenant Act 1987 s.24(4).
[728] Landlord and Tenant Act 1987 s.24(5). The court now order "remuneration" to be paid, either by the landlord or by some or all of the tenants (thereby resolving the problem presented by the lack of funds in *Evans v Clayhope Properties Ltd* para.2-117, n.688, above); but that term does not seem apt to cover expenditure, other than management fees (or litigation costs, perhaps); it would hardly seem to cover the reimbursement of the expenses of carrying out the necessary works by the manager. However, that lacuna might be filled by an order under the general words of s.24(4) and (11).
[729] Landlord and Tenant Act 1987 s.24(4).
[730] Landlord and Tenant Act 1987 s.24(6).
[731] See para.2-118, above.
[732] Landlord and Tenant Act 1987 s.24(7).
[733] Landlord and Tenant Act 1987 s.24(8).
[734] Landlord and Tenant Act 1987 s.24(9).

plication of any relevant person unless it is satisfied that the variation or discharge of the order will not result in a recurrence of the circumstances which led to the order being made and that it is just and convenient in all the circumstances to vary or discharge the order.[735]

No such order will be discharged by reason only that the landlord of the premises has become an exempt landlord, or a resident landlord, or that the premises have become a functional land of a charity.[736]

SECTION 15: OTHER EXAMPLES

Unlawful carrying on of a regulated activity or other breaches of financial   **2-121**
services relevant requirements and the Financial Services and Markets Act
2000. No person may carry on, or purport to carry on, a regulated activity in the United Kingdom, unless he is an authorised or exempt person[737] under the Financial Services and Markets Act 2000.[738] An activity is, for these purposes, a regulated activity if it is an activity of a kind specified by statutory instrument, carried on by way of business and relating to an investment[739] of a specified kind or so specified and carried on in relation to property of any kind.[740] Under the 2000 Act the Financial Conduct Authority and the Prudential Regulation Authority are given wide powers to apply to the court for injunctive relief and/or the making of restitution orders with regard to breaches of any "relevant requirement"[741] and in the case of market abuse. Although the Court's powers no longer expressly refer to the appointment of a receiver in the restitution order context,[742] it is suggested that the court's general power to appoint a receiver may be invoked in an appropriate case.

If a receiver is appointed in relation to a company which is, or has been, an authorised person; is, or has been, an appointed representative; or is carrying on, or has carried on, a regulated activity in contravention of the general prohibition, the Financial Conduct Authority or the Prudential Regulation Authority are entitled (a) to be heard on applications made under ss.35 or 63 of the Insolvency 1986 Act; (b) to make an application under ss.41(1)(a) or 69(1)(a) of the Insolvency Act 1986; (c) to receive from the person making it, a copy of the report made under s.48(1) or 67(1) of the Insolvency Act 1986. Further, a person appointed for the purpose by the appropriate authority is entitled: (a) to attend any meeting of creditors of the company summoned under any enactment; (b) to attend any meeting of a committee established under ss.49 or 68 of the 1986 Act; and (c) to make representations

---

[735] Landlord and Tenant Act 1987 s.24(9A).

[736] Landlord and Tenant Act 1987 s.24(10). For the definition of "exempt landlord" and "resident landlord", see nn.701, 702, para.2-118, above.

[737] See Financial Services and Markets Act 2000 Pt III.

[738] Financial Services and Markets Act 2000 s.19.

[739] Which includes any asset, right or interest: Financial Services and Markets Act 2000 s.22(4).

[740] Financial Services and Markets Act 2000 s.22 and Sch.2. See also e.g. Financial Services and Markets Act 2000 (Regulated Activities) Order 2001 (SI 2001/544); Financial Services and Markets Act 2000 (Regulated Activities) (Amendment) Order 2001 (SI 2001/3544).

[741] Widely defined and usually encompassing a requirement imposed by or under the 2000 Act or by any directly applicable Community regulation made under the markets in financial instruments directive or imposed by or under any other Act and whose contravention constitutes an offence which the Financial Conduct Authority or Prudential Regulation Authority has power to prosecute under the 2000 Act (see, e.g. Financial Services and Markets Act 2000 ss.380(6), 382(9)).

[742] Compare, e.g. former provision regarding breaches of prohibition on conducting investment business unless authorised or exempted as provided for by the Financial Services Act 1986 s.6.

as to any matter for decision at such a meeting.[743] If a receiver has been appointed in relation to a company, and it appears to the receiver that the company is carrying on, or has carried on, a regulated activity in contravention of the general prohibition, he or she must report the matter to the appropriate authority without delay.[744]

2-122 **Charities.** The principles relating to the preservation of property pending litigation apply as much to charities as to other bodies, where there is either:

(a) such dispute between the known officials themselves that they cannot carry on the business of their organisation in a proper manner; or

(b) that their identity is for any reason in dispute, so that it is not known for certain who is entitled to act on behalf of the body they should be managing.

In such cases, the court will interfere by the appointment of a receiver and, if required, a manager, pending the resolution of such disputes, or the ascertainment of the identity of the proper officials, to enable the business of the organisation to be properly conducted in the meantime.

Any appointment will be framed so as to last the shortest possible time. Thus, where such an appointment was sought in proceedings commenced by originating summons for the determination of the exact trusts affecting the charity and the precise identity of the trustees thereof, it was made only until after the substantive hearing of the originating summons, or further order in the meantime.[745] The charity in question was one which was responsible for running both a boys' and a girls' school. The trustees were directly responsible for running the girls' school, so that when the post of head teacher fell vacant, the receiver had power to advertise the vacancy, and, on taking proper advice, appoint a suitable person to that post[746] In the case of the boys' school, which was run by foundation governors, only some of whom were appointed by the trustees, others being appointed by the local education authority, it was held that the receiver had no similar power. He did, however, have power, either under the original order appointing him, or, if not, under powers which the court could confer upon him, to remove the existing foundation governors appointed by the trustees and to appoint others in their place.[747]

2-123 **Charities: acting by the Attorney-General.** Where the Attorney-General was suing the trustees of a charity over whose assets a receiver had been appointed, and sought an interlocutory injunction against one of the defendants to restrain him from disposing of various properties and bank accounts in his name, the question of a cross-undertaking in damages arose. Since the Crown was suing to assert proprietary rights of the charity, a cross-undertaking was appropriate. As there might be difficulty as to any possible right of funding any indemnity for the Attorney-General out of the assets of the charity, in the event that the cross-undertaking became effective, the court proposed to accept a cross-undertaking from the

---

[743] Financial Services and Markets Act 2000 s.363(5). Equivalent rights apply with regard to Limited Liability Partnerships see SI 2001/1090 regs 1, 6. The section is also effectively extended to Northern Ireland.

[744] Financial Services and Markets Act 2000 s.364.

[745] *Att.-Gen. v Schonfeld* (1979): unreported order of Walton J of 13 July 1979, referred to in further hearing [1980] 1 W.L.R. 1182.

[746] *Re Jewish Secondary School Movement's Trusts* (1979): unreported order of Megarry V-C of 24 October 1979, referred to in case note [1980] 1 W.L.R. 1182.

[747] *Att.-Gen. v Schonfeld*, n.745, above.

receiver, limited to such amount, if any, as the receiver himself was entitled and able to recover by way of indemnity from the funds of the charity.[748]

Enemies. Under the Trading with the Enemy Act 1939, the Board of Trade (now the Department of Trade and Industry), after report by an inspector appointed under s.3(1), had power to appoint a supervisor of any business carried on by the person named in the order, to secure compliance with the prohibition against trading with the enemy.[749] Such an appointment would displace a receiver appointed in a claim from the control of the business. The Board also had power, under s.7 of the Act, by order to vest any property of an enemy in the official called "the Custodian of Enemy Property".[750] After such an order had been made, but not previously, the Custodian became the assign of the enemy for the purpose of initiating or being a defendant in any proceedings relating to the property comprised in the order, including proceedings in which a receiver was sought.

A person who is an enemy cannot himself sue, but may be sued here.[751] There are many cases in which an enemy may be a necessary defendant, if no vesting order has been made. In a partnership, for instance, in which accounts are claimed, all the partners must be represented.[752] If one partner is an enemy, he must be made a defendant; but a receiver would be appointed without service or before an order dispensing with service. The test of enemy character, with regard to a right to sue in the Queen's courts, is residence or carrying on business in an enemy country or in a country under the control of the enemy.[753] A British national or other person in a country controlled by the enemy is an enemy for the purpose of this rule.

Apart from the above legislation, the appointment of a receiver at the instance of a manager here of an enemy's business was refused.[754]

2-124

Bailee. An interim receiver may be appointed in respect of a chattel in an action in which the owner sues for its return from a bailee, who claims a lien, and the receiver may be authorised to allow the owner to use the chattel.[755] In an action for return of a piano let on hire-purchase, the plaintiff was appointed receiver on his ex parte application, until hearing of a summons for delivery up.

2-125

Lien. The normal remedy of a person entitled to an equitable lien over the property of another, who cannot obtain satisfaction of his demand, is a judicial

2-126

---

[748] *Att.-Gen. v Wright* [1987] 3 All E.R. 579.

[749] See s.1. For definitions of "enemy" and "enemy territory", see ss.2 and 15. Section 3A of the Act contains a power, widely used in World War II, for the Board to make a restriction order or winding-up order in respect of any such business, and to appoint a controller to carry out the order.

[750] Trading with the Enemy Act 1939 s.7.

[751] See above, n.750, para.2–100, above.

[752] *Public Trustee v Elder* [1926] Ch. 776.

[753] *Porter v Freudenberg* [1915] 1 K.B. 857; *Sovfracht v Van Udens* [1943] A.C. 203. See as to companies and incorporated bodies, *Daimler Co v Continental Tyre Co* [1916] 2 A.C. 307; *The Pamia* (1943) 112 L.J.P. 34. This is so, even where the claimant is the subject of (e.g. as a company incorporated in) an allied country, occupied by an alien enemy power: see *Fibrose Spolka Akcynja v Fairbairn Lawson Combe Barbour Ltd* [1942] A.C. 32 HL (where the Crown granted the plaintiff a retrospective licence to sue).

[754] *Maxwell v Grunhut* (1914) 31 T.L.R. 79; *Re Gaudig and Blum* (1915) 31 T.L.R. 153.

[755] *Hatton v Car Maintenance Co* [1915] 1 Ch. 621. As to the extent and relinquishment of such a lien, see *Green v All Motors Ltd* [1917] 1 K.B. 625 *Reliance Motor Works v Pennington* [1923] 1 K.B. 127.

sale.[756] Pending sale, a receiver may of course be appointed.[757] There may also be cases—for example where the lien is an unpaid vendor's lien over real property which has now become part of a railway system[758]—where the appointment of a receiver can be obtained over the property subject to the lien, as being the only practicable means of enforcement.

2-127 **Interpleader.** The court or a judge may, in an interpleader under CPR 85, to try the right to goods seized in execution, order that, instead of a sale by the sheriff, a receiver and manager of the property is appointed.[759]

2-128 **Arbitration.** Unless otherwise agreed by the parties, the court has, for the purposes of and in relation to arbitral proceedings, the same power of making an order appointing a receiver as it has for the purposes of and in relation to legal proceedings.[760]

If the case is one of urgency, the court may, on the application of a party or proposed party to the arbitral proceedings, appoint a receiver if it thinks it necessary for the purpose of preserving evidence or assets. However, if the case is not one of urgency, the court is to act only on the application of a party to the arbitral proceedings (upon notice to the other parties and to the tribunal) made with the permission of the tribunal or the agreement in writing of the other parties. In any case the court shall act only if or to the extent that the arbitral tribunal, and any arbitral or other institution or person vested by the parties with power in that regard, has no power or is unable for the time being to act effectively.[761]

If the court so orders, an order made under these powers will cease to have effect in whole or in part on the order of the tribunal or of any such arbitral or other institution or person having power to act in relation to the subject matter of the order.[762]

2-129 **Pending foreign litigation.** The court has jurisdiction to appoint a receiver pending litigation in a foreign court.[763]

2-130 **Foreign bankruptcy.** The court will appoint the *curateur*, in a foreign bankruptcy, receiver of the land of the debtor in England with power to sell.[764] However in many cases the court will now have more appropriate powers to act

---

[756] *Hope v Booth* (1830) 1 B. & Ad. 498.
[757] *Bishop of Winchester v Mid-Hants Ry* (1867) L.R. 5 Eq. 17. cf. *Ponoka-Calmar Oils v Earl F Wakefield Co* [1960] A.C. 18 (receiver, appointed as part of statutory machinery for enforcement of lien, could not prejudice claim of lien-holder).
[758] *Munns v Isle of Wight Ry* (1870) L.R. 5 Ch. 414.
[759] *Howell v Dawson* (1884) 13 Q.B.D. 67.
[760] Arbitration Act 1996 s.44. The powers conferred by s.44 apply even if the seat of the arbitration is outside England, Wales or Northern Ireland or no seat has been designated or determined, although in certain circumstances the court may refuse to exercise any such power: see Arbitration Act 1986 s.2(3) and see also *Econet Wireless Ltd v VEE Networks Ltd* [2006] EWHC 1568 (Comm); [2006] 2 All E.R. (Comm) 989.
[761] Arbitration Act 1996 s.44.
[762] Arbitration Act 1996 s.44(6).
[763] *Transatlantic Co v Peitroni* (1860) Johns, 604; see too, *Evans v Puleston* [1880] W.N. 89, 127; *Law v Garrett* (1878) 8 Ch. D. 16.
[764] *Re Kooperman* [1928] W.N. 101. The report is silent as to the means of carrying out the conveyance, but it seems that a vesting order could be obtained under Trustee Act 1925 s.44, without the necessity of proceeding under Senior Courts Act 1981 s.30. cf. also *Re A Debtor (Order in Aid No.1 of 1979) Ex p. Viscount of the Royal Court of Justice* (1981) Ch. 384 (a Jersey "désastre" case, i.e.

under the EU Regulation on Insolvency Proceedings[765] or the Cross-Border Insolvency Regulations.[766]

Trade unions.   Prior to the Industrial Relations Act 1971, since the court could   **2-131** not enforce any agreement for the application of trade union funds in provision of benefit,[767] a receiver could not be appointed over the general funds, or funds collected for a special purpose, to prevent their application contrary to agreement.[768] The Trade Union Act 1871 was repealed by the 1971 Act, but it, in its turn, was repealed by the Trade Union and Labour Relations Act 1974, and that has been replaced by the Trade Union and Labour Relations (Consolidation) Act 1992, without, however, re-enacting the provisions of the 1871 Act s.4. It therefore appears that in such cases a receiver could now be appointed.

Where a trade union was held to be in contempt of court and was duly fined,[769] the trustees of its funds, who were under the rules of the union bound to obey its national executive committee, pursuant to their instructions sent its funds abroad in an effort to avoid payment; those trustees were removed on ex parte application as trustees, and a receiver of the union's property was appointed in their place. The order was later affirmed inter partes.[770]

---

the Jersey equivalent to a bankruptcy). See also para.6-51, n.240, below.
[765] See Ch.28.
[766] SI 2006/1030.
[767] Trade Union Act 1871 s.4.
[768] *Samson v London Vehicle Workers' Union* (1920) 36 T.L.R. 666; as to when an injunction could be granted, see *Amalgamated Society of Carpenters v Braithwaite* [1922] 2 A.C. 440.
[769] *Clarke v Heathfield* [1985] I.C.R. 203 CA, upholding the ex parte order granted by the court below.
[770] *Clarke v Heathfield (No.2)* [1985] I.C.R. 606.

CHAPTER 3

OVER WHAT PROPERTY A RECEIVER MAY BE APPOINTED

3-1   In determining whether or not property is of such a nature that the court will appoint a receiver of it, it is necessary to consider the nature of the applicant's title.

There is a considerable difference, according to whether the appointment is made to preserve the subject-matter of a suit, or by way of equitable execution. In the former case, the appointment extends over the whole subject-matter of the suit, real and personal, including both legal and equitable interests[1]; in the latter case, there are certain reasonably well-defined restrictions as to the property which will be subjected to the appointment, which are discussed in the latter part of this chapter.[2]

Where the application is made to preserve the subject-matter of the suit, it is most frequently made at the instance of an incumbrancer seeking to enforce his or her charge. In such cases, it must be shown that the property is capable of assignment, and that prima facie a valid assignment or charge has been made, for otherwise the applicant has no title to maintain the action.

3-2   **Property which is assignable.**   It is not proposed to attempt to specify every description of property which is, or is not, assignable. Present and future earnings,[3] present and future debts,[4] deposits with banks, possibilities and expectancies[5] are assignable: so are rights to indemnity.[6] In some cases, however, though the property is assignable, the instrument of assignment may contain provisions, invalid as offensive to public policy or otherwise, which invalidate the assignment.[7] The exclusion from assignability of future earnings, in the case of a bankrupt,[8] may no longer be a relevant issue since, under the Insolvency Act 1986, the future earn-

---

[1]   See *Davis v Duke of Marlborough* (1818) 1 Swans. 74, 83; 2 Swans. 108, 132.

[2]   See paras 3-13 ff, below.

[3]   *Holmes v Millage* [1893] 1 Q.B. 551; *Horwood v Millar's Timber and Trading Co Ltd* [1917] 1 K.B. 305. But an assignment by a member of a profession of future earnings was held to be void against a trustee in bankruptcy as to receipts after commencement of the bankruptcy; *Re De Marney* [1943] Ch. 126. See, to the contrary, the dictum of Atkinson J in *King v Michael Faraday and Partners Ltd* [1939] 2 K.B. 753, 760-761. If that represents the law, the remedy of a judgment creditor is *semble* by attachment of the debt.

[4]   *Soinco v Novokuznetsk Aluminium* [1998] QB 406; *Masri v Consolidated Contractors International Company SAL* [2009] Q.B. 450.

[5]   *Tailby v Official Receiver* (1888) 13 App. Cas. 523; *Re Lind* [1915] 1 Ch. 744; [1915] 2 Ch. 345.

[6]   Even before anything is due: *British Union Co v Rawson* [1916] 2 Ch. 476. See also *Bourne v Colodense* [1985] I.C.R. 291 and *Maclaine Watson & Co Ltd v International Tin Council* [1988] Ch. 1 (affirmed [1989] Ch. 253 CA).

[7]   *Horwood v Millar's Timber and Trading Co Ltd* n.3, above; *A Schroeder Music Publishing Co Ltd v Macauley* [1974] 1 W.L.R. 1308.

[8]   *Re De Marney*, n.3, above: but contrast *King v Michael Faraday and Partners Ltd*, n.3 above.

ings of a bankrupt are no longer caught by the relevant sections[9]; the trustee is, however, entitled to apply for an income payments order or to obtain an income payments agreement,[10] covering such portion of them as is not required for the support of the bankrupt and his family.[11]

Assignments contrary to public policy.   The assignment of certain forms of   **3-3**
property is void, in some cases, as contrary to public policy, in others as forbidden by statute.[12] Thus assignments of the following have been held to be void as contrary to public policy: the pay or half-pay of an officer in the army, navy, or air force[13]; the salary of a person holding a civil office in the public service[14]; the salary of a clerk of the peace, a freehold office connected with the administration of justice[15]; of a clerk of petty sessions in Ireland, as he or she is a public and judicial officer[16]; sums payable to an assistant parliamentary counsel to the Treasury.[17]

Pensions or half-pay involving any liability to future service are inalienable[18]; but where they are granted wholly in consideration of past services, they are alienable,[19] unless alienation is prohibited by statute.[20] The following have been held assignable: salary of a chaplain to a work-house[21]; of the office of Master Forester to a royal forest[22]; unascertained sums due from an insurance committee to a panel doctor[23]; a retiring annuity or pension payable to a covenanted member of the Indian Civil Service[24]; a pension payable to a member of the Royal Irish Constabulary without liability to serve again.[25] In an Irish case,[26] it was held in effect that arrears of a salary might be assigned; though possibly future payments were not assignable, but even if this decision be correct, arrears of a pension inalienable by statute cannot be assigned before they are actually paid over.[27]

Pensions, etc. unassignable by statute.   The following are unassignable by   **3-4**
statute: any benefit payable to civil servants and other comparable public

---

[9]   Insolvency Act 1986 s.283(1).
[10]   See n.9 above, s.310(1), (2).
[11]   Insolvency Act 1986 s.310A.
[12]   As to immunity from attachment, whilst in the hands of the Crown, see para.2-39, above.
[13]   See *Apthorpe v Apthorpe* (1887) 12 Probate Division 192; *Ex p. Huggins* (1882) 21 Ch. D. 85; *Re Mirams* [1891] 1 Q.B. 594.
[14]   *Cooper v Reilly* (1892) 2 Sim. 560. Append. (1830) 1 Russ. & M. 560, and see n.9, above. Quaere, as to the salary of a Member of Parliament: see *Hollinshead v Hazleton* [1916] 1 A.C. 428.
[15]   *Palmer v Bate* (1821) 6 Moo. 28; see *Palmer v Vaughan* (1818) 3 Swans. 173.
[16]   *McCreery v Bennett* [1904] 2 Ir.R. 69.
[17]   *Cooper v Reilly*, above, n.14: these fees were irrecoverable at law.
[18]   *Wells v Foster* (1841) 8 M. & W. 149; *Macdonald v O'Toole* [1908] 1 I.R. 386; and see *Knill v Dumergue* [1911] 2 Ch. 199. As to how far pensions and allowances under the Superannuation Act 1972 involve liability to future services, see *Macdonald v O'Toole*, above.
[19]   See *David v Duke of Marlborough* (1818) 1 Swans. 74, 79; *Dent v Dent* (1867) L.R. 1 P. 266; *Willcock v Terrell* (1878) 3 Ex.D. 323; *Manning v Mullins* [1898] 2 Ir.R. 34; *Knill v Dumergue*, n.18, above.
[20]   See below as to statutory prohibitions.
[21]   *Re Mirams* [1891] 1 Q.B. 594.
[22]   *Blanchard v Cawthorne* (1833) 4 Sim. 566.
[23]   *O'Driscoll v Manchester Insurance Committee* [1915] 8 K.B. 499.
[24]   *Knill v Dumergue*, nn.18-19, above.
[25]   See *Manning v Mullins*, n.19.
[26]   *Picton v Cullen* [1900] 2 Ir.R. 612. See *Price v Lovett* (1851) 20 L.J. Ch. 270.
[27]   *Crowe v Price* (1889) 22 Q.B.D. 429; *Jones v Coventry* [1900] 2 K.B. 1029.

employees, under a scheme made under s.1 of the Superannuation Act 1972[28]; pay and pensions and allowances granted to officers or men, or to widows or dependants of officers and men who have been in the naval,[29] military,[30] or air[31] service of the Crown; parliamentary pensions[32]; pensions payable to former UK representatives in the European Parliament[33]; pensions payable to members of the police force or their dependants[34]; to officers employed in the National Health Service[35]; superannuation allowance or gratuity to school teachers[36]; to officers and employees of local authorities[37]; to members of the fire service[38]; universal credit and jobseekers' allowance[39]; guaranteed minimum pensions[40]; any income related benefits[41]; child benefit[42]; pension payable to a retiring incumbent.[43] There are other historical examples of such restrictions, for example pension payable to an Irish town clerk.[44] A lump sum payable as compensation under the Superannuation Acts is in the same position as a pension.[45] Sums payable as compensation under the War Damage Act 1943 could be assigned or charged only with the permission in writing of the War Damage Commission.[46]

Money received for commutation of a pension was held not to come within the

---

[28] *Crowe v Price* (1889), s.5(1). The main current scheme is the Principal Civil Service Pension Scheme.

[29] See originally Naval and Marine Pay and Pensions Act 1865 s.4 but now Armed Forces Act 2006 s.356.

[30] See the previous provision in Army Act 1955 s.203 but now Armed Forces Act 2006 s.356.

[31] See the previous provision in Air Force Act 1955 s.203 but now Armed Forces Act 2006 s.356.

[32] The position is now subject to provision to be made by regulation: see Parliamentary and Other Pensions Act 1987 s.2 and Sch.1 para.9. For regulations see Parliamentary Pensions (Consolidation and Amendment) Regulations 1993 (SI 1993/3253) Pt P.

[33] European Assembly (Pay and Pension) Act 1979 s.4; amended by the Transfer of Functions (European Parliamentary Pay and Pensions) Order 2003 (SI 2003/2922) art.2; European Assembly (United Kingdom Representatives) Pension Order 1980 (SI 1980/1450) art.22 applying s.20(1) of the Parliamentary and other Pensions Act 1972; repealed with savings by the Parliamentary and other Pensions At 1987 ss.2(9), 6(2), Schs 2, 4.

[34] Police Pensions Act 1976 s.9; applied by Police and Justice Act 2006 s.48 Sch.3 para.5.

[35] National Health Service Pension Scheme Regulations 1995 (SI 1995/300) reg.T3.

[36] Superannuation Act 1972 s.9; Sch.3 para.9 (amended by the Pensions (Miscellaneous Provisions) Act 1990 ss.4(1), 8(3), (4), 11(2), (3), (4); Pension Schemes Act 1993 s.190; Sch.8, para.7; Financial Services and Markets Act 2000 (Consequential Amendments and Repeals) Order 2001 (SI 2001/3649) art.107; Teachers' Pensions Regulations 2010 (SI 2010/990) reg.122; see *Re Duckett Minister of Education v The Trustee* [1964] Ch. 398, CA. *(Minister of Education entitled to appeal against ultra vires order); Bank Mellat v Kazni (Secretary of State for Social Services intervening)* [1989] Q.B. 541, CA.

[37] Superannuation Act 1972 ss.7, 8, 12 (amended by the Pensions Miscellaneous Provisions Act 1990 s.10(1) (2), and Sch.7 para.5(1)); Local Government Pension Scheme Regulations 2013 (SI 2013/2356) reg.84.

[38] Fire Services Act 1947 s.26 (amended by Fire Services Act 1951 s.1) (both repealed with savings by the Fire and Rescue Services Act 2004 ss.52, 54, Sch.2); Firemen's Pension Scheme Order 1992 (SI 1992/129) Sch.2 r.N17 (not in force at the time of writing in England and Wales).

[39] Social Security Administration Act 1992 s.187(1).

[40] Pension Schemes Act 1993 s.159. There is an exception for an assignment of, or agreement to assign a policy of insurance or annuity contract, in accordance with conditions prescribed by regulations under that Act s.39, Sch.2: Social Security Act 1985 s.29(1).

[41] Social Security Administration Act 1992 s.187.

[42] Social Security Administration Act 1992 s.187.

[43] Church of England Pensions Regulations 1988 (SI 1988/2256) reg.29(2).

[44] Under Local Officers Superannuation (Ireland) Act 1896; *Brenan v Morrissey* (1890) 26 L.R. It. 618.

[45] See *Re Lupton* [1912] 1 K.B. 107 and cf. *Re Duckett Minister of Education v Trustee* (1964) Ch. 398, n.36 above: see also *Macdonald v O'Toole* [1908] 2 Ir.R. 386.

[46] War Damage Act 1943 s.23.

prohibition against alienation in s.203 of the Army Act 1955.[47] After money has been actually paid over by the paymaster, as an instalment of a pension, it loses the protection, and may be assigned or attached; but this does not include money credited to a pensioner's account at a bank, in respect of a warrant which has not been paid by the paymaster.[48]

Private unassignable pensions.   Sums payable under pension trust deeds are usu-   **3-5**
ally made wholly or partly unassignable by the terms of the deed. But if a private pension is unassignable, it may be possible for the court to order the mortgagor to execute an irrevocable power of attorney, enabling the receiver to receive the same.[49]

Collegiate fellowship.   Though, in one case,[50] a receiver over the profits of a fel-   **3-6**
lowship was refused, it was subsequently held that a receiver might be appointed of past and future appropriations in respect of the profits of a fellowship, the duties being so light that no questions of public policy could interfere with the validity of the assignment.[51] Similarly, a receiver has been appointed of the profits of a canonry of a collegiate church, to which no cure of souls belonged, but only the duty of a certain residence and of attendance on divine service, the performance of which duty by the canon was of no benefit to the public.[52]

Ecclesiastical benefices.   Formerly, there could not have been a receiver of the   **3-7**
profits of an ecclesiastical benefice, either at the instance of an assignee or a judgment creditor; for a beneficed clergyman was prohibited by the Benefices Act 1571 from charging the fruits of his living.[53] This Act was repealed by the Benefices Act 1803, and so the law remained, until the Benefices Act 1817, when the charging of ecclesiastical benefices was again prohibited, and the 1571 Act was revived: so that between the years 1803 and 1817 there was no law prohibiting a clergyman from charging his ecclesiastical benefice[54]; a receiver was accordingly on several occasions, in cases arising between those years, appointed over an ecclesiastical benefice.[55] The policy of the Benefices Act 1571, revived by the Benefices Act 1817, was not affected by the Judgments Act 1838, but the statute was repealed by the Statute Law Revision Act 1948 Sch.1. Consequently, the law appears to have been restored to the pre-1817 position.

Maintenance in family proceedings.   Sums ordered to be paid for the follow-   **3-8**
ing purposes have been held unassignable and consequently a receiver cannot be appointed over them; viz. maintenance pending suit ordered to be paid to a wife

---

[47]   *Crowe v Price* (1889) 22 Q.B.D. 429; see *Price v Lovell* [1851] 20 L.J. Ch. 270. See now Armed Forces Act 2006.
[48]   *Jones & Co v Coventry* [1909] 2 K.B. 1029; in the former case, the remedy is attachment, not equitable execution.
[49]   *James v Ellis* (1870), referred to in *Ambler v Bolton* (1872) L.R. 14 Eq. 427, 429.
[50]   *Berkeley v King's College* (1830) 10 Beav. 602.
[51]   *Feistel v King's College* (1847) 10 Beav. 491. Most fellowships now involve considerable duties.
[52]   *Grenfell v Dean and Canons of Windsor* (1840) 2 Beav. 544.
[53]   *Hawkins v Gathercole* (1855) 6 D.M. & G. 1; see *Long v Storie* (1849) 3 De G. & S. 308.
[54]   *Metcalfe v Archbishop of York* (1833) 1 M. & C. 553.
[55]   *Silver v Bishop of Norwich* (1816) 3 Swans. 112n.; *White v Bishop of Peterborough* (1818) 3 Swans. 109; *Metcalfe v Archbishop of York* n.54, above.

judicially separated[56]; a weekly sum ordered by a court of summary jurisdiction to be paid by a husband to a wife for her maintenance[57] maintenance ordered to be paid by a husband for the support of his divorced wife[58]; a voluntary allowance by the husband[59]; a sum payable under a bastardy order.[60]

The following have been held to be assignable, viz. sums payable to a wife under a separation deed,[61] and, semble, an annuity secured for a divorced wife.[62]

Arrears of maintenance are, it seems, assignable[63]; but a receiver would not be appointed over them, at all events during the life of the husband, since the enforcement of payment of such arrears is wholly in the discretion of the court in family proceedings,[64] the relationship of debtor and creditor not being created[65]; it is presumed that payment would only be enforced in favour of that person, for whose support the maintenance was ordered to be paid. The same appears to be the case with arrears of maintenance pending suit.[66]

For the procedure for appointing a receiver in family proceedings, where available, see paras 2-45, above, and 5-41, below.

3-9 **Other descriptions of property.** Many descriptions of property, over which a receiver will be appointed for purposes of preservation or to enforce a charge, are mentioned in the various sections of Ch.2; there is practically no limit in respect of the property in such cases; thus, a receiver has been appointed over public house licences,[67] heirlooms,[68] a motor car,[69] a newspaper,[70] profits of a solicitor's business.[71] Semble, a receiver may be appointed over a patent, whether being worked or not, at the instance of an assignee.[72] In some cases, certain property, e.g. uncalled capital,[73] will be excluded from the order appointing a receiver, where the applicant's charge can be made effective by other means; in other cases special powers are given to the receiver,[74] in accordance with the nature of the property.[75]

---

[56] *Re Robinson* (1884) 27 Ch. D. 160; see *Linton v Linton* (1885) 15 Q.B.D. 239; *Smith v Smith* [1923] P. 161.

[57] *Paquine v Snary* [1909] 1 K.B. 688; the order was under the Summary Jurisdiction (Married Women) Act 1895.

[58] *Watkins v Watkins* [1896] P. 222; *Smith v Smith*, n.56, above.

[59] *Walls Ltd v Legge* [1923] 2 K.B. 240.

[60] *Re Harrington* [1908] 2 Ch. 687.

[61] *Victor v Victor* [1912] 1 K.B. 247; and see *Clark v Clark* [1906] P. 331.

[62] Under the Matrimonial Causes Act 1973 s.30 as amended by the Family Law Act 1996 s.66(3) Sch.10.

[63] per Lindley LJ in *Watkins v Watkins*, n.58, above.

[64] See *Robins v Robins* [1907] 2 K.B. 13; *Ivimey v Ivimey* [1908] 2 K.B. 260; *Brydges v Brydges* [1909] P. 187; para.2-45, above.

[65] *Campbell v Campbell* [1922] P. 187; and see para.2-44, above.

[66] See *Smith v Smith*, see n.56, above. As to claims against the estate of the deceased husband, see para.2-45, above.

[67] *Charrington v Camp* [1902] 1 Ch. 376; *Leney & Sons Ltd v Callingham* [1908] 1 K.B. 79.

[68] *Earl of Shaftesbury v Duke of Marlborough* (1820) 1 Seton, Forms of Judgments and Orders, 7th edn, pp.734-735.

[69] *Hatton v Car Maintenance Co* [1915] 1 Ch. 621.

[70] *Kelly v Hutton* (1896) 17 W.R. 425; *Chaplin v Young* (1862) 6 L.T. 97.

[71] *Candler v Candler* (1821) Jac. 225.

[72] See *Edwards Co v Picard* [1909] 2 K.B. 903.

[73] See para.3-28, below.

[74] See especially Ch.9.

[75] e.g. *Leney & Sons Ltd v Callingham and Thompson*, n.67, above.

Ships. A receiver has been appointed of a ship,[76] of a ship and her gear,[77] of the   **3-10**
freight of a ship,[78] and of the machinery of a steam vessel.[79] So, also, a receiver may
be appointed, when an action of co-ownership is brought by the owner of one
moiety of a vessel against the owner of the other moiety.[80]

In a case where the legal title to a ship was in question, and the plaintiff had no
equitable as distinct from a legal title, a receiver was refused; but an order was made
by which the legal proceedings for ascertaining the title were accelerated, and the
court took possession of the ship, giving each party liberty to apply for its possession and use, upon giving security to deal with her as the court should direct.[81]

Rates and tolls. A receiver was refused of rates which were to be assessed by   **3-11**
commissioners at a future period, for until the assessment there was nothing to
collect.[82] There may be a receiver of the tolls chargeable in respect of turnpike or
toll roads, or of canal, railway, dock or market companies.[83] The extent to which a
receiver may be appointed over a statutory undertaking has been already dealt
with.[84]

Property abroad. It is not necessary, in order that the court may have jurisdic-   **3-12**
tion to appoint a receiver, that the property in respect of which he is to be appointed should be in England, or indeed, in any part of Her Majesty's dominions,[85]
though the extent to which the receiver may be able to obtain possession of the
property depends on the *lex loci*. Persons have been appointed to receive the rents
and profits of real estates and to convert, to get in and remit the proceeds of property
and assets, in cases in which the estate or property in question was located in
Ireland[86]; in the West Indies[87]; in India[88]; in Canada[89]; in China[90]; in Italy[91]; in
America[92]; in New South Wales[93]; in Jersey[94]; in Brazil[95]; and in Peru.[96] But the
court will not make such an order if it would be useless.[97] Although the court has
no power of enforcing its orders and decrees in places beyond its jurisdiction, the
receiver may be authorised to proceed abroad,[98] or to appoint an attorney, and a

---

[76] *Re Edderside* (1887) 31 S.J.744.
[77] *Compagnie du Sénégal v Woods & Co* [1883] W.N. 180; 53 L.J. Ch. 166.
[78] *Roberts v Roberts* (1854) Seton, p.772; *Burn v Herlofson* (1887) 56 L.T. 722.
[79] *Brenan v Preston* (1852) 2 D.M. & G. 813, 831; 10 Hare 334.
[80] *The Ampthill* (1880) 5 P.D. 224.
[81] *Ridgway v Roberts* (1844) 4 Hare 106.
[82] *Drewry v Barnes* (1826) 3 Russ. 94, 105; but see *Gibbons v Fletcher* (1853) 11 Hare 251.
[83] See Ch.2. s.6, above.
[84] Above, para.2-48 ff.
[85] *Houlditch v Lord Donegal* (1834) 8 Blight (N.S.) 301, 344.
[86] See n.82, above and *Bolton v Curre* [1834] W.N. 122; Seton p.776.
[87] *Bunbury v Bunbury* (1839) 1 Beav. 318; *Barkley v Lord Reay* (1843) 2 Hare 306.
[88] *Logan v Princess of Coorg*: Seton, p.776; *Keys v Keys* (1839) 1 Beav. 425.
[89] *Tylee v Tylee* (1853), Seton, p.777.
[90] *Hodson v Watson* (1788), Seton, p.776.
[91] *Hinton v Galli* (1854) 24 L.J. Ch. 121; *Drewry v Darwin* (1765), Seton, p.777.
[92] *Hanson v Walker* (1829) 7 L.J. Ch. 135.
[93] *Underwood v Frost* (1857), Seton, p.776.
[94] *Smith v Smith* (1853) 10 Hare App. 71.
[95] *Duder v Amsterdamsch Trustees Kantoor* [1902] 2 Ch. 322.
[96] *Re Huinac Copper Mines* [1910] W.N. 218.
[97] *Mercantile Investment Co v River Plate Trust* (1892) 2 Ch. 303.
[98] See Palmer's *Company Precedents*, Vol.3, Ch.61, p.647. The debenture holders consented.

party to the case who resists him or his attorney will be guilty of contempt.[99] A person will, however, not be appointed receiver of an estate which is out of the jurisdiction, unless he is within the reach of the court, or has submitted himself, or is amenable, to its jurisdiction.[100]

The course which the court usually adopts, where an estate is in a foreign country or otherwise out of the jurisdiction, is to appoint a receiver in this country, with power, if it be found expedient, to appoint an agent, with the approbation of the judge, in the country where the estate is situate, to collect the estate and remit the same to the receiver in this country.[101] The receiver or his agent will recover possession of the estate according to the laws of the country in which it is found.[102] The receiver will, when necessary, be empowered to sell lands abroad, according to a scheme approved by the judge.[103] Where a receiver in a debenture holder's action was unable to obtain possession of the property, because the courts of the country (Peru) in which it was situate refused to recognise any title other than that of the company, the court ordered the company to appoint attorneys to take possession on behalf of the receiver.[104]

This area was considered in detail by the Court of Appeal in *Masri v Consolidated Contractors International Company SAL*.[105] An order for the appointment of a receiver acts in personam and does not have proprietary effects. However, in deciding whether an order exceeds the permissible territorial limits it is important to consider: (a) the connection of the person who is the subject of the order with the English jurisdiction; (b) whether what they are ordered to do is exorbitant in terms of jurisdiction; and (c) whether the order has impermissible effects on foreign parties. As regards the latter two points, the provision of modified *Babanaft* provisions[106] in the order may have the result that the order will not exceed what is permissible. In the *Masri* case the court considered that the particular order to appoint a receiver was not objectionable with regard to relevant principles of private international law.

3-13   **Equitable execution.**   For the appointment of a receiver by way of equitable execution, see para.5-1, below. Where the appointment is sought by way of equitable execution, the property over which a receiver will be appointed is more restricted.

It is important to note that equitable execution is not like legal execution. It is equitable relief granted by the court where there is some hindrance which prevents or makes impractical legal execution. It is a form of equitable relief which has no proprietary effect. It is not limited to such property which may be taken in execu-

---

[99] *Langford v Langford* (1835) 5 L.J. Ch. 60.
[100] See *Houditch v Lord Donegal* (1834) 8 Blight (N.S.) 301; *Carron Iron Co v Maclaren* (1855) 5 H.L.Cas. 416; *Masri v Consolidated Contractors International Company SAL* [2009] Q.B. 450.
[101] *Anon. v Lindsay* (1808) 15 Ves. 91; *Keys v Keys* (1839) 1 Beav. 425; *Smith v Smith* (1853) 10 Hare App. 71; *Hinton v Galli*, n.91, above Seton, p.777.
[102] *Smith v Smith*, n.94, above. Consider *Re Maudslay, Sons & Field* [1900] 1 Ch. 602, 611: and *Re Derwent Rolling Mills Co* (1905) 21 T.L.R. 701.
[103] *Tylee v Tylee* (1853), n.89, above.
[104] *Re Huinac Copper Mines*, n.96, above: security is not required from the attorney.
[105] *Masri v Consolidated Contractors International Company SAL* [2009] Q.B. 450.
[106] *Babanaft International Co SA v Bassatne* [1990] Ch. 13. For an example of a situation which would go beyond the permissible limits of an appointment see *Taurus Petroleum Ltd v State Oil Marketing Co of the Ministry of Oil, Iraq* [2015] EWCA Civ 835 at [36]–[37].

tion but extends to whatever is considered in equity to be assets. It acts in personam.[107]

It is essential first to show that the property over which the appointment is required is capable of assignment. In addition, apart from execution against certain special types of assets, including land, as to which there are special statutory provisions,[108] and from cases of fraudulent conduct on the part of the judgment debtor or other special circumstances, it must also be shown that legal execution is impossible or impractical, owing to some impediment arising from the character in law of the judgment debtor's interest.[109] It is not sufficient to show that the property is inaccessible to legal execution[110]; the judgment creditor must go further, and show that there are certain difficulties arising from the nature of the interest of the debtor in the property, which make legal execution impossible or impractical, but which if removed would enable legal execution to issue.[111] The Judicature Acts made no difference in this respect: the court still applies the principles upon which the Court of Chancery formerly acted. In determining whether equitable execution can issue the courts have in recent years shown some flexibility in applying these principles to new situations.[112]

If it is proved that the judgment debtor is threatening or intending to deal with the property in such a manner as to amount to a fraudulent attempt to defeat the rights of creditors, or in some other analogous circumstances, a receiver may be granted, even over property susceptible to legal execution[113] as, for instance, where the debtor, a German company, was endeavouring to collect debts due to it and remove the proceeds from the jurisdiction.[114]

Restrictions on appointing receivers. In accordance with these principles, the court will not, except in special circumstances, appoint a receiver by way of equitable execution over property which can be reached by a writ of control, or attachment of debts[115]; nor over present or future earnings[116]; nor over money paid

3-14

---

[107] *Re Shepherd* (1889) 43 Ch.D. 131; *Bourne v Colodense Ltd* [1985] I.C.R. 291; *Masri v Consolidated Contractors International Company SAL* [2009] Q.B. 450; *Tasarruf Mevduati Sigorta Fonu v Merrill Lynch Bank and Trust Co (Cayman) Ltd* [2012] 1 W.L.R. 1721.

[108] Senior Courts Act 1981 s.37(4); Charging Orders Act 1979 s.2. See paras 3-14 ff, below. See para.3-2 ff, as to assignable property generally, and as to pensions and other property which are incapable of assignment.

[109] *Cruz City 1 Mauritius Holdings v Unitech Ltd* [2014] EWHC 3131 (Comm); *Holmes v Millage* [1893] 1 Q.B. 551; *Morgan v Hart* [1914] 2 K.B. 813, where the prior cases are reviewed.

[110] *Holmes v Millage*, n.109, above.

[111] per Cotton LJ in *Re Shephard* (1889) 43 Ch. D. 131; per Bowen LJ in (1889) 43 Ch. D. 131 at 137; *Holmes v Millage*, n.109, above; *Harris v Beauchamp Bros* [1894] 1 Q.B. 810.

[112] *Holmes v Millage*, n.109, above; *Edwards & Co v Picard* [1909] 2 K.B. 903; *Morgan v Hart*, n.109; *Masri*, n.107.

[113] See *Manchester and Liverpool District Banking Co v Parkinson* (1888) 22 Q.B.D. 173; *Harris v Beauchamp Bros*, n.111, above, at 806, 810, 811.

[114] *Goldschmidt v Oberrheinische Metallwerke* [1906] 1 K.B. 373. See also *Masri v Consolidated Contractors International Company SAL* [2009] Q.B. 450.

[115] See *Holmes v Millage, Morgan v Hart*, n.109, above. What is meant by special circumstances is that there is some hindrance or difficulty in using normal processes of execution. These may be practical or legal and it is necessary to take account of all the circumstances of the case: *Cruz City*, n.109 and *Masri*, n.107.

[116] *Holmes v Millage*, n.109, including directors' fees not earned; see *Hamilton v Brogden* [1891] W.N. 36. The courts have recently shown a willingness to extend the jurisdiction in this area and have permitted a receiver to be appointed over future debts in *Masri*, n.107.

for admission at a theatre[117]; nor over debts, merely because a security is about to be created over them[118]; nor over furniture of the debtor stored with that of other persons so as to be indistinguishable by the judgment creditor[119]; nor over a patent not being worked[120]; nor by way of equitable execution on a foreign judgment.[121]

On the other hand, where an unsuccessful plaintiff had a contractual right, which he refused to exercise, to have the costs awarded against him discharged by the trade union to which he belonged, to which he was entitled, a receiver was appointed at the instance of the successful defendant to enforce his rights against the union.[122] But where a body, against whom an award of damages had been made, had rights to be indemnified by its members, no such order was made; for this right was derived solely from the treaty by which it had been established, and a right of action founded on a treaty was not justiciable in the English courts.[123]

3-15   **Estates and interests in land and certain other assets.** The Administration of Justice Act 1956 abolished the writ of *elegit*,[124] and also the provisions of the Law of Property Act 1925, under which judgments entered up in Supreme Court operated as charges on land of the judgment debtor,[125] and it substituted a fresh system of execution against land and interests in land, legal or equitable.[126]

There were two main defects in the new system. First, it did not enable a charging order to be obtained over an interest of the debtor's in the proceeds of the sale of land[127]; secondly, as the making of such an order was a form of execution, in order to be valid as against a trustee in bankruptcy or liquidator, it had to be completed by seizure, or the appointment of a receiver, before bankruptcy or liquidation as the case might be.[128]

3-16   **The Charging Orders Act 1979 (as amended).** These defects were cured by the provisions of the Charging Orders Act 1979, which carried the system a great deal further, by including therein assets other than interests in land. The scope of the property, which may be made the subject of a charging order under this Act, extends to land, government stock,[129] stock[130] of any body (other than a building society[131])

---

[117]   *Cadogan v Lyric Theatres Ltd* [1894] 3 Ch. 338.

[118]   *Harris v Beauchamp Bros*, n.111. For a case involving a remarkable disregard of this principle, see *Re Swallow Footwear Ltd*, *The Times*, 23 October 1956.

[119]   *Morgan v Hart*, n.109, above. In *Hills v Webber* (1901) 17 T.L.R. 513, a receiver was appointed over the interest of the debtor, who was joint tenant of three houses of which only two were subject to a mortgage; but the circumstances were special.

[120]   *Edwards & Co v Picard* [1909] 2 K.B. 903; the proceeds of a patent being worked by a licensee could be reached by legal execution.

[121]   *Perry v Zissis* [1977] Lloyd's Rep. 607 CA.

[122]   *Bourne v Colodense* [1985] I.C.R. 291 CA. As to the assignability in general of rights of action, see *Trendtex Trading Corp v Credit Suisse* [1982] A.C. 679 HL.

[123]   *Maclaine Watson & Co Ltd v International Tin Council (No.2)* (1988) 3 W.L.R. 1190; sub nom. *MacLaine Watson v Department of Trade and Industry* [1989] A.C. 418; [1989] 1 All E.R. 523 HL: a receiver could not be appointed, in the premises. All the International Tin Council decisions were affirmed by the House of Lords at [1989] A.C. 418, HL.

[124]   Administration of Justice Act 1956 s.41.

[125]   Administration of Justice Act 1956 s.34(2).

[126]   Administration of Justice Act 1956 ss.35, 36.

[127]   *Irani Finance Ltd v Singh* [1971] Ch. 59, CA.

[128]   *Re Overseas Aviation Engineering (GB) Ltd* [1963] 1 Ch. 24 CA.

[129]   This means any stock issued by HM Government in the UK or any funds of, or annuity granted by, that Government: Charging Orders Act 1979 s.6(1).

incorporated within England and Wales, units of any unit trust,[132] in respect of which a register of the unit holders is kept at any place within England and Wales, and funds in court.[133] The charging order may be made in respect of any interest beneficially held by the debtor, in any asset of the kinds just enumerated, or under any trust.[134]

It may also be made in respect of any interest held by a trustee of a trust, if the interest is in such an asset as above, or is an interest under another trust, and either:

(i)   the judgment or order in respect of which the charge was imposed was made against that person as trustee of that trust; or

(ii)   the whole beneficial interest in the trust is held by the debtor unincumbered and for his own benefit; or

(iii)   in a case where there are two or more debtors, all of whom are liable to the creditor for the same debt, they together hold the whole beneficial interest under the trust, unincumbered and for their own benefit.[135]

Given the wide scope of a charging order, the appropriate court, whether High Court or county court, may, for the purpose of enforcing a judgment or order for the payment of money to the judgment creditor, impose, on any such property of the judgement debtor as may be specified in the order, a charge for securing the payment of any moneys due or to become due.[136] Where the charge is imposed on any interest in any asset other than land, such charge may be extended to any interest or dividend[137] payable in respect of such asset.[138] There is a power to set financial limits on the sum, payment of which may be secured by charging order.[139]

The Charging Orders Act 1979 (as amended) Procedure. Prior to the coming   3-17
into force, on 25 March 2002, of the Civil Procedure (Amendment No.4) Rules

---

[130]   This includes shares, debentures and any securities of the body concerned, whether or not constituting a charge on the assets of that body: Charging Orders Act 1979 s.6(1).

[131]   As defined in the Building Societies Act 1986; Charging Orders Act 1979 s.6(1), as amended by Sch.18 of that Act.

[132]   This means any trust established for the purpose, or having the effect, of providing for persons having funds available for investment, facilities for the participation by them, as beneficiaries under the trust, in any profits or income arising from the acquisition, holding, management or disposal of any property whatsoever: Charging Orders Act 1979 s.6(1).

[133]   Charging Orders Act 1979 s.2(2). Any of the securities referred to may in fact be standing in the name of the Accountant General. See s.6(3).

[134]   See n.133, above; s.2(1)(b). Combining this with Charging Orders Act 1979 s.2(2), above, *Irani Finance Ltd v Singh* n.24, above, is no longer law: see *National Westminster Bank Ltd v Stockman* [1981] 1 W.L.R. 67.

[135]   See n.133, above; s.2(1)(b). The Lord Chancellor, by statutory instrument, may amend these provisions by adding to, or removing from, the kind of asset for the time being referred to, any asset of a kind which in his opinion ought to be so added or removed. Any such order is subject to annulment in pursuance of a resolution of either House of Parliament: Charging Orders Act 1979 s.3(7), (8). The provisions numbered (iii) in the text give statutory force to the decision in *National Westminster Bank Ltd v Allen* [1971] 2 Q.B. 718.

[136]   Charging Orders Act 1979 s.1(1). The expression "moneys due or to become due" does not cover unassessed costs: *A & M Records Inc. v Darakdjian* [1975] 1 W.L.R. 1610.

[137]   In relation to unit trusts, this includes any distribution in respect of any unit: Charging Orders Act 1979 s.6(1).

[138]   Charging Orders Act 1979 s.2(3).

[139]   Charging Orders Act 1979 s.3A as inserted as from 17 May 2012 by Tribunals, Courts and Enforcement Act ss.94, 148(5).

2001,[140] charging orders practice and procedure were regulated by RSC Ord.50 and CCR Ord.31. Those surviving Orders were revoked by the new Rules, on the coming into force of CPR Pts 70–73. But those new Parts do not apply to enforcement proceedings which had already been issued before 25 March 2002.[141]

Under CPR r.73.3, application may be made for a charging order without notice, to be issued out of the court of the judgment, unless the claim has been transferred to another court. The application may be transferred to the district where the judgment debtor resides, or where he carries on business, or to some other more convenient court.

3-18   **The appropriate court for application.**   If the property to be charged is a fund in court, the appropriate court is the court in which that fund is lodged.[142] If other property is in question, and the order to be enforced is a maintenance order[143] of the High Court (or an order for costs made in family proceedings in the High Court), the application may be made either to the High Court or the family court.[144] If neither of the foregoing provisions applies, and the judgment or order is one of the High Court for a sum exceeding the county court limit,[145] the appropriate court is the High Court or the county court[146]; in all other cases it is the county court.[147]

3-19   **Nature of orders made.**   The court will usually make an "interim charging order" (formerly an order nisi) without a hearing, fixing a hearing date to consider making a final charging order.[148] In the High Court, the order may be made by a master.[149] It may be made either absolutely, or subject to conditions as to notifying the debtor, or as to the time when the charge is to become enforceable, or as to other matters.[150] Any such order is, in the first instance, an order to show cause, specifying the time and place for further consideration and imposing the charge until that time in any event.[151] On further consideration, the court will, unless it appears that there is sufficient contrary reason, make the order absolute, with or without modification.[152] Appeal from a final order lies, with permission, direct to the Court of Appeal.[153]

The power, however, is a discretionary power; before the court imposes the charge, it must consider all the circumstances of the case, including the personal circumstances of the debtor, and whether any other creditor of the debtor would be

---

[140]   SI 2001/2792. For a summary of the procedures, see Civil Court Practice CPR 70.
[141]   Such pre-existing proceedings continue to be governed by what were classified respectively as CPR Sch.1–RSC 49, and Sch.2–CCR 30.
[142]   Charging Orders Act 1979 s.1(2)(a).
[143]   This has the same meaning as in the Attachment of Earnings Act 1971 s.2(a); Charging Orders Act 1979 s.1(2); see s.1 and Sch.1 to the 1971 Act.
[144]   Charging Orders Act 1979 s.1(2)(b). If the order to be enforced is an order of the family court, the family court has jurisdiction.
[145]   This means the county court limit for the time being specified in an Order in Council under s.145 of the County Courts Act 1984; Charging Orders Act 1979 s.1(2), as amended by the Administration of Justice Act 1982 ss.34(3), 37 Sch.3 Pt II paras 2, 3, 6; and County Courts Act 1984 s.148(1) Sch.2 Pt II.
[146]   Charging Orders Act 1979 s.1(2)(c).
[147]   Charging Orders Act 1979 s.1(2)(d).
[148]   CPR r.73.4, replacing CPR Sch.1, RSC 49 and CCR 30, with effect from 25 March 2002.
[149]   *Barclays Bank Ltd v Moore* [1967] 1 W.L.R. 1201.
[150]   Charging Orders Act 1979, s.3(1); CPR r.73.4.
[151]   See CPR 73 generally as to procedure.
[152]   CPR r.73.8.
[153]   *Rainbow v Moorgate Properties Ltd* [1975] 1 W.L.R. 788.

likely to be unduly prejudiced by the making of the order.[154] If, for example, the court is aware that the debtor is in liquidation and is, or is likely to turn out to be, insolvent, the order should not be made.[155]

The provisions of the Land Charges Act 1972 (as regards unregistered land) and of the Land Registration Act 2002 (as regards registered land) apply in relation to any such order as they apply to other writs or orders affecting land, issued or made for the purpose of enforcing judgments.[156] Subject as aforesaid, they have the like effect, and are enforceable in the same manner, as an equitable charge created by the debtor by writing under his hand.[157] This is subject to the specific provisions regarding instalment orders set out in s.3(4A)–(4E). The ultimate remedy of the creditor will therefore be an order for sale,[158] and he or she is in the interim entitled to the appointment of a receiver.[159]

The final provision is that the execution effected by the charging order is regarded as completed, when the order is made, and not, as under the Administration of Justice Act 1956, only when a receiver had been subsequently appointed.[160]

The present position is therefore that, both as regards bankruptcy and liquidation, the execution is completed, in relation to goods,[161] by seizure and sale, or by the making of a charging order, and, in relation to land, by seizure,[162] the appointment of a receiver, or by the making of a charging order, and the attachment of a debt is completed by the receipt of that debt.[163]

In relation to which judgments, etc. may a charging order be made. These **3-20** provisions apply in relation to a judgement, order, decree or award (however called) of any court or arbitrator (including an foreign court of foreign arbitrator), which is or has become enforceable (whether wholly or to a limited extent), as if it were a judgement or order of the High Court, the family court or the county court as they apply in relation to a judgment or order of the High Court, family court or the county court.[164]

Whether or not a charge has been imposed on land by any such order,[165] the power of the High Court,[166] or the county court,[167] to appoint a receiver by way of equitable execution is extended to all legal as well as equitable estates and interests in land. This power is in addition to, and not in derogation from, any power of the court to appoint a receiver in any proceedings for enforcing any charge imposed

---

154 Charging Orders Act 1979 s.1(5): CPR 73, and n.154, below.
155 *Rainbow v Moorgate Properties Ltd*, n.153; *Roberts Petroleum Ltd v Bernard Kenny Ltd* [1983] 2 A.C. 192, HL cf. *Glass (Cardiff) Ltd v Jordean Properties Ltd* [1976] 120 S.J. 167, CA.
156 Charging Orders Act 1979 s.3(2).
157 Charging Orders Act 1979 s.3(4). The judgment creditor would therefore be entitled to be added as a party to any foreclosure action by a mortgagee of the land, but must take the action as he finds it: *Re Parabola Ltd* [1909] 2 Ch. 437.
158 *Matthews v Goodday* (1861) 31 L.J. Ch. 282.
159 In the proceedings brought for the enforcement of the charge.
160 Insolvency Act 1986 ss.183(3), 346(5).
161 "Goods" includes securities: Insolvency Act 1986 s.183(6).
162 However, with the abolition of the writ of *elegit*, there is no longer any such process as "the seizure of land".
163 See above, n.159. The expression "receipt of the debt" is inaccurate, since what is received is the money represented by the debt: see *George v Tompson's Trustee* [1949] Ch. 322 (under Bankruptcy Act 1914 s.40).
164 Charging Orders Act 1979 s.6(2).
165 Senior Courts Act 1981 s.37(4).
166 Senior Courts Act 1981 s.37(4).
167 County Courts Act 1984 s.107(1).

under the foregoing provisions.[168] Where an order has been made and is duly registered under the Land Charges Act 1972,[169] the provisions of that Act, which provide that an order appointing a receiver, and any proceedings pursuant to the order or in obedience thereto, shall be void against a purchaser unless the order is registered,[170] do not apply to an order appointing a receiver, made either in proceedings for enforcing the charge or by way of equitable execution.[171]

3-21   **Mortgagor.**   Receivers by way of equitable execution were, prior to 1926, appointed against a mortgagor over an equity of redemption.[172] Since the coming into force of the Administration of Justice Act 1956, there is statutory warrant for the appointment of a receiver in such a case.[173] It seems also that a receiver could be appointed over the balance of proceeds of sale in the hands of a mortgagee after satisfying his or her own incumbrance, at the instance of a judgment creditor of the mortgagor (seeing that the mortgagee is in the position of a trustee[174]), or over proceeds of sale under a pending contract at the instance of a judgment creditor of the vendor. The remedy by attachment is defective, as there is usually no ascertained debt due to the vendor before completion.

3-22   **Settled land.**   Where land is the subject-matter of a settlement within the meaning of the Settled Land Act 1925, the interests of the beneficiaries as such are equitable, and the property remedy of a judgment creditor has since 1925 been by way of equitable execution, even against the tenant for life; for the legal estate is vested in him as trustee[175] and is not therefore subject to his judgment debt.

3-23   **Trust of land.**   The interests of persons under a trust of land[176] are equitable, and a receiver has always been the appropriate remedy.[177] Such an appointment was held not to make the receiver a "person interested" in the proceeds of sale within s.30 of the Law of Property Act 1925, so as to enable him to apply for a sale of the property[178]; but the creditor himself is a "person interested" and can either himself apply for an order for sale, or his receiver can be authorised to take such proceedings in his name as may be necessary.[179]

3-24   **Miscellaneous.**   A receiver may be appointed: over the interest of a mortgagee in a theatre[180]; where a legal estate is outstanding;[181] where a fund in another court is

---

[168] See above, n.164.

[169] See s.6. As registration can only be made against the "estate owner" (see Charging Orders Act 1979 s.6(2) and definition of "land" in s.17(1)), it would appear that registration is only possible in the case of execution against a legal interest. In the cases of an equitable interest, notice is simply given to the trustees, as in the case of any other charge by a beneficiary.

[170] Land Charges Act s.6(4).

[171] Senior Courts Act 1981 s.37(5); County Court Act 1984 s.107(3).

[172] *Ex p. Evans* (1879) 13 Ch. D. 252; *Anglo-Italian Bank v Davies* (1878) 9 Ch. D. 275; *Smith v Cowell* (1880) 6 Q.B.D. 75.

[173] Charging Orders Act 1979 ss.2(1)(a)(i), (2)(a) and 3(4).

[174] See Law of Property Act 1925 s.105; *Thorne v Heard* [1895] A.C. 495.

[175] Settled Land Act 1925 s.107.

[176] Under the Trusts of Land and Appointment of Trustees Act 1996, replacing "trusts for sale".

[177] As in *Stevens v Hutchinson* [1953] Ch. 299.

[178] See n.73, above.

[179] *Levermore v Levemore* [1979] 1 W.L.R. 1277, applying *Re Shephard, Atkins v Shephard* (1889) 43 Ch. D. 131, 135, and 137, and distinguishing *Stevens v Hutchinson*, n.73, above.

[180] *Cadogan v Lyric Theatre* [1894] 3 Ch. 338.

payable to a judgment debtor[181] over the income of a trust fund[183]; and over a judgment debtor's interest in an outstanding charge upon land and subsisting policies of insurance.[184] A receiver may be appointed of a reversionary interest[185]; of a sufficient portion of a reversionary legacy to satisfy the claimant's debt[186]; but not over the debtor's share in an intestate's estate before a grant of administration,[187] nor over directors' fees.[188] The appointment over interests in partnership property is discussed in the previous chapter.[189]

The receiver can only affect the interest of the debtor.[190]

Cases in which a receiver will not be appointed. A receiver cannot be appointed to receive the interest of a fund, the disposal of which is in the absolute discretion of trustees or others. It must be clearly shown that there is something payable to the defendant in such a way as to make his or her interest assignable.[191] But where the judgment debtor is the sole object of a discretionary trust, it is apprehended that a receiver could always have been appointed.[192] Where the judgment debtor has control over a discretionary trust, where for example, a settlor who is also a potential beneficiary has a power of revocation, this is equivalent to ownership and so an appointment may be made.[193]

It has been held, in Ireland, that a receiver will not be appointed over a gratuity which has been awarded to a public servant, before it is paid over,[194] and the same would be the case with a gratuity which a private employer had expressed an intention to pay.[195] A receiver will not be appointed, where the effect of the appointment might be to destroy the property,[196] though the appointment of a receiver, without powers of management, may be obtained by the incumbrancer of a business, and the goodwill thus destroyed.[197]

Property of married women. Under the Law Reform (Married Women and Tortfeasors) Act 1935, and the Married Women (Restraint upon Anticipation) Act

3-25

3-26

---

[181] *Wells v Kilpin* (1874) L.R. 18 Eq. 298.
[182] *Westhead v Riley* (1884) 25 Ch. D. 413. Where the fund is in court, a charging order is now the appropriate remedy (Charging Orders Act 1979 s.2(2)(c)).
[183] *Oliver v Lowther* (1880) 28 W.R. 381; *Webb v Stenton* (1883) 11 Q.B.D. 518.
[184] *Beamish v Stephenson* (1886) 18 L.R. Ir. 319; see *Orr v Grierson* (1895) 28 L.R. Ir. 20.
[185] *Fuggle v Bland* (1883) 11 Q.B.D. 711; *Tyrell v Painton* [1895] 1 Q.B. 202; *Ideal Bedding Co v Holland* [1907] 2 Ch. 157.
[186] *Macnicoll v Parnell* (1887) 35 W.R. 773.
[187] *Mullane v Ahern* (1891) 28 L.R. Ir. 105; sed quaere.
[188] *Hamilton v Brogden* [1891] W.N. 36 (unpaid fees may be garnished (now subject to a third party debt order under CPR 72).
[189] See para.2-42, above.
[190] *Wills v Luff* (1888) 38 Ch. D. 197.
[191] *R. v Lincolnshire County Court Judge* (1887) 20 Q.B.D. 167; and see *Willis v Cooper* (1900) 44 S.J. 698, where the appointment of a receiver to secure the payment of untaxed costs was refused.
[192] See *Re Smith* [1928] Ch. 915; so too, where two joint judgment debtors are the only objects. A receiver may be appointed to enforce a charging order, which can now be made in such cases: Charging Orders Act 1979 ss.2(1)(b)(ii) and (iii) and 3(4). A receiver will not be appointed over property of no appreciable value: *Walls Ltd v Legge* [1923] 2 K.B. 240.
[193] *Tasarruf Mevduati Sigorta Fonu v Merrill Lynch Bank and Trust Co (Cayman) Ltd* [2012] 1 W.L.R. 1721; *JSC Mezhdunarodniy Promyshlenniy Bank v Pugachev* [2015] EWCA Civ139.
[194] *Timothy v Day* [1908] 2 Ir.R. 26; but see *Re Lupton* [1912] 1 K.B. 107. See also *Wells v Wells* [1914] P. 157 (barrister's fees).
[195] *Timothy v Day*, n.194, above at p.31.
[196] *Hamilton v Brogden*, above, n.188.
[197] See para.2-32, above.

1949, a married woman, as regards her property, and as regards the law of bankruptcy and the enforcement of judgments and orders, became in the same position as a *feme sole*: and property could no longer be held for her separate use.[198] Equitable execution against a married woman is obtainable in all cases on the same principles as against a man.

3-27   **Form of order.**   Both the application notice and order, in cases where the appointment is sought by way of equitable execution, should specify the property over which the receiver is sought, for the receiver will not be appointed over the debtor's property generally.[199] It appears that the debtor may be examined under the provisions of CPR r.71.2 in order to ascertain the nature of the property.[200] This does not amount to the enforcement of a judgment or order, for which leave is required under what is now the Reserve and Auxiliary Forces, etc. Act 1951.[201] Any special directions as to keeping accounts of different properties should be inserted in the order. Where the debtor was entitled to rent of furniture and a house let together, the house being in mortgage, the receiver was, as against the mortgagee, held entitled to the share of the rent apportioned to the furniture.[202]

COMPANIES

3-28   In the case of ordinary limited companies, questions can rarely, if ever, arise as to whether the property is or is not assignable. In the case of statutory undertakings, the extent to which a receiver can be appointed over the assets has been discussed in Ch.2, above.[203]

In the case of ordinary limited companies, the conditions necessary to the creation of a valid charge are mentioned above.[204] The accidental omission of an item from the particulars registered under what is now ss.859A and 859H of the Companies Act 2006, was held not to affect the security over, nor the receiver's right to take possession of, that item.[205] The title of the debenture holders was held not to be good against the trustee in bankruptcy in respect of assets, the assignment of which to the company was void as fraudulent or as an act of bankruptcy.[206] A receiver is a trespasser as regards such assets.[207]

Where the liquidator recovered money which had been paid to an unsecured creditor, on the ground of fraudulent preference, the debenture holder's charge, which had crystallised by the appointment of a receiver before the liquidation, was

---

[198]   See s.1 of the 1935 Act; s.1 of the 1949 Act. The life interest of a married woman is now directed to be held on protective trusts, which are a bar to legal or equitable execution.

[199]   *Hamilton v Brogden*, above, n.188.

[200]   *Hamilton v Brogden*, above, n.188. See also *Morgan v Hart* per Phillimore LJ [1914] 2 K.B. 183 at 191.

[201]   cf. s.3(9), proviso, and *Fagot v Gaches* [1943] K.B. 10 (a decision under the Courts (Emergency Powers) Act 1943).

[202]   *Hoare v Hove Bungalows* (1912) 56 S.J. 686, CA.

[203]   See Ch.2, para.2-48, above.

[204]   See paras 2-62 ff, above.

[205]   *National Provincial Bank v Charnley* [1924] 1 K.B. 431 (under Companies Act 1929 s.79).

[206]   Acts of bankruptcy were abolished by Insolvency Act 1986; but a debenture may be set aside as a transaction defeating creditors: see Insolvency Act 1986 ss.423-425.

[207]   *Re Simms* [1934] 1 Ch. 1.

held not to extend to that money, since at the date of crystallisation the company had no right whatever in respect of it.[208]

Assets to be excluded. If certain specific assets are excluded from the debenture holder's charge, they must be excluded from the order appointing a receiver.[209] In a case in which different sets of debentures specifically charged certain items, and all sets included a floating charge over the undertaking, different receivers were appointed over the respective specifically charged assets, one of whom was appointed manager.[210] The practice where foreign property is included has already been discussed.[211]

    It is the practice to exclude uncalled capital from a receivership order, even though it is included in the charge given by the debentures.[212]

    If there is a doubt as to the property over which the debenture holder's charge extends, an application notice may be filed, asking for an inquiry to bring out the relevant facts[213]; in the meantime, the receiver may be ordered to carry to a separate account funds representing property as to which the doubt exists. The fact that some things included in a general assignment cannot be ascertained does not affect the assignee's right to the remainder[214]; nor does the fact that the security is invalid as to certain items.[215]

3-29

Books and papers. When debentures charge all the property and assets of a company, including its uncalled capital, the order appointing a receiver usually directs that all books and documents relating to such property and assets be handed over to the receiver. But if the company is being wound up, the liquidator is entitled to the custody of such books and documents as relate to the management and business of the company and are not necessary to support the title of the holders of the debentures; the court will therefore order the delivery of these books and documents to the liquidator, on an undertaking by him to produce them to the receiver.[216] The court has no power to order instruments which have been deposited in the Land Registry to be delivered up to a receiver in a debenture holder's action, unless the property has been redeemed or sold.[217] Where title deeds are in the custody of trustees for debenture holders, the court may, for reasons of convenience, order them to be handed over to a receiver for the debenture holders, on his undertaking to re-deliver them; there is no hard-and-fast rule, the matter being one for the discretion of the court in each case.[218]

3-30

    Where an administrative receiver had obtained from the Registrar ex parte an order[219] that the liquidator of the company (already in office) should hand over to him all the company's books and records, a statement of his receipts and pay-

---

[208] *Re Yagerphone Ltd* [1935] 1 Ch. 392. Such preferences are no longer characterised as "fraudulent".
[209] In such a case as *Lemon v Austin Friars Investment Trust* [1926] Ch. 1 CA, the security, though operating as a debenture, would not have enabled a receiver to be appointed over the assets.
[210] See *Re Ind Coope Co* [1911] 2 Ch. 223.
[211] See paras 3-12 ff, above.
[212] See para.4-9, below, as to duties of a receiver in such a case.
[213] *Re Gregory, Love & Co* [1916] 1 Ch. 203.
[214] See *Imperial Paper Mills v Quebec Bank* (1913) 110 L.T. 91.
[215] See *Re North Wales Produce Co* [1922] 2 Ch. 340.
[216] *Engel v South Metropolitan Brewery Co* [1892] 1 Ch. 442.
[217] *Somerset v Lands Securities Co* [1849] 3 Ch. 464.
[218] *Re Ind Coope & Co* n.210, above.
[219] To which he was entitled, as office-holder, under Insolvency Act 1986 s.234.

ments, and all the money which he was retaining towards the liquidation costs, the order was set aside, as having been improperly obtained ex parte; the liquidator, however, was condemned in costs, for his contempt in having failed promptly to comply with the order, even though it had been wrongly made.[220]

Where mortgagors are seeking the delivery up by administrative receivers of documents in their possession relating to the company's affairs, which they assert to be the property of the company, it is a question whether documents created for and on behalf of the receivers ought to be considered as the property of the company, or of the receivers themselves.[221]

---

[220] *Re First Express Ltd* [1991] B.C.C. 782.
[221] *Gomba Holdings (UK) Ltd v Minories Finance Ltd.* [1988] 1 W.L.R. 1231; [1989] 1 All E.R. 261, CA.

Chapter 4

WHO MAY BE APPOINTED RECEIVER

Requirement of disinterested person: exceptions. A receiver must under CPR r.69.2(2) be an individual. A receiver appointed in a claim should, as a general rule, be an individual wholly disinterested in the subject-matter[1]; but it is competent for the court, upon the consent of the parties, and in a proper case without such consent, to appoint as receiver a person who is interested in the subject-matter of the claim, if it is satisfied that the appointment will be attended with benefit to the estate.[2] Accordingly, in a claim to dissolve a partnership, one of the partners is often appointed receiver.[3] In an urgent case, the plaintiff was appointed on his ex parte application.[4] So, also, a mortgagee in possession has been appointed receiver[5]; and, in an Irish case, the owner of incumbered lands which had been directed to be sold was appointed, the incumbrancers consenting, but no receiver's fees were allowed him.[6] Where the appointment is by way of equitable execution, it is not unusual to appoint the judgment creditor without salary.[7]

A party to the claim will not usually be appointed receiver, unless he undertakes to act without salary,[8] though in partnership cases a salary is sometimes allowed.[9]

When a party to the action is appointed receiver, he or she does not thereby lose any privilege belonging to him or her as such party,[10] nor are his or her rights as to receiver affected by his or her liabilities as a party.[11]

Exception in partnership cases. The appointment of a party as receiver, without the consent of the other parties is most frequently made in partnership cases, because in such cases it is likely to be for the benefit of the estate: if the partner actually carrying on the business has not been guilty of such misconduct as to have rendered it unsafe to trust him or her, the court sometimes appoints him or her receiver and manager, with or without salary according to circumstances.[12] It has been usual, however, to require him or her to give security duly to manage the

4-1

4-2

---

[1] See *Re Lloyd* (1879) 12 Ch. D. 447.

[2] See *Boyle v Bettws Llantwit Colliery Co* (1876) 2 Ch. D. 726: unpaid vendor appointed.

[3] See n.9, below.

[4] *Taylor v Eckersley* (1876) 2 Ch. D. 302; *Hyde v Warden* (1876) 1 Ex. D. 309; *Fuggle v Bland* (1883) 11 Q.B.D. 711.

[5] *Re Prytherch* (1889) 42 Ch. D. 590; and see *Davis v Barrett* (1884) 13 L.J. Ch. 304.

[6] *Re Golding* (1888) 21 L.R. Ir. 194.

[7] See *Pawley v Pawley* [1905] 1 Ch. 593.

[8] *Re Prytherch*, n.5, above; *Wilson v Greenwood* (1818) 1 Swans, 471, 483: *Hoffman v Duncan* (1853) 18 Jur.69; *Sargant v Read* (1876) 1 Ch. D. 600.

[9] See *Davy v Scarth* [1906] 1 Ch. 55.

[10] *Scott v Platel* (1847) 2 Ph. 229, 232.

[11] *Davy v Scarth*, n.9, above.

[12] *Wilson v Greenwood* (1818) 1 Swans, 471; see *Maund v Allies* (1839) 4 My. & C. 507; *Sheppard v*

partnership affairs, and to account for moneys received.[13] Where the appointment of a receiver is referred by the judge to the master, leave is sometimes given for each partner to propose himself or herself. If an independent person is appointed, he or she may be authorised to appoint a working partner as manager at remuneration.

4-3 **Appointment of trustee.** It is not according to the usual course of the court to appoint a trustee to be receiver, though a trustee with no active duties to perform, or with powers not yet exercisable, is sometimes appointed.[14] The court, on appointing a receiver of a trust estate, looks to the trustee to see that the receiver is doing his or her duty.[15] The two characters of trustee and receiver are rarely compatible, and, in addition to this, the appointment of a trustee to act as receiver is, unless he or she undertakes to act without remuneration, a violation of the rule of equity that a trustee cannot derive any benefit from the discharge of his or her duty as trustee. The court will even remove a receiver whose private interests are in conflict with his or her duties, notwithstanding that his or her acts may for the most part have been for the general good of the property, and that a majority in number and value of the incumbrancers on it may desire that he or she be retained.[16] The rule against appointing a trustee to be a receiver applies, whether the receiver is a sole trustee or is acting jointly with others.[17]

In special cases, however, where the appointment of a trustee to be receiver will be beneficial to the estate, as, for instance, where he or she has a peculiar knowledge of the estate, or no one else can be found who will act with the same benefit to the estate, the court will make the appointment.[18] The receiver may be required to undertake to act without remuneration. Remuneration is not usually allowed to a trustee acting as a receiver,[19] but there is no inflexible rule against the allowance of remuneration.[20]

Under special circumstances, a trustee may be appointed receiver with a salary. Where, for instance, a testator had appointed as trustee of his estates a person who for many years had been the paid receiver and manager of them, he was continued as receiver with salary, the tenant for life being an infant.[21] There appears to be less objection than in other cases to appoint a trustee for the purposes of the Settled Land Act 1925 to be receiver of an estate or to allow him or her remuneration, so long as there is a tenant for life of full age: for as trustee he or she has no duties as regards the management of the land.

Where a trustee is willing to act as receiver without salary, he or she will be allowed to propose himself or herself, but the judge is not bound to accept him or her.[22]

Oxenford (1855) 1 K. & J. 491; *Hoffman v Duncan* (1853) 18 Jur. 69 (retired partner, liable for debts); *Sargant v Read* (1876) 1 Ch. D. 600: see n.8, above.

[13] *Wilson v Greenwood*, n.12, above; *Blakeney v Dufaur* (1851) 15 Beav. 40; *Sargant v Read* (1876) 1 Ch. D. 600; *Collins v Barker* [1893] 1 Ch. 578.

[14] *Sutton v Jones* (1809) 15 Ves. 584, 587, 588. cf. *Tait v Jenkins* (1842) 1 Y. & C. Ch. Cas. 492.

[15] *Sykes v Hastings* (1805) 11 Ves. Jun. 363; *Sutton v Jones*, n.14, above; cf. *Craig v Att.-Gen.* [1926] N. Ir. 218.

[16] *Fripp v Chard Ry* (1835) 11 Hare 241, 260; cf. *Cookes v Cookes* (1865) 2 De. G.J. & S. 526, 530.

[17] *Anon. v Jolland* (1802) 8 Ves. 72.

[18] *Gardner v Blane* (1842) 1 Hare 381; *Powys v Blagrave* (1853) 18 Jur. 462.

[19] *Re Bignell, Bignell v Chapman* [1892] 1 Ch. 59.

[20] *Sutton v Jones*, n.14, above; *Pilkington v Baker* (1876) 24 W.R. 234.

[21] *Bury v Newport* (1856) 23 Beav. 30.

[22] *Banks v Banks* (1850) 14 Jur.659.

Party in a fiduciary position, etc. The rule, that the court will not sanction the appointment, as receiver, of a person whose duty it is to check and control the receiver, is extended to other persons besides trustees[23]; e.g. the next friend (now "litigation friend") of a minor, whose duty it is to watch the accounts and check the conduct of a receiver of the minor's estate[24]; or the solicitor of a party having the conduct of an action, because it will be his or her duty to check the receiver's accounts.[25]

4-4

Nor will an individual be appointed receiver whose position may cause difficulty in administering justice: thus a master in Chancery, whose duty it was to pass the accounts and check the conduct of a receiver, was held to be disqualified.[26]

Although a solicitor in a claim[27] cannot be appointed receiver of the estate in relation to which he or she is acting as solicitor, there is no general objection to the appointment of a solicitor to be receiver.[28] In one case,[29] the solicitor of a married woman was, on her application, appointed receiver of her separate estate, although a strong affidavit was made by her husband, seeking to show the unfitness of the solicitor for the office.

Considerations looked at in making the appointment. The person appointed ought to be one who, consistently with professional and other pursuits, can spare sufficient time for the duties the office.[30] Accordingly, in a case where a man proposed as receiver was a Member of Parliament and a practising barrister, and also resided at a very considerable distance from the estate, the court held that these circumstances, though not amounting to an absolute disqualification, formed sufficient grounds to render further consideration advisable.[31]

4-5

The court will not appoint as receiver a person whose privileges protect him or her from the ordinary remedies which it may become proper to enforce,[32] such as a peer[33]; or probably a Member of the House of Commons[34]; or a person under security to the Crown, having regard to the Crown's prerogative rights.[35]

Any party interested in the proceedings[36] may propose that some person other than the person proposed be appointed. A stranger to the action cannot propose a

---

23 See *Cookes v Cookes* (1865) 2 De G.J. & S. 526, 530.
24 *Stone v Wishart* (1817) 2 Madd. 64. In *Taylor v Oldham* (1822) Jac. 527. Lord Eldon refused to appoint the son of a next friend. For "litigation friends", acting on behalf of minors and mental health patients, see now CPR r.21.3, cf. PD 21.
25 *Garland v Garland* (1793) 2 Ves. Jr. 137; *Wilson v Poe* (1825) 1 Hogg. 322; cf. *Grundy v Buckeridge* (1853) 22 L.J. Ch. 1007; *Craig v Att.-Gen.* [1926] N.Ir. 218.
26 *Ex p. Fletcher* (1801) 6 Ves. 427.
27 *Garland v Garland*, n.25, above; *Re Lloyd* (1879) 12 Ch. D. 447.
28 See *Wilson v Poe*, n.25, above; *Della Cainea v Hayward* (1825) McClel. & Y. 272.
29 *Bagot v Bagot* (1873) 2 Jr. 1063.
30 *Wynne v Lord Newborough* (1808) 15 Ves. 283.
31 See n.30, above. Distance is of less significance nowadays.
32 *Att.-Gen. v Gee* (1813) 2 Ves. & B. 208.
33 *Att.-Gen. v Gee* (1813) 2 Ves. & B. 208.
34 See *Lord Wellesley's Case* (1831) W R. & M. 639; *Lechmere Charlton's Case* (1837) 2 Myl. & G. 316; *Re Armstrong Ex p. Lindsay* (1892) 1 Q.B. 327; cf. *Re Gent* (1888) 40 Ch. D. 190. In *Wiggin v Anderson*, unreported, March 16, 1982, Walton J appointed the plaintiff, who was a partner with the defendant, to be receiver, notwithstanding that he was a Member of Parliament; but the duties to be performed by him were not such that his parliamentary activities were likely to interfere therewith.
35 *Att.-Gen. v Day* (1817) 2 Madd. 246, 254; Daniell's *Chancery Practice*, 8th edn, pp.1470–1472): "Who may be appointed". These rights do not apply in bankruptcy: see Insolvency Act 1986 s.434.
36 *Att.-Gen. v Day*, n.35, above; *Bagot v Bagot* (1838) 2 Jr.1063.

receiver.[37] The most suitable person should be appointed, without regard to the party by whom he or she has been proposed.[38] In making the selection, the circumstances of the case and the interests of all parties must be taken into consideration[39]; but, other things being equal, that is, if the parties are equally interested, and the persons proposed on both sides are unobjectionable, the person proposed by the party having the conduct of the proceedings is usually preferred.[40] In the appointment of a receiver, considerable attention will be given to the recommendations of a testator.[41]

If an estate over which a receiver is to be appointed is in mortgage, preference will be given to the person proposed by the mortgagee, unless there is some substantial objection to the appointment, although a person proposed by the mortgagor may be more experienced in the duties of the office.[42]

A party to the action may propose himself or herself as receiver, if leave to that effect is given and embodied in the judgment or order[43]; but not otherwise,[44] unless leave be subsequently obtained on application notice at chambers.[45]

Under the old practice of the Court of Chancery, when the appointment of a receiver rested with the masters in Chancery, it was a settled rule not to entertain any objection to the report of the master which was not founded on principle.[46] Under the present practice, the Court of Appeal acts on the same principles; accordingly, it will not entertain an application bringing in question the decision of the judge as to the most suitable person to be appointed receiver, unless the appointment is open to some overwhelming objection in point of choice, or to some objection fatal in point of principle.[47]

4-6   **Objection on ground of partiality.**   It is a substantial objection to the appointment of a receiver that he or she has an undue partiality for one of the parties[48]; but if an order has been made without any objection on the part of any of the parties, giving liberty to one of the parties to propose himself or herself as receiver, the question is one not of principle, but of judicial discretion, with regard had to all the circumstances of the case; if the judge appoints the party proposing himself or herself, the Court of Appeal will not interfere with that selection.[49] The mere fact

---

[37] *Att.-Gen. v Day*, n.35, above.
[38] *L'Espinasse v Bell* (1821) 2 Jac. & W. 436. cf. *Att.-Gen. v Dyson* (1826) 2 Sim. & St. 528.
[39] *Wood v Hitchings* (1840) 4 Jr.858.
[40] *Wilson v Poe* (1825) 1 Hogg. 322; see 1 Hogg. 322; see *Baylies v Baylies* (1844) 1 Coll. C.C. 537; *Bord v Tollemache* (1862) 1 New Rep.177. Where a receiver had been appointed in two administration suits, the carriage of the order was given to the plaintiff who first gave notice of motion; *Hart v Tulk* (1849) 6 Ha. 611.
[41] *Wynne v Lord Newborough* (1808) 15 Ves. 283.
[42] *Wilkins v Williams* (1798) 3 Ves. 588; *Tillett v Nixon* (1883) 25 Ch. D. 238; see, too, *Bord v Tollemache*, n.40, above, where the deed contained a provision for the appointment of a receiver by the first mortgagee, and the suit for the appointment of a receiver was instituted by a second mortgagee.
[43] *Meaden v Sealey* (1849) 6 Hare 620; *Cookes v Cookes* (1865) 2 De G.J. & S. 526; Seton, 7th edn, pp.729, 739.
[44] *Davis v Duke of Marlborough* (1818) 2 Swans. 108.
[45] See, for a form of application notice, *Atkin's Court Forms* Vol.33, (2011 Issue), p.201; see Daniell's *Chancery Practice*, n.36, above.
[46] *Cookes v Cookes*, n.43, above; *Tharp v Tharp* (1857) 12 Ves. 317.
[47] *Cookes v Cookes*, n.43, above; *Perry v Oriental Hotels Co* (1870) L.R. 5 Ch. 420; *Nothard v Proctor* (1875) 1 Ch. D. 4.
[48] *Blackeway v Blakeway* (1833) 2 L.J. (n.s.) Ch. 74.
[49] *Cookes v Cookes*, n.43, above.

of the existence of disputes of differences between the parties to a claim does not debar the judge from appointing a party to the claim.[50]

Where a receiver has been appointed, the court will not remove him or her on the mere ground of being an illiterate person, in the absence of some weightier reason, such as mismanagement, dishonesty, or incompetency to manage the estate.[51]

In Company Cases

Statutory disqualifications. A body corporate is not qualified for appointment **4-7** as receiver of the property of a company[52] formed and registered under the Companies Acts.[53] Any such purported appointment is a nullity.[54] If an undischarged bankrupt,[55] or a person to whom a moratorium period under a debt relief order applies[56], or a person who is subject to a bankruptcy restrictions order or undertaking[57] or a person who is subject to a debt relief restrictions order or undertaking,[58] acts as receiver or manager of the property of a company on behalf of debenture holders, otherwise than under an appointment by the court, he or she becomes liable to imprisonment or a fine or both.[59]

No person against whom a disqualification order has been made, under the provisions of the Company Directors Disqualification Act 1986,[60] or in respect of whom a disqualification undertaking has been accepted,[61] may, without the leave of the court,[62] be a receiver or manager (but not including an administrative receiver)[63] of the property of a company for a period specified in such order or undertaking.[64] This

---

[50] *Cookes v Cookes*, n.43, above at 531.

[51] *Chaytor v Maclean* (1848) 11 L.T.(o.s.) 2.

[52] This expression, by s.29(1)(a) of Insolvency Act 1986, includes a receiver of part of the company's property, and a receiver only of the income arising from its property or from part thereof; and similarly in the case of a manager.

[53] Insolvency Act 1986 ss.30, 251 (as amended by SI 2007/2194); Companies Act 2006 s.1. The penalties for contravention are on conviction on indictment, a fine, and on summary conviction a fine not exceeding the statutory maximum: See Insolvency Act 1986 ss.30, 430, Sch.10.

[54] *Portman Building Society v Gallwey* (1955) 1 W.L.R. 96.

[55] Insolvency Act 1986 s.31(1)(a), as inserted by Enterprise Act 2002 s.257(3) Sch.21 para.1.

[56] Insolvency Act 1986 s.31(1)(aa), as inserted by the Tribunals, Courts and Enforcement Act 2007 s.108(3) Sch.20, Pt 1, paras 1, 2(1)(a).

[57] Insolvency Act 1986 s.31(1)(b) as inserted by Enterprise Act 2002, s.257(3) Sch.21, para.1. Insolvency Act 1986 s.31 only refers to bankruptcy restrictions orders but this expression includes bankruptcy restrictions undertakings: see Insolvency Act 1986 Sch.4A para.8.

[58] Insolvency Act 1986 s.31(1)(b), as amended by the Tribunals, Courts and Enforcement Act 2007 s.108(3), Sch.20 Pt 1 paras 1, 2(1)(b). Insolvency Act 1986 s.31 only refers to debt relief restrictions orders but this expression includes debt relief restrictions undertakings: see Insolvency Act 1986 Sch.4ZB para.8.

[59] Insolvency Act 1986 s.31 (as amended).

[60] Company Directors Disqualification Act 1986 s.1 (as amended).

[61] Company Directors Disqualification Act 1986 ss.1A, 8ZC, 8ZE, 9B.

[62] Company Directors Disqualification Act 1986 s.17 (as amended). Broadly, the court with jurisdiction is the court with winding up jurisdiction which made the disqualification order or (if there is no such court) the court with winding up jurisdiction regarding the company in relation to which the misconduct occurred.

[63] Company Directors Disqualification Act 1986 s.22(10), as inserted by the Insolvency Act 2000 s.5(3).

[64] Company Directors Disqualification Act 1986 s.1(1), as amended by Insolvency Act 2000 s.5.

period cannot exceed 15 years.[65] Such a person is absolutely prohibited from being an insolvency practitioner.

If any person acts in contravention of such an order or undertaking, he or she will, in respect of each offence, be liable on conviction on indictment to imprisonment for a term not exceeding two years, or a fine, or both or, on summary conviction, to imprisonment for a term not exceeding six months or to a fine not exceeding the statutory maximum or to both.[66]

In the case of companies, an accountant is very frequently appointed. It is only in special circumstances that the court will appoint the claimant in a debenture holder's action to be receiver, and then only, as a rule, subject to production of a witness statement or an affidavit that all the other debenture holders consent.[67] A director will not as a rule be appointed. Thus, a chartered accountant resident near Birmingham was appointed receiver and manager of a company, the assets of which were a building estate near London, though the appointment of the managing director was desired by another debenture holder.[68] A person entrusted with management over a statutory undertaking will sometimes be appointed.[69]

4-8   Qualification required for administrative receiver: licensed insolvency practitioner.   The term "administrative receiver" means: (a) a receiver or manager of the whole, or substantially the whole of the company's property, appointed by or on behalf of the holders of any debentures of the company secured by a charge which, as created, was a floating charge, or by such charge and one or more other securities, or a person who would be such a receiver or manager, but for the appointment of some other persons as the receiver or manager of part of the company's property[70]; or (b) a receiver appointed under Scottish law under s.51 of the Insolvency Act 1986 in a case where the whole (or substantially the whole) of the company's property is attached by the floating charge.[71] This office is considered in more detail below, in relation to the appointment of such a receiver out of court.[72]

Such an appointment is considered, for many purposes of the provisions of the Insolvency Act 1986, to signify the insolvency of the company.[73] There is also the concept of "the office-holder", being a person administering an insolvent company; this embraces for most purposes an administrative receiver, an administrator,[74] a provisional liquidator, and a liquidator.[75] Without prejudice to the position of the Official Receiver,[76] an office-holder must be a person who is qualified to act as an insolvency practitioner in relation to the company,[77] although if by some mischance a person other than an insolvency practitioner is appointed, his or her acts will be

---

[65] Company Directors Disqualification Act 1986 ss.2(3)(b), 3(5), 4(3), 5(5), 5A(6), 8ZA(4), 8ZD(5), 6(4), 8(4), 9A(9), 10(2). In some cases the period cannot exceed five years.
[66] Company Directors Disqualification Act 1986 s.13.
[67] See *Budgett v Improved Furnace Syndicate* [1901] W.N. 23.
[68] *Re Carshalton Park Estate Ltd* [1908] 2 Ch. 62, 66.
[69] *Ames v Birkenhead Docks* (1855) 20 Beav. 332; *Potts v Warwick & Birmingham Canal Co* (1853) Kay 142.
[70] Insolvency Act 1986 s.29(2).
[71] Insolvency Act 1986 s.251.
[72] See Ch.19 below.
[73] Insolvency Act 1986 s.247(1).
[74] See paras 14-1 ff, below.
[75] Insolvency Act 1986 s.233(1), and, in personal insolvency, the corresponding office-holder.
[76] Insolvency Act 1986 ss.388(5), 389(2).
[77] Insolvency Act 1986 ss.388(1)(a), 389(1).

valid.[78] He or she will, however, in that case be liable, if he or she acts an administrative receiver of the company, on conviction on indictment to imprisonment for a term not exceeding two years or a fine, or to both, or on summary conviction to imprisonment for a term not exceeding six months, or to a fine not exceeding the statutory maximum, or to both.[79]

Bases for qualification. Only an individual can be an insolvency practitioner.[80] **4-9**
He or she can only be qualified to act, if he is authorised so to do by virtue of membership of a professional body recognised by order of the Secretary of State.[81] Authorisation may now be in relation to companies only, individuals only, or as is far more common, full authorisation which allows the practitioner to act as officeholder in both types of insolvency.[82] It is no longer possible to be authorised directly by the Secretary of State.[83] The individual will not be qualified to act as an insolvency practitioner, unless there is in force at that time security for the proper performance of his or her functions, and that the security meets the prescribed requirements with respect to his or her so acting in relation to the company in question.[84] As to the general security requirements now to be complied with by receivers, see paras 5-18 ff, below.[85]

No person is qualified to act as an insolvency practitioner at any time, if at that time he or she has been adjudged bankrupt and has not been discharged; or, is subject to a moratorium under a debt relief order[86]; or is subject to a bankruptcy restrictions order or undertaking, which is in force or is subject to a debt relief restrictions order or undertaking which is in force[87]; or is subject to a disqualification order made, or a disqualification undertaking accepted, under the Company Directors Disqualification Act 1986,[88] or if he or she lacks capacity (within the meaning of the Mental Capacity Act 2005) to act as an insolvency practitioner.[89]

Receiver ceasing to be qualified. Where a person, previously qualified to act as **4-10**
an insolvency practitioner, ceases to be so qualified, either by the non-renewal of

---

[78] Insolvency Act 1986 s.232.

[79] Insolvency Act 1986 s.389(1), 430, Sch.10.

[80] Insolvency Act 1986 s.390(1).

[81] Insolvency Act 1986 ss.390(2), 390A. The bodies so recognised are:
The Chartered Association of Certified Accountants; The Insolvency Practitioners Association; The Institute of Chartered Accountants in England and Wales; The Institute of Chartered Accountants in Ireland; The Institute of Chartered Accountants in Scotland.
See the Insolvency Practitioners (Recognised Professional Bodies) Order 1986 (SI 1986/1764), made under Insolvency Act 1985, preserved by Insolvency Act 1986 s.437 Sch.11 Pt V para.23. The Law Society and the Law Society of Scotland ceased to be recognised professional bodies for these purposes in 2016 (see respectively SI 2016/403 and SI 2015/2067).

[82] Insolvency Act 1986 s.390A.

[83] See the now repealed Insolvency Act 1986 ss.390(2)(b).

[84] Insolvency Act 1986 s.390(3).

[85] The security requirements are dealt with in Pt 3 of, and Sch.2 to, the Insolvency Practitioners Regulations 2005 (SI 2005/524). The security must be by way of a bond which must cover certain specified types of loss.

[86] Insolvency Act 1986 s.390(4)(aa), inserted by the Tribunals, Courts and Enforcement Act 2007 s.108(3) Sch.20 Pt 1 paras 1, 6(1), (2).

[87] Insolvency Act 1986 s.390(5), inserted by the Enterprise Act 2002 s.257(3) Sch.21 para.4 and amended by the Tribunals, Courts and Enforcement Act 2007 s.108(3) Sch.20 Pt 1 paras 1, 6(1), (3).

[88] Note also express restriction on acting as an insolvency practitioner under the terms of a disqualification order or undertaking as defined in the Company Directors Disqualification Act 1986 ss.1, 1A, and 9B and the criminal penalty under s.13 of that Act.

[89] Insolvency Act 1986 s.390(4)(d).

qualification on its expiry,[90] or by a direct sanctions order of the court,[91] or by his or her suffering some change to status which disqualifies him or her,[92] he or she must immediately cease to act as an insolvency practitioner in any capacity.[93] The Court may then itself appoint a successor, or give directions as to the necessary steps for an appointment. Such a successor may be appointed from among the duly qualified partners in his or her own firm.[94]

4-11   **Liquidator.**   Where there is a winding-up, the court will generally take care, so as to avoid trouble and expenses, that the receiver and the liquidator shall be one and the same person, wherever that can properly be done[95]; though some judges have considered it undesirable that one person should fill both posts where the interests represented may conflict.[96] Where, after the making of an order to wind up a company and the appointment of a liquidator, the appointment of a receiver has been applied for by the plaintiffs in a debenture holder's action, the liquidator has frequently been appointed receiver,[97] but not if special circumstances rendered the appointment undesirable, e.g. if he or she has assumed a position of hostility to the debenture holders[98]; the discretion of the judge of first instance will seldom be interfered with by the Court of Appeal.[99] The consent of the debenture holders is in general a prerequisite: see below. Where a liquidator in a voluntary winding-up is also receiver, this fact may be sufficient ground for removing him from the former position on the application of creditors.[100]

4-12   **Effect of liquidation on receivership.**   A receiver who has been appointed before the commencement of the winding-up of a company is not displaced by the appointment of a liquidator; but the court may remove such a receiver after a winding-up order has been obtained, and may appoint the liquidator to act as receiver as well as liquidator.[101] This, however, is "only a prima facie rule of practice; if justice or

---

[90] Insolvency Act 1986 s.393(3); see now the Insolvency Practitioners Regulations 2005 (SI 2005/524): see also Insolvency Act 1986 s.19(2) Sch.B1 para.6 (Administrators); s.45(2) (Administrative receivers); s.62(2) (receivers).

[91] Insolvency Act 1986 s.391O. It is possible for the Secretary of State to revoke the recognition of a recognised professional body under s.391L which would also lead to individuals losing their insolvency practitioner qualification.

[92] See para.4-9, above.

[93] Insolvency Act 1986 s.389.

[94] *Re A.J. Adams (Builders) Ltd* [1991] B.C.C. 62; [1991] B.C.L.C. 359. For block transfer orders in this context see *Donaldson v O'Sullivan* [2009] EWCA Civ 879; [2009] 1 W.L.R. 924 and Practice Direction—Insolvency Proceedings, para.1.6. However, as regards the court's powers in relation to administrative receivers see *Re A & C Supplies Ltd* [1998] B.C.C. 708; [1998] 1 B.C.L.C. 603.

[95] *Re Joshua Stubbs* [1891] 1 Ch. 475, 482; but the court cannot appoint a receiver to replace one appointed out of court: see n.99, below.

[96] *Re Karamelli & Barnett Ltd* [1917] 1 Ch. 203 per Neville J: "The liquidator acts for and in the interests of the company, whereas the receiver and manager acts for and in the interests of the debenture-holders and not for the company": per Lawrence J in *Stead Hazel & Co v Cooper* [1933] 1 K.B. 840, 843.

[97] *Perry v Oriental Hotels Co* (1870) L.R. 5 Ch. 420; *Tottenham v Swansea Zinc Ore Co* [1884] W.N. 54; 53 L.J. Ch. 776.

[98] *Giles v Nuthall* [1885] W.N. 51; see, too, *Boyle v Bettws, etc. Colliery Co* (1876) 2 Ch. D. 726; and *Strong v Carlyle Press* [1893] 1 Ch. 268.

[99] *Giles v Nuthall*, n.98, above.

[100] *Re Karamelli & Barnett Ltd*, n.96, above.

[101] See n.84, above; *Campbell v Compagnie Générale* (1876) 2 Ch. D. 181.

convenience require it, the rule will be displaced".[102] It will be displaced, if there is only (as is, in fact, now normally the case) a small amount of unpaid capital (or more commonly none) to be got in. In such a case, the court will generally abstain from substituting the liquidator for a receiver, and will allow the receiver to continue to act[103]; or the appointment may be split, the receiver being only displaced as to uncalled capital.[104] If the assets of the company are not enough to pay the debenture holders, the court will not remove the receiver in favour of a liquidator who wishes to question the validity of the debentures.[105]

Relevance of consent of debenture holders. Where debenture holders still have a right under their security to appoint a receiver, a winding-up order, coupled with the appointment of a liquidator, does not interfere with this right, though it may prevent the receiver from doing things which he or she is authorised to do by the debenture deed, for instance, carrying on the business, or making a call. The court has never appointed the liquidator to act as receiver for debenture holders, except where the debenture holders have themselves come to court and asked for a receiver. In that case, the court, in the exercise of its discretion, will generally appoint the liquidator, as being the most suitable person.

    4-13

But where, under the terms of their security, the debenture holders still have a right to appoint their own receiver, and they insist on their right, they are entitled to an order giving their receiver liberty to take possession.[106] In such a case, the court has no discretion. A power of appointing a receiver conferred by a company's debentures must be exercised in good faith and only in the interest of the debenture holders; accordingly; where it had been exercised by the donee of the power (a debenture holder who was also a shareholder) in the interest of the shareholders the court interfered and appointed its own receiver[107]; so also where the appointment was made by means of the vote of a person who had assigned his debenture to the plaintiff and against the wishes of the latter.[108]

Where a receiver has been appointed out of court, the court often appoints that person. In such cases, the order should include a direction to the receiver to include, in the accounts to be brought in by him, all receipts, payments and liabilities incurred before his or her appointment in the action. If another person is appointed, liberty should be given by the order to the original receiver to apply to have his or her accounts taken in the action; in such a case, if the receiver is not agent for the company, he or she has a right of indemnity against the debenture holders.[109]

Appeal. Where a judge at first instance has, in the exercise of his or her discretion, refused to displace a receiver by a liquidator, the Court of Appeal will not, in

    4-14

---

[102] *British Linen Co v South American and Mexican Co* [1894] 1 Ch. 108, at 119; *Bartlett v Northumberland Avenue Hotel Co*, 53 L.T. 611. In the former case, the receiver was allowed to continue to act, in respect of certain assets particularly difficult to realise.

[103] *Re Joshua Stubbs*, n.88, above, at 483. See, too, *Re Vimbos Ltd* [1900] 1 Ch. 470, where all the assets, which were of considerable amount, were realised by a receiver appointed by debenture holders, shortly before the company went into liquidation.

[104] *British Linen Co v South American and Mexican Co*, n.95, above.

[105] *Strong v Carlyle Press* [1893] 1 Ch. 268.

[106] See *Re Henry Pound, Son and Hutchins* (1889) 42 Ch. D. 402.

[107] *Re Maskelyne British Typewriter* [1898] 1 Ch. 133.

[108] *Re Slogger Automatic Feeder Co* [1915] 1 Ch. 478.

[109] *Re Arctic Supplies* [1932] W.N. 79.

the absence of special circumstances to justify their so doing, interfere with the exercise of that discretion.[110]

4-15   Custody of books.   Where the receiver is not displaced, a question may arise between him or her and the liquidator as to the custody of the books of the company. In general, the liquidator is entitled to the custody of such of the books and documents of the company as relate to its management and business and are not necessary to support the title of the debenture holders.[111]

4-16   Official Receiver.   Where an application is made to the court to appoint a receiver on behalf of the debenture holders or other creditors of a company which is being wound up by the court in England, the Official Receiver may be so appointed.[112]

---

[110] *Re Joshua Stubbs*, n.95, above; *Bartlett v Northumberland Avenue Hotel Co* (1886) 53 L.T. 611; cf. *Giles v Nuthall*, n.98, above.

[111] See *Engel v South Metropolitan Brewing Co* [1892] 1 Ch. 442, cited above, para.3-30. In *Re Trading Partners Ltd* [2002] B.P.I.R. 606, liquidators of companies incorporated in the British Virgin Islands, applying under Insolvency Act 1986 s.426, were authorised to inspect the books and papers of the companies held by their English receivers (including limited access to the receivers' working papers).

[112] Insolvency Act 1986 s.32.

Chapter 5

MODES OF APPOINTING A RECEIVER OF THE COURT

Procedural changes. Until the coming into force of the Civil Procedure Rules   **5-1**
1998 ("the CPR"), the exercise of the statutory jurisdiction[1] of the High Court and
of the county court to appoint receivers, both generally and by way of equitable
execution, was regulated in the High Court by RSC Ords 30, 51 and 115, and in the
county court by CCR Ord.32. The processes used were writs, motions and originating summonses.

Those rules were also applicable to the special jurisdictions under the Criminal
Justice Act 1988, the Drug Trafficking Act 1994, the Criminal Justice (International
Co-operation) Act 1990, and the Terrorism Act 2000 ("the confiscation statutes").
Under the provisions of those statutes, enacted for the confiscation and the recovery
of the proceeds of crime, receivers could be appointed in aid of orders made by
courts of criminal trial, by way of restraint orders, charging orders, recovery orders
and confiscation orders over the property of an offender and his associates. RSC
Ord.115 was, and remains, entitled "Confiscation and Forfeiture in connection with
criminal proceedings". The Proceeds of Crime Act 2002 ("POCA") has largely
replaced the 1988 and 1994 Acts but they, and RSC Ord.115 remain applicable to
instances where the criminal acts in question were carried out prior to 24 March
2003 (SI 2003/333).

Although civil recovery claims commenced under POCA must be brought under
CPR Pt 8 in accordance with para.4.1 of the Civil Recovery Proceedings Practice
Direction, the court has power to order a case to proceed under Pt 7 where
appropriate. Under CPR r.3.3 the Queen's Bench Division (as from 3 May 2016)
has put in place a new Practice Note for the case management of POCA civil
recovery claims (for example in relation to confiscation orders).

Some parts of the CPR (and their accompanying Practice Directions) provide
detailed rules for terrorism-related litigation such as CPR Pt 76 (proceedings under
the Prevention of Terrorism Act 2005 which is now repealed but CPR Pt 76 remains
relevant to proceedings brought under the 2005 Act); CPR Pt 79 (proceedings under
the Counter-Terrorism Act 2008 and Pt 1 of the Terrorist Asset-Freezing etc. Act
2010); CPR 80 (proceedings under the Terrorism, Prevention and Investigation
Measures Act 2011 which replaced the 2005 Act); and CPR Pt 88 (proceedings
under the Counter-Terrorism and Security Act 2015).

The Family Proceedings Rules 1991 ceased to apply to family proceedings in
2011and were replaced by the Family Procedure Rules 2010 (SI 2010/2955) which,
in relation to the appointment of receivers, apply CPR Pt 69 to family proceedings:
see para.5-41, below.

Rules for receivers: CPR Pt 69 and PD 69.   CPR Pt 69, entitled "Court's power   **5-2**

---

[1]   Senior Courts Act 1981 s.37 (High Court); County Courts Act 1984 ss.38 and 107.

to appoint a receiver", with its attendant Practice Direction, (PD 69) effectively came into force on 2 December 2002.[2] RSC Ords 30 and 51 were revoked, so that CPR Pt 69 and PD 69 now cover the entire field, including receiverships under the confiscation statutes, but excluding those under special statutes: see below. For the regulation of procedures under the confiscation statutes, CPR Sch.1–RSC 115, was retained, with a new Practice Direction, RSC PD 115, entitled "Restraint Orders and Appointment of Receivers in connection with Criminal Proceedings and Investigations"; this regulates the practice and procedure relating to applications for restraint, charging and confiscation orders where the acts in question were carried out prior to 24 March 2003 (SI 2003/333).

5-3   **The Practice Guides.**   The Chancery Guide (2016) refers to "A Guide for receivers in the Chancery Division" which is available on request from the Chancery Operations Manager.[3] The Queen's Bench Guide (2017)[4] deals with the appointment of receivers by way of equitable execution. The Guide mentions that a receiver by equitable execution may be useful where, for example, there is a debtor with a life interest in a trust fund or where a third party debt order cannot be used to reach future debts which may become due to the judgment debtor. In such circumstances, the appointment of a receiver may be just and convenient.[5]

5-4   **The criminal confiscation statutes: application of CPR Pt 69.**   The confiscation statutes have largely been replaced by the Proceeds of Crime Act 2002 ("POCA"), which creates further jurisdictions, now civil as well as criminal, for the pursuit and recovery of the proceeds of crime. Subject to transitional provisions, from 23 March 2003,[6] Pt VI of the Criminal Justice Act 1988, and Pt I of the Drug Trafficking Act 1994, were largely repealed[7] by the Proceeds of Crime Act 2002, and (except for pending and transitional cases) all applications for restraint orders and the appointment of receivers are now brought in the Crown Court under Pt 2 of that Act. See para.5-30, below.

5-5   **The new procedures.**   CPR Pt 69 and PD 69, which came into force on 2 December 2002,[8] provide a brief but comprehensive code for the appointment and control of receivers by the High Court and the county court, in the exercise of the court's statutory powers.[9] The new Rules have made significant changes to the previous codes. See the Chancery Guide and the Queen's Bench Guide.

5-6   **Receivership jurisdictions not covered by CPR Pt 69.**   CPR Pt 69 and CPR PD 69 apply to all appointments by the courts of receivers, except:

---

[2]   Civil Procedure (Amendment) Order 2002 (SI 2002/2098) rr.1(b), 26 Sch.7; these rules only apply to applications to appoint receivers filed, and appointments made, after 2 December 2002.
[3]   It is also available on the gov.uk website.
[4]   At the time of writing para.23.11.
[5]   At the time of writing para.23.11.1.
[6]   Proceeds of Crime Act 2002 (Commencement No.5, Transitional Provisions, Savings and Amendment) Order 2003 (SI 2003/333). See generally Pinto and Evans, *Corporate Criminal Responsibility*, 3rd edn (Sweet & Maxwell, 2013) especially Ch.9: "Confiscation, Restraint and Receivership—The Criminal Confiscation Regime".
[7]   Provisions regarding certain overseas provisions remain in force.
[8]   See n.2, above.
[9]   See n.1, above.

(a) interim receivers[10] in bankruptcy[11];
(b) receivers of mortgaged property[12];
(c) receivers of the property of patients.[13]

Modes of appointment: applications may be made with or without notice. The court may appoint a receiver—a term which includes a manager,[14] (who must be an individual person)[15]—before proceedings have started, or in existing proceedings, or on or after judgment.[16] It may at any time terminate a receiver's appointment, and may appoint another receiver in his or her place.[17] Provision is made for the orders to be made and served upon such termination.[18] A master or a district judge has power to grant an injunction in connection with or ancillary to an order appointing a receiver by way of equitable execution.[19]

    Such applications are to be made in the first instance in private, and may be made, in cases of urgency (or on grounds of the necessity for secrecy), without notice to any other party.[20] Application is made by application notice, supported by written evidence, and where the appointment is by way of equitable execution, entitled in the name of the action in which the judgment or order was obtained.[21]

    Although the court may appoint a receiver before substantive proceedings have started, and may do so upon an application made without notice,[22] it will normally only hear such an application after being satisfied that the application notice seeking the appointment has been served on the respondents and the person to be appointed receiver.[23]

Time to apply. Application should be made as soon as it appears to be necessary or desirable to make it.[24] It should normally be made by filing in court the application notice with the written evidence and a draft of the order sought.[25] The application notice, if to be served, so as to constitute it an application made with notice, and therefore requiring a hearing date, should be served on the parties affected as soon as possible after it is filed and in any event not less than three days before the appointed hearing date.[26]

    If the notice cannot be formally served within that time-span, informal notifica-

5-7

5-8

---

10 Insolvency Act 1986 s.286; Insolvency Rules 2016 (SI 2016/1024) rr.10.49–10.54.
11 Interim receivers should not be confused with the Official Receiver although the Official Receiver may be appointed as an interim receiver.
12 Law of Property Act 1925 Pt III.
13 The provisions of the now repealed Mental Health Act 1984, s.99 permitted the appointment of a receiver over the property of a person who lacked capacity to make decisions. The replacement regime under the Mental Capacity Act 2005 and the Court of Protection Rules 2007 (SI 2007/1744) as supplemented by relevant PDs no longer provides for receivers to be appointed but has replaced that system with a system of appointing deputies.
14 CPR r.69.1(2).
15 CPR r.69.2(2).
16 CPR r.69.2(1).
17 CPR r.69.2(3).
18 CPR r.69.11.
19 CPR PD 2B, para.2.3(c); CPR PD 69, para.3.2.
20 CPR r.69.3(a); CPR PD 23, paras 1 and 2. For applications made without notice, see para.5-9, below.
21 CPR r.69.3(b).
22 CPR r.69.3(1).
23 CPR PD 69, para.2.1.
24 CPR PD 23A, para.2.7.
25 CPR rr.23.3, 23.6, 23.7.
26 CPR r.23.7(1)(b). For the calculation of this period, see CPR r.2.8(3). Saturdays, Sundays, Bank

tion should be given.[27] But this rule does not apply where the application requires secrecy.

Strict rules apply to the procedure where the application is not served, and is to be heard without notice: see below. The court may abridge the time for hearing.[28]

5-9   **Applications heard without notice.** Applications may in general be heard without notice to the party or parties affected, when one of the following circumstances applies[29]:

    (1)   cases of exceptional urgency;

    (2)   where the overriding objective of the CPR (see CPR r.1(1)) is best furthered thereby;

    (3)   where all parties consent;

    (4)   with permission of the court;

    (5)   where service cannot be effected before a fixed date for a hearing regarding other matters at which it is desired to make the application and there is not sufficient time to serve an application notice; in this event informal notice is to be given to the other parties and to the court, and the application is to be made orally; and

    (6)   where a court order, or a rule or practice direction permits.

Applications without notice may similarly be made for an interim injunction, not only in cases of urgency, but also where notice to the respondent would frustrate the injunction.

5-10   **Notice to be given of right to apply to set aside order.** Where the court has made any order on an application made without service of the application notice, copies of the order made, of the application notice and of any evidence in support, must (unless the court otherwise orders) be served on the person or persons against whom the order was made or had been sought; there must be included a statement of the party's right to apply to set the order aside, or to vary it.[30] Such an application must be made with seven days of the service of the order.[31]

5-11   **Telephone hearings of urgent applications.** Provision is made in the CPR for applications to be heard by telephone, connecting the court with all the parties. The facility is subject to strict conditions. Video-conferencing facilities may also be available.[32]

5-12   **Forms of application.** If application to the court to appoint a receiver is made before the commencement of substantive proceedings, it is generally to be made by application notice,[33] supported by written evidence.[34] If the appointment is sought, with or without a claim for an injunction, by way of substantive proceedings, ap-

---

Holidays, Christmas Day and Good Friday are days that do not count for this purpose.

[27]   CPR PD 23A, para.4.2.

[28]   CPR r.23.7(4).

[29]   CPR PD 23A, para.3; CPR r.23.4.

[30]   CPR r.23.9(3). The right is under CPR r.23.10.

[31]   CPR r.23.10(2)

[32]   CPR PD 23A, para.7. See also CPR PD 32, para.29.1 and Video Conferencing Guidance at CPR PD 32, Annex 3.

[33]   CPR PD 23A, para 2.1: Form N.244.

[34]   CPR r.69.3(b).

plication must be made by a Pt 7 or Pt 8 claim form.[35] If the appointment of a receiver and a related injunction are sought at the same time, the same claim form or application notice must be used for both claims.[36]

The written evidence to be relied upon must be filed with the application notice, and, in general, copies served with it on the other party or parties.

Form of written evidence to support application. Written evidence may now be given in the form of witness statements, verified by a statement of truth, in all proceedings, or by Statements of Case and application notices, in either case verified by a statement of truth,[37] except where affidavits or statutory declarations are specifically required, either by a statute, a rule, a practice direction, or by order of the court or where the court allows evidence to be given orally.[38]

5-13

Examples of such obligatory affidavits are those required on the application for a freezing (*"Mareva"*) injunction and a search (*"Anton Piller"*) order, or on applications for committal: see CPR Pts 25 and 52.

Contents of evidence to support application to appoint a receiver. The evidence to support the application, and to be filed with the application notice, must:

5-14

(1)   explain the reasons by the appointment is required; and
(2)   give details of the property which it is proposed that the receiver should get in, or manage, including estimates of its value, and of the amount of income it is likely to produce.[39]

If the application is for a receiver by way of equitable execution, details must also be given of:

(1)   the judgment which the applicant seeks to enforce;
(2)   the extent of the debtor's failure to comply with its terms;
(3)   the result of any steps already taken to enforce the judgment; and
(4)   why the judgment cannot be enforced by any other method[40]; see, as to the considerations relevant to the court making an order, para.5-35, below.

If the application asks that the receiver is to act without giving security, or before he or she has given security or has satisfied the court that he or she has security in place, the reasons why this is necessary must also be given.[41] For the practice on such applications, see para.5-32, below.

Identification of, and consent by, the proposed receiver. The evidence must identify the proposed receiver ("the nominee"), giving his or her name, address and position, and must include written evidence by a person who knows the nominee, stating that he or she believes the nominee to be a suitable person to be appointed, and the basis for that belief, and be accompanied by the nominee's signed consent in writing to act as receiver, if appointed.[42]

5-15

---

35   CPR Pts 7, 8.
36   CPR PD 69, para.3.1.
37   CPR r.32.6(2); CPR PD 32 paras 1.1 ff and 26 ff.
38   See CPR r.32.2.
39   CPR PD 69, para.4.1(1), (2).
40   CPR PD 69, para.4.1(3).
41   CPR PD 69, para.4.1(4).
42   CPR PD 69, para.4.2.

It is suggested that, in accordance with previous practice, other parties may submit other names to the court for appointment, instead of the nominee.

Although receivers appointed by the court rarely require to be qualified as licensed insolvency practitioners, the possession of such a qualification will no doubt be a strong factor in establishing the nominee's fitness for appointment, and in obtaining the court's approval.[43] Such a qualification also carries with it the possession of substantial continuous security, as required to be held by such a practitioner.

5-16   **Where no nominee is put forward, or nominee is not appointed.** If the applicant does not put forward any nominee, or the court declines to appoint the nominee, the court may order that a suitable person be appointed receiver, and may direct any party to nominate a suitable individual to be appointed. Any party so directed must file the same type of evidence in support of his or her nomination, as is required in respect of the original nominee, including the nominee's written consent.[44]

5-17   **Service of order appointing receiver and need for directions.** The applicant for the appointment must serve a copy of the order making the appointment, when made, on the person appointed as receiver, and, unless the court orders otherwise, on every other party to the proceedings, and on such other persons as the court may direct.[45] The Chancery Guide for Receivers also provides that a copy of Appendix C to the Guide, setting out notes on the main powers and duties of a receiver, should be passed to the receiver.

The Guide also points out that where an order has been made appointing a receiver, it is generally necessary to apply for directions, by application notice under CPR Pt 23. An application for directions should normally be made immediately after the making of the order appointing the receiver, especially where security has to be given within a limited time (see below). Only if the order appointing the receiver appoints him or her by name and gives full directions as to accounts and security will an application for directions not be necessary.

5-18   **Security to be given by receiver.** The court may (and almost invariably will) direct that, before a receiver begins to act, or within a specified time after his appointment, he must either: (a) give such security as the court may determine; or (b) file and serve on all parties to the proceedings evidence that he has already in force sufficient security, in either case sufficient to cover his liability for his acts and omissions as receiver.[46]

5-19   **Nature of security.** Unless the court directs otherwise, security will be given: (a) if the receiver is a licensed insolvency practitioner, by means of a bond, as obligatorily provided under the Insolvency Practitioner Regulations 2005, extended so as to cover appointment as a court-appointed receiver (see above); or (b) by a guarantee.[47]

5-20   **Former requirements as to security.** Under the old regime, security was

---

[43] For these qualifications, see Insolvency Act 1986 s.390A ff, and n.49, below.
[44] CPR PD 69, paras 4.3, 4.4.
[45] CPR r.69.4.
[46] CPR PD 69.5; CPR PD 69, para.7.1.
[47] CPR PD 69, para.7.2.

required to be given by evidence of the security provided by the guarantee society, which was to be filed in the office or registry of the court, and kept on record.[48] The new rules no longer include this provision.

Present requirements.   The present reference to, and permitted reliance upon, the   **5-21** insolvency practitioner's bond is new. Practitioners are required to maintain in force permanent security by bond, providing security in very large minimum amounts, sufficient to cover their professional liabilities in all their appointments.[49]

Where the court has given directions about security, then either: (a) written evidence by the receiver as to his bond, and the sufficiency of the cover, and that it includes appointment as a court-appointed receiver, must be filed in court; or (b) a guarantee should be prepared in a form, and entered into with a clearing bank or insurance company, in both cases as approved by the court.[50]

The "Guide for Receivers in the Chancery Division",[51] in the context of security, gives detailed guidance.

The order appointing a receiver will normally include directions in relation to security, and will specify the date by which security is to be given. It is therefore important to obtain an early date for the directions hearing after the order making the appointment. If security is not completed within the time specified the receivership may be terminated and it will then be necessary for an application to be made to renew it. To avoid this, if it seems likely that security will not be given in time an application should be made at the directions hearing for an extension of time to give security. When the amount of the security has been settled, a guarantee in the form provided in Appendix A of the Guide must (unless the receiver is a licensed insolvency practitioner covered by bond, which has been extended to cover the appointment) be prepared and entered into with one of the four main clearing banks or the insurance company listed in Appendix B to the Guide. The guarantee must then be engrossed and executed, i.e. signed by the receiver and signed and sealed by the bank or insurance company. It should then be lodged in Masters' Appointments Section, ground floor, Rolls Building, 7 Rolls Buildings, Fetter Lane, London EC4A 1NL. It will then be signed by the Master and endorsed with a certificate of completion of security and placed on the court file. Where security is given by bond, written evidence of the extended bond and the sufficiency of its cover must be filed at the above address in accordance with the requirements of PD 69, para.7.3(1). If the amount of the security given is subsequently increased or decreased, an endorsement is made to the original guarantee. See also para.5-29, below.

Failure to provide security: new regime.   If the receiver fails, by the date speci-   **5-22** fied, to give the required security, or to satisfy the court as to the existing security which he or she claims to have in force, the appointment does not automatically lapse, as it did previously (see below), but the court may terminate the appointment on that ground.[52] The provision that possession of the insolvency practitioner's

---

[48]   RSC Ord.30 r.4.2(4) (revoked).
[49]   Insolvency Act 1986 s.390A ff, and Insolvency Practitioner Regulations 2005 (SI 2005/524).
[50]   CPR PD 69, para.7.3.
[51]   Available on the gov.uk website.
[52]   CPR r.69.5(2).

permanent ongoing security (extended as necessary) will normally be sufficient should reduce the number of such failures.[53]

5-23 **Failure to provide security: old regime.** Where the court had ordered security to be given by a receiver, and he failed to provide it by the specified date, his appointment automatically lapsed, although it could be re-activated by an order re-appointing him, on the basis that the appointment should be deemed to have continued, notwithstanding the default.[54]

Where the security initially given by the receiver is not given in the form of an insolvency practitioner's bond, which is of very considerable global value, but is given in the form of a guarantee, based on an assessment of the believed value of the assets, then if the value of those assets significantly increases, further security ought to be provided.[55] Similarly, if the realisation worth of the security becomes diminished by reason of the happening of any event, the value ought to be proportionately increased.[56] The Chancery Guide to Receivers points out that if the amount of the security given is subsequently increased or decreased, an endorsement is made to the original guarantee

5-24 **Directions from the court, or applied for by receiver**   (see also para.5.17, above). The court may give directions to the receiver upon appointment, or at any time thereafter, relating to security (see above), and as to: (a) whether, and on what basis, the receiver is to be remunerated; (b) the preparation and service of accounts; (c) the payment of money into court; and (d) authority for him or her to carry on an activity, or to incur an expense.[57]

The receiver generally applies for directions, by filing an application notice.[58] If, however, the directions which the receiver seeks are unlikely to be contentious or important to the parties, he or she may apply to the court by letter, and the court may reply by letter, or may direct him or her to file an application notice. The receiver need not serve copies of such letters on the parties, unless the court so orders.[59]

5-25 **Receiver's remuneration.** See "Remuneration and expenses of a receiver" at para.10-1, below.

5-26 **Receiver's accounts.** The court will direct the receiver to render accounts at specific intervals, and will adjudicate on any objections to such accounts[60]: see "Receiver's accounts" at para.11-1, below. The Chancery Division Guide for Receivers provides that if directions as to the receiver's accounts have not been given in the order appointing the receiver, such directions must be obtained at the directions hearing.

5-27 **Court's powers to control receiver.** If a receiver fails to comply with any rule, practice direction or direction of the court, the court may summon him to attend a

---

[53] CPR PD 69, para.7.2.
[54] RSC Ord.30 r.2 (revoked).
[55] *Seton*, p.742.
[56] Events such as death or bankruptcy, or the insolvency of the guarantor or guarantee society.
[57] CPR r.69.6.
[58] CPR PD 69, para.8.1.
[59] CPR PD 69, paras.8.2 and 8.3.
[60] CPR r.69.8; CPR PD 69, para.10.

hearing, to explain the failure to comply.[61] At the hearing, the court may make such order as it considers appropriate, including: (a) terminating the appointment; (b) reducing his or her remuneration or disallowing it altogether; or (c) ordering him or her to pay the costs of any party.[62]

Application for discharge of receiver. The receiver or any party may apply for the receiver to be discharged, on completion of his duties.[63]

5-28

The Chancery Guide for Receivers provides that when a receiver has completed his duties, the receiver or any party should apply for an order discharging the receiver and cancelling the security.

Order discharging or terminating receiver's appointment. An order discharging, or terminating the appointment of, a receiver, may: (a) require the receiver to pay into court any money held by him or her; (b) specify the person to whom he or she must pay any money or transfer any assets in his or her possession; (c) make provision for the discharge or cancellation of any guarantee given by the receiver as security.[64] Any such order must be served on those persons who were required to be served with the order appointing the receiver: see above.[65] The Chancery Guide for Receivers provides that when an order for cancellation of a receiver's security has been made, any guarantee and the duplicate order appointing the receiver are endorsed to that effect. The endorsed guarantee and duplicate order should then be taken to the bank or insurance company by the solicitors for cancellation and return of any outstanding premium.

5-29

See also "Discharge of receiver" at para.12-1, below.

Receiverships under the criminal confiscation statutes. For details of the rules for commencing proceedings, see e.g. Pinto and Evans, *Corporate Criminal Responsibility* 3rd edn (Sweet & Maxwell, 2013), especially Chapter 9 "Confiscation, Restraint and Receivership – The Criminal Confiscation Regime".

5-30

Receiver by way of equitable execution: practice on application. The practice and procedure on applications for the appointment of a receiver (which includes a manager) by way of equitable execution of a judgment or order were first amended and codified by the revoking of the former rules, CPR Sch.1—RSC Ords 30 and 51, and then replaced by CPR Pt 69, and its Practice Direction, CPR PD 69, which came into force on 2 December 2002. These have been discussed above. The new Pt 69 applies both to the High Court and to the county court.

5-31

Jurisdiction to appoint such receivers is conferred on the judges both of the Queen's Bench Division and of the Chancery Division, and on the masters of those courts, and on the judges and district judges of the county courts. Masters in either division and district judges are given the power to grant injunctions in support of such receivers, so far as ancillary to, or incidental to, such execution.[66]

On the hearing of applications (as opposed to trial), except where a freezing

---

[61] CPR r.69.9(1).
[62] CPR r.69.9(1), (2).
[63] CPR r.69.10.
[64] CPR r.69.11(1).
[65] CPR rr.69.11(2) and 69.4.
[66] See n.19, above.

(*Mareva*) injunction or a search (*Anton Piller*) order,[67] is sought, or where the court directs, or a statute, rule or practice direction requires,[68] the necessary written evidence is to be given by witness statements (or Statements of Case or Application Notices), verified by a statement of truth, rather than by affidavits.[69]

5-32 **Application and evidence: details of the judgment and of the judgment debtor.** The application is again made by application notice. The written evidence is given by witness statement, verified by a statement of truth, and may include statements of case and the application notice, if so verified.[70] It must give details of:

    (a) the date and particulars of the unsatisfied judgment or order which the applicant is seeking to enforce;

    (b) the extent to which the judgment debtor has failed to comply with the judgment or order;

    (c) the result of any steps already taken to enforce the judgement or order (including any partial satisfaction) (the nature of the High Court Enforcement Officer's return (if any) should also be given.);

    (d) the reason why the judgment or order cannot be enforced by any other method, e.g. that the debtor appears to have no property on which execution can be levied.[71]

The evidence must also give details of the property which it is proposed that the receiver should receive, including any legal interests in land, estimates of the value of such property and of the income it is likely to produce, and the possible costs of the appointment.[72]

5-33 **Grounds of urgency.** Evidence, if available, should be given of:

    (a) any considerations of urgency for making the appointment;

    (b) of any known pecuniary difficulties of the debtor; and

    (c) if such be the case, of the judgment creditor's reasonable apprehension that the debtor may assign, or otherwise dispose of, such property as he has, unless restrained by injunction.[73]

The court may think it necessary to cause an enquiry to be made to ascertain the force of these factors, although this seems unlikely.[74]

5-34 **Details of the proposed receiver.** The written evidence must also include:

    (a) a statement of the name, address and position of the proposed receiver;

    (b) a statement by a person who knows the nominee and believes him or her to be a suitable person to be appointed receiver; and

    (c) the consent of the nominee to act as receiver, if appointed.[75]

---

[67] CPR PD 25A – Interim Injunctions, para.3.1.
[68] CPR r.32.15.
[69] See para.5-13, above.
[70] See para.5-13, above.
[71] CPR PD 69, para.4.1(3).
[72] CPR PD 4.1(2). See also *Lloyds Bank Ltd v Medway Upper Navigation Co* [1905] 2 K.B. 359.
[73] See the previous version of the Queens Bench Guide, para.12.7.
[74] As under RSC Ord.51 r.1 (revoked).
[75] CPR PD 69, para.4.2.

Relevant considerations for appointment of receiver by way of equitable execution.   The court, in considering whether to appoint a receiver to enforce a judgment by way of equitable execution, will have regard to:

    (1) the amount claimed by the judgment creditor;
    (2) the amount likely to be obtained by the receiver;
    (3) the probable costs of his appointment.[76]

A county court judge has jurisdiction to appoint a receiver by way of equitable execution, over both equitable[77] and legal estates[78] in land.

5-35

Dispensing with security: previous practice.   Although the requirement of security has always been a matter of discretion,[79] the court rarely dispenses with the usual security, even with the consent of the parties interested.[80] But if all the parties interested were competent, and agreed to appoint a receiver of their own authority and not by the authority of the court, the court might allow him or her to act without security.[81] Where a testator had by his will directed that a named person should be appointed receiver of his real and personal estates, stating that he intended by the appointment to give him a pecuniary benefit, the court appointed that person to be receiver and agent of the estates (the testator's only real estate being in the West Indies) on his own personal recognisance only.[82] Even in a case where the parties were not all competent to consent, the circumstance that the person proposed as receiver had been employed by the testator to manage his estates was held to be a reason for dispensing with sureties, and appointing him receiver of the estates on his own personal recognisance only.[83] But where some of the parties were not sui juris, and, therefore, incapable of giving consent, the court declined to dispense with the usual security.[84]

    Where no salary is to be given to the receiver, the court has dispensed with the security.[85] So, too, security has been dispensed with, where the party appointed receiver had only to incur expenditure.[86] Security was also dispensed with, where the order appointing a receiver was made merely for the purpose of creating a charge upon the debtor's property subject to prior incumbrances, and the receiver was not to go into possession or receive anything.[87] However, unless specific moneys received by the receiver are ordered to be paid by him or her to a named person, which is not the usual case, the appointment of a receiver does not create a charge.[88]

5-36

---

[76] See n.72, above.
[77] *R. v Selfe* [1908] 2 K.B. 121.
[78] County Court Act 1984 s.107.
[79] See CPR PD 69.
[80] *Manners v Furze* (1847) 11 Beav. 30.
[81] See n.80, above.
[82] *Hibbert v Hibbert* (1808) 3 Mer. 681.
[83] *Carlisle v Berkeley* (1759) Amb. 599; see too, *Wilson v Wilson* (1847) 11 Jur.793.
[84] *Tylee v Tylee* (1853) 17 Beav. 583.
[85] *Gardner v Blane* [1842] 1 Hare 381; *Re Prytherch* (1889) 42 Ch. D. 590; see, too, *Pilkington v Baker* (1876) 24 W.R. 234.
[86] *Hyde v Warden* (1876) 1 Ex.D. 309, 310; *Boyle v Bettws Llantwit Colliery Co* (1876) 2 Ch. D. 726; *Fuggle v Bland* (1883) 11 Q.B.D. 711.
[87] *Hewett v Murray* [1885] W.N. 53; 54 L.J. Ch. 572. For form of order appointing a receiver by way of equitable execution without security, see also (1877) 52 L.T. 380.
[88] *Re Whiteheart* (1971) 116 S.J. 75. See further para.6-4, below.

5-37   **Practice in the Queen's Bench Division.**   For the practice of the Queen's Bench Division on giving security, see further the Queen's Bench Guide at para.12.11.

5-38   **Notification of appointment.**   A copy of the judgment or order appointing a receiver must be served by the applicant on the receiver, and all other parties to the proceedings, unless the court orders otherwise, and on such other persons as the court may direct.[89]

5-39   **Form of order as to property.**   The order appointing a receiver should either state on its face the property over which the appointment is to extend, or refer to the pleadings or some document in the proceedings which describes the property.[90] In the case of mortgaged property, the description will follow the terms of the mortgage, and if the latter is in general terms, the order will be similarly expressed. In the case of a receiver by way of equitable execution, the property should be specified; the appointment will not be made over the debtor's equitable interests in general terms. The order will direct the receiver, by a specified date or at specified intervals,[91] to serve his or her accounts on specified persons, and to pay the balances due from him or her, as the court shall direct, or directions to this effect may be given in the order.[92]

  If the appointment of a receiver is over real or leasehold property, the order usually directs the parties on the record who are in possession, not as tenants but as owners, to deliver up to the receiver possession,[93] or to attorn tenant to the receiver at an occupation rent.[94] An order directing possession to be given to the receiver may, in a proper case, be obtained.[95] In a mortgagee's action, where the mortgagor is in possession, prima facie the proper order, on application being made for a receiver, is to order possession to be given to the receiver, though the court has a discretion and may allow the mortgagor to attorn tenant at an occupation rent.[96]

  The mortgagor is entitled to remain in occupation without payment of rent, until such an order is made.[97]

5-40   **Directions in order.**   If tenants are in possession of real or leasehold property over which a receiver is appointed, the order should direct them to attorn and pay their

---

[89] CPR r.69.4.
[90] *Seton*, 7th ed., p.738.
[91] CPR r.69.8 and CPR PD 69, para.10.
[92] CPR r.69.11.
[93] *Griffith v Griffith* (1751) 2 Ves. Sen.40, above n.1; *Everett v Belding* (1852) 22 L.J. Ch. 75; 1 W.R. 44; *Hawkes v Holland* [1881] W.N. 128; see, as to form of order, *Davis v Duke of Marlborough* (1818) 2 Swans. 108, 116; *Baylies v Baylies* (1844) 1 Coll.C.C. 548; *Edgell v Wilson* [1893] W.N. 145.
[94] *Re Burchnall, Walker v Burchnall* [1893] W.N. 171.
[95] *Ind. Coope & Co v Mee* [1895] W.N. 8; *Charrington & Co v Camp* [1902] 1 Ch. 386. In *Taylor v Soper* [1980] W.N. 121; 62 L.T. 828, North J refused in special circumstances to make an order for delivery up of possession before trial.
[96] *Pratchett v Drew* [1924] 1 Ch. 280; *Masters v Crouch* (1927) 63 L.J.N.C. 557: the plaintiff was a second mortgagee.
[97] See *Yorkshire Banking Co v Mullan* (1887) 35 Ch. D. 125; *Re Burchnall, Walker v Burchnall*, n.2, above.

rents in arrear and the growing rents to the receiver[98]; but this direction should be omitted where the estates are out of England or Wales.[99]

If the property over which a receiver is appointed is outstanding personal estate, the order should direct parties in possession of such estate to deliver up to the receiver all such estate, and also all securities in their hands for such estate or property, together with all books and papers relating thereto.[100]

The costs incurred with reference to the completion of the security of the receiver, and subsequent thereto where there is no bond, are in the first instance paid by the receiver, and will be allowed him or her in passing his or her first account.[101] Premiums paid by the receiver to a guarantee society which had become his or her surety, under modern practice, have usually been allowed.[102]

A receiver is sometimes appointed until judgment or further order, but very often no limit of time is fixed, though a limit is always fixed in the appointment of a manager. Where no limit of time is fixed in the order appointing a receiver, it is not necessary for the judgment to direct that he or she be continued[103]; but where he or she is appointed only until judgment or further order, then, if he or she is to continue to be receiver, further security may need to be given,[104] unless, as is usually the case, the security originally given is made applicable to any continuation of the appointment. Where the appointment is for a limited time, application to extend the appointment can be made by application notice before the time limit has expired: if the time has expired, an order may be obtained continuing and confirming the appointment.[105]

A fresh action in the Chancery Division by a creditor who had recovered judgment in the Queen's Bench Division was held to be prima facie so vexatious as to render him liable for the costs of such second action; but if the mere appointment of a receiver would not give him the remedy to which he was entitled, e.g. where there were accounts to be taken between him and the judgment debtor, or if it were necessary to take proceedings in the name of the person having the legal right to sue, the action for a receiver would properly be brought in the Chancery Division.[106]

Family proceedings: the jurisdiction. Applications for a receiver generally, and   **5-41** for a receiver by way of equitable execution, are made to the Family Division in the same manner as to the other Divisions of the High Court, or to the county court. They are, however, required still to be made in accordance with the Family Procedure Rules,[107] unless the context requires otherwise. The Family Procedure

---

[98] 1 Seton, 7th edn, p.762.

[99] 1 Seton, 7th edn, above, p.776.

[100] 1 Seton, 7th edn, above, p.725; *Truman v Redgrave* (1881) 18 Ch. D. 547; *Leney & Sons Ltd v Callingham* [1908] 1 K.B. 79. If necessary, a receiver will be ordered to keep separate accounts of real and personal estates: *Hill v Hibbitt* (1868) 18 L.T. 553.

[101] *Daniell's Chancery Practice*, p.1492. As to costs, where an ignorant person had been induced by the misrepresentations of the plaintiff to consent to act as receiver, and afterwards, on discovering the nature of the office, refused to enter into the recognisance, see *Hunter v Pring* (1845) 8 Ir.Eq.R. 102.

[102] See an article by Master Mosse in 101 L.J. 241: the direction of the judges therein mentioned cannot be traced.

[103] *Davies v Vale of Evesham Preserves* [1895] W.N. 105; 43 W.R. 646.

[104] *Brinsley v Lynton Hotel Co* [1895] W.N. 53; 2 Mans. 244.

[105] For a form of order in administration proceedings, see [1943] W.N. 71.

[106] *Proskauer v Siebe* [1885] W.N. 159.

[107] Family Procedure Rules 2010 (SI 2010/2955).

Rules specifically apply the CPR to family proceedings where the appointment of a receiver is sought.[108] CPR Pt 69 and PD 69 therefore apply.[109]

Application should normally be made by filing in court the application notice with the written evidence and a draft of the order sought.[110] The application notice, if to be served, so as to constitute it an application made with notice, and therefore requiring a hearing date, should be served on the parties affected as soon as possible after it is filed and in any event not less than three days before the appointed hearing date.[111]

An injunction in aid of the proposed relief may be applied for, without notice if a matter of urgency or confidentiality; but it cannot be granted as a free-standing entitlement, but only in support of a claim to enforce legal or equitable rights.[112] It may be granted on an application made without notice, on the applicant's undertaking, and the application adjourned for service.[113] A receiver may not be appointed by way of enforcement of maintenance for a wife,[114] but a receiver has been appointed over a marriage settlement of the spouses.[115] It appears now to be the view that a receivership is nowadays more rarely sought, in view of the advantages conferred by a charging order.[116]

Where an appointment of a receiver is made, it is made on condition that the receiver first gives security to the satisfaction of the court, unless it is otherwise directed.[117]

5-42   **The matrimonial home.** A judgment creditor in family proceedings can obtain the appointment of a receiver by way of equitable execution over the matrimonial home; such an order entitles the receiver to apply to register a land charge or caution against dealings with the respondent's share of, or interests in, the property, and will protect that share or those interests from any competing attachment by another judgment creditor; the receiver would also be entitled to attach an appropriate share of the proceeds of sale, if and when the property is sold. An injunction might in such a case be granted, if thought to be essential, to restrain the spouse from prejudicially dealing with his or her interests.[118] A question arises as to whether such a receiver could obtain an order for sale.[119] This remains doubtful; but there has been held to be jurisdiction to authorise such a receiver to bring proceedings in the name of the respondent for a sale under statutory powers.[120]

A receiver can only be appointed over property that is assignable; in family proceedings, this encounters problems with the respondent's rights under pension policies or plans, where in many cases the pension-holder's rights are expressly made unassignable by contract,[121] unless some right in the pension-holder can be identified by which he can be benefited, but which is not unassignable.

---

108   Family Procedure Rules 2010 (SI 2010/2955) r.33.22.
109   See paras 5-5 ff, above.
110   See paras 5-5 ff, above.
111   See paras 5-5 ff, above.
112   *Richards v Richards* [1984] A.C. 174, HL.
113   See *Bullus v Bullus* (1910) 102 LT 100.
114   *Walls Ltd v Legge* [1923] 2 K.B. 240 CA.
115   *Oliver v Lowther* (1880) 28 W.R. 381.
116   See the Charging Orders Act 1979, and Ch.6 below.
117   See paras 5-19 ff, above.
118   *Livermore v Livermore* [1979] 1 W.L.R. 1297.
119   See *Stevens v Hutchinson* [1953] Ch. 299.
120   Trusts of Land and Appointment of Trustees Act 1996 ss.14 ff.
121   *Field v Field* [2003] 1 F.L.R. 376.

The receiver's remuneration will usually be payable out of, and charged on, the assets he or she collects.[122]

Form of application.   In the case of mortgages, the practice as to mortgagees   **5-43**
generally is applicable.[123] In the case of debentures, the application for a receiver
is made by application notice in a debenture holder's action,[124] which must include
a claim to enforce the security by sale or foreclosure.[125] Permission to serve short
notice with the claim form is usually obtained, as the application is urgent.[126] The
action must be commenced by claim form, though an order for foreclosure could,
even under the old procedure, have been made on an originating summons at the
instance of debenture-holders.[127] If the claimant's debenture is one of a series, he
or she sues on behalf of himself or herself and all other debenture-holders of the
same series, and should specify as accurately as possible the class on behalf of
which he or she sues,[128] the company and a member of each class of debenture-
holders, subsequent to the series of the claimant on behalf of such class, being made
defendants.[129] A receiver may, however, be, and often is, appointed before all the
subsequent debenture-holders have become parties or represented.[130] If subsequent
debentures are secured by a trust deed, the trustees of that deed, having regard to
CPR r.19.7, sufficiently represent the debenture holders.[131] Where there is a
debenture trust deed to secure the claimant's series, the trustees should be made
defendants,[132] if not claimants. If one of several representative claimants withdraws
his or her retainer, he or she may be added as defendant.[133]

Representation of company: appearance "in person" by representative.   For   **5-44**
the practice rules on the company's right to appear by representative rather than by
a lawyer, see para.7-49, below.[134]

Service on company.   Service on a company registered in England and Wales   **5-45**
under the Companies Act 2006 may be effected by leaving it at, or sending it by

---

[122] See para.20-1, below.
[123] A debenture-holder, whose security consists of a floating charge ranking subsequent to a legal mortgage, is nevertheless a necessary party to an action by the legal mortgagee to enforce his or her security: *Wallace v Evershed* [1899] 1 Ch. 891.
[124] As to practice in such actions; *Seton*, 1953–1973; *Palmer's Precedents*, 30th edn, Vol.III.
[125] See *Gasson and Hallagan v Jell* [1940] Ch. 248; *Re Newport Construction Co Ltd* [1948] Ch. 217.
[126] No permission is now necessary for service with the claim form if full notice is given.
[127] *Oldrey v Union Works* (1895) 72 L.T. 627; *Sadler v Worley* [1894] 2 Ch. 170. An order for foreclosure cannot be made, unless all the debenture-holders are parties: see *Westminster Bank v Residential Properties Co* [1938] Ch. 639.
[128] *Marshall v South Staffordshire Tramways* [1895] 2 Ch. 36.
[129] Being added, if necessary, under CPR r.19.2. If any member of the class represented by the claim-ant wishes to appear, he or she must apply to be added as a defendant.
[130] See e.g. *Re Crigglestone Coal Co* [1906] 1 Ch. 523.
[131] Formerly RSC Ord.15 r.14 (revoked): see *Re Wilcox & Co Ltd* [1903] W.N.64.
[132] See *Cox v Dublin City Distillery* [1917] 1 Ir.R. 203.
[133] *Re Kent Coal Concessions Ltd* [1923] W.N. 328.
[134] A company may, in certain circumstances, appear in legal proceedings by a duly authorised representative, i.e. by an officer in appropriate employee: see CPR r.39.6. But see also, the Admiralty and Commercial Courts Guide. For judicial guidance see *Watson v Bluemoor Properties Ltd* [2002] EWCA Civ 1875; [2003] B.C.C. 382.

post (including registered post) to, the company's registered office.[135] Where a company registered in Scotland or Northern Ireland carries on business in England or Wales a claim form or other process may be served on the company by leaving it at, or sending it by post to, to the company's principal place of business in England or Wales, addressed to the company's manager or other head officer in England or Wales.[136]

A document may be served on an overseas company whose particulars are registered under s.1046 of the Companies Act 2006, by leaving it or sending it by post to: (1) the "registered address"[137] of any person resident in the United Kingdom who is authorised to accept documents on the company's behalf; or (2) if there is no such person as in (1), or such person refuses service or service cannot for any other reason be effected, any place of business of the Company in the United Kingdom.

In addition to these statutory provisions for service on a company, Pt 6 of the CPR contains detailed provisions for service of court proceedings under the CPR on companies which are alternatives to the methods provided for under the Companies Act 2006.[138] Service under the CPR is likely to be simpler and cheaper than under the legislation.

5-46 **Acting without security.** Liberty to act before security, on the claimant's undertaking to be responsible for the acts and defaults of the receiver, may be given. Immediate leave for the receiver to borrow and charge the assets to meet necessary expenses may be obtained, if the evidence shows clearly a case of extreme urgency, subject to providing particulars of the assets and the amount required. But, generally, the matter is more satisfactorily dealt with by the registrar or the judge in private.

It is common practice for an application for a receiver to be, by consent, treated as an application for judgment where all parties are present, and the order for the usual accounts and inquiries to be then made. On such an application, the company (or its liquidator) ought not to consent to a declaration of charge.[139]

The person who appoints a receiver or manager, or on whose application an order for a receiver or manager is made, must within seven days of the appointment, or the order, give notice to the Registrar of Companies.[140]

Such claims are now rare.[141] Debentures are almost invariably constituted by means of a trust deed with active trustees, who, if the situation warrants, will invariably appoint a receiver out of court. The receiver will, either under the provisions of the documents constituting the issue or by statute, normally have amply suf-

---

[135] Companies Act 2006 s.1139(1).

[136] Companies Act 2006 s.1139(4). Where process is served on the company under this provision the person issuing out the process must send a copy of it by post to the company's registered office: Companies Act 2006 s.1139(4).

[137] For these purposes a person's "registered address" means the address for the time being shown as a current address in relation to that person in the part of the register available for public inspection: Companies Act 2006 s.1139(3).

[138] CPR r.6.3(2) and see *Cranfield v Bridgegrove Ltd* [2003] EWCA Civ 656; [2003] 1 W.L.R. 2441, CA.

[139] See para.5-44, above.

[140] *Re Gregory, Love & Co Ltd* [1916] Ch. 203, 209; unless perhaps in special circumstances the indefeasible nature of the charge is absolutely clear; *Re Gregory, Love & Co Ltd* [1916] Ch. 203, 209. See also Companies Act 2006 s.859K.

[141] *Civil Court Practice* no longer prints the extensive notes on such actions which formerly appeared.

ficient powers to enable him to conduct the realisation of the company's assets for the benefit of the holders of the debentures, without any necessity for recourse to the courts.

Form of order. The practice on appointment as to security and generally is dealt   **5-47**
with in the earlier part of this Chapter.[142] After a winding-up order, permission of the court to bring or continue the action must be obtained, but this will be given to incumbrancers as a matter of course.[143]

In March 1900, the judges of the Chancery Division directed that the undertaking by the plaintiff (now the claimant) in a debenture-holder's action, on the appointment of a receiver who was to act at once, should extend to all liabilities which would be covered by the completed security, not only to the receipts of the receiver.[144]

Under direction, the order formerly included a direction that the receiver should forthwith pay the preferential debts out of any assets come to his or her hands which were subject to the floating charge. But having regard to the decision in *Re Glyncorrwg Colliery Co*,[145] the judges of the Chancery Division decided that the earlier practice was to be resumed, and that the order for payment of the preferential debts was to be omitted from the order appointing a receiver. There was inserted in the judgment an inquiry as to whether there were any such debts and, if so, which creditors were entitled to preferential payment, and what was due to them.[146] The judges also directed that there were clearly assets available for payment of preferential debts, application should be made to the master for a direction to the receiver to pay them.[147]

---

[142] See paras 5-18 and 2-48 ff, above.

[143] Insolvency Act 1986 s.130(2), (3); and see *Re Wanzer Ltd* [1891] 1 Ch. 305.

[144] *Re Debenture Holders' Actions* [1900] W.N 59.

[145] [1926] 1 Ch. 951.

[146] Under Insolvency Act 1986 ss.40 and 175, and Sch.6 (as amended); for form of order, see *Re Burradon Coal Co* [1929] W.N. 15, printed in *Supreme Court Practice* (1976), Vol.II, para.1481.

[147] Such debts were considerably reduced, when Enterprise Act 2002 Pt 10 s.251, came into force, repealing preferential debts due to the Crown. See further, para.7-62, below.

PART II: THE STRUCTURE OF COURT-APPOINTED RECEIVERSHIPS IN ENGLAND AND WALES

CHAPTER 6

EFFECT OF APPOINTMENT AND POSSESSION OF A RECEIVER

6-0   This chapter should be read in conjunction with Ch.5, dealing with the appointment of the receiver. In appointing a receiver, the court appoints an officer of its own, to take possession of the property over which he or she is appointed. The appointment, however, does not, without an express direction, effect any change in the possession of land, nor does it create an estate in, or (apart from statutory provisions) a charge in favour of, the receiver, or the person obtaining the appointment.[1] A receiver is an officer appointed to collect the rents and profits of real estate, or the income or capital of personal estate, upon the title of the parties to the action; the rights of those parties are not affected by the order, but the appointment operates as an injunction to prevent them from receiving the subject-matter of the order, or from dealing with it to the prejudice of other parties to the action. The rights of persons not parties are not affected by the order, but they cannot exercise those rights without the leave of the court. The above propositions will be illustrated in this chapter.

6-1   **Date from which appointment operates**   A receiver or manager duly appointed by the court, from the date of appointment, enjoys the status of an officer and representative of the court[2] but is not legally clothed with that character, or able to perform the duties of the office, until he or she has given security and that security has been perfected,[3] or accepted as already valid and sufficient,[4] except so far as he or she may be expressly authorised to act without security.

When, however, as may be done in urgent cases, an interim receiver is appointed[5] with liberty to act at once, with a direction that he or she give security within a specified time,[6] or satisfy the court that he or she already has adequate security in force,[7] or where he or she is appointed without security, he or she becomes an officer of the court, and is legally clothed with that character from the date of appointment,[8] though in the former case under the old law, the appoint-

---

1   As to when a charge is so created, see para.6-14, below.
2   *Aston v Heron* [1834] 2 My. & K. 390; *Owen v Homan* (1853) 4 H.L.C. 997, 1032; see *Davey v Scarth* [1906] 1 Ch. 55; *Boehm v Goodall* [1911] 1 Ch. 155; *Evans v Clayhope Properties Ltd* [1987] 1 W.L.R. 225.
3   *Defries v Creed* (1865) 34 L.J. Ch. 607; *Edwards v Edwards* (1876) 2 Ch. D. 291; *Re Sims & Woods Ltd* [1916] W.N. 233. See, too, *Ridout v Fowler* [1904] 1 Ch. 658; affirmed [1904] 2 Ch. 93 CA.
4   In the case of a receiver who is an insolvency practitioner, see CPR r.69.5(1)(b) and PD 69.
5   For in the case of a receiver who is an insolvency practitioner, see CPR r.69.5(1)(b) and PD 69.
6   For in the case of a receiver who is an insolvency practitioner, see CPR r.69.5(1)(b) and PD 69.
7   CPR PD 69, para.7.2(1).
8   *Taylor v Eckersley* (1876) 2 Ch. D. 302; (1877) 5 Ch. D. 740.

ment lapsed, unless security was completed within the specified time.[9] So, also, where the order appointing a receiver, with power to take possession, did not direct that he or she should give security, and the receiver took possession accordingly, the appointment was complete, even though he or she was subsequently continued as receiver by an order requiring security to be given.[10]

The termination, where security not given or not proved to be in force. However, under the CPR, if a receiver is now appointed on condition that he or she gives security, or satisfies the court as to the security he or she has in force, by a specified time, but fails to do so, the appointment does not *ipso jure* lapse, but the court may terminate it.[11]

6-2

The appointment of a receiver of the rents of land at the instance of a judgment creditor, though conditional on the receiver's giving security, or registration where necessary[12] operates as an immediate delivery of the land in execution; and, when the security is afterwards given, the order relates back accordingly.[13] But as regards personalty, it is settled law that, when the order is in the form of appointing a receiver upon his or her giving security, the appointment is not effectual, until the security is given. It is a conditional appointment, and the giving of security is a condition precedent.[14]

Nature of receiver's possession. The appointment of a receiver does not in any way affect the right to the property over which he or she is appointed. The court takes possession by its receiver, and that possession is that of all parties to the action, according to their titles[15]; the receiver does not collect the rents and profits by virtue of any estate vested in him or her, but by virtue of his or her position as an officer of the court, appointed to collect property upon the title of the parties to the action.[16] In appointing a receiver, the court deals with the possession only, until the right is determined, if the right be in dispute: or until the property is realised, if the appointment is made for that purpose.[17] If the appointment is made at the instance of encumbrancers, and the encumbrance is cleared off, the possession is restored to the party from whom it was taken.[18]

6-3

Receiver as officer of the court. Since the receiver is an officer of the court, any property of which he or she is in possession is strictly in the possession of the court. In a case where there were two claimants to furniture in the possession of the receiver, and the receiver succeeded in displacing the title of the first claimant, he

6-4

---

[9] See para.5-23, above.
[10] *Morrison v Skerne Ironworks Co* (1889) 60 L.T. 588; 33 S.J. 396.
[11] See CPR r.69.5(2).
[12] If a charging order imposing a charge on the land to enforce the judgment has been made and registered, further registration of the appointment of the receiver is unnecessary: Senior Courts Act 1981 s.37(5). See generally *Ashburton v Nocton* [1915] 1 Ch. 274, cf. para.3-15 ff.
[13] *Ex p. Evans* (1879) 13 Ch. D. 252; and see *Re Shephard* (1889) 43 Ch. D. 131.
[14] per Farwell J in *Ridout v Fowler*, n.3, above.
[15] See *Re Butler* (1863) 13 L.R. Ir. 156; *Bertrand v Davies* (1862) 31 Beav. 429.
[16] *Vine v Raleigh* (1883) 24 Ch. D. 238.
[17] As in the case of partnership, or usually at the instance of encumbrancers.
[18] *Sharp v Carter* (1735) 3 P. Wms. 375; *Skip v Harwood* (1747) 3 Atk. 564; *Wells v Kilpin* (1874) L.R. 18 Eq. 298; and see *Moss SS Co v Whinney* [1912] A.C. 254, HL. Where an order for the discharge of a receiver has been made, and he continues in possession after the date of his discharge, paying over the rents to the party entitled, his possession is the possession of that party: *Horlock v Smith* (1842) 11 L.J. Ch. 157.

was not thereafter allowed to set up the title of that claimant as an answer to the claim of the second claimant.[19]

6-5   **Receiver as agent of party entitled.**   In some cases, after the right has been determined, a receiver will be considered as receiver for the person entitled[20]: for instance, in an action for specific performance, where the purchaser was compelled to accept the title[21]; and conversely, where the appointment was due to the inability of the vendor to make out his title.[22]

6-6   **Benefit and loss due to acts of receiver.**   The acts of a receiver are for the benefit of all parties according to their titles: as, for instance, where he or she is ordered to keep up policies of insurance.[23] Conversely, if a loss arises from the action of a receiver, the estate must bear it, as between the parties to the action.[24] A claimant cannot claim damages for detention of goods while in the hands of a receiver, for any damage is due to the law's delay, not to a wrongful act of the defendant.[25]

6-7   **Effect as to possession.**   The appointment of a receiver does not of itself effect a change in the possession of land, nor does a receiver of the rents and profits of land take possession, unless the order directs him or her to do so.[26] If, therefore, one of the parties, for instance, a mortgagor, is in possession, the order should direct him or her to deliver up possession to the receiver, or to attorn tenant at a rent.[27]

Where the order did not direct possession to be given, it was held that the entry of a receiver upon the lands of a company did not effect any change in the occupation within s.16 of the Poor Rate Assessment and Collection Act 1869,[28] so as to exempt the property from the obligation to pay arrears of rates[29]; it appears that the same would be the case, where possession is ordered to be given.[30]

As an "office-holder",[31] an administrative receiver[32] of a company has a statutory right to require supplies of gas, electricity, water, electronic communication services and other goods and services (relating to point of sale terminals, computer hardware and software, information technology assistance, data storage and website

---

[19]   *Re Savoy Estate Ltd* [1949] Ch. 622. See para.7-35, below.
[20]   *Boehm v Wood* (1820) Turn. & R. at 345; *Re Butler*, n.15, above; *Rigge v Bowater* (1785) 3 Bro.C.C. 365.
[21]   *Boehm v Wood*, n.20, above; see also *Re Butler*, n.15, above.
[22]   *McCleod v Phelps* (1838) 2 Jur.962.
[23]   *Seymour v Vernon* (1864) 10 L.T. 58; see *Bertrand v Davies* (1862) 31 Beav. 429; *Frazer v Burgess* (1860) 13 Moo P.C. 314; *Defries v Creed* (1865) 34 L.J. Ch. 607.
[24]   *Hutchinson v Massareene* (1811) 2 Ball. & B. 49; see *Re London United Breweries* [1907] 2 Ch. 511.
[25]   *Peruvian Guano Co v Dreyfus Bros.* [1892] A.C. 166, HL.
[26]   *Ex p. Evans*, n.13, above.
[27]   See *Pratchett v Drew* [1942] 1 Ch. 280: cf. *Charrington v Camp* [1902] 1 Ch. 386.
[28]   Later replaced by s.18 of the General Rate Act 1967. For non-domestic rating see now Local Government Finance Act 1988 Pt III.
[29]   *Re Marriage, Neave & Co* [1896] 2 Ch. 663; *National Provincial Bank v United Electric Theatres Ltd* [1916] 1 Ch. 132; *Gyton v Palmour* [1945] K.B. 426.
[30]   See *Husey v London Electric Corp.* [1902] 1 Ch. 411; but see *Re Marriage, Neave & Co* n.29, above per Rigby LJ.
[31]   See Insolvency Act 1986 ss.233(1) and 234(1); for a consideration of this term, see para.21-4, below.
[32]   For the definition of "administrative receiver" see below. In s.72A, inserted into Insolvency Act 1986, by Enterprise Act 2002 s.250, the definition adopted is that in Insolvency Act 1986 s.251, i.e. as defined in Insolvency Act 1986 ss.29(2) and 251.

hosting to the company) without first having to pay outstanding charges.[33] In the case of an ordinary receiver, where of course such services are in any event less likely to be required, his appointment and entry did not create anything in the nature of a fresh occupation, under para.7 of Sch.2B to the Gas Act 1986, so as to enable the receiver to insist on a continued supply of gas, without payment of arrears due by the company.[34] Nor, in the like circumstances, could the receiver insist upon a further supply of electricity, without payment of the arrears.[35] The Postmaster-General—before his replacement by the British Telecommunications Corporation[36]—never claimed payment of the company's telephone account as a condition of continuing the telephone service to the receiver. A receiver appointed by the court was held not to be an "owner" within the Public Health Acts.[37]

Executors. Where possession was obtained by a receiver appointed in administra-   **6-8**
tion proceedings, the personal liability of the executors for rent was held to be suspended during the term of the receiver's possession.[38]

The appointment of a receiver formerly did not affect the executor's former right of retainer,[39] which he or she might therefore have exercised in respect of existing debts,[40] to the extent of assets in his or her hands when the order was made, though such assets had been handed to the receiver, but not in respect of assets collected by the receiver.[41] The appointment of a receiver in an administration action prevented a return of *nulla bona*, to a *fi. fa.* (now a writ of control) against an executor, from operating as a presumption of *devastavit*.[42]

Order removes parties from receipt of rents. Although the order does not   **6-9**
necessarily create a charge, or effect a change in the possession, it removes the parties to the action from the right to receive the rents and profits of property to which the order extends: for the order operates as an injunction.[43] It is a contempt of court, punishable by committal, for a judgment creditor to obtain payment of money, over which a receiver by way of equitable execution has been appointed, after service

---

[33] Insolvency Act 1986 s.233. For a more detailed consideration of the statutory provisions, see para.21-11, below.

[34] See *Paterson v Gas Light and Coke Co* [1896] 2 Ch. 476, and *Smith's Case* [1893] 1 Q.B. 323 (decided under s.18 of the Gas Light and Coke Companies Act 1872, and s.39 of the Gas Works Clauses Act 1971, respectively). cf. *Granger v South Wales Electricity Co* [1931] 1 Ch. 551, decided on the wording of a Special Act.

[35] Clause 27 of the Schedule to the Electric Lighting (Clauses) Act 1899, adopted by s.57 of the Electricity Act 1947. cf. *Granger v South Wales Electricity Co* [1931] 1 Ch. 551, decided on the wording of a Special Act. See now Pt 1 of the Electricity Act 1989 and the Utilities Act 2000.

[36] British Telecommunications Act 1981. See now Communications Act 2003 and the functions and powers of OFCOM.

[37] See s.4 of the Public Health Act 1875, now s.343 of the Public Health Act 1936; *Corporation of Bacup v Smith* (1890) 44 Ch. D. 395.

[38] *Minford v Carse* [1912] 2 Ir.R. 245.

[39] The right of retainer (formerly under the Administration of Estates Act 1925 s.34(2)) was abolished by the Administration of Estates Act 1971 s.10.

[40] *Re Beavan* [1913] 2 Ch. 595. The right is not affected by an order under s.421 of the Insolvency Act 1986 dealing with the insolvent estates of deceased debtors. See, under Bankruptcy Act 1883 generally, *Re Broad* (1911) 105 L.T. 719.

[41] *Re Harrison* (1886) 32 Ch. D. 395; *Re Jones* (1886) 31 Ch. D. 440.

[42] *Batchelar v Evans* [1939] Ch. 1007.

[43] *Tyrrell v Painton* [1895] 1 Q.B. 202; *Ideal Bedding Co v Holland* [1907] 2 Ch. 157.

of the order on him or her.[44] If a party is himself or herself appointed receiver, he or she is nonetheless excluded from the receipt in his or her own right of the rents and profits.[45]

6-10 **Right of receiver to rents.** The rents and profits of an estate over which a receiver has been appointed, including unpaid arrears, are, as regards parties to the action, bound from the date of the order[46]; but the appointment does not relate back to the date of the application,[47] though the right of a person, e.g. a first mortgagee whose rights have been interfered with by the appointment, dates back to an application for leave to take possession or appoint a receiver.[48] If a solicitor in the action has received rents without an authority from the court, he or she must pay them to the receiver, although they were received before the appointment was completed: the solicitor cannot claim a lien over them for costs.[49] The right of a prior mortgagee is discussed below.[50]

If the order directs tenants to pay their rents to the receiver, all rents due and unpaid at the time of the service of the order are bound. The tenants are not answerable in respect of rents which have accrued due and been paid prior to such service[51]; and a person entitled to receive the rents is bound, as from the date of the order, if he or she has notice of it.[52] A prepayment by the tenant to the mortgagor, before the due date, is invalid against a receiver who demands it before that date, whether the mortgage is legal or equitable; the prepayment is only good as to the amount due, not as to the remainder.[53] But a prepayment or release of rent, before the date of the mortgage or charge, is valid against a mortgagee or a receiver.[54] The receipt of rent by a receiver appointed in a mortgagee's action does not amount to a recognition of the tenancy, so as to prevent the mortgagee subsequently asserting his or her title paramount.[55]

6-11 **Effect on third parties.** Persons who are not parties to the order are not bound by it in this sense, that no action can be maintained against them, e.g. for rent, until something more has been done to make the order binding on them: a further order that they attorn tenant or pay their arrears to the receiver must be obtained.[56] If, however, after notice of the order, tenants pay their rents to a party bound by the

---

[44] Quaere whether a person paying the money with notice of the order is not also in contempt: or whether he or she obtains a valid receipt. See para.6-12, below.

[45] See *Ames v Birkenhead Docks* (1855) 24 L.J. Ch. 540, where the chairman of a statutory undertaking was appointed; *Davy v Scarth* [1906] 1 Ch. 55.

[46] *Lloyd v Mason* (1837) 2 My. & Cr.487; *Codrington v Johnston* (1838) 1 Beav. 520.

[47] per Lindley MR, in *Re Clarke* (1898) 1 Ch. 336, 339.

[48] See para.6-17, below.

[49] *Wickens v Townsend* (1830) 1 Russ. & M. 361; *Re Birt* (1883) 22 Ch. D. 604; *Re British Tea Table Co* (1909) 101 L.T. 707; see also paras 6-26, 6-27, below, as to lien.

[50] See para.6-17, below.

[51] See *Ashburton v Nocton* [1915] 1 Ch. 274; *Codrington v Johnstone*, n.46, above; *McDonnel v White* (1865) 11 H.L. 570; *Russell v Russell* (1853) 2 Ir.Ch. 574.

[52] *Hollier v Hedges* (1853) 2 Ir.Ch.R. 370; see *Eastern Trust Co v McKenzie, Mann & Co* [1915] A.C. 750, HL.

[53] *Ashburton v Nocton*, n. 51, above at 290; *Cook v Guerra* (1872) L.R. 7 C.P. 132, 136.

[54] See *Green v Rheinberg* (1911) 104 L.T. 149; see *Ashburton v Nocton*, n. 51, above; *Wakefield Bank v Yates* [1916] 1 Ch. 452.

[55] *Re O'Rourke's Estate* (1889) 23 L.R. Ir. 497.

[56] See *Seymour v Lucas* (1860) 1 Dr. & Sm. 177; and para.7-19, below, as to procedure. They may be ordered to pay the costs if they unreasonably refuse to pay to the receiver: *Re Potts* [1839] 1 Q.B. 648. As to determination of tenancies, and raising of rents, see para.6-10, above.

order, they will not obtain a valid receipt, since the order operates as an injunction.[57] The receipt of the receiver will be valid, if a receipt could have been given by a party bound by the order, but not otherwise.[58] The same rules will apply where a receiver has been appointed over personal estate at the instance of an encumbrancer, if the property is sufficiently specified in the order.[59] But where the property is not specified, for example, where a receiver is appointed against trustees over a trust estate, without specifying the trust investments they hold, the receipt by the trustees of money payable, e.g. on redemption of debentures, will be valid against the receiver[60]; for the company is entitled to deal with the persons holding the legal title, and not being affected by virtue of the property being alleged to be trust property.[61]

Receiver of equitable interest in personalty. The same principles apply, where   **6-12** a receiver has been appointed over equitable interests in personal estate at the instance of a judgment creditor; after notice of the order and request for payment, the person in whose *dominium* the fund is cannot obtain a valid receipt.[62] In one case,[63] it was in effect held that an order appointing a receiver over a debtor's current account at a bank did not prevent the bank, with notice of the order, from honouring cheques drawn by the debtor. But this decision can only be supported, if at all, on the ground that the order for a receiver was improperly made, as there was no bar to legal execution by garnishee proceedings (now entitled third party debt proceedings)[64] and the judgment creditor had therefore no equity to complain of the action of the bank.[65]

No estate in receiver. An order appointing a receiver does not of itself cause any   **6-13** estate to vest in the receiver.[66] Consequently, it does not cause a forfeiture, under a clause determining a life interest on the happening of any event, which would cause it to belong to or become vested in any other person than the life tenant, where nothing has been done under the order.[67] So too, where the gift over is limited to assigning or attempting to assign.[68] But an appointment of a receiver at the instance of a judgment creditor amounts to "a taking in execution by process of law", so as to cause a forfeiture conditioned to occur on the happening of that event.[69] A forfeiture will not be caused, where the life tenant merely requests a receiver, appointed over

---

[57] See para.6-10, above.
[58] For the receiver collects property upon the title of the parties: see *Preston v Tunbridge Wells Opera House* [1903] 2 Ch. 232; *Re Metropolitan Amalgamated Estates* [1912] 2 Ch. 497.
[59] For instance, where a receiver is appointed for debenture-holders over all the assets, debtors with notice cannot obtain a receipt from the company.
[60] See *Flegg v Prentis* [1892] 2 Ch. 428.
[61] *Tyrrell v Painton* [1895] 1 Q.B. 202; *Ideal Bedding Co v Holland* [1907] 2 Ch. 157; *Re Marquis of Anglesey* [1903] 2 Ch. 727; *Singer v Fry*, 84 L.J.K.B. 2025; *Ex p. Peak Hill Goldfield* [1909] 1 K.B. 430.
[62] *Eastern Trust Co v McKenzie, Mann & Co* [1915] A.C. 750.
[63] *Giles v Kruyer* [1921] 3 K.B. 23. The reasoning of the judgment appears to conflict with the judgments in *Re Marquis of Anglesey* and *Ideal Bedding Co v Holland*, n.61, above; *Re Pollard* [1903] 2 K.B. 41, on which it is founded, was a case of sequestration.
[64] See CPR Pt 72.
[65] This ground is not mentioned in the report.
[66] *Vine v Raleigh* (1883) 24 Ch. D. 243.
[67] *Re Beaumont* (1970) 79 L.J. Ch. 744; [1910] W.N.181; *Re Laye* [1913] 1 Ch. 298.
[68] See *Re Evans* [1920] 2 Ch. 304.
[69] *Blackman v Fysh* [1892] 3 Ch. 209.

the testator's estate, to pay a debt out of money due to the life tenant, for this request may refer to money then due.[70]

6-14 **When charge created.** The appointment of a receiver does not of itself create a charge,[71] unless specific moneys are ordered to be paid to a specific person.[72] However, as one effect of an agreement between the parties or of the terms of a statute, a charge may be created or rendered enforceable by the appointment. Thus the appointment of a receiver at the instance of debenture-holders causes the floating charge created by the debentures to crystallise into a specific enforceable charge.[73]

6-15 **Charge over land or interest in land.** Prior to the coming into force of the Administration of Justice Act 1956, an order appointing a receiver at the instance of a judgment creditor operated, when registered,[74] to create an equitable charge on every interest in land, legal and equitable, to or over which the judgment debtor was beneficially entitled at the date of entry or any time thereafter.[75] Under the present law, having regard to the repeal of the former statutory provisions, the obtaining of an order appointing a receiver, in a case where no charging order had been made under the Charging Orders Act 1979,[76] would not, even when registered,[77] appear to create any charge on the land.[78] Unless registered, the order would be void as against a purchaser of the land.[79] As already noticed, however, for the purposes of the Insolvency Act 1986, in relation both to corporate and to individual insolvency, the appointment of a receiver completes the execution.[80] If the judgment debtor has only an interest in land, no registration is possible,[81] but notice will of course be given to the trustees.

Where an order discharging a receiver appointed over the debtor's interest in leaseholds, at the instance of his trustee in bankruptcy, contained a provision that the order was not to prejudice the contention of the judgment creditor that he was a secured creditor, it was held that, on the execution being completed, the judgment creditor had no such interest as would entitle him to rank as a secured creditor.[82]

6-16 **No charge over interests in personalty.** Apart from such interests as are dealt with by the Charging Orders Act 1979, there never has been any statutory provision applicable to pure personal estate, corresponding to s.195(1) of the Law of

---

[70] *Durran v Durran* [1904] W. 184; 91 L.T. 187.
[71] *Campbell v Campbell* (1895) 72 L.T. 294.
[72] *Re Whiteheart* (1971) 116 S.J. 75.
[73] See para.6-58, below.
[74] Under Land Charges Act 1972 s.6(1).
[75] See Law of Property Act 1925 s.195, see n.78, below; and *Ashburton v Nocton* [1915] 1 Ch. 274, where the previous statutes were considered in great detail.
[76] See para.6-41, below.
[77] Under Land Charges Act 1972 s.6(1).
[78] Law of Property Act 1925 s.195 was (except for subs.(4)) repealed by Administration of Justice Act 1956 s.34(2).
[79] Land Charges Act 1972 s.6(4).
[80] Insolvency Act 1986 ss.183(3), 346(5).
[81] See the definition of "land" in Land Charges Act 1972 s.17(1).
[82] *Re Bueb* [1927] W.N. 299.

Property Act 1925.[83] The appointment, therefore, at the instance of a judgment creditor of a receiver over the debtor's personal property has never created a charge[84]; nor could the person who had obtained the order, by giving notice of it, obtain thereby a charge[85]; nor had, or has, the court jurisdiction to make a declaration of charge, when making the appointment.[86] But, as has been already stated,[87] the order operates as an injunction to prevent the debtor dealing with the property over which it extends.

Paramount claims. If the receivership order does not contain a direction for payment to the judgment creditor, the receiver holds the property, when it reaches his or her hands, *in medio*; it remains subject to all claims paramount to that of the judgment creditor at the date when the order is obtained. Subject to these claims, the court will order the receiver to pay the judgment creditor the amount of the debt owed, in priority to the claims of any person whose interests in the fund were acquired subsequently to the date of the order,[88] except those of persons whose claims may have priority by statute, e.g. a trustee in bankruptcy.[89] Thus, where a judgment creditor had obtained the appointment of a receiver over a consignment of copper, which was subject to a lien, and the debtors were subsequently adjudicated to be in judicial liquidation in France, it was held that the judgment creditor was entitled to the copper after the lien had been satisfied, in priority to the liquidator, though nothing had been received at the date of the liquidation: see also para.6-28, below.[90]

    6-17

Stop orders. Further, although a receivership order obtained by a judgment creditor does not create a charge on personal property over which the receiver is appointed, if that property cannot be taken in execution or made available by any other legal process, it prevents any subsequent mortgagee or judgment creditor from gaining priority, by means of a stop order, over the creditor obtaining the receivership order[91]; the mere omission to obtain a stop order does not postpone a judgment creditor, who has obtained a receivership order, to a person who subsequently

    6-18

---

[83] See para.6-11, above.

[84] *Re Potts* [1893] 1 Q.B. 648 (under Companies Act 1862); *Re Beaumont* [1910] W.N. 181; 79 L.J. Ch. 744; *Ideal Bedding Co v Holland* [1970] 2 Ch. 157; *Stevens v Hutchinson* [1953] Ch. 299.

[85] *Re Potts*, n.82, above; *Re Pearce* [1919] 1 K.B. 354; *Giles v Kruyer* [1912] 3 K.B. 23.

[86] *Flegg v Prentis* [1892] 2 Ch. 428. See per Farwell J in *Ridout v Fowler* [1904] 1 Ch. 658, 663. This case was affirmed at [1904] 1 Ch. 658, 663.

[87] See para.6-11, above, and *De Peyrecave v Nicholson* (1849) 42 W.R. 702; *Westhead v Riley* (1883) 25 Ch. D. 413.

[88] At all events if they had notice of it.

[89] See per Swinfen Eady J in *Re Marquis of Anglesey* [1903] 2 Ch. 727, 731, 732; per Kekewich J in *Ideal Bedding Co v Holland*, n.84, above; *Ex p. Peak Hill Goldfield Ltd* [1909] 1 K.B. 430, 437.

[90] *Levasseur v Mason and Barry* [1891] 2 Q.B. 73. The English Bankruptcy Acts had no application in this case: see *Re Pearce* [1919] 1 K.B. 354, 364. *Ridout v Fowler* [1904] 2 Ch. 93, cited above, n.86 (claim by judgment creditor of purchaser in respect of forfeited deposit), was decided against the creditor on the ground that the vendor's forfeiture of the deposit was contractual, by virtue of the purchaser's default, which was prior in date to the receivership order; and that certain money paid by the vendor was to secure possession of the land, not in part repayment of the deposit.

[91] See *Re Marquis of Anglesey*, n.89, above, at 731 per Swinfen Eady J. In that case, the receivership order was obtained over a judgment debtor's interest in residuary personal estate, partly in court there, and partly in the hands of an executor to whom notice of the order was at once given: at the date of the order, the residue was unascertained, and the fund in court was insufficient to pay the testator's creditors; the judgment creditor by obtaining the order did not obtain therefore either a charging order or a stop order.

obtains a stop order.[92] But an assignee for value of a debt has priority over a judgment creditor who obtains a receivership order, although the order is made before notice of the assignment has been given.[93]

6-19   **Cross-claim or set-off.** Inasmuch as a receivership order operates as an injunction and prevents the judgment debtor from dealing with the property comprised in it, he or she cannot utilise such property for purposes of a cross-claim, or by way of set-off against a third person. Thus, where the property consists of debentures of a company which had fallen due, the judgment debtor could not set them up to defeat a bankruptcy petition by the company, founded on a debt less in amount than the sum secured by the debentures.[94]

6-20   **Receiver not agent of creditor.** A receiver appointed at the instance of a creditor holds the goods of the debtor as agent, not for the creditor but for the court, in order that it may decide the right to them. Moreover, an order appointing a receiver of the goods of a debtor does not make a judgment creditor, who has obtained such an order, a secured creditor or a creditor holding any security within the meaning of s.248(1) and (2) (in relation to companies), and ss.285(4) and 383(2) (in relation to individuals) of the Insolvency Act 1986; the effect of those sections causes the term "a secured creditor" to mean a creditor who holds security over the property of the debtor, by way of mortgage, charge, lien or other security.[95] The order can only do so, if it charges the person, in whose hands the money is, not to deal with it, except by paying it to, or holding it for, the execution creditor.[96] Orders therefore directing the receiver, after making such payments as might be ordered, to accumulate the balance to form a fund for payment of the judgment debt, did not create a valid charge against the trustee in bankruptcy[97]: but an order directing payment of certain costs out of money in the hands of a receiver was held to amount to such a charge, unless the debtors had notice of an act of bankruptcy at the date of the order, followed by adjudication.[98]

6-21   **Miscellaneous.** The order does not create any charge, so as to give the creditor priority over other creditors, where the judgment debtor is a company in liquidation.[99] It was held not to constitute an execution, so as to entitle the executors of a deceased judgment creditor to apply for it under the then RSC Ord.46 r.2, in order to enforce a judgment obtained by their testator.[100] Nor does it cause the amount due to cease to be immediately payable, under the Insolvency Rules 2016,[101] so as to disentitle the judgment creditor from serving a statutory demand under s.268(1)(a) of the Insolvency Act 1986, in respect of the same debt.[102]

    The judgment creditor, after obtaining a receiver by way of equitable execu-

---

[92] See *Re Galland* [1886] W.N. 96; *Fahey v Tobin* [1901] 1 Ir.R. 516.

[93] *Re Bristow* [1906] 2 Ir.R. 215.

[94] *Ex p. Peak Hill Goldfield Ltd*, above, n.89.

[95] See *Re A. Debtor (No.310 of 1988)* [1989] 1 W.L.R. 452; see also the similar provisions under previous Bankruptcy Acts.

[96] per Swinfen Eady MR in *Re Pearce*, [1919] 1 K.B. 354.

[97] *Re Pearce*, n.94, above.

[98] *Re Gershon and Levy* [1915] 2 K.B. 527; as to the effect of a Scottish Bankruptcy, see Bankruptcy (Scotland) Act 2016, and *Singer v Fry* (1915) 113 L.T. 552.

[99] *Croshaw v Lyndhurst Ship Co* [1897] 2 Ch. 154; *Re Lough Neagh Ship Co.* [1896] 1 I.R. 29.

[100] *Norburn v Norburn* [1894] 1 Q.B. 448; see para.2-26, above: see now Pts 70 ff of the CPR.

[101] Insolvency Rules 2016 r.10.1.

[102] cf. under the Bankruptcy Act 1890, *Re Bond* [1911] 2 K.B.988; nothing had in fact come into the

tion, has a right, under CPR Pt 71,[103] to examine the debtor as to his or her means of satisfying the judgment, and also as to his or her dealings with property, against the removal of which an injunction had been granted, prior to the appointment.[104]

Bankruptcy of the debtor.   The title of the trustee in bankruptcy prevails over that   **6-22** of a receiver, appointed by way of equitable execution in respect of after-acquired property of the bankrupt, since s.307(4)(a) of the Insolvency Act 1986[105] only protects purchasers in good faith and for value, and without notice of the bankruptcy. That section overruled "the Rule in *Cohen v Mitchell*",[106] which had conferred protection on transactions, done by the bankrupt with after-acquired property, with a person who gave value in good faith, but had notice of the bankruptcy.

Where, in an action to enforce an agreement by the defendant to give a bill of sale of sundry chattels, an interim receiver of the chattels was appointed and he took possession, and very soon afterwards the defendant became bankrupt, it was held that the possession of the receiver had taken the chattels out of the order and disposition of the bankrupt at the time of his bankruptcy.[107] But the appointment of a receiver of the book debts of a trader, who was afterwards adjudicated bankrupt, did not take them out of his order and disposition, unless the appointment had been followed by notice to the book-debtors before the bankruptcy.[108]

In this connection, by s.344 of the Insolvency Act 1986, an assignment or charge, by a person engaged in any business, of present or future book debts, except debts due from specified debtors, or growing due under specified contracts, or debts included in a bona fide transfer of a business for value, or included in an assignment of assets for the benefit of creditors generally, is void against the trustee in bankruptcy, unless registered as a bill of sale.[109]

Since the receiver is not an agent of any party, but an officer of the court, a receiver appointed in a partnership action is not "a person having the control or management of the partnership business", upon whom a statutory demand under s.268(2) of the Insolvency Act 1986 could lawfully be served by a creditor of the firm.[110]

---

hands of the receiver; the court in bankruptcy may inquire whether the receivership order prevented payment of the debt.

[103] Replacing RSC Ord.48, revoked in relation to enforcement proceedings issued on or after 25 March 2002: see the Civil Procedure (Amendment No.4) Rules 2001 (SI 2001/2792).

[104] *Sturges v Warwick (Countess)* (1913) 30 T.L.R. 112; see now CPR r.72.1 as to procedure.

[105] Under the Bankruptcy Act 1914, *Hosack v Robins (No.1)* [1918] 2 Ch. 339, a case of a charging order. cf. *Re Fox* [1940] N.I. 42. Where the claim of the trustee is made against the assets of a deceased bankrupt, the claim may be defeated by an order for an insolvency administration (i.e. in bankruptcy), under Insolvency Act 1986 s.421, (as amended) and Administration of Insolvency Estates of Deceased Persons Order 1986 (SI 1986/1999, as amended) the trustee having then only a right of proof. Such an order may now be obtained after judgment in an administration action.

[106] (1890) 25 Q.B.D. 262 CA.

[107] *Taylor v Eckersley* (1877) 5 Ch. D. 740.

[108] *Rutter v Everett* [1895] 2 Ch. 872. In *Re Neal* [1914] 2 Ch. 910, Horridge J disagreed with Stirling J in *Rutter v Everett*, above, that, if bankruptcy supervened before notice could reasonably be given, the debts would not be in the order and disposition of the bankruptcy, considering that the assignee of the debt might well have given the notice before the application for a receiver; but this would not apply to an equitable chargee. The "order and disposition" clause in the Bankruptcy Act 1914 s.38(c), was repealed by Insolvency Act 1986, and not re-enacted.

[109] Reproducing Bankruptcy Act 1914 s.43.

[110] *Re Flowers & Co* [1897] 1 Q.B. 14 (concerning the service of a bankruptcy notice, under Bankruptcy

6-23   **Hire-purchase agreement.**   An ordinary hire-purchase agreement, in respect of machinery affixed to the land, confers an equitable interest in the land on the hirers-out, in priority to the interests of subsequent equitable encumbrancers, such as debenture-holders, and entitles them to enter and remove the thing hired, after the appointment of a receiver, on leave being obtained.[111]

6-24   **To whom money in the hands of a receiver belongs, on dismissal of action.**   When money comes into the hands of a receiver appointed in a foreclosure action, and no particular direction has been given for its application, it belongs prima facie to the claimant, who, accordingly, has a right to receive it, in the event of and upon the dismissal of the action.[112] An order for payment of money out of court may be made after the dismissal of an action.[113]

6-25   **Interpleader.**   A receiver cannot be compelled to interplead on the ground that his or her appointment is improper: he or she can appear for the purpose of asserting his or her right, and denying the right of any court, other than that which appointed him or her, to interfere with his or her possession.[114]

6-26   **Solicitor's charging order.**   The appointment of a receiver and manager does not necessarily amount to such a "preservation of property", as to entitle a solicitor to a charging order for his or her costs; for instance, where the attack, from which the property was preserved, was that of the party whose solicitor asks for the charging order.[115] The solicitor for a claimant in a partnership action is prima facie entitled to a charging order.[116] In an Irish case, the solicitor for a judgment creditor, who had been appointed receiver by way of equitable execution, over so much of a sum due to the defendant as would satisfy the debt and costs, was held entitled to a charge for costs over the amount payable to the judgment creditor.[117]

If a party changes solicitor, in the course of an action in which a receiver has been appointed, the former solicitor cannot assert, as against the receiver, an unlimited lien.[118]

6-27   **Persons with paramount rights.**   If persons with paramount rights, who are not parties to the action, are actually in possession of those rights, the appointment of a receiver does not prejudice them in the enjoyment of those rights.[119] But if they are not actually in such possession, then, after a receiver has been appointed, they must come to the court for leave to exercise those rights, in which case their application cannot be refused: see also para.6-18, above.[120]

6-28   **Receiver for puisne encumbrancer.**   Thus, if a puisne encumbrancer obtains the

---

Act 1914 s.1(1)(g)); and see *Boehm v Goodall* [1911] 1 Ch. 155; see para.6-0, above.
[111] *Re Morrison, Jones and Taylor Ltd* [1914] 1 Ch. 50; as to property in chattels, see *Whiteley Ltd v Hilt* [1918] 2 Ch. 808. See also as to effect of transactions relating to hire-purchase agreements. *Re George Inglefield Ltd* [1933] Ch. 1; *Transport and General Credit Corp. v Morgan* [1939] Ch. 531.
[112] *Paynter v Carew* (1854) 18 Jur.417; but the order should specifically deal with its application.
[113] *Wright v Mitchell* (1811) 18 Ves. 292. See now CPR r.40.6(3)(b)(v) and PD 40B, para.3.5.
[114] See *Russell v East Anglian Ry* (1850) 3 Mac. & G. 104 at 115, 122, 123.
[115] *Wingfield v Wingfield* [1919] 1 Ch. 462; but not where there is collusion, see at p.472.
[116] See para.6-41, below.
[117] *Duff v Taite* [1914] 2 Ir.R. 31: but only after completion of the order, *Wingfield v Wingfield*, n.115, above.
[118] *Dessau v Peters, Rushton & Co* [1922] 1 Ch.1, at 5 at q.v. for form of order.
[119] *Evelyn v Lewis* (1844) 3 Hare 472.
[120] See *Re Metropolitan Amalgamated Estates* [1912] 2 Ch. 497. See also paras 2-27, above and 12-6,

appointment of a receiver in an action to which a prior mortgagee is not a party, and such prior mortgagee is not actually in possession at the date of the order, the receiver can give a good discharge for rents accrued due, until service by the prior mortgagee of notice of application for liberty to take possession by himself or herself or a receiver[121]: it makes no difference that the prior mortgagee has, previous to the order, appointed a receiver who has never given notice to the tenants.[122] The prior mortgagee is entitled to rents paid or accruing after the date of the service of the notice to take possession. When permission is required, under what is now the Reserve and Auxiliary Forces, etc. Act 1951, the right of the prior encumbrancer to the rents was held to date from service of the originating summons asking for leave.[123]

Preserving the rights of prior encumbrancers. If the order made on the application of the puisne encumbrancer expressly reserves the rights of prior mortgagees, a prior mortgagee may, without application to the court, give notice to the tenants to pay their rents to him or her[124]; a tenant paying to him or her in obedience to such notice is not guilty of contempt of court, and can set up the payment against the receiver.

6-29

The order appointing a receiver should expressly preserve the rights of prior encumbrancers; but if it does not, the receiver cannot be displaced at the instance of a prior encumbrancer, without application to the court, nor is the prior encumbrancer entitled to rents received by the receiver before the date of the application for permission.[125] Thus, notice by a mortgagee, not a party, to tenants to pay their rents to him, was held to be ineffective to give him any title to those rents against the receiver and the parties to the action, where the order appointing the receiver did not preserve the rights of mortgagees,[126] for the appointment of a receiver is for the benefit of mortgagees only so far as they avail themselves of it.[127] So if a mortgagee, claiming under a title paramount to that under which the receiver has been appointed, suffers the receiver to pay away the surplus rents to the beneficial owner, or to apply them for purposes other than the satisfaction of his security, he is not entitled to a retrospective account of rents and profits.[128] Money in the hands of a receiver is not, as is the case of a sequestrator, "*in custodia legis*".[129]

Though a receiver appointed by an equitable mortgagee is entitled to rents as against a person obtaining a third party debt order (formerly a garnishee order), the

---

below.
[121] *Thomas v Brigstocke* (1827) 4 Russ. 64; *Preston v Tunbridge Wells Opera House* [1903] 2 Ch. 323, 325. As to dates in this report, see n.120, above at 501.
[122] *Re Metropolitan Amalgamated Estates*, n.120, above.
[123] *Re Belbridge Property Trust* [1941] Ch. 304, a decision under the Courts (Emergency Powers) Act 1939.
[124] *Underhay v Reid* (1887) 20 Q.B.D. 209; this case appears to cover the query raised in *Re Metropolitan Amalgamated Estates* n.120, above, as to the effect of such a reservation.
[125] See *Re Metropolitan Amalgamated Estates*, n.120, above.
[126] The suit was for establishing the will of the mortgagor: *Thomas v Brigstocke* (1827) 4 Russ. 65.
[127] *Gresley v Adderley* (1818) 1 Swans, 579; *Salt v Lord Donegal* (1835) Ll. & G. temp. Sug.91; *Penney v Todd* (1878) 26 W.R. 502; [1878] W.N.71. cf. *Piddock v Boultbee* (1867) 16 L.T. 837.
[128] *Gresley v Adderley*, n.127, above; *Thomas v Brigstocke*, n.126, above; *Flight v Camac* (1856) 4 W.R. 664.
[129] *Re Hoare* [1892] 3 Ch. 94; not following *Delaney v Mansfield* (1825) 1 Hogg. 234.

equitable mortgagee obtains no priority[130] by giving notice to tenants to pay their rents to him or her, nor by appointing a receiver who gives no notice to tenants.[131]

6-30   **Position of encumbrancers not parties.**   Where a receiver is appointed over an estate, encumbrancers who are not parties to the action may or may not avail themselves of the order appointing a receiver by applying to him or her. If they apply to him or her, they will be paid their interest, or, if he or she refuses or neglects to pay them, they may complain to the court of such neglect or refusal. But if they omit to apply for the interest, it is to be presumed that they are satisfied with the security they have, both for interest and also for principal. The court does not force payment upon them, nor does it set apart any portion of any rents and profits receivable by the receiver, to answer unclaimed interest. The balance is paid in by him or her, and is carried to the credit of the action, without any previous inquiry whether all encumbrancers have or have not been paid their interest.[132]

A direction given by the court to the receiver, to keep down the interest on encumbrances, does not have the effect of an appropriation of any rents and profits receivable by him or her to that specific purpose. It is given partly in justice to the encumbrancers, that they may not be injured by the act of the court in taking possession of rents and profits to which they had a right to resort for payment of their interest, and partly for the benefit of the estate itself, lest the encumbrancers, having their interest stopped, might be induced to take proceedings injurious to those who stand behind them.[133]

Where a receiver has been appointed under an order directing interest on prior encumbrances to be kept down, and has received rents with the knowledge of the first mortgagee, that mortgagee, upon afterwards taking possession, is entitled only to the rents in the receiver's hands, after deduction of the receiver's remuneration and expenses.[134]

6-31   **Interference with the possession of a receiver.**   When the court has appointed a receiver who is in possession, his or her possession is the possession of the court, and may not be disturbed without its permission.[135] If anyone disturbs the possession of the receiver, the court holds that person guilty of contempt of court, and liable to be imprisoned for the contempt.[136] The court will not allow the possession of its receiver to be interfered with or disturbed by anyone, whether claiming by title paramount to or under the right which the receiver was appointed to protect.[137]

---

[130] See para.6-11, above.

[131] *Vacuum Oil Co v Ellis* [1914] 1 K.B. 693. But now a second mortgage does have, usually, a legal estate, and can give an effective notice to tenants.

[132] *Bertie v Lord Abingdon*, (1817) 3 Mer. 560; *Penney v Todd*, n.127, above. cf. *Piddock v Boultbee*, n.127, above.

[133] *Bertie v Lord Abingdon*, see n.130, above. See, too, *Flight v Camac*, n.128, above.

[134] *Davy v Price* [1883] W.N. 226.

[135] *Angel v Smith* (1804) 9 Ves. 335; *Aston v Heron* (1834) 2 My. & K. 390; *Ames v Birkenhead Docks* (1855) 20 Beav. 332; *Defries v Creed* (1865) 34 L.J. Ch. 607. But cf. *Bell v Spereman* (1726) Sel.Cas.Ch. 59.

[136] *Fripp v Bridgewater Canal Co* (1855) 3 W.R. 356; *Lane v Sterne* (1862) 3 Giff.629; *Ex p. Hayward* [1881] W.N. 115. See, too, *Dixon v Dixon* [1904] 1 Ch. 161, where an injunction restraining interference with a receiver and manager was granted. As to form of order for committal for obstructing a receiver, see Seton, 7th edn, p.454.

[137] *Evelyn v Lewis* (1844) 3 Hare 472; *Russell v East Anglian Ry* (1850) 3 Mac. & G. 104, 114.

Libellous statements relating to a business carried on by a receiver and manager are a contempt, and may be punished by committal.[138]

When a receiver may be sued. But unless the receiver comes with clean hands, **6-32** he or she will not be granted an injunction to restrain any interference with him or her, for instance, by commercial rent arrears recovery (formerly the remedy of distress).[139] A person who thinks he or she has a right paramount to that of the receiver must, before he or she presumes to take any step of his or her own motion, apply to the court for permission to assert his or her right.[140] If the receiver has done anything wrong, the party who has suffered the wrong must apply to the court which appointed the receiver, and will get full justice done.[141] But where a claim cannot be made in the original action,[142] or in any other case where it is convenient to bring a separate action against the receiver, permission to bring an action must first be obtained from the court.[143] Where an action in the Queen's Bench Division was threatened by the owner of certain plant, against a receiver appointed in a debenture-holder's action to enforce a claim in respect of the user by the receiver of such plant, the court, upon motion in the debenture-holder's action, restrained any proceedings, otherwise than by way of claim therein.[144] Neville, J there said (at p.286):

> "It appears to me that a dispute of that kind is one which ... the Court will deal with itself, and that it will not allow its officer to be subject to an action in another Court with reference to his conduct in the discharge of the duties of his office, whether right or wrong. The proper remedy for anyone aggrieved by his conduct is to apply to this Court in the action in which he was appointed. If any wrong has been done by the officer, the Court will no doubt see that justice is done, but no one has a right to sue such an officer in another Court without the sanction of this Court".

A claim against a receiver and manager, appointed by the court in a partnership action, was held not proper to be heard as part of the partnership action, but had to be tried separately. The court has a discretion, whether or not to grant permission to sue its officer, to be exercised dependent on the reasonable prospects of success of the claim[145]; a disappointed bidder for a purchase from the receiver has no locus standi to claim against him or her on that account.[146] A receiver appointed to get in property, part of which he or she finds in the possession of another receiver, ought not to take proceedings to deprive the latter of such possession, without a direc-

---

[138] *Helmore v Smith* (1887) 35 Ch. D. 440. The contempt occasioned by abuse of the claimant in an action in which a receiver is appointed, is of a different nature, due to the fact that his evidence may be affected: see *Re Thomas Shipping Co.* [1930] 2 Ch. 368.

[139] *Jarvis v Islington BC* (1909) 73 J.P. 323.

[140] See n.137, above; *Hawkins v Gathercole* (1852) 1 Drew. 12; *Randfield v Randfield* (1860) 1 Dr. & Sm.310; *Ex p. Cochrane* (1875) L.R. 20 Eq.282; *Re Botibol* [1947] 1 All E.R. 26; and cases cited in n.127, above.

[141] *Ex p. Day* (1883) 48 L.T. 912; *L P Arthur (Insurance) Ltd v Sisson* [1966] 1 W.L.R. 1384; and para.6-53, below.

[142] A claim for an injunction against nuisance would be an example.

[143] *Re Botibol* [1947] 1 All E.R. 26.

[144] *Re Maidstone Palace of Varieties* [1909] 2 Ch. 282.

[145] *McGowan v Chadwick and Grant* [2001] E.W.C.A. Civ. 1751; [2003] B.P.I.R. 647 CA, para.[76], applying *Re Maidstone Palace of Varieties Ltd*, n.144, above.

[146] *McGowan v Chadwick and Grant*, n.145, above, at para.[84], following *Skyepharma Plc v Hyal Pharmaceutical Corp.* [2001] B.P.I.R. 163 (Ontario CA).

tion from the court.[147]

It is not competent for anyone to interfere with the possession of a receiver on the ground that the order appointing him or her ought not to have been made: persons who feel aggrieved by an order of the court may question its validity in proper proceedings, but while it lasts it must be obeyed.[148]

The court requires and insists that application be made to it, in order to take possession of any property of which its receiver has taken, or is directed to take, possession. The rule is not confined to property actually in the hands of a receiver: for the court will not permit anyone, without its sanction and authority, to intercept or prevent payment to the receiver of any property, within the territorial jurisdiction of the court, which he or she has been appointed to receive, although it may not be actually in his or her hands.[149]

6-33 **Foreign property.**   Where, however, the court appoints a receiver over property out of the jurisdiction, the receiver is not put in possession of such foreign property by the mere order of the court.[150] Something further has to be done, and, until that has been done in accordance with the foreign law, any person, not a party to the action, who takes proceedings in the foreign country for the purpose of establishing a claim upon the foreign property, is not guilty of a contempt of court, on the ground of interference with the receiver's possession or otherwise. In reference to such proceedings, no distinction can be drawn between a foreigner and a British subject.[151] In this connection, it is to be observed that the English court will recognise the validity of an equitable charge on foreign property, though such charge is not enforceable in the courts of that country.[152]

6-34 **Acts of interference.**   Any deliberate act, calculated to destroy property which is under the management of the court by means of a receiver and manager, is an interference with the receiver, although it may not induce the breaking of any contract. The object of the court is to prevent any improper interference with the administration of justice, and when anyone, whether a partner in a business, a party to the litigation, or a stranger, interferes with an officer of the court, the court will protect that officer.[153]

6-35 **Receiver not in actual possession.**   The rule, however, that the possession of a receiver may not be disturbed without permission of the court, does not apply, so far at least as third persons are concerned, until a receiver has been actually appointed, and is in actual possession. Until the appointment has been perfected, and the receiver is actually in possession, a creditor is not debarred from proceeding to

[147] *Ward v Swift* (1848) 6 Hare 309; *Ex p. Cochrane* n.140, above.
[148] *Russell v East Anglian Ry* (1850) 3 Mac. & G. 104, 117; cf. *Re First Express Ltd* [1991] B.C.C. 782 disobedience to an invalid order, until it is set aside, is punishable as a contempt.
[149] *Ames v Birkenhead Docks* (1855) 20 Beav. 332.
[150] See *Re Huinac Copper Mines* [1910] W.N. 218. cf. "Property in the UK" (comprised in a floating charge given by a company).
[151] *Re Maudslay, Sons & Field* [1900] 1 Ch. 602, 611.
[152] *Re Anchor Line (Henderson Bros)* [1937] Ch. 483. It can be enforced against property brought within the jurisdiction.
[153] per Swinfen Eady J in *Dixon v Dixon* [1904] 1 Ch. 161, 163. As to interference with business carried on by a receiver and manager, see para.6-31, above.

execution.[154] An execution creditor may, therefore, lawfully seize chattels, after an order has been made appointing a receiver on his giving security, but before the security has been given or possession taken.[155] In the case of equitable execution or the appointment of a receiver for debenture-holders, the order should if possible be obtained in a form to operate as from its date.

Property must be specified.   There is no disturbance of a receiver, unless the order for the appointment states, on the face of it, the property over which the receiver is appointed, so as to enable the property to be identified.[156]   **6-36**

Execution against shareholder-receiver.   Nor, again, was there disturbance of a receiver, in a case where, on the chairman of a railway company having been appointed receiver, a debenture-holder, who had recovered judgment against the company in respect of arrears of interest, successfully applied for leave to issue execution against the chairman, to the extent of the money remaining due in respect of his shares; the money which would be reached by the execution in such a case was money in the hands of an individual shareholder, and not part of the undertaking or profits of the company, of which a receiver had been appointed.[157]   **6-37**

Receiver in administration action.   The appointment of a receiver in an administration action does not prevent trustees, or parties in whom the property has become vested on the statutory trusts,[158] from selling all or any part of the property without the permission of the court.[159] The same is the case as regards the power of a tenant for life, in whose favour an assent has been made, to sell under the Settled Land Act 1925.[160]   **6-38**

Receiver of life tenancy.   Where a receiver had been appointed, under the old law, over the estate of a tenant for life, the remainderman was held entitled, on the death of the tenant for life, to go into possession, without making any application to the court.[161] The special, or, where the land ceases to be settled land, the general, personal representatives, who take the legal estates as trustees, would be in the same position; for the appointment would have been only over the equitable interest of the tenant for life.   **6-39**

Permission required even for first step.   To constitute disturbance of a receiver, it is not necessary that the person complained of should be about to turn the receiver out of possession. The court will not allow even the first step to be taken by anyone in an action, whether of ejectment[162] or otherwise,[163] against a receiver, without an application having been first made to the court for permission to take it. So, a lo-   **6-40**

---

[154] *Defries v Creed* (1865) 34 L.J. Ch. 607; *Edwards v Edwards* (1876) 2 Ch. D. 291.

[155] *Ex p. Evans* (1879) 13 Ch. D. 255 per James LJ.

[156] *Crow v Wood* (1850) 13 Beav. 271; para.6-12, above.

[157] *Re West Lancashire Ry* [1890] W.N. 165; 63 L.T. 56; under s.36 of the Companies Clauses Consolidation Act 1845.

[158] Under Law of Property Act 1925, Sch.I Pt IV.

[159] *Bernhardt v Galsworthy* [1929] 1 Ch. 549; but after an order has been made for administration of an estate or trust, the powers of the executors or trustees can only be exercised with the sanction of the court, which may be given generally as to a class of transactions, e.g. the creation of tenancies: see *Re Furness* [1943] Ch. 415.

[160] See n.146, above and *Cardigan v Curzon-Howle* (1885) 30 Ch. D. 531, 538.

[161] *Britton v M'Donnel* (1843) 5 Ir.Eq. 275; *Re Stack* (1862) 13 Ir.Ch.R. 213.

[162] *Hawkins v Gathercole* (1852) 1 Drew. 12, 18.

cal authority was not able, without the leave of the court, to distrain upon property in the hands of a receiver for money due to it.[164]

6-41   **Charging order.**   The form and effect of a charging order obtained by creditors of a partnership, after appointment of a receiver in a partnership action, has already been discussed.[165] This form of order does not override the right of the solicitor of the claimant in the partnership action to a charge for his or her costs[166]; but it was held to create a valid charge against the trustees in bankruptcy of the partners, unless the parties in whose favour it is made had notice of an available act of bankruptcy at the date of the order.[167]

6-42   **Remedies of landlord.**   It has already been pointed out[168] that persons with paramount rights, unless actually in possession of them at the appointment, must, after a receiver has been appointed, apply to the court for leave to put them into force unless the order preserves their powers: this applies to cases where a receiver has been appointed over the estate of a tenant in possession. The appointment of a receiver, as against the estate of a tenant, does not affect the rights of the landlord; but the landlord will not be permitted to exercise those rights without first obtaining the permission of the court. Before exercising the remedy of commercial rent arrears recovery (previously the remedy of distress), the landlord should come to the court and ask for authority to do so, notwithstanding the appointment of a receiver[169]; the landlord acquires no prior claim over other creditors to the proceeds of sale of chattels sold by the receiver after formal notice of his or her claim to rent.[170]

Similarly, where a partnership was trading from leasehold premises, the reversion to which was acquired by one partner personally, the fact that a receiver of the partnership assets had been appointed did not affect the right of the landlord-partner to apply to the court for relief, either by way of re-entry, or, if re-entry was refused, for an order that the receiver should pay the rent.[171] In the event, the receiver was directed to give up possession. The court also held that the fiduciary position of the landlord as a partner did not raise any equity preventing him from exercising his rights as landlord to the full.[172]

So, again, where, after a mortgagee of leasehold land has obtained the appointment by the court of a receiver, the lessor brings an action against the lessee and

---

[163] *Re Botibol* [1947] 1 All E.R. 26.
[164] See *Pegge v Neath District Tramways Co* [1895] 2 Ch. 508; *Reeve v Medway Upper Navigation Co* (1905) 21 T.L.R. 400: as to a person of unsound mind, see *Winkle v Bailey* [1897] 1 Ch. 123.
[165] See para.3-16, above.
[166] *Ridd v Thorne* [1902] 2 Ch. 344, 348.
[167] Under Bankruptcy Act 1914; acts of bankruptcy were abolished by Insolvency Act 1986; see *Re Gershon and Levy* [1915] 2 K.B. 527, 530. For the insolvency law now in force with respect to insolvent partnerships, see Insolvency Act 1986 s.420, and the Insolvent Partnerships Order 1994 (SI 1994/2421).
[168] See paras 6-17 and 6-28, above.
[169] *Sutton v Rees* (1863) 9 Jur. (N.S.) 456; see, too, *Walsh v Walsh* (1839) 1 Ir.Eq. 209. Where, however, a receiver is appointed over the estate of a superior landlord, and the lands are occupied by undertenants, the intermediate tenant may exercise commercial rent arrears recovery (formerly distress) upon the occupiers for rent, without any order for the purpose: *Furlong on Landlord and Tenant*, p.744.
[170] *Sutton v Rees*, n.169, above; see *Re JW Abbot & Co* [1913] W.N. 284.
[171] *Brenner v Rose* [1973] 1 W.L.R. 443; see also *Hand v Blow* [1901] 2 Ch. 721, 737.
[172] *Brenner v Rose*, n.169.

obtains judgment for recovery of the land, he or she (the lessor) cannot proceed to enforce the judgment, as against the receiver, by writ of possession, without first getting the leave of the court to do so.[173]

Application for leave to proceed. Persons whose rights are interfered with, by having a receiver appointed over property, in which they have an enforceable interest, may, on making a proper application to the court, obtain all that they can justly require.[174] The court will always take care to give to a party, who applies in a regular manner, protection of his or her rights, and will even assist him or her in asserting rights and having the benefit of them,[175] though the court does not profess to cure every inconvenience arising from its action in appointing a receiver.[176] An instance is the method adopted to enable creditors of a partnership business to obtain payment from the receiver without legal execution, which is discussed on other pages.[177]

6-43

The proper course for a person to adopt, who claims a right paramount to that of the receiver, or more precisely to that of the party who obtained the receiver, and who is prejudiced by having the receiver appointed, is to apply to the court for permission to proceed,[178] notwithstanding the possession of the receiver, or to come in and be examined *pro interesse suo*.[179] The former course is, usually, preferable. The application must be made by application notice,[180] and may be framed in the alternative, that the receiver may pay the amount of the claimant's demand, or that the latter may be allowed to proceed.[181] The application must be made in the action in which the receiver was appointed, and not, as a rule, in a fresh action against the person who obtained the appointment.[182] In some cases, however, a fresh action may be advisable, or even necessary.[183]

Action commenced without leave. If a party has, without the permission of the court, instituted proceedings at law to recover lands in the possession of a receiver,

6-44

---

[173] *Morris v Baker* [1903] 73 L.J. Ch. 143. cf. *Johns v Pink* [1900] 1 Ch. 296; para.19-9, below.

[174] *Russell v East Anglian Ry* (1850) 3 Mac. G. 104, 117.

[175] *Evelyn v Lewis* (1844) 3 Hare 472; *Hawkins v Gathercole* (1852) 1 Drew. 12; *Ex p. Cochrane* (1875) L.R. 20 Eq. 282; *Forster v Manchester and Milford Ry* (1880) 49 L.J. Ch. 454; [1880] W.N. 63; and see *Re Septimus Parsonage Co* (1901) 17 T.L.R. 420, where possession was given to trustees for debenture holders, though an action was pending by first debenture holders in which the appointment of a receiver was claimed.

[176] *Hand v Blow* [1901] 2 Ch. 721, 735; see, as to rights of lessors, para.7-29, below.

[177] See para.2-43, above.

[178] See para.6-42, above, as to encumbrancers.

[179] *Angel v Smith* (1804) 9 Ves. 335; *Russell v East Anglian Ry* (1850) 3 Mac. & G. 117; *Ex p. Cochrane* (1875) L.R. 20 Eq. 282. In a case where a receiver had been appointed in a suit instituted by encumbrancers, it was held that a judgment creditor might file a bill against the owner and the receiver to have his debt paid out of the surplus; and that the encumbrancers in the former suit need not be made parties to the latter: *Lewis v Lord Zouche* (1828) 2 Sim. 388; but now a third party debt order may be obtained: As to examinations pro interesse suo, see further, para.6-45, below.

[180] As to form of application notice, see CPR 23, Form N244 for form of examination *pro interesse suo*, see *Daniell's Chancery Forms*, 7th edn, p.778.

[181] *Brooks v Greathed* (1820) 1 Jac. & W. 176; *Potts v Warwick and Birmingham Canal Co.* (1853) Kay 142; *Russell v East Anglian Ry* (1850) 3 Mac. & G. 104.

[182] *Searle v Choat* (1884) 25 Ch. D. 723; see, too, *Ames v Richards* (1905) 40 L.J.N.c. 66. The receiver is seldom a necessary party: see *Smith v Effingham* (1839) 2 Beav. 232; (1843) 7 Beav. 357.

[183] See para.2-28, above.

the court may allow him or her to continue the action[184]: it may direct an inquiry whether it would be for the benefit of the parties interested that the receiver should defend the ejectment, and charge the expenses to his or her accounts.[185] Permission may equally be refused to continue the action.[186]

The court refused to restrain a person from prosecuting an action in a Scottish court, which amounted to interference with a receiver (although it had jurisdiction to do so), where the receiver had been added as a defendant in the Scottish action, and his rights and those of the plaintiff could most conveniently be determined in that action.[187]

6-45 **Inquiry as to personal interest (pro interesse suo).** Where a person has brought an action against a receiver, or has otherwise interfered with his or her possession without the permission of the court, the order restraining the irregular act may also give permission, or direct, that the author of it be examined pro interesse suo.[188]

The inquiry as to personal interest is conducted in the same manner as that in which it would be conducted, if the property were in the possession of sequestrators under a commission of sequestration.[189] If the court, on examining the title, is satisfied that the right of the claimant is clear, it will at once decide the matter in his or her favour, without directing an inquiry, and order the receiver to pay him or her what he or she claims,[190] or give the claimant leave to enforce his or her legal remedy, notwithstanding the possession of the receiver.[191] Thus, leave was given by the Court of Chancery to a judgment creditor, on his application, to issue legal execution against property in the possession of a receiver.[192]

So, also, where a person wishes to distrain on property in the possession of a receiver, the court, on being satisfied that the legal right of distress is paramount to the title of the party for whose benefit the receiver was appointed, will allow the distress to be made, either for rent,[193] or for rates or other money due to a local authority,[194] or for money due to a gas supplier, for which it has obtained a distress warrant under its statutory power.[195] Permission was given to distrain, notwithstanding the possession of a receiver, for a statutory penalty for breach of a condition in the very constitution of a public company, for instance, neglect by a tramway company to keep rails in repair[196]; but leave was refused to distrain for a penalty under the Highway Acts for failure to pay instalments to a local authority which by

---

184 *Gowar v Bennett* (1847) 9 L.T. 310; see *Aston v Heron* (1834) 2 My. & K. 397.
185 *Anon.* (1801) 6 Ves. 287.
186 See *Lees v Waring* (1825) 1 Hog. 216; cf. *Townsend v Somerville* (1824) 1 Hog. 99.
187 *Re Derwent Rolling Mills* (1905) 21 T.L.R. 81, 701.
188 See *Johnes v Claughton* (1822) Jac. 573.
189 *Daniell's Chancery Practice*, 8th edn, p.801.
190 *Dixon v Smith* (1818) 1 Swans. 457; *Russell v East Anglian Ry* n.179; *Randfield v Randfield* (1860) 1 Drew. & Sm. 310, per Kindersley V-C; see, too *Ex p. Thurgood* (1868) 18 L.T. 18, where damages for injuries sustained in a collision had been recovered against a railway company over which a receiver had been appointed.
191 Costs will usually be allowed to a successful applicant: *Eyton v Denbigh, etc. Ry* (1868) L.R. 6 Eq. 14, 488; see *Walsh v Walsh* (1839) 1 Ir.Eq.R. 209.
192 *Gooch v Haworth* (1841) 3 Beav. 428; *Potts v Warwick and Birmingham Canal Co*, n.181, above.
193 *Cramer v Griffish* (1840) 3 Ir.Eq.R. 230; *Russell v East Anglian Ry* n.179, above; *Sutton v Rees* (1863) 9 Jur. (n.s.) 456. The right of a landlord to exercise a right of commercial rent arrears recovery (formerly distress for rent), after the commencement of a bankruptcy, is limited by Insolvency Act 1986 s.347, to six months' rent. See *Ex p. Cochrane* (1875) L.R. 20 Eq. 282.
194 *Pegge v Neath District Tramways Co* [1895] 2 Ch. 508; and see *Winkle v Bailey* [1897] 1 Ch. 123.
195 *Re Adolphe Crosbie Ltd* (1909) 74 J.P. 25.
196 *Pegge v Neath District Tramways Co*, n.194, above; in this case the mortgage did not include the

agreement had taken over the roads which the company was under a statutory liability to repair.[197] Accordingly, where a company's goods had been mortgaged for more than their value to debenture-holders, who brought an action to enforce their rights and obtained the appointment of a receiver, and afterwards the company was ordered to be wound up, leave was given to the landlord of the house in which the goods were, to distrain, notwithstanding the appointment of the receiver, and notwithstanding the winding-up order, on the ground that, for all practical purposes, the goods were not the goods of the company but of the debenture-holders, as against whom the landlord was entitled to distrain.[198]

Attachment of moneys in hands of receiver.   A judgment creditor may obtain a   **6-46**
third party debt order (formerly a garnishee order), attaching money payable to the judgment debtor which is in the hands of a receiver,[199] but only such money as is actually in his or her hands when the order is obtained,[200] and not, it seems, money which has, by an order, been directed to be paid to the judgment debtor.[201] So, where a rentcharge created by a railway company under the Lands Clauses Consolidation Act 1845 had been reserved to a landowner, the court gave him liberty to distrain, notwithstanding that a receiver of the tools of the company had been appointed, in a suit instituted by the owner of a similar rentcharge on behalf of himself and all other owners of similar rentcharges who should come in and contribute to the expenses of the suit.[202] So also, in a case where it was held that a receiver ought not to have been appointed, leave was given to an execution creditor to levy, notwithstanding the appointment.[203]

Practice in Queen's Bench Division.   The procedure in equitable execution be-   **6-47**
ing founded on the equitable and not the common law jurisdiction of the court, the practice in the Queen's Bench Division follows that in the Chancery Division as nearly as circumstances will admit. Thus, where a prior encumbrancer applied to have an order appointing a receiver discharged, and for consequential relief, numerous affidavits were filed upon the application, and the matter was referred to a master of the Queen's Bench Division to report. Upon an application to set aside or vary the report, it was held that the court was bound to consider the objections to the report, and to go into the evidence, and to deal with the report as upon a motion to vary the certificate of a chief clerk[204] in the Chancery Division.[205]

Where the court is not satisfied that a receiver ought to have been appointed, the

---

chattels, and a receiver ought not to have been appointed over them; see *Reeve v Medway Upper Navigation Co* (1905) 21 L.T.R. 400.

[197] *Reeve v Medway Upper Navigation Co*, n.196, above.
[198] *Ex p. Purssell* (1887) 34 Ch. D. 646, 660, 662. See, too, *Re Harpur's Cycle Fittings Co* [1900] 2 Ch. 731 at 734, where no receiver had been appointed, but Wright J considered that that fact made no difference; and distinguishing *Re British Fuller's Earth Co* (1901) 17 T.L.R. 232 (followed in *Re Mayfair & General Property Trust Ltd* [1945] 2 All E.R. 523, where overseers were held to be not entitled to an order directing the receiver appointed in a debenture holder's action to pay to them the amount of rate due out of money in his hands.
[199] *Re Cowan's Estate* (1880) 14 Ch. D. 638.
[200] See *Webb v Stenton* (1883) 11 Q.B.D. 518, criticising some of the dicta in *Re Cowan's Estate*, n.199, above.
[201] *De Winton v Mayor of Brecon* (1859) 28 Beav. 200.
[202] *Eyton v Denbigh, etc. Ry* (1868) L.R. 6 Eq. 14, 488; 16 W.R. 1005; *Forster v Manchester and Milford Ry* (1880) 49 L.J. Ch. 454; [1880] W.N. 63.
[203] *Russell v East Anglian Ry* n.179; see *Fowler v Haynes* (1863) 2 N.R. 156.
[204] Now a master.

court may, so that the execution creditor may not suffer loss by the possession of the receiver, order that the receiver keep available for a certain period sufficient property to answer the demand. Or the court may make an order allowing the creditor to levy, unless the amount of his or her demand be paid into court to the credit of the action within a week from service of the order, the receiver to be at liberty to pay the amount in, and the money to remain in court, subject to further order.[206]

If encumbrancers come in for examination *pro interesse suo*, and upon inquiry their claim is made out, they are entitled to have rents and profits received and to be received by the receiver applied in payment of the costs of the application, and then of their encumbrances.[207]

If there is a doubtful question relating to land, and it is purely a matter of title, the court will give the claimant leave to sue for possession, taking care, however, to protect the possession by giving proper directions.[208] It is not the practice of the court, unless it is perfectly clear that there is no foundation for the claim, to refuse leave to try a right which is claimed against its receiver.[209]

In an old case, where a prior encumbrancer had delayed overlong in pursuing his remedies, the Court of Chancery refused his application that a receiver, who had been appointed at the instance of a second encumbrancer, should apply the rents according to their priorities; but leave was given to bring ejectment. The ground of the decision was that the prior encumbrancer had no right to come by petition for relief which he had sought in a suit previously commenced by him, but not proceeded with. No costs were given against the prior encumbrancer.[210]

6-48   **Committal, etc. for disturbance of receiver.**   A person who disturbs or interferes with the possession of a receiver is guilty of a contempt of court, and is liable to be committed.[211] In extreme or aggravated cases, the court will, for the purpose of vindicating its authority, order a committal,[212] but it does not ordinarily punish by actual committal.[213] The court is generally satisfied with ordering the party in contempt to pay the costs and expenses occasioned by his or her improper conduct, and the costs of the application to commit,[214] usually awarded on an indemnity basis. In some cases, an injunction restraining the interference may be an appropriate and sufficient remedy.[215] Thus, where the contempt consists in entering upon land in the possession of a receiver, or in bringing an action against a receiver, or against a person over whose property a receiver has been appointed, the practice of the court has been to grant an injunction, restraining the party in contempt from

---

[205] *Walmsley v Mundy* (1884) 13 Q.B.D. 807. This practice is obsolete.

[206] *Russell v East Anglian Ry*, n.177, above.

[207] *Walker v Bell* (1816) 2 Madd. 21; *Tatham v Parker* (1853) 1 Sm. & G. 506. For applications pro interesse suo, see para.6-45, above.

[208] *Empringham v Short* (1844) 3 Hare 461. See now CPR 55 and PD 55.

[209] *Randfield v Randfield* (1861) 3 De G.F. & J. 772; *Lane v Capsey* [1891] 3 Ch. 411.

[210] *Brooks v Greathed* (1820) 1 Jac. W. 176. See also *Wastell v Leslie* (1846) 15 Sim. 453.

[211] See para.6-31, above.

[212] *Broad v Wickham* (1831) 4 Sim. 511 (Application to commit a person for taking forcible possession against a receiver).

[213] For form of order to commit for interference with a receiver "in lunacy", see *Re Seaton* [1928] W.N. 307.

[214] *Russell v East Anglian Ry*, n.179, above: *Hawkins v Gathercole* [1852] 1 Drew, 12. A partner who had got in debts adversely to the receiver was ordered within a week to make an affidavit of the amount, and to pay that amount to the receiver, and in default to be committed: *Parker v Pocock* (1874) 30 L.T. 458.

[215] e.g. *Dixon v Dixon* [1904] 1 Ch. 161.

trespassing or prosecuting the action, as the case may be, at the same time ordering him or her to pay the costs of the application to commit.[216] In such a case,
whether the person bringing an action did or did not know that a receiver had been
appointed, or however clear his or her right may be, the court will restrain the
prosecution of the action, if it was brought without permission.[217] Where the agents
of the receiver in the cause, acting upon leave given by the court, took forcible possession of a house occupied by a servant of one of the defendants, an order was
made restraining that defendant from prosecuting an indictment against the
agents.[218] An action, however, against a person who professes to have acted under
the authority of a receiver, will not be restrained, unless it is clear that he or she has
really been acting under that authority.[219]

An application to commit a person for disturbing the possession of a receiver is
improper, if made long after the act complained of, and not for the protection of the
receiver's possession, but in order indirectly to compel payment of expenses, after
settlement of the question relating to the possession. The proper course is to make
directly any application for the payment of expenses or costs which may be war-
ranted by the circumstances.[220]

High Court enforcement officer, county court bailiff may not disturb posses-   6-49
sion of a receiver.   The court will not protect an enforcement officer who executes
process, after notice from a receiver that he or she is in possession.[221]

An enforcement officer[222] who seizes goods in the possession of a receiver is
guilty of a contempt of court,[223] and may be committed, even though the act is really the act of an employee, and there is no reason to infer that it is his or her
personal act. Where, however, under the previous enforcement regime, an under-
sheriff had seized goods in the possession of a receiver, the court, on the submission of the sheriff, abstained from committing him, but ordered him to withdraw
from possession, and to pay the costs.[224]

Where a sheriff had taken property, part of which was claimed by a receiver, the
latter was directed to give a list of the property claimed by him to the sheriff, who
was ordered to withdraw from possession of the specified property.[225]

An enforcement officer may also be restrained, if necessary, from compelling a
receiver to interplead, and may be ordered to pay the costs of proceedings instituted
for that purpose. If the execution creditor is before the court, he or she will be
restrained from proceeding against the enforcement officer in relation to the
property seized by him or her, or any property in the possession of the receiver. If

---

[216] *Johns v Claughton* (1822) Jac. 573; *Aston v Heron* (1834) 2 My. & K. 390; *Tink v Rundle* (1847)
10 Beav. 318; *Evelyn v Lewis* (1844) 3 Hare 472; *Ames v Birkenhead Docks* (1855) 20 Beav. 350;
(1855) 20 Beav. 350; *Bayly v Went* [1884] W.N. 197; 51 L.T. 765.

[217] *Evelyn v Lewis* (1844), n.214, above.

[218] *Turner v Turner* (1851) 15 Jur.218.

[219] *Birch v Oldis* (1837) Sau. & Sc. 146.

[220] *Ward v Swift* (1851) 6 Hare 309.

[221] *Try v Try* (1851) 13 Beav. 422; see, too, *Rock v Cook* (1848) 2 Ph. 691, where the sheriff entered
under a *fi. fa.* issued out of Chancery.

[222] Formerly a sheriff.

[223] *Lane v Sterne* (1862) 3 Giff. 629.

[224] *Russell v East Anglian Ry*, n.179, above.

[225] *Russell v East Anglian Ry*, n.179, above.

he or she is not before the court, this cannot be done, and the enforcement officer may come to the court for protection.[226]

The court may empower a claimant, who asserts a right against a receiver, to abate an obstruction. In such a case, the proper form of order is to give the claimant permission, notwithstanding the receivership, to pursue any remedies, or do any acts, that he or she may lawfully take or do to abate the obstruction.[227]

6-50   **Person, in the position of a receiver, appointed abroad.**   Before the English courts will recognise the status of a "receiver" appointed by a foreign court, they must be satisfied, in accordance with the English principles of conflict of laws, that the foreign court is one of competent jurisdiction.[228] They must, therefore, first be satisfied that there is a sufficient connection between the defendant and the jurisdiction in which the foreign receiver was appointed. There will be a sufficient connection, if the defendant submitted to the jurisdiction of the foreign court, in the proceedings in which the receiver was appointed.[229] But, if the defendant is a company, it is not sufficient that one of its subsidiary companies with assets in the foreign jurisdiction has appeared in the original action, in an attempt to have the original order set aside, and so submitted to the jurisdiction.[230]

It might, however, be sufficient if the defendant company had itself been incorporated under the laws of the country whose courts appointed the receiver, or of any state or territory thereof[231]; or, perhaps, although more debatably, if it could be demonstrated that, under the law of the country where it is in fact incorporated, the title of the foreign receiver would be recognised.[232] It might be sufficient if the defendant company had itself carried on business in the foreign country, or that the seat of its central management and control was located there.[233] This aspect of the jurisdiction may be affected, and extended, by the recast EU Regulation on Insolvency Proceedings and the Cross-Border Insolvency Regulations 2006.[234]

6-51   **Foreign creditors can always enforce claims in England.**   In any event, no order of a foreign court can destroy the rights of creditors of an English company to enforce their rights against the company under the laws of England. Hence, the English courts refused to recognise the title of a receiver, appointed by a United States court over the English subsidiary of a United States parent company, since the English company was registered and carried on business here, even though the English company had consented to the making of the order.[235]

In one case, the Securities and Exchange Commission of the United States obtained in proceedings in the American courts the appointment of a receiver over the assets of a holding company. By a further order of the court, their receiver was

---

[226] *Wilmer v Kidd* (1853) Seton, p.729.

[227] *Russell v East Anglian Ry*, n.179, above, at pp.120, 122.

[228] *Lane v Capsey* [1891] 3 Ch. 411.

[229] *Schemmer v Property Resources Ltd* [1975] Ch. 273 (under US law). See the valuable commentary on this case in *The Law of Receivers and Administrators of Companies*, Lightman & Moss, 4th edn (2007) at paras 32–016 to 32–019.

[230] See Dicey and Morris's *Conflict of Laws*, 11th edn, r.37 (Third Case), Vol.I, pp.436 ff; *Houlditch Donegall* (1834) 2 Cl. & Fin.470; *Schemmer v Property Resources Ltd*, n.229, above.

[231] See n.230, above, at 287F–G.

[232] See n.230, above, at 287G–H; *Macaulay v Guaranty Trust Co of New York* (1927) 44 T.L.R. 99; *North Australian Territory Co v Goldborough Mort & Co Ltd* (1889) 61 L.T. 716.

[233] *Schemmer v Property Resources Ltd*, n.229, above at p.287H.

[234] See Ch.28, below and n.230, above, cf. Dicey, above, r.37 (First Case).

[235] See n.236, below.

authorised to take proceedings in the United Kingdom to have himself appointed receiver of the assets of a subsidiary company of that holding company and its subsidiaries located in the United Kingdom. The receiver issued a writ against the defendant company (the subsidiary of the holding company), claiming the appointment of himself, or some other fit and proper person, as receiver, and suitable injunctions restraining the defendant and its subsidiary companies from parting with their liquid assets. The defendant subsidiary entered a conditional appearance to the writ, and moved for an order setting aside the order giving leave to serve outside the jurisdiction and staying all further proceedings in the action. The court, applying the above principles, granted the defendant company the relief it sought.[236]

If the appointment of the foreign "receiver" has been made by a court which, according to the principles of English conflict of laws, is a court of competent jurisdiction, the court may either recognise his or her title directly, by allowing him or her to sue for the assets over which he or she has been appointed receiver in his or her own name, or indirectly, by constituting a subsidiary receivership.[237]

The court will also recognise the right of a person, with powers analogous to those of a receiver, appointed by a foreign court of competent jurisdiction over the property of a person resident abroad, to give receipts for dividends on shares in a British company,[238] and to sue for a chose in action in his or her own name[239]; persons who unreasonably refuse to accept such receipts may be disallowed costs if an action is brought.[240] The *curateur* of a foreign bankrupt will be appointed receiver with power to sell immovables.[241] Where an order in aid was sought in the English Insolvency Court by the Viscount of Jersey, to enforce a Jersey administration of a debtor's estate *en désastre*, a receiver was appointed to get in the assets in England.[242]

Orders for transfer of assets abroad in the context of foreign proceedings. In a case where provisional liquidators were appointed by the English courts in relation to Australian insurance companies, the question arose as to whether, as requested by letters of request from the Australian court in which the companies were being wound up as principal liquidations, the English provisional liquidators should be ordered to remit to the Australian liquidators, assets collected by the English provisional liquidators after paying for the provisional liquidators' proper costs charges and expenses. The House of Lords[243] decided that the assets should be transmitted but for different reasons. Lord Hoffmann (with whom Lord Walker agreed) considered that the English courts have jurisdiction to remit assets abroad

6-52

[236] *Levy v International Resources Ltd* (1973) 117 S.J. 222 CA. *Schemmer v Property Resources Ltd*, n.229, above; see para.6-50, n.230, above.
[237] n.229, above, at 287E–F per Goulding J.
[238] *Lepage v San Paulo Coffee Estates Co* [1917] W.N. 216 (mandataire séquestre).
[239] *Macaulay v Guaranty Trust Co* [1927] W.N. 308; 44 T.L.R. 99.
[240] *Pélégrin v Coutts Co* [1915] 1 Ch. 696.
[241] *Re Kooperman* [1928] W.N. 101.
[242] *Re A Debtor (Order in Aid No.1 of 1979) Ex p. Viscount of the Royal Court of Jersey* [1981] Ch. 384: see also para.2-130, above.
[243] *HIH Casualty & General Insurance Ltd, McGrath v Riddell* [2008] UKHL 21; [2008] 1 W.L.R. 852. See also *Singularis Holdings Ltd v PricewaterhouseCoopers* [2015] A.C. 1675 where the common law power to assist a foreign court in overseas insolvency proceedings was held not to be exercisable where an equivalent order could not have been made by the court in which the foreign liquidation was proceeding; *New Cap Reinsurance Corp Ltd v Grant* [2011] EWHC 677 (Ch); *Rubin v Eurofinance SA* [2011] Ch. 133; *In the Matter Of Swissair, Schweizerische Luftverkehr-Aktiengesellschaft* (2009) [2009] EWHC 2099 Ch.

to be dealt with under the winding up laws of another jurisdiction, even if the distribution laws of that overseas liquidation varied from those of English law. It would be a question of discretion as to whether the variation was such as that the remission should be ordered. Lord Scott and Lord Neuberger considered that only s.426 conferred such a power. Lord Phillips agreed that s.426 conferred jurisdiction but decided it was unnecessary to resolve the wider issue dealt with by the other Law Lords—that is the position where s.426 did not apply because the overseas country in question is not designated for the purposes of that section. Leaving aside the question of jurisdiction, all of their Lordships agreed that as a matter of discretion it was appropriate to order that the assets be remitted.

6-53 **Action against receiver.** Nobody can bring an action against a receiver, in his or her capacity as such, without the permission of the court,[244] and if such action is brought without permission, its further prosecution will be restrained.[245] In general, a party to an action in which the receiver was appointed, may (like any other injured party) obtain any relief to which he or she is entitled against the receiver by applying in the action[246]; but there may be cases where, on such application being made, the court decides that the best course for disposing of the issue is for an action to be brought against the receiver. In such cases, it will give permission for the action to be brought.[247] Where, at the time when a receiver, by way of equitable execution, was appointed by the High Court, the debtor's property was legally, though not actually, in the possession of a receiver appointed by a county court having jurisdiction in bankruptcy, the equitable execution obtained by the judgment creditor was held to be ineffectual.[248]

A person who is not a party should apply by application notice in the action, for payment out of a fund in court, or by the receiver personally, of a debt due to him or her, where the receiver is personally liable for the debt and where it may be ultimately payable by subrogation out of the fund.[249]

6-54 **Effect of limitation acts.** The appointment of a receiver in an action will not prevent the operation of the Limitation Act 1980 against a rightful owner, who is out of possession and is not a party to the action,[250] nor will it interrupt the possession of a stranger, so as to prevent the statute from conferring a title on him or her.[251] Nor is a right to damages, which has already accrued, taken away by the appointment by consent, of a receiver.[252]

6-55 **Receiver not acting.** Where a receiver had been appointed at the instance of an

---

[244] *Re Maidstone Palace of Varieties Ltd* [1909] 2 Ch. 283; applied in *McGowan v Chadwick and Grant* [2001] EWCA. Civ 1758; [2003] B.P.I.R. 647, C.A.; see para.6-32, above.

[245] See n.244, above and n.208, above.

[246] *Searle v Choat* (1884) 25 Ch. D. 727. This applies to a receiver appointed in bankruptcy proceedings: see *Ex p. Cochrane* (1875) L.R. 20 Eq. 282; *Ex p. Day* [1883] 48 L.T. 912; [1883] W.N. 118. See, as to the insolvency jurisdiction of High Court and country courts, Insolvency Act 1986 ss.286, 287, and Insolvency Rules 2016 r.12.1 harmonising the 2016 Rules with the CPR 1998.

[247] *L.P. Arthur (Insurance) Ltd v Sisson* [1966] 1 W.L.R. 1384, explaining *Ex p. Day* n.244, above.

[248] *Salt v Cooper* (1880) 16 Ch. D. 544.

[249] *Re Earnest Hawkins & Co* (1915) 31 T.L.R. 247: the application was premature, as the receiver's account had not been taken. See also *Brocklebank v East London Ry* (1879) 12 Ch. D. 839; *Re Rylands Glass Co* (1905) 118 L.T.Jo. 87 (the report in 49 S.J. is not to be relied upon).

[250] *Harrison v Duignan* (1842) 2 Dr. & War. 295. cf. *Wrixon v Vize* (1842) 3 Dr. & War.123.

[251] *Groom v Blake* (1858) 6 Ir.C.L. 401; 8 Ir.C.L. 432. As to payment by a receiver taking the demand out of the Limitation Act, see para.7-46, below.

[252] *Dreyfus v Peruvian Guano Co* (1889) 42 Ch. D. 66; [1892] A.C. 166.

encumbrancer of a company, and no security was given and the receiver never acted, the action was stayed on the application of the Official Solicitor, on production of the company's consent.[253]

When sequestrators are in possession of land in question in an action, the appointment of a receiver of the rents and profits of the land will have the effect of discharging the sequestration.[254] Similarly, the appointment of a receiver in an action has been held to put an end to the power of a trustee appointed, for the benefit of creditors, to collect the rents.[255]

It is apprehended that if a receiver is appointed over the interest of tenant for life under the Settled Land Acts, the latter can exercise his or her statutory powers without the leave of the court.

COMPANIES

The general principles stated in the earlier part of this chapter, relative to the possession of a receiver, and the effect of the appointment, are equally applicable to receivers of the undertaking and property of a company. This section deals only with principles and decisions peculiarly applicable to such last-mentioned receivers: the early part of the chapter should be consulted on any points not mentioned in this section.

6-56

Representation of companies in court. The previous rules, requiring companies or other corporations to appear by counsel have been revoked. A company may now be represented at a hearing by an employee, who has been authorised to appear in court on its behalf, provided that the court gives permission.[256] Practice Direction 39A to CPR Pt 39 contains provisions dealing with companies appearing as litigants in person.[257]

6-57

Application for the court's permission may be obtained, on informal application made in advance, preferably to the judge who is to hear the case; but if that is not practicable or convenient, permission may be obtained from any judge by whom the case could be heard; notice need not be given to other parties. The judge who gives the permission should record it in writing, and supply a copy to the company, and to any other party who asks for one.[258] Permission should be given, unless there is some particular or sufficient reason why it should be withheld. The matters to be taken into account include the complexity of the issues, and the experience and position of the company's proposed representative.[259]

At any hearing, where a party which is a company is to be represented by an employee, a written statement shall be provided for the court, stating: (1) the full name of the company, as stated in its certificate of incorporation; (2) its registered number; (3) the position or office in the company held by the representative, and (4) the date on which, and the manner in which, the representative was authorised to act for the company, e.g. (date) written authority from managing director, or

---

[253] *Re Cornish Tin Lands Ltd* [1918] W.N. 377; costs ordered to be paid by plaintiff: "It was not for a receiver to be left in hand, on the chance that he might come in useful some day": Peterson J at 378.

[254] *Shaw v Wright* (1796) 3 Ves. 22, 24; *Reeves v Cox* (1849) 13 Ir.Eq.R. 247.

[255] *Donnel v White* (1865) 11 H.L.Cas. 570.

[256] CPR r.39.6.

[257] CPR PD 39A, para. 5.2 "Representation at hearings".

[258] CPR PD 39A, paras 5.4, 5.5.

[259] CPR PD 39A, para.5.3.

[date] Board resolution dated ...[260] The statement should presumably also include the copy of the judge's permission (see above).

A company may apply for permission to be assisted in court by the appointment of a "lay adviser" (often known as a "McKenzie friend").

6-58   **Nature of floating charge.** The appointment of a receiver, with or without powers of management, of the undertaking and property of a company, was previously most frequently made at the instance of debenture-holders or other persons having a floating security, with or without a specific charge on part of the property. The nature and effect of a floating security have been discussed at length in many cases: it may be shortly described as an equitable charge on the assets for the time being of a going concern, according to their varying condition, which remains dormant until the undertaking charged ceases to be a going concern, or until the person in whose favour the charge exists intervenes; this he or she may do, unless otherwise agreed, as soon as he or she pleases, after an agreed default event. As distinct from a specific charge, which fastens on definite or ascertained property, or property capable of being defined or ascertained, a floating charge is "ambulatory and hovers over the property until some event occurs, which causes it to settle and crystallise into a specific charge".[261]

So long as the charge remains floating, the company has a licence to deal with its business and all its assets in the ordinary course.[262] Accordingly, if it creates, in the ordinary course of business, an equitable interest in property in favour of a purchaser, by entering into a contract of sale, the subsequent appointment of a receiver on behalf of the holder of the floating charge will not prevent the purchaser obtaining specific performance of the contract of sale, if it would otherwise be a proper case for it to be granted.[263] But any "hiving-down" operation must respect the legal and equitable rights existing in and to the company's (or companies') property.[264] It conversely follows that the complete cessation by the company of its business (as, for example, as the result of a liquidation) will cause the charge to crystallise.[265] If the floating charge provides that such charge is to crystallise upon the giving of a notice by the debenture-holders, either in certain events or generally at any time, and whether in respect of all or part of the assets comprised in that notice, then the giving of a valid notice will have that precise effect.[266]

---

[260] CPR PD 39A, para.5.2.

[261] See per Lord Macnaghten in *Government Stock Co v Manila Ry* [1897] A.C. 81 at 86; *Illingworth v Houldsworth* [1904] A.C. 355; *De Beers Cons Mines Ltd v British South Africa Co* [1912] A.C. 52; *Re Standard Rotary Machine Co* (1906) 95 L.T. 829. For the extent to which the nature and existence of such a charge will be recognised in foreign jurisdictions, see Ch.24, below.

[262] *Re Standard Manufacturing Co* [1891] 1 Ch. 627 at 641 per Fry LJ; *Robson v Smith* [1895] 2 Ch. 118; *Re Crompton & Co Ltd* [1914] 1 Ch. 954; *Brunton v Electrical Engineering Corp* [1892] 1 Ch. 434; *George Barker (Transport) Ltd v Eynon* [1974] 1 W.L.R. 462.

[263] *Freevale Ltd v Metrostore (Holdings) Ltd* [1984] Ch. 199. It does not appear from the report that the sale was in the ordinary course of the company's business, nor that the debentures therein mentioned were secured only by a floating charge: but these incidents must follow, from the concession there made, that, apart from the appointment of a receiver, specific performance would undoubtedly have been granted. That decision was followed in *Ash and Newman Ltd v Creative Devices Technology Ltd* [1990] B.C.C. 97, based on a finding that the third party had acquired from the company an equitable interest in chattels, comparable to an equitable interest in land.

[264] *Telemetrix Plc v Modern Engineers of Bristol (Holdings) Plc* [1985] B.C.L.C. 213.

[265] *Re Crompton Co Ltd*, above, n.262.

[266] *Re Brightlife Ltd* [1987] Ch. 200.

A floating charge need not include all the assets[267]; but it must embrace both present and future property and, all property of a particular class,[268] which would, in the carrying on of the company's business, change from time to time.[269] So long as the charge remains floating, the company can not only deal with its business in the ordinary course, but can also, unless otherwise provided by the terms of the charge, create specific mortgages in priority to it,[270] and even if the creation of specific mortgages is forbidden, the specific mortgagee may have priority, if he or she takes without notice of the prohibition.[271] A charge, duly registered under ss.859A and 859H of the Companies Act 2006, even if taken with notice of an unregistered charge, enjoys priority.[272]

Crystallisation of floating charge. The appointment by the court of a receiver   **6-59**
over the whole or substantially the whole of a company's undertaking —who would almost invariably be an "administrative receiver"[273]—is one of the events which causes the floating charge to crystallise.[274] The order operates from the date when the appointment becomes effective.[275] The receiver becomes entitled to possession of the company's assets, and any interference with his or her possession is a contempt of court.[276] He or she takes, subject to all specific charges which have been validly created by the company in priority to the floating charge,[277] and to all rights of set-off acquired by debtors to the company in respect of dealings with it.[278]

But the title of the receiver prevails over that of execution creditors who have not completed their execution,[279] even though the debentures were not issued at the date of the execution, if there was a valid contract for their issue[280]; it is therefore good

---

[267] *Re Yorkshire Woolcombers' Assoc* [1903] 2 Ch. 284, affirmed, sub nom. *Illingworth v Houldsworth*, n.261, above.

[268] n.267, [1903] 2 Ch. 284 per Cozens-Hardy LJ.

[269] See n.267, at 295 per Romer LJ: see *National Provincial Bank of England v United Electric Theatres Ltd* [1916] 1 Ch. 132.

[270] *Re Colonial Trusts Corp* (1879) 15 Ch. D. 465; *Hamer v London City and Midland Bank* (1918) 118 L.T. 571.

[271] *Re Castell and Brown Ltd* [1898] 1 Ch. 315; *Re Valletort Sanitary Steam Laundry Co Ltd* [1903] 2 Ch. 654; see *Cox v Dublin Distillery* [1906] 1 I.R. 446.

[272] *Re Monolithic Building Co.* [1915] 1 Ch. 643, unless, of course, it is expressly made subject to the unregistered charge. That case was approved in *Midland Bank Trust Co Ltd v Green* [1918] A.C. 513; [1918] 1 All E.R. 153, HL.

[273] For the definition of "administrative receiver", see Insolvency Act 1986, s.29. As regards a different view, namely that the Court cannot appoint an administrative receiver as a matter of definition, see Lightman and Moss, *The Law of Administrators and Receivers of Companies*, 4th edn (2007), para.1–009(c).

[274] See *Robson v Smith* [1895] 2 Ch. 118; *Re Crompton Co. Ltd* [1914] 1 Ch. 954. As to when the appointment is made, above, Ch.2, ss.6 and 8.

[275] See para.6-1, above.

[276] See the earlier part of the chapter for these topics treated at length.

[277] As to what specific charges have priority, see above: debentures or charges issued before the appointment may be valid, even if issued after action brought, subject to the provisions of Insolvency Act 1986 ss.238–241, 244–246.

[278] *E. Nelson & Co v Faber* [1903] 2 K.B. 367; see also *Ex p. Peak Hill Goldfield Ltd* [1909] 1 K.B. 430. As to set-off in relation to transactions arising after the appointment of a manager, see para.9-13, below.

[279] *Re Opera Ltd* [1891] 3 Ch. 360; *Davey & Co v Williamson & Sons* [1898] 2 Q.B. 194; *Evans v Rival Granite Quarries* [1910] 2 K.B. 771.

[280] See *Simultaneous Colour Printing Co v Foweraker* [1901] 1 K.B. 771.

against a person who has obtained a third party debt order, either interim or final,[281] if the charge crystallises before actual payment.[282] The title of the receiver was held to prevail,[283] even over that of a creditor who had obtained a garnishee order absolute, before the debentures were issued to a person with notice of the order; but it is submitted that this case would not be followed.[284] Though the title of the receiver is good against an enforcement officer[285], where the execution has not been completed, the receiver cannot claim money paid in discharge or part discharge of the judgment creditor's debt, whether it is paid direct to the judgment creditor or to the enforcement officer to release the goods; he or she cannot claim such money in the hands of the enforcement officer,[286] nor can he or she claim money paid to the holder of the third party debt order, before crystallisation.[287]

6-60   **Property in the United Kingdom.**   A receiver appointed under the law of any part of the United Kingdom, in respect of the whole or part of any property or undertaking of a company, in consequence of the company having created a charge which, when created, was a floating charge, is entitled to exercise his or her powers in any other part of the United Kingdom, so far as their exercise is not inconsistent with the law applicable thereto.[288] Having regard to the wide powers which are automatically conferred upon a receiver under Scottish law (subject to their not being inconsistent with the instrument creating the charge),[289] such inconsistency is unlikely. The appointment will in Scotland be subject to:

(i)   the rights of persons who have effectually executed diligence (i.e. levied execution) on all or any part of the property of the company prior to the appointment of the receiver; and

(ii)   the right of any person who holds over all, or any part of, the property of the company, a fixed security or floating charge having priority over, or ranking *pari passu* with, the floating charge by virtue of which the receiver was appointed.[290]

There are no special problems in Northern Ireland, whose law closely follows English law.

---

[281] *Norton v Yates* [1906] 1 K.B. 112. This is the term for what used to be called "garnishee" orders, with "interim" replacing "nisi", and "final" replacing "absolute": see CPR 72 and PD 72.

[282] *Cairney v Back* [1906] 2 K.B. 746; see *Sinnott v Bowden* [1912] 2 Ch. 414.

[283] *Geisse v Taylor* [1905] 2 K.B. 658.

[284] For though a third party debt order creates no charge, it earmarks a debt to answer a particular claim, and prevents the creditor from assigning it, except subject to the third party debt order (see n.281, above). *Galbraith v Grimshaw* [1910] A.C. 508; see also, [1910] 1 K.B. 339 CA per Kennedy and Farwell LJJ: *Goetze v Aders* (1874) 2 Rettie 150.

[285] Previously known as a sheriff.

[286] *Robinson v Burnell's Vienna Bakery Co* [1904] 2 K.B. 624; *Heaton and Dugard v Cutting Bros* [1925] 1 K.B. 655. See, however, Insolvency Act 1986 s.184.

[287] *Robson v Smith* [1895] 2 Ch. 118.

[288] Insolvency Act 1896 s.72(1). "Receiver" here includes both a manager and a person who is appointed both receiver and manager: Insolvency Act 1986 s.72(2).

[289] Insolvency Act 1986 s.55 and Sch.2. By virtue of Sch.2 para.14, the receiver has power to carry on the business of the company—i.e. is a manager.

[290] Insolvency Act 1986 s.55(3).

Effect of winding up. By s.184(1), (2), of the Insolvency Act 1986, if notice is **6-61** served on an enforcement officer[291] that a provisional liquidator has been appointed or a resolution for winding up passed, before sale of the goods, or completion of the execution by receipt or recovery of the full amount of the levy,[292] the enforcement officer must deliver the goods, or any money seized or received in part satisfaction of the execution, to the liquidator, but the costs of the execution are a first charge on the goods or money so delivered. It is apprehended that the receiver's claim to the money or goods, if valid against the enforcement officer, would be unaffected.

Subsections (3) and (4) of s.184 (as amended) provide in effect that where, under an execution in respect of a judgment for more than £500,[293] goods of a company are sold or money paid to avoid sale, the enforcement officer is to retain the goods or money for 14 days, less costs of execution: if, within that time, notice is served on him or her of the presentation of a winding-up petition, or of the proposal of a resolution for winding up, which is followed by an order, or where the resolution is passed, the enforcement officer must pay the money to the liquidator, who may retain it against the execution creditor.[294] The concluding words of subs.(4) appear to leave the claim of the receiver for debenture-holders unaffected; the section may enable the receiver to establish his or her claim to the money against the liquidator, though he or she could not have done so against the execution creditor.[295] Finally, the rights conferred by those subsections upon the liquidator may be set aside by the court in favour of the creditor, to such an extent and subject to such terms as the court thinks fit.[296]

The debenture-holder's charge does not extend to an asset which does not form part of the company's property when the receiver is appointed, such as money recovered by the liquidator on the ground of voidable preference.[297] Nor does it extend to the proceeds of successful claims by the liquidator for "fraudulent trading", under s.213, or for "wrongful trading", under s.214; the sums so recovered are contributions to the company's assets.[298] But it does extend to money recovered from delinquent directors in misfeasance proceedings, under what is now s.212 of the Insolvency Act 1986.[299]

Fraudulent assignment. The holder of a floating charge may assert his or her **6-62**

---

[291] Formerly the sheriff.

[292] "Completion" means, in the case of goods, seizure and sale, or the making of a charging order under Charging Orders Act 1979 s.1; in the case of attachment, receipt of the debt; and in the case of land seizure, the appointment of a receiver, or the making of a charging order as aforesaid: Insolvency Act 1986 ss.183(3), 346(5). In the case of an equitable interest, it means the appointment of a receiver by way of equitable execution: *Re Overseas Aviation Engineering (GB) Ltd* [1963] Ch. 24, CA.

[293] The figure of £250 was increased to £500 by the Insolvency Proceedings (Monetary Limits) Order 1986 (SI 1986/1996) art.2 Sch. Pt II.

[294] See *Bluston and Bramley Ltd v Leigh* [1950] 2 K.B. 548, as to the form of notice required.

[295] See *Heaton and Dugard v Cutting Bros* [1925] 1 K.B. 655.

[296] Insolvency Act 1986 s.184(5), originally Companies Act 1948 s.326(3). See *Re Caribbean Products (Yam Importers) Ltd* [1966] Ch. 331 CA, and cases there discussed.

[297] Insolvency Act 1986 s.176ZB. For the previous case law which effectively reached this result see *Re Yagerphone Ltd* [1935] Ch. 392. As to voidable preferences, see now Insolvency Act 1986 s.239; *Peat v Gresham Trust* [1934] A.C. 252; and *Re M Kushler Ltd* [1943] Ch. 248 CA.

[298] Insolvency Act 1986 s.176ZB. For the earlier case law see *Re Anglo-Austrian, Printing etc. Co,* [1895] 2 Ch. 891; *Re Oasis Merchandizing Services Ltd* [1998] Ch. 170.

[299] *Re Produce Marketing Consortium Ltd* (1989) 5 B.C.C. 569; *Re Oasis Merchandizing Services Ltd,* n.298, above.

claim to property of which the company has disposed by a fraudulent transaction, if the assignee was a party to the fraud, since that would not be a dealing in the ordinary course of business.[300] But he or she cannot assert his or her claim to part only of the property comprised in his or her charge, before the whole security crystallises, and cannot therefore acquire priority, whether by giving notice to a debtor not to pay the debt to a third party debt claimant,[301] or by giving notice to trustees of a fund not to deal with it[302]; though the appointment of a receiver would have given priority in both these cases, by causing the charge to crystallise.

Where an assignment to the company is set aside as fraudulent, the receiver has no title against the trustee in bankruptcy of the assignor; and the trustee might apply in the action for permission to take possession of the property; but if he or she elects to treat the receiver as a trespasser, he or she cannot afterwards obtain an account of profits earned by the receiver.[303]

6-63 **Nature of possession of a receiver and effect on contracts.** The effect of the appointment of a receiver is to paralyse the powers of the company to deal with its property, so far as comprised in the charge under which he or she is appointed.[304] The legal persona of the company, however, still subsists, and its powers, in relation to the property comprised in the appointment, are delegated to the receiver by an appointment as manager, with whatever limitations may be imposed by the order[305]: the powers of the receiver in that event are discussed in Ch.9. The receiver is not prima facie of either the company or of the encumbrancers, but is an officer of the court exercising the company's powers as such, and as a principal.[306]

6-64 **Contracts of the company.** If the receiver is not also appointed manager, the contracts of the company involving work to be done or goods to be supplied by the company are terminated, since there is no longer any person in existence with power to carry those contracts into effect[307]; the other parties to such contracts may therefore claim damages for breach.[308]

6-65 **Contracts of employment.** There are certain contracts where the relationship is of a personal nature, such as contracts of employment, which are prima facie determined by the appointment by the court of a receiver, even though he or she is also appointed manager,[309] for the court's appointment changes the persona of the company as the employing authority. But where the appointment is of, or includes the appointment of, a manager or, a fortiori, of an administrative receiver, then the question of the subsequent "adoption" of current contracts of employment becomes highly material: see Ch.23, below.

---

[300] See *Williams v Quebrada Copper Co* [1895] 2 Ch. 751.
[301] *Evans v Rival Granite Quarries* [1910] 2 K.B. 979.
[302] *Re Ind. Coope & Co* [1911] 2 Ch. 223.
[303] *Re Simms* [1934] Ch. 1; a case of a receiver appointed out of court.
[304] *Moss SS Co v Whinney* [1912] A.C. 254 HL.
[305] *Parsons v Sovereign Bank of Canada* [1913] A.C. 160.
[306] See para.9-10, below.
[307] *Re Newdigate Colliery Co Ltd* [1912] 1 Ch. 468.
[308] See *Parsons v Sovereign Bank of Canada*, n.305, above; as to damages, see *Re Vic Mill Ltd* [1913] 1 Ch. 465.
[309] It seems that the only contracts of service definitely terminated by the appointment of the receiver are those of directors: *Parsons v Sovereign Bank of Canada* n.305, above; see also judgment of Moulton LJ in *Whinney v Moss SS Co* [1910] 2 K.B. 813: as to the position of directors, see *Welstead v Hadley*, (1906) 21 T.L.R. 165; *Measures Bros Ltd v Measures* [1910] 2 Ch. 248. See *Nokes v Doncaster Amalgamated Collieries* [1940] A.C. 1014.

The employee whose contract has been terminated by the appointment can claim damages for wrongful dismissal.[310] But if the receiver has continued to employ him or her at the same or increased wages for the residue of his or her term, the continuance in employment might amount to a waiver of the breach by the employee; but mere continuation in the service of the receiver does not necessarily waive the breach.[311] However, from the point of view of redundancy payments, if the employee is immediately re-engaged on the same terms by the receiver, then, for such purposes, the employment is regarded as continuous.[312] Moreover, if the receiver offers to renew the employee's contract of employment, or to re-engage him or her under a new contract of employment, but the employee refuses the offer, then he or she will not be entitled to a redundancy payment if he or she has unreasonably refused that offer.[313] And in considering whether he or she has unreasonably so refused, the fact that the receiver is now the employer in place of the former employer is not to be taken into account.[314]

There is a middle course between an employee continuing in his or her employment after the appointment of an administrative receiver, simply, as before the appointment, as an employee of the company, and being dismissed and re-engaged by the receiver. This is described in the Insolvency Act 1986, as the receiver "adopting" the contract of employment in the carrying out of his or her functions.[315] Although nothing done or omitted to be done within 14 days of the appointment will be sufficient to amount to "adoption",[316] if the receiver does "adopt" the contract he or she will thereafter be personally liable upon it, with entitlement to an indemnity out of the assets of the company to the extent of the "qualifying liabilities"; as prescribed by the Insolvency Act 1994; see Ch.23 below.

Direct re-engagement.   In cases of direct re-engagement by the receiver, or of **6-66** adoption by an administrative receiver, unless the receiver is able to transfer the undertaking, or part of the company's undertaking in which the employee is serving, to another person, or at the end of the day he is able to hand back its undertaking to the company as a going concern, he will, of course, be personally liable in respect of any redundancy payments which then fall to be made in respect of the employees,[317] with the usual right of recoupment of a proportion of such payments from the Secretary of State for Work and Pensions.[318] A covenant restricting

---

[310] *Measures Bros Ltd v Measures* n.309, above; and cf. *Re Gramophone Records Ltd* [1930] W.N. 42. If a new contract on equivalent terms with the receiver is implied, only nominal damages could be recovered: see *Brace v Calder* [1895] 2 Q.B. 261: see *Re English Joint Stock Bank* (1867) L.R. 3 Eq. 341; *Re Forster*, 19 L.R. Ir. 240, and cf. *Collier v Sunday Referee Co* [1940] 2 K.B. 647, as to the necessity for actual employment: as to quantum, cf. *Southern Foundries v Shirlaw* [1940] A.C. 701.

[311] See *Ex p. Pitt* [1923] 40 T.L.R 5.

[312] Employment Rights Act 1996 ss.182–190.

[313] See n.312, above.

[314] See n.312, above.

[315] Insolvency Act 1986 s.44(1)(b). Subject to interpretation by Insolvency Act 1986 s.44 subs.(2A), (2B) and (2C) inserted by Insolvency Act 1994 s.2. There is a similar provision in s.37 of the 1986 Act relating to receivers of a company's property who are not administrative receivers; but in this case, such a receiver has to be appointed under powers contained in an instrument.

[316] See n.315, above, s.44(2).

[317] See n.312, above.

[318] See Wages Act 1986 ss.27(1), (2), 32(2) and Sch.5 Pt. I.

the employee's employment after the termination of his employment cannot be enforced, when the appointment of a receiver has operated as a dismissal.[319]

6-67 **"Deemed insolvency" of company for certain purposes.** If an employer becomes insolvent, then, under the Employment Rights Act 1996, the employee himself,[320] and also the persons competent to act in respect of an occupational pension scheme or a personal pension scheme,[321] normally the trustees of the relevant scheme, have rights to be paid various sums by the Secretary of State for Work and Pensions out of the Redundancy Fund. For this purpose, "insolvency" is defined as happening not only when the company is wound up, whether compulsorily or voluntarily, but also where an administration order has been made,[322] or an administration appointment made,[323] or when a receiver or manager of its undertaking is duly appointed, or possession is taken, by or on behalf of the holders of any debentures secured by a floating charge, of any property of the company comprised in or subject to the charge, or a voluntary arrangement proposed for the purposes of Pt I of the Insolvency Act 1986, has been duly approved.[324]

As has already been noted, the appointment of the receiver will normally determine contracts of employment,[325] and in this case the right of the employee will crystallise on the appointment of the receiver. However, in a large number of cases the employee will be immediately re-engaged by the receiver, and in such cases the practical effect is that the employment will be terminated at some later date, and in such cases the rights of the employee crystallise at that date.

6-68 **The employment rights of the company's employees.** The rights under current legislation of the employees of companies in administration and under administrative receivership are complex and ongoing, and will not be further discussed in this work. Reference should be made to specialist works on employment protection legislation.[326]

6-69 **Third party insurance.** If the company is insured against liabilities to third parties and incurs any such liability, whether before or after the happening of any of the events hereinafter mentioned, then on the happening of any such event, its rights against the insurers under the contract are automatically transferred to and vested in the third party.[327]

The events are:

---

[319] *Measures Bros Ltd v Measures* [1910] 2 Ch. 248; see *General Bill Posting Co v Atkinson* [1909] A.C. 118.

[320] Employment Rights Act 1996 Pt 12.

[321] Pension Schemes Act 1993 Pt 7.

[322] Administration orders formerly made under Insolvency Act 1986 Pt II s.8; now, after the repeal of that Part, they are made under Insolvency Act 1986 Sch.B1 para.12: see also Ch.14, below.

[323] Under Insolvency Act 1986 Sch. B1 paras 14 and 22, see n.322, above and Ch.14, below.

[324] Insolvency Act 1986 s.4A.

[325] See para.6-63, above.

[326] See also Lightman and Moss, *The Law of Receivers and Administrators of Companies*, 4th edn (2007), Ch.26.

[327] Third Parties (Rights Against Insurers) Act 2010 s.1(1). The provisions of this Act are excluded, in the case of oil pollution by merchant shipping, by the Merchant Shipping Act 1995 s.165. The Act confers its own systems of rights against insurers.

(i)   a winding-up order or an administration order[328] or an administration appointment being made[329];

(ii)   a resolution for voluntary liquidation (otherwise than for the purposes of reconstruction or amalgamation) being passed;

(iii)   the appointment of a receiver or manager;

(iv)   possession being taken by or on behalf of debenture-holders of any property comprised in their floating charge; and

(v)   a voluntary arrangement, proposed for the purposes of Pt I of the Insolvency Act 1986 (as amended),[330] being approved under that part.[331]

It is correspondingly the duty of the liquidator, administrator, receiver or manager, or person in possession of the property, to give any person who claims that the company is under a liability to him or her such information as he or she may reasonably require for the purpose of ascertaining whether any rights have been so transferred to and vested in him or her, and for enforcing the same.[332] There appears to be not power to contract out of any of these provisions.[333]

Warranties given by a company on sale of its products to customers, and covered by insurance, are within the Act, so as to be enforceable by customers against the insurers directly.[334]

Petition to wind up. A debenture-holder who has brought an action to enforce **6-70** his or her security, and has obtained the appointment of a receiver, is not thereby precluded from presenting a petition to wind up the company.[335]

The appointment of a receiver, and payment into court of the proceeds of sale of property subject to the trusts of a debenture trust deed, do not necessarily determine the right of the trustees to remuneration and a lien therefor,[336] even though the trustees may have a specific power to appoint a receiver and delegate their powers to him or her.[337] The terms of the trust deed must be considered in each case.[338] The lien of a solicitor for trustees of a debenture trust deed has priority against the debenture-holders.[339]

Where two directors of a company, who were entitled to a share in certain sums payable for remuneration to the whole body of directors, had been appointed receivers and managers of the company's business, and had become entitled to remunera-

---

[328] See Ch.14, para.14-1, below.

[329] By Enterprise Act 2002 Sch.17 para.1(a), a reference in any pre-commencement instrument to the making of an administration order includes the appointment of an administrator under Insolvency Act 1986 Sch.B1 paras 14 and 22.

[330] See Ch.16, para.16-1 ff.

[331] See Third Parties (Rights against Insurers) Act 2010 Sch. 1.

[332] See n.331, above and Sch.3, para. 1A: The duty to give information correspond with the duty under CPR of parties to court proceedings in which an order for standard disclosure has been made.

[333] See n.332, above.

[334] *Re OT Computers Ltd* (2004) *The Times,* May 31, (CA) reversing [2003] All E.R. (D) 144, VC, applying *Tarbuck v Avon Insurance Ltd* [2001] 2 All E.R. 503.

[335] *Re Borough of Portsmouth Tramways Co* [1892] 2 Ch. 362.

[336] *Re Piccadilly Hotel Ltd* [1911] 2 Ch. 534.

[337] *Re British Cons Oil Corp* [1919] 2 Ch. 81.

[338] *Re Piccadilly Hotel Ltd*, n.336, above; *Re Anglo-Canadian Lands Ltd* [1918] 2 Ch. 287, distinguishing *Re Locke and Smith* [1914] 1 Ch. 687; *Re British Cons. Oil Corp*, above.

[339] *Re Dee Estates* [1911] 2 Ch. 85.

tion for so acting, it was held that they were nevertheless entitled to their remuneration as directors up to the date of a winding-up.[340]

The conduct of a debenture-holder's action may be taken from the claimant, if his or her interest in the subject-matter is adverse to that of other members of the class represented by him or her.[341]

---

[340] *Re South-Western of Venezuela Ry* [1902] 1 Ch. 701.
[341] *Re Services Club Estate Syndicate* [1930] 1 Ch. 78. See para.7-11, below.

CHAPTER 7

POWERS AND DUTIES OF A RECEIVER

The general duty of a receiver is to take possession of the estate, or other property, the subject-matter of dispute in the action, in the room or place of the owner thereof; and, under the sanction of the court, to do, as and when necessary, all such acts of ownership, in relation to the receipts of rents, compelling payment of them, management, letting lands and houses, and otherwise making the property productive, or collecting and realising it, for the benefit of the parties to be ultimately declared to be entitled thereto, as the owner could do if he or she were in possession.

It is the duty of a receiver, as soon as his or her appointment is effective or he or she is given leave to act, to require all tenants of freehold or leasehold property to pay their rents to the receiver, and, where the appointment is over the estate of a deceased person or the assets of a business or undertaking, to require all debtors to pay their debts to him or her. These topics, and the obligations of the receiver as to the application of money coming into his or her hands, are treated at length in this chapter.

Parties required to deliver up possession. Where parties to an action are directed by the order appointing a receiver to deliver up possession of such parts of the property as are in their holding, the receiver, as soon as his or her appointment is complete, should apply to them to deliver possession accordingly. If any of them refuse to do so, the receiver should report the refusal to the solicitor of the party having the conduct of the proceedings, who should then serve the refusing parties or party personally with the order directing possession to be delivered up.[1] A time within which the delivery of possession is to be made must be specified in the order, and the order must be indorsed in the manner prescribed by the CPR.[2]

If possession is still withheld from a receiver, application should be made, by application notice, for a writ of possession to put the receiver in possession pursuant to the order; the application should be supported by a witness statement verified by a statement of truth, or an affidavit, of service of the order, and of non-compliance.[3]

The writ may not be enforced unless a copy of it has been served on the person required to deliver up possession.[4] If thought fit, proceedings may be taken for contempt.

7-1

---

[1] *Green v Green* (1892) 2 Sim. 430.
[2] CPR rr.81.4 and 81.5; see, for the former procedure, see *Savage v Bentley* [1904] W.N. 89; 90 L.T. 641.
[3] CPR Pt 55, PD 55A, PD 55B and r.83.13. A writ of possession must be in Form 66 or 66A in PD 4, whichever is appropriate.
[4] *Savage v Bentley*, n.2, above. In the case of an order on a company, see CPR r.81.5 and also see *Benabo v Jay* [1941] Ch. 52; and *Iberian Trust v Founders Trust* [1932] 2 K.B. 87.

Where chattels are involved, a writ of delivery may be obtained.[5] A writ of delivery to recover the goods without alternative provision for recovery of the assessed value of those goods ("writ of specific delivery") may be used;[6] or alternatively a judgment or order for the delivery of any goods or payment of their assessed value may be enforced by for example a writ of delivery to recover the goods or their assessed value (or by order of the court, writ of specific delivery).[7]

If any party to the proceedings who is in possession of the property in question, or any part of it, is not ordered to deliver up possession to the receiver, he or she is not bound to do so; but he or she may be charged with an occupation rent for the property in his or her possession[8]; such occupation rent will be payable only from the date of demand of possession by the receiver, and not from the date of the order appointing the receiver.[9] A person in possession will not be ordered, on application before trial, to pay an occupation rent for a period antecedent to the order fixing the occupation rent.[10] If a party, e.g. a mortgagor, who has been ordered to deliver up possession to the receiver, offers to attorn tenant at an occupation rent with security, the direction of the court should be obtained before proceeding to enforce the order.[11]

7-2   If tenants in possession of real or leasehold estates, over which a receiver is appointed, are directed by the order to attorn to the receiver,[12] the receiver should, as soon as his or her appointment is complete, call on them to attorn accordingly.

The attornment to a receiver appointed by the court constitutes a tenancy by estoppel between the tenant and the receiver, which the court applies to the purposes of collecting and securing the rents until a judgment can be pronounced: the court takes care that the tenant shall be protected, both while the receiver continues to act, and also when, by the authority of the court, the receiver is withdrawn. The attornment creates a tenancy between the tenant and the receiver only, and does not enure for the benefit of the person who may ultimately be found to be entitled to the legal estate, so as to enable him or her to exercise the right of commercial rent arrears recovery (formerly the remedy of distress).[13]

If any tenant refuses to attorn to the receiver, the party prosecuting the order should serve him or her personally with a copy[14] of the order for the appointment of a receiver, and of the order or certificate completing the appointment,[15] and also with a notice in writing signed by the receiver, requiring him or her to attorn and pay.[16] If he or she still refuses to attorn, the tenant should be served with an application notice to attorn and pay within a limited time after service of the order to be made on the application.[17]

---

5   CPR r.83.14.
6   CPR r.83.14(1).
7   CPR r.83.14(2).
8   *Randfield v Randfield* (1861) 31 L.J. Ch. 113.
9   *Yorkshire Banking Co v Mullan* (1887) 35 Ch. D. 125.
10 *Lloyd v Mason* (1837) 2 My. & Cr 487, 488.
11 *Pratchett v Drew* [1924] 1 Ch. 280.
12 See para.6-10, above.
13 *Evans v Matthias* (1857) 7 E. & B. 590.
14 *Evans v Matthias* (1857) 7 E. & B. 510. For a case in which a tenant was not estopped by payment of rent to a receiver appointed under the statutory power, see *Serjeant v Nash, Field & Co* [1903] 2 K.B. 304.
15 See paras 5-39 and 5-30, above.
16 *Daniell's Chancery Practice*, 8th edn, p.1481.
17 For form of application notice and evidence, see CPR Pt 23 and PD 23A.

Tenant entitled to appear. The person served may appear to the application, and   **7-3** inform the court whether he or she is in possession as tenant or not.[18] If he or she does not appear, the order will be made upon proof by witness statement, or affidavit of service, of the application, orders, certificate, and notice to attorn, and proof by witness statement or affidavit of the refusal to attorn.[19] The order will be made without costs in cases where the tenant had reasonable grounds for refusing to attorn.[20]

A copy of the order, indorsed in the usual manner, is then served personally upon the person thereby directed to attorn.[21] If the person so served still refuses to attorn, a committal application for contempt may be made.[22]

Where the nature of the interest of a person, in possession of property over which a receiver has been appointed, does not clearly appear, it is not necessary to make him or her a party to the claim. The court will, upon allegation that he or she is a tenant, treat him or her as a tenant and require him or her to attorn, unless he or she can satisfy the court that he or she holds possession in some other character, and will fix him or her with an occupation rent.[23]

If a judgment creditor is in possession under a judgment, the court cannot order him or her to attorn.[24]

A solicitor to a party will be ordered to produce and deliver up to a receiver ap-   **7-4** pointed in an administration claim documents over which the solicitor has a lien for costs, on the ground that the solicitor has no higher right than his or her client to refuse production.[25] But the statutory provisions as to liens under the Insolvency Act 1986[26] have been held to protect, as against liquidators, a solicitor's lien for unpaid costs, exercisable over "documents which give a title to a property", which were held to include debentures, charges over land, a counterpart lease and share certificates.[27]

Rents in arrears. The receiver may obtain on application[28] an order for pay-   **7-5** ment of all arrears of rent due at the date of the appointment, even though the tenant may not have attorned: the tenant may be ordered to pay the costs of the application.[29] If the tenant pays rent due to a mortgagor before notice of the order, he or she will obtain a good receipt.[30]

---

[18]   *Reid v Middleton* (1823) T. & R. 455; *Hobhouse v Hollcombe* (1848) 2 De G. & Sm. 208.

[19]   *Daniell's Chancery Practice*, 8th edn, p.1481; *Hobson v Sherwood* (1854) 19 Beav. 575.

[20]   *Hobhouse v Hollcombe*, n.18, above. cf. *Hobson v Sherwood*, n.19 above.

[21]   *Daniell's Chancery Practice*, p.1481.

[22]   See CPR r.81.10.

[23]   *Reid v Middleton*, n.18 above.

[24]   *Davis v Duke of Marlborough* (1818) 2 Swans. 108.

[25]   *Re W Caudrey* (1910) 54 S.J. 444; following *Re Hawkes* (1898) 2 Ch. 1; and see *Re Rapid Road Transit Co* [1909] 1 Ch. 96; *Dessau v Peters, Rushton & Co* [1922] 1 Ch. 1, 5. As to the right of a receiver for debenture holders to money in the hands of a solicitor in respect of future costs, see *Re British Tea Table Co* (1909) 101 L.T. 707. As to position of a company director with regard to documents, see *Re Maville Hose* [1939] Ch. 32 (private examination).

[26]   Insolvency Act 1986 s.349(2).

[27]   *Re SEIL Finance Ltd (in liquidation)* [1992] B.C.C. 538, Morritt V-C (Lancaster); compare, in an administration case. *Euro-Commercial Leasing Ltd v Cartwright & Lewis* [1995] B.C.L.C. 618, where a solicitor's line, over his client company's funds, held on client's account, was held to prevail over the administrator's claim. See also *Withers LLP v Rybak* [2012] 1 W.L.R. 1748.

[28]   On notice to tenant: form, Atkin's *Court Forms*, Vol.33 (2011 Issue), para.237.

[29]   *Hobson v Sherwood* (1854) 19 Beav. 585; cf. *Re Potts* [1893] 1 Q.B. 648.

[30]   See further, para.6-10, above.

A person who admits a sum of money to be due from him or her to the estate cannot dispute the right of the receiver to collect it.[31]

Although a receiver is entitled to all arrears of rent as at the date of appointment, produce not converted into money, which has been separated from the estate before the date of the order, does not belong to the receiver over the land.[32]

7-6   **Duty of receiver to take proper receipts.**   When the order directs that the receiver shall keep down the interest of incumbrances, or make any other payments, he or she must, of course, comply with the order, and the sums so paid will be allowed in his or her accounts. The receiver must, however, take proper receipts from the persons to whom he or she makes the payments; for on any examination of the accounts, he or she will be subject to the rules to which all other accounting parties are subject, and accordingly will only be discharged if the accounts are in order.[33]

A receiver is only justified in paying to the person named in an order for payment, or on a power of attorney duly executed by that person. Express authority for payment in any other way must be shown by the receiver, on peril of being disallowed credit therefore on any examination of his or her accounts. A solicitor having the carriage of the proceedings has not as such, and in the absence of special authority, power to give a valid receipt for money ordered to be paid by a receiver to his or her client.[34]

7-7   **Distress (now the remedy of commercial rent arrears recovery).**   After a tenant has, by attorning to a receiver, created a tenancy between him and the receiver,[35] the receiver may distrain upon the tenant in his own name, without leave obtained from the court,[36] and may employ a bailiff for this purpose.[37] Before attornment, the receiver must distrain in the name of the person having the legal estate.[38] In *Brandon v Brandon*,[39] it was stated to be the practice for permission to distrain, without an order, for more than one year's arrears of rent. In that case, the motion was for the leave to distrain in the names of trustees in whom the legal estate was; apparently, if the tenant has attorned, the receiver may distrain without leave for all rent accrued due during the tenancy.[40]

At the instance of a purchaser who had been let into possession, a receiver was restrained from distraining for arrears of rent due from a former tenant, on the ground that receiver will not be permitted to utilise the legal estate so as to injure the person having the best title to it.[41]

---

[31] *Wood v Hitchings* (1840) 2 Beav. 289.
[32] *Codrington v Johnston* (1838) 1 Beav. 520. But the case is otherwise where the appointment, as in the case of a receiver for debenture holders, includes the whole of the assets.
[33] See CPR rr.69.8–69.11 and PD 69. See also *Daniell's Chancery Practice*, 8th edn, p.920.
[34] *Re Browne* (1886) 19 L.R. (Ir.) 132.
[35] See *Evans v Matthias* (1857) 7 E.B. 602.
[36] *Pitt v Snowden* (1752) 3 Atk. 750; *Bennett v Robins* (1832) 5 Car. & P. 379; see, too, *Morton v Woods* (1869) L.R 4 Q.B. 293. A receiver may employ a bailiff to make a distress: *Dancer v Hastings* (1826) 4 Bin.2, above. As to distress in cases where a receiver has been appointed by a mortgagee under the power conferred by Law of Property Act 1925, see para.19-20, below.
[37] *Birch v Oldis* (1837) Sau. & Sc. 146.
[38] *Hughes v Hughes* (1790) 3 Bro.C.C. 87; 1 Ves.Jun.161.
[39] (1821) 5 Madd. 473 per Leach MR.
[40] Where the arrears are of long standing, the receiver will be well advised to obtain a direction before distraining for the whole.
[41] *Re Powers* (1894) 39 W.R. 185.

Permission to exercise commercial rent arrears recovery (previously the remedy of distress).   Permission for the receiver to exercise the right to commercial rent arrears recovery ("CRAR" previously the remedy of distress) in the name of the person having the legal estate is obtained on application notice. If there is any doubt as to who has the legal right to the rent, the receiver should make an application to the court for directions;[42] but where there is no doubt as to who has the legal right to the rent, it is conceived that the leave of the court to exercise CRAR in the name of the person having the legal estate is not generally necessary.[43] Where, however, the person having the legal estate is a trustee, and objects to the exercise of CRAR, leave should be obtained, unless the objection is wholly unreasonable.[44]

7-8

Instead of applying that the receiver may have liberty to exercise CRAR in the name of the person having the legal estate, the receiver may obtain an order on application notice with notice to the tenants, for payment by the tenants notwithstanding that they may not have attorned,[45] or the receiver may apply that the tenants do attorn, and that CRAR may afterwards be exercised in his or her name. If the tenants oppose, on the ground of the pendency of a claim for the same rent commenced before the appointment of the receiver, the application may be ordered to stand over until the action has been tried.[46]

Where a receiver is appointed without prejudice to the rights of any prior incumbrancer, and, at the date of the order, an enforcement agent is in possession under CRAR, the landlord need not apply for permission to proceed with the CRAR.[47]

The abatement of an action in which a receiver has been appointed does not determine the appointment, nor suspend the receiver's authority to proceed against the tenants. The receiver's authority continues until an order is made for his or her removal.[48]

A receiver appointed, at the instance of the mortgagee, of an underlease was deemed to be "the landlord of the premises", within the meaning of that term in the now repealed s.1 of the Landlord and Tenant Act 1709 and, as such, was entitled to be paid by an execution creditor,[49] before the latter could proceed with his execution. It is likely that, as CRAR and the writ of control (used by most execution creditors) both use the same procedure, such primacy of the position of a landlord exercising CRAR would no longer be recognised. Whoever exercises their rights first, by seizure by enforcement agents, would have priority over the other.[50]

Where a receiver is appointed by the court to get in outstanding personal property,

7-9

---

[42] See CPR r.69.6 and PD 69, para.6.3. As to the form of order, see 1 Seton, 7th edn, p.763. The minute of the master is usually considered sufficient, without drawing up an order: *Daniell's Chancery Practice*, 8th edn, p.1487.

[43] *Pitt v Snowden* (1752) 3 Atk. 750; *Brandon v Brandon* (1821) 5 Madd. 473.

[44] *Della Cainea v Hayward* (1825) McClel. & Y. 272.

[45] *Hobson v Sherwood* (1854) 19 Beav. 575, para.7-1, above.

[46] *Hobson v Hollcombe* (1848) 2 De G. & Sm. 208.

[47] *Engel v South Metropolitan, etc. Co* (1891) W.N. 31 this authority may not survive the abolition of distress.

[48] *Newman v Mills* (1825) 1 Hog. 291; *Brennan v Kenny* (1852) 2 Ir. Ch. R. 282. For a case where a distress was rescued by a tenant, see *Fitzpatrick v Eyre* (1824) 1 Hog. 171.

[49] Semble, neither a receiver appointed over chattels in which the debtor had an equitable interest, nor the creditor, would be an execution creditor within the section: see *Norburn v Norburn* [1894] 1 Q.B. 448.

[50] See ss.71, 72 of, and Sch.12 to, the Tribunals, Courts and Enforcement Act 2007.

it is his or her duty to collect all that he or she can get in,[51] and to obtain directions for realisation.[52] A receiver of book debts was held to be obliged to give immediate notice of his appointment to the debtors, in order to take the debts out of the order and disposition of the creditor in the event of his becoming bankrupt.[53] A receiver for debenture-holders, whose debentures expressly or impliedly confer a power to create a charge in priority to the debentures, cannot obtain priority, in respect of a debt due to the company, over a person in whose favour a charge thereon has been created, and of whose charge he or she has knowledge, by giving prior notice to the debtor.[54]

An order appointing a receiver of outstanding personal estate generally contains a direction that the parties, in whose possession the same may be, shall deliver over to the receiver all securities in their possession for such outstanding personal estate, together with all books and papers relating thereto.[55] If parties, in whose hands such securities and papers are, refuse to deliver them up, the receiver should give notice of the refusal to the party conducting the proceedings, and the latter must take the necessary steps for enforcing the order.[56]

7-10   **Trust funds.**   Where the order does not describe the property, as for instance where the receiver is appointed generally over a trust fund invested in the names of trustees, it may be necessary to obtain a further order expressly referring to the property, to enable the receiver to obtain dividends or money payable on redemption of debentures: for a company does not have to have regard to equitable interests, and, apart from express order, only recognises the legal title of the trustees.

In the performance of his or her duties and the management of the estate generally, the receiver must have regard to the terms of the appointment. If he or she requires powers additional to those specifically given or implied thereby, he or she must obtain from the court permission to exercise such powers, as, for instance, power to carry on a business. Generally speaking, a receiver should not initiate or defend or compromise any proceedings, or do any other act liable to involve the estate in expenses, or liability; without obtaining specific authority,[57] which can be obtained on application notice supported by a witness statement or affidavit of the relevant facts.[58] If an agent for sale is appointed by a receiver without leave of the court, the court in its discretion may make him or her an allowance, even though he or she is not entitled to a commission.[59]

7-11   **Applications in respect of the estate.**   All applications to the court in respect of estates in the hands of a receiver should, as a general rule, be made by or on behalf of persons beneficially interested in the estate, and not by the receiver. The receiver

---

51   See para.7-2, above as to means of obtaining possession.
52   As to sale by receiver, see paras 7-48 ff, below; and as to the power of a receiver, appointed to wind up an Irish Loan Society, to compromise claims, see *O'Reilly v Connor* [1904] 2 Ir.R. 601.
53   *Rutter v Everett* [1895] 2 Ch. 872; *Re Neal* [1914] 1 K.B. 910. The "order and disposition" clause of Bankruptcy Act 1914 s.38, was abolished by Insolvency Act 1986.
54   *Re Ind Coope & Co; Fisher v The Company* [1911] 2 Ch. 223.
55   1 Seton, 7th edn, p.725.
56   *Daniell's Chancery Practice*, 8th edn, p.1481.
57   *Daniell's Chancery Practice*, n.56, above. The court will not empower a receiver to sue, unless it appears likely that some fruits may be derived from his doing so: *Dacie v John* (1824) McClel. 575.
58   See Atkin's *Court Forms*, Vol.33 (2011 Issue), para.235; take proceedings, para.235; defend proceedings, para.235; carry on business, para.235; pay debts, para.235; borrow, para.235; carry out repairs, para.235; and to grant of leases, para.235, for which also see para.7-19, below.
59   *Re National Flying Services* [1936] Ch. 271.

ought not, generally, to originate any proceedings in the action.[60] The conduct of the action is not nowadays given to a receiver,[61] and may be taken from the claimant, if his or her interest is adverse to other members of a class, e.g. of debenture-holders, whom he or she represents.[62] If, owing to any difficulty, an application to the court becomes necessary, the receiver should apply in the first instance to the party having the carriage of the order,[63] or if necessary, to any other party, to make the necessary application. If, after he or she has done so, no application is made, and no proper means are taken to relieve the receiver from his or her difficulty, or if the matter is so urgent that the purpose of the application would be defeated by any delay caused in applying to the parties,[64] he or she may apply and would be entitled to his or her costs.[65] Where a receiver had incurred costs in the execution of his duties, and the parties to the action had for a long time neglected to provide for them, he was able himself to apply by application notice for payment.[66]

The solicitor for the party having the conduct of the action should exercise a general supervision over the receiver, and protect the estate against irregularities by him or her; failure to do so may prevent the claimant from applying for recoupment out of the fund of expenditure rendered necessary by the irregularity.[67] **7-12**

Party receiver. Where a party to an action is appointed receiver, he or she is entitled to apply to the court as freely as if he or she were not holding that office.[68] **7-13**

Right to sue. A receiver acquires no right of action by virtue of his or her appointment: the receiver cannot sue in his or her own as receiver, e.g. for debts due to a company, or to parties over whose assets the receiver has been appointed; nor can the court authorise the receiver to do so.[69] In such cases, the receiver must maintain the claim in the name of the person or persons who would be entitled to sue[70] apart from the appointment.[71] A receiver may, however, acquire a right of action to sue in his or her own name: for instance, as the holder of a bill of exchange[72]; or as the assignee of a debt which has been actually assigned to the receiver; or by virtue of the receiver's possession,[73] as, for instance, to recover goods which have been in his or her possession, or to restrain the cutting off of a **7-14**

---

[60] *Miller v Elkins* (1825) 3 L.F. (o.s.) Ch. 128; *Parker v Dunn* (1845) 8 Beav. 497; Ex p. Cooper (1887) 6 Ch. D. 255. If the receiver of an estate proves a debt, without leave, against the estate of a bankrupt legatee, a debtor to the estate, he or she thereby discharges the debt, and entitles the legatee, on the annulment of his or her bankruptcy, to his or her legacy: *Armstrong v Armstrong* (1871) L.R. 12 Eq. 614.

[61] *Re Hopkins* (1881) 19 Ch. D. 61.

[62] *Re Services Club Estate Syndicate* [1903] 1 Ch. 78.

[63] *Windschuegel v Irish Polishes Ltd* [1914] 1 Ir.R. 33.

[64] cf. *Nangle v Lord Fingal* (1824) 1 Hog. 142.

[65] *Ireland v Eade* (1844) 7 Beav. 55; *Parker v Dunn*, n.60, above and see *Brenner v Rose* [1973] 1 W.L.R. 443, where the receiver applied by summons for directions in relation to an underlease.

[66] *Ireland v Eade*, n.65, above.

[67] *Craig v Att.-Gen.* [1926] N. Ir. 218.

[68] *Scott v Platel* (1847) 2 Ph. 229, 230.

[69] *Ex p. Sacker* (1888) 22 Q.B.D. 179; *Rodriguez v Speyer Bros.* [1919] A.C. 59, 75, 112.

[70] It must be remembered, that in partnership cases, one partner cannot sue or be sued in the name of the firm: *Meyer & Co v Faber* [1923] 2 Ch. 421.

[71] *Rodriguez v Speyer Bros* n.69, where the dicta to the contrary in *Rombach v Gent* (1915) 84 L.J.K.B. 1558, were criticised.

[72] *Ex p. Harris* (1876) 2 Ch. D. 423, explained in *Ex p. Sacker* (1888) 22 Q.B.D. 179.

[73] *Ex p. Sacker*, n.72, above.

supply of electric power to an hotel of which the receiver is in possession.[74] In all these cases, the receiver acquires a right of action in the court of his or her receivership, but not in consequence of it alone.[75] So, also, a receiver can sue in his or her own name on contracts under which he or she has contracted as principal, e.g. in carrying on a business.[76] As the receiver does not bring proceedings in his or her own name he or she may become the subject of an application for a third party costs order.[77]

7-15   **Receiver as petitioning creditor in bankruptcy.**   A receiver, is, on similar principles, a good petitioning creditor in respect of a judgment debt which has been assigned to him or her, although when received it would fall to be dealt with in the claim in which the receiver has been appointed[78]; but not in respect of specific sums ordered to be paid to him or her as receiver by a defendant, since he or she could not sue at law or in equity for such sums.[79]

7-16   **Claim by receiver of mortgaged property.**   After a receiver has been appointed by the court at the instance of a mortgagee, the court may direct such proceedings as it considers proper to be commenced or carried on by the receiver, at the expense of the mortgaged property; neither the mortgagor not the mortgagee has an absolute right to insist on, or to object to, an action being brought. Thus, in one case a company had commenced an action against its first mortgagees and a purchaser from them, to set aside as fraudulent a sale by the former to the latter. The purchaser, having subsequently acquired the interest of a holder of debentures for £10,000 in the company, commenced in his own name a debenture-holder's action against the company, and obtained the appointment of a receiver therein. The court, on the application of the company, ordered the receiver to carry on proceedings in the first action, upon the terms that his costs should be a first charge on the company's assets, notwithstanding the protest of the plaintiff in the second action (who was the purchaser's nominee) that assets over which the purchaser had, in effect, a first charge would be used to support a claim against him in another capacity.[80]

As has been already pointed out, if the receiver desires to bring an action, leave must be obtained, and the application is not made by the receiver but by a party.[81] The application is by application notice.[82] Permission to defend, compromise, or discontinue an action must be obtained in the same way. If the cause of action is one vested in the receiver personally, or if an action is brought against him or her personally, although he or she can sue or defend without permission, this will be at his or her own risk as to costs; he or she should therefore obtain permission.

Where it becomes necessary for the receiver to obtain permission to sue in the name of a third person such as a liquidator or a trustee in bankruptcy, he or she will

---

[74] *Husey v London Electric Supply Corp* [1902] 1 Ch. 411.
[75] Ex p. *Sacker*, n.72, above.
[76] See *Moss SS. Co v Whinney* [1912] A.C. 254.
[77] *Mills v Birchall* [2008] EWCA Civ 385; [2008] B.P.I.R. 607.
[78] *Re Macoun* [1904] 2 K.B. 700.
[79] Ex p. *Sacker*, n.72 above; cf. *Re North Bucks Furniture Depositories* [1939] Ch. 690, where a local authority, whose only specific remedy to recover rates was by distress, was held competent to petition for winding-up.
[80] *Viola v Anglo-American Cold Storage Co* [1912] 2 Ch. 305.
[81] See *Ward v Swift* (1848) 6 Hare 309.
[82] See Atkin's *Court Forms*, Vol.33 (2011 Issue), para.[235].

only be allowed to do so on giving the latter a complete indemnity, not one limited to assets in the hands of the receiver.[83]

Where a receiver is appointed to manage a partnership concern, he or she must **7-17** be guided by the terms of the order of appointment, keeping in mind the general maxim that, as his or her authority flows from the court, he or she must, in every case not covered by the terms of the order, act under a special order to be obtained from the court.

The court, by appointing a partner to be a receiver, protects his or her operations, and gives the receiver power to have recourse to the court for assistance and advice; but it does not enable the receiver to do anything, as against his or her partner, which the existing conventions or agreements between the parties do not justify.[84] The court has no power to clothe a receiver with an authority which would wholly transcend the nature of the original arrangement between the partners.[85] A partner appointed receiver is, like other receivers, an officer of the court and must act accordingly.[86] It is the duty of a partner to give such information to the receiver as may be necessary to enable him or her to collect the assets,[87] broadly corresponding to discovery in the claim. It is conceived that this duty could not be cut down by any provisions in the arrangements between the partners.

Where there was a conflict of interest between the receiver and the separate estate of a partner, whose trustee in bankruptcy the plaintiff was, it was held that the receiver ought not to be represented by the claimant's solicitor, but by the solicitor for the defendant.[88]

Other cases. It is not only in the case of a partnership, that it may become neces- **7-18** sary for the receiver to be advised by a separate, legal adviser, in order that he or she may hold an even hand between the various parties interested.[89] But the mere fact that the receiver consults a solicitor who is also a party, provided the advice is properly sought and properly given, does not necessarily invalidate a transaction with regard to which the advice is given, as against other parties.[90] If the receiver desires to employ a separate legal adviser, except in the matter of vouching the receiver's own accounts,[91] he or she should obtain the leave of the court, on his or her own application if necessary.[92]

That the receiver appointed in an action should be made a party to proceedings in it, is in some cases necessary. Thus, if the receiver pays money to the claimant's solicitors who are also his or her own solicitors, without any previous instructions as to the specific application of the money, it will be considered to be paid to them as the solicitors not of the claimant but of the receiver, and the receiver must be

---

[83] *Re Grenfell* [1915] H.B.R. 74; *Harrison v St Etienne Brewery Co* [1893] W.N. 108; *Re Westminster Syndicate*, 99 *L.T.* 924.

[84] *Nieman v Nieman* (1889) 43 Ch. D. 198.

[85] See n.84 above per Bowen LJ at p.205.

[86] See *Davy v Scarth* [1906] 1 Ch. 55.

[87] See *Ray v Ellis* (1912) 56 S.J. 724, where the application for a direction to the plaintiff to assist in preparing bills of costs due to a solicitor's business was refused in the circumstances: *Parsons v Mather & Platt Ltd* (1974) 9 December, CA, Appeal Court Judgments (Civil Division), No.392A.

[88] *Bloomer v Curie* (1907) 51 S.J. 277.

[89] See, e.g. *Viola v Anglo-American Cold Storage Co* [1912] 2 Ch. 305.

[90] See *Re Rogerstone Brick, etc. Co* [1919] 1 Ch. 110.

[91] As to which, see paras 11-1 ff, below.

[92] See para.7-17, above.

made a party to an application for payment into court of the money by the solicitors.[93]

7-19   **Power to lease.**   A direction to set and let is not now inserted in an order appointing a receiver over real or leasehold estate,[94] the judge, having power to give any direction in chambers as to the management of the estate,[95] however, in special circumstances, the order may include a direction for the granting of a specific lease, or the power to grant a class of tenancies.

A receiver cannot, without the sanction of the court, set or let even for a single year; the Court of Appeal has laid it down that no valid lease can be made by a receiver, without the sanction of the court.[96] The court can, however, give a general authority to let, or approve any lease which it considers necessary for the protection of, or making fruitful, the property over which a receiver is appointed,[97] even after the letting has in fact begun.[98] But even where the receiver is also appointed manager, he or she should still obtain the sanction of the court to a proposed lease. The duty of a receiver appointed to receive rents and profits of leasehold property includes the serving in due time, in accordance with the leases, of rent review notices, in order to maximise the obtainable return; failure to do so exposes the receiver to a claim for damages for negligence.[99]

7-20   **A Lease binding by estoppel only.**   If a receiver grants a lease without sanction, then as between the receiver and the person who takes the lease, the lease will be binding by estoppel.[100] As between the lessee, however, and the owner of the legal estate, the lease has, in the absence of special circumstances, no binding force, even though it may have been made with the sanction of the judge.[101] The powers of the receiver are limited to receiving proposals and making arrangements as to the leasing of the property over which he or she has been appointed receiver.[102] He or she has no power, by a lease made in his or her own name, to transfer the legal estate in the property, nor can such a power be given by the judge.[103] Leases should be granted in the name of the estate owner. Leases by a mortgagor or mortgagee, or under the Settled Land Act 1925 or other statute, may be granted in the name of the estate owner, by the person empowered to grant the same, whether he or she is the

---

[93] *Chater v Maclean* (1855) 1 Jur. (n.s.) 175; see, too, *Dixon v Wilkinson* (1859) 4 Drew. 614; 4 D. & J. 501; *Ind Coope v Kidd* (1894) 63 L.J.Q.B. 726.

[94] Under the former practice, a direction to let was included in the order: see *Thornhill v Thornhill* (1845) 14 Sim. 600.

[95] 1 Seton, 7th edn, p.725.

[96] *Wynn v Lord Newborough* (1797) 1 Ves. 164.

[97] *Anon.*, cited *arguendo* in *Stamford, etc. Banking Co v Keeble* [1913] 2 Ch. 96; *Re Cripps* [1946] Ch. 265; and see *Durnford v Lane* (1806) 2 Madd. Ch. Pr. (3rd edn) 302. Quaere, whether a receiver and manager of a land company could properly grant leases without express leave, where such grants were in the course of the ordinary business of the company: it is considered that a direction should be obtained.

[98] *Re Cripps*, above, n.97.

[99] *Knight v Lawrence* [1991] B.C.C. 411, VC the receiver appointed by a mortgagee had failed to serve rent review notices provided for by the leases, thereby falling below the standard of care required of receivers, which was owed to all persons interested in the property, and was held liable in damages.

[100] *Dancer v Hastings* (1826) 4 Bing. 2; 12 Moo. 34.

[101] See below.

[102] See *Gibbins v Howell* (1818) 3 Madd. 469; *Evans v Matthias* (1857) 7 E. & B. 602.

[103] Though he or she may be authorised to execute in the name of the estate owner, if a party.

estate owner or not.[104] The lease may be authorised to be executed by the receiver in the name of the property party.

A receiver should apply for liberty to re-let, before an existing lease expires and the property becomes vacant. If he or she neglects to do so, he or she may be visited with any loss which may arise.[105]

Where the court directs a receiver to give any person the option of being tenant of some particular item of property, it will generally reserve power to the receiver to inspect the state and condition of the property.[106]

In cases where the estate over which a receiver is appointed is out of the jurisdiction, it is usual to give the receiver more extensive powers of managing and letting than is usual in the case of estates situated in this country,[107] though in the latter case a general direction, so as to avoid numerous applications, is usually given readily. A reference to the master may be directed to inquire what should be the term, beyond which the receiver should not be permitted to let.[108]   **7-21**

A receiver must let the estate, over which he or she is acting as receiver, to the best advantage, and is bound to obtain the best terms.[109] He or she may not, either in his or her own name or through the medium of a trustee,[110] become tenant of any part of the estate over which he or she is acting as receiver.[111] He or she cannot raise the rents on slight grounds without the permission of the court,[112] not can he or she abate the rents, or forgive the tenants their arrears, without permission or the consent of all parties beneficially interested.[113]

Mode in which proposals for leases are dealt with. Applications with reference to property under the management of a receiver are made by application notice in private; proposals for the management and letting of the property may be made by any party interested.   **7-22**

Where a specific lease is to be sanctioned, the proposed tenant enters into a provisional agreement to become tenant or lessee of it, upon terms specified in the agreement, subject to the approval of the judge. An application notice for an order to carry the agreement into effect is then taken out by the claimant's solicitor and served on the parties interested. The application is supported by the production of the agreement and the witness statement, or affidavit, of a land agent or other competent person, stating the grounds on which, in his or her judgment, the agreement should be adopted. The power of a party to demise on the terms specified should also be shown by proper written evidence.

It is convenient to schedule the form of lease to the agreement, in which case no further order is required. Otherwise, on approval of the original agreement, either an order is made directing it to be carried into effect, and that the lease to be granted in pursuance thereof be settled by the judge, either absolutely, or in case the par-

---

[104] Law of Property Act 1925 s.8.
[105] *Wilkins v Lynch* (1823) 2 Moll. 499. As to liability in damages for negligence, see para.7-19, above, n.99.
[106] *Baylies v Baylies* (1844) 1 Coll. 545.
[107] *Morris v Elme* (1790) 1 Ves. Jun. 139.
[108] *Anon. v Lindsay* (1808) 15 Ves. 91.
[109] *Wynne v Lord Newborough* (1797) 1 Ves. 164
[110] See also para.7-48, below.
[111] *Meagher v O'Shaughnessy* (1826) cited Fl. & K. 207, 224; see, too, *Anderson v Anderson* (1846) 9 Ir. Eq. R. 23; *Eyre v M'Donnell* (1864) 15 Ir. Ch. R. 534. cf. *King v O'Brien* (1866) 15 L.T. 23.
[112] *Wynne v Lord Newborough* (1797) 1 Vest. 164; *Alven v Bond* (1841) Fl. & K. 196, 223.
[113] *Evans v Taylor* (1837) Sau. & Sc. 681.

ties differ; or, to save expense, the master indorses a minute of the approval on the application notice, and adjourns the matter until the draft lease has been brought in for approval. Upon the draft lease, or a certified copy of the order (if any) approving the agreement, being left at chambers, an application notice is taken out to settle the draft lease[114]; or, if no order has been drawn up, an appointment for this purpose is given. The application notice, or notice of the appointment, is then served on the parties interested. The application draft lease is then settled by the master, with the assistance, if necessary, of one of the conveyancing counsel, and is then engrossed in duplicate, and an affidavit is made, verifying the engrossment of the lease, and that of the counterpart, as being each a true and correct transcript of the draft as settled. A copy of this affidavit is left at chambers with the engrossments and draft.

The master then signs a memorandum of allowance in the margin of each engrossment, and issues the certificate of the result of the proceeding, which is completed in the usual way; or, if an order approving the agreement has been drawn up, an order is made approving the agreement and the lease. Where, as is often the case, the draft lease is settled in private, before an order approving the agreement has been drawn up, the order may include an approval of the engrossments, thereby saving the expense of a certificate, which, indeed, is often dispensed with, the master's memorandum of allowance, in the margins of the engrossments, being deemed sufficient evidence of the fact of the lease having been settled by the judge.[115]

Where, however, the property is shown to be most advantageously let on a number of weekly or quarterly, or even yearly tenancies, a general authority would be given, with limitations as to terms and rent.[116]

7-23   If the person who has agreed to take the lease wishes to rescind the contract, the correct course for that person is to apply to the court which sanctioned the contract for his or her release.[117]

7-24   **Power of receiver to give notice to quit.**   A receiver appointed by the court over lands, with a general authority to let the lands from year to year, has thereby an implied authority to determine such tenancies by regular notices to quit.[118] If a tenant holds over, after regular notice to quit given to him or her by a receiver, the court will give the receiver leave to sue the tenant for double the yearly value of the premises, under the Landlord and Tenant Act 1730 s.1.[119]

7-25   **Power to insure.**   A receiver of the rents and profits of real and leasehold estate may with propriety insure the property against damage by fire, either in his or her

---

[114] As to forms of application to approve of agreement to grant a lease, and of evidence in support, and form of application to settle a draft lease, see Atkin's *Court Forms*, Vol.33 (2011 Issue), para.235.

[115] As to form of evidence verifying engrossments of lease and counterpart, form of certificate of settlement of lease, and minutes of order approving an agreement and the lease to be issued in pursuance thereof, see *Daniell's Chancery Practice*, 8th edn, p.932.

[116] See *Anon. v Lindsay* (1808) 15 Ves. 91.

[117] *Grace v Boynton* (1877) 21 S.J. 631.

[118] *Doe v Read* (1810) 12 East. 57; *Crosbie v Barry* (1838) J. & C. 106; *Wilkinson v Colley* (1771) 5 Burr. 2694; *Jones v Phipps* (1868) L.R. 3 Q.B. 567. As to requirements of notices to quit, see *May v Borup* [1915] 1 K.B. 830; *Queen's Club, etc. Ltd v Bignell* [1924] 1 K.B. 117; *Dagger v Shepherd* [1946] K.B. 215; *Crate v Miller* [1947] K.B. 946 (date for which notice is given); and, as to agricultural tenancies, Agricultural Holdings Act 1986 ss.3, 25–33; cf. *Edell v Dulieu* [1924] A.C. 38.

[119] *Wilkinson v Colley*, n.118, above.

own name or in the names of trustees, and will be allowed in his or her accounts the premiums paid.[120]

A Rent review notices.   As to the duties of a receiver with respect to the giving of rent review notices: see para.7-17, above. **7-26**

Landlord and Tenant Acts 1927 and 1954.   A receiver of leasehold property should, in a proper case, procure an application to be made to the master for directions as to claiming compensation for improvements under Pt 1 of the Landlord and Tenant Act 1927; or a new lease under Pt 2 of the Landlord and Tenant Act 1954. The notice will be given on behalf of the tenant; an equitable chargee of the tenant, such as a debenture-holder, has a right to enforce the tenant's rights under the statute.[121] **7-27**

Anything authorised or required by the provisions of the Landlord and Tenant Act 1954, other than those relating to the supplying of information,[122] to be done at any time by, to or with the landlord, or a landlord of a specified description, is, if at that time the interest of the landlord is subject to a mortgage and a receiver has been appointed thereunder, authorised or required to be done by, to or with the mortgagee instead of that landlord.[123]

Miscellaneous notices.   Where a receiver of the landlord's interest has been served with any notices under these or any other Act (e.g. the Town and Country Planning Act 1990), he or she should at once cause an application to be made to the master by the claimant for directions. **7-28**

Power of receiver as to repairs.   A receiver appointed by the court may lay out small sums of money in customary repairs, or may allow the same to a tenant; but he or she may not apply money in repairs to any considerable extent without a previous application to the judge.[124] It was at one time a rule of the Court of Chancery that the receiver of an estate could not lay out money on it, without a previous order of the court.[125] The rule of the court is no longer so strict; a receiver may effect without permission small repairs estimated to cost not over £1,000[126] in any one accounting period. If the limit is exceeded, the master may allow the excess, if the receiver establishes (if necessary by means of an inquiry) that he or she has acted reasonably.[127] If the nature of the property is such that the normal expenditure is likely to be greater, application should be made by application notice for the limit to be increased in the particular case.[128] Where the receiver is appointed manager, he or she can, without permission expend money on such current repairs as are **7-29**

---

[120] *Re Graham* [1895] 1 Ch. 66, 71; as to employment of policy moneys in rebuilding, see *Sinnot v Bowden* [1912] 2 Ch. 414.

[121] *Gough Garages v Pugsley* [1930] 1 K.B. 615 (a decision under the 1927 Act).

[122] Under s.40(2) and (3).

[123] See s.67.

[124] *Waters v Taylor* (1808) 15 Ves. 10; *Ex p. Izard* (1883) 23 Ch. D. 75.

[125] *Tempest v Ord* (1816) 2 Mer. 55, 56.

[126] *Practice Direction*, 1 July 1985: see *Practice Direction (Chancery: Directions' Index) (No.1 of 1986)* [1987] 1 W.L.R.93.

[127] *Att.-Gen. v Vigor* (1805) 11 Ves. 563; *Tempest v Ord*, n.125, above; *Ex p. Izard*, n.124, above. cf. *Re Langham* (1837) 2 Ph. 299.

[128] *Practice Direction* [1970] 1 W.L.R. 520.

necessary for the purposes of the business. There is no need to stress here the potential liability upon a receiver who allows the premises to remain out of repair.[129]

If, from their extent, or the circumstances under which money for repairs is claimed, the receiver feels any difficulty in authorising them to be done, he or she should apply to the claimant's solicitor to obtain the sanction of the judge, which is obtained on application notice, supported by written evidence stating the nature and costs of the repairs and the reasons which lead to their being necessary: evidence by a surveyor may be required, if the repairs are extensive.[130]

7-30   If a receiver requires money to discharge his or her duties, the court will give him or her leave to borrow upon the security of the property in his or her hands. This power is most frequently exercised in the case of a receiver and manager appointed in debenture-holders claims.[131]

A receiver appointed under the previous mental health jurisdiction, who was plaintiff in an action relating to certain property of the patient, upon which were mortgages which the mortgagee was threatening to call in, was, on application being made in the action, authorised to borrow upon security of the patient's property sufficient money to pay a commission to a proposed transferee of the mortgages, as a consideration for his consenting to take the transfer.[132]

7-31   **Management of the estate.** An order may be obtained from the master authorising a receiver to cut and sell timber, and to employ it, if necessary, in repairs.[133] The court, before giving liberty to cut timber for repairs, may direct inquiries.[134] Where there is a receiver, a sale of timber is usually effected under his or her direction.[135] The receiver of an estate may obtain an order to grant a licence to win and get clay and brick earth on the estate, and to manufacture the same into bricks.[136] But the court has no jurisdiction, in a foreclosure action, to sanction the grant of a licence to work deposits of peat, which amount in effect to a sale of the surface by instalments, nor to sanction mining leases, other than such as are authorised by statute.[137]

An application by a person not a party to the action, for directions as to the management of real property by a receiver, may be made by application notice.[138]

7-32   **Estate of stranger.** Where the estate of a stranger has come into possession of the receiver in an action, and possession of it has been held by him or her with the acquiescence of such of the parties to the action as are not under disability, and without objection on behalf of any party under disability, the transaction is binding on all those parties; the stranger will be ordered to be compensated out of the fund in court in respect of any rents of the stranger's estate received by the receiver and not paid over to the stranger, and also in regard to any dilapidations during the receiver's possession, since the stranger has a right against the fund, by subroga-

---

[129] Consider *Solomons v Gertzenstein Ltd* [1954] 2 Q.B. 243.
[130] See 1 Seton, 7th edn, p.770; and, as to order giving the receiver liberty to spend money in repairs, *Seton*, 7th edn, p.765.
[131] See para.9-18, below where the matter is treated at length.
[132] *Chaplin v Barnett* (1911) 28 T.L.R. 256; this order was made under the former RSC Ord.29 r.2.
[133] 1 Seton, 7th edn, p.766.
[134] 1 Seton, 7th edn, p.770.
[135] 1 Seton, 7th edn, p.766.
[136] 1 Seton, 7th edn, p.766.
[137] *Stamford Banking Co v Keeble* [1913] 2 Ch. 96.
[138] *O'Hagan v North Wingfield Colliery Co* (1882) 26 S.J. 671; and see *Searle v Choat* (1884) 25 Ch. D. 723.

tion to the receiver's right of indemnity.[139] This may be ordered on the application of the stranger, although he or she be not a party to the action.[140]

Lessee committing waste.   After a receiver has been appointed, an injunction will   7-33
be granted on application notice to restrain a person, in possession under an agreement, from committing waste, though the latter is not a party to the action.[141]

Leaseholds generally.   As has already been pointed out, a receiver of leaseholds,   7-34
though not personally liable,[142] is bound in the first place, out of the sub-rents, to discharge the head-rent and outgoings payable to a lessor, for which the person whose estate is being dealt with by the court is actually liable to that lessor.

If, in consequence of the receiver's default, the head-lessor is compelled to institute proceedings for the recovery of the head-rent, the receiver is held liable for costs, if sub-rents have reached his or her hands. The sub-rents should be, in the first place, appropriated to the payment of the head-rent. If the receiver pursues a different course, and pays away sub-rents received without providing for the head-rent, choosing to speculate upon obtaining other funds wherewith to pay the latter, he or she does not act in accordance with the course of the court, and will be compelled by the court to pay personally any arrears of the head-rent.[143]

Leaseholds mortgaged by sub-demise.   But the above principle does not apply   7-35
where the receiver has been appointed at the instance of a mortgagee, between whom and the lessor or head-lessor there is no such privity as to make the mortgagee liable to pay rent or other outgoings to such lessor or head-lessor, as in the case of a mortgage by sub-demise or by way of legal or equitable charge[144]; the receiver there is not, any more than the mortgagee in whose right he or she was appointed, liable, whether in possession or not, to the lessor of head-lessor for rent or other outgoings. There is no equity entitling the lessor to claim rent, or damages for breach of (for instance) a repairing covenant in the lease, from the receiver by reason of his or her having occupied the mortgaged premises, even though he or she has, under an order of the court, sold off the mortgagor's goods and so in effect deprived the lessor of a remedy by CRAR (formerly distress): there is no principle of honour, honesty or justice requiring the court to interfere in such a case[145]; nor, if the receiver has sold the leaseholds, has the lessor any remedy against

---

[139] *Neate v Pink* (1851) 15 Sim. 450; explained in *Hand v Blow* (1901) 2 Ch. 721, 728: cf. *Brocklebank v East London Ry* (1879) 12 Ch. D. 839. Quaere, whether, if the fund remaining in court is insufficient, the stranger could recover from the parties into whose hands the money had come: see *Re Jones' Estates* [1914] 1 Ir.R. 188.

[140] *Neate v Pink* n.139, above.

[141] *Walton v Johnson* (1848) 15 Sim. 352; see, too, *Casamajor v Strode* (1823) 1 Sim. & St. 381.

[142] *Consolidated Entertainments Ltd v Taylor* [1937] 4 All E.R. 432.

[143] *Balfe v Blake* (1850) 1 Ir.Ch.R. 365; *Jacobs v Van Boolen* (1889) 34 S.J. 97. cf. *Re Mayfair and General Property Trust Ltd* (1945) 174 L.T. 1.

[144] In the case of sub-terms with a declaration of trust, subsisting at the commencement of Law of Property Act 1925, where the right of redemption was barred or the property had been sold, the head term vests in the mortgagee, unless he or she disclaims it before action: Law of Property Act 1925 Sch.I Pt III paras 3 and 7(a) and (m).

[145] *Hand v Blow* [1901] 2 Ch. 721. In *Neate v Pink* (1851) 15 Sim. 450, the court appears to have treated the relationship of landlord and tenant as subsisting in the circumstances between the lessor and the receiver, which thus gave the former a right by subrogation against the fund: see judgment of Stirling LJ in *Hand v Blow*, above. The receiver is not estopped by having paid one instalment of the rent:

the fund in court.[146] And the same principles apply to the use by the receiver of goods on hire to the mortgagor.[147]

But though payment of rent cannot be enforced against a receiver or the fund, where appointment is made, on the application of a mortgagee by sub-demise or an equitable incumbrancer, the receiver often needs to obtain permission to pay the rent in order to avoid CRAR (formerly distress) and safeguard goods on the premises. A receiver who has entered into a tenancy agreement is personally liable for the rent, and the lessor can claim against the fund by subrogation.[148]

7-36   If there is uncertainty as to the amount of rent due to the head-lessor, the receiver should cause an application to be made for directions; if he or she waits until the head-lessor makes an application on the subject, he or she may appear by his or her solicitor, state the facts, and have the court's order accordingly.

If the lessor has recovered judgment for possession, rent and mesne profits against the lessee, the lessor cannot recover rent from a person who is actually in possession, such as a receiver for debenture-holders of a company entitled in equity to the lease,[149] since the court will in a proper case direct its officer to do what is right and honourable.[150] Although it does not profess to cure all the inconveniences caused by the appointment of a receiver,[151] it will, it is submitted, not allow a receiver to retain rents from sub-tenants without paying a head-rent, even though there is no actual liability on the mortgagees to pay such a head-rent as between them and the head-lessor, since otherwise the sub-tenants would be exposed to CRAR (formerly distress) and forfeiture. In such a case, it seems, the head-rent would be ordered to be paid out of the funds,[152] if the receiver has elected to remain in possession and receive a profit rental under a lease, in respect of which the company was liable directly to the lessee, semble that the receiver will be ordered to pay to the lessor out of moneys in his or her hands the amount of dilapidations due on the determination of the lease, though the lessor may not be entitled as of right to such payment.[153]

7-37   **Abandonment of leaseholds.** Permission may be given to the receiver of a company to abandon unprofitable leaseholds, where neither the company nor the

---

Justice v James (1898) 15 T.L.R. 181.

[146] *Re JW Abbott & Co* [1913] W.N. 284; but, it is submitted, a reasonable sum in respect of the receiver's occupation would be paid to the lessor: see *Neate v Pink* n.57. cf. *Hay v Swedish, etc. Ry* (1889) 8 T.L.R. 775.

[147] *Hay v Swedish, etc. Ry*, n.146, above.

[148] See para.9-17, below.

[149] *Re Westminster Motor Garage Co* (1914) 84 L.J. Ch. 753. Debenture holders or trustees for debenture holders are not necessary parties to an action by the lessor involving forfeiture; they can by leave be added on terms, *Egerton v Jones* [1939] 2 K.B. 702.

[150] As to which, see *Hand v Blow*, n.145, above; *Re John Griffiths Cycle Corp.* [1902] W.N. 9 (refusal of application by successful appellants to House of Lords for receiver to pay money paid into court by him as security for costs of appeal to the Court of Appeal, and paid out to him, on appeal succeeding in the Court of Appeal); see also *Re Abdy* [1912] 2 K.B. 735; *Re Wigzell* [1921] 2 K.B. 835; *Scranton's Trustee v Pearse* [1922] 2 Ch. 87; *Re Savoy Estate Ltd* [1949] Ch. 622.

[151] Per Collins MR in *Hand v Blow*, n.145, above, and cases cited therein; *Re Levi* [1919] 1 Ch. 416: in most cases, the payment would be necessary to prevent forfeiture of a beneficial lease.

[152] See judgment of Stirling LJ in *Hand v Blow*, n.145, and cases cited therein; *Re Levi* n.151: in most cases, the payment would be necessary to prevent forfeiture of a beneficial lease.

[153] *Hand v Blow*, n.145, above; see *Re Levi*, n.151, above.

debenture-holders can benefit; the receiver may, however, be ordered to pay rent accrued due during the receiver's possession.[154]

Forfeiture of lease.   A mortgagee is not a necessary party to an action by a lessor against the lessee involving forfeiture, and if the mortgagee wishes to intervene he or she can be allowed to do so on terms[155]; it may sometimes be necessary for a receiver of leaseholds to obtain a direction as to applying for permission to intervene in such an action in the name of the mortgagee. Leave to serve a counter-notice under the Leasehold Property (Repairs) Act 1938, as amended,[156] may also be necessary.   **7-38**

Business Rates and Council Tax.   As local authorities normally have an adequate remedy by means of enforcement of liability orders (and indeed the potential threat of imprisonment for non-payment of council tax), a receiver will not in general be ordered to pay business rates or council, even if he or she has been receiving inclusive rentals from the tenants of the property.[157]   **7-39**

War Damage Act 1943.   For the position under this Act, see the 13th edn at pp.196–197 and the 17th edn at p.189.   **7-40**

Payment to avoid CRAR (formerly distress).   In the past, where a receiver for debenture-holders paid a debt due to the Crown to avoid distraint, it was held that he could not claim to be paid a sum, equal to the amount of the discharged debt, out of money, due from the Crown to the company, which had been assigned to third persons.[158] Such a decision would appear likely to apply to any payment made to avoid the exercise of CRAR or other enforcement action by the Crown.   **7-41**

Duty when tenants interfered with.   When the receiver is informed by tenants that defendants have interfered with the rents, it is his or her duty to move for a committal.[159] The interference of the owner of the inheritance with the rents does not exempt the receiver from being charged with the whole amount: in order to be discharged, the receiver must show what the owner of the inheritance received, or hindered the receiver from getting in.[160]   **7-42**

The receiver appointed in an action ought not to interfere in any litigation between the parties to it. If he does, he will not be allowed the costs of his intervention for such a purpose.[161]   **7-43**

Interest on incumbrances.   If a receiver is appointed at the instance of a puisne mortgagee or judgment creditor, it is no part of the receiver's duty without directions to apply any part of the rents in keeping down interest on prior   **7-44**

---

[154] cf. *Hay v Swedish, etc. Ry* (1889) 8 T.L.R. 775.

[155] *Egerton v Jones* [1939] 2 K.B. 702.

[156] See Landlord and Tenant Act 1954 s.51 and CPR r.56.2.

[157] *Re British Fuller's Earth Co* (1901) 17 T.L.R. 232; *Re Mayfair and General Property Trust Ltd* (1945) 174 L.T. 1. cf. *Tagg's Island Casino Co Ltd v Richmond LBC* (1967) R.A. 70.

[158] *Re Ind Coope & Co; Fisher v The Company* [1911] 2 Ch. 223; quaere, whether one debt could have been set off against the other before payment.

[159] *Anon.* (1829) 2 Moll. 499.

[160] *Hamilton v Lighton* (1810) 2 Moll. 499r.

[161] *Comyn v Smith* (1823) 1 Hog. 81.

incumbrances.[162] Where, however, the receiver is appointed over a trust estate, or in similar cases, and also where he or she is directed to keep down the interest on incumbrances, he or she ought, except under very special circumstances, so far as the rents and profits will go, pay them on account of the interest of the several incumbrancers in the order of their priority.[163] This rule applies where the receiver has been appointed over the interest of a tenant for life. He or she must keep down interest on incumbrances on the fee simple out of the rents.

7-45　**Trade fixtures.**　Trade machinery and fixtures,[164] a right to remove which belongs to a lessee as against the lessor, pass with the land to a mortgagee of the leasehold interest, who can sell them with the land, though he or she has no right to sever them from the land during the term; if, however, he or she severs and sells them apart from the land, they do not revest in the mortgagor, who has no right to the proceeds of sale, but only a possible claim for damages. Where, therefore, a receiver for debenture-holders had consented to a sale of the fixtures by a prior mortgagee, the debenture-holders had no claim to the proceeds of sale.[165] If the receiver of a business, carried on from leasehold premises during the term, sells machinery and plant, the tenant's right to which has been negatived by the terms of the lease, the landlord has a right to affirm the sale and recover the proceeds, without waiting for the end of the term.[166]

A mortgagee has a reasonable time to remove trade fixtures after the lease has determined. Therefore, where after the appointment of a receiver the lease was determined, under a proviso contained in it, by the lessee company going into voluntary liquidation, the receiver was entitled to a reasonable time for the sale on the premises and removal of the fixtures, notwithstanding a demand for immediate possession by the lessor.[167]

7-46　**Statute-barred debts.**　If a receiver has power to pay debts, he or she may pay an instalment of a debt, even though the effect of so doing may be to stop the Limitation Act 1980 from running.[168] But a payment made by a receiver, which is not authorised by the order of appointment, will not stop the statute from running[169]; nor, under the previous mental health regime would payment by a person administering the estate of a person of unsound mind, without an order appointing that person receiver.[170] A receiver must not pay statute-barred debts, if not specifi-

---

[162] A receiver appointed out of court must keep down interest on prior incumbrances: Law of Property Act 1925 s.109(8).

[163] See *Re Kearney* (1890) 25 L.R. Ir. 89.

[164] As to what are fixtures in the case of a theatre, see *Vaudeville Electric Cinema Co v Muriset* [1923] 2 Ch. 74.

[165] *Re Rogerstone Brick and Stone Co* [1919] 1 Ch. 110; the prior mortgage had been created with the express assent of the debenture holders, and it was considered that it would have been oppressive for the receiver to refuse his consent.

[166] *Re British Red Ash Collieries Ltd* [1920] 1 Ch. 326.

[167] *Re Glasdir Copper Works* [1904] 1 Ch. 819.

[168] *Re Hale, Lilley v Food* [1899] 2 Ch. 107; and see *Wandsworth Union v Worthington* [1906] 1 K.B. 420, where payment to guardians by a receiver, under an order in lunacy, of the income of the patient's estate (which was insufficient to discharge the sums due for maintenance) was held to take a claim for arrears of maintenance out of the statute.

[169] *Whitley v Lowe* (1858) 25 Beav. 421.

[170] *Re Beavan* [1912] 1 Ch. 196.

cally authorised to do so. If there is a doubt, the receiver should apply for directions.[171]

If a receiver, directed to keep down interest on a prior incumbrance, makes overpayments through a mistake of fact, such as ignorance of a proviso for a reduction of the rate on punctual payment, the person to whose prejudice the overpayments were made can recover them from the mortgagee, up to a period of six years before action.[172]

A receiver appointed on behalf of a mortgagee was held to be the "agent" of the mortgagor within the Real Property Limitation Act 1833 s.40, and a payment of interest by him stopped the running of the statute,[173] and the same is the case under s.30 of the Limitation Act 1980.

Receiver must not defend without leave.   It is not proper for a receiver to defend, without sanction, actions brought against him or her.[174] In the case where a receiver had, without the authority of the court, defended an action arising out of a distress (a remedy now abolished and replaced with CRAR) made by him upon a tenant of the estate for rent, and was unsuccessful, the court refused to allow him his costs of the action.[175] But if he or she successfully defends an action, without putting the estate to the expense of an application to the court, which he or she might have made for his or her own security, he or she will stand in the same position as to indemnity as if he or she had made that application.[176]   **7-47**

An application by the tenants of an estate, to restrain a receiver from doing acts which are within his or her authority, will be refused with costs; for they have no sufficient interest to support it.[177]

Sale.[178]   A receiver acquires no power of sale by virtue of his or her appointment; but in most cases the court has power to direct a sale of the property over which the receivership extends; for instance, where the appointment is made in an action for foreclosure, redemption or sale,[179] including, of course, debenture-holders' actions,[180] or in the administration of the estate of a deceased person. The court has power, under CPR r.25.1(c)(v), on the application of any party, to make an order for the sale of relevant property which is of a perishable nature or which for any   **7-48**

---

[171] See *Re Fleetwood and District Electric Light and Power Syndicate* [1915] 1 Ch. 486; and see *Hibernian Bank v Yourrel* [1919] Ir.R. 310.

[172] See *Re Jones' Estates* [1914] 1 Ir.R. 188. Money paid out of court under a mistake of fact may be ordered to be repaid: *Platt v Casey's Brewery* [1912] 1 Ir.R. 279.

[173] *Chinnery v Evans* (1864) 11 H.L.Cas. 115; cf. Law of Property Act 1925 s.109(2).

[174] *Anon.* (1801) 6 Ves. 287; *Swaby v Dickon* (1833) 5 Sim. 629. The receiver should not wait to apply for leave to defend an action until just before trial: *Anon.* (1801) 6 Ves. 287.

[175] *Swaby v Dickon* (1833) 5 Sim. 629; see *Re Montgomery* (1828) 1 Moll. 419.

[176] *Bristowe v Needham* (1847) 2 Ph. 190, 191. But whether he or she will, in any particular case, be indemnified in respect of the costs of defence will depend upon the nature of the claim; see *Re Dunn* [1904] 1 Ch. 648. If the possession of a tenant under a receiver is disturbed, and no application is made to the court to prevent the disturbance, the tenant is entitled to the costs of protecting his or her own possession: *Miller v Elkins* (1825) 3 L.J. Ch. 128.

[177] *Wynn v Lord Newborough* (1797) 1 Ves. 164.

[178] See CPR Pts 25 and 40. The receiver will not normally be directly concerned in any conveyance or transfer of ownership, but if he or she is, he or she will be doing so for this purpose as the nominee of the true owner.

[179] Law of Property Act 1925 ss.90, 91. Sale cannot be made of part of the surface, apart from the rest: see *Stamford, etc. Banking Co v Keeble* [1913] 2 Ch. 96.

[180] See *Palmer's Company Precedents*, 16th edn, Pt III, Ch.60; for an order for sale of a claim against directors, see *Wood v Woodhouse* [1896] W.N. 4.

other good reason it is desirable to sell quickly.[181] A sale may be ordered to enforce a charge over land under the Charging Orders Act 1979, even if a receiver has been appointed thereunder.[182]

In the case of statutory corporations formed to work a public undertaking, a sale of the undertaking cannot be ordered,[183] except where the statute under which the incorporation takes effect authorises a sale.[184]

In a debenture-holders' action, where the debenture-holders had a charge and the claimant was suing on behalf of himself and other debenture-holders, a sale could be ordered, before as well as after judgment, before all persons interested were ascertained, where the judge was of the opinion that there must eventually be a sale.[185] A sale out of court may be directed, if all parties are before the court or bound by the order. The sale is frequently ordered to be made by the receiver, and, if not directed to be made out of court, a conditional contract by the receiver will be approved by the judge.[186] The order will contain directions as to disposal of the purchase-money.

Subsequent incumbrancers should be added as parties under CPR r.19.4. Where a sale is ordered with the consent of prior incumbrancers in the form used in a creditor's action, informal notice may be given with a view to obtaining such consent.[187]

7-49   **Sale directed out of court.**   Where the court directs the sale out of court or with the approbation of the judge, the sale is often ordered to be by the receiver, especially where the whole of an undertaking is sold; but, except where chattels pass by delivery, the assurance of the property must be executed in the names of those persons in whom the property is vested.[188] The receiver as such has no power in his or her own name to convey the legal estate, which must always, where practicable, be conveyed by and in the name of the estate owner.[189] Where the contract is entered into subject to the approval of the court, and the receiver takes no step before the day fixed for completion to obtain such approval, the purchaser is entitled to repudiate the contract and recover any deposit.[190]

A receiver can sell the copyright of a book which had been assigned to the company, free from any author's lien for royalties, where such royalties had not,

---

[181] See notes to the *Civil Court Practice*, Pt 1, CPR 25.
[182] Law of Property Act 1925 s.90.
[183] *Re Woking UDC Act 1911* [1914] 1 Ch. 300; *Gardner v LC & D Ry* (1867) 2 Ch.App.201.
[184] See *Re Crystal Palace Co* (1911) 104 L.T. 898; sub nom. *Saunders v Bevan* (1912) 107 L.T. 70.
[185] See generally, as to sales in debenture holders' actions, *Palmer's Company Precedents*, 16th edn, Pt III, Ch.60.
[186] Unless all debenture holders subsequent to the claimant are parties, it is usual to direct a sale with the approbation of the judge that absent debenture holders may be brought in on the application to approve the conditional contract: *Re Crigglestone Coal Co* [1906] 1 Ch. 523. Formal notice of judgment is not normally served on the debenture holders of the same class, but notice is given them by circular letter or advertisement. If a debenture holder served with such notice of the proceedings (without formal notice of the judgment) wishes to attend, he or she must apply for leave: *Re W Mate & Sons Ltd* [1920] 1 Ch. 551.
[187] Direction of judges of the Chancery Division, 12 May 1909.
[188] See paras 7-18 and 7-19, above.
[189] See Law of Property Act 1925 ss.7(4), 8, 88, 89.
[190] *Re Sandwell Park Colliery Co Ltd* [1929] 1 Ch. 277.

by the original assignment, been charged as an unpaid vendor's lien, but were only secured by the covenant of the company.[191]

Where the receiver is appointed manager, he or she can carry out all such sales as are necessary for the ordinary conduct of the business over which he or she is appointed, but no sale of the permanent plant or assets should be made without permission of the court.

Sale through agent. Where the sale is effected through an agent whom the receiver has not obtained the permission of the court to employ, without any binding agreement as to the payment of commission, the court, in its discretion, may award him such compensation for the agent's services as it thinks right.[192] **7-50**

Conveyance of legal estate. Where the claimant or other party is a legal mortgagee, the order for sale may authorise him or her to convey the fee simple or term, under the powers conferred by the Law of Property Act 1925 s.92.[193] But where the order merely authorises the sale to be carried into effect, if the contract is entered into by the receiver, the legal mortgagee alone cannot convey the fee simple, or in the case of leaseholds the head-term which remains in the mortgagor.[194] The company or other mortgagor, and any other legal mortgagees, must concur in the conveyance, unless an order is made under s.91(7). The concurrence of parties to the action or persons bound by the order with only an equitable interest, such as second debenture-holders without a fixed legal charge, is not necessary, as they are bound by the order. Otherwise, if they are not parties to or bound by the order, their concurrence is necessary. If the claimant is an equitable mortgagee, or has a charge under the Charging Orders Act 1979, power to convey the legal estate can be obtained under ss.90 or 91 of the 1925 Act. **7-51**

Dissolved corporations: bona vacantia. If a company has been dissolved, before the contract for sale has been completed by conveyance, an order must be obtained under the Trustee Act 1925 s.44(ii)(c), for vesting in the purchaser any legal interest in land which was vested in the company[195]; or under s.51(1)(ii)(c) in the case of other property.[196] By s.1012 of the Companies Act 2006,[197] all property and rights vested in or held in trust for a dissolved company immediately before its dissolu- **7-52**

---

[191] *Barker v Stickney* [1919] 1 K.B. 121. As to sale of trademarks and right to use name, *Hart v Thurber Whyland* (1908) 32 R.P.C. 217; *Wood v Hall* (1916) 33 R.P.C. 16.

[192] *Re National Flying Services Ltd, Cousins v The Company* [1936] Ch. 271.

[193] See Law of Property Act 1925 s.92(7).

[194] Section 104 only applies where the sale is made by a mortgagee.

[195] As to the effect of a vesting order, see Law of Property Act 1925 s.9(1)(b). See *Re Strathblaine Estates Ltd* [1948] Ch. 228.

[196] See also Law of Property Act 1925 s.3(5). For a case of a patent, *Re Dutton's Patent* [1923] W.N.64. The law relating to dissolution as set out in the Companies Act 1985 was amended by Companies Act 1989 s.141(1), (2) and (3), and the period of limitation was extended by s.141(4). The law and procedure were further extensively amended by the Deregulation and Contracting-Out Act 1994, which inserted into Companies Act 1985 new ss.652A-652F. Dissolution powers are now exercisable by an administrator: see Insolvency Act 1986 Sch.B1 para.84 and para.16-68 below. The position was radically altered by Pt 31 of the Companies Act 2006. The Registrar of Companies now has an administrative power to restore companies to the register in certain circumstances following their having been struck off (see Companies Act 2006 ss.1024-1028). The court has a single statutory jurisdiction to restore to the register (Companies Act 2006 s.1029). This replaces the previous separate jurisdictions to restore to the register (see Companies Act 1985 s.653) and to declare dissolution void (see Companies Act 1985 s.651). In the case of applications to restore for the purposes of bringing proceedings against the dissolved company for damages for personal injury there is no

tion (including leaseholds, but not including property held by the company on trust for any other person) vest as bona vacantia in the Crown or the Duchy of Lancaster or the Duke of Cornwall, according to its location. Having regard to the exclusion of property held in trust for any person, the section does not apparently apply to property in which a bare legal estate is left in the company after receipt of the purchase-money. A vesting order under ss.44 or 51 of the Trustee Act can be applied for, and should be served on the Treasury Solicitor.[198] Those sections of the Trustee Act apply in the case of any dissolved corporation, while s.1012 of the Companies Act 2006 only applies to companies within the meaning of that Act.[199]

7-53   **Re-creation of an estate determined by dissolution.**   By s.181 of the Law of Property Act 1925, where, by reason of the dissolution of a corporation before or after the Act, a legal estate in any property has determined,[200] the court may by order create a corresponding estate and vest the same in the person who would have been entitled to a determined estate. Under the present practice, application for a vesting order should be made under the Trustee Act 1925 where that statute applies, and under s.181 of the Law of Property Act 1925, only where the former Act does not apply. It was formerly the practice to serve a petition for a vesting order in the case of leaseholds on the reversioner[201]; but under s.1012 of the Companies Act 2006, this is not now necessary in the case of a company within that Act, unless any question of forfeiture arises.

The former doubt[202] as to whether a debt due to a dissolved corporation vests in the Crown as bona vacantia was resolved, as regards companies formed and registered under the Companies Acts, by what is now s.1012, which plainly includes such debts. Leaseholds vest in the Crown as bona vacantia, apart from this section.[203]

7-54   **Alternatives to sale.**   Where sale is impracticable, or is not desired, the court may sanction a scheme of arrangement under Pt 26 of the Companies Act 2006; such

---

time limit on applications but otherwise the time limit is six years from the date of dissolution (see Companies Act 2006 s.1030(1), (4)).

[197] See previously s.654 of the Companies Act 1985, re-enacting s.354 of Companies Act 1948, itself re-enacting s.296 of Companies Act 1929, which, however, was held not to be retrospective; but the doctrine that bona vacantia vest in the Crown applies to leaseholds apart from the section: *Re Spencer Wells* [1933] 1 Ch. 29. The Crown has had, since July 1, 1948, power to disclaim any property so vesting: see CA 1948 s.355; Companies Act 1985 s.656 and now Companies Act 2006 s.1013 and, as regards the effect of crown disclaimer, ss.1014 and (in England and Wales) ss.1015-1019. As regards the effect of crown disclaimer in Scotland see ss.1020-1023. For the effect on bona vacantia of subsequent restoration to the register see the Companies Act 2006 s.1034.

[198] This was not formerly done in all cases: see *Re 9 Bomore Road* [1906] 1 Ch. 359.

[199] That is, companies formed and registered under the 2006 Act, or the Acts which it replaces, being Companies Act 1985, Companies Act 1948, Companies Act 1929, the Companies (Consolidation) Act 1908, Companies Act 1862, Companies Act 1989, and the Joint Stock Companies Acts (see Companies Act 2006 s.2). It had previously been held that the doctrine of bona vacantia did not apply in the case of an unregistered company: *Re Tierney* [1914] 1 Ir.R. 142. For the power of the court to restore to the register, see s.1029 of the 2006 Act.

[200] For a criticism of this, see *Re Strathblaine Estates Ltd* [1948] Ch. 228.

[201] *Re Albert Road, Norwood* [1916] 1 Ch. 289.

[202] See *Re Higginson & Dean* [1899] 1 Q.B. 325; *Hastings Corp. v Letton* [1908] 1 K.B. 378; *Re Hills* [1912] 107 L.T. 95 (as to which, see judgments in *Re Spencer Wells*, n.197, above); *Re Henderson's Nigel Co* (1911) 105 L.T. 370.

[203] *Re Spencer Wells* [1933] 1 Ch. 29 CA, and see n.202, above.

scheme need not be in the nature of a compromise[204]: but if it involves a reduction of capital, the provisions of the Act relative thereto must be observed.[205]

For a description of the scheme of arrangement procedure (in the case of administration), see para.16-55, below.

An order for sale does not prevent the court from subsequently approving a scheme of realisation involving the disposal of the assets for shares in a new company.[206] The report of the receiver may be an important factor to be considered with regard to the question of whether such scheme should be approved.[207]

Receiver may not purchase. A receiver, being in a fiduciary position, cannot directly or indirectly, without the permission of the court, bid at a sale for or purchase any of the property subject to the receivership, even though the sale is made by a mortgagee selling outside the claim.[208]

7-55

COMPANIES: ADMINISTRATIVE RECEIVERS

The Enterprise Act 2002. The prohibition imposed by the Enterprise Act 2002,[209] on any future appointment of an administrative receiver by the holder of a floating charge created on or after 15 September 2003, other than in the case of companies falling within certain excepted categories referred to as "special administration regimes", is confined to the power to make such an appointment exercisable by the floating charge holder. It does not restrict the court's powers to make such an appointment.[210]

7-56

Representation of companies in court. The previous rules, requiring companies or other corporations to appear by counsel, have been revoked. A company involved in litigation may now be represented at a hearing by an employee, who has been authorised to appear at trial or the hearing on its behalf, provided that the court gives

7-57

---

[204] *Re Guardian Assurance Co* [1917] 1 Ch. 431.

[205] *Re White Pass Ry* [1918] W.N. 323. See also *Practice Statement (Companies: Schemes of Arrangement)* [2002] 3 All ER 96.

[206] *Re Buenos Aires Tramways Ltd* (1920) 123 L.T. 748.

[207] It has become increasingly common for overseas companies to take advantage of the scheme of arrangement in recent years; see, e.g, *Re Global Garden Products Italy SpA* [2016] EWHC 1884 (Ch); *Re Metinvest BV* [2016] EWHC 1868 (Ch); *Re Van Gansewinkel Groep BV* [2015] EWHC 2151 (Ch); *Re Apcoa Parking Holdings GmbH* [2015] 2 B.C.L.C. 659; *Re Zodiac Pool Solutions SAS* [2014] B.C.C. 569; *Re Magyar Telecom BV* [2013] EWHC 3800 (Ch); *Re Primacom Holding GmbH (No.1)* [2011] EWHC 3746 (Ch) and (No.2) [2012] EWHC 164 (Ch); and *Re Rodenstock GmbH* [2012] B.C.C. 459.

[208] *Nugent v Nugent* [1908] 1 Ch. 546; *Alven v Bond* (1841) Fl. & K. 196; *Cary v Cary* (1804) 2 Sch. & Lef. 173. Semble, the receiver could not plead any statute of limitations: *Taylor v Davies* [1920] A.C. 636; and would be liable to account, if he or she resold and repurchased; see *Gordon v Holland* (1913) 108 L.T. 385.

[209] Enterprise Act 2002 Pt 10 s.250, inserting into Insolvency Act 1986 a new s.72A, subject to the exceptions prescribed in new ss.72B-72H.

[210] See Ch.14 below. As regards the Court's power to appoint administrative receivers, for a contrary view, see Gordon Stewart, *"Administrative Receivers and Administrators"* (CCH, 1987) and Blackburne J in *Re A & C Supplies Ltd* [1998] B.C.C. 708 regarding the court's power to appoint a replacement administrative receiver.

permission.[211] Extensive practice hearing directions have been given on the subject of companies appearing as litigants in person.[212]

Application for the court's permission may be obtained, on informal application made in advance, preferably to the judge who is to hear the case; but if that is not practicable or convenient, permission may be obtained from any judge by whom the case could be heard; notice need not be given to the other parties. The judge who gives the permission should record it in writing, and supply a copy to the company, and to any other party who asks for one.[213] Permission should be given, unless there is some particular or sufficient reason why it should be withheld. The matters to be taken into account include the complexity of the issues, and the experience and position of the company's proposed representative.'[214]

At any hearing, where a party which is a company is to be represented by an employee, a written statement shall be provided for the court, stating:

(1) the full name of the company, as stated in its certificate of incorporation;
(2) its registered number;
(3) the position or office in the company held by the representative; and
(4) the date on which, and the manner in which, the representative was authorised to act for the company, e.g. [date] written authority from managing director, or [date] Board resolution dated.[215]

The statement should presumably also include the copy of the judge's permission (see above).

Presumably, a company may also ask for permission to be accompanied by a "*McKenzie friend*" or lay adviser.

7-58   **Powers of administrative receivers.**   Under the Insolvency Act 1986, the powers conferred upon an administrative receiver[216] by the debentures by virtue of which he or she is appointed are deemed to include, except in so far as they are inconsistent with any of the provisions of those debentures, the extensive powers specified in Sch.1 to that Act.[217] Since, however, the powers of a receiver or receiver and manager appointed by the court do not in any way depend upon the powers conferred by the terms of the debenture under which the receiver is appointed, they are not applicable in the case of such receiver or receiver and manager. Hence, it follows that the powers and duties of court-appointed receivers or receivers and managers appointed over the undertaking of a company do not differ in principle from those of court-appointed receivers for other incumbrancers. In the ensuing pages, only those points are discussed which are peculiar to receivers of the property

---

[211] CPR r.39.6.
[212] CPR PD 39A.
[213] CPR PD 39A, paras 5.4 and 5.5.
[214] CPR PD 39A, para.5.3.
[215] CPR PD 39A, para.5.2.
[216] For the meaning of "administrative receiver", see para.20-12 and paras 21-1 ff, below.
[217] Insolvency Act 1986 s.42(1). For the powers specified in Sch.1, see paras 21-9 ff, below. The position appears to be otherwise in relation to receivers appointed by the court under Scottish Law: see Insolvency Act 1986 s.55 and St. Clair and Young, *The Law of Corporate Insolvency in Scotland*, 4th edn (W Green, 2011), Ch. 6. Having regard to the terms of Sch.1, if an administrative receiver is appointed out of court, then (unless the terms of the debenture are otherwise inconsistent therewith) he or she will as a matter of course have all the powers of a manager, and presumably would be expected to utilise them. Accordingly, if all that is required is the appointment of a receiver (and not a receiver and manager), an appointment by the court would be indicated.

of companies: the earlier portion of the chapter should be referred to in respect of their powers and duties, and Ch.9 in respect of their powers and duties as managers.

Statutory duties of receiver. A receiver[218] of the property of a company formed **7-59** and registered under the Companies Act 2006, or earlier Companies Acts, is subject to statutory obligations. As the prescribed part deduction in favour of unsecured creditors only applies to debentures created on or after 15 September 2003, no such deduction is likely in an administrative receivership which, by reason of the Enterprise Act 2002, will normally only be made in relation to debentures created before that date. However see Ch.21 below for the limited but important circumstances where administrative receivership is possible based on debentures dated after 15 September 2003.

(a) *Notice of appointment.* In the case of an administrative receiver, he or she must forthwith after appointment, i.e. as soon as reasonably practicable, send to the company and publish in the prescribed manner[219] a notice of the appointment, and, within 28 days after appointment, unless the court otherwise directs, send such a notice to all the creditors of the company,[220] so far as he or she is aware of their addresses.[221] Default exposes the receiver to a fine.[222]

(b) *Preferential debts.* If appointed on behalf of the holders of debentures secured by a charge which, as created, was a floating charge, he or she must pay the preferential debts. As the prescribed part deduction in favour of unsecured creditors only applies to debentures created on or after 15 September 2003, no such deduction is likely in an administrative receivership which, by definition, will normally only be made in relation to debentures created before that date.

(c) *Invoices, etc.* Every invoice, order for goods or services, business letter or order form (whether in hard copy, electronic or other form) issued by or on behalf of the company or the receiver or manager or the liquidator, and all the company's websites must contain a statement that a receiver or manager has been appointed.[223]

---

[218] See Insolvency Act 1986 s.29(1) for the meaning of "receiver" in this connection.

[219] Standard contents of such notices are listed in Pt 1 of Insolvency (England and Wales) Rules 2016 (SI 2016/1024).

[220] Insolvency Act 1986 s.46(1). This obligation does not apply in relation to the appointment of an additional administrative receiver to act with an existing administrative receiver, or in place of an administrative receiver dying or ceasing to act, unless it has not been complied with before such event: see s.46(2). If the company is being wound up, this obligation persists, notwithstanding that the administrative receiver and the liquidator may be one and the same person, with any necessary modifications: See s.46(3).

[221] The receiver would normally obtain the names and addresses of creditors from the books of the company and from the statement of affairs.

[222] If the administrative receiver without reasonable excuse makes default, he or she is liable on summary conviction to a fine not exceeding one-fifth of the statutory maximum, and on conviction after continued contravention to a daily default fine not exceeding one-fiftieth of the statutory maximum: See ss.46(4), 430, Sch.10. For the meaning of "statutory maximum" see Insolvency Act 1986 Sch.10. The statutory maximum means: (a) in England and Wales, the prescribed sum under the Magistrates' Court Act 1980 s.32; and (b) in Scotland, the prescribed sum under Sch.1 to the Criminal Procedure (Consequential Provisions) (Scotland) Act 1995.

[223] Insolvency Act 1986 s.39(1). Any officer, liquidator, receiver or manager who knowingly and wilfully authorises or permits a default in complying with this provision is liable on summary convic-

(d) *Register of debentures.* If the claim in which the receiver has been appointed is to enforce registered debentures or registered debenture stock, and these are numerous, the receiver may be directed by the court or a judge to open and keep a register of transfers and other transmissions of such debentures or stock (called "the receiver's register").[224]

(e) *Within three months* (or such longer period as the court may allow) after appointment, an administrative receiver must send to the registrar of companies, to any trustees for secured creditors of the company and, so far as he is aware of their addresses[225] to all such creditors (other than creditors who have opted out of receiving such notices under s.246C), a report.[226] This report must contain prescribed information as to the events which led up to the appointment.[227] It must also contain details of any disposal or proposed disposal of any company property, any carrying on or proposed carrying on of the company's business, the amounts of capital and interest payable to the appointing debenture holder, amounts payable to preferential creditors and the amount (if any) likely to be available to other creditors.[228]

(f) *Within three months* (or such longer period as the court may allow) an administrative receiver must also either send a copy of the report under (e) above[229] to all unsecured creditors of the company (other than opted-out creditors), so far as he or she is aware of their addresses or publish a notice, stating an address to which unsecured creditors can write for copies of the report to be sent to them free of charge.[230]

(g) *Where the company has gone or goes into liquidation,* an administrative receiver shall within seven days of sending the report under (e) above (or, if later, the nomination or appointment of the liquidator) send a copy of the report to the liquidator.[231]

7-60   **Enforcement of duties.**   If any receiver or manager makes default in filing, delivering, or making any return, account, or other document, or in giving any notice, as by law required, after a 14-day notice to make good the default, the registrar or a member or creditor may, without prejudice to any penalties imposed in respect of such default, apply by application notice for an order directing him or her to make good the default.[232]

7-61   **Statement of affairs.**   An administrative receiver shall forthwith after appointment require certain named persons connected with the company to make out and

---

tion to a fine not exceeding one-fifth of the statutory maximum; Insolvency Act 1986 ss.39(2), 430, Sch.10. As to the meaning of the expression "statutory maximum" See n.222, above.

[224] Such a register is distinct from the Register of Charges kept by the Registrar of Companies under Companies Act 2006 s.859L.

[225] The receiver would normally obtain the names and addresses from the books of the company and from the statement of affairs.

[226] Insolvency Act 1986 s.48(1).

[227] Insolvency Act 1986 s.48(1).

[228] See also Insolvency Rules 2016 r.4.13.

[229] See n.227 above; r.4.14.

[230] Insolvency Act 1986 s.48(2).

[231] Insolvency Act 1986 s.48(4).

[232] Insolvency Act 1986 s.41(1)(a), (2), (3). There is a similar remedy open to a liquidator, if the receiver fails to render proper accounts or to pay over balances due: Insolvency Act 1986 s.41(1)(b), (2), (3). The receiver may be ordered to pay the costs of any application: s.41(2). See CPR Pt 69 and PD 69.

submit to him or her a statement of affairs.[233] It is partly or wholly from such a statement that he or she will be enabled to compile the report he or she is obliged to give. Since the procedure in relation thereto is identical with the procedure in relation to such statement of affairs where such a receiver is appointed out of court, this subject is dealt with in Ch.22.

Preferential debts and costs of liquidation. The Insolvency Act 1986 provides that, where a receiver is appointed on behalf of the holders of any debentures of a company secured by a charge, which, as created, was a floating charge,[234] or possession is taken by or on behalf of such debenture holders, then, if the company is not being wound up, the debts which, under the provisions of s.386 of, and Sch.6 to, the Act[235] relating to preferential payments, are to be paid in priority to all other debts, must be paid out of the assets coming to the hands of the receiver or other person taking possession in priority to any claims for principal or interest in respect of the debentures.[236] As between themselves, ordinary preferential debts rank equally, and if the assets are insufficient to meet them, they abate to equal proportions accordingly. Only once ordinary preferential debts are paid, are secondary preferential debts paid and they also rank equally amongst themselves.[237] The most common type of ordinary preferential debt is limited sums of money owed to employees of the insolvent employer. Secondary preferential debts are comparatively rare in practice and are limited in scope to certain payments in excess of amounts covered by the Financial Services Compensation Scheme. The periods of time mentioned in Sch.6 are reckoned from the date of the appointment.[238] Any payments under the section are to be recouped so far as possible out of assets available for the general creditors.[239]

7-62

Where at the date of the receiver's appointment, the company is being wound up, the same debts, together with the costs of the winding-up, are given priority over the claims of debenture-holders under a charge which, as created, was a floating charge.[240] This only applies where either an order for winding-up has actually been made, or a resolution for its winding-up has been passed.[241]

Fixed charges not subordinated to preferential debts. These provisions have no application to the proceeds of a charge which was, from the first, fixed. Where the debentures contained both a fixed and a floating charge, and the debenture-

7-63

---

[233] Insolvency Act 1986 s.47.
[234] Insolvency Act 1986 s.251.
[235] Insolvency Act 1986 s.386 (which explains the meaning of ordinary preferential debts and secondary preferential debts), Sch.6, as amended.
[236] Insolvency Act 1986 s.40(1), (2). For the meaning here of "the debentures", see *Re H & K (Medway) Ltd, Mackay v IRC* [1997] 2 All E.R. 321.
[237] Insolvency Act 1986 ss.175(1A), (1B) and 386(1), (1A) and (1B).
[238] Insolvency Act 1986 s.387(4)(a).
[239] Insolvency Act 1986 s.40(3). "The scheme of s.94 is in broad outline to give preference to debts which would have been preferential under s.319 (of the Companies Act 1948) if an order had been made or a resolution passed for the winding-up of the company at the time of the appointment of a receiver or of possession being taken on behalf of the debenture holder": per Vinelott J in *Re Christonette International Ltd* [1982] 1 W.L.R. 1245, 1250D-E.
[240] Insolvency Act 1986 s.175(2)(b). Having regard to the change in the law, under which the assets available for preferential debts are those comprised in a charge which as created was a floating charge, the subsequent crystallisation of such charge is now immaterial. As to the former law, see *Re Christonette International Ltd*, n.239, above.
[241] *Re Christonette International Ltd*, n.239 above; and cf. *Re M C Bacon Ltd* [1991] Ch. 127 per Millett J, but cf. *Portbase Clothing Co Ltd* [1993] Ch. 388 per Chadwick J.

holders were paid in full out of the proceeds of sale of the assets comprised in the fixed charge, thus discharging the debenture, the surplus of the proceeds of sale of such assets remaining in the hands of the receiver were ordered to be paid to the liquidator,[242] and not to the preferential creditors,[243] as the person entitled to the mortgaged property.

It was formerly held that if the assets of the company were insufficient to satisfy its liabilities, the court could order the costs, charges and expenses incurred in the winding-up to be paid out of its assets, which for this purpose would include all assets comprised only in a charge, in such order of priority as it thought just.[244] However, in *Re Leyland DAF Ltd, Buchler v Talbot*[245] the House of Lords decided that although s.175(2)(b) of the 1986 Act made an incursion into the proprietary rights of debenture holders regarding preferential debts of an insolvent company, so that they were payable out of property comprised within a floating charge in priority to payment to the chargeholder, s.175(2)(b) did not authorise the liquidator's costs and expenses of a winding up to be paid out of the assets subject to a floating charge ahead of the chargeholder's claims. However, this reversal of the previously understood position was temporary. The Companies Act 2006 s.1282 inserted a new s.176ZA into the Insolvency Act 1986. Under that section the expenses of winding up in England and Wales, so far as the assets of the company available for payment of general creditors, are insufficient to meet them, have priority over any claims to property comprised in or subject to any floating charge created by the company. The priority thereby conferred is also over any payments to preferential creditors. However, the right to priority is subject to Insolvency Rules 2016 (rr.6.42–6.48 and 7.108–7.116). In broad terms, in the case of litigation expenses in excess of £5,000, the liquidator must have obtained authorisation in advance, or subsequent approval, by the floating chargeholder and any preferential creditors, for the incurring of expense in relation to certain specified categories of litigation. The court also has power to sanction such expenses in certain circumstances.

The detailed provisions regarding preferential debts are contained in Sch.6 (as amended) to the Insolvency Act 1986.

The preference given by s.175 is conferred in respect only of property subject to a charge which, as created, was a floating charge, and does not extend to property comprised in a specific charge[246]: and where debentures as created include both a floating and a fixed charge, the preference is limited to the assets not comprised in the fixed charge.[247] The fact that the floating security has crystallised before the commencement of winding-up as regards any property, does not entail that s.175 does not apply to that property[248]: the same would apply as regards s.40. If a secured creditor holds security for both preferential and non-preferential debts, he or she may appropriate the security as he or she pleases.[249]

The present practice is not to direct the receiver to pay the preferential debts forthwith, but to direct an inquiry, which is answered, if possible, before the other

---

[242] Pursuant to Law of Property Act 1925 s.105.
[243] *Re GL Saunders Ltd (In liquidation)* [1986] 1 W.L.R. 215.
[244] Insolvency Act 1986 s.156; *Re Barleycorn Enterprises Ltd* [1970] Ch. 465, but see n.240, above.
[245] [2004] 2 A.C. 298.
[246] See Ch.6 above, as to the nature of a floating charge.
[247] *Re Lewis Merthyr Consolidated Collieries* [1929] 1 Ch. 498.
[248] See, as to the former law *Re Griffin Hotel Co Ltd* [1941] Ch. 129.
[249] *Re William Hall (Contractors) Ltd* [1967] 1 W.L.R. 948.

inquiries directed by the judgment[250]; when possible the amounts of wage claims should be agreed with the workers' representatives. It is usual for workers to claim most of their rights to preferential claims initially from the Redundancy Payments Service set up under the Employment Rights Act 1996 and operated by the Insolvency Service and funded out of the National Insurance Fund. The Fund is thereafter subrogated to any rights the employees had against the insolvent employer.

Subject to any of the following express provisions, the Crown has no priority.[251]

Business Rates and Council Tax. These are no longer preferential.[252]　　　**7-64**

The relevant date. "The relevant date" determines the existence and amount of 　　**7-65**
a preferential debt.[253] If the appointment of the receiver antedates any order or resolution for winding-up, the date of such appointment is the relevant date.[254]

If the reverse is the position, and the winding-up is a compulsory winding-up, and the order was made immediately upon the discharge of an administration order, or the appointment of an administrator,[255] the relevant date is the date of the making of the administration order.[256] If the company is in compulsory liquidation and had not commenced to be wound up voluntarily before the date of the order, the relevant date is the date of the appointment, or first appointment, of a provisional liquidator, or, if no such appointment has been made, the date of the winding-up order; in any other case, the relevant date is the date of the passing of the resolution for the winding-up of the company.[257]

Crown debts. The preferences previously accorded to debts due to the Crown in 　　**7-66**
respect of debts due to the then Inland Revenue for unpaid PAYE income tax, and to the then Customs and Excise in respect of unpaid value added tax and other duties, and in respect of unpaid social security contributions, were repealed when the Enterprise Act 2002 came into force.[258]

These amendments leave in place as preferential debts those debts listed in the amended Sch.6 to the Insolvency Act 1986, namely unpaid contributions to occupational pension schemes, unpaid remuneration, etc. of employees, and unpaid

---

[250] See para.5-47, above.
[251] *Food Controller v Cork* [1923] A.C. 647. There is no set-off against the Crown: *Att.-Gen. v Guy Motors* [1928] 2 K.B. 78 except in respect of other Crown debts: *Re West End Networks Ltd (in liquidation) Secretary of State for Trade and Industry v Frid* [2004] UKHL 24; [2004] 2 B.C.L.C. 1, HL (VAT refund set-off against Crown's subrogated claim for employee protection. As to what are Crown debts, see *Metropolitan Meat Industry Board v Sheedy* [1927] A.C. 899. A fine constitutes a debt due to the Crown: *Re Pascoe* [1944] Ch. 310 (a bankruptcy case under Bankruptcy Act 1914); but fines are no longer provable in bankruptcy, although they remain provable in winding-up: Insolvency Rules 2016 r.14.2 but they have no priority under s.175. Betterment levy was abolished by the Land Commission (Dissolution) Act 1971 with effect from 22 July 1970 as a preferential debt, see Land Commission Act 1967 Sch.12 paras 17, 19.
[252] The preferential status, previously accorded by Companies Act 1948 ss.94 and 319, was repealed and not re-enacted by Insolvency Act 1986.
[253] Insolvency Act 1986 s.387(1).
[254] Insolvency Act 1986 s.387(4). This is true under both English and Scottish law Insolvency Act 1986 s.387(4).
[255] As to administration orders and extra-judicial appointments of administrators, see Pt III, Ch.14 below.
[256] Insolvency Act 1986 s.387(3)(a).
[257] Insolvency Act 1986 s.387(3)(b).
[258] Enterprise Act 2002 s.251(1) and (3), amending Insolvency Act 1986 s.386 and Schs 3 and 6.

levies on coal and steel production. Various debts owed in relation to payments made by the Financial Services Compensation Scheme have been added as ordinary and secondary preferential debts in recent years.

7-67 **Contributions to occupational pension schemes, etc.** These comprise any sum which is owed by the company, and is a sum to which Sch.4 to the Pension Schemes Act 1993 applies (contributions to occupational pension schemes and state scheme premiums).[259]

7-68 **Remuneration, etc. of employees.** This category comprises three heads:

(a) *Remuneration.* This comprises so much of any amount which is owed by the company to a person who is or has been an employee of the company, and is payable by way of remuneration in respect of the whole or any part of the period of four months next before the relevant date as does not exceed so much as may be prescribed by order[260] made by the Secretary of State.[261] This sum is at present £800.[262]

A sum is payable by the company to a person by way of remuneration in respect of any period, if it is paid as wages or salary (whether payable for time or for piece-work or earned wholly or partly by way of commission), in respect of services rendered to the debtor in that period, or is one of the following four items payable by the company in respect of that period.[263] These four items are:

(i) a guarantee payment under Pt III of the Employment Rights Act 1996 (employee without work to do);

(ii) any payment for time off under s.53 (looking for work, etc.) or s.56 (antenatal care) of the 1996 Act or under s.169 of the Trade Union and Labour Relations (Consolidation) Act 1992 (time off for carrying out trade union duties etc);

(iii) remuneration on suspension on medical grounds or on maternity grounds, under Pt VII of the 1996 Act; or

(iv) remuneration under a protective award made by an industrial tribunal under s.189 of the Trade Union and Labour Relations (Consolidation) Act 1992 (redundancy dismissal with compensation).[264]

Further, any remuneration payable by the company to a person, in respect of a period of holiday,[265] or of absence from work through sickness or other good cause, is deemed to be wages or (as the case may be) salary in respect of services rendered to the company in that period.[266]

---

[259] Sch.6 para.8, (as amended by the Pension Schemes Act 1993 s.190 and Sch.8, substituting references to Sch.4 to that Act for reference to the 1975 Act) see Insolvency (Amendment) Rules 2003 (SI 2003/1730) r.1(2).

[260] Any such order may contain such transitional provisions as may appear to the Secretary of State necessary or expedient, and shall be made by statutory instrument, subject to annulment in pursuance of a resolution of either House of Parliament: Insolvency Act 1986 s.386 Sch.6 para.16.

[261] Insolvency Act 1986 Sch.6 para.9.

[262] Insolvency Act 1986 s.386 Sch.6 para.13(1). The sum was prescribed by the Insolvency Proceedings (Monetary Limits) Order 1986 (SI 1986/1996) art.4.

[263] Insolvency Act 1986 s.386 Sch.6 para.13(2).

[264] Sch.6 para.13(2).

[265] Sch.6 para.15(a).

[266] Sch.6 para.15(a).

(b) *Accrued holiday remuneration.* An amount owed by way of accrued holiday remuneration in respect of any period of employment before the relevant date, to a person whose employment by the debtor had been terminated, whether before, on or after that date.[267]

Where a person's employment has been terminated by or in consequence of the company going into liquidation, or by or in consequence of the appointment of a receiver at the instance of debenture-holders secured by a charge which, as created, was a floating charge, holiday remuneration is deemed to have accrued to that person in respect of any period of employment if, by virtue of the contract of employment or of any enactment,[268] that remuneration would have accrued in respect of that period if the employment had continued until he or she became entitled to be allowed his or her holiday.[269]

The second and third paragraphs under (a) above also apply in this case.[270]

(c) *Other emoluments.* So much of any amount which is ordered (whether before or after the relevant date) to be paid to the company under the Reserve Forces (Safeguard of Employment) Act 1985, and is so ordered in respect of a default made by the company before that date in the discharge of its obligations under that Act, as does not exceed such amount as may be prescribed by order made by the Secretary of State.[271] This sum is at present £800.[272]

Advance to pay remuneration or accrued holiday remuneration. There was   **7-69** no provision in the 1908 Act corresponding to s.319(4) of the Companies Act 1948,[273] (now Insolvency Act 1986 s.386 Sch.6 para.11), under which preference was first given to a debt in respect of an advance made for the purpose of paying wages, salaries (now remuneration) or accrued holiday remuneration, and in fact applied for that purpose, to the extent to which the wages or salary or remuneration so paid would have been entitled to priority.[274] Presumably, the preference relates to the gross amount advanced, e.g. if a bank advances £200, £175 of which is paid to the employee, £15 being deducted as PAYE and £10 as Social Security contributions,[275] the bank will be entitled to preference for the full £200. While the 1908 Act was in force, it was held[276] that the effect of s.5 of the Mercantile Law Amendment Act 1856 was to entitle a person who had guaranteed a preferential debt to stand in the shoes of the creditor, and obtain the preference to which the debt so paid would have been entitled on a winding-up. This decision appears to be unaffected by para.11 of Sch.6. It applies to all preferential debts, not merely those to

---

[267] Sch.6 para.10.
[268] This includes an order or direction made under an enactment: Sch.6 para.14(3).
[269] Sch.6 para.14.
[270] Sch.6 para.15.
[271] Sch.6 para.12.
[272] Insolvency Proceedings (Monetary Limits) Order 1986 (SI 1986/1996) art.4.
[273] Replacing and extending Companies Act 1929 s.264(3).
[274] See *Re Primrose (Builders) Ltd* [1950] Ch. 561, for an unsuccessful attempt to question such priority on special facts, and *Re E J Morel* (1934) Ltd [1962] Ch.21 (successful); *Re James R Rutherford & Sons Ltd* [1964] 1 W.L.R. 1211 (unsuccessful); *Re Rampgill Mill Ltd* [1967] Ch. 1138 (unsuccessful).
[275] See para.7-68, above.
[276] *Re Lamplugh's Iron Ore Co* [1927] 1 Ch. 308.

which that subsection applies: but it applies only to payment made under a guarantee, not, as in the case of para.11, to a simple advance.

7-70   **Payment of certain debts by Secretary of State.** As to the subrogation of the Secretary of State to certain debts paid by him or her, see paras 6-66 and 7-63, above.

7-71   **Set-off of preferential against non-preferential debts.** Where such debts fall to be set-off, the "credit" may require to be set off rateably between the respective classes of debt.[277]

7-72   **Order of application of assets.** The effect of the Insolvency Act 1986 s.176ZA, is to make the costs and expenses of winding-up payable out of the assets not included in the debenture-holder's security, in priority to the preferential debts. If such assets do not suffice for payment of those debts, the balance is ultimately borne by the property subject to any charge which, as created, was a floating charge.[278]

The order of application of the assets, where the assets are deficient, is as follows:

(1)   costs of realisation, including costs of an abortive sale;
(2)   balance due to receiver, including remuneration and costs;
(3)   costs, charges and expenses of the trustees under the debenture trust deed (if any), including their remuneration[279];
(4)   costs of action;
(5)   preferential debts (first ordinary then secondary);
(6)   the fund for unsecured creditors ("the prescribed part") which, as explained above at para.7-59, is unlikely to be encountered in an administrative receivership[280]; and
(7)   debenture-holders with the benefit of a floating charge.[281] If the assets are insufficient to discharge the preferential debts in full, such debts abate in equal proportions (with ordinary preferential debts having priority over secondary preferential debts).[282]

7-73   **Distress, etc.** Section 128(1) of the Insolvency Act 1986, relating to the invalidity of any attachment, sequestration, distress (now defined for the purposes of the 1986 Act under s.436 as including the right to exercise commercial rent arrears

---

[277] See *Re Unit 2 Windows Ltd* [1985] 1 W.L.R. 1383 (a winding-up case; but the principle would seem to be applicable, by analogy, to a receivership without winding-up) but see *Turner v Inland Revenue Commissioners* [1993] B.C.C. 299.

[278] See analysis formerly in *Westminster Corp v Chapman* [1916] 1 Ch. 161. As to liquidator's costs and remuneration, see *Re Beni-Felkai Co* [1934] Ch. 406; *Re Wm Adler Co* [1935] 1 Ch. 138. See also Companies Act 1980 s.267, and *Re Barleycorn Enterprises Ltd* [1970] Ch. 465. However, see also *Re Leyland DAF Ltd, Buchler v Talbot* [2004] UKHL 9; [2004] 2 A.C. 298, subsequently reversed in effect by Insolvency Act 1986 s.176ZA.

[279] Whilst there can be no doubt as to the entitlement of the trustees for the debenture holders to their costs, charges, expenses and remuneration, in priority to the debenture-holders themselves, under a well-drawn debenture trust deed (see *Re Piccadilly Hotel Ltd* [1911] 2 Ch. 534), it is not clear why these should rank ahead of the preferential debts. In *Re Glyncorrwg Collieries Co Ltd* [1926] Ch. 951, Tomlin J simply referred to the terms of the trust deed, but this would hardly seem to be conclusive of the position.

[280] "The prescribed part", under s.176A of the Insolvency Act 1986, inserted by Enterprise Act 2002 s.262.

[281] *Re Glyncorrwg Collieries Co* n.279, above.

[282] Insolvency Act 1986 s.175(1A) and (1B).

recovery ("CRAR")) or execution put in force against the estate of effects of the company after the commencement of the winding-up, has no application to cases within s.40, where there is no winding-up.[283]

Where a winding-up was in progress, and the liquidator stated that the assets would not suffice for payment in full of the preferential debts, the lessor was restrained from proceeding with a distress for rent (a right now replaced by CRAR); the fact that the amount due on the debentures far exceeded the assets was held in the circumstances to be immaterial.[284]

Failure to pay preferential debts. If money is paid over to debenture-holders without providing for preferential debts, it may be recovered: the proper claimant is the liquidator in the name of the company.[285] The receiver is personally liable to creditors for failure to comply with the provisions of the section and the order directing payment of the preferential debts.[286]

7-74

Other rights and duties. The rights and duties of a receiver for incumbrancers with regard to rent[287] and attornment of tenants,[288] have already been discussed; also his or her right to possession.

7-75

A receiver for debenture-holders has no right to the rents in arrear, as against specific assignees of such arrears, when he or she goes into possession of property over which the debentures constituted only a floating charge; but the case is otherwise where the arrears of rent claimed by the specific assignees thereof are in respect of property specifically charged by the debentures.[289]

Leaseholds. The liability of a receiver appointed on behalf of equitable incumbrancers for the rent of leaseholds has already been dealt with.[290] A receiver appointed on behalf of debenture-holders is in the same position in this respect as a receiver appointed on behalf of a mortgagee by sub-demise: he or she is therefore under no contractual liability to pay rent under a lease to the company, though he or she may be in occupation[291]; though he or she may be compelled to pay arrears to avoid CRAR (formerly distress). If he or she enters into a fresh agreement for a tenancy or an agreement to pay arrears, he or she will be personally liable thereon, with a right to indemnity.

7-76

If the property is onerous and incapable of realisation, the receiver may apply for leave to abandon it, though there may be under-tenants. It may be made a term of the order that the receiver shall pay rent in respect of the period of occupation.

---

[283] *Herbert Berry Associates Ltd v IRC* [1977] 1 W.L.R. 1437 HL; (distress for taxes).

[284] *Re South Rhondda Colliery Co* [1928] W.N. 126. The application was made by originating motion: it would now be made by application notice. *Semble*, where there was no winding-up, the same principle would apply on the appointment of a receiver, and the receiver might apply either in the name of the company or of a preferential creditor.

[285] *Semble*, where there is no winding-up, the company would be the proper claimant: Westminster Corp v Chapman [1916] 1 Ch. 161.

[286] *Woods v Winskill* [1913] 2 Ch. 303; *Westminster Corp. v Haste* [1950] Ch. 442; *IRC v Goldblatt* [1972] Ch. 498.

[287] See paras 7-1 and 7-34, above.

[288] See para.7-2, above.

[289] *Re Ind Coope & Co; Fisher v The Company* [1911] 2 Ch. 223.

[290] The power of a liquidator to disclaim, under Insolvency Act 1986 s.178, is to be considered in this connection: as to which, see *Re Katherine et Cie* [1932] 1 Ch. 70. It may become necessary for the claimant in a debenture holder's action to apply for a vesting order.

[291] *Re JW Abbott & Co* [1913] W.N. 284; *Hay v Swedish, etc. Ry* (1892) 8 T.L.R. 775.

Where there are valuable tenants' fixtures such as trade machinery, permission to remove them should be applied for. In such cases, if the debentures do not exceed the value of the assets, the liability which the company will incur in damages for breach of covenants in the lease is a factor which will need to be taken into account.

7-77   **Debtors to the company.**   The receiver should at once give notice of the appointment to debtors to the company, and require them to pay their debts to the receiver, obtaining where necessary an order for that purpose. If an action to compel payment is necessary, it must be brought in the name of the company, or if a winding-up has begun, of the liquidator, on a complete indemnity to the latter.[292] The debenture-holders have the absolute right to insist on, or to prohibit, any action being brought; the court has a discretion to be exercised for the benefit of all the parties interested.[293]

7-78   **Uncalled capital.**   Where uncalled capital is included in the debenture-holders' security, the receiver may be given leave to use the name of the liquidator, on a complete indemnity to the latter, in order to recover the calls made by him or her.[294] It is necessary to apply to the court for directions to the liquidator to make the requisite calls, in order to enable the debenture-holders to obtain realisation.[295] In such cases, it is a usual and convenient practice for the liquidator to be appointed receiver. If the company is not in liquidation, then, if the uncalled capital is included in the security, the claimant should apply by application notice that the receiver may be authorised to make the call and recover the amount called up, with power if necessary to sue in the company's name. As previously pointed out, the order appointing a receiver excludes uncalled capital, and therefore special directions are required as to making the call and dealing with the proceeds.[296] If there is a doubt as to whether the uncalled capital is included in the security,[297] it may be necessary to issue an application notice to determine the point.[298]

7-79   **Sale.**   A sale is often effected by the receiver entering into a conditional contract subject to the approval of the court: an application notice is then issued by the claimant for an order confirming the contract and directing it to be carried into effect. A party with power to convey the legal estate may be authorised to convey the fee simple or the term; otherwise, the concurrence of the company and legal incumbrancers is required[299]: if any dispute arises as to the form of the conveyance, or if any party refuses to concur, an application notice is issued for an order that the conveyance be settled by the judge. Where sale by tender is directed, there is under the usual conditions no binding contract, until the sale has been confirmed by the order of the master. An offer received after the close of the date for tenders may therefore be accepted.

In the case of disposal of the assets on reconstruction or amalgamation, care should be taken to comply with the requirements of the Finance Acts and the Corporation Tax Acts.

---

[292] See, as to extent of the indemnity for costs, para.8-12, below.
[293] *Viola v Anglo-American Cold Storage Co* [1912] 2 Ch. 305.
[294] *Re Westminster Syndicate* (1908) 99 L.T. 924; form of order, *Stiebel's Company Law*, 3rd edn, Vol.I.
[295] *Fowler v Broad's Patent, etc. Co* [1893] 1 Ch. 724; see, as to master's certificate as to unpaid calls, *Madeley v Ross, Sleeman & Co* [1897] 1 Ch. 505.
[296] Also whether any additional security is to be given.
[297] See *Streatham Estates Co* [1897] 1 Ch. 15; *Re Handyside & Co* [1909] 131 L.T.J. 125.
[298] See *Re Gregory, Love & Co* [1916] 1 Ch. 203.
[299] After the winding-up, the company's seal, if any, must be affixed by the liquidator.

Powers and duties generally.   As already stated, the receiver should apply to the   **7-80**
court for permission to exercise all powers, not implied or expressly included in the
terms of the appointment, which he or she considers necessary to preserve the
property.

Thus, the receiver may be given power to appoint attorneys, to give up possession to prior mortgagees, to give up property generally to prior claimants, to give
up tenancies, to close a business, to compromise claims, to grant leases, to give
undertakings not to commit nuisances, to promote a Bill in Parliament, to pay out
certain debenture-holders, to repair, to pay off prior incumbrances, to go abroad to
arrange a sale of assets, and generally to exercise any power or authority which the
court can, under its statutory or general jurisdiction, direct or sanction.[300]

Application for directions.   The receiver may apply to the court at any time for   **7-81**
directions to assist in the carrying out of the functions as a receiver,[301] in addition
to those directions which may have already been given on appointment.[302]

The receiver will normally apply by filing an application notice[303]; but if the
directions sought are unlikely to be contentious or important to the parties, he or
she may apply by letter, and the court may reply by letter, or may summon the
receiver for an interview to receive oral directions. In such a case, the receiver need
not serve on the parties copies of the letter of application, or the court's letter of
reply, unless the court orders so to do.[304]

However, where the receiver has applied by letter, the court may order him or
her to file and serve an application notice.[305] After giving any directions, the court
may order the receiver to serve the application notice and the directions given, on
any person.[306]

Receivers appointed by mortgagees of a business.   It is the duty of receivers to   **7-82**
preserve the property entrusted to them. If, therefore, debenture-holders obtain the
appointment of a receiver over the actual assets of the business, apart from the
goodwill, it is no part of the duty of such receiver to preserve the goodwill: he or
she has to preserve the assets entrusted to him or her with a view to their most
favourable realisation: the receiver need not have regard to contracts entered into
by the company,[307] though it may become necessary to apply for certain powers of
management to preserve the assets which are in his or her possession. Where,
however, the receiver is also appointed manager, the goodwill forms part of the
property entrusted to his or her care, and the receiver must, in order to preserve it,
carry out contracts entered into by the mortgagor, unless authorised by the court to
disregard them.[308]

A receiver of the property of a foreign company, appointed by a foreign court of

---

[300] Forms of application, *Atkin's Court Forms* (2011 issue), Vol.33, paras 233 ff. Forms of order, 1 *Seton*,
    7th edn, p.762; *Palmer's Company Precedents*, 16th edn, Pt III, Ch.62.
[301] CPR r.69.6.
[302] CPR PD 69, paras 6.1-6.3.
[303] CPR PD 69, para.8.1.
[304] CPR PD 69, para.8.2.
[305] CPR PD 69, para.8.3.
[306] CPR r.69.6.
[307] See *Re Newdigate Colliery Co* [1912] 1 Ch. 468.
[308] See n.306, above and see Ch.9.

competent jurisdiction, can maintain an action in his or her own name[309] to recover money due to the company.[310]

---

[309] Semble, the company can be joined as co-claimant.

[310] *Macaulay v Guaranty Trust Co* [1927] W.N. 308: party costs were allowed to the defendant and ordered to be deducted. Semble, that where the debt and appointment are clearly established, the court may refuse to allow defendants their costs.

CHAPTER 8

LIABILITIES OF A RECEIVER

Liability under general law. In addition to the liabilities of a receiver dealt with **8-1** in this chapter, there are various statutes and statutory provisions under which a receiver, whose duties include the carrying on or the winding up of a business, may incur liability to penalties, e.g. Occupiers' Liability Act 1957, the Health and Safety At Work etc Act 1974, the Food Safety Act 1990, Licensing Act 2003. Further, a receiver may have to observe agreements with trade unions and other bodies regulating the conditions of employment of workpeople. It is therefore essential for a receiver, when concerned in carrying on a business, to obtain expert advice from persons experienced in similar businesses: see e.g. as to waste management licenses, para.8-15, below.

Liability to account. A receiver is liable to account for all money coming into **8-2** his or her hands, in the capacity of receiver, at any time, whether before or after the date of perfecting his or her security, and even after the appointment has lapsed.[1] The principle, that the appointment is merely conditional until his or her security is perfected, has no application where the question is as to his or her own liability, or that of his or her sureties, in respect of money received or expended by the receiver.[2]

Responsibility for losses. A receiver is responsible for any loss occasioned to the **8-3** estate over which the appointment is made, by reason of the receiver's wilful default.[3] If the receiver places money received in what he or she knows to be improper hands, the receiver will have to answer for the loss out of his or her own pocket.[4] A receiver, however, is not expected, any more than is a trustee or executor, to take more care of property than would a reasonably prudent person of business.[5] If a receiver deposits money for safe custody with a banker in good credit, to be placed to his or her account as receiver, he or she will not be answerable for the failure of the banker.[6] The money must, however, be deposited to the account of the receiver in that character, or be otherwise earmarked. If a receiver pays money, which comes into his or her hands as receiver, into a private account with a banker, and not into a separate account as receiver, or otherwise mixes up the

---

[1] For the form of the order in this case, see *Practice Note* [1943] W.N. 71.
[2] *Smart v Flood* (1833) 49 L.T. 467.
[3] *Re Skerrett's Minor* (1829) 2 Hog. 192.
[4] *Knight v Lord Plymouth* (1747) 3 Atk. 480.
[5] This is the standard required from persons in fiduciary positions in all cases: see *Speight v Gaunt* (1883) 9 App. Cas. HL.
[6] *Knight v Lord Plymouth*, n.4, above.

money which he or she collects as receiver with his or her own money, the receiver will be liable for the loss if the banker fails.[7]

8-4   **Parting with control of fund.**   If a receiver puts a fund out of his or her own control, so that other persons are able to deal with it, he or she is answerable for any loss that may ensue.[8] Accordingly, where the receiver, in order to obtain sureties, had agreed that the money, to be collected from the property over which he was receiver, should be handed over to a partner of one of the sureties, and should be deposited with bankers in the joint names of the sureties, and that all drafts upon the money so deposited should be written by the partner and signed by the receiver, it was held that the receiver was liable for the loss occasioned by the failure of the banking house in which the money had been deposited.[9] If, indeed, a receiver parts with control over the fund, by introducing the control of an irresponsible person who is unknown to the court, it is conceived that he or she will be answerable for any loss which may happen to the fund which he or she has so dealt with, not only where some particular peril in which he or she has placed the fund can be shown to have been the cause of the loss, but generally, where the receiver has not conducted himself or herself as a prudent person would have done.[10]

Where a receiver had paid money to the plaintiff's solicitor, with directions to pay it into court, which had not been done, the receiver was held liable for the loss, there being no sufficient evidence to show that the receiver had authority from the plaintiff to pay the money to the solicitor.[11] Where a receiver, appointed by way of equitable execution, pays money to the judgment creditor's solicitor instead of to the creditor, he or she will be liable if the money never comes to the creditor's hands.[12]

If a receiver is in default for not submitting accounts and paying any balances within the proper time, or if, not being in default, he or she derives a benefit by accepting interest on the balances which are from time to time in the hands of his or her banker, he or she is liable to make good any loss which may be occasioned by the bankruptcy of the banker, although the moneys may have been deposited to a separate account.[13]

A person who, having improperly assumed the character, neglects the duties of a receiver, while the parties interested consider him or her to be acting as a receiver, makes himself or herself responsible for any property which is lost through neglect.[14] If a solicitor in an action assumes the character of a receiver, and rents are paid to him or her in that character, he or she will be ordered to pay them over

---

[7]   *Wren v Kirton* (1805) 11 Ves. 377. As to following money which the receiver has mixed with money of his own, cf. *James Roscoe Ltd v Winder* [1915] 1 Ch. 62.

[8]   *Salway v Salway* (1831) 2 R. & M. 214.

[9]   *Salway v Salway*, n.8, above; *Salway v Salway* in the House of Lords, sub nom. *White v Baugh* (1835) 9 Bligh 181; 3 Cl. & Fin.44.

[10] *Salway v Salwayi*, n.8, above.

[11] *Delfosse v Crawshay* (1834) 4 L.J. Ch. 32; see, too, *Dixon v Wilkinson* (1859) 4 Drew. 614; 4D G. & J. 508.

[12] *Ind, Coope & Co v Kidd* (1844) 63 L.J. Q.B. 726.

[13] *Drever v Maudesley* (1844) 13 L.J. Ch. 433; 8 Jur.547; 3 L.T. 157; see, too, *Shaw v Rhodes* (1827) 2 Russ. 539; *Wilkinson v Bewick* (1853) 4 Jur. (N.S.) 101.

[14] *Wood v Wood* (1828) 4 Russ. 558.

to the real receiver, and can claim upon them either by virtue of an agreement with a party to the action, for costs.[15]

Moneys received "belong" to court.   All money which comes to the hands of a   **8-5**
receiver, by virtue of an order of the court entitling him or her to receive it, belongs in a sense to the court, and the receiver can only be discharged by applying it in accordance with an order.[16]

If a receiver has paid money to a wrong person, and is afterwards obliged by that person's mortgagees to pay the amount into court, and after due application thereof a surplus remains, the court will not pay over such surplus to the person to whom the former payment was wrongfully made, without satisfying the receiver's demands.[17] If, however, the wrongful payment is made by the receiver's agent, the receiver cannot have the benefit of the payment against the surplus, except subject to any liability of the agent to the person to whom the wrongful payment was made; and the accounts cannot be opened between those persons, on application by the executor of the receiver, praying for repayment from the person wrongfully paid, or, in default of such repayment, out of the rents of the estate over which the receiver was appointed.[18]

When ordered to pay costs.   A receiver may be ordered personally to pay costs   **8-6**
incurred by reason of his or her misconduct or neglect in the discharge of his or her duties.[19] The receiver will not, however, be held personally responsible if he or she has honestly done his or her best and has failed. If a receiver has not succeeded in getting in rents, it is his or her first duty to lay the state of affairs before the court, and to ask for guidance, under circumstances where the incumbrancers on the property can consult with the receiver and advise as to the best course to be pursued for their common interests.[20]

When the receiver conducts or takes over the company's proceedings.   A   **8-7**
receiver, who takes over the defence of proceedings already commenced by the company, may be personally liable for the adverse costs which may be incurred, if unsuccessful; but he or she may claim reimbursement of such costs as expenses of the receivership.[21] The cases recognise that injustice may be caused where litigation is conducted by a receiver on behalf of an insolvent company for the benefit of secured creditors. In an appropriate case a non-party costs order may be made against a receiver or against the secured creditor. A costs order against the receiver will be more readily made where the company is in liquidation and the receiver's agency has terminated (if such be the case) or where the successful party has not been able to obtain security for costs or adequate security for costs.[22]

Where a receiver of leases containing beneficial rent review clauses negligently

---

[15] *Wickens v Townshend* (1830) 1 Russ. & M. 361.
[16] See de *Winton v Mayor of Brecon* (1859) 28 Beav. 200.
[17] *Gurden v Badcock* (1842) 6 Beav. 157.
[18] See n.17, above.
[19] *Ex p. Brown* (1888) 36 W.R. 303.
[20] *Re St. George's Estate* (1887) 19 L.R. Ir. 566.
[21] *Anderson v Hyde* [1996] 2 B.C.L.C. 144.
[22] *Mills v Birchall* [2008] 1 WLR 1829.

failed to implement those clauses, he was held liable to the mortgagor for the losses sustained by the estate from his failure to collect the enhanced rents.[23]

8-8 **Breach of statutory duty.** A receiver is personally liable for breach of a statutory duty; e.g. if, with notice of a preferential claim, he or she exhausts the assets in making payments to other creditors, he or she is liable for damages in tort to the preferential creditors[24]: it would be difficult, if not impossible, for a receiver successfully to allege want of notice in such a case, as notice would be implied from the circumstances.[25] An inquiry is now ordered as to preferential debts.[26] Preferential debts were greatly reduced in volume, when Crown preferential debts were abolished by the Enterprise Act 2002.[27]

PERSONAL ACCOUNTABILITY OF A RECEIVER

8-9 **Attachment under the Debtors Acts.** A person who owes money, come to his or her hands as receiver, is in a fiduciary capacity within the meaning of the third exception to s.4 of the Debtors Act 1869.[28] He or she is liable to committal for breach of an order to pay such money, made after he or she has been discharged from being receiver. The mere fact that a defaulting receiver is unable to pay is not sufficient to induce the court to exercise the discretion given by the Debtors Act 1878, and to refuse leave to issue a committal.[29]

8-10 **Misconduct in the exercise of duties.** Although the court will not allow the possession of its receiver to be disturbed without its leave,[30] it will, in its discretion, if the misconduct of the receiver becomes the subject of proceedings in another court, either itself take cognisance of the complaint, or leave the matter to be dealt with in the other proceedings.[31] There is a clear and well-recognised distinction between cases where the jurisdiction of the court, or the validity or propriety of its orders or process, is disputed, and cases where the authority of the court is admitted, but redress is sought against its officer for irregularity or excess in the performance of its orders. In the former case, the court has no choice, but must draw the whole matter over to its own cognisance. In the latter case, the court has an indisputable right to assume the exclusive jurisdiction; but it may, if it thinks fit, refuse to interfere and may permit another court to proceed for punishment or redress.[32]

8-11 **Purchase by receiver.** A receiver is in a fiduciary capacity, and cannot, without the special leave of the court, purchase either directly, or indirectly in the name of a trustee for himself or herself, any property or interest in property over which he

---

[23] *Knight v Lawrence* (1991) B.C.C. 411, V.C.
[24] *Woods v Winskill* [1913] 2 Chr.303; *Westminster Corp. v Haste* [1950] Ch. 442; *I.R.C. v Goldblatt* [1972] Ch. 948; and cf. *Argylls Ltd v Coxeter* (1913) 29 T.L.R. 355.
[25] *Westminster Corp v Chapman* [1916] 1 Ch. 161; see further, para.7-74, above.
[26] See n.23, above.
[27] Enterprise Act 2002 s.251. See para.7-62, above.
[28] Relating to default by a person acting in a fiduciary capacity and ordered to pay any sum in his or her possession or under his or her control by a court of equity.
[29] *Re Gent* (1888) 40 Ch. D. 190.
[30] See paras 6-31, 6-48 and 6-56, above.
[31] See, further, para.6-32, above.
[32] *Aston v Heron* (1834) 2 My. & K. 390; see, too, *Chalie v Pickering* (1837) 1 Keen 749.

or she is receiver,[33] he or she must therefore account for any profit made through a purchase or other dealing.[34] A receiver is a trustee for the parties interested of any money due from him or her as a receiver and not accounted for, and could not, as against them, avail himself or herself of any Statute of Limitations, even when the receiver's final accounts have been passed and the receivership terminated.[35] The opinion has been expressed that a receiver is not within the protection of s.21 of the Limitation Act 1980.[36] It appears that a receiver cannot claim relief from personal liability under s.61 of the Trustee Act 1925, at least where he or she is paid.[37]

Personal liability and right to indemnity. A receiver appointed by the court is **8-12** an officer of the court: he or she is therefore not an agent for any other person, but a principal,[38] and as such is personally liable to all persons contracting with him or her, irrespective of the amount of assets in the receiver's hands, unless his or her personal liability is excluded by the express terms of the contract,[39] subject to a correlative right to be indemnified out of the assets in respect of all liabilities properly incurred.[40] A receiver is entitled to this indemnity, in priority even to the claims of persons who had advanced money under an order making the repayment of the advance a first charge on all assets,[41] and in priority to the costs of the action,[42] and subject only to the claimant's costs of realisation.[43] Questions as to a receiver's liability, and his or her right to indemnity in contract and in tort, occur most frequently where the receiver is also appointed manager, and are dealt with fully in Ch.9. A receiver's right to indemnity was held not to extend to the costs of an action, charging him with fraud, but successfully defended, where the acts complained of did not benefit the estate and were not in discharge of his duties.[44]

A receiver, appointed by the court at the instance of debenture-holders and mortgagees of a company, is personally liable as a principal in respect of contracts or engagements entered; but he or she is not personally liable in respect of breaches of contracts which were entered into by the company before the appointment.[45] A receiver of the assets of a company was not held personally liable to refund money paid to him in discharge of a debt, after he had paid the money into court, though the payment to the receiver was, without his knowledge, void as a fraudulent

---

33 See para.7-55, above.
34 See *Nugent v Nugent* [1908] 1 Ch. 546, and notes to *Fox v Mackreth* (1791) 2 White and Tudor, Cases in Equity.
35 *Seagram v Tuck* (1881) 18 Ch. D. 296.
36 *Re Cornish* [1896] 1 Q.B. 99 per Kay LJ at p.104, concerning the former s.8 of the Trustee Relief Act 1888, and later, s.19 of the Limitation Act 1939. The actual decision was that the Act did not apply to a trustee in bankruptcy. The observations of Lord Esher on this appear at variance with those of Lord Sterndale and Warrington LJ in *Re Richardson* [1920] 1 Ch. 438, 447. See, however, the judgment of Younger LJ at 449.
37 He or she is a paid trustee: see *Re Windsor Steam Coal co* [1929] 1 Ch. 151 per Lawrence LJ.
38 Except receivers of statutory undertakings: see para.9-20, below.
39 As to the contrary doctrine evolved by the American courts, see para.9-15, below.
40 *Burt, Boulton and Hayward v Bull* [1895] 1 Q.B. 276; *Re Glasdir Copper Mines* [1906] 1 Ch. 365; *Re A. Boynton Ltd* [1910] 1 Ch. 519; *Moss Steamship Co v Whinney* [1912] A.C. 271 per Lord Mersey; and see *Ex p. Izard* (1883) 23 Ch. D. 75, 79; *Re Brooke* [1894] 2 Ch. 600.
41 *Strapp v Bull, Sons & Co* [1895] 2 Ch. 1; *Re Glasdir Copper Mines* n.38, above; *Re A. Boynton Ltd*, n.38, above.
42 *Batten v Wedgwood Coal Co* (1885) 28 Ch. D. 317.
43 See *Re London United Breweries* [1907] 2 Ch. 511; and *Ramsey v Simpson* [1899] I I.R. 194.
44 *Re Dunn* [1904] 1 Ch. 648.
45 cf. *Re Botibol* [1947] 1 All E.R. 26; and *Airline Spares v Handley Page* [1970] Ch.193. See as regards leases paras 7-34 ff, above and paras 9-15 and 9-17, below.

preference.[46] However, the law as to voidable preferences has been substantially altered by the Insolvency Act 1986.[47] He or she can apply to enforce his indemnity by means of an application for directions.[48]

If a receiver appointed by the court is charged with trespass, the court has jurisdiction, if it thinks fit, to restrain the action and leave the intending claimant to claim in the proceedings in which the receiver was appointed.[49]

The "owner" made liable by s.38(4) of the Water Act 1945 did not include a constructive owner such as a receiver,[50] and the person liable under para.54 of Sch.3 to that Act[51] was the person who actually collected the rents; accordingly, where a mortgagor had appointed a collector who paid them first to the mortgagor and afterwards to a receiver, the collector and not the receiver was held liable to pay the water rate.[52]

Receiver's liability for Value Added Tax (VAT).

8-13   (a) *Liability of administrators and administrative receivers.* Regulation 9 of the VAT Regulations 1995 (as amended) provides (in part) that if a taxable person becomes bankrupt or incapacitated, "the Commissioners may, from the date on which he died or became bankrupt or incapacitated treat as a taxable person any person carrying on that business until some other person is registered in respect of the taxable supplies made or intended to be made by that taxable person in the course or furtherance of his business or the incapacity ceases, as the case may be; and the provisions of the [VAT] Act [1994] and of any Regulations made thereunder shall apply to any person so treated as though he were a registered person." Regulation 9(3) provides that "in relation to a company which is a taxable person, the references in paragraph 1 of this Regulation to the taxable person becoming bankrupt or incapacitated shall be construed as references to its going into liquidation or receivership or entering administration." Regulation 9(3) appears to have been intended to cover receivers appointed with respect to companies as administrative receivers.

When an administrative receiver begins to carry on the business of the company, he or she must within 21 days inform the HMRC that he or she has done so, and of the date when the receivership commenced.[53] HMRC is as-

---

[46] See *Re Morant & Co* [1924] 1 Ch. 79; cf. *Bissell v Ariel Motors* (1910) 27 T.L.R. 73. The term now employed is "voidable preference". The same rule would apply, even if the debt arose on a contract made by the receiver. Application could be made in the action by the trustee in bankruptcy for payment out of the fund.
[47] See Insolvency Act 1986 s.239 (companies winding up), and s.340 (bankruptcy); for the orders which may be made under these sections, after setting aside a voidable preference, see Insolvency Act 1986 ss.241, 342.
[48] *Re Therm-a-Stor Ltd* [1996] 1 W.L.R. 1338.
[49] See *Aston v Heron* (1834) 1 My. & K. 390; and n.30.
[50] *Metropolitan Water Board v Brooks* [1911] 1 K.B. 289 (a decision on s.4 of the Water Companies (Regulation of Powers) Act 1887). As to liability in respect of gas, electric, light, rates, etc. see para.6-7, above.
[51] The Water Act 1945 was finally completely repealed by the Water Act 1989.
[52] Decided on s.72 of the Waterworks Clauses Act 1847. References in the Water Act 1945 s.38, to "a water rate" included charges payable under Pt III of the Water Act 1973, and those in Sch.3 included a reference to any such charge for services, which included a supply of water for domestic purposes: Water Act 1973 s.40(2) and Sch.8 para.53.
[53] VAT Regulations 1995 (SI 1995/2518) reg.9(2).

sumed to have the power, in the case of corporate receiverships, to bring the current VAT period to an end.[54]

(b) *Liability of receivers appointed under statutory powers.* Regulation 9 does not, as a matter of construction, cover other receivers appointed in the exercise of statutory powers, such as the Law of Property Act 1925 s.109(8); the term "going into receivership" cannot be construed so as to include the appointment of such receivers.[55] Such a receiver accordingly has a discretion as to whether to pay over VAT monies received to HMRC; but although such a discretion exists, such receivers were held, initially, not to be entitled to exercise it, by refraining from making payment, since they would thereby be causing the company to commit a criminal offence,[56] although that sanction has since been repealed.[57] It has since been held that, notwithstanding that such a receiver has such a discretion, and there is no longer any criminal sanction, he or she would be acting dishonourably, towards those persons who had paid him the VAT payments, if he or she did not pay them over to HMRC.[58]

When the receiver is treated as "a taxable person". The effect of para.(1) of reg.9 appears to be this. If a company has a receiver appointed, the Commissioners may treat the receiver as a taxable person carrying on the company's business, with the consequence that all the obligations laid on taxable persons, under the general VAT legislation, will fall on the receiver. The Commissioners are, however, not obliged to treat the receiver as a taxable person. They may, presumably, continue to treat the company as the taxable person. Presumably, also, they cannot treat the receiver as a taxable person, unless the receiver actually carries on the company's business. Regulation 9(1) cannot apply, where some other person is registered as a taxable person in relation to the former business of the company. If the receiver is not acting as agent of the company, and elects to carry on the company's former business, then it would seem that he or she should cause himself or herself to be registered in respect of the business, since he or she will be the person carrying it on.   **8-14**

If the receiver is treated as a taxable person under reg.9(1), or is actually registered as a taxable person, he or she will be personally liable for VAT on the supplies made. The receiver must, in this situation, be certain that he or she can treat the VAT, for which he or she is liable, as an expense of the receivership having priority over creditors. If the receiver is an agent of the company, the Commissioners are perhaps unlikely to invoke reg.9(1) and the company will remain the taxable person. Nevertheless, although the receiver is not then under any personal liability to pay over to the Commissioners the VAT on supplies made by the company and received by it, nevertheless he or she ought so to do.[59]

Onerous property: waste management licences. The power of disclaiming onerous property, possession of which can impose personal liability on the manager   **8-15**

---

[54] VAT Regulations 1995 (SI 1995/2518) regs 25(3) and 30.
[55] See *Sargent v Commissioners of Customs and Excise* [1995] 1 W.L.R. 821 CA.
[56] *Re John Willment (Ashford) Ltd* [1980] 1 W.L.R. 173, per Brightman J.
[57] Finance Act 1985 s.31.
[58] *Sargent v Customs & Excise* [1995] 1 W.L.R. 821 CA (varying [1994] 1 W.L.R. 235 Judge Paul Baker QC).
[59] For a valuable analysis of the question, whether and if so when the receiver can be declared to be "a taxable person", see Lightman and Moss, *The Law of Receivers and Administrators of Companies*, 4th edn (2000), Ch.18.

of a business, and are exercisable by a liquidator or a trustee in bankruptcy,[60] has not yet been conferred on administrative receivers or administrators.[61]

---

[60] Insolvency Act 1986 ss.178 (companies) and 315 (bankrupts).
[61] As in the case of waste management licences: *Re Celtic Extraction Ltd* [2000] 2 W.L.R. 991; sub nom. *Official Receiver v Environment Agency* [1999] B.P.I.R. 986 CA.

Chapter 9

MANAGERS

Where a receiver is required for the purposes not only of receiving rents and profits, or of getting in outstanding property, but also of carrying on or superintending a trade, business or undertaking, he or she is called a manager, or more usually a receiver and manager. The appointment of a manager implies that he or she has power to deal with the property over which he or she is appointed manager, and to appropriate the proceeds in a proper manner.[1]

9-0

In what cases appointed. Where the court appoints a manager of a business or an undertaking, it in effect takes the management of it into its own hands; for the manager is an officer of the court. Managers, when appointed by the court, are responsible to the court, and can have no regard to orders from any of the parties interested in the business. The court will not usually assume the management of a business or undertaking, except in two cases. First, with a view to its winding-up and sale as a going concern, in which case the management ends with the sale,[2] and, secondly, with a view to deciding the proper constitution of the body to which the management should properly be entrusted, in which case the management ends with such determination.[3] The court may, however, appoint a person to manage the business of a testator pursuant to the trusts of his will, although no sale or winding-up is contemplated, for instance, where the legatee of the business is an infant.[4] The case of public undertakings is discussed on a later page.[5]

9-1

The court also has jurisdiction, upon application for interim relief, to authorise a receiver to exercise such powers of management as are necessary for the preservation of property which is the subject of litigation, and to which the applicant has made out a prima facie title.[6] Thus, where the application was made by a lessor in an action to recover possession of a licensed hotel, the lease of which contained covenants by the lessee to keep the premises continuously open as an hotel, and not

---

[1] *Sheppard v Oxenford* (1855) 1 K. & J. 491; *Re Manchester & Milford Ry* (1880) 14 Ch. D. 645, 653; *Truman v Redgrave* (1881) 18 Ch. D. 547; *Parsons v Sovereign Bank of Canada* [1913] A.C. 160.
[2] *Gardner v LC & D Ry* (1867) 2 Ch.App. 201, 211, 212 per Lord Cairns; *Whitley v Challis* [1892] 1 Ch. 64, 69; *Re Newdigate Colliery Co* [1912] 1 Ch. 468, 472; *Re Newport Construction Co; Barclays Bank v The Company* [1948] Ch. 217, 220.
[3] *Trade Auxiliary Company v Vickers* (1873) L.R. 16 Eq. 303; *AG v Schonfeld* (1979) J. 3729, Order of Walton J, 13 July appointment of receiver and manager of charity, until after hearing of originating summons to determine constitution of management. See further the report at [1980] 1 W.L.R. 1182 at 1184.
[4] See *Re Irish* (1888) 40 Ch. D. 49.
[5] See paras 9-20 and 9-23, below.
[6] *Leney & Sons Ltd v Callingham and Thompson* [1908] 1 K.B. 79. See especially, judgment of Farwell LJ; *Charrington v Camp* [1902] 1 Ch. 386; and see now CPR Pt 25. For procedures, see CPR Pt 23 and PD 23A.

to endanger the licences, the court, being satisfied that the licences were in jeopardy, owing to threats by the defendant lessee to close the hotel, appointed a receiver, directed the licences to be handed over to him, and authorised him to keep the premises open as an hotel, and to do all acts necessary to preserve the licences.[7] In such cases, the receiver is not given general powers of management, but such powers only as are necessary to preserve the property.

A manager may be appointed to carry on a private trade or business, with a view to effecting a sale or winding-up for the benefit of the persons interested. Thus, a manager was appointed to carry on the business of an intestate, there being no existing representative of his estate.[8] Where trustees have to manage a business, but are not themselves qualified to do so, and cannot agree on appointing a manager, the court may appoint a receiver and manager of the business[9]; but the more usual course would be to authorise the trustees to appoint a manager at a salary.

9-2   **Scope of Appointment.**   It may happen that the business which the receiver and manager is appointed to manage turns out to be unprofitable; or not to be capable of making sufficient profit to meet the normal costs of the receivership. In such a case, the court may, of course, authorise the receiver and manager to close down the business,[10] or may, alternatively, if such a course is feasible, simply curtail the duties which the receiver and manager would normally perform, so as to avoid further loss.[11]

9-3   **Partnership.**   The court has jurisdiction to appoint a manager of a partnership business, with a view to winding it up or selling it as a going concern,[12] and notwithstanding that the partnership has expired, pursuant to a provision contained in the partnership.[13] The appointment is made for the purpose of preserving the assets and nothing more: the court does not intend to throw any liabilities of an onerous nature upon the partners.[14]

9-4   **"Patients" under the Mental Health Act.**   Under the previous receivership regime under the Mental Health Act 1983, the judge[15] was able to authorise the receiver of the estate of the patient to carry on his or her trade or business.[16] The

---

[7]   *Leney & Sons Ltd v Callingham and Thompson* [1908] 1 K.B. 79, q.v. as to form of order.

[8]   *Steer v Steer* (1864) 2 Dr. & Sm. 311. See also *Blackett v Blackett* (1871) 19 W.R. 559; *Spencer v Shaw* [1875] W.N. 115; *Re Wright* (1888) 32 S.J. 721. As to manager of a newspaper, see *Chaplin v Young* (1862) 6 L.T. 97.

[9]   *Hart v Denham* [1871] W.N. 2 per Lord Romilly MR.

[10]   For an example, see the order of the Master of 1 November 1977 in *Fillippi v Antoniazzi* (1976) F. 2251, unreported, where it was ordered that the receiver and manager should be at liberty to cease trading forthwith.

[11]   See n.10, above and master's order of 12 May 1977, whereby it was ordered that the duties of the receiver and manager in relation to the supervision of the income and expenditure mentioned in the order appointing him should be limited to half-a-day's work per week.

[12]   See also Ch.2, paras 2-83 ff, above.

[13]   *Taylor v Neate* (1888) 39 Ch. D. 538.

[14]   per Chitty J in *Taylor v Neate* (1888) 39 Ch. D. 538, 545. See also *Boehm v Goodall* [1911] 1 Ch. 155.

[15]   i.e. the Judge of the Court of Protection, or, by direction, the Public Trustee: see paras 2-105 ff, above.

[16]   See the repealed Mental Health Act 1983 ss.93, 94, 96(1)(f), 99(1), 112. For the previous regime dealing with insolvent "patients", see Ch.2, para.2-107, above.

person so authorised was, for the purpose of estimating liability to persons dealing with him or her, the agent of the patient.[17]

Special manager in bankruptcy cases. By s.370 of the Insolvency Act 1986, ap- **9-5** plication may be made by an interim receiver (who will usually be the Official Receiver), or by the trustee of the bankrupt's estate, in any case where it appears to such person that the nature of the estate, property or business, or the interests of the creditors generally, so requires, for the appointment of any person to be the special manager of a bankrupt's estate, of the business of an undischarged bankrupt, or of the property or business of a debtor.[18] A special manager so appointed has such powers as may be entrusted to him or her by the court, which may give a direction that any provision in Pts VIII–XI of the Insolvency Act 1986, that has effect in relation to the Official Receiver, interim receiver or trustee, is to have the same effect in relation to the special manager, for the purpose of carrying out any of the functions of the official receiver, interim receiver, or trustee.[19]

A special manager so appointed must give such security as may be prescribed,[20] prepare and keep such accounts as may be prescribed,[21] and produce those accounts, in accordance with the Insolvency Rules 2016 to the Secretary of State or to such other persons as may be prescribed.[22]

The appointment will terminate if the bankruptcy petition is dismissed, or, if, an interim receiver having been appointed, is discharged without a bankruptcy order having been made.[23] If the interim receiver or the trustee is of opinion that the employment of the special manager is no longer necessary or beneficial to the estate, he or she must apply to the court for directions, and the court may order the appointment to be terminated.[24] The interim receiver or the trustee must make the same application, if the creditors decide that the appointment should be terminated.[25] Where, while acting as interim receiver under s.286, prior to a bankruptcy order[26] the Official Receiver was appointed special manager, but the petition was afterwards dismissed, the special manager was held entitled to be paid his expenses properly incurred and his remuneration out of his receipts; the debtor could not impugn any acts done by the manager in the proper conduct of the business.[27]

Special manager in winding-up cases. Where a company has gone into liquida- **9-6** tion, or a provisional liquidator has been appointed, the court may, on application by the liquidator or provisional liquidator, appoint any person to be the special

---

[17] *Plumpton v Burkinshaw* [1908] 2 K.B. 572.
[18] Insolvency Act 1986 s.370(1), (2). For the procedure on such appointment, see Insolvency Rules 2016 Pt 10 Ch.7. There is no appeal from a refusal to make such an application: *Re Whittaker* (1884) 1 Mom. 3(1) though sed quarae under the Insolvency Act 1986.
[19] Insolvency Act 1986 s.370(3), (4).
[20] As to security, see Insolvency Rules 2016 r.10.95 and Ch.6, above.
[21] See Insolvency Rules 2016 r.10.97.
[22] Insolvency Act 1986 s.370(5).
[23] Insolvency Rules 2016 r.10.98(1).
[24] Insolvency Rules 2016 r.10.98(2).
[25] Insolvency Rules 2016 r.10.98(3).
[26] See Insolvency Act, 1986 s.286, as to powers of interim receiver.
[27] *Re AB & Co (No.2)* [1900] 2 Q.B. 429; *Re A Bankruptcy Petition* (1900) 7 Mans. 132 (under Bankruptcy Act 1883). Accounts could be enforced under BA 1883, later BA 1914 s.105(5): see *Re Jones* [1908] 1 K.B. 204.

manager of the business or property of the company.[28] The application may be made in any case where it appears to them that the nature of the business or property of the company, or the interests of the company's creditors or contributories or members generally, require the appointment of another person to manage the company's business or property.[29]

The special manager has such powers as may be entrusted by the court, which may direct that any provision of the Insolvency Act 1986, that has effect in relation to the provisional liquidator or liquidator of a company, is to have the like effect in relation to the special manager, for the purposes of the carrying out by him or her of any of the functions of the provisional liquidator or liquidator.[30]

The special manager must give such security (or, in Scotland, caution) as may be prescribed[31]; prepare and keep such accounts as may be prescribed[32]; and produce those accounts in accordance with the rules to the Secretary of State or to such other persons as may be prescribed.[33]

The special manager's appointment terminates if the winding-up petition is dismissed, or, if a provisional liquidator having been appointed, the latter is discharged without a winding-up order having been made.[34] If the liquidator is of the opinion that the employment of the special manager is no longer necessary or profitable for the company, he or she must apply to the court for directions, and the court may order the termination of the appointment.[35] The liquidator must make the same application, if a resolution of the creditors is passed, requesting that the appointment be terminated.[36] This appointment implies the payment of reasonable remuneration.[37]

9-7 **On application of incumbrancers.**[38]   The court will appoint a manager upon the application of incumbrancers whose security includes the goodwill[39]; but unless the goodwill is included, a receiver only will be appointed,[40] though he or she may be given such powers of management as are necessary to preserve the property actually comprised in the security.[41] An incumbrancer with a charge upon the goodwill has an option either to have a receiver simply, or a receiver and manager.[42]

The legal mortgagees of a hotel, whose security comprised the trade fixtures, goodwill and business, obtained upon interlocutory motion the appointment of a

---

[28] Insolvency Act 1986 s.177(1). For the procedure on such appointment, see Insolvency Rules 2016 Pt 3 of Pt 5, Pt 5 of Pt 6 and Pt 12 of Pt 7.
[29] Insolvency Act 1986 s.177(2).
[30] Insolvency Act 1986 s.177(3), (4).
[31] See the Insolvency Rules 2016 rr.5.18, 6.38 and 7.94.
[32] Insolvency Rules 2016 rr.5.20, 6.40 and 7.96.
[33] Insolvency Act 1986 s.177(5).
[34] Insolvency Rules 2016 r.7.97(1) which applies in compulsory winding up. See r.6.41 for the position in a creditors' voluntary liquidation and r.5.21 in a members' voluntary liquidation.
[35] Insolvency Rules 2016 r.7.97(2) applicable in a compulsory winding up.
[36] Insolvency Rules 2016 r.7.97(3) applicable in a compulsory winding up.
[37] *Re US Ltd* (1983) 127 S.J. 748, which will be fixed by the court pursuant to Insolvency Rules 2016 r.7.93(5).
[38] As to managers appointed under the powers in an instrument, see Ch.18, below.
[39] *Truman v Redgrave* (1881) 18 Ch. D. 547.
[40] *Whitley v Challis* [1892] 1 Ch. 64; *Re Lease Hotel* [1902] 1 Ch. 332.
[41] Upon the principles illustrated in *Leney & Sons Ltd v Callingham and Thompson*, para.9-1, above.
[42] See para.2-32, above.

manager to carry on the business of a licensed victualler carried on in it.[43] So also a manager has been appointed at the instance of holders of a registered statutory mortgage of a steamship[44]; of collieries held under a lease containing working covenants[45]; and, on the application of the unpaid vendor, of the property of a company in liquidation.[46] In order that the goodwill may be included in the security, it need not be expressly mentioned: thus, where debentures issued by a hotel company charged "all its property and effects whatsoever," it was held that the goodwill of the business was included.[47]

Companies. The appointment of a manager was, at one time, very frequently made over the undertaking of an ordinary limited company, on the application of mortgages or debenture-holders whose security included the goodwill[48]; and it is well settled that the court will readily make such an appointment, in order to enable a beneficial realisation of the property comprised in the security to be effected.[49] For the appointment of a receiver only, without powers of management, must inevitably cause damage to or the destruction of the goodwill, which cannot be preserved for the benefit of the persons who have a charge upon it, unless a manager is appointed. Even where there is no goodwill of any saleable value, it is often necessary to carry on the business for a time, in order to facilitate the sale of the assets as a going concern. Where three sets of debentures had been issued, each of which created a charge on certain specific items in addition to a general floating charge, the court appointed a receiver in each of three actions brought by the different sets of debenture-holders, and appointed the receiver for the first debenture-holder manager.[50] A manager cannot, except under the express authority of a statute, be appointed of a public undertaking.[51]

9-8

Practice on Appointment. A manager is appointed for a definite period, usually of from one to six months; if a realisation is not likely to be effected at the expiration of that period, application must be made to the court before such expiration to continue the appointment.[52]

A manager must obey strictly the terms of the appointment: he or she will be disallowed items of expenditure incurred subsequent to the appointment, as well as remuneration for services after that date.[53]

The preceding chapters of this book, relative to the practice on the appointment of receivers and to its consequences, are equally applicable where the receiver is

9-9

---

[43] *Truman v Redgrave* (1881) 18 Ch. D. 547; see this case for form of order. See also *Ind Coope & Co v Mee* [1895] W.N.8.

[44] *Fairfield, etc. Co v London and East Coast SS Co* [1895] W.N. 64.

[45] *Campbell v Lloyds Bank* (1889) 58 L.J. Ch. 424; *County of Gloucester Bank v Rudry Coal Co* [1895] 1 Ch. 629.

[46] *Boyle v Bettws Llantwit Co* (1876) 2 Ch. D. 726.

[47] *Re Leas Hotel Co* [1902] 1 Ch. 332; but, semble a mortgage of land and buildings, on which experimental works were carried on, would not authorise the appointment of a manager to carry on similar works as a commercial enterprise: *Stamford, etc. Banking Co v Keeble* [1913] 2 Ch. 96, 102. But cf. *Britannia Building Society v Crammer* [1997] B.P.I.R. 596 (a nursing home).

[48] See *Re Leas Hotel Co* n.47, at 334, and para.2-77, above.

[49] See *Edwards v Standard Rolling Stock Syndicate* [1893] 1 Ch. 574; *Re Victoria Steamboats* [1871] 1 Ch. 158; *Re Leas Hotel Co* [1902] 1 Ch. 332. For form of order, see Seton, 7th edn, p.735.

[50] *Re Ind. Coope & Co* [1911] 2 Ch. 223.

[51] See paras 9-20, 9-25, below.

[52] Application made in private. See CPR Pt 25.

[53] *Re Wood Green & Hornsey Laundry Ltd* [1918] 1 Ch. 423.

appointed manager, with the exceptions mentioned below: and many of the topics dealt within the last two preceding chapters apply to managers. These chapters should therefore be consulted as to any matter not dealt with here.

9-10   Effect of appointment of manager.   The appointment of a receiver and manager over the assets and business of a company does not dissolve or annihilate the company, any more than the taking of possession by the mortgagee of the fee of land let to tenants annihilates the mortgagor. Both continue to exist; but the company is entirely superseded in the conduct of that business, and deprived of all power to enter into contracts in relation to that business, or to sell, pledge or otherwise dispose of the property put into the possession or under the control of the receiver and manager. The powers of the directors in this respect are entirely in abeyance, so far as that business of the company is concerned, and the relevant powers of the company are exercised by the receiver under the direction of the court.[54]

9-11   Existing general contracts.   The receiver and manager is the agent neither of the company nor of the debenture-holders, but owes duties to both. He or she is appointed to preserve the goodwill of the business and, subject to any directions made on appointment, it is therefore the receiver's duty to carry into effect contracts entered into by the company before the appointment.[55] Such contracts, unless they are contracts depending on personal relationships, remain valid and subsisting, notwithstanding the appointment of a receiver and manager. Special rules, however, apply to contracts of employment; see below.[56]

Any breach of such contracts will render the company, not the manager,[57] liable in damages, and will, moreover, destroy the goodwill of the business. In this respect, a manager differs from a receiver appointed over the assets without any power to carry on the business, who is under no obligation, and has no powers, to carry out these contracts, nor to have regard to preserving the goodwill, and whose appointment therefore operates to determine the contracts.[58]

A manager must not, without leave of the court, disregard contracts in order to benefit the debenture-holders, since this course would both destroy the goodwill and render the company liable in damages; nor must he or she pick and choose which contracts to carry out as being most profitable.[59] If, however, it can be shown that to fulfil the contracts will benefit neither the company nor the debenture-holders, as, for instance, where to disregard them does not affect the value of the goodwill, the court will, on the application of the receiver, allow him or her to refrain from carrying them into effect.[60] The same principles apply to managers of a business appointed at the instance of mortgagees.

---

[54]   per Lord Atkinson in *Moss SS Co v Whinney* [1912] A.C. 254, 263; *Parsons v Sovereign Bank of Canada* [1913] A.C. 160. No estate vests in the manager; any action or assurance is in the name of the company.

[55]   See *Re Newdigate Colliery Co* [1912] 1 Ch. 468; *Parsons v Sovereign Bank of Canada* [1913] A.C. 160; *R. v Board of Trade Ex p. St. Martin's Preserving Co Ltd* [1965] 1 Q.B. 603, 614.

[56]   These are discussed below, at para.9-12, and in Ch.23.

[57]   The manager might, however, be liable in tort if he or she took steps which effectively prevented the completion of a contract: see *Re Botibol* [1947] 1 All E.R. 26.

[58]   See paras 6-63 ff, above.

[59]   *Re Newdigate Colliery Co* n.55, above; *Moss SS Co v Whinney* [1912] A.C. 262.

[60]   *Re Thames Ironworks* [1912] W.N. 66; 106 L.T. 674; *Re Great Cobar Ltd* [1915] 1 Ch. 682. In the last-named case, it appears to have been considered that the fact that to disregard the contract might have involved a heavy claim for damages was immaterial. See, however, the judgment of Buckley LJ in *Re Newdigate Colliery Co* n.55, above. If the debenture-holders will not be substantially

The above principles were illustrated in a case in which the Court of Appeal refused to allow the manager, appointed over the undertaking and assets of a colliery company, to disregard contracts which had been entered into for the forward supply of coal, even though, owing to a rise in price, this course would have enabled the manager to obtain enhanced receipts of the extent of £200 per week.[61] In another case, a company had contracted to construct, for £60,000, certain ships which were unfinished at the date of the appointment of the receiver and manager, and in respect of which £20,000, part of the purchase price, had then been paid on account: the company had given to a bank a charge, which ranked in priority to the debentures, to secure £40,000 on the ships and on the unpaid balance of £40,000 to be received under the contract: it was proved that the cost of completing the ships would amount, without profit, to £50,000. In these circumstances, the court refused to sanction a borrowing by the receiver and manager for the purpose of completing the ships, and authorised him to discontinue work upon them, on the ground that no benefit would accrue, either to the company or the debenture-holders, from the completion of the contract, and that in the circumstances it was not shown that the goodwill would be injured.[62]

Contracts of employment.   With respect to contracts of employment, the law has   **9-12**
been substantially changed, both by case law and by statute, with respect to administrators and administrative receivers, but not so substantially for other receivers and managers. Where, as must almost invariably be the case, the manager has been appointed to carry on an existing business, he or she will have needed to retain the existing employees in paid employment. Before the litigation in *Powdrill v Watson and associated cases*,[63] there had grown up a practice of seeking to protect receivers and managers and administrators from their potential personal liability on contracts of employment, under which they offered the continuation of paid employment on the same, or substantially the same, terms as previously but with a unilateral disclaimer of personal liability.[64] But in those cases, which terminated in the House of Lords,[65] it was held that such attempts to retain the services of the workforce, but without acceptance of personal liability, were wholly ineffectual, and that such conduct, whether by the receiver and manager, the administrative receiver or the administrator, constituted "adoption" in law under the statute. The serious effects of this for office holders were somewhat mitigated by the rapid enactment of the Insolvency Act 1994[66]; but that only relieved administrators and administrative receivers. For a detailed examination of these developments, see Ch.23. As these cases and statutory provisions did not, and do not, apply to court-appointed receivers, it would appear that without any specific statutory provision providing for personal liability of a court-appointed receiver (such as Insolvency Act 1986

---

prejudiced, it would seem that liability in damages would be an important factor, if there is likely to be a surplus after satisfying the debenture holders. cf. *Airlines Airspares Ltd v Handley Page Ltd* [1970] Ch. 192 (receiver and manager appointed out of court), para.9-19, below.

[61]   *Re Newdigate Colliery Co* n.55, above.
[62]   *Re Thames Ironworks* [1912] W.N. 66; 103 L.T. 674, where money had been borrowed to complete other contracts.
[63]   [1995] 2 A.C. 394 HL, affirming, though varying, the order in *Powdrill v Watson* [1994] I.C.R. 395, CA.
[64]   The so-called "Specialised Mouldings" form of letter.
[65]   See n.63, above.
[66]   The Insolvency Act 1994 received the Royal Assent on 25 March 1994, retrospective to 15 March 1994.

s.44 in relation to administrative receivers or s.37 in relation to other receivers and managers appointed out of court) such a receiver will incur no personal liability on a company's employment contracts if such personal liability is expressly excluded by the receiver and manager.

9-13   **Contracts: set-off.**   Inasmuch as a manager is considered to be carrying out contracts entered into by the company, if he or she continues to supply goods for which contracts had been entered into by the company before the appointment, the persons to whom the goods are supplied can, in an action by the receiver or by assignees for the price, set off damages for subsequent breach of such contracts by the manager ceasing to carry them out.[67] Unless the receiver and manager has obtained leave to disregard such contracts, he or she will be presumed to have acted thereunder, and not on new contracts made by him or her.[68] However, the effect of the crystallisation of the charge produced by the appointment of the receiver is that, as each purchase price due to the company is ascertained, it is immediately assigned by way of equitable charge to the debenture-holders. Accordingly, if at the date when it arises there is no right to a set-off, no set-off can be made, as the parties (the debenture-holders: the company) are not the same.[69]

9-14   **Lien of creditors.**   Persons contracting with a receiver and manager, carrying on the business of a company, who are cognisant of the appointment,[70] must be taken to know that he or she is contracting as principal, not as agent for the company, whose powers are paralysed. Consequently, shippers could not, under a bill of lading under which goods were expressed to be consigned to the company, and which contained a provision that they were to have a lien on the goods shipped for previously unsatisfied freight due from the shippers or consignees, claim a lien on the goods against the receiver.[71]

A receiver and manager should, subject to any special directions of the court, carry on the business according to the general course adopted by the particular trade; he or she must not speculate,[72] and if he or she requires to do anything outside the ordinary course of business, must obtain the leave of the court.[73] He or she cannot, as a general rule, without the consent of the court, create any charge or lien on the property of the company for debts due from it, though it would appear that he or she could create a lien for unsatisfied freight or traffic charges due from him or her personally, where such a lien is in the ordinary course of business.[74] But if a receiver for a company purports to create a lien for unsatisfied freight due from the company, he or she cannot claim the goods without satisfying the lien, though the company, or the debenture-holders, might do so.[75]

Where an administration order had been made in respect of an aviation company,

---

[67]   *Parsons v Sovereign Bank of Canada* n.55, above; *Forster v Nixon's Navigation Co Ltd* (1906) 23 T.L.R. 138.
[68]   *Parsons v Sovereign Bank of Canada*, n.67, above.
[69]   *NW Robbie & Co Ltd v Witney Warehouse Co Ltd* [1963] 1 W.L.R. 1324.
[70]   See Insolvency Act 1986 s.39, discussed at para.7-59, above. This section was new in the Companies Act 1929.
[71]   *Moss SS Co v Whinney* [1912] A.C. 254. The decision really turned on the construction of the documents: See *Parsons v Sovereign Bank of Canada* [1913] A.C. 160, 167 and nn.67, 68.
[72]   *Taylor v Neate* (1888) 39 Ch. D. 544; and see *Re British Power, etc. Co (No.2)* [1907] 1 Ch. 528.
[73]   See para.7-71, above, as to obtaining permission.
[74]   *Moss SS Co v Whinney*, n.71, above.
[75]   *Moss SS Co v Whinney*, n.71, above per Lords Loreburn, Shaw and Mersey.

which then entered into a company voluntary arrangement, to whose supervisor a secured creditor had released an aircraft over which it had a charge, an unsecured aircraft repairs creditor obtained possession of the aircraft, and claimed a contractor's lien for its pre-administration indebtedness. This was disallowed, by reference to principle and to the relevant dates, and because the creditor had neither obtained the consent of the administrators, nor the leave of the court, to enforce his lien.

A solicitor's lien, over documents of title to property held on behalf of their client company, was held to be valid against an administrator.[76]

Liability of managers. Receivers and managers appointed by the court (except   **9-15**
the previous regime of so-called "receivers" appointed by the Court of Protection,[77] and probably also receivers and managers of statutory undertakings) are personally liable to persons dealing with them, in respect of liabilities incurred, or contracts entered into by them in carrying on the business,[78] unless the express terms of the contract exclude, as they may do, any personal liability[79]; but subject to a correlative right to be indemnified out of the assets in respect of liabilities properly incurred;[80] for receivers are not agents for any other person, but are principals,[81] and are not therefore assumed to pledge their personal credit. Their liability will not be displaced by the fact that in giving orders they sign as "receiver and manager".[82]

This principle, however, does not operate to render the receiver and manager personally liable in respect of sums which have been advanced pursuant to an order of the court,[83] making repayment of such sums a charge on the assets,[84] whether such sums are advanced by a party to the claim or by a stranger,[85] nor for breach of contracts entered into by the company.[86]

If the terms of the contract exclude the personal liability of the receiver, and limit the creditor's right to a claim against the assets,[87] the creditor can have no claim by subrogation against the assets,[88] though it is presumed he or she could follow money which he or she could earmark.[89] If the receiver, while negativing his or her personal liability, falsely represented that he or she had authority to contract, it is conceived that the creditor might claim damages against the receiver personally for breach of warranty of authority.

Where a receiver under the previous mental health jurisdiction was, by an order

---

[76] *London Flight Centre (Stansted) Ltd v Osprey Aviation Ltd* [2002] B.P.I.R. 115, and see Ch.20, below.

[77] See para.9-4, above.

[78] The American courts, starting from the same premises, have evolved a different doctrine, namely, that actions against the receiver are actions against the receivership, and that the receiver cannot be held liable beyond the assets in his or her hands. See *Clark on Receivers*, pp.839, 844; cf. *Bevan on Negligence*, 4th edn, pp.1468 ff.

[79] See below.

[80] See para.9-16, below.

[81] *Burt, Boulton and Hayward v Bull* [1895] 1 Q.B. 276; *Strapp v Bull, Sons & Co* [1895] 2 Ch. 1; *Re Glasdir Copper Mines* [1906] 1 Ch. 365; *Moss SS Co v Whinney* [1912] A.C. 254, 259, 271.

[82] *Burt, Boulton and Hayward, v Bull*, n.83, above. See *Moss SS Co v Whinney*, n.81.

[83] As to time and mode of enforcing the liability, see *Re Ernest Hawkins & Co* (1915) 31 T.L.R. 237.

[84] *Re A Boynton Ltd* [1906] 1 Ch. 519.

[85] *Re Glasdir Copper Mintes*, n.81 above; *Re A Boynton Ltd*, n.84, above.

[86] See para.9-11, above.

[87] See *Re British Power, etc. Co (No.2)* [1907] 1 Ch. 528.

[88] Unless the contract were a beneficial one, of which the debenture holders had obtained the benefit: see *Re British Power, etc. Co (No.2)* n.87, above.

[89] See *Sinclair v Brougham* [1914] A.C. 398.

made by the Court of Protection or the nominated judge, authorised to manage the business of the patient, he was not personally liable to creditors in respect of liabilities which he incurred in carrying on the business, unless he expressly or impliedly pledged his own credit; for he was regarded as agent for the patient.[90]

The position of receivers and managers appointed by debenture-holders or mortgagees under the powers of an instrument is discussed in Ch.20.

9-16   **Right to indemnity.**   A receiver and manager appointed by the court is entitled to be indemnified out of the assets against all liabilities properly incurred[91] by him or her in carrying on the business.[92] The receiver and manager is entitled to this indemnity (in addition to the rest of his or her costs, charges, expenses and remuneration) in priority to all other claims against the assets (except the costs of realisation),[93] even to the claims of persons who have advanced money to enable the business to be carried on, under an order of the court declaring the repayment of such advances a first charge on the assets,[94] and in priority to the costs of the action.[95] The receiver may waive these rights in this respect; but waiver will not be implied except in a plain case,[96] nor does the bankruptcy of others affect the receiver's rights. He or she will still be allowed to apply for a full indemnity, even after he or she has submitted his or her final account, if the assets are still undistributed.[97] But he or she has no lien in respect of potential future, as opposed to actual present, claims.[98]

Even where a receiver and manager has borrowed the whole of a specified sum, which borrowing has been authorised for the general purposes of the business, upon the security of a charge on the assets, he or she will be allowed an indemnity in respect of such further liabilities as he or she can, in the circumstances, justify as having been properly incurred. It is not, however, enough to show that the additional liabilities were incurred in the ordinary course of business; for it is prima facie the duty of the receiver and manager to obtain the leave of the court before incurring liabilities in excess of the sum specified. Thus, a receiver and manager of a motorcar business, who had exercised to the full extent a power given to him of borrowing a specified sum, was allowed indemnity in respect of the cost of supplying bodies of cars which had been ordered, and of the rent of business premises, but not in respect of the cost of cars for exhibition at a show, for this was a speculation; nor of an overdraft for sums borrowed and employed in carrying on the busi-

---

90   *Plumpton v Burkinshaw* [1908] 2 K.B. 572. See, as to the now repealed receivership regime of management of the affairs of mental health patients, paras 2-104 ff.
91   See *Re British Power, etc. Co* [1906] 1 Ch. 497; *Re British Power, etc. Co (No.2)*, n.87, above.
92   *Ex p. Izard* (1883) 23 Ch. D. 75, 79; *Strapp v Bull Co* [1895] 1 Ch. 1; *Re Glasdir Copper Mines* n.81, above; *Moss SS Co v Whinney* [1912] A.C. 254, 270; and see *Re Brooke* [1894] 2 Ch. 600.
93   See *Re London United Breweries* [1907] 2 Ch. 511; cf. *Bertrand v Davies* (1862) 31 Beav. 429; *Fraser v Burgess* (1806) 13 Moo. P.C. 314, but, as to priority of an executor's former right of retainer, see *Re Wester-Wemyss* [1940] Ch. 1.
94   *Strapp v Bull, Sons & Co* [1895] 2 Ch. 1; *Lathom v Greenwich Ferry* (1895) 72 L.T. 790; *Re Glasdir Copper Mines* [1906] 1 Ch. 365; *Re Boynton* [1910] 1 Ch. 519. The order ought, however, to state whether the charge is to be subject to the receiver's right of indemnity or not. See *Re Glasdir Copper Mines*, above.
95   *Batten v Wedgwood Coal & Iron Co* (1885) 28 Ch. D. 317; *Re London United Breweries* [1907] 2 Ch. 511.
96   See *Re Glasdir Copper Mines*, n.94.
97   *Levy v Davis* [1900] W.N. 174.
98   *Dyson v Peat* [1917] 1 Ch. 99.

ness, because leave to incur this liability might and should have been obtained from the court.[99]

The extent of this right to indemnity is limited to the amount of the assets; if these are insufficient, the receiver has no enforceable claim against the parties to the action in respect of indemnity or remuneration, even where he or she has been appointed under a consent order.[100] See further para.9-23, below.

Creditors of receiver who makes default. Where a receiver and manager has properly incurred liabilities in the discharge of his or her duties, his or her creditors, in the event of the receiver's failure to pay them, are entitled by subrogation to claim against the estate direct,[101] and can resort to funds carried to the separate account of a legatee of the testator, in the administration of whose estate the order appointing a receiver was made.[102] If the receiver and manager has become bankrupt, payment will be ordered direct to the creditors, not through the receiver's trustee in bankruptcy.[103] But a creditor could not issue execution against the assets on a judgment obtained against the receiver.[104] The creditors of a receiver and manager appointed by the court to carry on a business, authorised by a testator's will to be carried on, are entitled by subrogation to be paid out of the assets in priority to the trustees or their creditors.[105]

This right of the creditors to claim against the assets is limited to the amount of the receiver's indemnity; thus, where a receiver and manager had properly incurred liabilities to trade creditors to the extent of £900 in respect of which he was entitled to indemnity, and was in default to the estate to the extent of £400, it was held that the creditors could only claim against the assets to the extent of the receiver's net indemnity, i.e. £500, and that, therefore, as the estate would suffer no loss by the receiver's default, his sureties could not be compelled by the creditors to make good the £400 by which he was in default; accordingly, the creditors had no remedy, except their claim against the receiver personally, in respect of the £400.[106] In an earlier case,[107] the facts were similar, except that the sureties had paid into court the sum, for which the receiver and manager was in default, without contesting their liability; the court accordingly directed payment to be made direct to the creditors of the receiver and manager, who had become bankrupt, of the full amount of their debts. The judgment in this case must be read in the light of the fact that the estate would suffer no loss, because the sureties paid the amount of the deficiency; it cannot therefore be considered to conflict with the principles enunciated in the later case cited above.[108]

Borrowing by manager. If a receiver and manager requires money to enable a business to be carried no, the court will give him or her liberty to borrow upon the

9-17

9-18

---

[99] *Re British Power, etc. Co (No.2)* [1907] 1 Ch. 528.
[100] *Boehm v Goodall* [1911] 1 Ch. 155.
[101] *Re British Power, etc. Co* [1906] 1 Ch. 497; *Re British Power, etc. Co (No.2)* 1 Ch. 528; *Re London United Breweries* [1907] 2 Ch.511.
[102] *O'Neill v M'Grorty* [1915] 1 Ir.R. 1.
[103] *Re London United Breweries*, above, n.101.
[104] See *Jennings v Mather* [1902] 1 K.B. 1.
[105] See *Re Healy* [1918] 1 Ir.R. 366; *Re Oxley* [1914] 1 Ch. 604. Also *Burke v Whelan* [1920] 1 Ir.R. 200; *Re East* [1914] 111 L.T. 101.
[106] *Re British Power, etc. Co (No.3)* [1910] 2 Ch. 470. See *Re Johnson* (1880) 15 Ch. D. 548.
[107] *Re London United Breweries*, n.101, above.
[108] *Re British Power, etc. Co (No.3)*, above, n.106.

security of the property in his or her control, and as a first charge upon the whole undertaking, in priority even to debentures, where the money is required for preservation of the assets and the goodwill[109]; leave will not, however, be given if the borrowing will not benefit either the company or the debenture-holders[110]; thus, leave will not be given without a prior incumbrancer's consent, where there is a larger amount due on the prior incumbrance than the property is likely to realise.[111]

Where a receiver and manager, appointed in a debenture-holder's action, has been authorised to raise money, he or she has implied power to create a charge to secure the money in priority to existing debentures.[112] The order ought always to state whether the charge is, or is not, to be subject to the receiver's right of indemnity.[113] In order to secure the money raised, the receiver sometimes gives a certificate, sometimes a charge; or the amount may be raised on the security of debentures.[114] In a case where the receiver was authorised to borrow £700 and, not requiring all the money at once, he overdrew £500 from the bank and afterwards paid off the overdraft, it was held that he had not exhausted his borrowing powers to the extent of £500, but was still able to borrow the entire £700 without further leave.[115]

The claims of persons who have advanced money to receivers and managers, under an order of the court upon security of a charge on the assets, are, unless the order otherwise directs, postponed to the receiver's rights.[116] The receiver is under no personal liability for the sums advanced,[117] unless the contract provides otherwise.

Where a manager had contracted in part in excess of an authorised amount, with an express provision that he was not to be personally liable, an application by the creditor for payment out of assets, or by the receiver personally, was dismissed, as being capable of being dealt with on taking the receiver's accounts.[118]

9-19   **Torts.**   As a receiver is a principal, he or she appears to be personally liable, but with a right of indemnity against the assets, to third persons, not parties, in respect of torts committed by him or her, or by persons in his or her employment[119] in the ordinary course of their duties.[120] But, if the act complained of is done under the express directions of the court, it seems that the person aggrieved should not sue the receiver, but should apply in the action[121]; this is the more convenient course

---

[109] *Greenwood v Algeciras Ry* [1894] 2 Ch. 205.
[110] *Securities and Properties Corp v Brighton Alhambra* (1893) 62 L.J. Ch. 566. Form of application notice, CPR Pt 23, PD 23A.
[111] *Re Thames Ironworks* [1912] W.N. 66; 106 L.T. 674.
[112] *Latham v Greenwich Ferry Co* [1895] W.N. 77; 72 L.T. 790.
[113] See *Re Glasdir Copper Mines* [1906] 1 Ch. 365: form of order, See Seton, 7th edn, p.754.
[114] See Palmer's *Company Precedents*, 16th edn, Vol.III, Ch.58.
[115] *Milward v Avill and Smart* [1897] W.N. 162. The order should, however, clearly define the extent of the power to borrow: e.g. whether on terms that the outstanding loan or overdraft at any one time should not exceed a specified sum, or whether a single limited sum is to be borrowed.
[116] See para.9-17, above.
[117] *Re A Boynton Ltd* [1910] 1 Ch. 519.
[118] *Re Ernest Hawkins & Co* (1915) 31 T.L.R. 247.
[119] *Aston v Heron* (1834) 2 My. & K. 390. The English authorities are scanty: see *Re Dunn* [1904] 1 Ch. 648. The American cases are collected in *Clark on Receivers*, pp.785 ff; it must be remembered that the American doctrine of the limitation of the receiver's liability to the assets does not apply in England; see para.9-15, above.
[120] See *Lloyd v Grace, Smith & Co* [1912] A.C. 716; *Percy v Glasgow Corp* [1922] 2 A.C. 299.
[121] See para.6-31 ff, above; in such a case the court has jurisdiction to restrain a separate action.

in cases of alleged trespass.[122] If the act complained of was not specifically authorised, but was merely committed in the course of the receiver's duties, e.g. where his servant negligently injured a third person, the injured person could sue the receiver, and it seems, without leave of the court,[123] though it can never be improper to apply for such leave.[124] In all such cases, the receiver should apply for leave to defend, at the cost of the estate.[125]

Statutory undertaking.   The case of receivers of statutory undertakings appears to be an exception to the above doctrines, though the question can seldom arise, as the receiver cannot as a rule be appointed manager.[126] If, however, under the authority of a statute, such receiver is given powers of management,[127] it is submitted that he or she is not personally liable, except to the extent of assets in his or her hands, either in contract or tort. For the company or the undertakers derive an exclusive power to carry on a particular undertaking from their statute of incorporation, and it is submitted that the court has no power to authorise a receiver or anyone else to carry on the undertaking, except as agent for the undertakers.[128]   **9-20**

Liability in general.   With regard to parties to the action, the receiver is not liable for defaults of his or her employees and agents, if he or she has exercised due care.[129]   **9-21**

If an offence against the Food Safety Act 1990, or any similar statute, is committed during the receivership by a person in the employment of the receiver, the latter may be liable to prosecution[130]; it seems that the company can be made liable for the receiver's own acts in such a case.[131]

Indemnity.   If a receiver becomes liable for damages in tort, or is fined in respect of a criminal act, the right to indemnity depends upon whether the act, in respect of which damages were awarded or a fine was imposed, was done in the course of his or her duties, without any want of due care on his or her part: for instance, if the receiver is sued or prosecuted in respect of the negligence, fraud or criminality of an employed person, he or she is entitled to be indemnified, if he or she has been reasonably careful in employing that person[132]; but if, for example, the receiver employs a person who is wholly unqualified to do skilled work, it is conceived that he or she would not be entitled to be indemnified against damages recovered by a third person for negligence on the part of the employee. See also para.9-16, above.   **9-22**

Interference with manager.   Inasmuch as the property entrusted to him or her as manager includes the goodwill, the court will restrain deliberate acts calculated to destroy it, either by a party or a stranger. Inducing employees to leave a business   **9-23**

---

122 See *Re Maidstone Palace of Varieties* [1909] 2 Ch. 283.
123 See para.8-10, above.
124 cf. *Re Botibol* [1947] 1 All E.R. 26.
125 Otherwise he or she may not be indemnified against costs.
126 See below, para.9-25.
127 e.g. Railway Companies Act 1867 s.4; see above, paras 2-59 ff, above.
128 On similar principles, the court cannot authorise a sale of the undertaking, where the statute does not do so: *Re Woking Urban DC (Basingstoke Canal) Act 1911* [1914] 1 Ch. 300.
129 See para.8-3, above.
130 See *Jarvis v Islington Borough Council* (1909) 73 J.P. 323, cited at para.6-33, above; cf. *Booth v Helliwell* [1914] 3 K.B. 252.
131 *Jarvis v Islington BC*, n.130, above. cf. *R. v ICR Haulage Ltd* [1944] K.B. 551.
132 See para.9-16, above.

which is being carried on under the direction of the court, with a view to their employment in another business which is being started in opposition, and attempting to obtain a tenancy of a field which, to the knowledge of the person making the attempt, had been occupied in connection with the business, are such acts of interference, and will be restrained by injunction.[133] Deliberate acts of interference are a contempt of court and may be punished as such[134]; it is such an act of interference for one of the partners of the original business to start or conduct a competing business in such a way as improperly to injure the original business while under the control of the court, as, for instance, by representing by circulars that the latter business is no longer carried on.[135]

9-24   Interest must not conflict with duty.   A receiver and manager, being an officer of the court, must not place himself or herself in a position in which his or her interest will conflict with his or her duty: accordingly, where a receiver and manager had been appointed over the undertaking of a railway company, it was held that he could not enter into a partnership with the company, and use his own steamboat in conjunction with the company's traffic, by issuing through tickets for use on the steamboat and the company's railway.[136]

Receivers appointed by the court owe a fiduciary duty to the court, and to the estate over which they are appointed, to justify their professional charges for performing their functions in protecting the estate.[137]

9-25   Public company.   Although the court will, in the case of a private trade or business, appoint a manager, the case is different where a company has been incorporated, and empowered by the legislature, acting for the public interest, to construct and maintain an undertaking for a public purposes, and where the legislature has imposed powers and duties of an important kind on the company. Inasmuch as these powers and duties have been conferred and imposed on the company and on no other body of persons, the powers must be executed, and the duties discharged, by the particular company: they cannot be delegated or transferred. Accordingly, although the court may appoint a receiver, it will not appoint a manager of the undertaking of such a company at the instance of a debenture-holder; inasmuch as a debenture, in the form scheduled to the Companies Clauses Consolidation Act 1845, gives only a charge on the company's undertaking, not a right to interfere with the carrying on the business of the company, and no right is given to sell the undertaking.[138] Upon this ground the court refused to

---

[133] *Dixon v Dixon* [1904] 1 Ch. 161. The acts complained of were done by a defendant to the action. Acts of bona fide trade competition by strangers would not be restrained, although their effect might be to destroy the goodwill. cf. *Re Bechstein* (1914) 58 S.J. 864; and *Re William Thomas Shipping Co* [1930] 2 Ch. 368.

[134] *Taylor v Soper* (1890) 62 L.T. 828. See generally, as to interference with a receiver, Ch.6, above. But in the absence of such inclusive words, the goodwill may not be charged, and a manager cannot be appointed: *Britannia Building Society v Crammer* [1997] B.P.I.R. 242 (a 1990 decision) and see Ch.2, para.2-78.

[135] *King v Dobson* (1911) 56 S.J. 51.

[136] *Re Eastern & Midlands Ry* (1890) 45 Ch. D. 367; (1890) 90 L.T.J. 20.

[137] *Mirror Group Newspapers Plc v Maxwell* [1998] B.C.C. 324, 684, and see article by Lightman J in *Insolvency Intelligence* (1998) p.1.

[138] *Gardner v London, Chatham & Dover Ry* (1867) L.R. 2 Ch.App.201, 212, 215–217 per Lord Cairns; *Blaker v Herts and Essex Waterworks Co* (1889) 41 Ch. D. 399.

appoint a manager of a tramway company governed by the Tramways Act 1870,[139] and it would not, formerly, appoint a manager of a railway company.[140]

The reasoning upon which these decisions are founded appears not to apply where there is a specific power to sell conferred by the statute which effects the incorporation, as it sometimes the case with statutory companies.[141] If there is a power to sell, and therefore to cause the conduct and management to devolve on persons other than those specified by the statute, presumably a manager might be appointed.

Market, etc.   Although a receiver may be appointed of the tolls of a market, the court will not appoint a manager of a market belonging to a municipal corporation and regulated by statute, because this would amount to an administration of the affairs of a corporation.[142]   **9-26**

Property abroad.   Where a claim related to property situated overseas, which partakes of the nature of a trade, it is competent for the court to appoint a manager. In a case relating to a West Indian estate, it was said that a manager is appointed, not for the purpose of carrying on the management of the estate, but to enable the court to give relief, when the cause is heard.[143] Persons, for instance, have been appointed to manage landed property, to receive the rents and profits, and to convert, get in, and remit the proceeds of property and assets, in cases in which the property situate in India,[144] in the West Indies,[145] in Demerara,[146] and in Brazil.[147] Thus, where the whole undertaking of a limited company is situate abroad, the court may appoint a manager: managers have been appointed of railways in Venezuela,[148] mines in Peru,[149] a railway and mines in Chile.[150]   **9-27**

A person resident in England may be appointed manager, with authority to appoint an agent abroad in the country where the property is situate[151]; and sometimes a person resident in the country where the estate is situated has been appointed manager.[152] Where a receiver and manager, appointed over mines in Peru belonging to a limited company, was unable to obtain possession because the lex loci only recognised the title of the company, the court ordered the company to appoint two

---

[139] *Marshall v South Staffordshire Tramways Co* [1895] 2 Ch. 36, disapproving *Bartlett v West Metropolitan Tramways Co* [1893] 3 Ch. 437; [1894] 2 Ch. 286.

[140] *Gardner v LC & D Ry*, n.138, above, but see now para.2-59, above.

[141] See *Re Crystal Palace Co* (1910) 104 L.T. 251, 898; affirmed sub nom. *Saunders v Bevan* (1912) 107 L.T. 70. There is no power to direct a sale, unless it is specifically given by the statute; see *Re Woking Urban DC (Basingstoke Canal) Act 1911* [1914] 1 Ch. 300.

[142] *De Winton v Mayor, etc. of Brecon* (1859) 26 Beav. 533.

[143] *Waters v Taylor* (1808) 15 Ves. 10, 25 per Lord Eldon. See, too, *Sheppard v Oxenford* (1855) 1 K. & J. 491.

[144] *Logan v Princess of Coorg* (1860) Seton, 7th edn, p.776.

[145] Seton, 7th edn, p.778. See, too, *Barkely v Lord Reay* (1843) 2 Hare 306.

[146] *Bunbury v Bunbury* (1839) 1 Beav. 318; *Bentinck v Willink* (1845) 2 Hare 1; 67 E.R. 1.

[147] *Sheppard v Oxenford* (1855) 1 K. & J. 491; as to form of order, see that case at p.501. See, too, *Duder v Amsterdamsch Trustees Kantoor* [1902] 2 Ch. 132, 144, where the same persons were appointed receivers in two actions for enforcing different claims on the same property.

[148] *Re South Western of Venezuela Ry* [1902] 1 Ch. 701.

[149] *Re Huinac Copper Mines* [1910] W.N. 218.

[150] *Re Arauco Ltd* (1898) 79 L.T. 336.

[151] Seton, 7th edn, p.777; Palmer's *Company Precedents*, 16th edn, Vol.III, Ch.65.

[152] Seton, 7th edn, p.777.

attorneys to take possession on behalf of the receiver.[153] It is not the practice in such cases to direct the attorneys to give security.[154]

9-28   **Notice to registrar of companies.**   A person who obtains an order for the appointment of a receiver or manager of the property of a company, must within seven days give notice to the registrar of companies, who thereupon enters the fact upon the register of charges.[155]

9-29   **Restraint of trade.**   A purchaser of a business under a contract entered into by a receiver cannot insist upon the insertion in the conveyance of a covenant by the receiver against the carrying on by him or her of a competing business[156]: and it appears that he or she will not be entitled to restrain a receiver from carrying on such a business, although the latter must not make use of information obtained as receiver.[157] If a purchaser requires a restriction against the carrying on of a competing business to be entered into by the receiver, he or she must procure the insertion in the contract of a stipulation to this effect.

9-30   **Consignees.**   In cases where the manager of an estate must necessarily reside in the country where the estate is situated, it was formerly usual to add to the order directing the appointment of a manager an order for the appointment of a consignee or consignees resident in this country, to whom the produce of the property in question might be remitted, and by whom it might be disposed of.[158]

Under modern commercial practice, the appointment of a consignee can seldom be necessary or advisable, the produce being sold in situ or consigned to commercial agents. The present practice in such cases is to appoint a receiver in this country, with power to appoint attorneys, managers or local agents abroad, and with such directions as to disposal money in the hands of the latter as may be required in any particular case.[159]

The court, in dealing with property overseas, may provide against the inconveniences likely to arise from the death, absence, or incapacity of an existing manager, by appointing another person to act as manager in any of those events.[160]

---

[153] *Re Huinac Copper Mines*, n.149, above.
[154] per Warrington J in chambers, 18 January 1912: though in particular circumstances security may be ordered.
[155] Companies Act 2006 s.859K. Failure to give notice involves on summary conviction a fine not exceeding level 3 on the standard scale and, for continued contravention, a daily default fine not exceeding one-tenth of level 3 on the standard scale.
[156] *Re Irish* (1888) 40 Ch. D. 49, commented on in *Boorne v Wicker* [1927] 1 Ch. 667. cf. *Farey v Cooper* [1927] 2 K.B. 384.
[157] *Re Gent* (1892) 40 W.R. 267; *Re Irish*, n.156, above.
[158] Seton, 7th edn, p.778.
[159] See form of order, Palmer's *Company Precedents*, 16th edn, Vol.III, Ch.52.
[160] *Rutherford v Wilkinson* (1823), Seton, 7th edn, p.780; *Forbes v Hammond* (1819) 1 J. & W. 88.

CHAPTER 10

REMUNERATION AND EXPENSES OF A RECEIVER

Introduction. The principal rules for assessing and authorising the remuneration of a receiver appointed by the court are now contained in CPR 69, and its Practice Direction, PD 69. They were formerly contained in RSC Ord.30. There is a considerable amount of case law on those subjects, which, under the former procedures, has been examined by previous authors of this work, and in particular by Sir Raymond Walton. It has been thought to be helpful to practitioners to retain the major part of those examinations of the case-law, in this Chapter: see para.10-7, below.

10-1

A receiver may only charge for his or her services, if the court so directs, and specifies the basis on which the receiver is to be remunerated.[1] The court may specify the person who is to be responsible for paying the receiver, and the fund or property from which he or she is to receive remuneration.[2] For provisions applying to the remuneration of receivers appointed under the criminal confiscation statutes, the reader is directed to specialist texts such as Ch.9 of the third edition of *Corporate Criminal Responsibility* by Pinto and Evans.

If the court directs that the amount of the receiver's remuneration is to be determined by the court, he or she may not recover any remuneration for his or her services, without a determination by the court, for which the receiver or any party may at any time apply.[3]

Basis for application. Such an application for the determination of remuneration must be supported by written evidence, showing on what basis the remuneration is claimed, and that it is justified, and is in accordance with CPR 69, and also by a certificate, signed by the receiver, that he or she considers that the remuneration claimed is reasonable and proportionate.[4]

10-2

The court, before determining the amount of the remuneration, may require the receiver to provide further information in support of the claim, and may appoint an assessor to assist the court,[5] or refer the determination of the remuneration to a costs judge.[6]

General principles for calculating bases of remuneration. Unless the court directs otherwise, in determining the remuneration of a receiver, the court shall

10-3

---

[1] CPR 69.7(1); CPR PD 69, paras 9.1, 9.2. Subject to the overriding criteria in CPR 69.7 and CPR PD 69, para.9. The term "receiver" here includes a manager: CPR 69.1(2).
[2] CPR r.69.7(2).
[3] CPR 69.7(3).
[4] CPR PD 69, para.9.4.
[5] CPR PD 69 para 9.5.
[6] CPR 69.7(5).

award such sum as is reasonable and proportionate in all the circumstances, and which takes into account:

(a) the time properly given by the receiver and his or her staff to the receivership;

(b) the complexity of the receivership;

(c) any responsibility of an exceptional kind or degree, which falls on the receiver in consequence of the receivership;

(d) the effectiveness with which the receiver appears to be carrying on, or to have carried out, his or her duties; and

(e) the value and nature of the subject-matter of the receivership.[7]

The expenses incurred by a receiver in carrying out his or her functions are not dealt with as part of his or her remuneration, but are accounted for as part of the account for the assets which he or she has recovered.[8]

THE CASE-LAW

10-4 **Right to salary and allowances.** A receiver, unless it was otherwise ordered, or unless he or she consented to act without a salary, has always been allowed a proper salary, or has allowances made to him or her for the care and pains in the execution of his or her duties, such remuneration being fixed by reference to such scales or rates of professional charges as the court thought fit.[9] Even where the receiver consented to act without a salary, he or she was to be paid for services which proved beneficial to the estate, and which it was no part of his or her duty to perform, e.g. working as a mechanic in a business of which the receiver had, by the order appointing him, been constituted manager; though this is an indulgence, if the receiver so acts without directions as to payment.[10] Where the order appointing a receiver says nothing about remuneration, this does not amount to a decision that he or she is to have no remuneration, even though the receiver be a trustee, who as a general rule receives no remuneration.[11] The amount of a receiver's salary or allowance is usually not fixed until after the submission of the receiver's first account, and often, especially in the case of companies, not till later, when he or she will be allowed either a percentage of receipts, or a gross sum by way of salary.[12]

The remuneration of a receiver appointed by the High Court was formerly assessable by a Chancery master; it may now, since the introduction of the CPR, be determined by a costs judge,[13] or with an assessor to assist the court.[14]

An agreement by a trustee in bankruptcy for pooling his remuneration with the

---

[7] CPR 69.7(4).

[8] CPR PD 69, para.9.6. See also *Capewell v Customs and Excise Commissioners* [2006] C.P.Rep. 36 at 43 per Carnwarth J. The decision was reversed on other grounds by the House of Lords ([2007] UKHL 2; [2007] 1 W.L.R. 386).

[9] RSC Ord.30 r.3 (revoked). For the former position in relation to receivers appointed by the Court of Protection, see the now revoked Court of Protection Rules 1984 (SI 1984/2035) r.42. A special manager's remuneration in insolvency is fixed by the court: Insolvency Rules 2016 rr.5.17, 6.37 and 7.93.

[10] *Harris v Sleep* [1897] 2 Ch. 80.

[11] *Re Bignell v Chapman* [1892] 1 Ch. 59.

[12] *Daniell's Chancery Practice* (8th ed.), p.1485. It was formerly fixed by the Master, but was sometimes fixed and allowed by the taxing master, now the costs judge: *Silkstone, etc. Coal Co v Edey* [1901] 2 Ch. 652, 655.

[13] CPR 69.7(5) and PD 69. See also *Alliance Leicester Building Society v Edgestop (No.2)* [1995] 2 B.C.L.C. 506.

amount recovered in respect of a debt due to his employer or partner was void, since it might result in the creditor obtaining a preference,[15] since receivers must hold an even hand; since between creditors, the same rule appears to apply to them.

A receiver and manager will not be allowed remuneration for any period beyond the term of the appointment, unless an extension is made before it expires.[16]

Formerly, where the court appointed a receiver with a salary, he or she was obliged to pay out of his or her own pocket any expenses which might be incurred in giving security, whereas, if appointed without salary, he or she would have been allowed in his or her accounts expenses reasonably incurred for that purpose.[17] Now, such expenses, formerly allowed as a disbursement, are prescribed as forming no part of remuneration.[18]

Amounts to be allowed—scales of remuneration: Chancery Division.   There **10-5** have never been any settled scales governing the allowances to a receiver. According to an old rule in *Day v Croft*,[19] the allowance to a receiver of the rents and profits of a freehold or leasehold estate was, at that time, (1840) generally five per cent on the amount received. That allowance might, however, be increased, if there was any special difficulty in the collection; or it might be diminished; or a fixed salary might be allowed, where the rental was considerable.[20] The practice in the Chancery Division has been to allow remuneration on the basis of a quantum meruit, according to the time, trouble and degree of responsibility involved, as is now codified on CPR 69.7. However, as the Guide for Receivers in the Chancery Division recognises,[21] there may be cases where it is appropriate to fix remuneration by reference to some fixed scale or, for example, percentage of rents collected. A remuneration statement is required, setting out first a brief description of the work done by the receiver and secondly a time account.[22]

A receiver and manager appointed to wind up or carry on a partnership business has been, in the absence of express stipulation, entitled to a quantum meruit, even where he was himself a partner, irrespective of his liabilities to the partnership as a partner[23]; but the scale allowed to liquidators was not acceptable as a guide.[24]

Scales of remuneration: Queens Bench Division.   In the Queen's Bench Divi- **10-6** sion, the remuneration of a receiver by way of equitable execution had been governed by a Memorandum of the King's Bench Masters of June 1929. This ran as follows:

"Where a receiver is appointed by way of equitable execution, unless the court or a judge otherwise orders, the total amount to be allowed for costs of the receiver (including his remuneration, the costs of obtaining his appointment, of completing his security (if any),

---

14 CPR PD 69, para.9.5.
15 *Farmers' Mart Ltd v Milne* [1915] A.C. 106.
16 *Re Wood Green and Hornsey Laundry Ltd* [1918] 1 Ch. 423.
17 *Harris v Sleep*, n.10, above.
18 See CPR PD 69, para 9.6.
19 (1840) 2 Beav. 488.
20 1 *Seton*, 7th edn, p.739.
21 See para.10.
22 Form, *Atkin's Court Forms*, Vol.33 (2011 issue) para.[231]; *Palmer's Company Precedents*, 16th edn, Pt III, Ch.68.
23 *Davy v Scarth* [1906] 1 Ch. 55; and see para.10-12, below.
24 See *Prior v Bagster* [1887] W.N. 194. In *Re Carton Ltd* (1923) 39 T.L.R. 1994, remuneration was allowed to a liquidator in a voluntary winding-up on the scale applicable to a trustee in bankruptcy.

of passing his accounts, and of obtaining his discharge), should not exceed 10 per cent. of the amount due under the judgment or the amount recovered by the receiver whichever may be the lesser sum; provided that not less than £5 be allowed unless otherwise ordered, and that where the amount due under the judgment does not exceed £50 the plaintiff or party applying shall be made answerable and the usual security be dispensed with. The amount allowed shall, when required, be apportioned by the Master as between costs and remuneration respectively."[25]

In other cases, the practice of the Queen's Bench Division had been as follows:

(1) In the case of rent, a percentage varying from, say, 2–10 per cent was allowed on the gross rents collected, varying according to the amount of the rent and circumstances as follows:

  (a) If the rents were large and were payable yearly or half yearly, and no undue trouble arose owing to the state of repair or otherwise, 2 per cent or slightly over would be allowed.

  (b) If the rents were collected monthly or quarterly, 3–5 per cent would be allowed.

  (c) If collected weekly, from 7–10 per cent would be allowed.

In each of the above cases, the difficulties, trouble and labour involved would be taken into consideration, and although the percentage as above was taken as a guide, it was not slavishly followed, and was only used as a means to arrive at a quantum meruit or proper remuneration.

(2) In the case of dividends, a percentage of 1–3 per cent on the gross sums collected would be allowed, according to whether the dividends were numerous, or large or small; in exceptional cases the percentage might be reduced or increased—the percentage being only used to assist in arriving at the proper remuneration.

(3) In other cases, a quantum meruit allowance was made, according to time and trouble involved.

A receiver cannot claim remuneration until he or she has discharged sums for which the receiver is accountable under his or her security.[26]

10-7 **Costs, charges and expenses.** A receiver is entitled to be paid out of funds collected or realised by the receiver, his or her costs, charges, and expenses properly incurred in the discharge of ordinary duties, or in the performance of extraordinary services which have been sanctioned by the court.[27] Where a receiver has paid sums out of his or her own pocket in satisfaction of legacies, the receiver will not be reimbursed.[28]

It is not generally necessary for a receiver to make any special application to the court for the payment of his or her costs, charges, and expenses properly incurred in the discharge of the receiver's duties.[29]

---

[25] But see now CPR PD 69, para.9.6, above.

[26] See *Re British Power, etc. Co (No.3)* [1910] 2 Ch. 470.

[27] *Malcolm v O'Callaghan* (1837) 3 My. & Co. 52; and see below, para.10-11. In bankruptcy, a receiver is entitled to his or her costs next after the costs of realising the estate: *Ex p. Royle* (1875) 23 W.R. 908. As to costs of receiverships in the Queen's Bench Division, see (1890) 34 S.J. 74, 90.

[28] *Palmer v Wright* (1846) 10 Beav. 234; and see *Morison v Morison* (1855) 7 De G.M. & G. 214.

[29] *Fitzgerald v Fitzgerald* (1843) 5 Ir.Eq. 525; but he or she may do so personally, if it is necessary.

The payment of the costs, charges, and expenses, including the remuneration,[30] of a receiver appointed over an estate is not dependent on the sufficiency of the estate to bear all the costs. This right is not affected by the receiver's bankruptcy; but the sum due to him or her will not be paid out to the trustee in bankruptcy, but to the persons entitled by subrogation.[31] A receiver appointed over the assets of a company is entitled to be paid next after payment of the costs of realisation,[32] in priority to the claimant's costs and the costs of trustees of a debenture trust deed and preferential creditors,[33] and even in priority to persons advancing money under an order of the court on the terms that repayment is to be a first charge on the assets,[34] but not in priority to the prior charges.[35]

Unless the order otherwise provides, costs of realisation do not include costs of preservation,[36] nor of any step in the action.[37] The receiver's claim is, however, limited to the amount of the assets. The receiver has no claim against the parties personally if the assets are deficient, even though he or she may have been appointed under a consent order in a partnership action.[38]

Receiver's lien for remuneration and expenses. The receiver has a lien for his or her remuneration and expenses, and to secure his or her right of indemnity, which binds the assets bound by the receivership. Its existence is independent of the receiver's physical possession of any assets, and extends not merely over those assets in his or her actual possession, but also over all the assets so bound. Those rights do not terminate on the receiver's discharge, nor on the return or delivery of the assets to the parties entitled to them.[39]   **10-8**

Where the master, in an order for payment out of a fund in court, in an action for administration of the trusts of a debenture trust deed, had by inadvertence omitted an express direction for payment of the trustees' costs in priority to the plaintiff's costs and the receiver's remuneration, the order was varied in the winding-up of the company by inserting the requisite directions, and the registrar's order to that effect was confirmed on appeal: a wrong date in the certificate was also corrected.[40]

Under the old practice, where in a partnership action both partners were adjudicated bankrupt, and the fund was transferred to the trustee in bankruptcy, and possession was ordered to be given up by the receiver, it was held that there was no jurisdiction in bankruptcy to reconsider and reassess the receiver's remunera-

---

Form of application notice to be based on, Palmer's *Company Precedents*, 16th edn, p.697.
[30] *Re Glasdir Copper Mines* [1906] 1 Ch. 365.
[31] *Re London United Breweries* [1907] 2 Ch. 511.
[32] *Batten v Wedgwood, etc. Co* (1885) 28 Ch. D. 317; *Re London United Breweries*, n.31, above; *Re Glyncorrwg Colliery Co* [1926] Ch. 951. The claimant is entitled to his or her costs of realisation as between solicitor and client, if the estate is deficient for payment of the debentures in full: see *Re A. Boynton Ltd* [1910] 1 Ch. 519. As to cases where the liquidator's costs of realisation have priority to the debentures, see *Re Regent's Canal Ironworks* (1876) 3 Ch. D.411; *Johnston v Cox* (1882) 19 Ch. D. 17.
[33] *Re Glyncorrwg Colliery Co*, n.32, above.
[34] *Strapp v Bull, Sons & Co* [1895] 1 Ch. 1; *Re Glasdir Copper Mines*, n.30; *Re A. Boynton Ltd*, n.32, above.
[35] *Choudri v Palta* [1992] B.C.C. 787.
[36] *Lathom v Greenwich Ferry* (1895) 72 L.T. 790.
[37] *Re Callender's Paper Co* per Neville J in chambers, 18 January 1911.
[38] *Boehm v Goodall* [1911] 1 Ch. 155.
[39] *Mellor v Mellor* [1992] 1 W.L.R. 517.
[40] *Re City Housing Trust Ltd* [1942] Ch. 262. The priority of the remuneration was down to the date of the master's order only.

tion which had been allowed in passing his accounts in the action, there being no application to vary the certificate.[41]

A receiver appointed over mortgaged property,[42] who went into possession with a direction to keep down interest on incumbrances, and received the rents of the property with the knowledge of the mortgagee, was entitled to deduct his remuneration and expenses before paying over to a mortgagee the balance of rents in his hands to which the latter was entitled.[43]

If a receiver is directed to pay to a successful litigant costs of proceedings to which the receiver is a party, such costs will be payable in priority to the receiver's own claim for costs, charges, and expenses.[44] If, with permission of the court, a liquidator or the company brings, or defends, proceedings for the benefit of the debenture-holders, the costs of such proceedings will have priority over the claims of the debenture-holders[45]: but where a proceeding is brought by the liquidator of a company on an indemnity from the receiver, the liability to the liquidator for costs paid by him or her will, in default of any order to the contrary, have no precedence over other liabilities of the receiver.

Where the court gives a receiver authority to advance money for the benefit of the estate of which he or she is receiver, interest at five per cent was formerly allowed on the advance[46]; but this is not a fixed rule, and a lower rate may be fixed: the receiver is given a charge on the assets for that sum and interest. If a receiver advances money without such previous authority, he or she is entitled only to an indemnity out of the assets.[47]

A receiver has not such a vested right to the collection of money payable in respect of the receivership estate as to be entitled to prevent such money from being paid into court without passing through his or her hands, where poundage may be saved by a direct payment into court.[48]

The court has no jurisdiction to order a party to a proceeding to pay the remuneration and expenses of a receiver appointed in the proceeding, as part of the costs of and incidental to the proceeding.[49]

10-9 **Extraordinary expenses.** A receiver may be granted allowances, beyond a salary, for any extraordinary trouble or expense in the performance of his or her duties,[50] or in bringing actions, or in defending legal proceedings which have been brought against the receiver,[51] even though defended without leave,[52] though leave should always be obtained as soon as the action against the receiver is commenced.[53] Where, for example, an adverse application had been made against a receiver by a party to the cause, and had been refused with costs, the applicant

---

[41] *Re Kay and Lovell* [1941] Ch. 420.
[42] See also paras 7-34 to 7-35, above.
[43] *Davy v Price* [1883] W.N. 226.
[44] As is the case with a liquidator: *Re Pacific Coast Syndicate* [1913] 2 Ch. 26.
[45] See *Re Wrexham, Mold and Connah's Quay Co* [1990] 1 C. 261.
[46] *Ex p. Izard* (1883) 23 Ch. D. 75.
[47] *Ex p. Izard*, n.46, above.
[48] *Haigh v Grattan* (1839) 1 Beav. 201.
[49] *Re Andrews* [1999] 1 W.L.R. 1236, CA.
[50] *Potts v Leighton* (1808) 14 Ves. 273; *Harris v Sleep* [1897] 2 Ch. 80. Such expenses are specifically envisaged by CPR 69.7(4)(c): See para.10-4, above.
[51] *Bristowe v Needham* (1847) 2 Ph. 190; *Re WC Home & Sons Ltd* [1906] 1 Ch. 271. Distinguish *Re Dunn* [1904] 1 Ch. 648, below.
[52] *Bristowe v Needham*, n.51, above; the defence succeeded.
[53] *Anon.* (1801) 6 Ves. 287.

being wholly unable to pay those costs, it was held that the receiver was entitled to be indemnified, and to have his costs as between solicitor and client out of a fund in hand, although it belonged to incumbrancers.[54]

Again, where one of two partners in a business of agricultural implement makers, being the defendant in an action for dissolution of the partnership, had been appointed receiver and manager of the business without salary, he was allowed in his accounts, a weekly sum, as wages, for a period of 18 months during which he had worked as a common workman in the business of which he was the receiver. The Court of Appeal, however, pointed out that, in not asking for the wages at the time of his appointment, he had committed a technical irregularity, and had run a great risk of not getting any remuneration for his extraordinary services.[55] The costs of litigation undertaken, with the permission of the court, to preserve the assets are part of the receiver's costs of administration, and ought to be included in his or her accounts.[56]

Restrictions on receiver's rights or reimbursements or indemnity. If any extraordinary expenses have been incurred by the receiver without the approbation of the court,[57] allowances for them will not generally be sanctioned, unless the estate has been benefited thereby.[58] Accordingly, where a receiver, without the leave of the court, defended an action arising out of a distress for rent made by him, and had compromised it on the terms of the plaintiff abandoning it and each party bearing his own costs, he was not allowed his costs.[59] Nor was he allowed his costs of proceedings improperly taken and abandoned, although he acted bona fide and succeeded in subsequent proceedings.[60]   **10-10**

A receiver, appointed and acting in proceedings for the administration of an estate, is not entitled to indemnity in respect of the costs of defending a purely personal action against the receiver, having no relation to the estate, except so far as the acts complained of were done by the receiver while acting as an officer of the court: for no benefit to the estate can result from defending such an action.[61] Nor is the receiver entitled to litigate for the profit of the receivership; his or her only interest is in his or her remuneration.[62]

Expenses of foreign travel and other expenses and costs. The receiver of an estate is not entitled to be reimbursed the expenses of journeys to and residence in a foreign country, for the purpose of prosecuting proceedings before the tribunals of that country for the recovery of property belonging to the estate, unless he or she has the express sanction and authority of the court for such journeys and residence[63]; though if such proceedings are successful, and it appears that the success has been   **10-11**

---

[54] *Courand v Hanmer* (1846) 9 Beav. 3; distinguish *Re Dunn*, n.51, above.
[55] *Harris v Sleep*, n.50, above at 84, 85.
[56] *Re WC Horne & Sons Ltd*, n.51, above; these costs had been omitted from the receiver's accounts, and the solicitor was granted a charging order.
[57] *Harris v Sleep*, n.46, above; *Re Ormsby* (1809) 1 Ba. & Be. 189; *Ex p. Izard*, n.46, above; as to allowances to a receiver and manager in respect of liabilities incurred by the receiver, see Ch.9, paras 9-16 ff, above.
[58] *Bristowe v Needham*, n.52, above; *Malcolm v O'Callaghan* (1837) 3 My. & C. 52; and see *Viola v Angle-American Cold Storage Co* [1912] 2 Ch. 305 at 311.
[59] *Swaby v Dickon* [1833] 5 Sim. 629.
[60] *Re Montgomery* [1828] 1 Moll. 419.
[61] *Re Dunn*, n.51, above, at 655, 657.
[62] *Ex p. Cooper* (1887) 6 Ch. D. 255.
[63] *Malcolm v O'Callaghan*, n.58, above.

due to the presence of the receiver, the court may consider it inequitable for the parties to take the benefit of the receiver's exertions, without defraying the expenses.[64] The fact that some of the parties interested in the estate may have given the receiver authority furnishes no ground for the allowance by the court of such expenses out of the estate.[65]

If the property involved is small, the court may appoint a receiver without remuneration.[66]

If a trustee,[67] or party interested, asks leave to propose himself or herself as receiver, he or she will usually be required, if appointed, to act without salary.[68]

Where a receiver in an action is served with a proceeding in it, which makes no personal charge against the receiver, he or she should not appear, and will get no costs of appearance if he or she does.[69] In a case under the old practice, in which a receiver had incurred costs for which the parties had long neglected to provide, he was allowed to petition for the payment of them.[70]

If a receiver suffers any costs to accrue which ought to have been prevented, he or she may have to pay them out of his or her own pocket.[71]

The costs of drawing out a scheme of an estate over which a receiver has been appointed, and of the holdings of the tenants, are chargeable, if at all, as part of the receiver's costs, and not of the solicitor's; but no allowance will usually be made to the receiver for such an item, where he or she is paid by a percentage, though it may be necessary for the due performance of the receiver's duties.[72]

10-12　**Defaults by receiver.**　The receiver must obey the terms of orders made in the suit: thus, where a receiver was directed, by the order appointing him, to make a specified payment to a party to the suit, and without leave he paid the money to judgment creditors of that party, pursuant to a garnishee order, the creditors were ordered, on motion in the suit by the party aggrieved, to repay the money so paid to them, and a direction was also given that, in default of such repayment, the amount should be disallowed to the receiver on the passing of his account; and the receiver, and also the creditors, were held liable to pay the costs of the motion.[73]

In a case where the receiver's defaults in bringing in his accounts on the appointed days were known to the parties, and the accounts had been passed and poundage allowed without objection, no loss having been sustained by the receiver's fault, and no balance being due from him, the court would not afterwards listen to an application to strike out his allowance of poundage and costs at the instance of the parties who had the benefit of his services[74]; but the amount of the allowance made to a receiver may be reconsidered, where, though an objection was originally made to it, the particular circumstances of the case and the nature of the

---

[64]　*Malcolm v O'Callaghan*, at 58, n.58, above.
[65]　See n.64 at 61.
[66]　*Marr v Littlewood* (1837) 2 My. & C. 458.
[67]　*Sykes v Hastings* (1805) 11 Ves. 363; *Pilkington v Baker* (1876) 24 W.R. 234; above, Ch.4, para. 4-2.
[68]　See n.67, above.
[69]　*Herman v Dunbar* (1857) 23 Beav. 312. In *General Share Co v Wetley Brick Co* (1882) 20 Ch. D. 260, 267, an applicant, who had improperly served the receiver, was ordered to pay his costs of appearance, but the circumstances were peculiar.
[70]　*Ireland v Eade* (1844) 7 Beav. 55; application would now be by application notice in the action.
[71]　*Cook v Sharman* (1844) 8 Ir.Eq.R. 515.
[72]　See *Re Catlin* (1854) 18 Beav. 511.
[73]　*De Winton v Mayor, etc. of Brecon* (1859) 28 Beav. 200.
[74]　*Ward v Swift* (1848) 8 Hare 139.

items were not taken into consideration.[75] If a receiver is guilty of a breach of duty, he or she does not necessarily, as is the case with agents,[76] forfeit his or her remuneration, but the court will usually deprive him or her of it if any improper profit has been made.

Balances in hand.   A receiver who submits his or her accounts and pays his or   **10-13**
her balances regularly, is not entitled on that ground to make interest for his or her own benefit, out of money which comes into his or her hands, in the character of receiver, during the intervals between the times of passing the accounts.[77]

Receiver of life interest.   If it is necessary, not from the conduct of the parties,   **10-14**
but owing to the condition of the estate, to have a receiver appointed over the life interest of a tenant for life of real estate, it is the right of the remainderman to have the ordinary expenses incidental to the appointment paid out of the life interest.[78]

---

[75]   *Day v Croft* (1840) 2 Beav. 488. See *Re Carton Ltd* (1923) 39 T.L.R. 194.
[76]   See *Andrews v Ramsay* [1903] 2 K.B. 635; *Rhodes v Macalister* (1923) 29 Com.Cas. 19.
[77]   *Shaw v Rhodes* (1827) 2 Russ. 539. See, too, *Lonsdale (Lord) v Church* (1788) 3 Bro.C.C. 40.
[78]   *Shore v Shore* (1859) 4 Drew. 510.

CHAPTER 11

RECEIVER'S ACCOUNTS

11-1   As already explained,[1] prior to CPR Pt 69 coming into effect, the former rules regulating the appointment and control of receivers appointed by the High Court, and also by the county court, were contained in RSC Ords 31 (general receivers) and 51 (receivers by way of equitable execution). The power of appointment of receivers by the county court had been contained in CCR Ord.32 but that order had been revoked and the provisions of RSC Ord 30 extended to cover such appointments. The new Rules contained in CPR Pt 69 effectively came into force on 2 December 2002.[2]

11-2   **CPR Pt 69.**   The new provisions under the CPR are contained in CPR Pt 69 and PD 69, which deal with both types of receiver. As that Part and Practice Direction deal only briefly with the rendering and examining of a receiver's accounts,[3] it has been thought useful to retain, somewhat abridged, the commentary by Sir Raymond Walton on the previous procedures and the case-law.[4]

CPR Pt 69 and PD 69 now provide that the court may order a receiver to prepare and serve accounts,[5] directing him or her to do so either by a specified date, or at specified intervals,[6] and may specify the persons on whom he or she must serve the accounts.[7]

Under the Guide for Receivers in the Chancery Division it is provided that if directions as to accounts have not been given in the order appointing the receiver then directions must be obtained at the directions hearing.[8] Normally accounts are prepared half yearly and must be delivered within a month after the end of the ac-counting period.[9] Generally they are not required to be presented to the court un-less there is an objection under the procedure set out below.

Any person served with the accounts may apply for an order to inspect any docu-ment in the receiver's possession, relevant to such accounts[10]; but should not do so,

---

[1]   See para.5-1, above.
[2]   As a result of the Civil Procedure (Amendment) Rules, 2002 (SI 2002/2058), rr.1(2), 26; Schs 7 and 10, inserting the new Pt 69.
[3]   CPR r.69.8; PD 69, para.10.
[4]   See para.11-3, below, "Case Law".
[5]   See above, n.3.
[6]   CPR PD 69, para.10.1(1).
[7]   CPR PD 69, para.10.1(2).
[8]   CPR PD 69, para.11.
[9]   A Guide for Receivers in the Chancery Division, para.12.
[10]   CPR r.69.8(2).

until he or she has first asked the receiver to permit such inspection, without an order.[11]

Where the court makes such an order for inspection, it will normally direct the receiver to permit inspection within seven days after service of the order,[12] and to provide a copy of any documents the subject of the order within seven days after receiving a request for a copy from the party permitted to inspect them, provided that that party has undertaken to pay the reasonable cost of making and providing the copy.[13]

Accounts and objections thereto: orders for examination. Any party, within **11-3** 14 days of being served with the accounts, may serve notice on the receiver: (a) specifying any item in the accounts to which he or she objects; (b) giving the reason for such objection; and (c) requiring the receiver, within 14 days of the receipt of such notice, either to notify all the parties who were served with the accounts that the receiver accepts the objection, or, if he or she does not accept the objection, to apply for an examination of the accounts in relation to the disputed item.[14]

When the receiver applies for the examination of the accounts, he or she must at the same time file the accounts, and a copy of the notice served on him or her under the rule.[15] If the receiver fails to notify all parties who were served with the accounts that he or she accepts the objection or to apply for such an examination when required to do so, any party may apply to the court for an examination of the accounts in relation to the contested item.[16] At the conclusion of its examination of the accounts, the court will certify the result.[17]

CPR PD 40A, prescribing procedures for the court when inquiring into accounts, is applicable to such accounts.[18]

There is a general power for dealing with defaulting or recalcitrant receivers, including the imposition of penalties.[19] Where a receiver's appointment is terminated, orders may be made dealing with the financial consequences.[20]

Case-law. Under the former practice, there was no automatic scrutiny of the **11-4** receiver's accounts by the court; it was only if there were objections to his or her accounts that the court was involved at all. The receiver must now submit such accounts to such parties at such intervals, or on such dates, as the court may direct[21]; they are no longer required to be delivered to the judge's chambers. If, of course, the receiver should be unable to comply with the directions of the court, he or she can always apply for further time by an application in private.[22]

---

[11] CPR PD 69, para.10.2.
[12] CPR PD 69, para.10.3(1).
[13] CPR PD 69, para.10.3(2).
[14] CPR r.69.8(3).
[15] CPR r.69.8(4).
[16] CPR r.69.8(5).
[17] CPR r.69.8(6).
[18] See concluding wording to CPR r.69.8.
[19] CPR r.69.9.
[20] CPR r.69.9(2), (3).
[21] CPR PD 69 para.10.1. They are no longer required to be delivered to the judge's chambers as a matter of course, as previously, see *Kerr*, 15th edn, Ch.11.
[22] The application should properly be made by the party with the conduct, but if he or she refuses, the receiver may make it: In relation to respectively, an order on examining items in a receiver's account and an application notice for further time to serve account, see *Atkin's Court Forms*, Vol.33

11-5 **Form of accounts.** No form of accounts is prescribed by the CPR[23]; the title should correspond with that of the order appointing the receiver. The old practice was as follows. In the first account submitted, the receiver of an estate would state, in the column for observations, how each tenant held, and every alteration was to be noted in the subsequent accounts. In this column also was entered any remarks the receiver might think proper to make as to arrears of rent, state of repair, or otherwise.[24] If the account is drawn up in an irregular manner, the receiver may still, it is submitted, on the application of any person to whom the accounts have to be submitted, be ordered to draw it up in a proper form, and to pay the costs occasioned by the irregularity.[25]

Where a receiver appointed by debenture-holders out of court was subsequently appointed receiver in an action to enforce the security, his accounts as receiver were taken in the action from his first appointment: if a different person had been appointed in the action, the first receiver could have applied to have his account taken.[26] Under the CPR, the matter would be dealt with by the master directing such accounts from either receiver to be submitted as in the circumstances of the particular case seem appropriate.

11-6 **Verification and examination of accounts.** These processes are now provided for by CPR Pt 69, CPR PD 69A, para.10 and CPR PD 40A "Accounts, Inquiries etc". Examination of the accounts is limited to the item or items to which objection is taken.[27]

11-7 **Objections to the accounts: order for examination.** Whereas formerly there was no time limit specified, within which any party dissatisfied had to give notice of objection to any item in the accounts, notice must now be given within 14 days of service of the accounts.[28] CPR PD 40A deals with accounts and inquiries directed by an order generally. Paragraph 3 thereof deals with objections to the accounts and can be taken as a good indicator of the sort of objection that can be made under CPR r.69.8, as well as indicating the sort of detail that should be provided in the relevant written notice under that provision with a view to speeding up and assisting any eventual process under CPR PD 40A. CPR PD 40A provides that any party who seeks to contend that an accounting party (here, obviously the receiver) has received more than the amount which he or she has by his or her account admitted to have received, or that he or she should be treated as having received more than he or she has actually received, or that any item in the account is erroneous in respect of amount or that in any other respect the account is inaccurate must, on the taking of the account and unless the court otherwise orders, give him or her written notice thereof, stating, so far as he or she is able, the amount by which it is contended that the account understates the amount received by the accounting party, or the amount which it is contended that the accounting party should be treated as having received

---

(2011 Issue), paras 232 and 230.

[23] For the former practice, see *Atkin's Court Forms*, Vol.33 (1981 Issue), pp.236–238. As to separate accounts of real and personal estate, see *Hill v Hibbit* (1868) 18 L.T. 553. As to the accounts of an insolvency special manager, see Insolvency Rules 2016 (SI 2016/1024) rr.5.20, 6.40 and 7.96.

[24] *Daniell's Chancery Practice*, 8th edn, p.1492. If money has been paid to the receiver under protest, he or she ought to distinguish it from the rest: *Brownhead v Smith* (1837) 1 Jur.237.

[25] *Daniell's Chancery Practice*, 8th edn, p.1492. See *Bertie v Lord Abingdon* (1845) 8 Beav. 53, 60.

[26] *Practice Note* [1932] W.N. 51.

[27] CPR r.69.8 reproduces *Practice Direction (Chancery Chambers)* [1982] 1 W.L.R. 1189, para.29.

[28] CPR r.69.8(3).

more than he or she has actually received or the respects in which it is contended the account is inaccurate and in each case the ground on which the contention is made.

Once an objection remains unaccepted an application under CPR Pt 23 for an examination of the accounts in relation to any contested item will follow. The notice of objection will be filed by the court, and an appointment before the master or district judge will be given. At that first appointment appropriate directions as to the examination of the accounts should be sought. It will usually be necessary for the objecting party to support the objection by a witness statement, verified by a statement of a truth, or by an affidavit, which should be filed and supplied to the receiver in good time.

The receiver will usually file his or her accounts with the court, together with a witness statement, verified by a statement of truth, or an affidavit, verifying the item or items to which exception has been taken, or dealing with the alleged item or items of surcharging, as the case may, and exhibiting where appropriate the necessary vouchers in respect of any challenged expenditure.

Following the examination, by or on behalf of the court, of an item or items to which objection is taken, the master or district judge will certify the result, and an order may thereupon be made as to the incidence of any costs or expenses incurred.[29]

The previous practice, under which a receiver was entitled to employ his or her own solicitor to carry into chambers and pass (now prepare and serve) his or her accounts, and would be allowed the costs thereof, continues to apply to proceedings for the examination of an account, save where the master or district judge finds that the item or items, of which complaint is made, is or are improper for whatever reason. It is common practice to employ the solicitor of the party having the conduct of the proceedings to pass (now serve) the accounts.[30]

Costs.   Earlier practice was that the receiver, upon passing his or her accounts, **11-8** brought in also his or her bill of costs, which was then taxed,[31] and the amount included in his or her disbursements. On passing the first account, his or her costs of completing the appointment were also taxed and allowed.[32]

It may well happen that a receiver never has his or her accounts queried at all, so that no examination thereof by the court ever takes place. There is, however, now no provision dealing with the time at which the receiver should bring in his or her bill of costs. In these circumstances, the receiver should take advantage of any convenient opportunity, such as an examination of his or her accounts, to bring in his or her bill for it be assessed; but if no such natural opportunity readily arises, the receiver would be entitled to apply by application notice for this purpose, at any time after a reasonable time had elapsed (which will depend upon all circumstances of the case) from the last assessment.

The receiver is always entitled to charge in his or her accounts for the cost of supplying the copies of the accounts which he or she is directed to supply.

Costs of parties attending the examination of accounts.   Parties attending the **11-9** examination of a receiver's accounts recover costs from the receiver only after a

---

[29]   CPR r.44.3.
[30]   See *Dixon v Wilkinson* (1859) 4 Drew. 614; and see also *Bloomer v Curie* (1907) 51 S.J. 277.
[31]   The equivalent of what is now detailed assessment.
[32]   *Daniell's Chancery Practice*, 8th edn, p.1492, n.(m).

judgment or order disposing of the costs of the action, and showing who are or is entitled to costs out of the property in the receiver's charge; in other cases, the costs of the parties are costs in the action. Where the parties are entitled to have their costs paid by the receiver, such costs are assessed at chambers, and paid by the receiver and included in his or her account.[33] Sureties are not allowed costs of attending, except by order.[34] If a receiver occasions expenses or delay by making improper claims, he or she may be disallowed his or her costs, or even ordered to pay the costs of examining the account.[35]

Where an order referred it to the Taxing Master (now the Costs Judge) to tax the claimant's costs of an action, including the costs and remuneration of the receivers and managers appointed in the claim, and to certify the balance after making a certain deduction, it was held that the taxing master had no power to make a separate certificate for the costs alone.[36]

If a receiver includes in the bill of costs charges for work done in another capacity, which he or she allows the costs judge to deal with and to strike out without objection, he or she cannot afterwards recover the amount of the sums so struck out in an action brought for that purpose.[37]

11-10   Receiver must pay in moneys.   The court may fix the amounts and frequency of payments into court to be made by a receiver[38]; but arrangements are almost universally made between the parties and accepted by the court, for payment into solicitors' joint accounts, or otherwise out of court. Where the order appointing the receiver does direct payment into court, the Accountant General will only accept the deposit if provided with either a deposit schedule signed and authenticated by the court;[39] or a written request and a sealed copy of the court order authorising the deposit.[40]

Although a receiver is only bound to make payments at the periods appointed, he or she may at any time apply to the court to pay in money in his or her hands; and if, in the interim between dates on which payments are ordered to be made, he or she receives sums of such an amount as to make it worthwhile to lay them out, he or she ought to apply for leave to pay them into court so that they may be productive for the benefit of the estate.[41] The receiver will need to satisfy the terms of the Court Funds Rules 2011 in making any such payments.[42]

11-11   Receiver's liability for not paying money into court.   If the receiver keeps in his or her hands money which he or she has been directed to pay into court, it is no excuse to say that the circumstances of the estate made it necessary to keep such sums in hand, nor will it prevent the court from directing an inquiry as to what such

---

[33] *Daniell's Chancery Practice*, 8th edn, p.1492.

[34] *Dawson v Raynes* (1826) 2 Russ. 466; *Re Birmingham Brewery* (1883) 31 W.R. 415.

[35] See *Re Holton's Trust* (1919) 88 L.J. Ch. 444 (trustee).

[36] *Silkstone, etc. Coal Co v Edey* [1901] 2 Ch. 652; taxing masters are now titled "costs judges".

[37] *Terry v Dubois* (1884) 32 W.R. 415.

[38] RSC Ord.30 r.6. (revoked); now CPR r.69.11; PD 69, para.6.3(3).

[39] Court Funds Rules 2011 (SI 2011/1734) r.6(1)(a).

[40] Court Funds Rules 2011 (SI 2011/1734) r.6(10(b). Where securities are to be lodged, a special direction must be inserted in the order.

[41] *Shaw v Rhodes* (1827) 2 Russ. 539. For former practice, see *Atkin's Court Forms*, Vol.33 (1981 Issue), p.158.

[42] See also CPR Pt 37.

sums might or ought to have been reasonably laid out at interest.[43] Where the order appointing a receiver does not provide for the payment of moneys into court, or otherwise provide for their destination, the receiver will not be allowed to avail himself or herself of the omission, and to keep a balance in hand without interest, under a pretence of waiting for some party to the action to obtain an order upon him or her for payment in.[44] The receiver ought to apply by application notice, which should be served on the parties to the action, for an order for that purpose, and that the costs be allowed him or her in his or her next account; unless the receiver does so, the court might charge him or her with interest.[45]

Default by receiver. If a receiver fails to comply with any rule, practice direction or direction of the court including failing to submit any account,[46] or to attend for the examination of any such account, or to provide access to any books or papers, or to do any other thing which he or she is required to submit, provide or do, he or she may be required to attend court to explain the non-compliance. The court may then make any order it considers appropriate including terminating the appointment of the receiver, appointing a substitute and payment of costs; reducing the receiver's remuneration or disallowing it altogether and ordering the receiver to pay the costs of any party.[47] If the receiver submits his or her account, but does not attend when it is examined, on a hearing to explain his or her non-compliance the master or district judge may allow the sums with which the receiver has charged himself or herself, and disallow such of his or her payments as are objected to.[48] If the receiver neglects to obey the order for submission of an account, an order may be obtained on application notice,[49] which must be served on the receiver. If he or she does not appear, the order will be made on production of a witness statement, verified by a statement of truth, or an affidavit of service of the application notice, or, if the default consists in not making a payment into court, of the order under which the payment ought to have been made; and the Paymaster General's certificate of the default must be produced in support of the application.[50] **11-12**

Form of order made against receiver. The order, which is drawn up, must state specifically where the accounts are to be submitted,[51] and an indorsed copy must be served personally on the receiver without notice.[52] If personal service of the order cannot be effected, an order for service by an alternative method should be obtained, on an application by application notice, supported by witness statement or affidavit, and the last mentioned order must be served in conformity with the direc- **11-13**

---

[43] *Hicks v Hicks* (1734) 3 Atk. 274.
[44] *Potts v Leighton* (1808) 15 Ves. 273, 274. See, too, 1 Ba. & Be. 230.
[45] *Daniell's Chancery Practice*, 8th edn, p.1493. As to form of application notice, see *Atkin's Court Forms*, Vol.33 (2011 Issue), para.233.
[46] CPR rr.69.9 and 69.11.
[47] CPR r.69.9. *Daniell's Chancery Practice*, 8th edn, p.1493. As to form of order, see Seton, 7th edn, pp.773, 781.
[48] *Daniell's Chancery Practice*, 8th edn, p.1493.
[49] Form of order consequential on non-compliance by receiver, *Atkin's Court Forms*, Vol.33 (2011 Issue), para.244.
[50] *Daniell's Chancery Practice*, 8th edn, p.1493.
[51] e.g. "Room—of chambers of Mr. Justice B., situate at the Royal Courts of Justice, Strand, London." See *Practice Note* [1923] W.N. 344.
[52] See CPR r.81.6.

tions thereby given.[53] If, after such original or alternative service, the receiver neglects to obey the order, it may be enforced against by process of contempt. A similar course should be pursued against a receiver who is directed to pay his or her balance to the parties instead of into court, and neglects to do so. It is irregular to issue a writ of control (formerly a writ of *fi. fa.*) for such a balance.[54]

An order requiring a receiver to submit his or her accounts may be obtained by one of several joint receivers against another who is in default. For, even though joint receivers may be, by the terms of their appointment, required to account jointly, each of them must submit his or her own accounts of what he or she individually receives; and, where the court has found that one of them is in default, the order is as of course, as long as that finding stands.[55]

The receiver in an action may be ordered to submit accounts and pay over the balance, although the claim has been dismissed,[56] or the proceedings in it have been ordered to be stayed.[57]

A receiver who does not pay into court money which has been found to be due, and which he or she has been directed to pay, is liable to committal under s.4(3) of the Debtors Act 1869.[58]

In cases within CPR r.81.4, a writ of sequestration against the estate and effects of a receiver, for disobedience to an order of the court, may be issued, but only with the permission of the court.[59]

If the action has abated by reason of the death of the parties or otherwise, it appears that the receiver may obtain an order for assessment of his or her costs and payment of the balance into court without reviving the action, where revivor is impracticable.[60] In a proper case, a person may be appointed to represent the estate of a deceased party in the absence of a personal representative.[61]

11-14   **Disallowance of salary and charge of interest on unpaid balances.**   Where a receiver fails to submit any account, or to attend for the examination of any account, or fails to pay into court on the date fixed by the court any sum required to be so paid, the court may disallow any remuneration claimed by the receiver, and may, where he or she has failed to pay any such sum into court, charge him or her with interest, at the rate currently payable in respect of judgment debts,[62] or such other rate as it considers appropriate, on that sum while in his or her possession as receiver.[63]

In an old case, where a receiver of the personal estate of a testator had been appointed, and was in default, the Court of Chancery declined to charge him with interest on each sum from the time when it was received, but charged him as an

---

[53] CPR r.81.8 and see *Re Bell's Estate* (1870) L.R. 9 Eq. 172.
[54] *Whitehead v Lynes* (1865) 34 Beav. 161, 165; affirmed, 12 L.T. 332.
[55] *Scott v Platel* (1847) 2 Ph. 229, 230, 231.
[56] *Pitt v Bonner* (1833) 5 Sim. 577. See, too, *Hutton v Beton* (1863) 9 Jur. (n.s.) 1339.
[57] *Paynter v Carew* (1854) Kay App. 36, 44.
[58] *Re Gent* (1888) 40 Ch. D. 190.
[59] CPR r.81.20.
[60] cf. *Ballard v Milner* [1895] W.N. 14.
[61] CPR r.19.2.
[62] Currently 8% per annum. See Judgments Act 1838 s.17 (as amended).
[63] See CPR r.69.9.

executor would be charged, that is, by making yearly or half-yearly rests in the accounts.[64] The former practice was in substantial accordance with that decision.[65]

Remedies after discharge.   The remedies which have been indicated remain for   **11-15**
the most part available against a receiver, even after he or she has been discharged.[66] Where, however, default had been made by the executors of a deceased receiver, the sureties were only ordered to pay interest at four per cent.[67] A receiver may be surcharged on his or her accounts, notwithstanding that he or she has been discharged.[68]

A receiver may be charged with interest on money improperly kept in his or her hands, and not paid into court, or which he or she has failed to invest, as directed by the order appointing the receiver,[69] although the receiver has submitted accounts, and no party has expressed dissatisfaction; for this purpose an inquiry as to what money the receiver has received from time to time, and how long it was kept in his or her hands, may be directed.[70] In *Anon. v Jolland*,[71] Lord Eldon intimated that, if such a case should be brought before him, it would at least be a very grave question whether the receiver should be ordered to make good any loss which might have been occasioned from a difference in the price of government funds between the time when the receiver's balance was paid in, and the time when it ought to have been paid in.

Accounts in foreclosure action.   The mortgagor is entitled to credit for rents   **11-16**
received by the receiver appointed in a foreclosure action during the period between the date of the court's order and the day fixed for redemption. Where a receiver has been appointed, an interim order for foreclosure ought to provide that, in taking the account, the claimant should be charged with the amount (if any) paid into court by the receiver, and any sum in the receiver's hands at the date of the order, and with such a sum (if any) as claimant shall submit to be charged with, in respect of rents and profits come to the receiver's hands before final foreclosure order.[72] If this form of Order is used, the necessity for re-opening the foreclosure and ordering a fresh account will be avoided. If more is in fact received than the claimant submitted to be charged with, a fresh account may be verified by witness statement, verified by a statement of truth, or affidavit and vouched without further order; but the claimant should be careful to submit to be charged with a sufficient sum to cover all rents and profits. If the balance due from the receiver, after deducting outgoings, is less than the amount with which the claimant submitted to be charged, the foreclosure is not opened, the receiver's account being taken at once.[73]

If the interim order is not made in the above form, a fresh account will be directed

---

[64]   *Potts v Leighton* (1808) 15 Ves. 273.
[65]   See *Daniell's Chancery Practice*, 8th edn, p.1494.
[66]   *Harrison v Boydell* (1833) 6 Sim. 211.
[67]   *Clements v Beresford* (1864) 10 Jur. 771.
[68]   *Re Edwards* (1892) 31 L.R. Ir. 242. cf. *Re Browne* (1886) 19 L.Ir.132.
[69]   *Hicks v Hicks* (1744) 3 Atk. 276: See now CPR r.69.9(3).
[70]   *Fletcher v Dodd* (1789) 1 Ves. Jun.85: See *Hicks v Hicks* n.69, above.
[71]   (1802) 8 Ves. 72,73.
[72]   *Simmons v Blandy* [1897] 1 Ch. 19. This practice also obtains where the receiver has powers of management, e.g. of licensed premises. For earlier forms of order, *Smith v Pearman* (1888) W.R. 681; *Cheston v Wells* [1893] 2 Ch. 151.
[73]   So decided by Eady J in an unreported case. See also *Ellenor v Ugle* [1895] W.N. 161.

and a further time, usually one month, given for redemption,[74] though to save the expense of an account, a mortgagee has been allowed to verify the amount due by affidavit, after allowing for receipts down to the application.[75] If rents are received after the date fixed for redemption, the foreclosure is not re-opened, but an immediate order absolute is made[76]; and where the interim order provided that the plaintiff might apply for any moneys come to the hands of the receiver, who received rents after certificate, an order absolute was made, without further account or extending the time.[77]

After a receiver appointed in a foreclosure action had (under the old practice) brought in his final account, and the foreclosure had been made absolute, it subsequently appeared that the receiver had omitted some rents from his account, but it was nevertheless held that, in the absence of any evidence that the plaintiff in the foreclosure action had received any of the rents which the receiver had not accounted for, there was no reason why the foreclosure should be re-opened, merely because the receiver, who was not the plaintiff's agent, but an officer of the court, had made a mistake which was not discovered before it was too late.[78]

11-17   Accounts of deceased receiver.   An order may be obtained, on application notice, that the personal representatives of a deceased receiver be at liberty to submit his or her accounts and to lodge the balance in court.[79] In a case where, on the executors' application, liberty had been given them under the former practice to pass their accounts, and to pay in the balance, they were not allowed, after the lapse of many years, to object to the order on the ground of want of assets.[80]

The order cannot, however, be obtained without the consent of the personal representatives. If they do not consent, the court has no jurisdiction to order, in a summary way, that they shall submit and abide by the court's examination (if any) of the deceased receiver's accounts, and pay the balance out of his or her assets.[81] The proper course, subject to the remedy against the surety, is to sue the personal representatives for an account and administration.[82]

An admission by a receiver's executor of assets to answer what is due from the deceased receiver is sufficient to make the executor liable to pay such interest as the receiver's estate may be charged with, in respect of the rents retained in the deceased's estate.[83] But, if there has been undue delay by the parties, the executor will only be ordered to pay in the principal money and the costs of the application.[84]

---

[74]   *Jenner-Fust v Needham* (1886) 32 Ch. D. 582; *Peat v Nicholson* (1886) 34 W.R. 451; but see *Welch v National Cycle Works* (1886) 35 W.R. 127.
[75]   *Jenner-Fust v Needham*, n.74, above.
[76]   *National Building Society v Raper* [1892] 1 Ch. 54, following *Constable v Howick* (1858) 5 Jr. (n.s.) 331, and not following *Ross Improvement Commissioners v Usborne* [1890] W.N. 92.
[77]   *Coleman v Llewellin* (1887) 34 Ch. D. 143.
[78]   *Ingham v Sutherland* (1890) 63 L.T. 614.
[79]   For form of order, cf. Seton, 7th edn, p.736. See, too, 15 Sim. 483.
[80]   *Gurden v Badcock* (1842) 6 Beav. 157.
[81]   *Jenkins v Briant* (1834) 7 Sim. 171.
[82]   *Ludgater v Channell* (1851) 15 Sim. 482; 3 Mac. & G. 175.
[83]   *Foster v Foster* (1878) 2 Bro. C.C. 615; *Tew v Earl of Winterton* (1792) cited 4 Ves. 606, on a point not in the ordinary reports of that case.
[84]   *Gurden v Badcock*, n.80, above.

Putting recognisance in suit.   Where a receiver neglects to submit his or her ac-   **11-18** counts, or, having submitted them, fails to pay any amount required to be paid[85] within the time limited, and has been proceeded against for the contempt of court, the party prosecuting the contempt may proceed against the sureties. But he or she is not at liberty to sue the sureties, until he or she has taken proceedings against the receiver for the contempt, unless the receiver has become bankrupt, or it can be shown that proceedings against the receiver for contempt would be useless.[86]

If proceedings are to be taken against the sureties, leave is obtained on application, notice to be served on the receiver or his or her personal representatives and the sureties.

Upon the death of a receiver, the parties interested may apply to the court, either against his or her representatives or against his or her sureties; they should in the first place apply against both, to avoid the objection which, if either were omitted, the persons made respondents might raise to the absence of the persons omitted. The court, without deciding whether the representatives or the sureties are primarily liable, can make an order allowing the deceased receiver's guarantee to be enforced against his or her personal representatives and sureties.[87]

---

[85]   See CPR r.69.9(1).

[86]   *Smith, Chancery Practice*, p.1037. See, too, *Ludgater v Channell* (1851) 3 Mac. & G. 175 at p.176, n.(a).

[87]   *Ludgater v Channell*, n.86, at 179–181.

CHAPTER 12

DISCHARGE OF A RECEIVER

12-1   As already stated,[1] the rules regulating the appointment and control of receivers by the court were substantially amended and codified by CPR 69 and CPR PD 69, revoking and replacing RSC Ord.30, with effect from 2 December 2002, with respect to proceedings commenced on or after that date.[2] The new rules relating to the discharge of receivers are as follows.

The court is empowered to discharge a receiver, or to terminate the appointment, at any time, and to appoint another receiver in his or her place.[3] In particular, at the commencement of the appointment, the court may terminate it, if the receiver fails, by the date specified, to give the security which the court has required, or to satisfy the court as to the security which he or she has in force.[4]

The appointment may also be terminated, if the receiver is proved to have failed to comply with any rule, practice direction or direction of the court.[5]

When the court is discharging a receiver, or terminating the appointment, the court may require him or her to pay into court any money held by him or her, or to specify the person (e.g. a successor receiver), to whom the money must be paid over, or to transfer any assets still in his or her possession,[6] and to make provision for the discharge or cancellation of any guarantee given by the receiver as security.[7]

The receiver, or any party to the proceeding, may apply to the court for the receiver to be discharged on completion of his or her duties.[8]

12-2   **The case law.**   The case-law on these subjects, as analysed by Sir Raymond Walton, as slightly abridged and amended is set out below. Despite the updating of the rules, the principles applicable no doubt remain much the same.

12-3   **On his own application.**   Unless the order appointing or continuing a receiver, or a receiver and manager, contains a provision for discharge,[9] an application to the court is necessary in order to divest his or her possession.[10] The appointment of a receiver made previously to the judgment in the action will not be superseded by

---

1   See Ch.5, above.
2   Civil Procedure (Amendment) Rules 2002 (SI 2002/2058) rr.2, 26, and Sch.7.
3   CPR 69.2(3).
4   CPR 69.5(2). Under the former rules, if he or she did not complete the security by the date specified, the appointment terminated.
5   CPR 69.9(1) and (2).
6   CPR 69.11(1)(a).
7   CPR 69.11(1)(c).
8   CPR 69.10.
9   *Day v Sykes, Walkers & Co* (1886) 55 L.T. 733; [1886] W.N. 209.
10   *Thomas v Brigstocke* (1827) 4 Russ. 64; see now CPR 69.10.

the judgment, unless the receiver is appointed only until judgment or further order.[11] But an order to put a purchaser into possession is in itself a discharge of a previous order for a receiver, as to the lands mentioned in the subsequent order.[12]

As a general rule, where a receiver has been appointed and has given security, he or she will not be discharged upon his or her application, before completion of his or her duties, without showing some reasonable cause why the parties should be put to the expenses of a change,[13] otherwise he or she may have to pay the costs of the removal and of a appointment of a successor. If, however, the receiver can show reasonable cause for his or her discharge, such as ill-health, he or she may be discharged and allowed to deduct the costs of and incidental to the application for discharge out of any balance in his or her hands.[14] As an alternative, if his or her indisposition be only temporary, the receiver may obtain the leave of the court to appoint an attorney for a limited period.

A manager may be in a situation where, without the whole-hearted co-operation of some party to the action, which is not forthcoming and cannot be privately compelled, he or she is unable to function effectively as a manager. In these circumstances, it is proper for the manager to apply in the alternative to be discharged, or to have his or her functions restricted to those which it is possible to carry out.[15]

Similarly, if there proves to be no advantage in continuing to carry on a business, either because it cannot be run at a profit, or because the possible profits do not justify the expenses of managing it, the manager, may, and indeed should, make a similar application.[16]

A receiver ought not to make an application for discharge to come on with the further consideration of the action; for the court can, on the further consideration, discharge him or her without such an application. Accordingly, the costs of a separate application for discharge have been refused.[17]

On satisfaction of incumbrance. A receiver is generally continued until judg- **12-4**
ment in the action in which the appointment is made; but, if the right of the claimant ceases before that time, the receiver will be discharged at once.[18] But where the appointment is made in a foreclosure action at the instance of a claimant who is subsequently paid off, another incumbrancer may, on application, obtain leave to be added as claimant, in which case the receivership may be continued.[19] Similarly, if a receiver is appointed for the purpose of satisfying a number of claims, he or she will not be discharged merely on the application of a satisfied claimant, if some of

---

[11] See para.5-40, above.
[12] *Ponsonby v Ponsonby* (1825) 1 Hog. 321; *Anon.* (1839) 2 Ir. Eq. R. 416.
[13] *Smith v Vaughan* (1744) Ridg. temp. Hard. 251; cf. *Cox v M'Namara* (1847) 11 Ir. Eq. R. 356.
[14] *Richardson v Ward* (1822) 6 Madd. 266.
[15] *Parsons v Mather & Platt Ltd*, unreported, 9 December 1974 CA (Appeal Court Judgments (Civil Division) No.392A), where (in effect) the manager was relieved of his management duties and restricted to those of a pure receivership.
[16] See e.g. the master's order in *Fillippi v Antoniazzi* (1976) R. 2251 unreported of 1 November 1977, directing that the receiver and manager be at liberty to cease trading forthwith at the premises of the partnership business.
[17] *Stilwell v Mellersh* (1851) 20 L.J. Ch. 356.
[18] *Davis v Duke of Marlborough* (1818) 2 Swan. 108.
[19] See *Munster, etc. Bank v Mackey* [1917] 1 Ir.R. 49.

the other claims are still outstanding.[20] Proceedings may always be stayed without prejudice to the receivership.[21]

12-5   Continuance becoming unnecessary.   If, in the course of the proceedings, the continuance of a receiver becomes unnecessary, he or she will be discharged. Thus, where a receiver had been appointed in consequence of the misconduct and incapacity of trustees under a will, he was ordered to be discharged on the appointment of new trustees.[22] Again, where a receiver, who had been appointed in consequence of the executors of a testator's will having refused to act, moved away from the vicinity of the estates over which he had been appointed receiver, the court, on the consent of the other parties, and the executors expressing their willingness to act, made an order that the receiver should pass (now prepare and serve) his accounts.[23] A receiver will be discharged, when the object of the appointment has been fully effected,[24] as, for instance, when arrears of annuity, to obtain which the receiver was appointed, have been paid.[25] When the receivership has ceased to serve any valid purpose, it should be discharged without delay.[26]

12-6   Other causes for discharge.   A receiver is liable to be discharged for irregularity in carrying in his or her accounts, for conduct making it necessary to take proceedings to compel him or her to do so, and for so submitting the accounts that the amount of the balance in the receiver's hands cannot be ascertained.[27] So also, if his or her conduct has been such as to impede the impartial course of justice,[28] or to amount to a gross dereliction of duty,[29] or if the appointment as a receiver has been improper.[30]

It is conceived, however, that a charge of misbehaviour against a receiver, for suffering the owner of an estate, over which the receiver was appointed, to remain in part possession of it to the prejudice of the estate, will not be regarded by the court as a sufficient reason for discharging the receiver, for in such a case the parties themselves have caused the loss, by not compelling the owner, by the authority of the court, to deliver up possession to the receiver.[31]

Where a receiver becomes bankrupt, he or she will be discharged, and another receiver appointed.[32]

If a receiver has been wrongly appointed over property belonging to a person

---

[20] *Largan v Bowen* (1803) 1 Sch. & Lef. 296.
[21] *Damer v Lord Portarlington* (1846) 2 Ph. 34; *Paynter v Carew* (1854) 18 Jur. 417; *Murrough v French* (1827) 2 Moll. 497.
[22] *Bainbrigge v Blair* (1841) 3 Beav. 421, 423. It is otherwise where, on the appointment of new trustees, there are questions still outstanding: See *Reeves v Neville* (1862) 10 W.R. 335.
[23] *Davy v Gronow* (1845) 14 L.J. Ch. 134.
[24] *Tewart v Lawson* (1874) L.R. 18 Eq. 490. See, too, *Hoskins v Campbell* [1869] W.N. 59.
[25] *Braham v Lord Strathmore* (1844) 8 Jur. 567.
[26] *Capewell v Customes & Excise* [2004] EWCA Civ 1628; [2005] B.P.I.R. 1266 CA.
[27] *Bertie v Lord Abingdon* (1845) 8 Beav. 53.
[28] *Mitchell v Condy* [1873] W.N. 232.
[29] *Re St. George's Estate* (1887) 19 L.R. Ir. 566.
[30] *Re Lloyd* (1879) 12 Ch. D. 447; *Nieman v Nieman* (1889) 43 Ch. D. 198; *Re Wells* (1890) 45 Ch. D. 569; *Brenan v Morrissey* (1890) 26 L.R. Ir. 618.
[31] *Griffith v Griffith* (1751) 2 Ves.Sen. 400.
[32] *Daniell's Chancery Practice*, 8th edn, p.1479.

who is not a party to the action, he or she will be discharged, even though there has been an abatement of the claim by the death of a sole defendant.[33]

The court will discharge a receiver upon the application of a prior mortgagee who demands to go into possession as such by himself or herself or by his or her receiver.[34]

Where a receiver had been appointed in an administration suit, another person, who was willing to act at a lower salary, was ordered to be substituted for him, as receiver, on the application of a mortgagee of a tenant for life of the property.[35]

Property to be sold. Where estates, over which a receiver has been appointed, have been ordered to be sold, the receiver will be continued, until completion of the sale, in order that he or she may collect any arrears of rent.[36]   **12-7**

Balance due to receiver. The receiver of an estate will not be discharged until he or she has received from the estate any balance found due to him or her on passing his or her accounts.[37] In administration actions, a receiver may be discharged on passing his or her accounts, and be paid remuneration and costs, without waiting to see whether the estate is sufficient to pay all costs payable out of it.[38]   **12-8**

Application of one party only. A receiver, being appointed for the benefit of all the parties interested, will not be discharged on the application of that party only at whose instance he or she was appointed.[39]   **12-9**

Mode of application to discharge. The application to discharge a receiver appointed in a claim should be made by application notice[40]; the direction for discharge may be given in the judgment at the trial, or in the order upon further consideration.[41]   **12-10**

In the Queen's Bench Division, an application to discharge a receiver is made to the master by application notice,[42] which may be issued before or after submission of the receiver's final account. In the former case, the order is made, subject to the receiver complying with the usual Central Office regulations; in the latter, on production of the master's certificate, and proof that the receiver has complied with the directions therein.

Where, under the former procedure, a bond had been given up on application at the General Filing Department, it was to be delivered up on production of the master's order: see below.

---

[33] *Lavender v Lavender* (1875) 9 Ir.R.Eq. 593.
[34] *Re Metropolitan Amalgamated Estates* [1912] 2 Ch. 497; above, para.2-27.
[35] *Stanley v Coulhurst* (1868) W.N. 305.
[36] See *Quin v Holland* (1745) Ridg. temp. Hard. 295.
[37] *Bertrand v Davies* (1862) 3 Beav. 436.
[38] *Batten v Wedgwood, etc. Co* (1885) 28 Ch. D. 317.
[39] *Davis v Duke of Marlborough* (1812) 2 Swans. 108; *Bainbrigge v Blair* (1814) 3 Beav. 421, 423.
[40] *Atkin's Court Forms*, Vol.33 (2011 Issue), para.[243]; forms of order, 1 Seton, 7th edn, p.781; see also *Palmer's Company Precedents*, 16th edn, Pt III, Ch.69.
[41] 1 Seton, 7th edn, pp.781, 782.
[42] See now CPR 69.10.

12-11 Service and appearance. An application for the discharge of a receiver should be served on all the parties.[43] The service of it on the receiver should be personal, and such service will not be dispensed with, unless an order for alternative service is obtained.[44] But a receiver, though served, is not entitled to appear at the hearing of the application, unless some personal charge is made against him or her. If the receiver appears, he or she will not be allowed the costs of such an appearance,[45] except under special circumstances.[46] Those parties who are required to be served with notice include all those parties who were required to be served with the order appointing the receiver, and include any new parties, who have been added to proceedings since the date of the order.[47]

12-12 Form of order on discharge. If the receiver has not submitted his or her final account, nor paid over any balance shown thereby, or determined after examination to be due from him or her, the order discharging him or her will direct him or her to do so.

The order of discharge may be conditional on the performance of some act by the receiver, or be otherwise contingent on some future event. On proper evidence of compliance or of the happening of the event, the court will indorse on the order a direction that any guarantee given by the receiver is to be cancelled. On production of the order the guarantee is indorsed with the vacating note and delivered to the solicitor against his or her receipt.[48]

12-13 Effect of discharge. The court has power, by making an order for release and discharge, to protect the receiver from all liability for acts done in the course of his or her duties. This power should not be exercised without the court first investigating, or making provision for the investigation of, claims of which the court has notice. But the court is not obliged to wait until the end of the limitation period, before protecting its officer against such a claim, if the claimant, having had ample opportunity to do so, neglects to prosecute any claim.[49]

12-14 Notice to surety. Under the usual form of guarantee, the receiver is bound to give to the surety by post notice of the discharge: and within seven days thereafter, send the surety an office copy of the order discharging him or her.

In an Irish case, in which a receiver was discharged owing to gross dereliction of duty, the order discharging him disallowed his fees and poundage on all accounts not passed within the prescribed time, and directed him to pay interest on the balance (if any) from time to time in his hands, and to pay the costs of the motion to discharge him, of his own discharge, and of the appointment of his successor.[50]

---

43 *Daniell's Chancery Practice*, 8th edn, p.1499.
44 *Att.-Gen. v Haberdasher's Company* (1838) 2 Jr. 915.
45 *Herman v Dunbar* (1857) 23 Beav. 312.
46 *General Share Co v Wetley Brick Co* (1882) 20 Ch. D. 260, 267.
47 CPR 69.10, applying CPR 69.4: see *Shalso v Russo*, noted in Civil Court News (2005) November p.1.
48 CPR 69.11. This does not arise, where the receiver is a licensed insolvency practitioner and is covered by continuous security.
49 *IRC v Hoogstraten* [1984] 3 W.L.R. 933 at 944H.
50 *Re St. George's Estate* [1887] 19 L.R. Ir. 566.

IN COMPANY CASES

Administrative receivers; vacation of office. There are special rules dealing   **12-15**
with the vacation of office by administrative receivers.[51] Such a receiver must
forthwith vacate office, if he or she ceases to be qualified to act as an insolvency
practitioner in relation to the company.[52] Where he or she vacates office at any time,
his or her remuneration, and any expenses properly incurred, and any indemnity to
which he or she is entitled out of the assets of the company, will be charged on and
paid out of any property of the company which is in the receiver's custody or
control at that time, in priority to any security held by the person by or on whose
behalf he or she was appointed.[53]

Resignation of administrative receiver. When an administrative receiver   **12-16**
proposes to resign, he or she must give *at least five business days' notice*, stating
the date when the resignation is to take effect,[54] to: (i) his or her appointor; (ii) the
company, or, if it be in liquidation, the liquidator; and (iii) to the members of the
creditors' committee, if any.[55] If the administrative receiver dies in office, notice
must, *as soon as is reasonably practicable*, be give notice to the same persons (and
the registrar of companies).[56] The making of an administration order does not itself
terminate the appointment; but since an order can only be made, where an
administrative receiver is in office, with the consent of the appointor, the administrative receiver must vacate office,[57] and so his or her resignation will necessarily
follow.

Where an administrative receiver vacates office on completion of the receivership or by virtue of having ceased to be qualified as an insolvency practitioner, he
or she must also *as soon as reasonably practicable* give notice to: (i) his or her appointor; (ii) the company, or, if it be in liquidation, the liquidator; and (iii) to the
members of the creditors' committee, if any.[58]

Where an administrative receiver's office is vacated other than by death notice
must be delivered to the registrar of companies within 14 days of the vacation of
office.[59]

---

[51] An administrative receiver may now only be removed by the court: Insolvency Act 1986 s.45(1).
[52] Insolvency Act 1986 ss.45(2): for the meaning of "insolvency practitioner qualified to act in relation to the company," paras 4–8 to 4–9, above.
[53] Insolvency Act 1986 s.45(3).
[54] Insolvency Rules 2016 (SI 2016/1024) r.4.18(2).
[55] Insolvency Rules 2016 r.4.18(1).
[56] Insolvency Rules 2016 r.4.19(1).
[57] Insolvency Act 1986 Sch.B1 paras 39 and 41.
[58] Insolvency Rules 2016 r.4.20.
[59] Under Insolvency Rules 2016 r.4.21 notice under Insolvency Act 1986 s.45(4) may be given by
delivering the notice required by Companies Act 2006 s.859K(3).

CHAPTER 13

LIABILITIES AND RIGHTS OF RECEIVER'S SURETIES

13-1   **The new regime for security.**   Under the previous procedural rules,[1] security to be given by a receiver was to be provided, unless the court otherwise directed, by a guarantee[2]; this would be backed by one or more sureties, corporate or individual.

Under the CPR, such security is now to be given, unless the court otherwise directs, either: (a) where the receiver is a licensed insolvency practitioner,[3] by the bond which he or she is required to hold by way of continuous security, as a qualification for that status,[4] extended to cover appointment as a court-appointed receiver; or (b) by a guarantee; such guarantee must be in a form approved by the court, and with a clearing bank or an insurance company also approved by the court.[5]

13-2   **The case law.**   Where the security is being provided by the insolvency practitioner's bond, as so extended, no question will normally arise as to the liabilities and rights of sureties. But where a guarantee is given, then the previous case law on those subjects will still be relevant.

13-3   **Discharge of sureties.**   The sureties for a receiver will not be discharged at their own request. Where, therefore, an application was made to discharge a receiver on the ground of misconduct, and the sureties joined in the application, Lord Hardwicke held that no regard was to be had to their application, unless it was for the benefit of the estate, or unless there were special circumstances[6]; as, for instance, where underhand practice could be proved, and the person secured could be shown to have been connected with such practice.[7] In one case, a surety was discharged on his own application, where he had become surety in violation of his partnership articles.[8]

---

[1]   CPR Sch.1 – RSC Ords 30 and 115, revoked and replaced by CPR Pt 69 and CPR PD 69, with effect from 2 December 2002.
[2]   CPR Sch.1 – RSC Ord 30 r.2 (revoked).
[3]   Insolvency Act 1986 s.388 (as amended), and see Ch.22, below.
[4]   Insolvency Practitioners Regulations, 2005 (SI 2005/524).
[5]   CPR PD 69 para.7.2(1) and (2).
[6]   *Griffith v Griffith* (1871) 2 Ves.Sen. 400; as to application by a surety for his discharge, see *O'Keefe v Armstrong* (1852) 2 Ir.Ch.R. 115.
[7]   *Hamilton v Brewster* (1820) 2 Moll. 407 per Manners LC.
[8]   *Swain v Smith* (1827) Seton (7th ed.), p.775.

Fresh bond required.   Where a surety procures his or her discharge during the   **13-4**
continuance of the receivership, the receiver must enter into a fresh covenant with
new sureties.[9]

Where one of two sureties dies, or goes abroad, and the receiver is unable to
procure another surety, it has not been the practice to charge the receiver with the
expenses of his or her discharge, or the appointment of a new receiver.[10]

When a surety becomes bankrupt, or being a company enters into liquidation, the
receiver is usually required to procure a fresh guarantee. The order is now to be
made on application notice.[11]

The amount of security for which the surety is liable may be increased or reduced
in a proper case; for example, where part of the assets have been got in and disposed
of.[12]

If a yearly premium under the guarantee is not paid within 15 days (or such other
period specified) after the expiration of the first year, the surety can, under the
express terms of the guarantee, apply to be relieved from further liability.

Order on discharge.   In *Shuff v Holdway*,[13] an order was made on the applica-   **13-5**
tion of a surety, directing the receiver's accounts down to that time to be passed (as
it would now be, served), and that, on payment into court by the receiver, or by the
applicant, of the amount due from the receiver, the applicant should be discharged
as surety, and that the applicant should be at liberty to attend the taking (as it would
now be, examination) of the accounts; but he was ordered to pay the costs of the
application.

Attendance at taking of receiver's account.   A surety was held not to be entitled   **13-6**
without leave to attend at the examination of a receiver's accounts, except at his
own expense[14]; but leave may be given in a proper case, as, for instance, where the
sureties were likely to be called on to pay a balance[15]; and where a receiver had died
in insolvent circumstances, and his personal representative had consented to his
final account being taken in the suit to which he was appointed, liberty to attend was
given to the personal representative.[16]

Extent of liability of surety.   The surety is answerable, to the extent of the amount   **13-7**
of the guarantee, for whatever sum of money, whether principal, interest, or costs,
the receiver has become liable for to the estate which is being administered, including the costs of his her removal and of the appointment of a replacement receiver.[17]
This statement of the law was approved in *Re Graham, Graham v Noakes*,[18] by
Chitty J, from whose judgment it may be concluded that, in ascertaining the li-

---

[9] *Vaughan v Vaughan* (1743) 1 Dick. 90; *Bois v Betts* (1760), 1 Dick. 336.

[10] *Lane v Townsend* (1852) 2 Ir.Ch.R. 120. The surety has usually been a single company.

[11] *Daniell's Chancery Practice* (8th ed.), p.1500. As to form of application of notice, see *Daniell's Chancery Forms*, 7th edn, p.788.

[12] The form of guarantee provides for an increase by endorsement.

[13] 3 September 1857, cited in *Daniell's Chancery Practice*, 8th edn, p.1500; see also *O'Keefe v Armstrong* (1852) 2 Ir.Ch.R. 115.

[14] *Re Birmingham Brewery Co* (1883) 31 W.R. 315.

[15] *Dawson v Raynes* (1826) 2 Russ. 466.

[16] *Simmons v Rose*, 20 November 1860, cited in *Daniell's Chancery Practice*, 8th edn, p.1501.

[17] *Maunsell v Egan* (1846) 3 Jo. & Lat. 251; *Re MacDonaghs* (1876) 10 Ir.Eq.R. 269; *Smart v Flood* (1883) 49 L.T. 467. cf. *Watters v Watters* (1847) 11 Ir.Eq.R. 335.

[18] [1895] 1 Ch. 66 at 70.

ability of sureties, the court proceeds on the principle that the surety is liable (to the extent of the amount of the penalty or guarantee) for all sums of money which the receiver was properly liable to pay into court or to account for. Consequently, where a receiver of "rents and profits" of real estate had:

(1) insured some of the farm buildings in his own name, and received and misapplied the insurance moneys;

(2) received and not accounted for dividends on government funds in court, representing proceeds of sale of real estate; and

(3) received under an order of the court money representing personal estate to be spent in repairs, which money he had misappropriated;

it was held that the sureties had been properly charged in respect of those three items.[19]

Where a receiver had long been known to be bankrupt, during which time no steps were taken to compel the passing (as it would now be, service) of his accounts, the surety was excused from payment of interest.[20] On taking a defaulting receiver's account, the court does not necessarily exact from the surety the full amount of the sum mentioned in the guarantee.[21]

13-8   Surety not liable for loss to third persons.   The liability of the surety under the ordinary bond or guarantee is to make good the net loss, caused by the receiver's default, to the estate which is being administered, not to third persons. Where, therefore, a receiver and manager had properly incurred, and was entitled to be indemnified against, trade liabilities to the extent of £900, but was in default to the estate to the extent of £400, it was held that, inasmuch as the trade creditors could only claim against the estate up to the net amount of the receiver's indemnity, i.e. £500, the estate had suffered no loss by reason of the receiver's default, and that, consequently, the sureties could not be called upon to pay the £400.[22]

A receiver of the estate of a patient was not accountable as receiver to the Court of Protection, for rents and profits received after the death of the patient, and so his surety was not liable in respect of the receiver's default as to such rents and profits.[23]

A surety cannot come to the court for protection, unless there is an accrued liability enforceable against him or her, or semble, unless the receiver is threatening an act which will involve the surety in liability.[24]

13-9   Indemnity of surety.   If a surety has been called on to pay anything on account of the receiver, he or she is entitled to be indemnified for what has been so paid, out of the balance which may be coming to the receiver in the action. Therefore, where a receiver had borrowed money from his surety for the purpose of making sundry necessary payments, it was held that the surety was entitled to be repaid the amount which he had lent to the receiver out of a balance in court due to the receiver.[25] Upon the same principle, the value of shares belonging to a receiver in property which was being administered by the court was applied in making good

---

19   *Re Graham, Graham v Noakes*, n.18, above.
20   *Dawson v Raynes*, above, n.15; see also *Re Herricks* (1853) 3 Ir.Ch.R. 183.
21   per Chitty J in *Re Graham, Graham v Noakes*, n.18, above.
22   *Re British Power, etc. Co (No.3)* [1910] 2 Ch. 470; cited, at para.9-16, above. Quaere, whether this is still the case under the modern form of guarantee.
23   *Re Walker* [1907] 2 Ch. 120; and see *Re Bennett* [1913] 2 Ch. 318.
24   *Re Ledgard* [1922] W.N. 105.
25   *Glossup v Harrison* (1814) 3 Ves. & B. 134; Coop.61.

to his sureties a sum of money which they had been obliged to pay in consequence of his default, although those shares were not included in a security which the receiver had given to the sureties by way of indemnity.[26]

Right against co-surety. A surety who pays the debt of his or her principal has the same right against a co-surety as he or she has against the principal, and he or she will be permitted to claim contribution.[27] **13-10**

Application for stay, etc. Where an action is brought against a surety upon a guarantee, the proper course to pursue is to apply to the court by application notice served on the parties interested, in the claim to which the receiver was appointed, to stay the proceedings against the surety, offering at the same time to lodge what in court is due from the receiver, up to the amount of the guarantee.[28] The surety must pay the costs of the application, and of the proceedings in consequence of it.[29] If the receiver's account has not been prepared and served, the application notice should also ask for an inquiry as to what is due from the receiver. The court may, upon an application of this kind, allow the surety to pay the balance due from the receiver by instalments.[30] Payment by a surety to the solicitor conducting the proceedings is insufficient.[31] **13-11**

The practice on discharge of the receiver is dealt with in the preceding chapter.

---

[26] *Brandon v Brandon* (1859) 3 De G. & J. 24, 530, 531.
[27] *Re Swan's Estate* (1869) 4 Ir.R.Eq. 209.
[28] *Walker v Wild* (1816) 1 Madd; *Re Graham, Graham v Noakes*, n.18, above, at 70: *Daniell's Chancery Practice*, 8th edn, p.1501.
[29] *Walker v Wild*, above, n.28.
[30] See n.29, above.
[31] *Mann v Stennett* (1845) 8 Beav. 189.

PART III: ADMINISTRATION

CHAPTER 14

ADMINISTRATORS: JUDICIALLY AND EXTRA-JUDICIALLY
APPOINTED

SECTION 1: INTRODUCTION

14-1 **The creation of the administration order jurisdiction.** The administration order jurisdiction was originally recommended by the Insolvency Law Review Committee in its Report ("The Cork Report"),[1] and its proposals were ultimately given effect to by the enactment of Pt II of the Insolvency Act 1986. The new jurisdiction formed, with the parallel reform of administrative receivership, and the procedures for voluntary arrangements, the first instalments of the Government's newly-formulated programme of "Rescue Culture".[2] It had been one of the principal terms of reference of that Committee to advise as to possible alternatives to individual bankruptcy and insolvent winding-up, in order to reduce the economic and social damage resulting from avoidable insolvencies,[3] and the wasteful break-up of socially valuable, or economically productive, units or undertakings.

14-2 **The Enterprise Act 2002** In the 15 years of its operation, the original administration scheme generated much case-law. That scheme was wholly superseded (with transitional and other exceptions), and replaced by the provisions of Pt 10 of, and Schs 16 and 17 to the Enterprise Act 2002,[4] which came into force, as to its corporate insolvency provisions and certain other provisions, on 15 September 2004. That Act repealed the Insolvency Act 1986 Pt II (with limited exceptions), and replaced it by Sch.16 to the Act, now re-titled Insolvency Act 1986 Sch.B1. These enactments represented further instalments of "Rescue Culture". The legislative scheme enacted by that Schedule, and by the accompanying Insolvency (Amendment) Rules 2003 (which substituted a new Pt 2 of the Insolvency Rules 1986 for the original Pt 2 of those Rules), provided in much greater detail for the whole process of administration and its functioning, extending to 118 paragraphs and additional Schs 17 and 18. The Insolvency Rules 1986 have now been entirely replaced by the Insolvency Rules 2016 which were published on 25 October 2016 and took final effect on 6 April 2017. Part 3 of the new Insolvency Rules deals with administration as well as rules contained in the new so-called "common parts" of the 2016 Rules which apply to a range of insolvency regimes.

---

1 *Insolvency Law and Practice* (Cmnd 8558), paras 1538 ff; the former editor of this work was a member of the Committee.
2 *Productivity and Enterprise: Insolvency—A Second Chance* (DTI, TSO, 2002).
3 See n.1: "to suggest possible less formal procedures as alternatives to bankruptcy and company winding-up proceedings in appropriate circumstances, and to make recommendations".
4 Enterprise Act 2002 Pt 10; the corporate insolvency provisions, and some other provisions, came into force on 15 September 2003: the individual insolvency provisions, with which this work does not deal, came into force on 1 April 2004.

Duration of an administration. The statute limits the duration of an adminis-   **14-3**
trator's appointment, whether made judicially or extra-judicially, to 12 months.[5]
This period may be extended by the court,[6] or by the consent of creditors,[7] but only
before its expiry.[8] The court is not limited in its number of extensions; but the creditors can only consent to an extension once for a period not exceeding one year, and
not at all, if the court has already granted an extension.[9] Various qualifications attach to the consent of creditors.[10] Although the statute prohibits the extension of the
period after expiry, it has been so extended, exceptionally, at least once.[11] In the
absence of special circumstances, an application for the extension of administration should be made at least six weeks before the end of the administration.[12]

Validity of the appointment of an administrator. An administrator is ap-   **14-4**
pointed judicially by the court on an administration application, or extra-judicially
by the holder of "a qualifying floating charge",[13] or by the company or by its
directors.[14]

An appointment by order of the court is subject to judicial review of that order,
as it was under the old regime, where appointments were made on petition; but an
extra-judicial appointment is not so subject; see Ch.17, paras 17-3 ff.

An "administrator" means a person appointed to manage the company's affairs,
business and property.[15] As such, he is an officer of the court, whether or not appointed by the court.[16] He must be qualified as an insolvency practitioner, in relation to the company.[17] His acts as administrator are valid, in spite of a defect in his
appointment or qualification.[18] However, this does not apply where the defect
renders the appointment a nullity.[19] In such cases, the court has, on a number of occasions, made an order for the appointment of the administrator with retrospective

---

[5] Insolvency Act 1986 Sch.B1 para.76(1).
[6] Insolvency Act 1986 Sch.B1 paras 76(2), 77(1). For an example, see *Re Top Marques Car Rental*
[2006] EWHC 746 (Ch); [2006] B.P.I.R. 1328.
[7] Insolvency Act 1986 Sch.B1 paras 76(2), 78(4).
[8] Insolvency Act 1986 Sch.B1 paras 77(1) and 78(4)(c).
[9] Insolvency Act 1986 Sch.B1; Insolvency Act 1986 Sch.B1 paras 76(2)(b), 78(4)(a) and (b).
[10] Insolvency Act 1986 Sch.B1 para.78(1), (2).
[11] *Re TT Industries Ltd, Re Fibaflo Ltd* [2006] B.P.I.R. 597, HH Judge Norris, QC, Birmingham District
Registry; the application to extend was made before, but could not be heard until after, the expiry;
the judge gave useful directions for future applications. See also *Re Frontsouth (Witham) Ltd* [2011]
EWHC 1668 (Ch); [2011] B.C.C. 635. Cf. *Re Roches Leisure Services Ltd* [2005] EWHC 3148, Ch;
[2006] B.P.I.R. 453 per Rimer J; an old regime case.
[12] *Practice Direction* [2014] B.C.C. 502.
[13] For a definition, see paras 14-15 ff below.
[14] Insolvency Act 1986 Sch.B1 paras 12, 14, 22.
[15] Insolvency Act 1986 Sch.B1 para.1(1).
[16] Insolvency Act 1986 Sch.B1 para.5.
[17] Insolvency Act 1986 Sch.B1 para.6; see Insolvency Act 1986 Pt XIII, ss.388 ff (as amended).
[18] Insolvency Act 1986 Sch.B1 para.104.
[19] As in, for example, *Re Kaupthing Capital Partners II Master LP Inc* [2010] EWHC 836 (Ch); [2011]
B.C.C. 338. See also *Re Ceart Risk Services Ltd* [2012] EWHC 1178 (Ch); [2012] B.C.C. 592.
Although in *Re Blights Builders* [2006] EWHC 3549 (Ch); [2007] B.C.C. 712 Sch.B1 para.104 was
relied on in a case where it was arguable that the appointment was a nullity.

effect.[20] However, doubt has been expressed as to whether there is jurisdiction to make such an order or whether it is an appropriate course.[21]

14-5   **The "purpose of administration".**   "The purpose of administration" to be carried out by such a person is described thus[22]:

> (1)   *"Purpose of administration"* The administrator of a company must perform his functions with the objective of—
>   (a)   rescuing the company as a going concern, or
>   (b)   achieving a better result for the company's creditors as a whole than would be likely if the company were wound up (without first being in administration), or
>   (c)   Realising property in order to make a distribution to one or more secured or preferential creditors;
> (2)   Subject to sub-paragraph (4), the administrator of a company must perform his functions in the interests of the company's creditors as a whole;
> (3)   The administrator must perform his functions with the objective specified in sub-paragraph (1)(a), unless he thinks either
>   (a)   that is not reasonably practicable to achieve that objective, or
>   (b)   that the objective specified in sub-paragraph (1)(b) would achieve a better result for the company's creditors as a whole;
> (4)   The administrator may perform his functions with the objective specified in sub-paragraph (1)(c), only if
>   (a)   he thinks that it is not reasonably practicable to achieve either of the objectives specified in sub-paragraph (1)(a) and (b), and
>   (b)   he does not unnecessarily harm the interests of the creditors of the company as a whole."

The administrator of the company must perform his functions as quickly and efficiently as is reasonably practicable.[23]

Where the term "the purpose of administration" is used in the Insolvency Act 1986 Sch.B1, it means an objective specified in para.3 of that Schedule.

14-6   **The restrictions on making an administration order.**   The court may only make an administration order:

> (1)   where it is satisfied that the company or entity, in respect of which the application is made, is qualified to become, or is not disqualified from becoming, the subject of an administration application[24]; and

---

[20]   Under Insolvency Act 1986 Sch.B1 para.13(2)(a). See *Re G-Tech Construction Ltd* [2007] B.P.I.R. 1275. Such an order can only be made if the conditions of Sch. B1 para.11 are met at the time the order is made.

[21]   *Re Care Matters Partnership Ltd* [2011] EWHC 2543 (Ch); [2011] B.C.C. 957 in which Norris J expressed the view that Sch.B1 para.104 could apply to many such cases, indicating that many defective appointments should not be regarded as nullities; *Re Synergi Partners Ltd* [2015] EWHC 964 (Ch).

[22]   Insolvency Act 1986 Sch.B1 para.3.

[23]   Insolvency Act 1986 Sch.B1 para.4. His failure to perform his functions quickly and efficiently may expose him to removal: Insolvency Act 1986 Sch.B1 para.74(2) and (3).

[24]   Insolvency Act 1986 Sch.B1 para.9.

(2) where it is satisfied that the company is, or is likely (i.e. more likely than not) to become, unable to pay its debts[25]; and

(3) that an order is reasonably likely to achieve "the purpose of administration".[26]

The administrator's priorities.   As set out in para.14-9 above, the administrator's   **14-7**
"functions" are to be directed to "an objective" particularised into a set of priorities.[27] The prime object is to "rescue" the company as a going concern (an expression of the "Rescue Culture" terminology, and echoing the dicta of the House of Lords in *Powdrill v Watson*).[28] The administrator must pursue that objective, unless he thinks (a) that its achievement is not reasonably practicable, or (b) that he can achieve a better result for the company's creditors as a whole, otherwise than by an immediate winding-up.[29]

He may only pursue the third course, namely, realising property in order to make a distribution to one or more secured or preferential creditors,[30] and therefore necessarily having to embark on a break-up policy, if he thinks that it is not reasonably practicable to pursue either of the first two objectives, and that such a course will not *unnecessarily* harm the interests of the creditors as a whole.[31] The intention and the extent of the adverb "unnecessarily" in para.3(4)(b) are not clear: one must ask whether it is intended to reflect an objective decision, or a subjective one.

SECTION 2: THE JURISDICTIONS

Companies or bodies constitutionally qualified to become the subject of an   **14-8**
administration application.   The provisions of the original Pt II of the Insolvency Act 1986 were confined in their application to "companies" as defined by the Companies Act 1985 s.735, that is to say, companies formed and registered under that Act.[32]

This definition excluded UK companies incorporated under statute, or by royal charter, and industrial or friendly societies, or other quasi-corporate bodies, and all foreign-registered companies. The Insolvency Act 1986 s.8(5) (now repealed), also specifically excluded many insurance and banking companies.

Relaxation of restrictions entering administration.   Insolvent foreign-   **14-9**

---

[25] Insolvency Act 1986 Sch.B1 para.11(a); but this requirement does not control applications by a floating charge-holder, made under para.35: see para.14-19, below.

[26] Insolvency Act 1986 Sch.B1 para.11(b). In *Re AA Mutual International Insurance Co Ltd* [2004] EWHC 2430 Ch; [2005] 2 B.C.L.C. 8 it was held that in order for the court to consider the achievement of the purpose of the administration to be "reasonably likely" there must be "a real prospect" of the purpose being achieved. "A real prospect" does not equate with 50 per cent probability: *Re Trident Fashions (No.2) Ltd* [2004] EWHC 293, Ch; [2004] 2 B.C.L.C. 35, at [39] per Lawrence Collins J.

[27] Insolvency Act 1986 Sch.B1 para.3(1).

[28] [1995] 2 A.C. 394; [1995] 2 All E.R. 65, HL; note that the rescue is of the company, and not of the business alone—para.3(1)(a).

[29] Insolvency Act 1986 Sch.B1 para.3(2).

[30] Insolvency Act 1986 Sch.B1 para.3(1)(c).

[31] Insolvency Act 1986 Sch B1 para.3(4).

[32] Or under previous Companies Acts, as applied by the Insolvency Act 1986 s.251. The 1985 Act has now been almost wholly superseded by the Companies Act 2006, which, in s.1(1) applies to companies formed and registered under the Act, unless the context otherwise requires (and see s.1158 of the 2006 Act).

registered companies could overcome their disqualification from entering administration, if a court in a "relevant country"[33] requested a court in the UK to apply the UK's insolvency law to the company, which the UK court would generally be required to do, including the making of an administration order.[34]

The disqualification of insurance companies, banks and authorised institutions was lifted (under conditions) by orders made under the Financial Services and Markets Act 2000.[35]

Insolvent partnerships were given access to administration in 1994,[36] building societies in 1997,[37] and limited liability partnerships in 2001.[38] Access by insolvent partnerships to the benefits of administration has been widened, to equate them, mutatis mutandis, with the procedure in the case of companies. Members of an insolvent partnership can now appoint an administrator out of court, and so can the holder of a qualifying agricultural charge over a partnership's assets. But in the case of such appointments by or in respect of a partnership, the partnership must be proved to be actually unable to pay its debts, and not just reasonably likely to become so.[39]

14-10   Further extensions of jurisdiction: the EC Regulation on Insolvency Proceedings 2000 and the EU Regulation on Insolvency Proceedings 2015. The European Council Regulation on Insolvency Proceedings 2000 ("the EC Regulation") came into force in the UK on 31 May 2002.[40] This, inter alia, legislated for "insolvent companies or other legal persons".[41] Article 3 regulated the commencement of insolvency proceedings, i.e. "collective insolvency proceedings, which entail the total or partial divestment of a debtor and the appointment of a liquidator",[42] in every Member State of the European Union. The 2000 Regulation has now been superseded by the EU Regulation on Insolvency Proceedings 2015 the majority of which came into force on 26 June 2017 and applies to insolvency proceed-

---

[33]   Under the Co-operation of Insolvency Courts (Designation of Relevant Countries and Territories) Orders (SI 1986/2123, 1996/253 and SI 1998/2766), made under the Insolvency Act 1986 s.426 (as amended); for the current list of designated countries and territories.

[34]   *Re Dalhold Estates (UK) Pty Ltd* [1992] B.C.L.C. 621, and see *Hughes v Hannover Ruckversicherungs AG* [1997] 1 B.C.L.C. 497.

[35]   Financial Services and Markets Act 2000 (Administration Orders relating to Insurers) Order 2002 (SI 2002/1242) Sched. para.6 (now repealed by the Financial Services and Markets Act 2000 (Administration Orders relating to Insurers) Order 2010 (SI 2010/3023)).

[36]   Insolvent Partnerships Order 1994 art.6, Sch.2. For cases of an order made in respect of an insolvent partnership, see *Re H Smith & Sons Times*, 6 January 1999; *Re Greek Taverna* [1999] B.C.C. 153. The Insolvent Partnerships Order 1994 does not apply in Scotland, where insolvent partnerships are dealt with under the Bankruptcy (Scotland) Act 1985. Administration is not available to a Scottish partnership.

[37]   Building Societies Act 1997 s.39.

[38]   Limited Liability Partnerships Regulations 2001 and the Limited Liability Partnerships (Scotland) Regulations 2001 (SI 2001/128): see n.16 and, for an example of such an order, see *DKLL Solicitors v Revenue and Customs Commissioners* [2007] EWHC 2067, Ch; [2007] B.C.C. 908; [2008] 1 B.C.L.C. 112.

[39]   Insolvent Partnerships (Amendment) Order 2005 (SI 2005/1516), which came into force on 1 July 2005; see also the Insolvent Partnerships (Amendment) Order 2006 (SI 2006/622). These do not apply in Scotland.

[40]   See Ch.28, below.

[41]   EC Regulation 2000 art.3 para.1.

[42]   EC Regulation 2000 art.2(b). This term comprehensively described every "person or body whose function it is to administer or liquidate assets of which the debtor has been divested or to supervise the administration of their affairs." It is used in the Insolvency (Amendment) Rules 2003 and 2004.

ings opened on or after that date. For the terms of the Regulation, and a detailed treatment of the subject, see Ch.28, below.

As under the 2000 Regulation, art.3 of the 2015 Regulation provides for "insolvency proceedings" (a term which encompasses administrations, including judicial and extra-judicial appointments, in the UK)[43] to be classified as either "main proceedings", "secondary proceedings" or "territorial proceedings".[44] The courts of that Member State in which the debtor has or has had "the centre of his (or its) main interests"[45] are to exercise paramount jurisdiction for the commencement of such proceedings, and it is in those courts that proceedings concerning a debtor, whose centre of main interests is there situated, should prima facie be commenced. They are to be entitled "the main proceedings". If the debtor's COMI is not in England, on the basis of which "main proceedings" under the regulation could be opened, the presence of an "establishment" in England gives the English court jurisdiction to open insolvency proceedings in England but those proceedings will be restricted in effect to assets situated in England ("secondary" or "territorial" proceedings depending on whether they are opened subsequent or prior to the "main" proceedings).[46]

The concept of the "centre of main interests" is the place where the debtor conducts the administration of his interests on a regular basis and which is ascertainable by third parties".[47] The 2015 Regulation now codifies the rebuttable presumptions that apply when ascertaining COMI. In the case of a company, the place of the registered office shall be presumed to be the COMI in the absence of proof to the contrary. However, that presumption shall only apply if the registered office has not been moved to another Member State within the three-month period prior to the request for the opening of insolvency proceedings.[48] The ascertainment of the COMI is to be made on the basis of evidence, both as to its actual location, and as to the circumstances in which it was established there, or transferred there. Important factors are whether, and to what extent, the company's creditors were aware that that was the company's COMI, and dealt with the company there, and on what basis. Evidence given by or on behalf of the company may need to be accepted, in the absence of cross-examination. The 2015 Regulation addresses some of the matters which the court should take into account when determining COMI.[49] These matters largely follow the principles established in case-law under the 2000 Regulation. There is an emphasis on being alert to "fraudulent or abusive" forum shopping as opposed to a genuine relocation of COMI. The location of the COMI at the claimed place must have "an air of permanence". It is open to a debtor company (or a debtor) to move its or his COMI to another State, before the commencement of the insolvency proceedings, for acceptable reasons, and such a change is binding on, or against, the creditors. But the court must look critically at all the relevant facts, and be alert to identify changes to the COMI capable of giving rise to a suspicion of an attempt to defeat creditors.[50]

Time at which the location of the COMI is to be ascertained. The time for the   **14-11**

---

[43] EU Regulation 2015 art. 2(4) referring to Annex A.
[44] EU Regulation 2015 art.3 paras 1–4.
[45] See para.14-11 below.
[46] EU Regulation 2015 art.3 paras 2–4
[47] IA 1986 Sch.B1 para.111(1B). This was set out in the 2000 Regulation, Preamble, para.13. It is now contained in the 2015 Regulation art.3(1).
[48] EU Regulation 2015 art.3 para.1.
[49] EU Regulation 2015 Preamble paras 28–32.
[50] *Shierson v Vlieland-Boddy* [2005] EWCA Civ 974; [2005] B.P.I.R. 1170 CA, reversing [2004]

ascertainment of the location of the company's COMI is the date when the request to open insolvency proceedings is made, and not the date when the debt was incurred or the date of judgment.[51]

14-12 **Conferment of jurisdiction by EC Regulation 2000: instances.** There is a significant body of case-law of the question of COMI under the 2000 Regulation, including the following examples.

An American company registered in the State of Delaware, USA, which had never traded there, but had conducted its trading activities entirely in and from the UK, has been held to have its centre of main interests in the UK. The courts of the UK therefore had jurisdiction, under the 2000 Regulation, to make an administration order against the company.[52]

Where a businessman carried on business in many States of the European Union, but had his centre of main interests in Switzerland (not a member of the Union), the court held that it had no jurisdiction under the Regulation to make a bankruptcy order against him; but it held that it did have such jurisdiction, by virtue of his residence in England.[53]

England was found to be the COMI of an English subsidiary of a US parent company, and also the COMI of its own subsidiary companies which were incorporated in England, Germany and France. It was found that the management of the French and German companies was largely conducted in England notwithstanding that their registered offices were abroad and certain elements of their businesses were conducted abroad.[54] However, mere "parental control" has been held not to be sufficient for a company's COMI to be that of the jurisdiction of its parent company.[55]

Another Delaware-registered company was the subject of a decision to open insolvency proceedings (an administration application) as main proceedings under the EC Regulation, on the ground of its centre of main interests being located in England. It had operated there exclusively, and had represented to the applicant (its bankers) that its executive office was based in London. Although the administration prospects of success were not made out, the court made a winding-up order.[56]

Where a company registered in Jersey was held, on an administration application, to have conducted all its business activities in England, where two of its direc-

---

EWHC 2852, Ch, Mann J. This was a bankruptcy petition; the bankruptcy order, originally made on the ground of the debtor's COMI being in England, was set aside, but made de novo on the basis of the debtor having had an establishment in England. The decision was followed in *Re Collins & Aikman Europe SA*, unreported, 15 July 2005, Lawrence Collins J and *Official Receiver v Eichler* [2007] B.P.I.R. 1636. See article by Gabriel Moss QC, "Jurisdiction follows the sun: debtor moves his COMI to Spain" (2005) 18 *Insolvency Intelligence* 6.

[51] *Interedil Srl v Fallimento Interedil Srl* (C-396/09) [2012] B.C.C. 851; *Re Staubitz-Schreiber* (C-1/04) [2006] B.C.C. 639.

[52] *Re BRAC Rent-A-Car International Inc* [2003] 4 All E.R. 261, and see *Re Ci4Net.com.Inc* [2004] EWHC 1941 (Ch); [2005] B.C.C. 277; see Moss, Fletcher and Isaacs, *The E.C. Regulation on Insolvency Proceedings* (OUP, 2002). The first such case was *Re Enron Directo SA*, unreported, 4 July 2002, Lightman J noted at 15 *Insolvency Intelligence* (2002); *Shierson v Vlieland-Boddy*, see n.50.

[53] *Skjevesland v Geveran Trading Co Ltd* [2002] EWHC 2898 Ch; [2003] B.C.C. 391, affirming [2003] B.C.C. 209.

[54] *Re Daisytek-ISA Ltd* [2003] B.C.C. 562.

[55] *Re Eurofood IFSC Ltd* (C-341/04) [2006] B.C.C. 397.

[56] *Re Ci4net.com Inc, Re DBP Holdings Ltd* [2004] EWHC 1941 (Ch); [2005] B.C.C. 277.

tors lived (none living in Jersey), it was held to have its centre of main interests in England, and an administration order was made.[57]

Another Irish-based company (the subsidiary of an UK-based parent, already in administration) was held to have no establishment or substantial business activities in Eire, where it had been registered for extraneous reasons, and to have conducted from England (where its sole director lived) its world-wide business activities; its centre of main interests were held to be in England, and an administration order was made.[58]

Where a company registered in the Cayman Islands applied for an administration order, it was proved that its head office was in London, where its bank accounts were maintained, on which basis the court found that its centre of main interests was in the UK, and an administration order was made.[59]

Where a group of Cyprus-registered shipping companies had devolved their operations and management to a shipping agent in London, there was sufficient evidence to rebut the presumption that their centre of main interests was Cyprus and it was instead held to be in England.[60]

Special administration regimes excluded from administration. The regime for administration contained in Sch.B1 to the Act does not apply to the seven "special administration regimes" specified in the statute.[61] These are regulated by the provisions of the previous Pt II of the Insolvency Act 1986 (saved for this purpose from repeal), and by their own regulatory legislation.[62]   **14-13**

Companies excluded from administration by reason of their insolvency status, conditions or characteristics.   An administrator may not be appointed over a company which is already in administration,[63] nor, in general, over one which is in creditors' voluntary or compulsory winding-up.[64] But the holder of a qualifying floating charge (see para.14-19, below), may be entitled, under certain conditions, to apply to the court to appoint an administrator over a company in insolvent winding-up[65]; in addition, a compulsory or voluntary liquidator of the company may also apply to the court to appoint an administrator.[66] Administrators may not be appointed over a company which, without being duly qualified, has accepted a deposit under the Banking Act 1987, or over a company which effects or carries out contracts of insurance.[67]   **14-14**

Where there is an administrative receiver in office, the court must dismiss an

---

[57]   *Re Ci4net.com Inc, Re DBP Holdings Ltd,* see n.56, above.
[58]   *Re Aim Underwriting Agencies (Ireland) Ltd* [2004] EWHC 2114 (Ch); [2005] I.L.Pr. 22, applying *Re Brac Rent-A-Car International Ltd,* n.52, above; *Re Daisytek-Isa Ltd,* see n.90, above.
[59]   *Re Sendo Ltd* [2005] EWHC 1604 Ch; [2006] 1 B.C.L.C. 395.
[60]   *Re Northsea Base Investment Ltd* [2015] EWHC 121 (Ch); [2015] 1 B.C.L.C. 539.
[61]   Enterprise Act 2002 s.249(1); see *The Enterprise Act 2002, Explanatory Notes,* (2002) TSO, paras 647–652. Two more such special regimes have been added by statutory instrument.
[62]   Enterprise Act 2002 s.249(2), subject to any orders to the contrary made by the Treasury or the Secretary of State.
[63]   Insolvency Act 1986 Sch.B1 para.7.
[64]   Insolvency Act 1986 Sch.B1 para.8; but see also paras 37 and 38. See article, I L & P (2004) Vol.20, No.3, p.124.
[65]   Insolvency Act 1986 Sch.B1 para.37.
[66]   Insolvency Act 1986 Sch.B1 para.38.
[67]   Insolvency Act 1986 Sch.B1 para.9; but see also para.9(3).

administration application,[68] unless the appointor of the receiver consents to the making of the administration order,[69] or unless the court thinks that the security, by virtue of which the receiver was appointed, may fall to be released, discharged or avoided.[70]

SECTION 3: PERSONS ENTITLED TO APPLY FOR ADMINISTRATION ORDER

14-15 **Meaning of "qualifying floating charge".** A "qualifying floating charge in respect of a company's property", the holder of which has rights under these enactments, is defined in Sch.B1 para.14(2) thus:

"... a floating charge qualifies, if created by an instrument which:

(a) states that this paragraph applies to the charge;
(b) purports to empower the holder to appoint an administrator of the company;
(c) purports to empower the holder to make an appointment which would be the appointment of an administrative receiver, within the meaning of the Insolvency Act, 1986, s.29(2), or
(d) purports to empower the holder of a floating charge in Scotland to appoint a receiver who on appointment would be an administrative receiver."

14-16 **Meaning of qualifying floating charge-holder.** A person is the holder of such a floating charge over the company's property:

"if he holds one or more debentures secured:

(a) by such a charge relating to the whole or substantially the whole of the company's property,
(b) by a number of such charges which together relate to the whole or substantially the whole of the company's property or
(c) by charges and other forms of security which together relate to the whole or substantially the whole of the company's property and at least one of which charges is a qualifying floating charge." [71]

14-17 **The re-definition of "floating charge".**[72] In *Re Spectrum Plus Ltd, National Westminister Bank Plc v Spectrum Plus Ltd*,[73] it was held, at first instance[74] that

---

68 Insolvency Act 1986 Sch.B1 para.39(1).
69 Insolvency Act 1986 Sch.B1 para.39(1)(a).
70 Insolvency Act 1986 Sch.B1 para.39(1)(b), (c) and (d), which refer to the Insolvency Act 1986, ss.238–240 and 245; these enact the powers to set aside securities on insolvency grounds. The sub-paragraphs apply, whether the receiver was appointed before or after the administration application was made. The court had no jurisdiction to make an order where administrative receivers were in post, had not consented to the application being made and where there were no circumstances to suggest that security under which they had been appointed was likely to be set aside: *Chesterton International Group Plc v Deka Immobilien Inv GmbH* [2005] EWHC 656 Ch; [2005] B.P.I.R. 1103.
71 Insolvency Act 1986 Sch.B1 para.14(3).
72 The law discussed in this paragraph does not apply in Scotland insofar as it relates to the possibility of creating a fixed charge over book debts. In Scots law, it is not competent to create a fixed charge over a book debt without formal assignation of the debtor's obligation intimated to the debtor. Accordingly, the question of whether such a charge is fixed or floating does not arise in Scots law.
73 *Re Spectrum Plus Ltd, National Westminster Bank plc v Spectrum Plus Ltd* [2004] EWCA Civ 670; [2004] Ch. 337.
74 [2004] EWHC 9 Ch; [2004] 1 All E.R. 981; [2004] 1 B.C.L.C. 355, Morritt VC, dissenting from *Siebe Gorman & Co Ltd v Barclays Bank Ltd.* [1979] 2 Lloyd's Rep. 147, Slade J (which the Court

although a bank imposed restrictions on a company's ability to deal with its book debts, the company could use the proceeds of their book debts in the normal course of business, until the bank intervened, and that this situation, constituted a floating charge. The Court of Appeal, reversing this decision, held that when, as was the case here, the proceeds of the book debts had to be paid into an overdrawn account as soon as they were received, the title to them passed to the bank, and they could not be used by the company without the bank's consent. This constituted a fixed, and not a floating, charge. *Siebe Gorman & Co Ltd v Barclays Bank Ltd*[75] was rightly decided. The Court of Appeal further found that the form used in *Siebe Gorman* and also in *Spectrum Plus* had been widely used for many years, and that it could be contended that the form had become a fixed charge by customary usage.

The House of Lords reversed the decision of the Court of Appeal and overruled *Siebe Gorman*.[76] Whilst accepting that it was legally possible to create a fixed charge over book debts, the *Siebe Gorman* formula would only be effective where the chargeholder could demonstrate *factual* control over both the uncollected debts *and* their proceeds, once collected. On the facts, the chargor remained free to draw on the "blocked" account into which the charge holder required the debts to be paid, and this was inconsistent with the charge existing as a fixed charge, and entirely consonant with the well established characteristic of a floating charge that the chargor is free to withdraw the "asset" in question from the security unless and until the charge holder intervened.[77] The House of Lords accepted that it was possible to overrule longstanding decisions with prospective effect only, but refused to exercise that power in this instance.

The decision in *Spectrum Plus* was concerned with whether a particular form of debenture created a fixed or a floating charge over the book debts of the company in question, but the test of control is of general application.[78] Their Lordships did not attempt to prescribe what would amount to adequate chargeholder control, either in relation to the specific case of debts paid into a bank account or in relation to fixed charges over other classes of assets. It is notable that an application of the test of control has led to the result that a charge over real property described by the parties as floating was in fact a fixed charge.[79]

Company in insolvent winding up: administration application by floating charge-holder or by liquidator.   14-18   Where the company is in liquidation, and the holder of a qualifying floating charge would be entitled, but for the winding-up, to appoint an administrator, he may make an administration application to the court.[80] The liquidator may also make such an application.[81]

---

of Appeal affirmed).

[75] See n.95, above. Compare and contrast *Re Westmaze Ltd (in administrative receivership) Times*, 15 July 1998, CA, applying *Royal Trust Plc v National Westminster Bank Plc* [1996] B.C.C. 613.

[76] [2005] UKHL 41; [2005] 2 A.C. 680.

[77] Following *Re Brumark Investments Ltd* [2001] UKPC 28; [2001] 2 A.C. 710. In accordance with the opinion expressed in *Brumark*, the House of Lords overruled *Re New Bullas Trading Ltd* [1994] B.C.C. 36, where the Court of Appeal held that a charge over book debts which was expressed to be fixed in relation to the debts whilst uncollected but floating as regards the debts once collected was valid according to its terms. For a detailed discussion of the decision see A. Berg, "The cuckoo in the nest of corporate insolvency: some aspects of the *Spectrum* case" [2006] J.B.L. 22.

[78] See, e.g., *Re Cosslett Contractors Ltd* [1998] Ch.495.

[79] *Russell Cooke Trust Co Ltd v Elliott* [2007] EWHC 1443 Ch; [2007] 2 B.C.L.C. 637.

[80] Insolvency Act 1986 Sch.B1 para.37(2).

[81] Insolvency Act 1986 Sch.B1 para.38(1).

Whichever of them is the applicant, he must, in his witness statement,[82] state:

(i)　　the name and address of the liquidator, with full details of the insolvency proceedings, and the person who appointed him, and on what date;

(ii)　　the reasons why it has subsequently been considered appropriate to make an administration application; and

(iii)　　all other matters which would, in the applicant's opinion, assist the court in considering the need to make provision in respect of matters arising in connection with the liquidation.

The affidavit must also contain those details required by r.3.6(3) of the Insolvency Rules 2016.[83] Where the applicant is a charge-holder, he must set out sufficient evidence to satisfy the court that he is entitled to appoint an administrator, under Insolvency Act 1986 Sch.B1 para.14.[84]

On making an appointment upon such applications, the court shall discharge the winding-up order. It shall make provision for such matters as may be prescribed and may make other consequential provisions. It shall specify which of the powers under the Insolvency Act 1986 Sch.B1, shall be exercisable by the administrator, and Sch.B1 shall have effect with such modifications as the court may specify.[85]

14-19　**Appointments of the administrator made otherwise than by the court.**　The court's power of appointment is only one of three modes of appointment. Powers of direct extra-judicial appointment are vested in the holder of a qualifying floating charge,[86] and in the company or its directors[87]; but such power of *direct* appointment is not conferred on any of its creditors (other than as a qualifying floating charge-holder), nor on its compulsory or on its creditors' voluntary liquidator, nor on the magistrates' court's chief executive.

14-20　**Powers to apply for appointment: who may apply to the court.**　The persons entitled to apply to the court for an administration order are the same as those formerly authorised by Insolvency Act 1986, Pt II[88] (now, except for transitional provisions and for excepted regimes, repealed and replaced), namely the company itself or its directors, one or more creditors (including contingent and prospective creditors), including the holder of a qualifying floating charge,[89] and a magistrates' court's chief executive, or a combination of any of those[90]; to this original list has been added the supervisor of a corporate voluntary arrangement affecting the company.[91]

---

[82]　Insolvency Rules 2016 r.3.6(5).
[83]　Insolvency Rules 2016 r.3.6(5).
[84]　Insolvency Rules 2016 r.3.6(4).
[85]　Insolvency Act 1986 Sch.B1 paras 37(3), 38(2), and Insolvency Rules 2016 r.3.14.
[86]　Insolvency Act 1986 Sch.B1 para.14.
[87]　Insolvency Act 1986 Sch.B1 para.22.
[88]　Insolvency Act 1986 Pt II s.9(1) (repealed).
[89]　For the definition of "a qualifying floating charge", see para.14-19, above.
[90]　Insolvency Act 1986 Sch.B1 para.12(1). The magistrates' court will be enforcing a fine.
[91]　Insolvency Act 1986 Sch.B1 para.12(5) (added by Order below), and see Insolvency Act 1986 s.7(4)(b) which authorises the supervisor of a corporate voluntary arrangement to apply for an administration order, to be added to the list in para.12(1): see Enterprise Act 2002 (Insolvency) Order 2003 (SI 2003/2096) art.2(1), (2).

Making of administration application to the court: statutory   **14-21**
notices.   Application to the court by any of the above applicants for an administration order is no longer made by petition (as under the old Insolvency Act 1986 Pt II),[92] but by an "administration application",[93] with specified contents.[94] Notice of the making of the application must be given by the applicant, *as soon as is reasonably* practicable, to:

(i)   any person who has appointed, or is, or may be, entitled to appoint an administrative receiver of the company;

(ii)   any person who is, or may be, entitled to appoint an administrator of the company under the Insolvency Act 1986 Sch.B1 para.14; and

(iii)   such other persons as may be prescribed.[95]

An administration application may not be withdrawn without the permission of the court.[96] Where an administrator has been appointed by the court by order made on an administration application, the court has power to review, vary or discharge that order, if satisfied that the order, in the light of certain circumstances, should not have been made, thereby terminating the administrator's appointment.[97]

Section 4: Drafting the Application: Procedure

Procedure on application: drafting the application.   The procedure discussed   **14-22**
in this section does not apply in Scotland, where the procedure is governed by the Insolvency (Scotland) Rules 1986 (as amended), and by the Rules of the Court of Session and of the Sheriff Court, to which reference should be made for the detailed provisions.

The administration application must contain specified information,[98] and must be supported by a witness statement,[99] to be made by or on behalf of the applicant, deposing to prescribed matters.

Where the application is made by a company or by its directors, the witness statement must be made by one director, or by the company secretary.[100] An application by the supervisor of a company in a corporate voluntary arrangement is to be treated as an application made by the company once it has been served on the company.[101] An application by creditors is to be made, if by a single creditor, in his or its name, and if by several creditors, in the name of one of them, identifying those other creditors on whose behalf he or it is also applying.[102] The application must state the applicant's belief that the company is, or is likely to become, unable to pay its debts (except where the applicant is the holder of a qualifying floating charge,

---

[92]   Insolvency Act 1986 Pt II s.9 (repealed).
[93]   Insolvency Act 1986 Sch.B1 para.12(1).
[94]   Insolvency Rules 2016 r 3.3(2). Unlike the Insolvency Rules 1986, the new Rules do not prescribe forms but rather specify the content required in the application within the applicable Rule.
[95]   Insolvency Act 1986 Sch.B1 para.12(2); such persons are any enforcement agent or other officer, who, to the applicant's knowledge, is charged with distress or other legal process against the company or its property, and anyone who, to his knowledge, has distrained against the company or its property: see Insolvency Rules 2016 r.3.9.
[96]   Insolvency Act 1986 Sch.B1 para.12(3).
[97]   Insolvency Rules 2016 r.12.59.
[98]   Insolvency Rules 2016 r3.3.
[99]   Insolvency Rules 2016 r.3.6.
[100]   Insolvency Rules 2016 r.3.6(1).
[101]   Insolvency Rules 2016 r.3.5.
[102]   Insolvency Rules 2016 r.3.3(2).

who may be exempt from this requirement, under the Insolvency Act 1986 Sch.B1 para.35(2)).[103] The application for an administration order must be made to a judge.[104]

14-23 Where floating charge-holder intervenes with his own nominee for appointment. Where a qualifying floating charge-holder intervenes in the application by another party (not such a holder), requiring the appointment of his nominee by the court,[105] he must produce to the court the written consent of any prior floating charge-holder, a written statement by his nominee, and sufficient evidence that he is entitled to appoint an administrator under the Insolvency Act 1986 Sch.B1 para.14.[106]

14-24 Interposition of charge-holder's direct appointment. A qualifying floating charge-holder is entitled, notwithstanding that an administration application is pending before the court, to appoint an administrator himself and not through the court. If he does so, he must as soon as reasonably practicable send a copy of the notice of his appointment to the applicant in that application, and to the court to which it has been made.[107]

14-25 Interposition by prior floating charge-holder. Where a qualifying floating charge-holder has appointed an administrator under the powers conferred by Sch.B1 para.14, the holder of a prior qualifying floating charge may apply to the court for an order that the administrator so appointed should be replaced by his own nominee.[108]

Prior to that first appointment, the intending appointor must have notified any prior holder of his intention to make an appointment, or must have obtained his consent to the appointment.[109] It would appear that notice must be given even where the prior chargee's security is not currently enforceable.[110] This provision presumably covers the case of a prior holder who has not consented but took no steps to block the appointment at the time.

Such a substitution of administrator would require the prior holder-applicant and his nominee to possess respectively the same qualifications, and to follow the same procedure, as are required in the case of an original administration application.

14-26 Statement by the proposed administrator. There must be a statement by the proposed administrator (and by each of them, if more than one) known as a "consent to act" filed with the administration application.[111] This statement must include a statement that:

(a) he consents to accept appointment;
(b) he gives details of any prior professional relationship(s) that he has had with the company;

---

[103] Insolvency Rules 2016 r.3.3(2)(i).
[104] See para.14-36, below.
[105] Under Insolvency Act 1986 Sch.B1 para.36(1)(b).
[106] Insolvency Rules 2016 r.3.11(1).
[107] Insolvency Act 1986 Sch.B1 para.14; Insolvency Rules 2016 r.3.19.
[108] Insolvency Act 1986 Sch. B1 para.96.
[109] Insolvency Act 1986 Sch.B1 para.15(1). Failure to do so will render the appointment invalid; it cannot be validated retrospectively: *Re Eco Link Resources* [2012] B.C.C. 731.
[110] *Re OMP Leisure Ltd* [2008] B.C.C. 67.
[111] Insolvency Rules 2016 r.3.7(1).

(c) he is of the opinion that the purpose of administration is reasonably likely to be fulfilled.

The proposed administrator, in giving his opinion as to the favourable prospects of the scheme, must follow the Code on Guidance for expert evidence,[112] and in particular must be aware of possible conflicts of interest.[113]

The evidence in support of the application. The witness statement in support of the application must depose to the following matters[114]: **14-27**

(a) a statement of the company's financial position, stating (to the best of the applicant's knowledge and belief) the company's assets and its liabilities (including its contingent or prospective liabilities);

(b) details of any security known or believed to be held by creditors, and whether they empower the holders to appoint an administrative receiver or an administrator of the company, under the Insolvency Act 1986 Sch.B1 para.14, and whether an administrative receiver has been appointed;

(c) details (so far as known) of any insolvency proceedings in relation to the company, including any petition presented for its winding up;

(d) if more than one administrator is proposed to be appointed, details of the distribution of functions between them[115];

(e) the reason for the statement that the proceedings will be main, secondary, territorial or non-EC proceedings;

(f) any other matters which, in the opinion of those intending to apply for an administration order, will assist the court in deciding whether to make such an order,

(g) where the applicant is the holder of a qualifying floating charge, and relies on the Insolvency Act 1986 Sch.B1 paras 35 or 37, he shall depose to sufficient detail to satisfy the court that he is entitled to appoint an administrator under that Act, Sch.B1 para.14.[116]

Filing of the application. The application and all supporting documents must be filed with the court, with sufficient copies to be served on each of the persons (potentially very numerous) requiring to be "notified" (i.e. served).[117] **14-28**

Parties or persons to be "notified" or served.[118] **14-29**

(a) any person or persons who has/have appointed, or may be entitled to appoint, an administrative receiver of the company;

(b) any person or persons who is/are or may be entitled to appoint an administrator of the company (i.e. the holder of a qualifying floating charge over its property, or the company or its directors);

(c) any administrative receiver in office;

---

[112] See CPR Pt 35 and PD 35. The "Protocol for the instruction of Experts to give evidence in civil claims", replaced the former Code of Guidance and was in turn replaced by "Guidance for the instruction of experts in civil claims" which came into effect on 1 December 2014.

[113] *Re Colt Telecom Group pc (No.2)* [2002] EWHC 2815 Ch; [2003] B.P.I.R. 324: see at paras 80 ff.

[114] Insolvency Rules 2016 r.3.6(3).

[115] Insolvency Act 1986 Sch.B1 para.100(2).

[116] Insolvency Rules 2016 r.3.6(4).

[117] Insolvency Rules 2016 r.3.7

[118] Insolvency Act 1986 Sch.B1 para.12.2; Insolvency Rules 2016 r.3.8(3).

(d) the petitioner in any pending petition presented for the winding-up of the company, and any provisional liquidator appointed under such a petition;
(e) any Member State liquidator appointed in "main proceedings" in another EU State, affecting the company[119];
(f) the proposed administrator(s);
(g) the company (if not the applicant); and
(h) the supervisor of any corporate voluntary arrangement affecting the company.

Each copy of the application tendered to the court will be sealed by the court and issued to the applicant, endorsed with the date and time of filing, and with the venue (i.e. the date, time, and place of the hearing).[120]

14-30   Subsequent notice of any insolvency proceedings.   The applicant must file with the court notice of any insolvency proceedings affecting the company (anywhere in the world, if a company incorporated in England and Wales; in any EEA state if a company incorporated in an EEA state and in any member state other than Denmark if a company not incorporated in an EEA state) as soon as he is aware of them.[121]

14-31   Notice to execution officers.   The applicant must, as soon as reasonably practicable, give notice of the filing of the application to:

(a) any enforcement officer agent or other officer who, to the applicant's knowledge, is charged with distress or other legal process against the company or its property; and
(b) any person who to his knowledge has distrained against the company or its property.[122]

14-32   Service of the application.   Service may be effected as follows[123]:

(a) on the company itself (where not the applicant), by delivery of the documents to its registered office, unless such service is not practicable, when they may be delivered to the company's principal place of business[124];
(b) on any other person, by delivery of the documents to his proper address, which is an address notified as his address for service; if no such address has been so notified, then service may be effected by delivery to his usual or last known address[125]; and
(c) in the case of a person who is or has been an authorised deposit-taker, or who has appointed or may be entitled to appoint an administrative receiver, or an administrator, of the company, under the Insolvency Act 1986 Sch.B1 para.14, and has not notified an address for service, that person's proper address is the address of any office of that person where the applicant knows that the company maintains a bank account, or where no such office is

---

[119] See para.14-14, above and Ch.28, below.
[120] Insolvency Rules 2016 r.3.7(4).
[121] Insolvency Rules 2016 r.3.10.
[122] Insolvency Rules 2016 r.3.9.
[123] Insolvency Rules 2016 Sch 4 para.3.
[124] Insolvency Rules 2016 Sch 4 para.3(1)(a).
[125] Insolvency Rules 2016 Sch 4 para.3(1)(b) and (2)

known, the registered office of that person, or its or his usual or last known address[126];

(d) *alternatively*, in such other manner as the court may direct.[127]

Proof of service.   Service of the application shall be verified by a certificate of service verified by a statement of truth,[128] specifying the date on which, and the manner in which, service was effected which shall be filed with the court as soon as reasonably practicable after service, and *in any event not less than the business day before the hearing of the application.*[129]   **14-33**

Effect of floating charge holder's intervention.   Where an administration application has been made by a person other than a qualifying floating charge-holder, and is still pending, a floating charge-holder may himself appoint an administrator, under his extra-judicial powers (see para.14-47, below), which will render the pending application abortive. The court and the applicant have each the right to be supplied with copies of the notice of appointment.[130]   **14-34**

Section 5: The Hearing and the Order

Hearing of the application.   The following persons may appear or be represented on the hearing of the application: **14-35**

(a) the applicant;
(b) the company;
(c) one or more of its directors;
(d) any administrative receiver in office;
(e) any petitioner for the winding-up of the company (presumably this would include its provisional liquidator: see Sch.B1 para.12(2));
(f) the proposed administrator;
(g) any Member-State liquidator appointed in main proceedings under the EU Regulation 2015;
(h) any holder of a qualifying floating charge;
(i) any supervisor of a voluntary arrangement affecting the company; and
(j) with the permission of the court, any other person who appears to have an interest justifying his appearance.[131]

Applications which must be made before a judge.   All applications for an administration order must be listed before a judge. Applications for directions or case management, after any proceedings have been referred to or adjourned to a judge, must also be listed before the judge, except where liberty to apply to the Registrar or District Judge has been given.   **14-36**

All other applications relating to administration orders should be listed for initial hearing before a Registrar or District Judge. When deciding whether to hear the proceedings themselves, or to adjourn them to the judge, they should have regard to the following factors:

---

126 Insolvency Rules 2016 Sch 4 para.3(3) and (4).
127 Insolvency Rules 2016 Sch 4 para.1.
128 Insolvency Rules 2016 Sch 4 para.6.
129 Insolvency Rules 2016 r.3.8(4).
130 Insolvency Rules 2016 r.3.19(2).
131 Insolvency Rules 2016 r.3.12(1).

(a) the complexity of the proceedings;
(b) whether the proceedings raise new or controversial points of law;
(c) the likely date and length of the hearing; and
(d) public interest in the proceedings.[132]

14-37   **The merits of the application.**   Where there are real issues of fact and law concerning the alleged debt, on which the administration application is based, and which cannot be resolved at the hearing, case-law has held that the applicant fails to establish his locus standi.[133] However, in *Hammonds (A Firm) v Pro-fit USA Ltd*,[134] Warren J considered that there was no reason to apply the practice adopted in relation to disputed debts and cross claims in winding up petition hearings to administration applications. If the applicant could establish a good arguable case that a debt was due to him, he was a creditor for the purpose of the locus standi requirements of para.12 of Sch.B1.[135] Equally, where the company opposed the appointment of an administrator by the debenture-holder, on the ground that it bona fide disputed the debenture-holder's claim, it was held that such a dispute does not remove the debenture-holder's right to appoint an administrator; the realisation of securities could be seriously impeded if secured creditors could be held up by a disputed debt.[136] However if the debt is disputed and is covered by an arbitration clause, the court should not make an administration order but should require the dispute to be resolved by arbitration.[137]

14-38   **Competition between nominees for appointment.**   Where groups of creditors dispute between themselves as to the appropriate nominees, the choice of the largest group by value will usually prevail. However it may be outweighed by matters such as the nominees' prior relevant experience.[138]

Where, on the other hand, a company's directors preferred their own nominee over those of the trustee of a pension fund, the trustee's application was nevertheless granted, notwithstanding that the directors' nominees were already acting in relation to the company's subsidiary: the trustee was a substantial creditor of the company, and the best interests of the creditors demanded a rigorous and independent professional analysis by the administrators.[139] In *The Oracle (North West) Ltd v Pinnacle Financial Services Ltd*[140] Patten J was called upon to adjudicate between the company's choice of administrator and that of its largest creditor. The company's chargeholder and its other unsecured creditors were neutral on the matter. In deciding in favour of the creditor's nominee, the learned judge considered that "… (t)he court's role on an administration application is to attempt to provide the best solu-

---

[132] Practice Direction on Insolvency Proceedings 2014, para.3.
[133] *Re Simoco Digital UK Ltd*, sub nom *Thunderbird Industries LLC v Simoco Digital UK Ltd* [2004] EWHC 209 (Ch); Patten J; cf. *Swindon Town Properties Ltd v Swindon Town Football Club Ltd* [2003] B.P.I.R. 253.
[134] [2007] EWHC 1998 Ch; [2008] 2 B.C.L.C. 159; and see *L Ho*, (2007) 23 I.L. & P 146.
[135] This approach was followed in *Corbett v Nysir (UK) Ltd* [2008] EWHC 2670 Ch.
[136] *BCPMS (Europe) Ltd v GMAC Commercial Finance Ltd*, [2006] EWHC 3744 Ch; [2006] All E.R. (D) 285 (Feb) Lewison, J, applying *Rushingdale Ltd v Byblos Bank Plc* [1986] 2 B.C.C. 99509.
[137] *Fieldfisher LLP v Pennyfeathers Ltd* [2016] EWHC 566 (Ch).
[138] *Healthcare Management Services Ltd v Caremark Properties Ltd* [2012] EWHC 1693 (Ch).
[139] *GP Noble Trustees Ltd v Directors of Berkeley Berry Birch Plc* [2006] EWHC 982 Ch; [2007] B.P.I.R. 1271.
[140] [2008] EWHC 1920 Ch; [2009] B.C.C. 159.

tion in terms of setting up an administrative framework for the benefit of the creditors"[141] and, further, that the court should have regard to the wishes of the creditors.

Paramount discretion of the court. Under the old regime, the court hearing an administration petition exercised a very wide-ranging discretion as to whether to make or refuse the order.[142] This discretion is still conferred under the current regime.[143] The court must be alert to the possibility that the application may be unreasonable, unfeasible, or an abuse of process, or generally motivated by an "improper motive":[144] "It is in the public interest that there should be an effective sanction to deter this abuse. The effective sanction is rescission".[145] It is the absence of this judicial discretion in deciding on appointments, which renders the extra-judicial appointments potentially hazardous for creditors, and members.

14-39

Pre-packaged administrations A practice has developed known as a "pre-packaged" administration ("pre-pack"), a strategy whereby the prospective administrator of a company negotiates the sale of all or a part of the company's business prior to his appointment and, shortly after that appointment, executes the agreement.[146] The legal validity of the pre-pack has been questioned, but the strategy has been judicially sanctioned by the courts, who have made administration appointments where a pre-pack sale is contemplated. In *Re DKLL Solicitors v HM Revenue and Customs*[147] it was argued that the court should not make an administration order where it was known that a pre-pack was contemplated and the company's majority creditor opposed the proposed sale and would, if given the opportunity, vote against the administrator's (hypothetical) proposal to execute the agreement. Andrew Simmons QC disagreed: the court could authorise the implementation of proposals notwithstanding the objection of a majority creditor[148] and the critical question in the circumstances was whether it was reasonably likely that the objective of the administration would be achieved, and on the evidence there was no reason to believe that the pre-pack would not achieve the objective in question.

However, in *Re Kayley Vending Ltd*,[149] it was noted by HHJ David Cooke that in such applications "the court must be alert to see, so far as it can, that the procedure is at least not being obviously abused to the disadvantage of creditors ... . If it is, or may be, the court may conclude that it is inappropriate to give the pre-

14-40

---

[141] At para.[8].
[142] *Re Simoco Digital UK Ltd, sub nom. Thunderbird Industries LLC v Simoco Digital UK Ltd*, n.134 above.
[143] *Re Colt Telecom Group Plc (No.2)* [2002] EWHC 2815 Ch; [2003] B.P.I.R. 324, where the petition was stigmatised as being without substance; "it should never have been launched, being in reality a mere cash-gathering exercise"; cf. the submissions of the company in *Re Simoco Digital UK Ltd, Thunderbird Industries LLC v Simoco Digital UK Ltd*, n.134 above.
[144] *Re Colt Telecom Group Plc (No.2)* [2002] EWHC 2815, para.81, Ch.17, below.
[145] *Cornhill Insurance Plc v Cornhill Insurance Services Ltd* [1992] B.C.C. 97; see para.17-5, below.
[146] See, generally, Finch, Pre-packaged Administrations: Bargains in the Shadow of Insolvency or Shadowy Bargains? [2006] J.B.L. 568; Walton, Pre-Packaged Administrations: Trick or Treat? (2006) 19 Insolv. Int. 113. For an empirical analysis of the pre-pack trend, see Frisby, "*A Preliminary Analysis of Pre-Packaged Administrations*" (hereinafter "The Preliminary Report"), available on the R3 website at: *http://www.r3.org.uk*.
[147] [2007] EWHC 2067 Ch; [2007] B.C.C. 908.
[148] *Re Structures & Computers Ltd* [1998] B.C.C. 348 Ch D.
[149] [2009] EWHC 904 Ch.

pack the apparent blessing conferred by making the administration order."[150] The courts remain willing to make administration orders to facilitate prepacks.[151] However, following concerns and adverse comments on the practice, pre-pack transactions now come under a greater degree of scrutiny following the instigation of a non-statutory scheme for the regulation of pre-packs, contained in a "Statement of Insolvency Practice" ("SIP 16") issued by the Insolvency Service in January 2009 which has since been revised to increase information disclosure to creditors and compliance obligations.[152] In *Re Hellas Telecommunications (Luxembourg) II SCA*,[153] the court required provision of the same information as that required to be sent to creditors under SIP 16 on an application for an administration order in the context of a pre-pack sale.

14-41 **Costs.** If the court makes an administration order, the costs of the applicant, and of any persons whose costs are allowed by the court, are payable as an expense in the administration.[154]

14-42 **The making of the administration order.** If the court makes an administration order, (i.e. an order appointing one or more administrators), it shall include specified provisions,[155] according to the nature of the application.[156] For the orders which may be made, see below.

After making the order, the court shall as soon as reasonably practicable send two sealed copies of it to the applicant, who shall, as soon as reasonably practicable, send one of them to the administrator(s).[157] If the court makes an interim order, or any other order "as it thinks appropriate", it shall give directions as to which persons are to receive notice of it, and how this should be effected.[158]

14-43 **Time of commencement of administration order.** An administration order takes effect at the date and time appointed by the court, or if no date is appointed, then at the time that it was made.[159] As a matter of principle, the time for an administration order taking effect should rarely be postponed: see "Problems presented by interim or conditional orders", para.14-50, below.

14-44 **Orders which the court may make on an administration application.** On hearing an administration application, the court may make any of the following orders[160] (subject to Sch.B1 para.39)[161]:

    (a)   make the administration order sought;

---

[150] [2009] EWHC 904 at [24].
[151] For a recent example, see *Capital for Enterprise Fund A LP v Bibby Financial Services Ltd* [2015] EWHC 2593 (Ch), where a challenge to a pre-pack sale was unsuccessful.
[152] The revised SIP 16 came into force on 1 November 2015 and affects all administration appointments starting on or after that date.
[153] [2009] EWHC 3199 (Ch).
[154] Insolvency Rules 2016 r.3.12(2).
[155] Insolvency Rules 2016 r.3.13.
[156] Insolvency Rules 2016 r.3.13, 3.14.
[157] Insolvency Rules 2016 r. 3.15.
[158] Insolvency Rules 2016 r.3.15(3).
[159] Insolvency Act 1986 Sch.B1 para.13(2).
[160] Insolvency Act 1986 Sch.B1 para.13(1); and see also n.170, above.
[161] Insolvency Act 1986 Sch.B1 para.13(4); para.39 deals with the situation where there is an administrative receiver in office, which is a bar to appointing an administrator, unless the charge-holder consents, or the court thinks that his security may be held to be invalid or released on insolvency

(b) dismiss the application;

(c) adjourn the hearing, conditionally or unconditionally;

(d) make the interim order;

(e) treat the application as a winding-up petition, and make any order which it could make under the Insolvency Act 1986 s.125[162]; and

(f) make any other order which the court thinks appropriate.

An interim order may restrict the exercise of a power of the directors or of the company,[163] or make provision conferring a discretion on the court, or on a person qualified to act as an insolvency practitioner in relation to the company.[164]

Orders to be made when the company is in insolvent liquidation. Where the company is in insolvent liquidation, and an administration order is made, as it may be made, on the application either of the holder of a qualifying floating charge, or of the liquidator, (see para.14-18, above), the order of the court shall contain the following additional terms: **14-45**

(a) in the case of a liquidator appointed in a voluntary winding up, the removal of the voluntary liquidator from office;

(b) provisions for payment of the expenses of the winding up;

(c) such provision as the court thinks just relating to any indemnity given by the liquidator, the release of the liquidator, the handling or realisation of any of the company's assets in the hands of or under the control of the liquidator and other matters arising in connection with the winding up; and

(d) such other provisions if any as the court thinks just.[165]

Problems presented by the making of interim or conditional orders. The categories of order which it is open to the court to make are very wide. But the extensive inclusion therein of powers to adjourn, conditionally or unconditionally, and to make interim orders, or "any other order which the court thinks appropriate",[166] can create problems. The making of conditional orders requires considerable care, in exercising a jurisdiction whose orders have such a powerful impact on the company, its creditors, its members and other persons having dealings with the company. They fetter the rights of those parties, without giving them, and especially the creditors, the benefit of the administration having commenced, while affording the company (or the partnership) the protection of the moratorium,[167] without being subject to any of its detriments, save any expressly imposed by the order under Sch.B1 para.13(3).   **14-46**

SECTION 6: THE EXTRA-JUDICIAL APPOINTMENTS

Powers of extra-judicial appointment. In parallel with the courts' power to make an administration order on an administration application, Schedule B1 contains provision for extra-judicial appointment. These are exercisable by the   **14-47**

---

grounds: see para.14-33, above.

[162] A winding up order against a Delaware company was made under this provision, which has no counterpart in the "old" regime, in *Re Ci4Net.com.Inc* [2004] EWHC 1941 Ch; [2005] B.C.C. 277.

[163] Insolvency Act 1986 Sch.B1 para.13(3)(a).

[164] Insolvency Act 1986 Sch.B1 para.13(3)(b).

[165] Insolvency Rules 2016 r.3.14.

[166] Insolvency Act 1986 Sch.B1 para.13(1)(f).

[167] Insolvency Act 1986 Sch.B1 para.42–44.

holder of a qualifying floating charge, and by the company or its directors.[168] Each of these parties is now empowered, under very strict procedural conditions, to appoint an administrator. When so appointed, he becomes an officer of the court[169]; as such, he will exercise the same functions and have the same powers and duties as an administrator appointed by the court (except in two cases).[170]

In consequence of the conferment of this exceptional power of extra-judicial appointment on appointors other than the court, the exercise by them of that power is hedged round with a staged series of conditions, all of which must be strictly complied with; total compliance appears to be essential for the appointment "to take effect".

SECTION 7: PROCEDURES FOR MAKING EXTRA-JUDICIAL APPOINTMENTS

14-48 **Appointment by qualifying floating charge-holder: duty to give notice of intention to appoint.** The holder of a qualifying floating charge may only exercise his power to appoint an administrator of the company, after he has given *at least two business days' written notice* to the holder of any prior qualifying floating charge (viz. one created first, or by agreement to be treated as having priority,[171]) unless that prior holder has consented in writing to the making of the appointment.[172] Notice must be given even where the prior qualifying floating charge holder's charge is not currently enforceable.[173] An administrator may not be appointed by the holder of a qualifying floating charge, unless the charge is enforceable,[174] nor where a provisional liquidator, or an administrative receiver, is in office.[175] For the position where a prior qualifying floating charge-holder applies to the court to intervene to appoint his own nominee, see para.14-25, above.

14-49 **Exclusive rights accorded to floating charge-holders.** The floating charge-holder is granted several exclusive rights, not afforded to other applicants for an administration order, or other appointors, as stated below:

(a) *Over-riding power of appointment by floating charge-holder* Where a floating charge-holder receives notice that an administration application has been made (but an appointment thereunder has not yet been made) he may himself appoint an administrator. If he does so, he must, as soon as reasonably practicable, send a copy of his notice of appointment to the administration applicant and to the relevant court.[176]

This overriding power of appointment is exempt from the suspensory effect of the interim moratorium directed to prevent actions against the company and its

---

[168] Insolvency Act 1986 Sch.B1 paras 2, 14 and 22.
[169] Insolvency Act 1986 Sch.B1 para.5.
[170] Insolvency Act 1986 Sch.B1 paras 59–74, "Functions of Administrator"; the exceptions are made by paras 37(3) and 38(2).
[171] Insolvency Act 1986 Sch.B1 para.15(2); or, in Scotland, has priority under s.464(4)(b) of the Companies Act 1985.
[172] Insolvency Act 1986 Sch.B1 para.15(1).
[173] *Re OMP Leisure Ltd* [2008] B.C.C. 67.
[174] Insolvency Act 1986 Sch.B1 para.16.
[175] Insolvency Act 1986 Sch.B1 para.17.
[176] Insolvency Rules 2016 r.3.19.

property,[177] which comes into force when the administration application is filed, or when the notice of intention to appoint is given.[178]

(b)   Power to apply to appoint an administrator where the company is in liquidation   The fact of the company being in liquidation is a general bar to any application to appoint an administrator; but a floating charge-holder (and also the liquidator) is exceptionally entitled to apply to appoint an administrator of a company in insolvent liquidation.[179] See para.14-18, above.

(c)   Power to make an administration application, without proof of a company's insolvency   As an exception to the general bar, precluding the making of an administration order, except on proof that the company is unable, or is likely to become unable, to pay its debts, a floating charge-holder is entitled to make an application without such proof of the company's actual or prospective insolvency.[180]

(d)   Power to appoint administrator, to take effect out of court office hours   Although in general the extra-judicial appointment of an administrator only takes effect when notice of appointment is filed in court, the floating charge-holder is entitled, by the use of a special procedure, to appoint out of court business hours: see para.14-51, below.

Notice of appointment: by the floating charge-holder.   The holder of a qualifying floating charge who appoints an administrator must file with the court a notice of appointment, and the other prescribed documents.[181] The notice of appointment must identify the administrator(s), and must be accompanied by a statement by him/them that he/they consent(s) to the appointment, and that in his/their opinion the purpose of administration is reasonably likely to be achieved, and giving such other information and opinions as may be prescribed.[182] He/they is/are entitled to rely on information supplied by the directors, unless he/they has/have reason to doubt its accuracy.[183]   **14-50**

These documents include a statutory declaration made by or on behalf of the appointor that: (a) the appointor is the holder of a qualifying floating charge in respect of the company's property; (b) each floating charge relied on in making the appointment is (or was) enforceable at the date of the date of the appointment; and (c) the appointment is in accordance with the Insolvency Act 1986 Sch.B1 para.14.[184] Such a statutory declaration must be made within the prescribed period, viz. *not more than five business days before the notice of appointment is filed with the court.*[185] The charge relied upon must be a true floating charge, as now judicially redefined.[186]

Floating charge-holder's right to appoint out of court business hours.   An   **14-51**

---

[177]   Insolvency Act 1986 Sch.B1 para.44(7)(b).
[178]   Insolvency Act 1986 Sch.B1 para.44.
[179]   Insolvency Act 1986 Sch.B1 para.37(2).
[180]   Insolvency Act 1986 Sch.B1 para.35(2).
[181]   Insolvency Act 1986 Sch.B1 para.18(1): Insolvency Rules 2016 rr.3.17 and 3.18(1).
[182]   Insolvency Act 1986 Sch.B1 para.18(3).
[183]   Insolvency Act 1986 Sch.B1 para.18(4); Insolvency rules 2016 r.3.2.
[184]   Insolvency Act 1986 Sch.B1 para.18(2).
[185]   Insolvency Rules 2016 r.3.17(3).
[186]   See para.14-17, above.

extra-judicial appointment in general does not commence and take effect until the notice of appointment and the prescribed accompanying documents have been filed in court.[187] However, a floating charge-holder, who needs and wishes to make an appointment *to take effect out of court business hours*, is entitled to make such an appointment, and to file it with the court, while closed, by transmitting the notice by fax or email[188] to a telephone number/email address designated by Lord Chancellor.[189]

The appointor must ensure that the fax machine used to transmit the notice creates a fax transmission report detailing the time and date of the transmission, and a copy of the first page (or part of it) of the notice or that a hard copy of the email is created giving the time and date of the email and the address to which it was sent.[190] The appointment takes effect from the date and time of the fax transmission or email, as so recorded.[191] The copy of the faxed notice of appointment will be forwarded by the Court Service as soon as practicable to the court specified in the notice as having jurisdiction in the case, to be filed on the relevant file.[192]

The appointor must, *on the next occasion on which the court is open for business*, take to the court three copies of the faxed/emailed notice, the fax transmission report or hard copy email, and all the supporting documents, as prescribed for such filing out of court business hours.[193] He shall also attach a statement giving full reasons for the out of hours filing, including why it would have been damaging to the company and its creditors not to have so acted.[194]

The copies of the notice shall be sealed by the court, with the date and time when, according to the transmission report or hard copy of the email, the notice was faxed or emailed, and also the date when the accompanying documents were delivered to the court.[195] The date and time of the appointment shall be presumed (subject to a right of rebuttal) to be the date and time shown on the fax transmission report or hard copy of the email.[196]

The administrator's appointment *shall cease to have effect, if the filing of the document was not completed on the next occasion when the court was open.*[197]

The court shall send two sealed copies of the notice of appointment to the appointor, who shall, as soon as reasonably practicable, send one to the administrator.[198]

14-52   **Authority required for company or directors to appoint administrator.** To authorise a company or its directors to appoint an administrator, the company must have passed a resolution (it would appear that an ordinary resolution is suf-

---

[187] Insolvency Act 1986 Sch.B1 para.19. The fact that when the statutory declaration is made the charge itself is not enforceable will not invalidate the appointment, as the appointment takes effect when the documents are *filed*: see *Fliptex v Hogg* [2004] EWHC 1280 (Ch); [2004] B.C.C. 870.
[188] Insolvency Rules 2016 r.3.20.
[189] Insolvency Rules 2016 r.3.20(3). The fax number and email address are published on the Insolvency Service website, and will be made available in writing, on request.
[190] Insolvency Rules 2016 r.3.20(5).
[191] Insolvency Rules 2016 r.3.22(2).
[192] Insolvency Rules 2016 r.3.20(8).
[193] Insolvency Rules 2016 r.3.20(9).
[194] Insolvency Rules 2016 r.3.20(9)(d).
[195] Insolvency Rules 2016 r.3.20(10).
[196] Insolvency Rules 2016 r.3.22(3).
[197] Insolvency Rules 2016 r.3.22(2)(b).
[198] Insolvency Rules 2016 r.3.20(11),(12).

ficient[199]), or the directors[200] must have formally resolved, that such an appointment should be made. The notice of intention to appoint requires a statement that the notice is accompanied by a copy of the relevant document recording such a resolution or a record of the directors' decision.[201]

Appointment by a company or its directors: general restrictions on appointment.　An administrator may not be appointed by the court, nor an administration application made by a company or its directors, nor directly by a company or its directors, in any of the following circumstances:

14-53

(1)　during the period of 12 months, beginning with the date on which an earlier appointment of an administrator ceased to have effect[202];

(2)　where a moratorium, which has been current for a company under the Insolvency Act 1986 Sch.A1,[203] has ended on a date when no voluntary arrangement is in force in respect of that company, during the period of 12 months beginning with that date[204];

(3)　where a voluntary arrangement in respect of a company has been approved during a moratorium for the company under Sch.A1 (see above), and the arrangement has ended "prematurely" within the meaning of the Insolvency Act 1986 s.7B,[205] that is to say, that when it ceased to have effect, it had not been fully implemented in respect of all persons bound by the arrangement[206]; during the period of 12 months beginning with the date when it so ended;

(4)　where a petition for the winding-up of the company has been presented, or an administration application has been made, but in either case has not yet been disposed of, or where an administrative receiver of the company is in office.[207] However, an administrator can be appointed under para.22 if the petition for the winding up of the company was presented after the notice of intention to appoint was filed with the court under para.27 of Sch.B1 unless the petition was presented under a provision mentioned in para.42(4) of Sch.B1.[208]

Further restrictions on the power of appointment by a company or its directors.　Further to the above restrictions on the power to appoint, no appointment may be made, unless and until the appointor has complied with all the requirements set out in the Insolvency Act 1986 Sch.B1 paras 26 and 27, and either the *five business days' written notice* (of intention to appoint) has expired, or each of the persons to whom notice has been given has consented in writing to the

14-54

199　Under the Companies Act 2006 a unanimous informal agreement would also presumably be effective.

200　Or a majority of them: see Insolvency Act 1986 Sch.B1 para.105.

201　Insolvency Rules 2016 r.3.23(1)(j).

202　Insolvency Act 1986 Sch.B1 para.23(2).

203　Schedule A1 was inserted into the Insolvency Act 1986 by the Insolvency Act 2000 s.1A.

204　Insolvency Act 1986 Sch.B1 para.24(1).

205　Insolvency Act 1986 Sch.B1 para.24(2): the new s.7B was inserted into the Insolvency Act 1986 by the Insolvency Act 2000 Sch.2 para.10.

206　By virtue of the Insolvency Act 1986 s.5(2)(b)(i), or Sch.A1 para.37(2)(b)(i).

207　Insolvency Act 1986 Sch.B1 para.25.

208　Insolvency Act 1986 Sch. B1 para.25A, inserted by the Deregulation Act 2015 Sch.6 para.5.

appointment.[209] Furthermore, the statutory required by Sch.B1 para.27(2) must be made *not more than five business days* before the notice of appointment is filed with the court.[210]

Finally, no appointment may be made at all *after the expiry of 10 business days, beginning with the date when the notice of intention to appoint was filed.*[211]

14-55 **Appointment by a company or its directors: duty to give notice of intention to appoint.** Where a company or its directors intend to exercise its or their power to appoint an administrator, it or they must give *at least five business days' written notice* to:

- (a) any person who is or may be entitled to appoint an administrative receiver of the company[212];
- (b) any person who is or may be entitled to appoint an administrator of the company under the Insolvency Act 1986 Sch.B1 para.14[213]; and
- (c) such other persons as may be prescribed.[214] The persons prescribed are—
    - (i) any enforcement agent or other officer who is known, to the person giving the notice of intention to appoint, to be charged with distress or other legal process against the company;
    - (ii) any person so known to have distrained against the company or its property;
    - (iii) the supervisor of any corporate voluntary arrangement affecting the company; and
    - (iv) the company itself, if it is not the applicant.[215]

14-56 **The content of the statutory notices of intention to appoint.** Such notice must identify the proposed administrator, and be in the prescribed form.[216] Notice is to be given by service of the notice in accordance with the provisions of the Insolvency Rules 2016 Sch.1.[217] But such obligations to give notice do not apply, where there are none of the persons prescribed to receive notice: see para.14-60, below.

The appointor(s) must file with the court, *as soon as reasonably practicable*, a copy of his (their) notice of intention to appoint,[218] together with a statutory declaration made in the prescribed form and during the prescribed period, in the terms set out below.[219]

14-57 **Notices of appointment: by the company or its directors.** The company or its directors, which or who appoint an administrator, must file with the court a notice of appointment, together with the other prescribed documents.[220] The notice of appointment, and statements by the administrator, must contain the same informa-

---

209 Insolvency Act 1986 Sch.B1 para.28(1)(a) and (b).
210 Insolvency Rules 2016 r.3.23(6)(b).
211 Insolvency Act 1986 Sch.B1 para.28(2).
212 Insolvency Act 1986 Sch.B1 para.26(1)(a).
213 Insolvency Act 1986 Sch.B1 para.26(1)(b).
214 Insolvency Act 1986 Sch.B1 para.26(2).
215 Insolvency Rules 2016 r.3.23(4).
216 Insolvency Act 1986 Sch.B1 para.26(3).
217 Insolvency Rules 2016 r.3.23(5).
218 Insolvency Act 1986 Sch.B1 para.27(1).
219 Insolvency Act 1986 Sch. B1 para.27(2)., (3)
220 Insolvency Act 1986 Sch.B1 para.29(1).

tion as is prescribed for appointment by the floating chargeholder, above, and are to be drafted and made under the same conditions.[221]

The prescribed documents include a statutory declaration made by or on behalf of the appointor(s):

(a) that the appointor(s) is/are entitled to make the appointment under the Insolvency Act 1986 Sch.B1 para.22;
(b) that the appointment is in accordance with that paragraph; and
(c) that, so far as the deponent is able to ascertain, the statements made and the information given, in the statutory declaration filed with the notice of intention to appoint, remain accurate.[222]

Content of statutory notices of appointment. The notice of appointment must **14-58** identify the administrator, and must be accompanied by a statement by him, in the prescribed form, that he consents to the appointment, and that in his opinion the purpose of administration is reasonably likely to be achieved, and giving such other information as may be prescribed.[223]

The foregoing statutory declarations must be made in the prescribed form, and within the prescribed period, viz. *not more than five business days before filing the notice with the court*.[224] Very brief periods of time are prescribed for the giving and filing of such notices, for the making of such statutory declarations, and for the making of the appointment itself. Many steps must be taken "as soon as is reasonably practicable".

Contents of statutory declaration by intending appointor: (company or its **14-59** **directors).** The statutory declaration must be made by or on behalf of one of the intending appointor(s),[225] and within the prescribed period of *five business days before the notice is filed in court*.[226] It must state:

(a) that the company is, or is likely to become, unable to pay its debts;
(b) that it is not in liquidation;
(c) that so far as the maker of the witness statement or the deponent can ascertain, the appointment is not prevented by any of the factors or events prescribed by the Insolvency Act 1986 Sch.B1 paras 23–25; and
(d) to such additional effect, and giving such further information, as may be prescribed (see above).[227]

Where there is no person to whom notice of intention to appoint must be **14-60** **given.** Where no persons are entitled to receive such notices of intention to appoint, the statutory declaration prescribed to be made and filed *after* the appointment is made shall include the statements required to accompany a notice of intention to appoint, when given.[228]

---

[221] See para.14-50, above.
[222] Insolvency Act 1986 Sch.B1 para.29(2).
[223] Insolvency Act 1986 Sch.B1 para.29(3).
[224] Insolvency Rules 2016 r.3.24(3).
[225] Insolvency Act 1986 Sch.B1 para.27(1).
[226] Insolvency Rules 2016 r.3.23(6).
[227] Insolvency Act 1986 Sch.B1 para.27(2).
[228] Insolvency Act 1986 Sch.B1 para.30.

Times for appointment.

14-61   *(a)   By the floating charge-holder.*   The floating charge-holder's time for making his appointment is limited by his obligation to file the notice of appointment with the court *not later than five business days after the date of making of the statutory declaration*, which forms part of that notice.[229]

(b)   By the company or its directors.   The time for making an appointment made by the company or its directors is limited by two factors: first, it must be made *within 10 business days, beginning with the date of the filing with the court of the notice of intention to appoint*,[230] and secondly, *within five business days of the making of the statutory declaration*, which forms part of that notice.[231] It is not clear from what date the obligation to make the statutory declaration, which fixes the period within which the appointment must be made, is to be calculated, where no notice of intention to appoint has needed to be given.[232]

For the times of commencement of such appointments, see "Commencement of appointment", para.14-70 below.

Statements in the statutory declarations by appointors that are false, or are not reasonably believed to be true, may subject the maker to criminal penalties.[233]

14-62   **Commencement of appointment: (1) appointment by the court.**   The administration commences at the time appointed by the order, or where no time is appointed, at the time when it was made.[234] The giving of notice of the appointment by the court, although obligatory, does not affect that time: see para.14-43, above.

The applicant shall, as soon as is reasonably practicable send a sealed copy of the order appointing him to the administrator.[235] If the court, in appointing the administrator, makes any interim order, or any other "appropriate order", it shall direct which persons are to be given notice of such order, and in what manner.[236]

14-63   **Commencement of appointment: (2) statutory notices.**   The extra-judicial appointment of an administrator by an appointor (as distinct from an appointment made by an administration order) does not take effect solely by means of the physical act of making the appointment. It only takes effect legally when all the statutory obligations attendant thereon have been complied with, as to the filing and giving of notices of and relating to the appointment. There are other obligations as to notice, but these do not affect the statutory times of commencement. Accordingly, the respective appointments take legal effect as follows:

   (a)   *Appointment by the holder of a qualifying floating charge:* this appointment commences when the appointor has complied with all his obligations to file with the court a notice of appointment and other prescribed documents. The appointor shall also, as soon as is reasonably practicable,

---

[229] Insolvency Rules 2016 r.3.17(3).
[230] Insolvency Act 1986 Sch.B1 para.28(2).
[231] Insolvency Rules 2016 r.3.23(6).
[232] See para.14-64, above.
[233] Insolvency Act 1986 Sch.B1 paras 27(4), 29(7).
[234] Insolvency Act 1986 Sch.B1 para.13(2).
[235] Insolvency Rules 2016 r.3.15(2).
[236] Insolvency Rules 2016 r.3.15(3).

give notice (i) to the administrator, and (ii) to any other prescribed persons, of the appointment having so commenced, by virtue of his compliance with his obligations under the Insolvency Act 1986 Sch.B2 para.18, as to notices[237]:

(b) *Appointment by company or its directors:* this commences, when the appointor(s) has/have compiled with all of its/their obligations to file with the court a notice of appointment and other prescribed documents. The appointor shall also, as soon as is reasonably practicable, give notice (i) to the administrator, and (ii) to any other prescribed persons, of the appointment having so commenced, by virtue of its or their compliance with its or their obligations under the Insolvency Act 1986 Sch.B1 para.29.[238]

But if, before the company or the directors have completed the giving of the prescribed notices, an administrator is otherwise appointed, either by the court or by a floating charge-holder, they need not carry out, or complete, that giving of notices.

Making a statutory declaration which contains a statement that is false, or which is not necessarily believed to be true, constitutes an offence.[239]

Modes of giving notice to creditors. Notices to creditors must be sent by post; **14-64** notices by e-mail are not permitted.[240] But notifications to creditors have been allowed to be made by advertisements, instead of by circular.[241]

Remedies for impeachable or defective appointments. Where an order of appointment is made on application, the dissatisfied or aggrieved party is entitled to **14-65** apply for judicial review of the appointment[242]; but this, being a discretionary remedy, may well not be exercised, where too much time has elapsed since the order was made, the more so because there are other procedures for terminating the appointment and its effect.[243]

Indemnity in consequence of invalid appointments. Where the holder of a **14-66** qualifying floating charge purports to appoint an administrator, or where a company or its directors purport to appoint an administrator, and the appointment is in either case discovered to be invalid, the court may order a purported appointor to indemnify the appointee against any liability accruing to him solely by reason of that invalidity.[244]

It is to be noted that the draughtsman of Schedule B1 has taken steps to fix the intended appointee with personal responsibility for the validity of his appointment; for he is required to participate in the notice of his appointment, by adding

---

237 Insolvency Act 1986 Sch.B1 paras 19, 20.
238 Insolvency Act 1986 Sch.B1 paras 31, 32.
239 Insolvency Act 1986 Sch.B1 para.27(4).
240 *Re Sporting Options Plc (in administration)* [2004] EWHC 3128 (Ch); [2005] B.P.I.R. 435; [2004] All E.R. (D) 30 (Dec); see also article at 21 I L & P (2005), p.28. Although notice of appointment sent by email will be permitted if creditors have previously nominated email addresses to which communications should be sent: *Re Advent Computer Training Ltd* [2010] EWHC 459 (Ch); [2011] B.C.C. 44.
241 *Re A Licence-Holder & ors, Saville v Gerard* [2004] EWHC 1363 (Ch); [2005] B.C.C. 433.
242 See para.14-43 above.
243 See Ch.17, below.
244 Insolvency Act 1986 Sch.B1 para.21 (chargeholder); para.34 (company or directors).

to his statement of consent to be appointed his opinion that the purpose of administration is reasonably likely to be achieved (by his appointment).[245]

---

[245] Insolvency Act 1986 Sch.B1 paras 18(3), 29(3).

CHAPTER 15

THE ADMINISTRATOR IN OFFICE: POWERS AND DUTIES

SECTION 1: INTRODUCTION

Introduction. As described in Ch.14, the original Pt II of the Insolvency Act 1986 **15-1** ("the Act"), and Pt 2 of the Insolvency Rules 1986 (as amended), prescribed the previous procedures to be adopted when the court had appointed an administrator, referred to in this work as "the old regime". Those provisions have been repealed (except for special cases and transitional savings), and replaced by the new Sch.B1 and the Insolvency Rules 1986 have since been replaced by the Insolvency Rules 2016 ("the current regime").[1]

The circumstances in which the old regime will apply are transitional cases, where the administration proceedings had already commenced when the Enterprise Act 2002 came into force on 15 September 2003, and the other special cases referred to at para.14-13. For the administrator's powers and duties under the old regime, reference may be made to the 17th edition of this work, Ch.14, (with its Second Cumulative Supplement 1997). This chapter deals with the position under the current regime.

SECTION 2: INITIAL DUTIES OF THE ADMINISTRATOR

I: Notices and Stationery

Advertisement of the appointment. The administrator must advertise a notice **15-2** of his appointment in the *Gazette* as soon as reasonably practicable, and may also advertise it in any other way he thinks fit.[2] Those advertisements must contain the standard contents for notices set out in the Rules, as follows.

- A notice advertised in the *Gazette* must include the administrator's contact details and IP number, the name of any other person who may be contacted about the administration, the date of appointment,[3] and the company's registered office.[4]
- Any other notice must identify the administrator and his contact details.[5]
- In either case the notice must also identify the proceedings, the company's principle trading address (in the case of a *Gazette* advertisement, only if it is different from the registered office), any name under which the company

---

[1]   All references to the Insolvency Rules in this Chapter are to the Insolvency Rules 2016.
[2]   Insolvency Act 1986 Sch.B1 para.46(2)(b); Insolvency Rules 2016 r.3.27(1).
[3]   Insolvency Rules 2016 r.1.11(1).
[4]   Insolvency Rules 2016 r.1.12(1)(a).
[5]   Insolvency Rules 2016 r.1.15(2).

was registered in the 12 months before the appointment, and any other name under which it carried on business or under which any debt to a creditor was incurred.[6]

The notice itself must state that an administrator has been appointed, the date of the appointment and the nature of the business of the company,[7] and it must be authenticated and dated by the administrator.[8]

15-3 **Notice to creditors.** As soon as is reasonably practicable, the administrator must obtain a list of the company's creditors, and send a notice of his appointment to each creditor of whose claim and address he is aware.[9] The court may dispense with the requirement to send notices to creditors.[10] The required content of these notices is not specified, but it should probably replicate the notice to be advertised pursuant to para.46(2)(b) of Sch.B1.[11]

15-4 **Notice to other persons.** The administrator must send a copy of the notice of his appointment to the company as soon as reasonably practicable,[12] and to the registrar of companies. In the latter case the notice is to be sent within seven days of his appointment (if appointed by administration order) or receipt by him of the notice of appointment.[13] The notices must state that an administrator has been appointed, the date of the appointment, and the nature of the business of the company.[14] In addition the notice to be delivered to the registrar of companies must state the nature of the notice, identify the proceedings, state that the notice is given pursuant to para.46(4) of Sch.B1, give the administrator's contact details, give the date of appointment, and identify the person, body or court making the appointment.[15]

As soon as reasonably practicable after his appointment the administrator must also send a notice of his appointment to:

- any receiver of the company (administrative or otherwise);
- the petitioner in, and any provisional liquidator appointed in, a winding-up petition against the company;
- any enforcement officer, enforcement agent, or other officer known by him to be charged with distress or other legal process against the company or its property;
- any person known to him to have distrained against the company or its property;
- any supervisor of a voluntary arrangement involving the company.[16]

15-5 **Use of email or a website to give notice.** Notices may be sent to a creditor by email where that creditor has given actual or deemed consent for electronic delivery

---

6   Insolvency Rules 2016 rr.1.11(1), 1.12 and 1.16.
7   Insolvency Rules 2016 r.3.27(2).
8   Insolvency Rules 2016 r.3.27(5).
9   Insolvency Act 1986 Sch.B1 para.46(3).
10   Insolvency Act 1986 Sch.B1 para.46(7). The paragraph also speaks of applying a different period for sending notices, but this probably applies only to the "prescribed period" under para.46(5).
11   See para.15-2.
12   Insolvency Act 1986 Sch.B1 para.46(2)(a).
13   Insolvency Act 1986 Sch.B1 para.46(4) and (6).
14   Insolvency Rules 2016 r.3.27(2).
15   Insolvency Rules 2016 rr.1.29 and 1.30.
16   Insolvency Act 1986 Sch.B1 para.46(5); Insolvency Rules 2016 r.3.27(3).

of documents, has not revoked that consent before the notice is sent, and has provided an email address. A creditor is deemed to have given such consent where it has customarily communicated with the company by email before the commencement of the administration.[17]

Where the administrator is required to send a notice or other document to a person, he also may do so by making the document available on a website.[18] This may be done either in relation to specific documents, or generally in relation to all documents which must be delivered, save that the general delivery of documents by website is not available in respect of documents which must be personally delivered, notice of intention to declare a dividend pursuant to r.14.29, or a document which is not delivered generally[19] (i.e. to all members of a particular class).[20]

Where the administrator chooses to use a website to deliver a specific document, he must send to the relevant person a notice stating that the document is available to view and download on a website, and that any person who receives the notice may request a hard copy of the document.[21] Where he uses a website to deliver documents generally, the notice must state that all future documents will be made available for viewing on the website without notice to the recipient, that at any time the recipient may request a hard copy of any or all of the documents already on the website or to be placed on the website in future, and that the administrator will not be required to deliver those documents to the recipient unless requested to do so.[22] In either case the notice must give the web address and any password necessary, and the necessary contact details for making a request for hard copy documents.[23]

Any document delivered by means of a website must remain available on the website until the later of two months after the end of the administration or the release of the last person to hold office as administrator.[24]

Business stationery (in Sch.B1 para.45, "Publicity"). Every business document, that is to say, every invoice, order for goods or services, or business letter, issued by or on behalf of the company after it enters administration, or by or on behalf of the administrator, must state the name of the administrator and that the affairs, business and property of the company are being managed by him. This information must also appear on any website of the company.[25]   **15-6**

Offences. Failure by the administrator, without reasonable cause, to send out the notices required by para.46 of Sch.B1 constitutes an offence.[26] In addition, any authorisation of, or permission for, a contravention of the obligations relating to business stationary by the administrator, by an officer of the company, or by the company itself, constitutes an offence.[27]   **15-7**

---

[17] Insolvency Rules 2016 r.1.45.
[18] Insolvency Act 1986 s.246B(1).
[19] Insolvency Rules 2016 r.1.50(2).
[20] Insolvency Rules 2016 r.1.50(3).
[21] Insolvency Rules 2016 r.1.49(2).
[22] Insolvency Rules 2016 r.1.50(1).
[23] Insolvency Rules 2016 rr.1.49(2) and 1.50(1).
[24] Insolvency Rules 2016 r.1.51(2).
[25] Insolvency Act 1986 Sch.B1 para.45(1) and (3).
[26] Insolvency Act 1986 Sch.B1 para.46(9).
[27] Insolvency Act 1986 Sch.B1 para.45(2).

II: The Statement of Affairs

15-8 **Request for a Statement of Affairs.** As soon as is reasonably practicable after his appointment, the administrator must initiate the preparation of the statement of affairs. He must issue, to such of the "relevant persons" as he deems appropriate, notices requiring them to prepare to supply him with a statement of the company's affairs.[28]

The notice must be headed "Notice requiring statement of affairs" and, in addition to notifying the recipient of the obligation to prepare and return a statement of affairs, must also inform him of the names and addresses of any other persons to whom such a notice has been delivered, of the requirement to return the statement of affairs no later than 11 days after receipt of the notice, and of the penalty for non-compliance set out in para.48(4) of Sch.B1 and the duty to co-operate with the administrator imposed by s.235 of the Act.[29] In addition, the administrator must inform the recipient that a document for the preparation of the statement of affairs will be supplied if requested.[30] In practice it is sensible to enclose such a document with the notice from the outset.

As set out at para.15-14, the administrator may agree to extend time for return of the statement of affairs, or may revoke the notice of requirement to prepare the statement.

15-9 **Who are "relevant persons".** "Relevant persons" are (a) those who are or have been officers of the company; (b) those who have taken part in the formation of the company during the period of one year before the company entered administration; (c) the employees of the company during that period, whether employed through a contract of employment or a contract for services; and (d) those who are or have been during that period an officer or employee of a company.[31]

15-10 **Preparation of the statement of affairs.** The statement of affairs must be headed "Statement of affairs", identify the company, and state that it is a statement of the company's affairs on the date on which it entered administration.[32] It must give particulars of the property, debts and liabilities, the names and addresses of the company's creditors, and specifying the security (if any) held by each creditor and the date when it was granted.[33] This information must be given in accordance with the more detailed provisions of r.3.30(2)–(6). It should be noted that among these more detailed requirements are schedules of creditors, including their names and addresses, with any employee or consumer creditors to be included in separate schedules from other creditors.[34]

The statement of affairs must be verified by the relevant person by a statement of truth in accordance with the CPR,[35] and must be delivered to the administrator, with a copy,[36] within the period of 11 days beginning with the day when he received

---

[28] Insolvency Act 1986 Sch.B1 para.47(1).
[29] Insolvency Rules 2016 r.3.29(2).
[30] Insolvency Rules 2016 r.3.29(3).
[31] Insolvency Act 1986 Sch.B1 para.47(3) and (4).
[32] Insolvency Rules 2016 r.3.30(4)–(6).
[33] Insolvency Act 1986 Sch.B1 para.47(2).
[34] Insolvency Rules 2016 r.3.30(1).
[35] Insolvency Act 1986 Sch.B1 para.47(2)(a).
[36] Insolvency Rules 2016 r.3.29(4).

notice of the requirement[37] or any extended period agreed by the administrator or extended by the court as set out at para.15-14.

Statements of concurrence: the obligation to make. The administrator may   **15-11** require any relevant person or persons, in lieu of submitting a statement of affairs himself, to submit a "statement of concurrence", which is a statement that the maker agrees (subject to qualifications) with the statement of affairs being prepared by another relevant person.[38]

Where the administrator requires one or more people to deliver a statement of concurrence, he must inform the person who is required to prepare the statement of affairs of their identities, and that person must, in addition to delivering the statement of affairs to the administrator, send a copy of it to every person as to whom he has been informed that they are required to concur with it.[39]

The person required to make a statement of concurrence must do so within five business days beginning with the day on which he receives his copy of the statement of affairs, or such other period as the administrator may agree, and must verify it by a statement of truth.[40]

The right to qualify statement of concurrence. A person making a statement   **15-12** of concurrence with the statement of affairs is entitled to qualify it in respect of any matter stated therein, where he is not in agreement with the statement, or where he considers that it is erroneous or misleading, or where he is without the direct knowledge necessary for concurring with it.[41]

Filing the statement of affairs. When the submission of the statement of af-   **15-13** fairs and of any statements of concurrence has been completed, the administrator shall, as soon as reasonably practicable, send copies of these documents to the registrar of companies.[42] However, any schedules of creditors who are either employees (or former employees) of the company, or are consumers, must not be sent to the registrar[43]; nor should any parts of the documents which are covered by "an order of limited disclosure"[44] (as to which, see para.15-28).

Release from obligation to make statements, or extension of time. As stated   **15-14** above, the administrator is empowered to release a relevant person from the obligation to make a statement of affairs[45] imposed by the sending of the notice, either on his own initiative or at the request of the relevant person, and he is similarly

---

[37] Insolvency Act 1986 Sch.B1 para.48(1).
[38] Insolvency Rules 2016 r.3.31(2).
[39] Insolvency Rules 2016 r.3.31(3)–(4).
[40] Insolvency Rules 2016 r.3.31(6).
[41] Insolvency Rules 2016 r.3.31(5).
[42] Insolvency Rules 2016 r.3.32(1).
[43] Insolvency Rules 2016 r.3.32(2).
[44] Insolvency Rules 2016 r.3.32(3).
[45] Neither the Act nor the Rules specifically cover an extension of time, or release from the obligation, to make a statement of concurrence, as opposed to a statement of affairs. However, it seems likely that, for these purposes, a statement of concurrence required under Insolvency Rules 2016 r.3.31 is to be treated as a statement of affairs required under para.47 of Sch.B1, since there is no other provision of Sch.B1 which would empower the administrator to require one. It would follow that the provisions of para.48 of Sch.B1 and Insolvency Rules 2016 r.3.33 apply equally to statements of concurrence.

empowered to extend the time for making it.[46] That period may be so extended, whether before or after expiry.[47] If he refuses either request for a release or for an extension of time, the relevant person may apply to the court for relief.[48]

If, on such an application, the court forms the view that no sufficient cause is shown for it, it may dismiss the application without notice to any party other than the relevant person.[49] Otherwise, the court will fix a venue (i.e. a date, time and place) for the hearing.[50]

In that event, the relevant person must give notice of the application to the administrator at least 14 days before the hearing, stating the venue, with copies of his application and of any supporting evidence.[51] The administrator may appear and be heard on the application[52]; whether or not he appears, he may file in court a written report of any matters which he considers should be drawn to the court's attention,[53] sending a copy of any such report to the applicant, not later than five days before the hearing.[54]

The court will send sealed copies of any order made on the application to the applicant and to the administrator.[55] The applicant must in any event pay his own costs of the application, and, unless the court otherwise orders, no allowance towards them shall be made out of the estate.[56]

15-15   The expenses of the statement of affairs.   A relevant person who makes either a statement of affairs, or a statement of concurrence is entitled to be paid, as an expense of the administration, the expenses incurred thereby which the administrator considers reasonable. If the administrator decides that certain expenses were not reasonably incurred, this decision may be appealed to the court.[57]

15-16   Limited disclosure of confidential information.   Where the administrator thinks that it would prejudice the conduct of the administration, or that it might reasonably be expected to lead to violence against any person,[58] if the whole or part of the statement of affairs or any statement of concurrence were disclosed, he may apply to the court for an "order of limited disclosure" in respect of the statement, or of any specified part of it.[59] On such an application, the court may order that the statement, or the specified part, shall not be filed with the registrar of companies.[60] In that event, the administrator must then, as soon as reasonably practicable, send to the registrar the prescribed form, accompanied by a copy of the order of the court,

---

[46]   Insolvency Act 1986 Sch.B1 para.48(2); Insolvency Rules 2016 r.3.33(1).
[47]   Insolvency Act 1986 Sch.B1 para.107.
[48]   Insolvency Rules 2016 r.3.33(2).
[49]   Insolvency Rules 2016 r.3.33(3).
[50]   Insolvency Rules 2016 r.3.33(4).
[51]   Insolvency Rules 2016 r.3.33(5).
[52]   Insolvency Rules 2016 r.3.33(6)(b).
[53]   Insolvency Rules 2016 r.3.33(6)(a).
[54]   Insolvency Rules 2016 r.3.33(7).
[55]   Insolvency Rules 2016 r.3.33(8).
[56]   Insolvency Rules 2016 r.3.33(9).
[57]   Insolvency Rules 1986 r.2.32(1) and (2).
[58]   Insolvency Rules 2016 r.3.44.
[59]   Insolvency Rules 2016 r.3.45(1).
[60]   Insolvency Rules 2016 r.3.45(2).

and of so much of the statements of affairs or concurrence as is provided for by the order.[61]

Challenging limited disclosure and change of circumstances. If a creditor **15-17** seeks disclosure of a statement of affairs, or of a specified part of it, in respect of which an order of limited disclosure applies, he may apply to the court for an order that the administrator disclose the withheld material.[62] His application is required by the Rule to be supported by a witness statement.[63] He must give the administrator notice of his application at least three business days before the hearing.[64] The provisions of CPR Pt 31, relating to disclosure and inspection, do not apply to such applications.[65]

On such an application, the court may make any order for disclosure, subject to any conditions as to confidentiality, duration, the scope of the order in the event of any change of circumstances, or other matters as it thinks fit.[66]

If there is a material change of circumstances, rendering the limit on disclosure or any part of it unnecessary, the administrator must, as soon as reasonably practicable, apply to the court for the order to be rescinded or amended.[67] If the court makes such an order, the administrator must, as soon as reasonably practicable, deliver to the registrar of companies a copy of the order, together with a copy of the statement of affairs or statement of concurrence, to the extent provided by the order.[68]

III: The Administrator's Proposals

Duty to prepare statement of proposals for creditors. The administrator must **15-18** prepare and issue a statement of his proposals for achieving the purpose of administration.[69] This must be prepared and issued as soon as reasonably practicable, and in any event before the end of eight weeks after the company entered administration.[70] For the distribution of the statement of proposals, see para.15-24.

In exceptional circumstances the court may dispense with the requirement to prepare a statement of proposals.[71]

---

61   Insolvency Rules 2016 r.3.45(3).
62   Insolvency Rules 2016 r.3.46(1).
63   Insolvency Rules 2016 r.3.46(2).
64   Insolvency Rules 2016 r.3.46(3).
65   Insolvency Rules 2016 r.3.38(1).
66   Insolvency Rules 2016 r.3.46(4).
67   Insolvency Rules 2016 r.3.47(1).
68   Insolvency Rules 2016 r.3.47(2).
69   Insolvency Act 1986 Sch.B1 para.49(1).
70   Insolvency Act 1986 Sch.B1 para.49(5). Note that in the case of a pre-pack administration the report should be issued much sooner than this if possible: see para.15-21.
71   For example, in *Re UK Coal Operations Ltd* [2013] EWHC 2581 (Ch); [2014] 1 B.C.L.C. 471, the court dispensed with preparation of a statement of proposals where the company had been put into administration solely for the purpose of permitting it to go into CVL, which was due to happen within a matter of days after the making of the administration order (and, therefore, long before the obligation to deliver the proposals to creditors would arise).

15-19 Extension of time for proposals. This period may be extended by the court on the application of the administrator,[72] or by the administrator himself,[73] with the consent of each secured creditor of the company,[74] and the unsecured creditors (as a body).[75] The consent of the unsecured creditors is to be sought pursuant to the decision-making procedures set out in Pt 15 of the Rules (discussed at para.15-32 ff).[76] An extension may be granted by the court for any period, more than once, and after as well as before the expiry of the previous period.[77] However, an extension my be granted with the consent of creditors only for a maximum of 28 days, only where there has been no previous extension of time (whether by the court or creditors), and only where the initial period has not already expired.[78]

If such an extension is made by order of the court, notice of the extended period in the prescribed form must, as soon as is reasonably practicable, be sent to the registrar of companies, the creditors and every member of whose address the administrator is aware.[79] This notice must identify the proceedings, state the date to which an extension has been ordered, and contain the registered office of the company.[80]

No such notice is necessary in respect of extensions made by the administrator with the consent of creditors.

15-20 Required contents of statement of proposals. The statement of proposals must deal with the matters set out in the Sch.B1 of the Act, and in the Rules.[81] The administrator must give his reasons why (if such be the case) he thinks that the objectives mentioned in paras 3(1)(a) and (b) of Sch.B1 cannot be achieved.[82]

The proposals may also include a proposal for a voluntary arrangement under the Insolvency Act 1986 Pt I, and a proposal for a compromise or arrangement[83] with creditors or members to be sanctioned under the Companies Act 2006 Pt 26.

The detailed matters to be dealt with in the proposals are set out at rr.3.35 and 3.36, and include a copy or summary of the statement of affairs. It should be noted that r.3.36 requires the administrator to provide a significant amount of detail as to the pre-appointment costs, and that payment of these are not approval by the same decision which approves the proposals themselves.[84] Instead, payment of them must be separately approved under r.3.52.[85]

15-21 Pre-packs and the requirements of SIP 16. An administrator may sell the company's assets without the need to seek the permission of the court or the prior

---

72 Insolvency Act 1986 Sch.B1 paras 49(8) and 107(1)(a).
73 Insolvency Act 1986 Sch.B1 para.108(1).
74 Insolvency Act 1986 Sch.B1 para.108(2)(a).
75 Insolvency Act 1986 Sch.B1 para.108(2)(b).
76 Insolvency Act 1986 Sch.B1 para.108(3A).
77 Insolvency Act 1986 Sch.B1 para.107(2).
78 Insolvency Act 1986 Sch.B1 para.108(5).
79 Insolvency Rules 2016 r.3.37(2).
80 Insolvency Rules 2016 r.3.37(3).
81 Insolvency Act 1986 Sch.B1 para.49; Insolvency Rules 2016 r.3.35.
82 Insolvency Act 1986 Sch.B1 para.49(2)(b). Those objectives are (a) rescuing the company as a going concern and (b) achieving a better result for the company's creditors as a whole than would be likely if the company were wound up without first being in administration.
83 Insolvency Act 1986 Sch.B1 para.49(3)(a): see paras 16-5 to 16-57, below.
84 Insolvency Rules 2016 r.3.36(b)(ii). It would follow that they are also not automatically approved where the proposals contain a statement made pursuant to Insolvency Act 1986 Sch.B1 para.52(1).
85 See para.15-137.

approval of the creditors. Where this involves the sale of the whole, or substantially the whole, of a company's business and assets immediately upon the administrator's taking office—commonly referred to as a "pre-pack"—then the provisions of Statement of Insolvency Practice 16 ("SIP 16") will apply.

In addition to the duties owed by an insolvency practitioner, both before and after appointment as administrator, in relation to the transaction itself, SIP 16 sets out reporting obligations. In particular, they impose an obligation on the administrator to prepare a "SIP 16 report", which must be sent to all creditors within seven days of the transaction.[86] Save in exceptional circumstances, the SIP 16 report must include the details set out in the appendix to SIP 16. These include the following:

- details of the advising insolvency practitioner's and (if different) administrator's initial introduction;
- the reasons for pursuing a pre-pack rather than trading the business;
- details of the marketing activities undertaken and their effect;
- details relating to valuation of the sale assets;
- details of the assets sold, and the consideration for the sale; and
- in relation to a sale to a connected party,[87] details of any approach to the pre-pack pool and of any viability statement.

Where the administrator decides that exceptional circumstances justify withholding information which would ordinarily be included in the SIP 16 report, this too should be explained in the report. Commercial confidentiality can constitute such exceptional circumstances, though SIP 16 notes that in the case of a sale to a related party, this alone will not outweigh the need to provide creditors with information.[88] The administrator's statement of proposals should normally be sent to creditors at the same time as the SIP 16 report. Where it is impossible to do so, the proposals should include an explanation for the delay.[89] The SIP 16 report must also be included in the copy of the proposals filed with the registrar of companies.[90]

Protection for secured and preferential creditors. The administrator's proposals, whether original, modified or revised, may not include any action which affects the rights of a secured creditor[91] to enforce his security, or would result in a preferential debt being paid otherwise than preferentially, or in one preferential creditor receiving a smaller proportion of his debt than another.[92] But these restrictions do not preclude any action to which the relevant creditor consents, or a proposal for a voluntary arrangement under Pt I of the Act, or a scheme of arrangement under Pt 26 of the Companies Act 2006 (ss.895–901): see paras 16-5 and 16-57, below.[93] Equally, this restriction does not apply to a proposal for a cross- **15-22**

---

[86] SIP 16, para.17.
[87] Defined by reference to ss.249 and 435 of the Insolvency Act 1986.
[88] SIP 16, para.16.
[89] SIP 16, para.18.
[90] SIP 16, para.17.
[91] This is defined at s.248 of the Insolvency Act 1986 as, "a creditor of the company who holds in respect of his debt a security over property of the company." It was held in *Re Lomax Leisure Ltd* [2000] Ch. 502; [2000] B.C.C. 352 that this means a real security, as opposed to a metaphorical security such as a landlord's right to forfeit a lease by peaceable re-entry.
[92] Insolvency Act 1986 Sch.B1 para.73.
[93] Insolvency Act 1986 Sch.B1 para.73(2(a), (b), (c).

border merger within the meaning of reg.2 of the Companies (Cross-Border Mergers) Regulations 2007.[94]

15-23 Confidentiality of estimates. The Rules requires the administrator to give an estimate of the value of the company's net property, and of the value of "the prescribed part" of that property (for distribution among the unsecured creditors pursuant to s.176A of the Act), and to state whether he intends to make an application to the court relating to the distribution of that part.[95] But he is not required, in giving such estimates, to include any confidential information, the disclosure of which would seriously prejudice the commercial interests of the company.[96] If any such information is excluded from the calculations, this should be stated.[97]

15-24 Distribution of the statement of proposals. The administrator must send a copy of his proposals to the registrar of companies,[98] to every creditor of whose claim and address he is aware, other than an opted-out creditor,[99] and to every member of the company of whose address he is aware.[100] Those copies must be sent out as soon as is reasonably practicable and no later than eight weeks from the start of administration, subject to any extension of time obtained from the court or by agreement with the creditors.[101]

To discharge his obligation to send a copy to members, it will suffice if, within the same period, he publishes a notice undertaking to provide a copy of his proposals, free of charge, to any member who applies in writing to a specified address.[102] Such publication must take place once, in such manner as the administrator thinks most appropriate for ensuring that the notice comes to the attention of the members. It must identify the proceedings and contain the registered office of the company,[103] as well as the standard contents of any non-*Gazette* advertisement required by rr.1.15-1.18.

In common with other documents, the statement of proposals may be sent to creditors and members by email or published on a website.[104]

Together with the statement of proposals the administrator must send to the creditors a notice inviting them to decide whether a creditors' committee should be formed.[105]

If the administrator fails to make the required distribution of the statement of his proposals, he commits an offence.[106]

15-25 Deemed approval. An administrator may, in his statement of proposals, make a statement in accordance with para.52(1) of Sch.B1 to the effect that:

---

[94] Insolvency Act 1986 Sch.B1 para.73(2)(d).
[95] Insolvency Rules 2016 r.3.35(6).
[96] Insolvency Rules 2016 r.3.35(7).
[97] Insolvency Rules 2016 r.3.35(8).
[98] Insolvency Act 1986 Sch.B1 para.49(4)(a).
[99] Insolvency Act 1986 Sch.B1 para.49(4)(b). By s.246C of the Insolvency Act 1986 a creditor may opt out of receiving certain notices from the administrator.
[100] Insolvency Act 1986 Sch.B1 para.49(4)(c).
[101] See paras 15-19.
[102] Insolvency Act 1986 Sch.B1 para.49(6).
[103] Insolvency Rules 2016 r.3.37(1).
[104] See para.15-5.
[105] Insolvency Rules 2016 r.3.39(1). See further, Section 5, at para.15-82 ff below.
[106] Insolvency Act 1986 Sch.B1 para.49(7).

- the company has sufficient property to enable each creditor to be paid in full; or
- it has insufficient property to enable any distribution to be made to creditors, other than to the extent of the "prescribed part" for the benefit of the unsecured creditors (see Ch.31, below); or
- neither of the objectives specified in Sch.B1 to the Act, para.3(1)(a) or (b), can be achieved.

In such a case the proposals shall be deemed to have been approved by the creditors[107] unless the administrator is requested, by creditors holding at least 10% of the total debts of the company,[108] to seek the a decision of the creditors on the approvals.

Such a request must be made within eight business days of the date on which the proposals are delivered,[109] and in accordance with the provisions of r.5.8, dealt with at para.15-39. As to the timing of the decision, its costs, and security for those costs, see para.15-40, below.

Limited disclosure of the proposals. As with the statement of affairs, where the administrator thinks that the disclosure of information contained within the proposals is likely to prejudice the conduct of the administration or might reasonably be expected to lead to violence against any person, he may apply for an order limiting disclosure of the proposals. The procedure for making such an application, and for challenging or varying an order made on such an application, is the same as in relation to a statement of affairs.[110] It should be noted that where a variation of an order for limited disclosure of the statement of affairs has been made, and the administrator has already distributed a statement of his proposals to the creditors and members, he must provide the creditors with a copy of the revised statement of affairs, as now filed, or a summary of it.[111] **15-26**

Seeking the creditors' approval of the proposals. Unless the deemed approval provisions of para.52(1) of Sch.B1 of the Act apply, the administrator must seek a decision of the creditors as to whether they approve the proposals.[112] The initial decision date must be within 10 weeks from the commencement of administration,[113] unless varied pursuant to para.107 of Sch.B1.[114] The notice seeking the decision must accompany the proposals.[115] **15-27**

The administrator may seek the creditors' approval of the proposals by whichever qualifying decision-making procedure he thinks appropriate, save that he may not convene a physical meeting save at the request of the requisite number of creditors.[116] Alternatively, the administrator may make use of the deemed consent

---

[107] Insolvency Rules 2016 r.3.38(4).
[108] Insolvency Act 1986 Sch.B1 para.52(2).
[109] Insolvency Rules 2016 r.15.18(2).
[110] Discussed at paras 15-16.
[111] Insolvency Rules 2016 r.3.48(2).
[112] Insolvency Act 1986 Sch.B1 para.51(1).
[113] Insolvency Act 1986 Sch.B1 para.51(2). However, different timescales apply where the decision has been requested by creditors pursuant to Insolvency Act 1986 Sch.B1 para.52(2).
[114] Insolvency Act 1986 Sch.B1 para.51(4).
[115] Insolvency Rules 2016 r.3.38(2).
[116] Insolvency Act 1986 s.246ZE(2). See further, para.15-36.

procedure,[117] even where a decision of creditors has been specifically requested by creditors pursuant to para.52(2) of Sch.B1 of the Act.[118]

15-28 **The decision on the proposals.** The creditors may approve the administrator's proposals with or without modifications. However the administrator must consent to any modifications.[119] If he does not consent to an attempted modification then the creditors have the choice of approving the proposals without the modification or withholding approval. The creditors may also simply not approve the proposals.[120]

As soon as is reasonably practicable the administrator must report the decision to the court, the registrar of companies, the creditors, and any other person to whom a copy of the proposals was provided.[121]

15-29 **Revised proposals.** Where the administrator's proposals have been approved (with or without modifications), and the administrator proposes a revision to those proposals which he considers to be substantial,[122] he must send a statement to the creditors setting out the proposed revision.[123] As well as certain formal identifying information, that statement must contain a summary of the initial proposals, and the reasons for proposing a revision, details of the proposed revision, with details of the administrator's assessment of the likely impact of the proposed revision on creditors generally, or (as the case may be) on each class of creditors. Where a proposed revision relates to the ending of the administration by a creditors' voluntary winding up, the statement must also contain details of the proposed liquidator, as well as a statement of the creditors' power to nominate a different person as liquidator in accordance with para.83(7)(a) of Sch.B1 to the Act.[124] The statement of the proposed revision must be accompanied by a notice of the decision procedure prepared in accordance with r.15.8.[125] The deemed consent procedure may be used.[126]

In addition to sending the statement to creditors, the administrator must send a copy to the registrar of companies[127] and to the members.[128] In the latter case he will comply with the obligation by publishing a notice undertaking to provide a copy of the statement, free of charge, to any member who applies in writing to a specified address.[129] The requirements set out at para.15-24 in relation to the advertisement of the original proposals also apply to this advertisement. In either case the

---

[117] Pursuant to Insolvency Act 1986 s.246ZF. See further para.15-37.
[118] The deemed consent procedure may be used where the company's creditors are to make a decision: Insolvency Act 1986 s.246ZF(1). However, where a decision has been requested by the requisite number of creditors, it may be thought likely that the requisite number will also object to the use of the deemed consent procedure.
[119] Insolvency Act 1986 Sch.B1 para.53(1).
[120] This may be done either by actively voting against the proposals, or by simply not voting—they are not approved if no votes are received: see Insolvency Rules 2016 r.15.9(3).
[121] Insolvency Act 1986 Sch.B1 para.53(2); Insolvency Rules 2016 r.3.41(1). This would include no decision: see paras 15-30 and 15-35.
[122] Insolvency Act 1986 Sch.B1 para.54(1)(c).
[123] Insolvency Act 1986 Sch.B1 para.54(2)(b).
[124] Insolvency Rules 2016 r.3.42(2).
[125] Insolvency Rules 2016 r.3.42(1).
[126] Insolvency Rules 2016 r.3.42(3).
[127] Insolvency Rules 2016 r.3.42(6).
[128] Insolvency Act 1986 Sch.B1 para.54(2)(c).
[129] Insolvency Act 1986 Sch.B1 para.54(3).

statement must be sent within five business days of sending it to the creditors[130] (save that if it is advertised, that advertisement need only be made as soon as reasonably practicable).[131]

The outcome of the decision-making procedure must be reported in the same way as the outcome of the decision on the original proposals.[132] Default by the administrator in making such reports constitutes an offence.[135]

Where the creditors have failed to agree on the proposals, or the revised proposals.   Where either the initial creditors' meeting, or a subsequent creditors' meeting, has failed to approve the administrator's proposals, whether original or as revised, the administrator must report this to the court.[133] He is also obliged to make an application to court for directions.[134] The court may then make one or more of a number of orders: **15-30**

- it may provide that the appointment of an administrator shall cease to have effect, as from a specified time;
- it may adjourn the application hearing, conditionally or unconditionally;
- it may make an interim order;
- it may make an order on a subsisting petition for winding-up, which was suspended after a floating charge-holder had appointed the administrator;
- it may make such other order (including an order making consequential provision) as it thinks fit.[135]

The court may, in the exercise of its discretion under para.55(2), order the implementation of the rejected proposals, notwithstanding the opposition of the majority creditor of the company.[136] It may also order the winding up of the company, either voluntarily[137] or compulsorily,[138] whether or not a petition for winding up has been presented.

SECTION 3: DECISION-MAKING PROCEDURES FOR CREDITORS AND MEMBERS OF THE COMPANY IN ADMINISTRATION

General.   The process for creditors and members to make decisions in insolvency has been fundamentally altered by the Small Business, Enterprise and Employment Act 2015. This introduced ss.246ZE–246ZG to the Act, which prevent decisions from being taken at meetings unless one is specifically requisitioned by the minimum number of creditors or members (as the case may be). The rules relating to decision-making processes are at Pt 15 of the Rules. Save for the rules as to the value for which they can vote, the rules applying to decision-making by creditors   **15-31**

---

130 Insolvency Rules 2016 r.3.42(4) and (6).
131 Insolvency Rules 2016 r.3.42(5)(a).
132 Insolvency Rules 2016 r.3.43. See para.15-42.
133 Insolvency Act 1986 Sch.B1 para.55(1). This has the effect that the "decision" must be reported under paras 53(2) or 54(6) of Sch.B1 even where by reason of r.15.9(3), there has technically been no decision.
134 *Re BTR (UK) Ltd* [2012] EWHC 2398; [2012] B.C.C. 864. It has been suggested that an administrator may continue with his proposed course despite the refusal of creditors to approve it: see *Re Stanleybet UK Investments Ltd* [2011] EWHC 2820 (Ch); [2012] BCC 550 at [8]. However even if this is legally possible, it is doubtful whether it would be a practical solution.
135 Insolvency Act 1986 Sch.B1 para.55(2).
136 *DKLL Solicitors v Her Majesty's Revenue and Customs* [2007] EWHC 2067 Ch; [2007] B.C.C. 908.
137 *Re Stanleybet UK Investments Ltd* [2011] EWHC 2820 (Ch).
138 *Re Graico Property Co Ltd* [2016] EWHC 2827 (Ch); [2017] B.C.C. 15.

also apply to decision-making by members,[139] and the following paragraphs should be read accordingly.

I: Decision-Making Procedures

15-32   **Qualifying decision-making procedures.**   The Act now makes use of the concept of qualifying decision-making procedures. These are correspondence, electronic voting, virtual meeting, physical meeting, and "any other decision-making procedure which enables all creditors who are entitled to participate in the making of the decision to participate equally."[140] Where an administrator seeks a decision about any matter from the company's creditors or members, that decision may be made by any of the qualifying decision-making procedures he thinks fit, save that a physical meeting cannot be called unless the minimum number of creditors or contributories request one.[141]

15-33   **The decision date.**   The decision date is important for determining deadlines for the provision of notices by, and objections to, the administrator, as well as for determining the date on which a decision has actually been made. Where the decision is to be made at a meeting the decision date is the date of the meeting.[142] In other cases (including decisions made by the deemed consent procedure) the decision date is the date by which the decision is to be made, and (if made) it will be deemed to have been made at 23.59 on that date.[143]

15-34   **Notices of decision procedures.**   In all cases where the administrator seeks a decision of creditors, he must send out a notice at least 14 days in advance of the decision date.[144] In addition to the standard contents required of all notices, the notice must comply with the requirements of r.15.8(3). In particular it must give details of the decision to be made, a description of the decision-making procedure including (if applicable) details of the venue, the decision date, the date by which a creditor must deliver a proof of debt failing which his vote will be disregarded, and a statement of creditors' rights to appeal against decisions as to who may vote.[145] Unless the notice is given in respect of a physical meeting, it must also contain a statement that if creditors reaching the relevant threshold request it within five business days of receiving a copy of the notice then there will be a physical meeting instead.[146] The notice must be authenticated and dated by the administrator.[147]

It should be recalled that there is a general power for administrators to communicate notices to creditors by email or by advertising them on a website.[148] In addition, the court has the power to order that notice of a decision procedure is to be given by advertisement only. In doing so it must consider the relative cost of advertisement and individual notice, the assets available, and the extent of the interest of creditors and members. Any such advertisement must comply with the

---

[139]   Insolvency Rules 2016 r.15.2(3).
[140]   Insolvency Rules 2016 r.15.3.
[141]   Insolvency Act 1986 s.246ZE(2).
[142]   Insolvency Rules 2016 r.15.2(1)(a).
[143]   Insolvency Rules 2016 r.15.2(1)(b).
[144]   Insolvency Rules 2016 rr.15.2(2) and r.15.11(1).
[145]   Insolvency Rules 2016 r.15.8(3).
[146]   Insolvency Rules 2016 r.15.8(3)(k).
[147]   Insolvency Rules 2016 r.15.8(4)
[148]   See para.15-5.

requirements of r.15.8(3), and must also state that the court ordered notice to be given by advertisement only, and give the date of the order.[149]

Additional requirements for electronic voting or meetings. Additional requirements apply where the decision-making procedure is either electronic voting or a meeting. For a decision to be taken by means of electronic voting, the notice must also give the creditors any necessary information as to how to access the system, including any password needed.[150] It should also be noted that the Rules require that the voting system must enable a creditor to vote at any time between the notice being delivered and the decision date, and must not provide any creditor with information about other creditors' votes in the course of the vote. **15-35**

For a decision to be taken at a meeting (whether physical or virtual), the notice must contain a statement that the meeting may be suspended or adjourned by the chair of the meeting[151]; in the case of a virtual meeting, it must also provide the information necessary to access the meeting (such as telephone number, access code or password)[152]; and in the case of a physical meeting it must explain the administrator's discretion to permit somebody to attend the meeting remotely.[153] In either case the notice must contain a statement of the right to complain about a person's exclusion from the meeting,[154] be accompanied by a blank proxy form[155] and warn that the proxy must be delivered to the administrator before it may be used at the meeting.[156] Details of the meeting must also be advertised in the London *Gazette* and may be advertised in any other manner the administrator thinks fit.[157]

Requiring a physical meeting. A physical meeting must be called if, and only if, it is required by at least the minimum number of creditors.[158] The minimum number is 10% in value, 10% in number, or 10 in number.[159] Even where the decision is sought only from creditors of a particular class, creditors of any class count towards the minimum number.[160] The requests may be made any time before notice of the decision procedure (including the deemed consent procedure) has been sent out, but must be made no later than five business days after that notice was delivered.[161] **15-36**

Once requests from the minimum number of creditors have been received, the administrator must send out a further notice, complying with all the requirements of a notice of decision-making procedure, to convene the meeting.[162] This notice must be sent within three business days after the minimum number of requests have been received.[163]

The deemed consent procedure. Unless otherwise provided in the Act or the **15-37**

---

[149] Insolvency Rules 2016 r.15.12.
[150] Insolvency Rules 2016 r.15.4(a).
[151] Insolvency Rules 2016 r.15.5(b), r.15.6(3).
[152] Insolvency Rules 2016 r.15.5(a).
[153] Insolvency Rules 2016 r.15.5.
[154] Insolvency Rules 2016 r.15.8(3)(m).
[155] Insolvency Rules 2016 r.15.8(5).
[156] Insolvency Rules 2016 r.15.8(3)(l).
[157] Insolvency Rules 2016 r.15.13
[158] Insolvency Act 1986 s.246ZE(3)–(4).
[159] Insolvency Act 1986 s.246ZE(7).
[160] Insolvency Act 1986 s.246ZE(8).
[161] Insolvency Rules 2016 r.15.6(1).
[162] Insolvency Rules 2016 r.15.6(3).
[163] Insolvency Rules 2016 r.15.6(5).

Rules,[164] or by an order of the court, a decision need not be made by a qualifying decision-making procedure. Instead the administrator may make use of the deemed consent procedure.[165] To do so he must give the relevant creditors (other than opted-out creditors) or members (as the case may be) the necessary notice. In addition for the standard contents required of all notices of a decision procedure, the notice must also inform the creditors of their ability to object to use of the deemed consent procedure, and contain a statement that in order to object a creditor must deliver a notice to this effect to the administrator no later than the decision date, together with a proof of debt, failing which the objection will be disregarded, that it is the administrator's obligation to aggregate the objections to see if the threshold is met for objections, and as to the effect if that threshold is met.[166]

The relevant creditors are those who would be entitled to vote on the decision in a qualifying decision-making procedure[167] (and may, for instance, be limited to members of a class of creditors).[168] The threshold for a successful objection is 10% in value of the relevant creditors or members (as the case may be).[169] If this number of creditors or members object to the use of the deemed consent procedure then the decision is treated as not having been made and any future decision on the matter must be sought by means of a qualifying decision-making procedure.

While the Act does not envisage that creditors may require a physical meeting when the deemed consent procedure is used, it is clear from the Rules that this is the case.[170] It should be noted that the threshold for requiring a physical meeting is different from the threshold for objecting to the deemed consent procedure; that creditors who are not eligible to object to the deemed consent procedure may be eligible to require a physical meeting; and that the methods for ascertaining the value of creditors' claims is different in each case.

Remuneration decisions may not be taken by the deemed consent procedure.[171]

15-38   **Further creditors' decisions.**   In addition to seeking a decision on the proposals, and the administrator's own power to seek further creditors' decisions, he must seek a decision from the creditors if he is directed to do so by the court,[172] or he is requested to do so, in the prescribed manner, by creditors whose debts amount to at least 10% of the company's total debts.[173] Failure to summon such a meeting without a reasonable excuse constitutes an offence.[174]

15-39   **Procedure for requisitioning a decision of creditors.**   A request for a decision on the statement of proposals must be made and within eight business days of the date on which statement of proposals is delivered.[175] Any request for a decision of creditors—whether made in respect of the proposals pursuant to para.52(2) of

---

[164] It should be noted that the Rules frequently refer to the need to conduct a "decision procedure". This phrase is defined as a qualifying decision-making procedure (Insolvency Rules 2016 r.1.2(2)). Therefore where any rule requires this the deemed consent procedure may not be used.

[165] Insolvency Act 1986 s.246ZF(1).

[166] Insolvency Act 1986 s.246SF(3), Insolvency Rules 2016 r.15.7(2).

[167] Insolvency Act 1986 s.246ZF(7).

[168] Insolvency Act 1986 s.247ZF(9).

[169] Insolvency Act 1986 s.247ZF(6). For the rules as to how this must be calculated, see para.15-50.

[170] See, in particular, IR16 rr.15.6(1) and 15.8(3)(k)

[171] Insolvency Act 1986 s.246ZF(2).

[172] Insolvency Act 1986 Sch.B1 para.56(1)(b).

[173] Insolvency Act 1986 Sch.B1 para.56(1)(a).

[174] Insolvency Act 1986 Sch.B1 para.56(2).

[175] Insolvency Rules 2016 r.15.18(2).

Sch.B1 of the Act or more generally pursuant to para.56(1)—must include a statement of the purpose of the proposed decision and a list of the creditors concurring in the request, with the amounts of their individual debts, their individual written confirmations of their concurrence.[176]

The costs and timing of a requisitioned decision.   Once the administrator has   **15-40**
received a request for a decision from sufficient creditors, he may provide require payment of a sum as security for the costs of engaging in the decision-making procedure. If he wishes to require security, then he must send itemised details of the sum required within 14 days of the request.[177] The creditor, or creditors, requesting the meeting must then deposit this sum with the administrator, and he is under no obligation to act until it is so deposited. Once it has been deposited (or once the 14 days have elapsed with no request for security from the administrator), the administrator must then initiate the decision procedure within 28 days.[178] There is no reason in principle why the deemed consent procedure should not be used in an appropriate case.

It is for the creditors to decide whether the expenses of the requisitioned meeting should be paid out of the deposit or as an expense of the administration,[179] and in addition to the standard contents of any notice[180] the notice of the requisitioned decision must contain a statement that the creditors may make a decision as to these expenses.[181] Any surplus from the deposit is to be repaid to the person or persons who made it,[182] and conversely, where the creditors have not decided that the costs should be an expense of the administration and the deposit does not cover them in full, the creditor requesting the decision must pay the balance.[183]

II: The Conduct of Meetings

The chair.   The chair at any meeting summoned by the administrator must be   **15-41**
either the administrator himself,[184] or a person nominated by the administrator,[185] who must himself be qualified to act as an insolvency practitioner in relation to the company, or a person experienced in insolvency matters who is a member or employee of the administrator's firm or an employee of the administrator.[186] If, within 30 minutes from the time fixed for the meeting to commence, there is no person to act as chair, the meeting is adjourned to the same time and place of the week following, if that day is a business day, otherwise to the business day immediately following.[187] There can be a maximum of two adjournments on this basis.

---

[176] Insolvency Rules 2016 r.15.18(3).
[177] Insolvency Rules 2016 r.15.19(1).
[178] Insolvency Rules 2016 r.15.19(2).
[179] Insolvency Rules 2016 r.15.19(4)(a).
[180] See Insolvency Rules 2016 r.15.8(3).
[181] Insolvency Rules 2016 r.15.19(5).
[182] Insolvency Rules 2016 r.15.19(7).
[183] Insolvency Rules 2016 r.15.19(6).
[184] Insolvency Rules 2016 r.15.21(1)(a).
[185] Insolvency Rules 2016 r.15.21(1)(b).
[186] Insolvency Rules 2016 r.1.2(3).
[187] Insolvency Rules 2016 r.15.25(1).

After two adjournments, if there is again no chair within 30 minutes of the time fixed for the start of the adjourned meeting, then the meeting comes to an end.[188]

The chair has considerable discretion as to the conduct of the meeting. In particular the chair may permit a person who has given reasonable notice of his wish to attend to take part in a meeting; decide what intervention, if any, may be made by any person attending a creditors meeting who is not a creditor (and likewise, mutatis mutandis, for members); and decide what questions may be put to any officer or former officer of the company.[189]

Where the creditors' committee requires the administrator to attend a meeting with them, they may elect one of their number to be chairman, instead of the administrator: see para.15-82, below.

15-42 Quorum at meetings. The quorum for a meeting of creditors is one creditor entitled to vote.[190] For a meeting of members it is two, except in single member companies (when it is one).[191]

15-43 Attendance of directors etc. at meetings. If the administrator thinks that the attendance of an officer or former officer is required at a meeting, he must give 14 days' notice[192] to that officer, who is then obliged to attend the meeting.[193]

15-44 Adjournment and suspension of meetings. The meeting may be adjourned (more than once if necessary), if the chair thinks fit or if the meeting resolves to do so, but no adjournment can be to a date later than 14 days from the date when it was originally held, subject to the direction of the court.[194] Where the chair holds proxies for creditors or members, and is provided with important new information which ought to be reported to those creditors or members, he may be under an obligation to adjourn the meeting, even if it means obtaining an extension of time for the meeting from the court.[195]

15-45 Exclusion from meetings. It may occur that a person has taken all the steps necessary to attend a virtual meeting, or has been permitted by the administrator to attend a physical meeting remotely, but the arrangements put in place by the administrator do not enable that person to attend the whole of the meeting (an "excluded person").[196] If the chair becomes aware during the course of the meeting that a person is excluded from it, he may suspend the meeting for up to an hour without adjourning it.[197] Whether or not he chooses to suspend the meeting, the chair has the discretion continue the meeting, declare it void and convene it again,

---

[188] Insolvency Rules 2016 r.15.25(2).
[189] Insolvency Rules 2016 r.15.22.
[190] Insolvency Rules 2016 r.15.20(2)(a).
[191] Insolvency Rules 2016 r.15.20(2)(b).
[192] Insolvency Rules 2016 rr.15.2(2) and 15.14(4).
[193] Insolvency Rules 2016 r.15.14(1).
[194] Insolvency Rules 2016 r.15.23.
[195] *Cadbury Schweppes plc v Somji* [2001] 1 W.L.R. 615; [2001] 1 B.C.L.C. 498 at [25]. However some doubt was expressed in *Tradition(UK) Ltd v Ahmed* [2008] EWHC 2946 (Ch); [2009] B.P.I.R. 626 as to whether the chair would have authority to direct an adjournment on this basis, or would simply be under a duty to propose and vote for an adjournment as proxyholder (at [242]).
[196] Insolvency Rules 2016 r.15.36(1).
[197] Insolvency Rules 2016 r.15.36(4).

or declare it valid up to the point where the person was excluded and adjourn it.[198] A meeting which the chair decides to continue is valid unless the chair later decides to declare it void following a complaint, or the court directs otherwise.[199]

If a person has been excluded from a meeting, he may request an indication of what took place during the period of his exclusion,[200] provided that he does so by no later than 4pm on the business day following the day on which the exclusion took place.[201] The request must be made to the chair if it is made during the meeting; otherwise it must be made to the administrator.[202] So long as the chair or administrator (as the case may be) is satisfied that the person was excluded, he must provide the information as soon as practicable and not later than 4pm on the business day following the day on which the request was made.[203]

Complaints following exclusion from meetings. Where a person has been   **15-46** excluded from a meeting, that person and anybody else who attended the meeting and claims to have been prejudiced by the exclusion may make a complaint.[204] The request must be made to the chair if it is made during the meeting; otherwise it must be made to the administrator.[205] It must be made by 4pm on the business day following the exclusion,[206] unless it is made by the excluded person following a request for an indication of what took place at the meeting, in which case it must be made by 4pm on the business day after that indication is provided.[207]

If a complaint is made the chair or administrator (as appropriate) must determine whether there has been an exclusion and, if so, must take such action as he thinks fit to remedy the prejudice caused.[208] This action may include declaring the meeting void and holding it again.[209] If a vote took place during the exclusion and the excluded person asserts how he would have voted, then the chair or administrator must consider whether that vote would have changed the result of the vote.[210] If it would have, then he must amend the result of the vote as soon as reasonably practicable. The notice of the result must explain the change in the result and the reasons for it; and if notice has already been sent out a further notice of change must be delivered.[211]

The chair or administrator must provide notice of his decision to the complainant as soon as reasonably practicable.[212] If the complainant is not satisfied, he may apply to court for directions, provided that this application is made no more than two business days from the date of receiving the decision.[213]

Meetings of company incorporated outside England and Wales. In the case   **15-47**

---

[198] Insolvency Rules 2016 r.15.36(2).
[199] Insolvency Rules 2016 r.15.36(3). See para.15-46.
[200] Insolvency Rules 2016 r.15.37(1).
[201] Insolvency Rules 2016 r.15.37(2).
[202] Insolvency Rules 2016 r.15.37(3).
[203] Insolvency Rules 2016 r.15.37(4).
[204] Insolvency Rules 2016 r.15.38(1).
[205] Insolvency Rules 2016 r.15.38(2).
[206] Insolvency Rules 2016 r.15.38(3)(a).
[207] Insolvency Rules 2016 r.15.38(3)(b).
[208] Insolvency Rules 2016 r.15.38(4).
[209] Insolvency Rules 2016 r.15.36(3)(a).
[210] Insolvency Rules 2016 r.15.38(5) and (6). Where there is more than one excluded complainant the aggregate effect of their votes must be considered: Insolvency Rules 2016 r.15.38(7).
[211] Insolvency Rules 2016 r.15.38(6)(c) and (d).
[212] Insolvency Rules 2016 r.15.38(8).
[213] Insolvency Rules 2016 r.15.38(9).

of a meeting of the company itself (as opposed to a meeting of creditors or members called pursuant to the Act), if the company was not incorporated in England and Wales, but in another EEA state, the meeting must be conducted in accordance with the company's own constitution and with the laws of that state.[214] This provision governs the situation where, by virtue of the EC Regulation on Insolvency Proceedings, a company or other legal person, although registered or incorporated in another EEA state, enters administration in this country, in consequence of its centre of main interests being located in England and Wales. It should be noted that company meetings of companies incorporated outside the EEA are to be called and conducted in accordance with English law.[215]

III: Entitlement to Vote and Ascertaining Majorities

15-48   **Creditor's entitlement to vote.**   A creditor is only entitled to vote if he has delivered a proof of debt to the administrator no later than the decision date or, in the case of a meeting, 4pm on the business day before the meeting; and that proof has been admitted for the purposes of voting.[216] The administrator or (if different) chair is entitled to call for any document or evidence to be produced to substantiate the debt claimed in the proof if he thinks it is necessary.[217]

A vote may be cast only once in respect of each claim. The debt of a creditor and of a Member State liquidator are the same claim for these purposes,[218] as are the debt of a principal creditor and a guarantor of that debt.[219]

A proxy-holder may not vote at a meeting unless the administrator or chair has received the proxy form.[220]

15-49   **Valuing a creditor's vote.**   A creditor's vote is based on the net value of his claim as at the date of administration, after deducting any payments made to him after the company entered administration, and any allowable set-off.[221] Where a debt is wholly or partly secured, for voting purposes it is valued only to the extent that it is unsecured,[222] except where a decision has been requisitioned on proposals which contain a statement made pursuant to para.52(1)(b) of Sch.B1 of the Act.[223] A debt due under a hire purchase agreement is to be valued at the amount due and payable by the company on the date of administration, disregarding amounts due solely by reason of the fact of administration.[224]

Creditors with unliquidated debts, or debts of unascertained amount, may only vote, where the administrator or chair agrees to put on the debt an estimated value

---

[214] Insolvency Rules 2016 r.15.41(1)(b).
[215] Insolvency Rules 2016 r.15.41(1)(a).
[216] Insolvency Rules 2016 r.15.28(1). Under the 1986 Rules the administrator had a discretion to permit a creditor to vote even if the deadline for submitting a proof of debt had been missed (r.2.38(2)). It appears that the administrator no longer has such a discretion.
[217] Insolvency Rules 2016 r.15.28(4).
[218] Insolvency Rules 2016 r.15.31(7); see para.15-51.
[219] Until the principal debtor is discharged in full, only he may prove (and, therefore vote) the claim: *Mills v HSBC Trustee (CI) Ltd* [2011] UKSC 48; [2012] 1 A.C. 804.
[220] Insolvency Rules 2016 r.15.28(2).
[221] Insolvency Rules 2016 r.15.31(1)(a). As to set-off, see r.14.24, and see below at para.15-113.
[222] Insolvency Rules 2016 r.15.31(4) and (5).
[223] Insolvency Rules 2016 r.15.31(6(a).
[224] Insolvency Rules 2016 r.15.32.

for the purposes of entitlement to vote.[225] It has been held in the context of meetings to approve voluntary arrangements that in such a case the chair is under no independent duty to investigate the creditor's claim, but that he is obliged to examine such evidence as is produced to him in order to decide whether to attribute a value to it.[226] There does not seem to be any good reason why the position in administration should be different.

An administrator or chair may admit or reject a claim either in whole or in part. However a claim should only be rejected where it is clearly bad. Where there is any doubt the administrator or chair must mark the claim as objected to and admit it to vote in full.[227]

Valuing requests for physical meetings and objections to deemed consent procedure.   For the purpose of calculating whether the relevant threshold has been reached for the requisitioning of a physical meeting pursuant to s.246ZE(7) of the Act, or for objecting to the deemed consent procedure pursuant to s.246ZF(6) of the Act, the valuation provisions of r.15.31 also apply.[228] Where the administrator is aggregating objections to the deemed consent procedure he is entitled to presume that the value of relevant creditors claims is the value of claims by creditors who in his view would have been able to participate in a decision even if they have not yet met the criteria for entitlement to vote.[229]   **15-50**

Member State Liquidators' entitlements.   A Member State liquidator of the company appointed in another Member State pursuant to the EC Regulation on Insolvency Proceedings (see Ch.28, below), whether in main or secondary proceedings, is entitled to exercise all the rights of a creditor in the administration.[230] He is entitled to claim as a creditor to the extent of the debts owed by the company to creditors in the proceedings, in relation to which he holds office as liquidator.   **15-51**

However, where a creditor has lodged his claim in those insolvency proceedings he retains his ability to vote in the administration. If he does so and a Member State liquidator also votes in respect of the same debt, only the creditor's vote is to be counted.[231] Where a creditor has lodged his claim in more than one set of other Member State proceedings, and more than one Member State liquidator seeks to vote in respect of that claim, it is the Member State liquidator in the main proceedings who is entitled to vote.[232]

Requisite majority.   A decision is made by creditors if: **15-52**

---

[225] Insolvency Rules 2016 r.15.31(2).
[226] *Re Newlands (Seaford) Educational Trust (in administration)* [2006] EWHC 1511 Ch; [2007] B.C.C. 195 at [28].
[227] Insolvency Rules 2016 r.15.33; see too *Re a Debtor (No. 222 of 1990), Ex p. Bank of Ireland* [1992] B.C.L.C. 137; *Times,* 27 June 1991.
[228] Insolvency Rules 2016 rr.15.6(8) and 15.7(5). It may be noted that r.15.7(5) also requires the application of rr.15.32 and 15.33. It is not clear why a distinction should be drawn in the two cases. While the omission of reference to Rule 15.33 may have few practical effects, debts arising out of hire purchase agreements will very often have to valued differently in the two cases.
[229] Insolvency Rules 2016 r.15.7(4). Presumably this means that he may work on the basis that all creditors of whom he is aware would submit a proof if a decision were sought. In the case of requisitioning a physical meeting, it would seem that the administrator must make the same assumption until the decision date is reached or the 10% threshold is passed anyway.
[230] Insolvency Rules 2016 r.21.8; Regulation (EU) 2015/848 art.45.
[231] Insolvency Rules 2016 r.15.30(1).
[232] Insolvency Rules 2016 r.15.30(2).

- a majority in value of the votes cast are in favour or the proposed decision[233]; and
- not more than half in value of the creditors who, the best of the administrator's or chair's belief, are not connected with the company have voted against the decision.[234]

A person is "connected" with the company if he is a director, a shadow director, or an associate of it.[235] "Associate" is defined at s.435 of the Act. The associates of a company are any person or company with which it is partnership,[236] its employees,[237] including its directors (and any companies of which it is a corporate director),[238] any beneficiaries of a trust (or their associates) of which the company is a trustee, if the trust gives the company discretion which may be exercised in their favour,[239] and any person who has control of it, either alone or together with associates.[240] In addition to partners, employees, employers, trustees, beneficiaries and companies, a person's associates also include his husband, wife or civil partner,[241] his close relatives and those of his husband, wife or civil partner, and those relatives' husbands, wives or civil partners.[242]

A vote cast in a decision-making procedure which is not a meeting may not be changed subsequently.[243]

15-53 **Appeal against the admission and rejection of claims.** An appeal lies to the court, at the suit of any creditor, against any decision to admit or reject a claim to vote[244] (including in relation to aggregating objections to the deemed consent procedure).[245] Any such appeal must be made within 21 days of the decision.[246] In determining the appeal the court is not limited to the material which was before the administrator or chair, and in order to succeed it is not necessary to establish that the earlier decision was wrong.[247] However the court must determine what the posi-

---

[233] Insolvency Rules 2016 r.15.34(1).
[234] Insolvency Rules 2016 r.15.34(2).
[235] Insolvency Act 1986 s.249.
[236] Insolvency Act 1986 s.435(3).
[237] Insolvency Act 1986 s.435(4).
[238] Insolvency Act 1986 s.435(9).
[239] Insolvency Act 1986 s.435(6).
[240] Insolvency Act 1986 s.435(7). A person with "control" of a company is defined at s.435(10) as either being a person in accordance with whose instructions the directors are accustomed to act, or a person who is entitled to exercise or control the exercise of at least one third of the voting power at any general meeting of the company or of another company with control of the company, either alone or together with others. See *Unidare Plc v Cohen* [2005] EWHC 1410 (Ch) and, on aggregation of persons under s.435(10), see the tax case of *Kellogg Brown & Root Holdings (UK) Ltd v R&CC* [2010] EWCA Civ 118.
[241] Including former or reputed husbands, wives and civil partners: s.435(8). This does not include mere cohabitees, however long-standing: *Smurthwaite v Simpson-Smith and Mond (No.2)* [2006] B.P.I.R. 1483.
[242] Insolvency Act 1986 s.435(8). The close relatives are specified at s.435(8) as being a brother, sister, uncle, aunt, nephew, niece, lineal ancestor and lineal descendant.
[243] Insolvency Rules 2016 r.15.31(8).
[244] Insolvency Rules 2016 r.15.31(1).
[245] Insolvency Rules 2016 r.15.7(6).
[246] Insolvency Rules 2016 r.15.35(4).
[247] See *Power v Petrus* [2008] EWHC 2607 (Ch); [2009] B.P.I.R. 141 at [14].

tion was at the date of the decision, and events subsequent to the decision will not lead to an appeal being allowed.[248]

If the decision is reversed on appeal, or varied, or if a creditor's vote is declared invalid, the court may order that another decision procedure be initiated, or make such other order as it thinks fit.[249] If, for instance, it is clear that with the required variation a resolution would not have been approved, the court may simply overturn that decision without ordering a new meeting[250]; if the reversal would make no difference to the outcome of the decision-making procedure then the court may decline to make any order at all.[251]

Costs of appeal. The administrator or chair is not personally liable for costs   **15-54**
incurred by any person in relation to an appeal to the court for or against the admission or rejection of a claim unless the court so orders.[252] The court will not normally make such an order unless the administrator or chair has fallen so far below the proper standard to be expected of a professional person that it is appropriate to do so.[253]

Members' rights to vote. In the case of a decision-making procedure involving   **15-55**
members, the values to be ascribed to members' votes is the same as it would be in a general meeting of the company,[254] and the requisite majority is more than 50%.[255]

SECTION 4: THE PROCESS OF ADMINISTRATION

I: Management of the Company and its business

General. The powers and discretions conferred upon the administrator by virtue   **15-56**
of his appointment are identical, whether he is appointed by the court, or by a qualifying floating charge-holder or by a company or its directors.[256] References to "the administrator" apply, with necessary modifications, to the position where two or more administrators are appointed, to act jointly or concurrently. Such a multiple appointment must specify which (if any) functions are to be exercised by such persons acting jointly, and which (if any) are to be exercised by any or all of them individually.[257]

An offence of omission committed by "the administrator" is committed by each of those administrators who were appointed to act jointly, in respect of those func-

---

[248] *Power v Petrus* [2009] B.P.I.R. 141 at [17]. In *Re Shruth Ltd* [2005 EWHC] 1293 (Ch); [2007] B.C.C. 960 a creditor was not permitted to vote in respect of an unliquidated debt. By the time the appeal was heard, judgment had been obtained in respect of the debt so that it was now liquidated. It was held (at [26]) that the court was not entitled to take that into account.

[249] Insolvency Rules 2016 r.15.35(3).

[250] *Re a Debtor (No. 222 of 1990), Ex p. Bank of Ireland* [1992] B.C.L.C. 137; *Times*, 27 June 1991.

[251] *Power v Petrus* [2008] EWHC 2607 (Ch); [2009] B.P.I.R. 141 at [32].

[252] Insolvency Rules 2016 r.15.35(6).

[253] *Re a Debtor (No. 222 of 1990), Ex p. Bank of Ireland (No.2)* [1993] B.C.L.C. 233

[254] Insolvency Rules 2016 rr.15.2(4) and 15.39(a).

[255] Insolvency Rules 2016 r.15.39(b).

[256] Insolvency Act 1986 Sch.B1 para.1(1), except for some minor procedural variations.

[257] Insolvency Act 1986 Sch.B1 paras 100-103.

tions to which the offence or omission related; each of those persons may therefore be punished.[258]

15-57   **The administrator's status.**   The administrator must be a licensed insolvency practitioner, qualified to act as such in relation to the company. He is an officer of the court, regardless of whether he is appointed by the court or by a qualifying floating charge-holder, or the company or its directors. His acts are valid, regardless of any defect in his appointment or qualification. An act of the administrator is valid, in spite of any defect in his appointment or qualification.[259] Furthermore, a person who deals with an administrator in good faith and for value need not inquire whether he is acting within his powers.[260]

15-58   **General powers.**   The administrator is the agent of the company,[261] and is authorised to do anything necessary or expedient for the management of its affairs, business or property.[262] Any express authority conferred on him by other statutory provisions is without prejudice to the generality of that primary authority.[263]

The administrator also has the specific powers listed at Sch.1 to the Act. The primary of these is the power to take possession of, collect, and get in the property of the company.[264] Among the other powers listed are the power to raise or borrow money, if necessary by granting security over the company's property,[265] and the power to make any payment which is necessary or incidental to the performance of his functions.[266] He also has the power to sell the property of the company.[267] This gives him the right to assign any causes of action which are vested in the company even if such an assignment would ordinarily be void for champerty.[268]

15-59   **Powers of management and distribution.**[269]   The administrator's powers of management include the power to remove an existing director, and to appoint a director, either as a new appointment or to fill a vacancy.[270] Without his consent, no management power vested in the company (whether by enactment or by instrument) may be exercised by the company, or by any of its officers, which could

---

[258]   Insolvency Act 1986 Sch.B1. para.101(4).

[259]   Insolvency Act 1986 Sch.B1 para.104. Where the defect means that the administrator's actual appointment took place on a date after his purported appointment, this provision will validate his acts in the meantime: *Re Ceart Risk Services Ltd* [2012] EWHC 1178 (Ch); [2012] B.C.C. 592. The provision will not apply where the appointment is a nullity, although the court may order that the administrator be appointed with retrospective effect: *Re G-Tech Construction Ltd* [2007] B.P.I.R. 1275. However it should be noted that first-instance judges are now more likely to hold that there has been a defective appointment capable of being cured than that there has been no appointment at all: see the discussion in *Ceart* [2012] B.C.C. at [10]–[20]. See also para 14-4 above.

[260]   Insolvency Act 1986 Sch.B1 para.59(3).

[261]   Insolvency Act 1986 Sch.B1 para.69. The administrator's status as agent of the company does not always negative personal liability: see *Wright Hassall LLP v Morris* [2012] EWCA Civ 1472; [2013] B.C.C. 192.

[262]   Insolvency Act 1986 Sch.B1 para.59(1).

[263]   Insolvency Act 1986 Sch.B1 para.59(2).

[264]   Insolvency Act 1986 Sch.1 para.1.

[265]   Insolvency Act 1986 Sch.1 para.3.

[266]   Insolvency Act 1986 Sch.1 para.13.

[267]   Insolvency Act 1986 Sch.1 para.2.

[268]   *Re Park Gate Waggon Works Co* (1881) 17 Ch. D. 234.

[269]   As to distributions generally see para.15-102.

[270]   Insolvency Act 1986 Sch.B1 para.61.

interfere with the exercise of the administrator's powers.[271] He may call meetings of creditors of the company or of members,[272] and may obtain decisions from the creditors' committee by correspondence.[273]

Paragraph 65 of Sch.B1 also provides that the administrator may make "a distribution" (i.e. a payment) to a creditor of the company. While this would normally entail a payment made pari passu to all creditors of the same seniority, it was held in *Re HPJ UK Ltd*[274] that the provision could also be used to permit the making of a payment to only one unsecured creditor, where that payment was made in settlement of the creditor's claim in the administration at a discount, the administrators considered that the settlement would help them to conclude the administration to the advantage of the other creditors, and all the other creditors approved the making of the payment.

Paragraph 66 of Sch.B1 provides for a payment to be made other than in accordance with para.65 or para.13 of Sch.1 (the power to make payments necessary or incidental to the performance of the administrator's functions). This has been used to permit administrators to make payments to overseas creditors which are in excess of their entitlements under English Law, but instead in line with their entitlements under local law, thereby avoiding the risk of multiple insolvency proceedings.[275] Such a payment might also need to be made to an unpaid pre-administration creditor, to procure the restoration of essential goods or services to carry on the company's business.[276]

Taking control of the company's property. The administrator is entitled and obliged to take custody or control of all the property to which he thinks the company is entitled.[277] This includes property which has been sold to the company under a retention of title clause where the seller has not revoked the company's authority to sell the property.[278] Where a creditor claims that the company holds property subject to a retention of title claim, it is usually the creditor's, and not the administrator's, responsibility to identify this property.[279]　　　**15-60**

Any administrative receiver in office when the company enters administration must vacate office,[280] and any receiver of part of the company's property must vacate office, if the administrator requires him to do so.[281] In either case the receiver's remuneration is charged on any property in his custody or control immediately before he vacated office.[282]

Dealing with trust property. If the company holds property on trust for others,　**15-61**

---

[271] Insolvency Act 1986 Sch.B1 para.64(1).
[272] Insolvency Act 1986 Sch.B1 para.62.
[273] Insolvency Act 1986 Sch.B1 para.58; Insolvency Rules 2016 r.18.9: see para.15-91 below.
[274] [2007] B.C.C. 284.
[275] See *Re MG Rover Espana SA* [2006] B.C.C. 599; *Re Collins & Aikman Europe SA* [2006] EWHC 1343 Ch, [2006] B.C.C. 861; *Re MG Rover Belux SA/NV* [2007] B.C.C. 446.
[276] Although such a payment would almost certainly fall within Insolvency Act 1986 Sch.1 para.13.
[277] Insolvency Act 1986 Sch.1 para.1. In doing so the administrator is required to act with a "robustness of purpose": *Coyne v DRC Distribution Ltd* [2008] EWCA Civ 488; [2008] B.C.C. 612.
[278] A retention of title clause may operate so as to revoke this authority automatically upon the commencement of administration. Whether it does so in any particular case will be a question of construction: *Sandhu v Jet Star Retail Ltd* [2011] EWCA Civ 459.
[279] See *Blue Monkey Gaming Ltd v Hudson* [2014] All E.R. (D) 222 (Jun) at [154]. See also the discussion at para.15-70 ff.
[280] Insolvency Act 1986 Sch.B1 para.41(1).
[281] Insolvency Act 1986 Sch.B1 para.41(2).
[282] Insolvency Act 1986 Sch.B1 para.41(3).

that property is not the property of the company, as referred to at para.67 of Sch.B1 to the Act, and elsewhere. Therefore the administrator is not under an obligation to take that property into his custody or control, and ordinarily ought not to do so. In that way the company will continue to be the trustee of the property, and the administrator will not become trustee. Nevertheless, the administrator's power to do anything necessary or expedient for the purpose of managing the affairs of the company gives him some management powers in relation to trust property, since the distribution of the trust property is part of the company's "affairs".[283]

In some cases, it will be straightforward to ascertain what is and is not trust property. In a clear case it may be appropriate to apply to court for the appointment of a receiver over the trust property; in other cases it might be more appropriate to apply for directions as to the distribution of the trust fund.[284] Frequently the administrator will carry out a significant amount of work in identifying the trust assets or the beneficiaries. If that is the case then he may seek a "Berkeley Applegate" order permitting him to look to the trust fund for payment of his remuneration and expenses incurred in administering it.[285] However the court is unlikely to make such an order in respect of the costs of investigating the existence or validity of the trust,[286] where the administrator has been in the position of litigant claiming the asset,[287] or where the administrator has officiously and unsuccessfully interposed himself in a dispute between beneficiaries or putative beneficiaries.[288]

15-62 **Power to act before approval of Proposals.**   It is well established that, in appropriate circumstances, an administrator may sell the company's assets without the need to seek the permission of the court or the prior approval of the creditors.[289] This may encompass a sale of the whole, or substantially the whole, of a company's business and assets immediately upon the administrator's taking office.[290] Such a sale, commonly referred to as a "pre-pack", may be particularly appropriate where there will be limited or no funds to enable the administrator to trade the company following appointment, but a cessation of trading will impair the value of the company's business and assets.

Statement of Insolvency Practice 16 ("SIP 16") sets out the procedures to be followed by insolvency practitioners both before and after appointment, recognising that before administration the insolvency practitioner only advises the company (and not the directors or any other party potentially interested in the purchase), and that he may not eventually be appointed administrator. These procedures include ensuring that the marketing of the sale assets is as full as possible, and that a connected party purchaser is informed of the ability to approach the pre-pack pool for

---

[283] *Re Allanfield Property Insurance Services Ltd* [2015] EWHC 3721 (Ch); 2016] Lloyd's Rep I.R. 217.
[284] See *Re MF Global UK Ltd* [2013] EWHC 1655 (Ch); [2013] 1 W.L.R. 3874 for a helpful discussion of the relevant authorities and the basis on which the court may give directions to the administrator. The case itself is also an example of directions given to enable distribution of the trust fund when the identity of beneficiaries was not clear from the company's books and records.
[285] *Re Berkeley Applegate (Investment Consultants) Ltd (No.3)* (1989) 5 B.C.C. 803. Conversely, the liquidators were not entitled to claim that remuneration and expenses as an expense of the liquidation; see also *Re Eastern Captial Futures Ltd* [1989] B.C.L.C. 371.
[286] *Tom Wise v Fillimore* [1999] B.C.C. 129; *Green v Bramston* [2010] EWHC 3106 (Ch); [2011] B.P.I.R. 44.
[287] *Re Local London Residential Ltd (Liquidator's Costs)* [2004 EWHC 114 (Ch); 2004] 2 B.C.L.C. 72.
[288] *Gillan v Hec Enterprises Ltd* [2016] EWHC 3179 (Ch); [2017] 1 B.C.L.C. 340.
[289] *Re T&D Industries Plc* [2000] 1 W.L.R. 646; [2000] B.C.C. 956, *Re Transbus International Ltd (in Liquidation)* [2004] EWHC 932 (Ch); [2004] 1 W.L.R. 2654.
[290] *Re DKLL Solicitors* [2007] EWHC 2067 (Ch); [2007] 1 B.C.C. 908.

independent assessment of the transaction. The administrator should also ensure that an independent professional valuation has been obtained, or be prepared to explain why it was thought that none was necessary.

It should be noted that where a pre-pack sale has taken place, SIP 16 requires specific details relating to the pre-pack to be set out in a statement, which should be sent to creditors within seven days of the transaction and included in the administrator's statement of proposals.[291]

The moratorium. In order to enable the administration to achieve its purpose,[292] once a company goes into administration a moratorium applies to prevent steps from being taken against the company or its assets.[293] The moratorium on insolvency proceedings operates to prevent any winding up of the company, whether voluntarily or by the court, other than a winding-up petition presented by the Secretary of State on grounds of public interest,[294] by the Regulator (in relation to an SE) on just and equitable grounds,[295] or for the protection of the financial markets.[296] If such a petition is presented, the administrator must apply to court for directions.[297] Any winding up petition already presented against the company, other than one of the types already referred to, is either suspended (in the case of an out of court appointment) or dismissed (in the case of an appointment by court order).[298]

15-63

The moratorium on other legal process prevents the enforcement of security over the company's property,[299] the taking of any step to repossess goods in the company's possession under a hire-purchase agreement,[300] forfeiture of the company's premises by a landlord,[301] the institution of other legal process, including legal proceedings, execution or distress,[302] or the appointment of an administrative receiver.[303] Such steps may not be taken without the consent of the administrator or the permission of the court.

Lifting the moratorium. The administrator may give consent to any action which

15-64

---

[291] See para.15-21.

[292] *Re Atlantic Computer Systems Plc (No.2)* [1992] Ch. 505; [1990] B.C.C. 859.

[293] Insolvency Act 1986 Sch.B1 paras 42 and 43. Where an administration application is outstanding, or for a specified period after a notice of intention to appoint an administrator has been filed, para.44 creates an interim moratorium applying the provisions of paras 42 and 43.

[294] Insolvency Act 1986 Sch.B1 para.42(4)(a).

[295] Insolvency Act 1986 Sch.B1 para.42(4)(aa).

[296] Insolvency Act 1986 Sch.B1 para.42(4)(b).

[297] Insolvency Act 1986 Sch.B1 para.42(5).

[298] Insolvency Act 1986 Sch.B1 para.40.

[299] Insolvency Act 1986 Sch.B1 para.43(2). This will include exercising the right to stoppage in transit pursuant to s.44 of the Sale of Goods Act 1979, at least where this right is exercised as a necessary precursor to establishing a vendor's lien (see *Uniserve v Croxen* [2012] EWHC 1190 (Ch); [2013] B.C.C. 825.

[300] Insolvency Act 1986 Sch.B1 para.43(3). "Hire purchase agreement" is defined at para.111 of Sch.B1 as including a conditional sale agreement, a chattel leasing agreement and a retention of title agreement.

[301] Insolvency Act 1986 Sch.B1 para.43(4).

[302] Insolvency Act 1986 Sch.B1 para.43(6). A legal process includes criminal proceedings (see *Re Rhondda Waste Disposal Ltd* [2001] Ch. 57; [2000] B.C.C. 653) and involves something with a defined beginning and an ascertainable final outcome governed by a recognizable procedure, and can include regulatory procedures: see the discussion in *Re Frankice (Golders Green) Ltd* [2010] EWHC 1229 (Ch); [2010] Bus. L.R. 1608. An application to be joined as a defendant to proceedings commenced by the company is not caught by the moratorium: *Mortgage Debenture Ltd v Chapman* [2016] EWCA Civ 103; [2016] 1 W.L.R. 3048.

[303] Insolvency Act 1986 Sch.B1 para.43(7).

would otherwise be a breach of the moratorium on other legal process imposed by para.43 of Sch.B1 to the Act. There is no equivalent power in relation to the moratorium on insolvency proceedings imposed by para.42, as this would be inconsistent with the administration itself. Such consent may be given retrospectively, as may the permission of the court.[304]

The leading case on when the court will give permission to lift the moratorium remains *Re Atlantic Computer Systems Plc (No.2)*,[305] a case decided under the old regime. The court held that property "in the company's possession" included property which had been sublet by the company,[306] and it gave guidance for the approach of the court on permission applications made by lessors of land or goods, the key points of which are as follows[307]:

- It is for the person seeking permission to make out his case.
- If permission is unlikely to impede the achievement of the purpose of administration, then it should normally be given.
- In other cases the court will have to carry out a balancing exercise. Great weight is to be given to the proprietary interests of a lessor or secured creditor.
- It will normally be a sufficient ground for permission if significant loss would be caused to a lessor by refusal; but if significantly greater loss would be caused to others by grant of permission, that may outweigh the loss caused by a refusal. Various factors including the probability of the losses forecast and the conduct of the parties will often have to be taken into account.
- While para.43 does not give the court express power to refuse permission subject to conditions, it may do so by giving the administrator directions or by refusing permission conditional upon the administrator taking a certain step.[308]
- The guidance will also be relevant to cases where a secured creditor is seeking to enforce his security. There, an important consideration will often be whether the creditor is fully secured.

These principles are also relevant to the question of whether leave to commence legal proceedings should be given. There, in addition, it will be necessary for the applicant to establish that the court has jurisdiction to entertain the claim and that there is a seriously arguable case.[309]

Examples where the moratorium was lifted are: where a secured creditor wished to appoint receivers who would take steps to obtain planning permission over the

---

[304] *Re Colliers International UK Plc* [2012] EWHC 2942 (Ch); [2013] Ch. 422; *Fulton v AIB Group (UK) plc* [2014] NICh 8; [2014] B.P.I.R. 1169.

[305] [1992] Ch. 505; [1990] B.C.C. 859. This was approved in relation to the current regime in *Innovate Logistics Ltd v Sunberry Properties Ltd* [2008] EWCA Civ 1321; [2009] B.C.C. 164.

[306] [1992] Ch. 505 at 532.

[307] [1992] Ch. 505 at 542–544. The provisions of Insolvency Act 1986 Sch.B1 paras 70-72 will often be relevant as well: see para.15-70.

[308] The court gave the specific example of directing the administrator to pay current rent—a direction which now ought not to be necessary in normal circumstances following the decision in *Jervis v Pillar Denton Ltd* [2014] EWCA Civ 180; [2015] Ch. 87.

[309] *Re Polly Peck International plc (In administration) (No.2)* [1998] 3 All E.R. 812; [1998] 2 B.C.L.C. 185.

relevant property which the administrator was not in funds to pursue[310]; where solicitors wished to claim a charge on money recovered in litigation in which they had acted pre-administration[311]; where a landlord wished to commence forfeiture proceedings arising out of breach of a covenant not to assign and there would be no detriment to the administration[312]; where a creditor wished to advance a proprietary claim against a fund held by the company in administration[313]; where leave was sought to continue proceedings seeking injunctive relief and an account of profits where those proceedings had a proprietary basis and would not significantly impede the objective of the administration[314]; where a business tenant wished to continue its application for a new tenancy under the Landlord and Tenant Act 1954[315]; where a landlord wished to obtain specific performance of a pre-administration agreement to surrender a lease (together with payment our of a sum held in escrow)[316]; where a landlord wished to forfeit a lease and there was little real prospect that the administrators would be able to assign the lease at a premium to a tenant acceptable to the landlord[317]; and where the company held insurance which might cover the claim.[318]

By contrast, the moratorium was not lifted: where the claimant sought to challenge the validity of a patent which the administrators hoped to sell[319]; where the proceedings were a straight money claim and there would be no prejudice to the claimant for it to have its claim determined through the process of proof[320]; where a claimant under a retention of title agreement waited a year to seek the return of goods, by which time they had been sold to third parties[321]; or where a landlord wished to commence forfeiture proceedings arising out of breach of a covenant not to assign, but for it to do so might risk the recovery of substantial book debts.[322]

Protection of essential supplies. Where a company goes into administration and **15-65** the administrator requests (or concurs in a request) that essential supplies are continued after the commencement of the administration, the supplier may make it a condition of continuing to give the supply that the administrator personally guarantees payment in respect of that supply going forward,[323] but may not make

---

[310] *Re Rosshill Properties Ltd (in administration), Sinai Securities v Hooper* [2003] EWHC 910 Ch; [2004] 2 B.C.L.C. 575.

[311] *Hammonds v Thomas Muckle & Sons Ltd* [2006] B.P.I.R. 704.

[312] *Metro Nominees (Wandsworth) Ltd v Rayment* [2008] B.C.C. 40; *Lazari GP Ltd v Jervis* [2012] EWHC 1466 (Ch); [2013] B.C.C. 294.

[313] *Funding Corp Block Discounting Ltd v Lexi Holdings plc* [2008] EWHC 985 (Ch); [2008] 2 B.C.L.C. 596.

[314] *Magical Marking Ltd v Phillips* [2008] EWHC 1640 (Pat); [2008] F.S.R. 36.

[315] *Somerfield Stores Ltd v Spring (Sutton Coldfield) Ltd* [2009] EWHC 2348 (Ch); [2010] 2 B.C.L.C. 452.

[316] *Bristol Alliance Nominee No.1 Ltd v Bennett* [2013] EWCA Civ 1626; [2014] 1 E.G.L.R. 9.

[317] *Re SSRL Realisations Ltd* [2015] EWHC 2590 (Ch); [2016] 1 P.&C.R. 2

[318] *BAE Systems Pension Funds Trustees Ltd v Bowmer & Kirkland Ltd* [2017] EWHC 1200 (TCC), though permission was limited to service of the claim form in order to stop time running for the purposes of limitation.

[319] *Re Axis Genetics plc* [2000 B.C.C. 943; [2000] F.S.R. 448.

[320] *AES Barry Ltd v TXU Europe Energy Trading* [2004] EWHC 1757 (Ch); [2005] 2 B.C.L.C. 22.

[321] *Fashoff (UK) Ltd v Linton* [2008] EWHC 537 (Ch); [2008] B.C.C. 542.

[322] *Innovate Logistics Ltd v Sunberry Properties Ltd* [2008] EWCA Civ 1321; [2009] B.C.C. 164.

[323] Insolvency Act 1986 s.233(2)(a).

it a condition, or do anything to require, that outstanding charges for the period pre-administration are paid.[324]

In addition, any term of a contract for the supply of essential services whereby the contract terminates on or as a result of administration (either automatically or at the option of the supplier)[325] ceases to have effect once the company goes into administration.[326] Instead the supplier has the right[327] to terminate the contract with the consent of the administrator, the permission of the court, or if any supplies made after commencement of the administration are not paid within 28 days of becoming due[328]; and the right to terminate the supply if it gives written notice to the administrator that it requires him personally to guarantee payment of any charges in respect of the continuation of supply and that guarantee is not given within 14 days.[329]

Essential supplies are the supply of gas, electricity, water, communications services,[330] point of sale terminals, computer hardware and software, IT support services, data storage and processing, and website hosting.[331]

15-66   **Investigation of the company's affairs.**   As an office-holder[332] the administrator is entitled to take possession of any of the company's books and records which are held by a third party. If these are not delivered voluntarily, the court may order that they be provided to the administrator.[333]

It will frequently be the case that the administrator requires additional information which is not apparent from the face of the company's books and records in order to familiarise himself with the company's affairs. There is therefore an obligation on certain people to give the administrator such information about the company's business, dealings, affairs and property as he reasonably requires, and to attend a meeting with him at any time as be reasonably requires.[334] The people under this obligation are: the company's officers (past and present); those who were involved in its formation at any time within the year immediately preceding administration; its employees (including any former employees who were employed during the year immediately preceding administration); and any officers or employees (including any former officers or employees who held office or were employed during the year immediately preceding administration) of any company which is, or was within that year, an officer of the company in administration.[335] A failure to comply with this duty to co-operate is punishable by a fine.[336] However it is more usual for the obligation to be enforced by means of an application pursuant to s.236 of the Act.

---

[324] Insolvency Act 1986 s.233(2)(b).
[325] Insolvency Act 1986 s.233A(8).
[326] Insolvency Act 1986 s.233A(1). However, such a clause will still have effect to the extent that the termination event relied upon is an insolvency event other than administration or a voluntary arrangement, or the occurrence of a post-administration event: Insolvency Act 1986 s.233A(2).
[327] But only if the contract contains a clause which has ceased to have effect by reason of Insolvency Act 1986 s.233A(1): see s.233A(3).
[328] Insolvency Act 1986 s.233A(4).
[329] Insolvency Act 1986 s.233A(5).
[330] Insolvency Act 1986 s.233(3).
[331] Insolvency Act 1986 s.233(3A).
[332] Insolvency Act 1986 s.234(1).
[333] Insolvency Act 1986 s.234(2).
[334] Insolvency Act 1986 s.235(2).
[335] Insolvency Act 1986 s.235(3).
[336] Insolvency Act 1986 s.235(5).

This section gives the court the power to require any officer of the company, any person known or suspected to have property belonging to the company, and any other person it thinks is able to provide information as to the company's business, dealings, affairs or property,[337] to deliver up any books, papers or other records relating to the company or its business, dealings, affairs or property[338]; make a witness statement giving an account of his dealings with the company[339]; and attend court for oral examination.[340] If a person fails to attend court for examination when ordered to do so, he is liable to arrest.[341] However this is only if the order contains a penal notice and money has been tendered to cover reasonable travel expenses.[342]

The courts recognise that an order under s.236 of the Act is potentially oppressive to the person compelled to provide documents or information to the administrator. Any oppression must be balanced against the administrator's requirement for those documents or information[343]; and the administrator's requirements may go beyond simply reconstituting the knowledge of the company to the carrying out of his functions generally.[344] Where the administrator has made a firm decision to commence proceedings, an application for examination of the potential defendant will usually, though not always, be sufficiently oppressive to outweigh the administrator's interest in obtaining the information.[345] It is for the administrator to establish that he needs the information sought, and while his views will usually be given a good deal of weight[346] in anything but an obvious case it is not enough for him merely to assert that he needs the information without explaining why it is relevant or necessary.[347]

It is not a pre-requisite for obtaining an order for oral examination pursuant to s.236 that the person to be examined should first have been given the opportunity to co-operate, though it may be relevant to the exercise of discretion. It is relevant to the question of costs, however, since the court may only order that the administrator's costs of the examination be paid by the person being examined where that examination was necessarily because information was unjustifiably withheld.[348] Otherwise his costs of the examination must usually be paid as an expense of the administration.

Additional powers as an Office-Holder. As an office-holder the administrator **15-67** is also empowered to bring certain actions arising under the provisions of the Act.

---

[337] Insolvency Act 1986 s.236(2).
[338] Insolvency Act 1986 s.236(3).
[339] Insolvency Act 1986 s.236(3), (3A).
[340] Insolvency Act 1986 ss.236(2) and 237(4).
[341] Insolvency Act 1986 s.236(5).
[342] Insolvency Rules 2016 r.12.22(4).
[343] A useful discussion of the factors to be taken into account in carrying out this balancing exercise can be found in *Re British & Commonwealth Holdings plc (Nos.1&2)* [1992] Ch. 342 at 372; [1992] B.C.C. 172.
[344] *British & Commonwealth Holdings plc (Joint Administrators) v Spicer & Oppenheim*, Re British & Commonwealth Holdings plc (No.2) [1993] AC 426; [1992] B.C.C. 977. In *Re Pantmaenog Timber Co Ltd* [2003] UKHL 49; [2004] 1 A.C. 158 it was held that the relevant functions extend to the duty to prepare a report on the conduct of the directors of an insolvent company.
[345] *Cloverbay Ltd (Joint Administrators) v Bank of Credit and Commerce International SA (Re Cloverbay Ltd (No.2))* [1991] Ch 90; [1990] B.C.C. 414. A private examination was ordered even though proceedings had already been issued in *Shierson v Rastogi* [2002] EWCA Civ 1824; [2003] 1 W.L.R. 586.
[346] *Joint Liquidators of Sasea Finance Ltd v KPMG* [1998] B.C.C. 216; [1997] Lexis Citation 3701.
[347] *Re XL Communications Group plc* [2005] EWHC 2413 (Ch).
[348] Insolvency Rules 2016 r.12.22(1).

These actions are: to set aside a transaction at an undervalue[349]; to set aside a prefer-ence[350]; to set aside or vary an extortionate credit transaction[351]; to recover compensation for fraudulent[352] or wrongful trading[353]; to set aside a transaction defrauding creditors[354]; and in misfeasance against another administrator or former administrator.[355]

The administrator also has power to assign any of the above-mentioned claims.[356]

15-68 **Reporting to creditors.** The administrator must deliver a progress report to credi-tors in relation to each six month period of administration.[357] Each report must be delivered to creditors and to the registrar of companies within one month of the end of the period to which it relates.[358] In addition, where a person takes over the posi-tion of administrator, he must report to the creditors as soon as practicable about any matters he thinks they should be informed of.[359]

The required contents of a progress report are set out at r.18.3. In addition to information enabling the creditors to identify the proceedings and the office-holder, the report must contain details of the progress of the administration during the relevant period, together with a summary of receipts and payments.[360] It must also set out the basis fixed for remuneration (or the steps taken to fix a basis) together with details of the remuneration charged during the period of the report[361] (and additionally during preceding periods if it is the first report after the basis of remuneration has been fixed),[362] a statement of the expenses incurred during the period,[363] a statement setting out whether the expenses incurred are likely to exceed the estimate given to the creditors pursuant to r.18.16(4), together with the reasons for any excess,[364] and a statement of the creditors' rights to request further informa-tion about, or to challenge, the administrator's remuneration and expenses.[365]

In addition, where the administrator has included in the proposals a statement about pre-administration costs and expenses, the progress report must set out details of the amounts approved and the date of approval (if applicable),[366] and details of

---

[349] Insolvency Act 1986 s.238.
[350] Insolvency Act 1986 s.239.
[351] Insolvency Act 1986 s.244.
[352] Insolvency Act 1986 s.246ZA.
[353] Insolvency Act 1986 s.246ZB.
[354] Insolvency Act 1986 s.423.
[355] Insolvency Act 1986 Sch.B1 para.75. The provisions of s.212 which permit an office-holder to bring, in his own name, a misfeasance claim against directors and others do not apply to administrators. However that section does not give rise to any new cause of action, and there is no reason why an administrator could not cause the company to bring such a claim in its own name.
[356] Insolvency Act 1986 s.246ZD.
[357] Insolvency Rules 2016 r.18.6(1).
[358] Insolvency Rules 2016 r.18.6(4)
[359] Insolvency Rules 2016 r.18.6(3).
[360] Insolvency Rules 2016 r.18.3(1).
[361] Insolvency Rules 2016 r.18.4(1)(b)(i).
[362] Insolvency Rules 2016 r.18.4(1)(b)(ii).
[363] Insolvency Rules 2016 r.18.4(1)(d).
[364] Insolvency Rules 2016 r.18.4(1)(e); as to the estimate to be provided pursuant to r.18.16(4), see para.15–134.
[365] Insolvency Rules 2016 r.18.4(1)(f).
[366] Insolvency Rules 2016 r.18.5(1)(a).

any steps taken to obtain approval of any amounts not approved,[367] or a statement that the administrator will not seek approval for them.[368]

The administrator has to deliver a final progress report where the administration ends automatically,[369] it ends when its purposes have been achieved,[370] the court has made an order ending the administration,[371] the company moves from administration into creditors' voluntary liquidation,[372] or the company moves from administration to dissolution.[373] In addition to the standard terms to be included in a progress report, the final progress report must also include a summary of the proposals, any major amendments to or deviations from those proposals, the steps taken during the administration, and the outcome.[374]

Costs and expenses of administration. The costs and expenses of the administration are payable out of the company's property,[375] including any property subject to a floating (but not fixed) charge,[376] save that expenses associated with the prescribed part are payable out of the prescribed part.[377] They are payable in the order of priority set out at r.3.51(2).

15-69

Because expenses are payable in priority to all but fixed charge creditors' claims,[378] it will frequently be important to determine whether a particular claim is to be treated as a provable debt or an expense of the liquidation. Generally, where a liability arises as a result of an obligation entered into by the company before the commencement of administration, this will give rise to a provable debt and not an expense of the liquidation.[379] However, in the case of a statutory obligation, it is a matter of interpretation as to whether or not the obligation is to be treated as an expense of the administration.[380] Thus business rates are to be treated as an expense of the administration,[381] whereas the liability under the deemed contracts which arise pursuant to the Gas and Electricity Codes are not.[382]

Even where a claim is properly treated as a provable debt, it may be payable as an expense of the administration where and to the extent that it relates to property retained by the administrator for the purposes of the administration. Thus, rent is payable on the premises occupied by the company for the period of occupation for the purposes of the administration, irrespective of the precise dates on which the

---

[367] Insolvency Rules 2016 r.18.5(1)(b).
[368] Insolvency Rules 2016 r.18.5(2).
[369] Insolvency Rules 2016 r.3.55(2).
[370] Insolvency Rules 2016 r.3.56(4).
[371] Insolvency Rules 2016 r.3.59.
[372] Insolvency Rules 2016 r.3.60(3).
[373] Insolvency Rules 2016 r.3.61(4).
[374] Insolvency Rules 2016 r.3.53.
[375] Insolvency Act 1986 Sch.B1 para.99(3)(a). Property in the "custody or control" of the administrator means property which the administrator is entitled to take into his custody or control, and therefore extends to all of its property, subject to the effect of security given to creditors: see *Re MK Airlines Ltd* [2012] EWHC 1018 (Ch); [2014] B.C.C. 87.
[376] Insolvency Act 1986 Sch.B1 para.70, 99(3)(b).
[377] Insolvency Rules 2016 r.3.50(2).
[378] For the overall order of priority for payment out of the company's assets, see *Re Nortel GmbH, Bloom v Pensions Regulator* [2013] UKSC 52; [2014] A.C. 209 at [39].
[379] Insolvency Rules 2016 r.14.1(3)(b).
[380] *Re Nortel GmbH, Bloom v Pensions Regulator* [2014] A.C. 209 at [103].
[381] *Exeter City Council v Bairstow* [2007] EWHC 400 (Ch); [2007] B.C.C. 236.
[382] *Laverty v British Gas Trading Ltd* [2014] EWHC 2721 (Ch); [2014] B.C.C. 701.

liability to pay rent arises and the precise period to which that liability relates.[383] Similarly, the cost of gas and electricity supplies made under deemed contracts will be payable as an expense to the extent that the supplies were actually made for the benefit of the administration.[384]

II: Dealing with Property Subject to Security

15-70 **Property subject to a floating charge.**   Where property is subject to a floating charge, the administrator may dispose of it, or take action relating to it, as if it were not subject to the charge.[385] But the holder of the floating charge must have the same priority in respect of the proceeds of sale, or any property acquired by the administrator with those proceeds (whether directly or indirectly),[386] as he had with respect to the property disposed of.[387] For the purposes of this provision, as elsewhere in the Act, a charge is treated as a floating charge if it was created as a floating charge.[388] The question of whether, or when, a floating charge crystallised is therefore irrelevant for the purposes of the administrator's power to sell property.

15-71 **Property charged otherwise than by a floating charge.**   Where the property of the company includes property which is subject to a security other than the floating charge, the administrator is not free to dispose of it. However, if the administrator cannot obtain the consent of the secured creditor to a sale, the court may make an order enabling the administrator to dispose of it, as if it were not subject to the security.[389] Only the administrator is permitted to apply for such an order, and the court may only make the order if it thinks that the disposal of the property would be likely to promote the purpose of administration in respect of the company.[390] In addition, the court is obliged to make it a condition of any such order that the administrator must pay the secured creditor the net proceeds of disposal of the property, together with any additional sums required to bring the sale price up to market value.[391] The net proceeds of sale of the property payable to the secured creditor are the proceeds of sale after deduction of expenses including the administrator's own remuneration and expenses incurred in connection with the sale.[392]

On an application under para.71 of Sch.B1, the court must balance the prejudice to the secured creditor if the order is made against the prejudice to those interested in the promotion of the purposes of the administration if the order is not made.[393] The administrator must demonstrate in evidence that the terms of the disposal and

[383] *Jervis v Pillar Denton* [2014] EWCA Civ 180; [2015] Ch. 87.
[384] *Laverty v British Gas Trading Ltd* [2014] B.C.C. 701 at [63].
[385] Insolvency Act 1986 Sch.B1 para.70(1).
[386] Insolvency Act 1986 Sch.B1 para.70(3).
[387] Insolvency Act 1986 Sch.B1 para.70(2).
[388] Insolvency Act 1986 s.251.
[389] Insolvency Act 1986 Sch.B1 para.71(1).
[390] Insolvency Act 1986 Sch.B1 para.71(2).
[391] Insolvency Act 1986 Sch.B1 para.71(3). "Market Value" is defined at Insolvency Act 1986 Sch.B1 para.111(1) as the amount which would be realized on a sale of the property in the open market by a willing vendor. It is not necessary for this to be determined before an order permitting disposal is made (see *Re ARV Aviation Ltd* (1998) 4 B.C.C. 708). However the court must take proper steps to assess the value and not simply split the difference in any dispute (see *Stanley J Holmes & Sons Ltd v Davenham Trust Plc* [2006] EWCA Civ 1568; [2007] B.C.C. 485).
[392] *Townsend v Biscoe* [2010] WL 3166608.
[393] *Re ARV Aviation Ltd* (1998) 4 B.C.C. 708; [1989] B.C.L.C. 664, applied by the Court of Appeal to

the distribution of the proceeds will properly protect the secured creditors,[394] although it is not necessary for the market value of the property to be determined before an order is made.[395] If the administrator makes an application and fails, then he will normally ordered to pay the costs.[396] Where he acts unreasonably in making the application, he may be ordered to pay those costs personally.[397]

Where there is more than one security involved, monies shall be applied in the order of their respective priorities.[398]

The fact that an order has been made under this paragraph does not preclude a member or creditor from applying to court pursuant to para.74 of Sch.B1 on the ground that the administrator has or is proposing to act in such a way as is unfairly prejudicial to one or more members or creditors.[399]

Property subject to hire-purchase and other proprietorial agreements. Where 15-72 the property (including goods) of the company includes property subject to hire-purchase agreements, conditional sale agreements, chattel-leasing agreements or retention of title agreements,[400] the court may make an order enabling the administrator to dispose of it or them, as if all the rights of the owner under the agreement were vested in the company.[401] As with an order made in respect of charged property,[402] only the administrator is permitted to apply for such an order, and the court may only make the order if it thinks that the disposal of the property would be likely to promote the purpose of administration in respect of the company.[403] In addition, the court is obliged to make it a condition of any such order that the administrator must pay the secured creditor the net proceeds of disposal of the property,[404] together with any additional sums required to bring the sale price up to market value.[405] An application may only be made in respect of property which remains in the possession of the company.[406]

The fact that an order has been made under this paragraph does not preclude a

---

the current regime in *Rollings v O'Connell* [2014] EWCA Civ 639; [2014] All E.R. (D) 201 (May).

[394] *Re Capitol Films Ltd (in administration); Rubin v Cobalt Pictures Ltd* [2010] EWHC 3223 (Ch); [2011] 2 B.C.L.C. 359.

[395] *Re ARV Aviation Ltd* (1998) 4 B.C.C. 708. However the court must take proper steps to assess the value and not simply split the difference in any dispute: *Stanley J Holmes & Sons Ltd v Davenham Trust Plc* [2006] EWCA Civ 1568; [2007] B.C.C. 485.

[396] *Re Capitol Films Ltd (in administration); Rubin v Cobalt Pictures Ltd* [2010] EWHC 3223 (Ch) at [84]–[85].

[397] *Re Capitol Films Ltd (in administration); Rubin v Cobalt Pictures Ltd* [2010] EWHC 3223 (Ch) at [102].

[398] Insolvency Act 1986 Sch.B1 para.71(4).

[399] Insolvency Act 1986 Sch.B1 para.74(5)(b). As to such applications, see para.17-18.

[400] Insolvency Act 1986 Sch.B1 para.111.

[401] Insolvency Act 1986 Sch.B1 para.72(1).

[402] See para.15-71.

[403] Insolvency Act 1986 Sch.B1 para.72(2).

[404] In relation to an application under para.71 of Sch.B1 it has been held that "net proceeds of disposal" means the proceeds after the administrator's remuneration and expenses connected with the sale (*Townsend v Biscoe* [2010] WL 3166608). There is no equivalent authority in relation to relation to para.72, but there seems to be little reason why the same principle should not apply.

[405] Insolvency Act 1986 Sch.B1 para.71(3). "Market Value" is defined at Insolvency Act 1986 Sch.B1 para.111(1) as the amount which would be realized on a sale of the property in the open market by a willing vendor. It is not necessary for this to be determined before an order permitting disposal is made (see *Re ARV Aviation Ltd* (1998) 4 B.C.C. 708). However the court must take proper steps to assess the value and not simply split the difference in any dispute (see *Stanley J Holmes & Sons Ltd v Davenham Trust Plc* [2006] EWCA Civ 1568; [2007] B.C.C. 485).

[406] *Re Business Environment Fleet Street Ltd* [2014] EWHC 3540 (Ch); [2015] 1 W.L.R. 1167.

member or creditor from applying to court pursuant to para.74 of Sch.B1 on the ground that the administrator has or is proposing to act in such a way as is unfairly prejudicial to one or more members or creditors.[407]

15-73 **Procedure on application for permission to dispose.** Where an administrator applies to the court for permission to deal with property charged otherwise than by a floating charge, or the subject of a hire-purchase or analogous agreement, the court will endorse the application notice with a date, time and a venue for the hearing.[408] The administrator must, as soon as reasonably practicable, give notice to the holder of the security or (as the case may be) the owner of the property under the agreement.[409] Since the chargeholder or owner is the party interested in the application[410] it is advisable in any event to make them the Respondents, even though the Rules do not expressly require this.

15-74 **Reporting the making of the order for realisation.** Where the court makes such an order, it must send two sealed copies of the order to the administrator,[411] who must send a copy to the registrar of companies within 14 days of the making of the order[412] and also send a copy to the security holder or owner of the property.[413]

Failure by the administrator to send a copy to the registrar of companies constitutes an offence; but this is not expressed to be applicable to his failure to send a copy to the security holder or owner of the property in question.[414]

15-75 **Property subject to a lien or other possessory security.** Where property belonging to the company is subject to a lien or other possessory security, there is necessarily a different procedural approach, because the dispute between the administrator and creditor does not arise at the point where the administrator wishes to sell the property, but at the prior point at which he wishes to get in and take control of the property pursuant to s.234 of the Act. The creditor will likewise usually seek to safeguard his possessory security by means of an application pursuant to para.43(2)(b) of Sch.B1 of the Act.

Despite this difference in procedure, the court will take a similar approach to dealing with the dispute. It will generally not make an order for the delivery up of property subject to a possessory security unless it is satisfied that the secured creditor's rights are fully protected. This may extend to taking account of potential claims against the lien-holder by third parties for wrongful interference with their security interests.[415]

15-76 **Unenforceable securities.** Certain securities will not be enforceable against the administrator, so that they may be disregarded when dealing with any property which would otherwise be subject to them. Broadly speaking, there are three classes of such security: securities which have not been registered in accordance with the

---

[407] Insolvency Act 1986 Sch.B1 para.74(5)(b). As to such applications, see para.17-18.
[408] Insolvency Rules 2016 r.3.49(2).
[409] Insolvency Rules 2016 r.3.49(3).
[410] *Re Capitol Films Ltd (in administration); Rubin v Cobalt Pictures Ltd* [2010] EWHC 3223 (Ch); [2011] 2 B.C.L.C. 359 at [85].
[411] Insolvency Rules 2016 r.3.49(4).
[412] Insolvency Act 1986 Sch.B1 paras 71(4) and 72(4); Insolvency Rules 2016 r.3.49(5)(b).
[413] Insolvency Rules 2016 r.3.49(5)(a).
[414] Insolvency Act 1986 Sch.B1 paras 71(6) and 72(5).
[415] *Uniserve v Croxon* [2012] EWHC 1190 (Ch); [2013] B.C.C. 825.

provisions of the Companies Act 2006; certain floating charges created shortly before administration; and liens over the company's books and records.

The first class consists of securities which have not been registered pursuant to s.859A of the Companies Act 2006 within 21 days of their creation. All charges need to be registered, other than:

- a charge in favour of a landlord in relation to a cash deposit provided by way of security in connection with the lease of the land[416];
- a charge created by a member of Lloyds to secure its obligations[417];
- a security interest which arises by operation of law[418];
- security financial collateral arrangements within the meaning of reg.3 of the Financial Collateral Arrangements (No.2) Regulations 2003[419];
- security granted in favour of the Bank of England or other central bank[420]; and
- pledges and other possessory securities.[421]

By s.859H(3)(b) of the Companies Act 2006, such a security is void as against the administrator unless it has been registered within 21 days of creation or such longer time as the court may order.[422]

The second class consists of floating charges which were created within a "relevant time", the calculation of which depends on the status of the chargeholder. In the case of persons connected with the company, the charge is created at a relevant time if it is created within two years of the onset of insolvency[423]; otherwise the period is one year.[424] For persons unconnected with the company, there is the additional requirement that the company should have been insolvent at the time of the creation of the charge, or as a result of the transaction under which the charge is created,[425] unless the charge was created between the making of an administration application and the making of an administration order,[426] or between filing a notice of intention to appoint and appointment.[427]

In such a case, the floating charge is not necessarily invalid. Instead it is valid, but only to the extent that it secures money paid, or the value of goods or services supplied, at the same time as or after the creation of the charge[428]; the extent to

---

[416] Companies Act 2006 s.895A(6)(a).

[417] Companies Act 2006 s.895A(6)(b).

[418] *London and Cheshire Insurance Co Ltd v Laplagrene Property Co. Ltd* [1971] Ch.499; [1971] 1 All E.R. 766.

[419] SI 2003/3226.

[420] Banking Act 2009, s.252.

[421] Companies Act 2006 s.895A(7).

[422] Such an order may be made under Companies Act 2006 s.895F(3), but only if the failure to register the charge in time was accidental, if it is unlikely to prejudice the shareholders and creditors of the company, or if it is just and equitable to make the order on other grounds.

[423] Insolvency Act 1986 s.245(3)(a). The onset of insolvency is the date on which the administration application was made, the date on which the notice of intention to appoint was filed, or (where neither applies) the date of appointment.

[424] Insolvency Act 1986 s.245(3)(b).

[425] Insolvency Act 1986 s.245(4).

[426] Insolvency Act 1986 s.245(3)(c).

[427] Insolvency Act 1986 s.245(3)(d).

[428] Insolvency Act 1986 s.245(2)(a).

which the consideration for the charge was the reduction in a pre-existing liability of the company[429]; and interest.[430]

The third class consists of liens on the books, papers, or other records of the company: no such lien may be asserted so as to deny those books, papers and other records to the administrator.[431] Liens on title documents will, however, remain enforceable.[432]

15-77 **Potential liability in conversion.** An administrator will not be liable in conversion for merely retaining a third party's goods, unless and until he carries out a positive act of withholding those goods from the true owner.[433] Typically, this will be either a refusal to deliver them up when requested to do so, or a disposal of those goods. The administrator has a statutory defence to any claim in conversion where he disposes of property belonging to a third party and believes on reasonable grounds that he is entitled to do so.[434] However, that defence does not extend to any loss which is caused by the administrator's negligence. Where the administrator is notified of retention of title claims, and does not make an application pursuant to para.72 of Sch.B1, then he will be liable in conversion if those claims are subsequently made out.[435]

III: Directions and Court Control of the Administration

15-78 **General.** The administrator is expressly empowered to apply to court for directions.[436] A creditor or member is also expressly empowered to apply for an order controlling the administrator's conduct where the administrator is proposing to act, or is acting, in such a way as to unfairly harm that creditor' or member's interests,[437] or where the administrator is not acting as quickly or efficiently as is reasonably practicable.[438] In addition, while the Act does not expressly give creditors a general power to apply to court in order to control the administrator's actions, it has been held that the administrator is subject to the court's direction as its officer,[439] and that a creditor has standing to apply to court to exercise this jurisdiction.[440]

15-79 **Administrators' applications for directions.** The administrator is generally required to decide for himself questions of business, management and administra-

---

[429] Insolvency Act 1986 s.245(2)(b).
[430] Insolvency Act 1986 s.245(2)(c).
[431] Insolvency Act 1986 s.246(2).
[432] Insolvency Act 1986 s.246(3).
[433] *Barclays Mercantile Business Finance Ltd v Sibec Developments Ltd* [1992] 1 W.L.R. 1253; [1993] B.C.C. 148.
[434] Insolvency Act 1986 s.234(3). See *Euromex Ventures Ltd v BNP Paribas Real Estate Advisory and Property Management UK Ltd* [2013] EWHC 3007 (Ch); [2013] All E.R. (D) 106 (Oct) for an example where the office-holders were held to have acted reasonably in circumstances where the alleged owner had represented to them, on taking office, that the assets belonged to the company.
[435] *Hachette UK Ltd v Borders (UK) Ltd* [2009] EWHC 3487 (Ch).
[436] Insolvency Act 1986 Sch.B1 para.63.
[437] Insolvency Act 1986 Sch.B1 para.74(1). This provision also allows a creditor to seek redress after the event, a matter dealt with at para.17-18.
[438] Insolvency Act 1986 Sch.B1 para.74(2).
[439] *Re Atlantic Computer Systems Plc (No.2)* [1992] Ch. 505; [1990] B.C.C. 859.
[440] *Re Mirror Group (Holdings) Ltd* [1992] B.C.C. 972; [1993] B.C.L.C. 538.

tion, rather than seeking the court's direction or rubber-stamping.[441] If an administrator proposes to take a particularly momentous step, the court may give him directions to do so, but in giving those directions the court is limited to determining that the administrator's proposed course of action is both rational and a decision honestly reached.[442]

The court will give directions to assist the administrator in carrying out his functions in other jurisdictions, such as by setting out the extent of an English administrator's powers,[443] or by permitting distributions to be made to overseas creditors in accordance with their entitlements under local law rather than English insolvency law.[444] The court's power to give directions is constrained by para.68(3) of Sch.B1 to the Act,[445] and the court's inherent jurisdiction over the administrator as its officer cannot be utilised to extend his powers.[446] However, examples of actions which the court has sanctioned are the application of a cut-off date for submission of expenses claims,[447] and the carrying out of a scheme for making a distribution to members, which involved appointing a director who would in turn reduce the company's capital.[448]

Where the company holds trust property, the court has an inherent jurisdiction to give directions to the administrator as to the administration and distribution of the trust property.[449] The court does not have jurisdiction to vary the trust, but it does have jurisdiction to give the administrator directions as to the assumed factual basis on which the trust property is to be distributed.[450]

Applications by creditors and members. If the administrator is proposing to act, **15-80** is acting or has acted in a way which is unfairly prejudicial to any member or creditor[451] then that member or creditor may apply for an order controlling the administrator's conduct. On such an application the court may make any order it thinks fit.[452] The member or creditor must show both harm and that the harm is unfair.[453] However, it is not enough merely to show unequal or differential treatment: it must be shown that the unequal treatment which is not justified by sound commercial reasons relating to the purpose of the administration.[454] Further the complaint must relate to the member or creditor's interests qua member or credi-

---

[441] *Re T&D Industries Plc* [2000] 1 W.L.R. 646; [2000] B.C.C. 956, *RAB Capital Plc v Lehman Brothers International (Europe)* [2008] EWHC 2335 (Ch); [2008] B.C.C. 915, *Re MF Global UK Ltd* [2014] EWHC 2222 (Ch); [2014] Bus L.R. 1156.
[442] *Re Nortel Networks UK Ltd* [2014] EWHC 2614 (Ch) at [37].
[443] *Re MG Rover Espana SA & Ors* [2006] EWHC 3426 (Ch); [2006] B.C.C. 599.
[444] *Re MG Rover Espana SA & Ors* [2006] B.C.C. 599, *Re Collins & Aikman Europe SA* [2006] EWHC 1343 (Ch): [2006] B.C.C. 861.
[445] The court may only give directions consistent with any proposals which have been approved, unless none have been approved, the directions are required because of a change of circumstance since approval, or the directions are required because of a misunderstanding in relation to the proposals.
[446] *Re Lune Metal Products Ltd* [2006] EWCA Civ 1720; [2007] B.C.C. 217.
[447] *Re Nortel Networks UK Ltd* [2017] EWHC 1429; [2017] B.C.C. 325.
[448] *Re Lehman Brothers Europe Ltd* [2017] EWHC 2031 (Ch).
[449] *Re MF Global UK Ltd (No.3)* [2013] EWHC 1655 (Ch); [2013] 1 W.L.R. 3874 at [25].
[450] *Re MF Global UK Ltd (No.3)* [2013] 1 W.L.R. 3874 at [26], citing *Re Benjamin* [1902] 1 Ch. 723.
[451] Insolvency Act 1986 Sch.B1 para.74(1).
[452] Insolvency Act 1986 Sch.B1 para.74(3).
[453] *Re Lehman Brothers International (Europe); Four Private Funds v Lomas* [2008] EWHC 2869 (Ch); [2009] B.C.C. 632.
[454] *BLV Realty Organization Limited v Batten* [2009] EWHC 2994 (Ch); [2010] B.P.I.R. 277 at [22].

tor and not, for instance qua contracting party with the company.[455] On the other hand, unfairness does not necessarily involve differential treatment: where it can be shown that harm is caused by actions which are not commercially justified that may be unfair to all the creditors.[456]

A member or creditor may also apply to court for an order controlling the administrator's actions where he is not carrying out his functions as quickly or as efficiently as is reasonably practicable.[457]

The court also has an inherent jurisdiction over an administrator as officer of the court,[458] and a creditor[459] or member has standing to make an application pursuant to this inherent jurisdiction. However, if there is no unfairly harmful conduct within the scope of para.74 of Sch.B1 to the Act, the court will not interfere with the conduct of an office-holder unless the act complained of is either undertaken in bad faith or for a fraudulent purpose, or is an act which is "so utterly unreasonable and absurd that no reasonable man would have done it."[460]

15-81   **The rule in Ex parte James.**[461]   An additional ground for control of the administrator is the rule in *Ex parte James*. This is a principle that, where it would be unfair for an office-holder to take advantage of his legal rights as such, the court will order him not to do so.[462] It should be noted that this principle does not affect the scope or nature of the administrator's powers, but rather the way in which those powers should be exercised.[463]

SECTION 5: THE CREDITORS' COMMITTEE

15-82   **Establishment and functions of the Committee.**   The creditors may, if they think fit, establish a creditors' committee to exercise the functions conferred on it by the statutes and the rules.[464]

Where the administrator's proposals do not contain a statement made pursuant to para.52(1) of Sch.B1 to the Act, at the same time as he sends out the notice to approve the proposals the administrator must also send out a notice inviting the

---

[455] *BLV Realty Organization Limited v Batten* [2010] B.P.I.R. 277 at [24].
[456] *Re London & Westcountry Estates Ltd* [2014] EWHC 763 (Ch); [2014] Bus. L.R. 441, but compare *Re Coniston Hotel (Kent) LLP* [2013] EWHC 93 (Ch); [2015] B.C.C. 1.
[457] Insolvency Act 1986 Sch.B1 para.74(2).
[458] *Re Atlantic Computer Systems Plc (No.2)* [1992] Ch. 505; [1990] B.C.C. 859.
[459] *Re Mirror Group (Holdings) Ltd* [1992] B.C.C. 972; [1993] B.C.L.C. 538.
[460] *Re Edennote Ltd* [1996] B.C.C. 718; [1996] 2 B.C.L.C. 389, *Re Trident Fashions Plc (No.2)* [2004] EWHC 293 (Ch); [2004] 2 B.C.L.C. 35 at [39].
[461] *Re Condon, Ex p. James* (1873–74) L.R. 9 Ch. App. 609.
[462] The rule was summarised by Lord Neuberger PSC in *Re Nortel GmbH* [2013] UKSC 52; [2014] A.C. 209 at [122]. The rule was applied in *Re Lehman Brothers International Europe; Lomas v Burlington Loan Management Ltd* [2015] EWHC 2270 (Ch); [2015] B.P.I.R. 1162, where administrators were directed that they could not rely on waivers of statutory interest and non-provable claims contained in agreements agreeing the value of creditors' claims where the construction was unclear and none of the parties had considered the issue at the time the agreements were made. For examples where the rule was not applied, see *Expandable Ltd v Rubin* [2007] EWHC 2463 (Ch); [2009] B.C.C. 443 (disclosure of privileged documents refused); and *Re London Scottish Finance Ltd* [2013] EWHC 4047 (Ch); [2014] Bus. L.R. 424 (no obligation to repay money paid in discharge of consumer credit agreements which were unenforceable without leave of the court).
[463] *Re Lune Metal Products Ltd* [2006] EWCA Civ 1720; [2007] B.C.C. 217 at [35].
[464] Insolvency Act 1986 Sch.B1 para.57(1), (2); Insolvency Rules 2016 r.17.2.

creditors to decide whether a creditors' committee should be established.[465] The notice must also invite nominations for membership of the committee, specify a date by which those nominations must be received,[466] and state that nominations can only be accepted where the administrator is satisfied as to the nominee's eligibility.[467]

Whenever the administrator seeks a decision from creditors when there is no creditor's committee, he must send out a similar notice.[468] There is also no reason why creditors cannot requisition a decision for the purpose of establishing a committee if none is already established.

Nobody may be elected a member of the committee without his prior consent.[469] If the decision is made at a meeting that consent may be given at the meeting by a proxy-holder, unless the proxy expressly negatives this.[470] If the creditors decide that a committee should be established at a meeting of which the administrator is not the chair, the chair must deliver a notice of the decision to the administrator of this as soon as reasonably practicable, and, if applicable, inform him of the names and addresses of the persons elected to be members. If the creditors decide to establish a committee but do not decide on its composition at the same time, the administrator must then seek a further decision from them on this point.[471]

The general functions of such a committee are to assist the administrator in discharging his functions, and to act in relation to him in such manner as may be agreed from time to time.[472] The more specific functions are to apply for a replacement administrator where there is a vacancy and the administration was commenced by court order[473]; and to determine the time of the administrator's discharge from liability.[474]

Constitution of the Committee. The committee must consist of at least three, and **15-83** not more than five, creditors of the company, elected at the creditors' meeting.[475] Any creditor of the company is eligible to be a member of the committee, so long as he has proved for a debt[476] which is not fully secured,[477] and his proof has not been wholly disallowed for voting purposes or disallowed for the purpose of a distribution,[478] and he is not personally disqualified from membership.[479] A body corporate may be a member, but it must act through a representative[480]: see para.15-71.

The acts of the Committee, established for any administration, are valid,

[465] Insolvency Rules 2016 rr.3.38(1) and 3.39(1).
[466] Insolvency Rules 2016 r.3.39(2) and (3)(a).
[467] Insolvency Rules 2016 r.3.39(3)(b).
[468] Insolvency Rules 2016 r.3.39(4). This ensures that the invitation to form a creditor's committee is also sent out where a decision on the proposals is requisitioned pursuant to para.52(2).
[469] Insolvency Rules 2016 r.17.5(2).
[470] Insolvency Rules 2016 r.17.5(3).
[471] Insolvency Rules 2016 r.17.5(4).
[472] Insolvency Act 1986 Sch.B1 para.57(3); Insolvency Rules 1986 r.2.52(1).
[473] Insolvency Act 1986 Sch.B1 para.91(1)(a).
[474] Insolvency Act 1986 Sch.B1 para.98(2)(b): where the administrator was appointed by a floating charge holder or by the company and did not make a statement pursuant to para.52(1)(b) in the proposals.
[475] Insolvency Rules 2016 r.17.3(1).
[476] Insolvency Rules 2016 r.17.4(2)(a).
[477] Insolvency Rules 2016 r.17.4(2)(b).
[478] Insolvency Rules 2016 r.17.4(2)(c).
[479] By Insolvency Rules 2016 r.17.11, no member may be an undischarged bankrupt (though a bankrupt's trustee may be a member), or a person subject to a moratorium under a debt relief order.
[480] Insolvency Rules 2016 r.17.4(4).

notwithstanding any defect in the appointment, election or qualifications of any member, or of any committee member's representative or in the formalities of its establishment.[481]

15-84   **Formalities of establishment.**   The creditors' committee does not come into being, and accordingly cannot act, until the administrator has delivered a notice of its membership[482] to the registrar of companies.[483] The notice cannot be issued unless and until at least three of the persons who are to be members of it have agreed to act, and must contain a statement that the committee has been duly constituted, the identification details for any corporate member, and the name and address of any individual member.[484] It must be dated and authenticated by the administrator.[485]

As and when there is any change in the membership of the committee, the administrator must report the change to the registrar of companies as soon as reasonably practicable by delivering a notice[486] containing the dates of the original notice of constitution of the committee and of the latest such notice, a statement that the notice replaces the previous one, and the same identification details for the members of the current committee.[487] Unlike the first establishment of the committee, the change in membership will take effect before the notice is delivered.

15-85   **Meetings of the committee.**   Subject as follows, meetings of the committee are to be held when and where determined by the administrator.[488] The administrator must call a first meeting of the committee within six weeks after its first establishment.[489] Thereafter he must call a meeting if so requested by a member of the committee or his representative; such a meeting is to be held within 21 days of the request being received by the administrator.[490] He must also call a meeting for a specified date, if the committee has previously resolved that a meeting be held on that date.[491]

The administrator must give five business days' written notice of the venue (i.e. state, place and time) of any meeting to every member of the committee (or his representative designated for that purpose), unless in any case the requirement of notice has been waived by or on behalf of any member[492]; such waiver may be signified either at or before the meeting.[493] Where he thinks it appropriate the administrator may also arrange for remote attendance at the meeting,[494] and in that case his obligation to specify a venue is satisfied by specifying the arrangements for remote

---

[481]   Insolvency Rules 2016 r.17.27. For those formalities, see para.15–84. This provision does not prevent the court from enquiring as to the qualifications of the members of the committee in an appropriate case: *Re W&A Glaser Ltd* [1994] B.C.C. 199.
[482]   Insolvency Rules 2016 r.17.5(5).
[483]   Insolvency Rules 2016 r.17.5(9).
[484]   Insolvency Rules 2016 r.17.5(6).
[485]   Insolvency Rules 2016 r.17.5(7).
[486]   Insolvency Rules 2016 r.17.7(4).
[487]   Insolvency Rules 2016 r.17.7(2).
[488]   Insolvency Rules 2016 r.17.14(1).
[489]   Insolvency Rules 2016 r.17.14(2).
[490]   Insolvency Rules 2016 r.17.14(3)(a).
[491]   Insolvency Rules 2016 r.17.14(3)(b).
[492]   Insolvency Rules 2016 r.17.4(4).
[493]   Insolvency Rules 2016 r.17.4(5).
[494]   Insolvency Rules 2016 r.17.20.

attendance,[495] unless requested to specify a venue by a member of the committee within three business days of delivering the notice of the meeting.[496]

The chairman must be the administrator or a person nominated by the administrator,[497] who must himself be qualified to act as an insolvency practitioner in relation to the company, or a person experienced in insolvency matters who is a member or employee of the administrator's firm or an employee of the administrator.[498]

A meeting of the committee is quorate if due notice of it has been given to all the members, and at least two members are present or represented.[499]

Committee-members' representatives. A member of the committee may (and, **15-86** if it is a company, must),[500] in relation to the business of the committee, be represented by another person duly authorised by him for that purpose.[501] A person acting as a committee-member's representative must hold a letter of authority entitling him so to act (either generally or specially), and authenticated by or on behalf of the committee-member.[502] For this purpose, any proxy or any instrument conferring authority will, unless it contains a statement to the contrary, be treated as a letter of authority to act generally.[503] The chairman at any meeting of the committee may call on a person claiming to act as a committee-member's representative to produce his letter of authority, and may exclude him, if it is not produced or it appears that the authority is deficient.[504] No member may be represented by another committee member or their representative, a body corporate, a person who is an undischarged bankrupt, a person whose estate has been sequestrated and who has not been discharged, a person subject to a moratorium under a debt relief order, a person disqualified from acting as a company director, or a person who is subject to a bankruptcy or debt relief restrictions order (including interim order) or undertaking.[505] Where a member's representative signs any document on the member's behalf, the fact that he so signs must be stated below his signature.[506]

Committee's power to require information or attendance at meetings. The **15-87** Committee, on giving the administrator not less than seven days' notice, may require him to attend before it at any reasonable time, and to provide it with such information relating to the carrying out of his functions as it may reasonably require.[507] The notice to the administrator to attend must be accompanied by a copy of the resolution to require his attendance, and authenticated by a member of the committee[508] or his representative.[509] The date of the meeting is to be fixed by the committee for a business day, but the time and place is to be determined by the

---

495 Insolvency Rules 2016 r.17.20(6).
496 Insolvency Rules 2016 rr.17.20(8) and 17.21.
497 Insolvency Rules 2016 r.17.15.
498 Insolvency Rules 2016 r.1.2(3).
499 Insolvency Rules 2016 r.17.16.
500 Insolvency Rules 2016 r.17.4(4).
501 Insolvency Rules 2016 r.17.17(1).
502 Insolvency Rules 2016 r.17.17(2).
503 Insolvency Rules 2016 r.17.17(3).
504 Insolvency Rules 2016 r.17.17(4).
505 Insolvency Rules 2016 r.17.17(5).
506 Insolvency Rules 2016 r.17.17(6).
507 Insolvency Act 1986 Sch.B1 para.57(3).
508 Insolvency Rules 2016 r.17.22(2).
509 Insolvency Rules 2016 r.17.22(3).

administrator.[510] Where the administrator attends, the members of the committee may elect one of their number to be chairman, in place of the administrator or his nominee.[511]

15-88 **Resignation and Termination of membership.** A member of the committee may resign by notice in writing delivered to the administrator.[512]

Membership of the creditors' committee is automatically terminated, if the member becomes bankrupt, becomes the subject of a moratorium period under a debt relief order, is neither present nor represented at three consecutive meetings of the committee, (unless, at the third of those meetings, it is resolved that this provision is not to apply in his case), ceases to be a creditor other than for a fully secured debt, or has his proof wholly disallowed for voting purposes or rejected for the purposes of a distribution, or ceases to be, or is found never to have been, a creditor.[513] However, if the cause of termination is the member's bankruptcy, his trustee in bankruptcy will replace him as a member of the committee.[514] It follows that a representative must automatically cease to represent a member who becomes bankrupt. The same should not apply in the case of a company which goes into insolvency liquidation; in that case, unlike the case in bankruptcy, the company continues to be the creditor so the identity of the committee member does not change.

A member of the committee may be removed by a decision of the creditors on at least 14 days' notice.[515]

15-89 **Vacancies.** If there is a vacancy in the membership of the creditors' committee, it need not be filled, if the administrator and a majority of the remaining members of the committee so agree, provided that the total number of members does not fall below three.[516] The administrator may appoint any creditor (provided he is duly qualified to be a member of the committee) either to fill the vacancy or as an additional member, if a majority of the other members[517] of the committee agree to the appointment, and the creditor concerned consents to act.[518] If, out of a committee of five members, one ceases to be a member, the resultant committee of four members could produce stalemates; the administrator has no vote, or casting vote.

15-90 **Procedure at meetings of the Committee.** At any meeting, each member (whether present himself, or by his representative) has one vote,[519] and a resolution is passed when a majority of the members present or represented have voted in favour of it.[520] Every resolution passed must be recorded in writing, either

---

[510] Insolvency Rules 2016 r.17.22(4).
[511] Insolvency Rules 2016 r.17.22(5).
[512] Insolvency Rules 2016 r.17.10.
[513] Insolvency Rules 2016 r.17.11.
[514] Insolvency Rules 2016 r.17.11(a).
[515] Insolvency Rules 2016 r.17.12.
[516] Insolvency Rules 2016 r.17.8(2).
[517] Subject to there being at least two members: Insolvency Rules 2016 r.17.8(3)(a).
[518] Insolvency Rules 2016 r.17.8(3).
[519] Insolvency Rules 2016 r.17.18(1).
[520] Insolvency Rules 2016 r.17.18(2).

separately or as part of the minutes of the meeting. A record of each resolution must be authenticated by the chair and kept with the records of the administration.[521]

Resolutions by correspondence. The administrator may seek to obtain the agreement of members of the committee to a resolution by correspondence. If he does, he must send out to each member of the committee (or the member's representative designated for the purpose) a details of any proposed resolution on which a decision is sought,[522] set out in such a way that agreement with, or dissent from, each separate resolution may be indicated separately by the recipient.[523] Any member of the committee may require the administrator to summon a meeting of the committee to consider the matters raised by the resolution, but must do so within five business days of delivery of the proposed resolution.[524] In the absence of such a request, the resolution will be passed by the committee, if and when the administrator is given notice by a majority of the members that they agree with it.[525] A copy of every resolution so passed, and a note that the committee's agreement was obtained, must be kept with the records of the administration.[526]

15-91

Expenses of committee members. Subject as follows, the administrator must pay any reasonable travelling expenses directly incurred by members of the creditors' committee or their representatives in relation to their attendance at the committee's meetings, or otherwise on the committee's business, as an expense of the administration.[527] But this does not apply to any meeting of the committee held within six weeks of a previous meeting, unless the meeting in question is summoned at the instance of the administrator.[528]

15-92

Members' dealings with the company. Membership of the committee does not prevent a person from dealing with the company while the administration is ongoing, provided that any transactions in the course of such dealings are in good faith and for value.[529] The court may, on the application of any person interested, set aside any transaction which appears to it to be contrary to these requirements, and may make such other order as it thinks fit, including an order requiring a committee member dealing with the company to account for any profit obtained from, or to compensate the company for any losses which it may have incurred in consequence of, the transaction.[530]

15-93

Section 6: The "Prescribed Part"

Application of the Insolvency Act 1986 s.176A. The provisions of s.176A of the Act apply where a company is in administration and where it has a receiver ap-

15-94

---

[521] Insolvency Rules 2016 r.17.18(3).
[522] Insolvency Rules 2016 r.17.19(1).
[523] Insolvency Rules 2016 r.17.19(2).
[524] Insolvency Rules 2016 r.17.19(3).
[525] Insolvency Rules 2016 r.17.19(4).
[526] Insolvency Rules 2016 r.17.19(5).
[527] Insolvency Rules 2016 r.17.24(1).
[528] Insolvency Rules 2016 r.17.24(2).
[529] Insolvency Rules 2016 r.17.26(2).
[530] Insolvency Rules 2016 r.17.26(3).

pointed in respect of it.[531] However, no obligation under the section is imposed on a charge-holder who, instead of appointing a receiver, goes into possession of the charged property, whether personally or by an agent.[532]

The section only applies to floating charges created, after 15 September 2003.[533]

The provisions of the section do not apply if and in so far as they are "disapplied" by an order of the court under the section,[534] or by a voluntary arrangement in respect of the company, or by a compromise or arrangement with members and creditors, agreed under the Companies Acts.[535]

15-95 **Calculation of the prescribed part.** The prescribed part is calculated by reference to the value of the company's property which is available to floating charge holders – that is to say the value of the property which is subject to the floating charges, after deduction of preferential creditors' claims, the costs and expenses of the administration (other than those associated with the prescribed part itself),[536] and the costs of realising the property (defined in the Act as the "net property").[537]

The prescribed part is 50% of the first £10,000 of the company's net property, plus 20% of the remainder,[538] subject to a limit of £600,000.[539]

15-96 **The administrator's reporting obligations.** Except where he is proposing a CVA in relation to the company, the administrator must include in the statement of his proposals an estimate of the value of the company's net property and of the prescribed part.[540] He must also state whether or not he proposes to apply to the court under the Insolvency Act 1986 s.176A(5), to disapply the section, resulting in no distribution, and, if he does propose to do so, give his reasons. He may exclude from his estimates of value any information whose disclosure could seriously prejudice the commercial interests of the company,[541] but if that exclusion affects the calculation of the estimate the report must say so.[542]

The administrator is also required to give details of the prescribed part when he makes his final progress report,[543] when he gives notice that he is proposing to make a distribution to creditors,[544] and, if he intends to declare a dividend to unsecured creditors, when he gives notice declaring a dividend.[545]

---

[531] Insolvency Act 1986 s.176A(1).
[532] Under Companies Act 2006 s.754.
[533] Insolvency Act 1986 s.176A(8), (9); The Insolvency Act 1986 (Prescribed Part) Order 2003 (SI 2003/2097) ("The Prescribed Part Order"). A floating charge is a charge which was a floating charge when created: s.176A(9).
[534] Insolvency Act 1986 s.176A(5).
[535] Insolvency Act 1986 s.176A(4), and see Ch.16 above and Companies Act 2006 s.895 ff.
[536] These must be paid out of the prescribed part: Insolvency Rules 2016 r.3.50(2).
[537] Insolvency Act 1986 s.176(A)(6).
[538] Prescribed Part Order art.3(1).
[539] Prescribed Part Order art.3(2).
[540] Insolvency Rules 2016 r.3.35(6)
[541] Insolvency Rules 2016 r.3.35(7).
[542] Insolvency Rules 2016 r.3.35(8).
[543] Insolvency Rules 2016 r.18.3(2).
[544] Insolvency Rules 2016 r.14.29(3).
[545] Insolvency Rules 2016 r.14.35(4).

Payment of the prescribed part to the unsecured creditors. Unless the provi-   **15-97**
sions of s.176A of the Act do not apply,[546] the administrator must make the
prescribed part available for a distribution to unsecured creditors and set it aside for
that purpose. He must not distribute any part of the net property to the holder of a
floating charge, except to the extent that it exceeds either the prescribed part or the
amount required to satisfy the unsecured creditor's claims in full.[547]

Although the administrator is not normally authorised to make any distributions to unsecured creditors without the permission of the court, there is an exception for distributions of the prescribed part, which may be made without
permission.[548]

A distribution to unsecured creditors must be made to all of them, and the section may not be disapplied selectively.[549] Secured creditors are not entitled to share
in the distribution of the prescribed part, even in respect of an unsecured surplus[550]
unless they have surrendered their security, either explicitly[551] or through omitting
to mention it in a proof of debt.[552]

The Administrator does not require the permission of the court in order to
distribute the prescribed part.[553] The procedure for adjudicating on creditors' claims
in relation to, and for making a distribution of, the prescribed part are the same as
any other distribution.[554] However the costs of doing so must be borne out of the
prescribed part.[555]

Disapplying the prescribed part provisions. If the company's net property is   **15-98**
worth less than £10,000[556] and the administrator thinks that the cost of making a
distribution to unsecured creditors would be disproportionate to the benefits, then
the provisions requiring the prescribed part to be set aside for unsecured creditors
do not apply.[557]

Where the company's net property is above the statutory minimum, but the
administrator still thinks that the cost of making a distribution would be
disproportionate to the benefits, he may apply to the court for an order disapplying
the section.[558] Such an application was successful where the prescribed part was approximately £40,000, but creditors outside the company's group (with claims of approximately £500,000) would receive only £5,000 and the connected creditors

---

[546] See para.15–98.
[547] Insolvency Act 1986 s.176A(2).
[548] Insolvency Act 1986 Sch.B1 para.65(3)(a). See paras 15–102 ff for the procedure for making a
distribution to creditors.
[549] *Re Courts plc* [2008] EWHC 2339 (Ch); [2009] 1 W.L.R. 1499.
[550] *Re Permacell Finesse Ltd* [2007] EWHC 3233 (Ch); [2008] B.C.C. 208, *Re Airbase Services (UK)
Ltd* [2008] EWHC 124 (Ch); [2008] 1 W.L.R. 1516.
[551] *Re PAL SC Realisations 2007 Ltd* [2010] EWHC 2850 (Ch); [2011] B.C.C. 93.
[552] *Re JT Frith Ltd* [2012] EWHC 196 (Ch); [2012] B.C.C. 634.
[553] Insolvency Act 1986 Sch.B1. para.65(3)(a).
[554] See para.15–120 in relation to adjudicating on claims and para.15–102 ff in relation to making the
distribution.
[555] Insolvency Rules 2016 r.3.50(2).
[556] Insolvency Act 1986 s.176A(3)(a), Prescribed Part Order art.2.
[557] Insolvency Act 1986 s.176A(3).
[558] Insolvency Act 1986 s.176A(5). Since the costs involved in making the distribution are to be paid
out of the sum representing the prescribed part, the expense of making a distribution to very numerous creditors of small sums might be so disproportionate. For the relevant tasks for which costs are
to be borne, see *Re International Sections Ltd* [2009] EWHC 137 (Ch); [2009] B.C.C. 574.

agreed that the provision should be disapplied.[559] However an application failed where the prescribed part as only £18,500, which would reduce to £3,400 once the cost of adjudicating on proofs and making distributions was deducted, and creditors would receive 1.5p in the pound.[560] Where the prescribed part was only £5,699 and the costs of adjudicating claims were estimated at £5,000, leaving a dividend of 0.2p in the pound, the court refused to disapply the section, but directed the administrators simply to pay out claims without investigating them, permitting a distribution of 1.8p in the pound.[561] In a case where the prescribed part was £96,000 and the cost of distribution was estimated at £25,000, leading to a dividend of between 0.083p and 0.51p in the pound, the court refused an application, holding that the overall sum was still substantial, even if the dividend rate was low.[562]

15-99 **Making an application under s.176A(5).**   An application to disapply the prescribed part provisions may be made by the administrator without serving notice on any other party,[563] unless there is another office-holder acting in relation to the company (such as a Member-State liquidator, empowered as a creditor under the EC Regulation on Insolvency Proceedings).[564] In such cases, the other office-holders must be notified of the application.[565]

The application must be supported by a witness statement made by the administrator,[566] which must state the type of insolvency proceeding involved; provide a summary of the financial position of the company; set out the information which substantiates the administrator's view that the cost of making a distribution to the unsecured creditors would be disproportionate to the benefits; and give the details (including address) of any other office-holder acting in relation to the company.[567]

15-100 **Notice of orders made under s.176A(5).**   Where the court has made an order under s.176A(5) of the Act disapplying the prescribed part, it must, as soon as reasonably practicable, send a sealed copy to the administrator and to any other office-holder acting in relation to the company.[568]

As soon as reasonably practicable the administrator must give notice of the order to every creditor, unless the court directs him otherwise;[569] he must publish a notice in the *Gazette*[570]; and he must send a copy to the registrar of companies.[571] If one ground for making the order is that there is a very large number of small creditors, that might justify a direction not to give notice to the creditors, but the court may instead direct that such notice be given by publishing a notice stating that the court has made an order disapplying the section.[572]

---

[559] *Re Hydroserve Ltd* [2007] EWHC 3026 (Ch); [2008] B.C.C. 175.
[560] *Re International Sections Ltd* [2009] EWHC 137 (Ch); [2009] B.C.C. 574.
[561] *QMD Hotels Ltd Administrators, Noters* [2010] CSOH 168; [2012] B.C.C. 794.
[562] *Joint Administrators of Castlebridge Plant Ltd, Noters* [2015] CSOH 65; [2017] B.C.C. 87.
[563] Insolvency Rules 2016 r.12.15(1).
[564] See Ch.28, below.
[565] Insolvency Rules 2016 r.12.15(2).
[566] Insolvency Rules 2016 r.12.14(1).
[567] Insolvency Rules 2016 r.12.14(2).
[568] Insolvency Rules 2016 r.12.16(1).
[569] Insolvency Rules 2016 r.12.16(2).
[570] Insolvency Rules 2016 r.12.16(4).
[571] Insolvency Rules 2016 r.12.16(5).
[572] Insolvency Rules 2016 r.12.16(3).

SECTION 7: DISTRIBUTION BY ADMINISTRATOR

General.   The order of priority for payment out of a company's assets has been   **15-101**
summarised by the Supreme Court as follows.

(1)   Fixed charge creditors;
(2)   Expenses of the insolvency proceedings;
(3)   Preferential creditors;
(4)   Floating charge creditors;
(5)   Unsecured provable debts;
(6)   Statutory interest;
(7)   Non-provable liabilities; and
(8)   Shareholders.[573]

The administrator has a general power to make distributions to creditors, or to a single creditor.[574] But that general power is initially restricted to the making of a distribution to a secured or a preferential creditor,[575] or a distribution of the prescribed part[576]; any distribution which includes any other category of creditor requires the permission of the court.[577]

I: When the Administrator May Make a Distribution

Distributions to secured creditors from proceeds of charged property.   The   **15-102**
Administrator does not need the permission of the court to make a distribution to a secured creditor out of the net proceeds of charged property.[578] However any such distribution is, in the case of property charged under a floating charge, subject to any deduction for the costs and expenses of the administration,[579] the obligation to deduct and set aside the prescribed part,[580] and the obligation to pay preferential claims out of the proceeds of assets securing floating charges[581] where the company's unsecured assets are insufficient to discharge them.[582]

While para.65 makes explicit reference to s.175 of the Act, it does not mention s.176ZA, which makes liquidation expenses payable out of floating charge realisations in priority to the floating charge holder's debt. Therefore, provided that assets securing a floating charge are realised and distributed while the company remains in administration, the liquidation expenses will not be payable out of these realisations.

Permission to make a distribution to unsecured creditors.[583]   Paragraph 65(3)   **15-103**
of Sch.B1 to the Insolvency Act 1986 gives no explicit guidance on how the court should exercise its discretion as to whether or not to grant permission to the

---

[573]   *Re Nortel GmbH, Bloom v Pensions Regulator* [2013] UKSC 52; [2014] A.C. 209 at [39].
[574]   Insolvency Act 1986 Sch.B1 para.65(1). For the Administrator's power to make a distribution other than pari passu, or to make payments in the course of the administration, see para.15-59.
[575]   Insolvency Act 1986 Sch.B1 para.65(3).
[576]   Insolvency Act 1986 Sch.B1 para.65(3)(a).
[577]   Insolvency Act 1986 Sch.B1 para.65(3)(b).
[578]   Insolvency Act 1986 Sch.B1 para.65(3).
[579]   Insolvency Act 1986 Sch.B1 paras 70 and 99(3)(b).
[580]   Insolvency Act 1986 s.176A(2).
[581]   That is to say, charges which were floating charges when created: Insolvency Act 1986 s.251.
[582]   Insolvency Act 1986 s.175; Sch.B1 para.65(2).
[583]   For payment of the prescribed part, see para.15-94 ff.

administrator to make a distribution other than to secured or preferential creditors. In *Re GHR Realisations Ltd*[584] it was held that when determining whether or not to grant permission, the court should predominantly have regard to the interests of the company's creditors as a whole, and that the court must consider whether the payment of a dividend is consistent with the administrator's functions and duties and with his proposals. The court also considered the possibility that a distribution in liquidation would adversely or beneficially affect any classes of creditor.

A longer list of potential considerations was set out in *Re MG Rover Beluxl SA/ NV*.[585] These were the following:

- The matter is to be judged at the time when permission is sought.
- The court must be satisfied that the proposed distribution is conducive to the then current objectives of the administration.
- The court must be satisfied that the distribution is in the interests of the company's creditors as a whole.
- The court must be satisfied that proper provision has been made for secured and preferential creditors.
- The court must consider what are the realistic alternatives to the proposed distribution sought by the administrators, consider the merits and demerits of adopting a course other than that proposed by the administrators and assess whether the proposed distribution adversely affects the entitlement of others.
- The court must take into account the basis on which the administration has been conducted so far as the creditors are concerned, and in particular whether the creditors have approved (or not objected to) any proposal concerning the relevant distribution.
- The court must consider the nature and terms of the distribution.
- The court must consider the impact of the distribution upon any proposed exit route from the administration.[586]

Frequently permission will be granted where the only purpose of exiting administration via a liquidation would be to effect a distribution to creditors.[587]

II: Debts Which May be Claimed, and Their Quantification

15-104 **Meaning of "debt" and "liability".** The definitions of "debt" and "liability" for the purposes of administration (and winding up) are set out at r.14.1. They may be summarised as follows.

- "Debt" means any debt or liability to which the company is subject on the relevant date,[588] or to which it becomes liable after that date by reason of

---

[584] [2005] EWHC 2400 Ch; [2006] B.C.C. 139.
[585] [2006] EWHC 1296 (Ch); [2007] B.C.C. 446 at [7].
[586] The relevant passages of both *Re GHE Realisations Ltd* [2006] B.C.C. 139; and *Re MG Rover Beluxl SA/NV* [2007] B.C.C. 446 were approved in *Re Nortel Networks UK Ltd* [2015] EWHC 2506 (Ch); [2015] All E.R. (D) 05 (Sep).
[587] As in *Re GHE Realisations Ltd* [2006] B.C.C. 139.
[588] Insolvency Rules 2016 r.14.1(3)(a).

any obligation incurred before that date,[589] and any interest specifically provided for by the Rules.[590]

- In order for a liability in tort to be provable in the administration it is sufficient that all the elements necessary to establish the cause of action exist at the relevant date; there is no need for actionable damage to have been suffered by that date.[591]
- It is immaterial whether the debt or liability is present or future, whether it is certain or contingent, or whether its amount is fixed or liquidated, or is capable of being ascertained by fixed rules or as a matter of opinion, and references to "owing a debt" are to be read accordingly.[592]
- "Liability" means a liability to pay money or money's worth, including any liability under any enactment, any liability for breach of trust, any liability in contract, tort or bailment, and any liability arising out of an obligation to make restitution.[593]

The "relevant date" is the date the company went into administration, unless the administration was immediately preceded by a liquidation, in which case it is the date on which it went into liquidation.[594]

For a liability to be a contingent liability within the meaning of r.14.1(3)(b), and therefore provable in the administration, the company must have taken, or been subjected to, some step or combination of steps which had some legal effect (such as putting it under some legal duty or into some legal relationship), and which resulted in it being vulnerable to the specific liability in question. If that is established then it is also necessary to consider whether it is consistent with the regime under which the liability arises to conclude that it is a contingent debt for the purposes of proof.[595] In many cases contingent liabilities will arise as a result of a contract entered into by the company before the relevant date, where there is little difficulty in showing that they are provable. Other examples of contingent liabilities include a liability to contribute to a pension scheme arising out of a contribution notice issued by the Pensions Regulator,[596] a liability under a costs order made in litigation commenced before the relevant date,[597] and a protective award made after liquidation in respect of a pre-liquidation breach of the obligation to consult with employee representatives before terminating employment contracts.[598]

Non provable and postponed debts.   Some debts which otherwise fall within the   **15-105**
definition of "debt" set out in r.14.1 may not be proved for. These include an obliga-

---

[589] Insolvency Rules 2016 r.14.1(3)(b).
[590] Insolvency Rules 2016 r.14.1(3)(c). See para.15-111.
[591] Insolvency Rules 2016 r.14.1(4).
[592] Insolvency Rules 2016 r.14.1(5).
[593] Insolvency Rules 2016 r.14.1(6).
[594] Insolvency Rules 2016 r.14.1(3).
[595] *Re Nortel GmbH* [2013] UKSC 52; [2014] A.C. 209 at [77]. It was this last limb of the test which led the Supreme Court to conclude that the right which arises in a liquidation to claim a contribution from members pursuant to s.150 of the Insolvency Act 1986 is not provable by an administrator as a contingent liability: *Re Lehman Brothers International (Europe) (In Administration)* [2017] UKSC 38; [2017] 2 W.L.R. 1497 at [152]–[158].
[596] *Re Nortel GmbH* [2014] A.C. 209 at [85].
[597] *Re Nortel GmbH* [2014] A.C. 209 at [89], overruling *Glenister v Rowe* [2000] Ch. 76; [1999] 3 All E.R. 452.
[598] *Haine v Day* [2008] EWCA Civ 626; [2008] B.C.C. 845.

tion arising under a confiscation order made under s.1 of the Drug Trafficking Offences Act 1986, s.1 of the Criminal Justice (Scotland) Act 1987, s.71 of the Criminal Justice Act 1988, or Pts 2, 3 or 4 of the Proceeds of Crime Act 2002.[599] In addition a claim for a restitution order under s.382(1)(a) of the Financial Services and Markets Act 2000 is postponed until all other claims[600] have been paid in full with interest, unless the order is also made pursuant to s.382(1)(b) of that Act (i.e. that somebody has suffered a loss as a result of, or been adversely affected by, a contravention).[601]

It is possible for a creditor to subordinate its claims by contract with the company. The effect of any such subordination will depend on the precise wording of the contract. Where a debt was subordinated to all obligations other than "obligations which are not payable or capable of being established or determined in the insolvency of the borrower" it was held that this subordinated the debt not only to provable claims, but also to interest on those claims and to non-provable claims.[602]

15-106 The rule against double proof. In certain cases debts owed to two or more creditors will be treated as one single debt, and only one of them will be permitted to prove. This is the rule against double proof.

The rule arises most often in the context of guarantors and other sureties. When a surety pays the principle debtor's debt, he will usually have a right of indemnity against the principle debtor.[603] Even if the surety has not discharged the principal debt before the commencement of the administration, his indemnity claim will still be a provable debt, as a contingent liability. However, where any part of the principal debt subsists, the creditor will be permitted to prove for the full amount of the debt (and not just the outstanding balance).[604] The surety's right to an indemnity is treated as a claim for the same debt as the creditor, and so the surety will not be permitted to prove for its claim until the creditor has been paid in full.[605]

Likewise, where a creditor has proved for a debt, and a Member State liquidator proves for the same debt, there can be only one distribution in respect of that debt. Unless the creditor has assigned his right to dividend, or has requested that his dividend be paid to that liquidator, the dividend must be paid to that creditor.[606]

15-107 The Contributory Rule. Under the provisions of s.74 of the Act, in a winding up a company's members are liable to contribute to its assets an amount sufficient for payment of its debts and liabilities,[607] the expenses of the winding up, and to adjust the rights of the contributories among themselves. This is subject to various limitations, the most important of which being that, in the case of a company limited

---

[599] Insolvency Rules 2016 r.14(2)(2).

[600] Presumably this means provable claims.

[601] Insolvency Rules 2016 r.14(2)(4).

[602] *Re Lehman Brothers International (Europe) (In Administration)* [2017] UKSC 38; [2017] 2 W.L.R. 1497 at [135]–[147].

[603] *Re A Debtor (No.627 of 1936)* [1937] Ch. 156; [1937] 1 All E.R. 1.

[604] *Re Sass, Ex p. National Provincial Bank* [1896] 2 Q.B. 12; 65 L.J.Q.B. 481.

[605] *Re Kaupthing Singer & Friedlander Ltd (No.2)* [2011] UKSC 48; [2012] 1 A.C. 804.

[606] Insolvency Rules 2016 r.14.32(4).

[607] Including non-provable debts, but excluding any interest payable on provable debts: *Re Lehman Brothers International (Europe) (In Administration)* [2017] UKSC 38; [2017] 2 W.L.R. 1497 at [56] and [63].

by shares, a member's liability cannot exceed the amount unpaid on his shares.[608] Similarly, s.150 of the Act gives the court the power to make calls on a company's members when a winding up order has been made in respect of it, a power which is delegated to the liquidator.[609]

It is a rule in liquidations, often referred to as "the Contributory Rule", that a claimant may recover nothing as a creditor until his liability to the company as a contributory has been discharged.[610] Although there is no similar power which permits an administrator to make calls on contributories,[611] the Contributory Rule still applies,[612] though with necessary adjustments to take into account the fact that the call cannot be made until the company enters liquidation. The administrator must assess the contributory's likely liability and its likely dividend, and retain the lower of these two figures.[613]

Interest.

(a) Proving for Interest A proof of debt may include an amount in respect of   **15-108** interest accrued before the relevant date[614] where:

- it was agreed, either when the debt was contracted, or subsequently, that it would bear interest[615]; or
- although there was no agreement that the debt would bear interest—
  - the debt is due by virtue of a written instrument and payable at a certain time which has elapsed—in which case interest may be proved for from that time up to the relevant date[616]; or
  - written demand for payment has been made by or on behalf of the creditor, giving notice that interest would become payable from the date of the demand until payment—in which case interest is payable from the date of the demand until the relevant date.[617]

Where it was agreed that the debt would accrue interest, it may be proved for at the contractual rate. Where this is not the case, it may be proved for at the rate specified in the Judgments Act 1938 s.17, on the date of the company's entry into administration,[618] unless a lower rate was specified in a written demand.[619]

(b) Statutory Interest Where there is a surplus after the payment in full of the

---

608 Insolvency Act 1986 s.74(2)(d).
609 Insolvency Act 1986 s.160(1)(d); Insolvency Rules 2016 r.7.86.
610 *Re Overend Gurney & Co; Grissel's Case* (1866) L.R. 1 Ch. App. 528; *Re Kaupthing Singer & Friedlander Ltd (No.2)* [2011] UKSC 48; [2012] 1 A.C. 804.
611 *Re Lehman Brothers International (Europe) (In Administration)* [2017] 2 W.L.R. 1497 at [175]; and see para.15-95.
612 *Re Lehman Brothers International (Europe) (In Administration)* [2017] 2 W.L.R. 1497 at [179].
613 That is, retaining the dividend in full where the contribution is likely to exceed it, and paying out the difference where it is not: *Re Lehman Brothers International (Europe) (In Administration)* [2017] 2 W.L.R. 1497 at [180].
614 Defined in Insolvency Rules 2016 r.14.1(3): see para.15-95.
615 Insolvency Rules 2016 r.14.23(1).
616 Insolvency Rules 2016 r.14.23(3).
617 Insolvency Rules 2016 r.14.23(4) and (5).
618 Insolvency Rules 2016 r.14.23(6). The current rate is 8%: Judgment Debts (Rate of Interest) Order 1993 art.2 (SI 1993/564).
619 Insolvency Rules 2016 r.14.23(5).

proved debts, statutory interest is payable on those debts,[620] all debts being treated equally for this purpose.[621] This interest is payable at the higher of the Judgments Act rate or the rate otherwise applicable to the debt[622] and for the period between the relevant date and the discharge of those proved debts.[623] Where the contractual rate provides for compound interest, statutory interest is also payable at that compound rate.[624] For the purpose of calculating statutory interest, distributions to creditors are to be appropriated first to discharge of the proved debts and not to statutory interest that has accrued on them at the date of distribution,[625] and no interest is payable on the statutory interest itself.[626]

Where the company goes into liquidation before statutory interest is paid by the administrators, the creditors lose their right to receive it, and cannot claim it from the liquidator.[627]

15-109   **Foreign currency debts.**   A debt incurred or payable in a currency other than sterling must be claimed in that currency.[628] The administrator must convert the debt into sterling at the exchange rate prevailing on the relevant date.[629] He must notify the creditor of the exchange rate applied when he next communicates with the creditors,[630] and if the creditor considers that the rate is unreasonable he may apply to court for determination of the rate.[631]

No claim (provable or otherwise) lies in respect of losses made by foreign currency creditors as a result of currency market movements between the relevant date and the date of distribution.[632]

15-110   **Periodical payments.**   In the case of rent or other payments of a periodical nature, the creditor may prove for any amounts due and unpaid up to the relevant date.[633] In the case of a periodical payment then accruing due, but not yet become due, the creditor may prove for such an amount as would have fallen due on that date had

---

[620] Insolvency Rules 2016 r.14.23(7)(a).

[621] Insolvency Rules 2016 r.14.23(7)(b).

[622] The rate otherwise applicable does not include a judgment rate on a debt in respect of which the creditor has obtained judgment after the relevant date: *Re Lehman Brothers International (Europe) (in administration)* [2015] EWHC 2269 (Ch); [2016] B.C.C. 239 at [183]. Where contractual interest begins to run on a provable debt at some time after the relevant date, then the applicable rate of statutory interest for that period is 0% (if the contractual rate applies), and in order to determine whether the Judgments Act rate or the contractual rate applies, the total interest payable over the whole period to the distribution must be compared: *Re Lehman Brothers International (Europe) (in administration)* [2016] EWHC 2131 (Ch); [2017] B.C.C. 1.

[623] Insolvency Rules 2016 r.14.23(7)(c). This is the applicable period even in relation to debts which, at the relevant date, were future or contingent, but which became due prior to the distribution: *Re Lehman Brothers International (Europe) (in administration)* [2016] B.C.C. 239 at [225].

[624] *Re Lehman Brothers International (Europe) (in administration)* [2016] B.C.C. 239 at [22].

[625] Thus the common law rule in *Bower v Marris* (1841) Cr. & P. 351 does not apply: *Re Lehman Brothers International (Europe) (in administration)* [2016] B.C.C. 239 at [128]–[154].

[626] *Re Lehman Brothers International (Europe) (in administration)* [2016] B.C.C. 239 at [165]–[167].

[627] *Re Lehman Brothers International (Europe) (In Administration)* [2017] UKSC 38; [2017] 2 W.L.R. 1497 at [112], [124]–[127].

[628] Insolvency Rules 2016 r.14.21(1).

[629] Insolvency Rules 2016 r.14.21(2). The relevant date is defined in Insolvency Rules 2016 r.14.1(3)

[630] Insolvency Rules 2016 r.14.21(3)

[631] Insolvency Rules 2016 r.14.21(4) and (5).

[632] *Re Lehman Brothers International (Europe) (In Administration)* [2017] UKSC 38; [2017] 2 W.L.R. 1497 at [112].

[633] Insolvency Rules 2016 r.14.22(1). The relevant date is defined in Insolvency Rules 2016 r.14.1(3): see para.15-95.

the payment accrued from day to day.[634] The balance must be claimed as a future debt.[635]

Future, contingent, and uncertain debts.   A creditor for a debt which had not   **15-111**
yet fallen due for payment on the relevant date,[636] whether because it is due in the
future or is a contingent debt, or for a debt with is uncertain, may prove for it as if
payable then, but subject to a reduction to take into account accelerated payment,
or contingencies.

Where a creditor has proved for a debt payable in the future, there is no discount
to be applied to the distribution if the debt has fallen due for payment before the
date of the declaration of a dividend. Where, however, at the date of the declaration of a dividend the debt remains payable in the future,[637] the dividend must be
discounted at the rate of 5% per annum, compounded yearly, for the period between
the relevant date and the date when payment of the debt would otherwise be due.[638]

Where a debt, by reason of it being subject to a contingency, or for any other
reason, does not have a certain value, the administrator must make an estimate of
its value.[639] This estimate must be revised to take into account a change in
circumstances or new information,[640] and the creditor must be informed of the
original estimate and any revision to it.[641] The current estimate is the amount provable in respect of the debt.[642]

Discounts.   All trade and other discounts, which would have been ordinarily avail-   **15-112**
able to the company (other than a discount for early settlement) must be deducted
from the debt as proved.[643]

Insolvency set-off.   Unlike in a liquidation, insolvency set-off does not take place   **15-113**
automatically. Instead it takes place when the administrator gives notice of his intention to make a distribution to creditors.[644] Insolvency set-off applies where there
have been mutual dealings between the company and any creditor proving or claiming to prove for a debt in the administration. The set-off requires the account to be
taken as at the date when the administrator gave notice of his intention to make a
distribution.[645] However, future debts, contingent debts, and debts of uncertain or
unliquidated amounts are to be taken into account.[646] These debts, and any which
are in foreign currency, periodical, or interest bearing are to be calculated in the

---

[634] Insolvency Rules 2016 r.14.22(2).
[635] See para.15-111.
[636] The relevant date is defined in Insolvency Rules 2016 r.14.1(3)
[637] Insolvency Rules 2016 r.14.44(1).
[638] Insolvency Rules 2016 r.14.44(2).
[639] Insolvency Rules 2016 r.14.14(1).
[640] Insolvency Rules 2016 r.4.14(2). The Rule is expressed permissively. However the hindsight
       principle is of mandatory application and if the administrator does not revise the estimate the court
       will do so on the application of an interested party: see *MS Fashions Ltd v Bank of Credit & Com-
       merce International SA* [1993] Ch. 415; [1993] B.C.C. 360, and the discussion in *Re MF Global
       Trader UK Ltd* [2013] EWHC 92 at [48]–[52].
[641] Insolvency Rules 2016 r.14.14(3).
[642] Insolvency Rules 2016 r.14.14(4).
[643] Insolvency Rules 2016 r.14.20.
[644] Insolvency Rules 2016 r.14.24(1).
[645] Insolvency Rules 2016 r.14.24(2).
[646] Insolvency Rules 2016 r.14.24(7).

same way as in the distribution itself.[647] Where there are joint and several debtors of the company, a set-off available to one is available to all of them,[1010] and a claim by one branch of the Crown must be set off against a debt due to another branch.[648]

Only the balance on the account is provable in the administration or payable by the other party to the administrator.[649] If there is a balance due to the company after application of the set-off, interest is payable (if the debt attracts interest) on this balance from the date at which the account is taken to the date of payment.[650] A balance payable to the administrator as a result of a contingent or future debt owed to the company is payable in full and without discount, but only when the debt actually becomes due.

15-114 **Debts which may not be the subject of insolvency set-off.** A debt may not be set off if it does not arise out of mutual dealings. The requirement of mutuality means that the debts must be owed between the same parties and in the same right. Thus a debt owed to the company personally cannot be set off against a debt claimed from the company as trustee for another.[651] Where a debtor claims to be the beneficiary of a claim against the company held on trust by another, the court will only allow the set-off where the beneficial interest is established by clear evidence and without the need to take an account.[652] However a secured debt and an unsecured debt may be "mutual".[653] The requirement for dealings operates to exclude debts arising out of such claims as conversion[654] or breach of fiduciary duty.[655]

Set off is not available to a creditor where the obligation under which the debt arises was incurred, or (in the case where the debt has been acquired by the creditor, by assignment or otherwise) where the agreement for acquisition of the debt was made:

- after the company entered administration;[656]
- when the creditor had notice that:
  — an application for an administration order was pending[657]; or

---

[647] Insolvency Rules 2016 r.14.24(8). This rule is modified in the case of a close-out netting provision under a financial collateral arrangement: see Financial Collateral Arrangements (No.2) Regulations 2003 (SI 2003/3226) reg.12(4).

[648] *Secretary of State for Trade and Industry v Frid* [2004] UKHL 24; [2004] 2 A.C. 506 at [26]–[29].

[649] Insolvency Rules 2016 r.14.24(3) and (4).

[650] *Re Kaupthing Singer & Friedlander Ltd (in administration)* [2009] EWHC 2308 (Ch); [2010] Bus. L.R. 428. This was reversed in part in the Court of Appeal ([2010] EWCA Civ 518; [2011] B.C.C. 555), but not on this point.

[651] *Secretary of State for Trade and Industry v Frid* [2004] UKHL 24; [2004] 2 A.C. 506 at [26]. However the court is entitled to look into the arrangements between the company and creditor to see if mutuality survives the apparent imposition of a trust: *Re ILG Travel Ltd* [1996] B.C.C. 21 at 49.

[652] *Bank of Credit and Commerce International SA (in liquidation) v Prince Fahd Bin Salman Abdul Aziz Al-Saud* [1997] B.C.C. 63; [1997] 1 B.C.L.C. 457.

[653] *Re ILG Travel Ltd* [1996] B.C.C. 21 at 48.

[654] *Smith (Administrator of Cosslett (Contractors) Ltd) v Bridgend County Borough Council* [2001] UKHL 58; [2002] 1 A.C. 336.

[655] *Manson v Smith* [1997] 2 B.C.L.C. 161.

[656] Insolvency Rules 2016 r.14.24(6)(a) and (e)(i).

[657] Insolvency Rules 2016 r.14.24(6)(b)(i) and (e)(ii).

> — that notice had been given of the intention to appoint an administrator[658];

- in the case where a winding-up immediately preceded the administration,
  > — during that winding-up[659]; or
  > — at a time when the creditor had notice that a decision of creditors had been sought on the appointment of a liquidator pursuant to s.100 of the Act, or that a winding-up petition was pending.[660]

Insolvency set off may not be claimed in respect of a debt which has been rejected for proof,[661] or where the debt cannot be proved because of the rule against double proof.[662] However it is not right to say that a debt is not available for set-off merely because it cannot be proved.[663]

The set-off provisions are mandatory, and may not be contracted out of.[664] Nor does the court have any discretion to disapply them.[665] However they will not apply to close-out netting arrangements in circumstances where the other party has no notice of the company's winding up or administration.[666]

III: Provisions Relating to Secured Creditors

Secured creditors: general. Ordinarily a secured creditor will look first to the security for satisfaction of his claim. However it is frequently the case that the security does not cover the full extent of the debt. In that case the secured creditor may realise or value his security and prove for the balance, or he may give up his security and prove for the full debt.[667] The last of these courses will also permit the secured creditor to share in the distribution of the prescribed part.[668]   **15-115**

Valuing the security. A secured creditor must value his security in any proof of debt lodged for the purposes of the distribution.[669] This valuation may be altered subsequently, with the agreement of the administrator or the permission of the court.[670] If the secured creditor has previously valued his security for the purposes of an application for the administration order or a notice of intention to appoint or if he has voted in respect of the unsecured balance of his debt,[671] any re-valuation   **15-116**

---

658 Insolvency Rules 2016 r.14.24(6)(b)(ii) and (e)(iii).
659 Insolvency Rules 2016 r.14.24(6)(d) and (e)(v).
660 Insolvency Rules 2016 r.14.24(6)(c) and (e)(iv).
661 *Bank of Credit & Commerce International (Overseas) Ltd v Habib Bank Ltd* [1999] 1 W.L.R. 42; [1998] 2 B.C.L.C. 459.
662 *Re Fenton* [1931] 1 Ch. 85; *Secretary of State for Trade and Industry v Frid* [2004] UKHL 24; [2004] 2 A.C. 506 at [13].
663 *Re Lehman Brothers International (Europe) (In Administration)* [2017] UKSC 38; [2017] 2 W.L.R. 1497 at [167]–[170].
664 *National Westminster Bank Ltd v Halesowen Presswork & Assemblies Ltd* [1972] A.C. 785; [1972] 1 All E.R. 641.
665 *Re Bank of Credit & Commerce International SA (No.10)* [1997] Ch. 213; [1996] B.C.C. 980.
666 Financial Collateral Arrangements (No.2) Regulations 2003 (SI 2003/3226) reg.12.
667 Insolvency Rules 2016 r.14.19; *Moor v Anglo Italian Bank* (1879) 10 Ch. D. 681.
668 See paras 15-94 ff.
669 Insolvency Rules 2016 r.14.4(1)(g).
670 Insolvency Rules 2016 r.14.15(1).
671 Insolvency Rules 2016 r.14.15(2).

of his security by agreement with the administrator must be notified to the other creditors within five days.[672]

If a security which has been valued in a proof of debt is subsequently realised (whether or not at the instance of the administrator), the net amount realised must be treated in all respects as an amended valuation by the secured creditor, and he will be able to prove for the balance.[673]

15-117 Surrender, where security not disclosed. If the creditor omits to disclose his security in his proof of debt, he must surrender his security for the general benefit of creditors, unless the court relieves him, on the ground that the omission was inadvertent, or the result of an honest mistake.[674] In that event, the court may require or may allow his proof of debt to be amended, on such terms as may be just.[675]

Third parties' rights in rem, arising by virtue of the EC Regulation on Insolvency Proceedings, are protected from the impact of this rule.[676]

15-118 Where valuation disputed. Where the administrator is dissatisfied with the valuation of the creditor's security, or with its revaluation,[677] he may require any property comprised in the security to be offered for sale.[678] If the administrator and secured creditor cannot agree the terms of such a sale shall, the court has power to give directions.[679] If the sale is by auction, the administrator on behalf of the company, or the creditor on his own behalf, may appear and bid.[680]

15-119 Redemption by administrator. The administrator may at any time give notice to a secured creditor that he proposes to redeem the creditor's security at the value put on it in his proof 28 days after the date of the notice.[681] The creditor may then revalue his security in accordance with r.14.15[682] within 21 days, or such longer period as the administrator may allow.[683] If the creditor succeeds in revaluing his security, the administrator may only redeem it at the new value.[684] The cost of transferring the security is payable as an expense of the administration.[685]

A secured creditor may at any time give notice in writing to the administrator, requiring him to elect whether or not to exercise his power to redeem at the current valuation.[686] The administrator then has *three months* in which to exercise the power to redeem or to determine not to exercise it.[687]

---

[672] Insolvency Rules 2016 r.14.15(3).
[673] Insolvency Rules 2016 r.14.19(1). See para.15-127 for the effect of such a revaluation after a distribution has taken place.
[674] Insolvency Rules 2016 r.14.17(1).
[675] Insolvency Rules 2016 r.14.17(2).
[676] Insolvency Rules 2016 r.14.17(3).
[677] Unless this revaluation was with the court's permission: Insolvency Rules 2016 r.14.18(4).
[678] Insolvency Rules 2016 r.14.18(1).
[679] Insolvency Rules 2016 r.14.18(2).
[680] Insolvency Rules 2016 r.14.18(3).
[681] Insolvency Rules 2016 r.14.17(1).
[682] See para.15-116.
[683] Insolvency Rules 2016 r.14.17(2).
[684] Insolvency Rules 2016 r.14.17(3).
[685] Insolvency Rules 2016 r.14.17(4).
[686] Insolvency Rules 2016 r.14.17(5).
[687] Insolvency Rules 2016 r.14.17(6).

IV: Procedure for Proving Debts and Adjudicating Claims

Notice of proposed distribution. Where the proposed distribution will be a first **15-120** distribution, the administrator must also advertise the distribution in the *Gazette* stating his intention to declare a first dividend and the time and place for delivery of proofs of debt,[688] unless the intended distribution is only to preferential creditors,[689] or he has previously gazetted a notice inviting creditors to prove their debts.[690] The administrator may also advertise notice of a first distribution in any other manner he thinks fit.[691]

In all cases, the administrator must deliver a notice of his intention to make a distribution to all the creditors,[692] unless the proposed dividend is only for preferential creditors (in which case notice only need be delivered to preferential creditors).[693]

This notice must state that the administrator intends to make a distribution to creditors within two months of the last date for lodging proofs of debt; state whether the proposed distribution is interim or final; and give details of the date and place for delivering proofs of debt (the date must be the same for all creditors and must be at least 21 days after the date of the notice).[694] In addition, where a distribution is to be made to unsecured creditors the notice must also state the value of the prescribed part, to be distributed to unsecured creditors, unless there is no prescribed part or the court has directed that such a distribution need not be made.[695]

If the company has any "small debts"—which are any debts of not more than £1,000 each[696]—the administrator may choose to treat it as proved and admitted for the purposes of a dividend.[697] If so the notice sent to any small creditor must state of the amount of the debt the administrator believes to be owed to the creditor according to the company's accounting records; state that he will treat it as proved for the purposes of dividend unless the creditor advises him that the amount is incorrect or no debt is owed; require the creditor to notify the administrator by the last day for proving if either of these is the case, and advise him that if he advises that the amount of the debt is incorrect he must also submit a proof of debt.[698] The statement of the amount of the debt may be a schedule of all small debts which the administrator intends to treat as proved so long as it includes the one owed to the creditor.[699]

The proof of debt. In order to recover a debt, a creditor is obliged to deliver a **15-121**

---

[688] Insolvency Rules 2016 r.14.28(1). While the Rules do not explicitly say so, the first distribution to unsecured creditors must be gazetted even where there has been a previous distribution to preferential creditors: such a distribution would be classed as "a first distribution", and the importance of gazetting creditors in advance of declaring a dividend is made clear by r.14.28(4).

[689] In which case the administrator has a discretion whether or not to do so: Insolvency Rules 2016 r.14.28(2).

[690] Insolvency Rules 2016 r.14.28(4).

[691] Insolvency Rules 2016 r.14.28(3).

[692] Insolvency Rules 2016 r.14.29(1). Notice must be delivered even to opted-out creditors: Insolvency Act 1986 s.246C(2)(a).

[693] Insolvency Rules 2016 r.14.29(2).

[694] Insolvency Rules 2016 r.14.30.

[695] Insolvency Rules 2016 r.14.29(3). See para.15-94 ff in relation to disapplying the prescribed part provisions.

[696] Insolvency Rules 2016 r.14.1(3).

[697] Insolvency Rules 2016 r.14.31(1).

[698] Insolvency Rules 2016 r.14.31(2).

[699] Insolvency Rules 2016 r.4.31(3).

proof of debt to the administrator[700] unless the court orders otherwise,[701] or the creditor has already proved in a winding up which immediately preceded the administration (in which case the creditor is deemed to have proved in the administration).[702] In addition, a creditor is deemed to have proved for a "small debt"—which is to say a debt of no more than £1,000[703]—where the administrator has delivered to the creditor a notice of intention to make a distribution which complies with the provisions of r.14.31,[704] and the creditor has not notified the administrator that the debt is incorrect or not owed.[705]

The proof of debt must be made by, or under the direction of, the creditor, be dated and authenticated by the creditor or by a person authorised by him, and set out the creditor's name and address. It must state the total amount of his claim (including any VAT) as at the relevant date,[706] less any payments made after that date in relation to the claim, any discounts,[707] or any set-off,[708] and state whether the claim includes outstanding uncapitalised interest. The proof must also provide particulars of how and when the debt was incurred, particulars of any security (including the date on which it was given and the value put on it by the creditor) or retention of title claimed by the creditor, and the name, address and authority of the person signing the proof (if other than the creditor).[709] Supporting documents must be specified in the proof,[710] but need not be submitted with the proof, until called for by the administrator.[711]

All proofs must be made available by the administrator, while in office and so long as they are in his possession, for inspection by any creditor who has delivered a proof (unless that proof has been wholly rejected or withdrawn) or contributory, or his representation, at all reasonable times on any business day.[712]

15-122 **Admission or rejection of proofs.** The administrator must admit or reject all proofs submitted to him, or make such provision with respect to them as the thinks fit, within 14 days of the last date for proving.[713] Despite that period of limitation, the administrator may deal with late proofs, if he thinks fit.[714]

The administrator may make provision with respect to a proof, by setting aside sufficient funds to pay the proof if admitted, pending determination (for instance where there is an outstanding request either for documentary evidence in support or further information relating to the debt).[715]

A proof may be admitted for dividend for the whole amount claimed, for only

---

[700] Insolvency Rules 2016 r.14.3(1).
[701] Insolvency Rules 2016 r.14.3(1)(a).
[702] Insolvency Rules 2016 r.14.3(2)(a).
[703] Insolvency Rules 2016 r.14.1(3).
[704] As to which, see para.15-119.
[705] Insolvency Rules 2016 r.14.3(3).
[706] The relevant date is defined in Insolvency Rules 2016 r.14.1(3).
[707] See para.15-105.
[708] See para.15-112.
[709] Insolvency Rules 2016 r.14.4(1).
[710] Insolvency Rules 2016 r.14.4(1)(i).
[711] Insolvency Rules 2016 r.14.4(2) and (3).
[712] Insolvency Rules 2016 r.14.6. The right to inspect proofs does not extend to the documents delivered with or in support of a proof: *MG Rover Dealer Properties Ltd v Hunt* [2012] B.P.I.R. 590; [2013] B.C.C. 698.
[713] Insolvency Rules 2016 r.14.32(1).
[714] Insolvency Rules 2016 r.14.32(2).
[715] Insolvency Rules 2016 r.14.39.

part of it, or wholly rejected.[716] Where a proof is rejected, in whole or in part, the administrator must provide a written statement of his reasons for such rejection to the creditor as soon as reasonably practicable.[717] Rule 14.8(1) provides that a creditor may appeal against the administrator's decision that his claim is not a preferential debt. There is no longer any obligation on the creditor to state in the proof of debt whether or not he claims to have a preferential debt, and so, it would seem to follow, no obligation on the administrator to deal with this issue in any statement to the creditor as to the admission or rejection of the claim. Nevertheless, this is clearly a matter which an administrator will frequently have to determine, most obviously where the distribution is to be to preferential creditors only. Where this is the case, it would seem sensible for the administrator to include in his statement to the creditor whether he has accepted the claim as preferential and, if not, why not.

Even where the decision whether a proof should be admitted or rejected is a difficult one, it is a decision which the administrator should take himself. Only in exceptional circumstances, such as where a developing area of law is involved, should he seek directions from the court rather than leaving it for the creditors to pursue the statutory appeal mechanism set out in the Rules.[718]

Appeal against rejection of proof.   Any creditor or contributory who is dissatis- **15-123**
fied with the administrator's decision to admit or reject a proof, or with his decision to agree to the revaluation of a security,[719] may appeal that decision to the court.[720] Where the party appealing is the creditor whose proof was rejected, the appeal must be made within 21 days of the creditor receiving the administrator's statement notifying him of the rejection.[721] Where it is another creditor or a contributory, it must be made within 21 days of becoming aware of the decision.[722]

Where an application to the court is made by way of appeal, the court must fix a venue for the hearing,[723] and the applicant must give at least 14 days' notice,[724] both to the administrator and to the creditor whose proof is the subject of the application (if not himself).[725] On receipt of the notice, the administrator must file with the court a copy of the proof in dispute, and (if appropriate) a copy of his statement of his reasons for its rejection.[726]

As with an appeal against an administrator's decision to admit or reject a claim for voting purposes, an appeal pursuant to r.14.8 is not a true appeal. The court is not limited to the material which was before the administrator; and it is not relevant

---

[716] Insolvency Rules 2016 r.14.7(1).
[717] Insolvency Rules 2016 r.14.7(2).
[718] *Re Chinn, Parker v Nicholson* [2015] EWHC 3881 (Ch); [2015] All E.R. (D) 278 (Nov)—the decision concerns the admission or rejection of claims for voting purposes, but the reasoning is equally applicable to the admission or rejection of proofs for the purposes of a distribution.
[719] Pursuant to Insolvency Rules 2016 r.14.15: see para.15-116.
[720] Insolvency Rules 2016 r.14.8(1) and (3).
[721] Insolvency Rules 2016 r.14.8(2). This time limit may be extended pursuant to the court's case management powers under CPR r.3.1(2)(a), which is applied to time limits under the Rules by Insolvency Rules 2016 Sch.5 para.3. The application will be treated as an application for relief from sanctions pursuant to CPR r.3.9: *Re Lehman Brothers International (Europe)* [2014] EWHC 1687 (Ch); [2014] Bus. L.R. 1186.
[722] Insolvency Rules 2016 r.14.8(3).
[723] Insolvency Rules 2016 r.14.8(4).
[724] Insolvency Rules 2016 r.12.9(3).
[725] Insolvency Rules 2016 r.14.8(5).
[726] Insolvency Rules 2016 r.14.8(6).

(save as to costs) whether or not the administrator reached the wrong conclusion on the material before him.[727]

15-124 Withdrawal, variation or exclusion of proof of debt. The administrator and the creditor may at any time agree to a variation of the amount of a proof of debt,[728] and a creditor may withdraw a proof of debt by delivering written notice to the administrator.[729]

Where the administrator thinks that a proof of debt was improperly admitted, or ought to be reduced, he may apply to the court to exclude it or reduce it in amount.[730] If the administrator declines to interfere in the matter, a creditor can apply to the court for the same relief.[731]

The court must fix a venue for the hearing, and the applicant must give at least 14 days' notice[732] to the creditor, and to the administrator.[733]

On such an application, the applicant bears the burden of showing that the proof was improperly admitted. It is not necessary for to show that the administrator made a mistake of fact, or that there was any moral impropriety.[734] There is no time limit for the making of such an application, but where the application is made by a creditor or contributory outside the 21-day time limit for an appeal pursuant to Rule 14.8, then it will presumably be necessary either to show a change of circumstances or to show circumstances which would justify an extension of time for such an appeal.

15-125 Declaration of dividend. Subject to there being no grounds for its postponement, the administrator must declare the intended dividend within the two-month period after the last date for submitting proofs of debt, as specified in his notice of intention to make a distribution.[735]

When calculating the dividend he must make provision for any debts which have not yet been determined, or any disputed claims.[736] Where any of the company's property cannot be readily or advantageously sold, it may be distributed in specie with the permission of the creditors' committee or (if there is none) the creditors.[737]

When declaring a dividend, the administrator must deliver a notice that he is doing so to all creditors,[738] save where the distribution is made to preferential creditors only (in which case it need be delivered only to those preferential creditors who have proved for their debts).[739] This notice may be sent out with the dividend payment itself.[740]

It must state the amounts raised from the sale of assets, indicating (so far as practicable) the amounts raised from the sale of particular assets; payments made

---

[727] *Re Kentworth Constructions (Practice Note)* [1960] 1 W.L.R. 646; [1960] 2 All E.R. 655, *Caldwell v Jackson* [2000] All E.R. (D) 1975; [2001] B.P.I.R. 966. In relation to costs, see para.15-131.
[728] Insolvency Rules 2016 r.14.10(2).
[729] Insolvency Rules 2016 r.14.10(1).
[730] Insolvency Rules 2016 r.14.11(1)(a).
[731] Insolvency Rules 2016 r.14.11(1)(b).
[732] Insolvency Rules 2016 r.12.9(3).
[733] Insolvency Rules 2016 r.14.11(3).
[734] *Re Globe Legal Services Ltd* [2002] B.C.C. 858.
[735] Insolvency Rules 2016 r.14.34(1).
[736] Insolvency Rules 2016 r.14.39.
[737] Insolvency Rules 2016 r.14.13.
[738] Insolvency Rules 2016 r.14.35(1). This notice must be delivered even to opted-out creditors: Insolvency Act 1986 s.246C(2)(a).
[739] Insolvency Rules 2016 r.14.35(5).
[740] Insolvency Rules 2016 r.14.35(2).

by the administrator in carrying out his functions; provisions made for any unsettled claims, and a statement of funds retained for a specific purpose; the total amount (in money) of the dividend, and the rate of dividend; and whether and if so when, any further dividend is expected to be declared.[741] In addition, where the distribution is to be made to unsecured creditors, the notice must also state the value of the prescribed part (unless there is no prescribed part or the court has disapplied the provisions of s.176A of the Act).[742]

An administrator is not personally liable for payment of a dividend.[743] However where the administrator does not pay a dividend the court does have jurisdiction to order him to pay it (from the company's assets), and also to pay interest and costs from his own pocket.[744] Where the company's assets are insufficient for payment of the dividend, and where this arises through the fault of the administrator, then the company may have a misfeasance claim against him, but absent special circumstances individual creditors would not.[745]

Postponement or cancellation of a dividend.   If an appeal has been made against **15-126** the administrator's decision on a proof, or there is an outstanding application to exclude or reduce a proof, the administrator is not allowed to declare a dividend without the permission of the court.[746] If the challenge will not be determined within the period of two months from the last date for submitting proofs of debt, and he does not obtain the court's permission to make a distribution anyway, he must postpone or cancel the dividend.[747] He may also postpone the dividend if the nature of the company's affairs gives rise to real complexity in admitting or rejecting proofs.[748]

Once the administrator has postponed or cancelled the declaration of a dividend, he will have to send out a new notice under r.14.29 before he can declare a dividend in the future.[749]

Late or altered proofs: the effect on dividends.   Where a creditor's proof is **15-127** revised (whether by a variation of the debt claimed or of the value of a security) it will not be permitted to disturb a dividend already paid to other creditors, and any shortfall will have to be made up through later distributions. However, an overpayment can be recouped immediately.

Therefore, where the amount of a creditor's proof is increased,[750] or where a secured creditor's security is revalued and the revaluation produces an increase in

---

[741] Insolvency Rules 2016 r.14.35(3).

[742] Insolvency Rules 2016 r.14.35(4).

[743] Insolvency Rules 2016 r.14.45(1). See also *Re Lomax Leisure Ltd* [2007] EWHC 2508 (Ch); [2008] B.C.C. 686, where liquidators attempted to pay a dividend by means of cheques, which were stopped once they learned of an extant appeal against their decision on a proof. It was held that the cheques were not supported by consideration and that the liquidators had no personal liability to the creditors to pay the dividend they had declared.

[744] Insolvency Rules 2016 r.14.45(2).

[745] *Kyrris v Oldham* [2004] EWCA Civ 1506; [2004] B.C.C. 111.

[746] Insolvency Rules 2016 r.14.34(2).

[747] Insolvency Rules 2016 r.14.33(1). While the rule is phrased permissively, the only alternative is declaration of the dividend pursuant to r.14.34.

[748] Insolvency Rules 2016 r.14.33(2).

[749] Insolvency Rules 2016 r.14.33(3): see para.15-119.

[750] Insolvency Rules 2016 r.14.40(1)

his unsecured claim,[751] after a dividend has been paid, he is not entitled to disturb the general distribution already made.[752] Likewise, where a creditor lodges a proof of debt after the declaration of the dividend, he may not disturb the dividend (whether or not it has already been paid).[753] Instead, in each case the creditor becomes entitled to be paid the amount of any additional dividend to which he is entitled out of any funds available for a further distribution and in priority to the payment of any further general dividend.[754]

By contrast, where, after a dividend has been paid, a proof of debt is withdrawn or expunged, its amount is reduced, or any security is revalued up so as to reduce the unsecured claim, the creditor is liable to repay to the administrator any amount overpaid to him by way of dividend as soon as reasonably practicable.[755]

15-128 Assignment or re-direction of dividend. A creditor entitled to a dividend may give notice to the administrator to pay his dividend to another person, or that he has assigned his entitlement to another person.[756] The notice must specify the name and address of the person to whom payment is to be made[757]; the administrator must make payment in accordance with the notice.

15-129 Final dividends, and notices of no or no further dividend. Where the administrator intends to distribute a sole or final dividend, after the last date for proving set out in the notice of intention to declare a dividend he must pay the remuneration and expenses incurred in the administration and in any winding up which immediately preceded the administration. He must then distribute the remaining assets of the company without making provision for any claim not already proved for.[758]

If the administrator gives notice to creditors that he is unable to declare a dividend, or any further dividend, he must state in the notice either that no funds have been realised, or that the funds realised have already been distributed, used or allocated for defraying the expenses of the administration. This notice may form part of a progress report.[759]

15-130 Disqualification from dividend. If a creditor contravenes any provision of the Act or the Rules relating to the valuation of securities, the court may, on the administrator's application, order that the creditor be wholly or partially disqualified from participation in any dividend.[760]

15-131 Costs. A creditor's costs of proving his debt (including documentary expenses) are to be borne by the creditor.[761] The costs of verifying the quantum of the debt

---

[751] Insolvency Rules 2016 r.14.41(1) and (3).
[752] Insolvency Rules 2016 rr.14.40(1)(a) and 14.41(4).
[753] Insolvency Rules 2016 r.14.40(1)(b).
[754] Insolvency Rules 2016 rr.14.40(2) and 14.41(3).
[755] Insolvency Rules 2016 rr.14.40(4) and 14.41(2).
[756] Insolvency Rules 2016 r.14.43(1).
[757] Insolvency Rules 2016 r.14.43(2).
[758] Insolvency Rules 2016 r.14.38(1)(b).
[759] Insolvency Rules 2016 r.14.37.
[760] Insolvency Rules 2016 r.14.42.
[761] Insolvency Rules 2016 r.14.5(a).

are borne by the administrator, as an administration expense,[762] as are the costs of calculating the dividend and making the distribution.[763]

The administrator is not personally responsible for the costs of any person in respect of an appeal against his decision on a proof, unless the court otherwise orders.[764] This mirrors the position in relation to appeals against the valuation of claims for voting purposes,[765] and it has been held that the court will not normally make such an order unless the administrator or chair has fallen so far below the proper standard to be expected of a professional person that it is appropriate to do so.[766] A similar approach has been taken in relation to a successful appeal of a liquidator's decision on a proof of debt, where the liquidator was not ordered to bear the costs because he was not found to be acting for his own personal benefit or wholly for the purpose of advancing a proposed misfeasance claim.[767]

Distributions to members. Neither the Act nor the Rules contain any power **15-132** permitting the administrator to make a distribution to members. In the event that there is a surplus remaining after payment of the creditors in full, the usual practice is to put the company into members' voluntary liquidation. However where a distribution to members was likely to be beneficial to a company's creditors, the court was prepared to give directions sanctioning the carrying out of a scheme for making a distribution to members, which involved appointing a director who would in turn reduce the company's capital to enable the distribution of an interim dividend in accordance with the Companies Act 2006.[768]

SECTION 8: REMUNERATION OF ADMINISTRATOR

General entitlement to remuneration. The administrator is entitled to remunera- **15-133** tion for his services as office holder.[769] The bases upon which his remuneration may be fixed are:

- as a percentage of the value of the property with which he has had to deal;
- by reference to the time which he and his staff have properly given in attending to matters arising during the administration; and
- as a set amount.[770]

The administrator's remuneration may be fixed by one or by a combination of these bases, and it may be fixed on a different basis for different tasks or types of work.[771]

In determining the basis for the administrator's remuneration, the following mat-

---

[762] Insolvency Rules 2016 r.14.5(b).
[763] Though note that any of the administrator's costs which relate to distribution of the prescribed part are to be borne by the prescribed part: Insolvency Rules 2016 r.3.50(2).
[764] Insolvency Rules 2016 r.14.9(2).
[765] Insolvency Rules 2016 r.15.35(6).
[766] *Re a Debtor (No. 222 of 1990), Ex p. Bank of Ireland (No.2)* [1993] B.C.L.C. 233.
[767] *Re Burnden Group* [2017] EWHC 406 (Ch); [2017] B.P.I.R. 585.
[768] *Re Lehman Brothers Europe Ltd* [2017] EWHC 2031 (Ch).
[769] Insolvency Rules 2016 r.18.16(1). It was held that the predecessor to this rule, which referred to remuneration for the administrator's services "as such", did not permit remuneration to be fixed for work that the administrators do after they have ceased to hold office (for instance, at the request of liquidators): *Maxwell v Brookes* [2014] B.P.I.R. 1395; [2015] B.C.C. 113. It is doubtful that the rewording of the Rule has altered the position.
[770] Insolvency Rules 2016 r.18.16(2).
[771] Insolvency Rules 2016 r.18.16(3).

ters must be taken into account:

- the complexity (or otherwise) of the case;
- any respects in which, in connection with the company's affairs, there falls on the administrator any responsibility of an exceptional kind or degree;
- the effectiveness with which the administrator appears to be carrying out, or to have carried out, his duties as such; and
- the value and nature of the property with which he has to deal.[772]

The administrator is entitled to draw agreed remuneration during the course of the administration.[773]

15-134 **Initial information to creditors.** The statement of proposals sent by the administrator to the creditors must contain a statement of the basis on which he proposes that this remuneration should be fixed.[774] In addition, before the decision fixing his remuneration is taken (and usually also in the statement of proposals) the administrator must set out details of the work he proposes to undertake and the expenses he expects to incur in doing so.[775] If he is proposing that his remuneration should be fixed (wholly or partly) on a time-spent basis, then he must also provide a fees estimate.[776]

This fees estimate must set out:

- details of the work the administrator and his staff expect to do;
- the hourly rate or rates he and his staff propose to charge;
- the time he anticipates each part of the work will take;
- whether the administrator anticipates that it will be necessary to seek further approval of fees; and
- if so, the reasons why it will be necessary to seek further approval of the fees.[777]

The references to seeking further approval of fees are, presumably, references to the procedure for seeking remuneration in excess of the fees estimate[778] and suggest that the fees estimate should include details of contingencies which have not been budgeted for in the estimate and may cause the estimate to be exceeded.

The fees estimate provided by the administrator may extend to the estimated fees of a subsequent liquidation should the administrator be appointed liquidator.[779] Where the company exits administration by going into winding up (compulsory or voluntary) and the administrator is appointed liquidator, his remuneration as liquidator is treated as having been fixed on the same basis as it was in the administration.[780] There is no provision for the liquidator to supply a further fees estimate in that case, and it is not clear from the Rules whether as liquidator he would be bound by the estimate supplied when he was administrator. Given that the

---

[772] Insolvency Rules 2016 r.18.16(9).
[773] *Spring Valley Properties v Harris* [2001] B.C.C. 796; [2001] B.P.I.R. 709.
[774] Insolvency Rules 2016 r.3.35(9).
[775] Insolvency Rules 2016 r.18.16(7).
[776] Insolvency Rules 2016 r.18.16(4). It is important that the fee estimate is accurate, since the administrator may not draw remuneration in excess of the estimate without permission of the creditors (see para.15-139).
[777] Insolvency Rules 2016 r.1.2(2).
[778] See para.15-139.
[779] Insolvency Rules 2016 r.18.16(5).
[780] Insolvency Rules 2016 r.18.20(5).

consequences of exceeding the fees estimate are that he may not draw further remuneration without the creditors' permission, it would be a sensible precaution to include likely liquidation fees in the initial estimate where possible.

Further information for creditors.   The administrator must include in each **15-135** progress report sent to creditors details of the remuneration charged during the period of the report[781] (and additionally during preceding periods if it is the first report after the basis of remuneration has been fixed),[782] a statement of the expenses incurred during the period,[783] a statement setting out whether the expenses incurred are likely to exceed the estimate given to the creditors pursuant to r.18.16(4), together with the reasons for any excess,[784] and a statement of the creditors' rights to request further information about, or to challenge, the administrator's remuneration and expenses.[785]

Procedure for fixing remuneration.   It is the creditors' committee which has **15-136** primary responsibility for agreeing the basis of the administrator's remuneration.[786] Where there is no creditors' committee, or it does not make a determination, the remuneration may be fixed by a decision of the creditors,[787] unless the administrator has made a statement under para.52(1)(b) of Sch.B1 in his proposals.[788] In that case his remuneration may be fixed by the consent of each secured creditor of the company, together with (where preferential creditors are to receive a dividend) a decision of the preferential creditors.[789] The decision of the creditors or preferential creditors (as the case may be) must be reached through a qualifying decision-making procedure, and not by the deemed consent procedure.[790]

If the administrator's remuneration is not fixed by the creditors (whether by committee or otherwise), he is required to apply to court to fix his remuneration,[791] though he must first take steps to agree his remuneration with the creditors.[792] Such an application must be made within 18 months of the commencement of the administration,[793] and it will be dealt with in accordance with the provisions of Pt 6 of the Practice Direction on Insolvency Proceedings.

The Rules make no provision for the fee estimate to be agreed by creditors or

---

[781]   Insolvency Rules 2016 r.18.4(1)(b)(i).
[782]   Insolvency Rules 2016 r.18.4(1)(b)(ii).
[783]   Insolvency Rules 2016 r.18.4(1)(d).
[784]   Insolvency Rules 2016 r.18.4(1)(e); as to the estimate to be provided pursuant to r.18.16(4), see para.15-134.
[785]   Insolvency Rules 2016 r.18.4(1)(f).
[786]   Insolvency Rules 2016 r.18.18(2)
[787]   Insolvency Rules 2016 r.18.18(3).
[788]   That there are likely to be insufficient funds for distribution to unsecured creditors other than out of the prescribed part.
[789]   Insolvency Rules 2016 r.18.18(4).
[790]   Insolvency Act 1986 s.246ZF(2). For qualifying decision-making procedures, see para.15-32 ff.
[791]   Insolvency Rules 2016 r.18.23(1).
[792]   Insolvency Rules 2016 r.18.23(2).
[793]   Insolvency Rules 2016 r.18.23(3). This time limit may be extended pursuant to the court's case management powers under CPR r.3.1(2)(a), which is applied to time limits under the Rules by Insolvency Rules 2016 Sch.5 para.3. Since the administrator is not permitted to draw remuneration until the basis of his remuneration is fixed, an application for an extension of time should be treated as an application for relief from sanctions: cf. *Re Lehman Brothers International (Europe)* [2014] EWHC 1687 (Ch); [2014] Bus. L.R. 1186; and *Re Calibre Solicitors Ltd* [2015] B.P.I.R. 435.

fixed by the court.[794] It would follow that the creditors have no power unilaterally to vary the fee estimate provided by the administrator. Where they disagree with this estimate, therefore, their remedy is to refuse to agree the basis on which remuneration is to be fixed. However, there seems to be no reason why the fee estimate could not be varied by agreement between the administrator and creditors as part of the process of agreeing the basis of remuneration, or by directions given by the court when making an order fixing remuneration.

15-137 Pre-administration costs. Where the administrator has included in the proposals a statement about pre-administration costs and expenses,[795] it is for the creditors' committee to determine whether these are payable and, if so, in what amount.[796] Where there is no creditors' committee, the committee does not make a decision, or the insolvency practitioner whose fees are sought is unhappy with the decision,[797] then the decision may be sought from the creditors as a whole or (if a statement under para.52(1)(b) has been made) each secured creditor and the preferential creditors if the administrator thinks it likely that a distribution will be made to them.[798] If the insolvency practitioner whose fees are being sought is not the administrator and he requests it, the administrator must call a meeting of the creditors' committee or seek a decision of creditors by a qualifying decision-making procedure, and must give notice of that meeting or decision procedure within 28 days of the request.[799] Should the administrator fail to do so the other insolvency practitioner may apply to court for an order requiring him to do so.[800]

15-138 Review or increase of remuneration. Where the administrator considers that his remuneration has been fixed at too low a rate or on an inappropriate basis, he must first seek to increase it by a decision of the creditors if it was fixed by the creditors' committee.[801] If it was not fixed by the creditors' committee,[802] or if the creditors refuse to increase the remuneration,[803] then he may apply to court to increase his remuneration. Such an application will be dealt with in accordance with the provisions of Part 6 of the Practice Direction on Insolvency Proceedings.

Once the basis of the administrator's remuneration has been fixed, he may request that the basis be changed if there is a material and substantial change in the circumstances which were taken into account in fixing it.[804] Such a request must be made, in the first instance, to the body previously responsible for fixing the remuneration.[805] If that body was the creditors' committee, and the committee refuses the variation, he may then seek a decision of the creditors. If the creditors

---

[794] They do not fall within the scope of matters to be determined set out in Insolvency Rules 2016 r.18.16(8).
[795] Insolvency Rules 2016 r.3.35(1)(a).
[796] Insolvency Rules 2016 r.3.52(1).
[797] Insolvency Rules 2016 r.3.52(2).
[798] Insolvency Rules 2016 r.3.52(3).
[799] Insolvency Rules 2016 r.3.53(4).
[800] Insolvency Rules 2016 r.3.52(8).
[801] Insolvency Rules 2016 rr.18.24(a) and 18.25(2).
[802] Insolvency Rules 2016 r.18.28(2)(b) and (c).
[803] Insolvency Rules 2016 r.18.28(2)(a).
[804] Insolvency Rules 2016 r.18.29(1).
[805] Insolvency Rules 2016 r.18.29(2). However if the administrator's remuneration was previously fixed by the secured creditors or the secured and preferential creditors because his proposals contained a statement pursuant to Sch.B1 para.52(1)(b), and the company now has sufficient funds to make a distribution to unsecured creditors other than just out of the prescribed part, then the request must

or, in any other case the body previously responsible for fixing the remuneration, refuse then the administrator may apply to court for such a variation.[806] If there is a variation it takes effect from the date of the administrator's request.[807]

Exceeding the fees estimate.   The administrator is not allowed to draw any **15-139** remuneration in excess of the fees estimate without the permission of the body which fixed his remuneration.[808] A request for permission must specify the following:

- the reasons why the administrator has exceeded, or is likely to exceed, the fees estimate;
- the additional work he has undertaken or proposed to undertake;
- the hourly rate or rates he proposes to charge for each part of that additional work;
- the time that the administrator expects that the additional work will take;
- whether he anticipates that it will be necessary to seek further approval; and
- if so, the reasons it will be necessary.

The Rules do not make provision for the position where the creditors refuse to permit remuneration to be drawn in excess of the fees estimate, and there is no explicit power for the administrator to apply to court in that case. However, it is likely that the court will attempt to fill this obvious lacuna, by treating the question as an application to increase remuneration pursuant to r.18.24.

Apportioning remuneration between office-holders.   Where there are joint **15-140** administrators, it is for them to agree on the division of the global sum; any dispute between them is to be settled by the creditors' committee or the decision of the creditors, or, by an order of the court.[809]

Where a new administrator is appointed in place of a previous administrator, the decisions already made in respect of remuneration continue to have force until they are varied in accordance with the Rules.[810] Where the basis set was a fixed fee, the former administrator may request the body responsible for fixing the remuneration to determination of the share of this fixed fee which is payable to him, and what share is payable to the new administrator.[811] The former administrator has 28 days from the day when he ceased to hold office in order to make this request. If he fails to do so the new administrator may make the request.[812]

Whichever makes the request must deliver a copy of it to the other,[813] and the other will then have 21 days to deliver a notice of intent to make representations.[814] No decision can be made during this 21-day period or, where a notice of intent has

---

be made to the creditors' committee or (in their absence) the creditors.

[806] Insolvency Rules 2016 rr.18.28(2) and 18.29(3).
[807] Insolvency Rules 2016 r.18.29(5).
[808] Insolvency Rules 2016 r.18.30(1) and (2). However if the administrator's remuneration was previously fixed by the secured creditors or the secured and preferential creditors because his proposals contained a statement pursuant to Sch.B1 para.52(1)(b), and the company now has sufficient funds to make a distribution to unsecured creditors other than just out of the prescribed part, then the request must be made to the creditors' committee or (in their absence) the creditors.
[809] Insolvency Rules 2016 r.18.17.
[810] Insolvency Rules 2016 r.18.31.
[811] Insolvency Rules 2016 r.18.32(2).
[812] Insolvency Rules 2016 r.18.32(3).
[813] Insolvency Rules 2016 r.18.32(6).
[814] Insolvency Rules 2016 r.18.32(7).

been delivered, the party who delivered it has been given the opportunity to make representations. If either party is dissatisfied with the decision he may seek a decision of the creditors (where the original body determining the request was the creditors' committee) or apply to court.[815]

15-141 **Creditors' challenge to excessive remuneration or expenses.** Any secured creditor, or an unsecured creditor who has the support of at least 10% in value of the unsecured creditors (including himself) or who has the permission of the court,[816] may apply to the court for an order that the administrator's remuneration be reduced on the grounds that it is excessive, that the basis of his remuneration be changed, or that expenses be disallowed on the grounds that they are excessive.[817] It is unlikely that the court would give permission to an unsecured creditor to bring such a challenge unless it was satisfied that it had a real prospect of success[818] and that there was a possibility of a distribution to the unsecured creditors. If the administrator relies on his own costs and expenses to show that there is no such possibility, then he will have to provide a proper breakdown of them (or at least so much of them as is susceptible to challenge).[819] An application must be made within eight weeks after receipt of the progress report or final report which report the charging of the remuneration of expenses which are challenged.[820]

If the application is made without the need to seek the court's permission and the court thinks that no sufficient cause is shown for reduction, it may dismiss the application without a hearing.[821] Otherwise, the court must fix a venue for a hearing,[822] and the applicant must serve the application and any evidence in support on the administrator, at least 14 days before the hearing.[823]

On the application the court may reduce the amount of remuneration the administrator is entitled to charge.[824] It may instead reduce any fixed rate or amount, or change the basis of the administrator's remuneration,[825] though it may only do so in relation to the period covered by the report in question.[826] It may also disallow expenses as expenses of the administration (with the result that the administrator will have to pay them personally),[827] and order any excess remuneration or expenses to be repaid to the company.[828]

Unless otherwise ordered by the court, the costs of such an application shall be paid by the applicant, and are not payable as an administration expense.[829]

15-142 **The court's approach to remuneration applications: principles.** The court's

---

[815] Insolvency Rules 2016 r.18.32(9).
[816] Insolvency Rules 2016 r.18.34(2).
[817] Insolvency Rules 2016 r.18.34(1), rr.18.36(4) and r.18.37(4).
[818] Compare Insolvency Rules 2016 r.18.37(1).
[819] *Mattu v Toone* [2015] EWHC 3506 (Ch); [2016] B.P.I.R. 408.
[820] Insolvency Rules 2016 r.18.34(3). This time limit may be extended pursuant to the court's case management powers under CPR r.3.1(2)(a), which is applied to time limits under the Rules by Insolvency Rules 2016 Sch.5 para.3: see *Re Calibre Solicitors Ltd* [2015] B.P.I.R. for an extension of time in the context of a challenge to remuneration.
[821] Insolvency Rules 2016 r.18.37(1).
[822] Insolvency Rules 2016 rr.18.36(2) and 18.37(2).
[823] Insolvency Rules 2016 rr.18.36(3) and 18.37(3).
[824] Insolvency Rules 2016 rr.18.36(4)(a) and 18.37(4)(a).
[825] Insolvency Rules 2016 rr.18.36(4)(b), (c) and 8.37(4)(b), (c).
[826] Insolvency Rules 2016 rr.18.36(5) and 18.37(5).
[827] Insolvency Rules 2016 rr.18.36(4)(d) and 18.36(4)(d).
[828] Insolvency Rules 2016 rr.18.36(4)(e) and 18.37(4)(e).
[829] Insolvency Rules 2016 rr.18.36(6) and 18.37(6).

approach to all remuneration applications (whether they are applications to fix remuneration, vary it or challenge it)[830] is set out at Pt 6 of Practice Direction— Insolvency Proceedings. This sets out the principles to be derived from the Rules and from authority and it (or its predecessors) have been judicially approved on several occasions.[831] It sets out the principles on which the court will approach such applications.

- "Justification": it is for the administrator to justify his remuneration, and he should be prepared to provide full particulars of the basis for and nature of his claim. This is an aspect of the administrator's status as fiduciary.[832]
- "The benefit of the doubt": if there is any doubt as to the appropriateness, fairness or reasonableness of the administrator's claim to remuneration, it should be resolved against him.
- "Professional integrity": the court should give weight to the fact that the administrator is a member of a regulated profession and an officer of the court. This is particularly relevant where the complaint is that the administrator has carried out unnecessary tasks, or has performed tasks with excessive diligence.[833]
- "The value of the service rendered": the administrator's remuneration should reflect the value of the service rendered and not simply remunerate him for time expended. This is a principle which tends to merge with "proportionality of remuneration".
- "Proportionality": this principle is subdivided—
  - "Proportionality of information": the court and the parties must consider what information it is proportionate to require the administrator to provide, given the level of his fees subject to dispute, the nature, extent and complexity of the issues dealt with or to be dealt with, and the value of the assets in the administration. However this principle does not mean that the administrator need only provide timesheets without explaining why steps were carried out.[834]
  - "Proportionality of remuneration": similarly the remuneration should be proportional to these matters, also taking into account any risk undertaken by the administrator and the efficiency with which he has conducted the work. As well as the value of the assets in question the court will recognise the importance of the administrator's statutory obligations[835] and other matters not necessarily reflected in the value of realisations (such as disclaimers or dealing with creditors' claims), and the extent to which the conduct of directors or others has made his task more difficult and time consuming.[836]
- "Professional Guidance": the court is entitled to have regard to statements

---

[830] Practice Direction –Insolvency Proceedings, para.21.1.1.

[831] *Simion v Brown* [2007] EWHC 511 (Ch); [2007] B.P.I.R. 412; *Hunt v Yearwood Grazette* [2009] EWHC 2112 (Ch); [2009] B.P.I.R. 810; *Brook v Reed* [2011] EWCA Civ 331; [2012] 1 W.L.R. 419 at [41]–[48].

[832] *Mirror Group Newspapers v Maxwell (No.1)* [1998] B.C.C. 324; [1998] 1 B.C.L.C. 638.

[833] See, for example, *Re Super Aguri F1 Ltd* [2011] B.C.C. 452; [2011] B.P.I.R. 256 at [41].

[834] *Hunt v Yearwood Grazette* [2009] B.P.I.R. 810 at [17]–[24].

[835] *Simion v Brown* [2007] B.P.I.R. 412 at [26].

[836] *Barker v Bajjonn* [2008 B.P.I.R. 771; *Re Super Aguri F1 Ltd* [2011] B.C.C. 452, and see the discussion at *Brook v Reed* [2012] 1 W.L.R. 419 at [50]–[51].

of practice promulgated by regulatory and professional bodies, and the administrator's compliance with them.

- "Timing of the application": the court will take into account whether the application should have been made earlier, and the reasons for any delay.

The court's task on an application is to balance these principles.[837]

15-143 **The court's approach to remuneration applications: procedure.** Practice Direction—Insolvency Proceedings requires an administrator to provide a significant amount of information. This includes the following:

- The administrator must provide a narrative description and explanation of—
  - the background to, relevant circumstances of and reasons for the appointment;
  - the work undertaken or to be undertaken overall, breaking the description down into individual tasks or categories of task;
  - the reasons why it is or was considered necessary or beneficial to carry out each task, in the manner in which it was carried out;
  - the amount of time spent or to be spent and why it is considered fair, reasonable and proportionate; and
  - what has been or is likely to be achieved, the benefits from the work in question, and what remains to be achieved.
- He must provide a statement of the total of number of hours worked or to be undertaken in respect of which remuneration is sought (or in dispute), with a breakdown of those hours by individual staff member and individual task or category of task. Where appropriate and proportionate[838] he must also give details of the following in relation to the work which is subject to the application—
  - the proportion of what has already been done to what remains to be done; and
  - the proportion of work carried out or to be carried out by each member or grade of staff.
- He must provide a statement of the total amount to be charged for the work done or to be done which is subject to the application, including—
  - a breakdown of those amounts by individual member of staff and by task or category of task;
  - details of time spent or to be spent and remuneration charged or to be charged (or what would have been charged if remuneration were on a time spent basis) in respect of each task as a proportion of the whole.
- He must provide details of each individual engaged on the matter, including their experience, training, qualifications and level of seniority.
- He must provide details of the steps taken or to be taken to avoid duplication and to ensure that work is carried out by staff of the appropriate level of seniority.
- He must provide details of the individual rates charged by him and his staff, including a general explanation of the policy adopted in fixing rates and recording time spent, and the reasons for any increase applied during the

---

[837] *Brook v Reed* [2012] 1 W.L.R. 419 at [49].
[838] See *Hunt v Yearwood Grazette* [2009] B.P.I.R. 810 at [17]–[24] for the dangers of relying on proportionality to avoid provision of information.

period, and, in the unusual case where remuneration is sought in respect of secretaries, cashiers and other administrative staff, an explanation of why those costs should be regarded as overhead costs.
- He must provide details of any remuneration previously fixed or approved.
- He must explain what consultation has taken place with any persons he considers to have an interest in the assets under his control, or explain why there has been no such consultation. If there was a consultation, then the administrator must state the number and value of those consulted, as well as their proportion (in both number and value) to the total number of people with an interest in those assets.[839]

In addition, where the administrator seeks remuneration on a basis other than time spent, he must explain why and justify any rates suggested. He must also provide a comparison with the amount which would be charged by reference to the other available bases of remuneration.[840] The court may permit the administrator to draw remuneration on account while an application is pending.[841] Subject to any other order the court makes, the costs of remuneration applications are to be paid as an expense of the administration.[842]

The court's approach to remuneration applications: principles. The court's **15-144** approach to all remuneration applications (whether they are applications to fix remuneration, vary it or challenge it)[843] is set out at Pt 6 of Practice Direction—Insolvency Proceedings. This sets out the principles to be derived from the Rules and from authority and it (or its predecessors) have been judicially approved on several occasions.[844] It sets out the principles on which the court will approach such applications:

- "Justification": it is for the administrator to justify his remuneration, and he should be prepared to provide full particulars of the basis for and nature of his claim. This is an aspect of the administrator's status as fiduciary.[845]
- "The benefit of the doubt": if there is any doubt as to the appropriateness, fairness or reasonableness of the administrator's claim to remuneration, it should be resolved against him.
- "Professional integrity": the court should give weight to the fact that the administrator is a member of a regulated profession and an officer of the court. This is particularly relevant where the complaint is that the administrator has carried out unnecessary tasks, or has performed tasks with excessive diligence.[846]
- "The value of the service rendered": the administrator's remuneration should reflect the value of the service rendered and not simply remunerate

---

[839] Practice Direction—Insolvency Proceedings, para.21.4.2.
[840] Practice Direction—Insolvency Proceedings, para.21.4.3.
[841] Practice Direction—Insolvency Proceedings, para.21.4.7.
[842] Practice Direction—Insolvency Proceedings, para.21.4.8, though this conflicts with the position set out in Rules 18.36 and 18.37 which deal with challenges to administrators' remuneration.
[843] Practice Direction—Insolvency Proceedings, para.21.1.1.
[844] *Simion v Brown* [2007] EWHC 511 (Ch); [2007] B.P.I.R. 412; *Hunt v Yearwood Grazette* [2009] EWHC 2112 (Ch); [2009] B.P.I.R. 810; *Brook v Reed* [2011] EWCA Civ 331; [2012] 1 W.L.R. 419 at [41]–[48].
[845] *Mirror Group Newspapers v Maxwell (No.1)* [1998] B.C.C. 324; [1998] 1 B.C.L.C. 638.
[846] See, for example, *Re Super Aguri F1 Ltd* [2011] B.C.C. 452; [2011] B.P.I.R. 256 at [41].

him for time expended. This is a principle which tends to merge with "proportionality of remuneration".

- "Proportionality": this principle is subdivided—
  - "Proportionality of information": the court and the parties must consider what information it is proportionate to require the administrator to provide, given the level of his fees subject to dispute, the nature, extent and complexity of the issues dealt with or to be dealt with, and the value of the assets in the administration. However this principle does not mean that the administrator need only provide timesheets without explaining why steps were carried out.[847]
  - "Proportionality of remuneration": similarly the remuneration should be proportional to these matters, also taking into account any risk undertaken by the administrator and the efficiency with which he has conducted the work. As well as the value of the assets in question the court will recognise the importance of the administrator's statutory obligations[848] and other matters not necessarily reflected in the value of realisations (such as disclaimers or dealing with creditors' claims), and the extent to which the conduct of directors or others has made his task more difficult and time consuming.[849]
- "Professional Guidance": the court is entitled to have regard to statements of practice promulgated by regulatory and professional bodies, and the administrator's compliance with them.
- "Timing of the application": the court will take into account whether the application should have been made earlier, and the reasons for any delay.

The court's task on an application is to balance these principles.[850]

15-145 The court's approach to remuneration applications: procedure. Practice Direction—Insolvency Proceedings requires an administrator to provide a significant amount of information. This includes the following:

- The administrator must provide a narrative description and explanation of—
  - the background to, relevant circumstances of and reasons for the appointment;
  - the work undertaken or to be undertaken overall, breaking the description down into individual tasks or categories of task;
  - the reasons why it is or was considered necessary or beneficial to carry out each task, in the manner in which it was carried out;
  - the amount of time spent or to be spent and why it is considered fair, reasonable and proportionate; and
  - what has been or is likely to be achieved, the benefits from the work in question, and what remains to be achieved.
- He must provide a statement of the total of number of hours worked or to be undertaken in respect of which remuneration is sought (or in dispute), with a breakdown of those hours by individual staff member and individual

---

847 *Hunt v Yearwood Grazette* [2009] B.P.I.R. 810 at [17]–[24].
848 *Simion v Brown* [2007] B.P.I.R. 412 at [26].
849 *Barker v Bajjonn* [2008 B.P.I.R. 771; *Re Super Aguri F1 Ltd* [2011] B.C.C. 452, and see the discussion at *Brook v Reed* [2012] 1 W.L.R. 419 at [50]–[51].
850 *Brook v Reed* [2012] 1 W.L.R. 419 at [49].

task or category of task. Where appropriate and proportionate[851] he must also give details of the following in relation to the work which is subject to the application—

— the proportion of what has already been done to what remains to be done; and

— the proportion of work carried out or to be carried out by each member or grade of staff.

- He must provide a statement of the total amount to be charged for the work done or to be done which is subject to the application, including—

— a breakdown of those amounts by individual member of staff and by task or category of task; and

— details of time spent or to be spent and remuneration charged or to be charged (or what would have been charged if remuneration were on a time spent basis) in respect of each task as a proportion of the whole.

- He must provide details of each individual engaged on the matter, including their experience, training, qualifications and level of seniority.

- He must provide details of the steps taken or to be taken to avoid duplication and to ensure that work is carried out by staff of the appropriate level of seniority.

- He must provide details of the individual rates charged by him and his staff, including a general explanation of the policy adopted in fixing rates and recording time spent, and the reasons for any increase applied during the period, and, in the unusual case where remuneration is sought in respect of secretaries, cashiers and other administrative staff, an explanation of why those costs should be regarded as overhead costs.

- He must provide details of any remuneration previously fixed or approved.

- He must explain what consultation has taken place with any persons he considers to have an interest in the assets under his control, or explain why there has been no such consultation. If there was a consultation, then the administrator must state the number and value of those consulted, as well as their proportion (in both number and value) to the total number of people with an interest in those assets.[852]

In addition, where the administrator seeks remuneration on a basis other than time spent, he must explain why and justify any rates suggested. He must also provide a comparison with the amount which would be charged by reference to the other available bases of remuneration.[853]

The court may permit the administrator to draw remuneration on account while an application is pending.[854] Subject to any other order the court makes, the costs of remuneration applications are to be paid as an expense of the administration.[855]

---

[851] See *Hunt v Yearwood Grazette* [2009] B.P.I.R. 810 at [17]–[24] for the dangers of relying on proportionality to avoid provision of information.

[852] Practice Direction—Insolvency Proceedings, para.21.4.2.

[853] Practice Direction—Insolvency Proceedings, para.21.4.3.

[854] Practice Direction—Insolvency Proceedings, para.21.4.7.

[855] Practice Direction—Insolvency Proceedings, para.21.4.8, though this conflicts with the position set out in rr.18.36 and 18.37 which deal with challenges to administrators' remuneration.

CHAPTER 16

CONVERSION FROM ADMINISTRATION INTO OTHER FORMS OF
PROCEEDING

SECTION 1: INTRODUCTION

16-1   **The nature and purpose of administration (current regime).**   An administration, whether brought into being by a judicial appointment or by an extra-judicial
one, is intended to be no more than a temporary mode for the company to assume.
Unlike the former procedure, it has fixed periods for its permitted duration[1]; it is
intended to be, and should be, terminated, when it is no longer required,[2] or when
it does not or cannot function in accordance with the statute, and/or with the
administrator's proposals, or with the wishes of a majority of the creditors.

The appointment is intended to assist those responsible for and interested in the
company and its assets to achieve, so far as practicable, "the purpose of
administration".[3] If it cannot do so satisfactorily, or at all, then it must be terminated,
unless it has been, or can be, converted into another form of insolvency
administration. Such possible conversions are envisaged by the provisions as to the
administrator's proposals.[4]

The administrator's proposals may include a proposal that the company should
enter into a voluntary arrangement ("an administration-arrangement", employing
the standard procedure, modified for use by companies in administration[5]), or into
a compromise, or a scheme of arrangement,[6] with its creditors. The provisions of
the Insolvency Act 1986 relating to company voluntary arrangements and the Recast
Insolvency Regulation[7] apply in Scotland, but Pt VIII of the Act which deals with
individual insolvency arrangements applies only in England and Wales. In Scotland,
the insolvency or bankruptcy of an individual or a partnership is governed by the
Bankruptcy (Scotland) Act 2016 (repealing the Bankruptcy (Scotland) Act 1985).
This includes provision for a bankrupt individual to grant a voluntary trust deed for

---

[1]   Insolvency Act 1986 Sch.B1 para.76, capable of extension under the same provision for a period of
     up to one year (as amended by the Small Business, Enterprise and Employment Act 2015 from 26
     May 2015, an increase from six months) by consent or for a specified period on the application of
     the administrator.
[2]   *Re Railtrack Plc (No.2)* [2003] EWHC 1526 (Ch); [2003] All E.R. (D) 38 (Oct).
[3]   Insolvency Act 1986 Sch.B1 para.3.
[4]   Insolvency Act 1986 Sch.B1 para.49(3)(a) and (b). See below for such conversions.
[5]   Insolvency Act 1986 Pt I (as amended by Enterprise Act 2002) ss.1(3), 2(1), 3(1), 4A, 5(3), (4),
     6(2)(c); Insolvency Rules 1986 as amended by Insolvency (Amendment) Rules 2003, (SI 2003/
     584) rr.11, 10–12., and Pts 3, 4 and 5 generally: see para.16-5, below.
[6]   Companies Act 2006 Pt 26; Insolvency Act 1986 s.5(3)(a). If such an order is made, presumably the
     administrator ceases to have any further function to perform: see para.16-58, below.
[7]   And before it the European Council Regulation on Insolvency Proceedings 2000. See para 16.2,
     below.

behoof of his creditors, whose effect is approximately equivalent to an individual voluntary arrangement under English law.

If the administration cannot succeed on its own terms, and with its own resources, and cannot effectively be replaced by a voluntary arrangement or a scheme of arrangement, then the administrator, applying in the name of the company, or the supervisor of an ineffective arrangement, may put the company into a winding-up, preferably a creditors' voluntary winding-up, being considerably less expensive than a compulsory winding-up.[8] In the final analysis, in the absence of assets, he can take steps to cause the company to be dissolved.[9]

The insolvency rules referred to in this chapter in relation to voluntary arrangements, and the conversion from administration to winding up and the conversion from administration to dissolution referred to in ss.4 and 6, do not apply in Scotland where the position is governed by the Insolvency (Scotland) Rules 1986 (as amended).

The impacts of the Recast Insolvency Regulation and the prior EC Regulation on Insolvency Proceedings 2000.   Under the EC Insolvency Regulation 2000 and the Recast Regulation, in parallel with the powers of the administrator, and of his supervisor of an arrangement, if the company has part of its enterprise in another Member State, which constitutes its centre of main interests, and where it has been put into some form of insolvent administration (thereby constituting the "main insolvency proceedings" under the Recast Regulation[10]), the Member-State liquidator in those proceedings can exercise in the UK the rights and powers of a creditor,[11] and can himself apply to put the company in administration here into a creditors' voluntary winding-up,[12] or a compulsory winding-up.[13] It is to be noted that under the EC Insolvency Regulation 2000 it was not permitted for secondary proceedings to have a purpose other than winding up or bankruptcy, such that an IVA, CVA or administration commenced was not able to continue as such following the opening of main proceedings in another Member State. Such procedures were required to covert to winding up or bankruptcy. Under the Recast Regulation there is no equivalent restriction on secondary proceedings and so an IVA, CVA or administration can continue as secondary proceedings.   **16-2**

Conversions distinguished from terminations.   The foregoing "conversion" procedures must be distinguished from the end of the administration, in consequence either: **16-3**

(i)   of orders made by the court, that the appointment of the administrator shall cease to have effect, made on various grounds, either on the application of the administrator, or of the supervisor of an administration-arrangement,[14] or

---

8   In compulsory winding-up administrations, there are substantial charges levied on the assets recovered, payable to the Official Receiver: For the benefits to the creditors of a creditors' voluntary winding-up, see *Re Oakhouse Property Holdings Ltd* [2003] B.P.I.R. 469 per Rimer J at 470.
9   See para.16-71, below.
10   Insolvency Act 1986 Sch.B1 para.84; Recast Regulation art.3, see Ch.28, below.
11   Insolvency Rules 2016 r.21.8: see para.16-68, below.
12   Insolvency Rules 2017 rr.21.1 to 21.8: see para.16-63, below.
13   EC Regulation art.37.
14   Insolvency Act 1986 Sch.B1 para.79.

      (ii)   on the application of one or more creditors.[15]

These terminations are dealt with in Ch.17 below.

16-4   **Contents of Chapter.** This Chapter deals, in s.2, with voluntary arrangements, (para.16-5), in s.3, with schemes of arrangement, (para.16-57), in s.4, with winding-up, (para.16-64), in s.5, with pre-commencement cases, that is to say, where the relevant proceedings relating to the insolvent company had been commenced before the first commencement date under the Enterprise Act 2002, namely 15 September 2003, and in s.6 with dissolution (paras 16-71 and 16-72).

SECTION 2: COMPANY VOLUNTARY ARRANGEMENTS IN ADMINISTRATION

16-5   **General.** Voluntary arrangements, both in respect of insolvent companies and partnerships,[16] and of insolvent individuals, were introduced by the Insolvency Act 1986, Pts I and VIII, respectively. Initially, arrangements had to be proposed and conducted by licensed insolvency practitioners,[17] performing the duties of nominee and supervisor. But by the Insolvency Act 2000, this requirement was scaled down to a person suitably qualified, as a member of a professional body recognised by the Secretary of State for this purpose, in respect of whom there was in force security to the prescribed amount[18] for the proper performance of his functions, with respect to the particular arrangement.[19] By the Deregulation Act 2015 s.390A of the Insolvency Act 1986 was added allowing for the partial authorisation of insolvency practitioners.

    Under the Insolvency Act 1986 Pt II (repealed), the prospective approval of a company voluntary arrangement by its creditors and members was one of the four specific statutory "purposes", to achieve which the court might make an administration order.[20] The acceptability by the court, hearing an administration petition, depended on its view of the merits of the proposals, and the likelihood of the creditors and members approving the proposed arrangement by the requisite majorities.[21] It should be noted that a company voluntary arrangement could, and still can, be proposed and operated as a "stand-alone" procedure, without the contemporaneous use of an administration, but the use of administration coupled with such an arrangement was attractive because it triggered the coming into force of a broad moratorium[22] preventing creditor actions against the company without the administrator's consent or the permission of the court. In the absence of such a moratorium, the arrangement was at risk of individual actions in the period before proposals had been put to creditors and approved by them.

---

15 Insolvency Act 1986 Sch.B1 para.81.
16 Insolvency Act 1986 ss.1–7, 252–263; Insolvency Rules 2016 Pts 2 and 7.
17 Insolvency Act 1986 s.388 (as since amended).
18 Insolvency Act 1986 s.390(3), and see the Insolvency Practitioners Regulations, 2005 (SI2005/ 524).
19 Insolvency Act 2000 s.4, which was brought into force on 1 January 2003, by the Insolvency Act 2000 (Commencement No.1 and Transitional Provisions) Order 2001 (SI 2001/766).
20 Insolvency Act 1986 s.8(3)(b) (repealed except for old regime).
21 See *Re Land & Property Trust Plc (No.2)* [1991] B.C.C. 466; [1991] B.C.L.C. 849; and cf. *Re Consumer & Industrial Press Ltd* (1988) 4 B.C.C. 68; [1988] B.C.L.C. 177; and *Re Rowbotham Baxter Ltd* [1990] B.C.C. 113; [1990] B.C.L.C. 397.
22 See paras 15-63 ff, above.

The Insolvency Act 2000, s.1, which came into force on 1 January 2003,[23] to some extent addresses that problem by introducing a "CVA with moratorium" procedure for small companies.[24] The Insolvency Service has consulted on the possibility of extending this procedure to all companies, rather than just "small" ones.[25] the limitation remains in place.

A Voluntary arrangement as an "administration purpose". In the Enterprise Act 2002 Pt 10 (which for corporate insolvency purposes came into force on 15 September 2003), the "purposes of administration" were recast. They no longer specifically include the actual prospect of a voluntary arrangement.[26] Instead, the proposals to be submitted to the creditors may include a *proposal* that the company should enter into a voluntary arrangement.[27] That Act, by Sch.16 (now Insolvency Act 1986 Sch.B1), extended the company voluntary, arrangements code, as originally enacted in the Insolvency Act 1986 Pt I, for the purposes of arrangements proposed by an administrator.

16-6

Compliance with EC Regulation. Proposals for a company voluntary arrangement now need to contain a statement, in compliance with the Recast Regulation (and previously the EC Regulation 2000) stating whether the Regulation will apply to the proposed arrangement as an insolvency proceeding, and if so, whether the proceeding will constitute "main proceedings", "secondary proceedings" or "territorial proceedings": see para.16-2, above and Ch.29, below.

16-7

The Rules. Part 2 of the Insolvency Rules 1986 (as amended), which dealt with, inter alia, company voluntary arrangements within administration, was wholly revoked (except for the old regime).[28] It was replaced by a new Pt 2, containing, inter alia, the rules relating to administration proceedings, entitled "Administration Procedure".[29] These rules were likewise replaced in the Insolvency Rules 2016.

16-8

Changes from the old regime to the current. Not many changes, by way of amendment or addition, were made by the Enterprise Act 2002 Pt 10, to the company voluntary arrangements code, as originally enacted by the Insolvency Act 1986 Pt I.

16-9

Nominees and supervisors of voluntary arrangements are no longer obliged to be licensed insolvency practitioners; they may now be suitably qualified and authorised practitioners: see para.16-12, below.

An important addition was the requirement, in all insolvency proceedings, to comply with the EC Regulation, by a statement whether the Regulation applies, and if so whether the proceedings are main, secondary or territorial: see para.16-7 above and Ch.28, below.

---

[23] Insolvency Act 2000 (Commencement No.3 and Transitional Provisions) Order 2002 (SI2002/2711).

[24] Insolvency Act 1986 s.1A, and see below at paras 16-9 ff.

[25] *Encouraging Company Rescue: A Consultation* (The Insolvency Service, June 2009).

[26] Insolvency Act 1986 Sch.B1 para.3(1). As to the new and single purpose of administration, see para.14-9, above.

[27] Insolvency Act 1986 Sch.B1 para.49(3)(a); they may also include proposals for a composition or a scheme of arrangement under Companies Act 2006 Pt 26; Insolvency Act 1986 Sch.B1 para.49(3)(b).

[28] The "old" Pt 2 will continue to have some residual application to those remaining administrations commenced under the "old" regime (i.e. prior to 15 September 2003).

[29] See amending Insolvency Rules 1986 r.1.3(2), as further amended by Insolvency (Amendment) Rules 2004 (SI 2004/584); Insolvency Rules 2016 rr.2.2 and 2.3.

"Small companies" and insolvent partnerships (of limited size) can benefit from the complex moratorium provisions inserted by the Insolvency Act 2000 into the Insolvency Act 1986, and expanded upon in Sch.A1 to the Act (Insolvency Act 2000 Sch.1, and as subsequently amended).

The problem previously arising, when the creditors' meeting and the members' meeting arrive at different decisions, was solved by a procedure permitting a member to apply to the court for a ruling that the members' meeting's decision should prevail: see para.16-36, below.

Creditors who did not attend a creditors' meeting are bound by its decisions, if they would have been authorised to vote thereat, had they received notice of it.[30]

16-10   **Differences between the two voluntary arrangement codes.**   The principal point to be borne in mind in dealing with company voluntary arrangements is that, although they are legislated for in terms almost wholly identical with those employed in the setting up of an individual arrangement, and the case-law on voluntary arrangements is in general equally applicable to both categories of proceeding,[31] there are nonetheless significant differences. A company voluntary arrangement does not, in general terms, qualify, during the initial stages of setting it up, for the benefit of a moratorium, to protect it and the company's assets from the enforcement proceedings available to its creditors, comparable with the moratorium conferred on the debtor and his assets under an individual voluntary arrangement, as soon as it has been initiated, by the effect of the making of an interim order,[32] reinforced by the court's powers to stay proceedings after the application for the order is filed and before it is heard.[33] What has so far been conceded to insolvent companies generally is a moratorium procedure, confined to "small companies",[34] and to comparably limited insolvent partnerships[35] (see para.16-9, below).

There must also be held, in the case of a company voluntary arrangement (and comparably for an insolvent partnership), two meetings, one for the creditors and the other for the members (or partners).[36] Finally, the limited period of 28 days, within which a creditor (or, in the case of a company or partnership arrangement, a member) who is dissatisfied either with the results of, or the conduct of, the meetings of creditors and/or members, must file a "challenge" to the approval or disapproval of the debtor's or debtor company's proposals, may, in the case of a debtor's individual arrangement, be extended by the court, but may not be so extended in the case of company or partnership arrangement.[37]

16-11   **The moratorium provisions in administration.**   The Insolvency Act 1986 Pt I (as amended by the Insolvency Act 2000), provides a limited access to moratorium

---

[30]   Insolvency Act 1986 s.5(2).
[31]   *Re Bishopsgate Investment Management Ltd* [1993] Ch.1 CA. Insolvency Act 1986 s.252(2); but the making of such an order is no longer obligatory.
[32]   Insolvency Act 2000 s.3 and Sch.3 para.7, inserting into Insolvency Act 1986 a new s.256A.
[33]   Insolvency Act 1986 s.254(1) and (2).
[34]   Insolvency Act 1986 s 1A.
[35]   Insolvent Partnerships Order 1994 (SI 1994/2421) art.5 and Sch.1.
[36]   Insolvency Act 1986 s.3; they may be held together.
[37]   Power to extend time is conferred in individual cases under Pt VIII by Insolvency Act 1986, s.376, which does not apply to company cases under Pt I. But no limitation period applies to applications to set aside the arrangement on the grounds of fundamental invalidity. See below: para.16-44, Sch.B1 paras 42–44, for the moratoria, see Sch.B1 paras 42–44, and para.16-13, below. See also *Re Beloit Walmsley Ltd* [2008] B.P.I.R. 1445.

protection, in the form of s.1A, and Sch.A1 (enacted as Sch.1 to the Insolvency Act 2000, and as subsequently amended). But that limitation in respect of moratorium protection is removed by the provisions of the Insolvency Act 1986 Sch.B1, when the arrangement is being proposed within the context of an administration, because the administrator, and his supervisor in the case of an arrangement, are fully and automatically protected by the provisions of the Insolvency Act 1986. An interim moratorium comes into effect, when an administration application is filed in court, and when notice of intention to appoint an administrator extra-judicially is filed in court.[38] The final moratorium comes into effect when the company enters administration, by virtue of the appointment of the administrator taking effect.[39] The effectiveness of the operation of the moratorium provisions may be called into question, by the possible uncertainty of the exact time of its commencement[40]; see Ch.15.

Where an application is made to sue a company in administration for a simple monetary debt, permission will only be given in exceptional circumstances; the administrator must be free to run the company, free from unnecessary litigation.[41] Solicitors have been given permission to commence proceedings against a company in administration, seeking a declaration that they were entitled to a charge for their fees over a property recovered by them for the company.[42] Leave to forfeit a lease was granted where it would not have an adversely affect the purpose of the administration.[43]

The qualification of the nominee and supervisor. The relaxation, under the general law, referred to above,[44] of the original requirement, that the officers in charge of an arrangement must be licensed insolvency practitioners, so as to permit of their being, in the case of an individual arrangement, persons similarly qualified at a lower level, is not relevant in the case of an administrator, for he must himself be a licensed insolvency practitioner.[45] But if he proposes, as nominee and/or supervisor, persons other than himself, they must presumably hold the same qualification.   **16-12**

Moratorium facilities for small companies: position of subsidiaries. Where an administrator applies for a company voluntary arrangement, the company's assets are already automatically protected against hostile activity from creditors, by the appointment of the administrator.[46] It may however occur that the company in administration has subsidiaries, which are not protected automatically by the administration moratorium enjoyed by their parent company. If it is desired that they   **16-13**

---

38 Insolvency Act 1986 Sch.B1 para.44.
39 Insolvency Act 1986 Sch.B1 paras 42–43.
40 Insolvency Act 1986 Sch.B1 para.44(2)(b) (Five days), (4)(b) (10 days).
41 *Re Divine Solutions Ltd* [2003] EWHC 1931 Ch; [2004] 1 B.C.L.C. 373; [2004] B.C.C. 325; see also *Enron Metals & Commodity Ltd v HIH Casualty & General Insurance Ltd (in provisional liquidation)* [2005] EWHC 485 Ch (unreported): the claim was held to have had no real prospects of success; permission was refused. See also *Re Nortel Networks UK Ltd, Unite (The Union) v Nortel Networks UK Ltd* [2010 EWHC 826 (Ch); [2010] B.C.C. 706.
42 *Hammonds v Thomas Muckle & Sons (Buildei) Ltd* [2006] B.P.J.R. 704, 1111 Judge Langan QC, Leeds District Registry.
43 *Lazari GP Ltd v Jervis* [2012] EWHC 1466 (Ch); [2013] B.C.C. 294.
44 See para.16-9.
45 Insolvency Act 1986 Sch.B1 para.6.
46 See para.16-11, above. For a case where a creditor applied unsuccessfully for permission to sue the company in administration, see *Re Divine Solutions Ltd* [2003] EWHC 1931 Ch; [2004] B.C.C. 373.

should propose voluntary arrangements with their creditors (some of whom may also be creditors of the parent company for the same debts), they may need to apply for the "small companies" moratorium, if their capital and financial status qualify them for it.[47]

16-14   The Recast Insolvency Regulation.   The Recast Insolvency Regulation came into force on 26 June 2017. Before that, the European Council Regulation on Insolvency Proceedings 2000,[48] was brought into force on 31 May 2002, together with a number of statutory instruments applying its provisions to UK law; they apply to all forms of insolvency proceedings. The procedural consequences and obligations imposed by the Regulations are examined in Ch.28, below. An important source of guidance is the "*Virgos-Schmit Report*"[49]; it is frequently cited.

16-15   The company voluntary arrangement.   The prospective approval by a company's creditors of proposals for a company voluntary arrangement under Pt I of the Insolvency Act 1986, was the second of the four statutory purposes for which an administration petition might be presented, and an administration order made.[50] The introduction of the voluntary arrangements code was made by that part of the Act, with respect to insolvent companies,[51] including thereunder unregistered companies and insolvent partnerships, under Pt V of the Act.[52] The English court has jurisdiction to sanction a scheme of arrangement if a company is liable to be wound up and there is sufficient connection with the jurisdiction.[53]

16-16   Company voluntary arrangement: procedures.   The procedures for the preparation and filing of the statutory documentation, the summoning and holding of the meetings of creditors and of members, the voting rights at such meetings, and appeals in respect of such voting, and the initiation and conduct of proceedings brought by way of "challenge" to proposals approved thereat[54] (which in the case of a company may be brought by a dissatisfied creditor, a member or contributory, or by the nominee or the administrator or the liquidator), are all enacted in substantially the same form and language for both codes.[55] Relevant decisions on the practice and the construction of the sections made under one code are therefore applicable in cases brought under the other code.[56] The procedural aspects of company voluntary arrangements in Scotland are dealt with in Pt 1 of the Insolvency (Scotland) Rules 1986 (as amended).

---

[47]   Insolvency Act 1986 s.1A and Sch.A1, as inserted by Insolvency Act 2000 s.3 and Sch.1, as subsequently amended. A "small company" for this purpose is one defined by Companies Act 2006 s.382: see Insolvency Act 1986 Sch.A1 para.3(2).

[48]   European Council Regulation No.1246/2000 of 29 May 2000, [2000] OJ L160/1: see Europa Website (publications) *http://europa.eu/* [Accessed 21 November 2017] see Ch.28.

[49]   Dated 8 July 1996, relating to inter-state jurisdiction: see Ch.28 below, and *The EC Regulation on Insolvency Proceedings 2000* by Moss, Fletcher and Isaacs, Sweet & Maxwell (2002).

[50]   See n.26.

[51]   See n.26.

[52]   Insolvency Act 1986 Pt 1 ss.1–7; see Insolvency Act 1986 ss.220, 221; Insolvent Partnerships Order 1994 (SI 1994/2421); revoking IPO 1986). The Insolvent Partnerships Order 1994 does not apply in Scotland.

[53]   *Re Rodenstock GmbH* [2011] EWHC 1104 (Ch); [2011] Bus. L.R. 1245.

[54]   See paras 16-39 ff, below.

[55]   See para.16-8, above.

[56]   *Re Bishopsgate Investment Management Ltd* [1993] Ch.1 CA.

Proposals for company voluntary arrangements: fundamental **16-17**
characteristics. A company voluntary arrangement, under Pt I of the Insolvency
Act 1986 (as amended), is a proposal made by or in the name of the company to
its creditors and members for a composition in satisfaction of its debts, or a scheme
of arrangement of its affairs.[57] Such an arrangement may fairly be perceived as akin
to a commercial contract, and is to be construed generally by reference to the same
factors. However, the proposals for such an arrangement are usually put together
in some haste, and should therefore be construed in a practical fashion.[58]

An essential feature of such an arrangement is that it must provide for some
person, denominated "the nominee", to act in relation thereto, in the course of its
preparation and placing before the meetings of creditors and members, and to act
in relation thereto, if it is approved, either as trustee or otherwise, for the purpose
of supervising its implementation,[59] from which point he (or some other person) is
termed "the supervisor". An administrator may make such a proposal[60]: he may
propose himself, or some other duly qualified person, as the nominee,[61] and later
the supervisor.[62]

The proposal must provide[63] a short explanation why, in his opinion, a voluntary
arrangement under Pt I of the Insolvency Act 1986 (as amended) is desirable, and
give reasons why the company's creditors may be expected to concur with such an
arrangement.[64]

The matters to be stated or dealt with in the proposal. The following matters **16-18**
must all be stated, or otherwise dealt with, in the proposal, so far as is known to the
proposer[65]:

(a) the company's assets, with an estimate of their respective values;
(b) which assets are charged and the extent of the charge;
(c) which assets are to be excluded from the CVA;
(d) particulars of any property to be included in the CVA which is not owned
    by the company, including details of who owns such property, and the terms
    on which it will be available for inclusion[66];
(e) the nature and amount of the company's liabilities;
(f) how the company's liabilities will be met, modified, postponed or otherwise
    dealt with by means of the CVA and in particular:[67]
    (i)   how preferential creditors[68] and creditors who are, or claim to be,
           secured will be dealt with, with the amounts of their respective

---

57 Insolvency Act 1986 s.1(1).
58 *County Bookshops Ltd v Grove* [2002] EWHC 1160 Ch; [2002] B.P.I.R. 772, citing *Re Brelec Instal-
    lations Ltd* [2001] B.P.I.R. 772; sub nom. *Welsky v Brolec Installations Ltd* [2002] 2 B.C.L.C. 576:
    see para.16-27, below.
59 Insolvency Act 1986 s.1(2).
60 Insolvency Act 1986 s.1(3)(a).
61 Insolvency Act 1986 s.2(1); Insolvency Rules 2016 r.2.4.
62 For the office of "supervisor", see n.74, below.
63 Insolvency Rules 2016 r.2.3 (directors' proposal); r.2.3(1) (administrator's proposal).
64 Insolvency Rules 2016 rr.2.2(c) and 2.3.
65 Insolvency Rules 2016 r.2.3(1), as applied to administrators by Insolvency Rules 2016 r.2.3(3).
66 Insolvency Rules 2016 r.2.3(1)(d).
67 Insolvency Rules 2016 r.2.3(1)(f).
68 Insolvency Rules 2016 r.2.3(1)(e) and (f). For the meaning of "preferential creditors", see the
    Insolvency Act 1986 ss.4(7), 386(1) and Sch.6. The preferential debts in respect of money owed to
    the Inland Revenue for income deducted at source; VAT, car tax, betting and gaming duties and social
    security were repealed when Enterprise Act 2002 Pt 10 s.251, which came into force on 15

claims, and how it is proposed to deal with them and with other creditors who are, or claim to be, secured,

  (ii) how creditors who are connected with the company will be dealt with,[69]

  (iii) if the company is not in administration or liquidation whether, if the company did go into administration or liquidation, there are circumstances which might give rise to claims under s.238 (transactions at an undervalue), s.239 (preferences), s.244 (extortionate credit transactions), or s.245 (floating charges invalid), and

  (iv) where there are circumstances that might give rise to such claims, whether, and if so what, provision will be made to indemnify the company in respect of them;

(g) the amounts proposed to be paid to the nominee by way of and expenses;

(h) identification and contact details for the supervisor[70];

(i) confirmation that the supervisor is qualified to act as an insolvency practitioner in relation to the company and the name of the relevant recognised professional body which is the source of the supervisor's authorisation;

(j) how the fees and expenses of the supervisor will be determined and paid;

(k) the functions to be performed by the supervisor;

(l) where it is proposed that two or more supervisors be appointed a statement whether acts done in connection with the CVA may be done by any one or more of them or must be done by all of them;

(m) whether any, and if so what, guarantees have been given in respect of the company's debts, specifying which of the guarantors are persons connected with the company;

(n) whether any, and if so what, guarantees are proposed to be offered for the purposes of the CVA and, if so, by whom and whether security is to be given or sought;

(o) the proposed duration of the CVA;

(p) the proposed dates of distributions to creditors, with estimates of their amounts;

(q) whether the proceedings will be main, territorial or non-EC proceedings with reasons[71];

(r) how the business of the company will be conducted during the CVA;

(s) details of any further proposed credit facilities for the company, and how the debts so arising are to be paid;

(t) the manner in which funds held for the purposes of the CVA are to be banked, invested or otherwise dealt with pending distribution to creditors;

(u) how funds held for the purpose of payment to creditors, and not so paid on the termination of the CVA, will be dealt with;

September 2003, leaving as preferential only claims for the remuneration and other entitlements of employees. See further, Ch.7 and below.

[69] See Insolvency Act 1986 s.435.

[70] The "supervisor" is the person who is, for the time being, whether as trustee or otherwise, supervising the carrying out of the arrangement: Insolvency Act 1986 ss.1(2), 7(2). The supervisor will be the administrator or his nominee, or a replacement therefore: see the Insolvency Act 1986 ss.2(4), or 4(2).

[71] See paras 16-2, 16-7, above; and Ch.28, below.

(v)   how the claim of any person bound by the CVA by virtue of s.5(2)(b)(ii) or para.37(2)(b)(ii) of Sch.A1 will be dealt with;

(w)   where the proposal is made in relation to a company that is eligible for a moratorium (in accordance with paras 2 and 3 of Sch.A1) with a view to obtaining a moratorium under Sch.A1, the address to which the documents referred to in para.6(1) of that Schedule must be delivered; and

(x)   any other matters that the proposer considers appropriate to enable members and creditors to reach an informed decision on the proposal.

Where an administrator makes the proposal he must also include so far as is known:

(a)   an estimate of—
    (i)   the value of the prescribed part,[72] and
    (ii) the value of the company's net property (as defined by s.176A(6)); and

(b)   a statement as to whether the administrator or liquidator proposes to make an application to the court under s.176A(5) and if so the reasons for the application; and

(c)   details of the nature and amount of the company's preferential creditors.

Information may be excluded where it could serious prejudice the commercial interests of the company, but if it affected the calculation of the estimate, the proposal must include a statement to that effect.

Where administrator is not proposed as nominee.   If the administrator is   **16-19** proposing another person as nominee, he must give that person written notice of his proposal, together with a copy of such proposal,[73] and a copy of the company's statement of affairs.[74] If he agrees to act he must deliver a notice of that consent to the proposer as soon as reasonably practicable. He must cause a copy of the notice to be endorsed with the date of receipt, and the period of 28 days, within which he must make his report to the court,[75] will run from that date.[76]

With the agreement in writing of the nominee, the administrator's proposal may be amended in one of two cases. The first is where: (a) no steps have been taken to obtain a moratorium; (b) the nominee is not the liquidator or administrator of the company; and (c) the nominee's report has not been filed with the court; the second is where (a) the proposal is made with a view to obtaining a moratorium; and (b) the nominee's statement under para.6(2) of Sch.A1 (nominee's opinion on prospects of CVA being approved etc.) has not yet been submitted to the directors.[77] It is inferred that any deficiencies cannot thereafter be amended by the proposing debtor (i.e. the administrator) or the nominee.[78]

Provision of material for nominee's report.   If it appears to the nominee that he   **16-20**

---

[72]   For "the prescribed part", see para.15-94 ff, below, and Insolvency Act 1986 s.176A (inserted by the Enterprise Act 2002 s.252).

[73]   Insolvency Act 1986 s.2(3)(a). Insolvency Rules 2016 r.2.4 and as to contents r.2.3.

[74]   Insolvency Act 1986 s.2(3)(b): Insolvency Rules 2016 r.1.12(5).

[75]   See "Nominee's report to the court", para.16-21, below.

[76]   Insolvency Rules 2016 r.2.4(4). The copy of the notice so endorsed must be returned by the nominee to the administrator forthwith, at an address specified by him in the notice for that purpose.

[77]   Insolvency Rules 2016 r. 2.2.

[78]   See under the former provisions *RC v Bland and Sargent* EWHC 1068 Ch; [2003] B.P.I.R. 1274.

cannot properly prepare his report on the basis of information in the proposal and the statement of affairs, he may call on the administrator to provide him with:

(a) more information about the circumstances in which, and the reasons why, a CVA is being proposed;

(b) particulars of any previous proposals which have been made in respect of the company under Pt I of the Insolvency Act 1986; and

(c) any further information with respect to the company's affairs which the nominee thinks necessary for the purposes of his report.[79]

The nominee may also call on the administrator to inform him, with respect to any person who is, or, at any time in the two years preceding the nominee receiving the proposal has been, a director or officer of the company, whether and in what circumstances, whether in those two years or previously, that person has been concerned in the affairs of any other company or limited liability partnership, whether incorporated in England and Wales or not, which has become the subject of insolvency proceedings, or has himself been adjudged bankrupt, been the subject of a debt relief order, or entered into an arrangement with his creditors.[80]

For the purpose of enabling the nominee to consider the proposal and to prepare his report on it, the administrator must give him access to the company's accounts and records.[81]

16-21 **Nominee's report to the court.** Where the proposed nominee is not the administrator, there is an intermediate stage in the procedure.[82] This involves the submission to the court, *within 28 days after he has been given notice of the proposal for a voluntary arrangement*,[83] of a report.[84] This must state, first, whether, in his opinion, the proposed voluntary arrangement has a reasonable prospect of being approved and implemented, whether meetings of the company and of its creditors should be summoned to consider the proposal,[85] and if so, the date on which and the time and place at which he proposes that the meetings should be held.[86]

With such a report, the nominee must deliver a copy of the proposals, with authorised amendments, if any,[87] and a copy, or summary, of the company's statement of affairs.[88] The report must state why the nominee considers the proposal does or does not have a reasonable prospect of being approved and implemented, and why the creditors should or should not be invited to consider the proposal.[89]

The court will cause the nominee's report to be endorsed with the date on which it is filed in court.[90] The nominee must send a copy of his report and of his comments (if any) to the company.[91]

If the nominee fails to submit such report within the permitted 28 days, the court

---

[79] Insolvency Rules r.2.8.
[80] Insolvency Rules 2016 r.2.8(3).
[81] Insolvency Rules 2016 r.2.8(4).
[82] Insolvency Act 1986 s.2(1).
[83] See para.16-19, above.
[84] Insolvency Act 1986 s.2(2).
[85] Insolvency Act 1986 s.2(2)(a) and (b).
[86] Insolvency Act 1986 s.2(2)(c). The date on which the meetings are to be held must not be less than 14, nor more than 28, days from the date of filing the report: Insolvency Rules 2016 r.2.27.
[87] See para.16–19, above.
[88] Insolvency Rules 2016 r.2.9.
[89] Insolvency Rules 2016 r.2.9(2).
[90] Insolvency Rules 2016 r.2.9(2).
[91] Insolvency Rules 2016 r.2.9.

may, on an application made by the administrator, direct that the nominee be replaced as such by another person duly qualified as an insolvency practitioner.[92] The nominee is entitled to *at least five business days' notice of any such application.*[93]

Duties of nominee to the court as to report. The administrator, as nominee **16-22** under the proposed arrangement (or such nominee as he may appoint), must, in his report to the court on the debtor company's proposals, assert that the proposals are likely to succeed; the report must be entirely fair and frank, and if he cannot make such a report, he must not recommend the holding of the meeting.[94] Codes of best practice are being established for the guidance of insolvency practitioners.[95] He cannot amend the proposed arrangement, for the purpose of curing any deficiencies, after he has made his report to the court.[96]

Summoning of meetings: notices. Where the nominee is not the administrator, **16-23** and it has been reported to the court[97] that the necessary meetings should be summoned, the person making the report must, unless otherwise directed by the court, summon those meetings for the time, date and place proposed in the report.[98]

Where the nominee is the administrator, he must summon meetings of the company and of its creditors to consider the proposals for such a time, date and place as he thinks fit.[99]

In fixing the venue for the creditors' meeting and the company meeting, the administrator must have regard to the convenience of those invited to attend.[100] The meetings may be held on the same day and in the same place, but the creditors' meeting must be fixed for a time in advance of the company meeting.[101] With every notice summoning every meeting, there must be a copy of the proposal; a copy of the statement of affairs, or if the nominee thinks fit a summary including a list of creditors with the amount of their debts; the nominee's comments on the proposal, unless the nominee is the administrator or liquidator.[102] The notice to members where members are to consider the proposal at a meeting must include a blank proxy and the notice must specify the purpose of and venue for the meeting.[103] If the meetings of creditors and members are not held on the same day, they must be

---

[92] Insolvency Act 1986 s.2(4), but subject to the permitted lower qualification: para.16-5, above.
[93] Insolvency Rules 2016 r.2.10(1).
[94] *Re Greystoke (A Debtor)* [1996] 2 B.C.L.C. 459; [1997] B.P.I.R. 24 (an individual voluntary arrangement case). See also *Shah v Cooper* [2003] B.P.I.R. 1018.
[95] The Association of Business Recovery Professionals (R3, formerly the Council of the Society of Practitioners of Insolvency) has issued a "Statement of Practice on Individual Voluntary Arrangements", which was judicially approved and adopted by Lindsay J in *Re Greystoke (A Debtor)*, n.103. It has since provided revised statements of practice for both Individual and Company Voluntary Arrangements. A similar code of practice has also been published by the Insolvency Practitioners Association.
[96] See n.85, above.
[97] For the nominee's report, see para.16-21, above.
[98] Insolvency Act 1986 s.3(1).
[99] Insolvency Act 1986 s.3(2).
[100] Insolvency Rules 2016 r.2.26(2).
[101] Insolvency Rules 2016 r.28.2.
[102] Insolvency Rules 2016 r.2.25.
[103] Insolvency Rules 2016 r.2.26.

held within five business days of one another.[104] For the procedure where the two meetings arrive at different decisions, see para.16-36, below.

Notices calling the meetings must be delivered to each creditor at least seven days before the day fixed for the meeting[105]; and in the case of members must be delivered to all the members, to every officer or former officer of the company whose presence the nominee thinks is required, and all other directors of the company at least 14 days before the day fixed for the meeting.[106]

The notice to members must identify the proceedings; state the venue for the meeting; state the effect of the following: (a) r.2.35 about members' voting rights, (b) r.2.36 about the requisite majority of members for passing resolutions, (c) r.15.35 about rights of appeal, and (d) be accompanied by—(i) a copy of the proposal, (ii) a copy of the statement of affairs, or if the nominee thinks fit a summary including a list of creditors with the amounts of their debts, (iii) the nominee's comments on the proposal, unless the nominee is the administrator or liquidator, and (iv) details of each resolution to be voted on.[107] For creditors, the nominee must deliver to each creditor a notice in respect of the decision procedure which complies with r.15.8 so far as is relevant. The notice must also: (a) be accompanied by—(i) a copy of the proposal, (ii) a copy of the statement of affairs, or if the nominee thinks fit a summary including a list of creditors with the amounts of their debts, and (iii) the nominee's comments on the proposal, unless the nominee is the administrator or liquidator; and (b) state how a creditor may propose a modification to the proposal, and how the nominee will deal with such a proposal for a modification.[108] Notice must be delivered to every present or former officer of the company whose presence the convener thinks is required and that person is required to attend the meeting,[109] on at least 14 days' notice from the date of delivery of the notice.[110]

16-24 **Chair of the meeting.** At both meetings, and at the combined meeting, the chair will be the nominee or an appointed person.[111]

A proxy-holder at a meeting must not vote for a resolution which would directly or indirectly place the proxy-holder or any associate of the proxy-holder in a position to receive any remuneration, fees or expenses from the insolvent estate; or fix or change the amount of or the basis of any remuneration, fees or expenses receivable by the proxy-holder or any associate of the proxy-holder out of the insolvent estate. However, a proxy-holder may vote for such a resolution if the proxy specifically directs the proxy-holder to vote in that way.[112]

16-25 **Voting rights of creditors.** Every creditor who was given notice of the credi-

---

[104] Insolvency Rules 2016 r.2.28(3).
[105] Insolvency Act 1986 s.3(3) provides that the persons to be summoned are "every creditor of the company of whose claim and address the person summoning the meeting is aware." For the question of who is a "creditor" for this purpose, see *Re T & N Ltd* [2005] EWHC 2870 Ch; [2006] 1 W.L.R. 1728.
[106] Insolvency Rules 2016 r.2.30.
[107] Insolvency Rules 2016 r.2.25(3).
[108] Insolvency Rules 2016 r.2.25(5).
[109] Insolvency Rules 2016 r.15.14.
[110] Insolvency Rules 2016 r.15.2(2).
[111] Insolvency Rules 2016 r.2.34.
[112] Insolvency Rules 2016 r.16.7.

tors' meeting[113] is entitled to vote at the meeting.[114] Votes are calculated according to the amount of the creditor's debt, as at the date of the administration order.[115] A creditor claiming to vote in respect of a debt for an unliquidated amount, or any debt whose value is not ascertained, shall be entitled to vote, if the convenor or chair decides to put upon it an estimated minimum value for the purpose of entitlement to vote and admits the claim for that purpose.[116] See "Contingent debts and liabilities" and "Unliquidated debts or debts of unascertainable amount", paras 16-27 and 16-28, below.

At the creditors' meeting, the convenor or chair has power to admit or reject a creditor's claim for the purpose of the entitlement to vote, and the power is exercisable with respect to the whole or any part of the claim.[117] The decision on a creditor's entitlement to vote is subject to appeal to the court by any creditor, contributory or by the debtor.[118] If the chair or convenor is in doubt whether a claim should be admitted or rejected, he must mark it as objected to, and allow the creditor to vote, subject to his vote being subsequently declared invalid, if the objection to the claim is sustained.[119] If on appeal the decision is reversed or varied, or the creditor's vote is declared invalid the court may order another meeting to be summoned, or make such other order as it thinks just.[120]

Limitations on court's power to intervene by way of appeal or "challenge". In **16-26** a CVA the court may only make an order if it considers that the circumstances which led to the appeal gave rise to unfair prejudice or material irregularity.[121] An application to the court by way of appeal may not be made later than 21 days after the decision date, but in the case of a proposed CVA the appeal may not be made after the end of the period of 28 days beginning with the day on which the first of the reports required by s.4(6) or para.30(3) of Sch.A1 was filed with the court.[122] The power to extend time for appeal with respect to any of the events, or orders made, is not available in the case of company arrangements, but is restricted to individual arrangements.[123] The decision-maker is not, in general, personally liable for any costs incurred by any person in respect of such an appeal.[124]

However, under the old rules, where the nominee-chairman of the meeting of creditors in an individual voluntary arrangement[125] was found, on the hearing of a

---

[113] See para.16-23, above.
[114] Insolvency Rules 2016 r.15.28(5).
[115] Insolvency Rules 2016 r.15.31.
[116] Insolvency Rules 2016 r.15.31(2).
[117] Insolvency Rules 2016 r.15.33(2).
[118] Insolvency Rules 2016 r.15.35 For an unsuccessful challenge see *Re Newlands (Seaford) Educational Trust Ltd* [2006] EWHC 1511 Ch; [2007] B.C.C. 195.
[119] Insolvency Rules 2016 r.15.33.
[120] Insolvency Rules 2016 r.15.35(3).
[121] See para.16-39, below.
[122] See "Decisions of meetings", para.16-34, below. Insolvency Rules 2016 r.15.35
[123] Time was extended in *Tager v Westpac Banking Corpn* [1997] 1 B.C.L.C. 313; [1997] B.P.I.R. 543, under the Insolvency Act 1986 s.376; but in *Re Bournemouth & Boscombe Athletic Football Club Co Ltd* [1998] B.P.I.R. 183, that section was held to be confined to those parts of the Insolvency Act 1986 dealing with individual insolvency, and did not apply to corporate cases. But this time-limitation does not apply to applications to revoke the approval, on the ground of the invalidity of the arrangement.
[124] Insolvency Rules 2016 r.15.35(6).
[125] Under the Insolvency Act 1986 Pt VIII. The provisions are substantially the same in both Parts.

"challenge",[126] to have wrongfully excluded substantial creditors, and to have seriously misconducted himself, both in reporting on the debtor's proposal, and in the conduct of the meeting, including his exclusion of those creditors, the court, after revoking the approval of the proposal, ordered that the nominee-chairman should personally pay a substantial proportion of the costs of the successful appellants, apparently on the basis of his being guilty of breaches of statutory duties, notwithstanding the immunity ostensibly conferred on him by the rules.[127] An insolvency practitioner was held partly responsible in costs in *AB Agri Ltd v Curtis* [2016] B.P.I.R. 1287.

16-27   Contingent debts and liabilities.   These terms, when used in, or considered in the context of, a company voluntary arrangement, are not a term of art, nor defined by the Companies Acts. Their meaning depends partly on the language employed in the arrangement, when dealing with the various categories of the company's creditors—where they are, in the usual course of drafting collectively referred to as "actual, contingent or prospective creditors"—and partly on the context in which they are applied in relation to differing sets of facts. Questions as to their actual meaning cannot be answered by reference to authorities, or as a matter of abstract principle.[128]

The terms were sought to be defined (in the context of a Revenue case) thus: "contingent liabilities ... must mean sums, payment of which ... will only become payable if certain things happen, and which otherwise will never become payable".[129] Another definition was adopted by the Court of Appeal in these terms: "The term, 'contingent creditor' must, I think, denote a person towards whom, under an existing obligation, the company may or will become subject to a present liability, upon the happening of a future event or at some future date".[130] However, the Supreme Court has since spoken of the principle that every debt or liability capable of being expressed in money terms should be eligible for proof and that: "The notion that all possible liabilities within reason should be provable helps achieve equal justice to all creditors."[131]

16-28   Unliquidated debts or debts of unascertainable amount.   The terms of the original Insolvency Rules 1986 r.1.17(3), which were identical with those of the original r.5.17(3), relating to individual insolvency, gave rise to judicial differences of opinion, as to the process by which the chair was to "agree an estimated minimum value" to be placed on such debts, for the purpose of the creditor voting, and whether he had to "agree" it with the creditor, and as to the position when he did not, or could not do so.[132] The position was clarified by the Court of Ap-

---

[126] Insolvency Act 1986 s.262.

[127] *Re A Debtor (No.222 of 1990)* [1992] B.C.L.C. 137, Harman J; *(No.2)* [1993] B.C.L.C. 233 (judgment on costs); sed quaere: see *Re Cranley Mansions Ltd*, n.135, below.

[128] *County Bookshops Ltd v Grove* [2002] EWHC 1160 Ch.: [2002] B.P.I.R. 772, para.[49], where the following cases are discussed: see also para.16-18, above.

[129] *Re Sutherland (dec'd) Winter v IRC* [1963] AC 235 HL per Lord Reid.

[130] *Re William Hockley Ltd* [1962] 1 W.L.R. 555 at 558, adopted in *Glenister v Rowe* [2000] Ch.76 CA, per Mummery LJ at [83].

[131] *Bloom v Pensions Regulator* [2013] UKSC 52.

[132] In *Re Cranley Mansions Ltd* [1994] 1 W.L.R. 1610, Ferris J held that the creditor had to agree the figure with the chairman, and as she had not done so, she was not entitled to vote, and accordingly was not bound by the arrangement. In *Re Bradley-Hole (A Bankrupt) Ex p. Knight* [1995] 1 W.L.R.

peal[133]; the term "agree" did not refer to a bi-lateral consensual arrangement with the creditor, but to the chairman making his own best, personal, assessment of a figure, not nominal but realistic, at which the creditor should be admitted to vote, a figure which the creditor was entitled to challenge on appeal.[134] Any dispute as to the estimated figure being too low was material, only if the higher figure contended for would displace the majority opinion. The figure so selected in no way prejudiced the creditor's figure for his eventual proof of debt.[135]

In consequence of these controversies, the rules were amended to provide that such a creditor should be entitled to vote his debt at a figure of £1, unless the chairman agrees a higher value.[136] Now the position is that the creditor is entitled to vote as long as there is an estimated minimum value.

Where the amount of a major creditor's claim was known to the debtor, and was included in the proposals, but not referred to in that creditor's proxy form for the meeting, and the claim to vote was rejected on that ground, this was held to be a material irregularity, and the creditors' approval of the arrangement was revoked.[137]

Voting rights of members.   Members of the company at their meeting vote according to the rights attaching to their shares respectively in accordance with the articles. A member's shares include any other interest that person may have as a member of the company. The value of a member for the purposes of voting is determined by reference to the number of votes conferred on that member by the company's articles.

16-29

Requisite majorities (creditors).   At the creditors' meeting, for any resolution to pass approving any proposal or modification thereof, extending or further extending a moratorium, or bringing a moratorium to an end before the end of the period of any extension, there must be a *majority in excess of three-quarters in value of the creditors present in person or by proxy and voting on the resolution*.[138] The same applies in respect of any other resolution proposed at the meeting, but by submitting *one-half for three-quarters*.[139]

16-30

Debt claimed.   A creditor is entitled to vote where a proof has been properly delivered to the convenor, and was received by the convener not later than the decision date, or in the case of a meeting, 16.00 on the business day before the meeting, or later where the chair is content to accept the proof; and if the proof has been admitted for the purposes of entitlement to vote. A creditor's voting rights are calculated according to the amount of each creditor's claim but where a debt is

16-31

1097, Romer J dissented from this construction, with whom Knox J agreed in *Doorbar v Alltime Securities Ltd (No.1)* [1995] 1 B.C.L.C. 216, and *(No.2)* (reported as *Re A Debtor (No.162 of 1993)* [1995] 2 B.C.L.C. 513) where their views were upheld by the Court of Appeal, see n.36, overruling Ferris J on this point.

[133] *Doorbar v Alltime Securities Ltd (Nos 1 & 2)* [1996] 1 W.L.R. 456; [1996] 2 All E.R. 948 CA, whose judgment on this point is summarised in the text.

[134] See Insolvency Rules 2016 r.15.35), and see *Re Newlands (Seaford) Educational Trust Ltd* [2006] EWHC 1511 Ch; [2007] B.C.C. 195.

[135] This is for the supervisor to determine in the course of administration of the arrangement: see para.16-36, above.

[136] Insolvency Rules 1986 rr.1.17(3) and 5.21(3) substituted by Insolvency (Amendment) Rules (No.2) 2002.

[137] [2003] EWHC 2394 Ch, [2004] B.P.I.R. 208, applying *Re Hoare* [1997] B.P.I.R. 683.

[138] Insolvency Rules 2016 r.15.34(3).

[139] Insolvency Rules 2016 r.15.34(1).

wholly secured its value for voting purposes is nil and where a debt is partly secured its value for voting purposes is the value of the unsecured part. However, the value of the debt for voting purposes is its full value without deduction of the value of the security where the administrator has made a statement under para.52(1)(b) of Sch.B1 and the administrator has been requested to seek a decision under para.52(2); and where, in a proposed CVA, there is a decision on whether to extend or further extend a moratorium or to bring a moratorium to an end before the end of the period of any extension.[140]

In a proposed CVA or IVA a decision is not made if more than half the total value of the unconnected or non-associated creditors vote against it.[141]

The decisions of the convenor are subject to appeal by any creditor or member of the company, and the same provisions apply as in the case of appeals in relation to the establishment of creditors' voting rights.[142]

16-32   **Requisite majorities (members).**   Subject to the limitations set out below, and to any express provision made in the articles, at a company meeting any resolution will be regarded as passed, if voted by *more than one-half in value of members present in person or by proxy and voting on the resolution*.[143] The value of members is determined by reference to the number of votes conferred on each member by the company's articles. In determining therefore whether a majority for any resolution has been obtained, there must be left out of account any vote cast by members whose shares carry no voting rights.

16-33   **Procedure to obtain agreement on the proposal.**   The chair may (and must if it is so resolved) adjourn a meeting for not more than 14 days, but subject to any direction of the court. Further adjournment must not be to a day later than 14 days after the date on which the meeting was originally held (subject to any direction by the court). But in a case relating to a proposed CVA, the chair may, and must if the meeting so resolves, adjourn a meeting held under para.29(1) of Sch.A1(1) to a day which is not more than 14 days after the date on which the moratorium (including any extension) ends.[144] However, if the chair of a meeting to remove the liquidator or trustee in a creditors' voluntary winding up, a winding up by the court or a bankruptcy is the liquidator or trustee or the liquidator's or trustee's nominee and a resolution has been proposed for the liquidator's or trustee's removal, the chair must not adjourn the meeting without the consent of at least one-half (in value) of the creditors attending and entitled to vote.[145]

16-34   **Decisions of meetings.**   Such meetings, so held as aforesaid,[146] will decide whether to approve the proposed voluntary arrangement, with or without modifications.[147] The modifications may include one conferring the functions, proposed to be conferred on the nominee, on other insolvency practitioner or other

---

[140] Insolvency Rules 2016 r.15.34(3).
[141] Insolvency Rules 1986 r.1.19(5).
[142] Insolvency Rules 1986 r.1.19(7). See "Voting rights of Creditors", para.16-29, above.
[143] Insolvency Rules 1986 r.1.20(1).
[144] Rule 15.23.
[145] Rule 15.24.
[146] See para.16-23, above.
[147] Insolvency Act 1986 s.4(1).

suitably qualified person[148]; but the must not include any modification by virtue of which proposal ceases to be a "voluntary arrangement", as previously defined.[149]

Except with the concurrence of the creditor affected, the meeting may not approve any proposal or modification, which either:

(a) affects the right of a secured creditor to enforce his security[150];

(b) provides that any preferential debt[151] of the company is to be paid otherwise than in priority to such of its debts as are not preferential[152];

(c) provides that any ordinary preferential debt of the company is to be paid otherwise than in priority to any secondary preferential debts that it may have;[153] or

(d) provides that a preferential creditor of the company is to be paid an amount in respect of a preferential debt that bears to that debt a smaller proportion than is borne to another preferential debt, by the amount that is to be paid in respect of that debt.[154]

Actions after meetings. After the conclusion of either meeting, the chair must make a report[155] to the following effect: **16-35**

(a) stating whether the proposal was approved or rejected, and whether by the creditors alone or by both the creditors and members and, if approved, with what (if any) modifications;

(b) listing the creditors and members who voted or attended or who were represented at the meeting or decision procedure (as applicable) used to consider the proposal, setting out (with their respective values) how they voted on each resolution;

(c) identifying which of those creditors were considered to be connected with the company;

(d) if the proposal was approved, stating with reasons whether the proceedings are main, territorial or non-EC proceedings; and

(e) including such further information as the nominee or the chair thinks it appropriate to make known to the court.

A copy of this report must be filed in court *within four days of the meeting being held*, and the court will order such copy to be endorsed with the date of filing.[156] Immediately after the filing of the report, the chair must send notice of the result of each meeting to all the persons who were invited to consider the proposal or who

[148] Insolvency Act 1986 s.4(2). For other qualified persons, see Insolvency Act 2000 s.4.
[149] Insolvency Act 1986 s.4(2).
[150] Insolvency Act 1986 s.4(3). See, for the question of what is to be treated as security, *March Estates Plc v Gunmark Ltd* [1996] 2 B.C.L.C. 1; and *Razzaq v Pala* [1998] B.C.C. 66, but see also *Thomas v Ken Thomas Ltd* [2006] EWCA Civ 1504; [2007] B.P.I.R 959. See also *Re The Cotswold Co Ltd* [2009] 2 B.C.L.C. 371.
[151] For the meaning of "preferential debts" and "preferential creditors", see the Insolvency Act 1986 Pt XII s.386 (considered at para.7-62, above); Insolvency Act 1986 s.4(7), and see *IRC v Wimbledon FC* [2004] EWCA Civ 655; [2004] B.C.C. 638.
[152] Insolvency Act 1986 s.4(4)(a).
[153] Insolvency Act 1986 s.4(4)(aa).
[154] Insolvency Act 1986 s.4(4)(b).
[155] Insolvency Act 1986 s.4(5); Insolvency Rules 1986 r.1.24(1).
[156] Insolvency Act 1986 s.4(6); Insolvency Rules 1986 r.1.24(3).

were given notice of such meeting as aforesaid.[157]

16-36 **Where the decisions at the two meetings differ.** Where the decisions at the creditors' meeting and at the company meeting differ, the decision at the creditors' meeting shall primarily prevail.[158]

However, in that event, any member of the company who is dissatisfied may apply to the court for an order that the decision at the company meeting should prevail.[159] This provision offers some protection for the members, in the event that the creditors behave in a wholly unreasonable manner, to the prejudice of the interests of the members.

A member seeking to obtain this relief must apply to the court *within 28 days of the date of the creditors' meeting, or,* if the decision of the company meeting was taken at a later date, *within 28 days of that date.*[160] At the hearing of the application, the court may order that the decision at the company meeting shall prevail, or make such other order as it thinks fit.[161]

The applicant shall serve sealed copies of the order made on his application on the proposer and supervisor of the arrangement,[162] and also one copy to the company, at its registered office if the directors are the proposer[163] and, *within five business days of the date of the order,* an office copy on the registrar of the companies.[164] The supervisor (or the proposer where there is no supervisor) shall, *as soon as reasonably practicable,* deliver a notice that the order has been made to all persons who had received a notice to vote on the matter or who are affected by the order.[165]

16-37 **Resolution appointing person, other than the nominee, to be supervisor.** If, at either meeting, a resolution is moved for the appointment of some person other than the nominee to be the supervisor, there must be produced to the chair, at or before the meeting, that person's written consent to act (unless he is at the meeting and signifies his consent then and there), and confirmation that he is qualified to act as an insolvency practitioner in relation to the company.[166] Likewise if in response to the notice a member or creditor proposes that a person other than the nominee be appointed as supervisor, that person's consent to act and confirmation of being qualified to act as an insolvency practitioner in relation to the company must be delivered to the nominee by the deadline in the notice of the decision by correspondence or by the decision date (as the case may be).[167]

[157] Insolvency Rules 1986 r.1.24(4).
[158] Insolvency Act 1986 s.4A(2)(b), as inserted by Insolvency Act 2000 s.2 and Sch.2.
[159] Insolvency Act 1986 s.4A(3).
[160] Insolvency Act 1986 s.4A(4): if the company is a regulated company under Insolvency Act 1986 Sch.A1 para.44(18), the Financial Services Authority is entitled to be heard on the application: Insolvency Act 1986 s.4A(5).
[161] Insolvency Act 1986 s.4A(6).
[162] Insolvency Rules 1986 r.1.22A(2)(a).
[163] Insolvency Rules 1986 r.1.22A(2)(b).
[164] Insolvency Rules 1986 r.1.22A(5).
[165] Insolvency Rules 1986 r.1.22A(4).
[166] Insolvency Rules 1986 r.1.22(3).
[167] Rule 2.33.

Effect of approval: power to discharge the administration order or
appointment. Upon each meeting having approved the proposed voluntary arrangement,[168] either with the same modifications, or without modification,[169] it will
take effect as if made by the company at the creditors' meeting,[170] and will bind
every person who, in accordance with the Insolvency Rules 2016, had notice of, and
was entitled to vote at, that meeting,[171] whether or not he was present or represented
thereat, as if he were a party thereto.[172] The court may also by order either (i)
discharge the administration order, or (ii) give such directions with respect to the
conduct thereof as it thinks appropriate for facilitating the implementation of the
approved voluntary arrangement.[173] But *no such order may be made at any time*
before the end of a period of 28 days, beginning with the first day on which the
reports of the results of the two meetings[174] have been made to the court,[175] or at
any time when an application challenging the decisions,[176] or an appeal in respect
of such an application, is pending, or at any time within which such an appeal may
be brought.[177]

16-38

Challenge to the decisions of the meetings. There are two specific grounds upon
which an application may be made to the court to challenge the decisions of the
meetings. They are, first, that the voluntary arrangement approved as such meetings "unfairly prejudices" the interests of a creditor, member, or contributor of the
company.[178] Secondly, that there was some "material irregularity" at or in relation
to either of the meetings.[179] The persons who may apply on such grounds are the
administrator[180]; the nominee, or any person who has replaced him[181]; any person
entitled in accordance with the Insolvency Rules 2016, to vote[182] at either of the
meetings[183]; and any person who would have been entitled to vote at the creditors'
meeting if he had had notice of it.[184] *The application must be made within a period*
of 28 days, beginning with the first day on which each of the required reports[185] has
been made to the court. In the case of any person who was not given notice of the
creditors' meeting, the period is 28 days beginning with the day he became aware
that the meeting had taken place.[186] The power to extend time for appeal with

16-39

---

168 See "Decisions of Meetings", para.16-34, above.
169 Insolvency Act 1986 s.5(1).
170 Insolvency Act 1986 s.5(2)(a); unless the court has ordered the company meeting decision to prevail:
     see para.16-37, above.
171 See text to paras 16-25 ff, above.
172 Insolvency Act 1986 s.5(2)(b).
173 Insolvency Act 1986 s.5(3).
174 See para.16-35, above.
175 Insolvency Act 1985 s.5(4)(a).
176 See "Challenge to the decisions of the meetings", para.16-39, below.
177 Insolvency Act 1986 s.5(4)(b).
178 Insolvency Act 1986 s.6(1)(a).
179 Insolvency Act 1986 s.6(1)(b).
180 Insolvency Act 1986 s.6(2)(c).
181 Insolvency Act 1986 s.6(2)(b): for replacement of the nominee, see para.16-19, above.
182 See para.16-25, above.
183 Insolvency Act 1986 s.6(2)(a).
184 Insolvency Act 1986 s.6(2)(aa).
185 Insolvency Act 1986 s.6(3)(a).
186 Insolvency Act 1986 s.6(3)(b).

respect to any of the events, or orders made, is not available in the case of company arrangements, but is restricted to individual arrangements.[187]

16-40   Orders which the court may make on a successful challenge.   If, on any such application, the court is satisfied as to either ground, it may make one of both of the following orders. First, it may revoke or suspend the approvals given by the meetings, or, in a case where there has been a material irregularity at or in relation to either of the meetings, any approval given by the meeting in question.[188] Secondly, it may give a direction to any person for the summoning of further meetings to consider any revised proposal which the person who made the original proposal may make, or in a case of material irregularity, of a further company or creditors' meeting to reconsider the original proposal.[189] If, after having given such direction, the court is satisfied that the person who made the original proposal does not intend to submit a revised proposal, the court must revoke the direction, and revoke or suspend any approval given at the previous meetings.[190]

In a case where the court has given any such direction in relation to the summoning of further meetings, or has revoked or suspended an approval on either of the two possible grounds,[191] it may give such supplemental directions as it thinks fit and, in particular, directions with respect to things done since the meeting under any voluntary arrangement approved by the meeting.[192]

Except in pursuance of the above provisions, an approval given at a meeting duly summoned will not be invalidated by any irregularity at or in relation to the meeting.[193]

16-41   Alternative grounds for revocation of the creditors' approval.   The terms of the Insolvency Act 1986, in providing for the entry by corporate and individual debtors into voluntary arrangements,[194] might appear, on first impression, to provide that arrangements approved by the requisite majorities of creditors and members, or of creditors, were capable of "challenge" only on the specific grounds, discussed above, of (i) unfair prejudice to one or more creditors, or members, or (ii) a material irregularity in relation to the meetings, or the meeting,[195] for it is specifically enacted, in each Part of the Act, that an agreement cannot be invalidated by any irregularity at the meetings, or the meeting, other than as prescribed.[196]

16-42   Arrangements and schemes must comply with statutory requirements.   But the basis of the jurisdiction for a corporate or individual debtor to enter into an arrangement capable of being valid and binding on creditors is that the arrangement must provide either for a composition with the creditors, or for a scheme of arrange-

---

[187] There is no power to extend this period under the Insolvency Act 1986 s.376: see para.16-26, n.126, above.

[188] Insolvency Act 1986 s.6(4)(a).

[189] Insolvency Act 1986 s.6(4)(b).

[190] Insolvency Act 1986 s.6(5). Cf. an individual voluntary arrangement case, *Re A Debtor (No.83 of 1988)* [1990] 1 W.L.R. 789, sub nom. *Re Cove (A Debtor)* [1990] 1 All E.R. 949.

[191] See para.16-39, above.

[192] Insolvency Act 1986 s.6(6).

[193] Insolvency Act 1986 s.6(7); but see paras 16-44 ff, below.

[194] Insolvency Act 1986 ss.6(1), 253(1).

[195] Insolvency Act 1986 ss.6(1) (read with s.4A, inserted by Insolvency Act 2000 s.2 and Sch.2) and 262(1).

[196] Insolvency Act 1986 ss.6(7), 262(8).

ment of its affairs.[197] If it does not provide for either of these, it is a nullity and will be revoked or set aside.[198]

Where a corporate arrangement provided for no payment to its creditors, it was held to be invalid under the first head, but was held nevertheless to amount to a scheme of arrangement of its affairs, and to be valid.[199] But in a later individual arrangement case, the Inland Revenue successfully contended that a defective arrangement provided neither for a composition nor a scheme, and it was accordingly held to be a nullity and revoked.[200] Its defects could not be validly cured by amendments to the arrangements proposed, after the nominee had reported to the court favourably on the original proposals.[201]

The aggrieved creditor had failed to mount a challenge to the approval within the permitted 28 days[202]; but its subsequent application to set aside the arrangement as invalid was treated as not subject to that time-limitation.[203]

Proceedings after order made on successful challenge or invalidation. When **16-43** the court makes any such order of revocation or suspension, on a successful challenge or finding of invalidation, the person who obtained the order must serve sealed copies of it on the proposer and the supervisor (if different)[204]; *within five business days of the making of the order*, he must also deliver a copy of it with a notice which must contain the date on which the voluntary arrangement took effect, to the registrar of companies.[205] If the order includes a direction that action be taken (under s.6(4)(b) or (c) or under para.38(4)(b) or (c) of Sch.A1), the applicant must deliver a notice that the order has been made to the person who is directed to take such action.[206]

The proposer must, as soon as reasonably practicable, deliver a notice that the order has been made to all of those persons to whom a notice to consider the matter was delivered or who appear to be affected by the order.[207] He must also within five business days of delivery of a copy of the order (or within such longer period as the court may allow), deliver (if applicable) a notice to the court advising that it is intended to make a revised proposal to the company and its creditors, or to invite re-consideration of the original proposal.[208] But it would seem that the latter course may not be open to the court, in the case of the arrangement being held to be a nullity.[209]

Case-law on challenge procedure: "unfair prejudice" and "material **16-44** **irregularity".** The term "unfair prejudice"[210] is not defined in the Act or the Rules. It has been held, in challenge proceedings under individual voluntary ar-

---

[197] See para.16-4, above.
[198] Under Insolvency Act 1986 ss.6(6), 262(4).
[199] *Re Adam and Partners Ltd, IRC v Adam & Partners Ltd* [2000] 1 B.C.L.C. 222; [2000] B.P.I.R. 986 CA, affirming in part [1999] B.P.I.R. 868.
[200] *IRC v Bland and Sargent* [2003] EWHC 1068 Ch; [2003] B.P.I.R. 1275.
[201] See *IRC v Bland and Sargent* [2003] EWHC 1068 Ch; [2003] B.P.I.R. 1275.
[202] Insolvency Act 1986 s.6(3).
[203] See n.230 at paras [32], [53].
[204] Rule 2.40(2).
[205] Rule 2.40(6).
[206] Rule 2.40(4).
[207] Rule 2.40(5)(a).
[208] Insolvency Rules 1986 r.1.25(4)(b).
[209] See 16-42, above.
[210] Insolvency Act 1986 s.6 (company), s.262 (individual).

rangements,[211] not to apply to the debtor's landlord's dissatisfaction with an approved proposal for the sale of the lease, which he was, despite the approval, entitled to forfeit, although his debt for rent arrears would be modified by the approved proposal.[212] Misconduct was committed by the chairman of the creditors' meetings (who was the nominee's supervisor), summoned to approve an individual voluntary arrangement, with respect to incompetent preparation of the proposal and improper conduct of the meeting; he had wrongly disallowed claims by substantial creditors; such conduct was held to constitute both unfair prejudice to the interests of those creditors, and also material irregularities at or in relation to the meeting.[213]

In *Sisu Capital Fund v Tucker*[214] it was held that an arrangement was not unfairly prejudicial purely because the applicant creditors might have fared better under a scheme of arrangement with creditors. Nor is it necessarily unfairly prejudicial for an arrangement to specify different treatment of members of the same class.[215] In *Prudential Assurance Co Ltd v PRG Powerhouse Ltd*[216] proposals to release a parent company from guarantees given in relation to premises let to its subsidiary were approved by the requisite majorities: this was held to be unfairly prejudicial to the landlord of the tenant to whom the guarantees had been given.[217] It was not unfairly prejudicial to permit "football creditors" to vote in the CVA of a football club.[218]

As far as a challenge based on material irregularity is concerned, the case law has predominantly concerned the chairman of the creditors' meeting estimation of the value of claims for the purposes of voting at such meeting.[219] However, in *Re Trident Fashions Plc (in Administration) (No.2)*,[220] it was held that, whilst the failure of the administrators to disclose at the meeting called to approve the company voluntary arrangement the fact that certain offers had been made for the company's business constituted an irregularity, the irregularity was not a *material* one: even had the offers in question been disclosed, there was no real prospect that the subsequent approval would have been affected.[221] In *Rowbury v Official Receiver*[222] an IVA was revoked on the basis of a material irregularity due to a failure to suspend the creditors' meeting pending clarification of a proxy vote. In *Re Gatnom Capital & Finance Ltd*,[223] the challenge succeeded as the transactions purportedly founding the debts of certain creditors were shams.

16-45 **Effect on administrator's appointment of approval of arrangement.** Where a company which proposes a voluntary arrangement is in administration, and the arrangement is approved, the court may make one or both of the following orders. It may:

---

211 Under Insolvency Act 1986 s.262.
212 *Re Naeem (A Bankrupt) (No.18 of 1988)* [1990] 1 W.L.R. 48. See also *McMullen & Sons Ltd v Cerrone* [1994] B.C.C. 25; *Mytre Investments Ltd v Reynolds* [1995] 3 All E.R. 588.
213 *Re a Debtor (No.222 of 1990)* [1992] B.C.L.C. 137; (No.2) [1993] B.C.L.C. 233.
214 [2005] EWHC 2170 Ch; [2006] B.P.I.R. 154.
215 *Re Cancol Ltd* [1996] 1 All E.R. 37.
216 [2007] EWHC 1002 Ch; [2008] 1 B.C.L.C. 289.
217 See the similar case of *Mourant & Co Trustees Ltd v Sixty UK Ltd (in admin.)* [2010] EWHC 1890 (Ch).
218 *Revenue and Customs Commissioners v Portsmouth City Football Club Ltd (In Administration)* [2011] B.C.C. 149.
219 See, e.g. *Re Cranley Mansions* [1994] B.C.C. 576; *Re Sweatfield Ltd* [1997] B.C.C. 744; *Re Newlands (Seaford) Educational Trust Ltd* [2006] EWHC 1511 (Ch); [2007] B.C.C. 195.
220 [2004] EWHC 293 Ch; [2004] 2 B.C.L.C. 35.
221 See also I.L. & P. 2004, 20(2), 75.
222 [2015] EWHC 2276 (Ch).
223 [2010] EWHC 3353 (Ch).

(a) by order provide for the appointment of the administrator to cease to have effect, and/or

(b) give such directions with respect to the conduct of the administration as it thinks appropriate, for facilitating the implementation of the voluntary arrangement.[224]

But it may not make any such or order or orders (i) *before the end of 28 days*, beginning with the first day on which each of the reports of the meetings, which are required to be made to the court, was filed; and (ii) at any time when an application to challenge the decisions taken at the meetings, or an appeal in respect of any such application to challenge, is pending, or at any time within which such an appeal may be brought.[225]

If the court does make such an order under (a) above, causing the appointment of the administrator to cease to have effect, it must result in the administrator ceasing to be responsible for any of the outstanding administration business, so that the supervisor would become wholly in charge, unless the court had also given directions, under (b) above, to keep the administrator partially in control.

Implementation of arrangement: the supervisor's functions. The person who is for the time being carrying out, in relation to the voluntary arrangement, the functions conferred on the nominee, or his replacement,[226] is termed "the supervisor" of the voluntary arrangement.[227] If a person other than the administrator is appointed as supervisor, the administrator must forthwith do all that is required for putting the supervisor into possession of the assets included in the arrangement.[228] The supervisor must then, on taking possession of the assets, discharge any balance due to the administrator by way of remuneration, or on account of fees, costs, charges and expenses properly incurred and payable under the Insolvency Act 1986, or the Insolvency Rules 2016, and any advances made in respect of the company, together with interest.[229] Alternatively, the supervisor must, before taking possession, give the administrator a written undertaking to discharge any such balance out of the first realisation of assets.[230] The administrator will then have a charge on such assets in respect of such sums until they have been discharged, subject only to the deduction from realisations by the supervisor of the proper costs and expenses of such realisation.[231] The supervisor must also, from time to time, out of the realisation of assets, discharge all guarantees properly given by the administrator for the benefit of the company, and must pay all the administrator's expenses.[232]

16-46

Supervisor's right to ask court for directions. The supervisor is generally entitled to ask the court for directions, as to the performance of his functions, or as

16-47

---

[224] Insolvency Act 1986 s.5(3); the reports are to be made under Insolvency Rules 1986 r.1.24. The same procedure applies where the company is in liquidation.

[225] Insolvency Act 1986 s.5(4).

[226] See para.16-37, above.

[227] Insolvency Act 1986 s.7(1), (2).

[228] Insolvency Rules 1986 r.1.23(1).

[229] Insolvency Rules 2016 r.2.39(3): the rate of interest is that specified in the Judgments Act 1838 s.17, as at the date when the administration order was made, or the administrative appointment took effect.

[230] Insolvency Rules 2016 r.2.39(3).

[231] Insolvency Rules 2016 r.2.39(4).

[232] Insolvency Rules 1986 r.1.23(5).

to his dealings with the creditors.[233] These may include directions as to how, and by what procedures, different classes of creditors are to establish their claims.[234] The directions sought must not, if given, be such as to invalidate the arrangement as approved, or to alter its terms.[235] But directions have been given, which had the effect of including, among parties benefiting under the arrangement, a class of creditors (having claims of damages) who were not originally included.[236] But the supervisor must not abuse this right, by asking the court for directions on matters which it is his duty to decide for himself, in particular as to matters of commercial judgement.[237]

16-48 **When supervisor is required to keep accounts.** Where the arrangement authorises or requires the supervisor:

  (a) to carry on the business of the company or to trade on its behalf or in its name; or
  (b) otherwise to administer or to dispose of any of its funds;

he must keep accounts and records of his acts and dealings in and in connection with the arrangement, including in particular records of all receipts and payments of money.[238] He must preserve any such accounts and records which were kept by another person who has acted as supervisor of the CVA in his possession. He must then include in any report referred to at para.16–50 below include or accompany with the receipt a summary of receipts and payments or state that there are no such receipts or payments.

16-49 **Supervisor's duty to file and serve reports.** The supervisor must deliver reports on the progress and prospects for the full implementation of the CVA, the first report covering the period of 12 months commencing on the date on which the CVA was approved and a further report for each subsequent period of 12 months, delivered within the period of two months after the end of the 12-month period, sent to the registrar of companies; the company; the creditors bound by the CVA; the members; and if the company is not in liquidation, the company's auditors (if any) for the time being.

The court may, on application by the supervisor, dispense with the sending of reports or summaries as aforesaid to members of the company, either altogether, or on the basis that the availability of such reports or summaries to members is to be advertised by the supervisor in a specified manner.[239]

16-50 **Matters arising during implementation.** If any of the company's creditors or any other person is dissatisfied by any act, omission, or decision of the supervisor, he or they may apply to the court; and on such application the court may confirm,

---

[233] Insolvency Act 1986 s.7(4)(a).
[234] Insolvency Act 1986 s.7(4)(a) See, for example, *Re Federal Mogul Aftermarket UK Ltd* [2008] EWHC 1099 Ch; [2008] B.P.I.R. 846 (directions sought as to quantification of claims under the Pensions Act 1995). Other examples include *Re Energy Holdings (No.3) Ltd* [2010] B.P.I.R. 1339; and *TXU Europe Group plc* [2011] EWHC 2072 (Ch).
[235] *Re Alpha Lighting Ltd* [1997] B.P.I.R. 141.
[236] *Re FMS Financial Management Services Ltd* (1989) 5 B.C.C. 191.
[237] *Re Enron Direct Ltd* [2003] EWHC 1437 Ch; [2003] B.P.I.R. 1133.
[238] Insolvency Rules 1986 r.1.26(1).
[239] Insolvency Rules 1986 r.1.26(5)(a).

reverse, or modify any act or decision of the supervisor, give him directions, or make such other order as it thinks fit.[240]

Equally, the supervisor may apply the court for directions in relation to any particular matter arising under the voluntary arrangement.[241]

The court may, whenever it is expedient to appoint a person to carry out the functions of the supervisor, and if it is inexpedient, difficult or impracticable for any appointment to be made without the assistance of the court, make an order appointing a person qualified to act as an insolvency practitioner or authorised to act as supervisor, either in substitution for the existing supervisor, or to fill a vacancy.[242] Such power is exercisable so as to increase the number of persons exercising the functions of the supervisor, or, where there is more than one person exercising those functions, so as to replace one or more of those persons.[243]

Production of accounts and records to the Secretary of State. The Secretary   **16-51**
of State at any time, whether during the course of the arrangement or after its completion or termination, require the supervisor to produce for inspection his records and accounts,[244] and copies of summaries and reports furnished by him under the Insolvency Rules 2016.[245] The Secretary of State may require production either at the premises of the supervisor or elsewhere; it is the duty of the supervisor to comply with any such requirement.[246] The Secretary of State may require any such accounts and records to be audited; and the supervisor must give the Secretary of State such further information and assistance as he needs for the purpose of any such audit.[247]

Fees, costs, charges and expenses. The fees, and expenses that may be incurred,   **16-52**
for any of the purposes of the voluntary arrangement, are: fees for the nominee's services agreed with the company (or, as the case may be, the administrator or liquidator) and disbursements made by the nominee before the decision approving the CVA takes effect; and fees or expenses which are sanctioned by the terms of the CVA, or where they are not sanctioned by the terms of the CVA would be payable, or correspond to those which would be payable, in an administration or winding up.[248]

Completion or termination of the arrangement. *Not more than 28 days after*   **16-53**
the full implementation or termination of the arrangement, the supervisor must deliver to all creditors and members of the company who are, or were, bound by the arrangement, a notice that it has been fully implemented, or (as the case may

---

[240] Insolvency Act 1986 s.7(3).
[241] Insolvency Act 1986 s.7(4)(a); see para.16-49, above. In general, a supervisor is included among the persons who may apply to the court for a winding-up or administration order: see Insolvency Act 1986 s.7(4)(b) and Sch.B1 para.12(5). In the circumstances considered, there is in existence an administration order, the effect of which is to prevent the making of any order or the passage of any resolution, for winding-up: see Insolvency Act 1986 s.11(3)(a) (pre-Enterprise Act 2002); Insolvency Act 1986 Sch.B1 paras 42(2), (3) and 44(5).
[242] Insolvency Act 1986 s.7(5).
[243] Insolvency Act 1986 s.7(6).
[244] Insolvency Rules 1986 r.1.27(1)(a).
[245] Insolvency Rules 2016 r.2.42.
[246] Insolvency Rules 2016 r.2.42(1).
[247] Insolvency Rules 2016 r.2.42(2).
[248] Insolvency Rules 2016 r.2.43.

be) that it has terminated, with the date the CVA took effect.[249] With the notice, he must send a copy of his report, summarising all receipts and payments made by him in pursuance of the arrangement, and explaining, in relation to its actual implementation, any departures from the proposal, as it actually took effect.[250] If the CVA has been terminated, it must set out the reasons. He must also, *within the same period of 28 days*, send to the registrar of companies and to the court copies of the notice and of the report; he is not entitled to vacate office until after such copies have been sent.[251] The report must include a statement of any amount paid to unsecured creditors by virtue of the application of the s.176A Insolvency Act 1986.[252]

16-54 **The termination of arrangements.** Voluntary arrangements may be terminated by a decision of the supervisor that the company has not adhered to the conditions in the proposal as approved by the creditors and the members; a properly drawn set of proposals should specify what actions the supervisor should take in certain events of the failure of the arrangement, such as to put the company in liquidation.[253] The directors of the company may themselves decide, in such an event, to put the company into liquidation.[254]

16-55 **Reasons for termination.** In the case of a termination of the arrangement by decision of the supervisor, he must explain the reasons why the arrangement has terminated.[255] His final report must also include a statement of the amount paid (if any) to unsecured creditors, in respect of "the prescribed part" of the company's net assets.[256]

16-56 **Offences committed in relation to a voluntary arrangement.** A person who is a past or present officer, including a shadow director,[257] of a company commits an offence if he makes a false representation or commits any other fraud, for the purpose of obtaining the approval of the company's members or creditors to a proposal for any voluntary arrangement.[258] He will be liable on conviction on indictment to imprisonment, or a fine, or both, or on summary conviction to imprisonment, or a fine not exceeding the statutory maximum, or both.[259]

SECTION 3: CONVERSION FROM ADMINISTRATION TO SCHEME OF ARRANGEMENT

16-57 **Introduction.** The following notes are intended to provide the practitioner and the administrator with a general outline of the scheme of arrangement jurisdiction:

---

[249] Insolvency Rules 2016 r.2.44.
[250] Insolvency Rules 2016 r.2.44(2)(b).
[251] Insolvency Rules 2016 r.2.44(4). See form CVA4.
[252] Insolvency Rules 2016 r.2.44(2)(d). For the provisions of s.176A (the "prescribed part"), see para.15-94 ff.
[253] Insolvency Act 1986 s.7(4)(b).
[254] Insolvency Act 1986 s.124(1).
[255] Insolvency Rules 2016 r.2.44(2)(c).
[256] See Insolvency Act 1986 s.176A, and see 15-94ff, below.
[257] A "shadow director" is a person in accordance with whose directions or instructions (other than advice given in a professional capacity) the directors of the company are accustomed to act: but so that a person is not deemed a shadow director by reason only that the directors act on advice given by him in a professional capacity: Insolvency Act 1986 s.251, reproducing Companies Act 2006 s.251.
[258] Insolvency Act 1986 s.6A (inserted by Insolvency Act 2000 s.2 and Sch.2) and Sch.10.
[259] Insolvency Act 1986 s.6A(4).

more detailed practice guidance will be found in works on company law. Reference is made below to recent decisions on issues of principle and practice.

Provision was made by the Companies Act 1985 (as amended)[260] for a company[261] to propose a compromise or arrangement (generally referred to generically as a "scheme of arrangement") with its creditors or any class of its creditors, or its members, or any class of its members. The Companies Act 1985 has since been largely superseded by the Companies Act 2006, with Pt 26 of the new Act containing substantially similar provisions as far as arrangements and reconstructions are concerned. The administrator of a company in administration is empowered to propose such a scheme of arrangement to the creditors in the administration and to the members of the company,[262] and may include a proposal for such a scheme of arrangement in the statement of his proposals which he places before those creditors, and communicates to the members.[263]

Submission of the scheme to the court. The administrator applies to the court, by application notice, for an order to hold the appropriate meetings of creditors and members (or, as the case may be, of appropriate meetings of different classes of creditors or members).[264] On the hearing of the application, the court will not investigate the merits of the proposed scheme, unless it is one of which no court could reasonably approve.[265] What determines the definition of a class, is the existence of common rights, not of common interests.[266]

16-58

A foreign-registered company, which is classified as an "unregistered company",[267] is eligible to propose a scheme, on the following conditions: (a) where the company has a sufficient connection with England and Wales; (b) where the persons interested are resident within the court's jurisdiction; and (c) where the proposed scheme could be of benefit to those interested in the company.[268]

Majorities required for approval of scheme. Where the majority in number of

16-59

---

[260] Companies Act 1985 s.425, as amended by the Insolvency Act 1985 s.109(1) and Sch.6, and by the Enterprise Act 2002 Sch.17 para.5 (with effect from September 2003), to regulate the new administration jurisdictions.

[261] A company here means any company liable to be wound up under the Insolvency Act 1986: Companies Act 2006 s.895(2)(b). However, under s.900 of the Companies Act 2006 the court is empowered to facilitate a reconstruction or amalgamation, and under that section "company" means any company formed and registered under the Act (s.895(2)(a) of the Companies Act 2006, and see also s.1(1)).

[262] Insolvency Act 1986 Sch.B1 para.49(3)(b), replacing Insolvency Act 1986 s.9(3)(c) (repealed).

[263] Insolvency Act 1986 Sch.B1 para.49(3)(b).

[264] Companies Act 2006 s.896(2)(d).

[265] *Re Telewest Communications Plc* [2004] EWHC 924 Ch; [2004] B.C.C. 342. The main dispute between the parties was over the currency exchange rates adopted in the scheme. See also *Re City General Insurance Ltd*, unreported, 3 October 2002 where *Re Hawk Insurance Ltd* [2000] 2 B.C.L.C. 48 CA, was discussed. The scheme was not contrary to public policy not to the provisions of the Human Rights Act 1998 s.6. See also *My Travel Group Plc* [2004] EWHC 2741 Ch; [2005] 1 W.L.R. 2365.

[266] *Re Telewest Communications plc* [2004] EWHC 924 Ch; [2004] B.C.C. 342. See also *Re Equitable Life Assurance Co* [2002] B.C.L.C 510; and *Re Co-Operative Bank plc* [2013] EWHC 4072 (Ch).

[267] Insolvency Act 1986 ss.220 and 221 Sch.B1 para.111(1), applying the EC Regulation on Insolvency Proceedings 2000 art.3; see *Re Pan-Atlantic Assurance Co Ltd* [2003] EWHC 1696, Ch; [2003] 2 B.C.L.C. 678.

[268] *Re Drax Holdings Ltd Re Inpower Ltd* [2003] EWHC 2743 Ch; [2004] 1 All E.R. 903; [2004] 1 B.C.L.C. 10; the companies were registered in the Cayman Islands and Jersey respectively. The applications were unopposed. See also *Re Sovereign Marine & General Insurance Co Ltd* [2006] EWHC 1335 Ch; [2006] B.C.C. 774.

the creditors or members, or of the classes of creditors or of members, representing a majority of three-fourths in value, voting in person or by proxy, agrees to the
proposed compromise or arrangement, and it is sanctioned by the court, it becomes
binding on all creditors or members, or on all classes of creditors or of members,
and is also binding on the company.[269]

16-60   **Prescribed procedures for summoning a meeting or meetings.**   When the meetings are ordered to be summoned, every notice sent to a creditor or member must
be accompanied by a statement explaining the effect of the compromise or arrangement, and in particular, stating any material interest of the directors of the company
(whether as directors or as members or as creditors of the company or otherwise),
and the effect on those interests of the compromise or arrangement, in so far as it
is different from its effect on the like interests of other persons.[270]

Where the compromise or arrangement affects the rights of debenture holders of
the company, the statement shall give the like explanation as respects the trustees
of any deed for securing the issue of the debentures as it is required to give as
respects the company's directors.[271]

Directors and trustees for debenture holders are under a statutory duty to give
notice to the administrator, on behalf of the company, of such matters relating to
themselves as may be necessary for the purposes of the notices.[272]

Where the notice summoning the meeting is given by advertisement, the
advertisement must include a statement to the same effect as above, or must contain
a notification of the place at which, and the manner in which, creditors entitled to
attend the meeting, or meetings may obtain copies of the statement. Any creditor
so applying in the required manner is entitled to receive a copy of the statement free
of charge.[273]

16-61   **Practice directions.**   The current directions are contained in a *Practice Statement*, issued on 15 April 2002,[274] and intended to avoid the waste of costs and court
time.[275] Its purpose is to identify issues concerning the composition of classes of
creditor ("creditor issues") and issues concerning the type of meetings to be ordered
("meetings issues"), and thereby to facilitate their solution early in the
proceedings.[276]

The jurisdiction will continue to be exercisable either by a judge or a registrar,
but applications involving substantial schemes will be listed for hearing before a
judge. The judge who first hears the application should, where possible, retain carriage of the case throughout.[277]

In considering whether or not to order meetings of creditors ("meetings orders"),

---

[269] Companies Act 2006 s.899(3).
[270] Companies Act 2006 s.897(1), (2).
[271] Companies Act 2006 s.897(3).
[272] Companies Act 2006 s.898(1).
[273] Companies Act 2006 s.897(4).
[274] *Practice Statement (Companies: Schemes of Arrangement)*, 15 April 2002; [2002] 3 All E.R. 96,
Morritt V-C, replacing *Practice Note* by Eve J [1934] W.N. 142.
[275] As arose in, e.g. *Re Hawk Insurance Co* [2000] 2 B.C.L.C. 480 CA.
[276] See, Practice Statement, n.282.
[277] See n.282, para.3.

the court will consider whether more than one meeting is required, and if so their appropriate composition.[278]

Directions for the solution of creditors' meetings issues may include orders giving anyone affected by a meeting order a limited time in which to apply to vary or discharge them.[279]

The order sanctioning the scheme.   The order of the court sanctioning the   **16-62**
scheme does not take effect, until an office copy of it is delivered to the registrar of companies.[280] A copy of the order must also be affixed to every copy of the company's memorandum (or comparable instrument defining its constitution), which is issued by the company after the date of the order.[281]

Defaults in carrying out the statutory obligations by the administrator, the directors or the trustees for debenture holders, constitute an offence.[282]

SECTION 4: CONVERSION FROM ADMINISTRATION TO WINDING-UP

Introduction.   An administration may under the current regime, be converted into   **16-63**
a winding-up, voluntary or compulsory, with greater facility than under the old regime, both at the initiation of the administration, during its life, and at the end of its life: for the old regime in this field, see s.5, para.16-69, below.

Pre-administration.   Although not an instance of an administration proceeding   **16-64**
to a winding-up, it might be convenient here to draw attention to the court's power, on hearing an administration application, to treat it as a winding-up petition, and to make a winding-up order, or any other order which it could make on a petition under the Insolvency Act 1986 s.125.[283] In that event, the winding-up is deemed to commence on the making of the order. The court's very wide-ranging powers enable it to make any necessary consequential orders.[284]

This provision has solved a problem which arose under the old regime, that although the effect of a voluntary winding-up resolution could be achieved in an administration, no compulsory winding-up could be made, in view of the statute, without the presentation of a petition.[285]

Post-administration.   Once the company enters into administration, it may be put   **16-65**
into winding-up, compulsory or voluntary, by the use of a number of different procedures briefly summarised below.

(a)   As part of administrator's proposals   The administrator may, in the proposals to the creditors, include a proposal that the company go into a creditors' voluntary winding-up, In that event, he must give details of the proposed liquidator, and must inform the creditors that they may nominate, a person other than himself, as liquidator, provided that they do so after the receipt of the proposals and

---

[278]   See n.282, para.5.
[279]   See n.282, para.6.
[280]   Companies Act 2006 s.899(4).
[281]   Companies Act 2006 s.901(3).
[282]   Companies Act 2006 s.901(5).
[283]   Insolvency Act 1986 Sch.B1 para.13(1)(e).
[284]   Insolvency Act 1986 Sch.B1 para.13(1)(f).
[285]   *Re Brooke Marine Ltd* [1988] B.C.C. 546.

before they have been approved.[286] Where applicable, the declaration required by s.231 of the Insolvency Act 1986 shall be made.

(b)   As a procedure for terminating an unsuccessful administration   Where the administrator thinks that the purpose of administration cannot be achieved, or that the company should not have entered administration, or he is required by a creditors' meeting to apply, he may apply to the court for the appointment of the administrator to terminate. On such an application, the court, in the exercise of its wide-ranging powers, may make a winding-up order, or order that the company take steps to go into creditors' voluntary winding-up.

This provision also covers the position, where, in an administration order case, the administrator thinks that the purpose of administration has been sufficiently achieved. For those procedures, see the Insolvency Act 1986 Sch.B1 para.79 and para.17–28ff, below.

(c)   As a procedure for terminating a successful administration   Where the administrator is satisfied that distributions will be made to, or have been set aside for, the creditors, he may take steps, by virtue of which the company goes into creditors' voluntary winding-up. For this procedure, see the Insolvency Act 1986 Sch.B1 para.83, and para.17–34, below.

(d)   As a remedy for an aggrieved creditor   Where an aggrieved or dissatisfied creditor applies to the court for an order that the appointment of the administrator shall cease to have effect, on the ground that the applicant for the administration order, or the appointor of the administrator, had an improper motive, the court, in the exercise of its wide-ranging powers, may order that the company be compulsorily wound-up, or shall take steps to go into creditors' voluntary liquidation, with any necessary consequential orders. For this procedure, see the Insolvency Act 1986 Sch.B1 para.81, and paras 17–09 ff, below.

16-66   On the application of the supervisor.   Where the supervisor is of the opinion that the voluntary arrangement cannot proceed, in accordance with its approved provisions, to a satisfactory conclusion, or has been terminated,[287] he may apply for it to be wound up. He is empowered so to apply,[288] but is not authorised to present a petition in his own name as supervisor,[289] but only, it would seem, in the name of the company.[290] It must be expressed to be the petition of the company by the office-holder.[291]

Where the directors of a company, which was subject to a voluntary arrange-

---

[286] Rule 3.35(1)(j).

[287] For termination of voluntary arrangements, see para.16-54, above.

[288] Insolvency Act 1986 s.7(4)(b); he is empowered to apply, even where he is no longer carrying out his functions, e.g. where the arrangement has been revoked or otherwise terminated: *Re Arthur Rathbone Kitchens Ltd* [1998] B.C.C. 450.

[289] He is not included in the list of persons entitled to present a winding-up petition: Insolvency Act 1986 s.124.

[290] If, at the time of making a winding-up order, the supervisor is still in office, the court may appoint him to be liquidator: Insolvency Act 1986 s.140(2). It is not clear whether this rule can still apply, if the arrangement had been revoked, so that there was no longer any arrangement in existence, of which he could be regarded as being still, in law, the supervisor.

[291] Rule 7.27(1).

ment, petitioned for and obtained an order for its winding-up, this was held not to terminate the arrangement, or the interests of the creditors who had approved it.[292]

On the application of a Member-State liquidator. When the Member-State liquidator has been appointed, with respect to the company in main proceedings in insolvency commenced in a Member State of the European Union other than the United Kingdom, he is clothed with all the powers of a creditor of the company.[293]   **16-67**

Mutual obligations and rights of the supervisor and the Member-State liquidator. Where the supervisor of an arrangement is obliged to give notice to, or to provide copy documents (including orders of court) to the court, to the registrar of companies or to the Official Receiver, he must also give notice, or provide copy documents, as appropriate, to any Member-State liquidator in office in relation to the company.[294]   **16-68**

These obligations are without prejudice to the obligations imposed by the EC Regulation to co-operate and communicate information.[295] The obligations are mutual: the insolvency practitioner in the main insolvency proceedings and the insolvency practitioner in secondary insolvency proceedings concerning the same debtor shall cooperate with each other to the extent such cooperation is not incompatible with the rules applicable to the respective proceedings. Such cooperation may take any form, including the conclusion of agreements or protocols.[296] The insolvency practitioners shall as soon as possible communicate to each other any information which may be relevant to the other proceedings, in particular any progress made in lodging and verifying claims and all measures aimed at rescuing or restructuring the debtor, or at terminating the proceedings, provided appropriate arrangements are made to protect confidential information. They shall also explore the possibility of restructuring the debtor and, where such a possibility exists, coordinate the elaboration and implementation of a restructuring plan; and shall coordinate the administration of the realisation or use of the debtor's assets and affairs. In this regard, the insolvency practitioner in the secondary insolvency proceedings shall give the insolvency practitioner in the main insolvency proceedings an early opportunity to submit proposals on the realisation or use of the assets in the secondary insolvency proceedings.[297]

SECTION 5: WINDING-UP PROCEDURES IN PRE-COMMENCEMENT CASES

Under the old regime. "Pre-commencement cases" are those where the administration process had begun before 15 September 2003, when the current regime came into force.[298]   **16-69**

Under the old regime, as already indicated (see para.16-64, above) a company

---

[292] *Re Excalibur Airways Ltd* [1998] 1 B.C.L.C. 436; [1998] B.P.I.R. 598, distinguishing *Re Arthur Rathbone Kitchens Ltd*.

[293] Recast Insolvency Regulation arts 21, 45; Insolvency Rules 2016 rr.21.3 and 21.8.

[294] Insolvency Rules 2016 r.21.7(1)(b).

[295] Insolvency Rules 2016 r.21.7(2).

[296] EC Regulation, n.1, art.41(1).

[297] Recast Insolvency Regulation art.41(2).

[298] See Enterprise Act 2002 (Commencement No.4 and Transitional Provisions and Savings) Order 2003 (SI 2003/730) art.2.

subject to an administration order could not be put into compulsory winding-up, without the presentation of a winding-up petition.[299]

The company, by its administrator, or (with his leave) its directors, was technically competent to convene meetings of its members and of creditors to pass resolutions for creditors' voluntary winding-up.[300] But this course was prohibited by the existence of the administration order, and the moratorium which is brought into force.[301]

Accordingly, various procedures were judicially devised, so as to permit a company in administration to enter into creditors' voluntary winding-up. The first of these was for the company to pass a members' resolution to that end, conditionally on its not taking effect until an order had been made, discharging the administration order.[302] This procedure was held to be invalid, since the company had no power to pass such a conditional resolution.[303] Accordingly, an alternative procedure was devised, whereby the court made a "conditional order", discharging the administration order, which order would not be drawn up until the winding-up resolution had been passed and logged in court.[304]

As part of this procedure, the court had held itself to be empowered to order the administrator to pay the company's preferential creditors on the same basis, as to the relevant dates, as if the creditors' voluntary winding-up was a compulsory winding-up.[305]

In view of the accepted invalidity of the former procedure, the latter procedure has been adopted and accepted. A recognised form of order, "a *Norditrak* order", has been established and recognised.[306]

SECTION 6: CONVERSION FROM ADMINISTRATION INTO DISSOLUTION

16-70 Procedure. If the administrator thinks that the company has no property which might permit a distribution to creditors, he must give notice to that effect to the registrar of companies, attaching a copy of a final progress report.[307] The court however is empowered to disapply that provision, thereby relieving the administrator of that obligation.[308] If he is obliged to give the notice and gives it, the notice must identify the proceedings, and he must also, as soon as reasonably practicable, file copies of the notice and the report with the court,[309] and send a copy of the notice to each creditor, of whose claim and of whose address he is aware,[310] and in addition to all persons to whom notice of the appointment was delivered.[311]

16-71 Registration of notice leads to dissolution. Upon receipt of the notice, the

---

[299] *Re Brooke Marine Ltd* [1988] B.C.C. 546.
[300] Insolvency Act 1986 s.95.
[301] Insolvency Act 1986 s.11(3)(a) (repealed, except for old regime).
[302] *Re Powerstore (Trading) Ltd* [1998] B.C.C. 305; *Re Mark One (Oxford Street) Plc* [1998] B.C.C. 984.
[303] *Re Norditrak (UK) Ltd* [2000] 1 W.L.R. 343; [2000] B.C.C. 441.
[304] *Re Mark One (Oxford Street) Plc*, n.310, above, approved and followed in *Re Wolsey Theatre Ltd* [2001] B.C.C. 145; and *Re UCT (UK) Ltd* [2001] 1 CH 436; see also *Re Oakhouse Property Holdings Ltd* [2003] B.P.I.R. 469.
[305] See *Re Mark One (Oxford Street) Plc*, n.310.
[306] See n.311, adopted in *Re Oakhouse Property Holdings Ltd* at 470G.
[307] Insolvency Act 1986 Sch.B1 para.84(1): Insolvency Rules 2017 r.3.61(4).
[308] Insolvency Act 1986 Sch.B1 para.84(2).
[309] Insolvency Act 1986 Sch.B1 para.84(5)(a).
[310] Insolvency Act 1986 Sch.B1 para.84(5)(b).
[311] Insolvency Rules 2016 r. 3.61(3).

registrar will register it.[312] On the registration of the notice, the appointment of the administrator ceases to have effect.[313] At the end of three months from the date of the registration of the notice, the company is deemed to be dissolved.[314] The administrator, or another interested person, may apply to the court to extend that period, at the end of which dissolution will take place; on such an application, the court may extend the period, or suspend it, or disapply that provision.[315] In that event, the administrator, if the applicant, shall, as soon as reasonably practicable, send a copy of the court's order to the registrar of companies.[316] If he is not the applicant, the court will itself send a copy to the administrator.[317]

If the administrator fails to file with the court, or to send to the creditors, a copy of his notice regarding the company's lack of property to permit a distribution to creditors, and of his final progress report, he commits an offence.[318]

Problems presented by the cessation of the administrator's **16-72**
appointment.   These provisions appear to present difficulties, in that since the filing of the notice with the registrar results in the appointment of the administrator *ipso jure* ceasing to have the effect, he would prima facie then cease to have either the authority or the resources to comply with the remainder of his obligations flowing therefrom.

However, Sch.B1 appears to be based throughout on the proposition that despite the administrator's appointment having ceased to have effect, he continues to have the authority, and to be under certain obligations, to continue to perform at least some his functions.[319]

Paragraph 84, and the amended rules, do not however authorise the court to undo the effect of the original giving of notice to the registrar. Accordingly, if the court does make an order having the effect that the company does not proceed, or ceases to proceed, to dissolution, it would need to re-appoint the administrator, or to appoint a new administrator, to take charge of it.

There is of course the general power in the court, within six years of the dissolution of a company, to revoke its dissolution.[320] However, the company is deemed to have continued in existence on the basis that it was not dissolved, but the administration period cannot be retrospectively extended.[321]

---

[312]   Insolvency Act 1986 Sch.B1 para.84(3).
[313]   Insolvency Act 1986 Sch.B1 para.84(4).
[314]   Insolvency Act 1986 Sch.B1 para.84(6).
[315]   Insolvency Act 1986 Sch.B1 para.84(7).
[316]   Insolvency Act 1986 Sch.B1 para.84(8).
[317]   Insolvency Rules 2016 r.3.61(5).
[318]   Insolvency Act 1986 Sch.B1 para.84(9).
[319]   Throughout the provisions of Sch.B1, dealing with the cessation, on one ground or another, of the administrator's appointment to have effect, he remains liable to perform functions, e.g. filing a final progress report; see Insolvency Rules 2016 r.3.56.
[320]   Companies Act 2006 ss.1029, 1030.
[321]   *Re People's Restaurant Group Ltd*, unreported, 30 November 2012.

CHAPTER 17

ENDING ADMINISTRATION

SECTION 1: INTRODUCTION

17-1   **The current regime and the scope of this Chapter.**   This chapter principally addresses the termination of an administration and the circumstances in which the appointment of the administrator "ceases to have effect",[1] both on a non-contentious and on a contentious basis, whether the administration was commenced by an administration order made by the Court or by an appointment made out of court.

The circumstances in which the appointment of administrator may be set aside on the basis of some technical defect in the appointment, or on the grounds that there has been a failure properly to comply with the statutory formalities (possibly with the consequence that the appointment is invalid ab initio) are considered separately at para.14-4.

The present administration regime is contained in Sch.B1 to the Insolvency Act 1986 and is the product of the far-reaching amendments to the Insolvency Act 1986, inserted by s.248(1) and (2) of the Enterprise Act 2002, with effect from 15 September 2003.[2] As explored below, certain of the authorities under the old (pre-Enterprise Act) regime may nonetheless continue to provide useful guidance. The relevant procedural regime in relation to administrations in England and Wales is contained in the Insolvency (England and Wales) Rules 1986

The provisions of Sch.B1 extend to Scotland[3] with certain modifications.[4] Those modifications to Sch.B1 do not impact upon the contents of this chapter. The relevant procedural regime in respect of administration in Scotland is contained in the Insolvency (Scotland) Rules 1986[5] (as amended).

17-2   **Termination of the effect of the appointment is to be distinguished from the termination of administrator's appointment.**   Paragraph 1(2) of Sch.B1 to the Insolvency Act 1986 provides that:

"For the purposes of this Act—

   (a)   a company is "in administration" while the appointment of an administrator of the company has effect,

---

[1]   The term is used in Insolvency Act 1986 at s.140(1) and at Sch.B1 paras 1(2)(c), 74(4)(d), 76(1), 79(1), 80(3), 81(1), 82(3)(a), 83(6)(a), 84(4), 85(1)(a), 86(1), 98(1) and 99(1).
[2]   See the Enterprise Act 2002 (Commencement No.4 and Transitional Provisions and Savings) Order 2003 (SI 2003/2093). For a more detailed consideration of the pre-Enterprise Act 2002 regime and an in-depth analysis of the differences between the old regime and the present one, the reader is referred to previous editions of this work.
[3]   Insolvency Act 1986 s.440.
[4]   Insolvency Act 1986 Sch.B1 paras 112–115.
[5]   SI 1986/1915.

(b)   a company "enters administration" when the appointment of an administrator takes effect,

(c)   a company ceases to be in administration when the appointment of an administrator of the company ceases to have effect in accordance with this Schedule, and

(d)   a company does not cease to be in administration merely because an administrator vacates office (by reason of resignation, death or otherwise) or is removed from office." (Emphasis added)

The critical phraseology adopted in the legislation makes it clear that the point at which an administration ends is when the appointment of the administrator "ceases to have effect".[7] Importantly, it should be noted that neither the removal of the administrator (or administrators, if more than one), nor his death nor his resignation will, *of itself*, cause the appointment "to cease to have effect".[6]

Ending administration: two categories—contentious and non-contentious.   The procedures by which an administration may be ended fall broadly into two categories: **17-3**

(1)   There are those procedures that involve attacks by dissatisfied or aggrieved creditors (and also in some cases, by members) on the administration itself, either with or without an attack on the conduct of the administrator personally. These procedures may (but will not inevitably) lead to the ending of the administration and can conveniently be described for the purposes of this chapter as "contentious" procedures.

(2)   There are those procedures which are essentially capable of being characterised as being events in the ordinary course of administration. Those procedures can be described, for the purposes of this chapter, as "non-contentious".

Vacation of office (resignations, removals and replacements).   For completeness, the resignation, removal, death and replacement of the administrator are briefly addressed below. It must be stressed that in none of these cases does the administration per se cease to have effect.   **17-4**

Section 2: Contentious Procedures: remedies for Unsatisfactory
Appointments

The old regime and the current regime.   Under the pre-Enterprise Act regime, an administration appointment could only be made by the court, on the hearing of a petition, supported by sworn evidence and usually, supported also by a report prepared by the proposed administrator himself, addressing the viability of the administration.[7] Interested parties could appear and object.[8] The court had a wide discretion whether to appoint, and if so, who to appoint.[9] Thus, at this initial stage, the process of getting a company into administration was the subject of early   **17-5**

---

6   Insolvency Act 1986 Sch.B1 para.1(1)(d).

7   Insolvency Rules 1986 r.2.2 (repealed).

8   Insolvency Act 1986 Pt II, ss.8 and 9 (repealed, except for old régime). See also *Re Farnbrough Aircraft.com Ltd* [2002] EWHC 1224 (Ch); and *Re Chelmsford City Football Club (1980) Ltd* [1991] B.C.C. 133.

9   *Re Rowbotham Baxter Ltd* [1990] B.C.C. 113; [1990] B.C.L.C. 397; and see *Re Tasbian Ltd (No.2)* [1990] B.C.C. 322.

judicial scrutiny and this, in turn, reduced the scope for the making of inappropriate or unjustified appointments.

By contrast, under Sch.B1, whilst appointments can still be made in-court on application,[10] a key feature is the power to appoint an administrator *out* of court, vested in a qualifying floating charge-holder, and in the company or its directors.[11] In these cases, there are no judicial safeguards in place at the critical appointment stage.

17-6   **Remedies for unsatisfactory appointments under the old régime.**   Under the old régime, the principal remedy was contained in r.7.47[12] of the Insolvency Rules 1986. This conferred jurisdiction upon the Court to review, vary or rescind any order made by it in its insolvency jurisdiction (which would include an administration order).[13]

Accordingly, where it was contended that an appointment was unsatisfactory, and should be either varied or set aside altogether, an application could be made to the court under r.7.47 for that very purpose.[14] The right to make such an application was not confined to a creditor or a member but could be made by any party with a sufficient interest.

17-7   **Old regime: review by the Court and the Cornhill Insurance and Dianoor Jewels decisions.**   The leading decisions under the old régime on the question of the court's power (under its review jurisdiction) to set aside improper or inappropriate appointments are *Cornhill Insurance Plc v Cornhill Financial Services Ltd*[15] and *Re Dianoor Jewels Ltd.*[16]

In the *Cornhill Insurance* case, a company selling insurance business, as the tied agent of the Applicant insurance company, to which it was heavily indebted, transferred all its insurance-selling business to a shell company, owned by its proprietors. That company was intended to act as a tied agent for a different insurance company. Having procured the discharge of all its debts, other than its debt to the Applicant, the Respondent company presented a petition for an administration order. This was heard at short notice, ex parte, with no creditors or members being present or represented. An administration order was made.

On learning of the appointment, the Applicant applied for orders that it be joined as a party opposing the petition, for the petition to be reheard and for the administration order to be reviewed and set aside under r.7.47 of the Insolvency Rules 1986. The Applicant contended that the order and the appointment seriously prejudiced its rights as a major unpaid and unsecured creditor. The judge set the order aside, on the grounds of what he held to have been serious non-disclosures by the

---

10   By (amongst others) the company, its directors and one or more creditors, see Sch.B1 para.12(1).

11   Insolvency Act 1986 Sch.B1 paras 14 and 22.

12   Repealed. See now para.17.8, below and r.12.59(1) of the Insolvency Rules 2016.

13   See para.17-7 below. Note: r.7.47 applies only in England and Wales. While there is no equivalent to r.7.47 in Scotland, the Court of Session has inherent jurisdiction under its nobile officium to grant a remedy in the circumstances discussed.

14   As in *Cornhill Insurance Plc v Cornhill Financial Services Ltd* [1992] B.C.C. 818; [1992] B.C.L.C. 914, HH Judge Micklem and CA, and in *Re Dianoor Jewels Ltd* [2001] 1 B.C.L.C. 450; [2001] B.P.I.R. 234. See also the discussion in *Re Farnbrough Aircraft.com Ltd* (see n.8) as to what may constitute a sufficient interest under the old regime.

15   See n.14; at first instance, per HH Judge Micklem at 820.

16   See n.14.

petitioner as to the true facts of the Respondent company's position and circumstances.[17] The Respondent company appealed.

The Court of Appeal upheld the order setting aside the administration order. It did so, not on the grounds of non-disclosure,[18] but because the application for administration was wholly misconceived. The company's true intention was held to have been not (as the statute required) that its business should be administered by the administrator for the benefit of its creditors generally, but that the value of that business should pass to the shell company for no consideration.

In *Re Dianoor Jewels Ltd*,[19] an administration order had been made on a petition presented by the three directors of a company on the grounds of its insolvency. The petition was presented for the then statutory purposes of the protection of the company and the interests of its creditors.

The wife of one of the directors (who was himself the principal shareholder), who was not herself a creditor or member of the company, applied, as a party aggrieved by the order, to set it aside and terminate the administration, on the grounds that the company was not insolvent, and that the petition was an abuse of process. She contended that the order was intended to frustrate the enforcement of orders made for her benefit in the Family Division, in ancillary proceedings between her and her husband—in particular, an order for the sale for her benefit of (supposed) assets of the company.

Applying the *Cornhill Insurance* decision, the Court held that the petition was well-founded, in that the company was proved to be unable to pay its debts and that the petition was correctly directed towards the achievement of the statutory purposes of administration. The fact that the directors of the company, or one of them, had had a private purpose in presenting the petition (to prevent the enforcement of the orders for the benefit of the applicant wife), did not amount to an abuse of process justifying the setting aside of the administration order.

It should be noted that whilst the applicant in *Re Dianoor Jewels Ltd* (see above) was neither a creditor nor a member of the company, she was nevertheless held to be entitled to apply to set aside an order that she claimed prejudiced her interests or rights.

As addressed below, under the current regime, the Court retains its powers of review in the case of in-court appointments. Hence, in those cases, the *Cornhill* and *Dianoor* decisions under the old regime will remain directly relevant (if not, strictly, binding).

That said, although these decisions have no direct bearing on the subject of unsatisfactory extra-judicial appointments, they may nonetheless provide some guidance on the subjects of non-disclosure, and on question of "improper motive" (see paras 17-10 ff, below)

The present régime and the availability of review by the Court.   In the case   **17-8**
of in-court appointments, the review remedy is still available; it is now contained in r.12.59(1) of the Insolvency (England and Wales) Rules 2016. It can be invoked

---

[17] See n.14.

[18] For an example of serious non-disclosure see *Astor Chemical Ltd v Synthetic Technology Ltd* [1990] B.C.C. 977 at 107–8. In the same field, where an unsatisfactory administration order was set aside on the application of the administrator himself, on the ground that, in his opinion, there had been serious non-disclosure by the company in the course of the application see *Re Sharps of Truro Ltd* [1990] B.C.C. 94; see para.17-29, below.

[19] See n.15.

by any person demonstrating a sufficient interest.[20] In review cases (and in the absence of any known authority under the current regime), it is likely that the *Cornhill Insurance* and *Dianoor Jewels* cases will continue to provide useful guidance to carry considerable weight.

The review remedy is not available in the case of out-court appointments. In such cases, the aggrieved applicant's rights of recourse fall broadly into two categories:

(1) an attack on the appointment itself, under para.81 of Sch.B1 to the Insolvency Act 1986 for an order ending administration on the grounds of "improper motive" on the part of the appointor (available only to a creditor); and

(2) an attack on the administrator's conduct of the administration under para.74 of Sch.B1 (available only to a creditor or a member) or under para.75 (available to the official receiver, the administrator,[21] the liquidator, a creditor or a contributory).

These remedies are also available in the case of in-court appointments. But in both categories, the onus is a heavy one. The reality is that if the administration per se was viable at the outset and remains viable, the Court will be unlikely to bring it to an end.

17-9   **Paragraph 81 of Sch B1: Appointment of administrator ordered to cease to have effect, due to the presence of an "improper motive".**   This remedy was introduced by the Enterprise Act 2002 amendments with effect from 15 September 2003. A creditor of a company (but note, *not* a member), may apply to court for an order providing that the appointment of an administrator of the company is "to cease to have effect at a specified time".[22] It is the order that the appointment of the administrator shall cease to have effect which ends the administration.

Such an application *must* allege "an improper motive", (a) in the case of an administrator appointed by administration order, on the part of the applicant for the order, or (b) in any other case, on the part of the person or persons who made the appointment (i.e. a floating charge-holder, the company or its directors).[23] It will be noted from the express language of para.81(1) that the remedy is a discretionary one. Even if an "improper motive" is made out, the Court "may" make an order effectively bringing the administration to an end. It does not have to do so.

Perhaps surprisingly, prior to the judgment on 17 January 2017 in *Re FREP (Knowle) Ltd (in administration)*,[24] the construction and ambit of this provision had not been the subject of any detailed judicial scrutiny by the Courts of England and Wales.[25] The *FREP* case is considered in detail below at para.17-14.

17-10   **The meaning of "improper motive"**   "Improper motive" is not a term of art and

---

[20] As to what may constitute a sufficient interest, see *Patley Wood Farm LLP v Brake* [2016] EWHC 1688 (Ch). Under the old regime, see: *Re Farnbrough Aircraft.Com Ltd; Re Chelmsford City Football Club (1980) Ltd* [1991] B.C.C. 133.

[21] The present incumbent, presumably against either his predecessor or a joint appointee.

[22] Insolvency Act 1986 Sch.B1 para.81(1).

[23] Insolvency Act 1986 Sch.B1 para.81(2)(a), (b).

[24] [2017] EWHC 25 (Ch). (sub nom. *Thomas v Frogmore Real Estate Partners GP1 Ltd*) (*FREP*).

[25] For consideration of the equivalent provision in the Northern Irish legislation (art.82 of the Insolvency (Northern Ireland) Order 2005), see *Cursitan v Keenan* [2011] NICh 23, followed in *FREP*. See also the obiter observations of HHJ Thornton QC in *Jackson v Thakrar* [2007] EWHC 626 (TCC) at [808]ff.

the phrase does not appear elsewhere in the legislation. There is no guidance as to its meaning in any of the material published by the government departments and agencies which sponsored the amendments to the 1986 legislation—principally the White Paper, *Insolvency–A Second Chance* published by the Department of Trade and Industry in July 2001 and a subsequent paper from the same department delivered on 14 January 2002, entitled *An update on the Corporate Insolvency Proposals*. Likewise, there is no assistance to be found in *Explanatory Notes* on the Enterprise Act 2002[26] and no debate is recorded in *Hansard* in the course of Parliament's deliberations over the Enterprise Bill in both Houses.[27]

Needless to say, it is not easy to predict, let alone analyse, the possible motives which a floating charge-holder, or a company or its directors, may have had for applying for the appointment of an administrator, or for appointing one themselves. There may be a single motive, or a plethora of them, good, bad, or mixed.

In the light of the *FREP* decision, it is now open to doubt whether the construction of the phrase "improper motive", and the relevant inquiry for the Court when determining the presence or absence of such a motive, necessarily engages the identification of subjective criteria such as the presence or absence of "desire" or "intention".

These phrases of course do feature elsewhere in the legislation, most notably (in the case of "desire") in the provisions concerning voidable preferences under ss.239–242 of the Insolvency Act 1986. But it remains to be seen whether the case-law under those provisions (and indeed their predecessors) will provide any direct, or even useful, analogies. This case law is considered below for completeness.

Possible analogies between "improper motive" and s.239 of the Insolvency Act 1986 (voidable preferences). 17-11 Under s.239, the transaction by which a creditor was preferred will not be set aside by the court, unless the company which carried out the transaction, was *"influenced by a desire"* to produce the effect of putting the beneficiary of the transaction "into a position which, in the event of the company going into insolvent liquidation, will be better than the position he would have been in if that thing had not been done".[28]

The predecessor to s.239 was s.44 of the Bankruptcy Act 1914 (which also applied to insolvent companies until the enactment of s.615 of the Companies Act 1985). Section 44 of the 1914 Act concerned what were then known as transactions by way of "fraudulent preference", where the legislation used the expression "with the view of".[29]

On the subject of "mixed motives", in a "fraudulent preference" case under the 1914 Act, Lord Evershed MR said:

"Whether the word used be 'intention', or some other word, since it is notorious that human beings are by no means always single-minded, the intention to prefer which must be proved is the principal or dominant intention. There may also be a valid distinction, for present purposes, between an intention to prefer and the reason for forming and executing that intention".[30]

Section 239 and the current "preference" test. Section 239 does not use the 17-12

---

[26] *Enterprise Act 2002: Explanatory Notes* (DTI, TSO, 2002).
[27] *Jackson v Thakrar* [2008] 1 All E.R. 601 at 807, discussed in *FREP* at [42]–[44].
[28] Insolvency Act 1986 s.239(5).
[29] Bankruptcy Act 1914 s.44; Companies Act 1985 s.615.
[30] *Re Cutts Ex p. Bognor Mutual Building Society v Cutts' Trustee* [1956] 1 W.L.R. 728 CA, at 773–4. See also *Muir Hunter on Personal Insolvency* (Issue 35) 2004 at para.3–3280.

1914 Act's simple "with the view of" formulation. Instead, it adopts the more specifically "operational" phrase "influenced by the desire to".

When construing that expression, the courts have consistently rejected the former judicial constructions of the word "view", as a guide to the meaning of the word "desire". The leading authority remains the judgment of Millett J in *Re MC Bacon Ltd*; a liquidator is not required to prove that the "desire" to produce the specified outcome was the dominant motivating feature; proof that the transaction was "influenced by the desire" will suffice.[31] "'Intention' is objective, desire is subjective' ... A man may choose the lesser of two evils without desiring either. A man is not to be taken as *desiring* all the necessary consequences of his actions".[32]

17-13   **Mixed motives.** In the *Dianoor Diamonds* case, Blackburne J held that the presence of "mixed motives" for the presentation of an administration petition did not, *ipso jure*, invalidate the administration order made on that petition. His approach on the question of motive(s) is instructive.

He acknowledged the (possible or actual) presence in the minds of the directors of a "private purpose", namely to frustrate the applicant's enforcement of her orders against the supposed assets of the company. However, he held however that the presence of such a purpose would not vitiate either the petition or the administration order made on it, if (as he found to be the case) the petition was technically in order, and was correctly directed to the carrying out of the statutory purposes:

> "The question [of setting the order aside] does not arise, where, as here, the objective requirements of [the statute] have been sufficiently demonstrated, and the company is, or is likely to become, unable to pay its debts, and the court considers that the making of an administration order would be likely to achieve one or more of the statutory purposes, and *where there has been no material non-disclosure* [emphasis supplied], and where the evidence strongly suggests that, so far from suffering from the making of the administration order, the company's creditors will or may be gravely disadvantaged, if an order is not made ...".

Adopting this approach, the rule might be formulated thus; no matter what the motives of the appointor, if the appointment is good for the company and for the general body of its creditors, it should be treated as valid.[33] A similar approach was adopted by the Court in the context of a bankruptcy petition alleged to have been an abuse of process.[34] This formulation is consistent with the judgment in the *FREP* case, in which *Dianoor Jewels* was cited.

17-14   **The FREP case: what constitutes "improper motive" under para.81 of Sch.B1?**   The essential facts of the case were broadly as follows. Three companies (the "FREP Companies") were substantially indebted to the Nationwide Building Society under the terms of an amended and restated Facility Agreement dated 5 April 2012. The FREP Companies' liabilities to the Building Society were secured by debentures containing qualifying floating charges. In due course, the Building

---

[31]   [1990] 1 B.C.C. 78 at [87].

[32]   See n.31.

[33]   Such a rule leaves outstanding Blackburne J's qualification, concerning non-disclosure, emphasised above. The relevance of this factor must depend on the relevance of the material not disclosed; but such non-disclosure must be *material* to be significant for the decision, i.e. in the instant case, it would have needed to impair the judge's findings as to the formal propriety of the petition.

[34]   *Maud v Abbar Block SARL* [2015] EWHC 1626 (Ch); *Re Maud* [2016] EWHC 2175 (Ch).

Society made demand under the Facility Agreement and, on 7 November 2016, appointed Mr Thomas and Mr Kendall as administrators (out of court) in respect of all three companies.

As at the time these appointments were made, the FREP Companies had (as claimants) been in litigation against the Building Society (as defendant) for some 18 months prior. Indeed, as of 7 November 2016, a 10-day trial was only three months away. The essence of the FREP Companies' claims against the Building Society was that it had acted in breach of contract and in bad faith in disposing of its economic interest in the loans that were the subject of the Facility Agreement to a company called Promontoria Carlisle Ltd.

The relationship between the Building Society and Promontoria was governed by the terms of a Funded Participation Agreement dated 28 January 2015. By the terms of that agreement, the Building Society was required to act promptly in accordance with any reasonable directions given by Promontoria in relation both to the Facility Agreement and to the debentures. In accordance with those provisions and at Promontoria's direction, the Building Society made demand of the Companies, and proceeded to appoint the administrators.

The Company's other major creditor (Frogmore Real Estate Partners GP1 Ltd, an associated company) promptly applied for an order under para.81(1), that the appointments should cease to have effect on the grounds of an improper motive on the part of the Building Society as appointor. The core allegation was that the Building Society had been motivated by a wish to stifle or impede the ongoing litigation that the Companies had brought against it.

The Application was dismissed. The Deputy Judge (Philip Marshall QC) considered the Northern Irish decision in *Cursitan v Keenan*[35] which he considered provided the proper approach both as to the interpretation of para.81(1) and as to the proper exercise of the Court's discretion. At [46] and [47] of his judgment he said:

> "[46] In *Cursitan's case* [2011] NICh 23 the court was concerned with the appointment of an administrator by a bank creditor. It was alleged that the bank had been motivated by an improper purpose, namely that of frustrating litigation against the bank and seeking to benefit from certain distribution and control provisions. The legislation under consideration was the Insolvency (Northern Ireland) Order 2005 and in particular article 82, which, as mentioned above, largely mirrors paragraph 81 of Schedule B1 to the 1986 Act. McCloskey J concluded that a concession, that the appointment of administrators could be vitiated if motivated by an improper purpose, was rightly made. The court also concluded that a reasonable and objective evaluation of the evidence confirmed that frustrating and obstructing litigation formed part of the bank's thinking. Nevertheless the administration provisions had been formulated 'against a background of commercial realities and permissible commercial tactics of aggression' and the bank's motivation and conduct fell to be evaluated accordingly and were unobjectionable. The court also concluded that there was no disharmony between the bank's motivation and conduct and the statutory purpose of administration.
>
> [47] At paragraph 48, McCloskey J stated:
>
> > 'This analysis and conclusion may also be reached by a somewhat different route. I have already concluded that the (proposed) administrator was sufficiently informed to form the requisite statutory opinion. Thus the purpose of the administration was capable of being fulfilled from the outset, in harmony with the statutory regime. It seems to me that this will normally be the main touchstone for the court. In the abstract, it is unclear

---

[35] See n.25.

whether a conclusion and finding of this kind in any case could be undermined by evidence that the appointor was motivated by a purpose incompatible with the statutory objective enshrined in paragraph 4(1). Such a conclusion would not, in my view, follow as a matter of course. Thus, again in the abstract, an aggressive and, indeed, malevolent motivation would not, per se, undermine the (proposed) administrator's statutory statement of opinion. While I find that there was some hard commercial motivation in the Bank's conduct in the present case, I am of the opinion that this falls short of either constituting an improper purpose of a sufficiently vitiating nature or leading to the conclusion that the administrator had insufficient grounds for making his statutory statement of opinion'."

The judge then proceeded to summarise the relevant principles as follows:

"[48] In my judgment, the approach adopted in *Cursitan's case* [2011] NICh 23 has much to commend it and provides a proper approach to the interpretation and exercise of the discretion granted to the court under paragraph 81 of Schedule B1:

(1) It is important to note that the statute does not provide that establishing an improper motive on the part of the appointor of an administrator will ordinarily lead to an order requiring the administration to cease. Rather the legislation requires improper motive on the part of appointor to feature simply for the jurisdiction to be engaged. Thereafter the court has a wide discretion (as reflected in the variety of the forms of relief possible).

(2) It also seems to me invidious to attempt to pinpoint precisely what form the motivation must take for the statutory jurisdiction to be invoked. It will be sufficient that there was a motive that is not in harmony with the statutory purpose of administration and was causative of the decision to appoint. Whether it was primary or secondary will be immaterial so long as it was causative of the decision. However, if there is no disharmony (even if the motive is not actually the achievement of a statutory purpose) it is difficult to see why the motive then must be treated as improper or as a material matter militating towards termination of the administration.

(3) Most importantly, whilst it is conceivable that establishing an improper motive on the part of the appointor might lead to the court terminating the administration, the court will, before doing so, have regard to the nature of administration as a process which potentially affects other parties. If the statutory purpose of administration would be likely to be achieved, notwithstanding the motives of the appointor, like McCloskey J in *Cursitan's case*, it seems to me that this would normally be the main touchstone for the court. The existence of an improper motive may become of relative insignificance in such circumstances, particularly where the appointor's improper objective was not actually achieved.

[49] In arriving at these conclusions I have noted the observations in the principal textbooks on the provision, including the commentary in Lightman & Moss, *The Law of Administrators and Receivers of Companies*, 5th ed. (2014), para.27–028 (note 193) where it is stated that:

'It may seem that the "improper motive" test is a charter for any disaffected party to impugn the administrator's appointment: but one would hope and expect that the courts would take a robust view and confine this remedy to those situations where there is clear impropriety on the part of the appointor. In particular, it is submitted that it should be confined to cases of abuse of the administration procedure rather than used as a means of trying to frustrate those cases where the purpose of administration is reasonably likely to be achieved.'

[50] For the reasons set out above, in my judgment, where paragraph 81 of Schedule B1 is invoked it is unlikely to lead to an order that the administration cease where the statutory purposes could properly be achieved irrespective of the appointor's motivations.

For this reason I do not envisage that it could in practice be used for the purpose of frustrating administration in the manner feared."

Thus, it will be noted that in the Deputy Judge's judgment, the principal question was whether the statutory purpose of the administration would be likely to be achieved, irrespective of the motives of the appointor. This would "normally be the main touchstone for the court".[36] There would have been no disharmony between the Building Society's motivation (even if it had been proved to be an improper one, which was not the case) and the statutory purpose of the administration.

The questions of the subjective intention and state of mind of the appointor were not addressed in the judgment—but it is clear from the judgment as a whole that those considerations are most unlikely to be material, still less determinative.

The crucial evidential role of the administrator. The key player in a para.81 **17-15** application is bound to be the appointed administrator. At the pre-appointment stage, he is required, whether appointed in or out of court, to state his belief that "the purpose of administration is reasonably likely to be achieved".[37] In the *FREP* case, one of the joint administrators had submitted a witness statement setting out the background to his appointment and explaining that in his view, the purpose of the administration (the sale of three charged properties so as to produce a return to the Building Society) was and remained reasonably likely to be achieved. This carried significant weight with the court.

Indeed, it is not easy to see how any application alleging an improper motive under para.81 could succeed in circumstances where the administrator has credibly, honestly and reasonably confirmed that the statutory purposes was and is still achievable, in the absence evidence of his connivance in some malign strategy or his negligent failure to apply his professional judgment.

"Improper motive" on the part of others. It is clear from the language of the **17-16** statute that any operative "improper motive" must be that of the applicant or appointor—the statute requires the improper motive to have existed "on the part of" the applicant or the appointor.[38]

In this regard, the ordinary rules relating to attribution (or indeed vicarious responsibility) will not necessarily automatically apply. Hence, in the *FREP* case, the Deputy Judge found that if Promontoria had had an improper motive and this had been known to the Building Society "who had nonetheless gone along with its instructions, it might have been argued that that motive should be attributed to [the Building Society]".[39] However, absent any such circumstances, it could not be said that the Building Society had an improper motive by taking into account the views of another party with whom it was contractually bound to consult.

Applications under Sch.B1 para.81: procedure. The procedure is contained in **17-17** rr.3.58 and 3.59 of the Insolvency (England and Wales) Rules 2016. Where a creditor applies to the court for an order ending the administration under para.81, he must serve copies of his application on the administrator, and also on the applicant for

---

[36] See also [51] and the discussion of the *Dianoor Jewels* case.
[37] Insolvency Rules 2016 r.3.3(2)(i) and Insolvency Act 1986 Sch.B1 paras 14(3)(b) and 29(3)(b).
[38] Insolvency Act 1986 Sch.B1 para.81(2)(a) or (b).
[39] See [54].

the appointment or on the appointor(s) (as the case may be). Where the appointment was made by a floating charge-holder, a copy must be served on him.[40]

Such service is to be made *not less than five business days before the date fixed for the hearing*. Each of the persons served with a copy of the application may appear at the hearing.[41]

On the hearing of the application, the court may (i) adjourn the hearing, conditionally or unconditionally, (ii) dismiss the application, (iii) make an interim order, or (iv) make any order which it thinks appropriate (whether in addition to or instead of the order applied for).[42] It should be noted that these procedural rules are subject to the Court's wide case management powers under r.12.11 of the 2016 Insolvency Rules. Hence, the Court could in an appropriate case direct that there be cross-examination. Indeed, in the *FREP* case, the Court made an order for the cross-examination of the Building Society's principal witness, the relevant issue of fact for cross-examination being the question of the Building Society's true motive.

Where the court makes an order "ending the administration", the court must send a copy of the order to the parties prescribed by r.3.59(a)–(c), including the administrator. The administrator in turn must then deliver a copy of the order to the registrar[43] of companies together with his final progress report.[44]

17-18   Challenge to administrator's conduct of the company: relief for unfair harm under para.74 of Sch.B1.   A creditor, or a member, of the company in administration may apply to the court, claiming that the administrator (a) is acting, or has acted, "so as unfairly to harm" the interests of the applicant (whether alone or in common with some or all other members or creditors), *alternatively*, (b) that he proposes to act in a way which would unfairly harm the interests of the applicant (whether alone or in common with some or all of the other members or creditors).[45]

In addition, or alternatively, a creditor or a member may apply to the court, claiming that the administrator is not performing his functions as quickly or as efficiently as is reasonably practicable.[46]

The predecessor to this provision under the pre Enterprise-Act old regime was s.27(1) of the Insolvency Act 1986. This empowered creditors and members of the company to petition the court for an order that the administrator had managed, or proposed to manage the company's affairs business and property in a manner which was or would be *unfairly prejudicial* to the interests of creditors or members generally or to some part of its creditors or members.

17-19   The Court's powers on applications under para.74.   The Court's powers under paras 74(3) and 74(4) are wide and are listed non-exhaustively. The court may grant the relief sought; it may dismiss the application; it may adjourn the hearing conditionally or unconditionally; it may make an interim order; it may make such

---

40   Insolvency Rules 2016 r.3.58(1).
41   Insolvency Rules 2016 r.3.58(2).
42   Insolvency Act 1986 Sch.B1 para.81(3).
43   As for the standard content of notices to be delivered to the registrar of companies, see rr.1.19–1.26 of the Insolvency (England Wales) Rules 2016.
44   For progress reports in administration, winding up and, see Insolvency (England Wales) Rules 2016 r.18.3. For the additional contents of a final progress report see r.3.53 and para.17-47, below.
45   Insolvency Act 1986 Sch.B1 para.74(1).
46   Insolvency Act 1986 Sch.B1 para.74(2).

other order "as it thinks appropriate".[47] Importantly, by para.74(4)(d), the Court may "provide for the appointment of the administrator to cease to have effect".

Other consequential orders may (a) regulate the administrator's exercise of his functions; (b) require him, to do, or not to do, a specified thing; (c) require a creditors' meeting to be held for a specified purpose.[48]

By para.74(5), relief may be granted whether or not the action complained of is within the administrator's powers and whether or not that action was taken in reliance upon an order previously made under paras 71 or 72 of Sch.B1.

It should be noted that the Court may grant relief under this provision even after the administration has come to an end.[49]

Limitations on the jurisdiction under para.74. An order may not be made **17-20** under para.74, if it would prevent (a) the implementation of a voluntary arrangement under the Insolvency Act 1986 Pt I; (b) a compromise or arrangement sanctioned by the court under Pt 26 of the Companies Act 2006; (c) a cross-border merger within the meaning of reg.2 of the Companies (Cross-Border Mergers) Regulations 2007;[50] or (c) proposals, or revised proposals, approved by a creditors' meeting, held more than 28 days before the application for an order under para.74 is made.[51]

Cases on para.74 Paragraph 74 of Sch.B1 uses the notion of *unfair harm*, rather **17-21** than unfair prejudice to the interests of creditors and members, which was the touchstone under the old regime.[52] It is important to note that for the jurisdiction to be engaged, it is not necessary to prove that the administrator's act is perverse or unreasonable. To adopt such a test in place of the statutory test of unfairness would plainly be wrong.[53] The harm in question must be a tangible detriment[54] and there must be unfairness.[55]

Where an administrator, having taken legal advice, wrongly rejected a creditor's proof, para.74 was held not to apply. The aggrieved creditor could appeal to the court on the rejection of proof and moreover, the administrator's view was that there would be sufficient funds in a subsequent liquidation to meet the creditor's claim if it was later held to be valid. Therefore, it was held that the creditor was not unfairly harmed by the rejection.[56]

---

[47] Insolvency Act 1986 Sch.B1 para.74(3).
[48] Insolvency Act 1986 Sch.B1 para.74(4).
[49] *Re Coniston Hotel (Kent) LLP* [2013] EWHC 93 (Ch).
[50] See SI 2007/2974.
[51] See para.74(6).
[52] Whether or not "unfair harm" is to be interpreted any differently to "unfair prejudice" remains to be seen. For a discussion on the question of "unfairness" and its meaning under the old regime (s.27 of the Insolvency Act 1986, repealed), see *Re Charnley Davies Ltd* [1990] B.C.C. 605 per Millett J at 624–625.
[53] *Hockin v Marsden* [2014] EWHC 763 (Ch).
[54] For an example under the Northern Irish equivalent of para.74, see *Curistan v Keenan* (sub nom. Re Sheridan Millenium Ltd) [2013] NiCH 13.
[55] See for example, *Re Nortel GMBH* [2013] UKSC 52 at [121]–[122]; *Holgate v Reid* [2013] EWHC 4630 (Ch). By contrast, the power to remove an administrator under para.88 does not require proof of unfair conduct on his part. For a discussion on the question of "unfairness" and its meaning under the old regime, see *Re Charnley Davies Ltd* [1990] B.C.C. 605 per Millett J at 624–625.
[56] For a further unsuccessful challenge, *SISU Capital Fund Ltd v Tucker* [2005] EWHC 2170 (Ch); [2006] B.C.C. 463.

In *Re Lehman Brothers International Europe (In Administration)*[57] Blackburne J considered the scope of para.74 in some detail. The applicants in this extremely complex case had requested information from the administrators on the status of certain securities transferred to the company as collateral for future advances. The court had previously given directions to the administrators in relation to the establishment of a "Trust Property Team" to identify and deal with all such similar securities which might be subject to proprietary claims, and proposals had been put to, and approved by creditors, which related in part to the identification and return of the "trust property".

The administrators refused to provide the further information requested by the applicants, and this refusal was held by Blackburne J not to constitute unfair harm for the purposes of para.74: whilst harm might be caused to the applicants, it could not be said to be *unfair*. It was necessary to have regard to the context of administration, and in particular to the administrator's obligation to manage the affairs of the company with a view to achieving the purpose of the administration.[58] Where the administrators' actions were in accordance with the provisions of the Act, with approved proposals, and with directions given by the court, there was no room to find that any harm caused to creditors was unfair.[59] In the present case, the administrators should not be required to divert resources in order to provide the information requested.[60]

Actions taken by administrators in the interests of creditors as a whole will not per se be open to challenge simply because they affect an individual creditor differently,[61] but the decision of the Court of Sessions in *Re Chester West and Chester Borough Council (Petitioners)*[62] is an example of an instance in which unfair harm caused to one creditor, notwithstanding the benefit to the remaining creditors as a whole, was sufficient to engage the jurisdiction under para.74.

17-22 **Paragraph 74(4)(d) of Sch.B1 and the inclusion of the power to end the administration contrasted with the power to remove the administrator under para.88.** As noted above, para.74(4)(d) also confers jurisdiction upon the Court to end the administration altogether by making an order providing for the appointment of the administrator ceasing to have effect.

This singular power—whereby the administration is brought to an end—is, as a matter of first impression, a curious one to be included in provisions ostensibly intended to provide a remedy for the deficiencies of the administrator personally, rather than against the administration itself. Plainly, however, there will be situations in which the exercise of this ostensibly draconian power will be the appropri-

---

[57] *Re Lehman Brothers International Europe (In Administration)* [2008] EWHC 2869 (Ch); [2009] 1 B.C.L.C. 161.
[58] *Re Lehman Brothers International Europe (In Administration)* [2008] EWHC 2869 (Ch); [2009] 1 B.C.L.C. 161, [38] of the judgment.
[59] *Re Lehman Brothers International Europe (In Administration)* [2008] EWHC 2869 (Ch); [2009] 1 B.C.L.C. 161, [39].
[60] See also *Re Lehman Brothers International Europe (In Administration)* [2008] EWHC 2869 (Ch); [2009] 1 B.C.L.C. 161. In that case, there was a dispute about whether claims had been released by a "claims resolution agreement". As a matter of the proper construction of the agreement, the Court found that they had not been but if they had been relief would have been granted, either on the grounds of unfairness under para.74 or by reference to the rule in *Ex parte James* (1873–1874) L.R 9 Ch.App 609.
[61] *Re Zegna III Holdings Inc* [2009] EWHC 2994 (Ch).
[62] [2011] B.C.C. 174.

ate remedy; for example, where the administrator has been found guilty of misconduct, but cannot readily be replaced by any available substitute, or where he has left the administration in such a state of disarray, or impecuniosity, that no other licensed insolvency practitioner could be expected to agree to take over the office, or where the administration itself is not viable (because its purpose cannot be achieved).

Where, conversely, on a para.74 application, the Court has found the administrator's conduct to amount to (actual or prospective) "unfair harm" but the administration itself nonetheless remains viable, rather than ending the administration altogether, the obvious remedy is for the Court to order the removal of the administrator from office and for him to be replaced under para.88 of Sch.B1.

The distinction between the process of ending an administration and that of removing the office holder, and their respective effects is clearly stated in Sch.B1; in para.2(d): "a company does not cease to be in administration, merely because an administrator vacates office (by reason of resignation, death or otherwise) or is removed from office".[63]

The power to make an order for the removal of an administrator under para.88 is a wide one and is significantly more flexible than the jurisdiction under para.74, where the threshold of establishing "unfair harm" is a high one.[64] The power of removal under para.88 is not dependent upon a finding of misconduct, or personal fault, or criticism, albeit that "good or sufficient cause" must be shown.[65] The relevant procedure governing applications under para.88 is contained in r.3.65 of the Insolvency (England and Wales) Rules 2016. The grounds on which the order is requested must be stated in the application itself.

In *Clydesdale Financial Services v Smailes*,[66] an application to remove an administrator under para.88 was coupled with an application under para.74. A creditor objected to the terms of a "pre-pack" sale of the company's business completed by the administrator immediately after his appointment. In particular, the valuation of the business was questioned by the applicant. David Richards J considered that the pre-administration dealings prior to the sale were sufficiently "opaque" so as to require further investigation but that investigation could not be conducted by the incumbent administrator, who had been closely involved in the transaction itself (including at the pre-appointment stage). It was held that the administrator should therefore be removed from office and that a replacement administrator should be appointed. Hence, the para.88 application[67] succeeded, from which it followed that the Court did not consider it necessary to proceed to decide the para.74 limb of the application.[68]

---

[63] This distinction was emphasised by David Richards J in *Clydesdale Financial Services v Smailes*, [2009] B.C.C. 810 at [15].

[64] *Re St Georges Property Services (London) Ltd* [2011] EWCA Civ 858 per Mummery LJ at [29]–[32].

[65] *Re St George's Property Services (London) Ltd* [2011] EWCA Civ 858 at [33].

[66] [2009] B.C.C. 810.

[67] The costs of an application under para.88 where the hearing was superseded by a winding up order were held payable as an administration expense in *Coyne v DRC Distribution Ltd* [2008] EWCA Civ 488; [2008] B.C.C. 612.

[68] Contrast *SISU Capital Fund Ltd v Tucker* [2005] EWHC 2170 (Ch); [2006] B.C.C. 463 where the application to remove the office holders failed.

17-23   **The extent of the Court's powers under para.74 to control the administrator's actions.**   The fact that an administrator's actions are lawful and within his powers will not per se preclude the Court from intervening to regulate his conduct. Lawful and intra vires conduct may nonetheless be conduct which amounts to unfair harm.

This is clear enough from the wording of the statute. The jurisdiction under para.74 to control and regulate the actions of the administrator is exercisable by the court whether or not the action complained of is, or would be, within the administrator's powers under Sch.B1, or was taken, or was to be taken, in reliance on an order (a) made under para.71, in respect of property charged otherwise than by a floating charge, or (b) made under para.72, in respect of goods in the company's possession under a hire-purchase agreement,[69] (for those powers, see Ch.15, paras 15-85 ff, above).

By paras 71 and 72 of Sch.B1, the court may permit the administrator to dispose of certain assets (in essence, non-floating charge assets and hire purchase property), as if they were not subject to security or to the hire-purchase agreement (as the case may be).

Applications for such orders must be made on notice to those who have the relevant proprietary rights.[70] Hence, those parties' rights of objection would prima facie fall to be ventilated at an early stage within the framework of their opposition, as respondents, to the administrator's application under paras 71 or 72 (as the case may be).[71] However, plainly such complaints can also separately be litigated (and possibly even re-litigated) within the framework of an "unfair harm" application under para.74.

17-24   **Where the administrator is charged with "misfeasance" under para.75 of Sch.B1.**   Under the old pre Enterprise Act régime, creditors or members of the company who were aggrieved by the conduct, or misconduct, of an administrator "who had misapplied or retained, or become accountable for, any money or other property of the company or been guilty of any misfeasance or breach of any fiduciary or other duty in relation to the company" had their remedy against the administrator Pt IV s.212 of the Insolvency Act 1986 (entitled "Summary Remedy against Delinquent Directors, Liquidators, etc."). The inclusion of administrators within s.212 was however repealed by the Enterprise Act 2002,[72] in its reconstruction of the administration jurisdiction. By the replacement regime, similar remedies are provided expressly in the case of administrators by para.75 of Sch.B1, which is simply entitled "Misfeasance".

The categories of conduct or misconduct covered by Sch.B1 para.75 are, overall, the same as those contained in the Insolvency Act 1986 s.212; but they are differently arranged. In neither provision is "misfeasance" defined. However, in s.212, "misfeasance" was bracketed with "breach of any fiduciary or other duty in relation to the company", whereas in para.75, "misfeasance" appears in a separate sub-

---

[69]   Insolvency Act 1985 Sch.B1 para.74(5).

[70]   Insolvency (England and Wales) Rules 2016 r.3.49. But see *Re Capitol Films Ltd* [2010] EWHC 3223 (Ch) where the administrator was found to have acted unreasonably and was ordered to pay the fixed charge holder's costs on the indemnity basis.

[71]   See, for example, *Stanley J Holmes & Sons Ltd v Davenham Trust Plc* [2006] EWCA Civ 1568.

[72]   Enterprise Act 2002 s.278 and Sch.26.

paragraph, as if intended to function as a sweeping-up category. The expression "Misfeasance" is, however, adopted as the stand-alone title to para.75.

The case-law under the Insolvency Act 1986 s.212, will generally apply, but, mutatis mutandis, appropriately differentiating between the tasks and responsibilities of company officer, administrative receivers and liquidators, and those of an administrator.

Misfeasance proceedings under para.75: procedure.   The court may, on the application of specified persons, or classes of person, examine the conduct of a person (i) who is, *or purports to be*, or (ii) who has been, or *has purported to have been*, the administrator of a company.[73] Those persons who may apply are the Official Receiver, the liquidator of the company, the administrator (presumably the current administrator who is proceeding against a "purported" or a former office-holder or a joint appointee), and a creditor[74] or contributory of the company.[75]   **17-25**

The right of a contributory to apply for relief under this para.is not dependent on his obtaining the permission of the court to do so, nor upon his having to show that he would personally benefit from the success of his application.[76]

The cause of action derives from an allegation that the administrator, or the former *or purported* administrator,[77] has misapplied or retained, or has become accountable for, money or other property of the company, or has breached a fiduciary or other duty in relation to the company, or has been guilty of misfeasance.[78] An application in respect of an administrator, who has been discharged from liability under Sch.B1 para.98, may only be made with the permission of the court.[79] Such a discharge does not however prevent the court from exercising its powers over a former administrator under para.75.[80] This was also the case with misfeasance claims under the Insolvency Act 1986 s.212, where liability would subsist notwithstanding that the administrator had been released under s.20.

On a successful application under para.75, the court may order the respondent to repay, restore or account for the money or property, to pay interest, and to contribute a sum to the company's property by way of compensation for breach of duty or misfeasance.[81]

No procedural rules have been made, specifically regulating proceedings under para.75. Such proceedings will be regulated by the provisions under Ch.3 of the Insolvency (England and Wales) Rules 2016.

Remedies under para.75: an order for the payment of compensation or an order for the administrator's removal?   Paragraph 75(4) prescribes a list of discretionary remedies, whereby the Court may order the respondent "(a) to repay,   **17-26**

---

73   Insolvency Act 1986 Sch.B1 para.75(1).
74   But note, in the absence of a special relationship of appropriate proximity, an administrator does not owe a duty to care to a particular creditor: *Charalambous v B & C Associates* [2009] EWHC 2601 (Ch).
75   Insolvency Act 1986 Sch.B1 para.75(2).
76   Contrast the provisions of the Insolvency Act 1986 s.212(5).
77   Insolvency Act 1986 Sch.B1 para.75(5).
78   Insolvency Act 1986 Sch.B1 para.75(3).
79   Insolvency Act 1986 Sch.B1 para.75(6). For a discussion of the interlay between para.75 and para.98 of Sch.B1 see *Re Angel Group Ltd* [2015] EWHC 3624 (Ch).
80   Insolvency Act 1986 Sch.B1 para.98(4)(b).
81   Insolvency Act 1986 Sch.B1 para.75(4).

restore or account for money or property; (b) to pay interest; (c) to contribute a sum to the company's property by way of compensation for breach of duty or misfeasance".

Thus, prima facie, the jurisdiction is a compensatory one, which does not engage the possibility of an order either for the removal of the administrator or for terminating the administration. It will be noted that unlike para.74(3)(e), there is no "catch-all" provision in s.75 whereby the Court is given the jurisdiction to make whatever other order is may consider to be appropriate.

It will of course not inevitably follow that a finding of misfeasance will justify the removal of an administrator from office, still less the making of an order ending the administration per se. Each case will be fact sensitive. If, however, the conduct of the administrator has been such as to render the administration unviable, it is suggested that the court could be persuaded to order that the administration should cease to have effect, pursuant to its inherent jurisdiction or (in the case of an in-court appointment, pursuant to its powers of review). The safer course, however, would be to couple an application under para.75 with a claim for relief under para.74 (ending the administration) and/or para.88 (removing the administrator), subject to the caveat that the exercise by the Court of its jurisdiction to end the administration under para.74(4)(d) is dependent on the Court being satisfied that there has been "unfair harm" within the meaning of that provision. A finding of misfeasance will not of itself necessarily amount to unfair harm.[82]

SECTION 3: NON-CONTENTIOUS PROCEDURES

17-27   **Paragraph 76(1) of Sch.B1: "Automatic end of administration".**   Where the permitted statutory duration of the appointment of an administrator, either the initial period of one year,[83] or that period as extended, either by order of the court (under para.77 of Sch.B1) or by the consent of qualified creditors (in accordance with para.78),[84] expires, his appointment ceases to have effect and the administration terminates in all respects[85] and cannot be renewed.[86] This finite one-year period is a product of the Enterprise Act 2002 amendments (doubtless in the light of concerns, both judicial and otherwise, as to unduly protracted administrations).

Where the appointment of the administrator automatically ceases to have effect and he is not required by any other rule to give notice of that fact, he must, as soon as reasonably practicable, and in any event *within five business days of the date when the appointment ceased to have effect*, file "a notice of automatic end of administration", with the court accompanied by a final progress report, containing those matters which are prescribed by the relevant rule.[87] Copies of the notice and of the final progress report must be sent to the registrar of companies,[88] and also to

---

[82]   See *McCausland v Drenagh Farms Ltd* [2014] NICh 31. It does not follow that an administrator who has acted negligently has also acted unfairly. See also *Re Conisten Hotel (Kent) LLP* [2013] EWHC 93 (Ch).

[83]   Insolvency Act 1986 Sch.B1 para.76(1).

[84]   Insolvency Act 1986 Sch.B1 para.76(2).

[85]   Subject to the administrator's duty to file his final progress report.

[86]   Neither by order of the court: Insolvency Act 1986 Sch.B1 para.77(1)(b); nor by consent of creditors: para.76(1).

[87]   Insolvency (England and Wales) Rules 2016 r.3.55. Form AM20 must be used.

[88]   Insolvency (England and Wales) Rules 2016 r.3.55(2).

the directors and all other persons to whom notice of the administrator's appointment was delivered.[89]

Failure to comply with these reporting obligations is an offence.[90]

For the period of administration, and its extension, see para.14-8, above.

Paragraph 79(1) of Sch.B1: court providing for the appointment of the administrator to cease to have effect from a specified time. This provision confers jurisdiction upon the Court to end the administration, on the application of the administrator. Sub-paragraphs (2) and (3) impose differing mandatory obligations upon the administrator to make such an application, depending upon whether the appointment was made out of court or in court and depending upon whether the purpose of the administration is sufficiently achieved or is not considered to be achievable. However, it is clear that the exercise of the Court's jurisdiction to make an order under para.79(1) (or indeed ancillary or alternative orders under para.79(4)) is not confined to the circumstances listed in para.79(2) and (3). Hence, in *Re J Smith's Haulage Ltd*[91] the Court used its power under this provision to enable the administration to be replaced by a compulsory winding up (see further para.17-36, below). 17-28

Paragraph 79(2) of Sch.B1. Administrator appointed in court or out of court applying to terminate administration, where its purpose cannot be achieved, or on other prescribed grounds. By para.79(2) of Sch.B1, where, in the case of an appointment made either in-court or out of court, (a) the administrator "thinks"[92] that the purpose of administration cannot be achieved in relation to the company, or (b) he thinks that the company should never have entered administration at all, or (c) he has been required so to do by a duly summoned creditors' meeting, he must apply to the court for an order that his appointment shall cease to have effect.[93] 17-29

An order, under limb (b) would be appropriate, for example, should it transpire that the company was (and is) able to pay its debts, or because the facts presented to the court on an in-court application, were wrong and did not justify an appointment.[94]

Paragraph 79(3) of Sch.B1: Administrator appointed in-court applying to terminate administration, where its purpose is sufficiently achieved. By para.79(3) of Sch.B1, where the administrator was appointed on an in-court application, and he "thinks"[95] that the purpose of administration "has been sufficiently achieved" in relation to the company, he must apply to the court for an order that his appointment shall cease to have effect from a specified time. 17-30

Orders under para.79(1) and (4). In addition to, or as an alternative to making an order under para.79(1) providing for the appointment of the administrator to cease to have effect from a specified time, the Court has further powers. These are 17-31

---

89 Insolvency (England and Wales) Rules 2016 r.3.55(6).
90 Insolvency (England and Wales) Rules 2016 r.3.55(7).
91 [2007] B.C.C. 135.
92 For the meaning of "thinks", see *Unidare Plc v Cohen* [2006] Ch. 489, [2005] EWHC 1410 (Ch).
93 Insolvency Act 1986 Sch.B1 para.79(2).
94 As was the case in *Re Sharps of Truro Ltd* [1990] B.C.C. 94, a decision under the old regime, in which the administrator did himself apply on that ground.
95 For the meaning of "thinks", see *Unidare Plc v Cohen* [2006] Ch 489; [2005] EWHC 1410 (Ch).

listed (non-exhaustively) in para.79(4). On any such application (whether under para.79(2) or (3)), the court may do any of the following: adjourn the hearing conditionally or unconditionally, dismiss the application, make an interim order, or make any other order it thinks appropriate, whether in addition to or consequential to the order applied for.[96]

As stated, the exercise of the jurisdiction under para.79(1) and (4) is not confined to the circumstances listed in para.79(2) and (3).[97] In *Re Graico Property Co Ltd (In Administration)*,[98] the Court used its wide powers under para.79(4) to make a winding up order on ending the administration, without requiring the presentation of winding up petition. In *Re TM Kingdom Ltd*,[99] the administrator's application was made (and granted) in order to allow the company to enter into a creditors' voluntary liquidation and so take advantage of the then favourable treatment afforded to companies in liquidation as regards business rates on unoccupied property.[100]

17-32 **Paragraph 79 of Sch.B1: procedure for applications.** Where the administrator applies to the court under para.79, he must attach to his application (i) a progress report for the period since his last report, or since the company entered administration, and (ii) a statement of what he thinks should be the next steps for the company to take (if applicable). If he makes the application at the request of a creditors' meeting, he must attach to his application a statement, indicating (with reasons) whether or not he agrees with their request.[101]

Where he is not making the application at the request of a creditors' meeting, he must give advance notice in writing to the applicant upon whose application the administration order was made in court, or to the appointor in the case of an out of court appointment, and to the creditors *at least seven days before the date when he intends to apply*.[102] He must also attach to his application a statement that he has notified the creditors, with copies of their responses (if any).[103]

If he is making the application to the court in conjunction with the presentation of a petition to wind-up the company, he must notify the creditors if he intends to seek appointment as liquidator.[104]

Where, on such a para.79 application, the court makes an order ending the administration, the administrator must notify the registrar of companies, the directors and "all other persons to whom notice of the administrator's appointment was delivered", attaching a copy of the order, and of his final progress report.[105] For the administrator's final progress report, see para.17-47 above.

17-33 **Paragraph 80 of Sch.B1: termination of effect of out-of-court appointment, when objective achieved.** In the case of an out of court appointment, by para.80(2), where the administrator thinks that the purpose of administration has

---

[96] Insolvency Act 1986 Sch.B1 para.79(4).
[97] *Re TM Kingdom Ltd* [2007] B.C.C. 480.
[98] [2016] EWHC 2827 (Ch).
[99] [2007] EWHC 3272 (Ch); [2007] B.C.C. 480.
[100] See also *Re J Smiths Haulage Ltd* [2007] B.C.C. 135.
[101] Insolvency (England and Wales) Rules 2016 r.3.57.
[102] Insolvency (England and Wales) Rules 2016 r.3.57(2)(a).
[103] Insolvency (England and Wales) Rules 2016 r.3.57(2)(b).
[104] Insolvency (England and Wales) Rules 2016 r.3.57(3).
[105] Insolvency (England and Wales) Rules 2016 r.3.59. Form AM25 must be used.

been sufficiently achieved in relation to the company,[106] he may file with the court a notice in the prescribed form (called "the notice to end administration"[107]), containing prescribed information.[108] This notice must be accompanied by a second copy of the notice itself[109] and with the final progress report[110] (see para.17-47, below).

The court then endorses each of the two copies with the date and time of filing, seals one copy and delivers that sealed copy to the administrator.[111]

By para.80(3), once the procedural requirements under para.80(2) have been satisfied, the administrator's appointment ceases to have effect.

By para.80(4), the administrator must within the prescribed period of five business days send a copy of the notice and of his final progress report to every creditor of the company of whose address he is aware, other than an opted out creditor.[112]

Within the same timeframe, the administrator must send a copy of the notice and of the final progress report to all other persons (that is to say other than creditors and the registrar of companies) to whom notice of the administrator's appointment was delivered.[113]

An administrator who fails, without reasonable excuse, to give notice to the creditors in accordance with para.80(4), commits an offence.[114] However, by r.3.56(10) of the Insolvency (England and Wales) Rules 2016, the administrator will be taken to have complied with his duty under para.80(4) if *within five business days after filing the notice with the court* he gazettes a notice[115]: (i) stating that the administration has ended (and the date on which it ended); (ii) undertaking to provide a copy of the notice of the end of administration to any creditor of the company who applies to him in writing; and (iii) specifying the address to which to write.[116]

Paragraph 83 of Sch.B1: moving from to creditors' voluntary liquidation.   This provision contains a straightforward and cost-effective procedure whereby a company can move seamlessly from liquidation into administration.[117] It is available whether the administrator was appointed in court or out of court.

    17-34

In his initial statement of his proposals to the creditors under para.49 of Sch.B1, the administrator may include a proposal that the company shall go into creditors'

---

[106] *Nimmo and Fraser, Joint Administrators of Station Properties Ltd* [2013] CSOH 120 for an example of this procedure being used when the company in question had been restored to solvency.

[107] Insolvency Act 1986 Sch.B1 para.80(2).

[108] Insolvency (England and Wales) Rules 2016 r.3.56(1)–(3).

[109] Insolvency (England and Wales) Rules 2016 r.3.56(5).

[110] Insolvency (England and Wales) Rules 2016 r.3.56(4).

[111] Insolvency (England and Wales) Rules 2016 r.3.56(6).

[112] Insolvency (England and Wales) Rules 2016 r.3.56(7).

[113] Insolvency (England and Wales) Rules 2016 r.3.56(9).

[114] Insolvency Act 1986 Sch.B1 para.80(6).

[115] See rr.1.10 and 1.11 of the Insolvency (England Wales) Rules 2016 with regard to the standard contents of gazette notices and the use of such notices as evidence.

[116] Insolvency (England and Wales) Rules 2016 r.3.56(10). See also rr.1.10 and 1.11 of the Insolvency (England Wales) Rules 2016 with regard to the standard contents of gazette notices and the use of such notices as evidence.

[117] By stark contrast to the position under the pre-Enterprise Act 2002 regime in which there was no procedural equivalent, resulting in a cumbersome process, see for example: *Re Powerstore Trading Ltd* [1998] B.C.C. 305; *Re Mark One (Oxford Street) plc* [1998] B.C.C. 984.

voluntary liquidation, as a specific objective.[118] He may alternatively decide to make the move to that status at the end of his administration.[119]

Where the administrator "thinks"[120] that the total amount which each secured creditor is likely to receive has been paid to him or set aside for him, and that a distribution will be made to unsecured creditors (if there are any),[121] he "may" send (i.e. it is in his discretion[122]) a notice to the registrar of companies, stating that Sch.B1 para.83, applies to the company.[123] The registrar of companies must then register that notice.[124]

The administrator must attach to that notice a final progress report, which must include details of the assets to be dealt with in the liquidation.[125] He must then file with the court a copy of that notice,[126] and send a copy of it to each creditor of whose claim and address he is aware.[127] He must also send a copy of the notice and a copy of the final progress report, to all those persons (if there are any) other than creditors who received notice of his appointment.[128]

It is the registration of the notice by the registrar that causes the appointment of the administrator to cease to have effect. This is the operative date[129] upon which the administration ends and is supplanted by a creditors' voluntary liquidation. When that notice has been registered, and the appointment of the administrator has ceased to have effect, "the company shall be wound up, as if a resolution for voluntary winding-up, under s.84 of the Act, had been passed on the day[130] on which the notice was registered".[131]

The liquidator in that voluntary winding-up will be the person nominated by the creditors in the prescribed manner,[132] and within the prescribed period, or, if no such person has been nominated, it will be the former administrator.[133]

Note: in a notice dated 21 June 2013, Companies House directed that the filing of a notice of conversion under para.83 must also be supplemented by notice of appointment of a liquidator, and subsequently gazetted[134] (England and Wales only).

---

[118] Insolvency (England and Wales) Rules 2016 r.3.35(j)(ii).
[119] Under Insolvency Act 1986 Sch.B1 para.83.
[120] As to which see n.95, above.
[121] Insolvency Act 1986 Sch.B1 para.83(1)(a), (b).
[122] *Re Ballast Plc* [2004] EWHC 2356 (Ch).
[123] Insolvency Act 1986 Sch.B1 para.83(3). Form AM222.
[124] Insolvency Act 1986 Sch.B1 para.83(4).
[125] Insolvency (England and Wales) Rules 2016 rr.3.53 and 18.3.
[126] Insolvency Act 1986 Sch.B1 para.83(5)(a).
[127] Insolvency Act 1986 Sch.B1 para.83(5)(b); the sending to them of the final progress report must follow from their having received notice of the administrator's appointment.
[128] Insolvency (England and Wales) Rules 2016 r.3.55.
[129] Insolvency Act 1986 Sch.B1 para.83(6). See *E-Squared Ltd* [2006] EWHC 532 (Ch); and *Re Globespan Airways Ltd* [2012] EWCA Civ 1159. Even if the administration would otherwise automatically have expired due to effluxion of time by the time the notice is received, the effect of the sending of the notice is such as to automatically extend the administration, pending the registration of the notice. See also *Re Property Professionals Ltd* [2013] EWHC 1903 (Ch).
[130] Note the use of "on the day", rather than "at the time". From this it follows that the liquidation commences as of the preceding midnight.
[131] Insolvency Act 1986 Sch.B1 para.83(6)(b).
[132] Insolvency Act 1986 Sch.B1 para.83(7)(a).
[133] Insolvency Act 1986 Sch.B1 para.83(7)(b). See *Hobbs v Gibson* [2010] EWHC 3676 (Ch). But see also *Re Angel Group Ltd* [2015] EWHC 3624 (Ch) in which the Court found an alternative procedural route for the appointment of a new liquidator, despite the fact that there was no such power under para.83.
[134] See rr.1.10 and 1.11 of the Insolvency (England Wales) Rules 2016 with regard to the standard

Paragraph 84 of Sch.B1: administration moving to dissolution. This provi- **17-35**
sion has no counterpart in the pre-Enterprise Act 2002 regime. It applies to
administrators appointed both in court and out of court.

By para.84(1), if the administrator thinks that the company has no property which
might permit a distribution to creditors (i.e. any distribution to any creditors), he
"shall" send a notice to that effect to the registrar of companies,[135] which the
registrar shall register.[136] On the registration of such a notice, the appointment of
the administrator ceases to have effect.[137] The administrator shall, as soon as reasonably practicable, file a copy of the notice with the court, and send a copy to every
creditor of whose claim and address he is aware.[138] By para.84(6), at the end of the
three months from the date of registration of the notice, the company is deemed to
be dissolved.[139]

As a matter of first impression, it might be thought that this provision will only
apply if there were never any assets in hand in the first place. This is not the case,
however. The para.84 procedure is commonly used as a convenient route for exiting an administration after the administrator has distributed all assets that he is able
to and has nothing left in hand for that purpose.[140] In other words, para.84(1) should
be construed as extending to a scenario in which there is no remaining property
which might permit a further distribution to its creditors.[141]

The administrator, having committed himself by giving the notice to the registrar
of companies, cannot change his mind and then withdraw that notice. However, he
can apply to the court "to dis-apply the sub-paragraph in respect of the company".[142]
In other words, notwithstanding the mandatory language of para.84(1), the
administrator can apply to court for an order effectively exempting him from what
would otherwise be the mandatory requirement to file for dissolution. This might
be the appropriate course if, for example, there was a possibility of future recoveries via a liquidation.

By para.84(7), the administrator or another interested party, may apply to the
court to extend or suspend the prescribed period of three months, or to dis-apply
para.84(6) altogether.[143]

Notice of any such order relating to the extension or suspension of the period

---

contents of gazette notices and the use of such notices as evidence.

[135] Insolvency Act 1986 Sch.B1 para.84(1); Insolvency (England and Wales) Rule 2016 r.3.61. Form AM23.

[136] Insolvency Act 1986 Sch.B1 para.84(3).

[137] Insolvency Act 1986 Sch.B1 para.84(4).

[138] Insolvency Act 1986 Sch.B1 para.84(5).

[139] Insolvency Act 1986 Sch.B1 para.84(6). Should it be necessary (say if further assets come to light), the Court's power to declare the dissolution void under ss.1029 ff of the Companies Act 2006 can be invoked. But note, an order declaring the dissolution void would not entail the retrospective exten-sion of the administration period (*Re the Peoples Restaurant Group Ltd*, unreported, 30 November 2012).

[140] See *Re Hellas Telecommunications (Luxembourg) II SCA* [2011] EWHC 3176 (Ch), where the court determined that the company could not be dissolved under para.84 and directed instead that it should be wound up. This was because it was found that there were assets available for distribution and because a liquidator should be appointed to conduct investigations.

[141] *Re Preston & Duckworth Ltd* [2006] B.C.C. 133; and *Re GHE Realisations Ltd* [2005] EWHC 2400 (Ch).

[142] Insolvency Act 1986 Sch.B1 para.84(2).

[143] Insolvency Act 1986 Sch.B1 para.84(7).

prior to dissolution taking effect, or to the dis-applying of the paragraph, or to the dissolution taking effect, must be given to the registrar of companies.[144]

An administrator commits an offence[145] if he fails to give notice of dissolution to the court and to each creditor of whose address he is aware (other than an opted out creditor).

In the case of a company which went into administration on or after 15 September 2003, its last administrator may, after the expiry of one year from its dissolution, destroy all books, papers and records of the company. If the Secretary of State requests him to give particulars of any money in his hands or under his control, or dividends or other sums of money due to any person or member or former member of the company, he must supply these particulars within 14 days.[146]

17-36   **Compulsory winding up.**   By para.21 of Sch.2 to the Insolvency Act 1986, an administrator has the power to defend or present a winding up petition. A petition presented by an administrator will be presented in the name of the company and, in addition to seeking winding up order, the petition must seek an order that the administration of the company ceases to have effect.[147]

The petition may also include an application under s.140 of the Insolvency Act 1986 for an order that the outgoing administrator be appointed as liquidator.

Given the availability of an exit from administration by way of creditors' voluntary liquidation under para.83 (if the administrator thinks that there are assets available for distribution) or dissolution under para.84 (if there are thought to be no such assets), it is likely that the compulsory winding up route will be adopted in cases where the asset position is uncertain, or where an investigation and possibly recovery proceedings are thought to be appropriate or necessary.

17-37   **Special cases possibly resulting in the termination of the administration.**   There are two special cases where the appointment of the administrator may be ordered to cease to have effect, on grounds not related either to the actual progress of the administration itself or to the conduct of the administrator himself.

(1) Where the administrator's proposals have not been approved   Paragraph 55 of Sch.B1 applies where the administrator reports to the Court[148] either that the initial creditors' meeting has failed to approve the proposals which he presented to it, or that a creditors' meeting has (subsequently) failed to approve a revision to those proposals. By para.55(2), the court may in such a case make an order providing that the appointment of the administrator shall cease to have effect from a specified time.[149] Whilst the administrator is not expressly mandated by the express language of the statute to apply to court for directions, it has been held that it is implicit in the language of para.55(2) that he must do so, in the event that his proposals (or a revision to them) have not been approved.[150]

---

[144] Insolvency Act 1986 Sch.B1 para.84(8).
[145] Insolvency Act 1986 Sch.B1 para.84(9).
[146] Insolvency (Amendment) Regulations 2005 (SI 2005/512) art.6, inserting new art.3A, and art.8, inserting new art.36A, in the Insolvency Regulations 1994 (SI 1994/2507).
[147] Rule 7.27(2)(e) of the Insolvency (England and Wales) Rules 2016. See also r.7.32.
[148] Insolvency Act 1986 Sch.B1 para.53(2).
[149] Insolvency Act 1986 Sch.B1 para.55(2)(a).
[150] *Re BTR (UK) Ltd* [2012] EWHC 2398 (Ch); and *Re Pudsey Steel Services Ltd* [2015] B.P.I.R. 1459.

The powers conferred upon the Court under para.55(2) are wide. They include—in addition to the power to direct that the administration shall cease to have effect at a specified time—the power to make a winding up order on a petition that has been suspended under para.40(1)(b) and the power to make any other order that the court thinks appropriate.[151]

In *Parmeko Holdings Ltd*,[152] the Court held that there was no need for directions to be given to the administrators whose proposals had not been approved and that they could continue in office and manage the affairs of the company at their discretion. In *Re Stanleybet UK Investments Ltd*,[153] the administrators sought an order that the administration should be terminated in favour of a creditors' voluntary liquidation, following the rejection of their proposals. The Court made that order, pointing out that considerable weight should be given to the professional views of the appointed office holders. In *Re BTR (UK) Ltd*, the Court made a winding up order of its own motion.

(2)   Where a winding-up order is made on "public interest petition"   Although in general, once an administration appointment has taken effect, no winding-up petition may be presented, nor any winding-up order made,[154] there are three exceptions to that rule. A winding-up petition may be presented against a company which is in administration (i) by the Secretary of State on grounds of "public interest"[155]; (ii) by the Secretary of State under s.124B of the Insolvency Act 1986 where it is sought to wind up an SE ("Societas Europaea") whose registered office is in Great Britain[156]; and (iii) by the Financial Conduct Authority, on grounds of conduct constituting a contravention of a general prohibition, or of inability to pay debts, or on just and equitable grounds.[157]

A winding up order made on a public interest petition will not necessarily bring the administration to an end (as would be the case with an administrator's winding up petition, see para.17-36, above).

In the event of a winding-up order being made, or a provisional liquidator being appointed, on such a petition, the court may order either (a) that the appointment of the administrator shall cease to have effect, or (b) that it shall continue to have effect. In the latter case, the court may also specify which powers are to be exercisable by the administrator (and presumably also necessarily specifying those powers which are to be exercised by the liquidator or provisional liquidator), and may order that the provisions of Sch.B1, will continue to have effect in relation to the administration, with specified modifications.

Section 4: Resignations, Deaths and Departures

The departure of the administrator.   The appointment of the administrator, as   **17-38**
the holder of an office, as distinct from its legal effect on the status of the company,

---

[151] In *DKLL Solicitors v Revenue and Customs Commissioners* [2007] EWHC 2067 (Ch); [2007] B.C.C. 908 it was suggested that the court could order the implementation of proposals notwithstanding the objection of a majority creditor.
[152] [2014] B.C.C. 159.
[153] [2011] EWHC 2820.
[154] Insolvency Act 1986 Sch.B1 para.42(2), (3).
[155] Insolvency Act 1986 Sch.B1 para.42(4)(a).
[156] Insolvency Act 1986 Sch.B1 para.42(4)(aa), and see SI 2004/2326 reg.73(4)(c).
[157] Insolvency Act 1986 Sch.B1 para.42(4)(b).

may be terminated by his resignation (as distinct from his removal by order of the court), by the loss of his qualification as an insolvency practitioner in relation to the company,[158] or by death.

17-39 Resignation: para.87(1) of Sch.B1   Paragraph 87(1) of Sch.B1 provides that an administrator may resign only in prescribed circumstances. By para.87(2), where the administrator is entitled to resign, he may only do so by notice in writing (a) to the court (where he has been appointed by the Court), (b) or to the holder of the floating charge by virtue of which he was appointed, (c) or to the company (if he was appointed by the company), or (d) to the directors (if he was appointed by the directors). The prescribed circumstances are set out in r.3.62 of the Insolvency (England and Wales) Rules 2016. An administrator may only resign *without* the permission of the court on prescribed grounds,[159] namely (a) ill-health, or (b) intention to cease to be in practice as an insolvency practitioner, or (c) some conflict of interest, or change of personal circumstances, which precludes, or makes impracticable, the further discharge by him of the duties of administrator. To resign on other grounds requires the permission of the court.[160]

17-40 Procedure for resignation: notice of intention to resign and notice of intention to apply for permission to resign.   Where the administrator does not require the permission of the court to resign,[161] he must give at least five business days' notice[162] of his intention to resign. Where he does require permission, he must give at least five business days' notice of his *intention* to apply for permission to resign.[163] Rule 3.63(4) of the Insolvency (England and Wales) Rule 2016 lists those persons to whom such notice must be given. Where the administrator was appointed by a qualifying floating charge-holder, or by the company, or by the company's directors, he must give notice to the respective appointor(s).[164] Amongst other things, the notice must contain the date with effect from which the administrator intends to resign or (where the court's permission is needed) to date on which he intends to file his application for permission to resign.[165]

He must also give such notice of intention to resign or to apply to the court for permission to resign (i) to any continuing administrator, and (ii) to the creditors' committee (if there is one).[166] If there is neither such an administrator in office, nor such a committee in being, he must give such notice to the company itself and to and its creditors.[167] He must also give such notice to any Member-State liquidator who has been appointed in relation to the company.[168]

Where he was appointed by the holder of a qualifying floating charge, he must

---

[158] But note para.89(1) of Sch.B1 which provides that "the administrator of a company shall vacate office if he ceases to be qualified to act as an insolvency practitioner in relation to the company". The wording of this provision rather suggests that in these circumstances, the office of administrator is automatically vacated and that no positive act (i.e. a resignation) is required.

[159] Insolvency Act 1986 Sch.B1 para.87(1); Insolvency (England and Wales) Rules 2016 r.3.62(1).

[160] Insolvency (England and Wales) Rules 2016 r.3.62(2).

[161] Insolvency (England and Wales) Rules 2016 r.3.62(1).

[162] Insolvency (England and Wales) Rules 2016 rr.3.63(1) (2), (3) and 3.64.

[163] Insolvency (England and Wales) Rules 2016 r.3.63(1)(b).

[164] Insolvency (England and Wales) Rules 2016 r.3.63(4)(e).

[165] Insolvency (England and Wales) Rules 2016 r.3.63(3).

[166] Insolvency (England and Wales) Rules 2016 r.3.63(4)(b).

[167] Insolvency (England and Wales) Rules 2016 r.3.63(4)(c).

[168] Insolvency (England and Wales) Rules 2016 r.3.63(4)(d).

give such notice of his intention to resign or his intention to apply for the court's permission to resign (i) to the holders of any prior qualifying floating charges, (ii) to the person who appointed him, and (iii) to the holder of the floating charge, by virtue of which he was appointed.[169]

Where he was appointed by the company or the directors, he must give such notice of intention to resign to the appointor and to all holders of a qualifying floating charge.[170] In addition, by r.3.64, a copy of the notice must be delivered to the registrar of companies and filed with the court. Where the administrator was appointed in court, notice of resignation under para.87(2)(a) must be given by filing the notice with the court.[171]

Application for permission to resign: parties. Where the administrator needs **17-41**
the permission of the court to resign, there is no provision requiring him to serve his application on any of the parties to whom notice of intention to apply has to be given, or on any other party. Nor does the notice of intention to apply require him to give any details of the grounds on which the application for permission to resign may be based, other than the prescribed grounds.

It is to be assumed that any of the recipients of that notice would, however, be entitled to attend the hearing and to be heard.

Loss of qualification as insolvency practitioner: para.89 of Sch.B1. By para.89 **17-42**
of Sch.B1, where the administrator ceases to be qualified as an insolvency practitioner in relation to the company, he immediately ceases to be legally entitled to act as the administrator of a company,[172] and vacates office.[173] If he lost his qualification in consequence of a bankruptcy order being made against him[174] it is not clear whether, if he were to succeed in an appeal against the bankruptcy order, he would be entitled to resume his office; presumably not, for his place would have already been filled.

An administrator who has ceased to be qualified must give notice in writing of that fact as follows: where he was appointed by the court, to the court; where he was appointed by a qualifying floating-charge holder, to him; where he was appointed by the company or its directors, to it or to them.[175] He must also give notice in writing to the registrar of companies.[176]

A curious feature of the Insolvency Act 1986 Sch.B1 para.89, and is that it imposes no time limit on giving notice of what would seem to be a crucial event in the administration, not even in the elsewhere ubiquitous terms, "as soon as reasonably practicable".

Failure to give the required notices is an offence.[177]

Death of the administrator. Where the administrator dies, a notice of the fact and **17-43**
date must be filed with the court as soon as reasonably practicable by (a) the surviv-

---

[169] Insolvency (England and Wales) Rules 2016 r.3.63(4)(e).
[170] Insolvency (England and Wales) Rules 2016 r.3.63(4)(f).
[171] Insolvency (England and Wales) Rules 2016 r.3.64(4). The relevant form is form AM15.
[172] Insolvency Act 1986 ss.388 and 390.
[173] Insolvency Act 1986 Sch.B1 para.89(1).
[174] Insolvency Act 1986 s.390(4), (5).
[175] Insolvency Act 1986 Sch.B1 para.89(2).
[176] Insolvency (England and Wales) Rules 2016 r.3.66.
[177] Insolvency Act 1986 Sch.B1 para.89(3).

ing administrator, (b) a member of his firm, (c) an officer of his company, or (d) a personal representative.[178] If no such notice has been filed within 21 days following the administrator's death, any other person may file the notice.[179] Notice must also be given by the person who gives such notice to the registrar of companies, containing prescribed particulars.[180]

17-44 **Supplying vacancy in the office of administrator: Sch.B1 paras 91–95.** These provisions apply in circumstances where the administrator has died, has resigned, has been removed from office under para.88 or has vacated office under para.89.[181] The filling of that vacancy differs in procedure, depending upon whether the administrator was appointed in court[182] or out of court.[183]

17-45 **Substitutions: Sch.B1 paras 96 and 97.** In the case of an administrator having been appointed by a qualifying floating charge-holder, a *prior* qualifying floating charge-holder has the right to apply to the court to replace that administrator by his own nominee, actually *displacing him* while he is still in office, and not merely filling a vacancy.[184]

Where an administrator has been appointed by a company or its directors, a creditors' meeting may replace him, i.e. displace him while still in office, provided that there is no holder of a qualifying floating charge in relation to the company's property.[185] It should be noted that this power is vested in a creditors' meeting, and not a creditors' committee.[186]

17-46 **Modes of replacement of the administrator.** Where the administrator was appointed in court by an administration order, an application to the court to replace him may be made by the creditors' committee (if there is one), by the company, by the directors of the company, by one or more creditors, or by any person, appointed to act jointly or concurrently with the previous administrator, who is still in office[187]; but the creditors' committee claim to replace the administrator will in general prevail.[188]

However, the company, the directors, one or more creditors or a joint office-holder may only apply if there is no creditors' committee, or where the existing creditors' committee, or a remaining administrator, is not taking reasonable steps to make a replacement of the administrator, or the court considers it right, for any other reason, to allow the application to be made.[189]

Where the appointment was made by a qualifying floating charge-holder, that holder may appoint a replacement administrator; but see above at para.17-45, as to the rights of intervention of a prior holder.

---

178 Insolvency Act 1986 Sch.B1 para.90(a); Insolvency (England and Wales) Rules 2016 rr.3.67(1) and 3.67(2).
179 Insolvency (England and Wales) Rules 2016 r.3.67(3).
180 Insolvency (England and Wales) Rules 2016 r.3.67(4).
181 See para.90 of Sch.B1.
182 See para.91 of Sch.B1
183 See paras 92–94 of Sch.B1.
184 Insolvency Act 1986 Sch.B1 para.96.
185 Insolvency Act 1986 Sch.B1 para.97.
186 Insolvency Act 1986 Sch.B1 para.97(2).
187 Insolvency Act 1986 Sch.B1 para.91(1).
188 Insolvency Act 1986 Sch.B1 para.91(2).
189 Insolvency Act 1986 Sch.B1 para.91(2).

Where the appointment was made by the company or its directors, the company, or its directors, may respectively make the replacement appointment.[190] To be entitled to do so, it or they need to obtain the consent of each person who is the holder of a qualifying floating charge.[191] If such consent is withheld, it or they may apply to the court for permission to make the replacement.[192]

The administrator's final progress report.   In most of the procedures considered in this chapter, the termination of the administration, howsoever achieved, requires the outgoing administrator to prepare, file and distribute his "final progress report". This is a term of art. The "final progress report" falls to be distinguished from the six-monthly "progress report" which the administrator is required routinely to file during the term of the administration.[193]   **17-47**

This "final progress report" is regulated by two groups of procedural rules. Rule 18.3(1), (4) and (5) of the Insolvency (England and Wales) Rules 2016 prescribe the minimum contents of all progress reports in administration, winding up and bankruptcy. Rules 3.53 and 18.3(2) list those additional matters which must be addressed in a "final progress report" in an administration.

The basic contents of all progress reports are prescribed by r.18.3 and broadly comprise:

(a)   identification details for the proceedings;
(b)   identification and contact details for the office holder;
(c)   date of appointment and any changes to it;
(d)   details of progress over the period covered by the report, including a summary of receipts and payments over that period;
(e)   information relating to remuneration[194] and expenses;
(f)   information as to any distributions made if applicable;
(g)   details of what remains to be done; and
(e)   any other information that might be relevant to the creditors.

In addition, by r.3.53, the "final progress report" must include a summary of the administrator's proposals, any major amendments to, or deviations from them, the steps taken during the administration, and the outcome. If there has been a prescribed part distribution to unsecured creditors pursuant to s.176A of the Insolvency Act 1986, by r.18.3(2), the amount so paid must be stated in the final receipts and payments account.

---

[190]   Insolvency Act 1986 Sch.B1 paras 93(1) and 94(1).
[191]   Insolvency Act 1986 Sch.B1 paras 93(2)(a) and 94(2)(a).
[192]   Insolvency Act 1986 Sch.B1 paras 93(2)(b), 94(2)(b).
[193]   Insolvency (England and Wales) Rules 2016 rr.18.2, 18.3 and 18.6.
[194]   In accordance with r.18.4 of the Insolvency (England and Wales) Rules 2016.

PART IV: RECEIVERS APPOINTED OUT OF COURT

CHAPTER 18

RECEIVERS APPOINTED UNDER AN AGREEMENT

18-1   **Appointment of receivers out of court.** In many instances the appointment of a receiver, or a receiver and manager, is effected without resort to the courts. Such appointments are made:

    (a)   under an agreement between persons interested in the property over which the appointment is made; or

    (b)   under the provisions of a statute.

A receiver so appointed is the agent of the parties or one of them, according to the terms of the agreement or statute under which the appointment is made. By statute, however, the receiver may become personally liable to persons contracting with him,[1] and, as is the case with all other agents, he may in certain circumstances in any case become liable as a principal to persons dealing with him.[2]

18-2   **Comparison with appointment by the court.** The appointment of a receiver out of court does not entail the costs of proceedings, and formalities such as affidavits of fitness and provision of security, which are involved in appointments by the court. Further, additional powers may be conferred upon a receiver appointed out of court, either directly or by enlargement of the statutory powers, such as the right to grant options to purchase.

    There is no obligation on the person having the power to appoint a receiver out of court to make such an appointment: he is fully entitled to resort instead to such other remedies as he may have.[3]

18-3   **Conditions for appointment.** The conditions specified in the mortgage, or otherwise implied by statute, must be complied with before any valid appointment of a receiver can be made. Mortgages usually make the power of appointment exercisable so soon as the principal money becomes payable, or the interest is in arrear for a specified number of days, or so soon as interest in arrear or principal is not paid on demand. Frequently, the principal money is made payable on demand, and the power of appointment is exercisable on non-compliance with such a demand.

    Discussion between the mortgagor and mortgagee regarding realisation of the

---

[1]   See Insolvency Act 1986 ss.37(1) and 44(1), and Ch.20, below.
[2]   See para.20-32, below.
[3]   *Reeves v White* (1852) 17 Q.B. 995.

mortgaged property may result in a suspension or variation of the right to appoint a receiver, or postpone the mortgagor's liability to pay.[4]

Demand: sum to be demanded. Any demand required to be made of the mortgagor should make demand in the terms specified in the mortgage, and where, in the mortgage, the mortgagor agrees to pay on demand all monies owing the mortgagor may simply demand payment of the monies secured in those terms.[5] In most cases, the question of repayment is wholly academic, the mortgagor being unable to make repayment. Should the mortgagor be in a position to pay, there is probably a duty upon the mortgagee, on request by the mortgagor, to name a realistic sum as being due, on receipt of which (if necessary on account) no appointment of a receiver would be made.[6]

18-4

Time allowed for payment. Following demand, the mortgagor has to be given a reasonable opportunity of implementing whatever reasonable mechanics of payment he may need to employ to discharge the debt.[7] In the case of an amount which the mortgagor is likely to have, if he has it at all, in a bank account, he needs to be given such time as is reasonable in all the circumstances to enable him to contact his bank and make the necessary arrangements for the sum in question to be transferred from his bank to the creditor (allowing, if appropriate, for bank opening hours).[8] Where it is clear to the mortgagee that the mortgagor is unable to pay the amount owing, a period of about one hour between the making of the demand and the appointment of a receiver has been held to be acceptable.[9] If, moreover, the mortgagor has admitted to the mortgagee that the necessary monies are not available, the mortgagee need not allow any time at all to elapse before appointing a receiver.[10]

18-5

A mortgagee is not entitled to appoint a receiver if his security is in jeopardy unless he has the benefit of an express provision to that effect.[11] In the absence of such a provision, his remedy is to apply to the court for the appointment of a receiver.[12]

Charge document executed under hand. A power to appoint a receiver may validly be contained in a charge under hand only, notwithstanding that he may, in consequence, not be in a position to execute deeds on the mortgagor's behalf. But he may thereby be given power to enter into the mortgagor's property, without first obtaining the permission of the court. Such a charge operates as an agreement to execute a mortgage by deed, and the mortgagor could be compelled to execute conveyances.[13]

18-6

---

[4] *Ahmad v Bank of Scotland Plc* [2014] EWHC 4611 (Ch).
[5] *Bank of Baroda v Panessar* [1987] Ch. 335; *Bunbury Foods Pty Ltd v National Bank of Australasia Ltd* [1984] HCA 10; *Humphrey v Roberts* (1866) 5 S.C.R. (N.S.W.) 376 at 385–387; *Campbell v Commercial Banking Company of Sydney* (1879) 2 L.R. (N.S.W.) 375 at 385; *Clyde Properties Ltd v Tasker* [1970] N.Z.L.R. 754 at 757–758; *MIR Brox. Projects Pty Ltd* [1980] 2 N.S.W.R. 907 at 926.
[6] *Bank of Baroda v Panessar* [1987] Ch. 335 at 347.
[7] *Bank of Baroda v Panessar* [1987] Ch. 335.
[8] *Sheppard & Cooper v TSB Bank plc* [1996] 2 All E.R. 654 at 659.
[9] *R.A. Cripps & Son Ltd v Wickenden* [1973] 1 W.L.R. 944.
[10] *Sheppard & Cooper Ltd v TSB Bank plc (No.2)* [1996] 2 All E.R. 654; *Quah v Goldman Sachs International* [2015] EWHC 759 (Comm).
[11] *Cryne v Barclays Bank Plc* [1987] B.C.L.C. 548.
[12] See Ch.2, s.4, above.
[13] *Byblos Bank S.A.L. v Al-Khudhairy* (1986) 2 B.C.C. 99549.

18-7 **Matters to be considered by proposed receiver.** Any receiver who is proposed to be appointed out of court should, for his own protection, and prior to accepting the appointment, satisfy himself as to:

(a) the validity of the document (if any) under which the power to appoint him is said to arise[14]; and whether its execution was duly authorised[15]; and, if it contains a charge which is registrable under the Companies Act 2006, that the necessary formalities have been complied with[16]; if not, application should be made to the court without delay to obtain permission to file particulars with the registrar of companies out of time.[17]

(b) the validity of the appointment itself;

(c) whether he is suitably qualified;

(d) who, under the terms of the documents in question, is his principal;

(e) the extent of the powers conferred upon him; and

(f) the nature and extent of the property over which he has been appointed.

If there is any flaw in his appointment, not only will the receiver be unable to enforce any claims to priority over other parties interested in the property,[18] but he may be liable in trespass to any person whose rightful possession he disturbs,[19] although such person will have the option of treating the receiver either as a trespasser or as his agent.[20]

If the validity of his appointment is challenged, it is for the receiver to justify it: the maxim *omnia praesumuntur rite esse acta* does not apply.[21]

If, however, the appointment is subject to conditions which are not justified by the terms of the power to appoint (e.g. that all the receiver's payment instructions are to be countersigned by a designated person), but the owner of the property with knowledge of such provisions allows him to take possession and to act as receiver without objection, the owner will be taken to have assented to and sanctioned such conditions.[22]

18-8 **Who may be appointed.** Except in the case of companies, where there are certain restrictions, and in some cases the necessity for the receiver to have certain qualifications, there are no special limitations upon who may be appointed as a receiver. However, although the primary duty of a receiver is always to the person appointing him,[23] he also owes duties to the person over whose property he is ap-

---

[14] See *AJ Brush v Ralli Bros. (Securities)* (1967) 117 New L.J. 212, where the debenture under which a receiver was appointed was attacked as being part of a moneylending transaction.

[15] *Evans v Tiger Investments Ltd* [2002] 2 B.C.L.C. 188, as to authority to grant the debenture under which a receiver was appointed.

[16] See Companies Act 2006 s.859A.

[17] See Companies Act 2006 s.859F.

[18] Cf. *Kasofsky v Kreegars* [1937] 4 All E.R. 374.

[19] *Re Simms* [1934] Ch. 1.

[20] *Ex p. Vaughan* (1884) 14 Q.B.D. 29; *Re Simms*, n.19, above. See also *Wood v Wood* (1828) 4 Russell 558.

[21] *Kasofsky v Kreegars*, n.18, above: the maxim means "the presumption of regularity of administration in all respects".

[22] *Gosling v Gaskell and Grocott* [1897] A.C. 575 per Lord Herschell at 591, and per Lord Davey at 595.

[23] *Re B Johnson & Co (Builders) Ltd* [1955] Ch. 634; *Gomba Holdings (UK) Ltd v Homan* [1986] B.C.L.C. 331 at 336i-337a per Hoffmann J.

pointed receiver, and to anybody else (such as a guarantor of that person's debt)[24] who may be adversely affected by his actions.[25] Accordingly, a person with the power to appoint a receiver should take care to appoint a competent person to that office (and may indeed have a duty to take such care[26]), and the person appointed should, before accepting it, be confident of his ability to discharge the duties of that office.

Method of appointment. The method of appointment must comply with any 18-9 formalities required by the mortgage. If none is specified, the method of appointment is simply by means of an instrument in writing, as under the Law of Property Act 1925,[27] executed by the person designated so to do in the mortgage.[28] If the receiver is to have the power to execute a deed in the name of the mortgagee, then, like any other agent appointed for this purpose, he must be appointed by deed.[29]

It is not possible to presume the appointment of a receiver, where no such written appointment has been made. Therefore, where a mortgagee, by writing, appointed a person to act as receiver before he was entitled to do so, but did not reappoint him after an event took place which would have entitled him to make such an appointment, even though the receiver continued to act, it was held he had not been validly appointed.[30]

Time of appointment. Except in the case of companies,[31] the appointment of a 18-10 receiver takes effect when the document of appointment is handed to the receiver by a person having authority to do so, in circumstances from which it may fairly be said that he is appointing a receiver, and the receiver accepts the proffered appointment.[32] The delivery of the document of appointment gives the receiver knowledge, or means of knowledge, as to who the debtor is (if he does not know already), and acceptance may be tacit.[33] The date which the document effecting the appointment bears is irrelevant, save as evidence where the date of delivery or acceptance of the appointment is otherwise unknown.[34] There is no objection to the appointment being prepared and left ready, until it is required to be brought into effect in the manner indicated above.[35]

Requirement for appointee's consent Nobody can be forced to accept the office of a receiver. If a person has been appointed as a receiver, or been purported 18-11

---

24 *Standard Chartered Bank v Walker* [1982] 1 W.L.R. 1410. See also *Knight v Lawrence* [1991] B.C.C. 411 VC; *Rottenberg v Monjack* [1992] B.C.C. 688; and *China and South Seas Bank Ltd v Tan* [1990] 1 A.C. 536. As to liability for alleged negligence in the appointment, see *Shamji v Johnson Matthey Bankers Ltd* [1991] B.C.L.C.36.

25 See para.18-33, below.

26 See *Shamji v Johnson Matthey Bankers Ltd*, n.24, above, at p.283c–e (counsel's submission, apparently accepted by Hoffmann J).

27 Law of Property Act 1925 s.109: see Ch.19, below.

28 As to a possibly invalid deed taking effect as an appointment in writing, see *Windsor Refrigerator Co Ltd v Branch Nominees Ltd* [1961] Ch. 375 CA.

29 *Berkeley v Hardy* (1826) 5 B. & C. 355.

30 *R Jaffé Ltd (in liquidation) v Jaffé* [1931] N.Z.L.R. 195.

31 See Chs 20 to 26, below.

32 *R.A. Cripps & Son Ltd v Wickenden*, n.9, above, at 953F–G per Goff J; *Windsor Refrigerator Co Ltd v Branch Nominees Ltd*, n.28, above.

33 *R.A. Cripps & Son Ltd v Wickenden*, n.9 above, at 954C per Goff J.

34 *R.A. Cripps & Son Ltd v Wickenden*, n.9, above, at 954D per Goff J.

35 *R.A. Cripps & Son Ltd v Wickenden*, n.9, above, at 954D per Goff J; *Windsor Refrigerator Co Ltd v Branch Nominees Ltd*, n.28, above, at 395 per Lord Evershed MR and at 397 per Harman LJ.

to be appointed as a receiver, he may, at any time before acceptance of the office[36] but not after such acceptance,[37] refuse it. Such refusal should be notified to the appointor without delay, and in cases where his appointment has been notified to the registrar of companies[38] the registrar should forthwith be informed of such refusal.[39]

18-12 **What duty of care does an appointor owe?** If the mortgagee is contractually entitled to exercise a right to appoint a receiver, it does not, when deciding whether to exercise such right, owe any duty of care to the mortgagor, or to any guarantors of its liabilities, although it may, having to decided to exercise it, owe a duty to exercise the right in good faith.[40] But mortgagees who act in what they consider, in good faith, to be their own interests, can exercise their contractual right to appoint a receiver without regard to its effect upon the mortgagor or any guarantor. Accordingly, the mortgagee may delay, or accelerate, the appointment of a receiver, in the light of what it perceives to be its own best interests.[41]

The receiver, when preparing for a sale of mortgaged property, is entitled to have primary regard for the wishes of the mortgagee, and is not required to incur, at the instance of the mortgagor, any expenses, such as expenses incurred in the obtaining of planning permission, or in negotiating leases, which the mortgagor considers would be advantageous for the sale.[42]

If the power to appoint a receiver has become exercisable by reason of the mortgagor being wound up, it cannot be exercised solely upon this ground without the leave of the court.[43]

Where the power is conferred on trustees, or one or more of a class of creditors all ranking pari passu, such a power is a fiduciary power, to be exercised by the appointor in good faith in the interests of all the class of creditors.[44]

It is no objection to the validity of the appointment of a receiver that an incorrect reason for the appointment was given at that time, if in fact there existed a proper ground for the making of the appointment.[45]

It sometimes happens that the mortgagor invites the mortgagee to appoint a receiver, even though the specified conditions have not been fulfilled. In such cases, the invitation and appointment are together thought to constitute pro tanto a contractual variation in the terms of the mortgage. Similarly, if the mortgagor acquiesces in the appointment, although the specified conditions have not been fulfilled, it may be held to have accepted the validity of the appointment.[46]

18-13 **Appointments by agreement.** An appointment may be made wholly under the terms of an agreement in cases such as the appointment of a receiver to wind up a

---

[36] Cf. *Robinson v Pett* (1734) 3 P.W. 249.
[37] Cf. *Re Lister* [1926] Ch. 149.
[38] Under Companies Act 2006 s.859K(2).
[39] Cf. Companies Act 2006 s.859K(3).
[40] *Shamji v Johnson Matthey Bankers Ltd* [1986] B.C.L.C. 278 at 284 per Hoffmann J.
[41] *Shamji v Johnson Matthey Bankers Ltd* [1986] B.C.L.C. 278.
[42] *Silven Properties Ltd v Royal Bank of Scotland plc* [2003] EWCA Civ 1409; [2004] 1 W.L.R. 997 CA, affirming [2002] EWHC 1976 Ch; [2003] B.P.I.R. 171 (a Law of Property Act 1925 case.): see also *The Grosvenor (Mayfair) Estate v Edward Erdman Property Investment Ltd* [1996] E.G.C.S. 83; [1996] N.P.C. 69.
[43] Law of Property Act 1925 s.110.
[44] *Re Maskelyne British Typewriter Co* [1898] 1 Ch. 133.
[45] *Byblos Bank S.A.L. v Al-Khudhairy*, n.13, above.
[46] Cf. para.20-10, below.

partnership business. Another such case is where a person, entitled to payment out of a fund not yet in existence, such as gate money to be paid for admission, is given power to appoint a receiver over the receipts.

In all such cases, the agreement defines the rights, duties and obligations of the receiver. If the agreement contains no express provision for remuneration of the receiver, remuneration may be claimed on the basis of a quantum meruit.[47]

Appointment over a business.   Where a receiver is appointed, whether at the instance of a mortgagee or otherwise, to carry on a business, the problems which will confront him are in many respects similar to those which confront an administrative receiver of a company's undertaking, which are dealt with in Ch.21-26, although an administrative receiver is subject to many statutory obligations, and entitled to certain statutory privileges, which do not apply in the case of an ordinary receiver.[48]   **18-14**

Appointments by mortgagors.   In the case of equitable mortgages, the mortgagor may appoint a person to collect and deal with the rents and profits in the same manner as provided in the case of receivers appointed by mortgagees under the Law of Property Act 1925[49] or otherwise; the receiver's powers may be defined by reference to the statute. It is usual and advisable in such cases for the mortgagor to obtain the approval by the mortgagee of the person appointed. A person so appointed is in all respects the agent of the mortgagor, even if appointed by deed by the mortgagee.[50] An appointment should be made by deed if the person appointed is authorised to take proceedings in the name of the mortgagee or mortgagor.   **18-15**

Where a life-tenant appointed a receiver over rents, with a direction to the tenants to pay rents to such receiver, to secure payment of an annuity, this was held to create an equitable charge in priority to subsequent incumbrancers with notice.[51]

Appointments by mortgagees other than under agreement or statute.   Appointments by mortgagees are normally made either under an agreement entitling such appointment or under the statutory power[52]; but sometimes a mortgagee in possession of his own authority appoints an agent to collect rents. A person so appointed is the agent of the mortgagee, who remains accountable as a mortgagee in possession.[53]   **18-16**

Property to which appointment extends.   Clearly, the receiver can have no title to property which does not belong to the person over whose property the appointment purports to extend, or which is not comprised in the documents from which his title derives.   **18-17**

Under most modern forms of memoranda of association, the company has express power to charge all its assets, and even where it has not the Companies Act

---

[47]   "Justified remuneration" was said in *Prior v Bagster* [1887] W.N. 194 to be prima facie on the same scale as receivers appointed by the court; see now CPR r.69.7 and Ch.10, above.
[48]   See Ch.21, below.
[49]   See para.19-2, below.
[50]   See *Jefferys v Dickson* (1866) 1 Ch.App.183, 190; *Law v Glenn* (1866-67) L.R. 2 Ch.App. 634 at 640; *Gosling v Gaskell and Grocott* [1897] A.C. 575.
[51]   *Cradock v Scottish Provident Institution* [1893] W.N. 146; affirmed [1894] W.N.88.
[52]   See Ch.19, below.
[53]   *Leith v Irvine* (1833) 1 Mylne & Keen 277, 286.

2006 will normally produce this result.[54] These provisions resolve such difficulties as the finding that a power to charge the company's "funds or property" did not authorise a charge on uncalled capital,[55] whereas power to charge the "company's property and rights" did.[56]

However, no appointment can legally extend to property to which the mortgagor has no legal or equitable title, nor to property held upon trust by the mortgagor for third persons.[57] Apart from trusts created by agreement, trusts may also be created by statute.[58]

Where a second receiver is, or has already been, appointed over the same property by another mortgagee, the respective entitlements of the receivers will depend upon the priority position as between the charges under which the receivers were appointed.[59]

18-18 **Where money advanced is impressed with a trust.** Money advanced to the mortgagor for a particular purpose may be impressed with a trust so that, if the money is not utilised in the manner contemplated, it is thereafter to be held on trust for the person making the advance.[60] Similarly, a person who has paid money under a mistake of fact may be entitled to trace the same in the hands of the recipient, who thus may be a trustee for him.[61] In both classes of case, the title of the receiver cannot be better than the title of the mortgagor.

18-19 **Where mortgagor in possession of goods not owned by him.** Given the flexibility of the law in relation to the time of transfer of the property in specific or ascertained goods, which is simply the time at which the parties to the contract of sale intend it to be transferred,[62] it is possible for a mortgagor to be in possession of goods to which he has no title whatsoever.[63] Doubtless a power of sale, or of otherwise dealing with such goods, must be implied, if not expressly provided for; but it is then possible for the supplier, by apt provisions in the contract, to provide that the mortgagor is, as regards such sales or dealings, to stand in a fiduciary position towards him. The result is that the mortgagor may be a trustee of the proceeds of sale, and possibly also of the proceeds of other dealings (e.g. sale of a product

---

54 Companies Act 2006 s.39 confers virtually unlimited capacity upon a company as far as external parties are concerned. Further, s.40 provides that the authority of its directors to enter into obligations on the company's behalf is deemed to be free of any limitation under the company's constitution.

55 *Re The British Provident Life and Fire Assurance Society, Stanley's Case* (1864) 4 De G.J. & S. 407.

56 *Howard v Patent Ivory Manufacturing Company* (1888) L.R. 38 Ch. D. 156.

57 *Aluminium Industrie Vaassen BV v Romalpa Aluminium Ltd* [1976] 1 W.L.R. 676, CA. See *Re Kayford Ltd (in liquidation)* [1975] 1 W.L.R. 279, for a trust of money paid by customers in advance.

58 See, e.g., Estate Agents Act 1979 s.13.

59 *Bass Breweries Ltd v Delaney* [1994] B.C.C. 851.

60 *Barclays Bank Ltd v Quistclose Investments Ltd* [1970] A.C. 567 HL (where all the earlier cases are collected): money advanced to pay dividend which was never paid. See also *Carreras Rothmans Ltd v Freeman Mathews Treasure Ltd* [1985] Ch. 207 (monies paid to company to meet debts owed by it to third parties, held on trust for such third parties); *Re Kayford Ltd (in liquidation)*, n.57, above (money paid for goods in advance); *Re EVTR Ltd* [1987] B.C.L.C. 646 CA (original purpose of loan (purchase of machinery) not wholly carried out: failure of contract revived original trust pro tanto). See, also, *Re Farepak Food and Gifts Ltd* [2006] EWHC 3272 Ch; [2008] B.C.C. 22 (money paid towards redeemable vouchers could be held by the recipient company on constructive trust).

61 *Chase Manhattan Bank NA v Israel-British Bank (London) Ltd* [1981] Ch. 105.

62 Sale of Goods Act 1979 s.17. This may work both ways; the mortgagor may be in possession of goods which he has sold to a third party, the title to which has clearly passed to such third party.

63 In the *Romalpa* case (see n.57, above) title was only to pass when the mortgagor had met all that was owing to the supplier, "no matter on what grounds".

containing the goods supplied), for the original supplier.[64] Such trust monies can be disposed of in any way so as to affect the supplier's title thereto. The consequences of the combination of these two principles in a suitably drafted contract may, as was the position in the leading case, be very serious from the point of view of an apparently secured creditor.[65]

Receiver's obligations under retention of title agreements. Where goods, equipment or materials in the mortgagor's possession are subject to effective retention of title agreements, the receiver and the mortgagee are bound by the terms of those agreements, to the same extent as the mortgagor, as to the legal and equitable rights retained by the unpaid supplier, including any exclusive jurisdiction clause for the determination of disputes.[66] It is the practice, either in case of such disputes or for the accommodation of the receiver, for him to enter into personal undertakings to pay for any goods or materials used, or any equipment retained, which avoids the necessity for the retention of title owner to enforce his rights to his property by injunction. Any payments made by the receiver under such undertakings are covered by his rights of indemnity.[67]   **18-20**

Retention of title: an unregistered charge? A retention of title arrangement may create a charge created by the mortgagor and so be void, in the case of a company mortgagor which is in liquidation or administration, unless it is the subject of the required filing of particulars with the registrar of companies.[68] The principle behind the retention of title cases has been generalised into the proposition that, if material subject to a retention of title clause has been incorporated in, or used as material for, other goods, it is to be assumed that the newly-manufactured goods are owned by the buyer, subject to a charge in favour of the seller, unless the use of the material has left it in a separate and identifiable state, in which case it is possible for the seller to retain ownership of it.[69]   **18-21**

An even simpler example of a contract which on its true construction effected a charge was one where a contract for repair provided that the repairer was to be entitled to the ownership of any article for which it had supplied parts, pending payment therefor.[70]

Equally, of course, the appointment will not extend to any property the title to which has passed away from the mortgagor, although physical possession thereof

---

[64] Following the principle of *Re Hallett's Estate* (1880) 13 Ch. D. 696, the supplier is allowed to trace the goods supplied into their proceeds. The courts have not been quick to find that such a trust has in fact been created: see *Hendy Lennox (Industrial Engines) Ltd v Grahame Puttick Ltd* [1984] 1 W.L.R. 485; and *Re Andrabell Ltd (in liquidation)* [1984] 3 All E.R. 407.
[65] See n.64, above.
[66] See n.64, above.
[67] *Lipe Ltd v Leyland DAF Ltd* [1993] B.C.C. 385.
[68] Companies Act 2006 s.859H; *Clough Mill Ltd v Martin* [1985] 1 W.L.R. 111 CA; *John Snow & Co Ltd v DBG Woodcroft & Co Ltd* [1985] B.C.L.C. 54. For a case where the incorporated goods nevertheless retained their identity, see *Hendy Lennox (Industrial Engines) Ltd v Grahame Puttick Ltd* [1984] 1 W.L.R. 485.
[69] *Specialist Plant Services Ltd. v Braithwaite Ltd.* [1987] B.C.L.C. 1 CA, a decision difficult to reach in the *Romalpa* case. See also *Re CKE Engineering Ltd (in administration)* [2007] B.C.C. 975: the case contemplates that a tenancy in common may arise in the case of "mixed" goods (in this case galvanized zinc) as between the title retainer and the company.
[70] *Re Leyland DAF Ltd, Talbot v Edcrest Ltd* [1994] B.C.C. 166.

is still retained; but it will extend to any property which the mortgagor itself has sold with the benefit of a valid retention of title clause.[71]

18-22 **Rights of third parties over property to which the appointment extends.**   The receiver, having been appointed to collect and get in assets of the mortgagor as the mortgagor's agent, can only collect and get in those assets subject to any contractual rights of third parties in relation to those assets created before his appointment, such as an equitable interest in land created by a contract of which specific performance will be granted.[72] Further, the assets will be subject to any limitations (such as a freezing injunction) on a mortgagor's power to deal with those assets, or any of them, which existed at the date of his appointment.[73] Provided, however, that the rights of the mortgagee in relation to the assets so frozen took priority to those of the person who obtained the freezing injunction (which is almost invariably the case), such injunction would be discharged on application by the mortgagee, although it would not have been discharged on the application of the receiver.[74]

18-23 **Order for sale of goods needing to be sold quickly.**   If a supplier who has reserved title to goods which it is desirable to sell quickly refuses to agree to the receiver re-selling, and sues him or threatens to sue, the receiver may be able to obtain from the court an order under the CPR for the sale of such goods.[75]

18-24 **Where a company is bound by a freezing injunction.**   Where a claimant suing a mortgagor (with other defendants) obtained a freezing injunction against the mortgagor, in support of a judgment obtained against it, a receiver subsequently appointed by a mortgagee over the assets of the mortgagor bound by the injunction was held to be entitled, on his own application, to have the injunction discharged, on the ground that the mortgagee's rights took precedence over those of the judgment creditor.

The relief granted on that application would seem to have been justified by treating the receiver (who was constituted by the debenture as the mortgagor's agent) as being, ad hoc and pro tanto, the agent of the mortgagee.[76]

18-25 **Enforcement of third party's contractual rights by injunction.**   Where a party had, by virtue of a contract with the mortgagor, acquired for value pre-emption rights with respect to some of the company's specialised process machinery, and an administrative receiver of the mortgagor's assets declined to recognise that as a contractual liability of the mortgagor, the court granted the party an injunction restraining the receiver from offering the machinery for sale in derogation of those rights; the court held that the party had, by contract, acquired an equitable interest

---

[71]   Subject to the operation of s.25 Sale of Goods Act 1979; see *Re Highway Foods International Ltd* [1995] B.C.C. 271.

[72]   *Freevale Ltd v Metrostore (Holdings) Ltd* [1984] Ch. 199. See also *The Real Meat Co Ltd* [1996] B.C.C. 254.

[73]   *Cretanor Maritime Co Ltd v Irish Marine Management Ltd* [1978] 1 W.L.R. 966 CA at 975; the decision on this point of Mann J in *Taylor v Van Dutch Marine Holding Ltd* [2017] EWHC 636 Ch, which appears to be to the contrary, was made without the *Cretanor Maritime* decision being cited and should therefore, to that extent, probably be considered per incuriam.

[74]   See n.72 above.

[75]   CPR 25.1(c)(v); PD 25A.

[76]   *Capital Cameras Ltd v Harold Lines Ltd* [1991] 1 W.L.R. 54; [1991] 3 All E.R. 389, Harman J, distinguishing *Cretanor Maritime Co Ltd v Irish Marine Management Ltd*, n.73, above.

in the machinery, for breach of which contractual right damages would be no adequate remedy.[77]

Protection. The court will, if necessary, grant an injunction against any person bound by the appointment to prevent interference with a receiver appointed out of court.[78] **18-26**

Fiduciary position. A receiver stands in a fiduciary position towards those by whom, or on whose behalf, he is appointed.[79] Inasmuch as he will be in control and receipt of assets belonging to a third party, he will also owe a duty not to act negligently to such party.[80] He is absolutely disqualified from purchasing the property of those towards whom he stands in such a position[81] without the usual safeguards.[82] Further, his appointment to an office of such responsibility presupposes that he will discharge his duties with "punctilious rectitude".[83] **18-27**

Realisation. Mortgages as a rule confer upon the receiver a power to sell the property comprised in the security. In the absence of such a power, an ordinary receiver has no power to sell. The sale must instead be effected by the mortgagee under the statutory power, contained in s.101 of the Law of Property Act 1925. **18-28**

A receiver empowered to get in assets of the mortgagor can for this purpose sue in the mortgagor's name without the mortgagor's consent. Thus, where a contract for sale of land has been entered into by the mortgagor, he may sue for rescission and return of the deposit or alternatively for specific performance.[84]

The exercise by a receiver of a power to sell mortgaged property has been held, where the mortgagor is in default, not to contravene art.1 of the First Protocol to the European Convention on Human Rights.[85]

Conveyances and transfers. A mere power to sell does not enable the receiver to convey the legal estate: but express power to do so in the name of the mortgagor or, in the case of specific legal mortgages, of the mortgagee is usually conferred. **18-29**

Where a charge created by a security document is only equitable, e.g. a floating charge, the mortgagor must concur to convey the legal estate.

Who should convey on a sale. Where a charge document creates a legal mortgage, the conveyance of property can be made by the mortgagee. But in that case the contract for sale should be entered into by the mortgagee, and not by the receiver in his own name: the power conferred by s.104 of the Law of Property Act 1925 on a mortgagee to convey the whole legal estate on sale applies where the mortgagee exercises the power of sale, and not where the receiver as agent for the **18-30**

---

[77] *Ash & Newman Ltd v Creative Devices Technology Ltd* [1991] B.C.L.C. 403, applying *Freevale Ltd v Metrostore (Holdings) Ltd*, n.72, above (claim based on an equitable interest in land), and distinguishing *Airlines Airspares Ltd v Handley Page Ltd* [1970] Ch. 193 (where no such immediate equitable interest in land or chattels had been created).

[78] *Bayly v West* [1884] 51 L.T. 764. *Re Magadi Soda Co Ltd* [1925] 94 L.J. Ch. 217 at 219 per Eve J.

[79] See the judgments in *R. v Board of Trade Ex p. St Martins Preserving Co Ltd* [1965] 1 Q.B. 603.

[80] *Re Magadi Soda Co Ltd* n.78, above, at 219.

[81] *Nugent v Nugent* [1908] 1 Ch. 546.

[82] *Re Magadi Soda Co Ltd*, n.78, above, at 219.

[83] *Re Magadi Soda Co Ltd*, n.78, above, at 219.

[84] *M Wheeler & Co v Warren* [1928] Ch. 840.

[85] *Horsham Properties Group Ltd v Clark* [2008] EWHC 2327 (Ch).

mortgagor sells. Where the conveyance is in the name of the mortgagor, the mortgagee with a legal mortgage must concur to surrender his term or release his charge. For like reasons, a second mortgagee must concur or release his charge if the sale is expressed to be made by the mortgagor.

If the receiver or mortgagee attempts to sell before the power of sale has become exercisable, an injunction can be obtained[86]; so too, if the sale is at such a gross undervalue as to be fraudulent.[87] But a sale by a mortgagee will not be restrained on mere proof that it is at an undervalue[88]; this is without prejudice to the right of the mortgagor to claim damages in respect of a negligent sale,[89] or of a guarantor to set up such a sale as a complete or partial defence to any claim under the guarantee.[90]

A clause protecting a purchaser against irregularities may be effective.[91]

18-31 **Mortgagee not liable for disbursements made by receiver.** One effect of the receiver being agent of the mortgagor is that the mortgagee is not liable in respect of money paid away improperly by the receiver, the mortgagee being liable only for money which reaches his hands.[92] Nor does receipt of rent by the receiver necessarily create a tenancy by estoppel as between the tenant and the mortgagee.[93] The mortgagee may however create, by virtue of his legal estate in the land, the relationship of landlord and tenant between himself and a tenant of the mortgagor, whose tenancy is not binding upon him, without previously terminating the receivership.[94] The mortgagor may recover from the mortgagee sums paid to the latter by the receiver in excess of the sums due under a mistake of fact for a period of six years before action.[95]

Where the statutory powers are extended by the mortgage deed, the mortgage should expressly provide that the receiver is to be regarded as agent for the mortgagor. In the absence of an express provision, he may be held to be agent for the mortgagee. It is a question of construction in each case.[96]

---

[86] *Hickson v Darlow* [1883] 23 Ch. D. 690; *Seton*, 7th edn, p.719.
[87] As to set-off, where a sale is improperly made, see *Ellis & Co's Trustee v Dixon-Johnson* [1924] 2 Ch. 451; [1925] A.C. 48.
[88] See *Waring v London & Manchester Ass. Co* [1935] Ch. 310, and see *Reliance PBS v Harwood-Stamper* [1944] Ch. 362 (a building society case, where the provisions were reviewed) and *Leon v York-o-Matic Ltd* [1966] 1 W.L.R. 1450.
[89] *Cuckmere Brick Co v Mutual Finance* [1971] Ch. 949 CA; see *Silven Properties Ltd v Royal Bank of Scotland plc*, n.42, above, and see para.18-34, below.
[90] *Standard Chartered Bank v Walker* [1982] 1 W.L.R. 1410. This was discussed in *Silven Properties Ltd v Royal Bank of Scotland plc*, see para.18-34, below.
[91] See *Dicker v Angerstein* [1876] 3 Ch. D. 600; *Selwyn v Garfit* (1888) 38 Ch. D. 273. As to inquiries with regard to notices, see *Life, etc., Corp v Hand in Hand Society* [1898] 2 Ch. 230.
[92] *Re Della Rocella's Estate* [1892] 29 L.R. Ir. 464.
[93] *Serjeant v Nash* [1903] 2 K.B. 304; *Lever Finance Ltd v Needleman's Trustee* [1956] Ch. 375; *Stroud Building Society v Delamont* [1960] 1 W.L.R. 431; *Chatsworth Properties Ltd v Effiom* [1971] 1 W.L.R. 144. Quaere, whether it ever does. But if a mortgagee appoints a receiver in respect of rent due under tenancies not otherwise binding upon him, he may thereby waive any right to treat the tenants as trespassers.
[94] *Stroud Building Society v Delamont*, n.93, above; *Chatsworth Properties Ltd v Effiom*, n.93, above.
[95] *Re Jones' Estate* [1914] 1 Ir.R. 188.
[96] See paras 19-29 ff, below.

Death, bankruptcy or winding up of mortgagor. The death, bankruptcy or **18-32** winding up[97] of the mortgagor does not affect the statutory powers: the receiver becomes agent for the mortgagor's successor-in-title, so far as to enable him to exercise the statutory powers.[98] But the bankruptcy or winding up of the mortgagor determines the power of the receiver to impose any personal liability on the mortgagor or his estate.[99] The receiver can still carry on a business, but he becomes personally liable to persons dealing with him, subject to any right of indemnity against the mortgagee.[100]

Since the receiver is agent for the mortgagor it appears that, for so long as the receiver is in receipt of the rents, time cannot run against the mortgagor under the Limitation Act 1980, even if the rents are insufficient for payment in full of the interest on the mortgage loan. Equally, payments made by the receiver will prevent the Limitation Act 1980 running in favour of the mortgagor.[101]

Receiver's liability to the mortgagor and others. The mortgagor can maintain **18-33** an action for an account against the receiver as his agent.[102] Notwithstanding the relationship of principal and agent, however, the mortgagor cannot dismiss the receiver, since, for valuable consideration, he has committed the management of his property to an attorney with whose appointment he cannot interfere.[103]

Nevertheless, a receiver owes a duty of good faith to the mortgagor in respect of his acts whilst in possession of the mortgaged property or its produce.[104] Receivers under an agricultural charge were held liable to the farmer-mortgagor for their negligent conduct of his livestock business, in failing to obtain proper commercial discounts off the cost of pig-feed purchased for the feeding of the livestock. The Court of Appeal held that a receiver and manager, managing mortgaged property in the form of a business, owes duties to the mortgagor and to third parties interested in the equity of redemption.[105] The equity of redemption need not, for this purpose, have any commercial value.[106] These duties are not limited to a duty of good faith, the extent and scope of the duties depending on the facts of the case. Subject to his primary duty to obtain payment in full of the mortgage debt and interest, he must manage the property with due diligence, which includes the taking of reasonable steps to do so profitably.[107]

On the same basis, a receiver was appointed by a mortgagee of rents and profits receivable under leases containing rent-review clauses who failed to issue rent-review notices thereunder (which he had power to do), whereby increased rents

---

[97] See Ch.23, below, as to the necessity of obtaining permission of the court to take possession in this case.
[98] *Re Hale* [1899] 2 Ch. 107 at 117.
[99] *Thomas v Todd* [1926] 2 K.B. 511.
[100] See para.20-39, below.
[101] *Portman Building Society v Gallwey* [1955] 1 All E.R. 227.
[102] *Jefferys v Dickson* (1865-66) L.R. 1 Ch.App. 183 at 190.
[103] *Gaskell v Gosling* [1896] 1 Q.B. 669 at 692 per Rigby LJ (dissenting), upheld on appeal [1897] A.C. 575 HL.
[104] *Medforth v Blake* [2000] Ch. 86 CA; *Purewal v Countrywide Residential Lettings Ltd* [2015] EWCA Civ 1122.
[105] *Medforth v Blake*, n.104, above.
[106] *Raja v Austin Gray* [2002] EWCA Civ 1965.
[107] *Medforth v Blake*, n.104, above.

would have become payable, was liable in damages to the mortgagors for the sums thereby lost to the mortgaged estate.[108]

If a receiver is proposing to exercise any of his powers negligently (e.g. a sale at one price, when a better offer is available for acceptance) or if he is causing unnecessary injury to the property, he may be restrained from such exercise by the court.[109]

A receiver's duty to obtain the best price reasonably obtainable extends to a duty to a guarantor of the mortgage debt, because of the guarantor's obvious interest that the debt should be paid so far as possible out of the proceeds of sale.[110] Similarly, if the mortgagee interferes, so as to procure the receiver to take a course of action in relation to a sale, such as putting pressure upon him to effect a speedy sale, with the result that the sale takes place at an undervalue, he will be unable to recover the full amount of any shortfall from the guarantor.

A receiver does not owe duties to a bankrupt mortgagor. The receiver's duties are owed instead to the trustee in bankruptcy.[111]

18-34 **Receiver's duties to mortgagor in equity.** A line of authorities considering the duties of a mortgagee, and any receiver appointed by him, have sought to protect the mortgagor against both carelessness on the part of the mortgagee or receiver and too ruthless a pursuit of the mortgagee's interests. In *Palk v Mortgage Services & Funding Plc*,[112] the Court of Appeal declared, obiter, that a mortgagee is not entitled, while preserving his own interests, to conduct himself in a way which unfairly prejudices the mortgagor, such as by taking possession of the mortgaged premises but keeping them empty, hoping that the market will improve. He must not sell hastily, nor at a knock-down price only sufficient to satisfy his own debt. In that case, however, the mortgagee was held not to be in breach of any duty of care to the mortgagor by leasing the mortgaged property instead of selling it. The court differed from the decision in *Re B Johnson & Co (Builders) Ltd*,[113] and did not follow the Privy Council decision in *Downsview Nominees Ltd v First City Corp Ltd*.[114]

The law was thoroughly reviewed, and the position authoritatively stated, in *Silven Properties Ltd v Royal Bank of Scotland plc*.[115] The Court of Appeal reviewed a large number of past decisions, disapproving several, and approving or following others. With respect to the organisation of the sale, *Palk v Mortgage Services Funding Plc*[116] was followed. The *Cuckmere Brick Co Ltd v Mutual Finance Ltd*[117] line of cases was also followed, and *Knight v Lawrence*[118] was approved. The court enunciated the following principles:-

---

[108] *Knight v Lawrence* [1991] B.C.C. 411 VC. The mortgagors were held not to have been guilty of contributory negligence, in not having taken the necessary action themselves.

[109] *Hanson v Derby* (1700) 2 Vern. 392; cf. *Kemohan Estates v Boyd* [1967] N.I. 27.

[110] *Standard Chartered Bank v Walker*, n.90, above, overruling *Barclays Bank Ltd v Thienel* (1978) 247 E.G. 385; *Latchford v Beirne* [1981] 3 All E.R. 705; *American Express International Banking Corp. v Hurley* (1986) 2 B.C.C. 98993.

[111] *Purewal v Countrywide Residential Lettings Ltd* [2015] EWCA Civ 1122.

[112] [1993] Ch. 330 CA.

[113] [1955] Ch. 634 CA.

[114] [1993] A.C. 295 PC (on appeal from New Zealand).

[115] [2003] EWCA Civ 1409; [2003] B.P.I.R. 1409.

[116] [1993] Ch. 330 CA.

[117] [1971] Ch. 949 CA.

[118] [1993] B.C.L.C. 215.

(a)   A receiver owes no duty in contract or in tort to the mortgagor, but owes a fiduciary duty of care in equity to the mortgagor and also to anyone else interested in the equity of redemption.

(b)   A receiver has no right to remain passive if to do so would be damaging to the interests of the mortgagor or the mortgagee. In the absence of a provision to the contrary in the mortgage or his appointment, the receiver must be active in the protection and preservation of the property over which he is appointed.

(c)   The receiver is not managing the mortgagor's property for the benefit of the mortgagor, but managing the security, which is the property of the mortgagee, for the benefit of the mortgagee.

(d)   Not merely does the receiver owe a duty of care to the mortgagee as well as the mortgagor, but his primary duty in exercising powers of management is to try to bring about a situation in which the secured debt is repaid.

(e)   A receiver's management duties will ordinarily impose on him no general duty to exercise a power of sale. But a duty may arise if, for example, mortgaged goods are perishable and a failure to do so would cause loss to the mortgagor and mortgagee.

(f)   In selling mortgaged property, the receiver is under a duty to obtain the best price reasonably obtainable.

(g)   The receiver is entitled to sell mortgaged property in the condition which it is in, and in particular without awaiting or effecting any increase in value or improvement in the property.

(h)   A receiver who takes steps to investigate and (for a period) to proceed with an application for planning permission in respect of mortgaged property is at all times free to halt those steps and exercise his right to proceed with an immediate sale of the property as it is.

(i)   In the case of a breach of the receiver's duty, the appropriate relief is an order that the receiver should account to the persons interested in the equity of redemption for what he would have held as receiver but for his default.

Silven Properties was followed in *Den Norske Bank ASA v Acemex Management Co Ltd*,[119] where it was held that, in the case of the sale of a ship, the mortgagee was entitled to sell at a time and in a place of its own choosing where some other course, such as letting the ship proceed on its voyage, involved certain risks. In *Bell v Long*,[120] the court accepted that no breach of duty occurred when a mortgagee chose to sell certain properties on a portfolio basis, given that the market in question was an uncertain one and the offer received and accepted was a competitive one.

Receipt of rents, etc.   The receiver has power to demand and recover all the   **18-35**
income of which he is appointed receiver. This includes the income arising from trust property, where the interest therein of the mortgagor is included in the mortgage, to the extent of the income to which the mortgagor is entitled in possession, and includes income arising under the statutory trusts from an undivided share to which the mortgagor is entitled, but the receiver has no effective title to this income until notice has been given by him or the mortgagee to the trustees requir-

---

[119]   [2003] EWCA Civ 1559; [2004] 1 Lloyd's Rep. 1.
[120]   [2008] EWHC 1273 Ch; [2008] 2 B.C.L.C. 706.

ing payment.[121] If the mortgagor has leased land together with chattels (e.g. furniture) and the mortgage only extends to the land, the rent must be apportioned between the land and the chattels.[122]

18-36 Notice to tenants. The receiver must give notice to tenants to pay their rents to him. Until he does so, they can, even though aware of the appointment, obtain a valid receipt from the mortgagor.[123] If a receiver has been appointed by the court at the instance of a subsequent incumbrancer, a receiver appointed by a prior incumbrancer cannot claim the future rents without the permission of the court, unless the order, as it usually does and should do, has expressly reserved his right to do so.[124]

As long as a receivership continued, and the receiver's notice to tenants of his appointment had not been withdrawn, no valid distress (the predecessor of commercial rent arrears recovery) could be levied except by the receiver, or by some person including the mortgagor, authorised by him.[125] In the absence of such authority, a mortgagor was restrained by injunction from distraining for rent due from a tenant of part of mortgaged property, even though the receiver may have been negligent in collecting the rents.[126] The fact that rent was payable in advance did not prevent a distress, nor would distress be restrained on that ground after a winding-up order.[127] If a receiver appointed by mortgagees distrained under the statutory power after the title of the mortgagees had come to an end, he could be sued by the tenant, and be made personally liable in damages, on the ground of wrongful distress.[128] The same principles are likely to apply in relation to the commercial rent arrears recovery procedure.

18-37 Position of monies pending payment. Monies in the hands of the receiver do not, until payment over by him to the mortgagee, cease to belong to the mortgagor. If, therefore, the receiver disappears, together with the rents and profits which he has collected, even if those rents and profits exceed the amount of the interest payable, the mortgagor is still liable on his covenants to the mortgagee.[129]

18-38 Application of residue. A mortgagee must pay any balance in his hands, after satisfaction of his claim, to the person entitled to receive it. For this purpose, he must keep proper accounts and produce them to the person so entitled.[130] He cannot invoke a limitation period and pay a prior-ranking mortgagee only six years' interest.[131]

The person to whom the surplus is payable is usually the mortgagor[132] or his personal representatives, or his or their assignees if he or they retain the right to pos-

---

[121] See *Re Pawson's Settlement* [1917] 1 Ch. 541.
[122] See *Salmon v Matthews* (1841) 8 M. & W. 827; *C Hoare & Co v Hove Bungalows* (1912) 56 S.J. 686.
[123] *Vacuum Oil Co Ltd v Ellis* [1914] 1 K.B. 693.
[124] See paras 6-18, 6-28 and 6-29, above.
[125] *Woolston v Ross* [1900] 1 Ch. 788.
[126] *Bayly v Went* (1884) 51 L.T. 764.
[127] *Venner's Electrical Cooking and Heating Appliances, Limited v Thorpe* [1915] 2 Ch. 404.
[128] *Serjeant v Nash, Field & Co* [1903] 2 K.B. 304.
[129] *White v Metcalf* [1903] 2 Ch. 567 at 571; *Re Della Rocella's Estate* [1892] 29 L.R. Ir. 464 at 468.
[130] *Smiths Ltd v Middleton* [1979] 3 All E.R. 842 at 846b per Blackett-Ord V-C.
[131] *Re Thompson's Mortgage Trusts* [1920] 1 Ch. 508.
[132] It was, in consequence, held in Ireland that fidelity bond insurance taken out by a mortgagee, concerning the statutory application by a receiver of his receipts, enures for the benefit of the

session[133] or, if a subsequent incumbrancer has appointed a receiver or become mortgagee in possession, such receiver or incumbrancer. If the mortgagee who appointed the receiver holding a surplus is himself mortgagee in possession, the surplus would be payable to him (without an express direction under s.109(8)(v) of the Law of Property Act 1925): but it is advisable to give an express direction, and it is essential if such mortgagee is not in possession.

In the case of a mortgage of a life interest or other determinable interest, part of the money, not only the surplus in the hands of the receiver, may on the death of the mortgagor represent money to which neither the mortgagor's personal representatives nor his incumbrancers are entitled, e.g. money representing rents paid in advance in respect of a period which determined only after the death of the mortgagor. Where the tenant for life was tenant for life under the Settled Land Act 1925, it seems that a valid receipt for the proportion attributable to the period after his death might be obtained from his personal representative, as his receipt for the rents was a discharge to the tenants: but in the case of land subject to a trust for sale, or personalty, the apportioned part should be paid to the trustees of the settlement.

If the receiver is in doubt as to whom the surplus should be paid, or if the mortgagor cannot be found, and there is no action pending, the receiver might have the point determined under CPR Pt 64, or he might perhaps pay the money into court under s.63 of the Trustee Act 1925

Timber.   The statutory power to cut and sell timber and other trees, conferred by   **18-39**
s.101(1)(iv) of the Law of Property Act 1925 on a mortgagee in possession, does not, apart from express provision in the mortgage, become exercisable on the appointment of a receiver, nor can it be delegated to a receiver if exercisable. It is thought that if the power has been exercised by the mortgagee the proceeds of the timber become applicable as rents and profits; and, having regard to the definition of "income" in s.205(1)(xix) of the Law of Property Act 1925, read with ss.101(1)(iii) and 109(3), that they are payable to the receiver, whether the contract is made before or after his appointment, as regards money unpaid at the date of the appointment. But the purchaser of the timber will require an express direction from the mortgagee before paying the receiver.

Businesses and book debts.   In some cases, book debts are included in a   **18-40**
mortgage made by an individual, and power is conferred on a receiver to carry on a business. In all cases where book debts are included and power is conferred on the receiver to collect such debts, or to get in other money in the nature of capital which is included in the mortgage, notice should be given to the debtors or other persons liable to the mortgagor, or holding the property in trust for him, requiring the debt or other money to be paid to the receiver. The title of the mortgagee and the receiver was held to prevail over that of a garnishor, where the assignment to

---

mortgagor: *Kenny v Employers' Liability Association* [1901] 1 Ir.R. 301.

[133] *White v Metcalf*, n.129, above; *Turner v Walsh* [1909] 2 K.B. 484, explained in *Schalit v Joseph Nadler, Ltd* [1933] 2 K.B. 79. As to what are costs, charges and expenses of the mortgage, see *Re Smith's Mortgage* [1931] 2 Ch. 168, where costs of the successful defence of an action by the mortgagor, claiming to have purchased at an auction, were held not to be payable out of the proceeds of sale.

the mortgagee was before the date of the judgment or after judgment and before service of what is now termed an "interim third party debt order".[134]

In such cases, where the goodwill of a business is expressly or impliedly included in the security, but the stock-in-trade and chattels are not included, the latter must be acquired by purchase from the mortgagor or third persons: but this will be done by the mortgagee, not the receiver. In such cases, it is usually convenient to apply to the court for a receiver in order to obtain directions which will protect the mortgagee.

Where the mortgage confers an express power on the receiver to take possession and carry on a business, it usually appoints the mortgagee or his substitutes as attorneys, to do everything necessary to obtain a transfer: but if it does not, application for the appointment of a receiver should be made to the court.[135]

Where a mortgage authorised the mortgagee to appoint a receiver with power to carry on a business as agent for the mortgagor, it was held that the payment by the receiver of an instalment of a trade debt of the mortgagor operated to raise an implied promise to pay the balance and so to prevent the debt from becoming statute-barred.[136]

18-41 **Foreign property.** In the case of property situated outside the jurisdiction, the statutory powers to collect rents are ineffective. In such cases, the mortgage usually contains provisions for the appointment of the receiver as attorney, or confers powers on him to appoint attorneys to take all necessary steps for collection of rents or recovery of the mortgaged premises. The method by which those steps are taken in any particular case depends upon the law of the country in which the property is situated. Here again, in the absence of such provisions, it is necessary to apply to the court.[137]

18-42 **Discharge of receiver.** A receiver is entitled to a discharge on the termination of his receivership, and as a practical matter it may often be necessary for the mortgagee, or other appointor, to give the receiver an indemnity against all claims which might be made against him arising out of the receivership.

The receiver obtains his discharge from the person or persons who originally appointed him, or in any other way prescribed in his appointment. Apart from express provision, except in the case of an administrative receiver,[138] there are no prescribed formalities, but the receiver usually obtains a release, and frequently a release and an indemnity.

---

[134] See *Hirsch v Coates* [1856] 25 L.J.C.P. 315; *Wise v Birkenshaw* [1860] 29 L.J.Ex. 240; *Glegg v Bromley* [1912] 3 K.B. 474.
[135] See para.9-2, above.
[136] *Re Hale* [1899] 2 Ch. 107. The death of the mortgagor did not affect the power of appointment, and the payment by the receiver operated as if made by his principal the executrix.
[137] See para.3-12, above.
[138] See below, Ch.20.

CHAPTER 19

RECEIVERS APPOINTED UNDER STATUTORY POWERS

Law of Property Act 1925 Pt III. The principal statutory provisions regarding **19-1**
the appointment of a receiver are contained in Pt III of the Law of Property Act
1925, and relate to appointments by mortgagees.[1] There is an express provision[2]
enabling those statutory provisions to be varied or extended by the mortgage deed,
with the like incidents, effects and consequences as if the extension or variation had
been contained in the Act.

Appointment of receiver by mortgagee. By s.101(1)(ii) of the Law of Property **19-2**
Act 1925, a mortgagee whose mortgage is by deed[3] has powers to the like extent
as if the powers had been expressly conferred by the mortgage, at any time after
the mortgage money has become due,[4] to appoint a receiver of the mortgaged
property or any part thereof or, if the mortgaged property consists of an interest in
income or a rentcharge or an annual or other periodical sum, to appoint a receiver
of that property or any part thereof.

Unless there is express provision to the contrary in the mortgage deed,[5] the appointment cannot be made until the mortgagee has become entitled to exercise the
statutory power of sale,[6] that is, unless and until:

   (a)   notice has been served on the mortgagor, or one of several mortgagors,
requiring payment of the mortgage money and there has been default in payment of the money or any part thereof for three months after service;

   (b)   some interest under the mortgage is in arrear and unpaid for two months
after becoming due; or

   (c)   there has been a breach of some provision contained in the mortgage deed
or in the Act on the part of the mortgagee or some other person concurring
in the mortgage, other than the covenant for payment of the mortgage
money or interest.[7]

The statutory power of appointment did not apply to mortgages executed before

---

[1]   For other statutory provisions, see Chs 20, 21, below.

[2]   Law of Property Act 1925 s.101(3).

[3]   Charges registrable under Class A (other than a land improvement charge registered after 31
December 1969), and Class B of the Land Charges Act 1972 s.2(1), (2), (3), if for securing money,
take effect as if they were legal mortgages created by deed, and Law of Property Act 1925 s.101 applies accordingly: see Land Charges Act 1972 s.4(1).

[4]   See *Twentieth Century Banking Corporation Ltd v Wilkinson* [1977] Ch. 99 per Templeman J at
104D–E.

[5]   Law of Property Act 1925 s.101(4).

[6]   Law of Property Act 1925 s.109(1).

[7]   Law of Property Act 1925 s.103.

1882, and applies only if and so far as a contrary provision is not contained in the mortgage deed, and it has effect subject to the provisions of that deed.[8]

The statutory provisions apply to all mortgages or charges by deed, whether legal or equitable.[9]

Apart from express provision, an equitable mortgagee has no right to possession, and can therefore only obtain the rents and profits by means of a receiver[10]: but a subsequent-ranking mortgagee under a legal mortgage now has a legal estate and, subject to the rights of the prior mortgagees, has a right to possession.

A mortgagee of an undivided share in land under a mortgage made before 1926 has the power to appoint a receiver to receive the share of the rents and profits arising under the statutory trusts imposed by the Law of Property Act 1925, from the trustees in whom the land is vested.[11]

Where the mortgage is under hand and the mortgagee has no other power, application must be made to the court if the appointment of a receiver is required, unless the mortgagor concurs in the appointment.

19-3   **Limitations on property subject to appointment.**   Where a mortgage by a mortgagor carrying on a business was only of the real property (a nursing home) where the business was carried on and not also of the business of nursing carried on there, the business and its chattels therefore not being mortgaged, the appointment of a receiver and manager of the business was refused by the court.[12]

19-4   **Method of appointment where pending action.**   Where there is a pending action between the mortgagee and the mortgagor relating to the mortgage, it is preferable that the court should be asked to appoint the receiver, rather than that the mortgagee should exercise his right to effect the appointment out of court.[13]

19-5   **Time for appointment.**   In many cases, the mortgage deed provides that the appointment of a receiver may be made at an earlier date than is provided by the statute. In the case of debentures and other commercial charges, it is usual to provide that the appointment may be made as soon as the principal money has become payable, or if interest is more than a specified number of days in arrear, or as soon as payment of principal or interest has been demanded and default has been made for a specified number of days.

In some cases, a receiver is appointed on the execution of the mortgage[14] (for example, where the mortgage is of short leaseholds or other property held or existing for a limited period, or where the principal is to be repaid by short-dated instalments). In such cases, it was formerly the practice to make the appointment by a separate deed which could be produced to tenants: but as mortgage deeds are now short, it seems simpler to execute the mortgage in duplicate, in order that a counterpart may be handed to the receiver.

In the case of mortgages made after 1925, a power to appoint a receiver or a

---

8   Law of Property Act 1925 s.101(4) and (5).
9   Law of Property Act 1925 s.205(1)(xvi).
10   *Vacuum Oil Co v Ellis* [1914] 1 K.B. 693. The court may apparently let an equitable mortgagee into possession: *Barclays Bank Ltd v Bird* [1954] Ch. 274.
11   Law of Property Act 1925 s.102. Note the position where all the undivided shares are vested in the same mortgagees to secure the same debt. See Sch.I Pt IV para.1(7).
12   *Britannia Building Society v Crammer* [1997] B.P.I.R. 596.
13   *Tillett v Nixon* (1883) 25 Ch. D. 238.
14   As in *The United Realization Company Ltd v Commissioners of Inland Revenue* [1899] 1 Q.B. 361.

power of sale expressed to be exercisable by reason of the mortgagor being adjudicated bankrupt or, being a company, being wound up cannot be exercised solely on the ground of the happening of any of those events, without the permission of the court.[15] If any other event has occurred which renders the power exercisable, permission is not required, even if bankruptcy or winding up has supervened.

An appointment under the statutory power may be made by a mortgagee in possession[16]: and it is submitted that the appointment determines his liability to account, as mortgagee in possession, as regards such part of the property as is let,[17] except where he retains actual possession.

Mortgagor a company.   Where the mortgagor is a company, there are additional requirements and provisions under the Companies Act 2006 and the Insolvency Act 1986 to which attention must be paid. These are dealt with in Chs 20 to 26.   **19-6**

Who may be appointed.   The statute empowers the mortgagee to appoint "such person as he thinks fit" to be receiver.[18] In exercising his power of appointment, the mortgagee is acting in a fiduciary relationship to the mortgagor. He should not, therefore, appoint any person who is incompetent or unable to act with responsibility. The statutory power is apparently wide enough to authorise the mortgagee to appoint himself.[19] In a case where the appointment was made under an express power, the mortgagee himself was not allowed remuneration.[20] But it is difficult to see how, if he can appoint himself as receiver, he could be deprived of the 5 per cent commission to which he is entitled under the express provisions of s.109(6) of the Law of Property Act 1925. Where the mortgagee was a company, and extended powers of management were conferred, it was held that there was no such fiduciary relationship between its directors and the mortgagor as to disentitle one of such directors to remuneration for his services as receiver.[21]   **19-7**

Mode of appointment.   A receiver under the Law of Property Act 1925 is appointed by writing[22] under the hand of the mortgagee[23]: the receiver may in like manner be removed by the mortgagee and a new receiver appointed in his place.[24] The instrument of appointment (and presumably also those of removal and fresh   **19-8**

---

[15] Law of Property Act 1925 ss.110 and 205(1)(i).

[16] *Tillett v Nixon*, n.13, above; *County of Gloucester Bank v Rudry* [1895] 1 Ch. 629.

[17] Notwithstanding dicta to the contrary in *Re Prytherch* (1889) 42 Ch. D. 590: see *Anchor Trust v Bell* [1926] Ch. 805, 817, where, however, the mortgagee's possession was wrongful.

[18] Law of Property Act 1925 s.109(1).

[19] Sed quaere, whether such an appointment would not conflict with the principle that a mortgagee is entitled to nothing more than principal, interest and costs. In *Mace Builders (Glasgow) Ltd v Lunn* [1987] Ch. 191 CA, Sir John Donaldson MR, at 197B, remarked: "It must be emphasised that we are not concerned with the particular consequences of the defendant's having combined the roles of managing director, debenture holder and receiver."

[20] *Nicholson v Tutin* (1857) 3 Kay & J. 159: including one of several mortgages.

[21] Per Cozens-Hardy MR and Buckley LJ in *Bath v Standard Land Co* [1911] 1 Ch. 618, 626, 646, disapproving *Kavanagh v Workingman's Benefit Building Society* [1896] 1 Ir.R. 56. It is not unusual for a building society mortgage to contain an express provision authorising an official of the society to be appointed receiver: but, semble, this power exists without express provision.

[22] As to a possibly invalid deed taking effect as an appointment in writing, see *Windsor Refrigerator Co. Ltd v Branch Nominees Ltd* [1961] Ch. 375.

[23] Law of Property Act 1925 s.109(1).

[24] Law of Property Act 1925 s.109(5).

appointment) may be prepared in advance and left until required.[25] An appointment may be made in like manner on the death of a receiver.[26]

The appointment takes effect when the instrument of appointment is handed to the receiver in such circumstances that the fact of the appointment is communicated to him and he accepts the appointment.[27] The date of the instrument of appointment is irrelevant.[28]

The instrument of appointment may include a delegation by the mortgagee to the receiver of the powers of leasing and accepting surrenders of leases or any specified lease exercisable by the mortgagee,[29] a direction to insure the mortgaged property or any part thereof,[30] and a direction to apply the balance of any money remaining after providing for the payments referred to in sub-paras (i)-(iv) of s.109(8) in or towards discharge of the principal money owing to the mortgagee.[31] These matters or any of them can, however, be dealt with by separate directions after the appointment. Where extended powers are conferred by the mortgage, it may be desirable to deal with them in the appointment.

In the case of a transfer of a registered charge of registered land by the original mortgagee, the power of appointment remains in him until the transferee is registered. Any person ostensibly appointed receiver by the transferee prior to such registration is merely his own agent.[32]

If it is considered necessary to appoint the receiver to be attorney, e.g. to execute a conveyance in the name of the mortgagee, his appointment as receiver must be by deed, if his appointment as attorney is included therein.[33] But where the mortgage contains an express delegation to a receiver of a power to execute a deed and convey in the name of the mortgagor, the appointment can be made under hand; the execution as a deed by the mortgagor of the mortgage containing such a provision is sufficient.

19-9 **Priorities.** If appointed by a subsequent-ranking mortgagee, the receiver is displaced if a prior-ranking encumbrancer appoints a receiver. If a receiver has been appointed by the court of a judgment creditor at the instance of a puisne incumbrancer, a prior incumbrancer can appoint a receiver under the statute, but, unless the order appointing a receiver expressly reserves the rights of subsequent incumbrancers, application must be made to the court for discharge of its receiver.[34] The statutory receiver is entitled only to rents unpaid at the date of service of the application notice for discharge.[35]

19-10 **Effect of appointment.** A receiver appointed under the Law of Property Act 1925

---

[25] *Windsor Refrigerator Co. Ltd v Branch Nominees Ltd*, n.22, above.
[26] *Re Hill* [1920] W.N. 386.
[27] *R.A. Cripps & Son Ltd v Wickenden* [1973] 1 W.L.R. 944 at 953 per Goff J.
[28] *R.A. Cripps & Son Ltd v Wickenden*, n.27, above.
[29] Law of Property Act 1925 ss.99(19), 100(13).
[30] Under Law of Property Act 1925 s.109(7).
[31] Law of Property Act 1925 s.109(8)(v).
[32] *Lever Finance Ltd v Needleman's Trustee* [1956] Ch. 375.
[33] As the mortgagee's power of sale is not fiduciary (see *Kennedy v de Trafford* [1897] A.C. 180), semble it can be delegated; but as to building societies, see *Reliance Permanent Building Society v Harwood-Stamper* [1944] Ch. 362. See also *Cuckmere Brick Co Ltd v Mutual Finance Ltd* [1971] Ch. 949, as to the duty not to exercise the power negligently.
[34] See *Re Metropolitan Amalgamated Estates, Ltd* [1912] 2 Ch. 497; *Underhay v Read* (1887) 20 Q.B.D. 209.
[35] *Thomas v Brigstocke* (1827) 4 Russ. 64; *Preston v Tunbridge Wells Opera House, Ltd* [1903] 2 Ch. 323, 325; *Re Metropolitan Amalgamated Estates, Ltd*, n.34, above.

is deemed to be the agent of the mortgagor, who is liable for his acts and defaults, unless the mortgage deed otherwise expressly provides (which it seldom, if ever, does).[36] He has power to demand and recover all the income of which he is appointed receiver, in the name of the mortgagor or the mortgagee, to the full extent of the interest which the mortgagor could dispose of, and to give effectual receipts and to exercise any powers delegated to him by the mortgagee pursuant to the Act.[37] The appointment does not prevent the mortgagee from suing for the mortgage debt.[38]

The effect of the appointment is to determine the interest in possession of the mortgagor. The title of the receiver therefore prevails over that of a receiver for a judgment creditor, whether such receiver be appointed with or without the creation of a charge, which would of course be a subsequent charge only.[39] Thus, a landlord who, under the practice prior to 1957, had obtained possession under an *elegit* on a judgment for the rent,[40] was entitled after a receiver had been appointed by a mortgagee to distrain for rent accrued due thereafter, on the ground that his interest by *elegit* had been determined by the appointment.[41]

As the receiver is agent for the mortgagor, there is no change of occupation if the receiver obtains possession, so as to entitle the receiver to insist on entering into a new agreement for supply of water, gas or electric power without payment of arrears.[42]

But where the mortgagor is in occupation, a receiver appointed under the Law of Property Act 1925 has no power to recover possession against him by force of his own title: he has only a right to recover the rents, although if he can recover possession he can let, if the power to do so has been delegated to him.[43] If the mortgage deed confers on the receiver a right to take possession, presumably he can claim possession against the mortgagor: but if he does not, the mortgagee must either himself claim possession,[44] and thus assume the liability of a mortgagee in possession, or commence foreclosure proceedings and obtain the appointment of a receiver and apply for an order for possession to be given to the receiver, or that the mortgagor attorn tenant at a rent.[45]

After the appointment, the mortgagor is presumably unable to carry out commercial rent arrears recovery without the receiver's authority, even if the receiver neglects or refuses to do so.[46] If the receiver sues in the name of the mortgagor, the tenant can maintain a counterclaim against the mortgagor, e.g. on covenants by the mortgagor in the lease.

---

[36] Law of Property Act 1925 s.109(2): see para.19-12, below.

[37] Law of Property Act 1925 s.109(3).

[38] *Lynde v Waithman* [1895] 2 Q.B. 180, 184, 188; *Poulett v Hill* [1893] 1 Ch. 277.

[39] The permission of the court will be required for the receiver appointed out of court to displace the possession of the receiver appointed by the court, unless the order otherwise provides.

[40] *Elegits* were abolished on 1 January 1957; see now Charging Orders Act 1979 s.3; Senior Courts Act 1981 s.37(4).

[41] *Johns v Pink* [1900] 1 Ch. 296.

[42] See *Wellworth Cash & Carry (North Shields) Ltd. v North Eastern Electricity Board* (1986) 2 B.C.C. 99265.

[43] Under s.99(19).

[44] Under CPR Pt 55. See also PD 55A.

[45] It is submitted that if the receiver, after delegation of the power to him, creates a tenancy the tenant could claim possession against the mortgagor.

[46] *Bayly v Went* (1884) 51 L.T. 764; *Woolston v Ross* [1900]1 Ch. 788.

19-11 Powers which can be delegated by mortgagee. The powers which can be delegated to the receiver by the mortgagee include:

(a) Power to create leases or tenancies, which may in the case of agricultural or occupation leases be for a term not exceeding 21 years, or, provided that the mortgage was made after 1925, not exceeding 50 years, and in the case of building leases not exceeding 90 years, or where the mortgage has been made after 1925, 999 years. All leases must take effect in possession within 12 months, and the best rent must be reserved and no fine taken.[47] Leases must contain a covenant for payment of rent, and a proviso for re-entry if rent is in arrear for any period not exceeding 30 days. A counterpart must be executed by the lessee.[48] The lease must, if practicable, be granted in the name of the mortgagee,[49] since if covenants, other than the usual qualified covenant for quiet enjoyment, are entered into by the lessor there is no power without express authority to bind the mortgagor by such covenants. In general, the mortgagee's power to lease only applies to legal mortgages— apart from express provision in the mortgage, an equitable mortgagee is not entitled to possession,[50] and is therefore not within subs.(2) of s.99. It follows that a receiver appointed by an equitable mortgagee cannot usually create a lease, for he can do so only in the same manner as if the mortgagee, his appointor, were in possession.[51]

(b) Power to accept surrenders for the purpose of enabling new leases to be granted.[52]

(c) Power to insure up to two-thirds of the sum required to rebuild, unless there is a provision in the mortgage deed that no insurance is required, or unless insurance is kept up by the mortgagor in accordance with the mortgage deed or under an agreement with the mortgagee up to the full amount specified above.[53]

19-12 Agency for mortgagor. The agency of the receiver for the mortgagor is a statutory recognition of the previous conveyancing practice of making the mortgagee's appointee the agent of the mortgagor.[54] The agency is, however, a real one:

"[The receiver] must be faithful to [the mortgagor]; he must act in his interest; he must protect him against claims which are not sustainable; he must not assume liabilities which cannot be enforced against his principal".[55]

The receiver is agent of the mortgagor only, however, for so long as his appoint-

---

[47] In the case of a building lease, a peppercorn rent for any period up to five years is permissible: Law of Property Act 1925 s.99(10). The power to create leases and tenancies does not apply to any mortgages still extant and made before 1882.
[48] Law of Property Act 1925 s.99. The section also applies to agreements for lease, s.99(17).
[49] Law of Property Act 1925 ss.7(4) and 8.
[50] Cf. n.10, above.
[51] Law of Property Act 1925 s.99(19).
[52] Law of Property Act 1925 s.100, q.v. as to conditions to be observed.
[53] Law of Property Act 1925 ss.109(7) and 108, q.v. as to application of insurance money.
[54] *Jefferys v Dickson* (1865-66) L.R. 1 Ch.App. 183; *Gosling v Gaskell and Grocott* [1897] A.C. 575.
[55] *Hibernian Bank v Yourell (No.2)* [1919] 1 Ir.R. 310 at 312 per O'Connor MR. For an example of an action against a receiver for an account and damages for breach of duty and negligence brought by his principal (in this case a company), see *Smiths Ltd v Middleton* [1986] 1 W.L.R. 598, which was applied in *Rottenberg v Monjack* [1992] B.C.C. 688; see also para.19-15, below.

ment by the mortgagee is effective, and, accordingly, he ceases to be such agent when that appointment is superseded by one made by the court. Thus, where a receiver was appointed by a mortgagee of leaseholds, and was subsequently appointed by the court as receiver of the same leaseholds, the ground landlord could not claim to be paid ground rent out of money in the hands of the receiver as representing the property of the mortgagor.[56]

Receipts of rents, etc   The receiver may proceed by action, commercial rent arrears recovery, or otherwise, in the name of either the mortgagor or the mortgagee, to the full extent of the estate or interest which the mortgagor could dispose of.[57] He can give effectual receipts for such income.[58] Generally, he may exercise any powers which may have been delegated to him by the mortgagee, pursuant to the Law of Property Act 1925.[59] These do not include a power to forfeit a lease for nonpayment of rent.   **19-13**

Notice to tenants.   Section 141(2) of the Law of Property Act 1925 provides that any rent, covenant or right to possession reserved by or contained in a lease is capable of being recovered, enforced and taken advantage of by the person from time to time entitled, subject to the term, to the income of the land leased. It deals with procedure only, and means that a person entitled to the rent, to the exclusion of all others, may sue. This does not entitle a beneficiary to sue without joinder of the trustee, or to carry out commercial rent arrears recovery.[60] Where, therefore, the mortgagor is a beneficiary under a trust for him, the receiver cannot carry out commercial rent arrears recovery in his name.   **19-14**

A person paying money to the receiver is not concerned to inquire whether any event has happened to authorise the receiver to act.[61]

Removal or death of receiver.   The receiver may be removed and a new receiver may be appointed, from time to time, by the mortgagee by writing under his hand.[62] By analogy with the time of appointment,[63] removal presumably takes effect at the time of communication of the removal to the receiver.   **19-15**

If money stands to the credit of a receiver at a bank as agent for a mortgagor, it is doubtful whether the bank is bound to transfer the account to a new receiver on the demand of the latter.[64]

If the receiver is discharged or dies and a new receiver is appointed in his place without undue delay, the receivership is regarded as continuous.[65] If, after the death of a receiver, the mortgagor attempts to collect rent before the mortgagee has had an opportunity of appointing a new receiver, he might be restrained by injunction. A tenant would be well advised to withhold the rent in such circumstances: it is doubtful whether he would obtain a valid receipt from the mortgagor.

---

[56] *Hand v Blow* [1901] 2 Ch. 721.
[57] Law of Property Act 1925 s.109(3).
[58] See n.57, above.
[59] See n.57, above.
[60] *Schalit v Joseph Nadler Ltd* [1933] 2 K.B. 79.
[61] Law of Property Act 1925 s.109(4).
[62] Law of Property Act 1925 s.109(5).
[63] See para.18-10, above.
[64] See *Société Coloniale Anversoise v London and Brazilian Bank* [1911] 2 K.B. 1024. In a proper case, an injunction and an order for transfer could be obtained in an action against the first receiver, the company or other mortgagor, with or without the mortgagee being claimant.
[65] *Re White's Mortgage* [1943] Ch. 166.

19-16 **Application of monies received.** The statutory provisions as to the application by the receiver of monies in his hands define the rights as between the mortgagor and the mortgagee, and the mortgagee and puisne incumbrancers.[66] They do not enable a third person to maintain an action against a receiver for arrears.[67] They impose a statutory duty upon the receiver pursuant to which the mortgagee can maintain an action against the receiver for an account of the money that comes to his hands and its application.[68] The mortgagor could also maintain an action, since the receiver is his agent, but at his own risk as to costs. In an Irish case, where the receiver had given a bond to the mortgagee, the mortgagor was held entitled to maintain an action against the surety, joining the mortgagee as obligee of the bond as co-claimant, to recover a sum equal to that which the receiver had failed to pay to the mortgagee, and which had in consequence been raised by sale of part of the mortgaged property. It is considered that where a receiver with monies in his hands negligently omits to make payments, e.g. for sums analogous to council tax, the mortgagor might sue for damages thereby caused.

Where neither mortgagor nor mortgagee has any interest in the making of a proposed payment, then, since the creditor cannot enforce payment, the receiver may safely disregard the order of application set out in s.109(8) if he is so minded. It was doubtless for this reason that Brightman J in *Re John Willment (Ashford) Ltd*[69] was prepared to concede that in many cases a receiver may indeed have a discretion under that provision.

19-17 **Mode of application of monies in hand.** The statutory mode of application, directed by s.109(8) of the Law of Property Act 1925,[70] of monies in the receiver's hands, is as follows:

> (a) "In discharge of all rents, taxes, rates, and outgoings whatever affecting the mortgaged property."

This includes arrears of rents and taxes, business rates and council tax assessed upon the property, water and sewerage charges, and payments for gas and electric power, and possibly also telecommunications services. As already stated, s.109 does not enable the persons or incorporated bodies who are entitled to these payments to maintain an action against the receiver.[71] The receiver is usually required to pay arrears of charges for water, gas and electric power if the supplies are to be continued.

The statutory provisions may be varied by agreement between the mortgagee and the mortgagor, but not by a direction given by the mortgagee alone.[72]

Neither para.(i) nor para.(iii) of s.109(8) authorises the receiver to pay an unsecured debt of the mortgagor, even though incurred, e.g. for repairs executed on the instruction of the receiver.[73] Any such payment, in the absence of agreement, could only be justified if the payment were made on the direction of the mortgagee out of monies payable to him under s.109(8)(v).

---

[66] Law of Property Act 1925 s.109(8). *Yourell v Hibernian Bank, Limited* [1918] A.C. 372 at 386, 387 per Lord Atkinson.

[67] *Liverpool Corporation v Hope* [1938] 1 K.B. 751; see also *Re John Willment (Ashford) Ltd* [1980] 1 W.L.R. 73 and *Sargent v Customs and Excise Commissioners* [1994] 1 W.L.R. 235.

[68] *Leicester Permanent Building Society v Butt* [1943] Ch. 308; *Smiths Ltd v Middleton (No.1)* [1979] 3 All E.R. 842, at 845, 846 per Blackett-Ord V-C.

[69] [1980] 1 W.L.R. 73 at 77.

[70] See *Yourell v Hibernian Bank, Limited*, n.66, above.

[71] See n.66, above.

[72] *Yourell v Hibernian Bank, Limited*, n.66, above.

[73] See *White v Metcalf* [1903] 2 Ch. 567.

Where, however, the mortgage conferred wide powers to carry on a business and pay outgoings, the payment by the receiver of an instalment of a trade debt of the mortgagor was sufficient to raise an implied promise by the executrix of the mortgagor, who was dead at the date of the appointment,[74] to pay the balance, and thus prevent the debt from becoming statute-barred.[75]

(b) "In keeping down all annual sums or other payments and the interest on all principal sums, having priority to the mortgage in right whereof he is receiver."

Under the corresponding provision of the Conveyancing Act 1881, the receiver was held not entitled to justify a payment in reduction of principal[76]: but now a direction in writing by the mortgagee under para.(v) would justify such a payment.

Statute-barred interest can be paid either by the receiver or by the mortgagee out of money paid to him by the receiver.[77]

(c) "In payment of his commission, and of the premiums on fire, life, or other insurances, if any, properly payable under the mortgage deed, or under this Act, and the cost of executing necessary or proper repairs directed in writing by the mortgagee."

The rate of commission (which includes remuneration and all costs, charges and expenses incurred by the receiver[78]) is such rate (not exceeding 5% on the gross amount of all monies received[79]) as is specified in his appointment, and, if no rate is specified, then that rate on such amount, or such other rate as the court thinks fit to allow on an application by the receiver made for that purpose.[80] If the mortgage fixes the rate, it cannot be varied by the appointment. The rate will only be varied by the court in exceptional circumstances, as for example where the expense and difficulty of collecting the rents has been seriously increased. The application by the receiver can be made in foreclosure or redemption proceedings.[81]

Where the receiver has paid off the mortgagee's debt before drawing his remuneration, and assets remain in his hands unrealised, the company may be entitled to restrain further realisations, until a dispute as to the amount of his remuneration has been determined.[82]

Premiums include premiums on insurances of the mortgaged property subsisting at the date of the appointment or effected under s.108 of the Law of Property Act 1925, and on life or other policies comprised in the mortgage.

Repairs include any necessary or proper repairs, even though the mortgagee could not execute them without making himself liable as being in possession. The

---

74 See definition of "mortgagor" in Law of Property Act 1925 s.205(1)(xvi).
75 *Re Hale* [1899] 2 Ch. 107.
76 *Yourell v Hibernian Bank, Limited*, n.65, above. This defect was, however, cured by the assent of both parties.
77 *Hibernian Bank v Yourell (No.2)* [1919] 1 Ir.R. 310.
78 This does not include the mortgagee's costs of the appointment.
79 It would appear from this that, if a power of sale is conferred by the mortgage upon a receiver, and he exercises such power, he will be entitled to a percentage of the sale price; aliter, if a sale is effected by the mortgagee under the statutory power.
80 Law of Property Act 1925 s.109(6). Such an application is only required where the receiver wishes to obtain a rate of remuneration in excess of 5%: *Marshall v Cottingham* [1982] Ch. 82.
81 Semble, in the absence of such proceedings, it could be made by application notice, to which the mortgagor and mortgagee would be respondents.
82 *Rottenberg v Monjack* [1992] B.C.C. 688: see para.18-33, above.

cost of repairs arranged by the receiver will not be allowed him, in his accounts as against the mortgagee, unless the same are executed on the written instructions of the mortgagee.[83] If verbally directed by the mortgagee, the expenditure by the receiver might be justified against the mortgagee, but not against the mortgagor; nor can they be justified against the mortgagee if paid on the mortgagor's direction.

(d) "In payment of the interest accruing due in respect of any principal money due under the mortgage."[84]

By virtue of this provision, a receiver appointed by a mortgagee is bound to pay any arrears of interest due to the mortgagee at the date of his appointment, as well as interest accruing due subsequently,[85] but not statute-barred arrears.[86]

In cases in which a mortgagee receives, or is owed, sums in respect of interest from the mortgagor net of income tax, the mortgagee, and perhaps also a receiver, can apply an adequate part of the proceeds of the mortgaged property in payment of tax on the amount receivable as interest.[87]

(e) "In or towards discharge of the principal money if so directed in writing by the mortgagee."[88]

This direction may be given in the instrument of appointment, or at any time while the receiver retains money in his hands. Many mortgages made before 1926 contained an express power to the same effect as this direction.

19-18 Position of monies pending payment. The monies in the hands of the receiver do not, until payment over by him to the mortgagee, cease to belong to the mortgagor. If, therefore, the receiver disappears, together with the rents and profits which he has collected, even if those rents and profits exceed the amount of the interest payable, the mortgagor is still liable on his covenants to the mortgagee.[89]

19-19 Application of residue. The residue of the money received by the receiver is payable to the person who, but for the possession of the receiver, would have been entitled to receive the income of which the receiver was appointed, or who is otherwise entitled to the mortgaged property.[90] A mortgagee must pay any balance in his hands, after satisfaction of his claim,[91] to the person entitled to receive it. For this purpose, he must keep proper accounts and produce them to the person so entitled.[92] He cannot invoke a limitation period and pay a prior-ranking mortgagee only six years' interest.[93]

19-20 Sale. In the absence of express provisions in the mortgage, the receiver has no power to sell or convey, nor can an equitable mortgagee convey the legal estate un-

---

83 See n.66, above.
84 Law of Property Act 1925 s.109(8)(iv).
85 *National Bank v Kenny* [1898] 1 Ir.R. 197.
86 *Hibernian Bank v Yourell (No.2)*, n.77, above.
87 *Hollis v Wingfield* [1940] Ch. 335; see *Howell v IRC* [1939] 2 K.B. 597.
88 Law of Property Act 1925 s.109(8)(v).
89 *White v Metcalf*, n.72, above, at 571; *Re Della Rocella's Estate* [1892] 29 L.R. Ir. 464 at 468.
90 Law of Property Act 1925 s.109(8).
91 As to costs, charges and expenses of the mortgagee deductible from sale proceeds under Law of Property Act 1925 s.105, see *Re Smith's Mortgage* [1931] 2 Ch. 168 (costs of the successful defence of an action by the mortgagor not deductible).
92 *Smiths Ltd v Middleton* [1979] 3 All E.R. 842, 846b per Blackett-Ord V-C.
93 *Re Thompson's Mortgage Trusts* [1920] 1 Ch. 508.

less the charge is by deed and expressed to be by way of legal mortgage.[94] But in an action brought for realisation of the security, or for redemption or foreclosure, the court may order or direct a sale, and may make a vesting order in favour of the purchaser, or alternatively create and vest in the mortgagee a mortgage term sufficient to enable him to carry out the sale.[95] Debentures and other equitable mortgages often confer on a receiver power to sell the mortgaged property, and to convey the legal estate in the name of the mortgagor or mortgagee, and usually exclude the restriction imposed by s.103 as to the time for exercise of such power. An irrevocable power of attorney so conferred is unaffected by the death, disability, bankruptcy or winding up of the mortgagor.[96]

Upon a sale of freehold or leasehold property, the mortgagee cannot convey the legal estate in fee simple or for a term of years under the Law of Property Act 1925 s.104 unless the contract is entered into by him. Where the contract has been entered into by the receiver, the concurrence of the mortgagee is essential, unless the receiver has express power to convey in his name, as well as in the name of the mortgagor. On a sale by the receiver upon whom the statutory powers of a mortgagee are conferred by reference, minerals may be severed and conveyed, and reserved easements may be granted and restrictions imposed on land retained or the land sold.[97]

Power to appoint—rentcharges and similar charges. By s.122 of the Law of Property Act 1925, power is conferred on a person entitled to a rentcharge or other annual sum (not being rent incident to a reversion),[98] charged on or issuing out of another rentcharge or other annual sum charged on land or payable out of the income of land, to appoint a receiver over the rentcharge or annual sum on which his rentcharge is charged if any instalment of the latter is in arrear and unpaid for 21 days. The provisions of the Act relating to the appointment, powers, remuneration and duties of a receiver appointed by a mortgagee apply to such a receiver.[99]   **19-21**

The remedies of a person entitled to a rentcharge, created under the Improvement of Land Act 1864 or any special Improvement Act, are limited to the remedies given by s.121 of the Law of Property Act 1925.[100] He cannot appoint a receiver, but after a legal mortgage has been created under s.121(4), the mortgagee could do so.

Charges under other statutes. Powers of appointing a receiver to enforce certain statutory charges[101] are conferred on local authorities by s.212(3) of the Highways Act 1980 and by other statutes.   **19-22**

---

94 *Swift 1st Limited v Colin* [2011] EWHC 2410 (Ch).
95 Law of Property Act 1925 ss.90 and 91.
96 Powers of Attorney Act 1971 s.4.
97 In the case of mortgages made before 1912, those provisions do not apply. An order can instead be obtained under the Law of Property Act 1925 s.92.
98 I.e. payable under a sub-lease.
99 These provisions are in substitution for the remedies conferred on the holder of a rentcharge by Law of Property Act 1925 s.121, which include powers to carry out commercial rent arrears recovery and enter into possession: they are given because the holder of a sub-rentcharge has no power to carry out commercial rent arrears recovery.
100 See Law of Property Act 1925 s.207(c).
101 As to priority over all other charges, see *Paddington Borough Council v Finucane* [1928] Ch. 567.

19-23   Extension of statutory powers.   As already indicated,[102] the statutory powers given to a receiver by the Law of Property Act 1925, which are limited to the collection and application of income arising from the mortgaged property, are inappropriate where property such as book debts or a business are included in the security. In such cases, the mortgage or debenture usually confers an express power on the receiver to collect and get in the book debts and to carry on the business. In the absence of such an express power, application should be made to the court for the appointment of a receiver, as an appointment out of court is ineffective. The cases relating to the carrying on by a receiver appointed by a mortgagee of a business are almost invariably cases where the mortgagor is a company, and are dealt with in Chs 20 to 26. In other cases, the provisions of the Bills of Sale Acts usually render such charges inappropriate or invalid.

19-24   Armed forces—restriction on appointment of receiver.   Under the provisions of the Reserve and Auxiliary Forces (Protection of Civil Interests) Act 1951, a person is not entitled, in the cases to which Pt I of that Act applies,[103] without permission of the appropriate court, to exercise any remedy which is available to him by way of (among other things) taking possession, appointment of a receiver of any property, re-entry upon any land or realisation of any security.[104] The restriction does not affect the mortgagee's power of sale of land or an interest therein where the mortgagee is in possession at the relevant date,[105] or has appointed a receiver who is in possession or in receipt of the rents and profits at that date.[106] Where a receiver who has been appointed and is in possession or in receipt of the rents and profits on the relevant date dies or is removed after that date, permission is not required to appoint another in his place, if the appointment is made with reasonable promptness. If there is a substantial interval, the appointment will be regarded as a new one and leave will be required.[107]

Where, as was formerly a common practice, a receiver approved by the mortgagee was appointed by the mortgage itself or a contemporaneous deed, the case was outside the Reserve and Auxiliary Forces (Protection of Civil Interests) Act 1951, even if the receiver was not to act until interest was in arrear and at all events if no notice or requirement by the mortgagee was necessary before he could act, since in such cases no step was taken by the mortgagee to exercise any remedy.[108]

19-25   Rent Act 1977.   Although the provisions contained in the Rent Act 1977 restricting the enforcement of a mortgagee's remedies[109] were amended to exclude "controlled" mortgages by the Housing Act 1980, the provisions entitling a mortgagor under a "regulated" mortgage to apply to the court for relief in certain

---

[102] See para.18-40, above.
[103] See Reserve and Auxiliary Forces (Protection of Civil Interests) Act 1951 s.3 (being, broadly, periods of military service of certain types, specified in Sch.1 to that Act).
[104] Reserve and Auxiliary Forces (Protection of Civil Interests) Act 1951 s.2(2)(a).
[105] For definition, see Reserve and Auxiliary Forces (Protection of Civil Interests) Act 1951 s.3(10).
[106] Reserve and Auxiliary Forces (Protection of Civil Interests) Act 1951 s.2(2), proviso.
[107] *Re White's Mortgage* [1943] Ch. 166.
[108] But if the receiver's power is conferred by reference to Law of Property Act 1925, permission might be required before giving a direction under s.109(8)(v): the mortgage deed or contemporaneous deed can, however, make express provision for the application of the surplus.
[109] Rent Act 1977 ss.129–136 and Sch.19.

circumstances still apply, in respect of mortgages created before certain dates, the latest of which is 14 August 1974.[110]

On any such application, the court, if satisfied that, by reason of the circumstances and of the operation of the Rent Act 1977 the mortgagor would suffer severe financial hardship, may make such order limiting the rate of interest, extending the time for the repayment of the principal money or otherwise varying the terms of the mortgage or imposing any limitation or condition on the exercise of any right of remedy (which clearly includes the appointment of a receiver), as the court thinks appropriate.[111] The court may revoke any such order by a subsequent order.[112]

---

[110] Rent Act 1977 ss.129(2), 131 and 132.

[111] Rent Act 1977 s.132(2). Where an order is made, the court can, if appropriate, on the application of the mortgagee, apportion the mortgage money between dwelling-houses and other land, in which case the mortgage will take effect as if it were two separate mortgages: Rent Act 1977 s.132(3), (4).

[112] Rent Act 1977 s.132(5).

CHAPTER 20

RECEIVERS APPOINTED OVER PROPERTY OF A COMPANY
(OTHER THAN ADMINISTRATIVE RECEIVERS)

20-1   Receivers of company property—ordinary receivers and administrative receivers.   This chapter deals with those points which are specific to ordinary receivers appointed out of court over property owned by companies, such points being additional to those set out in Ch.18, above. It does not deal with receivers who constitute "administrative receivers".[1]

Administrative receivers are receivers of all or substantially all the property of a company appointed by the holder of a floating charge (with or without any fixed charges in addition to the floating charge).[2] Such charges are typically comprised in the security document now generally called a debenture. Administrative receivers of companies can be appointed only in very limited circumstances,[3] namely under charges granted prior to 15 September 2003 and under charges which are granted on or after that date and which relate to the situations, and satisfy the criteria, specified in ss.72B–72GA of the Insolvency Act 1986.[4]

This chapter therefore applies only to receivers appointed under fixed charges granted by companies or under floating charges in the (relatively unusual) situation where the appointment does not, for some reason, relate to all or substantially all the property of the company. In this chapter, accordingly, references to the position where a receiver is appointed under a floating charge presuppose that the receiver is not appointed over all or substantially all the property of the company (and is therefore not an administrative receiver).

20-2   The meaning of "receiver" in the Insolvency Act 1986.   Any reference in the Insolvency Act 1986 to a receiver or manager, or merely a receiver, of the property of a company includes, unless the context otherwise requires, a receiver or manager, or a receiver, of part only of that property, and a receiver only of the income arising from the property of the company or from part of that property.[5] Any reference in that Act to the appointment of a receiver or manager under powers contained in

---

[1]   Administrative receivers are dealt with in Chs 21–26, below.
[2]   Insolvency Act 1986 s.29(2).
[3]   Insolvency Act 1986 s.72A. Entities other than companies are not affected; Insolvency Act 1986 s.72A and *Re Dairy Farmers of Britain Ltd* [2009] EWHC 1389 (Ch) (which related to an industrial and provident society).
[4]   Those situations relate to: capital market arrangements and investments, public-private partnership projects, utility projects, urban regeneration projects, certain project finance situations, financial market charges, registered social landlords, certain water and sewerage companies, protected railway companies, and entities with air traffic control licences (such list being subject to any additions or amendments made by the Secretary of State).
[5]   Insolvency Act 1986 s.29(1)(a).

an instrument includes an appointment made under powers which, by virtue of any enactment, are implied in and have effect as if contained in an instrument.[6]

The application of the Insolvency (England and Wales) Rules 2016. The Insolvency (England and Wales) Rules 2016 provide that:

    20-3

(a) rule 4.1, which regulates the appointment of receivers and acceptance of appointment, applies to all receivers to whom the Insolvency Act 1986 Pt III (Receivership) applies (other than receivers in Scottish receiverships);

(b) rules 4.23 and 4.24, which relate to the distribution of the prescribed part of a company's net property, apply to all receivers appointed under a floating charge other than administrative receivers.[7]

Power of appointment: mortgages and charges In the case of a mortgage or charge created by a company, the statutory power of appointing a receiver applies, as in the case of any other mortgage or charge.[8] But in general, although the powers of such a receiver are the same as in any other case, he will be subject to additional statutory duties and liabilities.[9]

    20-4

If the prescribed particulars of a mortgage or charge are not duly filed with the registrar of companies, then it, and any appointment of a receiver made thereunder,[10] will become invalid as between the company and the mortgagee or chargee, and as against a liquidator or administrator and all other creditors of the company, if the company subsequently goes into liquidation or administration.[11] A proposed receiver should accordingly ensure that the document under which he is proposed to be appointed has been registered.[12] A certificate of registration of a charge out of time was conclusive, where it was issued pursuant to a valid order, even where it contained certain mistakes.[13]

A chargee may appoint a receiver notwithstanding that the chargor company has gone into liquidation.[14]

Power of appointment: under debentures and other instruments containing floating charges. In this chapter, "debenture" is used to mean security documents containing fixed charges and a floating charge (in the modern sense).

    20-5

Where a company issued debentures creating a charge by deed, the debenture-holders were entitled, even in the absence of any express provision, to rely on the statutory power to appoint a receiver, at any time after the security had crystallised, provided that they all concurred in the appointment.[15]

Assignment of debentures: tacking. The assignment of a debenture by the holder conveys to the assignee no greater rights than the assignor possesses at the

    20-6

---

6 Insolvency Act 1986 s.29(1)(b).
7 Insolvency (England and Wales) Rules 2016 r.4.22.
8 See Ch.19, above, "Receivers appointed under statutory powers".
9 See para.20-25, below: "Enforcement of duties".
10 *Burston Finance Ltd v Speirway Ltd* [1974] 1 W.L.R. 1648 at 1657. See also *Cheltenham & Gloucester Plc v Appleyard* [2004] EWCA Civ 291.
11 Companies Act 2006 s.859H.
12 Companies Act 2006 s.859A.
13 *Exeter Trust Ltd v Screenways Ltd* [1991] B.C.L.C. 888.
14 *Re Henry Pound, Son, & Hutchins* (1889) 42 Ch. D. 402; *Re Potters Oils Ltd. (No.2)* [1986] 1 W.L.R. 201.
15 See *Deyes v Wood* [1911] 1 K.B. 806.

date of the assignment. Where all the monies borrowed and accrued due under an "all monies debenture" had been repaid by the borrower, and contingent liabilities thereby secured had been discharged, the borrower had acquired an indefeasible right of redemption, which was binding on the assignee. The assignee could not, without the consent of the borrower, tack his pre-existing debts owed by the borrower on to the assigned debenture, so as thereby to obtain security for them; he could neither demand payment of them, nor validly appoint an administrative receiver for non-payment.[16]

20-7 **Method of appointment.** The method of appointment must comply with any formalities required by the security document. If none is specified, the method of appointment is simply by means of an instrument in writing, executed by the person designated so to do in the security document.[17] If the receiver is to have the power to execute a deed in the name of the chargee, then, like any other agent appointed for this purpose, he must be appointed by deed.[18] There is no objection to the appointment being prepared in advance, since it will only take effect when communicated to the receiver.[19]

The appointment is deemed to be made at the time at which the person appointed, or someone on his behalf, receives the instrument of appointment,[20] provided that the appointment is accepted by the appointee before the end of the next business day.[21] If the acceptance is not in writing, written confirmation of it by the appointee or on his behalf must be given to the appointor within five business days.[22] The acceptance or confirmation of acceptance must contain prescribed information.[23] Further provisions in relation to the appointment of two or more persons as joint receivers or managers are contained in the Insolvency (England and Wales) Rules 2016.[24]

It is not possible to presume the appointment of a receiver, where no such written appointment has been made. Therefore, where a chargee, by writing, appointed a person to act as receiver before he was entitled to do so, but did not reappoint him after an event took place which would have entitled him to make such an appointment, even though the receiver continued to act, it was held he had not been validly appointed.[25]

20-8 **Who may be appointed?** A body corporate may not be appointed receiver of the property of a company.[26] Any such purported appointment is a nullity.[27] Such a body acting as receiver is liable, on conviction on indictment, to a fine and, on summary conviction, to a fine not exceeding the statutory maximum.[28] If the chargee is not a

---

[16] *OBG Ltd v Allan* [2001] B.P.I.R. 1111.
[17] Law of Property Act 1925 s.109. As to a possibly invalid deed taking effect as an appointment in writing, see *Windsor Refrigerator Co Ltd v Branch Nominees Ltd* [1961] Ch. 375 CA.
[18] *Berkeley v Hardy* (1826) 5 B. & C. 355.
[19] *Windsor Refrigerator Co Ltd v Branch Nominees Ltd*, n.17, above.
[20] Insolvency Act 1986 s.33(1)(b).
[21] Insolvency Act 1986 s.33(1)(a).
[22] Insolvency (England and Wales) Rules 2016 r.4.1(3).
[23] Insolvency (England and Wales) Rules 2016 r.4.1(4).
[24] Insolvency (England and Wales) Rules 2016 r.4.1.
[25] *R Jaffé Ltd (in liquidation) v Jaffé* [1931] N.Z.L.R. 195.
[26] Insolvency Act 1986 s.30.
[27] *Portman Building Society v Gallwey* [1955] 1 All E.R. 227.
[28] Insolvency Act 1986 ss.30, 430 and Sch.10.

body corporate, there does not appear to be any objection to a chargee appointing himself receiver.[29]

Although there is no prohibition as such against the appointment of an undischarged bankrupt, or a person who has been discharged from bankruptcy but is subject to a bankruptcy restrictions order or undertaking,[30] such a person who acts as receiver or manager of the property of a company on behalf of a chargee commits a criminal offence.[31] He is liable, on conviction on indictment, to imprisonment for a term not exceeding two years or a fine, or both, or, on summary conviction, to imprisonment for a term not exceeding six months or a fine not exceeding the statutory maximum, or both.[32]

Disqualification from acting as a director is bar to appointment. A person against whom a disqualification order has been made, or who has given a disqualification undertaking under the Company Directors Disqualification Act 1986, may not, during the duration of the order, be a receiver or manager of a company's property without the permission of the court.[33] The Act specifies numerous conditions authorising, and one condition requiring, the court to make a disqualification order, and empowering it to accept a disqualification undertaking. These are not dealt with further in this work.

20-9

Contravention of the terms of an order or undertaking under the Company Directors Disqualification Act 1986 is punishable, on conviction on indictment, by imprisonment for a term not exceeding two years, or a fine, or both, or, on summary conviction, by imprisonment for a term not exceeding six months or a fine not exceeding the statutory maximum, or both.[34]

Invalid appointment: estoppel. Where an appointment is discovered to be invalid, whether by virtue of the invalidity of the instrument of appointment or otherwise, the court may order the person by whom, or on whose behalf, the appointment was made, to indemnify the person appointed against any liability which arises solely by reason of the invalidity of the appointment.[35] Such an order could cover, in particular, the personal liability of the person appointed under contracts entered into by him in purported performance of his function as receiver[36] and claims by the company against him for damages for trespass.[37]

20-10

The principle of estoppel applies in relation to invalid appointments. If the company through its directors has recognised the appointment as valid, thus encouraging the receiver to commit further acts of what would otherwise be trespass, it may be estopped as against him from later contending that his appoint-

---

[29] See *Mace Builders (Glasgow) Ltd v Lunn* [1987] Ch. 191 CA per Sir John Donaldson MR at 197A–B: "we are not concerned with the particular consequences of the defendant's having combined the roles of managing director, debenture-holder and receiver".
[30] Insolvency Act 1986 Sch.4A para.8.
[31] Insolvency Act 1986 s.31(1).
[32] Insolvency Act 1986 s.430 and Sch.10. For the meaning of "statutory maximum", see para.7-59, n.222, above.
[33] Company Directors Disqualification Act 1986 s.1(1).
[34] Company Directors Disqualification Act 1986 s.13.
[35] Insolvency Act 1986 s.34.
[36] See para.20-31, below.
[37] See para.20-32, below.

ment, and hence his acts as receiver, were invalid.[38] Further, in most cases the invalidity will be a technical matter (e.g. failure to give the company a sufficient length of notice of required repayment), and in consequence one which the appointor will be able to correct, such that if the appointment were challenged the appointor would be in a position to make a fresh appointment. In such circumstances, the company may, by unequivocal recognition of the position of the receiver,[39] but not otherwise,[40] be equally estopped as against the appointor.

20-11   **Notice of appointment.** Notice of the appointment in the prescribed form must be given by the person making the same to the registrar of companies within seven days of the appointment[41]; the notice is then noted in the charges register. If default is made in complying with this requirement, the appointor is liable on summary conviction to a fine not exceeding level 3 on the standard scale and, for continued contravention, a daily default fine not exceeding one-tenth of level 3 on the standard scale.[42]

20-12   **Notification that receiver or manager appointed.** After an appointment, every invoice, order for goods or services, business letter or order form issued by or on behalf of the company or the receiver or manager or a liquidator of the company must contain a statement that a receiver or manager has been appointed.[43] The same statement must appear on all the company's websites.[44]

If default is made, the company, and any of the following persons who knowingly and wilfully authorises or permits the default, namely any officer of the company, any liquidator of the company, and any receiver or manager, are liable on summary conviction to a fine not exceeding one-fifth of the statutory maximum.[45]

20-13   **Effects of appointment.** The effect of an appointment out of court is, as regards the crystallisation of a floating charge into a fixed charge,[46] and as regards the consequences in relation to judgment creditors,[47] the same as in the case of an appointment by the court. However, there is no objection in principle to a provision in a debenture whereunder a floating charge may be crystallised merely by the giving of a notice.[48] But if such notice is given, it will not automatically have the effect of crystallising a floating charge ranking in priority to it.[49]

On crystallisation of a floating charge, the powers of the company and its directors to deal with the property comprised in the appointment[50] (both property subject to the crystallised floating charge and property subject to a fixed charge), except in

---

38 *Save Acoustics Ltd v Pimms Furnishing Ltd* 11 January 1985, unreported, 1985; *Bank of Baroda v Panessar* (1987) Ch. 335.
39 *Bank of Baroda v Panessar*, see n.38, above.
40 *R Jaffé Ltd (in liquidation) v Jaffé* [1931] N.Z.L.R. 195 (wrongfully appointed receiver continued to act, after the date when he could have been validly appointed, but was not).
41 Companies Act 2006 s.859K. The prescribed form is Form MR01.
42 Companies Act 2006 s.859K(6) and (7).
43 Insolvency Act 1986 s.39(1)(a).
44 Insolvency Act 1986 s.39(1)(b).
45 Insolvency Act 1986 ss.39(2), 430 and Sch.10.
46 See *Kasofsky v Kreegars* [1937] 4 All E.R. 374; and para.6-59, above.
47 See *Cairney v Back* [1906] 2 K.B. 746.
48 *Re Woodroffes (Musical Instruments) Ltd* [1985] 2 All E.R. 908; *Re Brightlife Ltd* [1987] Ch. 200.
49 *Re Woodroffes (Musical Instruments) Ltd*, n.48, above.
50 As to the property comprised in the appointment, see para.20-14, below.

accordance with the charge, are paralysed; for although, under charges in the usual form, the receiver is agent for the company, the company's powers are delegated to the receiver so far as regards carrying on the business or collecting the assets; and frequently so as to enable the receiver as attorney to convey a legal estate.[51] However, the actual powers depend on the terms of the instrument. If, for example, they give no sufficient power to carry on the business, it may be necessary to apply to the court to make the appointment, or for a vesting order to vest the legal estate in a purchaser.[52]

The rights of the receiver against execution creditors are governed by the same principles as in the case of an appointment by the court.[53]

In other respects, the effect of the appointment differs from that of an appointment by the court; persons with paramount rights, such as prior encumbrancers, can exercise those rights without leave; for the receiver appointed out of court is not an officer of the court, but an agent of the company or of the chargee.

Property in Great Britain comprised in a floating charge. A receiver appointed under the law of either part of Great Britain (England and Wales or Scotland) in respect of the whole or part of any property or undertaking of a company, and in consequence of the company having created a charge which, as created, was a floating charge, may exercise his powers in the other part of Great Britain, so far as their exercise is not inconsistent with the law applicable there.[54]   **20-14**

Having regard to the wide powers conferred by statute upon receivers appointed in Scotland, whether in or out of court,[55] it is extremely unlikely that the charge would contain any powers which would not be valid under Scots law. However, the appointment will be subject to:

(a)   the rights of any person who has effectually executed Scots-law diligence (i.e. levied execution) on all or any part of the property of the company prior to the appointment of the receiver; and

(b)   the rights of any person who holds, over all or any part of the property of the company, a fixed security or floating charge having priority over, or ranking pari passu with, the floating charge by virtue of which the receiver was appointed.[56]

A person who engages in a transaction with a receiver appointed pursuant to a floating charge granted by a company which the Court of Session has power to wind up was held to be not concerned to enquire whether the receiver is acting within his powers.[57] It is not clear to what extent this provision applies in relation to receivers of the property of a company incorporated in England and Wales owning property in Scotland.

---

[51]   *Re Emmadart Ltd* [1979] Ch. 540; see also *Watts v Midland Bank plc* (1986) 2 B.C.C. 98961 and *Newhart Developments Ltd v Co-operative Commercial Bank Ltd* [1978] Q.B. 814, as to continuing powers of the company.

[52]   Law of Property Act 1925 ss.91, 92; Trustee Act 1925 s.44(ii)(c), where a corporation has been dissolved.

[53]   See paras 2-53 ff, above.

[54]   Insolvency Act 1986 s.72(1). "Receiver" here includes a receiver and manager: see s.72(2). For an example of the section's operation, see *Norfolk House Plc (in receivership) v Repsol Petroleum Ltd* 1992 S.L.T. 235.

[55]   Insolvency Act 1986 s.55 and Sch.2.

[56]   Insolvency Act 1986 s.55(3).

[57]   Insolvency Act 1986 s.55(4), and see *Iona Hotels Ltd, Petitioners* [1991] S.L.T. 11.

There should be no particular problem so far as property in Northern Ireland is concerned.

20-15 **Property comprised in appointment.** It is purely a matter of construction of the instrument of charge as to what property of the company[58] is comprised in the charge, and of the appointment as to what property is included therein. Under all forms of floating charge, however, the company is at liberty to create other charges and other similar rights, at least in the ordinary course of business, ranking in priority to the floating charge, even after it has crystallised. If a receiver appointed under a floating charge nevertheless obtains possession of property which is subject to such a charge or other right, he must account for it to the prior incumbrancer.[59]

The terms "book debts and other debts", used in an instrument of charge, are not apt to include cash standing to the credit of a company at its bank.[60]

Monies recovered in respect of misfeasance claims, even if recovered by a liquidator, are general assets of the company usually covered by a debenture.[61] Monies recovered by a liquidator or administrator on the ground of preference, on the other hand, are recovered for the benefit of the creditors as a whole: they do not fall within the scope of assets of the company comprised in a debenture.[62]

There may be statutory rights, e.g. the right to detain an aircraft for unpaid fees and charges, which are exercisable against the chattel concerned, irrespective of the existence of a fixed charge, and the exercise of which a receiver is therefore powerless to prevent.[63]

20-16 **Nature of receiver's possession** Any occupation of premises of the company enjoyed by a receiver will normally be enjoyed by him solely in his capacity as agent for some other party. Although it is possible for him to take independent possession of the premises as principal, such cases will be comparatively rare.[64] If the receiver is, as he usually is, expressly made an agent of the company,[65] then the mere fact that he enters upon the premises of the company for the purpose of managing and carrying on a business does not normally mean that the company has been dispossessed or has ceased to occupy the premises.[66] His occupation as agent for the company is the company's occupation, and there will have been no change of possession.[67] The cases already referred to[68] which illustrate the proposition that, unless directed by the order appointing him actually to take possession, a receiver

---

58 See paras 18-17 ff, above, as to property held by the company on trust as bailee.
59 *Re Arauco Co* (1898) 79 L.T. 336; *Re Anglo-Austrian Printing and Publishing Union* [1895] 2 Ch. 891.
60 *Northern Bank Ltd v Ross* [1990] B.C.C. 883 CA, following *Re Brightlife Ltd* [1987] Ch. 200.
61 *Re Zucco, Ex p. Cooper* (1874-75) L.R. 10 Ch. App.510; *Willmott v London Celluloid Co* (1886) 31 Ch. D. 425, affirmed 34 Ch. D. 147; *Re Yagerphone Ltd* [1935] Ch. 392.
62 *Channel Airways Ltd v Manchester Corpn* [1974] 1 Lloyd's Rep. 456; see also *Bristol Airport v Powdrill* [1990] Ch. 774. In the former case, the lien claimed by the airport was founded on a private Act, and was held not strictly to constitute a lien; in the latter case, it was founded on the Civil Aviation Act 1982, s.88; but that statutory lien was equally held not to be effective per se against an administrator.
63 See n.62, above.
64 *Ratford and Hayward v Northavon District Council* [1987] Q.B. 357 at 379G.
65 *Ratford and Hayward v Northavon District Council*, n.64, above, at 374 and 375.
66 *Ratford and Hayward v Northavon District Council*, n.64, above, at 376E-F. See also *Brown v City of London Corporation* [1996] 1 W.L.R. 1070.
67 See n.69, below.
68 See n.64, above.

appointed by the court is not in occupation for rating purposes strongly support this approach.

On the other hand, it may be shown, either from the terms of the receiver's appointment[69] or from what he has actually done,[70] or from both together, that he has actually taken possession adversely to the company. Since the decision in *Ratford and Hayward v Northavon District Council*,[71] however, it is clear that unusual circumstances are required to produce such a result; in the usual case, the receiver is not in possession otherwise than as agent for the company, or, if he is an agent for the chargee, for such chargee.

Position of receivers of property of a company. The position and powers of   **20-17**
such receivers are derived from and depend upon the contract between the parties expressed by the authorising instrument, as modified by statute.[72] Except where the context of the statute otherwise requires, the provisions of the Insolvency Act 1986 relating to receivers and managers of the property of a company apply also to a receiver or manager of part only of that property, and to a receiver only of the income arising from that property or from part of it.[73] Further, any reference in that Act to the appointment of a receiver or manager under powers contained in an instrument includes a reference to an appointment made under powers which, by virtue of any enactment (such as the Law of Property Act 1925), are implied in and have effect as if contained in the instrument.[74]

But a person so appointed is not a "manager" of the company (as distinct from property of the company) as defined in the definitions section[75] of the Companies Act 2006. On a similar basis, he could not have been made liable for misfeasance under s.333 of the Companies Act 1948 by unsecured creditors or contributories, to whom in any event he owes no duty.[76] This did not mean that, in properly constituted proceedings, he could never be made liable to the company.[77]

Limited appointment. In some cases, on an application by holders of a floating   **20-18**
charge for the appointment of a receiver, the court has excluded from the appointment property which is valueless to the holders of that charge, such as property charged up to its full value to specific chargees. It follows that, on an appointment by a chargee out of court, any particular items of property may be excluded, and that the charge is not crystallised but continues to float as regards that property.

---

[69] As in *Richards v Overseers of Kidderminster* [1896] 2 Ch. 212 (terms of debenture construed as including a provision entitling the receiver to take possession adversely to the company). The same result was apparently reached in *Meigh v Wickenden* [1942] 2 K.B. 160 DC, on the terms of the debenture, after a somewhat inadequate analysis of the legal position. This was a Factories Act case, where the receiver was held to be the occupier.

[70] *Taggs Island Casino Hotel Ltd v Richmond-upon-Thames LBC* [1966] 14 R.R.C. (interim relief on the basis that the receiver had, as he asserted, taken possession); *Banister v Islington LBC* [1972] 71 L.G.R.D.C. (similar finding). If not explicable on this basis, both these cases, and also *Meigh v Wickenden*, n.69, above are in clear conflict with *Ratford and Hayward v Northavon District Council* and *Brown v City of London Corporation*, n.66, above.

[71] See n.64, above, at 366.

[72] See especially Insolvency Act 1986 ss.29-42, and *R. Jaffé Ltd (in liquidation) v Jaffé* [1931] N.Z.L.R. 195 at 198-199.

[73] Insolvency Act 1986 s.29(1)(a).

[74] Insolvency Act 1986 s.29(1)(b).

[75] Companies Act 2006 s.1173.

[76] *Re B Johnson & Co (Builders) Ltd* [1955] Ch. 634.

[77] See para.18-34, above.

Where the appointment is to relate to part only of the property covered by a floating charge, the power to appoint a receiver may need to authorise expressly an appointment over a part only of such property, as is the case with the statutory power.[78] The point has, however, not been expressly determined.[79] Further, if the chargee excludes from the appointment any particular item of property, this may preclude it from afterwards extending the appointment to the excluded item.

20-19   **Validity of unregistered charge against company.** It has long been held that the failure to file particulars of a charge with the registrar of companies, although rendering it invalid against a liquidator and other creditors (and now also an administrator), does not render it invalid against the company whilst it is a going concern. The House of Lords has now held that an unregistered charge becomes invalid against the company if it subsequently goes into administration.[80] A charge given by a construction company to the building employer became invalid against the company in administration, with the result that, by directing a third party to remove the company's plant, purporting to be charged thereby, from the construction site, the building employer committed a conversion of the company's assets.

20-20   **Regularity of appointment.** A receiver appointed by a chargee should, before accepting the appointment, satisfy himself that the appointment is properly made in accordance with the provisions of the charge, and duly registered[81] and, where there is more than one chargee, that the requisite majority has concurred. If there is any flaw in his appointment, or if the charge under which he is appointed does not constitute a valid charge,[82] he may find himself liable as a trespasser to the liquidator in a subsequent winding up, the administrator in a subsequent administration,[83] or the trustee in bankruptcy of a vendor to the company[84]; although as an alternative the liquidator, administrator or trustee may elect to treat him as their agent.[85]

20-21   **Subsequent insolvency: avoidance of floating charge.** If a floating charge becomes invalid on the insolvency of the company (meaning, in this case, its going into administration or liquidation[86]) under s.245 of the Insolvency Act 1986, the prior appointment of a receiver is not void ab initio, and his acts prior to liquidation or administration are unaffected.[87] If, before such insolvency takes place, he has realised assets and paid off the debenture-holder out of such proceeds, the

---

[78] See Law of Property Act 1925 s.101(1)(iii).

[79] The decision in *Evans v Rival Granite Quarries, Ltd* [1910] 2 K.B. 979 is not to the contrary, but only negatived the right of the holder of a floating charge to claim any particular item against, e.g., a judgment creditor, until the security had been crystallised into a fixed charge by the accepted method.

[80] *Smith (Administrator of Cosslett (Contractors) Ltd) v Bridgend County Borough Council* [2001] UKHL 58; [2002] 1 All E.R. 292 HL.

[81] See Companies Act 2006 ss.859A–859H.

[82] As in *Rolled Steel Products (Holdings) Ltd v British Steel Corporation* [1986] Ch. 246 CA, where, the debenture being held to have been issued, to the knowledge of the holder, by the directors in breach of their fiduciary duties, the receiver was held accountable to the liquidator in respect of the assets he had collected. See also *Evans v Tiger Investments Ltd* [2002] 2 B.C.L.C. 185.

[83] *Smith (Administrator of Cosslett (Contractors) Ltd) v Bridgend County Borough Council* [2001] UKHL 58; [2002] 1 All E.R. 292 HL.

[84] See *Re Goldburg (No.2)* [1912] 1 K.B. 606; cf. *Re Simms* [1934] Ch. 1. See, however, paras 20-32, 20-33, below.

[85] *Ex p. Vaughan* [1884] 14 Q.BD. 25; *Re Simms*, n.84, above.

[86] Insolvency Act 1986 s.245(1).

[87] *Mace Builders (Glasgow) Ltd v Lunn* [1987] Ch. 191 CA.

debenture-holder will not be liable to repay any monies so received.[88] Transactions effected under the authority of the charge, before the commencement of the insolvency, are unaffected by the section. But subject thereto, on the insolvency of the company, the receiver will be accountable to the administrator or liquidator for all property then remaining in his hands, and he cannot properly act thereafter. The receiver may also be liable as a trespasser where the company has no title to property included in the security, e.g. where a sale to it is set aside as a fraud on the creditors of the vendor.[89]

Preferential debts.[90]   The obligation of a receiver appointed out of court to discharge the preferential debts out of assets subject to a charge which, as created, was a floating charge, in priority to the claims of the chargee, is the same as in the case of a receiver appointed by the court.[91] All such assets are in any event to be regarded as assets of the company for the purposes of the Insolvency Act 1986 s.156, under which, if the assets of the company are insufficient to satisfy its liabilities in a winding up, the court can order the costs, charges and expenses incurred in the winding up to be paid out of its assets in such order of priority as the court thinks just.   **20-22**

The expenses of a winding up are payable out of assets subject to a floating charge (including monies to which the preferential creditors are entitled), so far as the company's uncharged assets are insufficient to meet them.[92] However, this general rule is subject to the provisions of the Insolvency (England and Wales) Rules 2016 rr.6.44(2) and 7.112, which deal with "litigation expenses": essentially, where a liquidator proposes to commence, or has commenced, legal proceedings under ss.212, 213, 214, 238, 239, 244 or 423 of the Insolvency Act 1986, the expenses of such litigation will only take priority over the floating charge holder if the expenses are "approved" by that charge holder.

If the receiver fails to comply with the statutory obligations, he becomes personally liable in damages to the affected preferential creditors.[93] Where a receiver transfers monies that should have been paid to preferential creditors to a chargee, and the chargee is aware that there are unpaid preferential creditors, the chargee is also liable to account to the preferential creditors.[94]

The right of recoupment out of the general assets not subject to the chargee's charge[95] would, it seems, be enforceable by the receiver by application notice in the winding up.

Priority of preferential debts, where deficiency of assets.   Before there can be any return to the chargee under a floating charge, provision must have been made for: **20-23**

(a)   the costs of realisation, including the costs of any abortive sale and the costs of carrying on a business of the company with a view to a sale;

---

[88]   *Mace Builders (Glasgow) Ltd v Lunn* [1987] Ch. 191 at 199H per Sir John Donaldson MR.
[89]   *Re Simms*, n.84, above.
[90]   See Insolvency Act 1986 s.386 and Sch.6.
[91]   Insolvency Act 1986 s.40(1), (2).
[92]   Insolvency Act 1986 s.176ZA.
[93]   *Woods v Winskill* [1913] 2 Ch. 303; *Westminster Corporation v Haste* [1950] Ch. 442; *Inland Revenue Commissioners v Goldblatt* [1972] Ch. 498.
[94]   *Inland Revenue Commissioners v Goldblatt*, n.93, above.
[95]   Under Insolvency Act 1986 s.40(3). See, e.g. *Re Yagerphone Ltd* [1935] Ch. 392 (money recovered in respect of a fraudulent preference, and not therefore falling within the debenture).

(b) the amount due to the receiver, including his remuneration, costs and indemnity[96];
(c) the costs, charges and expenses of any trustee for the chargee[97];
(d) the expenses of any contemporaneous liquidation[98]; and
(e) the preferential debts of the company.[99]

Although there appears to be no direct decision on the matter, it is considered that the above is also the proper order of priority in the event of a deficiency of assets, since the position of a receiver appointed out of court has, by virtue of Insolvency Act 1986 s.37(1)(b), so far as concerns the entitlement to an indemnity, been approximated to that of a receiver appointed in court. Accordingly, if items (1)–(4) exhaust the available funds, then the preferential debts do not fall to be paid.

If the assets are insufficient to satisfy its liabilities, the court can order the costs, charges and expenses incurred in the winding up to be paid out of its assets in such order of priority as the court thinks just.[100] This, however, is subject to the overriding consideration that, if at any stage, after taking items (1)–(4) into consideration, the receiver has in his hands sufficient monies to enable him to discharge the preferential debts, either wholly or in part, then if he employs such monies in any other manner (as, for example, in further trading) he does so entirely at his own risk. Accordingly, if he continues to carry on a business of the company, and as a consequence loses such monies in the course of such trading, he will be personally liable to the disappointed preferential creditors, and the extent of his indemnity (which in the circumstances posed may well become enforceable) will not be relevant, so far as they are concerned.[101]

20-24 **Receivership accounts.** Every receiver or manager of a company's property appointed under powers contained in an instrument (other than an administrative receiver) must deliver to the registrar of companies for registration accounts of his receipts and payments.[102] These accounts must be delivered within one month (or such longer period as the registrar may allow) after the expiration of twelve months from the date of his appointment, and of every subsequent period of six months, and also within one month after he ceases to act as receiver or manager.[103]

The accounts must be in the form of an abstract, showing receipts and payments during the relevant period of 12 months, or six months, or, where he has ceased to act, receipts and payments from the end of the period of 12 or six months to which the last preceding abstract related.[104] If there is no such abstract, then the period covered must be from the date of appointment to the date of his ceasing to act[105]; there must be shown the aggregate amount of his receipts and payments during all preceding periods since his appointment.[106]

A receiver or manager who makes default in complying with these require-

---

96 As to the receiver's indemnity, see para.20-44, below.
97 But see n.279 in Ch.7, above.
98 Insolvency Act 1986 s.176ZA.
99 *Re Glyncorrwg Colliery Co Ltd* [1926] Ch. 951.
100 Insolvency Act 1986 s.156.
101 *Woods v Winskill*, n.93, above.
102 Insolvency Act 1986 s.38(1). The appropriate form is F.497 in the Companies (Forms) Regulations 1985 (SI 1985/854) Sch.3.
103 Insolvency Act 1986 s.38(2).
104 Insolvency Act 1986 s.38(3).
105 See n.104, above.
106 See n.104, above.

ments is liable on summary conviction to a fine not exceeding one-fifth of the statutory maximum, and on conviction after continued contravention to a daily default fine not exceeding one-fiftieth of the statutory maximum.[107]

The receiver, both as agent of the company under the terms of his appointment and also as an accounting party to the company,[108] is additionally under a duty to keep and to produce to the company, when required, full accounts of his dealings with the company's assets.[109]

The receiver is not a debtor to the company in respect of such sums as may ultimately prove to be the balance in his hands due to it, after discharge of the debenture-holders' claims, preferential debts, and any other proper payments, even though his accounts show that something will probably be due. Consequently, such sums cannot be the subject of a third party debt order.[110]

Enforcement of duties. If any receiver or manager of a company makes default **20-25** in filing, delivering or making any return, account or other document, or in giving any notice, in each case as is by law required from a receiver, after a 14-day notice to make good the default, the registrar or any member or creditor may apply for an order directing the receiver or manager to make good the default within such time as may be specified in the order,[111] without prejudice to any penalties incurred in respect of such default.[112] The same provision applies if the receiver fails, on request from a liquidator, to render proper accounts of his receipts and payments and to vouch them and pay over the amount properly payable.[113] The application in this case is by the liquidator.[114] The application is by application notice[115]; the receiver or manager may be ordered to bear all the costs of and incidental to the application.[116]

Other statutory obligations. There are other statutory obligations, according to **20-26** the nature of the trade or business which is carried on. Thus, for example, a receiver carrying on a business was liable as occupier to penalties under s.155 of the Factories Act 1961[117] (and is likely to be similarly liable under the Health and Safety at Work etc. Act 1974).

For the receiver's duty to distribute among the unsecured creditors "the prescribed part of the company's net assets" before making payment to the chargee under a floating charge, see paras 15-94 ff, above.

Application for directions. A receiver or manager of the property of a company **20-27**

---

[107] Insolvency Act 1986 ss.38(5), 430 and Sch. 10.
[108] Law of Property Act 1925 s.109(8).
[109] *Smiths Ltd v Middleton* [1979] 3 All E.R. 842; *Re B Johnson & Co (Builders) Ltd*, n.76, above, at 661–662 per Jenkins LJ; *R. v Board of Trade, Ex p. St Martins Preserving Co Ltd* [1965] 1 Q.B. 603 at 614 per Phillimore LJ. See also *Rottenberg v Monjack* [1992] B.C.C. 688.
[110] *Seabrook Estate Co Ltd v Ford* [1949] 2 All E.R. 94.
[111] Insolvency Act 1986 s.41(1)(a), (2).
[112] Insolvency Act 1986 s.41(3).
[113] Insolvency Act 1986 s.41(1)(b).
[114] Insolvency Act 1986 s.41(2).
[115] See CPR Pt 23.
[116] Insolvency Act 1986 s.41(2).
[117] *Meigh v Wickenden* [1942] 2 K.B. 160 (a Factories Act case). Personal liabilities and obligations are now imposed on those conducting noxious trades, such as waste disposal businesses: see *Re Celtic Extraction Ltd* [2000] 2 W.L.R. 991. See also *Lawson v Hosemaster Machine Co Ltd* [1966] 2 All E.R. 944 CA at 951.

appointed under the powers contained in any instrument,[118] or the persons by whom or on whose behalf he was so appointed, may apply to the court[119] for directions in relation to any particular matter arising in connection with the performance of his functions.[120] On such an application the court may give such directions, or may make such order declaring the rights of persons before the court or otherwise, as the court thinks just.[121] The matters in relation to which the court may give directions are broad, and include, for example, the liability to a receiver of an indemnifier,[122] the level of fees payable to a receiver,[123] and the construction of the definition of the term "insolvency event" in an agreement under which the receivers had been appointed.[124]

20-28   **Liability in respect of property.**   A receiver may incur many liabilities in respect of the property comprised in the security, more especially as regards the supply of gas, water, electricity and telecommunications charges, business rates, and value added tax.[125]

(a)   *Gas, water, electricity and telecommunications:* Where the receiver is agent for the company, there is no change in the occupier of the premises, and consequently an ordinary receiver is as a rule not entitled to enter into a fresh agreement for any such supply, and can be required to discharge any arrears if he requires the supply to be continued.[126] Where he is agent for the chargee, the position is exactly the same as if he were appointed by the court.[127]

(b)   *Business rates:* Charge documents usually make provision for the payment of business rates, council tax, taxes and other outgoings by the receiver. But, as in the case of the similar provisions in s.109(8) of the Law of Property Act 1925, this only defines the position as between the company and the chargee; it does not, ipso facto, entitle the rating authority to sue the receiver.[128]

The actions of a receiver and manager, whether appointed by the court or by a charge-holder, in managing the company's business, do not, without more, amount to rateable occupation of the company's premises by the receiver; they cannot found a claim for rateable occupation by him, since any occupation by him as agent for the company is occupation by the company.[129] Nor is a receiver liable for business rates assessed on unoc-

---

[118] This includes a reference to an appointment made under powers which, by virtue of any enactment, are implied in, and have effect as if contained, in an instrument; Insolvency Act 1986 s.29(1)(b).

[119] I.e. the court having jurisdiction to wind the company up: Insolvency Act 1986 s.251.

[120] Insolvency Act 1986 s.35(1).

[121] Insolvency Act 1986 s.35(2).

[122] *Re Therm-a-Stor Ltd* [1996] 1 W.L.R. 1338.

[123] *Munns v Perkins* [2002] B.P.I.R. 120.

[124] *Re Cheyne Finance plc* [2007] EWHC 2402 Ch; [2008] 2 All E.R. 987.

[125] As to VAT, see Ch.28, below.

[126] See *Re Marriage, Neave & Co* [1896] 2 Ch. 663; *Paterson v Gas Light and Coke Company* [1896] 2 Ch. 476.

[127] See para.6-7, above.

[128] *Liverpool Corporation v Hope* [1938] 1 K.B. 751 CA; *Re John Willment (Ashford) Ltd* [1980] 1 W.L.R. 73.

[129] *Rees v Boston Borough Council* [2001] EWCA Civ 1934, [2002] 1 W.L.R. 1304, where the authorities were extensively examined, including *Re Marriage, Neave & Co* n.129, above, and *Ratford and*

cupied business premises.[130] A receiver may, however, by his express acts or by the terms of his appointment, take up occupation in such a capacity as will justify his being held personally liable for such occupation[131]; "the question whether a person is an occupier or not within the rating law is a question of fact, and does not depend on legal title".[132]

(c) *Landlord and Tenant Act 1954:* Anything authorised or required by the provisions of the 1954 Act, other than those relating to the supplying of information,[133] to be done at any time by, with or to the landlord, or a landlord of a specified description, is, after the appointment of a receiver, authorised or required to be done by, with or to the mortgagee who has appointed the receiver instead of that landlord.[134] It follows that, if a mortgagee goes into possession, or appoints a receiver, between the making of an application by the tenant for a new lease and the hearing of such application, the mortgagee must be added as a respondent. If this step is not taken, the court has no jurisdiction.[135]

(d) *London Building Acts 1930–1939:* A receiver would appear to be an "owner" for the purposes of Pt V, but not Pt XII, of the London Building Acts (Amendment) Act 1939.[136]

Receiver as agent for the company Charge documents usually provide in express terms that the receiver is to be agent for the company, as in the case of the statutory power. Where this provision is omitted, it may be inferred from the terms of the instrument that an ordinary receiver is agent for the chargee, as, for instance, where he is given power to carry on a business, or other powers largely in excess of those conferred on receivers by statute.[137] When this is the case, the chargee will be itself personally liable to persons dealing with the receiver, and also to the receiver for his remuneration.[138]   **20-29**

Where debentures specifically incorporated certain of the provisions relating to receivers contained in the Conveyancing Act 1881, but also conferred large additional powers, including the power to carry on the business and to sell, the Court of Appeal held that there was sufficient contrary intention, within s.24(2) of the Conveyancing Act 1881 (now s.109(2) of the Law of Property Act 1925), to prevent the receiver being agent for the company, and that he was agent for the debenture-holders, and therefore entitled to recover his remuneration from them.[139] But the omission to state in the charge document, in express terms, that the receiver is to

---

Hayward v Northavon District Council [1987] Q.B. 357 CA.

[130] *Brown v City of London Corporation* [1996] 1 W.L.R. 1070, distinguishing *Sargent v Customs & Excise* [1995] 1 W.L.R. 821 CA; see also *Re Nolton Business Centres Ltd* [1996] 1 B.C.L.C. 400.

[131] See e.g. *Richards v Overseers of Kidderminster* [1896] 2 Ch. 212 (terms of debenture).

[132] *Holywell Union Assessment Committee v The Halkyn District Mines Drainage Company* [1895] A.C. 117 HL per Lord Herschell, LC at 125. See the article by Professor Ian Fletcher, "Rateable Occupation and Administrative Receivership", (2003) *Insolvency Intelligence* No.4, at p.25.

[133] Landlord and Tenant Act 1954 s.40(2), (3).

[134] Landlord and Tenant Act 1954 s.67. See *Meah v Mouskos* [1964] 2 Q.B. 23.

[135] *Meah v Mouskos*, n.134, above.

[136] *Solomons v R. Gertzenstein Ltd* [1954] 2 Q.B. 243.

[137] *Re Vimbos, Ltd* [1900] 1 Ch. 470; *Robinson Printing Co Ltd v Chic Ltd* [1905] 2 Ch. 123; *Deyes v Wood* [1911] 1 K.B. 806.

[138] *Robinson Printing Co Ltd v Chic Ltd*, n.137, above.

[139] *Deyes v Wood*, n.137, above.

be the agent of the company does not necessarily prevent him from being so.[140] The question is one of construction in each case.

For an analysis of the unusual character of such an agency, see *Silven Properties Ltd v Royal Bank of Scotland plc*.[141]

20-30 **Reality of agency.** Although the receiver is bound, at the conclusion of the receivership, to account strictly to the company for his receipts,[142] and is liable to it in respect of any misfeasance or breach of trust,[143] the company is not entitled to current information from him, as the receivership proceeds, unless it can establish that it is information which is required for some specific purpose. Even then, the receiver is entitled to put the interests of the chargee first, and to refuse any information which he thinks might be adverse to its interests.[144] In substance, he is only bound to give information which no reasonable receiver could possibly refuse, or alternatively if it appears that his refusal to give it must necessarily be the result of bad faith.[145]

20-31 **Effect of appointment on contracts: "adoption".** The appointment of a receiver with powers of management does not normally affect or terminate contracts, other than certain types of contract of employment, as to which see generally Ch.23, below. In the case of certain contracts current at the date of his appointment which he elects to cause the company to fulfil, then, in default of provision to the contrary, he will, like a receiver appointed by the court, be deemed to be carrying out contracts already entered into by the company. If he supplies goods or services in pursuance of such contracts, persons to whom he supplies such goods or services can set off damages for subsequent breach against the price.[146]

This is commonly and conveniently, if inaccurately, spoken of as the receiver "adopting" the contract; merely by causing the company to carry it out, he does not render himself personally liable thereon, as would be the case with a contract entered into *de novo*. At any rate, unless to disregard the contract would adversely affect the realisation of the assets, or would seriously affect the trading prospects of the company in a case where it will probably continue to trade, the receiver is not under any obligation to "adopt" the contract (except when he is actuated by bad faith) and he may safely disregard it.[147] Specific performance of a normal trading contract will very rarely be ordered against the company[148]; it is otherwise in the

---

[140] *Cully v Parsons* [1923] 2 Ch. 512; distinguishing *Deyes v Wood*, n.137, above; *Central London Electricity v Berners* [1945] 172 L.T. 289.

[141] [2003] EWCA Civ 1409; [2003] B.P.I.R. 1429 CA and para.18-34 above.

[142] See *Brown v Cork* [1986] P.C.C. 78, [1986] F.L.R. 1181 CA, as to the distribution of a surplus in the hands of the receiver, referable to overpayments arising from the realisation of debentures given by surety companies among such companies, without reference to the state of accounts between the surety companies *inter se*.

[143] See e.g. *Smiths Ltd v Middleton (No.1)* [1979] 3 All E.R. 842, applied where a company, whose debenture had been paid off, disputed the receiver's claim to remuneration; see also *Rottenberg v Monjack* [1992] B.C.C. 688.

[144] *Re B Johnson & Co (Builders) Ltd*, n.76, above.

[145] See n.143, above, and see *Gomba Holdings (UK) Ltd v Homan* [1986] 3 All E.R. 94.

[146] See paras 20-41, 20-42, below.

[147] *Airlines Airspares Ltd v Handley Page Ltd* [1970] Ch. 193; *Lathia v Dronsfield Bros Ltd* [1987] B.C.L.C. 321. In any event, the receiver would appear to owe no duty *to the other contracting party* to "adopt" the contract. See *Ardmore Studios (Ireland) Ltd v Lynch* [1965] Ir.R. 1.

[148] *Macleod v Alexander Sutherland Ltd*, 1977 S.L.T. (Notes of Recent Decisions) 44, but see *Land*

case of a contract under which the other party has already acquired an equitable interest in specific property.[149]

Generally, the powers and duties of a receiver depend on the instrument under which he is appointed and the terms of his appointment. Prima facie, it is his duty to preserve the goodwill, where he is authorised to carry on a business, although he owes no duty to the unsecured creditors or contributories of the company to preserve either a business or the goodwill of the company.[150] It is thought that, provided the preferential debts are provided for, he would be justified in paying an unsecured debt accrued due before his appointment, where payment is necessary to ensure continuation of a supply of goods essential to the company's business.[151] But he must not pay statute-barred debts. If, as is sometimes the case, he is appointed receiver of a business without any powers of management, his duty is to close down the business and collect the assets.

Liability of receiver to third persons in tort. If the receiver interferes with the   **20-32**
rights of third parties,[152] however innocently, he is personally liable as a trespasser, and the company (or the chargee, as the case may be) are in the same position as if he had acted within the scope of his authority. Thus, where a receiver and manager of the undertaking of a company had been appointed by debenture-holders, and subsequently the assignment by the vendor to the company of the whole of the assets was set aside as fraudulent, within the Fraudulent Conveyances Act 1571 (see now ss.423–425 of the Insolvency Act 1986[153]) in such circumstances that the title of the trustee in bankruptcy of the vendor related back, the receiver and the debenture-holders were held liable as trespassers in respect of all such parts of the property in question as had come into the hands of the receiver. An inquiry was directed as to the amount of such property: the receiver and the debenture-holders were, however, only liable in respect of the property which had belonged to the bankrupt, and not in respect of assets into which it had by sale been converted.[154]

Trustee in bankruptcy treating receiver as his agent. As an alternative to the   **20-33**
situation described in para.20-32, the trustee in bankruptcy in the situation pertaining in *Re Goldburg*[155] could have treated the receiver as his agent, adopted all his acts, claimed the final balance in his hands as the result of all his transactions, and required him to account accordingly.[156] But on this footing, apart from any separate claims arising out of misconduct, the receiver would have been entitled to bring losses as well as profits into account. If the receiver in such a situation recovers book debts, the trustee in bankruptcy may properly have no claim thereto, since he

---

Rover Group Ltd v UPF (UK) Ltd [2002] EWHC 3183 QB; [2003] 2 B.C.L.C. 222 (injunction awarded to allow a customer of the company in receivership to receive supplies until it had resourced).

[149] *Freevale Ltd v Metrostore (Holdings) Ltd* [1984] Ch. 199.

[150] *Re B Johnson & Co (Builders) Ltd*, n.76, above; *Kernohan Estates v Boyd* [1967] N.I. 27.

[151] Cf. *Re Hale* [1899] 2 Ch. 107.

[152] cf. *Re Botibol* [1947] 1 All E.R. 26; and *Said v Butt* [1920] 3 K.B. 497.

[153] Replacing s.172 of Law of Property Act 1925.

[154] *Re Goldburg* [1912] 1 K.B. 606; cf. *Re Gunsbourg* [1920] 2 K.B. 426; *Re Herman* [1915] H.B.R. 41; *Re Dombrowski* [1923] 92 L.J. Ch. 415.

[155] See para.20-32.

[156] *Re Simms*, n.84, above, at 27 per Lawrence LJ.

will have a claim for the debt against the original debtor, who has simply paid the wrong person.[157]

In a similar case, where the trustee in bankruptcy elected to treat the receiver as a trespasser,[158] he was not allowed to claim an account of profits against the receiver in respect of contracts completed by him.[159] A receiver who had been managing director of the company, when sued with the company, was held not entitled to refuse to produce material documents in an action in which fraudulent conspiracy between the defendants was alleged, though he asserted that he now held the documents as agent for the debenture-holders.[160]

20-34 **Vicarious liability to third persons in tort.** All employees engaged by a manager for the purpose of continuing a business will be employees of his principal (whether the company, debenture-holders, or their trustees) and not employees of the manager himself.[161] It is therefore apprehended that a manager will be vicariously liable in tort only to third parties in the same classes of case in which directors would be liable[162]: that is to say, only where he has either (i) directly or by necessary implication authorised the tort committed, or (ii) been otherwise privy thereto.[163] It is not in every case essential to show that he knew the acts in question were tortious, or that he was reckless as to whether they were tortious or not, unless knowledge in itself is an ingredient of the tort complained of: the extent of his personal involvement in the company's tort must be carefully examined.[164] Each case will depend upon its own particular facts.[165] Apart from the above classes of case, the principal of the tortious employee and such employee himself will alone be liable.

20-35 **Liability of receiver's principal.** Assuming the receiver has a principal (i.e. the company or the chargee, as the case may be), such principal is liable to third persons in respect of frauds, deceits, concealments, misrepresentations, torts, negligences, or other malfeasances, misfeasances or omissions of duty by the receiver in the course of the performance of the receiver's duties, but not for acts done outside the agency, unless ratified or subsequently adopted.[166]

20-36 **Liability to third persons in contract.** The powers of the receiver as regards the making of contracts will be governed by the terms of the charge under which he is appointed and the terms of his appointment, subject always to (i) the fact that, as

---

[157] *Re Simms*, n.84, above at 33 per Romer LJ.
[158] *Re Simms*, n.84, above.
[159] *Re Simms*, n.84, above.
[160] *Fenton Textile Association v Lodge* [1928] 1 K.B. 1.
[161] *Owen & Co v Cronk* [1895] 1 Q.B. 265 per Lord Esher at 272.
[162] See *Cargill v Bower* (1878) 10 Ch. D. 502; *Rainham Chemical Works v Belvedere Fish Guano Co* [1921] 2 A.C. 465 per Lord Buckmaster at 475, 476; *Performing Rights Society Ltd v Ciryl Theatrical Syndicate* [1924] 1 K.B. 1; *British Thomson-Houston Co v Sterling Accessories Ltd* [1924] 2 Ch. 33; *Mentmore Manufacturing Co Ltd v National Merchandising Manufacturing Co Inc* [1978] 89 D.L.R. (3d) 195; *Hoover Plc v George Hulme (Stockport) Ltd* [1984] 8 F.S.R. 565; *White Horse Distillers Ltd v Gregson Associates Ltd* [1984] R.P.C. 61.
[163] *Stone v Cartwright* (1795) 6 T.R. 411.
[164] *C Evans Ltd v Spritebrand Ltd* [1985] 1 W.L.R. 317.
[165] *Wah Tat Bank Ltd v Chan Cheng Kum* [1975] A.C. 507 per Lord Salmon at 514–515.
[166] See *Lloyd v Grace, Smith Co* [1912] A.C. 716; *Percy v Glasgow Corporation* [1922] 2 A.C. 299.

agent of the company, he cannot of course exceed the company's own powers,[167] and (ii) s.37(1) of the Insolvency Act 1986, which provides that a receiver or manager appointed out of court, under powers contained in an instrument (other than an administrative receiver), will, to the same extent as if he had been appointed by order of the court, be personally liable on any contract entered into by him in the performance of his functions,[168] except in so far as the contract otherwise provides. He will also be personally liable under any contract of employment "adopted" by him in the performance of his functions,[169] save, however, that he will not be taken to have adopted a contract of employment by reason of anything done or omitted to be done within 14 days after his appointment.[170]

What amounts to the "adoption" of an employment contract. The question of what amounts to the "adoption" of a contract of employment may be a matter of difficulty. Clearly, mere inaction in relation thereto cannot be sufficient: otherwise, a receiver might find himself personally liable upon a contract of employment of which he did not know, and might never have been able to discover any details of during the 14-day period referred to in para.20-36 (for example, in the case of an employee working wholly abroad). **20-37**

Nor can mere knowledge of the existence of the employees, and the fact that they are employed by the company, it is submitted, amount to "adoption". Otherwise, a receiver anxious to carry on a business of the company, with a view to its sale as a going concern, might well be placed in an impossible position. Some positive act of adoption is required.[171] Notice given by the receiver to employees that he is not adopting their contracts of employment has been held to be ineffective.[172]

Where an administrator had been informed that the company's operations in France were conducted through its French subsidiary, the rights of whose employees were regulated by French employment law, he later discovered that they were in fact employees of the company, and therefore might have claims against him. On his application, the court held that there was no evidence that he had in any way adopted their contracts of employment.[173]

In so far as the receiver is personally liable in the above manner on any contract, he is entitled in respect of that liability to an indemnity out of the assets.[174] But this provision does not limit any right of indemnity which he would have had apart from it, nor does it limit his liability in respect of contracts entered into without authority, or confer upon him an indemnity in respect of such liability.[175]

Effect of ratification. If a receiver ratifies a contract which has been ostensibly **20-38**

---

[167] Companies Act 2006 s.40(1) (validating any transaction, decided upon by the directors, in favour of a person dealing with the company in good faith) does not apply, but see the extensive powers conferred on the receiver by Insolvency Act 1986 Sch.1.
[168] For an example of personal liability, see *Re Mack Trucks (Britain) Ltd* [1967] 1 W.L.R. 780. Presumably he could, if so required, sue personally (and not in the name of the company) to enforce such a contract: see *Kettle v Dunster and Wakefield* [1928] 138 L.T. 158.
[169] Insolvency Act 1986 s.37(1)(a).
[170] Insolvency Act 1986 s.37(2). In relation to "adoption" of contracts, see para.20-31, above. In relation to the receiver's right of indemnity, see para.20-44, below.
[171] *Powdrill v Watson* [1995] 2 A.C. 394 HL.
[172] *Powdrill v Watson*, n.171, above.
[173] *Re Antal International Ltd* [2003] EWHC 339 Ch; [2003] B.P.I.R. 1067, applying *Powdrill v Watson*, n.171, above, on an application for directions under Insolvency Act 1986 s.14 (as amended).
[174] Insolvency Act 1986 s.37(1)(b).
[175] Insolvency Act 1986 s.37(3).

made on behalf of the company by a person acting without the receiver's authority, such a ratification does not result in a novation of the contract (which would entail his becoming personally liable thereon); since the receiver is never a party to the contract, the relevant statutory provisions have no operation; ratification will have the normal result of relating back to the date of the contract.[176]

The statutory provision assimilating the position of a receiver appointed out of court to that of one appointed by the court[177] made a radical departure in the law, since previously a receiver was not in general[178] personally liable in contract; such liability was the liability of his principal, whether the company or the chargee. There is, however, nothing in the section to exclude the liability of the receiver's principal, and accordingly the third party would seem to have a choice of defendants to sue.

20-39   **When receiver becomes liable for debts.**   If the receiver is an agent for the company, neither a trustee for chargees who appointed him, nor a chargee itself, are under any personal liability for debts incurred by him in carrying on a business.[179] If the receiver continues to carry on the business after his agency for the company has determined, he does not in a normal case[180] become an agent for the chargee[181] but becomes a principal.[182]

Where the receiver has incurred personal liability in respect of which he is entitled to indemnity, his creditor cannot, on a judgment against him, issue execution against the company's assets,[183] but can apply for payment out of the assets of the company, by way of subrogation.[184] Although the receiver is not personally liable in respect of the contracts of the company made before his appointment, like any other agent he may be liable to repay money received by him under a mistake of fact, or under a voidable contract, unless before proceedings are brought he has accounted to his principal, which he may do by payment into his receivership account.[185]

20-40   **Contractual liens.**   If, under a contract made by the company in the ordinary course of business[186] before the appointment of a receiver who is the agent of the company under a floating charge, the other contracting party obtains the right to a general lien over goods belonging to the company, that right may be exercised after the appointment of the receiver over any goods of the company which come properly[187] into the hands of such other party thereafter.[188] It is immaterial that the lien so conferred had not become exercisable before the appointment of the receiver,

---

[176] *Lawson v Hosemaster Machine Co Ltd* [1966] 1 W.L.R. 1300.
[177] Insolvency Act 1986 s.37.
[178] Cf. *Thomas v Todd* [1926] 2 K.B. 511.
[179] *Gosling v Gaskell and Grocott* [1897] A.C. 575; *Cully v Parsons* [1923] 2 Ch. 512.
[180] See *Re S Brown Co (General Warehousemen) Ltd* [1940] Ch. 961; but note the comments thereon in *Re Wood* [1941] Ch.112.
[181] *Gosling v Gaskell and Grocott*, n.179, above.
[182] *Thomas v Todd*, n.178, above. For a case where, on special facts, the receiver was held to be the agent of the company in liquidation, see *Re Northern Garage Ltd sub nom. Re Newton v Cattermoles (Transport) Ltd's Contract* [1946] Ch. 188.
[183] See *Jennings v Mather* [1902] 1 K.B. 1.
[184] *Re Rylands Glass Co* [1905] 118 L.T.J. 87.
[185] *Bissell v Ariel Motors* [1910] 27 T.L.R. 73.
[186] See *Robson v Smith* [1895] 2 Ch. 118 at 124.
[187] *George Barker Ltd v Eynon* [1974] 1 W.L.R. 462 at 466F.
[188] *Robson v Smith* [1895] 2 Ch. 118, n.186, above.

since the right to the lien pre-dated the appointment.[189] The only way in which, otherwise than by agreement, the receiver could prevent the lien from attaching would be by ensuring that no goods of the company, available to satisfy the lien, fell into the hands of such party.[190]

Contracts: set-off. The position in relation to set-off is in general the same, whether the receiver is appointed in or out of court.[191] The principles applicable are those relating to the right of set-off as against an equitable assignee.[192] Either (i) the charge document contains a fixed charge upon all the future property of the company, thus assigning in equity the benefit of any contractual debt due to the company to the chargee immediately upon its coming into existence, or (ii) the charge document contains a floating charge upon all the future property of the company, in which case the crystallisaton of the floating charge produces the same equitable assignment, by way of charge, in favour of the chargee.[193]

20-41

Obviously, in either case, if, at the date of the assignment, the debtor has a cross-claim against the company of such a nature that it can be set off, no matter how such claim originated, set-off is permissible in the absence of an express agreement to the contrary.[194] Nor will knowledge or notice of the existence of any uncrystal-lised floating charge alter the position.[195] Further, if subsequently the debtor becomes entitled to cross-claims arising out of the same contract as the assigned claim, which may happen whether the receiver "adopts" the contract or elects not to cause the company to carry it out, these will afford a valid set-off, no matter when they arise.[196]

The law of set-off in insolvency has been significantly changed and restated.[197]

Set-off under different contracts. Where, however, the claims arise under one contract, and the cross-claim which it is sought to set off arises subsequent to the appointment of the receiver, and under a different contract, the position is more complex. The general rule is undoubtedly that set-off is not, in general, pos-sible[198]; this is so, even though the receiver, in order to recover the claim, will have

20-42

---

[189] *George Barker Ltd v Eynon*, n.187, above, at 473B–C and 475G.

[190] *George Barker Ltd v Eynon*, n.187, above, per Stamp LJ at 471H; see also *London Flight Centre (Stansted) Ltd v Osprey Aviation Ltd* [2002] B.P.I.R. 1115, (2003) Insolvency Lawyer 60 and *Hammonds v Thomas Muckle & Sons Ltd* [2006] B.P.I.R. 704.

[191] See *NW Robbie & Co Ltd v Witney Warehouse Co Ltd* [1963] 1 W.L.R. 1324 at 1340 per Russell LJ.

[192] *NW Robbie & Co Ltd v Witney Warehouse Co Ltd*, n.191, above and see *Rother Iron Works Ltd v Canterbury Precision Engineers Ltd* [1974] Q.B. 1; *Security Trust Co v The Royal Bank of Canada* [1976] A.C. 503.

[193] See n.192, above. Where it was provided by statute that only an absolute assignment of a Crown debt was valid, an assignment pursuant to the crystallisation of a floating charge did not prevent set-off: *Clarkson Co Ltd v The Queen* [1979] 94 D.L.R. (3d) 348.

[194] *Phoenix Assurance Co Ltd v Earls Court Ltd* (1913) 30 T.L.R. 50 CA; *Rother Iron Works Ltd v Canterbury Precision Engineers Ltd*, n.192, above.

[195] *Biggerstaff v Rowatt's Wharf Ltd* [1896] 2 Ch. 93; *Re Roundwood Colliery Co Ltd* [1987] 1 Ch. 373 CA.

[196] *Young v Kitchin* [1878] 3 Ex.D. 127; *Government of Newfoundland v Newfoundland Ry Co* (1888) 13 App. Cas. 199; *Parsons v Sovereign Bank of Canada* [1913] A.C. 160 HL; *Lawrence v Hayes* [1927] 2 K.B. 111.

[197] *Re West End Networks Ltd (in liquidation); Secretary of State for Trade & Industry v Frid* [2004] UKHL 24; [2004] 2 B.C.L.C. 1; (VAT refund set-off against redundancy claims).

[198] *Biggerstaff v Rowatt's Wharf Ltd*, n.195, above; *Lynch v Ardmore Studios (Ireland) Ltd* [1966] Ir.R.

to sue in the name of the company, against which the cross-claim lies.[199] This, however, is not an inflexible rule; and where the two contracts under which the claim and cross-claim respectively arise are between the debtor and the company, and the second contract is intimately connected with the first, set-off will be allowed, notwithstanding that the claim under the second contract arises only after the equitable assignment.[200] Although the limits of the doctrine are not easy to discern, in general set-off will be allowed if the debtor can show some equitable ground for being protected against the receiver's demands.[201] It is of course possible for the parties (if neither is insolvent) to make an agreement not to raise a set-off.[202]

A receiver cannot claim to set off damages for breach of contract against monies validly assigned absolutely to a person in contractual relationship with the company; his only remedy is by way of an action for damages for breach of contract.[203]

20-43 **Third party insurance.** The principles applicable to third-party insurance are the same as in the case of a receiver appointed by the court.[204]

20-44 **Extent of receiver's indemnity.** If the receiver becomes liable to third persons in respect of acts done or contracts entered into by him in the course of his duties as receiver, he is entitled to indemnity out of the assets subject to the charge,[205] unless he has forfeited such right by improper conduct; such indemnity extends to his costs as between solicitor and client. He is not, however, entitled to a lien in respect of possible future claims.[206]

If the receiver is placed in a position in which he is liable to pay money to a third person, he is entitled to be indemnified by his principal, though the latter is not relieved from liability.[207]

20-45 **Leasehold property.** After the appointment of a receiver out of court, the remedies of the landlord of properties leased to the company are unaffected: the landlord can carry out commercial rent arrears recovery or re-enter if the rent is not paid by the receiver. He can also sue the company for the rent: but this remedy is generally useless, as the judgment cannot be enforced against the property of the company which is subject to the chargee's charge. It may therefore be to the advantage of the chargee for the receiver to abandon leasehold property which is burdensome and of no value.[208] The receiver cannot safely adopt this course unless it is clear that the assets are insufficient to discharge the security; and in all

---

133; *Business Computers Ltd v Anglo-African Leasing Ltd* [1977] 1 W.L.R. 578.

[199] *Watson v Mid-Wales Ry Co* [1867] L.R. 2 C.P. 593; *Re Pinto Leite and Nephews* [1929] 1 Ch. 221, 233; *NW Robbie Co Ltd v Witney Warehouse Co Ltd*, n.191, above.

[200] As in *Collins v Jones* [1830] 10 B. & C. 777; *McKinnon v Armstrong Bros & Co* [1877] 2 App. Cas. 531.

[201] *Rawson v Samuel* [1841] Cr. & PH. 161; *Barrett's Case (No.2)* (1865) 4 De G.J. & S. 756; *Handley Page Ltd v Customs & Excise* [1970] 2 Lloyd's Rep.459.

[202] *Kettle v Dunster and Wakefield* [1928] 138 L.T. 158.

[203] *Ashby, Warner & Co Ltd v Simmons* [1936] 2 All E.R. 697 (interpleader proceedings by the fund-holder).

[204] See para.6-69 above.

[205] Insolvency Act 1986 s.37(1)(b) (in relation to contracts entered into by the receiver).

[206] *Dyson v Peat* [1917] 1 Ch. 99.

[207] *Adams v Morgan* [1924] 1 K.B. 751.

[208] The receiver has no right of disclaimer, such as is vested in the liquidator, with permission of the

cases the approval of the chargee should be obtained. Apart from this, the power of sale conferred on mortgagees authorises surrender of a lease for proper consideration. It is considered that a receiver with power to carry on a business can accept surrenders of leases and tenancies, apart from the power conferred by s.100 of the Law of Property Act 1925 on mortgagees.

The receiver can, in the name of the company, exercise the right to claim renewal of a lease under Pt II of the Landlord and Tenant Act 1954.[209]

Conveyances and transfers. A mere power to sell does not enable the receiver to convey the legal estate: but express power to do so in the name of the company or, in the case of specific legal mortgages, of the mortgagee is usually conferred: this power is not affected by a winding up.

20-46

Where a charge created by a security document is only equitable, e.g. a floating charge, the company must concur to convey the legal estate.

An ordinary receiver is not usually in a position to cause a company seal to be affixed to a document, as the receiver is bound by the provisions of the articles relating to the use of the company seal, which normally provide that it is only to be used with the authority of the directors or a duly authorised committee of the directors.[210]

Normally, however, a suitable power of attorney will be conferred upon the receiver by the charge document, and he will be able to convey the property of the company in its name by exercising such power. If it does, he can convey in the name of the company by signing the name of the company in the presence of an attesting witness.[211]

When may the receiver become liable to the company? The long-standing general principle is that the receiver owes no general duty of care to the chargor company, but only a duty to act towards him in good faith, without fraud or bad faith, but the position is dependent on the particular facts present in any individual case. Various types of negligent act or omission in the conduct of a sale of the charged assets may expose the receiver to liability, and may also expose the chargee to liability if he has sought to direct, or has influenced the judgment of, the receiver.[212] In two leading cases, the Privy Council appears to have displayed inconsistent approaches to the subject (partially accounted for possibly by differences in the facts).[213]

20-47

Power to carry on business. Power to carry on a business is usually conferred on a receiver, but an ordinary receiver has no such power apart from express provision.[214] His powers are also limited by the powers of the company, as stated in the memorandum of association.

20-48

Power to borrow. It seems that a power to carry on a business implies a power

20-49

---

court, under s.178 of the Insolvency Act 1986, as to which see *Re Katherine et Cie* [1932] 1 Ch. 70.

[209] *Gough's Garages v Pugsley* [1930] 1 K.B. 615 (a decision under the Landlord and Tenant Act 1927).

[210] *Industrial Development Authority v Morgan* [1978] Ir.R. 159.

[211] Law of Property Act 1925 s.74(3). The purchase-money is expressed to be paid to the receiver.

[212] As the chargee may thereby constitute the receiver his agent: *American Express International Banking Corp v Hurley* [1985] 3 All E.R. 564.

[213] *Tse Kwong Lam v Wong Chit Sen* [1983] 1 W.L.R. 394 PC; *Downsview Nominees Ltd v First City Bank* [1993] A.C. 395 PC followed in *Silven Properties Ltd v Royal Bank of Scotland plc* [2003] EWCA Civ 1409; [2003] B.P.I.R. 1429 CA; and see para.18-34 above.

[214] See *Bompas v King* [1886] 33 Ch. D. 279, as to his powers and his indemnity.

to borrow[215] and to give creditors the benefit of his right to indemnity out of the charged assets, and that the receiver may pledge charged assets as security for loans made to him, at all events if he has a power to sell.[216] It is a question of construction, in each particular case, whether he is authorised to borrow money on the security of the assets in priority to the chargee. Thus where he was authorised "to make such arrangements as he might think expedient," he was held to have such a power.[217] For his own protection, he should see that the terms of his appointment give him an express power to borrow and to create charges for loans. If they do not, and it is imperative that he should raise money, he should apply to the court for directions.[218]

Although an ordinary receiver is generally treated as agent for the company, the acts of the receiver may bind the chargee; thus, where the receiver consented to a prior mortgage of leaseholds, including certain fixed plant, in a sale of chattels over which the debenture-holders' security extended, it was difficult, if not impossible, for the debenture-holders to obtain damages for severance, as the consent of the receiver was in their own interests.[219]

20-50   **Calls.**   If the company is not in liquidation, an ordinary receiver must apply to the court for directions as to the calling up of unpaid share capital,[220] which will presumably be given, as in the corresponding case of a receiver appointed by the court. If the company is in liquidation, the proper person to get in uncalled capital is the liquidator, and if he does not do so the receiver should apply for an order directing him to do so.[221]

Where a shareholder, before liquidation, had advanced money to the company, to which he also owed unpaid calls, he could not rely on his loan agreement with the company to entitle him to set off his loan indebtedness against the amount of his unpaid calls.[222]

20-51   **The receiver as a party to litigation.**   In litigation concerning the company, the receiver is not normally a necessary or proper party. As the agent of the company, his acts or inactions are acts or inactions of the company, and he bears no personal responsibility to any party who may be injured as a result. Thus, if the result of his actions or inactions is simply that the company does not perform a contract with a third party, that party's right of action is simply against the company.[223] However, there are cases in which the receiver, still in his capacity as an agent for the company, threatens to deal with property in a manner inconsistent with the equitable rights of others, such as, for example, by selling property which is, to his knowledge, held by the company on trust for a third person, or in or over which a third party has equitable rights which will be destroyed by the sale. In such a case,

---

[215] See *Ex p. City Bank* (1868) 3 Ch.App.758; *General Auction Co v Smith* [1898] 3 Ch. 432.
[216] *Robinson Printing Co v Chic Ltd* [1905] 2 Ch. 23; *Deyes v Wood* [1911] 1 Ch. 806. In the former case, it was held that the power to charge did not extend to debts accruing due after discharge.
[217] *Robinson Printing Co v Chic Ltd*, n.216, above.
[218] Under Insolvency Act 1986 s.35(1).
[219] See *Re Rogerstone Brick and Stone Co* [1919] 1 Ch. 110.
[220] Under Insolvency Act 1986 s.35.
[221] *Fowler v Broad's Patent Night Light Company, Ltd* [1893] 1 Ch. 724; *Re Westminster Syndicate Limited* (1908) 99 L.T. 924.
[222] *Re Pinecord Ltd, Bennett v Rolph* [1995] B.C.C. 483.
[223] *Airlines Airspares Ltd v Handley Page Ltd* [1970] Ch. 193; *Telemetrix Plc v Modern Engineers of Bristol (Holdings) Ltd* [1985] B.C.L.C. 213; *Lathia v Dronsfield Bros. Ltd* [1987] B.C.L.C. 321.

this amounts to tortious conduct, or a threat of such conduct, which not only renders the receiver a proper party to an action but will also render him liable to an award of costs against him.[224]

There is also a statutory power, but subject to rules of court, to order a receiver to pay the costs of an action by the company instigated by him or brought against the company, even though he is not a party thereto.[225]

Liquidation of company at instance of receiver. An ordinary receiver is entitled   **20-52**
to present a winding-up petition, as incidental to the preservation and protection of the assets over which he has been appointed receiver; but he is not entitled to an order *ex debito justitiae*, only as a matter of discretion.[226] It is in general desirable that the petition should be brought to the notice of those who might be concerned to oppose it.

Remuneration. The remuneration payable to the receiver is usually fixed by the   **20-53**
mortgage, by reference to and incorporating s.109(6) of the Law of Property Act 1925. That section will normally apply without express mention.

The commission for which provision is made by that subsection is therein stated to be not only in respect of the receiver's remuneration, but also in satisfaction of all costs, charges and expenses incurred by him as receiver. If, however, as is the common practice, the mortgage varies and extends the relevant sections (ss.99–109 inclusive) of the Law of Property Act 1925, and makes specific provision for the discharge of costs, charges and expenses otherwise than out of the receiver's commission, then such provision will take effect according to its terms, since, in such a case, the receiver is appointed not merely under the Law of Property Act 1925 but under a mortgage which incorporates and extends its provisions.[227]

As to the power of the court to fix the receiver's remuneration, see para.25-19, below.

---

[224] In *Telemetrix Plc v Modern Engineers of Bristol (Holdings) Ltd*, n.223, above, Peter Gibson J observed, at 217a, that "in asking for costs against the receivers, as well as against the company, counsel for the plaintiffs made it plain that it is not suggested that the receivers and managers should be personally liable for costs". In substance, the plaintiffs were seeking priority for their costs over the debenture holders.

[225] Senior Courts Act 1981 (formerly Supreme Court Act 1981) s.51(1) and CPR r.46.2; see *Aiden Shipping Co Ltd v Interbulk Ltd* [1986] A.C. 965 HL.

[226] *Re Emmadart Ltd* [1979] Ch. 540 (the object was to gain exemption from rates in respect of vacant premises).

[227] *Marshall v Cottingham* [1982] Ch. 82.

PART V: ADMINISTRATIVE RECEIVERS

CHAPTER 21

APPOINTMENT, STATUS AND POWERS OF AN ADMINISTRATIVE RECEIVER

21-1   Introduction.   The "administrative receiver" is a statutory construct. Section 29(2) of the Insolvency Act 1986 provides:

"In this Chapter 'administrative receiver' means—

(a)   a receiver or manager of the whole (or substantially the whole) of a company's property appointed by or on behalf of the holders of any debentures of the company secured by a charge which, as created, was a floating charge, or by such a charge and one or more other securities; or

(b)   a person who would be such a receiver or manager but for the appointment of some other person as the receiver of part of the company's property."

An administrative receiver is one of the types of receiver appointed out of court, the principal other types being receivers appointed under the provisions of the Law of Property Act 1925 (LPA Receivers) and receivers appointed under the terms of fixed charges (fixed charge receivers). When the Enterprise Act 2002 Pt 10 s.250[1] came into force on 15 September 2003 it prohibited the holders of floating charges created on or after that date from exercising any rights to appoint administrative receivers.[2] Those rights will continue to be exercisable however by holders of pre-existing instruments.

21-2   Current Relevance.   The appointment of an administrative receiver is therefore now only possible in relation to most companies under a floating charge created before 15 September 2003. It is also possible in relation to eight excepted categories of undertaking listed in the statute,[3] with respect to which the power to appoint administrative receivers will continue to attach to debenture or other floating charge securities, created by them after 15 September 2003. The excepted categories mainly concern specialist financing and are considered at para.21–6, below. However it would be a mistake to see these categories as irrelevant or of historical interest only. They include public-private partnerships, which continue to be favoured by government to deliver large infrastructure projects, as well as significant capital market arrangements, and projects designed for regulated utility businesses.

Where administrative receivership remains available, it can be an attractive op-

---

[1]   Brought into force by the Enterprise Act 2002 (Commencement No.4 and Transitional Provisions and Savings) Order 2003 (SI 2003/1730) art.3; and see Insolvency Act 1986 s.72A.

[2]   Insolvency Act 1986 s.72A(4); and see SI 2003/1832, 21-6.

[3]   Enterprise Act 2002 s.250, inserting ss.72A–72H into Insolvency Act 1986.

tion for lenders, with considerable advantages in particular in terms of tax (capital gains tax and corporation tax are not payable as an expense in an administrative receivership, as opposed to administration and liquidation).

History. The Companies Act 1948 recognised the special position of a person   **21-3**
who had been appointed to be receiver or manager of the whole, or substantially the whole, of the property of a company registered in England, without attaching any specifically distinctive name to such a person.[4] The Insolvency Act 1985 elaborated on this concept and attached the name of "administrative receiver" to a person who was a receiver or manager of the whole, or substantially the whole, of a company's property, appointed by or on behalf of the holder of any debentures of the company secured by a charge which, as created, was a floating charge, or by such a charge and by one or more other securities.[5] Nor would a person so appointed cease to be an administrative receiver, if a receiver had been appointed of some part only of the company's property.[6] This concept was carried on into the Insolvency Act 1986.[7]

The main objectives behind the creation of the new status were:

(i)   to secure that a person entrusted with such a responsible position is a suitably qualified person[8];

(ii)   to ensure that he has sufficient powers to enable him to operate with maximum efficiency[9];

(iii)   to ensure that he supplies the relevant authorities with sufficient information concerning the directors of the company, so that applications for their disqualification can in a proper case be considered[10]; and

(iv)   to ensure that the position of unsecured creditors of the company was no longer overlooked.[11]

Context. Obviously the usual case in which an administrative receiver is ap-   **21-4**
pointed is one in which the financial position of the company is, at the least, uncertain. Accordingly, except in so far as the context otherwise requires, "insolvency" in the provisions of the Insolvency Act 1986 relating to a company includes (in addition to the appointment of a liquidator) the appointment of an administrative receiver, the approval of a voluntary arrangement, the making of an administration order[12] and the extra-judicial appointment of an administrator.[13] However, it is important to note that an administrative receiver is appointed to realise property for the benefit of the security-holder alone. Administrative receivership is in essence an enforcement mechanism in relation to the property covered by the charge that gave rise to the appointment. The administrative receiver owes his primary duties to his appointor alone. The procedure is not a collective one,

---

[4]   Companies Act 1948 s.372, which simply defined such a person as "the receiver".
[5]   Insolvency Act 1985 s.45(2).
[6]   Insolvency Act 1985 s.45(2)(b).
[7]   Insolvency Act 1986 s.29(2). By s.250 of that Act, this definition applies throughout the Parts of the Act that govern corporate insolvency.
[8]   See para.21-16ff, below.
[9]   See para.21-19 ff, below.
[10]   Under the Company Directors Disqualification Act 1986 (as amended) ss.6, 7.
[11]   See Ch.22. The Administrative Receiver; Relationship with unsecured creditors.
[12]   Insolvency Act 1986 s.247(1).
[13]   Under Insolvency Act 1986 Sch.B1 paras 14 or 22.

conducted in the primary interests of creditors as a whole. It is thus not a "collective insolvency proceeding" and accordingly not covered by the EU Regulation on Insolvency Proceedings 2015.[14] Although by statute he is an agent of the company,[15] that description is "apt to give a somewhat false impression" as the agency is primarily a device to protect the mortgagee, and to insulate the mortgagee from liability for the administrative receivers' acts and omissions.[16] Further, although an administrative receiver is an office-holder and must be an insolvency practitioner, he is not an officer of the court and a number of statutory powers are not available to him (for example the power to set aside antecedent transactions, or enforce a statutory moratorium).

21-5 **White Paper restricting administrative receivership.** In July 2001 the Government published a White Paper called *Productivity and Enterprise: Insolvency – A Second Chance.*[17] It referred to the existence of concerns that: (i) "the large number of administrative receivership appointments in the early 1990s may have represented precipitate behaviour on the part of lenders, causing companies to fail unnecessarily", (ii) "as to the extent to which administrative receivership as a procedure provides adequate incentives to maximise economic value", and (iii) about "whether it provides an acceptable level of transparency and accountability to the range of stakehold- ers with an interest in a company's affairs, particularly creditors".[18] The Government also noted that the administrative receiver's principal obligation was towards his appointor and that international insolvency law was based on collective procedures. The Government's stated view was that:

> "on the grounds of both equity and efficiency, the time has come to make changes which will tip the balance firmly in favour of collective insolvency proceedings – proceedings in which all creditors participate, under which a duty is owed to all creditors and in which all creditors may look to an office holder for an account of his dealings with a company's assets. It follows that we believe that administrative receivership should cease to be a major insolvency procedure."

The White Paper proposed that administrative receivership be restricted to floating charges granted in transactions in the capital markets.[19]

By the time of the Enterprise Act 2002 the exceptions had been broadened to include a number of other specialist financing arrangements and to floating charges created before that Act came into force.

APPOINTMENT

21-6 **Permissible situations for an appointment.** As a result of the Enterprise Act 2002 there are now two situations where the holder of a floating charge may appoint an administrative receiver. The first is where the charge was created before 15 September 2003.[20] The second is where the company falls within one of the eight exceptions set out in Insolvency Act 1986 ss.72B–72GA. As already noted, these

---

[14] EU 2015/848.
[15] Insolvency Act 1986 s.44(1)(a).
[16] *Edenwest Limited v CMS Cameron McKenna (a firm)* [2012] EWHC 1258 (Ch).
[17] http://webarchive.nationalarchives.gov.uk/+/http:/www.insolvency.gov.uk/cwp/cm5234.pdf [accessed 20 August 2017].
[18] Paragraphs 2.1 and 2.2.
[19] Paragraph 2.5.
[20] Insolvency Act 1986 s.72A(4)(a).

mainly concern situations where specialist financing is employed. The White Paper recognised that the right to appoint an administrative receiver played an important role in capital market transactions and proposed to exempt those situations from the prohibition to be brought into force.[21] The list of exemptions was increased to eight situations by the time the Enterprise Act 2002 came into force:

(1) A capital market arrangement[22];
(2) Public-private partnerships[23];
(3) Utility projects including "step-in rights"[24];
(4) Urban regeneration projects including "step-in rights"[25];
(5) Project finance including "step-in rights"[26];
(6) Financial market companies[27];
(7) Registered social landlords[28];
(8) Protected Railway companies.[29]

These exceptions may be added to or removed or amended by an order (to be made by statutory instrument) of the Secretary of State or the Treasury.[30]

These categories of undertaking, and the meanings of the terms employed, are defined in considerable detail in Sch.2A to the Act[31] and are now discussed in turn. The question of whether a situation falls within an exemption is to be answered at the time the administrative receiver comes to be appointed.

(a) Capital Market Exception   An administrative receiver may be appointed "in pursuance of" an agreement which is or forms part of a capital market arrangement, so long as (a) a party incurs a debt of at least £50 million under the arrangement (or when the agreement was entered into was expected to incur a debt of that amount), and (b) the arrangement involves the issue of a "capital market investment".[32] Similar wording to the first of these conditions is found in s.72E(2)(a) (the "project finance" exception) and was discussed in *Feetum v Levy*,[33] in which the High Court (Lewison J) and the Court of Appeal held that where an expectation of a debt was relied on it must be an expectation of the debt arising under the financing agreement and at the date of that agreement as opposed to an expectation arising at the date of another, perhaps earlier agreement. The wording in this exception is not identical, as the party is to incur the debt "under the arrangement", but if an expected debt is relied on it must exist "when the agreement was entered into". The agreement (i.e. the charge) is just one part of the capital market arrangement.

Paragraphs 1 and 2 of Sch.2A define "capital market arrangement" and "capital

---

21   Paragraph 2.18.
22   Insolvency Act 1986 s.72B.
23   Insolvency Act 1986 s.72C.
24   Insolvency Act 1986 s.72D.
25   Insolvency Act 1986 s.72DA.
26   Insolvency Act 1986 s.72E: for a failed attempt to bring an appointment within this section, see *Feetum v Levy* [2005] EWCA Civ 1601; [2006] Ch. 585, discussed later in this paragraph.
27   Insolvency Act 1986 s.72F.
28   Insolvency Act 1986 s.72G.
29   Insolvency Act 1986 s.72GA.
30   Insolvency Act 1986 s.72H. The exceptions contained in ss.72DA and 72GA (above) were added using this power.
31   As inserted by Enterprise Act 2002 s.250(2) and Sch.8.
32   Insolvency Act 1986 s.72B(1).
33   [2005] 1 W.L.R. 2576 and [2006] Ch. 585, CA.

market investment". The former is a securitisation that involves certain defined investments (such as contracts for differences), or involves a grant of security to the issuer or to a trustee acting for the holders of the debt instrument, or involves one party guaranteeing another party's performance obligations, or one party providing security in respect of another party's performance obligations. The latter refers to debt instruments which are, or are designed to be, rated, listed or traded, or are particular types of bond or commercial paper.

A very similar exception applies to exempt capital market companies from eligibility for a CVA moratorium, albeit with a debt level of only £10 million.[34]

(b)   Public-private partnership ("PPP")   An administrative receiver may be appointed over a "project company" of a PPP project which includes "step in rights". The High Court in *Feetum v Levy*[35] gave a broad meaning to the term "project" and there was no appeal from that conclusion. The High Court refused to limit it to construction and engineering projects financed by project finance. It applied the Oxford English Dictionary definition of "project" to hold that a scheme to acquire and exploit software for delivering video and sound in taxicabs was a "project".

A "project company" is defined in para.7 to Sch.2A as one which exclusively carries out one of five defined roles for the purpose of the project (holding property, carrying out the project (including through agents) or being responsible for doing so, financing the project, or acting as holding company for a company engaged in these roles).

A PPP project is defined in s.72C(2) of the Insolvency Act 1986 as a project whose resources are provided "partly by one or more public bodies and partly by one or more private persons" or is designed wholly or mainly to assist a public body to discharge a function. "Resources" are broadly defined, to include funds but also "professional skill".[36] "Public body" means a body which exercises public functions and any further bodies specified by the Secretary of State.[37]

Critically, the project must include "step-in rights". The Court of Appeal in *Feetum v Levy*[38] considered this phrase, and its definition at para.6 of Sch.2A. This defines such rights as the conditional entitlement of the party providing finance to the project to assume responsibility for carrying out all or part of the project, or make arrangements to carry it out. The Court of Appeal deliberately eschewed any attempt at defining "step-in rights", but held that a power to appoint administrative receivers was not a "step-in right".

Project companies of PPP projects are also exempt from eligibility for a CVA moratorium.[39]

(c)   Utility Project   If a project is a "utility project" and includes "step-in rights" then an administrative receiver may be appointed over a project company forming part of that project.[40] A utility project is a project designed wholly or mainly for the

---

[34]   Insolvency Act 1986 Sch.A1 paras 4A and 4D–4G.
[35]   [2005] 1 W.L.R. 2576 at 2584.
[36]   Insolvency Act 1986 Sch.2A para.8.
[37]   Insolvency Act 1986 Sch.2A para.9.
[38]   [2006] Ch. 585 at 608.
[39]   Insolvency Act 1986 Sch.A1 para.4B.
[40]   Insolvency Act 1986 s.72D.

purpose of a regulated business, which is defined[41] to include businesses carried on in industries such as gas, electricity, water, public electronic communications, sewage and railways.

(d) Urban regeneration projects   An administrative receiver may be appointed over a project company of a project designed wholly or mainly to carry out urban regeneration work outside Northern Ireland, and which includes "step-in rights".[42]

(e) Project Finance   This is the exception specifically considered in *Feetum v Levy*.[43] It requires a project company (not necessarily the same as the company to whom the administrative receiver is appointed[44]) to be "financed" and for the project to have "step-in rights".[45] The finance must take the form of a debt of at least £50 million, which must be incurred under an agreement (not necessarily the agreement under which the administrative receiver is appointed[46]) or be expected to be incurred under that agreement. It appears that the nature of the project is immaterial.

(f) Financial Market   This exception allows the use of particular financial market charges to appoint an administrative receiver: market charges, system-charges and collateral security charges in relation to trading in the financial markets such as foreign exchange.[47]

(g) Social Landlord   This exception applies to a company which is a registered social landlord.[48]

(h) Certain Special Administration Regime Companies   This exception applies to certain companies subject to special administration regimes, comprising water and sewerage companies, protected railway companies and those with air traffic control licences.[49]

Pre-conditions for appointment.   The statutory definition of an "administrative receiver"[50] requires the appointment to be: **21-7**

(i)   of a receiver or manager,
(ii)   over the whole or substantially the whole of the property of "a company", and
(iii) made by or on behalf of the holders of a debenture or debentures secured by a charge which, as created, was a floating charge. It is sufficient that the security is a floating charge "and one or other securities".[51]

It is specifically provided that if a person would have been such a receiver or manager but for the appointment of another person as receiver of part of the

---

41   Insolvency Act 1986 Sch.2A para.10.
42   Insolvency Act 1986 s.72DA.
43   [2005] 1 W.L.R. 2576 and [2006] Ch. 585, CA.
44   [2005] 1 W.L.R. 2576 at 2584H.
45   Insolvency Act 1986 s.72E.
46   [2005] 1 W.L.R. 2576 at 2584H–2585A.
47   Insolvency Act 1986 s.72F.
48   Insolvency Act 1986 s.72G.
49   Insolvency Act 1986 s.72GA.
50   Insolvency Act 1986 s.29(2).
51   Insolvency Act 1986 s.29(2)(a).

company's property, he will still be an administrative receiver.[52] This may occur where a person uses a prior charge to appoint a receiver over part of the company's property.

(a)   Receiver or manager   The distinction between a receiver and a manager was explained by Sir George Jessell MR in *Re Manchester & Milford Railway Company*,[53] stating that traditionally the receiver took the income and the manager carried on the business. The distinction is now of limited use given that most debentures grant the appointee the power to receive income and manage the relevant asset.

(b)   The whole or substantially the whole of the company's property   There is no statutory definition of what is meant by "substantially" in this context nor is there any authority on its meaning. Its cognate "substantial" in other legislation has been criticised as being a word of no fixed meaning, and so an unsatisfactory adjective for carrying the idea of some ascertainable proportion of the whole.[54] It is probably best interpreted as importing a test of value (the test was declared failed in a case where 90% of the value of the company's property had been released from the relevant charge, although without explaining whether value was the reason for the declaration).[55] There is no absolute certainty as to the time at which the question of substantiality is to be considered: as the result of sales of the company's property, followed by partial repayment of the debentures, the receiver may after a while no longer be the receiver of substantially the whole of the company's property. The relevant date must therefore be the time of appointment. Presumably, however, "once an administrative receiver, always an administrative receiver."

There is a statutory definition of "company" for the purposes of this section. It means "a company registered under the Companies Act 2006 in England and Wales or Scotland".[56] This definition was added with effect from 1 October 2009 by the Companies Act 2006 (Consequential Amendments, Transitional Provisions and Savings) Order 2009.[57] This would appear to exclude appointments of administrative receivers over the property of a foreign company, as occurred under the old law in *Re International Bulk Commodities Ltd*.[58] It also excludes appointments over industrial and provident societies.[59] Section 1(1) of the Companies Act 2006 defines a company formed and registered under that Act as including those formed and registered under earlier Companies Acts.

(c)   By or on behalf of the holders of any debentures   This would appear to rule out the possibility of a court-appointed administrative receiver, as he would not be appointed "by or on behalf of" a debenture holder. There is no authority on whether

---

[52]   Insolvency Act 1986 s.29(2)(b).
[53]   (1880) 14 Ch. D 645 at 653 CA.
[54]   *Re AE Terry's Motors Ltd v Rinder* [1948] S.A.S.R. 167 per Mayo J at 180; *Re Palser v Grinling* [1948] A.C. 291. In *Palmer v Moloney* [1999] S.T.C. 890, CA it was described by Aldous LJ as importing a "jury-type question to be decided on the facts of each case".
[55]   *Scottish & Newcastle plc, Petitioners* [1993] B.C.C. 634.
[56]   Insolvency Act 1986 s.28(1).
[57]   SI 2009/1941.
[58]   [1993] Ch. 77.
[59]   *Re Dairy Farmers of Britain Limited* [2009] EWHC 1389 (Ch).

the court can appoint an administrative receiver, although in *Re A&C Supplies Ltd*[60] Blackburne J stated that the court could not appoint a replacement administrative receiver on the removal of an existing one.

(d)   Floating charge   The charge must have been a floating charge at the time of its creation.[61] Two leading cases are particularly relevant to the task of identifying a floating charge, as is one long-standing description.

The description comes from Romer LJ in *Re Yorkshire Woolcombers Association Ltd*,[62] who identified three characteristics of a floating charge:

(1)   it is a charge on a class of assets of a company present and future;

(2)   that class is one which, in the ordinary course of the business of the company, would be changing from time to time; and

(3)   "by the charge it is contemplated that, until some future step is taken by or on behalf of those interested in the charge, the company may carry on its business in the ordinary way as far as concerns the particular class of assets."

The two leading cases are *Agnew v Commissioner of Inland Revenue (Re Brumark Investment Ltd)*[63] and *Re Spectrum Plus Ltd (in liquidation)*.[64] Both cases concerned charges over book debts. In *Re Spectrum Plus* the fact that the debenture stated that it granted the bank a fixed charge was not determinative; in fact the charge was held to be a floating charge as it did not restrict the company's use of the proceeds of collections of book debts (c.f. requiring payment into a blocked account). That case also includes a description of the history of the floating charge. In both of these cases the third of Romer LJ's characteristics was described as the essential condition of a floating charge.

As regards the first of Romer LJ's characteristics, there is no need for the company to have un-charged assets to which the floating charge can attach at the time the charge is created. Nor does it matter that there is an unsatisfied prior fixed charge which prevents the company acquiring such assets in the future until that charge is satisfied.[65] However in that case Arden LJ described it as an open question whether a charge which is executed when a company has no property and in circumstances where no party to it intends that the company should acquire property to fall within it, is a valid floating charge.[66]

As regards the second and third characteristics, it is key that the charge should not interfere with the company's freedom to deal with the charged assets in the ordinary course of its business. In *Driver v Broad*[67] Kay LJ considered that there was no distinction between a debenture which expressly gives the company liberty to dispose of the charged property "in the ordinary course of its business" and one that does not, on the basis that the concept was inherent in the phrase "floating

---

60   [1998] B.C.C. 708.
61   Insolvency Act 1986 ss.29(2)(a) and 251.
62   [1903] 2 Ch. 284 at 295.
63   [2001] 2 A.C. 710 PC.
64   [2005] 2 A.C. 680 HL.
65   *Saw (SW) 2010 Ltd v Wilson (as joint administrators of Property Edge Lettings Ltd)* [2017] EWCA Civ 1001, following *Re Croftbell Limited* [1990] B.C.C. 781.
66   *Saw (SW) 2010 Ltd v Wilson (as joint administrators of Property Edge Lettings Ltd)* [2017] EWCA Civ 1001 at [49].
67   [1893] 1 Q.B. 744.

charge." In *Ashborder BV v Green Gas Power Ltd*[68] Etherton J reviewed a number of authorities on this issue. He declined to formulate a test for determining whether a transaction fell within the ordinary course of a company's business for the purpose of a floating charge, but drew nine conclusions from the case-law:

> "(1) The question whether a particular transaction is within the ordinary course of a company's business in the context of a floating charge is a mixed question of fact and law; (2) it is convenient to approach the matter in a two-stage process; (3) first, to ascertain, as a matter of fact, whether an objective observer, with knowledge of the company, its memorandum of association and its business, would view the transaction as having taken place in the ordinary course of its business; and, if so (4) secondly, to consider whether, on the proper interpretation of the document creating the floating charge, applying standard techniques of interpretation, the parties nonetheless did not intend that the transaction should be regarded as being in the ordinary course of the company's business for the purpose of the charge; (5) subject to any such special considerations resulting from the proper interpretation of the charge document, there is no reason why an unprecedented or exceptional transaction cannot, in appropriate circumstances, be regarded as in the ordinary course of the company's business; (6) subject to any such special considerations, the mere fact that a transaction would, in a liquidation, be liable to be avoided as a fraudulent or otherwise wrongful preference of one creditor over others, does not, of itself, necessarily preclude the transaction from being in the ordinary course of the company's business; (7) nor does the mere fact that a transaction was made in breach of fiduciary duty by one or more directors of the company; (8) such matters in (6) and (7) may, however, where appropriate and in all the circumstances, be among the factors leading to the conclusion that the transaction was not in the ordinary course of the company's business;(9) transactions which are intended to bring to an end, or have the effect of bringing to an end, the company's business are not transactions in the ordinary course of its business."[69]

21-8   **The floating charge must be valid.**   As with any corporate transaction, the grant of the floating charge must comply with the general law regulating the validity of a company's dealings with third parties. Thus the charge may be held invalid on the grounds that it was executed by persons without authority to do so,[70] is illegal, is a substantial property transaction within the meaning of s.190 of the Companies Act 2006, or supports a debenture that does not incorporate all the agreed terms and is signed by or on behalf of both parties.[71]

Invalidity may also result from an application by a liquidator or administrator of the company, in reliance on Insolvency Act 1986 s.245 (avoidance of floating charges created within 12 months of the onset of insolvency, or two years if the charge is connected with the company, save to the extent of the value of any goods and services provided in consideration for it), s.238 (transactions at an undervalue), s.239 (preferences), s.244 (extortionate credit transactions), or s.127 (charges created after the presentation of a winding-up petition).

---

68   [2005] EWHC 1517 (Ch); [2005] 1 B.C.L.C. 623.
69   At [227]. The Court of Appeal expressly accepted the last of these conclusions as a correct statement of the law in *Sandhu (t/a Isher Fashions UK) v Jet Star Retail Ltd (in administration)* [2011] EWCA Civ 459.
70   Though note the protection for unconnected persons dealing in good faith with a company provided by s.40(1) of the Companies Act 2006.
71   Law of Property (Miscellaneous Provisions) Act 1989 s.2.

The particulars of a floating charge must be delivered to the registrar for registration.   In relation to charges created before 6 April 2013, a charge over property was invalid against a liquidator, administrator or creditor unless registered within 21 days of its creation.[72] Since that date the requirement has altered so that the company or anyone interested in the charge is now obliged to deliver to the registrar of companies a "statement of particulars" and a certified copy of any instrument creating the charge. Where the charge is one of a series of debentures entitling their holders to pari passu distribution, then a certified copy of one of the debentures may also be required.[73] Non-registration (pre-6 April 2013) and non-delivery (under the current law) still leaves the charge valid against the company while it is a going concern. However any administrative receiver considering appointment under a non-compliant charge of property should ask the debenture-holder to seek an extension of time to provide the necessary documents to the registrar, under Companies Act 2006 s.859F(3).[74]   **21-9**

The charge must be enforceable.   Debentures usually make the power of appointment exercisable once the principal is payable (often on demand) or interest is in arrear and demanded. The terms of the debenture must be complied with. Note that there is no implied right to appoint an administrative receiver on the ground that the security is in jeopardy; such a right must be an express term of the debenture.[75] If a wrong reason was given for the appointment at the time it was made, but a proper ground for making it did exist at that time, then the appointment is valid.[76]   **21-10**

Appointment made in bad faith.   An appointment may also be challenged on the grounds that it was not made in good faith, or for the purpose of satisfying the debt.[77] There is no need for "purity of purpose", i.e. for the lender to be motivated only by the purpose of recovering the debt. In the event of several purposes that include a "proper" purpose then the appointment will still be valid.[78] Circumstances in which an appointment has been successfully challenged on this basis are rare. They include a case where receivers were appointed for the purpose of disrupting an existing receivership[79] and where a mortgage of a property was obtained and then exercised in order to enable the landlord of the property to evade the statutory protection given to the property's tenants by the Rent Acts.[80]   **21-11**

The company may be estopped from challenging the appointment if it allowed

---

[72] Companies Act 2006 s.874(1). *Re Cosslett Contractors Ltd* [1998] 2 W.L.R. 131 *and Smith (Administrator of Cosslett (Contractors) Ltd v Bridgend City BC* [2002] 1 A.C. 336 (holding that non-registration rendered the charge void as against the company in administration).

[73] Companies Act 2006 ss.859A and 859B.

[74] For charges created before 6 April 2013, the equivalent time extension provision is Companies Act 2006 s.873.

[75] *Cryne v Barclays Bank* [1987] B.C.L.C. 548.

[76] *Byblos Bank SAL v Al-Khudairy* [1987] B.C.L.C. 232 at 249 per Nicholls LJ. Applied in *Brampton Manor (Leisure) Limited v J McLean* [2006] EWHC 2983 (Ch). In both of these cases the existence of the "proper" ground only came to light well after the appointment, in the latter case as a result of disclosure during legal proceedings challenging the appointment.

[77] Lord Templeman in *Downsview Nominees Ltd v First City Corporation Ltd* [1993] A.C. 295 at 312F–G.

[78] *Cukurova Finance International Ltd v Alfa Telecom Turkey Ltd* [2013] UKPC 2; and *Meretz v ACP Ltd* [2007] Ch. 197.

[79] *Downsview Nominees Ltd v First City Corporation Ltd* [1993] A.C. 295.

[80] *Quennell v Maltby* [1979] 1 W.L.R. 318.

the bank to consider the appointment was valid. Such an estoppel would also be effective against a guarantor of the company's liabilities.[81] In *Bank of Baroda v Panessar* the company not only failed to object to the appointment for almost the entire duration of the receivership, but had also dealt with the receivers on the footing that they had been validly appointed.

21-12   Consequences of defective appointment. Where there was no power to appoint at all, the appointment is simply invalid.[82] In those circumstances the administrative receivers are technically trespassers and the appointor may be liable as a joint tortfeaser. In such circumstances the administrative receivers will not be liable for the torts of procuring a breach of contract or causing loss by unlawful means as long as they act in good faith and without unlawful means or an intention to cause loss.[83]

Where there was a power to appoint, but a defect in the manner of the appointment, Insolvency Act 1986 s.232 renders the acts of the administrative receiver valid regardless. This provision is not restricted to defects which are discovered after to the appointment, as is the case with directors of a company.[84]

21-13   Consequences of defective appointment: Indemnity from appointor. Section 34 of the Insolvency Act 1986 provides that where the appointment of an administrative receiver (or other receiver or manager) is discovered to be invalid (whether due to invalidity in the instrument under which he was appointed or otherwise) then the court may order the appointor to indemnify the receiver against any liability arising solely by reason of the invalidity of the appointment.

21-14   The office holder. The Insolvency Act 1986 introduced the concept of an "office-holder", that class of persons whose duty it is to cope with the insolvency of the company.[85] This title may relate to an administrative receiver, an administrator, the supervisor of a voluntary arrangement, a liquidator, or provisional liquidator, the Official Receiver, or some of these persons, according to the precise provisions of the relevant sections.[86] As office-holder, an administrative receiver is entitled to supplies of gas, electricity, water and telecommunication services, without having to pay any accrued charges before the date of his (or his first predecessor's) appointment[87]; he is entitled to apply to the court for the delivery up of the company's property from any person having it in his possession[88]; he is entitled to receive co-operation from officers of the company and certain others[89]; and he may apply to the court for the examination of those who appear to have information relating to the company.[90] Unlike certain other office-holders, an administrative receiver is not entitled to challenge transactions at an undervalue, or extortionate credit transac-

---

[81] *Bank of Baroda v Panessar* [1987] Ch. 335 at 353, applying *Habib Bank Ltd v Habib Bank A.G. Zurich* [1981] 1 W.L.R. 1265 at 1285.
[82] *Morris v Kanssen* [1946] A.C. 459; *Rolled Steel Products (Holdings) Ltd v British Steel Corpn* [1986] Ch. 246.
[83] *OBG Ltd v Allan* [2008] 1 A.C. 1
[84] Companies Act 2006 s.161.
[85] Insolvency Act 1986 s.234(1).
[86] Insolvency Act 1986 ss.230, 233(1), 234(1), 235(1), 236(1), 238(1), 239(1) and 246(1).
[87] Insolvency Act 1986 s.233.
[88] Insolvency Act 1986 s.234.
[89] Insolvency Act 1986 s.235.
[90] Insolvency Act 1986 s.236.

tions, or voidable preferences, under the provisions of the Insolvency Act 1986,[91] or to override any valid lien on the company's books.[92] Nor may he propose a voluntary arrangement for the company under the Insolvency Act 1986 Pt I.[93]

Provisions of general application.   Many of the provisions which have already **21-15** been discussed in relation to ordinary receivers apply equally to administrative receivers. Thus, the obligation on the person making the appointment to notify the registrar of companies[94]; the disqualification of bodies corporate from appointment[95]; the potential liability of the person making the appointment for an invalid appointment[96]; the right of the receiver to apply to the court for directions[97]; the court's power to fix the receiver's remuneration[98]; the necessity for notification that a receiver or manager has been appointed[99]; the necessity for payment of preferential debts out of assets subject to a charge which, as created, was a floating charge[100]; and the enforcement of the duty to make returns[101]; all these apply as well to an administrative receiver and his appointment as they apply to an ordinary receiver and his appointment.

Who may be appointed.   Only a person qualified to act as an insolvency **21-16** practitioner in relation to the company may be appointed[102]; any person not so qualified who acts as such is liable, on conviction on indictment, to imprisonment for up to two years, or to a payment of a fine, or both, or on summary conviction to imprisonment for up to six months, or to payment of a fine not exceeding the statutory maximum, or both.[103] On ceasing to be so qualified, he vacates his office.[104]

Only a natural person can be qualified to act as an insolvency practitioner[105]; and qualification involves the satisfaction of three sets of conditions, two positive and one negative. The first is that he must be authorised to act under the provisions of Insolvency Act 1986 s.390A. This and its accompanying sections were introduced by the Deregulation Act 2015. They provide for "partial authorisation" to act as an insolvency practitioner (i.e. only in relation to companies, or only in relation to individuals) and for "full authorisation". In either case the person must be authorised to act as an insolvency practitioner by virtue of his membership of a professional body recognised by the Secretary of State for this purpose, and be permitted so to act, by or under the rules of that body.[106] Or, alternatively, he must hold an authorisa-

---

[91] Insolvency Act 1986 ss.238(1), 244 and 239.
[92] Insolvency Act 1986 s.246(1).
[93] Insolvency Act 1986 s.1(3).
[94] Companies Act 2006 s.859K.
[95] Insolvency Act 1986 s.30.
[96] Insolvency Act 1986 s.34.
[97] Insolvency Act 1986 s.35.
[98] Insolvency Act 1986 s.36.
[99] Insolvency Act 1986 s.39.
[100] Insolvency Act 1986 s.40.
[101] Insolvency Act 1986 s.41.
[102] Insolvency Act 1986 ss.230(2), 388(1)(a), (4) and 390.
[103] Insolvency Act 1986 s.389(1), 430 Sch.10. For the meaning of "statutory maximum," see para.7-58, n.28, above.
[104] Insolvency Act 1986 s.45(2).
[105] Insolvency Act 1986 s.390(1): see also Insolvency Act 1986 s.30 (a body corporate is not qualified for appointment as a receiver).
[106] Insolvency Act 1986 s.390A(2)and (3).

tion granted by the Department of Enterprise, Trade and Investment in Northern Ireland for that purpose.[107]

The second condition is that there must be in force, at the time when the administrative receiver purports to act as such, due security for the proper performance of his functions, and that such security meets the prescribed requirements with respect to his so acting in relation to the company concerned.[108]

The third condition is that he is not qualified to act if, at that time, he has been adjudged bankrupt and has not obtained his discharge[109]; or is the subject of a bankruptcy restrictions order (interim or final), a debt relief restrictions order, or a moratorium period under a debt relief order[110]; or is subject to a disqualification order made, or has given a disqualification undertaking which has been accepted, under the Company Directors Disqualification Act 1986[111]; or lacks capacity (within the meaning of the Mental Capacity Act 2005) to act as an insolvency practitioner.[112]

Where a firm of insolvency practitioners had accepted instructions from a bank to report upon a company's affairs, on condition that they accepted no office in its management, it was held that they were precluded from accepting appointment as administrative receivers of the company.[113]

21-17 Method of appointment and time of commencement of receivership. Basically, the method of appointment, and the time from which it is effective, are the same as in the case of an ordinary receiver. However, additional requirements are imposed by the Insolvency Rules 2016. The administrative receiver, whether appointed alone or jointly with one or more others, must, if he accepts the appointment, accept in writing or confirm his acceptance in writing to the appointor *within a period of five business days*.[114] If two or more persons are appointed jointly, each of them must confirm acceptance on his own behalf; but the appointment will become effective only when all those jointly appointed have complied with this requirement.[115] Joint appointments will often be desirable.[116] In confirming such acceptance, the appointee must state the time and date of his receipt of notice of the appointment, and the time and date of his acceptance.[117] Such confirmation need not be given personally: it may be given on the appointee's behalf by a person whom he has authorised to give it.[118]

Where the advance secured by the debenture is repayable on demand, once the demand has been made and not complied with, no time need be given to the debtor company to make repayment beyond the time required to arrange the "mechanics of payment". A receiver may be appointed as soon as an hour after the demand, or

---

[107] Insolvency Act 1986 s.390A(2)(b).
[108] Insolvency Act 1986 s.390(3).
[109] Insolvency Act 1986 s.390(4)(a): see also Insolvency Act 1986 s.31.
[110] Insolvency Act 1986 s.390(5). To like effect is Insolvency Act 1986, s.31, which disqualifies bankrupts from acting as administrative receivers.
[111] Insolvency Act 1986 s.390(4)(b).
[112] Insolvency Act 1986 s.390(4)(d).
[113] *Sheppard & Cooper v TSB Bank Plc* [1997] 2 B.C.L.C. 222 CA.
[114] Insolvency Rules 2016 r.4.1(3).
[115] Insolvency Rules 2016 r.4.1(2).
[116] *Daniels v Deville* [2008] EWHC 1810 (Ch) per Lindsay J at [197]: "it is, of course, a commonplace that more than one administrative receiver of a particular firm is appointed at any one time. It is done in order to avoid delays or vacancies should an appointee die or fall ill or otherwise be away from his office."
[117] Insolvency Rules 2016 r.4.1(4).
[118] Insolvency Rules 2016 r.4.1(5).

less if the borrower has indicated it cannot pay.[119] The appointment may be by means of an instrument of appointment previously prepared.[120]

If an appointment or nomination relates to more than one person, or has the effect that the office of administrative receiver is to be held by more than one person, then the appointor must declare whether any act required or authorised under any enactment to be done by the administrative receiver is to be done by all or any one or more of the persons for the time being acting as such.[121]

Publicity of appointment: notices.   Since the objects of the following provisions will already have been achieved, they do not apply in relation to the appointment of an administrative receiver to act with an existing receiver, or in place of an administrative receiver dying or ceasing to act, except to the extent to which they may not already have been fully complied with.[122]   **21-18**

On appointment, the administrative receiver must forthwith send to the company, and publish in the prescribed manner, a notice of his appointment.[123] Further, within 28 days after his appointment, he must, unless the court otherwise directs, send such a notice to all the creditors of the company, so far as he is aware of their addresses.[124]

The notice has to contain the following matters:

(i)   the registered name of the company, as at the date of the appointment, and its registered number;

(ii)   any other name under which the company has been registered in the 12 months preceding that date;

(iii)   any name under which the company has traded at any time in those 12 months, if substantially different from its then registered name;

(iv)   the name and address of the administrative receiver, and the date of his appointment;

(v)   the name of the person by whom the appointment was made;

(vi)   the date of the instrument conferring the power under which the appointment was made, and a brief description of the instrument;

(vii)   a brief description of the assets of the company (if any), in respect of which the person appointed is not made the receiver.[125]

He must further cause notice of his appointment to be advertised once in the *London Gazette*, and once in such newspaper as he thinks most appropriate for ensuring that it comes to the notice of the company's creditors; such advertisement must state that an administrative receiver has been appointed, the date of the appointment, the name of the appointor and the nature of the business of the company.[126]

Where the company is the employer in relation to an occupational pension scheme established under a trust, the administrative receiver must give notice of his

---

[119] *Sheppard & Cooper v TSB Bank plc* [1996] 2 All E.R. 654 at 659; *R.A. Cripps & Son Ltd v Wickenden* [1973] 1 W.L.R. 944, applied in *Quah Su-Ling v Goldman Sachs International* [2015] EWHC 759 (Comm).

[120] *Windsor Refrigerator Co Ltd v Branch Nominees Ltd* [1961] Ch. 375 CA.

[121] Insolvency Act 1986 s.231(1), (2).

[122] Insolvency Act 1986 s.46(2).

[123] Insolvency Act 1986 s.46(1)(a). For the prescribed manner, see Insolvency Rules 2016 r.4.5(2).

[124] Insolvency Act 1986 s.46(1)(b).

[125] Insolvency Rules 2016 r.4.5(1).

[126] Insolvency Rules 2016 r.4.5(2)(c).

appointment to the trustees of the scheme, the Pensions Regulator and the Pension Protection Fund.[127]

POWERS

21-19   Powers and privileges.   The powers conferred on the administrative receiver by the debentures by virtue of which he was appointed are to be deemed to include[128]— save to the extent to which they are inconsistent with any of the provisions of those debentures—the following powers:

(1)   Power to take possession of, collect and get in the property of the company and, for that purpose, to take such proceedings as may seem to him expedient. Where any person has in his possession or control any property, books or papers or records to which the company appears to be entitled, the court[129] may require that person forthwith, or within such period as it may direct, to pay, deliver, convey, surrender or transfer the same to the administrative receiver.[130]

(2)   Power to sell or otherwise dispose of the property of the company by public auction or private contract or, in Scotland, to sell, feu, hire out or otherwise dispose of the property of the company by public roup or private bargain.

(3)   Power to raise or borrow money and grant security therefor over the property of the company.

(4)   Power to appoint a solicitor or accountant or other professionally qualified person to assist him in the performance of his functions.

(5)   Power to bring or defend any action or other legal proceedings in the name and on behalf of the company.[131]

(6)   Power to refer to arbitration any questions affecting the company.

(7)   Power to effect and maintain insurances in respect of the business and property of the company.

(8)   Power to use the company's seal. A debenture need not be under seal; the charge thereby conferred may be an equitable one, so that this provision (and the one following) is not one which could have been conferred except by statute, since authority to use the seal must otherwise be conferred by a document under seal.[132]

(9)   Power to do all acts and to execute in the name and on behalf of the company any deed, receipt or other document.

(10)   Power to draw, accept, make and indorse any bill of exchange or promissory note in the name and on behalf of the company.

(11)   Power to appoint any agent to do any business which he is unable to do

---

[127]   Pensions Act 1995 s.22 and Pensions Act 2004 s.120. The obligation to inform the trustees is also highly likely to be triggered by the duty on employers to notify trustees of events of material significance to the exercise of their functions (the Occupational Pension Schemes (Scheme Administration) Regulations 1996 (SI 1996/1715) reg.6(1)(b)).

[128]   Insolvency Act 1986 s.42(1), (2); Sch.1.

[129]   "The court" means the court having jurisdiction to wind up the company: Insolvency Act 1986 s.251.

[130]   Insolvency Act 1986 s.234(1), (2).

[131]   This includes the right to apply to lift or vary a freezing or other injunction imposed on the company: see *Capital Cameras Ltd v Harold Lines Ltd* [1991] 1 W.L.R. 54, where the court observed that once administrative receivers had been appointed, there was no longer any risk of dissipation of the company's assets.

[132]   *Steiglitz v Egginton* (1815) Holt N.P. 141.

himself or which can more conveniently be done by an agent and power to employ and dismiss employees.

(12) Power to do all such things (including the carrying out of works) as may be necessary for the realisation of the property of the company.

(13) Power to make any payment which is necessary or incidental to the performance of his functions.

(14) Power to carry on the business of the company.

(15) Power to establish subsidiaries of the company.

(16) Power to transfer to subsidiaries of the company the whole or any part of the business and property of the company. This is an extremely useful power, as such a transfer is frequently part of a tax-saving scheme which it is the duty of the administrative receiver to adopt, if it can be legitimately effected.[133]

(17) Power to grant or accept a surrender of a lease or tenancy of any of the property of the company, and to take a lease or tenancy of any property required or convenient for the business of the company.

(18) Power to make any arrangement or compromise on behalf of the company.

(19) Power to call up any uncalled capital of the company. This again is an extremely useful provision, since apart therefrom the proper persons to get in the uncalled capital are, while the company is a going concern, the persons indicated by the articles of the company.[134] This, for all practical purposes, means the directors of the company, who, of course, are unable to delegate their powers to a receiver (or anyone else), unless there is power so to do conferred by the articles.[135] Even if power to delegate is so conferred and exercised, this would be of no effect after liquidation, since on liquidation the court or the liquidator obtains a statutory power to get in the uncalled capital, which cannot be delegated.[136]

(20) Power to rank and claim in the bankruptcy, insolvency, sequestration or liquidation of any person indebted to the company, and to receive dividends, and to accede to trust deeds for the creditors of any such person.

(21) Power to present or defend a petition for the winding-up of the company.

(22) Power to change the situation of the company's registered office.

(23) Power to do all other things incidental to the exercise of the foregoing powers.

Property available to an administrative receiver. The property available to the   **21-20** administrative receiver under a floating charge includes only that property in which

---

[133] *Lawson v Hosemaster Machine Co Ltd* [1966] 1 W.L.R. 1300.

[134] See, e.g., the Companies Act 1985 Table A, as contained in The Companies (Tables A–F) Regulations 1985 (SI 1985/805) art.12. This Table will continue to apply to notwithstanding the coming into force of the Companies Act 2006: see Companies Act 2006 (Commencement No.8, Transitional Provisions and Savings) Order 2008 (2008/2860). New model articles, to take account of that Act, were drafted (see The Companies (Model Articles) Regulations 2008 (SI 2008/3229)), and came into force on 1 October 2009. Interestingly, the new model articles prescribe that all shares be fully paid up (SI 2008/3229 art.21), so that there is no room in the remainder of the model articles to allocate a power to make calls. However, the provisions of the draft model articles are not mandatory, and may be either excluded or modified as those forming the company think fit (Companies Act 2006 s.20).

[135] *Re Howard's Case* (1866) 1 Ch.App. 561.

[136] Insolvency Rules 2016 r.7.86: *Fowler v Broad's Patent Night Light Co* [1893] 1 Ch. 724.

the company has a beneficial interest, and does not include that to which the company has recorded title, but in which it has no beneficial interest.[137]

In *Lipe Ltd v Leyland DAF Ltd*[138] it was held that where administrative receivers dealt with goods that were subject to a valid retention of title clause the result would be an unsecured claim against the company for damages for the tort of conversion. The Court of Appeal noted how worthless this might prove, and said that it was customary for administrative receivers to offer a personal undertaking to pay the value of goods used or sold and subject to a valid retention of title clause. This undertaking would be supported by the administrative receiver's indemnity out of the assets of the company.[139]

Where a company before administration had paid trust monies into its general banking account, which was in credit, the beneficiaries were held entitled to follow their funds there; the payments in could not be impeached as a voidable preference[140]: but where a company before receivership was found to have paid trust monies into an account which was in debit, the beneficiaries had no right to trace into the general funds of the company.[141]

Where the charge includes a covenant to insure the subject matter, and a policy is written, the charge extends to include the proceeds of the policy, when paid.[142]

21-21   Power to dispose of charged property.   Where an administrative receiver wishes to dispose of any "relevant property",[143] which is subject to a charge ranking in priority to the charge under which he was appointed,[144] as if it were not subject to such charge (so as to avoid the necessity of obtaining the concurrence of the holder of that charge), he may apply to the court for leave to do so.[145] When the administrative receiver applies for such an order, the court will fix a venue for the hearing of the application, and the administrative receiver must then forthwith give notice of the venue to the person who holds the security.[146] If the court is satisfied that such disposal, with or without other assets, would be likely to promote a more advantageous realisation of the company's assets than would otherwise be effected, the court may grant such authorisation.[147] If it does, the administrative receiver must forthwith give notice of the making of the order to the holder of the security.[148] The court will send two sealed copies of the order to the administrative receiver, who

---

[137] *Sharp v Woolwich Building Society* [1997] B.C.L.C. 603, 41.
[138] [1993] B.C.C. 385.
[139] Insolvency Act 1986 s.44(1)(c).
[140] *Re Lewis' of Leicester Ltd* [1995] B.C.C. 524.
[141] *Re Style Financial Services Ltd v Bank of Scotland* 23 May 1995 (Inner House).
[142] *Colonial Mutual General Insurance Co v ANZ Banking Group (NZ) Ltd* [1995] 1 W.L.R. 1140, PC.
[143] This comprises not only the property of which he is the receiver, but also any property of which, but for the appointment of some other person as receiver of part of the company's property, he would be the receiver: Insolvency Act 1986 s.43(7).
[144] Insolvency Act 1986 s.43(2).
[145] Insolvency Act 1986 s.43(1).
[146] Insolvency Rules 2016 r.4.16(3).
[147] There is no case law on this provision, but it is thought that the court must be satisfied that there is a reasonable prospect that the disposal of the property will promote a better realisation of the company's assets: see, e.g. *Re Harris Simons Construction Ltd* [1989] 1 W.L.R. 368.
[148] Insolvency Rules 2016 r.4.16(4). The appropriate form is Form REC3.

must then send one of them to the holder of the security,[149] and also, within 14 days of the making of the order, an office copy thereof to the registrar of companies.[150]

It is a condition of any such order that the net proceeds of the disposal, and, where those proceeds are less than such amount as is determined by the court to be the net amount which would be realised on a sale of the property in the open market by a willing vendor, such further sums as would be required to make good the deficiency, are to be applied in discharging the sums secured by the security.[151] Where such a condition relates to two or more securities, that condition must require that the net proceeds of the disposal, and any such sums as are mentioned above, are to be applied towards discharging the sums secured by those securities in the order of their priorities.[152]

Company voluntary arrangements. An administrative receiver does not possess the power to propose a company voluntary arrangement.[153]   **21-22**

Overriding provision. Notwithstanding the width of the powers noted above, it is further provided that a person dealing with the administrative receiver in good faith and for value is not concerned to inquire whether the receiver is acting within his powers.[154]   **21-23**

This provision brings the position very much into line with that of a person who deals in good faith with the directors of a company.[155]

Status of administrative receiver. The administrative receiver is deemed to be the company's agent, unless and until it goes into liquidation.[156] It appears this may prevent him being liable under s.2(1) of the Misrepresentation Act 1967, as he is not a party to contracts that he enters into.[157] Nevertheless, he will be personally liable on any contract entered into by him in the carrying out of his functions (except in so far as the contract otherwise provides), and on any contract of employment adopted by him in the carrying out of those functions.[158] He is not, for this purpose, to be regarded as having adopted a contract of employment by reason of anything done or omitted to be done by him within 14 days after his appointment.[159]   **21-24**

CONDUCT OF AN ADMINISTRATIVE RECEIVERSHIP

Websites and invoices etc. Once the administrative receiver has been appointed, the company's websites and each of its invoices, orders and business letters must state that a receiver has been appointed.[160]   **21-25**

Supplies of utilities. Where the administrative receiver requires either a supply   **21-26**

---

[149] Insolvency Rules 2016 r.4.16(4).
[150] Insolvency Act 1986 s.43(5), with a penalty for non-compliance provided for by s.43(6).
[151] Insolvency Act 1986 s.43(3).
[152] Insolvency Act 1986 s.43(4).
[153] Insolvency Act 1986 s.1(1) and (3).
[154] Insolvency Act 1986 s.42(3).
[155] Companies Act 2006 s.40(1).
[156] Insolvency Act 1986 s.44(1)(a).
[157] *Phoenix International Life Sciences Inc v Rilett* [2001] B.C.C. 115.
[158] Insolvency Act 1986 s.44(1)(b).
[159] Insolvency Act 1986 s.44(2).
[160] Insolvency Act 1986 s.39.

of gas,[161] a supply of electricity,[162] a supply of water by a water undertaker,[163] or a supply of communication services by a public electronic communications service or a person who carries on a business which includes giving such supplies,[164] or a supply of specified IT goods or services for the purpose of enabling of facilitating anything to be done by electronic means[165] in respect of a period after the date of his appointment (or, if he was appointed in succession to another administrative receiver, the date on which the first of his predecessors was appointed), he is entitled to receive it, upon condition that he himself personally guarantees the payment of any charges in respect of the supply.[166] The supplier is not entitled to make it a condition of the giving of such supply that any outstanding charges in respect of a supply given to the company prior to the date of his appointment are paid.[167] Note that administrative receivers do not benefit from the further protection for essential supplies that was introduced from 1 October 2015 by s.233A of the Insolvency Act 1986. That section provides that where a company enters administration or a CVA and receives supplies of the "essential supplies" listed above under a contract entered into on or after 1 October 2015, clauses in that contract that would allow the supplier to terminate or take any other step because of the administration or CVA have no effect.

21-27   **Contracts.**   The appointment of an administrative receiver will not automatically terminate the company's existing contracts, unless the contract terms themselves provide for this. However the administrative receiver is under no duty to cause the company to perform the contract. He is entitled to cause the company to frustrate a contract that he has made clear he will not adopt, at least where to do so would not impede realization of the company's assets or seriously affect any future trading prospects that it has.[168] He is under no liability for inducing a breach of contract unless he acts in bad faith or outside the scope of his authority.[169]

However in an appropriate case the court can order specific performance of a contract by a company in administrative receivership. This may occur in relation

---

[161] Insolvency Act 1986 ss.233(1)(b), (3)(a) and (aa): see also the Gas Act 1986 s.7A for the definition of a supplier of gas.

[162] Insolvency Act 1986 ss.233(1)(b), (3)(b) and (ba). See also Pt 1 of the Electricity Act 1989.

[163] Insolvency Act 1986 ss.233(1)(b), (3)(c)–(cc); in Scotland, a water authority.

[164] Insolvency Act 1986 ss.233(1)(b), (3)(d) and (e); "communications services" do not include electronic communications to the extent that they are used to broadcast or otherwise transmit programme services within the meaning of the Communications Act 2003: Insolvency Act 1986 s.233(5)(d).

[165] Insolvency Act 1986 ss.233(1)(b), (3)(f). The specified goods and services are: point of sale terminals, computer hardware and software, information, advice and technical assistance in connection with the use of IT, data storage and processing and website hosting (Insolvency Act 1986 s.233(3A)).

[166] Insolvency Act 1986 s.233(2)(a), (4)(b).

[167] Insolvency Act 1986 s.233(2)(a), (b).

[168] *Airlines Airspares v Handley Page* [1970] Ch. 193.

[169] *Welsh Development Agency Ltd v Export Finance Co* [1992] B.C.C. 270, applying the rule in *Said v Butt* [1920] 3 K.B. 497 that an agent is not liable for the tort of inducing a breach of contract where the contract is one between his principal and a third party, as long as the agent acts bona fide and within the scope of his authority. This rule was recently applied to administrators, on the basis that their position vis-a-vis the company's contracts was materially indistinguishable from administrative receivers, in *Lictor Anstalt v Mir Steel UK Ltd* [2011] EWHC 3310 (Ch). That case also considered the possibility of the defence of justification being available to administrators who sold assets in breach of contract while discharging their statutory functions. The judge (David Richards J) found considerable force in that argument, but declined to accept it on a summary judgment application where there was no authority on the point and no findings of fact.

to a contract for the grant of an interest in land,[170] but there is no need for a proprietary interest to exist before specific performance will be ordered.[171] The court will perform a balancing exercise in deciding whether to enforce a third party's contractual rights against the company in administrative receivership. It may be relevant that the debenture under which the appointment was made was granted with actual knowledge of the contractual arrangements that are sought to be enforced. It is unlikely that an order would be made if it caused the company to trade at a loss.[172] Where the court makes an order for specific performance, it is submitted it should include a proviso to the order that the administrative receivers are not personally liable for such performance.

The position as regards employment contracts is discussed in Ch.23 below.

Administrative receivers may exploit the company's existing contractual rights in the way that they consider best furthers their duties and functions. In *Re Transtec Automotive Campsie Ltd*,[173] Jacob J held that administrative receivers could demand a revised price for goods from the customers of a company in administrative receivership that was based on what could be demanded if the customer sought the goods elsewhere. The customer, Ford, accused the administrative receivers of blackmail but the court disagreed.

Where the administrative receiver enters into contracts in the carrying out of his functions he will, save where the contract excludes this (as is common) be personally liable on those contracts.[174] In respect of all such personal liability, he is entitled to an indemnity out of the assets of the company.[175] However, this provision does not limit any right of indemnity which he would have apart from it (hence it is common for him also to seek an indemnity from the appointor). Nor does it limit his liability on contracts entered into or adopted without authority, nor confer any right to indemnity in respect of that liability.[176]

INFORMATION GATHERING

Statement of affairs. An administrative receiver must require any one or more **21-28** of a number of persons to make out and submit to him a statement as to the affairs of the company.[177] The form and contents of this statement is prescribed by the Insolvency Rules 2016,[178] but in essence it has to show:

(i)   particulars of the company's assets, debts and liabilities;

---

[170] *AMEC Properties v Planning Research & Systems plc* [1992] B.C.L.C. 1149 CA.

[171] *Ash & Newman v Creative Devices Research* [1991] B.C.L.C. 403 (where the court restrained a company in administrative receivership from disregarding pre-emption rights under a pre-existing contract, where the administrative receiver would not suffer harm as a result), applied in *Land Rover Group Ltd v UPF (UK) Ltd (in administrative receivership)* [2002] EWHC 3183 (QB).

[172] *Land Rover Group Ltd v UPF (UK) Ltd* [2002] EWHC 3183 (QB); [2003] 2 B.C.L.C. 222.

[173] [2001] B.C.C. 403, approved in *Land Rover Group Ltd v UPF (UK) Ltd* [2002] EWHC 3183 (QB); [2003] 2 B.C.L.C. 222.

[174] Insolvency Act 1986 s.44(1)(b).

[175] Insolvency Act 1986 s.44(1)(c).

[176] Insolvency Act 1986 s.44(3).

[177] Insolvency Act 1986 s.47(1), (3): Insolvency Rules 2016 r.4.16. The notice requiring the statement is Form 3.1B in Insolvency Rules 1986 r.12.7. The persons so required to make the statement are referred to as "deponents"; Insolvency Rules 2016 r.4.16. Such a statement does not connote a promise to pay nor acknowledge a continuing indebtedness, and is therefore ineffective as an acknowledgement under the Limitation Act 1980 s.29(5): see *Re Overmark Smith Warden Ltd* [1982] 1 W.L.R. 1195.

[178] Insolvency Rules 2016, r.4.16.

(ii)   the names and addresses of its creditors;
(iii)   the securities held by them respectively; and
(iv)   the dates when those securities were respectively given.[179]

The persons from whom such information may be demanded are:

(i)   those who are or who have been officers[180] of the company;
(ii)   those who have taken part in the company's formation, at any time within one year before the date of his appointment;
(iii)   those who are in the company's employment or have been in its employment within that year, and are in his opinion capable of giving the information required;
(iv)   those who are or have been within that year officers or in the employment of a company which is, or within that year was, an officer of the company.[181]

Where any such information has been demanded, it must be supplied by the person from whom it has been demanded within a period of 21 days, beginning with the day after that on which the prescribed notice of the requirement was given to them by the administrative receiver.[182] The prescribed notice must inform the person to whom it is addressed:

(i)   of the names and addresses of all others (if any) to whom the same notice has been sent;
(ii)   of the date by which the statement must be delivered;
(iii)   of the penalties for non-compliance; and
(iv)   of the application to him, and to each of the others to whom the notices are addressed, of the statutory provisions relating to the provision of information and attendance upon the administrative receiver.[183]

On request, the administrative receiver must furnish each such person with a document for the preparation of the statement of affairs.[184]

21-29   **Verification and delivery of statement of affairs.**   The statement has to be verified by statement of truth,[185] and the administrative receiver may require any of the other persons liable to make the statement of affairs to submit a statement of concurrence, stating that he concurs therein.[186] Such a statement of concurrence may be qualified, where the maker of it is not in agreement with the statement of affairs, or he considers the statement to be erroneous or misleading, or he is without the direct knowledge necessary for concurrence.[187]

The statement must be delivered to the administrative receiver by the person

---

[179] Insolvency Act 1986 s.47(2); Insolvency Rules 2016 r.4.7. The form of the statement of affairs is Form 3.2 in Insolvency Rules 1986 Sch.4.
[180] For the meaning of "officer", see Insolvency Act 1986 s.251; Companies Act 2006 s.1173.
[181] Insolvency Act 1986 s.47(3).
[182] Insolvency Act 1986 s.47(4). If a person without reasonable excuse fails to comply with this obligation, he is liable on conviction or indictment to a fine, or on summary conviction to a fine not exceeding the statutory maximum, and on conviction after contravention to a daily default fine not exceeding one-tenth of the statutory maximum: Insolvency Act 1986 ss.47(6), 430 and Sch.10.
[183] Insolvency Rules 2016 r.4.6(2).
[184] Insolvency Rules 2016 r.4.6(3).
[185] Insolvency Act 1986 s.47(2).
[186] Insolvency Rules 2016 r.4.8(2).
[187] Insolvency Rules 2016 r.4.8(5).

making the statement of truth (or by one of them, if more than one), together with a copy of the verified statement of affairs, and every statement of concurrence must be similarly delivered by the person who makes it, together with a copy.[188] These documents must be kept as part of the records of the receivership.[189]

A person making the statement of affairs or statement of concurrence must be allowed by the administrative receiver, and paid out of his receipts, any expenses incurred by him in so doing which the administrative receiver thinks reasonable.[190] Any decision by the administrative receiver in this regard is subject to appeal to the court.[191]

Modification of obligations in relation to statement of affairs.   The administrative receiver, if he thinks fit, may at any time release a person who would otherwise be under an obligation to provide a statement of affairs from that obligation.[192] He may, either when giving notice to submit a statement of affairs, or subsequently, extend the period of 21 days for compliance.[193] He may act either on his own discretion or at the request of any person so obliged.[194] Where, being requested to exercise such discretion, he has refused to exercise either power, the court, if it thinks fit, may itself exercise it.[195]   **21-30**

Applications to release: procedure.   Where an application is made to the court, it may dismiss it, if it thinks that no sufficient cause has been shown for the application, but it must not do so, unless the applicant has had an opportunity to attend the court for a hearing, of which he has been given at least seven days' notice.[196] If the court does not then dismiss it, it will fix a venue for it to be heard, and give notice to the applicant accordingly.[197] The applicant must then, at least 14 days before the hearing, send to the receiver a notice stating the venue, accompanied by a copy of the application and of any evidence in support.[198] The receiver may appear and be heard on the application, and, whether or not he appears, may file a written report of any matters which he considers ought to be drawn to the court's attention.[199] If such a report is filed, a copy of it must be sent by the receiver to the applicant not later than five days before the hearing.[200] The applicant's costs of the application must be paid by him, and, unless the court otherwise orders, no allowance towards them must be made out of the assets under the receiver's control.[201]   **21-31**

Sealed copies of any order will be sent by the court to the applicant and to the receiver.[202]

Further information-gathering powers.   As noted above, the administrative   **21-32**

---

[188] Insolvency Rules 1986 rr.4.7(6) and 4.8(6) .
[189] Insolvency Rules 1986 r.4.9.
[190] Insolvency Rules 1986 r.4.11(1).
[191] Insolvency Rules 1986 r.4.11(2).
[192] Insolvency Act 1986 s.47(5)(a).
[193] Insolvency Act 1986 s.47(5)(b).
[194] Insolvency Rules 2016 r.4.10.
[195] Insolvency Act 1986 s.47(5). As to the application to the court, see Insolvency Rules 2016 r.4.10(2).
[196] Insolvency Rules 2016 r.4.10.
[197] See n.152, above.
[198] Insolvency Rules 2016 r.4.10.
[199] Insolvency Rules 2016 r.4.10.
[200] See n.154, above.
[201] Insolvency Rules 2016 r.4.10.
[202] Insolvency Rules 2016 r.4.10.

receiver is entitled to apply to the court for the delivery up of the company's property, books, papers or records from any person having them in his possession[203]; he is entitled to receive co-operation from officers of the company and certain others[204]; and he may apply to the court for the examination of those who appear to have information relating to the company.[205] Guidance on the responsibility of the administrative receiver for the company's books and records is given in SIP 17. This notes that if the books and records are to be removed from the directors, a detailed receipt for all records that the administrative receiver takes should be drawn up and signed by a director. It is also noted that if the administrative receiver changes the company's registered office to his firm's address, this will trigger a requirement to move the statutory records to that address also.

An administrative receiver is entitled to require the company to hand over any of its documents; but this power is exercisable solely for the purposes of his functions as administrative receiver. He cannot, for example, obtain from the company confidential and sensitive documents, not for the purpose of using them as administrative receiver, but of passing them to the debenture-holder, for use in its litigation against the company's guarantors.[206] In those circumstances, the company's sole director was held to be entitled to sue the debenture-holder in the name of the company, without the leave of the administrative receiver, for the return of the documents from the receiver.[207] It follows that even where documents are obtained for the purpose of the administrative receivers' own functions, they cannot later be passed to the debenture holder without considering whether that onward disclosure serves the interests of the company.[208] That is not to say however that administrative receivers cannot waive a company's confidentiality and privilege in appropriate circumstances by disclosure to an appointor.[209]

DEALINGS WITH PROPERTY

21-33   It has been noted above (para.21–20) that the property available to the administrative receiver under a floating charge includes only that property in which the company has a beneficial interest. Where an administrative receiver deals with property that does not fall within that category, or falls outside the charge, he is strictly speaking a trespasser but may rely on the rule in *Said v Butt*.[210] In the case of tangible property only, he may also rely on the defence in Insolvency Act 1986 s.234(3) and (4).[211]

In order to realise property, the administrative receiver may rely on powers under the debenture, such as a power to execute documents in the name of the company,[212]

---

[203] Insolvency Act 1986 s.234.
[204] Insolvency Act 1986 s.235. The categories specified are very wide: and, for a tantalising application relating to this section which states that the office-holder may invite third parties to participate in an interview to be conducted under s.235 see *Re Madoff Securities International Ltd* [2009] EWHC 442 (Ch); [2009] 2 B.C.L.C. 78.
[205] Insolvency Act 1986 s.236.
[206] *Sutton v GE Capital Commercial Finance Ltd* [2004] 2 B.C.L.C. 662 CA.
[207] *Sutton v GE Capital Commercial Finance Ltd*, above, applying *Newhart Developments Ltd v Co-operative Commercial Bank Ltd* [1987] Q.B. 814 CA.
[208] *Sutton v GE Capital Commercial Finance Ltd* [2004] 2 B.C.L.C. 662 CA at [38]–[39].
[209] *Sutton v GE Capital Commercial Finance Ltd* [2004] 2 B.C.L.C. 662 CA at [40].
[210] [1920] 3 K.B. 497. See n.168 above.
[211] Discussed in *Welsh Development Agency Ltd v Export Finance Co* [1992] B.C.C. 270.
[212] Used, after liquidation, in the context of real property in *Barrows v Chief Land Registrar Times,* 20

or an express power of sale, or a power of attorney granted by the debenture. Note that the last of these does not survive a liquidation of the company. Further, the powers granted by Insolvency Act 1986 Sch.1 include power to use the company's seal and to execute any deed in the name of the company.

As the administrative receiver is an agent of the company, and not of the debenture holder, he is not able to release company property from the debenture if he sells it. The purchaser therefore needs to secure that release from the debenture-holder, and also the release of any other charges over the property (unless Insolvency Act 1986 s.43 applies).

The Land Registry has published guidance on its website on the process of applying for registration of property based on a disposition by an administrative receiver.

On liquidation, the status of the administrative receiver as agent of the company terminates but he retains powers bestowed by the debenture itself.[213]

Unlike a liquidator, an administrative receiver has no power to disclaim onerous property. It may be possible for the debenture holder to release such onerous property from its charge, but failing this it will be necessary to move the company into liquidation to allow disclaimer or to "hive down" the property into a newco in order to effect a restructure. Care should be taken regarding any regulatory consequences of such a hive down, which is likely to have the effect of removing financial support and may therefore trigger regulatory consequences.[214]

An administrative receiver owes duties to all those interested in the equity of redemption when selling property, namely to act in good faith and obtain the best price reasonably obtainable at the time when they decide to sell. They have free rein in choosing the time and manner of the sale.[215]

LITIGATION

The administrative receiver may apply to court for directions in relation to any **21-34** matter in connection with the performance of his functions. The court may give directions, or make declarations of the rights of persons appearing before it, or otherwise.[216] Note that the person appointing the administrative receiver may also apply. This power has been used in relation to remuneration[217] and for guidance as to which debts a receiver should take into account when determining whether a company was unable to pay its debts as they fell due.[218]

The issue of when an administrative receiver may institute proceedings in the name of the company, and when the board of directors may do so, is considered at paras 23–22 to 23–29, below.

The court has jurisdiction to order costs against administrative receivers in relation to proceedings brought by or against the company. However such orders are

---

October 1977.

[213] *Sowman v David Samuel Trust Ltd* [1978] 1 All E.R. 616.

[214] Consider Pensions Act 2004 s.43 if financial support is removed from the employer of an occupational pension scheme.

[215] *Downsview Nominees Ltd v First City Corp Ltd* [1993] A.C. 295 PC; *Medforth v Blake* [2000] Ch. 86; *Raja v Austin Gray (a firm)* [2002] EWCA Civ 1965.

[216] Insolvency Act 1986 s.35.

[217] *Munns v Perkins* [2002] B.P.I.R. 120.

[218] *Re Cheyne Finance plc* [2007] EWHC 2402 (Ch).

rare. In *Dolphin Quays Developments Limited v Mills*[219] the High Court refused an application for costs against receivers where a company's claim failed, on the basis that there was no evidence of exceptional circumstances or impropriety in their conduct of the claim and as they acted throughout as agents of the company. The court considered two cases in which a non-party costs order had been made against receivers,[220] but noted that in neither case was the receiver acting as agent of the company because of a subsequent liquidation. The decision was affirmed by the Court of Appeal,[221] which considered it important in the exercise of a court's discretion to order such costs to consider whether adequate security for costs would have been available. The court noted that where the company was the defendant to the claim, security for costs was not available, but said that the circumstances in which it may be appropriate to order costs against the receiver of such a company did not arise on the appeal.[222]

MAKING PAYMENTS

21-35 **Duty to distribute a "prescribed part" of net assets among unsecured creditors.**   Under the Enterprise Act 2002 Pt 10,[223] liquidators, provisional liquidators, administrators and any receiver of a company which has given a floating charge over the whole or substantially the whole of its assets after a prescribed date, must distribute among the unsecured creditors of the company a "prescribed part" (a percentage or an aggregate of percentages) of the company's net assets available for satisfying the amounts due to the charge-holder.[224]

REPORTING REQUIREMENTS

21-36 **Report by administrative receiver.**   The administrative receiver must, within three months, or such extended period as the court may allow, after his appointment,[225] send to the registrar of companies, to any trustees for secured creditors of the company, and, so far as he is aware of their addresses, to all such creditors, a report on the company's affairs.[226] The report must also be made available to unsecured creditors.[227] Such report must deal with the events leading up to his appointment, so far as he is aware of them; the disposal or proposed disposal by him of any property of the company, and the carrying on, or proposed carrying on, by him of any business of the company; the amounts of principal and interest payable to the debenture-holders by whom or on whose behalf he was appointed, and the

---

[219] [2007] EWHC 1180 (Ch).
[220] *Bacal Contracting Ltd v Modern Engineering (Bristol) Ltd* [1980] 2 All E.R. 655; and *Anderson v Hyde* [1996] 2 B.C.L.C. 144.
[221] [2008] 1 W.L.R. 1829.
[222] [2008] 1 W.L.R. 1829 at [88].
[223] Under Enterprise Act 2002 Pt 10 s.253, which came into force on 15 September 2003, inserting into Insolvency Act 1986 a new s.176A.
[224] Insolvency Act 1987 s.176A(2).
[225] The provisions of the Insolvency Act 1986 s.46(2) equally apply in the case of an appointment to act with an existing receiver, or in the place of an administrative receiver dying or ceasing to act: Insolvency Act 1986 s.48(7).
[226] Insolvency Act 1986 s.48(1). The report may also need to be sent to the Financial Conduct Authority or the Prudential Regulation Authority, if the company is or was an authorised person or representative, or carrying on regulated activities (Financial Services and Markets Act 2000 s.363(4)).
[227] Insolvency Act 1986 s.48(2).

amounts payable to preferential creditors; and the amount (if any) likely to be payable for the payment of other creditors.[228] It must also include a summary of the statement of affairs submitted to him, and his comments (if any) upon it.[229]

Report to include "prescribed part" information. The administrative receiver's   **21-37**
report under s.48(1) shall also state, to the best of his knowledge and belief:

(i)   an estimate of the value of the prescribed part (whether or not he proposes to make an application under s.176A(5) or whether s.176A(3) applies); and

(ii)   an estimate of the value of the company's net property.

Nothing in this rule is to be taken as requiring any such estimate to include any information, the disclosure of which could seriously prejudice the commercial interests of the company. If such information is excluded from the calculation the estimate shall be accompanied by a statement to that effect. The report shall also state whether, and if so why, the receiver proposes to make an application to court under s.176A(5).[230]

General restrictions on disclosure in report.   However, the report is not required   **21-38**
to include any information the disclosure of which would seriously prejudice the carrying out by the administrative receiver of his functions.[231] If he thinks it would, he may apply to the court for an order of limited disclosure in respect of the statement, or a specified part of it.[232] The court may then order that the statement, or the specified part of it, should not be open to inspection otherwise than with the leave of the court.[233] But subject to any such order of the court, the copy of the report to be sent to the registrar of companies must have attached thereto copies of the statement of affairs and of any affidavits of concurrence.[234] However, any such order may include directions as to the delivery of documents to the registrar of companies and the disclosure of relevant information to other persons.[235]

He must further, within three months, or such longer period as the court may allow, after his appointment, either send a copy of the report to all unsecured creditors of the company, so far as he is aware of their addresses, or publish in the same newspaper as his appointment was advertised, a notice stating an address to which unsecured creditors[236] of the company should write for copies of the report to be sent to them free of charge.[237] The question of the consideration of this report by the unsecured creditors is discussed later.[238]

---

[228]   Insolvency Act 1986 s.48(1).
[229]   Insolvency Act 1986 s.48(5).
[230]   Insolvency Rules 2016 r.4.13.
[231]   Insolvency Act 1986 s.48(6).
[232]   Insolvency Rules 2016 r.4.12.
[233]   Insolvency Rules 2016 r.4.12.
[234]   Insolvency Rules 2016 r.4.13 If not submitted before the copy of the report is sent to the registrar, they must be sent as soon as received. As to the statements of affairs and of concurrence, see paras 21-28 ff, above.
[235]   Insolvency Rules 2016 r.4.12.
[236]   Although the Insolvency Act 1986 s.48(2) refers to "unsecured creditors", provision is made by Insolvency Rules 2016 rr.15.31 and 15.9 for secured creditors to vote at the subsequent meeting of unsecured creditors, to the extent of the sum in respect of which they are not completely secured. The Act and the Rules therefore appear to be at variance.
[237]   Insolvency Act 1986 s.48(2). Any such notice must be published in the newspaper in which the receiver's appointment was advertised: Insolvency Rules 2016 r.4.14. The court will not so direct,

Where the company has gone, or goes into liquidation, the administrative receiver must, within seven days after sending his report to the registrar of companies, or, if later, the nomination or appointment of the liquidator, send a copy of the report to the liquidator; and if this takes place before the time limited for compliance with the sending of copies of the report to the unsecured creditors, he is not then required so to do.[239]

Failure to comply with the above provisions without reasonable excuse renders the receiver liable on summary conviction to a fine not exceeding one-fifth of the statutory maximum[240] and on conviction after continued contravention to a daily default fine not exceeding one-fiftieth of the statutory maximum.[241]

21-39 **Reports on conduct of directors.** With a view to furnishing the Secretary of State with sufficient information to enable him to decide whether proceedings should be taken under the Company Directors Disqualification Act 1986 against any directors of the company, duties are imposed upon an administrative receiver in relation to reporting the relevant facts.[242] The administrative receiver must prepare a report about the conduct of each person who is or has been a director of the company at any time in the three years before the appointment of the administrative receiver. The report must describe any conduct of the person which may assist the Secretary of State in deciding whether to disqualify them from acting as a company director.

The report must be sent to the Secretary of State within three months of the administrative receiver's date of appointment (unless the Secretary of State considers a longer period is appropriate). If further relevant information comes to light, the administrative receiver must provide it to the Secretary of State as soon as reasonably practicable.

21-40 **Abstract of receipts and payments.** The administrative receiver must, within two months after the end of 12 months from the date of his appointment, and of every subsequent period of 12 months, send to the registrar of companies, to the company, and to the person by whom he was appointed, and to each member of the creditors' committee (if any), the requisite account of his receipts and payments as administrative receiver.[243] He must also send such an account to the same persons within two months after he ceases to act as administrative receiver.[244]

The accounts are to be in the form of an abstract showing receipts and payments during the relevant period of 12 months,[245] or, where the administrative receiver has ceased to act, receipts and payments during the period from the end

---

unless the report states the receiver's intention to apply therefor, and a copy of the report is sent to the persons named, or such a notice is published, not less than 14 days before the hearing of the application: Insolvency Act 1986 s.48(3). The report or notice (as the case may be) must comply with certain requirements such as the venue for the hearing of the application: Insolvency Rules 2016 r.4.13.

[238] See paras 22-1 ff, below.
[239] Insolvency Act 1986 s.48(4).
[240] Insolvency Act 1986 s.48(8).
[241] Insolvency Act 1986 s.48(8).
[242] Company Directors Disqualification Act 1986 s.7A(2)(c). The same responsibility is also placed upon the official receiver, the liquidator, and an administrator: Company Directors Disqualification Act 1986 s.7A(9).
[243] Insolvency Rules 2016 r.4.17.
[244] Insolvency Rules 2016 r.4.17.
[245] Insolvency Rules 2016 r.4.17(4). The appropriate form is REC2.

of the last 12-month period to the time when he so ceased, or if there has been no previous abstract, then during the whole period he has as acted as receiver.[246]

The provision is without prejudice to the administrative receiver's duty to render accounts otherwise than as aforesaid.[247]

Summary remedy against delinquent administrative receivers. In common **21-41** with others who may at any time have been in a position of control, if it appears in the course of the winding-up of a company that an administrative receiver has misapplied or retained, or become accountable for, any money or other property of the company, or been guilty of any misfeasance or breach of any fiduciary or other duty in relation to the company, he is liable to the imposition of a summary remedy.[248] On the application of the Official Receiver, of the liquidator, or of any creditor, or, with the leave of the court,[249] of any contributory (a right which is exercisable, notwithstanding that he may well not benefit from any order the court may make) the court may examine into the conduct of the administrative receiver, and compel him to repay, restore or account for the money or property or any part of it, with interest at such rate as the court things just.[250] Alternatively, the court may order him to contribute such sum to the company's assets by way of compensation in respect of the misfeasance or breach of fiduciary or other duty as the court thinks just.[251]

Criteria to be applied in assessing the allegations of negligence by administra- **21-42** **tive receivers.** In adjudging whether an administrative receiver has been guilty of actionable negligence, the same principles would appear to be applicable as have been applied to receivers appointed under statutory powers.[252] It is perhaps notable that s.212(2) is expressed to apply to liquidators and is silent regarding administrative receivers. It provides that the phrase "misfeasance or breach of any fiduciary or other duty in relation to the company" includes any misfeasance or breach of duty in connection with the carrying out of functions "as liquidator" of the company.

---

[246] Insolvency Rules 2016 r.4.17(4). If he makes default, he is liable on summary conviction to a fine not exceeding one-fifth of the statutory maximum and on conviction after continued contravention to a daily default fine not exceeding one-fiftieth of the statutory maximum: Insolvency Rules 1986 r.4.17(6).

[247] Insolvency Rules 2016 r.4.17(5). For an action under the general law for an account (and also damages for breach of duty and negligence), see *Smiths Ltd v Middleton* [1986] 1 W.L.R. 598.

[248] Insolvency Act 1986 s.212(1)(b).

[249] Insolvency Act 1986 s.212(5).

[250] Insolvency Act 1986 s.212(3)(a).

[251] Insolvency Act 1986 s.212(3)(b).

[252] See *Knight v Lawrence* [1991] B.C.C. 411, [1991] B.C.L.C. 215, VC (a Law of Property Act receiver case); *Medforth v Blake* [2000] Ch. 86; [1999] 3 W.L.R. 922: receivers owe equitable duties to act in good faith and, subject to their primary duty to see the debt and interest repaid from the property over which they were appointed, they owed duties to manage that property with due diligence.

CHAPTER 22

ADMINISTRATIVE RECEIVER'S RELATIONSHIP WITH THE UNSECURED CREDITORS

22-1   Introduction.   Although the administrative receiver's primary concern will be the debt owed to the debenture-holder, it will also be necessary to consider the position of other unsecured creditors. This is in part due to the provisions requiring such creditors to receive a report regarding the administrative receivership (save "opted-out creditors") and to be able to vote on forming a creditors committee. However it is also possible for such creditors to seek priority over the debenture-holder's claim by asserting a right to set-off, or by relying on steps taken to enforce a judgment such as obtaining a charging order. Finally, although it is clear that the administrative receiver owes no duties to the company's unsecured creditors,[1] those creditors still have the ability to cause difficulties for an administrative receiver (for example causing the liquidator in any subsequent liquidation to challenge the administrative receiver's remuneration[2]).

22-2   Set off.   The position in relation to set-off is in general the same, whether a receiver is appointed in or out of court,[3] and whether or not as an administrative receiver. Rules of "insolvency set-off" as provided for in Insolvency Rules 2016 r.14.24 in the case of administration do not apply. The principles applicable are those relating to the right of set-off as against an equitable assignee.[4] This is because a debenture will usually contain a floating charge over all the future property of the company, in which case the crystallisation of the floating charge produces an equitable assignment over the benefit of any contractual debt due to the company, by way of charge in favour of the debenture holders.

   If, at the date of the assignment (i.e. the crystallisation of the charge), the debtor has a cross-claim against the company of such a nature that it can be set off, no matter how such claim originated, set-off is permissible in the absence of an express agreement to the contrary. The Court of Appeal considered this issue in 1972[5] and held that where a receiver was appointed at a time that the company owed money to a supplier and had also entered a contract with the supplier to provide it with certain goods, which were delivered after the appointment, then the supplier was

---

[1]   *Lathia v Dronsfield Brothers Ltd* [1987] B.C.L.C. 321, mentioned with approval in *International Leisure Ltd v First National Trustee Co Ltd* [2013] Ch 346.

[2]   Insolvency Act 1986 s.36.

[3]   See per Russell LJ in *NW Robbie & Co Ltd v Witney Warehouse Co Ltd* [1963] 1 W.L.R. 1324 at 1340.

[4]   *NW Robbie & Co Ltd v Witney Warehouse Co Ltd* [1963] 1 W.L.R. 1324; *Rother Iron Works Ltd v Canterbury Precision Engineers Ltd* [1974] Q.B. 1; *Security Trust Co v The Royal Bank of Canada* [1976] A.C. 503.

[5]   *Rother Iron Works Ltd v Canterbury Precision Engineers Ltd* [1974] Q.B. 1.

entitled to effect a set off. The company argued there was no mutuality as the latter contract gave rise to a chose in action against the supplier that was caught by the floating charge. The Court held that the debenture-holder could not be put in a better position than the company, and that only the net claim became subject to the debenture as at the date of crystallisation.

Nor will knowledge or notice of the existence of any uncrystallised floating charge alter the position.[6] Further, if subsequently the debtor becomes entitled to cross-claims arising out of the same contract as the "assigned" claim, which may happen whether the receiver "adopts" the contract or elects not to cause the company to carry it out, these will afford a valid set-off, no matter when they arise.[7]

Set-off under different contracts. Where, however, the claim arises under one contract, and the cross-claim which it is sought to set off arises subsequent to the appointment of the receiver, and under a different contract, the position is more complex. The general rule is undoubtedly that set-off is not, in general, possible[8]; this is so, even though the receiver, in order to recover the claim, will have to sue in the name of the company, against which the cross-claim lies.[9] This, however, is not an inflexible rule; and where the two contracts, under which the claim and cross-claim respectively arise, are between the debtor and the company, and the second contract is intimately connected with the first, set-off will be allowed, notwithstanding that the claim under the second contract arises only after the equitable assignment.[10] Although the limits of the doctrine are not easy to discern, in general set-off will be allowed if the debtor can show some equitable ground for being protected against the receiver's demands.[11] It is of course possible for the parties (if neither is insolvent) to make an agreement not to raise a set-off.

22-3

Enforcement. In the circumstances provided for by the applicable Civil Procedure Rules, unsecured creditors may enforce judgment debts by means of charging orders, third party debt orders or writs of fieri facias. A debenture-holder may need to move quickly in order to crystallise any floating charge and appoint a receiver in these cases.

22-4

(1) *Charging Orders.* A debenture-holder should be able to obtain priority to a judgment creditor with an interim charging order, but is unlikely to do so once the order has been made final. Only a final order gives an indefeasible right over the property in question. Even a final order may be set aside however, on the application of any person interested in property to which the charge relates. A debenture-holder would appear to satisfy that test.[12]

(2) *Third party debt orders.* Unlike a final charging order, a final third party debt order results in no security interest for the judgment creditor. Thus where a

---

6   *Biggerstaff v Rowatt's Wharf Ltd* [1896] 2 Ch. 93.
7   *Young v Kitchin* [1878] 3 Ex.D. 127; *Government of Newfoundland v Newfoundland Ry Co* (1888) 13 App. Cas. 199; *Parsons v Sovereign Bank of Canada* [1913] A.C. 160, HL; *Lawrence v Hayes* [1927] 2 K.B. 111.
8   *Biggerstaff v Rowatt's Wharf Ltd* [1896] 2 Ch 93; *Lynch v Ardmore Studios (Ireland) Ltd* [1966] Ir.R. 133; *Business Computers Ltd v Anglo-African Leasing Ltd* [1977] 1 W.L.R. 578.
9   *NW Robbie & Co Ltd v Witney Warehouse Co Ltd* [1963] 1 W.L.R. 1324.
10 *McKinnon v Armstrong Bros & Co* [1877] 2 App. Cas. 531.
11 *Rawson v Samuel* [1841] Cr. & PH. 161; *Barrett's Case (No.2)* (1865) 4 De G.J. & S. 756; *Handley Page Ltd v Customs & Excise* [1970] 2 Lloyd's Rep. 459.
12 Charging Orders Act 1979 s.3(5). On the indefeasible nature of a final charging order, see *Roberts Petroleum Ltd v Bernard Kenny Ltd* [1983] 2 A.C. 192.

receiver is appointed after the making of a final third party debt order but before payment pursuant to that order, the debenture-holder with a floating charge over the debt was entitled to that debt in place of the judgment creditor.[13]

(3) *Writs of fi. fa.* This method of execution also gives rise to no security.[14] Accordingly it is suggested that until payment is made to the judgment creditor as a result of the seizure of goods pursuant to the writ, the debenture-holder can crystallise his security and thus obtain priority. All of this assumes that no automatic crystallisation clause is in place which takes effect on the making of such a writ.

22-5 Meetings and Committees. As originally enacted and as remained in force until 25 May 2015, the Insolvency Act 1986 provided at section 48(2) for the administrative receiver to convene a meeting of the unsecured creditors of the company at which he should lay before them a report into certain prescribed matters including disposals and proposed disposals of company property, plans to carry on the business of the company, and the amount (if any) likely to be available to pay unsecured creditors. The current regime still requires such a report, as set out in para.21–36, above. However the requirement for the administrative receiver to convene a meeting of unsecured creditors was removed with effect from 6 April 2017 by the Small Business, Enterprise and Employment Act 2015.[15]

The current position is that the administrative receiver must send a copy of the report to all unsecured creditors save those who have opted out of receiving documents about the administrative receivership,[16] or must publish a notice stating the address to which unsecured creditors should write for copies of the report to be sent to them free of charge.[17] If this latter route is adopted, the method of publication must be gazetting and advertising in such manner as the administrative receiver thinks fit.[18]

Whether the administrative receiver opts to send the report to creditors, or to publish the notice described above, the report or notice must be accompanied by a further notice that invites the creditors to decide whether a creditors committee should be established if sufficient creditors are willing to be members of the committee.[19] This notice must also invite nominations for membership of the committee, such nominations to be received by the administrative receiver by a date to be specified in the notice. It must state that any nominations (a) must be delivered to the administrative receiver by the specified date; and (b) can only be accepted if the administrative receiver is satisfied as to the creditor's eligibility under Insolvency Rules 2016 r.17.4.[20]

If the creditors decide to use this power to establish a creditors' committee, its purpose is stated to be that of exercising "the functions conferred on it by or under" the Insolvency Act 1986.[21] That Act gives power to such a committee to require the

---

[13] *Cairney v Back* [1906] 2 K.B. 746.
[14] *Davey & Co v Williamson & Sons Ltd* [1898] 2 Q.B. 194.
[15] Schedule 9(1) para.12(4).
[16] For the rules on opting out see Insolvency Rules 2016 rr.1.37–1.39.
[17] Insolvency Act 1986 s.48(2).
[18] Insolvency Rules 2016 r.4.14.
[19] Insolvency Rules 2016 r.4.15(1).
[20] Insolvency Rules 2016 r.4.15(2)–(3).
[21] Insolvency Act 1986 s.49(1).

administrative receiver to attend before it, and to furnish information relating to the carrying out by him of his functions.[22]

Detail on the constitution, role and conduct of any creditors committee is given in the Insolvency Rules 2016 Pt 17. These rules apply equally to creditors committees formed in an administration, liquidation and bankruptcy. The only additional functions, however, which are thereby conferred upon the creditors' committee are those of assisting the administrative receiver in discharging his functions, and of acting in relation to him in such a manner as may be agreed with him from time to time.[23] There is a separate provision whereunder the receiver is bound to send annual accounts of his receipts and payments to each member of the creditors' committee.[24]

The administrative receiver is also now under a duty to the unsecured creditors with respect to the "prescribed part" of the company's net assets for distribution among the unsecured creditors.[25]

Whilst these provisions go a long way towards giving unsecured creditors of the company an opportunity to keep in touch with the course of an administrative receivership, it depends very much upon the use which the creditors and the administrative receiver feels they are able to make of the rules relating to a creditors' committee, as to whether such a body fulfils any other useful function. One weakness in the provisions is that the unsecured creditors' committee must be established as a result of notices sent out towards the beginning of the administrative receivership if at all. Subsequent dissatisfaction with the information provided by the receiver will not be curable by the device of establishing such a committee later.

Control over and accountability of receiver. The precise relationship between the administrative receiver and the creditors' committee, in the matter of his accountability (or lack of accountability) to the committee, is left regrettably vague by the Insolvency Act and the Insolvency Rules.[26] Although the committee (if appointed) is (i) empowered to require the receiver to attend before it, and to furnish it with such information relating to the carrying out of his functions as it may reasonably require,[27] and (ii) required to assist him in discharging his functions, and to act in relation to him on an agreed basis,[28] it is nowhere indicated who is, in the final analysis, to have the overriding power of decision.

The only provision made by the Act or the Rules for complaints to be made to the court of the administrative receiver's acts or omissions is confined to the misapplication of, or accountability for, funds, or for misfeasance or breach of a fiduciary or other duty to the company.[29] This provision would not seem to avail the committee, if it wishes to challenge the receiver solely in relation to his financial or administrative decisions, whether in general or in particular, where such grave improprieties do not arise, though the committee's concerns may be very weighty. Unlike the debenture holder by whom the administrative receiver was appointed,

22-6

---

[22] Insolvency Act 1986 s.49(2).
[23] Insolvency Rules 2016 r.17.2.
[24] Insolvency Rules 2016 r.4.17
[25] Insolvency Act 1986 s.176A.
[26] Insolvency Act 1986 s.49(1); Insolvency Rules 2016 r.17.22.
[27] Insolvency Act 1986 s.49(2).
[28] Insolvency Rules 2016 r.17.2.
[29] Insolvency Act 1986 s.212(1).

unsecured creditors do not have standing to make an application to court for directions as to the performance of the administrative receiver's functions.[30]

It is now appropriate to consider the detailed provisions of the Act and the Rules in relation to decisions to be taken by creditors and the creditors' committee, if one is established.

SECTION 1: DECISIONS BY CREDITORS

22-7   **Convening the meeting.**   It has already been noted that the administrative receiver is bound to send a copy of his report to all unsecured creditors of the company, advising them where they may obtain copies thereof, free of charge.[31] He must also invite them to decide whether a creditors committee should be established if sufficient creditors are willing to be members of it. The administrative receiver must also invite nominations for membership of the committee, to be received by a fixed time and only to be accepted if the administrative receiver is satisfied as to the creditor's eligibility to be a member of the creditors' committee.[32]

The process whereby creditors decide whether a creditors committee should be established is a "decision procedure" for the purposes of the Insolvency Rules 2016.[33] It must therefore take place in accordance with Insolvency Act 1986 ss.246ZE and 246ZF and Pt 15 of the Insolvency Rules 2016. It may be conducted by means of the deemed consent procedure in s.246ZF, unless the court orders otherwise, since nothing in the Act, rules or other legislation requires the decision to be taken in any particular way.[34] If deemed consent is obtained that a committee should not be formed, no further steps need be taken. However if 10 per cent of the unsecured creditors, by value, object then the decision must be sought again but this time by means of a "qualifying decision procedure". This means a procedure prescribed or authorised under para.8A of Sch.8 to the Insolvency Act 1986,[35] which in turn provides for procedures by means of correspondence, electronic voting, virtual meeting and physical meeting.

These provisions will also apply to any decisions that the administrative receiver needs from the company's creditors. He must give them at least 14 days' notice of decision procedures and notices seeking deemed consent.[36]

A creditors committee in administrative receivership must have at least three members and no more than five.[37] Accordingly, it is suggested that if three or more nominations of eligible creditors are received by the administrative receiver within the time specified, the administrative receiver will need to seek a decision from the creditors as to the committee's membership.[38]

---

[30] Insolvency Act 1986 s.35.
[31] See para.22-5, above.
[32] Insolvency Rules 2016 r.4.15, with the requirements for eligibility given by r.17.4. These require the creditor to have proved for a debt that is at least partly unsecured. That sits uncomfortably with the fact that administrative receivers have no power to make distributions to unsecured creditors, and thus no need to call for proofs of debt. The old rules required potential members of the creditors' committee simply to give details in writing of the value of their claim and have it admitted for voting purposes (Insolvency Rules 1986 rr.3.16(2) and 3.11).
[33] Insolvency Rules 2016 r.17.5(1).
[34] Insolvency Act 1986 s.246ZF(1).
[35] Insolvency Act 1986 s.246ZE(11).
[36] Insolvency Rules 2016 r.15.11(1).
[37] Insolvency Rules 2016 r.17.3(1).
[38] Insolvency Rules 2016 r.17.5(4).

SECTION 2: THE CREDITORS' COMMITTEE

Constitution of committee. Where the creditors decide to establish a creditors' committee,[39] such committee will consist of at least three and not more than five creditors of the company elected at the meeting.[40] Any creditor of the company is eligible as a member, provided his claim has not been rejected for voting purposes.[41] A body corporate may be a member of the committee, but it can only act as such by a representative duly appointed as such.[42]

22-8

Formalities of establishment. The creditors' committee does not come into being, and accordingly cannot act, until the administrative receiver has delivered a notice of its membership to the registrar of companies.[43] No person may act as a member of the committee, unless and until he has agreed to do so[44]; and the receiver's notice of membership may not be issued, until at least three of the persons who are to be members of it have agreed to act.[45] If, after its initial constitution, there is any change in its membership, the receiver must also deliver or file a notice of that change to the registrar of companies.[46]

22-9

Functions and meetings of the committee. The function of the committee is to assist the administrative receiver in discharging his functions, and to act in relation to him in such manner as may be agreed from time to time.[47]

22-10

The receiver must call the first meeting of the committee not later than six weeks after its establishment.[48] He must call a meeting if it is requested by a member of the committee or his representative to be held, and where the committee has previously resolved that a meeting be held on a particular date, on that date.[49] He must also call a meeting, if requested by a member of the committee or his representative, within 21 days of receipt of the request.[50] He may also call meetings where and when he himself determines.[51]

The receiver must give five business days' notice of the venue of any meeting to every member (or his representative designated for that purpose), unless in any case the requirement of notice has been waived by or on behalf of a particular member; waiver may be signified either at or before the meeting.[52]

Since the administrative receiver must report to the creditors regarding the "prescribed part" of the company's net assets which are to be distributed among the

---

[39] See para.22-1, above.
[40] Insolvency Rules 2016 r.17.3
[41] Insolvency Rules 2016 r.17.3
[42] Insolvency Rules 2016 r.17.3(4): see para.22-13, "Committee members' representations".
[43] Insolvency Rules 2016 r.17.5(5). The appropriate form of certificate is Form COM1.
[44] Such agreement may be given by his proxyholder or representative under the Companies Act 2006 s.363, present at the meeting establishing the committee, unless the relevant proxy or authorisation states to the contrary: see the Insolvency Rules 2016 r.17.5(3).
[45] Insolvency Rules 2016 r.17.5(5).
[46] Insolvency Rules 2016 r.17.7.
[47] Insolvency Rules 2016 r.17.2.
[48] Insolvency Rules 2016 r.17.14(2).
[49] Insolvency Rules 2016 r.17.14(3)(b).
[50] Insolvency Rules 2016 r.17.14(3)(a).
[51] Insolvency Rules 2016 r.17.14(1).
[52] Insolvency Rules 2016 r.17.14(4).

unsecured creditors,[53] and must explain why (if such be the case) that he is opposed to making such a distribution,[54] the committee will presumably be entitled to require him to discuss this subject with them.

22-11 The chairman of meetings. Save in a case where the committee has resolved to require the attendance of the receiver before them (in which case the committee may elect one of their number to be the chairman),[55] the chairman at any meeting of the committee will be the administrative receiver, or an "appointed person".

22-12 Quorum. A meeting is duly constituted if all members have either been given due notice or, if not, have waived its receipt, and at least two members are present or represented.[56]

22-13 Committee members' representatives. A member of the committee may, in relation to the business of the committee, be represented by another person duly authorised by him for that purpose.[57] A person so acting must hold a letter of authority entitling him so to act either generally or specially and signed by or on behalf of the committee-member.[58] The chairman of the meeting may call on any person claiming so to act to produce his letter of authority, and may exclude him if it appears that his authority is deficient.[59]

No member may be represented by a body corporate, an undischarged bankrupt, a disqualified director, or any person who is subject to a bankruptcy restrictions order (interim or final) or a bankruptcy restrictions undertaking.[60]

No person may, on the same committee, act at one and the same time as a representative of more than one member of the committee, or act both as a member of the committee and as representing another member.[61]

Where a representative signs any documents on the member's behalf, this fact must be stated below his signature.[62]

22-14 Cessation of membership. Membership is automatically terminated, if the member:

(i) becomes bankrupt or is a person to whom a moratorium period under a debt relief order applies; or

(ii) is neither present nor represented at three consecutive meetings, unless at the third of those meetings it is resolved that he should continue as a member; or

(iii) ceases to be, or is found never to have been, a creditor.[63]

However, if the cause of termination is the member's bankruptcy, his trustee in

---

[53] Under s.176A of the Insolvency Act 1986, as inserted by Enterprise Act 2002 s.252: see Chs 21 and 31.
[54] See n.75, above.
[55] See Insolvency Rules 2016 r.17.22(5).
[56] Insolvency Rules 2016 r.17.16.
[57] Insolvency Rules 2016 r.17.17(1).
[58] Insolvency Rules 2016 r.17.17(2).
[59] Insolvency Rules 2016 r.17.17(4).
[60] Insolvency Rules 2016 r.17.17(5).
[61] Insolvency Rules 2016 r.17.17(5)(b).
[62] Insolvency Rules 2016 r.17.17(6).
[63] Insolvency Rules 2016 r.17.11.

bankruptcy will replace him as a member of the committee.[64]

A member may be removed by resolution of a meeting of which at least 14 days' notice of intention to move such a resolution has been given.[65]

A member may resign by notice in writing delivered to the receiver.[66]

Vacancies. Provided that the number of members does not fall below three, the vacancy need not be filled, if the administrative receiver and the majority of the remaining members so agree.[67] If not, the administrative receiver may appoint any creditor who is duly qualified to be a member to fill the vacancy, provided a majority of the other members of the committee agree to the appointment, and the proposed appointee consents to act.[68]   **22-15**

Proceedings at meetings. At any meeting, each member, whether present by himself or his representative, has one vote, and a resolution is passed when a majority of the members present or represented vote in favour.[69] Every resolution passed must be recorded in writing, either separately or as part of the minutes of the meeting.[70] A record of each resolution must be signed by the chairman and kept as part of the records of the receivership.[71]   **22-16**

There is no provision for the chairman himself to have either an original or a casting vote: in the event of a tie, the motion will therefore fail to be carried.

Resolutions by correspondence. The receiver may seek to obtain the agreement of members of the committee to a resolution by sending to every member, or his representative designated for this purpose,[72] a copy of the proposed resolution.[73] In this case, he must send out to every member or his representative a statement, incorporating the resolution to which their agreement is sought, and all resolutions, if more than one, being set out in such a way that agreement with or dissent from, each separate resolution may be indicated by the recipient on the copy sent to him.[74]   **22-17**

Any member of the committee may, within seven business days from the date of the administrative receiver sending out a resolution, require him to summon a meeting of the committee to consider the matters raised in the resolution.[75] In the absence of any such request, the resolution will be deemed to have been passed by the committee, if and when the receiver is notified in writing by a majority of the members that they concur with it.[76]

A copy of every resolution passed under this provision and a note that the com-

---

[64]   Insolvency Rules 2016 r.17.11(a).
[65]   Insolvency Rules 2016 r.17.12.
[66]   Insolvency Rules 2016 r.17.10.
[67]   Insolvency Rules 2016 r.17.8(2)(a) and (b).
[68]   Insolvency Rules 2016 r.17.8(3)(a) and (b).
[69]   Insolvency Rules 2016 r.17.18(1).
[70]   Insolvency Rules 2016 r.17.18(3).
[71]   Insolvency Rules 2016 r.17.18(3).
[72]   See para.21-17, above.
[73]   Insolvency Rules 2016 r.17.19(1).
[74]   Insolvency Rules 2016 r.17.19(2).
[75]   Insolvency Rules 2016 r.17.19(3).
[76]   Insolvency Rules 2016 r.17.19(4).

mittee's concurrence was obtained must be kept with the records of the receivership.[77]

22-18   Information from the administrative receiver.   Where the committee resolves, as they are statutorily entitled to do,[78] to require the attendance of the administrative receiver before them, the notice to him must be accompanied by a copy of the resolution and authenticated by a member of the committee.[79] The meeting at which the administrative receiver's attendance is required must be fixed by the committee for a business day, and must be held at such time and place as the administrative receiver determines.[80]

Where the administrative receiver so attends, the members of the committee may elect one of their number to be chairman of the meeting, in place of the administrative receiver or any nominee of his.[81]

22-19   Expenses of members.   The administrative receiver must, out of the assets of the company, defray any reasonable travelling expenses directly incurred by members of the committee or their representatives in relation to their attendance at the committee's meetings, or otherwise on the committee's business, as an expense of the receivership.[82] But this obligation does not apply to any meeting of the committee held within three months of a previous meeting, unless called by the administrative receiver himself.[83]

22-20   Members' dealing with the company.   Membership of the committee does not prevent a person from dealing with the company while the administrative receiver is acting, provided that any transactions in the course of such dealings are entered into in good faith and for value.[84] The court may, on the application of any person interested, set aside any transaction which appears to it to be contrary to this provision, and give such consequential directions as it thinks fit for compensating the company for any loss which it may have incurred in consequence of the transaction.[85]

22-21   Formal defects.   The acts of the creditors' committee established for any administrative receivership are valid notwithstanding any defect in the appointment, election or qualifications of any member of the committee or any committee-member's representative or in the formalities of its establishment.[86]

---

[77]   Insolvency Rules 2016 r.17.19(5).
[78]   Insolvency Act 1986 s.49(2).
[79]   Insolvency Rules 2016 r.17.22(2).
[80]   Insolvency Rules 2016 r.17.22(4).
[81]   Insolvency Rules 2016 r.17.22(5).
[82]   Insolvency Rules 2016 r.17.24(1).
[83]   Insolvency Rules 2016 r.17.24(2).
[84]   Insolvency Rules 2016 r.17.26(2).
[85]   Insolvency Rules 2016 r.17.26(3).
[86]   Insolvency Rules 2016 r.17.27.

CHAPTER 23

ADMINISTRATIVE RECEIVER'S RELATIONSHIP WITH THE
COMPANY AND ITS STAFF: CONTRACTS OF EMPLOYMENT;
RESIDUAL POWERS OF THE DIRECTORS

General. This chapter will deal first, in s.1, with the general employment rights   **23-1**
of the existing workforce; in s.2, with the position and rights of managerial staff;
in s.3, with the residual powers of the Board as against the receiver, in relation to
the recovery of assets of the company and the initiation of litigation, and in s.4 with
the particular issue of occupational pension schemes.

SECTION 1: CONTRACTS OF EMPLOYMENT OF EMPLOYEES GENERALLY

Administrative receiver. Prior to the Insolvency Act 1986, the receiver and   **23-2**
manager for debenture-holders (as he was then termed) acted wholly as agent of the
company.[1] In continuing existing employees in employment, as he was practically
bound to do, at least to some extent, so as to maintain the business of the company
as a going concern, he incurred no personal liability, except where he dismissed the
employees, and immediately re-employed them.[2] The strict application of the then
applicable law and procedure resulted (in the absence of such dismissal and re-
employment) in the employees being left with no means of effectively enforcing
their creditors' rights as unpaid employees, whether contractual or statutory, either
against the receiver, or against the necessarily insolvent company. In a liquidation,
if its assets should prove to be wholly charged, or wholly subject to preferential
debts, their rights of proof might be valueless, while the receiver's right of recoupment for moneys laid out by him, in respect of wages paid, was not available to
recoup wages earned but not yet paid.[3]

The unfairness of this situation was highlighted by the decision of the Court of
Appeal, in *Nicol v Cutts*.[4] This coincided with the passage through Parliament of
the Insolvency Bill (later the Insolvency Act 1985), which was regarded as a major
exercise in the new statutory domain of "rescue culture".[5] The decision led to the
hurried insertion in the Bill of stringent new provisions to safeguard the rights of
employees in these situations. These were enacted in the Insolvency Act 1986 as
s.19(5) (dealing with the position of the newly-created administrators), and as
s.44(1)(b) and (2), dealing with the position of administrative receivers.

---

[1] E.g. *Griffiths v Social Services Secretary* [1974] Q.B. 468.
[2] As occurred in *Re Mack Trucks (Britain) Ltd* [1967] 1 W.L.R. 780, where the receiver incurred
    substantial personal liability by so doing. This case led to the practice of the issuing of "*Specialised
    Mouldings*" type letters disclaiming liability; see 23-4, below.
[3] See *Nicol v Cutts* [1985] B.C.L.C. 322, CA.
[4] [1985] B.C.L.C. 322, CA.
[5] See *Powdrill v Watson*, n.14, below, at 411 ff, 445, 449: see para.23-6, below.

23-3   The consequences of Nicol v Cutts.   The effects of this decision were (i) by s.44(1)(b)(2), to render the administrative receiver, although generally acting as agent of the company,[6] personally liable in respect of contracts of employment adopted by him, provided that he should not be taken to have adopted such a contract by reason of anything done or omitted by him during the 14 days after his appointment; (ii) in the case of the administrator, to provide, by virtue of s.19(5), that by virtue of his adoption (although deemed to be the company's agent),[7] or by any predecessor of his in office, of the employees' contracts, all debts and liabilities, incurred while he was administrator under such contracts, were to be charged on and paid out of the assets in his custody or control, in priority to his own remuneration and expenses, with the like proviso that his acts and omissions, during his first 14 days in office, should not cause him to have adopted any such contracts.

23-4   The "Specialised Mouldings" letters.   The burdens imposed on, and the financial hazards created for, the administrative receiver and the administrator by these sections, when they retained the employees of an undertaking in employment, led to the devising and the widespread use of what became known as the "*Specialised Mouldings* letter", so called from an unreported case, but in principle deriving from a much earlier decision, under the Companies Act 1948.[8] This was a standard letter which had come to be adopted and was used by administrative receivers and administrators to send to the employees, for the purpose of avoiding (as they believed) the legal "adoption" of the employees' current contracts of employment. The letter stated that the existing contracts would be continued on the same basis as previously, but that the receiver (or the administrator) was not adopting the contracts, and was assuming no personal liability in relation to the employees' continued employment.[9]

The first reported cases on the operation of the new sections appear to have been the applications by administrators in *Paramount Airways Ltd (in administration) (No.3)*.[10] In that case, airline pilots obtained a declaration that they were entitled to a charge on the assets in the administration (ranking in priority to the administrators' own charge for remuneration and expenses), to cover debts and liabilities arising on their contracts of employment, which it was contended that the administrators had "adopted".[11] That decision was affirmed by the Court of Appeal, sub nom. *Powdrill v Watson*.[12] Two other cases had been decided by Lightman J to the same effect, in each case against administrative receivers on similar facts, and where *Specialised Mouldings* type letters had also been used. Combined appeals were then

---

[6]   Insolvency Act 1986 s.44(1)(a).
[7]   Insolvency Act 1986 s.14(5) (repealed); re-enacted as Insolvency Act 1986 Sch.B1 para.69.
[8]   13 February 1987, Harman J (unreported), a receivership case. The last limb of the letter was held to be wholly ineffective: see *Powdrill v Watson* in the Court of Appeal, n.14, below.
[9]   The issue of the letter to the employees was intended to exclude the financial risks to the receiver which had arisen in *Re Mack Trucks (Britain) Ltd*, n.2, above.
[10]   [1993] 2 B.C.L.C. 118. This was the name of the company, whose case went to the House of Lords as *Powdrill v Watson*: see para.23-6, below. The "*Specialised Mouldings*" type of letter had been used there, in the receivership form, though incorrectly, as it was an administration.
[11]   Under Insolvency Act 1986 s.19(5).
[12]   [1994] I.C.R. 305; [1994] 2 All E.R. 513, CA.

brought before the House of Lords by the administrators and receivers, covering the Court of Appeal decision, and the two decisions of Lightman J.[13]

Powdrill v Watson: the decision.   The House dismissed all three appeals, through varying the orders made by the Court of Appeal and by Lightman J, and remitted the latter cases to the Chancery Division.[14] It held that, regard being had to the mischief aimed at by Parliament, namely the need for better protection of employees of insolvent enterprises, and as a necessary part of the rescue culture, a contract of employment was "adopted" for the purpose of the Insolvency Act 1986 ss.19(5) and 44(1)(b), wherever the conduct of the administrator or of the administrative receiver, in continuing the employees in paid employment, amounted to an election to treat a continued contract of employment with the company as giving rise to a separate liability in the administration or the receivership. The contract must inevitably be regarded as having been adopted, where the administrator or the administrative receiver caused the company to continue the employment of employees for more than 14 days after his appointment.

23-5

That consequence could not be avoided by the office-holder's unilateral statements to the employees, disclaiming any personal liability; nor could the *Specialised Mouldings* type of letter effect such a disclaimer. Furthermore, the contract could only be adopted as a whole, and not solely in respect of certain liabilities. The employees' contracts had therefore on the facts been conclusively adopted.[15]

Powdrill v Watson: its extent.   With respect to the quantum and types of claims falling within this ruling, in the *Paramount Airways (No.3)/Powdrill v Watson* case, priority as against the administrators was restricted to such liabilities under adopted contacts as had been incurred during the administrators' tenure of office; but those liabilities would still include wages, pension contributions and a proportion of holiday pay accruing during the contractual period of notice, or damages for failure to give such notice. The same entitlements and restrictions applied to the employees as against the administrative receivers in the other two cases.[16]

23-6

The House of Lords emphasised that the newly-enacted statute, the Insolvency Act 1994 (see below), would afford no protection to claims accrued against administrators and administrative receivers, in respect of contracts of employment adopted by them prior to the date of its commencement, viz. 15 March 1994. Employees, whose rights accrued prior to that date, and whose entitlements to remuneration and other benefits had not been recognised, would therefore seem to have had rights of action against the administrator or administrative receiver, under whom they were employed.

The reform of the law: the Insolvency Act 1994.   Immediately following the Court of Appeal judgment in *Powdrill v Watson*, which was delivered on 22 February the Insolvency Bill 1994 was presented to Parliament,[17] for the purpose of remedying the far-reaching and potentially damaging effects of that decision; it was

23-7

---

[13] [1994] I.C.R. 399A; [1994] 4 All E.R. 300.

[14] [1995] 2 A.C. 395 HL, sub nom. *Powdrill v Watson, Talbot v Cadge, Talbot v Grundy*; the two latter cases were leapfrog appeals.

[15] See n.14, at 450.

[16] See n.14, at 451.

[17] See n.14, at 443.

designed to define and to restrict the debts and liabilities which it would cause to fall directly upon administrative receivers, and indirectly on administrators. The Bill received the Royal Assent on 24 March 1994, being entitled the Insolvency Act 1994; it was only marginally retrospective, commencing on 15 March 1994, and therefore not applying to contracts adopted prior to that date.[18]

23-8   **The effect of the Insolvency Act 1994.**   The Act extended a limited protection to administrators and administrative receivers, by defining and restricting the liabilities to which they became exposed, by virtue of their adoption of contracts of employment, on and after 15 March 1994[19]; it did not however extend any similar relief to receivers, or receivers and managers who were not administrative receivers, who remained therefore personally liable on all contracts which, within the criteria of *Powdrill v Watson*, they had adopted, on or after that date.

With respect to administrative receivers, the Act, by s.2, amended s.44 of the Insolvency Act 1986, by inserting, in subs.(1)(b) the words "to the extent of any qualifying liability".

23-9   **"Qualifying liability": its meaning and extent.**   The term "qualifying liability" is defined[20] in terms which may conveniently be combined to read: "a liability to pay a sum by way of wages or salary or contribution to an occupational pension scheme,[21] which is incurred while the administrative receiver is in office, and is in respect of services rendered wholly or partly after the adoption of the contract". The effect of these provisions is to liberate the administrative receiver from accumulated pre-appointment liabilities, actual or contingent, including claims for unfair dismissal.[22]

The terms "wages or salary" include wages or salary payable in respect of a period of holiday, or absence from work through sickness or other good cause, which are to be deemed to be wages or salary in respect of services rendered in that period[23]; "a sum payable in lieu of holiday" is deemed to be in respect of services rendered in the period by reference to which the holiday entitlement arose.[24] Until 25 May 2015 the Act provided that this sum included any sums which, if paid, would have been treated by social security as earnings in respect of that period.[25] That provision was repealed by the Deregulation Act 2015,[26] as the employment contracts to which it related have ceased to be legally permissible. These were "year-in-hand' schemes, under which an employee earned holiday entitlement for the year ahead. Social security legislation provided that this holiday was counted as being accrued in the year it was earned. "Year in hand" schemes are no longer legally possible since the coming into force of the Working Time Regulations

---

[18] *Powdrill v Watson*, above, n.14.
[19] This was the day before the delivery of the judgment in the House of Lords: see n.14.
[20] Insolvency Act 1986 s.44(2A) (as amended).
[21] This term is not defined in the Act, but presumably refers to such schemes as are defined and regulated by the Pension Schemes Act 1993.
[22] See *Powdrill v Watson* at first instance, [1994] 2 B.C.L.C. 118 at 132e per Evans-Lombe J.
[23] Insolvency Act 1986 s.44(2C)(b).
[24] Insolvency Act 1986 s.44(2C). For problems over holiday pay entitlement, see *Re A Company (No. 005174 of 1999)* [2000] 1 WLR 502; at 508.
[25] Insolvency Act 1986 Sch.B1 paras 99(6), 44(2D).
[26] Deregulation Act 2015, s.19 and Sch 6 para.26.

1998.[27] Deductions from wages or salary for PAYE and National Insurance contributions also fall within the category of qualifying liabilities as they form an integral part of the employer's contractual liability.[28]

The initial period of 14 days after appointment, during which administrative receivers are not to be taken to have adopted any contract by reason of anything done or omitted, remains unchanged.[29]

In the case of an administrative receiver, sums payable in respect of a liability arising from services rendered partly before and partly after the adoption of the contract are to be apportioned, so that his liability only extends to the latter period.[30]

Liabilities held not to be "qualifying". Sums due to employees, or former employees, of the company in respect of statutory liabilities for payments on account of redundancy, or by way of compensation for unfair dismissal, are not "wages or salary",[31] and are therefore not qualifying liabilities, entitled to preferential payment;[32] nor are they "expenses" or "necessary disbursements", ranking for preferential payment under those heads.[33] Administrators have similarly been held not to be liable to employees, or former employees, for sums due in respect of "protective awards"[34] or in respect of awards of pay in lieu of notice. Judges at first instance had differed on the issue of liability[35]: the Court of Appeal ruled that there was no liability under either head,[36] except in respect of payments by way of "garden leave".[37]

23-10

What does "adoption of the contract" mean in practical terms? The Act nowhere defines the meaning of the "adoption" of a contract of employment, so that its meaning still needs to be deduced, both for pre-Act adoptions and post-Act adoptions, from the relevant factors identified in the House of Lords judgment.[38]

23-11

The mere continuation in employment by the company does not lead inexorably to the conclusion that the contract of employment has been adopted by the administrator or the receiver. It is a question of fact in each case. The initial 14-day period, at the conclusion of which the office-holder comes on risk, cannot justly be regarded as commencing until he actually becomes aware (or should reasonably have become aware) of the existence and the terms of employment of the relevant employees. It is only when he becomes so aware, or ought to have become

---

27 Explanatory Notes to the Deregulation Bill 2015, paras 599-600.

28 *Inland Revenue Commissioners v Lawrence* [2001] B.C.C. 633, CA.

29 Insolvency Act 1986 s.44(2).

30 Insolvency Act 1986 s.44(2)(b), giving statutory effect to the dicta in *Powdrill v Watson* (in the HL) n.14, above, at 451, adopting what was there described as a "forced construction" of the statute.

31 Under Sch.B1 para.99.

32 *Re Allders Department Stores Ltd (in administration)* [2005] EWHC 172 Ch; [2005] 2 All E.R. 122; [2005] B.C.C. 289. See also *Re Leeds United Football Club Ltd* [2007] EWHC 1761 Ch; [2008] B.C.C. 11.

33 See Insolvency Rules 2016 r.3.50.

34 Under the Trade Union and Labour Relations Act 1992 s.189.

35 In *Huddersfield Fine Worsteds Ltd and Re Globe Worsteds Ltd* [2005], All E.R. (D) 387 (Jul); Peter Smith J had decided in favour of liability; in *Re Ferrotech Ltd and Re Granville Technology Ltd* [2005] All E.R. (D) 45 (Aug), Etherton, J had decided against liability.

36 The cases cited in the footnote above were decided by the Court of Appeal under those titles in [2005] EWCA Civ 1072; [2005] 4 All E.R. 886 CA, reversing Peter Smith, J and affirming Etherton J. The expression "a period" in IA 1986 Sch.B1 para.99(6), must be construed as "such period".

37 Applying the dicta of Lord Browne-Wilkinson in *Delaney v Staples* [1992] 1 A.C. 687, HL. See also, on protective awards, *Haine v Day* [2008] EWCA Civ 626; [2008] B.C.C. 845.

38 See *Powdrill v Watson*, n.14, above, at 448–450.

so aware, that his subsequent conduct determines whether he has adopted their contracts or not.[39]

23-12   **"Deemed insolvency" for benefit of employees.**   The appointment of an administrative receiver by or on behalf of the holders of debentures of any property comprised in the charge produces a "deemed insolvency", conferring certain rights on its employees.[40] So too does the appointment of an administrator (whether by the court or extra-judicially) or of a receiver.[41]

The effect of this "deemed insolvency" is as follows. The Secretary of State shall pay out of the National Insurance Fund to each employee the amount of his outstanding[42] debts from the company in certain specified categories, up to a statutory maximum for debts referable to periods of time (currently £489 per week[43]):

(a)   Up to eight weeks arrears of pay, which category includes guarantee payments, payments for time off on trade union duties, remuneration for time when suspended from work on medical grounds and protective awards[44];

(b)   Liabilities during the notice period required by s.86 of that Act, or for failure to give such a notice period[45];

(c)   Holiday pay for up to six weeks' holiday, where accrued over the 12 months before the appointment of the administrative receiver or the date of termination of the employment contract, if later[46];

(d)   Any basic award for unfair dismissal[47];

(e)   Any reasonable sum to reimburse fees or premiums paid by an apprentice or articled clerk.[48]

23-13   **Statutory minimum period of notice to determine employment.**   The Employment Rights Act 1996 lays down minimum periods of notice to determine contracts of employment, basically by reference to the length of continuous service of the employee concerned. Where there is a succession to the trade, business, or undertaking of one employer, employment with the previous employer is regarded for this purpose as if it were employment with the successor.[49] Accordingly, for this purpose employment with the company and then with the receiver, whether as agent for the company, as agent for the debenture-holders, or as principal, or by any succession

---

[39]   *Re Antal International Ltd* [2003] EWHC 1939 Ch; [2003] B.P.I.R. 1067; the employees in question were incorrectly represented to the administrators as being employed by a subsidiary company, whereas in fact they were employed by the main company; the administrators were held not to have adopted the contracts; applying *Powdrill v Watson* per Lord Browne-Wilkinson, n.14, above at 449.

[40]   Employment Rights Act 1996, s.182-183.

[41]   Employment Rights Act 1996. The approval of a corporate voluntary arrangement under Pt I of the 1986 Act produces the same result.

[42]   As at the "appropriate date", defined in Employment Rights Act 1996 s.185 as the latest of (i) the appointment of the administrative receiver (described as the date of insolvency); and (ii) termination of employment, save that arrears of pay and holiday pay must be outstanding on the date of insolvency and a basic award may be claimed even when the award postdates the termination of the employment contract and the date of insolvency.

[43]   Employment Rights Act 1996 s.186.

[44]   Employment Rights Act 1996 s.184(1)(a) and (2).

[45]   Employment Rights Act 1996 s.184(1)(b).

[46]   Employment Rights Act 1996 s.184(1)(c). For the "appropriate date" see s.185.

[47]   Employment Rights Act 1996 s.184(1)(d).

[48]   Employment Rights Act 1996 s.184(1)(e).

[49]   Employment Rights Act 1996.

of these capacities, counts as one continuous period of employment. It does not matter that the employment is under a succession of contracts.[50]

Although the receiver will not normally be concerned with the position which arises where, by the process known as "hiving down", he causes the trade, business, or undertaking of the company to be transferred to a subsidiary company; such company will be an "associated company" of the original company, and the status of employment will for this purpose continue unbroken by this change of employers.[51]

Redundancy pay. Further, employees where an administrative receiver has been **23-14** appointed over property of their employer are entitled to claim redundancy payments (or payments made under agreements to refrain from claiming redundancy payments) from the Secretary of State. These are paid out of the National Insurance Fund, with the Secretary of State then subrogated to the claims of the employees and able to bring claims against the employer.[52] Redundancy pay is calculated by reference to continuous periods of employment. A contract of employment is treated as terminated by the employer, for the purposes of such payments, when any rule of law operates so as to terminate the contract under which the employee is employed.[53] Accordingly, prima facie, if any contract of service is terminated by the appointment of a receiver or an administrator, or by the liquidation of the company, or by the sale of the business of the company, a redundancy payment will fall to be made by the employer.

However, in such a situation if, by agreement with the employee, the person who immediately after the change is "the owner" of the business (the company by its agent the administrative receiver, or the debenture-holders acting through the receiver as their agent) renews the employee's contract of employment, with the substitution of that new owner for the previous owner, or re-engages him under a new contract of employment, those provisions of the 1996 Act which apply in the case of a dismissal and re-engagement by a current employer will also apply. The result will be that the employee will not be regarded as dismissed for the purpose of the 1996 Act.[54]

Offer of re-engagement. Further, if a purchaser of the business offers to renew **23-15** the employee's contract of employment, with the substitution of the new owner as employer in the place of the previous owner, or to reengage him under a new contract of employment, the relevant provisions of the Employment Rights Act 1996,[55] will have effect, in relation to that offer, as they would have had effect in relation to the like offer made by the previous owner. The effect is that, if the contract is offered to be continued, without any change apart from the identity of the employer, or otherwise if the offer constitutes an offer of suitable employment in relation to the employee, and in either case the employee refuses that offer, he will lose his right to a redundancy payment. Conversely, if at the end of his service the employee becomes entitled to a redundancy payment, this will only be in respect

---

[50] *Re Mack Trucks (Britain) Ltd*, n.2, above.
[51] Employment Rights Act 1996.
[52] Employment Rights Act 1996 ss.166-167.
[53] Employment Rights Act 1996 ss.135 and 162, discussed in *Lassman v Secretary of State for Trade and Industry* [2000] I.C.R. 1109, CA.
[54] Employment Rights Act 1996 s.138.
[55] Employment Rights Act 1996 s.138 and 145.

of service with his current employer, save where the business or undertaking in which he is employed has been transferred from one employer to another, or he has been taken into employment by an associated company.

23-16   Transfer of Undertakings Regulations.   The administrative receiver may decide to transfer the company's business at a time that employees are still engaged in it, or perhaps outsource the provision of services that it receives. This is likely to result in the application of the Transfer of Undertakings (Protection of Employment) Regulations 2006.[56] These Regulations apply to a "relevant transfer", which is defined to include "a transfer of an undertaking, business or part of an undertaking or business situated immediately before the transfer in the United Kingdom to another person where there is a transfer of an economic entity which retains its identity".[57] It also includes a "service provision change", under which activities are transferred from a client to a contractor, or vice versa, or between contractors, where the activities do not consist mainly of supplying goods to the client and are carried out by an organised group of employees in Great Britain whose purpose is the carrying out of those activities and which is intended to carry on doing so after the transfer, other than in the short term.[58].

Regulation 4 provides that contracts of employment of transferring employees are not terminated by a relevant transfer, that the transferor's rights, powers, duties and liabilities in connection with those contracts are transferred to the transferee, and that acts and omissions of the transferor pre-transfer are deemed those of the transferee post transfer.

Regulation 7(1) provides protection in the event that employees are dismissed because of a relevant transfer:

> "(1)   Where either before or after a relevant transfer, any employee of the transferor or transferee is dismissed, that employee shall be treated for the purposes of Part X of the 1996 Act (unfair dismissal) as unfairly dismissed if the sole or principal reason for his dismissal is–
>
> (a)   the transfer itself; or
>
> (b)   a reason connected with the transfer that is not an economic, technical or organisational reason entailing changes in the workforce ...".

The Regulations recognise that in insolvency the need to protect employee rights is likely to be in tension with the interests of creditors in maximising recoveries from the company's assets. Thus reg.8 provides for exceptions to the above Regulations in the event the transferor has entered "relevant insolvency proceedings". These are defined in reg.8(6), with a further definition given in reg.8(7). The effect of these is that "relevant insolvency proceedings" comprise insolvency proceedings opened in relation to the transferor and under the supervision of an insolvency practitioner. If such proceedings were instituted "with a view to the liquidation of the assets of the transferor" then regs 4 and 7 will not apply. If they were not so instituted then the employment contracts will still transfer to the transferee, but reduces the liabilities that fall on it.

---

[56]   SI 2006/246 (as amended). The European legislative background to the Regulations and their interrelationship with insolvency processes is explored in *Key2Law (Surrey) LLP v De'Antiquis* [2012] B.C.C. 375.

[57]   SI 2006/246 reg.3(1)(a).

[58]   SI 2006/246 reg.3(1)(b) and (3)

In *Secretary of State for Trade and Industry v Slater*,[59] Elias J explained "the rationale behind reg.8" as follows:

"13.   The scheme of the 2006 Regulations is broadly this. Typically, where there is a transfer of an undertaking, reg.4 provides that the employees are automatically transferred to the transferee with the latter taking over all the liabilities of the transferor.

14.   Regulation 7 provides that any dismissal will be automatically unfair unless it is for an economic, technical or organisational reason connected with the transfer. However, it is recognised that to apply these principles to insolvent businesses would discourage potential purchasers of the business from acquiring the business. That would be to the detriment of the employees.

15.   Regulation 8 therefore aims to relieve transferees of the burdens which would otherwise apply in certain defined circumstances.

16.   Essentially this is done in two quite distinct ways. The most extensive exception from the effect of the Regulations is created by reg.8(7) (which is intended to reflect the provisions of art.5(1) of Directive 2001/23). This provides that where the insolvency proceedings are analogous to bankruptcy proceedings and have been instituted with a view to liquidation of the assets, then neither reg.4 nor 7 applies at all. There is no transfer of staff to the transferee and no claim for unfair dismissal against him (although other provisions of the Regulations, such as the information and consultation regulations, continue to operate).

17.   A narrower exception is carved out where regulation 8(6) applies. This applies to insolvency proceedings where the purpose is not with a view to liquidation of assets. This does not altogether exclude, but it does modify, the effects of regs 4 and 7. It means that the transferee does not pick up all of the liabilities which would otherwise transfer to him.

18.   Regulation 8(3) has the effect of making the Secretary of State liable for all the obligations still outstanding at the date of the transfer which are caught by Pt XII of the 1996 Act [the Employment Rights Act 1996]. There is a deemed dismissal at that stage for purposes of fixing those liabilities even though there has been no actual dismissal. However, to the extent that the liabilities exceed the statutory limits, liability transfers to the transferee.

19.   Regulation 8(5) has the effect of making the insolvency fund rather than the transferee liable to meet any redundancy liabilities. (These will typically arise where there are dismissals for redundancy which are not for economic, technical or organisational reasons. The issue does not arise here.)"

As this quotation makes clear, the issue in relation to a transfer by an administrative receiver will be whether an administrative receivership is a "relevant insolvency proceeding". If so, a further issue might be whether it is instituted with a view to the liquidation of the assets of the company.

It is suggested that the latter is relatively easily answered: an administrative receiver is not appointed with a view to the liquidation of the assets of the transferor. While that may occur as a result of the appointment, it is perfectly possible for a company to come out of administrative receivership as a going concern, with certain assets realised in order to pay off the secured debt and interest.[60] It is only really sensible to talk of an administrative receivership being instituted with a view to the repayment of the debt of the debenture-holder, plus interest.

---

[59]   [2008] B.C.C. 70; [2008] I.C.R. 54.
[60]   Similar reasoning led the Court of Appeal to hold that administration was not a process instituted with a view to the liquidation of company's assets for the purposes of reg.8(7) in *Key2Law (Surrey) LLP v D'Antiquis* [2012] B.C.C. 375.

The former question is more difficult. An administrative receiver must be an insolvency practitioner, and administrative receivership is a form of "insolvency" within the meaning of Insolvency Act 1986 s.247.

However the Regulations are intended to give effect to Council Directive EC/2001/23 on the transfer of undertakings. That Directive refers to "insolvency proceedings" in art.5(2), which is the source of reg.8. It does not define the term, but it is notable that the EC Regulation on Insolvency Proceedings 2000 (No.1346/2000) does define insolvency proceedings as "collective" insolvency proceedings. It is clear that description does not apply to an administrative receivership. It is certainly arguable that the framers of the EC Directive did not intend to afford increased protection to insolvency processes that were conducted in the interests of one creditor, and that they would have had in mind the definition of insolvency proceedings from the EC Regulation of the previous year. In *Key2Law LLP* Warren J saw a "close parallel" between winding up proceedings as defined by the EC Regulation and insolvency proceedings falling within reg.8(7). While reg.8(6) is a broader category, it might be thought surprising if it included a process that did not fall within the EC Regulation's category of insolvency proceedings at all.

If administrative receivership is held to be a relevant insolvency proceeding for the purposes of the Regulations then the question may arise whether the dismissal of employees by the administrative receiver is automatically unfair under reg.7(1). This will apply if the sole or principal reason for the dismissal is the transfer of a relevant undertaking, unless the reason is an economic, technical or organisational one entailing changes in the transferor's workforce. This provision was considered by the Court of Appeal, albeit in an earlier form, in *Crystal Palace FC Limited v Kavanagh*.[61] The case concerned dismissals by administrators, and the Court of Appeal stressed the importance of the rescue culture when saying that courts should take care before characterising dismissals by administrators as manipulations of the TUPE regime. However administrative receivers may take some comfort from the Court of Appeal's distinction between the ultimate objective of an administrator, which will almost always be a transfer as part of a business sale, and the reason for a particular dismissal, which may well be cost-cutting in order to continue to trade for the time being. This latter reason is likely to fall within the "economic, technical or organisational" proviso to reg.7(1).

23-17 Position where the receiver is the agent of the company. The general rule in this case is that, unless and until the contract has been adopted, the appointment has no effect whatsoever upon a contract of service, which continues as before the appointment.[62] It has already been noted that the appointment of a receiver out of court produces a deemed insolvency of the company, which event has certain consequences as regards the discharge of various claims by employees by the Secretary of State for Work and Pensions, and the vesting of the employees' rights in the Secretary of State accordingly.[63] Subject to this possibility, and to the necessity of ensuring that all preferential payments are properly made before any distributions to the debenture holder, the administrative receiver can limit his personal involvement in employment matters.

23-18 The position of additional staff and re-engaged staff. If the receiver person-

---

[61] [2013] EWCA Civ 1410; [2014] B.C.C. 644.
[62] *Re Foster Clark Ltd.'s Indenture Trusts* [1966] 1 W.L.R. 125; *Re Mack Trucks (Britain) Ltd* [1967] 1 W.L.R. 780; *Griffiths v Social Services Secretary* [1974] Q.B. 468.
[63] See 23-12, above.

ally engages additional staff, or dismisses and re-engages existing staff, or adopts any contract of employment, or causes the company to enter into a fresh contract with existing staff, he will be personally liable on that contract, in addition of course to the liability of his principal, the company, as if he were the direct employer.[64]

Position where the receiver is not the agent of the company. If the receiver is   **23-19**
not the agent of the company when appointed (either because the debenture does not so provide, or because it does, but he is nevertheless appointed after the liquidation of the company),[65] or if he subsequently ceases to be such agent, but only because the company has gone into liquidation, then his appointment, or such liquidation, produces the result that the company is deemed to have become insolvent and all the employees of the company are discharged, as is the case with the appointment of a receiver by the court. For the purposes of redundancy pay, as well as the general law of employment, such discharge is the act of the company, not of the receiver.[66]

If the receiver then re-engages any of the employees, he will do so either on behalf of the debenture-holders as his principal, or on his own behalf as principal. Such re-engagement will normally be effective, both to extinguish any claim against the company itself for damages for wrongful dismissal,[67] and to extinguish any immediate claim in respect of redundancy payment.[68]

SECTION 2: THE MANAGEMENT OF THE COMPANY

Directors and other officers of the company. The appointment of an administra-   **23-20**
tive receiver by debenture-holders has no effect whatsoever upon the position in law of the principal officers of the company, viz. the directors and the secretary; and that is so, whether the receiver is the agent of the debenture-holders, or of the company, or (as would be the case, where an appointment was made after the company was in liquidation)[69] is himself a principal. The corporate structure of the company remains unimpaired,[70] and although the management and control of the assets comprised in the appointment is thereby taken completely out of the hands of the officers of the company, they remain in office as such officers, with all the usual statutory duties to discharge: as Brightman J said:

> "The appointment of a receiver for debenture-holders suspends the powers of the directors over the assets in respect of which the receiver has been appointed, so far as it is requisite to enable the receiver to discharge his functions ... The authority of a receiver is not however coterminous with the authority of the board of directors. The powers of the receiver stem from (i) the powers contained in the memorandum and articles of association of the company to create mortgages and charges, coupled with (ii) the particular

---

[64] Insolvency Act 1986 s.37(1) (ordinary receivers); s.44(1)(b) (administrative receivers). In the case of administrators, such a liability is confined to a prior charge over the assets in their hands: see s.1, above. The contract may "otherwise provide", but this rarely happens in practice: *Re Mack Trucks (Britain) Ltd* [1967] 1 W.L.R. 780.

[65] See Ch.24, below.

[66] Employment Rights Act 1996 s.183.

[67] cf. *Reid v Explosives Co* (1887) 19 Q.B.D. 264 (receiver appointed by the court re-engaging an employee: no damages against the company for breach of contract).

[68] Employment Rights Act 1996 s.138.

[69] *Re Barton Manufacturing Company Ltd* [1998] B.C.C. 827 at 828.

[70] *Hawkesbury Development Co Ltd v Landmark Finance Pty Ltd* (1969) 92 W.N. (NSW) 199, 209 per Street J.

powers which have been conferred on a duly appointed receiver, pursuant to the due exercise of the company's borrowing powers".[71]

23-21   **The employment position of the managers of the company.**   The appointment of the administrative receiver must, of necessity, terminate the employment of a person occupying any managerial position which is of such a nature as to impinge upon the rights of the receiver to manage the company as he thinks fit. Where the contract of employment cannot subsist together with the receiver's appointment, the employment will be automatically terminated, and once again, apart from the question of discharge of any preferential claims, the receiver will not be under any liability; for he will not have himself employed the person concerned, and is therefore not at risk of adopting his contract.[72] However, such discharge will not necessarily follow automatically from the mere description of the appointment held; the terms of the relevant contract must be scrutinised to determine whether there is, in reality, any inconsistency between the terms of that contract and the functions and duties of the receiver.

SECTION 3: THE RELATIONSHIP BETWEEN THE RECEIVER AND THE BOARD OF DIRECTORS

23-22   **Residual duties of the Board.**   The Board of Directors of the company may also, in some situations, still have active duties to perform, for example, where the security under which the receiver is appointed does not extend to the entirety of the assets of the company, or where property, which is held by the company in trust or as bailee for third parties, is not caught by the terms of the security. A major example of his category of property is any property in the possession of the company, subject to a valid retention of title clause.[73] Control of all such property remains with the directors, upon whom falls the active duty of ensuring that the company carries out its duties as trustee.

The directors continue to owe fiduciary duties to the company notwithstanding the appointment of an administrative receiver, and these duties may be enforced by means of litigation brought by the company.[74]

It has been held that the directors should not be liable to creditors for misfeasance for failing to place a company that was in receivership into liquidation so that distributions could be made to unsecured creditors before their debts became statute-barred. This was on the basis that management of the company's assets was no longer in their hands.[75]

23-23   **Residual powers of the Board of Directors.**   The board's powers over the assets caught by the debenture are clearly removed by the appointment of an administrative receiver. Lord Hoffmann described the position of a receiver appointed under a debenture that appointed him "agent for the company" in carrying

---

[71] *Re Emmadart Ltd.* [1979] Ch. 540 per Brightman J at 544, citing *Newhart Developments Ltd v Cooperative Commercial Bank Ltd* [1978] Q.B. 814 and *Lawson v Hosemaster Machine Co* [1966] 1 W.L.R. 1300 CA.

[72] *Griffiths v Social Services Secretary*, n.63, above.

[73] *Aluminium Industire Vaassen BV v Romalpa Aluminium Ltd* [1976] 1 W.L.R. 676; [1976] 2 All E.R. 552, and see paras 18-20 ff, above.

[74] *Simtel Communications Ltd v Rebak* [2006] 2 B.C.L.C. 571.

[75] *Re Joshua Shaw & Sons* (1989) 5 B.C.C. 188.

on its business: "the receiver replaces the board as the person having authority to exercise the company's powers".[76]

However the Board retains certain residual powers, in particular in relation to property that the administrative receiver does not control. The Board is entitled to convene a general meeting of the company with a view to putting it into voluntary liquidation, although the receiver may do so himself, and if he does, the company is not entitled to do so.[77] A minority shareholders' action cannot be brought against the debenture holder and its receiver, for such an action, if otherwise sustainable, can only be brought in the name of the company itself.[78] It has been held by the Court of Appeal that the Board may itself take proceedings, in the company's name to enforce a cause of action which the receiver, for whatever reason, does not wish to pursue.[79] This decision, which has been criticised,[80] is considered below.

What causes of action are the Board entitled to pursue? Depending on the   **23-24**
terms of the debenture, and the fixed and floating charges created thereby, the company may have charged to the debenture-holder all those rights of and to property, and all causes of action, which are vested in the company, and which the company is entitled to enforce. If so, it is the administrative receiver and the debenture-holder who are prima facie contractually entitled, and the only persons prima facie legally entitled, to enforce any of those rights; strictly speaking, the receiver should enforce them in the name of the debenture-holder, but by a long-established custom, he enforces them in the name of the company. It is therefore, again strictly speaking, only those rights which are *not* vested in the debenture-holder, and are therefore *not* enforceable solely by the administrative receiver, which the directors can properly be regarded as entitled to enforce themselves, in the name of the company. Note that causes of action may fall outside the charge either because they were never included, or because they have been released by the debenture-holder from the charge.

There may be causes of action that both the administrative receivers and the board are entitled to pursue.[81] It is suggested that in such circumstances the board may pursue the cause of action where to do so does not threaten the interests of the debenture-holder qua debenture holder. If the administrative receiver objects to the board litigating a cause of action that falls within the debenture-holder's security it is suggested that the board may only continue where the administrative receiver is acting in breach of his equitable duty owed to those interested in the equity of redemption to act in good faith and for the proper purpose of dealing with the charged property so as to achieve repayment of the secured debt and interest.[82]

Where the receiver has acted improperly, in breach of his duties to the company as its agent, and to the company's detriment, the Board has been held entitled to sue; for plainly the receiver cannot, in such a situation, bring proceedings against himself

---

[76]   *Village Cay Marina Limited v Acland* [1998] B.C.C. 417, PC, at [422].

[77]   See Ch.25, below.

[78]   *Watts v Midland Bank Plc* [1986] B.C.L.C. 15.

[79]   *Newhart Developments Ltd v Cooperative Commercial Bank Ltd* [1992] Q.B. 814 CA; *Watts v Midland Bank Plc*, n.82, where the mortgagor was held entitled to sue the receiver, in respect of an improper exercise of his powers.

[80]   *Tudor Grange Holdings Ltd v Citibank v N.A.* [1992] Ch. 53 CA.

[81]   For example a claim for breach of directors' duties committed during an administrative receivership which extended to conducting the company's business: *Simtel Communications Ltd v Rebak* [2006] 2 B.C.L.C. 571.

[82]   *Medforth v Blake* [2000] Ch. 86.

(except, presumably, by applying to the court for directions as to whether he had done wrong), although it would be open to the debenture-holder itself to sue him.[83] Such a claim against the administrative receiver by the debenture-holder is not barred by the rule in *Johnson v Gore Wood & Co*[84] against reflective loss, as the administrative receiver's primary duty was owed to the debenture-holder. The company's loss was secondary and only comprised the amount of damage that exceeded the sums required to satisfy the secured debt and interest.[85].

23-25 **Newhart Developments Ltd v Cooperative Commercial Bank Ltd: its effect.** In this case, the company had granted a debenture to a bank, and had entered into a financing agreement with a banking subsidiary of the debenture-holder, which was to provide the whole finance for the company's property developments. The development projects did not prosper, and the banking subsidiary withdrew its financial support; the debenture-holder then appointed a receiver and manager. The directors of the company, being of the opinion that the banking subsidiary was in breach of its contract with the company, commenced proceedings in the company's name for damages. The defendant bank applied to strike out the action, on the ground that it had been commenced without the knowledge or consent of the receiver, pleading that "he alone is entitled to the proceeds of the action". The company successfully appealed against an order to strike out.

The Court of Appeal held that the appointment of the receiver does not divest the directors of the power to institute proceedings, where to do so does not prejudice the position of the debenture-holder, by jeopardising the assets subject to his charge. If the receiver, in the exercise of his discretion, chooses to ignore a right of action capable of constituting an asset, or decides that it would be unprofitable from the point of view of the debenture-holder to pursue it, or refrains from taking proceedings for other reasons, it is open to the directors to sue to enforce that right of action in the interests of the company, that is to say, of its creditors and its members; it is indeed their duty to do so.[86] It was, however, incumbent on directors, desiring to bring such proceedings in the name of the company, to provide an adequate indemnity as to the costs.[87]

23-26 **Criticisms of the Newhart decision.** That decision, was criticised by Browne-Wilkinson V-C (as he then was),[88] who pointed out that any justification, based on the receiver's embarrassment at being obliged to sue his appointor, the debenture-holder, could be met by an application to the court for directions; it is, however, respectfully submitted that in this, no doubt extremely rare, type of case, the receiver cannot reasonably be expected himself to sue his own appointor, or to be directed to do so, for good practical reasons, which include both the likely exist-

---

[83] *International Leisure Ltd & Citibid Securities Ltd v First National Trustee Co* [2013] Ch. 346. See also *Watts v Midland Bank Plc* [1986] B.C.L.C. 15; and *American Express v Hurley* [1985] 3 All E.R. 564 at 571. In the latter case the receiver was held negligent on a claim brought by a guarantor of the company's debt to the debenture-holder, leading to findings that the debenture holder was liable for the receiver's negligence when acting as his agent but that he would be entitled to an indemnity from the receiver for that liability.

[84] [2002] 2 A.C. 1.

[85] *International Leisure Ltd & Citibid Securities Ltd v First National Trustee Co* [2013] Ch. 346.

[86] Per Shaw LJ at 819.

[87] In the Newhart case, the directors had provided such indemnities against costs: see also *L Lascomme v VDT* [1994] 1 L.R.M. 227.

[88] In *Tudor Grange Holdings Ltd v Citibank NA*, see n.84, above.

ence of legal professional privilege, conflicts of interest, and the long-standing relationships between banks and finance-houses and their regular panels of administrative receivers. While it would indeed seem to be plain that, in such a case as this, the receiver must have a duty to apply to the court for directions,[89] it is submitted that the directions which he seeks should not be that he should himself take the proceedings.

Possible solution by way of assignment. On such an application, where the court is satisfied that this type of problem has arisen, and that there is a substantial interest to be preserved, the court could be requested to direct the receiver to assign the cause of action to the directors, for them to litigate in the company's name, against comprehensive indemnities and an appropriate cross-assignment to the receiver of the whole or part of the proceeds of the action, such as is now the established practice in bankruptcy.[90] Difficulties might need to be overcome as to whether the receiver would provide the claimants with the documents essential for the conduct of the action.[91] If the suggested analogy with the bankruptcy case-law is an acceptable guide, it will be seen that, in the event of the trustee in bankruptcy refusing to take proceedings to enforce a cause of action likely to accrue to the benefit of the bankrupt's estate (and therefore suing directly or indirectly for the bankrupt's benefit), the court has power to direct the trustee to assign the cause of action, in this case also against satisfactory indemnities, and the allotment to the estate of a share of the proceeds.[92]

23-27

Where such an assignment has been made, by a liquidator or a trustee in bankruptcy, on terms of the assignor receiving a share of the proceeds of the action to enforce the claim, if successful, the defendant sometimes applies to challenge the assignee's right to sue to recover the claim, on the ground that the assignment is champertous. Such defences have usually been unsuccessful.[93] It has been held in the House of Lords that an assignment of a cause of action by a company, which was ineligible for legal aid, to an individual who was eligible, for the purpose of suing thereon, was not void or unenforceable on that ground.[94]

Which causes of action might the Board normally seek to pursue? The distinction between those acts or omissions by the administrative receiver in his conduct of the business of the company, and his realisation of its assets, which lie *within* the exclusive powers of the receiver and his appointor, the debenture-holder or other mortgagee, and for which he is not accountable to the company, and those which lie *outside* those powers, and for which the receiver remains accountable to the company as mortgagor for any unjustifiable injury to them, is difficult to determine with any precision. The cardinal principle by which the court should, it is submitted, be guided must be to respect and enforce the former category of

23-28

---

[89] Insolvency Act 1986 s.35.

[90] See *Hunt v Aziz* [2011] EWCA Civ 1239 at [11].

[91] But see *Gomba Holdings UK Ltd v Homan* [1986] 1 W.L.R. 1301, where the receiver was held entitled to withhold from the company information needed to prosecute an action, of a character contrary to the interests of the debenture-holder.

[92] The directors might justly claim a share of the proceeds for the company, freed from the charge, as a compensation for their assumption of the financial risks of the litigation.

[93] But it succeeded, on special facts, in *Grovewood Holdings Ltd v James Capel & Co Ltd* [1995] Ch. 80; but this decision was doubted in *Re Oasis Merchandising Services Ltd* [1995] 2 B.C.L.C. 493, CA at 504.

[94] *Norglen Ltd (in liquidation) v Reeds Rains Prudential Ltd* [1999] 2 A.C. 1, HL.

rights, and to define as precisely as possible the latter category. A useful comparison and distinction between the two categories is exemplified by the selling by the receiver of the charged property; he is not accountable for his, or his appointor's decision, *when* to make the sale,[95] but he is accountable for *how much* the price should be and to a certain extent how the sale is set up and conducted.[96] More debatable decisions often arise as to the receiver's decision to close down the company's business, thereby destroying the goodwill; much may depend on the current circumstances of the business, and its foreseeable future.[97] Where the administrative receiver engages professional advisers, such as valuers, the ordinary position is that he will not enter into such an engagement on behalf of the company.[98] This is because he owes the company no duty beyond the equitable duty identified in *Cuckmere Brick*. As regards that duty however, the law imposes strict liability on the administrative receiver to ensure that reasonable care is taken by the adviser engaged by the receiver in connection with the sale. The company (and others interested in the equity of redemption) may sue the administrative receiver if that does not occur, but is unlikely to be owed any duties by the advisers.[99]

As a condition for pursuing the company's causes of action while an administrative receiver is appointed it will usually be necessary for the board to give indemnities to the company in respect of costs.[100]

23-29 **Limitations on the powers of administrative receivers.**   The extent of, and the limitations on, the powers of an administrative receiver were further examined and defined in a case where an administrative receiver, in office, had required the company to deliver up to him important and sensitive documents, which he had then passed to the debenture-holder's solicitors. This he had done, not in the exercise of his functions as receiver, but for the purpose of assisting the debenture-holder in its other proceedings against the guarantors of the company's indebtedness. The company applied for an injunction to restrain this course of action.

The Court of Appeal held that the receiver had improperly exercised his powers, and had infringed the company's right to privacy and its legal professional privilege. It was ordered that the documents be returned to the receiver, to be held by him for the sole purpose of use in his functions of getting in, protecting and realising the assets comprised in the charge. The company, by its sole director, had brought the proceedings for the injunction. The receiver had contended that the proceedings were invalid, as not having been authorised by him. But the Court of Appeal held that the directors of a company under administrative receivership were entitled, without the authority of the receiver, to bring any proceedings, which did not threaten the interests of the debenture-holder.[101]

---

[95] *Bank of Cyprus (London) Ltd v Gill* [1988] 2 Lloyd's Rep. 51; *Routestone Ltd v Minories Finance Ltd* [1997] 21 E.G. 148; but only where the power to sell has validly arisen: see *Hickson v Darlow* (1883) 23 Ch. D. 690.

[96] As to how he may be accountable for the manner in which the sale is conducted: see *Silven Properties Ltd v Royal Bank of Scotland* [2003] EWCA Civ 1409; [2003] B.P.I.R. 1429, CA, affirming [2002] EWHC 1976 (Ch), affirming [2003] B.P.I.R. 171.

[97] See *Downsview Nominees Ltd v First City Corp.* [1993] A.C. 295, PC, where the whole of the law on this subject was reviewed, and *Medforth v Blake* [2000] Ch. 86.

[98] *Edenwest Ltd v CMS Cameron McKenna (a firm)* [2013] B.C.C. 152 at 164.

[99] *Raja v Austin Gray (a firm)* [2003] B.P.I.R. 725.

[100] *Enigma Technique Ltd v RBS* [2005] EWHC 3340 (Ch).

[101] *Sutton v GE Capital Commercial Finance Ltd, Anglo-Petroleum Ltd v GE Capital Commercial*

Section 4: Pensions

An increasingly important issue in corporate insolvency is the presence of an oc- **23-30** cupational pension scheme either supported by the insolvent company as its employer (or as one of its participating employers), or within the corporate group of which the company forms part. Administrative receivership is an insolvency event for the purpose of reporting requirements under the pensions legislation. It is also a trigger event for a statutory debt due from the employer to a defined benefit occupational pension scheme where its employer enters insolvency. The following paragraphs set out certain aspects of the pensions landscape with which the administrative receiver will have to deal. However reference should be made to the specialist works for fuller treatment of these and other pensions issues which arise in insolvency generally, in particular the role of the Pension Protection Fund ("PPF").

The notification requirements imposed on the administrative receiver once appointed have been identified in Ch.21 above, being found under ss.22 and 23 of the Pensions Act 1995 and s.120 of the Pensions Act 2004. The company is also obliged to inform the trustees of the scheme of "the occurrence of any event relating to the employer which there is reasonable cause to believe will be of material significance in the exercise by the trustees or managers or professional advisers of any of their functions".[102] It is hard to imagine that the appointment of an administrative receiver will not trigger this obligation.

On receiving notice that an insolvency practitioner has commenced acting in relation to an employer company the Pensions Regulator may use an express power found in s.23 of the Pensions Act 1995 to appoint an independent trustee of the pension scheme, who will then be the only scheme trustee able to use powers vested in the trustees.[103]

The appointment of an administrative receiver over a sole employer of a defined benefit pension scheme will be an "insolvency event" for the purposes of Pensions Act 1995 s.75. This will trigger a debt (which is provided to be unsecured and non-preferential) from the employer company to the trustees of the scheme.[104] The amount of the debt is the difference between the scheme's assets and its liabilities (i.e. its deficit), with the liabilities calculated on the basis of the cost of buying them out with annuities. This "buy out" basis is the most expensive of the funding bases in use and deficits calculated under s.75 of the Pensions Act 1995 are likely to exceed most other unsecured creditor claims in an administrative receivership.

Certain categories of unpaid contributions to an occupational pension scheme form preferential debts which must be paid out of the assets coming into the hands of the administrative receiver before he makes payments to the debenture-holder.[105] The categories are set out at Sch.4 to the Pension Schemes Act 1993:

(a) Sums owed on account of an earner's contributions to an occupational pension scheme that were deducted from earnings in the four months immediately preceding the appointment of the administrative receiver;

Finance Ltd [2004] EWCA Civ 316; [2004] 2 B.C.L.C. 662 CA, applying *Newhart Developments Ltd v Co-operative Commercial Bank Ltd* [1978] Q.B. 814.
[102] The Occupational Pension Schemes (Scheme Administration) Regulations 1996 (SI 1996/1715) reg.6(1)(b).
[103] Pensions Act 1995 s.25.
[104] Pensions Act 1995 s.75(4).
[105] Insolvency Act 1986 s.40(2) and Sch.6 para.8, in turn cross-referring to Pension Schemes Act 1993 Sch.4.

(b) sums owed on account of an employer's contributions to a Northern Ireland
     salary related contracted-out scheme which were payable in the 12 months
     immediately preceding the appointment. Such contracted out salary related
     schemes were abolished in England and Wales by the Pensions Act 2014.
(c) Sums payable where the state second pension is restored to an employee,
     in Northern Ireland.

CHAPTER 24

EXTRA-TERRITORIAL EXTENT OF FLOATING CHARGES AND OF RECEIVERSHIPS

Extra-territoriality. By the term "extra-territoriality" is here meant the recogni- **24-1**
tion by, and the enforceability in, foreign jurisdictions (i) of a floating charge created in the United Kingdom, and specifically under the laws of England or of
Scotland, and (ii) of receivers appointed under such a floating charge, normally out
of court, although many of the relevant principles are equally applicable to an appointment by the court. This chapter does not consider the position of companies
incorporated outside the UK, nor of insurers and financial institutions incorporated
within the UK but whose insolvencies are governed by specific EU Directives.

The following issues are considered:

(1) exercise of receivers' powers within the UK;
(2) exercise of powers outside the UK under the Insolvency Act 1986;
(3) non-application of the EU Insolvency Regulation and UNCITRAL Model
     Law;
(4) exercise of powers outside the UK by means of recognition of receiver-
     ships overseas;
(5) assistance from English courts by orders in personam.

Powers within the UK. Section 7 of the Administration of Justice Act 1977 **24-2**
provides that a receiver appointed under the law of any part of the UK may exercise
their powers in any other part of the UK as long as they were appointed receiver
over the whole or any part of any property or undertaking of a company, and in
consequence of the company having created a charge which, as created, was a floating charge. In this provision, "receiver" includes a manager and a person appointed as receiver and manager. The section is subject to the important caveat that
the exercise of the receiver's powers must not be inconsistent with the law of the
part of the UK where they are sought to be exercised. Section 72 of the Insolvency
Act 1986 provides for the same mutual exercise of receivers' powers, but only
between England and Scotland. There is no express exclusion of administrative
receivers in either section, unlike for example in Insolvency Act 1986 s.37, and it
is suggested that these sections apply to administrative receivers. Such receivers
must be receivers or managers in order to satisfy the definition of "administrative
receiver" in s.29(2)(a).

The requirement to register charges has been considered in Ch.21 above in relation to English companies. Scottish companies are covered by the same legislation, as Companies Act 2006 s.859A(7) states that "company", for the purposes of
that part of that Act, means UK-registered companies. Charges that must be
registered include rights in security constituted under the law of Scotland. For
further information on registration requirements applicable to Scottish companies,

see *Palmer's Company Law*, para.13.402. A charge that had been granted by a Scottish company over property located in England, but which had not been registered in accordance with the predecessor to these provisions, was held unenforceable by an English court.[1]

It should also be noted that Insolvency Act 1986 s.426 applies to orders made by courts in any part of the UK in the exercise of jurisdiction relating to "insolvency law", which is defined in s.426(10) to include administrative receivership. Courts having jurisdiction in relation to "insolvency law" in the UK are to afford each other mutual assistance,[2] and enforce orders made in relation to insolvency law as if made in that part of the UK.

24-3   **Powers outside the UK: use of Insolvency Act 1986.**   An administrative receiver may make use of the powers to get in the company's property and obtain information regarding the company that are found in Insolvency Act 1986 ss.234, 235 and 236. There is no authority on the extra-territorial effect of ss.234 or 235, but the extra-territoriality of s.236 has been considered twice at first instance in recent years. In *Re MF Global UK Limited*[3] David Richards J held that an order could not be made against a company outside the jurisdiction, following a case on s.25 of the Bankruptcy Act 1914.[4] However in *Re Omni Trustees Ltd*[5] HHJ Hodge declined to follow the MF Global UK case and considered that s.236 was structured differently to the Bankruptcy Act 1914 provision that was considered in that case. In *Re Mid East Trading Ltd, Phillips v Lehman Brothers*[6] the Court of Appeal held that an order could be made under section 236 in relation to documents situated overseas. Once a person is in the jurisdiction they can be restrained from leaving pending an examination under s.236.[7]

24-4   **EU Insolvency Regulation and UNCITRAL Model Law.**   As noted in Ch.21, an administrative receivership is not a collective insolvency process. For this reason it is not listed in Annex 1 to the EU Insolvency Regulation as an insolvency process for the purpose of that Regulation and an administrative receiver will therefore not be able to rely on any of the provisions for mutual assistance and recognition between member states of the European Union that are set out in that Regulation. For the same reason administrative receivers cannot seek assistance overseas in reliance on provisions of foreign law that enact the UNCITRAL Model Law. This is because art.1 provides that the Model Law applies to requests for assistance from foreign courts of foreign representatives in connection with "foreign proceedings". These are defined in art.2(a) as: "a collective judicial or administrative proceeding in a foreign State, including an interim proceeding, pursuant to a law relating to insolvency in which proceeding the assets and affairs of the debtor are subject to control or supervision by a foreign court, for the purpose of reorganization or liquidation". Administrative receivership is not a collective proceeding nor does it have the requisite purpose of reorganisation or liquidation.

---

[1]   *Arthur D Little Ltd (in administration) v Ableco Finance LLC* [2003] Ch. 217 at [22]–[24].
[2]   Insolvency Act 1986 s.426(4).
[3]   [2015] EWHC 2319 (Ch).
[4]   *Re Tucker (a bankrupt)* [1990] Ch. 148, CA.
[5]   [2015] EWHC 2697 (Ch).
[6]   [1998] B.C.C. 726.
[7]   *Re a Company (003318 of 1987)* (1987) 3 B.C.C. 564; [1988] P.C.C. 9.

Obtaining assistance overseas: recognition of charge and receivership in a foreign court. In seeking to act overseas it is likely that an administrative receiver will be forced to obtain recognition of his powers from the foreign court.[8] This will require the charge to be recognised as valid and as extending to the property situated overseas that is in question. This should be governed by the law of the debenture,[9] likely to be English law, and as a matter of English law a floating charge covering all assets of a company will be construed as including assets overseas.[10]

24-5

However the effectiveness of the charge in relation to property overseas will depend on the law of the place where that property is situated, namely the *lex situs*, The charge may be ineffective for not being registered in accordance with that law, or be repugnant to it, or be unenforceable under it for other reasons.

Orders in personam. If a foreign court of the country where the assets are situated refuses to recognise a receiver appointed by the English court, the Court of Appeal has said that the English court will, in an appropriate case, do what it can to render the appointment effective by orders in personam against persons who are subject to the jurisdiction of its court.[11] It is suggested that the same should apply in the case of administrative receivers who, whilst not appointed by the court, nonetheless are office-holders and afforded a certain status under statute.

24-6

---

8 The Court of Appeal used this as an analogy with the freezing order jurisdiction in *Derby & Co Ltd v Weldon (No.6)* [1990] 1 W.L.R. 1139 at 1150.
9 *Re Anchor Line (Henderson Brothers) Ltd* [1937] Ch. 483.
10 *British South Africa Co v De Beers Consolidated Mines Ltd* [1910] 1 Ch. 353.
11 *Derby & Co Ltd v Weldon (No.6)* [1990] 1 W.L.R. 1139, 1150, CA.

CHAPTER 25

RELATIONSHIP BETWEEN ADMINISTRATIVE RECEIVERSHIP AND
OTHER INSOLVENCY PROCESSES

25-1   Introduction.   This chapter considers the place of administrative receivership in
the wider context of other insolvency processes that may be available to a company.
It notes where administrative receivership is prevented by a company being in
another insolvency process (as in the case of administration), where administrative receivership may coexist with another insolvency process (liquidation) and the
potential effects of insolvency processes on each other in these circumstances.

25-2   Administration.   An application to the court for an administration order must be
notified as soon as reasonably practicable to any administrative receiver of the
company and to any person entitled to appoint one.[1] An administrator may not be
appointed out of court by a company or its directors without five business days'
written notice being given to anyone who may be entitled to appoint an administrative receiver.[2] Similarly, an administrator may not be appointed out of court by the
holder of a qualifying floating charge without giving two business days' written
notice to the holder of any prior qualifying floating charge (unless they have
consented in writing to the appointment).[3]

Once an administrative receiver has been appointed, no out of court application
for an administration order may be made.[4]

An administration application may be made to court when an administrative
receiver is in office, but the court must dismiss the application unless either (i) the
person by whom the administrative receiver was appointed (or on whose behalf he
was appointed) consents to such an order, or (ii) the court thinks that the security
under which the administrative receiver was appointed is susceptible to challenge
in a subsequent administration. This must be due to a potential challenge as a
transaction at an undervalue, a preference, or a floating charge securing past
indebtedness and created within 12 months of the administration application being made (or 24 months if the chargee is connected to the company).[5] The court
must dismiss the application even where the administrative receiver was appointed after the application was made.[6] Such an appointment is not prevented by

---

1   Insolvency Act 1986 Sch.B1 para.12(2)(a) and (b).
2   Insolvency Act 1986 Sch.B1 para.26(1)(a).
3   Insolvency Act 1986 Sch.B1 para.15(1).
4   Insolvency Act 1986 Sch.B1 paras 17(b) and 25(c).
5   Insolvency Act 1986 Sch.B1 para.39(1). In *Chesterton International Group plc v Deka Immobilien
     Inv GmbH* [2005] EWHC 656 (Ch) the court applied this provision and held that there was no discre-
     tion to make an administration order unless one of the exceptions set out in para.39(1) applied.
6   Insolvency Act 1986 Sch.B1 para.39(2).

the interim moratorium that results from the making of an administration application or the filing of a notice of intention to appoint an administrator out of court.[7]

The making of an administration application when an administrative receiver is already in office will not result in an interim moratorium until the person by whom the administrative receiver was appointed (or on whose behalf he was appointed) consents to the making of an administration order.[8]

If the court is persuaded to make an administration order despite the presence of an administrative receiver, then the administrative receiver must vacate office.[9] This is in contrast to a receiver, who may continue in post with the administrator's consent.[10]

Once a company has entered administration an administrative receiver may not be appointed.[11]

CVA. The directors of a company may not propose a CVA when the company is **25-3** in administration or being wound up.[12] There is no such restriction where an administrative receiver is in office, although the debenture-holder may well be the company's source of funding and thus have a vital role to play in deciding whether a CVA will be viable. Unlike an administrator or liquidator, an administrative receiver may not propose a CVA.[13]

A company is ineligible for a CVA moratorium if an administrative receiver is already in office.[14] However the presence of a CVA moratorium prevents any administrative receiver of the company being appointed.[15] Further, the presence of a CVA moratorium means that no notice to crystallise an uncrystallised floating charge, or having the effect of restricting the disposal of property of the company, may take effect until the moratorium comes to an end.[16] The Insolvency Act 1986 also curtails the ability of a debenture-holder to crystallise a floating charge when steps are being taken to obtain a moratorium. Any provisions in the debenture that would provide for crystallisation on the occurrence of a company obtaining a moratorium or doing anything with a view to obtaining a moratorium (including any preliminary decision or investigation) is void.[17]

The approval of a CVA may not affect the right of a secured creditor of the company to enforce its security, except with the secured creditor's consent.[18]

Receivership. The court has jurisdiction to appoint a receiver despite the prior **25-4** appointment of a receiver out of court.[19]

Liquidation. An administrative receiver and a liquidator may hold office at the **25-5** same time, and either may be appointed first. The Insolvency Act 1986 even envis-

---

[7] Insolvency Act 1986 Sch.B1 para.44(7)(c).
[8] Insolvency Act 1986 Sch.B1 para.44(6).
[9] Insolvency Act 1986 Sch.B1 para.41(1).
[10] Insolvency Act 1986 Sch.B1 para.1(2).
[11] Insolvency Act 1986 Sch.B1 para.43(6A).
[12] Insolvency Act 1986 s.1(1).
[13] Insolvency Act 1986 s.1(3).
[14] Insolvency Act 1986 Sch.A1 para.4(1)(c).
[15] Insolvency Act 1986 Sch.A1 para.12(1)(e).
[16] Insolvency Act 1986 Sch.A1 para.13.
[17] Insolvency Act 1986 Sch.A1 para.43.
[18] Insolvency Act 1986 s.4(3).
[19] *Re Maskelyne British Typewriter Co* [1898] 1 Ch. 133, applied in *Bass Breweries Ltd v Delaney* [1984] B.C.C. 851; *Re Slogger Automatic Feeder Company, Limited* [1915] 1 Ch. 478.

ages that in certain circumstances the same individual may be the liquidator and administrative receiver.[20]

25-6 **Appointment of receiver no bar to winding up.** A winding-up order must in general not be refused on the ground that the assets of the company have been charged to an amount equal to or in excess of their value, or that the company has no assets.[21] It follows that the court can make a winding-up order, even though an administrative receiver is in office, and although no benefit accrues to the creditors by the order. Thus, a winding-up order was made where the receiver was incurring large liabilities[22]; and again where the business was being carried on in the interests of the debenture-holders, and though the majority of the unsecured creditors opposed.[23] Conversely, if the debenture-holder who has appointed the receiver can show any benefit to himself which might arise as the result of liquidation, he may himself petition for an order.[24] Indeed, where the receiver has power to do what is incidental to his right to possession of the assets, he may himself present a petition in the name of the company for liquidation, on the "just and equitable" ground, if thereby the assets of the company will be protected from depletion.[25] He has no right to such an order *ex debito justitiae*; the matter lies in the discretion of the court, which will be concerned to ensure that all persons who might wish to oppose the petition are aware of its presentation.[26] An administrative receiver is given an express power to present (or defend) a winding-up petition.[27] There is also no legal impediment to the company going into voluntary liquidation.[28]

25-7 **Effect of winding up on appointment of receiver.** An administrative receiver may be appointed where a company has already entered liquidation.[29] Lack of delivery of particulars of the charge under which the appointment was made, as required by s.859A of the Companies Act 2006, is not a matter of which the company, whilst a going concern, can complain. But a charge whose particulars have not been so delivered to the registrar is made void (so far as the conferment of any security is concerned) not only against other creditors, but also against the liquidator or administrator of the company.[30] For this reason, no person will normally accept appointment as administrative receiver under an unregistered charge (the position before 6 April 2013) or one whose particulars and associated documents have not been delivered (the position from 6 April 2013),[31] although if

---

[20] Insolvency Act 1986 s.46(3).
[21] Insolvency Act 1986 s.123(2).
[22] *Re Chic Ltd* [1905] 2 Ch. 345.
[23] *Re Clandown Colliery* [1915] 1 Ch. 369.
[24] *Re Borough of Portsmouth Tramways Co* [1892] 2 Ch. 362.
[25] *Re Emmadart Ltd* [1979] Ch.540. In that case, the company was liable for rates in respect of unoccupied property, unless it could claim exemption under Rating (Exemption of Unoccupied Property) Regulations 1967 (SI 1967/954) reg.2, as being subject to a winding-up order.
[26] See n.23, above.
[27] Insolvency Act 1986 s.42 and Sch.1 para.21.
[28] Insolvency Act 1986 s.84.
[29] *Re Henry Pound & Son, Hutchins* (1889) 42 Ch.D 402, a case on receivers. The case of *Re Potters Oils Ltd (No.2)* [1986] 1 W.L.R. 201 was also a case where a receiver was appointed after the appointment of a liquidator, leading to a challenge to the receiver's fees.
[30] Companies Act 2006 s.859H.
[31] Debenture-holders who have actually seized chattels under an unregistered charge may be in a better position than a receiver who does not seize them as their agent: see *Re Toomer* (1883) 23 Ch. D.

he does so he may safely act until liquidation,[32] when he must account to the liquidator for all the assets then in his hands.

An order or resolution for winding up may, as a result of the application of s.239 of the Insolvency Act 1986, (relating to preferences), or s.245 of that Act, (relating to the possible invalidity of floating charges), have the effect of invalidating either the whole, or a portion, of the charges in respect of which the receiver has been appointed, and hence, either pro tanto or wholly, his appointment. Since s.239 relates to charges given within a period of up to two years, as does s.245 in relation to floating charges with "connected" persons, before "the onset of insolvency",[33] no receiver who is appointed within such period of two years will usually be willing to act before such time limits have expired, without either the most searching inquiry into the circumstances surrounding the giving of the charge, or more usually, an indemnity from the debenture-holder. Of course such an indemnity is now implied in the case of the appointment of an administrative receiver.[34]

Receiver's powers unabated by winding-up.   Subject to the foregoing, neither **25-8** the making up of a winding-up order—nor, still less, the passing of a resolution to wind up—displaces the receiver appointed by the debenture-holders, or in any way terminates his powers under the debenture.[35] It is undecided whether it has any effect on the powers that are deemed to be included in the debenture by Insolvency Act 1986 s.42(1). It is suggested that those powers too are unaffected by the company entering liquidation, but that they must be used for the proper purposes of the administrative receivership, namely the realisation of property covered by the debenture in order to repay the debenture-holder's debt and interest.[36] Where those powers are inconsistent with the powers and functions of a liquidator it is possible to argue that they are of no effect.

As noted, a winding up order does not prevent the debenture-holders from appointing a receiver, if one has not already been appointed[37]; but after the making of a winding-up order, the receiver must apply to the liquidator, or to the court in the winding-up, for liberty to take possession of any property of which he is not then

---

254; *Wrightson v McArthur and Hutchisons (1919) Ltd* [1921] 2 K.B. 807; *Mercantile Bank of India Ltd v Chartered Bank of India, Australia and China* [1937] 1 All E.R. 231. If the receiver acts quickly enough in realising the assets and paying off the debentures, so that they are paid off by the commencement of the liquidation, s.245 of the Insolvency Act 1986 will have no application: *Mace Builders (Glasgow) Ltd v Lunn* [1987] Ch. 191, CA.

[32]   *Burston Finance Ltd v Speirway* [1974] 1 W.L.R. 1648 per Walton J at 1657E.

[33]   Where there is an administration order (or an administrator is appointed extra-judicially), or the company has gone into liquidation immediately upon the discharge of such an order, the onset of insolvency occurred on the date of the presentation of the petition upon which the administration order was made. If the company goes into liquidation at any other time, it means the date of the commencement of the winding up: Insolvency Act 1986 ss.240(3), 245(1) (as amended). Where an administrator has been appointed extra-judicially, the date is the date when the notice of intention to appoint was filed with the court.

[34]   See Insolvency Act 1986 s.44(1)(c), by virtue of which an administrative receiver is entitled to an indemnity out of the assets of the company in respect of any contracts entered into by him in the carrying out of his functions (unless the contract otherwise expressly provides), and in respect of any contract of employment adopted by him. As to the adoption of contracts of employment, see Ch.23, above.

[35]   *Gough's Garages Ltd v Pugsley* [1930] 1 K.B. 615 per Romer LJ at p.626; *Sowman v David Samuel Trust Ltd* [1978] 1 W.L.R. 22.

[36]   The Court of Appeal emphasised the importance of the proper purpose of administrative receiver's powers in *Sutton v GE Capital Commercial Finance* [2004] EWCA Civ 315.

[37]   See n.29, above.

in possession.[38] A receiver or manager must also, at any time whether during or after his tenure of office, when so required by the liquidator, render proper accounts of his receipts to the liquidator, vouch the same, and pay over to the latter the amount properly payable to him.[39] In default, the court may make an order, on the application of the liquidator, for this to be done within a specified time, and may order that all costs of and incidental to the application should be borne by the receiver or manager, as the case may be.[40]

25-9   Agency of administrative receiver for company.   On the commencement of the liquidation, the agency of the administrative receiver for the company determines.[41] If he continues to carry on business after such determination, he does not, in a normal case,[42] become an agent for the debenture-holders.[43] In this case, the debenture-holder will, as principal, be liable for his actions and equally, as principal entitled (subject to any express term in the appointment), to an indemnity from the administrative receiver in respect of any loss caused by his negligence.[44] In all other cases, he becomes a principal.[45] Thus, he will become personally liable on all contracts into which he enters, to the exclusion of the company. He will of course be entitled to a right of indemnity (except as to contracts entered into without authority) out of the assets in his hands.[46] After the commencement of a winding up, he should if possible obtain authority from the debenture-holders to continue to carry on business as their agent, unless he decides to cease to trade, or effects a "hive down" of the company's business to a subsidiary.

25-10   Where the administrative receiver's agency is terminated.   This determination of his agency entails that he can no bind the company personally by acting in its name as its agent. However he retains his powers under the debenture. Goulding J stated as follows in *Sowman v David Samuel Trust Ltd*[47]:

> "Winding up deprives the receiver, under such a debenture as that now in suit, of power to bind the company personally by acting as its agent. It does not in the least affect his powers to hold and dispose of the company's property comprised in the debenture, including his power to use the company's name for that purpose, for such powers are given by the disposition of the company's property which it made (in equity) by the debenture itself. That disposition is binding on the company and those claiming through it, as well in liquidation as before liquidation, except of course where the debenture is vulnerable under section 95 or section 322 of the Companies Act 1948 or is otherwise invalidated by some provision of law applicable to the winding up."

The provisions of s.127 of the Insolvency Act 1986, which avoid any disposition

---

[38] In *Re Potters Oils Ltd (No.2)* [1986] 1 W.L.R. 201 it was said by Hoffmann J that the receiver would be entitled to that leave as of right (at [206]).

[39] Insolvency Act 1986 s.41(1)(b).

[40] Insolvency Act 1986 s.41(1)(b), (2); CPR r.69.8; Financial Services and Markets Act 2000 s.363(3).

[41] Insolvency Act 1986 s.44(1)(a), reflecting the position at common law regarding all receivers: *Gosling v Gaskell* [1897] A.C. 575 HL; *American Express International Banking Corp v Hurley* [1985] 3 All E.R. 564.

[42] See *Re S Brown & Co (General Warehousemen) Ltd* [1940] Ch. 961; but note the comments thereon in *Re Wood* [1941] Ch. 112.

[43] *Gosling v Gaskell* [1897] A.C. 575.

[44] *American Express International Banking Corp. v Hurley*, n.22, above.

[45] *Thomas v Todd* [1926] 2 K.B. 511. For a case where, on special facts, the receiver was held to be the agent of the company in liquidation, see *Re Northern Garage Ltd* [1946] Ch. 188.

[46] Insolvency Act 1986 s.37(1)(b), (3).

[47] [1978] 1 W.L.R. 22 at 30.

of the property of a company after the commencement of the winding up, do not apply to a disposition of property under a power in the debenture: the relevant "disposition" in such a case is of course the original charge under which the administrative receiver has been appointed.[48]

If, however, part of the assets of the company, over which the receiver is appointed, consists of shares in a subsidiary company which is put into compulsory liquidation, the provisions of this section will apply to any disposition of the assets of the subsidiary.[49]

Administrative Receiver's possession of company property. As regards the property of the company charged to the debenture-holder, including (if charged) its undertaking, this remains in the control of the receiver, who will continue to manage and deal with it as a principal.[50] It would appear that the receiver is entitled not merely to possession of all the physical assets of the company (as regards which he would be in the same position as debenture-holders who had validly seized their security), but is also solely entitled to all choses in action, such as the benefit of contracts with the company existing at the date of the winding up.[51] For enforcing such rights, if required, he may sue in the name of the company.[52]   **25-11**

On the other side of the coin, his liability to keep accounts and produce them to the company, now represented by the liquidator, will continue at any rate as long as there is any possibility that there may be a surplus in his hands for which he will be accountable to the company.

Nature of receiver's status. Although an administrative receiver in office at the same time as a liquidator is technically the principal, he is not of course acting on his own behalf. He is still acting as receiver of the company, and his possession and control is throughout for the benefit of the debenture-holders and the company, to the extent of their respective interests in the assets he holds. It has been held, in consequence, that for the purposes of legislation governing employment, if the receiver transfers the business of the company to a third party, that transfer may be regarded as a transfer from the company, and not from the receiver himself personally, thus ensuring technical continuity of the employment.[53]   **25-12**

---

[48] *Sowman v David Samuel Trust Ltd* [1978] 1 W.L.R. 22, 30C per Goulding J cf. the position under ss.239, 245, para.25-7, above.

[49] See *Clifton Place Garage Ltd* [1970] Ch. 477. But in that case, it was not the assets of the company itself which were involved, but the assets of a subsidiary, which was not charged by the debenture. See *Re Margart Ltd* [1985] B.C.L.C. 314 at 319. Insolvency Act 1986 s.127, was amended by Enterprise Act 2002 Sch.17 para.15, to cover administrator's acts while a winding-up petition was suspended under Insolvency Act 1986 Sch.B1 para.40.

[50] See *Gosling v Gaskell* [1897] A.C. 575, HL.

[51] *Gough's Garages Ltd v Pugsley* [1930] 1 K.B. 615 (right to apply for new lease under Landlord and Tenant Act 1927 s.5, a right charged by company; receiver accordingly entitled to enforce that right in name of company, notwithstanding liquidation).

[52] See n.54, above.

[53] *Deaway Trading Ltd v Calverley* [1973] I.C.R. 546 (a decision of the NIRC under the Contracts of Employment Act 1963 Sch.1 para.10(2), and the Employment Protection (Consolidation) Act 1978 s.151). It is not, however, clear why the court did not simply regard the appointment of the receiver in that case as effecting a transfer of the business to him. See now The Transfer of Undertakings (Protection of Employment) Regulations 2006 (SI 2006/246) regs 4, 7, and the Employment Rights Act 1996. See Ch.23 above.

Effect of termination of agency.

25-13 (a) *Contracts*   The receiver will be entitled to the benefit of all contracts entered into by the company, as well before as after his appointment, and entitled to enforce the same. For this purpose, he may if necessary use the name of the company in litigation.[54] It is not considered that liquidation has any effect on rights of set-off.

However, all contracts of personal service with the company will be terminated, as if the appointment was one made by the court.[55] Moreover, for the purposes of redundancy payments, such termination is treated as a termination by the company.[56] Such an automatic termination of contracts of employment, in consequence of the winding-up of the company having terminated the administrative receiver's agency for the company, does not apply to contracts which the receiver has adopted.[57]

(b) *Further contracts*   Since the business of the company is likely to have been transferred to a subsidiary company, whose operations will in principle be entirely unaffected by the liquidation of the original company, the question of contracts entered into by the receiver after liquidation has rarely been considered by the courts. Since the receiver is now a principal, the company cannot be affected in any way by any loss which may be incurred as a result of any such contract. For the same reason, since the receiver is no longer an agent for the company, he is not bound by the doctrine of ultra vires (in so far as that is still a live issue): on the other hand, his appointment by the debenture-holders or trustees will have been for the purpose of managing the business of the company and not for any wider purpose. Accordingly, he will owe them a duty not to do anything which he could not have done whilst an agent for the company.

(c) *Torts of employees*   The maxim *respondeat superior* will now apply in its full force to the receiver.

25-14 **Completion of conveyances.**   Although there is no doubt as to the receiver's power to sell the property of the company after liquidation, some doubt has been expressed as to the manner of completion of conveyances after this event. It is, of course, clear that if the debenture contains a power of attorney conferred upon the debenture-holders themselves, then such power will not be revoked by the liquidation, either because an authority coupled with an interest is irrevocable,[58] or because of the express provisions of the Powers of Attorney Act 1971.[59]

But if a power of attorney is given simply to the receiver himself, then it may be argued that neither of the foregoing rules will ensure the continuance of the power, because the benefit thereby secured is not a benefit to the donee himself—the receiver—but to the debenture-holders.[60]

On the other hand, it may well be argued that in any event the ordinary power, conferred upon the receiver by any well-drawn debenture, to sell the assets in the

---

[54] See n.52, above.
[55] See *Reid v Explosives Co Ltd* (1887) 19 Q.B.D. 264.
[56] Employment Rights Act 1996. See generally, Chs 18 and 23, above.
[57] Under s.44(1)(b) of the Insolvency Act 1986.
[58] *Smart v Sandars* (1848) 5 C.B. 895 at 917.
[59] See s.4 of that Act, and *Sowman v David Samuel Trust Ltd* [1978] 1 W.L.R. 22.
[60] See per Goulding J in *Sowman v David Samuel Trust Ltd*, n.60, above, at 31A–C.

name of the company, and to complete such sale by the execution of a conveyance or transfer, will itself survive liquidation in the same way as all the other powers conferred upon the receiver.[61] In the further alternative, it may well be that the trustees for debenture-holders may be entitled to exercise the usual statutory power of a mortgagee under the Law of Property Act 1925 s.104,[62] even in a case where their mortgage is only equitable.[63]

It is submitted that, where this latter power is clearly available—that is to say, where the debenture-holder or trustees for debenture-holders are in the position of legal mortgagees or charges—this is the proper course to take. As a suitable alternative, of course, there can be no doubt as to the proper course to take, if a valid power of attorney has been conferred upon them. In all other cases, it is submitted, the power of the receiver to convey in the name of the company must survive liquidation, as being a necessary incident to the completion of sales made in exercise of his power of sale, which beyond all question survives liquidation.

Litigation brought or continued by receiver. There is no doubt that a receiver **25-15** may continue, after liquidation, litigation which was properly commenced in the name of the company before liquidation, whether it was originally commenced by the company itself,[64] or by the receiver.[65] It is also apparent, from the way in which the court approached the question in the case which decided the latter point, that, provided that the chose in action represented by the right to litigate can fairly be regarded as within the scope of the assets comprised in the appointment of the receiver, there is no legal obstacle to the receiver bringing an action after the liquidation, but in the name of the company.[66] Where a freezing injunction was obtained against the company by a plaintiff, prior to the appointment of the receiver, this did not bind the assets of the company to the detriment of a debenture-holder, the creation of whose security predated the grant of the injunction.[67]

Incidence of costs of litigation. Since, in most cases of liquidation, there will be **25-16** genuine reason to believe that the company will be unable to pay the costs of the defendant, if successful in his defence, the defendant will normally be able to obtain an order for security for costs.[68] Quite apart from this possibility, however, since the incidence of costs is always in the discretion of the court,[69] the court may well, in the case of a claim originally started by the company, seeing that the continuation of the claim is obviously primarily intended to ensure for the benefit of the debenture-holders, order that the costs incurred after the date of the winding-up order should be paid by the receiver.[70] In this case, such costs will be allowed as

---

[61] See above at 31C–F.

[62] See above at 31G–H.

[63] *Sowman v David Samuel Trust Ltd*, n.60, above; *Barrows v Chief Land Registrar, Times,* 20 October 1977.

[64] *Bacal Contracting Ltd v Modern Engineering (Bristol) Ltd* [1980] 2 All E.R. 655.

[65] *Gough's Garages Ltd v Pugsley* [1930] 1 K.B. 615.

[66] See n.66, above per Greer LJ at 621, and per Romer LJ at 625–626.

[67] *Capital Cameras Ltd v Harold Lines Ltd (National Westminster Bank intervening)* [1991] 1 W.L.R. 54; [1991] 3 All E.R. 389 per Harman J, distinguishing *Cretanor Maritime Co Ltd v Irish Marine Ltd* [1978] 1 W.L.R. 966, CA.

[68] CPR r.25.13(2)(a) and (b).

[69] Senior Courts Act 1981 s.51(1).

[70] Senior Courts Act 1981 s.51(1).

part of his expenses as such.[71] The balance of the costs will then represent an unsecured claim against the company.[72]

In a case where the litigation has throughout been conducted by the receiver on behalf of the company, whether commenced before or after the liquidation, the court has jurisdiction to order the receiver to pay all the costs, both those incurred before as well as those incurred after the liquidation. However this is not a jurisdiction that will commonly be exercised. The Court of Appeal considered it in *Dolphin Quay Development Ltd v Mills*,[73] and affirmed the decision of the Chancellor[74] not to order costs against receivers appointed under a fixed charge and (in one case) as an administrative receiver ("the receivers"). The receivers had unsuccessfully pursued a claim in the name of the company, acting as its agents as they were entitled to do under the relevant debenture and pursuing a contractual right of the company. The defendant to the claim made no application for security for costs, which the court considered to be his appropriate protection in such circumstances, but when the claim failed he sought costs from the receivers as non-parties in reliance on Senior Courts Act 1981 s.51(3). This failed, on the basis that the receivers had not been the "real party" to the litigation but merely the company's agent. They had no interest in the outcome of the claim (an argument based on the fees they would earn from conducting the claim was rejected).

25-17   **Calls.**   The proper person to get in uncalled capital charged by a debenture is the liquidator,[75] and if he does not do so the receiver may apply in the liquidation for an order directing him to do so.[76]

25-18   **Preference.**   Where money has been recovered by an administrator or the liquidator from a creditor on the ground of a voidable preference made at a relevant time,[77] the receiver for debenture-holders has no title to the money, which belongs to the general body of creditors.[78] But moneys recovered in misfeasance proceedings are included in the debenture-holders' security.[79]

25-19   **Variation of remuneration.**   The remuneration payable to the receiver or manager is usually fixed by the debentures or the debenture trust deed, by reference to and incorporating s.109(6) of the Law of Property Act 1925. This section would normally apply, without express mention. By s.36 of the Insolvency Act 1986, the court may, upon the application of the liquidator, fix the amount to be paid by way of remuneration to an administrative receiver (or other receiver),[80] and may vary or amend the order upon the application of the liquidator or the receiver or

---

[71] *Bacal Contracting Ltd v Modern Engineering (Bristol) Ltd*, n.65, above; *S. & M Hotels Ltd v Family Housing Association* [1979] CA Transcripts 132, not following the dictum of Shaw LJ in *Newhart Developments Ltd v Co-operative Commercial Bank Ltd* [1978] Q.B. 814 at 819, to the contrary.

[72] See, by analogy with the position in bankruptcy where a trustee in bankruptcy continues a claim begun by the bankrupt before his appointment, the Supreme Court decision of *Gabriel v BPE Solicitors* [2015] UKSC 39.

[73] [2008] 1 W.L.R. 1829.

[74] [2007] 4 All E.R. 503.

[75] *Fowler v Broad's Patent, etc. Co* [1893] 1 Ch. 724.

[76] *Re Westminster Syndicate Ltd* (1908) 99 L.T. 924.

[77] Insolvency Act 1986 ss.239 and 240.

[78] *Re Yagerphone Ltd* [1935] Ch. 392.

[79] *Re Anglo-Austrian Printing, etc. Union* [1895] 2 Ch. 891.

[80] Insolvency Act 1986 s.36(1).

manager.[81] Where no previous order has been made under this section, the power of the court extends to fixing such remuneration for a period before the making of the order or the application[82]; it is exercisable, notwithstanding that the receiver or manager has died or has ceased to act before the making of the order or the application[83]; and it extends to requiring the receiver or his personal representative to account for the whole or any part of any remuneration paid to or retained by him in respect of any period before the making of the order, in excess of the sum so fixed by the court.[84] However, this last power is not to be exercised as respects any period before the making of the application for the order, unless, in the court's opinion, there are special circumstances making it proper for the power to be exercised.[85]

Where the receiver had paid off the debenture-holder's debt before drawing his own remuneration, and the remaining funds would not suffice to pay that remuneration (the amount of which was disputed by the company) without realising further assets, the receiver was restrained by injunction from realising any further assets, until the dispute as to the amount or scale of his remuneration had been determined.[86]

Good faith in exercise of power to fix remuneration. The power conferred by **25-20** the Law of Property Act 1925 to fix the receiver's remuneration must be exercised in good faith: to that extent there is a qualified duty of care owed by the debenture-holders to the company.[87] But the Insolvency Act 1986 s.36, is confined to cases where the remuneration can clearly be seen to be excessive, and is not intended to ensure a routine taxation by the court.[88]

The amount allowed depends upon the circumstances of each case. There is no hard-and-fast rule as to the amount to be allowed, either to a receiver or a liquidator.

The application by the liquidator, whether in a compulsory or a voluntary winding up, is by application notice in private. In either case, the application notice must be served on the receiver.

Where an administrative receiver, in a Scottish case, was sued by the debenture-holder, claiming damages for having negligently continued the company's trading, he defended the claim, contending that under the debenture the company alone was responsible for his acts and defaults; he also counter-claimed for payment of his remuneration: it was held that he was not a party to the debenture, and acquired no third-party rights thereunder. He was accordingly held liable for his own acts and defaults, and, in the absence of any specific agreement, could only look to the assets of the company for his remuneration.[89]

Custody of books and papers. The liquidator will be entitled to the custody of **25-21**

---

[81] Insolvency Act 1986 s.36(3).
[82] Insolvency Act 1986 s.36(2)(c).
[83] Insolvency Act 1986 s.36(2)(b).
[84] Insolvency Act 1986 s.36(2)(b).
[85] Insolvency Act 1986 s.36(2).
[86] *Rottenberg v Monjack* [1992] B.C.C. 688: the company was required to put up a substantial sum to secure its cross-undertaking in damages; *Smiths Ltd v Middleton* [1979] 3 All E.R. 842; and *Gomba Holdings (UK) Ltd v Homan* [1986] 1 W.L.R. 1301 were applied. See also, as to the fixing of the receiver's remuneration, and his right to demand an indemnity, *Re Therm-a-Stor Ltd, Morris v Lewis* [1996] 1 W.L.R. 138, and *Munns v Perkins* [2002] B.P.I.R. 120, where the receiver sought directions as to his rate of remuneration.
[87] *Re Potters Oils Ltd (No.2)* [1986] 1 W.L.R. 201; the application was unsuccessful.
[88] In *Munns v Perkins*, above, remuneration was approved at the rate of 4.2% of the value of the assets realised.
[89] *Hill Samuel & Co Ltd v Laing* [1991] B.C.C. 665 (Inner House); (previous proceedings were reported

such books and documents of the company as relate to its management of the statutory books of the company, and of all other books and documents of the company as relate to the management and business of the company and are not necessary to support the title of the debenture-holders. It is thought that, by analogy with the position which obtains where a receiver is appointed by the court, the liquidator must produce such books to the receiver when requested. Where an administrative receiver is appointed after an insolvent winding-up has commenced, any application by the receiver for the delivery up by the liquidator of any books, papers or property can be made in reliance on Insolvency Act 1986 s.234 and should be made inter partes.[90]

---

at [1988] 4 B.C.C. 9; 1988 S.L.T. 454).

[90] *Re First Express Ltd* [1991] B.C.C. 782.

CHAPTER 26

TERMINATION OF ADMINISTRATIVE RECEIVERSHIP

Termination of the administrative receivership: general.   As seen in the   **26-1**
preceding chapter, an administrative receiver appointed by a debenture-holder may,
if the court thinks fit, be removed by the court (but only by the court). Administrative receivers may also resign, vacate office on ceasing to be qualified, or vacate
office on death. Further, on the making of an administration order,[1] or the extra-
judicial appointment of an administrator and its taking effect, any administrative
receiver of the company must vacate office.[2] Finally the position regarding dissolution will be noted.

Removal.   Only the court can remove an administrative receiver. Accordingly, no   **26-2**
provision in the debenture whereunder he was appointed, authorising his removal
by the appointor, or by anybody else other than the court, will be effective. This is
in contrast to the position of receivers, where appointors may remove as long as they
comply with the terms of the debenture.[3] Just as his appointment takes effect only
when communicated to the receiver, so also (in the absence of any special provision) notice of removal, under a power to remove, is effective only when received
by him.[4] To the extent to which it is his duty to have paid preferential debts, a
receiver who is removed from office must ensure that these are discharged, or that
he retains sufficient assets in his hands to meet them, before he parts with the assets.
Alternatively (see below), his removal may be accompanied by another appointment, under such circumstances that the receivership may properly be regarded as
continuous, in which case he will be justified in transferring the whole of the assets in his hands, save as mentioned below, to the new receiver. If he does not either
ensure payment of the preferential debts, or else that the receivership may properly
be regarded as continuous, he will be personally liable to any disappointed
preferential creditor whose debt he ought to have discharged.[5]
   Having regard to the personal liability imposed upon all receivers by statute in
respect of their own contracts (save insofar as such contracts may provide, which
is unusual, to the contrary), an administrative receiver who has been removed will,

---

[1]   See Ch.14 above.
[2]   Insolvency Act 1986 Sch.B1 para.41(2).
[3]   In *IRC v Goldblatt* [1972] Ch. 498 the debenture-holder revoked a receiver's appointment as part
   of a scheme to procure the company's assets were transferred to the debenture-holders without paying preferential tax claims. The court found the receiver was liable to the preferential creditor as
   constructive trustee, and that the debenture-holder came under the statutory duty to pay preferential
   debts with the company's assets, and breached it.
[4]   *Windsor Refrigerator Co Ltd v Branch Nominees Ltd* [1961] Ch.375, CA per Donovan LJ at 398.
[5]   *IRC v Goldblatt* [1972] Ch. 498. The debenture holder who procured the removal of the receiver was
   also held liable.

like any other agent who has properly made himself liable in respect of his principal's contracts, have a lien on the assets in his hands against all such liabilities personally incurred by him.[6]

Removal of an administrative receiver may occur on the application of other debenture-holders, or of the appointor, in favour of its own receiver.[7] The court may not appoint a replacement administrative receiver on such an application[8]; this will have to be done by the debenture-holder out of court.

26-3 Displacement. A receiver appointed by or on behalf of subsequent debenture-holders will be displaced by the appointment of a receiver by or on behalf of prior debenture-holders.

26-4 Resignation. An administrative receiver may resign his office by giving notice.[9] He must give at least five business days' notice of his intention to do so to his appointor and to the company, or, if it is then in liquidation, its liquidator, specifying the date on which he intends his resignation to take effect. This notice must also be given to members of the creditors committee (if any).[10]

Then, within 14 days after his vacation of office, he must send a notice to that effect to the registrar of companies.[11]

26-5 Cessation of qualification. The administrative receiver will similarly vacate office, if he ceases to be qualified to act as an insolvency practitioner in relation to the company[12]; this will be without prejudice to the validity of any acts which he may have carried out, after he ceased to be so qualified.[13] In this event, he must forthwith give notice of his vacation of office to the liquidator of the company, if it is in liquidation, and to the members of the creditors' committee, if there is one.[14] Within 14 days, he must also send a notice to that effect to the registrar of companies.[15]

26-6 Death. If the administrative receiver dies, a notice of that fact and of the date of death must be delivered as soon as reasonably practicable to: the appointor, the registrar of companies, to the company, or, if it is then in liquidation, to its liquidator and to members of the creditors' committee (if any).[16] The notice must be delivered by any one of: a surviving joint administrative receiver, a member of the deceased's firm (if any), an officer of the deceased's company (if any) or a personal representative of the deceased. If none of these individuals have delivered the notice within 21 days of the death then any other person may do so.[17] This expanded list of individuals replaced a requirement under the Insolvency Rules 2016 for the appointer to deliver the notice. Form REC5 must be used.

---

6   Insolvency Act 1986 ss.44(1)(c) and 45(3)(b).
7   Insolvency Act 1986 s.45(1).
8   *Re A&C Supplies Ltd* [1998] B.C.C. 708.
9   Insolvency Act 1986 s.45(1).
10   Insolvency Rules 2016 r.4.18.
11   Insolvency Act 1986 s.45(4).
12   Insolvency Act 1986 s.45(2).
13   Insolvency Act 1986 s.232; Sch.B1 para.104.
14   Insolvency Rules 2016, r.4.20.
15   Insolvency Act 1986 s.45(4).
16   Insolvency Rules 2016 r.4.19(1).
17   Insolvency Rules 2016 r.4.19(2).

If, after the death of a receiver, the company attempted to deal with its assets before the debenture-holders had an opportunity of appointing a new receiver, the company could clearly be restrained by injunction from so acting. In the normal case, an appointment will be promptly made in replacement, and the receivership can then be regarded as continuous,[18] but provision will of course have to be made to ensure the indemnification of the receiver's estate against all liabilities personally incurred by him.

Continuity of receivership.   Although the only directly relevant decision relates to a special statutory situation,[19] where a new receiver is appointed, in the place of a receiver who has died or been removed, without undue delay, the receivership may be regarded as continuous.[20] This is particularly important as regards any undischarged statutory duties, such as the duty to discharge preferential debts.[21] If these have not been discharged prior to the death or removal, then his personal representatives or the receiver himself, as the case may be, will, if the receivership can be regarded as being continuous, but not otherwise, be justified in accounting to the new receiver in respect of the entirety of the assets in his hand (save for such portion thereof as is required for his protection against contractual claims), leaving it to the new receiver to complete the statutory obligations in this regard.

26-7

If, however, the receivership cannot be regarded as continuous,[22] he cannot safely take this course. Nor, if no further receiver is to be appointed, can he simply take the course of accounting to the company, without first discharging all preferential debts, and distributing, if required, the "prescribed part" to the unsecured creditors.[23]

Duty to cease to act.   If, at any stage of his management of the company, the receiver has in his hands sufficient moneys to discharge all the debts of the company which he is bound to discharge[24], all possible claims which could be made against him and in respect of which he is entitled to an indemnity, his own remuneration, and all moneys secured by the instrument pursuant to which he was appointed, it will be his duty to cease to act with all due expedition; this should confine his further activities to taking the necessary steps to conclude his administration. This has been held not to include realising further properties in order to pay remuneration in circumstances where the company's directors argued that sufficient money had already been realised for that purpose and where an inquiry for that purpose would be needed.[25] If he continues to act, any accounts will be taken against him thereafter with annual rests from the date when he had sufficient moneys in his hands to cover all such amounts.[26] His continuance in possession of the company's assets thereafter might also be regarded by the courts as wrongful, since his appointment is only for the purpose of enabling the encumbrancers, entitled to the

26-8

---

18   See para.26-7 below.
19   *Re White's Mortgage* [1943] Ch. 166 (appointment of receiver requiring leave under the Courts (Emergency Powers) Act 1939).
20   Insolvency Act 1986 s.46(2): see also s.62(6).
21   See para.26-2, above.
22   In *Re White's Mortgage*, n.20, above, a delay of 10 months was held to break the continuity of the receivership.
23   Under Insolvency Act 1986 s.176A, inserted by Enterprise Act 2002 s.253.
24   He is entitled to remain in place so long as there is a contingent liability secured by the debenture: *OBG Ltd v Allan* [2001] B.P.I.R. 1111.
25   *Rottenberg v Monjack* [1992] B.C.C. 688.
26   *Foxcraft v Wood* (1828) 4 Russ. 487.

benefit of the instrument under which he was appointed, to recover their debt; once this purpose has been achieved, there is no ground for his continuance in office. The effect would be that thereafter he would be in the position of trespasser.[27]

For various reasons, the receiver may have sufficient moneys in his hands for the above purpose, but may not be in a position to settle all possible claims which could be made against him and in respect of which he is entitled to an indemnity. He should then request his appointor to apply for his discharge, and should retain sufficient moneys to answer his indemnity, and account at once for any balance to the company. Alternatively, he may (but cannot be forced to) accept an indemnity from the company which may (but cannot be compelled to) offer such indemnity.

He will also, of course, vacate office on the completion of his receivership: in this case notices must be given as if he had vacated office in consequence of ceasing to be qualified as an insolvency practitioner.[28]

When he vacates office, his remuneration, any expenses properly incurred by him, and any indemnity to which he is entitled out of the assets of the company, will be charged on and paid out of any property of the company which is in his custody or under his control at that time in priority to any security held by his appointor.[29]

26-9   **Administration.**   An administrative receiver will automatically vacate office on the making of an administration order[30]; but no such order is made without the consent of his appointor,[31] unless the security whereunder he was appointed is considered by the court to be liable to be set aside as being at an undervalue, or a voidable preference, or an invalid floating charge.[32]

26-10   **Accounts upon administrative receiver ceasing to act.**   Within two months (or such extended period as the court may allow) after ceasing to act as administrative receiver, he must send to the registrar of companies, to the company and to his appointor, and to each member of the creditors' committee (if there is one), the requisite account of his receipts and payments as receiver.[33]

26-11   **Balance in accounts due to company.**   The duty of the receiver to keep accounts and make them available for inspection by the company, as and when required, has already been noted. But whereas the receiver is not a debtor to the company in respect of any intermediate balance which might appear from his accounts to be due to the company, he will be a debtor to the company in respect of the final balance, after discharging all preferential debts and so forth, shown by his accounts to be due to the company. It follows that this balance can be the proper subject of a third party debt order.[34]

26-12   **Remuneration, expenses and indemnity on vacation of office.**   Where a receiver or manager appointed under powers contained in an instrument, whether or not an

---

27 cf. *Ashworth v Lord* (1887) 36 Ch. D. 545.
28 Insolvency Rules 2016 r.4.20.
29 Insolvency Act 1986 s.45(3).
30 Formerly under Insolvency Act 1986 s.11(1)(b) (repealed): now under Insolvency Act 1986 Sch.B1 paras 39(1)(a), 41(1).
31 Formerly under n.19, s.9(3)(a) (repealed); now under Insolvency Act 1986 Sch.B1 para.39(1)(b), (c), (d).
32 Under ss.238, 239, 245 Insolvency Act 1986.
33 Insolvency Rules 2016, r.4.17.
34 As envisaged by the judgment in *Seabrook Estate Co Ltd v Ford* [1949] 2 All E.R. 94 at 97.

administrative receiver, vacates office, his remuneration,[35] expenses properly incurred by him, and any indemnity to which he is entitled out of the assets of the company, are charged on, and are to be paid out of any property of the company which is in his custody or under his control at that time, in priority to any charge or other security held by the person by or on whose behalf he was appointed.[36]

Withdrawal of receiver before payment off of debenture holders in full. If a receiver is withdrawn by consent, before the debenture-holders have been paid off in full, any floating charge comprised in their security, having once crystallised, will not re-float automatically, and can only be made so to do by express agreement. A more difficult question is whether, after the withdrawal of a receiver, the debenture-holders are still entitled to a fixed equitable charge on the assets so released to the company; in principle, there appears to be no reason why this charge should not continue to attach to any assets which belonged to the company at the date of crystallisation, and which have not been disposed of during the receivership. The charge would not attach to assets of the company acquired subsequently to the date of crystallisation.[37] The practical results of this position are so inconvenient that it is thought that an intention to waive the fixed charge will readily be implied.

26-13

Destination of books and papers. The ownership of documents in the possession of a receiver at the end of the receivership may vest in the company, or in the debenture-holders, or may remain with the receiver, depending on their nature. All documents generated by or received by the receiver pursuant to his duty to manage the business of the company, or to dispose of its assets, vest in the company. This includes "ordinary correspondence" sent or received by the companies in the conduct of their affairs.[38] Documents containing advice and information about the receivership, or about the companies brought into existence by the receiver for the purpose of enabling him to advise the debenture-holders, belong to them, despite being produced by administrative receivers who were at all times agents of the company. Notes, calculations, working papers and memoranda prepared by the receiver, not pursuant to any duty to prepare them, but better to enable him throughout to discharge his professional duties, belong to the receiver.[39]

26-14

Dissolution of the company (otherwise than under the Insolvency Act 1986 ss.202–204). Where the liquidator in a compulsory winding up gives notice to the registrar that the final meeting has been held,[40] or the Official Receiver (as liquidator) gives notice that the winding-up is complete, the registrar will register that notice, and on the expiry of three months thereafter, the company will be dissolved.[41] The Official Receiver, or any other person who can satisfy the Secretary of State of his interest, may apply to the Secretary of State for a deferment of the

26-15

---

[35] As to the court's power to fix his remuneration, see para.25-19, above.
[36] Insolvency Act 1986 s.45(3) (administrative receivers).
[37] *Re Yagerphone* [1935] Ch. 392. The passage in the test was criticised by Russell LJ in *NW Robbie & Co Ltd v Witney Warehouse Co Ltd* [1963] 1 W.L.R. 1324 at 1338; but he omitted to observe that it is dealing with the position of future assets, acquired after: (i) a crystallisation of the charge; and (ii) a subsequent withdrawal of the receiver. It is still submitted that future assets fall within the scope of the floating charge only.
[38] *Gomba Holdings (UK) Ltd v Minories Finance Ltd* [1988] 1 W.L.R. 1231 at 1234.
[39] *Gomba Holdings (UK) Ltd v Minories Finance Ltd* [1988] 1 W.L.R. 1231 at 1234.
[40] Insolvency Act 1986 s.205.
[41] Insolvency Act 1986 s.205(2).

dissolution.[42] But these provisions do not oblige the liquidator or the Official Receiver to give the administrative receiver, being still in office, any notice, although it is the Official Receiver's practice to advise the receiver, and on the receiver's request to apply for a deferment of the dissolution.[43]

However, there is no obligation on an outside liquidator to give any such notice to the administrative receiver (except pursuant to an individual agreement), nor is there any provision as to the giving of notice of dissolution after voluntary winding up, with respect to which the court has power, on the application of the liquidator or any person appearing to be interested, to defer the dissolution.[44]

Due to the lack of any obligation to notify the administrative receiver of a proposed dissolution, it is suggested that written requests are made to any liquidator appointed when the administrative receiver is in office, seeking their agreement to give the administrative receiver notice of any proposal to dissolve the company.

26-16   **Early dissolution of the company (Insolvency Act 1986 ss.202–204).** Under certain conditions, the Official Receiver, if he is the liquidator of the company, may at any time apply to the registrar of companies for the early dissolution of the company.[45] Basically, he must be of the opinion that the realisable assets of the company are insufficient to cover the expense of winding-up and that the affairs of the company do not require any further investigation.[46] Before making any such application, the official receiver must give at least 28 days' notice of his intention to do so (inter alios) an administrative receiver.[47]

If no application to the Secretary of State is made, as below, the Official Receiver will make his application to the registrar of companies, who will forthwith register it; and, at the end of the period of three months beginning with the day of the registration of the application, the company will be dissolved.[48] However, the Secretary of State may, on the application of the Official Receiver or any other person who appears to the Secretary of State to be interested, give directions under the following provisions.

If a notice that the Official Receiver is proposing to apply as aforesaid is given, the administrative receiver may apply to the Secretary of State for directions.[49] The grounds of any such application must be either:

(i)   that the realisable assets of the company are sufficient to cover the expenses of the winding-up; or

(ii)   that the affairs of the company do require further investigation; or

(iii)   that for any other reason the early dissolution of the company is inappropriate.[50]

The Secretary of State may then give such directions, making such provisions as he thinks fit, for enabling the winding-up of the company to proceed as if no such

---

[42]   Insolvency Act 1986 s.205(3); by subs.(4), there is an appeal against his decision.
[43]   See (1995) 8 Insolvency Intelligence, Pt 11, p.56.
[44]   Insolvency Act 1986 s.201.
[45]   Insolvency Act 1986 s.202.
[46]   Insolvency Act 1986 s.202(1), (2).
[47]   Insolvency Act 1986 s.202(3).
[48]   Insolvency Act 1986 s.202(5).
[49]   Insolvency Act 1986 s.203(1).
[50]   Insolvency Act 1986 s.203(2).

notice had been given by the Official Receiver.[51] He may, in a case where no such application was made originally, so that the company will be dissolved on the expiry of the three-month period, defer the date of the dissolution of the company for such period as he thinks fit.[52]

There is an appeal to the court from any such decision of the Secretary of State.[53] It is the duty of the person on whose application any directions are given, or in whose favour an appeal with respect to an application for such directions is determined, within seven days after the giving of the directions or the determination of the appeal, to deliver to the registrar of companies for registration a copy of the directions or determination.[54] The Secretary of State will send the applicant two copies of his direction,[55] and, following an appeal, the court will send two sealed copies of its order to the person in whose favour the appeal was determined.[56] In each case, one of those copies is the document which is to be sent to the Secretary of State.[57]

If a person without reasonable excuse fails to deliver any copy as aforesaid, he is liable on summary conviction to a fine not exceeding one-fifth of the statutory maximum, and, on conviction after continued contravention, to a daily default fine not exceeding one-fiftieth of statutory maximum.[58]

---

[51] Insolvency Act 1986 s.203(3)(a).
[52] Insolvency Act 1986 s.203(3)(b).
[53] Insolvency Act 1986 s.203(4).
[54] Insolvency Act 1986 s.203(5).
[55] Insolvency Rules 2016 r.7.119(2).
[56] Insolvency Rules 2016 r.7.119(4).
[57] Insolvency Rules 2016 r.7.119.
[58] Insolvency Act 1986 ss.203(6), 430 and Sch.10.

PART VI: TAXATION

PART VII: CROSS-BORDER PROCEEDINGS

CHAPTER 27

THE TAXATION OF RECEIVERS AND ADMINISTRATORS

27-1   Introduction.   UK tax law does not contain a set of rules given over exclusively to the tax treatment of receivers and administrators. Instead, any analysis must proceed from first principles, occasionally assisted by case law and a handful of specific provisions to be found scattered across the tax code. It is also fair to say that this is an area that is heavily dominated by practice.

Until the Enterprise Act 2002 reforms took effect the taxation of receivers and administrators had much in common. After those reforms, however, the tax treatment of administrators came to have more in common with that of liquidators than of receivers. This shift has impacted on the area of taxation in insolvency in two significant respects: first, it affects the practical choice of which insolvency procedure to adopt from a tax point of view; secondly, it has increased the amount of tension that exists between the tax rules and the policy underlying the insolvency law.

SECTION 1: RECEIVERS APPOINTED BY THE COURT

27-2   Core provision.   The central section that governs the tax liabilities of a court-appointed receiver is s.75 of the Taxes Management Act 1970 ("TMA 1970"), which provides:

> "By s.77 of the TMA 1970 this section is applied in relation to capital gains tax, subject to certain modification."

27-3   Origins of TMA 1970 s 75.   This provision has a considerable history, having been around in one form or another since Henry Addington's Act of 1803.[1] The substance of the section has remained essentially the same since its first incarna-

---

[1]   (43 Geo. III C.122) the original section, s.XC of the 1803 Act, read: "And be it further enacted, that the receiver or receivers appointed by the Court of Chancery, or by any other Court in Great Britain, having the direction and control of any property in respect whereof a duty is charged as last mentioned, whether the title to such property shall be uncertain or not, or subject to any contingency or not, or be depending, or be not ascertained by reason of any dispute or other cause, shall be chargeable to the said duties in a like manner and to the like amount, as would be charged if the said property was not under the direction and control of such Court, and the title thereto was certain, and not subject to any contingency whatever; and every such receiver shall be answerable for doing all such matters and things as shall be required to be done by virtue of this Act, in order to the assessing the duties granted by this Act and paying the same". It is possible, however, to identify a provision dealing with court receivers that dates back even further still. Section LXXXIV of the Duties on Income Act 1799, the Act which introduced the first income tax in Great Britain, dealt with the imposition of tax in circumstances where the title to income was uncertain for any reason. Where that was the case the person chargeable was the person in receipt of the income, whether on his own account or for another; and where the income in question was under the "control or direction" of

[564]

tion, with only two changes of significance taking place in the meantime. First, the specific reference to the Court of Chancery was removed when the provision moved from the Income Tax Act 1842 to the Income Tax Act 1918,[2] presumably as a result of the advent of the Supreme Court of Judicature Act 1873 and the expansion of the jurisdiction to appoint receivers. The second, and perhaps more important, change made was to the hypothetical basis on which the receiver was taxed. Section 75 of the TMA 1970 directs that a court appointed receiver is to be assessed and charged to tax as if the property in question were not under the direction and control of the court. Until 1918, however, the provision also postulated that the title to the property in question was certain, and directed that any contingency to which the property in question was subject was to be ignored.

Construction and effect.   But tracing the origins of s.75 of the TMA 1970 is   **27-4** much easier than interpreting it, a task recently described by one judge as "exceptionally difficult".[3] The problem stems from the closing words of the section and the fact that it is not clear how they are intended to affect the tax position of the receiver. This was one of the matters that fell to be determined by the court in *Re Piacentini*, which involved a receiver appointed under s.77 of the Criminal Justice Act 1988 to realise the assets of an individual who had been tried for and convicted of tax fraud. The receiver's actions had given rise to a capital gains and/or income tax liability and so she sought directions from the court as to whether she was assessable to tax in respect of realisations made and whether such tax was payable as an expense of the receivership within the meaning of s.81(5) of the 1988 Act. The question of liability turned on the proper interpretation of TMA 1970 s.75. On the subject of construing the closing words of the section Lightman J said:

> "The difficulty is to understand the import of the final words of s 75(1): 'if the property were not under the direction and control of the court'. It may mean 'as if no receiver had been appointed at all' or 'as if the receivership was an out of court appointment'. If the liability to assessment of the court appointed receiver is to be approached on the assumed premise that there is no receivership, then necessarily there can be no liability on the part of the receiver. On the other hand, if the court appointed receiver is to be treated as an out of court receiver, it is plain that, since in the ordinary case the receiver is the agent of the company or debenture holder, he is subject to no liability, (a proposition for which counsel cited Lightman and Moss, *The Law of Receivers and Administrators of Companies* (3rd edn, 2000) paras 13-013 and 13-017)."

The judge thus considered that the words "if the property were not under the direction and control of the court" could have one of two effects. They could either absolve the receiver of any liability because the section operates on the hypothesis that there is no receiver; or it could treat the receiver as if he or she were a receiver appointed otherwise than by the court. The first of these two interpretations is very difficult to square with the remainder of the section, which clearly posits that the receiver shall be "assessable and chargeable with tax"; had it been intended that the receiver would not be subject to tax at all then the section could easily have said that.

---

any Court of Equity, or any other court, then upon application by the receiver, the court was to give directions as to the amount and payment of the tax. This provision also covered agents and trustees, but it seems that it formed the basis for s.XC of the 1803 Act.

2   See s.XLIII, Income Tax Act 1842, and General Rule 15, Income Tax Act 1918.

3   *Re Piacentini* [2003] S.T.C. 924 at 930 per Lightman J.

It appears that Lightman J preferred the second interpretation, and in doing so he declined to follow the only other authority that touched on the issue in hand, *IRC v Thompson*.[4] That case involved the assessment to tax of a receiver of a company appointed pursuant to a debenture. Counsel in the case made reference to a former incarnation of s.75 of the TMA 1970 in support of his submission that the receiver was properly assessable to tax on the income of the company. Lawrence J regarded that what went on to become s.75 contemplated that a receiver other than a receiver appointed by the court would be assessed and charged in the ordinary course, being the person who received the income, and that the provision had been introduced for the purpose of providing that a receiver appointed by the court shall be assessed and charged in the same way.[5] However, Lightman J considered that in his holding the receiver "received" the income. Lawrence J in *Thompson* had failed to have full and proper regard to the agency of the receiver; this upset his conclusion as to the position of out of court receivers and, consequently, his reasoning as to court-appointed receivers could not stand.

In the judgment of Lightman J, s.75 was founded on the same erroneous premise (i.e. that out of court receivers are subject to a charge) that founded the views expressed by Lawrence J on the predecessor section. Accordingly, Lightman J concluded that s.75 misfired and could have no effect or application at all. Moreover, common sense required that where there is a realisation by the receiver the tax liability (whether for capital gains or income tax) should remain that of the defendant alone, and that the receiver should not be assessable.

It is submitted, however, that the conclusion that s.75 is without effect or application can, and ought to be, avoided, and that the better interpretation is that s.75 does impose liability on court-appointed receivers in respect of income received by or capital gains accruing to him.

It is well-established as a matter of general law that a court-appointed receiver is, generally speaking, not an agent or trustee in respect of either party to the action; rather the receiver is an officer of the court, and his or her possession is strictly the possession of the court (see para.6-8, above). Accordingly, if one applies the reasoning in *Re Piacentini* and focuses on the representative capacity of the receiver then it follows that any tax liability that results from the actions of the receiver will lie with the court that appointed him or her. However, a court cannot be assessed to tax relating to property under its control, and so s.75 of the TMA 1970 makes the receiver liable as if the property were not under the direction and control of the court. In other words, the section makes the receiver subject to tax as if he was acting on his own account rather than as "the hand of the Court".[6] This was the thrust of Lawrence J's observations in *IRC v Thompson*, and this interpretation is also consistent with those parts of the tax code that imposes liability on those in receipt of income.[7] Moreover, it is submitted that this interpretation is more consistent with the history of the section. As set out above, in addition to the proviso that the receiver is to be taxed as if the property was not under the direction and control of the court, older versions of the section also contained the stipulation that title to the property in question was to be assumed to be certain and that any contingency to which the property in question was subject was to be ignored. This indicates that

---

4   20 T.C. 422.
5   20 T.C. 422 at 430.
6   As the status of a receiver was described in *Wilkinson v Gangadhar Sirkar* (1871) 6 B.L.R. 486, Ind.
7   For example, under s.8 of the ITTOIA 2005, which imposes liability for the charge to tax on trading income on the person receiving or entitled to the profits.

the receiver was intended to be taxed in his own right in the normal way, with anything that might conflict with such treatment being disregarded.

It is, therefore, submitted that the overall effect of the section is to make court-appointed receivers assessable and chargeable to tax as if the receiver were acting as principal.

Income Tax. The section is concerned only with the Income Tax Acts,[8] and by extension, to capital gains tax. It, therefore, does not have application to companies that are within the scope of the charge to corporation tax. However, receivers appointed in respect of companies that are not within the ambit of the corporation tax charge, and so are potentially subject to income tax, are within the scope of the section.   **27-5**

Capital Gains. As mentioned, s.75 TMA 1970 is applied to capital gains, with necessary modifications, by s.77(1) of the TMA 1970. However, it is provided by subs.(2) that the extension in subs.(1) shall not affect the question of who is the person to whom chargeable gains accrue, or who is chargeable to capital gains tax, so far as that question is relevant for the purposes of any exemption, or of any provision determining the rate at which capital gains tax is chargeable.   **27-6**

VAT. It is considered that, in line with his position under the general law, a court-appointed receiver supplies his services to the Court that appointed him, rather than to any particular concerned party. In the only case to consider the point the VAT Tribunal concluded only that the receiver did not supply his services to the firm that had petitioned for his appointment so that the firm was not entitled to recover input tax[9]; the Tribunal did not go on to decide to whom the supplies had actually been made.   **27-7**

Section 2: Out of Court Receivers

Income and Corporation Tax. The out of court receiver is the agent of one or more of the parties concerned according to the terms of the agreement or statute under which the appointment is made (see para.18-1, above). As a consequence of this the receiver is not, generally, liable for the taxes arising on the income or gains of the property in relation to which he is appointed. It was common ground that this was the case in *Re Mesco Properties*. Rather like administrative receivers, however, there are instances where an out of court receiver will be required to deduct or withhold tax, for example, where interest is paid to a person abroad.[10]   **27-8**

VAT. Receivers in receipt of payments of VAT are obliged to pay such amounts over to HMRC and not to their principal following the Court of Appeal's decision in *Sargent v Customs and Excise Commissioners*.[11] In that case a receiver appointed over rental properties received sums in respect of rent, an element of which represented VAT. The Commissioners considered that the receiver was obliged to   **27-9**

---

8   Which are defined for the purposes of the Taxes Act 1988 as "the enactments relating to income tax, including any provisions of the Corporation Tax Acts [as defined] which relate to income tax": s.831(1)(b) of the TA 1988.

9   *Re M & TJ Lister* LON/92/1336 (9972).

10   Under Pt 15 of ITA 2007.

11   [1995] S.T.C. 398.

account to them for VAT, whilst the bank that had appointed the receiver instructed him to pay the same sums over to it. The receiver, therefore, sought directions from the Court as to how he should proceed. The Court of Appeal held, first, that the Commissioners were not entitled to treat the receiver as the "taxable person" under what is now reg.9 of the VAT Regulations 1995,[12] and secondly that following the earlier decision in *Re John Willment (Ashford) Ltd*,[13] that although in theory a receiver appeared to have a discretion under s.109(8) of the LPA 1925 as to whether or not to pay over VAT to the Commissioners, on grounds of public policy there was in fact no such discretion. Thus the receiver was obliged to account to the Commissioners for the VAT he had collected on the rents.

SECTION 3: ADMINISTRATORS

27-10   **Introduction.**   The advent of the Enterprise Act 2002 had profound effects on the taxation of administrations. Before that point there was a considerable degree of overlap between the tax treatment of administrations and administrative receiverships. But after the EA 2002 reforms it is fair to say that, in terms of tax consequences, administration now has much more in common with liquidation than receivership.

The changes to the tax position brought about by the Enterprise Act came in two forms: the first set made direct amendments to the tax code and was effected by the Finance Act 2003. As a result both entry into[14] and exit from[15] administration now causes the company's current accounting period to end and a new one to begin; and secondly, once appointed, the administrator now becomes the proper officer of the company for the purposes of the Taxes Acts.[16] The second set of changes consisted of amendments to the general law that were made by the EA 2002 itself. Perhaps the two most important alterations under this head were the abolition of the Crown preference for pre-appointment tax liabilities[17] and the provision of a set order of priorities of administration expenses.[18]

27-11   **Accounting Periods.**   Before the Enterprise Act 2002 reforms, the entry of a company into administration had no effect on its accounting periods; whereas the commencement of the winding up of the company caused, and still does cause, the company's accounting period to end and a new 12-month cycle of accounting periods to begin. In this sense administration was more like administrative receivership than liquidation. But once it had been determined that tax arising during the course of the administration would be a prescribed expense it also became necessary to provide a means to quantify accurately the size of the tax liability for the period of the administration. Accordingly, the rules on corporation tax accounting periods were altered to provide that the entry of a company into, and exit of a company from, administration would each trigger the cessation of an accounting

---

[12]   Discussed above in the context of administration.
[13]   [1979] S.T.C. 286.
[14]   See now s.10(1)(i) of the Corporation Tax Act 2009.
[15]   See now s.10(1)(j) of the Corporation Tax Act 2009.
[16]   s.108(3) of the Taxes Management Act 1970.
[17]   The Crown preference was abolished by s.251 of the Enterprise Act 2002.
[18]   Insolvency (England and Wales) Rules 2016 r.3.51.

period, thus creating a discrete period that corresponds almost exactly[19] to the period during which the company is in administration.

These amendments had a significant impact on the use of trading losses incurred by the company in the lead up to its entry into administration. In essence it was the case that trading losses made by the company prior to being put into administration could not be used against capital profits that accrued to the company once it was in administration. The upshot is that, in a case where the administrator of a company with pre-administration trading losses realised an asset standing at a capital gain, HMRC became entitled to more corporation tax than would have been the case before the EA 2002 reforms.[20] This effect was exacerbated by the fact that the additional tax is also now expressly an expense of the administration. Whether or not these further consequences were intended is unclear.

Under the Finance Bill 2017–2019, which was due to receive Royal Assent imminently at the time of writing, the corporate loss relief rules change significantly, with effect from 1 April 2017. The two most significant changes are to permit post-31 March 2017 trading losses carried forward to be set off against total profits and surrendered as group relief but, subject to a group-wide de minimis allowance of £5 million, to permit only 50% of profits to be sheltered by carried forward losses. These changes may over time to some extent ameliorate the effect of the 2002 reforms on capital gains.

Entering Administration. As just mentioned, it is now the case that an accounting period comes to an end upon a company entering administration.[21] The ending of the accounting period is treated as happening immediately before the day on which the company enters administration.[22] So, for example, if an administrator is appointed in respect of Alpha Ltd on 1 May 2017 the company's accounting period will end for tax purposes on 30 April 2017. Provided that Alpha Ltd remains within the scope of the charge to corporation tax a new accounting period will begin immediately after the end of the previous one.[23] **27-12**

Section 10(3) of the Corporation Tax Act 2009 provides that for the purposes of the section a company enters administration either:

(a) when it enters administration under Sch.B1 to the Insolvency Act 1986; or

(b) when it is subject to a corresponding procedure, other than one under that Act.

The first limb, thus, requires reference to be made to Sch.B1, which stipulates that a company enters administration for the purposes of the Insolvency Act 1986 when

---

[19] There is a slight mismatch between the insolvency and the tax rules which means that, technically speaking, there is likely to be a small period of time during which a new "administration accounting period" will have begun for tax purposes but the administration itself will not actually have commenced. This phenomenon arises because, as will be seen in the next section, it is stipulated in the CTA 2009 that an accounting period is to be treated as ending immediately before the day on which the company enters administration, i.e. immediately before the day on which the appointment of the administrator takes effect. However, for insolvency law purposes, the appointment of an administrator can take effect part way through a day.

[20] The effect of this may be mitigated by the effect of the administration enabling the company to claim terminal loss relief which permits losses to be carried back for up to three years and so potentially recover tax previously paid (CTA 2010 s.39).

[21] s.10(1)(i) of the CTA 2009.

[22] s.10(2) of the CTA 2009.

[23] s.9(1)(b) of the CTA 2009.

the appointment of the administrator takes effect.[24] Where there has been a court appointment this takes effect at the time specified in the order, or, if no such time has been specified, at the time the order is made.[25] It is important to note that it is possible for an order to be made under para.13(2) with retrospective effect,[26] and it appears to follow that were such an order is made the company's accounting periods will be also be retrospectively affected. If the appointment is by a charge-holder or by the company or its directors then the appointment will be effective when their respective notice and filing requirements have been met.[27] It is, therefore, within the power of the appointer to determine when the appointment, and consequently when the change to the company's accounting periods, will take place, and this can be useful when it comes to tax planning.

The second limb is aimed at non-UK insolvency procedures that correspond to administration. The question of precisely when the company in question has entered that procedure will be a matter of the applicable foreign law.

27-13   Accounting Periods—During Administration.   Once a company is in administration the usual rules on accounting periods still apply. This means that an accounting period will also end on the occurrence of any of the following: the ending of 12 months from the beginning of the accounting period[28]; an accounting date of the company[29]; if there is a period for which the company does not make up accounts, the end of that period[30]; the company starting or ceasing to trade[31]; if the company carries on only one trade, coming, or ceasing to be, within the charge to corporation tax in respect of that trade[32]; if the company carries on more than one trade, coming, or ceasing to be, within the charge to corporation tax in respect of all the trades it carries on[33]; the company becoming, or ceasing to be, UK resident[34]; the company ceasing to be within the charge to corporation tax[35]; the company ceasing to be in administration.[36]

This can commonly give rise to a series of very short accounting periods where, for example, the company's normal accounting date falls soon after the commencement of the administration, and this is followed closely by the cessation of the company's business. This, in turn, can create additional compliance burdens since the administrator, as the proper officer, is obliged to make a return for each accounting period.[37]

27-14   Accounting Periods—Ending Administration.   An accounting period will end

---

[24]   Sch.B1, IA 1986 Sch.B1 para.1(2)(b).
[25]   Sch.B1 IA 1986 Sch.B1 para.13(2).
[26]   *Re G-Tech Construction* [2007] B.P.I.R. 1275; *Re Derfshaw Ltd* [2011] EWHC 1565 (Ch); *Re Pettit (as joint administrators of Bradford Bulls (Northern) Ltd (In Administration) and others* [2016] EWHC 3557 (Ch); *Mond v Syneri Partners Ltd* [2015] EWHC 964 (Ch).
[27]   IA 1986 Sch.B1 para.19 (in the case of appointment by charge-holder) and IA 1986 Sch.B1 para.31 (in the case of appointment by the company or its directors).
[28]   s.10(1)(a) of the CTA 2009.
[29]   s.10(1)(b) of the CTA 2009.
[30]   s.10(1)(c) of the CTA 2009.
[31]   s.10(1)(d) of the CTA 2009.
[32]   s.10(1)(e) of the CTA 2009.
[33]   s.10(1)(f) of the CTA 2009.
[34]   s.10(1)(g) of the CTA 2009.
[35]   s.10(1)(h) of the CTA 2009.
[36]   s.10(1)(j) of the CTA 2009.
[37]   Finance Act 1998 Sch.18 para.5.

once the company ceases to be in administration.[38] Section 10(4) of the Corporation Tax Act 2009[39] provides that for the purposes of the section a company ceases to be in administration either:

(a) when it ceases to be in administration under Sch.B1 to the Insolvency Act 1986; or

(b) when a corresponding event occurs, other than under that Act.

Under Sch.B1 a company ceases to be in administration when the appointment of an administrator of the company ceases to have effect in accordance with the Schedule[40]; but, a company does not cease to be in administration merely because an administrator vacates office (by reason of resignation, death or otherwise) or is removed from office.[41]

The general rule under Sch.B1 is that the appointment of an administrator shall automatically cease to have effect at the end of the period of one year beginning with the date on which it takes effect.[42] However, the administrator may apply to the court for an order extending his term of office for a specified period, and the administrator's term of office may be extended by consent for a specified period not exceeding one year.[43] In addition, an appointment will cease where:

(a) the administrator thinks that the purpose of the administration has been sufficiently achieved in relation to the company and he files a notice in the prescribed form[44]; or

(b) where the court makes an order on the application of a creditor[45]; or

(c) where the company moves into a creditors' voluntary liquidation following the delivery of a notice by the administrator[46]; or

(d) where the administrator thinks that that the company has no property which might permit a distribution to the creditors and serves a notice to that effect on the registrar of companies.[47]

SECTION 4: CONSEQUENCES OF ACCOUNTING PERIODS CHANGES

Beneficial Ownership During Administration. The orthodox position in the context of winding up is that the onset of liquidation divests the company of beneficial ownership of its assets. This has various taxation consequences, particularly in relation to group relief and the efficacy of hive downs. The key authority for this proposition is the decision of the House of Lords in *Ayerst (Inspector of Taxes) v C & K (Construction) Ltd*.[48] By contrast, there is no equivalent authority in the context of administration and it is accepted, correctly, by HMRC

27-15

---

[38] s.10(1)(j) of the CTA 2009.
[39] Formerly s.12(7ZA) of the ICTA 1988.
[40] IA 1986 Sch.B1 para.1(2)(c).
[41] IA 1986 Sch.B1 para.1(2)(d).
[42] IA 1986 Sch.B1 para.76(1).
[43] IA 1986 Sch.B1 para.76(2).
[44] IA 1986 Sch.B1 para.80.
[45] IA 1986 Sch.B1 para.81.
[46] IA 1986 Sch.B1 para.83.
[47] IA 1986 Sch.B1 para.84.
[48] [1975] 3 W.L.R. 16.

that the appointment of an administrator does not affect the company's beneficial ownership of its shares.[49]

27-16   Status of the Administrator Following Appointment. Once appointed the administrator acts as the company's agent.[50] As a matter of tax law the administrator will become the "proper officer" of the company and will, therefore, have responsibility for doing everything to be done by the company under the Taxes Acts and service on a company of any document under or in pursuance of the Taxes Acts may be effected by serving it on the administrator as proper officer.[51] Where two or more persons are appointed to act jointly or concurrently as the administrator of a company then the proper officer will be either such one of them as is specified in a notice given to the Board, or where no such notice is given to the Board then it will be such one or more of those persons as the Board may designate as the proper officer.[52] In contrast to the position in liquidation, it is permissible for a company in administration still to act through such other person as may for the time being have the express, implied or apparent authority of the company to act on its behalf; accordingly the administrator may look to the company's duly authorised officers to carry out the relevant activities while he is in position as the proper officer.

27-17   Pre-appointment Liabilities. An administrator does not assume any personal liability for pre-appointment tax liabilities, which will rank as unsecured claims.[53] However, without the consent of the administrator, the directors should not exercise any management power.[54] Note too that although s.130 of the FA 2008 provides for general Crown set-off of taxation, HMRC cannot set off post-administration credit against a pre-administration liability owed to them.[55]

27-18   Taxation During the Currency of the Appointment. In common with the position in liquidation, tax has now been made now an expense of the administration for which the administrator must account. The list of administration expenses can be found in r.3.51 of the Insolvency (England and Wales) Rules 2016, which reads as follows:

"The expenses of the administration are payable in the following order of priority—expenses properly incurred by the administrator in performing the administrator's functions; the cost of any security provided by the administrator in accordance with the Act or these Rules; where an administration order was made, the costs of the applicant and any person appearing on the hearing of the application whose costs were allowed by the court; where the administrator was appointed otherwise than by order of the court, the costs and expenses of the appointor in connection with the making of the appointment and the costs and expenses incurred by any other person in giving notice of intention to appoint an administrator; any amount payable to a person in respect of assistance in the preparation of a statement of affairs or statement of concurrence; any allowance made by order of the court in respect of the costs on an application for release from the obligation to submit a statement of affairs or deliver a statement of concurrence; any necessary

---

[49]   *Company Taxation Manual 06030.*
[50]   IA 1986 Sch.B1 para.69.
[51]   TMA 1970 s.108(1), (3)(a).
[52]   TMA 1970 s.108(4).
[53]   cf. the position in pre-Enterprise Act administrations when the Inland Revenue (as was) ranked as a preferential creditor in respect of VAT and PAYE liabilities.
[54]   IA 1986 Sch.B1 para.64.
[55]   FA 2008 s.131.

disbursements by the administrator in the course of the administration (including any costs referred to in Articles 30 or 59 of the EU Regulation and expenses incurred by members of the creditors' committee or their representatives and allowed for by the administrator under rule 17.24, but not including any payment of corporation tax in circumstances referred to in sub-paragraph (j) below; the remuneration or emoluments of any person who has been employed by the administrator to perform any services for the company, as required or authorised under the Act or these Rules; the administrator's remuneration the basis of which has been fixed under Part 18 and unpaid pre-administration costs approved under rule 3.52; and the amount of any corporation tax on chargeable gains accruing on the realisation of any asset of the company (irrespective of the person by whom the realisation is effected)."

Of obvious importance for tax purposes are rr.3.51(2)(g) and 3.51(2)(j). Under r.3.51(2)(g) the term "necessary disbursement" covers corporation tax other than on chargeable gains accruing on the realisation of any company asset (irrespective of who makes the realisation). It is also considered that all VAT, PAYE and NICs liabilities will be considered "necessary disbursements" for these purposes.

It is worth noting that the priority of the administrator's remuneration[56] lies between "any necessary disbursements" and corporation tax on chargeable gains; it is quite possible to envisage situation in which an administrator might want to arrange the tax affairs of the company so that any gain will be of a capital, rather than income, nature so as to ensure that there are sufficient funds to meet his remuneration. Such a scenario raises interesting questions both of tax law and the nature of an administrator's duties, and it should also be borne in mind in this connection that the court may, in the event of the assets of the company being insufficient to satisfy its liabilities, make an order as to the payment out of the assets of the expenses incurred in the administration in such order of priority as the court thinks just.[57]

Group Relationships and Administration. As mentioned, it is not considered **27-19** that a company loses beneficial ownership of its assets when it enters administration. Accordingly a company in administration does not lose beneficial ownership of its subsidiaries, as occurs in liquidation. It is the case, however, that HMRC have argued that a group relationship is severed above the company in administration on the basis that degrouping provisions in s.154 of the Corporation Tax Act 2010 are triggered by the administrator's appointment. The relevant parts of the legislation provide:

"**154.**–(1) This section applies if, apart from this section, one company ('the first company') and another company ('the second company') would be members of the same group of companies.

(2) For the purposes of this Part the companies are not members of the same group of companies if—

(a) one of the companies has surrenderable amounts for an accounting period; ("the current period"), and

(b) arrangements within subsection (3) are in place.

(3) Arrangements are within this sub-section if they have any of the following effects (but see sections 155A and 155B).

---

56   Insolvency (England and Wales) Rules 2016 r.3.51(2)(i).
57   r.3.51(3).

Effect 1   At some time during or after the current period, the first company or any successor of it—

    (a)   could cease to be a member of the same group of companies as the second company and

    (b)   could become a member of the same group of companies as a third company (see sub-section (4)).

Effect 2   At some time during or after the current period a company (other than the first or second company) has or could obtain, or persons together (other than those companies) have or could obtain, control of the first company but not of the second company.

Effect 3   At some time during or after the current period, a third company could start to carry on the whole or part of a trade that at a time during the current period is carried on by the first company and could do so—

    (a)   as the successor of the first company, or

    (b)   as the successor of another company which is not a third company and which started to carry on the whole or a part of the trade during or after the current period."

The definition of "control" is that found in s.1124 of the Corporation Tax Act 2010,[58] which provides that:

"in relation to a body corporate (A), control means the power of a person (P) to secure—

(a) by means of the holding of shares or the possession of voting power in relation to that or any other body corporate; or

(b) as a result of any powers conferred by the articles of association or other document regulating that or any other body corporate,

    that the affairs of company A are conducted in accordance with P's wishes."

"Arrangements" here are defined as meaning arrangements of any kind whether or not in writing.

The first limb of s.154 will be met if the administrator has arranged to transfer shares in one group company to a company outside the group. This is straightforward and it ought to be apparent where this has occurred.

The application of the second limb is more difficult, however. HMRC are known to argue that control of the company in administration is lost by the shareholders, who are no longer able to secure that the affairs of the company are conducted in accordance with their wishes. Thus, HMRC argue, in the case of a two company group where the subsidiary is in administration, the shareholders of the parent company can be said still to control the parent but not its subsidiary; accordingly, say HMRC, the group is severed above the level of the subsidiary.

But this argument, if correct, leads to arbitrary results. For example, if the parent company itself went into administration then the second limb of s.154(3) would not be met because it would not be the case that the shareholders of the parent controlled that company but not its subsidiary; accordingly the two companies would still be grouped. Similarly, if the parent company owned not one but two subsidiaries, both of which were in administration, then again the s.154(3) test would not be met as regards the two subsidiaries since the shareholders of the parent would not have control of either of them: thus they would remain grouped.

---

[58]   Corporation Tax Act 2010 s.117(2).

HMRC's interpretation may have some force on a literal interpretation but on a purposive construction it might have been thought that such a result was not intended by Parliament when enacting this legislation. It is also not immediately clear how the event of a group company entering administration can be within the mischief of these provisions, which were understood at the time to have been aimed at preventing avoidance.

However HMRC's position was strengthened by the First Tier Tribunal decision in *Farnborough Airport Properties*[59] where the "arrangements" legislation, i.e. s.154 was found to deny group relief between two companies where the surrendering company, otherwise an indirect 75% subsidiary of a common parent company of the claimant companies (the appellants), was placed into receivership under a debenture which gave both fixed charges and a floating charge which crystallised on appointment of a receiver and conferred extensive powers on the receiver to run the company in receivership. Arguments based on *Pepper v Hart*,[60] and purposive construction[61] were unsuccessful.

Similarly arguments to the effect that "arrangements" should be given a restrictive interpretation were unsuccessful, in part because of the statutory "carve out" for certain types of security arrangements to be ignored until enforcement[62]. Therefore, the argument, at the appeal before the Upper Tribunal in *Farnborough* (which would now have to be made before the Court of Appeal) was unsuccessful, would have to turn on whether the administrators powers still permit sufficient control to remain in the shareholders, acting via the directors, to sidestep s.154. In particular one issue must be whether the administrator obtain or could obtain control[63] within s.1124: it is interesting to note that HMRC maintain the exact opposite stance in their SDLT Manual, namely that the appointment of an administrator does not result in a change of control.

VAT in Administration.   Regulation 9 of the VAT Regulations 1995 provides that: **27-20**

"If a taxable person dies or becomes bankrupt or incapacitated, the Commissioners may, from the date on which he died or became bankrupt or incapacitated treat as a taxable person any person carrying on that business until some other person is registered in respect of the taxable supplies made or intended to be made by that taxable person in the course or furtherance of his business or the incapacity ceases, as the case may be; and the provisions of the Act and of any Regulations made thereunder shall apply to any person so treated as though he were a registered person. Any person carrying on such business shall, within 21 days of commencing to do so, inform the Commissioners in writing of that fact and of the date of the death, the date of the bankruptcy order, or of the nature of the incapacity and the date on which it began. In relation to a company which is a taxable person, the references in paragraph (1) above to the taxable person becoming bankrupt or incapacitated shall be construed as references to the company going into liquidation or receivership or entering administration."

This regulation, therefore, entitles HMRC to treat an administrator carrying on the business of the company as a taxable person. Moreover, upon entering office an

---

[59] *Farnborough Airport Properties Company Limited, Farnborough Properties Company Limited v HMRC* [2016] UKFTT431.
[60] Admission of Parliamentary material where there is ambiguity etc: *Pepper v Hart* [1993] A.C. 593.
[61] i.e that the legislation was an anti-avoidance provision.
[62] See s.155B of the CTA 2010.
[63] See the discussions in [58]–[71] of *Farnborough*.

administrator is obliged to give written notice of his appointment to the Commissioners. The appointment of the administrator does not, however, affect the VAT registration of the company itself.

Where HMRC chooses to treat the administrator as the taxable person, he will have responsibility for dealing with the post-appointment VAT affairs of the company, including making VAT returns, making payments and maintaining and producing records. However, it is expressly provided in reg.30 of the 1995 Regulations that:

> "Where any person subject to any requirements under this Part dies or becomes incapacitated and control of his assets passes to another person, being a personal representative, trustee in bankruptcy, receiver, liquidator or person otherwise acting in a representative capacity, that other person shall, if the Commissioners so require and so long as he has such control, comply with these requirements, provided that any requirement to pay VAT shall only apply to that other person to the extent of the assets of the deceased or incapacitated person over which he has control; and save to the extent aforesaid this Part shall apply to such a person, so acting, in the same way as it would have applied to the deceased or incapacitated person had that person not been deceased or incapacitated."

Accordingly, it is considered that an administrator, who acts in a representative capacity,[64] will not be liable to account for VAT beyond the extent of the assets under his control; it is also considered that VAT will fall within the head of "necessary disbursements" in r.3.51(2)(g) of the Insolvency (England and Wales) Rules 2016.

SECTION 5: ADMINISTRATIVE RECEIVERS

27-21 **Introduction.** The Enterprise Act largely abolished administrative receivership as a form of insolvency proceeding with effect for debentures executed on or after 15 September 2003. Today there are a dwindling number of appointments of administrative receivers being made and the procedure will eventually disappear from all but the few very specific contexts in which it has been preserved. As described above, after the Enterprise Act reforms the taxation of administrative receiverships is now quite distinct from that of administrations, but this can have its advantages, for example where a "pre-pack" procedure is required.

27-22 **Effect of Appointment.** Unlike the appointment of an administrator, the appointment of an administrative receiver is essentially a non-event in tax terms: it will not cause a change in the accounting periods of the company,[65] which continues to be liable to corporation tax, nor will it affect who is the "proper officer" of the company for tax purposes.[66] In addition, the beneficial ownership of the company's assets remains intact and it is not considered that group relationships are disturbed.

---

[64] i.e. as agent of the company: IA 1986 Sch.B1 para.69.

[65] Although, of course, the accounting periods of the company will still begin and end in accordance with the standard provisions mentioned above.

[66] See s.108(3) of the TMA 1970; however, the administrative receiver may have the authority of the company to make returns on its behalf.

Liability for Tax During the Appointment. An administrative receiver, who will **27-23** be deemed to be acting as agent for the company,[67] is generally not liable for the taxes arising on the income or gains of the company in relation to which he is appointed. Exceptions to this general proposition are encountered in circumstances where tax is required to be deducted or withheld from out-going payments. The most common examples of this are payments of rent, royalties or interest by the administrative receiver on the company's behalf.

The position of the administrative receiver as regards VAT is similar to that of an administrator.

---

[67] See s.44 of the IA 1986.

Chapter 28

THE EU REGULATIONS ON INSOLVENCY PROCEEDINGS AND THE CROSS-BORDER INSOLVENCY REGULATIONS 2006

Section 1: The EU Regulations on Insolvency Proceedings

28-1   **Introduction.**   The EU Insolvency Regulations of 2000 and 2015 are part of UK insolvency law, and their provisions apply to most UK domestic insolvency procedures. The 2015 Regulation,[1] also known as the Recast Insolvency Regulation, is an amended version of the 2000 Regulation[2] and it applies to insolvencies which commence on or after 26 June 2017. The 2000 Regulation continues to apply to insolvencies which commenced before 26 June 2017.

28-2   **The 2015 Regulation.**   The 2015 Regulation was made by the Parliament and the Council of the European Union and came into force formally on 26 June 2015, and applies to insolvencies which commence on or after 26 June 2017. Both the 2015 Regulation and the predecessor 2000 Regulation aim to provide for the efficient and effective functioning of cross-border insolvency proceedings in the European Union.[3] A number of statutory instruments came into force in the UK to supplement the 2000 Regulation and to align the existing UK law with its provisions. These included the following:

    (a)   the Insolvency Act 1986 (Amendment) Regulations 2002;
    (b)   the Insolvency Act 1986 (Amendment) (No.2) Regulations 2002;
    (c)   the Insolvency (Amendment) Rules 2002;
    (d)   the Administration of Insolvent Estates of Deceased Persons (Amendment) Order 2002; and
    (e)   the Insolvent Partnerships (Amendment) Order 2002.

Additional statutory instruments have been made in order to accommodate the 2015 Regulation.

In an increasingly "globalised" business world, cross-border insolvencies, where insolvency proceedings can be commenced concurrently against the same corporate or individual debtor in more than one EU member state, which or who has been carrying on business in more than one member state, had been presenting increasing problems. The insolvency laws of the Member States differ markedly from one

---

[1]   Regulation (EU) 2015/848, printed at [2015] OJ L141/19 and accessible at *http://eur-lex.europa.eu*.
[2]   Council Regulation (EC) No.1346/2000, printed at [2000] OJ L160/1 and accessible at *http://eur-lex.europa.eu*. Explanatory notes in relation to the 2000 Regulation, provided by the Insolvency Service, were appended to the Insolvency Act 1986 (Amendment) Regulations 2002 (SI 2002/1037).
[3]   See 2015 Regulation, Preamble, para.3.

another, and not infrequently demonstrated a built-in discrimination, favouring national creditors over foreign creditors.

In very broad terms, the 2015 Regulation and its predecessor focus on the assignment of insolvency jurisdiction between Member States of the EU and on the recognition of such jurisdiction. They do not harmonise the substantive insolvency laws of the Member States. On the whole they provide for the local law under which proceedings are opened to be the governing law, but with limited exceptions in specific situations.

Both the 2015 Regulation and the predecessor 2000 Regulation are long and complex documents, with lengthy and significant Preambles, and will here be described only in general procedural outline. There are several substantive differences between the two Regulations. To the extent that they differ from each other, this chapter describes the position only under the 2015 Regulation. Where proceedings are involved, the relevant Regulation should be studied in detail, with the assistance of works dedicated to their impact on cross-border insolvency proceedings within the European Union.[4]

The jurisdictional extent of the EU Regulations. Denmark opted out of the   **28-3**
provisions of the 2000 Regulation, so that Danish involvement in multi-state insolvency did not fall within the 2000 Regulation.[5] The same position applies in respect of the 2015 Regulation.[6] For present purposes therefore, references to the impact of the 2015 and 2000 Regulations and EU Member States should be treated as references to the 26 Member States to which the respective Regulation applies (excluding Denmark).

The 2015 and 2000 Regulations only apply where the "centre of main interests" (or "COMI") of the debtor is situated in a member state of the EU.[7] If the debtor's COMI is outside the EU, the EU Regulations will not have effect and the other existing domestic law of the relevant member state (including its conflict of law rules) will continue to apply. The EU Regulations also do not deal with assets or creditors located outside the EU (save insofar as they are dealt with as part of an EU-based insolvency process) nor collective insolvency proceedings which are initiated outside the EU, even if the debtor has its COMI within the EU. This can give rise to potential problems where groups of companies are involved. The mere relationship of parent-subsidiary and the parental control over a subsidiary implied from such relationship will not of itself, automatically and without more, be determinative of the COMI of the subsidiary.[8]

The 2015 Regulation applies only to public collective proceedings based on laws relating to insolvency for rescue, debt adjustment, re-organisation or liquidation.[9] It does not, therefore, apply to receiverships in the UK, nor to solvent liquidations.

---

4   See, e.g., Lightman and Moss, *The Law of Receivers and Administrators of Companies*, 6th edn (2017).
5   2000 Regulation, Preamble, para.33. See also *Re the Arena Corporation Ltd* [2003] EWHC 3032 Ch; [2004] B.P.I.R. 375 (not dealt with on appeal at [2004] EWCA Civ 371; [2004] B.P.I.R. 415). Portugal entered a derogation with respect to arts 26 and 37 of the 2000 Regulation (OJ C183 of 30 June 2000, p.1).
6   2015 Regulation, Preamble, para.88.
7   See 2015 Regulation, Preamble, para.25.
8   *Re Eurofood IFSC Ltd* [2006] Ch. 508. However note also e.g. *Re MG Rover Espana SA* [2006] B.C.C. 599; and *Re MG Rover Belux SA/NV* [2007] B.C.C. 446. See also *Re Stanford International Bank Ltd* [2009] EWHC 1441 (Ch) (a case under the Cross-Border Insolvency Regulations 2006).
9   2015 Regulation art.1, as amplified by art.2 and Annex A. Note that it appears that, although not

The latter are dealt with by the Brussels Convention.[10] The 2015 Regulation further does not apply to schemes of arrangement, or to winding-up petitions brought in the public interest on the just and equitable ground, even if the company is insolvent.[11] Also excluded from its scope are certain collective insolvency proceedings in relation to entities of particular types, namely insurance undertakings, credit institutions, investment firms and other firms, institutions and undertakings to the extent that they are covered by Directive 2001/24/EC, and also collective investment undertakings.[12]

28-4   UNCITRAL Model Law.   The UNCITRAL Model Law on Cross Border Insolvency follows in large part the scheme of the 2000 Regulation. It was adopted into British law by the Cross-Border Insolvency Regulations 2006,[13] which are considered in more detail in Section 2, below. Article 3 of Sch.1 to those Regulations provides that, to the extent that the Model Law conflicts with an obligation of the United Kingdom under the 2000 Regulation, the requirements of the 2000 Regulation are to prevail.

28-5   The United Kingdom.   The component parts of the United Kingdom are treated as one jurisdiction for the purposes of the EU Regulations, and that jurisdiction also includes the self-governing colony of Gibraltar.

28-6   The Virgos-Schmit Report.   An important guide to the construction of the 2000 Regulation was the "Virgos-Schmit Report".[14] This was produced by two international law experts, and published in 1996 with reference to the EU Convention on Insolvency Proceedings of 1995 (which was never fully signed and was superseded by the 2000 Regulation). It was later revised. Although it enjoyed no official legal standing, the report was widely cited in relation to the 2000 Regulation, particularly in cases where the cross-border operation of the 2000 Regulation was in issue, as in the decisions referred to at para.28-24, below. Its relevance in the case of the 2015 Regulation is diminished, owing to the significant differences between the two Regulations, but it is expected that it will continue to be referred to in relation to matters which are common to both Regulations.

28-7   The debtor's centre of main interests ("COMI").   The EU Regulations prescribe three levels of insolvency jurisdiction and procedure, designed to control, and so far as practicable to harmonise, insolvency proceedings which involve, or are capable of involving, cross-border problems and conflicts. Paramount jurisdiction in insolvency proceedings is assigned to the state in which the insolvent debtor (corporate or individual) has its or his "centre of main interests" (generally abbreviated to COMI).

A debtor's centre of main interests is defined as "the place where the debtor

---

listed in Annex A, insolvent partnerships (see SI 2002/1308) and the administration of the insolvent estates of deceased persons are also covered.

[10]   *Re Cover Europe Ltd* [2002] 2 B.C.L.C. 61.

[11]   *Re Marann Brooks CSV Ltd* [2003] B.C.C. 239 (decided in relation to the 2000 Regulation).

[12]   2015 Regulation art.1(2). As to the expression "collective investment undertaking", see *Financial Services Authority v Dobb White & Co* [2003] EWHC 3146 Ch. See also EC Directives 2001/17 and 2001/24, and SIs 2004/353 and 2004/1045.

[13]   SI 2006/1030.

[14]   EU Council Document No.6500/96, DRS 8 (CFC), Brussels, 3 May 1996. See also M. Virgos, *European Community Convention on Insolvency* (Kluwer, 1998).

conducts the administration of its interests on a regular basis and which is ascertainable by third parties".[15] In the case of a company or a partnership, the location of the centre of main interests is, unless the contrary is proved, presumed to be the location of its registered office, provided that the registered office has not "been moved" from one member state to another within the three months prior to the request for the opening of insolvency proceedings.[16] In the case of an individual debtor, the presumption is in favour of the principal place of business of an individual carrying on a business or profession, and the habitual residence of any other individual.

There have been numerous decisions involving findings that a corporate debtor's centre of main interests was located elsewhere than in its state of registration. Other decisions have involved a consideration of what analogous principles apply for determining that fact in the case of an individual multi-state debtor.

Meaning of a debtor's "establishment". If a debtor operates in a member state   **28-8**
other than that in which he or it has his or its COMI, each place from which it operates is described as an "establishment" if it comprises a "place of operations where the debtor carries out or has carried out in the three-month period prior to the request to open main insolvency proceedings a non-transitory economic activity with human means and assets".[17]

The three categories of insolvency proceedings. With respect to the business   **28-9**
activities of the debtor in the state of its or his centre of main interests, the business activities carried on at "establishments" located in other Member States or outside the EU take second place.

Insolvency proceedings commenced in the state where the debtor's centre of main interests is located are termed within the 2015 Regulation "main proceedings".[18]

Insolvency proceedings commenced in another state before the commencement of main proceedings are termed "territorial proceedings"; they may be opened in that state only if the debtor has an establishment there, and are limited in their extent to local creditors and locally-situated assets.[19]

Insolvency proceedings commenced in another member state after the commencement of main proceedings are termed "secondary proceedings". The same term is also applied to territorial proceedings if main proceedings have been subsequently commenced elsewhere.[20]

---

[15] 2015 Regulation art.3(1); also defined in Insolvency (England and Wales) Rules 2016 r.1.2. As regards creditors' voluntary liquidation of a foreign company, see *Re TXU Europe German Finance BV* [2005] B.C.C. 90. A company incorporated outside the EU with a COMI within the EU was governed by the 2000 Regulation: *Re BRAC Rent-a-Car International Inc* [2003] EWHC 128 Ch; [2003] 1 W.L.R. 1421.

[16] 2015 Regulation art.3(1). A partnership does not have, in the UK, a registered office. The equivalent place prescribed for the purposes of the service of insolvency proceedings is its principal place of business, see e.g. Insolvency Act 1986 s.123 as modified for the purposes of winding up by the Insolvent Partnerships Order 1994 Sch.4 para.7(a) (SI 1994/2421).

[17] 2015 Regulation art.2(10). See *Telia AB v Hillcourt (Docklands) Ltd* [2002] EWHC 2377 (Ch); [2003] B.C.C. 856 and contrast *Shierson v Vlieland-Boddy* [2005] EWCA Civ 974; [2005] B.C.C. 949 (both decided in relation to the 2000 Regulation).

[18] 2015 Regulation art.3(1).

[19] 2015 Regulation art.3(4).

[20] 2015 Regulation art.3(3).

28-10   **Conditions to be satisfied for the opening of territorial proceedings.**   Territorial proceedings may be opened only where:

- (a) main proceedings cannot be opened because of the conditions laid down by the domestic law of the state where the debtor's centre of main interests is located;
- (b) the claim of the creditor who wishes to open insolvency proceedings arises from or is in connection with the operation of an establishment situated in the member state where the opening of territorial proceedings is requested; or
- (c) the opening of territorial proceedings is requested by a public authority which, under the law of the member state within which the establishment is situated, has the right to request the opening of insolvency proceedings.[21]

28-11   **Conditions to be satisfied for the opening of secondary proceedings.**   Secondary proceedings may be opened in a member state only if:

- (a) main proceedings have already been validly opened in the state where the debtor has its COMI;
- (b) the debtor has an establishment in the state of the proposed secondary proceedings; and
- (c) the debtor has assets located in that state.[22]

The office-holder in main proceedings has considerable rights and powers to intervene in secondary proceedings as a creditor, including the right to convert those proceedings into proceedings of any other type listed in Annex A to the 2015 Regulation.[23]

28-12   **Law applicable to insolvency proceedings.**   The general principle is that the law which is applicable to insolvency proceedings and their effects is the law of the member state within the territory of which the proceedings are opened (the "state of the opening of the proceedings").[24] That law determines the conditions for the opening of the proceedings, their conduct and their closure. However, there are a number of exceptions. The opening of insolvency proceedings is not to affect:

- (a) "rights in rem" in property which belongs to the debtor and which is situated within the territory of another member state[25];
- (b) rights of creditors to set-off where permitted by the law applicable to the insolvent debtor's claim[26];
- (c) sellers' reservation of title rights where, at the time of the opening of proceedings, the asset is situated within the territory of a member state other than the state of the opening of proceedings[27];
- (d) contracts relating to immovable property, which (subject to one exception)

---

[21] 2015 Regulation art.3(4).
[22] 2015 Regulation arts 3(3), 34; also defined in Insolvency (England and Wales) Rules 2016 r.1.2.
[23] 2015 Regulation art.51; also Insolvency (England and Wales) Rules 2016 r.21.3.
[24] 2015 Regulation art.7. As regards the effect on arbitration proceedings, see *Syska v Vivendi* [2009] EWCA Civ 677.
[25] 2015 Regulation art.8; see para.30-26, below.
[26] 2015 Regulation art.9.
[27] 2015 Regulation art.10.

are governed by the law of the member state within the territory of which the immovable property is situated[28];

(e)   the rights and obligations of the parties to a payment or settlement system or a financial market, which are governed solely by the law applicable to that system or market[29];

(f)   contracts of employment, which (subject to one exception) are to be governed by the law applicable to the same[30];

(g)   the rights of debtors (and certain third party purchasers) in immovable property, a ship or an aircraft subject to registration in a public register, which are to be determined by the law under whose authority the register is kept[31];

(h)   certain European patents and Community trade marks and similar rights[32];

(i)   rights to set aside prior acts in insolvency where there is no means to challenge the transaction under the law of the member state governing the act in question[33];

(j)   pending lawsuits and arbitral proceedings in other Member States.[34]

The titles of national insolvency proceedings and national insolvency   **28-13**
administrators.   To make the EU-wide insolvency jurisdiction intelligible and workable, in respect of each of the 26 Member States to which the 2015 Regulation applies the Regulation contains lists of the forms of insolvency proceedings covered by the Regulation in each state, using its official title in that state's language (Annex A), and lists of the types of insolvency administrators in each state, using their official titles in the respective state's language (Annex B).

The English version of the 2000 Regulation[35] used the term "liquidator" to refer to all such insolvency administrators[36] (whether an individual or a body). The selected term was changed, for the English version of the 2015 Regulation, from "liquidator" to "insolvency practitioner". The term "insolvency officer-holder" (or "insolvency officer") would clearly have been preferable. The Insolvency Act 1986 and the Insolvency (England and Wales) Rules 2016 continue to use the term "member state liquidator" to refer to such a person or body.[37] It will be convenient, for the purposes of discussing the Regulations here, to apply to those many, and variously-entitled, insolvency administrators the generic statutory description of "office-holder" used in the Insolvency Act 1986 for insolvency officers generally.[38]

It appears that the lists of the United Kingdom's proceedings and appointments

---

28   2015 Regulation art.11.
29   2015 Regulation art.12.
30   2015 Regulation art.13.
31   2015 Regulation arts 14, 17.
32   2015 Regulation art.15.
33   2015 Regulation art.16.
34   2015 Regulation art.18. As regards arbitration proceedings see *Syska v Vivendi* [2009] EWCA Civ 677.
35   2015 Regulation art.2(5).
36   Insolvency Rules 1986 r.13.13(11); "temporary administrator", provided for in 2015 Regulation art.52, is defined in Insolvency (England and Wales) Rules 2016 r.1.2. See also Insolvency (England and Wales) Rules 2016 r.21.
37   Insolvency Act 1986 s.251 and Insolvency (England and Wales) Rules 2016 r.1.2 (both as amended by the Insolvency Amendment (EU 2015/848) Regulations 2017 (SI 2017/702)).
38   See Insolvency Act 1986 ss.230 ff.

are not complete; they do not refer to the insolvency of partnerships[39] or of deceased persons or the respective office-holders, but those proceedings appear to be covered by both EU Regulations. As noted above, the EU Regulations do not apply at all to receiverships, whether the receiver is court-appointed or chargee-appointed, and whether administrative or non-administrative, nor to schemes of arrangement or solvent liquidations.

28-14 **Meaning of "court" and "judgment opening insolvency proceedings" within the 2015 Regulation's ambit.**   The term "court" is used to refer to the judicial body, or any other competent body, of a member state who or which is empowered to "open" (i.e. commence) insolvency proceedings, to confirm such an opening, or to take decisions in the course of such proceedings.[40] The term therefore encompasses not only courts in the normal sense but also other bodies.

The term "judgment opening insolvency proceedings" includes the decision of any court to open such proceedings, to confirm the opening of such proceedings, or to appoint an office-holder.[41]

28-15 **The position and powers of the office-holder.**   The office-holder appointed by the relevant authority in main proceedings may exercise, in another member state, all the powers conferred on him by the law of the state where the main proceedings were opened, so long as no other insolvency proceedings have been opened in the other member state, nor any preservation measures taken there, further to a request for the opening of insolvency proceedings in that state.[42] He may, in particular, remove assets of the debtor from the territory of the member state where they are situated,[43] subject to the rights of creditors with special interests, such as a creditor with the benefit of reservation of title rights relating to such assets.[44]

The office-holder appointed in territorial proceedings in a member state may, in another member state, claim, through its courts or out of court, that movable assets of the debtor have been removed to that state, after the opening of the proceedings, and may bring an action to set such removal aside.[45]

The office-holder may exercise all the rights and powers of a creditor of the company, and is required to be served with copies of all proceedings and notices with which a creditor is to be served. He may, in particular, in England and Wales attend any court insolvency proceeding relating to the company, held in public or in private, and may inspect the court file of the proceedings.[46]

28-16 **Proof of the office-holder's appointment.**   Proof of the office-holder's appointment, conferring on him the powers under the 2015 Regulation, is established by

---

[39] All types of English-law partnership fall within the ambit of the 2015 Regulation. Whilst this is not expressly stated in the 2015 Regulation, provision on this basis was nonetheless made in English law, with respect to the 2000 Regulation, by way of, e.g., the Insolvent Partnerships (Amendment) Order 2002 (SI 2002/1308). As at the date of this edition, there has been no amendment of the Insolvent Partnerships Order 1994 to cater for the 2015 Regulation.

[40] 2015 Regulation art.2(6).

[41] 2015 Regulation art.2(7).

[42] 2015 Regulation art.21 (2000 Regulation art.18).

[43] 2015 Regulation art.21(1) (2000 Regulation art.18(1)), subject to arts 8 and 10 (2000 Regulation arts 5 and 7).

[44] 2015 Regulation art.10 (2000 Regulation art.7).

[45] 2015 Regulation art.21(2) (2000 Regulation art.18(2)).

[46] Insolvency (England and Wales) Rules 2016 rr.21.7 and 21.8.

a certified copy of the original decision appointing him, or by any other certificate of the court which has jurisdiction.[47] Apart from the provision of any necessary translation of the document into the language, or one of the languages, of any other member state in which he intends to act, no other legalisation of his appointment is required.[48]

Confirmation of office-holder's appointment in creditors' voluntary winding up.   With respect to the United Kingdom, it was considered that the appointment of a liquidator by creditors in a creditors' voluntary winding up lacked sufficient formality for the purposes of the 2015 Regulation.[49]   **28-17**

Provision is, however, made for such a liquidator to obtain from the court an order "confirming" the creditors' voluntary winding up.[50]

His application must be made in writing, and supported by a witness statement stating:

(a)   his name;
(b)   the name and registered number of the company;
(c)   the date of the winding-up resolution;
(d)   that the application is accompanied by copies of all necessary documents; and
(e)   whether the winding-up proceedings will be main proceedings, secondary proceedings or territorial proceedings.[51]

This procedure is also available to confirm the conversion of the administration of a company into a voluntary winding up.[52]

Two copies of the application must be filed, together with one copy of the winding-up resolution (or the notice of conversion from administration to winding up), the evidence of his appointment as office-holder, and the company's statement of affairs (or specified information from the administrator's statement of proposals).[53] The court (which for this purpose may include a member of the court staff) may deal with the application without a hearing, and, if it confirms the winding up, it is to affix the court's seal to the application.[54]

Notice to office-holders and creditors in other Member States of creditors' voluntary winding up   Where a court in England and Wales has made an order confirming a creditors' voluntary winding up,[55] the liquidator shall give notice of the order to any office-holder as soon as reasonably practicable,[56] and the liquidator or the court shall immediately inform known foreign creditors of the company.[57]   **28-18**

Rights of office-holders   An office-holder may exercise all the rights and powers conferred on him by the law of the member state where the proceedings were   **28-19**

---

47   2015 Regulation art.22 (2000 Regulation art.19).
48   2015 Regulation art.22 (2000 Regulation art.19).
49   The procedure has an informality rarely, if ever, found in the other Member States.
50   Insolvency (England and Wales) Rules 2016 r.21.4.
51   Insolvency (England and Wales) Rules 2016 r.21.4(3).
52   Insolvency (England and Wales) Rules 2016 r.21.4(1).
53   Insolvency (England and Wales) Rules 2016 r.21.4(4).
54   Insolvency (England and Wales) Rules 2016 r.21.5.
55   See para.28-17, above.
56   Insolvency (England and Wales) Rules 2016 r.21.6(1).
57   Insolvency (England and Wales) Rules 2016 r.21.6(2); 2015 Regulation art.54.

opened in any other member state, provided that no proceedings have been opened there and no steps have been taken to preserve the debtor's assets there, and, in other proceedings, may exercise all the rights of a creditor of the company and is required to be served with copies of all proceedings and notices with which a creditor is to be served.[58] He may in particular, in England and Wales, participate in any court insolvency proceedings relating to the company, in public or in private, and may inspect the court file of the proceedings.[59]

28-20   Obligations of office-holders to co-operate.   The office-holders in each of the three sets of proceedings are under a duty to co-operate with each other and to communicate to one another information relevant to the other proceedings, including, in particular, information as to any progress made in lodging and verifying the creditors' claims, and all measures aimed at rescuing or restructuring the debtor or at terminating the proceedings.[60]

The office-holders in main proceedings and secondary proceedings must explore the possibility of restructuring the debtor and, if there is such a possibility, co-ordinate with each other in preparing and implementing a restructuring plan. The office-holders must also co-ordinate in relation to "the administration of the realisation or use of the debtor's assets and affairs", and the office-holder in the secondary proceedings must give the office-holder in the main proceedings an early opportunity of submitting proposals for the realisation or use of the assets in the secondary proceedings.[61]

For the situation where proceedings, or requested proceedings, relate to two or more members of a group of companies, the 2015 Regulation introduced a framework for co-operation between office-holders and between courts and, additionally, a procedure called "group coordination proceedings".[62]

28-21   Publication and registration in other Member States of the opening of insolvency proceedings.   The office-holder is obliged to request that notice of the judgment opening insolvency proceedings, and also, where appropriate, the decision appointing him, be published in any other member state where the debtor has an establishment, in accordance with that state's publication procedures, specifying the office-holder appointed, and stating into which category of proceedings under the 2015 Regulation the proceedings fall.[63]

Where the debtor has an establishment registered in a public register of a member state or the debtor owns immovable property located in a member state and, in either case, that member state requires the publication of the opening of insolvency proceedings in the land register, the company register or any other public register, such publication shall be effected by the office-holder.[64]

The office-holder may also request that information on the opening of the main

---

[58] 2015 Regulation arts 21, 45(3).
[59] Insolvency (England and Wales) Rules 2016 r.21.8.
[60] 2015 Regulation art.41.
[61] 2015 Regulation art.41(2).
[62] 2015 Regulation arts 56–77.
[63] 2015 Regulation art.28(1) (2000 Regulation art.21(1) plus amendment).
[64] 2015 Regulation art.29(1).

proceedings is registered in the land register, the company register and any other public register in any other member state.[65]

Recognition of insolvency proceedings. Any judgment in a member state open-   28-22
ing main insolvency proceedings, and any appointment of an office-holder in such proceedings, must be recognised throughout the EU in every member state to which the 2015 Regulation applies. No order by way of *exequatur* is any longer required to give effect to a cross-border insolvency proceeding.[66] The effects of territorial proceedings may not be challenged in other Member States.[67] The judgment open-ing main proceedings in one member state shall produce the same effect in any other member state as it produces under the law of the former state, unless the 2015 Regulation otherwise provides, or territorial proceedings have been opened in that other member state or secondary proceedings are subsequently opened there.[68]

Insolvency jurisdiction extended by the EU Regulations. The EU Regula-   28-23
tions have had the effect of considerably extending the potential areas of insolvency jurisdiction of domestic insolvency courts within the states of the European Union (with the exception of Denmark).

The insolvency jurisdiction of domestic courts in any member state now extends to insolvent companies (including partnerships) and other legal persons (a term which includes individual debtors) whose "centre of main interests" is proved to be located in that state, regardless of the location elsewhere of their place of incorporation, registration, business or residence.[69]

**Cases of non-acceptance of the EU Regulations' jurisdictional   28-24
rules.** Acceptance by the Member States of the extended jurisdiction, by virtue of which "their companies" are put into insolvency proceedings by the courts of another member state on the ground of the location there of their centre of main interests, has not been uniform. There were cases, under the 2000 Regulation, where the insolvency courts of a member state opened insolvency proceedings against a company or other legal person when insolvency proceedings involving that company or legal person had already been opened in another member state which constituted main proceedings.

In one case, a number of companies in an international group, including three German companies and one French company, were put into administration by an English court, such administration constituting main proceedings.[70] Subsequently, insolvency proceedings, not purporting to be territorial or secondary proceedings, were opened in French and German insolvency courts, with respect to the French company and two of the three German companies, notwithstanding the existing main proceedings in England. The judgments opening the French and German proceedings were eventually reversed on appeal, but not before the office-holder in the French proceedings had effected a sale of the business of the French company.

Another case concerned the Irish subsidiary of an Italian company. Eurofoods

---

[65] 2015 Regulation art.29(2).
[66] An *exequatur* ("executive instrument") was formerly widely required to validate the order of a foreign court for the purposes of its enforcement.
[67] 2015 Regulation art.20(2) (2000 Regulation art.17(2)).
[68] 2015 Regulation art.20(1) (2000 Regulation art.17(1)).
[69] 2015 Regulation art.3(1).
[70] [2003] B.C.C. 562.

was the subject of a winding-up petition in the Irish court and a provisional liquidator was appointed: this step constituted the opening of main proceedings. Notwithstanding the opening of those proceedings, an Italian court which had already opened insolvency proceedings against the Italian parent company of Eurofoods then opened insolvency proceedings against the Irish subsidiary, refusing to recognise the jurisdiction of the Irish court. The case was ultimately referred by the Irish Supreme Court to the European Court of Justice, which gave significant rulings on (1) the presumption laid down in art.3(1) of the 2000 Regulation, (2) the time of the opening of proceedings, (3) the duty to recognise main proceedings opened by the courts of another Member State (even if believed to have been opened without jurisdiction) and (4) the scope of the right of a member state under art.26 of the 2000 Regulation (now art.33 of the 2015 Regulation) to refuse to recognise insolvency proceedings opened in another state on the basis of the former state's public policy.[71]

Such instances of conflict as between the courts of different Member States may now be less likely to occur as a result of the arrangements relating to "group coordination proceedings" introduced in the 2015 Regulation.[72]

28-25 **The effect of the EU Regulations on domestic insolvency proceedings.** In order to comply with the jurisdictional and procedural requirements of the 2000 Regulation, substantial amendments were made to a number of statutes, rules, regulations and forms in England and Wales.[73]

Every insolvency court process, or analogous documentary act, which brings into being collective insolvency proceedings must now include a statement on oath or by way of statement of truth as to whether the debtor to whom the proceedings relate is or is not a member of one of the exempted categories of debtor to which the 2015 Regulation does not apply, and, if that Regulation does apply to the debtor, using prescribed forms and stating whether the proceedings being commenced thereby constitute main proceedings, territorial proceedings or secondary proceedings. These rules and forms include all types of insolvency petition, an administration application, notices of the appointment of an administrator (by a floating charge holder, the company or its directors), and proposals for a company voluntary arrangement or an individual voluntary arrangement.

28-26 **Recognition by the EU Regulations of floating charges.** An important concession to the security laws of the "Anglo-Saxon jurisdictions" is the recognition by the EU Regulations of the floating charge over property situated in a different member state. Previously, the "civil law" states of the EU have tended to refuse to recognise the floating charge, in the English-law form, when it is sought to enforce such a charge over property of a debtor situated within their territories, on the grounds that it was a fraud on creditors, to be avoided on the principles of the "*actio Pauliana*".

---

[71] *Re Eurofood IFSC Ltd* [2004] IESC 45.
[72] 2015 Regulation arts 56–77.
[73] Insolvency Act 1986 (Amendment) Regulations 2002 (SI 2002/1037); Insolvency Act 1986 (Amendment) (No.2) Regulations 2002 (SI 2002/1240); Insolvency (Amendment) Rules 2002 (SI 2002/1307); Insolvent Partnerships (Amendment) Order 2002 (SI 2002/1308); Administration of Insolvent Estates of Deceased Persons Order 2002 (SI 2002/1309).

The recognition is made in these terms[74]:

"The opening of insolvency proceedings shall not affect the rights in rem of creditors or third parties in respect of tangible or intangible, moveable or immoveable assets, both specific assets and collections of indefinite assets as a whole which change from time to time, belonging to the debtor which are situated within the territory of another member state at the time of the opening of proceedings."

The rights of holders of floating charges are thus specifically protected.[75] Such rights, however, and the legal acts creating them, are nonetheless subject to domestic laws of Member States relating voidness, voidability or unenforceability, on the ground that they are detrimental to the general body of creditors.[76]

Office-holder's power to convert existing insolvency proceedings into another form. An office-holder in main proceedings may request that the courts of a member state which has opened secondary proceedings convert those secondary proceedings into one of the other forms of insolvency proceedings listed in Annex A.[77] **28-27**

Form and content of application to convert. An application in England and Wales for the conversion of an administration or a company voluntary arrangement into a winding up requires evidence by way of witness statement, made by or on behalf of the office-holder: **28-28**

(a) stating that main proceedings have been opened in another Member State;
(b) stating the applicant's belief that the conversion would be most appropriate as regards the interests of the local creditors and coherence between the main and secondary insolvency proceedings;
(c) advising whether, in his opinion, the company should enter voluntary or compulsory winding up; and
(d) stating all other matters which in his opinion would assist the court in deciding whether to make the order and, in that event, what consequential provision would need to be made.[78]

If an order is made for the company to go into voluntary winding up, the order may provide that it be wound up as if a resolution for voluntary winding up were passed on the day on which the order is made.[79]

A similar procedural requirement applies in the case of insolvency proceedings relating to individuals.

SECTION 2: THE CROSS-BORDER INSOLVENCY REGULATIONS 2006

The Model Law on Cross-Border Insolvency. The Cross-Border Insolvency Regulations 2006[80] ("the 2006 Regulations") enact in England and Wales a code based upon the Model Law on Cross-Border Insolvency ("the Model Law"). The **28-29**

---

74 2015 Regulation art.8(1) (2000 Regulation art.5(1)).
75 2015 Regulation art.8(2) (2000 Regulation art.5(2)).
76 2015 Regulation art.8(4) (2000 Regulation art.5(4)).
77 2015 Regulation art.51. Portugal entered a derogation with respect to arts 26 and 27 of the 2000 Regulation (which relate to secondary proceedings).
78 Insolvency (England and Wales) Rules 2016 r.21.2.
79 Insolvency (England and Wales) Rules 2016 r.21.3.
80 SI 2006/1030.

Model Law was adopted by the UN Commission on International Trade Law (UNCITRAL) in May 1997 and, later that year, agreed to by the General Assembly of the UN. The Model Law is precisely that, a set of rules which may be adopted and adapted by domestic legislation.

The 2006 Regulations were made under the power conferred by s.14 of the Insolvency Act 2000. They import into law in England and Wales, and also Scotland, the Model Law in the form set out in Sch.1 to the 2006 Regulations, which is "the Model Law with certain modifications to adapt it for application in Great Britain". That version of the Model Law may be considered together with the Model Law itself and other relevant UNCITRAL documents for the purposes of ascertaining its meaning and effect.[81]

The Model Law is not a harmonising instrument. It is a set of rules which are designed to deal with the recognition of foreign insolvency proceedings and to assist in situations in which co-operation and co-ordination as between different jurisdictions should make those proceedings more effective. It has been adopted in 45 jurisdictions.

Unlike the 2000 and 2015 EU Regulations,[82] there is no higher authority outside Great Britain which can make binding determinations in relation to the meaning of the Model Law as adopted in Great Britain, though the decisions of other courts on the meaning of the Model Law in general will no doubt be of great persuasive authority. Schedule 2 to the Regulations deals with various procedural matters arising from the application of the Model Law as enacted in the form set out in Sch.1.

28-30 **The 2006 Regulations: scope.** Unlike the 2000 and 2015 EU Regulations,[83] there is no reciprocity involved in the adoption of the Model Law. Persons from states which have not adopted the Model Law may rely on the Model Law within Great Britain even though a person from Great Britain would have no equivalent rights in that other state. The Model Law is also largely permissive, rather than reducing the jurisdiction of the British courts.

As noted above, art.3 of Ch.I in Sch.1 to the 2006 Regulations provides that, to the extent that the Model Law conflicts with an obligation of the United Kingdom under the 2000 and 2015 EU Regulations, the requirements of the 2000 and 2015 EU Regulations shall prevail.

However, where there is a conflict between the general provisions of British insolvency law and the 2006 Regulations then the 2006 Regulations prevail.[84] Similarly, although the common law rules about recognition of overseas office-holders may not be ousted by the 2006 Regulations, it should be used only to supplement, not to trump, the 2006 Regulations.[85]

In any case there may be the possibility of invoking s.426 of the Insolvency Act or the 2006 Regulations. The 2006 Regulations do not apply in respect of a list of

---

[81] 2006 Regulations reg.2(2).

[82] See Section 1 of this chapter.

[83] See Section 1 of this chapter.

[84] 2006 Regulations reg.3(2).

[85] If it is established that an office-holder has been properly appointed in the place of incorporation of a corporation, with the power and duty to collect assets on behalf of all creditors, then, barring exceptional circumstances, the office-holder should be left to carry out his function without outside interference from others and a receiver with competing collection duties should not normally be recognised: *Re Stanford International Bank Ltd* [2010] EWCA Civ 137.

specialised insolvency proceedings, largely relating to public utilities, banks and related entities and insurance companies.[86]

In broad terms, the 2006 Regulations apply where (i) assistance is sought within Great Britain by a foreign court or representative in connection with a foreign proceeding, (ii) assistance is sought from a foreign state in connection with a proceeding under British insolvency law, and (iii) a foreign proceeding and a British insolvency proceeding in respect of the same debtor are taking place concurrently, or creditors or other interested persons have an interest in requesting the commencement of, or participating in, a proceeding under British insolvency law.[87]

The structure of the version of the Model Law set out in Sch.1 to the 2006 Regulations is as follows:

(a) Ch.1 art.5 permits a British insolvency office-holder to act in a foreign state on behalf of a proceeding under British insolvency law as permitted by the applicable foreign law;

(b) Ch.II deals with access to the British courts by foreign representatives and creditors;

(c) Ch.III deals with recognition of foreign proceedings and the relief to be granted;

(d) Ch.IV deals with co-operation with foreign courts and foreign representatives;

(e) Ch.V deals with concurrent proceedings.

Some key concepts. A number of concepts used in the Model Law are identical, **28-31** or very similar, to those used in the 2000 and 2015 EU Regulations[88]:

(a) "Establishment" is defined as any place of operations where the debtor carries out a non-transitory economic activity with human means and assets or service;

(b) "Foreign main proceeding" means a foreign proceeding taking place in the state where the debtor[89] has his centre of main interests. For the purposes of the 2006 Regulations, "centre of main interests" has been held to have the same meaning as in the 2000 EU Regulation, and therefore should presumably now be construed in accordance with the 2015 EU Regulation[90];

(c) "Foreign non-main proceeding" means a foreign proceeding, other than a foreign main proceeding, taking place in a state where the debtor has an establishment. It is to be noted that the Model Law as adopted does not draw a distinction between different types of non-main proceeding, as the 2000 and 2015 EU Regulations do (territorial and secondary proceedings).

Chapter II: Access to British courts. Article 9 confers a right of direct access **28-32** to the British courts on a foreign representative without the need for a formal recognition process. Article 10 limits the effects of any submission to the jurisdiction flowing from any such application being made pursuant to the 2006 Regulations. Without undergoing a formal recognition process, a foreign representa-

---

[86] 2006 Regulations Sch.1 art.1(2).
[87] 2006 Regulations Sch.1 art.1(1).
[88] The definitions are set out in 2006 Regulations Sch.1 art.2.
[89] It appears that the debtor need not be an entity known to English law: *Rubin v Eurofinance* [2012] UKSC 46.
[90] *Re Stanford International Bank Ltd* [2010] EWCA Civ 137.

tive appointed in a foreign main proceeding or non-main proceeding is given locus to commence a British insolvency proceeding if the conditions for commencing the proceeding are otherwise met.[91] As regards proceedings under British law, a foreign representative is entitled to participate, but only where the foreign proceeding has first been recognised.[92] Foreign creditors are given the same right to commence and participate in British insolvency proceedings as British creditors, and the ability to object to foreign claims on the grounds solely that they are tax-based claims or social security authority claims is removed. In addition, foreign creditors are to receive notification of insolvency proceedings under British law.[93]

28-33   **Chapter III: Recognition of foreign proceedings.**   Chapter III deals with the recognition of foreign proceedings.[94] Essentially, an application for recognition is to be accompanied by (i) a certified copy of the decision of the foreign court commencing the foreign proceeding and appointing the foreign representative, (ii) a certificate from the foreign court affirming the existence of the foreign proceeding and of the appointment of the foreign representative, or (iii) any other evidence acceptable to the court of the existence of the foreign proceeding and of the appointment of the foreign representative. There must also be a statement identifying all foreign proceedings, proceedings under British insolvency law and requests under s.426 of the Insolvency Act 1986 in respect of the debtor, in so far as known to the foreign representative. English translations are required where applicable.[95]

If recognition is granted,[96] the recognition must identify whether it is recognition of a foreign main proceeding or a foreign non-main proceeding. The main effect of this distinction is that recognition of a foreign main proceeding results in an immediate stay of proceedings and freezing of assets,[97] whereas the recognition of a foreign non-main proceeding gives the court a discretion to grant certain relief, including a stay on proceedings and the freezing of assets.[98] This discretion as regards relief, which is wider than that taking effect automatically on recognition, also applies in respect of a foreign main proceeding. Included among the powers of the court is a power to entrust the distribution of assets situated within Great Britain to the foreign representative, provided that the court is satisfied that the interests of creditors in Great Britain are adequately protected.[99]

Pending determination of the application, the court has various interim powers

---

91   2006 Regulations Sch.1 art.11.
92   2006 Regulations Sch.1 art.12.
93   2006 Regulations Sch.1 arts 13, 14.
94   The proceedings have to be "pursuant to a law relating to insolvency". In a case where a receiver was appointed by the Texas court as a protective measure, to prevent detriment to investors, and where the underlying cause of action which led to the making of the order had nothing to do with insolvency, no allegation of insolvency had featured in the applicant's complaint and the powers and duties imposed on the receiver were duties to gather in and preserve assets, not to liquidate or distribute them, the Court of Appeal held that the receivership did not qualify as a foreign proceeding and the receiver could not be recognised as a foreign representative under the 2006 Regulations: *Re Stanford International Bank Ltd* [2010] EWCA Civ 137.
95   2006 Regulations Sch.1 art.15(4). See also Sch.2 paras 2–5 and the guidance in *Re Rajapaske (Note)* [2007] B.P.I.R. 99.
96   2006 Regulations Sch.1 art.17.
97   2006 Regulations Sch.1 art.20. Examples of cases in which the power of the court to lift a stay has been considered include *Seawolf Tankers Inc v Pan Ocean Co Ltd* [2015] EWHC 1500 (Ch) and *Ronelp Marine Ltd v STX Offshore and Shipbuilding Co* [2016] EWHC 2228 (Ch).
98   2006 Regulations Sch.1 art.21.
99   See, e.g., *Re Swissair Schweizerische Luftverkehr-Aktiengesellschaft* [2009] EWHC 2099 (Ch).

to grant provisional relief.[100] Once the foreign proceeding is recognised, the foreign representative has standing to make applications in connection with pre-insolvency transactions which may be impugned on the grounds of undervalue or preference under the Insolvency Act 1986 and to intervene in any proceedings in which the debtor is a party.[101]

Chapter IV: Co-operation. Chapter IV contains provisions requiring and facilitating co-operation between foreign courts or foreign representatives and the British courts and British insolvency office-holders. The Model Law is not designed, however, to provide for the reciprocal enforcement of judgments, and the 2006 Regulations cannot therefore be utilised for the enforcement of a foreign judgment against a third party.[102]   **28-34**

Chapter V: Concurrent proceedings. Chapter V contains provisions dealing with concurrent proceedings. Once a foreign main proceeding is recognised as such, then any proceeding under British insolvency law will be limited to assets located in Great Britain. Otherwise, there are detailed provisions regarding the co-ordination of any British insolvency proceedings and any foreign insolvency proceedings.   **28-35**

---

[100] 2006 Regulations Sch.1 art.19.
[101] 2006 Regulations Sch.1 arts 23, 24.
[102] *Rubin v Eurofinance SA* [2012] UKSC 46.

INDEX